# Financial Accounting

## for Undergraduates

**Kenneth R. Ferris**

*W.P. Carey School of Business*
*Arizona State University*

**James S. Wallace**

*The Peter F. Drucker and Masatoshi Ito*
*Graduate School of Management*
*Claremont Graduate University*

FINANCIAL ACCOUNTING FOR UNDERGRADUATES, First Edition, by Kenneth Ferris and James Wallace

ISBN 978-1-934319-63-5

**Bookstores & Faculty:** To order this book, contact the company via email **customerservice@cambridgepub.com** or call 800-619-6473.

**Students & Retail Customers:** To order this book, please visit the book's Website and order directly online.

Printed in Canada.
10 9 8 7 6 5 4 3 2 1

# About the Authors

**KENNETH R. FERRIS** is a Professor in the W.P. Carey School of Business at Arizona State University. He received a B.B.A. and an M.B.A. from The George Washington University and an M.A. and a Ph.D. from The Ohio State University. He previously served on the faculties of Northwestern University, The Claremont Graduate University, Southern Methodist University, and Thunderbird School of Global Management, In addition, he has taught at numerous academic institutions in Australia, Hong Kong, Japan, and New Zealand. Professor Ferris is the author or co-author of eleven books, over fifty academic and professional publications, and over eighty case studies. He previously served as a director of several NYSE listed companies and is active in executive education programs around the world.

**JAMES S. WALLACE** is an Associate Professor at The Peter F. Drucker and Masatoshi Ito Graduate School of Management at The Claremont Graduate University. He received his B.A. from the University of California, Santa Barbara, his M.B.A. from the University of California, Davis, and his Ph.D. from the University of Washington. Professor Wallace also holds a CPA certification from the state of California. He previously served on the faculty of the University of California, Irvine and has served as a visiting professor at the University of California, San Diego. Professor Wallace's work has appeared in leading academic journals including the Journal of Accounting and Economics, the Journal of Corporate Finance, and Information Systems Research, along with leading applied journals such as the Journal of Applied Corporate Finance, the Journal of Accountancy, Issues in Accounting Education and Accounting Horizons. Prior to his career in academics, Professor Wallace worked in public accounting and in industry with a Fortune 500 company. He has done consulting work with numerous companies in multiple industries.

# Preface

**W**elcome to *Financial Accounting for Undergraduates.* We wrote this book to satisfy the needs of students taking their first financial accounting course by providing a high quality, contemporary, and engaging textbook at an affordable price. *Financial Accounting for Undergraduates* is written for students who want to understand how financial statements are prepared and how the information in published financial reports is used. This book is the product of extensive market research including focus groups, market surveys, manuscript reviews, and interviews with faculty from across the country.

## TARGET AUDIENCE

*Financial Accounting for Undergraduates* is intended for use in the first financial accounting course at the undergraduate level; one that balances the preparation of financial statements with their interpretation and use. This book teaches students how to read, analyze, and interpret financial accounting data to make informed business decisions.

We believe students become more engaged in the course when they see how the content pertains to their everyday lives. Once engaged in the course, students perform much better and enjoy the class more. Furthermore, we believe accounting is a discipline best learned by doing. Unlike some other disciplines, accounting needs to be practiced. Consequently, we took great care to incorporate a number of pedagogical devices and real examples that show students the relevance of financial accounting to their lives and that help students succeed in the course.

## RELEVANCE

### "Why do I need to study financial accounting?"

Students frequently ask this or similar questions. The extent to which they feel accounting is relevant to their daily lives will often determine how much effort they put into the course. The following features are used throughout the book to convey the relevance of accounting to their lives and society.

#### REAL DATA AND EXAMPLES

Today's students must be skilled in using real financial statements to make business decisions. Through their exposure to various financial statements, students will learn that, while financial statements do not all look the same, they can readily understand and interpret them to make business decisions. In each chapter, we incorporate a wide range of examples using real companies that students know. In addition, the **Extending Your Knowledge** section in the assignments of each chapter requires students to use the financial statements of **Columbia Sportswear Company** and **The Timberland Company**.

---

**EYK2-2.** **Comparative Analysis Problem: Columbia Sportswear Company vs. The Timberland Company**

The financial statements for **Columbia Sportswear** can be found in Appendix A and **The Timberland Company**'s financial statements can be found in Appendix B at the end of this textbook.

COLUMBIA SPORTSWEAR
COMPANY

THE TIMBERLAND COMPANY

**Required**

*a.* Calculate for each company the following ratios for 2009:
 1. Current ratio
 2. Debt-to-total-assets ratio
 3. Return on sales
*b.* Comment on the companies' relative profitability, liquidity, and solvency.

---

## ACCOUNTING IN PRACTICE

These boxed inserts help bridge the gap between the classroom and what students encounter in the real world. **Accounting In Practice** illustrations document situations a reader is likely to encounter and present the choices that companies make in reporting financial results.

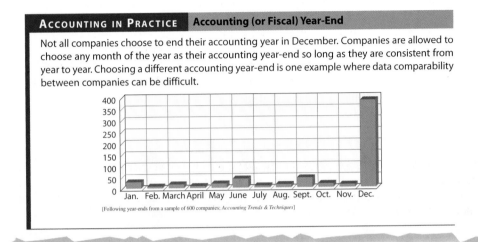

**ACCOUNTING IN PRACTICE**    **Accounting (or Fiscal) Year-End**

Not all companies choose to end their accounting year in December. Companies are allowed to choose any month of the year as their accounting year-end so long as they are consistent from year to year. Choosing a different accounting year-end is one example where data comparability between companies can be difficult.

[Following year-ends from a sample of 600 companies; *Accounting Trends & Techniques*]

## FORENSIC ACCOUNTING

**Forensic Accounting** is the one of the fastest growing areas in the practice of accounting. These boxed inserts help students understand how financial accounting knowledge can be used to aid in the prevention of financial accounting errors and the detection of fraud.

**FORENSIC ACCOUNTING**    **Fraudulent Reporting**

 Verifying that the sum of the debit account balances from the general ledger is equal to the sum of the credit account balances is not sufficient to guarantee accuracy of financial records. The infamous accounting scandal at **WorldCom** provides a case in point. To inflate its net income, WorldCom improperly "capitalized expenses"—that is, they inappropriately debited property, plant, and equipment, an asset account, when they should have debited an expense account. While the sum of the debit account balances on WorldCom's books did equal the sum of the credit account balances, assets were overstated and expenses were understated by almost $7 billion. WorldCom's CEO Bernard Ebbers, the mastermind of its fraudulent accounting, was convicted of conspiracy to commit fraud, securities fraud, and making false filings with the SEC. Mr. Ebbers was sentenced to 25 years in prison.

## CORPORATE SOCIAL RESPONSIBILITY

Increasingly, companies have found that "doing good" leads to a more successful, profitable enterprise. These boxed inserts help students understand how corporate social responsibility is being embraced by forward-thinking enterprises as part of their long-term business models.

**CORPORATE SOCIAL RESPONSIBILITY**    **Investing with a Social Conscience**

Not all investors are singularly focused on the financial performance of businesses they invest in. For a segment of the investing community, corporate social responsibility goes hand in hand with financial performance in choosing an investment. **Socially responsible investing (SRI)**, also known as sustainable investing, considers a firm's environmental stewardship, consumer protection, human rights, and diversity, along with its financial performance. Investments in SRI funds are near $3 trillion and have grown in recent years at a pace almost six times greater than the growth of professionally managed investments.

# SUCCESS

Financial accounting can be challenging—especially for students lacking business experience or previous exposure to business courses. To help students succeed in the course, we include many features that provide direction to students and require them to recall and apply the financial accounting techniques and concepts described in each chapter.

## PUTTING EACH CHAPTER IN CONTEXT

Often, students lose sight of the big picture. The Past/Present/Future feature provides students with an overview of where the chapter fits within the whole course.

| PAST | PRESENT | FUTURE |
|---|---|---|
| Chapters 1 and 2 described the environment of financial accounting. They also introduced the financial statements and basic analysis of them. | This chapter explains the accounting system, including transaction analysis, the system of debits and credits, and the journalizing of transactions. | Chapter 4 describes accounting adjustments, the construction of financial statements, and the period-end closing process. |

## MAPPING EACH CHAPTER

Each chapter begins with an overview that visually depicts the layout of the chapter.

## YOUR TURN!

**Your Turn** boxes are integrated throughout each chapter as a means of reinforcing the material just presented. Solutions are provided at the end of the chapter so students can check their work.

### Your Turn!    2.2

The following information is available from the financial statements of the Philips Company.

|  | 2010 | 2009 |
|---|---|---|
| Net sales | $120,000 | $110,000 |
| Net income | 20,000 | 15,000 |
| Cash provided by operating activities | 25,000 | 22,000 |
| Expenditures on property, plant, and equipment | 7,000 | 6,000 |
| Current assets | 75,000 | 65,000 |
| Current liabilities | 50,000 | 45,000 |
| Total assets | 220,000 | 190,000 |
| Total liabilities | 150,000 | 145,000 |

Compute the following ratios and comment on any trends observed between 2009 and 2010: (1) return on sales, (2) current ratio, (3) debt-to-total-assets ratio, and (4) free cash flow.

**The solution is on page 96.**

## A.K.A. BOXES

**A.K.A.** (Also Known As) boxes inform students of commonly used alternative terms that they may encounter.

**Stockholders' equity** refers to the ownership (stockholder) claims on the assets of the business. Stockholders' equity represents a *residual claim* on a business's assets; that is, it is a claim on the assets of a business that remain after all liabilities to creditors have been satisfied. For this reason, stockholders' equity is sometimes referred to as a business's **net assets**, where net assets equal the difference between the total assets and total liabilities. In equation format,

**A.K.A.** The accounting equation is also called the *balance sheet equation.*

## HINTS

Helpful suggestions are inserted in the margin as **Hints** to help students understand difficult concepts.

**Hint:** A contra account is increased and decreased in the opposite way of its controlling account. Also, the normal balance of a contra account is opposite to the normal balance of its controlling account.

The **contra accounts** are so named because they are used to record reductions in, or offsets against, a controlling account. The Accumulated Depreciation account has a normal credit balance and appears in the balance sheet as a deduction against its related asset account balance. Use of the contra account Accumulated Depreciation allows the original cost of the related asset to be reported in the company's balance sheet, followed by the accumulated amount of depreciation taken to date. Users of financial statements want to see both of these amounts so that they can estimate how much of an asset has been used up and how much remains to benefit the business in future periods.

## TAKEAWAYS

These in chapter summaries ensure that students grasp key concepts before proceeding to the next topic.

| | | Concept | ➡ | Method | ➡ | Assessment |
|---|---|---|---|---|---|---|
| TAKEAWAY 2.1 | | Can a company meet its short-term obligations? | | Current assets and current liabilities from the balance sheet.<br><br>Current ratio = $\dfrac{\text{Current assets}}{\text{Current liabilities}}$ | | A larger current ratio implies greater liquidity and a greater ability to pay short-term obligations. |

# ETHICS

In today's post-Sarbanes-Oxley world, ethical decision making has never been more pertinent to business and students studying accounting. We discuss ethics where appropriate in the text, and we have included at least one assignment in each chapter that raises an ethical issue. Assignments involving ethics are identified by the icon in the margin.

### ETHICS AND ACCOUNTING

Ethics deals with the values, rules, and justifications that govern one's way of life. Although fundamental ethical concepts such as right and wrong, good and evil, justice and morality are abstract, many issues in our daily lives have ethical dimensions. The way that we respond to these issues defines our ethical profile. In both our personal and professional lives, our goal is to act ethically and responsibly.

Ethical behavior has not always been the rule in business. Business history reveals un-

# INTERNATIONAL FINANCIAL REPORTING STANDARDS (IFRS)

The convergence of U.S. GAAP and International Financial Reporting Standards (IFRS) is in process. Our introductory students should be prepared for this eventuality with a basic understanding of the similarities and differences in the current reporting requirements and methods under U.S. GAAP and IFRS. Consequently, we incorporate discussions that examine these similarities and differences where appropriate throughout the book in IFRS Alert! boxes. In addition, the financial statements for Tesco, PLC are included in Appendix C at the end of the book. Each chapter includes an IFRS assignment related to Tesco. The IFRS icon identifies those assignments.

**IFRS ALERT!**

Under IFRS, LIFO is *not* generally accepted. Further, under U.S. GAAP inventory may not be revalued above its acquisition cost. IFRS permits inventory to be revalued upwards if the inventory's fair value appreciates above acquisition cost. When inventory is revalued upward under IFRS a parallel increase is made to an equity account called Asset Revaluation Reserve. To illustrate, assume that **Tesco**'s ending inventory at year-end is valued on its books at 2,669 million British pounds. Also assume that a review by management concluded that the fair value of its inventory had appreciated to 3,000 million British pounds. Under IFRS, we make the following journal entry to revalue inventory:

| | | |
|---|---|---|
| Inventories | 331 | |
|     Asset revaluation reserve | | 331 |
|     *To write up inventory to its fair market value.* | | |

| A | = | L | + | SE |
|---|---|---|---|---|
| +331 | | | | +331 |

Appendix C at the end of this book presents the IFRS financial statements of Tesco. Tesco's asset revaluation reserve is in the equity section of its balance sheet.

## THINKING GLOBALLY

In addition to **IFRS Alert!** boxes, these **Thinking Globally** inserts emphasize the similarities and differences between the United States and other countries that are not necessarily related to reporting standards.

> **THINKING GLOBALLY**
>
> Companies measure their operating performance using the currency of their principal place of business. The **Johnson & Johnson Company**, a well-known maker of baby shampoo and Band-Aids, is headquartered in New Jersey, and reports its financial results using the U.S. dollar. On the other hand, **Moet Hennessy-Louis Vuitton**, the luxury goods manufacturer, is headquartered in Paris, France, and reports its financial results using the euro. Some companies prepare "convenience translations" of their financial statements in the currency and language of other countries so that potential foreign investors can more readily understand the company's financial performance and condition.

# SUPPLEMENT PACKAGE

## FOR INSTRUCTORS

**Instructor CD-ROM:** This convenient supplement provides the text's ancillary materials on a portable CD-ROM. All the faculty supplements that accompany the textbook are available, including PowerPoint, Solutions Manual, Test Bank, and Computerized Test Bank.

**Solutions Manual:** Created by the authors, the *Solutions Manual* contains complete solutions to all the assignment material in the text.

**PowerPoint:** The PowerPoint slides outline key elements of each chapter.

**Test Bank:** The test bank includes multiple-choice items, matching questions, short essay questions, and problems.

**Excel Templates**: We provide Excel spreadsheets for assignments. These spreadsheets will save time in data entry and allow students to dedicate additional time to learning the material. The Excel spreadsheets are identified by the Excel icon.

**Website:** All instructor materials are accessible via the book's Website (password protected) along with other useful links and marketing information. **www.cambridgepub.com**

**Blackboard Cartridge:** A full complement of online material is available for incorporation with your Blackboard course management system.

## FOR STUDENTS

**Student Study Guide:** This saleable study aid provides students with additional resources to master the course. It includes chapter outlines, chapter summaries, multiple choice questions, and additional exercises.

**Excel Templates:** We provide Excel spreadsheets for assignments. These spreadsheets will save students' time in data entry and allow them to dedicate additional time to learning the material. The Excel spreadsheets are identified by the Excel icon.

**Website:** Practice quizzes and other useful links are available to students free of charge on the book's Website.

# ACKNOWLEDGMENTS

This book benefited greatly from the valuable feedback of focus group attendees, reviewers, students, and colleagues. We are extremely grateful to them for their help in making this project a success.

Markus Ahrens *St. Louis Community College*
David Ambrosini *Cabrillo College*
Matthew Anderson *Michigan State University*
James Bannister *University of Hartford*
Debbie Benson *Kennesaw State University*
Lydia Botsford *DeAnza College*
Rada Brooks *University of California—Berkeley*
Marilyn Brooks-Lewis *Warren County Community College*
Amy Browning *Ivy Tech Community College*
Sandra Byrd *Missouri State University*
Jeffrey Byrne *Indiana University—Southeast*
Betty Chavis *California State University—Fullerton*
Alan Cherry *Loyola Marymount University*
Leslie Cohen *University of Arizona*
Nancy Coster *Loyola Marymount University*
John Coulter *Western New England College*
Alan Falcon *Loyola Marymount University*
Julie Finnegan *Mendocino College*
Carolyn Galantine *Pepperdine University*
Lisa Gillespie *Loyola University*
Bruce Gunning *Kent State University*
Bob Hartman *University of Iowa*
Rosemary Hayward *Cabrillo College*
Haihong He *California State University—Los Angeles*
Cynthia Hollenbach *University of Denver*
Steven Hornik *Central Florida University*
Stephen Jablonsky *Colorado State University*
Marianne James *California State University—Los Angeles*
Ching-Lih Jan *California State University—Northridge*
Catherine Jeppson *California State University—Northridge*
Thomas Kam *Hawaii Pacific University*
Kathryn Kapka *University of Texas—Tyler*
Jocelyn Kauffunger *University of Pittsburgh*
Christine Kloezeman *Glendale Community College*
John Koeplin *University of San Francisco*
Christopher Kwak *De Anza College*
Cathy Larson *Middlesex Community College*
Doug Larson *Salem State University*
Greg Lauer *North Iowa Area Community College*

Ron Lazer *University of Houston*
Elliott Levy *Bentley College*
Zining Li *Southern Methodist University*
Siyi Li *University of Illinois*
Christine Li *College of Marin*
Lihong Liang *Syracuse University*
Emily Lindsay *American University*
Ariel Markelevich *Suffolk University*
Dawn Massey *Fairfield University*
Michele Matherly *Xavier University*
Allison McLeod *University of North Texas*
Jeff McMillan *Clemson University*
Michael Meyer *University of Notre Dame*
Michelle Moshier *SUNY—Albany*
Tracie Nobles *Austin Community College*
Sarah Nutter *George Mason University*
Kimberly Perkins *Austin Community College*
Marietta Peytcheva *Lehigh University*
Gary Pieroni *University of California—Berkeley*
Allan Rabinowitz *Pace University*
Maria Roxas *Central Connecticut State University*
Albert Schepanski *University of Iowa*
Arnold Schneider *Georgia Tech University*
Steve Sefcik *University of Washington*
Cathy Sevigny *Bridgewater State University*
Carol Shaver *Louisiana Tech University*
John Shon *Fordham University*
Gregory Sinclair *San Francisco State University*
Eric Slayter *Cal Poly--San Luis Obispo*
Nancy Snow *University of Toledo*
John Suckow *Lansing Community College*
Diane Tanner *University of North Florida*
Linda Tarrago *Hillsborough Community College*
Sheri Trumpfheller *University of Colorado—Colorado Springs*
Joan Van Hise *Fairfield University*
Marcia Viet *University of Central Florida*
Robert Walsh *University of Dallas*
Susan Wright *DeKalb Technical College*

In addition, we are extremely grateful to George Werthman, Jill Fischer, Jocelyn Mousel, Rich Kolasa, Debbie Golden, Terry Mc-Quade, and the entire team at Cambridge Business Publishers for their encouragement, enthusiasm, and guidance. Feedback is always welcome. Please feel free contact us with your suggestions or questions by emailing them to: Ken_and_Jim@cambridgepub.com.

Ken Ferris            Jim Wallace
Phoenix, AZ           Claremont, CA
                      March 2011

# Brief Contents

# Contents

CHAPTER **3**

Processing Accounting
Information  98

**(Ac)counting Stars  99**

Accounting Cycle  100

Analyzing Transactions  101
   Accounting Equation Expanded  102
   Transactions and the Accounting Equation: An
     Illustration  102
   Transaction Summary  106
   Your Turn! 3.1  106

CHAPTER **4**

Accrual Basis of Accounting  158

**Making Dough  159**

Accrual Basis of Accounting  160
   Revenue Recognition Principle  160
   Expense Recognition (Matching) Principle  161

Adjusting Accounts  162
   Unadjusted Trial Balance  162
   Types of Adjustments  163
   Allocating Previously Recorded Assets to
     Expenses  163

**CHAPTER 5**

# Accounting for Merchandising Operations  220

## CHAPTER 6

## Accounting for Inventory  266

## CHAPTER 7

## Internal Control and Cash  316

**CHAPTER 8**

# Accounting for Receivables  362

**MGM Resorts International—Managing Credit for Bigger Profits  363**

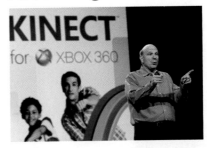

# CHAPTER 11

## Stockholders' Equity   498

**Starbucks—The Corporate Form of Organization   499**

**Nature and Formation of a Corporation   500**

Advantages of the Corporate Form of Organization   500

Disadvantages of the Corporate Form of Organization   502

Accounting for Stockholders' Equity in Alternative Organizational Forms   503

Your Turn! 11.1   503

**Par Value Stock and No-Par Value Stock   503**

**Types of Capital Stock   504**

Common Stock   504

Preferred Stock   505

Your Turn! 11.2   508

**Stock Issuances for Cash   508**

Noncash Stock Issuances   509

Your Turn! 11.3   509

**Stock Splits   510**

**Treasury Stock   510**

Accounting for Treasury Stock   510

Your Turn! 11.4   511

# CHAPTER 12

## Statement of Cash Flows   542

**Home Depot: A Company with a Vision   543**

**Cash and Cash Equivalents   544**

**Activity Classifications in the Statement of Cash Flows   545**

Operating Activities   546

Investing Activities   546

Financing Activities   546

An Illustration of Activity Classification Usefulness   547

**Noncash Investing and Financing Activities   547**

**Using the Statement of Cash Flows   548**

**Cash Flow from Operating Activities   549**

Your Turn! 12.1   550

# CHAPTER 13

## Analysis and Interpretation of Financial Statements   592

**Procter & Gamble   593**

# APPENDIX A

## Columbia Sportswear Company: Annual Report and Social Responsibility Report   A-1

# Financial Accounting and Business Decisions

## PRESENT

This chapter explains business formation, the use and users of accounting, the types of activities companies pursue, and financial statements that report on business.

## FUTURE

The next few chapters more fully explain financial statements, including how they are prepared, constructed, analyzed, and interpreted.

## LEARNING OBJECTIVES

1 **Explain** business organization and its three forms. (p. 4)

2 **Indicate** who uses accounting information. (p. 5)

3 **Describe** business activities. (p. 9)

4 **Explain** the accounting process and generally accepted accounting principles. (p. 10)

5 **Describe** the accounting equation and each financial statement. (p. 12)

6 **Explain** additional disclosures that accompany financial statements. (p. 20)

7 Appendix 1A: **Discuss** international accounting principles and their formulation. (p. 23)

# WHAT THE NUMBERS MEAN

If it's true that accounting is the language of business, then this textbook is crucial to your future livelihood. All of us confront accounting issues in our daily lives. We must control our cash and other assets, we must monitor our paychecks and our expenses, we must purchase items that fit within our budgets, and we must use accounting data in making business decisions.

It is no surprise then that accounting knowledge ranks near the top of what employers look for when hiring new workers. It is also no surprise that students with accounting knowledge perform better than those that do not understand the basics of accounting. This book provides the fundamental knowledge for future success in business and life.

**Columbia Sportswear Company** (Columbia.com), a maker of clothing for dedicated lovers of the greater outdoors, must also rely upon accounting for its success. It uses financial reports to judge its performance and that of its managers. It uses accounting controls to monitor its inventory. It uses accounting data to assess the wisdom of payments, and their amounts, to shareholders. Consequently, accounting not only impacts our lives, but also the business activities of all

companies worldwide. We even witness national and international politicians using accounting data to justify or reject key economic and governmental policies.

Columbia Sportswear states the following about its products: "We enjoy the outdoors . . . which means we know what you need. We know that being cold and wet is no fun. Blue eyes may be sexy, but blue lips aren't. And, while a sunny day is excellent, sunburn sucks." The authors of this book might state: "We enjoy success . . . which means we know what you need. Being in a red dress may be sexy, but being in the red isn't. And, while a huge sales day is excellent, out-of-stock product isn't."

So, just as Columbia Sportswear makes products to protect and aid us in the greater outdoors, this book protects and aids us in our financial lives. No matter how small or large your business, or how small or large your nest egg, accounting skills benefit us throughout our careers and lives.

This first chapter introduces us to many basic relations and principles underlying financial accounting reports. It also identifies many key users of accounting information and how that information is useful in businesses globally.

## BUSINESS ORGANIZATION

The three principal forms of business organization are the sole proprietorship, the partnership, and the corporation. Although each of these organizational forms is treated as an accounting entity, only the corporation is viewed under the law as a legal entity separate and distinct from its owners.

A **sole proprietorship** is a business owned by one person; it is the most common of the three forms of business organization. A **partnership** is a voluntary association of two or more persons for the purpose of conducting a business. Partnerships and sole proprietorships differ principally with respect to the number of owners.

The primary advantage of the sole proprietorship is its ease of formation. As the only owner, the sole proprietor makes all of the decisions affecting the business. This organizational form also enjoys certain income tax advantages relative to a corporation in that the income of that business is not taxed; instead, its income is included as part of the owner's income that is reported to the taxation authorities.

Partnerships are also easy to establish. Because a partnership involves multiple owners, the partners should establish the rights and obligations of each partner to avoid any misunderstandings that might lead to disputes and lawsuits. An advantage of the partnership form over the sole proprietorship is the broader skill set that multiple partners can bring to a business. Partnerships also enjoy the same income tax advantage as sole proprietorships.

A **corporation**, on the other hand, is a legal entity created under the laws of a state or the federal government. The owners of a corporation receive shares of stock as evidence of their ownership interest in the business, and consequently, they are referred to as **stockholders** (or *shareholders*). Since corporations are a separate legal entity, they must pay income taxes on any earned profits. This leads to a situation of double taxation because the income of the corporation is taxed and stockholders also pay taxes on dividends they receive from the corporation. The corporation is the dominant organizational form in terms of the volume of business activity conducted in the United States and worldwide.

While most businesses start off as either a sole proprietorship or as a partnership, they often outgrow these organizational forms and convert to the corporate form. For example, the **Columbia Sportswear Company** was incorporated in 1961 after beginning as a sole proprietorship in 1931. Two primary reasons for converting a sole proprietorship or a partnership to the corporate form of business are the ease of raising capital to grow the business and the protection afforded to stockholders against personal liability. A third advantage of the corporate form is the relative ease of selling ownership shares. Stock exchanges, such as the **New York Stock Exchange (NYSE)**, exist to enable stockholders to readily buy and sell their ownership shares. No such exchanges exist for sole proprietors or partners, and thus, selling an ownership interest in a sole proprietorship or a partnership is a more difficult, time-consuming event.

| **Proprietorship** | **Partnership** | **Corporation** |
|---|---|---|
| • One owner controlled | • Shared owner control | • All types of owner control |
| • Business not taxed, but owner taxed | • Business not taxed, but owners taxed | • Business taxed **and** owners taxed |
| • Not legal entity | • Not legal entity | • Separate legal entity |
| • Limited life | • Limited life | • Unlimited life |

### Your Turn!　　1.1

Identify two characteristics for each of the three principal forms of business organizations.

1. sole proprietorship
2. partnership
3. corporation

**The solution is on page 48.**

## ACCOUNTING INFORMATION AND ITS USE

In today's society, many individuals and agencies are involved in the economic life of a business. The information needs of these parties are fulfilled, in part, by accounting information. Information users are classified by their relation to a business as either *internal users* or *external users*.

LEARNING OBJECTIVE 2

**Indicate** who uses accounting information.

### INTERNAL USERS OF ACCOUNTING

A major function of accounting is to provide the internal management of a company with the data needed for decision making and the efficient management of the business. While managers have an interest in the information reported to external users, managers also require various other types of information, such as the cost of its products, estimates of the income to be earned from a sales campaign, cost comparisons of alternative courses of action, and long-range budgets. Because of the strategic nature of much of this information, it is usually only available to a company's top-level management. The process of generating and analyzing such data is referred to as **managerial accounting**. Exhibit 1-1 illustrates the various types of accounting information that are required by a company's internal users.

| EXHIBIT 1-1 | Accounting Information Needs of Internal Users |
|---|---|
| **User Group** | **Accounting Information Needed to Address Questions such as:** |
| Marketing Department | What is the optimal price to sell **Motorola's** Droid phone to maximize the company's sales revenue? |
| | Was the promotional campaign by **Twentieth Century-Fox Film Corporation** successful in promoting the company's film "Avatar"? |
| Human Resources Department | How will a five percent wage increase for all employees at **Costco** affect the company's profitability? |
| | What will the impact be on expenses for **Dell** if the company switches its healthcare insurance provider? |
| Management team | How much is the Olive Garden restaurant chain contributing to the overall profitability of its parent company, the **Darden Restaurant Group**? |
| | What is the projected profitability of the **General Motors'** Chevrolet brand for the coming year? |
| Finance Department | Is there sufficient cash available for **Hewlett Packard** to buy back a large amount of its outstanding common stock? |
| | Will **General Electric** have sufficient cash flow to pay its short-term expenses? |

## EXTERNAL USERS OF ACCOUNTING

An important function of the accounting process is to accumulate and report accounting information that details a business's results of operations, cash flows, and financial position. By U.S. law, publicly owned businesses must publish financial statements annually and quarterly. The subset of accounting that produces these publicly available financial statements is referred to as **financial accounting**.

Financial accounting information serves a variety of users. Potential investors and investment professionals need financial data to compare prospective investments to determine which, if any, should be invested in, and at what price. Creditors must consider the financial strength of a business before lending it funds, and stockholders must evaluate whether to remain invested in a business, buy more shares, or sell their existing shares of stock.

The financial statements issued by a company are the main source of financial information for these external users. Because financial statements are often used to evaluate the management team running the business, their objectivity is sometimes called into question because the reports are prepared by the management team itself. To establish the validity of financial statements, most businesses have their financial data audited by an independent public accountant. The independent public accountant, or independent auditor, examines the financial statements and recommends any changes or improvements that are warranted. The independent auditor then expresses a professional opinion as to whether the financial statements are fairly presented "in conformity with generally

---

**ACCOUNTING IN PRACTICE** **The Big Four**

Independent auditors are licensed by the state in which they do their auditing work and are identified as **certified public accountants (CPAs)**. To qualify as a CPA, an individual must pass a rigorous examination that is administered nationally and must meet the educational and work experience requirements set by each state to ensure high standards of accounting and auditing performance. The four largest U.S. public accounting firms, referred to as the *Big Four*, have offices located throughout the world and employ thousands of auditors. These firms are **PricewaterhouseCoopers, Deloitte and Touche, Ernst & Young**, and **KPMG, LLP**.

accepted accounting principles." External users have greater confidence in financial statements that have been audited by an independent, certified public accountant.

There are many other external users of a company's accounting information. For example, a business's customers may want information to help them determine if a company like **Maytag** will be able to honor its product warranties. Labor unions require information to determine the level of pay raises that they can demand from companies like **United Parcel Service**. Exhibit 1-2 illustrates the kind of accounting information that is required by a company's external users.

| EXHIBIT 1-2 | Accounting Information Needs of External Users |
| --- | --- |
| **User Group** | **Accounting Information Needed to Answer Questions such as:** |
| Potential investors and stockholders | How does the profitability of **Target** compare to that of **WalMart**? |
| | How does **Bank of America Corporation** compare with **Wells Fargo & Company** in terms of firm size? |
| Creditors and lenders | Will **Delta Airlines** be able to repay its creditors in a timely fashion? |
| | Is it safe to provide a bank loan to the **Federal Express Corporation**? |
| Taxation authorities and regulators | Is **Time Warner Inc.** reporting the proper amount of taxable income? |
| | Is **Duke Energy**'s rate hike justified by its operating costs? |

## Your Turn!   1.2

1. Are financial statements the primary output of managerial or financial accounting? Explain.
2. Identify at least two internal users and explain why they need accounting information.
3. Identify at least two external users and explain why they need accounting information.

**The solution is on page 48.**

### ETHICS AND ACCOUNTING

**Ethics** deals with the values, rules, and justifications that govern one's way of life. Although fundamental ethical concepts such as right and wrong, good and evil, justice and morality are abstract, many issues in our daily lives have ethical dimensions. The way that we respond to these issues defines our ethical profile. In both our personal and professional lives, our goal is to act ethically and responsibly.

Ethical behavior has not always been the rule in business. Business history reveals unethical activities such as price gouging of customers, using inside information for personal gain, paying bribes to government officials for favors, ignoring health and safety regulations, selling arms and military equipment to aggressor governments, polluting the environment, and issuing misleading financial information. Recent accounting scandals at such companies as **Enron**, **Worldcom**, and **AIG** have again brought ethics to the forefront.

Increasingly, business managers recognize the importance and value of ethical behavior by their employees. It is now commonplace for businesses to develop written codes of ethics to help guide the behavior of employees. Similarly, professional organizations of accountants have written ethics codes. The **American Institute of Certified Public Accountants** (AICPA), for example, has a professional code of ethics to guide the conduct of its member CPAs. Similarly, the **Institute of Management Accountants** (IMA) has written standards of ethical conduct for accountants employed in the private sector.

Unethical behavior that results in misleading financial statements such as those at Enron and WorldCom have the potential to erode public confidence and trust in accounting information. In response to this decline in public confidence, the U.S. Congress passed the **Sarbanes-Oxley Act** in 2002 with the goal of restoring investor trust by reducing the likelihood of future accounting scandals. Among the many changes required by this legislation is that a company's top management must certify in writing the accuracy of its reported financial statement information, and these executives risk criminal prosecution for fraudulent certification. In addition, companies must now report on the internal controls put into place to help deter errors in the financial reporting process and to detect them should they occur.

---

**FORENSIC ACCOUNTING** **Accountant as Detective—CSI in Real Life**

 Law enforcement personnel are not the only people who perform criminal investigations. A branch of accounting known as **forensic accounting** is vitally important in many types of criminal investigations, from financial statement fraud, to money laundering, to massive investment frauds such as the one perpetrated by Bernard Madoff (who is currently serving a 150-year prison sentence). Unlike law enforcement personnel, forensic accountants are involved both before and after the commission of a crime.

---

Accountants face several unique ethical dimensions as a result of their work. These dimensions include the following:

1. The output produced by accountants have financial implications for individuals, as well as businesses. These situations generate considerable pressure on the accountant to "improve" the reported results. The amount of income taxes to be paid by an individual or business, the amount of a bonus to be received by an employee, the price to be paid by a customer, and the amount of money to be distributed to a business's owners are examples of situations in which the financial implications can lead to efforts to influence the outcome. *Ethical behavior mandates that accountants ignore these pressures.*

2. Accountants have access to confidential, sensitive information. Tax returns, salary data, details of financial arrangements, planned acquisitions, and proposed price changes illustrate this type of information. *Ethical behavior mandates that accountants respect the confidentiality of information.*

3. A criticism of U.S. business practices is that they are too "bottom-line" (that is, short-term profit) oriented. This orientation can lead to unethical actions by management to increase reported short-term profits. Because accountants measure and report a firm's profit, they must be particularly concerned about these ethical breakdowns. *Both accountants and management must recognize the importance of a long-run perspective.* Studies indicate that, over the long term, successful companies and ethical practices go hand in hand.

---

**Your Turn!** **1.3**

As an accountant for the Madoff Corporation, you are responsible for measuring and reporting the company's net income. It appears that actual results are going to be less than was expected by Wall Street analysts. Your supervisor has asked that you report some of next period's sales revenue early so that the current period's net income will be in line with analyst expectations. You know that reporting revenue like this represents a violation of generally accepted accounting principles. He states that you will not really be doing anything wrong because the sales revenues are real—the company will just be reporting the revenue earlier than accounting guidelines allow. What should you do?

**The solution is on page 48.**

# ACTIVITIES OF A BUSINESS

Every business, regardless of its organizational form, its industry, or its size, is involved in three types of business activities—financing, investing, and operating. The financial accounting system is designed to keep track of each of these activities and to communicate the results of the activities to financial statement users.

## FINANCING ACTIVITIES

Before a company can begin operations, a company must acquire money to support its operations. Employees need to be hired, buildings constructed, raw materials purchased, and machinery put in place. Companies can obtain the necessary funds to undertake these activities in several ways. These **financing activities** are generally categorized as either debt financing or equity financing.

**Debt financing** involves borrowing money from sources such as a bank by signing a note payable or directly from investors by issuing bonds payable. The individuals or financial institutions that lend money to companies are called their **creditors**. Debt financing involves an obligation to repay a creditor both the amount initially borrowed, called the **principal**, and an interest fee for the use of the funds.

**Equity financing** involves selling shares of stock to investors. In contrast to creditors who lend money to a business and expect to receive that money back with interest, investors that purchase shares of stock are actually buying an ownership interest in the company. Investors hope that their stock will increase in value so that they can earn a profit when the stocks are sold. The owners of a company's stock may also receive dividend payments when the company decides to distribute some of its net income.

## INVESTING ACTIVITIES

For a company to undertake its business, it needs to purchase certain long-term resources necessary to conduct its business, such as a printing press purchased by a printing company. The purchase of these resources is known as **investing activities**. Companies can obtain the money needed to make an investment in such items as land, buildings, and equipment from either the financing activities discussed above or from any excess cash accumulated from running the business profitably.

Investing activities involve acquisition and disposition of items such as factories, office furniture, computer and data systems, and delivery vehicles, to carry out the business plans. These items are referred to as *assets*. Investing decisions regarding these assets are known as *asset management*.

**A.K.A.** Land, buildings, and equipment is often referred to as property, plant, and equipment, or simply PP&E.

## OPERATING ACTIVITIES

The day-to-day activities of producing and selling a product or providing a service are referred to as **operating activities**. Operating activities are critical for a business because if a company is unable to generate income from its operations it is very likely that the business will fail. If creditors and stockholders do not believe that a company will be able to generate a profit, they are unlikely to provide the financing needed to start, or maintain, its operations.

Exhibit 1-3 provides a summary of the three types of business activities. Arrows are pointing both toward, and away from, operating activities. This is because financing and investing activities are necessary to carry out a company's operating activities; however, if a company's operating activities generate excess cash, then the excess cash can be used to either finance additional investments or repay the company's creditors.

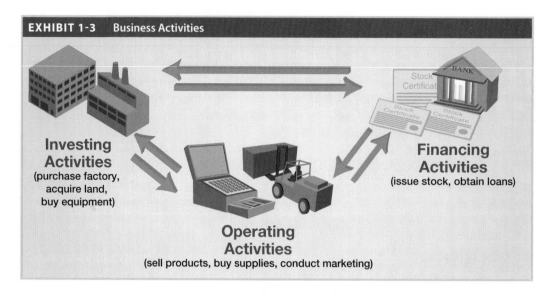

**EXHIBIT 1-3    Business Activities**

**Investing Activities** (purchase factory, acquire land, buy equipment)

**Financing Activities** (issue stock, obtain loans)

**Operating Activities** (sell products, buy supplies, conduct marketing)

---

**Your Turn!**                                                                1.4

Classify each of the following activities as a financing, investing, or operating activity.

1. Receiving a loan from a bank.
2. Selling merchandise online.
3. Purchasing a delivery truck.
4. Purchasing merchandise for resale to customers.
5. Issuing shares of stock in exchange for cash.
6. Paying employee salaries.

**The solution is on page 48.**

---

# THE ACCOUNTING PROCESS

**Accounting** is *the process of measuring economic activity of an entity in monetary terms and communicating results to users.* The accounting process consists of two principal activities—measurement and communication.

The measurement process must (1) identify the relevant economic activities of a business, (2) quantify these economic activities, and (3) record the resulting measures in a systematic manner. Measurement is done in monetary terms. In the United States, measurements are stated in U.S. dollars. In other countries, measurements are expressed in the local currency. In Mexico, for example, measurements are stated in pesos, and in most European countries, they are stated in euros.

**THINKING GLOBALLY**

Companies measure their operating performance using the currency of their principal place of business. The **Johnson & Johnson Company**, a well-known maker of baby shampoo and Band-Aids, is headquartered in New Jersey, and reports its financial results using the U.S. dollar. On the other hand, **Moet Hennessy-Louis Vuitton**, the luxury goods manufacturer, is headquartered in Paris, France, and reports its financial results using the euro. Some companies prepare "convenience translations" of their financial statements in the currency and language of other countries so that potential foreign investors can more readily understand the company's financial performance and condition.

The purpose of accounting is to provide useful financial information, and the communication process is extremely important. Accordingly, the accounting process

(1) prepares financial reports to meet the needs of the user and (2) helps interpret the financial results for that user. To provide reports that serve users effectively, managers must be aware of how these users are likely to apply the reports. The needs of the various users differ; as such, there are different types of accounting reports. Managers employ various techniques to help users interpret the content of reports. These techniques include the way the report is formatted, the use of charts and graphs to highlight trends, and the calculation of ratios to emphasize important financial relations. Exhibit 1-4 portrays the accounting process.

**EXHIBIT 1-4**

Measuring Economic Activity

Communicating Economic Results

## GENERALLY ACCEPTED ACCOUNTING PRINCIPLES

It is important that financial statements be prepared under a set of rules that is understood by the users of reports. Imagine if every business were free to determine exactly how it measured and communicated its financial health and operating performance. How would a user of this information be able to compare one company's results to another if each played by a different set of rules? Financial statement users who rely on accounting data expect that all companies will follow the same standards and procedures when preparing their statements. These standards and procedures are called **generally accepted accounting principles**.

Generally accepted accounting principles (GAAP) are not immutable laws like those in the physical sciences. Instead, they are *guides to action* that can (and do) change over time. Sometimes specific accounting principles must be altered or new principles formulated to fit a changing set of economic circumstances or changes in business practices. For instance, there existed no generally accepted accounting principles to account for the emerging dot.com companies; and consequently, the business community had to create a set of guidelines for companies such as **Amazon.com** and **eBay** to measure and communicate their financial results.

The most prominent organization concerned with the development of generally accepted accounting principles in the United States is the **Financial Accounting Standards Board (FASB)**. The FASB is a nongovernmental entity whose pronouncements establish U.S. GAAP. The FASB consists of a five-member board and follows a process that allows for input from interested parties as it considers a new or changed accounting principle. A new or changed principle requires the support of at least a majority of the board members.

Accounting principles, however, do differ among countries of the world. Energized by the continuing growth of international business, efforts are underway to create greater uniformity in worldwide accounting principles.

**A.K.A.**    Generally accepted accounting principles are often referred to as GAAP (pronounced like the clothing store "Gap").

# FINANCIAL STATEMENTS

**LEARNING OBJECTIVE 5**

**Describe** the accounting equation and each financial statement.

## BALANCE SHEET

There are four basic financial statements: the balance sheet, the income statement, the statement of retained earnings, and the statement of cash flows. Each financial statement begins with a heading. The heading provides the name of the company, the name of the financial statement, and the date or time period of the statement.

The **balance sheet** is a listing of a firm's assets, liabilities, and stockholders' equity as of a given date, usually the end of an accounting period. The balance sheet depicts a framework called the **accounting equation**. The accounting equation states that the sum of a business's economic resources must equal the sum of any claims on those resources. That is, a business obtains resources that it utilizes in its operations from outside sources, principally creditors and stockholders, who maintain claims on those resources. Consequently, the accounting equation can be written as:

**A.K.A.**  The balance sheet is also referred to as the statement of financial position.

$$\text{Economic resources of a company} = \text{Claims on economic resources}$$

Assets refer to a company's resources, liabilities refer to creditor claims on those resources, and stockholders' equity refers to owner claims on those resources. Using these terms, the accounting equation can be reformulated as:

$$\text{Assets} = \text{Liabilities} + \text{Stockholders' equity}$$

This equation states that the firm's assets equals the sum of its liabilities plus its stockholders' equity—see Exhibit 1-5. Throughout the accounting process, the accounting equation must always remain in balance.

**Hint:** Only resources that can be expressed in monetary terms are included among the assets reported on the balance sheet. There exist some assets that cannot be expressed in monetary terms, such as the value of a company's workforce, and, therefore, are not reported on a balance sheet.

| **EXHIBIT 1-5** | **Accounting Equation for a Business** | | | | |
|---|---|---|---|---|---|
| **Economic Terms** | Economic Resources | = | Creditor Claims on Resources | + | Stockholder (Owner) Claims on Resources |
| **Business Terms** | Assets | = | Liabilities | + | Stockholders' Equity |

**Assets** are the economic resources of a business that can be expressed in monetary terms. Assets take many forms. Cash is an asset, as are claims to receive cash payments from customers for goods or services provided, called accounts receivable. Other types of assets include inventory, supplies, land, buildings, and equipment. The key characteristic of any asset is that it represents a probable future economic benefit to a business.

**Liabilities** are the obligations or debts that a business must pay in cash or in goods and services at some future time as a consequence of past transactions or events. For example, a business can borrow money and sign a promissory note agreeing to repay the borrowed amount in six months. The business reports this obligation as a liability called notes payable. Similarly, if a business owes money to various suppliers for goods or services already provided, it is called accounts payable, or if it owes wages to its employees for work already performed, it is called wages payable. The business reports these obligations on its balance sheet.

**Stockholders' equity** refers to the ownership (stockholder) claims on the assets of the business. Stockholders' equity represents a *residual claim* on a business's assets; that is, it is a claim on the assets of a business that remain after all liabilities to creditors have been satisfied. For this reason, stockholders' equity is sometimes referred to as a business's **net assets**, where net assets equal the difference between the total assets and total liabilities. In equation format,

> **A.K.A.** The accounting equation is also called the *balance sheet equation.*

$$\textbf{Assets} - \textbf{Liabilities} \ = \ \textbf{Stockholders' equity}$$

and,

$$\textbf{Net assets} \ = \ \textbf{Stockholders' equity}$$

Exhibit 1-6 shows the balance sheet for WebWork, Inc., which illustrates the typical format for a balance sheet. Total assets ($84,560) are equal to the sum of liabilities ($42,210) and stockholders' equity ($42,350). This equality must always exist as required by the accounting equation.

> **Hint:** Final totals in the financial statements are double underlined. Follow this format whenever asked to prepare a financial statement.

| EXHIBIT 1-6 | Balance Sheet for WebWork, Inc. |
|---|---|

**WEBWORK, INC.**
**Balance Sheet**
**December 31, 2011**

| Assets | | Liabilities | |
|---|---|---|---|
| Cash | $40,590 | Accounts payable | $ 2,850 |
| Accounts receivable | 1,490 | Interest payable | 300 |
| Office supplies | 1,530 | Wages payable | 810 |
| Prepaid rent | 9,000 | Unearned revenue | 2,250 |
| | | Notes payable | 36,000 |
| Office equipment, net | 31,950 | Total liabilities | 42,210 |
| | | **Stockholders' Equity** | |
| | | Common stock | 30,000 |
| | | Retained earnings | 12,350 |
| | | Total stockholders' equity | 42,350 |
| Total assets | $84,560 | Total liabilities and stockholders' equity | $84,560 |

| Concept ⟶ | Method ⟶ | Assessment |
|---|---|---|
| What form of financing does a company use to finance its assets? | The balance sheet provides information regarding the various forms of financing, both debt financing and equity financing.<br><br>Compare the amount of liabilities appearing on the balance sheet to the amount of stockholders' equity appearing on the balance sheet. | A higher ratio of liabilities to equity implies a higher use of creditor financing, and vice versa. Creditor financing is viewed by users as more risky for the business. |

**TAKEAWAY 1.1**

## INCOME STATEMENT

The **income statement** reports the results of operations for a business for a given time period, usually a quarter or a year. The income statement lists the revenues and expenses

> **A.K.A.** The income statement is also called the statement of operations, the statement of income, and the earnings statement.

of the business. **Sales revenue** are increases to a company's resources that result when goods or services are provided to customers. The amount of sales revenue earned is measured by the value of the assets received in exchange for the goods or services delivered.

**Expenses** are decreases in a company's resources from generating revenue. Expenses are generally measured by the value of the assets used up or exchanged as a result of a business's operating activities. Common examples of expenses include the cost of the items sold, referred to as cost of goods sold, selling expenses, marketing expenses, administrative expenses, interest expense, and income taxes.

When sales revenue exceeds total expenses, the resulting amount is called **net income**; when total expenses exceed sales revenue, the resulting amount is called a net loss. Exhibit 1-7 shows the income statement for WebWork. It reported net income of $12,850 for December because its revenue exceeded its expenses by that amount.

| **EXHIBIT 1-7** | **Income Statement for WebWork, Inc.** | |
|---|---|---|
| | **WEBWORK, INC.** | |
| | **Income Statement** | |
| | **For Month Ended December 31, 2011** | |
| Revenue | | |
| Fees revenue............................................................ | | $19,150 |
| Expenses | | |
| Wage expense ............................................... | $ 2,430 | |
| Supplies expense ........................................... | 1,320 | |
| Rent expense ................................................ | 1,800 | |
| Depreciation expense...................................... | 450 | |
| Interest expense ............................................ | 300 | |
| Total expenses........................................... | | 6,300 |
| Net income........................................................... | | $12,850 |

| | Concept | ⟶ | Method | ⟶ | Assessment |
|---|---|---|---|---|---|
| **TAKEAWAY 1.2** | Is a company profitable? | | The income statement reports a company's performance for a given period of time.<br><br>Compare reported sales revenue to reported expenses. | | Reported sales revenue in excess of reported expenses yields net income, implying a profitable company. If expenses exceed revenue, the company is operating at a net loss. |

### STATEMENT OF RETAINED EARNINGS

The **statement of retained earnings** reports the events causing an increase or decrease in a business's retained earnings during a given time period. The statement starts with retained earnings as of the beginning of the period, then reports the events causing increases and decreases in retained earnings, and concludes with retained earnings at the end of the period. Retained earnings reflect the amount of a company's net income that is retained in the business for corporate use, rather than distributed to stockholders as a dividend. Retained earnings are increased when operations produce net income and decreased when operations produce a net loss. Retained earnings also decrease when a company pays a dividend to its stockholders.

For December, the retained earnings of WebWork increased by $12,850 due to net income, while it decreased by $500 due to a dividend payment to stockholders. At the end of December, the company's retained earnings totaled $12,350—see Exhibit 1-8. Many companies present their statement of retained earnings as part of a more inclusive financial statement called the **statement of stockholders' equity**, which we explain in Chapter 2. The statement of stockholders' equity presents information on all of the events causing a change in stockholders' equity during a given time period, including changes to retained earnings.

| EXHIBIT 1-8 | Statement of Retained Earnings for WebWork, Inc. |
|---|---|

**WEBWORK, INC.**
**Statement of Retained Earnings**
**For Month Ended December 31, 2011**

| | |
|---|---:|
| Retained earnings, December 1, 2011 | $     0 |
| Add: Net income | 12,850 |
| | 12,850 |
| Less: Dividends | 500 |
| Retained earnings, December 31, 2011 | $12,350 |

| Concept ➝ | Method ➝ | Assessment |
|---|---|---|
| What portion of a company's current period net income is distributed to its stockholders, and what portion is retained in the company? | The statement of retained earnings reports both a company's net income and the amount of dividends distributed to stockholders.  Compare the company's dividends to its net income. | A higher ratio of dividends to net income implies that a company is distributing more of its net income to its stockholders, whereas a lower ratio of dividends to net income implies that a company is retaining more of its income for other purposes, such as growing its business. |

**TAKEAWAY 1.3**

## STATEMENT OF CASH FLOWS

The **statement of cash flows** reports a business's cash inflows and cash outflows during a given period of time. The cash flows are grouped into the three business activities of operating, investing, and financing. The cash flow from operating activities reveals the cash spent on operating expenses and the cash received from the sale of goods or services. The cash flow from investing activities includes the cash payments and receipts when a business buys and sells long-term assets that it uses in its operations. The cash flow from financing activities reports the issuances and repurchases of shares in a business and the amounts borrowed and repaid to creditors.

The statement of cash flows for WebWork is in Exhibit 1-9 and reveals that its cash increased by $40,590 in December, and that the principal source of this cash was issuance of shares of stock ($30,000) and bank borrowings ($36,000). The cash flow from operations was positive and the cash flow from investing was negative for the company during December (negative cash flows from investing activities is not unusual for a start-up company).

| EXHIBIT 1-9 | Statement of Cash Flows for WebWork, Inc. |
|---|---|

**WEBWORK, INC.**
**Statement of Cash Flows**
**For Month Ended December 31, 2011**

| | | |
|---|---:|---:|
| **Cash flows from operating activities** | | |
| Cash received from clients | $19,910 | |
| Cash paid to employees and suppliers | (1,620) | |
| Cash paid for rent | (10,800) | |
| Cash provided by operating activities | | $ 7,490 |
| **Cash flows from investing activities** | | |
| Purchase of furniture and equipment | (32,400) | |
| Cash used by investing activities | | (32,400) |
| **Cash flows from financing activities** | | |
| Stock issued | 30,000 | |
| Borrowing from bank | 36,000 | |
| Cash dividends | (500) | |
| Cash provided by financing activities | | 65,500 |
| Net increase in cash | | 40,590 |
| Cash at December 1, 2011 | | 0 |
| Cash at December 31, 2011 | | $40,590 |

| Concept | → | Method | → | Assessment |
|---|---|---|---|---|
| **TAKEAWAY 1.4** | What are the major sources and uses of a company's cash? | The statement of cash flows reports a company's sources and uses of cash separated into three activities: operating, investing, and financing.

Identify a company's sources and uses of cash as reported in the statement of cash flows. | | Sources of cash are reported as positive numbers and uses of cash are reported as negative numbers. Larger positive numbers represent major cash sources and larger negative numbers represent major cash uses. |

## RELATIONS AMONG THE FINANCIAL STATEMENTS

Exhibit 1-10 indicates that the income statement, the statement of retained earnings, the balance sheet, and the statement of cash flows complement one another. That is, the financial statements *articulate*. To illustrate, refer to the financial statements of WebWork in Exhibit 1-11. Observe that Ⓐ, the company's net income (or net loss) for a period is an input to the statement of retained earnings, and that Ⓑ, the ending retained earnings is an input to the balance sheet. The statement of cash flows Ⓒ explains the change in the cash balance on the balance sheet for a period. When financial statements are prepared, the sequence suggested by these relations is customarily followed; that is, (1) the income statement is first prepared, followed by (2) the statement of retained earnings, then (3) the balance sheet, and finally (4) the statement of cash flows.

**EXHIBIT 1-10    Financial Statement Links across Time**

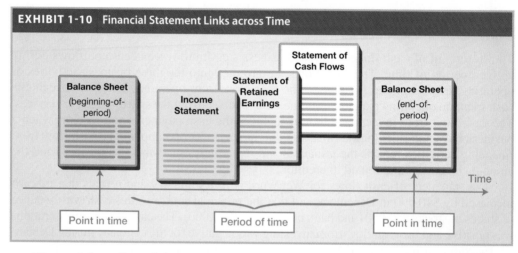

Three of these financial statements present information covering a specific period of time: the income statement, the statement of retained earnings, and the statement of cash flows. For this reason, these financial statements are referred to as **period-in-time statements**. In contrast, the balance sheet reports information as of a specific date. The balance sheet, therefore, is referred to as a **point-in-time statement**.

## Your Turn!    1.5

Kanzu Corporation started business on January 1, 2011. The following information was compiled by Kanzu as of December 31, 2011.

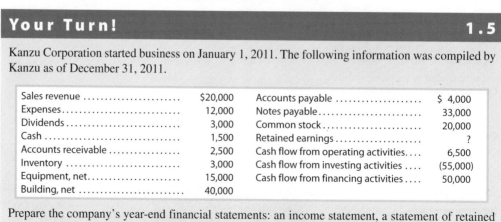

| | | | |
|---|---|---|---|
| Sales revenue | $20,000 | Accounts payable | $ 4,000 |
| Expenses | 12,000 | Notes payable | 33,000 |
| Dividends | 3,000 | Common stock | 20,000 |
| Cash | 1,500 | Retained earnings | ? |
| Accounts receivable | 2,500 | Cash flow from operating activities | 6,500 |
| Inventory | 3,000 | Cash flow from investing activities | (55,000) |
| Equipment, net | 15,000 | Cash flow from financing activities | 50,000 |
| Building, net | 40,000 | | |

Prepare the company's year-end financial statements: an income statement, a statement of retained earnings, a balance sheet, and a statement of cash flows.

**The solution is on page 49.**

**EXHIBIT 1-11   Financial Statements for WebWork, Inc.**

| WEBWORK, INC.<br>Income Statement<br>For Month Ended December 31, 2011 | | |
|---|---|---|
| **Revenue** | | |
| Fees revenue............. | | $19,150 |
| **Expenses** | | |
| Wage expense ............ | $ 2,430 | |
| Supplies expense ......... | 1,320 | |
| Rent expense ............. | 1,800 | |
| Depreciation expense..... | 450 | |
| Interest expense .......... | 300 | |
| Total expenses......... | | 6,300 |
| Net income................. | | $12,850 |

| WEBWORK, INC.<br>Statement of Retained Earnings<br>For Month Ended December 31, 2011 | |
|---|---|
| Retained earnings, December 1, 2011 .......... | $      0 |
| Add: Net income ............................. | 12,850 |
| | 12,850 |
| Less: Dividends................................ | 500 |
| Retained earnings, December 31, 2011......... | $12,350 |

| WEBWORK, INC.<br>Balance Sheet<br>December 31, 2011 | | | |
|---|---|---|---|
| **Assets** | | **Liabilities** | |
| Cash ...................................... | $40,590 | Accounts payable ............................ | $ 2,850 |
| Accounts receivable ....................... | 1,490 | Interest payable ............................. | 300 |
| Office supplies ........................... | 1,530 | Wages payable .............................. | 810 |
| Prepaid rent.............................. | 9,000 | Unearned revenue ......................... | 2,250 |
| | | Notes payable.............................. | 36,000 |
| Office equipment, net ..................... | $31,950 | Total liabilities............................ | 42,210 |
| | | **Stockholders' Equity** | |
| | | Common stock............................. | 30,000 |
| | | Retained earnings .......................... | 12,350 |
| | | Total stockholders' equity.................... | 42,350 |
| Total assets............................... | $84,560 | Total liabilities and stockholders' equity ....... | $84,560 |

| WEBWORK, INC.<br>Statement of Cash Flows<br>For Month Ended December 31, 2011 | | |
|---|---|---|
| **Cash flows from operating activities** | | |
| Cash received from clients............................................. | $19,910 | |
| Cash paid to employees and suppliers ................................. | (1,620) | |
| Cash paid for rent ................................................... | (10,800) | |
| Cash provided by operating activities................................. | | $ 7,490 |
| **Cash flows from investing activities** | | |
| Purchase of furniture and equipment ................................. | (32,400) | |
| Cash used by investing activities....................................... | | (32,400) |
| **Cash flows from financing activities** | | |
| Stock issued ........................................................ | 30,000 | |
| Borrowing from bank................................................. | 36,000 | |
| Cash dividends....................................................... | (500) | |
| Cash provided by financing activities ................................. | | 65,500 |
| Net increase in cash .................................................. | | 40,590 |
| Cash at December 1, 2011 ............................................. | | 0 |
| Cash at December 31, 2011 ............................................. | | $40,590 |

# ACTUAL FINANCIAL STATEMENTS— COLUMBIA SPORTSWEAR

Let's look at the financial statements of **Columbia Sportswear Company**. The actual Columbia financial statements are in Appendix A at the end of this book and are summarized here in Exhibits 1-12 through 1-15. Columbia reports more than one year of data in its financial statements. This enables users to observe trends in financial position and operating performance. Columbia's reported numbers are rounded to the nearest thousand dollars. For example, cash appears on the balance sheet as $386,664 when the exact amount as been rounded to $386,664,000.

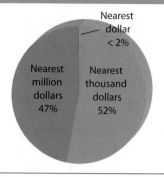
## COLUMBIA SPORTSWEAR—INCOME STATEMENT

Columbia's income statement is presented in Exhibit 1-12. The statement begins with the business's name, statement title, and time period or date to which the statement applies. For Columbia, total revenue in 2009 is reported to be $1,254,510,000 (remember amounts are rounded to the nearest $1,000). Next, Columbia subtracts a series of expenses totaling $1,187,489,000, yielding net income of $67,021,000. This is a decrease of $28,026,000 from Columbia's 2008 net income of $95,047,000. It looks like Columbia's management team will need to answer to the company's stockholders to justify a 29.5 percent decline ([95,047 − 67,021]/95,047) in net income.

**EXHIBIT 1-12**    Columbia Sportswear Income Statement

**COLUMBIA SPORTSWEAR COMPANY**
**Income Statement**
**For Years Ended December 31, 2009, and December 31, 2008**

| (In thousands) | 2009 | 2008 |
|---|---|---|
| Revenue | | |
| Sales......................................................... | $1,244,023 | $1,317,835 |
| Other revenue ..................................................... | 10,487 | 13,524 |
| Total revenue.................................................. | 1,254,510 | 1,331,359 |
| Expenses | | |
| Cost of sales ......................................................... | 719,945 | 750,024 |
| Selling, general, and administrative........................................ | 444,715 | 430,350 |
| Other expenses ....................................................... | | 24,742 |
| Income tax expense.................................................... | 22,829 | 31,196 |
| Total expenses..................................................... | 1,187,489 | 1,236,312 |
| Net income........................................................... | $ 67,021 | $ 95,047 |

**CORPORATE SOCIAL RESPONSIBILITY**    **Reporting on Triple Bottom Line**

Companies worldwide are focused on more than just the bottom line. Research has shown that financial responsibility goes hand in hand with social responsibility. This is labeled a "virtuous cycle" in which financial success provides the means to act socially responsible, and acting socially responsible increases a company's financial performance; in a sense doing good and doing well reinforce each other. Companies also know that it is very difficult to manage things that are not measured. Financial statements are not well suited for measuring social performance. To aid in the pursuit of socially responsible behavior, accountants have developed a **triple bottom line** framework in which the single bottom line of financial performance is supplemented with a social bottom line and an environmental bottom line. The triple bottom line standard for urban and community accounting has been ratified by the United Nations and has become widely used in public sector accounting.

## COLUMBIA SPORTSWEAR—STATEMENT OF RETAINED EARNINGS

Columbia's statement of retained earnings appears in Exhibit 1-13. We extracted Columbia's statement of retained earnings from its statement of stockholders' equity to emphasize two important concepts: (1) the relation between the income statement and the balance sheet and (2) the components of retained earnings. Retained earnings represents the net income of a business that has not been distributed to stockholders in the form of dividends. Retained earnings are increased when a business earns an income and that income is not distributed. Retained earnings are decreased when a company has a loss or when it pays a dividend.

Columbia's statement of retained earnings in Exhibit 1-13 begins with its ending retained earnings from 2008 of $942,609,000. Its net income of $67,021,000 from 2009 is added. Can you find this amount on Columbia's income statement in Exhibit 1-12? Next, the portion of these earnings that was distributed to Columbia's stockholders in 2009 as a dividend ($13,238,000) is subtracted to yield an ending retained earnings balance of $996,392,000 as of December 31, 2009. Can you find this amount on Columbia's balance sheet in Exhibit 1-14?

| EXHIBIT 1-13 | Columbia Sportswear Statement of Retained Earnings |
|---|---|

**COLUMBIA SPORTSWEAR COMPANY**
**Statement of Retained Earnings**
**For Year Ended December 31, 2009 (in thousands)**

| | |
|---|---:|
| Retained earnings, December 31, 2008............................................... | $ 942,609 |
| Add: Net income ...................................................................... | 67,021 |
| | 1,009,630 |
| Less: Dividends and other............................................................. | 13,238 |
| Retained earnings, December 31, 2009............................................... | $ 996,392 |

## COLUMBIA SPORTSWEAR—BALANCE SHEET

Columbia's balance sheet is shown in Exhibit 1-14 and reports the company's assets, liabilities, and stockholders' equity. Columbia's assets totaled $1,212,883,000 at year-end

| EXHIBIT 1-14 | Columbia Sportswear Balance Sheet |
|---|---|

**COLUMBIA SPORTSWEAR COMPANY**
**Balance Sheet**
**December 31, 2009, and December 31, 2008**

| (In thousands) | 2009 | 2008 |
|---|---:|---:|
| **Assets** | | |
| Cash ......................................................................... | $ 386,664 | $ 230,617 |
| Investments................................................................. | 22,759 | 22,433 |
| Accounts receivable ........................................................ | 226,548 | 299,585 |
| Inventories.................................................................. | 222,161 | 256,312 |
| Prepaid expenses........................................................... | 32,030 | 29,705 |
| Property, plant, and equipment, net......................................... | 235,440 | 229,693 |
| Other assets................................................................ | 87,281 | 79,891 |
| Total assets................................................................ | $1,212,883 | $1,148,236 |
| **Liabilities and Stockholders' Equity** | | |
| Liabilities | | |
|     Accounts payable ..................................................... | $ 102,494 | $ 104,354 |
|     Accrued liabilities .................................................... | 67,312 | 58,085 |
|     Income taxes payable ................................................. | 26,714 | 29,130 |
|     Other liabilities....................................................... | 19,135 | 12,577 |
|     Total liabilities ...................................................... | 215,655 | 204,146 |
| Stockholders' Equity | | |
|     Common stock........................................................ | 836 | 1,481 |
|     Retained earnings..................................................... | 996,392 | 942,609 |
|     Total stockholders' equity ............................................ | 997,228 | 944,090 |
| Total liabilities and stockholders' equity ..................................... | $1,212,883 | $1,148,236 |

2009, with the largest asset being cash of $386,664,000. Looking at total assets reveals that Columbia's size remained about the same from 2008 to 2009, with total assets growing by about $65 million, or approximately 5.6 percent.

Columbia's balance sheet indicates that the company principally depends on stockholders' equity to finance its operations since liabilities totaled only $215,655,000 at 2009 year-end, or less than 18 percent of total assets. Columbia has been quite profitable in the past and its board of directors has chosen not to distribute much of its net income.

## COLUMBIA SPORTSWEAR—STATEMENT OF CASH FLOWS

Columbia's statement of cash flows is in Exhibit 1-15. This statement shows that Columbia's cash balance increased during 2009 by $156,047,000, from $230,617,000 on December 31, 2008, to $386,664,000 on December 31, 2009. Can you find these ending cash balances on Columbia's balance sheet in Exhibit 1-14?

The statement of cash flows reveals how Columbia acquired its cash and how it was used. We see that its day-to-day operations generated $214,372,000 of cash. So if Columbia's operations generated all this cash, why did its cash balance only go up by $156,047,000? The statement reveals that uses of cash included $33,043,000 for capital expenditures and $22,331,000 for payment of dividends.

We devote considerable time to understanding and analyzing financial statements such as those of Columbia's in later chapters. However, before we end our current discussion we need to consider other information that is presented in a company's annual report along with the financial statements to help a user understand a company's financial statements and its performance.

| EXHIBIT 1-15 | Columbia Sportswear Statement of Cash Flows | | |
|---|---|---|---|
| **COLUMBIA SPORTSWEAR COMPANY** Statement of Cash Flows For Years Ended December 31, 2009, and December 31, 2008 | | | |
| (In thousands) | | 2009 | 2008 |
| Cash flows from operating activities | | | |
| Cash receipts from operating activities.................................... | | $1,327,547 | $1,321,923 |
| Cash payments for operating activities.................................... | | (1,113,175) | (1,176,993) |
| Cash provided by operating activities .................................. | | 214,372 | 144,930 |
| Cash flows from investing activities | | | |
| Net sales (purchases) of investment securities............................. | | (142) | 59,228 |
| Net capital expenditures ................................................. | | (33,043) | (47,528) |
| Cash provided (used) by investing activities ........................... | | (33,185) | 11,700 |
| Cash flows from financing activities | | | |
| Repurchase of common stock ........................................... | | (7,313) | (80,377) |
| Cash dividends paid...................................................... | | (22,331) | (22,098) |
| Other financing activities................................................ | | 4,504 | (15,488) |
| Cash used in financing activities....................................... | | (25,140) | (117,963) |
| Net increase in cash ...................................................... | | 156,047 | 38,667 |
| Cash at beginning of year................................................. | | 230,617 | 191,950 |
| Cash at end of year ....................................................... | | $ 386,664 | $ 230,617 |

# ADDITIONAL INFORMATION

**LEARNING OBJECTIVE 6**

**Explain** additional disclosures that accompany financial statements.

Columbia Sportswear Company, like all publicly traded companies in the United States, must file an **annual report** called a Form **10-K** with the U.S. Securities and Exchange Commission (SEC). Some companies also mail a less detailed version of their annual report to their stockholders. The four financial statements explained in this chapter are essential components of this report. Additional components of the annual report are the Management Discussion and Analysis, the notes to the financial statements, and the auditor's report.

## MANAGEMENT DISCUSSION AND ANALYSIS

The **Management Discussion and Analysis**, or MD&A, contains management's interpretation of the company's recent performance and financial condition. This interpretation helps financial statement users gain a context within which to place their own analysis and interpretation of the numbers that appear in the financial statements.

The MD&A is also where a company's management provides its opinion regarding what the future holds for its business. Discussions of future opportunities and risks are called "forward-looking" and are helpful to any financial statement user interested in learning about such things as potential new markets for the company's products or potential new competitors. Obviously these forward-looking statements are subjective in nature, and the statement users must do an independent analysis of the financial statements.

The following is a short excerpt from Columbia's MD&A.

**Strategy and Outlook**

Our business, like other branded consumer product companies, is heavily dependent upon discretionary consumer spending patterns. Our net sales volumes have been negatively affected by the volatility of the global economy and its impact on consumer purchasing behavior, and retailers' behavior related to advance orders, order cancellations, and seasonal reorders. The current macro-economic environment has caused tightening of credit for some of our wholesale customers, independent distributors, and consumers and a significant slowing of retail sales. This has resulted in, and could continue to cause, a more cautious approach by many of our wholesale customers and independent distributors when placing advance orders for seasonal products and reducing, delaying delivery of, or cancelling advance orders placed in earlier periods. We expect our retail revenues to partially offset some of this anticipated wholesale revenue decline.

## NOTES TO FINANCIAL STATEMENTS

A skilled financial statement user wants to know more than just the bare numbers reported in financial statements. That user also wants to know assumptions and estimates that were used in preparing the statements, the measurement procedures that were followed, and the details behind certain summary numbers. **Notes to the financial statements**, which are both quantitative as well as qualitative, provide a great deal more information than just the numbers alone. For example, notes usually contain a description regarding how the company determined the value of its inventory, a detailed chart to explain the property, plant, and equipment account, and a description of any pending lawsuits. No analysis of the annual report is complete without a careful reading of the notes to the financial statements. The following is a short excerpt from Columbia's notes:

**Accounts receivable**  Accounts receivable have been reduced by an allowance for doubtful accounts. The Company makes ongoing estimates of the uncollectability of accounts receivable and maintains an allowance for estimated losses resulting from the inability of the Company's customers to make required payments. The allowance for doubtful accounts was $9,542,000 and $7,369,000 at December 31, 2008 and 2007, respectively.

## AUDITOR'S REPORT

The report of the independent auditor, commonly referred to as the **auditor's report**, describes the activities undertaken by a company's independent auditor and reports that auditor's opinion regarding whether the financial statements fairly present the results of the company's operations and financial health. A short excerpt from the auditor's report included with Columbia Sportswear's annual report follows. **Deloitte & Touche**, which is Columbia's independent auditor, reports that the financial statements of Columbia are, in its opinion, fairly presented. The independent auditor has intentionally avoided using language such as the statements are "correctly presented" or are "exactly correct." As we will see in subsequent chapters, the financial statements are prepared only after the management team makes a number of assumptions, estimates, and accounting policy decisions. As a consequence, it is inappropriate to describe the statements as being right or wrong since the reported numbers are dependent on the accounting policies selected and the assumptions and estimates made by management.

---

**Report of Independent Registered Public Accounting Firm**

In our opinion, such consolidated financial statements present fairly, in all material respects, the financial position of the Company as of December 31, 2008 and 2007, and the results of its operations and its cash flows for each of the three years in the period ended December 31, 2008, in conformity with accounting principles generally accepted in the United States of America. Also, in our opinion, such a financial statement schedule, when considered in relation to the basic consolidated financial statements taken as a whole, presents fairly, in all material respects, the information set forth therein.

*DELOITTE & TOUCHE LLP*

---

## Your Turn!                                                                1.6

Match each of the items in the left column with the appropriate annual report component where we would find that item, from the right column.

1. An opinion regarding the fair presentation of financial statements.
2. Information regarding the procedures followed to value a company's assets.
3. A discussion of new markets that a company plans to enter.

a. Management Discussion and Analysis
b. Notes to the Financial Statements
c. Auditor's report

**The solution is on page 49.**

---

### WORKING WITH THE TAKEAWAYS

You have just learned that you inherited a large sum of money. You know that it is important to invest this money wisely, and you have decided to invest in the shares of several different companies. One of those companies is the Columbia Sportswear Company.

**Required**

Answer the following questions regarding your potential investment in Columbia Sportswear shares:

a. Should you request financial statements from the company, and if so, which ones?
b. Is it important that the financial statements be audited by an independent auditor? Explain.
c. What does each of the four financial statements tell you about Columbia's financial health or operating performance?

**Solution**

a. You should request an annual report from Columbia Sportswear containing the income statement, the statement of retained earnings, the balance sheet, and a statement of cash flows. Alternatively, you can download this data directly from the company's Website or from the SEC site.
b. It is important that these statements be audited by an independent auditor such as Deloitte and Touche, the auditors of Columbia's financial statements. The auditor is able to provide a level of assurance that the financial statements are presented fairly and can be relied upon for investment decision-making purposes.
c. Each of the four financial statements provides different information that, taken together, provides a more complete view of the financial condition and operating performance of the company. The income statement reports revenues and expenses—that is, information regarding the company's profitability. The statement of retained earnings provides information regarding the company's decision as to how much net income will be distributed to its stockholders and how much will

be retained in the company. The balance sheet reports Columbia's assets, liabilities, and stockholders' equity to help you evaluate the company's financial position. Finally, the statement of cash flows reports the company's sources and uses of cash to help you determine the company's ability to generate future cash flow and details how those cash flows are likely to be used.

# APPENDIX 1A: International Accounting Principles

A topic of considerable importance to the world's financial community is the development and implementation of a global set of accounting principles. The phrase **international accounting principles** refers to a set of accounting guidelines that are acceptable for the preparation of financial statements worldwide. Two major reasons for interest in a global set of accounting principles are (1) to improve the operational efficiency of international capital markets and (2) to reduce the information-generating costs of multinational companies.

LEARNING OBJECTIVE 7

Appendix 1A:
**Discuss** international accounting principles and their formulation.

## IMPROVE THE OPERATIONAL EFFICIENCY OF INTERNATIONAL CAPITAL MARKETS

Accompanying the movement to a global economy has been the development of an international capital market. A U.S. company in need of funds, for example, can seek financing in one or more foreign countries, or a foreign company can seek financing in the United States. Similarly, a U.S. investor can invest in foreign securities, or a foreign investor can invest in U.S. securities. The movement of capital across borders is sizable, amounting to trillions of dollars each year.

At present, there exist differences in the accounting principles used by some countries. For example, while the United States follows U.S. GAAP, the United Kingdom follows the International Financial Reporting Standards (IFRS) promulgated by the International Accounting Standards Board (IASB). These differences create barriers to, and cause inefficiencies in, the operation of the international capital market. For example, some foreign companies are unwilling to offer their securities in the United States because they do not want to incur the costs of restating their financial data using U.S. accounting principles. In 2007, the SEC decided to allow foreign companies desiring to raise capital in the United States to file their financial reports with the agency using IFRS. Nonetheless, a concern for foreign companies is the unwillingness of U.S. investors to buy shares in companies whose financial data they might not fully understand. U.S. investors and lenders effectively incur extra costs as they adjust their analyses to compensate for the lack of comparability in the underlying accounting principles. Lenders may even increase the rate of interest charged to borrowers to compensate for the uncertainty created by the use of different, and not completely understood, accounting principles. A set of international accounting principles, understood, applied, and interpreted consistently throughout the world would eliminate these types of problems and encourage the flow of capital across borders.

Even the existence of large amounts of capital currently flowing into the international capital market does not reduce the need for increased harmonization of accounting principles throughout the world. Accounting's role in the allocation of resources in capital markets is to provide investors and creditors with relevant and reliable financial information so that informed decisions can be made as to where resources should be allocated. If the underlying accounting data are not comparable across countries, as is currently the case, then it is likely that investors and creditors are not making optimal resource allocation decisions.

### Reduce Costs of Multinational Companies

A multinational company can have subsidiary units located outside the firm's home country. To the extent that each country in which a subsidiary is located has different accounting principles, the multinational's cost of generating accounting information is increased. For example, a different accounting system must be established for each country in which the firm operates so that local reporting requirements can be met, company personnel must be trained in the similarities and differences in accounting principles used by subsidiary units, and subsidiary financial data must be converted to the home country accounting principles whenever the data from all units are to be merged into one overall set of consolidated financial statements. The costs associated with these activities would be eliminated with the implementation of a global set of international accounting principles.

## OBSTACLES TO INTERNATIONAL ACCOUNTING PRINCIPLES

Getting a set of international accounting principles identified and accepted by different countries is a difficult task. For example, after nearly 30 years of debate, the member countries of the European

Union (EU) finally agreed that, beginning in 2005, all EU companies would adopt IFRS for purposes of preparing their consolidated financial statements. Among the obstacles that the EU faced for 30 years included (1) cultural differences, (2) differences among countries as to who establishes accounting principles, and (3) nationalistic tendencies of accounting principle-setting bodies.

## Cultural Differences

Countries differ in terms of their economic environment, political structure, and language. These differences contribute to the diversity in accounting principles among countries, and this diversity makes it more difficult to agree on a common set of principles.

An economic environment with a high rate of inflation, for example, may adopt an accounting principle that requires inflation adjustments to the financial statements, whereas a country with a low inflation rate may not require such adjustments. As an illustration, Mexican accounting principles require inflation adjustments to the financial statements produced by Mexican companies, but U.S. principles do not. Similarly, an economy dominated by publicly held corporations, such as the United States, may require accounting principles that are not needed in an economy influenced by small, family-owned businesses, such as Italy.

Some political systems place more emphasis on private ownership of property than do other systems, and this can lead to differences in accounting principles. The relation between tax law and accounting principles also differs among countries. In some countries, tax returns must conform to financial statements, such as in Germany and Japan, whereas in other countries, such as Canada and the United States, tax returns and financial statements can differ significantly.

Language differences can also create problems in establishing a uniformly understood set of international accounting principles. Accounting contains many technical terms and not all languages can easily assimilate the fine points of technical definitions. Also, the interpretation of certain concepts, such as the *timeliness* of reporting or the *reliability* of data, can differ among countries.

## Differences in National Principle-Setting Bodies

The nature of the professional group with primary responsibility for formulating accounting principles varies from one country to the next. The group can be a committee in the private sector, such as the Financial Accounting Standards Board in the United States and the Accounting Standards Committee in Canada, or it can be a governmental body (in Germany, for example, Parliament sets accounting standards through the Ministry of Finance), or it can be a combined effort of a private-sector committee and a governmental body. The group's membership can consist only of accountants or it can be a mix of accountants and non-accountants. A governmental body containing bureaucrats is likely to have a different perspective regarding appropriate accounting principles than is a private-sector committee composed of accountants and representatives of the financial community. The variety among countries in the nature and composition of accounting principle-setting bodies contributes to the problem of achieving agreement on international accounting principles.

## Nationalistic Tendencies of Principle-Setting Bodies

To achieve a set of international accounting principles that is acceptable to all countries, each country's principle-setting body will have to compromise its views. These compromises can be difficult to achieve. For example, although U.S. GAAP permits the use of last-in, first-out (LIFO) for purposes of valuing inventory, LIFO is not generally accepted under IFRS. (We will discuss the LIFO method in later chapters.) Thus, before the United States could fully adopt IFRS, the FASB would need to resolve this inconsistency in practice. Further, the appropriate role for a nation's accounting principle-setting body once international principles are in place is still open to question. A strong national principle-setting group, for example, would not want its role to be only that of advocate for its country's interests at the international level. Concerns about compromise and future roles create a tendency in principle-setting bodies to resist, or slow down, the movement toward international harmonization of accounting principles. For substantial progress toward international harmonization to occur, nationalistic attitudes will need to be modified.

## INTERNATIONAL ACCOUNTING STANDARDS BOARD

Although several organizations are working to increase international harmonization in accounting, the organization that has taken the lead in formulating international accounting principles is the *International Accounting Standards Board (IASB)*. Organized in 1973 as the International Accounting Standards Committee, and headquartered in London, the IASB's membership now covers more than 100 professional accounting organizations from more than 100 countries. The IASB has no authoritative status in any country, nor does it have any enforcement powers. Instead, the IASB depends on its members to persuade the principle setters in their home countries that financial statements should comply with IFRS.

The IASB is governed by a 14-member board, and standards must be approved by at least 75 percent of the board's members. Like U.S. GAAP, IFRS permits a range of acceptable practice rather than specifying a single accounting principle for each situation. For the most part, the practices allowed by IFRS are compatible with generally accepted accounting principles (GAAP) in the United States. Notable exceptions include LIFO and the IFRS use of market value to value assets versus the use of the cost principle under U.S. GAAP. Other differences between IFRS and U.S. GAAP are identified in the individual chapters that follow.

## SUMMARY OF LEARNING OBJECTIVES

**Explain business organization and its three forms. (p. 4)**                     LO1

- There are three primary organizational forms that a business can take. They are the sole proprietorship, the partnership, and the corporation.
- A sole proprietorship consists of a single owner. It is the most common form of business and the easiest to establish.
- A partnership is similar to a sole proprietorship except that there is more than one owner. Partnerships are also relatively easy to establish. An advantage of the partnership form over the sole proprietorship is the broader set of skills and resources that multiple partners can bring to an enterprise.
- A corporation is the most complex of the three organizational forms. The advantages of the corporate form of business include the ease of transferring ownership interests and the ease of raising funds. Another advantage is the limited liability protection it offers its owners. A disadvantage of the corporate form is the possibility of double taxation of the company's net income.

**Indicate who uses accounting information. (p. 5)**                     LO2

- Accounting information is important to both internal and external users.
- The process of generating and analyzing data for internal management use is referred to as managerial accounting.
- Financial accounting produces publicly available financial statements for external users including investors, creditors, taxation authorities, regulatory agencies, labor unions, and customers.
- Generally accepted accounting principles (GAAP) are the standards and procedures that guide the preparation of financial statements.
- The Financial Accounting Standards Board (FASB) is an organization in the private sector that has responsibility for formulating generally accepted accounting principles in the United States.

**Describe business activities. (p. 9)**                     LO3

- Companies engage in three types of business activities: operating, investing, and financing.
- Operating activities consist of selling products or providing services to generate sales revenue and using economic resources to manufacture goods or provide services.
- Investing activities consist of those activities needed to provide the infrastructure to run a company's operations. Also included in this activity category are investments of excess cash.
- Financing activities consist of both debt financing and equity financing. Debt financing involves the procurement of a bank loan, whereas equity financing involves the sale of shares of stock to investors.

**Explain the accounting process and generally accepted accounting principles. (p. 10)**                     LO4

- Accounting is the process of measuring the economic activities of an enterprise in money terms and communicating the results to interested parties.
- The basic purpose of accounting is to provide financial information that is useful in making economic decisions.

**Describe the accounting equation and each financial statement. (p. 12)**                     LO5

- The accounting equation, Assets = Liabilities + Stockholders' Equity, is the fundamental framework within which accounting analysis takes place.
  - Assets are the economic resources of a business that can be expressed in money terms.
  - Liabilities are the obligations that a business must pay in money or services in the future as a consequence of past transactions or events.
  - Stockholders' equity is the residual interest of the owners in the assets of a business.

- *Income statement:* Presents a company's sales revenues and expenses for a period of time.
- *Statement of retained earnings:* Reports the financial events causing a change in retained earnings during a period of time, and commonly includes net income and dividends.
- *Balance sheet:* Presents a company's assets, liabilities, and stockholders' equity as of a given date.
- *Statement of cash flows:* Reports a company's cash inflows and outflows during a period of time.

**LO6** **Explain additional disclosures that accompany financial statements. (p. 20)**
In addition to the basic financial statements, the annual report includes Management Discussion and Analysis, notes to the financial statements, and an auditor's report.

- The Management Discussion and Analysis (MD&A) provides management with an opportunity to both analyze past performance and discuss future opportunities and concerns involving a company.
- The notes to the financial statements provide both a quantitative and a qualitative description of a company's financial statements and explain the numbers reported in those financial statements.
- The auditor's report, issued by an independent auditor, provides a degree of assurance that a company's financial statements are presented fairly and can be relied upon for decision-making purposes.

**LO7** **Appendix 1A: Discuss international accounting principles and their formulation. (p. 23)**
- Two major reasons for interest in international accounting principles are:
  - to improve the operational efficiency of international capital markets
  - to reduce the information-generating costs of multinational companies.
- Obstacles to international accounting principles include:
  - cultural differences
  - differences among countries as to who establishes accounting principles
  - nationalistic tendencies of accounting principle-setting bodies.
- International Accounting Standards Board (IASB) has taken the lead in formulating international accounting principles.

## TAKEAWAY: SUMMARY CHART

| | Concept | Method | Assessment |
|---|---|---|---|
| **TAKEAWAY 1.1** | What form of financing does a company use to finance its assets? | The balance sheet provides information regarding the various forms of financing, both debt financing and equity financing.<br><br>Compare the amount of liabilities appearing on the balance sheet to the amount of stockholders' equity appearing on the balance sheet. | A higher ratio of liabilities to stockholders' equity implies a higher use of creditor financing, and vice versa. Creditor financing is viewed by users as more risky for the business. |
| **TAKEAWAY 1.2** | Is a company profitable? | The income statement reports a company's performance for a given period of time.<br><br>Compare reported sales revenue to reported expenses. | Reported sales revenue in excess of reported expenses yields net income, implying a profitable company. If expenses exceed revenue, the company is operating at a net loss. |
| **TAKEAWAY 1.3** | What portion of a company's current period net income is distributed to its stockholders, and what portion is retained in the company? | The statement of retained earnings reports both a company's net income and the amount of dividends distributed to stockholders.<br><br>Compare the company's dividends to its net income. | A higher ratio of dividends to net income implies that a company is distributing more of its net income to it stockholders, whereas a lower ratio of dividends to net income implies that a company is retaining more of its income for other purposes such as growing its business. |

| What are the major sources and uses of a company's cash? | The statement of cash flows reports a company's sources and uses of cash separated into three activities: operating, investing, and financing.<br><br>Identify a company's sources and uses of cash as reported in the statement of cash flows. | Sources of cash are reported as positive numbers and uses of cash are reported as negative numbers. Larger positive numbers represent major cash sources and larger negative numbers represent major cash uses. | TAKEAWAY 1.4 |

## GLOSSARY OF KEY TERMS

**10-K** The report filed annually with the U.S. Securities and Exchange Commission by publicly held companies that reports the financial position and operating performance of the company (p. 20).

**Accounting** The process of measuring the economic activity of a business in money terms and communicating those financial results to interested parties. The purpose of accounting is to provide financial information that is useful in economic decision making (p. 10).

**Accounting equation** An expression of the equivalency of the economic resources and the claims upon those resources of a business, often stated as Assets = Liabilities + Stockholders' Equity (p. 12).

**Annual report** A report filed with the U.S. Securities and Exchange Commission by publicly held companies that reports the financial position and operating performance of the company. A less detailed version is mailed to the company's stockholders (p. 20).

**Assets** The economic resources of a business that can be expressed in money terms (p. 12).

**Auditor's report** The report of the independent auditor that describes the activities undertaken by a company's outside auditor and reports the auditor's opinion regarding whether the financial statements fairly present the results of the company's operations and financial health (p. 21).

**Balance sheet** A financial statement showing a business's assets, liabilities, and stockholders' equity as of a specific date (p. 12).

**Certified public accountant (CPA)** A professional designation given to an accountant who has fulfilled stringent licensing requirements (p. 6).

**Corporate social responsibility** The practice that considers how a corporation's behavior affects its various stakeholders to ensure an adherence to ethical standards (p. 18).

**Corporation** A legal entity created under the laws of a state or the federal government. The owners of a corporation receive shares of stock as evidence of their ownership interest in the company (p. 4).

**Creditor** An individual or financial institution that lends money or services to a company with the expectation of receiving repayment in the future (p. 9).

**Debt financing** A source of financing for a company involving the use of debt, such as a bank loan or the issuance of bonds (p. 9).

**Equity financing** A source of financing for a company involving the sale of shares of common stock (p. 9).

**Ethics** An area of inquiry dealing with the values, rules, and justifications that govern an individual's way of life or a corporation's behavior (p. 7).

**Expenses** Decreases in stockholders' equity incurred by a firm during the process of generating its sales revenues (p. 14).

**Financial accounting** The area of accounting dealing with the preparation of financial statements showing a business's results of operations, financial position, and cash flow (p. 6).

**Financial Accounting Standards Board (FASB)** A private, not-for-profit organization whose task is to develop generally accepted accounting principles in the United States (p. 11).

**Financing activities** Cash flow activities that include obtaining cash by issuing debt, the repayment of debt, obtaining cash by the issuance of common stock, the repurchase of stock, and the payment of dividends (p. 9).

**Forensic accounting** A branch of accounting that involves investigations that result from actual or anticipated disputes such as criminal activity (p. 8).

**Generally accepted accounting principles (GAAP)** A set of standards and procedures that guide the preparation of financial statements (p. 11).

**Income statement** A financial statement reporting a business's sales revenue and expenses for a given period of time (p. 13).

**International Accounting Standards Board (IASB)** An independent accounting standard-setting agency whose purpose is to develop international financial accounting standards (p. 12).

**International accounting principles** A set of accounting guidelines that are acceptable for the preparation of financial statements worldwide (p. 23).

**International Financial Reporting Standards (IFRS)** An international set of accounting standards, interpretations, and the framework for the preparation and presentation of financial statements used in many countries (p. 12).

**Investing activities** Cash flow activities involving the acquisition and disposition of the infrastructure of a company, including land, buildings, and equipment. Also included are cash flows for investments in shares of other companies (p. 9).

**Liabilities** The obligations or debts that a business must pay in money or services at some time in the future as a consequence of past transactions or events (p. 13).

**Management Discussion and Analysis (MD&A)** Part of the annual report that contains management's interpretation of the company's recent past performance along with discussion of possible future opportunities and risks (p. 21).

**Managerial accounting** The accounting activities carried out by a firm's accounting staff primarily to provide management with accounting data for decisions related to a firm's operations (p. 5).

**Net assets** The difference between a business's assets and liabilities. Net assets are equal to stockholders' equity (p. 13).

**Net income** The excess of a business's sales revenues over its expenses (p. 14).

**New York Stock Exchange (NYSE)** A marketplace, located in New York City, for the buying and selling of corporate shares (p. 5).

**Notes to the financial statements** The annual report section following the four financial statements that includes a description of the assumptions and estimates that were used in preparing the statements, the measurement procedures that were followed, and the details behind the summary numbers (p. 21).

**Operating activities** Cash flow activities that are associated with the day-to-day operations of a business, for example the cash received from sales revenues and the cash paid for operating expenses (p. 9).

**Partnership** A voluntary association of two or more persons for the purpose of conducting a business (p. 4).

**Period-in-time** A financial statement accumulating information for a specific period of time; examples include the income statement, the statement of stockholders' equity, the statement of retained earnings, and the statement of cash flows (p. 16).

**Point-in-time** A financial statement presenting information as of a particular date; the balance sheet is a point-in-time statement (p. 16).

**Principal** As it relates to debt financing, the amount initially borrowed from the creditor (p. 9)

**Sales revenues** Increases in stockholders' equity that result when a firm provides goods or services to its customers (p. 14).

**Sarbanes-Oxley Act (SOX)** A set of legislative rules enacted in 2002 to provide stricter guidance over corporate behavior. The legislation was a reaction to the infamous accounting scandals at Enron and WorldCom (p. 8).

**Sole proprietorship** A form of business organization in which one person owns the business (p. 4).

**Statement of cash flows** A financial statement showing a business's cash inflows and outflows for a specific time period, classified into operating, investing, and financing activities (p. 15).

**Statement of retained earnings** A financial statement that presents information regarding the events causing a change in retained earnings during a period, including net income and dividends (p. 14).

**Statement of stockholders' equity** A financial statement presenting information regarding the events that cause a change in stockholders' equity during a period. The statement presents the beginning balance, additions to, deductions from, and the ending balance of stockholders' equity for the period (p. 14).

**Stockholder** An owner of a corporation as a result of the purchase of the corporation's shares of stock; also known as a shareholder (p. 4).

**Stockholders' equity** The residual interest of a company's stockholders in the assets of a business; equal to the difference between the company's assets and liabilities (p. 13).

**Triple bottom line** A form of reporting that captures an expanded set of measures in addition to traditional financial reporting. The three bottom lines include economic, ecological, and social (p. 18).

## COMPREHENSIVE PROBLEM

You have been approached by Janet Jones about helping her assemble a set of December 31 financial statements for her new business. Janet began the operations of her bakery shop on January 1, 2011. Janet decided that she did not want to risk any personal liability resulting from operating the business; consequently, she organized the bakery, called Sweet Pleasures, as a corporation.

### Required

Use the format of Exhibits 1-6 through 1-9 to prepare an income statement, statement of retained earnings, balance sheet, and statement of cash flows for Sweet Pleasures as of December 31, 2011. Use the account titles and balances provided below. Be sure to use proper underlining and double underlining.

| | | | |
|---|---|---|---|
| Sales of goods | $200,000 | Dividends | $ 10,000 |
| Cash | 99,000 | Bank loan payable | 20,000 |
| Rent expense | 16,000 | Accounts receivable | 40,000 |
| Interest payable | 1,600 | Cash received from operating activities | 160,000 |
| Issuance of common stock | 50,000 | Cash payments for operating activities | 94,000 |
| Insurance expense | 20,000 | Salary expense | 40,000 |
| Purchase of equipment | 27,000 | Borrowing from bank | 20,000 |
| Equipment, net | 27,000 | Interest expense | 1,600 |
| Common stock | 50,000 | Administrative expense | 18,000 |
| Cash dividends paid | 10,000 | | |

### Solution

| SWEET PLEASURES CORPORATION |
|---|
| **Income Statement** |
| **For Year Ended December 31, 2011** |

| | | |
|---|---|---|
| Revenue | | |
| Sales of goods | | $200,000 |
| Expenses | | |
| Rent expense | $16,000 | |
| Insurance expense | 20,000 | |
| Salary expense | 40,000 | |
| Administrative expense | 18,000 | |
| Interest expense | 1,600 | |
| Total expenses | | 95,600 |
| Net income | | $104,400 |

**SWEET PLEASURES CORPORATION**
**Statement of Retained Earnings**
**For Year Ended December 31, 2011**

| | |
|---|---:|
| Retained earnings, January 1, 2011............................................... | $     0 |
| Add: Net income ..................................................................... | 104,400 |
| | 104,400 |
| Less: Dividends...................................................................... | 10,000 |
| Retained earnings, December 31, 2011............................................ | $ 94,400 |

**SWEET PLEASURES CORPORATION**
**Balance Sheet**
**December 31, 2011**

| Assets | | Liabilities | |
|---|---:|---|---:|
| Cash ..................... | $ 99,000 | Bank loan payable............................. | $ 20,000 |
| Accounts receivable ...... | 40,000 | Interest payable .............................. | 1,600 |
| Equipment, net........... | 27,000 | Total liabilities................................ | 21,600 |
| | | **Stockholders' Equity** | |
| | | Common stock ................................ | 50,000 |
| | | Retained earnings ............................ | 94,400 |
| | | Total stockholders' equity.................... | 144,400 |
| Total assets.............. | $166,000 | Total liabilities and stockholders' equity ......... | $166,000 |

**SWEET PLEASURES CORPORATION**
**Statement of Cash Flows**
**For Year Ended December 31, 2011**

| | | |
|---|---:|---:|
| Cash flow from operating activities | | |
| Cash received from operating activities ................................ | $160,000 | |
| Cash payments for operating activities................................. | (94,000) | |
| Cash provided by operating activities ............................... | | $66,000 |
| Cash flow from investing activities | | |
| Purchase of equipment................................................. | (27,000) | |
| Cash used by investing activities ........................................ | | (27,000) |
| Cash flow from financing activities | | |
| Borrowing from bank.................................................... | 20,000 | |
| Issuance of common stock ............................................. | 50,000 | |
| Cash dividends paid..................................................... | (10,000) | |
| Cash provided by financing activities................................ | | 60,000 |
| Net increase of cash ..................................................... | | 99,000 |
| Cash at January 1, 2011................................................... | | 0 |
| Cash at December 31, 2011 ............................................... | | $99,000 |

# SELF-STUDY QUESTIONS

(Answers to Self-Study Questions are at the end of this chapter.)

1. Which form of business organization is characterized by limited liability?   **LO1**
   a.  Sole proprietorship
   b.  Partnership
   c.  Corporation
   d.  Both sole proprietorship and partnership

2. Which of the following processes best defines accounting?   **LO4**
   a.  Measuring economic activities
   b.  Communicating results to interested parties
   c.  Preventing fraud
   d.  Both a and b.

**LO4**    **3.** Generally accepted accounting principles are:
- *a.* A set of guidelines to aid in the financial reporting process
- *b.* A set of laws to prevent financial fraud
- *c.* A set of standards for ethical conduct
- *d.* A set of voluntary "best business practices"

**LO2**    **4.** To which area of accounting are generally accepted accounting principles primarily relevant?
- *a.* Managerial accounting
- *b.* Financial accounting
- *c.* Tax accounting
- *d.* Financial reporting to all regulatory agencies

**LO3**    **5.** Which of the following is not one of the three types of business activities?
- *a.* Investing
- *b.* Financing
- *c.* Marketing
- *d.* Operating

**LO5**    **6.** If assets total $70,000 and liabilities total $40,000, how much are net assets?
- *a.* $30,000
- *b.* $40,000
- *c.* $70,000
- *d.* $110,000

**LO5**    **7.** What are increases in resources that a firm earns by providing goods or services to its customers?
- *a.* Assets
- *b.* Revenues
- *c.* Expenses
- *d.* Liabilities

**LO6**    **8.** Which of the following items is not required to be included as part of a company's annual report?
- *a.* Notes to the financial statements
- *b.* Management discussion and analysis
- *c.* Detailed history of the company
- *d.* Auditor's report

**LO2**    **9.** Which of the following situations presents ethical challenges to accountants?
- *a.* Pressure by superiors to produce a "good" number
- *b.* Avoiding the disclosure of confidential information
- *c.* An emphasis on short-term results
- *d.* All the above present ethical challenges to accountants

**LO1**    **10.** Match the following organizational attributes in the left column with the organizational form in the right column that the attribute is most often associated with.

| | |
|---|---|
| 1. Tax advantages | *a.* Sole proprietorship |
| 2. Unlimited liability | *b.* Partnership |
| 3. Shared control | *c.* Corporation |
| 4. Most complex to set up | |
| 5. Easiest to raise a large amount of funds | |
| 6. Single owner | |

**LO5**    **11.** The financial statements of Bower Company contain the following. How much is its net income?

| | |
|---|---:|
| Accounts payable | $10,000 |
| Revenues | 17,000 |
| Accounts receivable | 12,000 |
| Expenses | 9,000 |
| Cash | 5,000 |

- *a.* $15,000
- *b.* $8,000
- *c.* $17,000
- *d.* 7,000

**LO4**    **12.** If Ross Company reports its year-end total liabilities to be $75,000, and its year-end stockholders' equity to be $85,000, how much is Ross Company's year-end total assets?
- *a.* $10,000
- *b.* $160,000
- *c.* $85,000
- *d.* cannot be determined from the given information

13. Huff Company began the year with a retained earnings balance of $20,000, reported net income  LO5
for the year of $60,000, and reported ending retained earnings of $70,000. How much dividends
did Huff Company report for the year?
   a. $150,000                              c. $10,000
   b. $20,000                               d. $30,000

## DISCUSSION QUESTIONS

1. Define *accounting*. What is the basic purpose of accounting?
2. What is the distinction between *financial* accounting and *managerial* accounting?
3. Who are some of the outside groups that may be interested in a company's financial data and what
   are their particular interests?
4. What are *generally accepted accounting principles* and what organization has primary responsibility for their formulation in the United States?
5. What are the main advantages and disadvantages of the corporate form of business?
6. What role does financial accounting play in the allocation of society's financial resources?
7. What is the accounting equation? Define *assets, liabilities,* and *stockholders' equity.*
8. What are the three principal business activities and how do they differ?
9. What is meant by corporate social responsibility?
10. What is the difference between generally accepted accounting principles (GAAP) and international
    financial reporting standards (IFRS)?
11. What are *revenues* and *expenses*?
12. What is the purpose of an income statement? The statement of retained earnings? The balance
    sheet? The statement of cash flows?
13. What is a *period-in-time statement*? Give three examples.
14. What is a *point-in-time statement*? Give one example.
15. On December 31, the Miller Company had $700,000 in total assets and owed $220,000 to credi-
    tors. If the corporation's common stock amounted to $300,000, what amount of retained earnings
    should appear on its December 31 balance sheet?
16. What are three aspects of the accounting environment that may create ethical pressure on an
    accountant?
17. What type of information might you find in the Management Discussion and Analysis section
    (MD&A) of the annual report?
18. What is the purpose of having the financial statements audited by an independent auditor?
19. Determine whether the following statements are true or false and explain why:
    a. The accounting process is only interested in communicating economic activity.
    b. There are few potential users of accounting information.
    c. Financial accounting is primarily used to communicate to outside users.
    d. Auditors ensure the validity of a company's financial statements.

## SHORT EXERCISES

**SE1-1. Forms of Business Organization**  LO1
Match the following forms of business organization with the set of attributes that best describes
that form of business: sole proprietorship, partnership, or corporation.
   a. Shared control, unlimited liability, tax advantages, increased skills and resources
   b. Best for raising large amounts of funds, double taxation, limited liability, easiest to trans-
      fer ownership interests
   c. Sole ownership, easiest to establish, tax advantages, unlimited liability

**SE1-2. Accounting Processes**  LO4
Identify the following processes as either measuring or communicating.
   a. Prepare financial statements for the entity
   b. Identify relevant economic activities of the entity
   c. Record relevant economic activities of the entity
   d. Interpret financial results of the entity
   e. Quantify relevant economic activities of the entity

**LO2**  **SE1-3.**  **Types of Statements**

Match the following type of report with the most likely statement user: management, taxation authority, regulatory agency, or investor.

a.  Financial statements
b.  Tax return
c.  Annual budget
d.  Special report on a bank's financial health

**LO4, LO7**  **SE1-4.**  **Accounting Organizations**

Match the following organizations with the set of accounting guidelines: Financial Accounting Standards Board (FASB), International Accounting Standards Board (IASB).

a.  Generally accepted accounting principles (GAAP)
b.  International financial reporting standards (IFRS)

**LO3**  **SE1-5.**  **Business Activities**

Match the following activities with the type of activity: Operating, Investing, Financing.

a.  Day-to-day business activities
b.  Purchase of land for a new warehouse
c.  Sale of merchandise inventory
d.  Obtain a new bank loan
e.  Payment of dividends
f.  Invest excess cash
g.  Purchase office supplies
h.  Sell old equipment that is no longer needed

**LO5**  **SE1-6.**  **Financial Statement Items**

Identify the financial statement in which each of the following items would appear: income statement (IS), statement of retained earnings (SRE), balance sheet (BS), or statement of cash flows (SCF).

a.  Assets
b.  Revenues
c.  Cash flow from investing activities
d.  Stockholders' equity
e.  Expenses
f.  Net change in cash
g.  Net income
h.  Liabilities

**LO6**  **SE1-7.**  **Annual Report Components**

Which of the following would not be part of the notes to the financial statements in a company's annual report?

a.  Qualitative information about potential lawsuits
b.  Additional information about the reported total of notes payable
c.  Details about potential new products to be introduced during the next year
d.  Details of estimates used to compute the expected amount of warranty expense

**LO2**  **SE1-8.**  **Sarbanes-Oxley Act**

The Sarbanes-Oxley Act of 2002 was enacted to help restore confidence in financial reporting. Which of the following was not part of the legislation?

a.  Severe penalties for fraudulent reporting
b.  A requirement for certification of the financial statements by top management
c.  A new statement of social responsibility
d.  A report on controls to help prevent and detect errors in the reporting process

**LO4, LO7**  **SE1-9.**  **Financial Accounting and Generally Accepted Accounting Principles**

Answer the following multiple-choice questions:

1.  What is not a primary function of financial accounting in society?
    a.  Provide comedy material for late-night talk shows.
    b.  Aid in the proper allocation of financial resources in a free enterprise economic system.
    c.  Aid users to make better investing decisions.

   2. IFRS refers to:
     *a.* A random set of letters.
     *b.* A set of standards and procedures that form guidelines for international financial accounting.
     *c.* A set of standards and procedures that form guidelines for international managerial accounting.
   3. GAAP:
     *a.* Is the distance between two objects.
     *b.* Is a set of guidelines for preparing managerial reports in the United States.
     *c.* Is a set of guidelines for preparing financial reports in the United States.

**SE1-10. Cash Flow Activity Classification**                         **LO3**
Classify each activity as financing, investing, or operating:

   1. Repay a loan from a bank.
   2. Sell merchandise from a storefront operation.
   3. Dispose of an old delivery truck.
   4. Pay rent on a company warehouse.
   5. Repurchase shares of stock from stockholders.
   6. Pay utilities.

**SE1-11. Using the Basic Accounting Equation**                     **LO5**
Use the basic accounting equation to answer the following:

*a.* Kendrick Company has total assets of $100,000 and total liabilities of $60,000. How much is the company's total stockholders' equity?
*b.* Gassol Company has total liabilities of $80,000 and total stockholders' equity of $75,000. How much total assets does the company have?
*c.* If Brown Company's total assets increased by $15,000 during the year, and its total liabilities decreased during the same year by $10,000, what was the change in the company's total stockholders' equity?

**SE1-12. Using the Basic Accounting Equation**                     **LO5**
Henderson Company had beginning-of-the-year total assets of $200,000 and total liabilities of $120,000.

*a.* If during the year total assets increased by $25,000 and total liabilities increased by $30,000, what is the end-of-year total stockholders' equity?
*b.* If during the year total assets increased by $50,000 and total liabilities decreased by $10,000, what is the end-of-year total stockholders' equity?
*c.* If during the year total liabilities increased by $20,000 and total stockholders' equity increased by $30,000, what are the end-of-year total assets?

**SE1-13. Financial Statements**                                      **LO5**
Indicate which statement you would examine to locate the following items: balance sheet (BS), income statement (IS), statement of retained earnings (RE), or statement of cash flows (CF).

*a.* Expenses for the period
*b.* Cash at year-end
*c.* Cash used to purchase new equipment
*d.* Dividends for the period

**SE1-14. International Accounting**                          **LO7**
Which of the following is not usually cited as an obstacle to international accounting principles?    **(Appendix 1A)**

*a.* Differences among countries as to who establishes accounting principles
*b.* Nationalistic tendencies of accounting principles-setting bodies
*c.* Different currencies among countries
*d.* Cultural differences

## EXERCISES—SET A

**E1-1A. Forms of Business Organization**                         **LO1**
Match the following organizational attributes in the left column with the organizational form in the right column. More than one organizational form may be associated with a given attribute.

1. Unlimited liability
2. Full control
3. Business income combined with owner(s) income for income tax purposes.
4. Relatively more difficult to establish
5. Easier to raise funds

a. Sole proprietorship
b. Partnership
c. Corporation

**LO4** **E1-2A.** **Accounting Process**
Establish the correct sequence of steps in the accounting measurement process.

a. Record in a systematic fashion
b. Identify relevant economic activity
c. Quantify economic activity

**LO2** **E1-3A.** **Types of Accounting**
Identify the type of accounting associated with each type of report: Managerial, Financial, Tax, combination as needed.

a. Budget for internal use by management
b. Tax return for state income taxes
c. Audited financial statements
d. Special reports for regulators of a public utility

**LO5** **E1-4A.** **Corporate Social Responsibility**
Which of the following is not part of the triple bottom line reporting framework?

a. Economic bottom line
b. Social bottom line
c. Competitive bottom line
d. Environmental bottom line

**LO4, LO7** **E1-5A.** **Generally Accepted Accounting Principles**
Identify whether the following statements are true or false:

a. U.S. GAAP is universally accepted in all countries in the world.
b. U.S. GAAP is established by the IASB.
c. Once established, U.S. GAAP is rarely, if ever, modified.
d. The international counterpart to the FASB is the IASB.

**LO3** **E1-6A.** **Business Activities**
Identify each of the following activities as operating (O), investing (I), or financing (F):

a. Payment of employee salaries
b. Repayment of a loan
c. Issuance of common stock
d. Purchase of equipment to manufacture a company's products
e. Sale of merchandise inventory
f. Investment of excess cash in the shares of another company

**LO5** **E1-7A.** **The Accounting Equation**
Determine the missing amount in each of the following cases:

| Assets | Liabilities | Stockholders' Equity |
|---|---|---|
| $200,000 | $85,000 | ? |
| ? | $32,000 | $28,000 |
| $93,000 | ? | $52,000 |

**LO5** **E1-8A.** **Determining Net Income**
The beginning and ending balances of retained earnings for the year were $30,000 and $35,000, respectively. If dividend payments from stockholders' equity exceed new capital contributions during the year by $3,000, determine the net income or net loss for the year.

a. $8,000 net loss
b. $14,000 net income
c. $2,000 net income
d. $8,000 net income

**E1-9A. Determining Retained Earnings and Net Income**                    LO5

The following information appears in the records of Bock Corporation at year-end:

| | | | |
|---|---|---|---|
| Accounts receivable | $23,000 | Retained earnings | $    ? |
| Accounts payable | 11,000 | Supplies | 9,000 |
| Cash | 8,000 | Equipment, net | 138,000 |
| Common stock | 110,000 | | |

a.  Calculate the balance in retained earnings at year-end.

b.  If the amount of the retained earnings at the beginning of the year was $30,000, and $12,000 in dividends is paid during the year, calculate net income for the year.

**E1-10A. Determining Stockholders' Equity**                    LO1, LO5

Determine the following:

a.  The stockholders' equity of a sole proprietorship that has assets of $450,000 and liabilities of $326,000.

b.  The assets of a corporation that has liabilities of $400,000, common stock of $200,000, and retained earnings of $185,000.

**E1-11A. Financial Statements**                    LO5

Karl Flury operates a golf driving range. For each of the following financial items related to his business, indicate the financial statement (or statements) in which the item would be reported:

a.  Accounts receivable
b.  Cash received from the sale of land
c.  Net income
d.  Cash invested in the business by Flury
e.  Notes payable
f.  Supplies expense
g.  Land
h.  Supplies

**E1-12A. Omitted Financial Statement Data**                    LO5

For the following four unrelated situations, A through D, calculate the unknown amounts appearing in each column:

| | A | B | C | D |
|---|---|---|---|---|
| **Beginning** | | | | |
| Assets | $28,000 | $12,000 | $28,000 | $    ? |
| Liabilities | 18,600 | 5,000 | 19,000 | 9,000 |
| **Ending** | | | | |
| Assets | 30,000 | 26,000 | 34,000 | 40,000 |
| Liabilities | 17,300 | ? | 15,000 | 19,000 |
| **During Year** | | | | |
| Sales revenue | ? | 23,500 | 18,000 | 24,000 |
| Expense | 8,500 | 21,000 | 11,000 | 17,000 |
| Dividends | 3,000 | 1,500 | ? | 3,000 |

**E1-13A. Other Components of the Annual Report**                    LO6

Identify where the following items will appear in a company's annual report: Management Discussion and Analysis (MD&A), notes to the financial statements, or the auditor's report.

a.  A comment that the financial statements appear to be fairly presented
b.  A discussion about new competition likely to occur next year
c.  A quantitative summary of notes payable appearing on the balance sheet
d.  The "secret" ingredients in the company's special sauce

**E1-14A. Ethics**                    LO2

In each of the following cases, (a) identify the aspect of the accounting environment primarily responsible for the ethical pressure on the accountant and (b) indicate the appropriate behavioral response for the accountant.

1.  James Jehring, a tax accountant, is preparing an income tax return for a client. The client asks Jehring to take a sizable deduction on the tax return for business-related travel even

though the client states that he has no documentation to support the deduction. "I don't think the IRS will audit my return," declares the client.

2. Willa English, an accountant for Dome Construction Company, has just finished putting the numbers together for a construction project on which the firm is going to submit a bid next month. At a social gathering that evening, a friend casually asks English what Dome's bid is going to be. Ms. English knows that the friend's brother works for a competitor of Dome.

3. The manager of Cross Department Store is ending his first year with the firm. December's business was slower than expected, and the firm's annual results are trailing last year's results. The manager instructs Kyle Tarpley, the store accountant, to include sales revenues from the first week of January in the December data. "This way, we'll show an increase over last year," declares the manager.

**LO7**
**(Appendix 1A)**

**E1-15A. International Accounting Principles**

The worldwide acceptance of a global set of international accounting principles will provide certain benefits.

*a.* Which group has taken the lead in developing a set of international accounting principles?

*b.* Identify and briefly discuss two major benefits that would result from the adoption of a global set of international accounting principles.

**LO7**
**(Appendix 1A)**

**E1-16A. International Accounting Principles**

Identify whether the following statements are true or false.

1. U.S. GAAP and IFRS are essentially the same, with few significant differences.
2. IFRS is accepted as GAAP in every country of the world.
3. The SEC allows foreign companies to file their annual reports using IFRS.
4. LIFO is generally accepted under IFRS.

# EXERCISES—SET B

**LO1**

**E1-1B. Forms of Business Organization**

Match the following organizational attributes in the left column with the organizational form in the right column. More than one organizational form may be associated with a given attribute.

| | |
|---|---|
| 1. Limited liability | *a.* Sole proprietorship |
| 2. Shared control | *b.* Partnership |
| 3. Double taxation | *c.* Corporation |
| 4. Easiest to form | |
| 5. Easier to transfer ownership | |

**LO4**

**E1-2B. The Accounting Process**

Establish the correct sequence of steps in the accounting measurement process.

*a.* Quantify economic activity
*b.* Identify relevant economic activity
*c.* Record in a systematic fashion

**LO2**

**E1-3B. Types of Accounting**

Identify the type of accounting associated with each type of report: Managerial, Financial, Tax, combination as needed.

*a.* Cost report for a new product
*b.* Tax return for federal income taxes
*c.* Unaudited financial statements requested for a bank loan
*d.* Special report for banking regulators

**LO5**

**E1-4B. Corporate Social Responsibility**

Which of the following is not part of the triple bottom line reporting framework?

*a.* Social bottom line
*b.* Environmental bottom line

c. Economic bottom line

d. Efficiency bottom line

**E1-5B. Generally Accepted Accounting Principles**   LO4, LO7

Identify whether the following statements are true or false.

a. GAAP can differ from one country to another.

b. U.S. GAAP is established by the FASB.

c. U.S. GAAP is a guide to action that may change over time.

d. At this time there is no international counterpart to the FASB.

**E1-6B. Business Activities**   LO3

Identify each of the following activities as operating (O), investing (I), or financing (F).

a. Payment of rent on the company headquarters

b. Repurchase of the company's common stock

c. Obtain a long-term bank loan

d. Sale of an empty warehouse

e. Delivery of consulting service

f. Sale of short-term investments

**E1-7B. The Accounting Equation**   LO5

Determine the missing amount in each of the following cases:

| Assets | Liabilities | Stockholders' Equity |
|---|---|---|
| $300,000 | ? | $170,000 |
| $ 80,000 | $32,000 | ? |
| ? | $40,000 | $ 49,000 |

**E1-8B. Determining Net Income**   LO5

The beginning and ending balances of retained earnings for the year were $45,000 and $52,500, respectively. If dividends paid from stockholders' equity exceed new capital contributions during the year by $4,500, determine the net income or net loss for the year:

a. $12,000 net loss

b. $21,000 net income

c. $3,000 net income

d. $12,000 net income

**E1-9B. Determining Retained Earnings and Net Income**   LO5

The following information appears in the records of the Jones Corporation at year-end:

| | | | |
|---|---|---|---|
| Accounts receivable | $ 40,000 | Retained earnings | $ ? |
| Accounts payable | 19,000 | Supplies | 27,000 |
| Cash | 17,000 | Equipment, net | 108,000 |
| Common stock | 210,000 | | |

a. Calculate the amount of retained earnings at year-end.

b. If the amount of the retained earnings at the beginning of the year was $60,000, and $25,000 in dividends is paid during the year, calculate net income for the year.

**E1-10B. Determining Stockholders' Equity**   LO5

Determine the following:

a. The stockholders' equity of a sole proprietorship that has assets of $750,000 and liabilities of $300,000.

b. The assets of a corporation that has liabilities of $170,000, common stock of $85,000, and retained earnings of $74,000.

**E1-11B. Financial Statements**   LO5

Kattie Klein operates a bakery. For each of the following financial statement items related to her business, indicate the financial statement (or statements) in which the item would be reported:

a. Accounts payable

b. Cash received from the sale of equipment

c. Net loss

  *d.*   Cash invested in the business by Klein

  *e.*   Notes receivable

  *f.*   Rent expense

  *g.*   Building

  *h.*   Inventory

**LO5** **E1-12B. Omitted Financial Statement Data**

For the following four unrelated situations, A-D, calculate the unknown amounts appearing in each column:

|  | A | B | C | D |
|---|---|---|---|---|
| **Beginning** | | | | |
|  Assets | $42,000 | $18,000 | $42,000 | ? |
|  Liabilities | 27,900 | 7,500 | 28,500 | 13,500 |
| **Ending** | | | | |
|  Assets | 45,000 | 39,000 | 51,000 | 60,000 |
|  Liabilities | 25,950 | ? | 22,500 | 28,500 |
| **During Year** | | | | |
|  Sales revenue | ? | 35,250 | 36,000 | 36,000 |
|  Expense | 12,750 | 31,500 | 16,500 | 25,500 |
|  Dividends | 4,500 | 2,250 | ? | 4,500 |

**LO6** **E1-13B. Other Components of the Annual Report**

Identify where the following items will appear in a company's annual report: Management Discussion and Analysis (MD&A), notes to the financial statements, the auditor's report, or not disclosed.

  *a.*   A comment that the statements are presented in conformity with generally accepted accounting principles

  *b.*   A discussion about new products to be introduced next year

  *c.*   A quantitative summary of property, plant, and equipment appearing on the balance sheet

  *d.*   The salaries of every employee

**LO2** **E1-14B. Ethics**

In each of the following cases, (a) identify the aspect of the accounting environment primarily responsible for the ethical pressure on the accountant and (b) indicate the appropriate behavioral response for the accountant.

 1. Jenny Jones, a tax accountant, is preparing an income tax return for a client. The client asks Jones to omit some income she received for consulting services because the amount was paid in cash. "I don't think the IRS will audit my return," declares the client. "And even if they do, what are the chances they would catch this?"

 2. Fred French, an accountant for Top Electronics Company, has just finished estimating the cost for a new iPod device that the company plans to introduce. Cost estimates help the company to determine the price they can charge for new products. At a social gathering that evening, a friend casually asks Fred what Top's cost for the iPod device came out to be. Fred knows that the friend's brother works for a competitor of Top Electronics.

 3. The manager of Jazz Department Store is ending his first year with the firm. December's business was slower than expected, and the firm's annual results are below Wall Street's expectations. The manager instructs Chris Green, store accountant, to record some of December's expenses in the following year. "This way, we'll meet Wall Street's expectations," declares the manager.

**LO7** **E1-15B. International Accounting Principles**

**(Appendix 1A)**

Although there are benefits to the worldwide acceptance of a global set of international accounting principles, several obstacles will have to be overcome before such acceptance could occur.

   Identify and briefly discuss three obstacles to the worldwide acceptance of a global set of international accounting principles.

## PROBLEMS—SET A

**P1-1A. Forms of Business Organization**    LO1

Presented below are four independent situations:

*a.* Kali Kane, a senior in college looking for summer employment, decided to start a dog-walking business. Each morning and evening she picks up a group of dogs and walks them around the city park.

*b.* Brothers Joe and Jay Simmons each owned a separate electronics repair shop. They decided to combine their talents and resources in order to expand the amount of business they could undertake.

*c.* Three chemists at a large engineering company decided to start their own business based on an experimental chemical process they had developed outside the company. The process had the potential to be very successful; however, it was quite dangerous and could result in large legal problems.

*d.* Jack Prince ran a small, but successful holistic healing spa. The spa has gained a strong reputation beyond the community where it is located. Jack decided to open a chain of similar spas across the state to capitalize on his reputation. This will require a substantial investment in supplies and employee training. In addition, since Jack will not be able to closely supervise each location, he is worried about potential liability.

**Required**

Explain the form of organization that would be best in each situation—sole proprietorship, partnership, or corporation. Explain what factors you considered important in each situation.

**P1-2A. Financial Statements**    LO5

While each of the financial statements is likely to aid in any business decision, it is often the case that a particular financial statement may be best suited to help in a particular decision. Consider each decision below independently:

*a.* You are trying to determine whether a particular firm is a good investment. You understand that share price increases are impacted heavily by a company's earnings potential.

*b.* You are employed in the lending department of a large bank. You are trying to determine if you should lend to a potential customer. If you do make the loan you are especially concerned that the company will have sufficient collateral in the event that it is unable to repay the loan.

*c.* You wish to invest in a firm that provides you with a steady source of income. You especially want a firm that pays out a large part of its net income as dividends.

*d.* You are trying to determine if a particular firm will have sufficient cash flow in order to keep expanding without relying too heavily on external sources of financing.

**Required**

Determine which of the financial statements contains the most useful information to help in your decision. Explain what information you used from each statement to help you make your decision.

**P1-3A. Balance Sheet**    LO5

The following balance sheet data are for Normandy Catering Service, a corporation, at May 31, 2011:

| | | | |
|---|---|---|---|
| Accounts receivable | $18,300 | Accounts payable | 5,200 |
| Notes payable | 20,000 | Cash | 12,200 |
| Equipment, net | 55,000 | Common stock | 42,500 |
| Supplies | 16,400 | Retained earnings | ? |

**Required**

Prepare a balance sheet for Normandy as of May 31, 2011.

**P1-4A. Statement of Retained Earnings and Balance Sheet**    LO5

The following is balance sheet information for Lynch Janitorial Service, Inc., at the end of 2010 and 2011:

ASSIGNMENTS

| | December 31, 2011 | December 31, 2010 |
|---|---|---|
| Accounts payable | $ 6,000 | $ 9,000 |
| Cash | 23,000 | 20,000 |
| Accounts receivable | 42,000 | 33,000 |
| Land | 40,000 | 40,000 |
| Building, net | 250,000 | 260,000 |
| Equipment, net | 43,000 | 45,000 |
| Mortgage payable | 90,000 | 100,000 |
| Supplies | 20,000 | 18,000 |
| Common stock | 220,000 | 220,000 |
| Dividends | 10,000 | 0 |
| Retained earnings | ? | ? |

**Required**

a. Prepare a balance sheet as of December 31 of each year.

b. Prepare a statement of retained earnings for 2011. (*Hint:* The increase in retained earnings is equal to the net income less the dividend.)

**LO5** **P1-5A.** **Income Statement and Balance Sheet**

On March 1, 2011, Amy Dart began Dart Delivery Service, which provides delivery of bulk mailings to the post office, neighborhood delivery of weekly newspapers, data delivery to computer service centers, and various other delivery services using leased vans. On February 28, Dart invested $15,000 of her own funds in the firm and borrowed $6,000 from her father on a six-month, non-interest-bearing note payable. The following information is available at March 31:

| | | | |
|---|---|---|---|
| Accounts receivable | $9,700 | Delivery fees earned | $19,300 |
| Rent expense | 1,500 | Cash | 12,900 |
| Advertising expense | 900 | Supplies | 6,500 |
| Supplies expense | 2,700 | Notes payable | 6,000 |
| Accounts payable | 1,200 | Insurance expense | 800 |
| Salaries expense | 6,300 | Common stock | 15,000 |
| Miscellaneous expense | 200 | Retained earnings | ? |

**Required**

a. Prepare an income statement for the month of March.

b. Prepare a balance sheet as of March 31, 2011.

**LO5** **P1-6A.** **Statement of Cash Flows**

Shown below is selected information from the financial records of Mantle Corporation as of December 31:

| | | | |
|---|---|---|---|
| Inventory | $ 72,000 | Cash purchase of equipment | $ 27,000 |
| Cash collected from customers | 330,000 | Buildings, net | 440,000 |
| Equipment, net | 125,000 | Sales revenue | 475,000 |
| Retained earnings | 275,000 | Cash paid for operating activities | 210,000 |
| Cash dividends paid | 42,000 | Principal payments on existing note payable | 47,000 |
| Salary expense | 110,000 | Common stock | 155,000 |

**Required**

a. Determine which of the above items will appear on the statement of cash flows and then prepare the statement for Mantle Corporation for the year ended December 31, 2011.

b. Comment on the adequacy of Mantle's operations to provide cash for its investing and financing activities.

**LO2** **P1-7A.** **Ethics**

In each of the following cases, (a) identify the aspect of the accounting environment primarily responsible for the ethical pressure on the accountant and (b) indicate the appropriate behavioral response that the accountant should take.

1. Patricia Kelly, an accountant for Wooden Company, is reviewing the costs charged to a government contract that Wooden worked on this year. Wooden is manufacturing special

parts for the government and is allowed to charge the government for its actual manufacturing costs plus a fixed fee. Kelly notes that $75,000 worth of art objects purchased for the president's office is buried among the miscellaneous costs charged to the contract. Upon inquiry, the firm's vice president replies, "This sort of thing is done all the time."

2. Barry Marklin, accountant for Smith & Wesson partnership, is working on the 2011 year-end financial data. The partnership agreement calls for Smith and Wesson to share the firm's 2011 net income equally. In 2012, the partners will share the net income 60 percent to Smith and 40 percent to Wesson. Wesson plans to cut back his involvement in the firm. Smith wants Marklin to delay recording sales revenue from work done at the end of 2011 until January 2012. "We haven't received the cash yet from those services," declares Smith.

3. The St. Louis Wheelers, a professional football franchise, just signed its first-round draft pick to a multiyear contract that is reported in the newspapers as a four-year, $20 million contract. Johanna Factor, the Wheelers' accountant, receives a call from an agent of another team's first-round pick. "Just calling to confirm the contract terms reported in the papers," states the agent. "My client should receive a similar contract, and I'm sure you don't want him to get shortchanged."

**P1-8A.** **Income Statement, Statement of Retained Earnings, and Balance Sheet**

LO5

Napolean Corporation started business on January 1. The following information was compiled by Napolean's accountant on December 31, 2011:

| | | | |
|---|---|---|---|
| Sales revenue | 30,000 | Building, net | 60,000 |
| Expenses | 18,000 | Accounts payable | 6,000 |
| Dividends | 4,500 | Notes payable | 49,500 |
| Cash | 2,250 | Common stock | 30,000 |
| Accounts receivable | 3,750 | Retained earnings | ? |
| Inventory | 4,500 | | |
| Equipment, net | 22,500 | | |

**Required**

a.  You have been asked to assist the accountant for the Napolean Corporation in preparing year-end financial statements. Use the above information to prepare an income statement, statement of retained earnings, and a balance sheet as of December 31, 2011.

b.  Comment on the decision to pay a $4,500 dividend.

**P1-9A.** **Ethics**

LO2

As the accountant for Minkow Corporation, you are responsible for reporting the company's profit. It appears that the company's actual results are much better than was expected by Wall Street analysts. Your supervisor has requested that you report some of next period's expenses now so that this period's profits will be in line with analyst expectations. He states that you are not really doing anything wrong since the reported results will be more conservative. In addition, this will make it easier to make next year's numbers. What should you do?

# Problems—Set B

**P1-1B.** **Forms of Business Organization**

LO1

Presented below are four independent situations:

a.  Dino Owens, a photography major in college, decided to start a photography business specializing in weddings and similar occasions. Dino is still able to go to school full-time as all of his jobs are on weekends or holidays.

b.  Joe Thursday and Jay Lightfoot each owned a separate detective agency. They decided to combine their talents and resources in order to expand the amount of business they could undertake.

c.  Three business school professors at a large university decided to start their own consulting business based on their combined talents. They feel that the insurance they can obtain will satisfy any possible legal issues they may face. They plan to use one of the professor's home office to meet clients, so start-up costs should be minimal.

d.  Vera Gold runs a small, but successful beauty salon. The salon has gained a strong reputation beyond the community where it is located. Vera has decided to open a chain of

ASSIGNMENTS

similar salons across the state to capitalize on her reputation. This will require a substantial investment in facilities and supplies. In addition, since Vera will not be able to closely supervise each location, she is worried about potential liability.

**Required**

Explain the form of organization that would be best in each situation—sole proprietorship, partnership, or corporation. Explain what factors you considered important in each situation.

**LO5** **P1-2B.** **Financial Statements**

While each of the financial statements is likely to aid in any business decision, it is often the case that a particular financial statement may be best suited to help in a particular decision. Consider each decision below independently:

a. You are trying to determine whether a particular firm is a good investment. You want to invest in a firm that has strong revenue growth.

b. You are employed as a financial analyst for a large investment firm. You are trying to assess the riskiness of a particular investment opportunity. You understand that the more debt a firm has relative to its stockholders' equity, the riskier the firm is.

c. You are trying to determine how much of a firm's net income it distributes to its stockholders.

d. You are trying to determine how a particular firm was able to finance its large expansion during the year.

**Required**

Determine which of the financial statements contains the most useful information to help in your decision. Explain what information you used from each statement to help you make your decision.

**LO5** **P1-3B.** **Balance Sheet**

The following balance sheet data are for Bettis Plumbing Contractors, Inc., as of June 30, 2011:

| | | | |
|---|---|---|---|
| Accounts payable | $ 8,900 | Common stock | $100,000 |
| Cash | 14,700 | Retained earnings | ? |
| Supplies | 30,500 | Notes payable | 30,000 |
| Equipment, net | 98,000 | Accounts receivable | 9,200 |
| Land | 25,000 | | |

**Required**

Prepare a balance sheet as of June 30, 2011.

**LO5** **P1-4B.** **Statement of Retained Earnings and Balance Sheet**

Balance sheet information for Jordan Packaging Service at the end of 2011 and 2010 is as follows:

| | December 31, 2011 | December 31, 2010 |
|---|---|---|
| Accounts receivable | $22,800 | $17,500 |
| Accounts payable | 1,800 | 1,600 |
| Cash | 10,000 | 8,000 |
| Equipment, net | 32,000 | 27,000 |
| Supplies | 4,700 | 4,200 |
| Notes payable | 25,000 | 25,000 |
| Dividends | 12,000 | 0 |
| Common stock | 5,000 | 5,000 |
| Retained earnings | ? | ? |

**Required**

a. Prepare a balance sheet as of December 31 of each year.

b. Prepare a statement of retained earnings for 2011. (*Hint:* The increase in retained earnings is equal to the net income less the dividend.)

**LO5** **P1-5B.** **Income Statement and Balance Sheet**

The records of R. Levy, Interior Decorator, show the following information for the year-end December 31, 2011:

| | | | |
|---|---|---|---|
| Notes payable...................... | $ 4,000 | Supplies........................... | $ 6,100 |
| Decorating fees earned.............. | 67,600 | Cash ............................... | 4,200 |
| Supplies expense................... | 9,700 | Accounts receivable ................ | 10,600 |
| Insurance expense.................. | 1,500 | Advertising expense................ | 1,700 |
| Miscellaneous expense ............. | 200 | Salaries expense................... | 30,000 |
| Common stock..................... | 11,600 | Rent expense....................... | 7,500 |
| Retained earnings ................. | ? | Accounts payable ................. | 1,800 |

**Required**

*a.* Prepare an income statement for the year.

*b.* Prepare a balance sheet as of December 31, 2011.

**P1-6B. Statement of Cash Flows**

Shown below is selected information from the books of Mays Corporation as of December 31, 2011:

| | | | |
|---|---|---|---|
| Inventory ........................... | $144,000 | Cash purchase of equipment......... | 127,000 |
| Cash collected from customers........ | 660,000 | Buildings, net........................ | 880,000 |
| Equipment, net...................... | 250,000 | Sales revenue ....................... | 950,000 |
| Retained earnings ................... | 550,000 | Cash paid for operating activities ..... | 420,000 |
| | | Principal payments on existing | |
| Cash dividends paid ................. | 84,000 | note payable..................... | 127,000 |
| Salary expense ..................... | 220,000 | Common stock..................... | 310,000 |

**Required**

*a.* Determine which of the above items will appear on the statement of cash flows and then prepare the statement for Mays Corporation for the year ended December 31, 2011.

*b.* Comment on the adequacy of Mays' operations to provide cash for its investing and financing activities.

**P1-7B. Ethics**

In each of the following cases, (a) identify the aspect of the accounting environment primarily responsible for the ethical pressure on the accountant and (b) indicate the appropriate behavioral response that the accountant should take:

1. Kenneth Mills, an accountant for the Riley Company, is reviewing costs charged to a big government contract to supply logistical support. The contract specifies that Riley is entitled to its cost plus 10 percent extra for profit. Kenneth notices that gardening services at the home of the company president, Stu Riley, are included under miscellaneous expenses. The company's vice president, Slick Lowe, tells you not to worry about this since the government expects a little bit of fancy accounting to be included in all of its contracts.

2. Sergio Salles, an accountant for the law partnership Dewy and Suem, is working on the year-end financial statements. Currently the two partners, Dewy and Suem, each receive one-half of the firm's net income. Next year the allocation will change to a two-thirds, one-third split since Suem will be taking considerable time off to do pro bono work, something Dewy never does. Dewy suggested to Salles that he delay booking a large partial settlement the partnership received in December until January of next year when they will receive the final cash payment. Dewy commented that it would be "cleaner" to keep it all together.

3. Pete Freely is the accountant for a large professional services firm. Part of his responsibility is to complete payroll tax reports based on the salaries paid to all the employees. Pete received a call from a friend at a search firm that specializes in personnel such as those employed at Pete's place of employment. Pete's friend casually asked how much certain employees were making, explaining he wanted to be able to calibrate market wages for work he was doing.

**P1-8B. Financial Statements and Other Components**

Match each of the items in the left column with the appropriate annual report component from the right column:

1. The company's total assets
2. An opinion regarding whether the financial statements followed GAAP
3. Information regarding the estimates used in the financial statements
4. The use of cash during the period
5. The company's total expenses for the period
6. A discussion of potential risks that a company may encounter in the future
7. The amount of a company's earnings that are distributed to the company's stockholders

   a. Income Statement
   b. Statement of Retained Earnings
   c. Balance Sheet
   d. Statement of Cash Flows
   e. Management Discussion and Analysis (MD&A)
   f. Notes to the Financial Statements
   g. Auditor's report

# SERIAL PROBLEM: KATE'S CARDS

**SP1.** Kate Collins has always been good at putting together rhymes for any occasion. Recently, Kate's financial assistance for college was cut back due to budget problems in the state where she lives. Kate determined that the best way to raise enough money to stay in school and still have enough time for her studies was to start a greeting card business. She feels that this will not only help her to raise money, but it will supplement what she is learning at school as a business major.

Kate decided that she would start small and work out of her dorm room, designing the cards on a new Apple iMac that she was planning to purchase. Kate also decided to offer classes in greeting card design to other aspiring greeting card producers. After much thought, Kate decided to name her business "Kate's Cards."

**Required**

a. What form of business—sole proprietorship, partnership, or corporation—should Kate choose? Discuss why the organizational form that you selected is most appropriate for Kate.
b. What accounting information will Kate need to run her business?
c. What balance sheet accounts—assets, liabilities, and stockholders' equity—and income statement accounts—revenues and expenses—will Kate likely need to use?
d. Should Kate use her personal bank account or open a separate business bank account?
e. Kate will also be using her computer for schoolwork. She recalls from her business studies that it is important to keep her personal records and her business records separate. How should she account for these things while running Kate's Cards?

## EXTENDING YOUR KNOWLEDGE

### REPORTING AND ANALYSIS

COLUMBIA SPORTSWEAR COMPANY

**EYK1-1.** **Financial Reporting Problem: Columbia Sportswear Company**
Simplified financial statements for the **Columbia Sportswear Company** are reported in Exhibits 1-12 through 1-15.

**Required**
Refer to Columbia Sportswear's financial statements to answer the following questions:

a. How much did Columbia's total assets increase or decrease from December 31, 2008, to December 31, 2009?
b. How much did Columbia's cash increase or decrease from December 31, 2008, to December 31, 2009, and how much cash did Columbia report on its December 31, 2009, balance sheet?
c. How much accounts receivable and accounts payable did Columbia report on December 31, 2009? Does it appear that Columbia is able to collect from its customers as well as pay its own bills?
d. Did Columbia experience revenue growth in 2009?

*e.* Was Columbia profitable in 2009? How does the company's 2009 profit compare to 2008?

**EYK1-2.** **Comparative Analysis Problem: Columbia Sportswear Company vs. The Timberland Company**

Simplified financial statements for the **Columbia Sportswear Company** are reported in Exhibits 1-12 through 1-15 and **The Timberland Company**'s financial statements are presented in Appendix B at the end of this book.

COLUMBIA SPORTSWEAR
COMPANY
THE TIMBERLAND COMPANY

**Required**

1. Based on the information in these financial statements, compare the following for each company as of December 31, 2009:
   *a.* Total assets
   *b.* Total revenue
   *c.* Net income
   *d.* Cash flow from operations
2. From this information, what can you conclude about the relative size and operating performance of each company?

**EYK1-3.** **Business Decision Problem**

Paul Seale, a friend of yours, is negotiating the purchase of an exterminating company called Total Pest Control. Seale has been employed by a national pest control service and knows the technical side of the business. However, he knows little about accounting, so he asks for your assistance. The owner of Total Pest Control, Greg Krey, provided Seale with income statements for the past three years, which showed an average net income of $72,000 per year. The latest balance sheet shows total assets of $285,000 and liabilities of $45,000. Seale brings the following matters to your attention:

1. Krey is asking $300,000 for the firm. He told Seale that because the firm has been earning a 30 percent return on stockholders' equity, the price should be higher than the net assets reported on the balance sheet. (Note: The return on stockholders' equity is calculated as net income divided by total stockholders' equity.)
2. Seale noticed that there was no salary expense reported for Krey on the income statements, even though he worked half-time in the business. Krey explained that, because he had other income, he withdrew only $18,000 each year from the firm for personal use. If he purchases the firm, Seale will hire a full-time manager to run the firm at an annual salary of $36,000.
3. Krey's tax returns for the past three years report a lower net income for the firm than the amounts shown in the financial statements. Seale is skeptical about the accounting principles used in preparing the company's financial statements.

**Required**

*a.* If Seale accepts Krey's average annual income figure of $72,000, what would Seale's percentage return on stockholders' equity be, assuming that the net income remained at the same level and that the firm was purchased for $300,000?
*b.* Should Krey's withdrawals of $18,000 per year affect the net income reported in the financial statements? What will Seale's percentage return be if he takes into consideration the $36,000 salary he plans to pay a full-time manager?
*c.* Could there be legitimate reasons for the difference between net income as shown in the financial statements and net income as reported on the tax returns, as mentioned in point 3? How might Seale obtain additional assurances about the propriety of the company's financial statements?

**EYK1-4.** **Financial Analysis Problem**

Todd Jansen is deciding among several job offers. One job offer he is considering is in the marketing department at Columbia Sportswear. Before he makes his decision, he decides to review the financial reports of the company.

**Required**

Use the Columbia Sportswear annual report located in Appendix A at the end of this book to answer the following questions:

*a.* Were the financial statements of Columbia audited? If so, what firm performed the audit?

*b.* What was the amount of Columbia's 2009 net income? How does this compare with 2008 net income?

*c.* How much cash was provided or used for investing activities? What were the major sources and uses of cash from investing activities?

*d.* How much were accrued liabilities in 2009? What makes up this balance?

*e.* What are some of the more significant estimates used in the preparation of the company's financial statements?

*f.* To what amount are the financial statements rounded?

## CRITICAL THINKING

**EYK1-5.** **Accounting Research Problem**

GENERAL MILLS, INC.

Go to this book's Website and locate the annual report of **General Mills, Inc.** for the year ending May 30, 2010 (fiscal year 2010).

**Required**

*a.* Refer to the company's balance sheet.
1. What form of business organization does General Mills use? What evidence supports your answer?
2. What is the date of the most recent balance sheet?
3. For the most recent balance sheet, what is the largest asset reported? the largest liability?

*b.* Refer to the company's income statement.
1. What time period is covered by the most recent statement of earnings?
2. What total amount of sales revenues did General Mills generate in the most recent period? What is the change in sales revenues from last year to the current report year?
3. What is the net income (i.e., net earnings) for the most recent period?

*c.* Refer to the company's statement of cash flows.
1. For the most recent period, what is the amount and trend of the cash flow from operating activities?
2. For the most recent period, what is the amount and trend of the cash flow from investing activities?
3. For the most recent period, what is the amount and trend of the cash flow from financing activities?

**EYK1-6.** **Accounting Communication Activity**

Jasper Simmons is an intern for the Newby Company. He knows the company's balance sheet is supposed to balance, but he is not having much luck getting it to balance. Jasper knows that you are taking a course in accounting so he asks for your help. Jasper provides you with the following balance sheet that is currently out of balance:

| NEWBY COMPANY | | | | |
|---|---|---|---|---|
| **Balance Sheet** | | | | |
| **December 31, 2011** | | | | |
| **Assets** | | **Liabilities** | | |
| Cash . . . . . . . . . . . . . . . . . . . . . | 15,000 | Inventory . . . . . . . . . . . . . . . . . . . . . . . . . . . . . . . . | 20,000 | |
| Accounts receivable . . . . . . . | 30,000 | Notes payable . . . . . . . . . . . . . . . . . . . . . . . . . . . . | 38,000 | |
| Equipment, net . . . . . . . . . . . | 28,000 | **Stockholders' Equity** | | |
| Accounts payable . . . . . . . . . | (22,000) | Dividends . . . . . . . . . . . . . . . . . . . . . . . . . . . . . . . . . | (11,000) | |
| | | Common stock . . . . . . . . . . . . . . . . . . . . . . . . . . . . . | 10,000 | |
| | | Retained earnings, beginning of year. . . . . . . . . . | 10,000 | |
| Total . . . . . . . . . . . . . . . . . . . . | 51,000 | Total . . . . . . . . . . . . . . . . . . . . . . . . . . . . . . . . . . . . . . | 67,000 | |

In addition, Jasper provides you with a correct income statement that reports a net income for 2011 of $24,000.

**Required**

*a.* Prepare a corrected balance sheet for the Newby Company.

*b.* Write a memo to Jasper explaining what he did wrong.

*c.* In the memo explain the purpose of the balance sheet.

**EYK1-7.**    **Accounting Ethics Case**

Jack Hardy, CPA, has a brother, Ted, in the retail clothing business. Ted ran the business as a sole proprietor for 10 years. During this 10-year period, Jack helped Ted with various accounting matters. For example, Jack designed the accounting system for the company, prepared Ted's personal income tax returns (which included financial data about the clothing business), and recommended various cost control procedures. Ted paid Jack for all of these services. A year ago, Ted expanded the business and incorporated. Ted is president of the corporation and also chairs the corporation's board of directors. The board of directors has overall responsibility for corporate affairs. When the corporation was formed, Ted asked Jack to serve on its board of directors. Jack accepted. In addition, Jack now prepares the corporation's income tax returns and continues to advise his brother on accounting matters.

Recently, the corporation applied for a large bank loan. The bank wants audited financial statements for the corporation before it will decide on the loan request. Ted asked Jack to perform the audit. Jack replied that he cannot do the audit because the code of ethics for CPAs requires that he be independent when providing audit services.

**Required**

Why is it important that a CPA be independent when providing audit services? Which of Jack's activities or relationships impair his independence?

**EYK1-8.**    **Corporate Social Responsibility Problem**

Go to the **Columbia Sportswear Company** Website and find the section on their commitment to corporate responsibility. This section can be found near the bottom of their home page under the section "About Us."

**Required**

Answer the following questions.

*a.*   How does Columbia describe the company's efforts at corporate responsibility?

*b.*   What is the stated purpose of Columbia's sustainability efforts?

*c.*   What environmental initiatives has Columbia embarked upon?

*d.*   Why do you think that Columbia makes these efforts to be a good corporate citizen? Why do you think they devote so much space on their Website to promote these efforts?

**EYK1-9.**    **Forensic Accounting Problem**

Go to the Association of Certified Fraud Examiners Website and find their description of a forensic accountant. This can be found under the Career Center tab, Career Advantages of a CFE, then click on "How does the CFE support your career?" Finally click on Career Profiles and then Forensic Accountant.

**Required**

Answer the following questions.

*a.*   What type of engagements do forensic accountants work on?

*b.*   What are some of the useful skills that a forensic accountant should possess?

*c.*   How might your knowledge learned from this course help you to become a forensic accountant?

**EYK1-10.**   **Analyzing IFRS Financial Statements**

Tesco PLC is the world's third largest retailer. Tesco is based in the United Kingdom but also maintains operations in the United States. Tesco's IFRS financial statements are presented in Appendix C at the end of this book. After reviewing the company's financial statements, consider the following questions:

*a.*   What is Tesco's largest asset account on its 2009 balance sheet? What percentage of total assets does this asset represent?

*b.*   Is Tesco principally debt financed or equity financed in 2009? What percentage of Tesco's assets is financed with debt?

*c.*   Is Tesco profitable in 2009? What percentage of the company's sales revenue in 2009 is represented by its "profit for the year," or its net income?

*d.*   How much is Tesco's cash flow from operating activities in 2009? How does Tesco's profit for the year (net income) compare with its cash flow from operating activities?

## ANSWERS TO SELF-STUDY QUESTIONS:

1. c, (p. 5)  2. d, (p. 10)  3. a, (p. 11)  4. b, (p. 11)  5. c, (p. 9)  6. a, (p. 13)  7. b, (p. 14)  8. c, (p. 20)
9. d, (pp. 7–8)  10. (pp. 4–5)

1. Sole proprietorship and partnership
2. Sole proprietorship and partnership
3. Partnership
4. Corporation
5. Corporation
6. Sole proprietorship

11. b, (p. 14)  12. b, (p. 13)  13. c, (p. 15)

## Your Turn! Solutions

**Solution 1.1**

Sole proprietorship: Easiest to set up, owner controlled, and tax advantages.
Partnership: Relatively easy to establish, larger skill set, and tax advantages.
Corporations: Easiest to raise capital, easiest to transfer ownership, and protection against personal liability.

**Solution 1.2**

1. The financial statements are the primary output of financial accounting. External users require information on a business's performance and financial position. This is the type of information provided by the financial statements.
2. Internal users include management, the marketing department, the human resources department, and the finance department, among others. Each of these groups require data for decision making.
3. External users include, among others, investors, lenders, and regulators. These external groups require accounting information to help them make decisions regarding a company's performance and financial position.

**Solution 1.3**

Your supervisor is asking you to participate in the preparation of fraudulent financial statements. This is not only unethical; it is also illegal and could subject you to criminal prosecution. By reporting the sales revenue early, the financial statements will mislead users into thinking the company is doing better than it actually is. This in turn may lead them to make erroneous investment decisions. You should not follow your supervisor's request. Instead you should explain to your supervisor why reporting sales revenue prior to when it is earned is unethical. If your supervisor continues to pressure you, you should report your supervisor's request to a higher level of management in the company.

**Solution 1.4**

1. Financing
2. Operating
3. Investing
4. Operating
5. Financing
6. Operating

**Solution 1.5**

| KANZU CORPORATION<br>Income Statement<br>For Year Ended December 31, 2011 | |
|---|---:|
| Sales revenue | $20,000 |
| Expenses | 12,000 |
| Net income | $ 8,000 |

| KANZU CORPORATION<br>Statement of Retained Earnings<br>For Year Ended December 31, 2011 | |
|---|---:|
| Retained earnings, January 1 | $ 0 |
| Add: Net income | 8,000 |
| | 8,000 |
| Less: Dividends | 3,000 |
| Retained earnings, December 31 | $5,000 |

**KANZU CORPORATION**
**Balance Sheet**
**December 31, 2011**

| Assets | | Liabilities | |
|---|---:|---|---:|
| Cash | $ 1,500 | Accounts payable | $ 4,000 |
| Accounts receivable | 2,500 | Notes payable | 33,000 |
| Inventory | 3,000 | Total liabilities | $37,000 |
| Building, net | 40,000 | **Stockholders' Equity** | |
| Equipment, net | 15,000 | Common stock | 20,000 |
| Total assets | $62,000 | Retained earnings | 5,000 |
| | | Total stockholders' equity | 25,000 |
| | | Total liabilities and stockholders' equity | $62,000 |

| KANZU CORPORATION<br>Statement of Cash Flows<br>For Year Ended December 31, 2011 | |
|---|---:|
| Cash flow from operating activities | $ 6,500 |
| Cash flow from investing activities | (55,000) |
| Cash flow from financing activities | 50,000 |
| Net increase in cash | 1,500 |
| Cash at January 1, 2011 | 0 |
| Cash at December 31, 2011 | $ 1,500 |

**Solution 1.6**

1. c
2. b
3. a

CHAPTER

# Understanding Financial Statements

| PAST | PRESENT | FUTURE |
|---|---|---|
| Chapter 1 described the need for accounting, its various users, and the basic set of financial statements. | This chapter introduces classified financial statements, some key ratios computed from those statements, and the conceptual framework for GAAP. | Chapter 3 explains the accounting system for recording, reporting, and analyzing financing, investing, and operating activities. |

## LEARNING OBJECTIVES

**1** **Describe** a classified balance sheet. (p. 52)

**2** **Discuss** use of a balance sheet and ratios to assess liquidity and solvency. (p. 57)

**3** **Discuss** use of the income statement and ratios to assess profitability. (p. 59)

**4** **Explain** the components of the statement of stockholders' equity. (p. 61)

**5** **Explain** use of the statement of cash flows to help assess solvency. (p. 62)

**6** **Discuss** the development of generally accepted accounting principles and the conceptual framework. (p. 64)

**7** **Describe** the concepts, principles, and constraints of financial accounting. (p. 66)

# IDENTIFYING A WIN-WIN COMPANY

After a visit to one of **Apple**'s many retail stores, you will likely find it hard to believe that the company ever faced financial difficulties. The company has a cult-like following for its products including its Macintosh computer, the iPod, the iPhone, and the iPad. Things have not always been so good for the company that was established by Steve Jobs, Steve Wozniak, and Ronald Wayne. In fact, Apple suffered crippling financial losses and record low stock prices in the mid-1990s. Steve Jobs, who left the company in 1985 to start another business, was brought back to Apple in 1997 as chief executive officer (CEO). Over the next few years, Jobs was able to return the company to profitability.

Being a profitable company has allowed Apple to benefit from what some refer to as a virtuous cycle in which the company is able to both do good financially and do good socially. The company's solid financial resources provide the ability to do good, whereas doing good helps the company do well financially.

Apple realizes that a win-win situation can be obtained through its commitment to social responsibility. For example, Apple's Website explains how important it is to follow sound environmental policies to conserve natural resources. An example of this philosophy is demonstrated by its innovative packaging of the company's fourth-generation iPod nano that is 32 percent lighter and uses 54 percent less packaging than the first-generation iPod nano, saving both natural resources and money.

But what if we decide to consider investing in a company like Apple? How should we go about determining whether Apple is a good investment? We first want to do some research to determine if the company is profitable and financially sound. In this, and future chapters, we will begin to accumulate the financial skills needed to evaluate the financial health and operating performance of companies such as Apple.

# CLASSIFIED BALANCE SHEET

A **classified balance sheet** presents the assets and liabilities of a business in separate subgroups. Such classification aids our financial analysis and business decision making. Exhibit 2-1 presents a list of the typical components of a classified balance sheet. A company need not use all of the components, and each company will use only those components necessary to report its financial position. Exhibit 2-1 shows that a company's assets are commonly classified into two subgroups: current assets and long-term assets. Similarly, liabilities are classified into two subgroups: current liabilities and long-term liabilities. Classified balance sheets are presented by most businesses. In those industries in which the normal operating cycle exceeds one year, such as the financial services industry and the wine industry, classified balance sheets are rarely presented.

| EXHIBIT 2-1 | Typical Components of a Classified Balance Sheet | | |
|---|---|---|---|
| **Assets** | | **Liabilities and Stockholders' Equity** | |
| **Current Assets** | | **Current Liabilities** | |
| | • Cash and cash equivalents | | • Accounts payable |
| | • Accounts receivable | | • Accrued expenses payable |
| | • Inventory | | • Short-term notes payable |
| | • Other current assets | | • Other current liabilities |
| **Long-Term Assets** | | **Long-Term Liabilities** | |
| | • Property, plant, and equipment | | • Long-term notes payable |
| | • Intangible assets | | • Other long-term liabilities |
| | • Other long-term assets | **Stockholders' Equity** | |

## CURRENT ASSETS

**Current assets** consist of cash and other assets that will be converted into cash or used up within the normal operating cycle of a business or one year, whichever is longer. The

**normal operating cycle** of a business is the average period of time between the use of cash to deliver a service or to buy goods for resale and the subsequent collection of cash from customers who purchase those services or products. For most businesses, the normal operating cycle is less than one year. For example, the normal operating cycle for a grocery store chain like **Safeway** might be as short as a week or two, on average, and even only a day or two for perishable products like bread and fresh sliced vegetables.

Current assets are listed on a classified balance sheet in the order of their expected liquidity. **Liquidity** is determined by the ability of an asset to be readily converted into cash. Exhibit 2-1 lists four examples of current assets in the order of their expected liquidity: cash, accounts receivable, inventory, and other current assets. Accounts receivable and inventory are converted into cash as part of the normal operations of a business; that is, inventory is sold for cash or on credit (accounts receivable) that is subsequently collected as cash from customers. Other current assets, such as supplies, are consumed during the normal operating cycle rather than converted into cash, and thus, represent the least liquid of the current assets. The following excerpt shows the current asset section of **Apple**.

| APPLE INC.<br>Balance Sheet (Partial)<br>September 25, 2010 (in millions) | |
| --- | --- |
| **Current assets** | |
| Cash | $11,261 |
| Accounts receivable | 5,510 |
| Inventory | 1,051 |
| Other current assets | 23,856 |
| Total current assets | $41,678 |

## LONG-TERM ASSETS

Long-term assets are assets that the company does not expect to convert into cash within the next year or use up during the course of the normal operating cycle, whichever is longer. Long-term assets include property, plant, and equipment, intangible assets, and other long-term assets.

### Property, Plant, and Equipment

**Property, plant, and equipment** consists of the land, buildings, equipment, vehicles, furniture, and fixtures that a company uses in its day-to-day operations. Investments into property, plant, and equipment, or PP&E, are often referred to as *capital expenditures* or capital investments. The following excerpt shows the PP&E section of **Apple**.

| APPLE INC.<br>Balance Sheet (Partial)<br>September 25, 2010 (in millions) | | |
| --- | --- | --- |
| Property, plant, and equipment | | |
| Land and buildings | $1,471 | |
| Equipment | 3,733 | |
| Leasehold improvements | 2,030 | $7,234 |
| Less: accumulated depreciation and amortization | | 2,466 |
| Total property, plant, and equipment | | $4,768 |

### Intangible Assets

**Intangible assets** consist of brand names, copyrights, patents, and trademarks that a company acquires. These assets are referred to as "intangible" because, unlike buildings and equipment, they lack a physical presence. But, like buildings and equipment, intangible assets enable a company to generate revenue from its customers who recognize the quality associated with products bearing a brand name or trademark. The following excerpt shows the intangible asset section of **Apple**.

| APPLE INC. Balance Sheet (Partial) September 25, 2010 (in millions) | |
| --- | --- |
| Intangible assets | |
| Goodwill......................................................................... | $ 741 |
| Acquired technology............................................................ | 242 |
| Trademarks ...................................................................... | 100 |
| Total intangible assets ..................................................... | $1,083 |

## Other Long-Term Assets

Other long-term assets consist of resources that a company consolidates into a single miscellaneous category. We discuss and illustrate the various types of assets that comprise this category of assets in later chapters. The following excerpt shows the other asset section of **Apple**.

| APPLE INC. Balance Sheet (Partial) September 25, 2010 (in millions) | |
| --- | --- |
| Other long-term assets | |
| Long-term marketable securities .............................................. | $25,391 |
| Other assets .................................................................... | 2,263 |
| Total other long-term assets................................................. | $27,654 |

## CURRENT LIABILITIES

**Current liabilities** consist of liabilities that must be settled within the normal operating cycle or one year, whichever is longer. Exhibit 2-1 lists four types of current liabilities: accounts payable, accrued expenses payable, short-term notes payable, and other current liabilities. Accounts payable reflects the amounts owed for inventory that was purchased from suppliers on credit. Accrued expenses payable include wages, utilities, interest, income tax, and property taxes that are legally owed by a company but which have not yet been paid. Short-term notes payable represent the financing that a company receives from its lenders for large inventory purchases and for inventory purchases that a company does not expect to pay off for more than 90 days. Other current liabilities consist of current obligations that the company aggregates into a single miscellaneous category. One example is the advance payments received from customers (deferred revenue), such as for goods under a layaway plan that will be earned as revenue within the normal operating cycle or one year, whichever is longer. The following excerpt shows the current liabilities section of **Apple**.

| APPLE INC. Balance Sheet (Partial) September 25, 2010 (in millions) | |
| --- | --- |
| Current liabilities | |
| Accounts payable ............................................................... | $12,015 |
| Deferred revenue ............................................................... | 2,984 |
| Accrued expenses................................................................ | 5,723 |
| Total current liabilities ..................................................... | $20,722 |

## LONG-TERM LIABILITIES

**Long-term liabilities** consist of debt obligations not due to be settled within the normal operating cycle or one year. Long-term notes payable and bonds payable are two examples of long-term liabilities. Other long-term liabilities include unfunded employee retirement plans that will be funded by the company in the future. The following excerpt shows the long-term liabilities section of **Apple**.

**A.K.A.** Long-term liabilities are also referred to as noncurrent liabilities.

| APPLE INC. Balance Sheet (Partial) September 25, 2010 (in millions) | |
| --- | --- |
| Long-term liabilities | |
| Deferred revenue | $1,139 |
| Deferred tax liabilities | 4,300 |
| Other liabilities | 1,231 |
| Total long-term liabilities | $6,670 |

## STOCKHOLDERS' EQUITY

**Stockholders' equity** is the residual ownership interest in the assets of a business after its liabilities have been paid off. The stockholders' equity of a corporation is divided into two main categories: amounts invested by stockholders (common stock) and the cumulative net income of a business that has not yet been distributed to its stockholders as a dividend (retained earnings). The following excerpt shows the stockholders' equity section of **Apple**.

**A.K.A.** Stockholders' equity is also referred to as shareholders' equity.

| APPLE INC. Balance Sheet (Partial) September 25, 2010 (in millions) | |
| --- | --- |
| Stockholders' equity | |
| Common stock | $10,668 |
| Retained earnings | 37,169 |
| Other equity | (46) |
| Total stockholders' equity | $47,791 |

## PRESENTATION FORMAT

There are two generally accepted formats for presenting a classified balance sheet—the account form and the report form. Exhibit 2-2 presents the account form of a classified balance sheet for **Apple** as of September 25, 2010. For the **account form**, assets are displayed on the left side and liabilities and stockholders' equity are displayed on the right side. For the **report form**, assets are displayed at the top, with liabilities displayed below the assets,

**Hint:** According to *Accounting Trends and Techniques,* a recent survey of 600 large U.S. companies shows that 88% use the *report form* for their balance sheet while 12% use the *account form.*

---

**IFRS ALERT!**

Go to Appendix C at the end of this book and review the classified balance sheet of **Tesco PLC**. Tesco is the world's third largest retailer and is based in the United Kingdom. Tesco prepares its classified balance sheet using IFRS. After reviewing Tesco's balance sheet, prepare a list of differences between Tesco's IFRS balance sheet and Apple's U.S. GAAP balance sheet in Exhibit 2-2. Differences include: (a) Tesco utilizes the report form; (b) Tesco presents noncurrent assets before its current assets—that is, it lists the company's assets in reverse order of liquidity; (c) Tesco calculates net assets by subtracting total liabilities from total assets; and (d) Tesco uses slightly different labeling for some of its balance sheet accounts, for instance common stock is referred to as "share capital."

and stockholders' equity displayed below liabilities. Apple's 2010 balance sheet in report form is presented in Exhibit 2-3. The report form is the more widely used format.

---

**EXHIBIT 2-2   Account Form of a Classified Balance Sheet**

**APPLE INC.**
**Balance Sheet**
**September 25, 2010, and September 26, 2009**

| (in millions) | 2010 | 2009 | | 2010 | 2009 |
|---|---|---|---|---|---|
| **Assets** | | | **Liabilities** | | |
| **Current assets** | | | **Current liabilities** | | |
| Cash.................. | $11,261 | $ 5,263 | Accounts payable .................. | $12,015 | $ 5,601 |
| Accounts receivable......... | 5,510 | 3,361 | Other current liabilities............ | 8,707 | 5,905 |
| Inventory .................. | 1,051 | 455 | Total current liabilities .......... | 20,722 | 11,506 |
| Other current assets........ | 23,856 | 22,476 | **Long-term liabilities.**.............. | 6,670 | 4,355 |
| Total current assets ....... | 41,678 | 31,555 | Total liabilities .................. | 27,392 | 15,861 |
| **Long-term assets** | | | **Stockholders' Equity** | | |
| Property, plant and equipment .............. | 4,768 | 2,954 | Common stock ...................... | 10,668 | 8,210 |
| Intangible assets............ | 1,083 | 453 | Retained earnings ................... | 37,169 | 23,353 |
| Other long-term assets...... | 27,654 | 12,539 | Other equity ........................ | (46) | 77 |
| Total long-term assets..... | 33,505 | 15,946 | Total stockholders' equity ........ | 47,791 | 31,640 |
| **Total assets**.................. | $75,183 | $47,501 | **Total liabilities and stockholders' equity** .............. | $75,183 | $47,501 |

---

**EXHIBIT 2-3   Report Form of a Classified Balance Sheet**

**APPLE INC.**
**Balance Sheet**
**September 25, 2010, and September 26, 2009**

| (in millions) | 2010 | 2009 |
|---|---|---|
| **Assets** | | |
| **Current assets** | | |
| Cash......................................................... | $11,261 | $ 5,263 |
| Accounts receivable......................................... | 5,510 | 3,361 |
| Inventory ................................................... | 1,051 | 455 |
| Other current assets......................................... | 23,856 | 22,476 |
| Total current assets ...................................... | 41,678 | 31,555 |
| **Long-term assets** | | |
| Property, plant and equipment ............................... | 4,768 | 2,954 |
| Intangible assets ............................................ | 1,083 | 453 |
| Other long-term assets....................................... | 27,654 | 12,539 |
| Total long-term assets...................................... | 33,505 | 15,946 |
| Total assets................................................. | $75,183 | $47,501 |
| **Liabilities** | | |
| **Current liabilities** | | |
| Accounts payable ............................................ | $12,015 | $ 5,601 |
| Other current liabilities...................................... | 8,707 | 5,905 |
| Total current liabilities ................................... | 20,722 | 11,506 |
| **Long-term liabilities.**....................................... | 6,670 | 4,355 |
| Total liabilities ........................................... | 27,392 | 15,861 |
| **Stockholders' Equity** | | |
| Common stock............................................... | 10,668 | 8,210 |
| Retained earnings ........................................... | 37,169 | 23,353 |
| Other equity ................................................ | (46) | 77 |
| Total stockholders' equity................................... | 47,791 | 31,640 |
| Total liabilities and stockholders' equity ...................... | $75,183 | $47,501 |

**Your Turn!** 2.1

The President of Musicland Company requests that you prepare a classified balance sheet in account form for the company. The following financial data are available from the company's accounting records as of December 31, 2011.

| | | | |
|---|---|---|---|
| Cash | $ 300 | Accounts payable | $ 2,500 |
| Accounts receivable | 3,000 | Other current liabilities | 2,000 |
| Inventory | 12,200 | Long-term notes payable | 20,000 |
| Other current assets | 1,500 | Stockholders' equity | 17,500 |
| Property, plant, & equipment, net | 25,000 | | |

The solution is on page 96.

# WORKING WITH FINANCIAL STATEMENTS

Chapter 1 introduced the basic financial statements. We now extend that discussion by demonstrating how financial statements are used to address questions about a company's operating performance and financial health.

## ANALYSIS BASED ON RATIOS

If Apple's net income in 2010 totaled $14,013 million, would we conclude that the company had a good year or a bad year? While $14,013 million is a large number, some frame of reference is needed before we can conclude that this amount represents a good, bad, or mediocre level of operating performance. For example, $14,013 million is a phenomenal performance if the company had only $1 million to operate with during the year. But it is not exceptional if the company had $100,000 million to operate with during the year.

Investment professionals use a variety of methods to get a better understanding of how to interpret a net income number like $14,013 million. One such method involves ratio analysis. **Ratio analysis** expresses the relation of one relevant accounting number to another relevant accounting number through the process of division. The result of the division is expressed as a percentage, a rate, or as a proportion.

To illustrate how a ratio can provide additional meaning to Apple's net income of $14,013 million, we can divide Apple's net income by its total assets of $75,183 million, which is known as its **return on assets (ROA)**. The result is 18.6 percent and tells us that Apple earned a rate of return of 18.6 percent on each dollar of assets invested in the business in 2010. We can also compare this return with that of other technology companies to help us evaluate Apple's performance.

Although a single number like Apple's net income is difficult to interpret in isolation, a single ratio is also difficult to interpret without some point of reference or benchmark. Business professionals often use one of two techniques to further their understanding of ratios. **Trend analysis** is a process in which we compare a company's results, or the results of a ratio, over time. This technique helps the financial statement user identify any readily observable trends in a company's performance. **Benchmarking analysis** is where the analyst compares a company's performance or a ratio to that of its competitors or to an industry average. Under benchmarking analysis, we are trying to compare or benchmark a company's performance against similar companies or against an industry standard. Trend analysis and benchmarking analysis are powerful tools to place a company's results into a meaningful context.

## WORKING WITH THE BALANCE SHEET

The balance sheet helps users evaluate how financially healthy a company is. The balance sheet also provides information on how the company finances the acquisition of its assets,

**LEARNING OBJECTIVE 2**

**Discuss** use of a balance sheet and ratios to assess liquidity and solvency.

with debt or with equity. Exhibit 2-2 presented a simplified version of Apple's balance sheet.

Terms such as liquidity and solvency refer to the financial well-being of a company. For a company to remain in business it must be able to pay its bills when they come due. Before a bank such as **Bank of America** will commit to extend a loan to a company like Apple, it needs to assess the likelihood that it will be repaid the amount borrowed and be paid the interest due on the amount borrowed, both in a timely manner. This assessment involves evaluating Apple's *liquidity*, the ability to pay obligations that come due in the current year, and *solvency*, the ability to pay obligations over the long term.

## Liquidity

**Liquidity** refers to a company's ability to pay its short-term financial obligations. It depends on several factors, including the level of cash a company has and how quickly it can generate cash from operations or its assets.

### CURRENT RATIO

One widely-used measure of a company's liquidity is the **current ratio**. The current ratio is defined as current assets divided by current liabilities. Current assets provide a measure of the cash available and expected to be generated in the current period. Current liabilities provide a measure of the cash that will be needed in the current period to pay existing or expected obligations.

$$\text{Current ratio} = \frac{\text{Current assets}}{\text{Current liabilities}}$$

A current ratio greater than one implies that a company has more cash and current assets than needed to pay off its current obligations, and a ratio less than one implies the opposite. While this interpretation is overly simplistic, it does provide an easily understood assessment of a company's liquidity. In general, the greater the current ratio, the more liquid a company is, and the less concern a lender has in extending a loan to the company.

| **EXHIBIT 2-4** Current Ratio | | |
|---|---|---|
| **(in millions)** | **2010** | **2009** |
| Apple . . . . . . . . . . . . . . . . . . . . . . . . . . . . . . . . . . . . . . . . . . . . . . . . . . . . . . . | $\frac{\$41,678}{\$20,722} = 2.01{:}1$ | $\frac{\$31,555}{\$11,506} = 2.74{:}1$ |
| Dell . . . . . . . . . . . . . . . . . . . . . . . . . . . . . . . . . . . . . . . . . . . . . . . . . . . . . . . . | $\frac{\$24,245}{\$18,960} = 1.28{:}1$ | $\frac{\$20,151}{\$14,859} = 1.36{:}1$ |

The current ratio for both Apple and for Dell is in Exhibit 2-4. Both Apple and Dell report current ratios greater than one in 2010 and 2009; however, Apple reports a larger current ratio than does Dell in both years. Based on this ratio, we would conclude that Apple is more liquid than Dell, although each company appears to be sufficiently liquid to satisfy currently due obligations.

**TAKEAWAY 2.1**

| Concept ⟶ | Method ⟶ | Assessment |
|---|---|---|
| Can a company meet its short-term obligations? | Current assets and current liabilities from the balance sheet.<br><br>$\text{Current ratio} = \frac{\text{Current assets}}{\text{Current liabilities}}$ | A larger current ratio implies greater liquidity and a greater ability to pay short-term obligations. |

## Solvency

Lenders often provide loans that have repayment terms that extend over several years. In such cases the lender is interested in evaluating a company's solvency. **Solvency** refers to a company's ability to pay its long-term financial obligations. It depends on several factors, including the level of assets a company has. Solvency, therefore, is a measure of a company's ability to survive over the long term. (Both liquidity and solvency are important indicators of financial health; but, a company must first be liquid. If a company is unable to pay its bills in the short term, it is irrelevant whether it is solvent in the long term.)

### DEBT-TO-TOTAL-ASSETS RATIO

In general, the more debt a company uses to finance its assets and day-to-day operations, the riskier it is. This follows because the amount borrowed and the interest on that amount must be paid on a regular schedule. If a company is unable to meet the cash outflows required to satisfy its debt repayment schedule or meet its regular interest payments, a lender can legally demand immediate repayment of a loan, potentially forcing a company into bankruptcy if it is unable to repay that amount. The **debt-to-total-assets ratio**, calculated as total liabilities divided by total assets, provides a measure of this risk and is one ratio used to assess a company's solvency.

$$\text{Debt-to-total-assets ratio} = \frac{\text{Total liabilities}}{\text{Total assets}}$$

The greater the debt-to-total-assets ratio, the greater is a company's risk of not being able to pay its interest payments or principal repayments on a timely basis, and the lower is the company's solvency. Like the current ratio, the debt-to-total-assets ratio should not be used in isolation. There are many factors that must be considered when judging a company's solvency.

| EXHIBIT 2-5 | Debt-to-Total-Assets Ratio | | |
|---|---|---|---|
| **(in millions)** | | **2010** | **2009** |
| Apple ........................................................... | | $\frac{\$27,392}{\$75,183} = 36.4\%$ | $\frac{\$15,861}{\$47,501} = 33.4\%$ |
| Dell ............................................................. | | $\frac{\$28,011}{\$33,652} = 83.2\%$ | $\frac{\$22,229}{\$26,500} = 83.9\%$ |

Exhibit 2-5 shows the debt-to-total-assets ratio for Apple and Dell. This exhibit reveals that in 2010, Dell used considerably more debt to finance its assets than did Apple (83.2 percent versus 36.4 percent). Consequently, Dell would be considered a riskier, less solvent company. A lender such as **Citibank** would likely be more concerned about the solvency of Dell than the solvency of Apple.

| Concept → | Method → | Assessment |
|---|---|---|
| Can a company meet its long-term obligations? | Total assets and total liabilities from the balance sheet.<br><br>Debt-to-total-assets ratio = $\frac{\text{Total liabilities}}{\text{Total assets}}$ | A larger ratio implies reduced solvency and a reduced ability to repay outstanding obligations over the long term. |

TAKEAWAY 2.2

## WORKING WITH THE INCOME STATEMENT

Apple generates income by selling computers, iPads, iPods, iPhones, peripherals, and downloads from its iTunes store. The company's income statement provides a report detailing how much net income Apple was able to generate from these activities. A review of a company's income and its components is called profitability analysis. Apple's net income of $14,013 million for the year ended September 25, 2010, indicates that Apple was able to sell these products at a price that exceeded the cost of manufacturing. Apple's income statement, presented in Exhibit 2-6, also shows that the company's profitability increased from 2009 to 2010.

LEARNING OBJECTIVE 3

**Discuss** use of the income statement and ratios to assess profitability.

| **EXHIBIT 2-6**  Income Statement | | |
|---|---|---|
| **APPLE INC.** | | |
| **Income Statement** | | |
| **For Years Ended September 25, 2010, and September 26, 2009** | | |
| **(in millions)** | **2010** | **2009** |
| Revenues | | |
| Net sales..................................................... | $65,225 | $42,905 |
| Expenses | | |
| Cost of goods sold ........................................ | 39,541 | 25,683 |
| Selling, general, and administrative expenses ..................................... | 7,144 | 5,156 |
| Income tax expense........................................ | 4,527 | 3,831 |
| Total expenses ............................................ | 51,212 | 34,670 |
| Net income................................................. | $14,013 | $ 8,235 |

Apple's net income increased by $5,778 million, from $8,235 in 2009 to $14,013 in 2010. One of Apple's competitors is **Dell Inc.**, an online retailer of personal computers. During a similar period, Dell's net income fell by nearly $1 billion, from $2,478 million to $1,433 million. This suggests that Apple outperformed one of its leading competitors during a difficult economic period. How was that possible? Perhaps Apple's success reflects its superior product line or possibly its greater diversity in products offered for sale. Alternatively, it might reflect the superior operating acumen of Apple's management team.

## MEASURES FOR PROFITABILITY ANALYSIS

There are many ways to measure a company's success. One such measure is profitability. Profitability indicates whether or not a company is able to bring its products or services to the market efficiently, and whether it produces products or services that are valued by the market. The more profitable a company is, the better are its long-term prospects. Consistently unprofitable companies are on a path to failure.

### Return on Sales

It is somewhat unfair, and potentially misleading, to compare two companies of differing size on the basis of net income. A larger company is expected to generate a larger net income. But a large net income does not necessarily indicate that a company is performing more efficiently than a company with a smaller net income. One measure that facilitates a comparison of the profitability between companies of different size is the return on assets ratio, which we already explained. Another useful measure is the **return on sales (ROS) ratio**, calculated as net income divided by net sales.

$$\text{Return on sales} = \frac{\text{Net income}}{\text{Net sales}}$$

Exhibit 2-7 shows the calculation of return on sales for both Apple and Dell. Apple is a bit larger than Dell based on sales generated in 2010 ($65,225,000,000 for Apple versus $52,902,000,000 for Dell). Apple also generates much more income than Dell ($14,013,000,000 for Apple versus $1,433,000,000 for Dell in 2010). This translates into a much higher return on sales for Apple (21.5 percent for Apple versus 2.7 percent for Dell in 2010). An ROS of 21.5 indicates Apple has 21.5 cents left over for each dollar of sales revenue after subtracting all of its expenses. This is almost eight times as much as Dell, which generates just 2.7 cents for each dollar of sales revenue. This result suggests that Apple is a more profitable company than Dell, possibly because it is able to command a premium price for its products and/or because it runs a more efficient operation than does Dell.

| EXHIBIT 2-7 | Return on Sales | | |
|---|---|---|---|
| **(in millions)** | | **2010*** | **2009** |
| Apple........................................................ | | $\dfrac{\$14,013}{\$65,225} = 21.5\%$ | $\dfrac{\$8,235}{\$42,905} = 19.2\%$ |
| Dell.......................................................... | | $\dfrac{\$1,433}{\$52,902} = 2.7\%$ | $\dfrac{\$2,478}{\$61,101} = 4.1\%$ |

\* One of the difficulties encountered in benchmarking is that companies often have different fiscal year-ends. Apple's year-end occurs in September, while Dell's year-end occurs in January.

| Concept | ⟶ | Method | ⟶ | Assessment |
|---|---|---|---|---|
| How much net income does a company generate from each dollar of sales revenue? | | Net sales and net income from the income statement. $$\text{Return on sales} = \frac{\text{Net income}}{\text{Net sales}}$$ | | A larger ratio indicates that a company is more profitable on each sales dollar; this is because it commands a premium price for its products and/or is more operationally efficient. |

TAKEAWAY 2.3

## WORKING WITH THE STATEMENT OF STOCKHOLDERS' EQUITY

Chapter 1 introduced the statement of retained earnings, which summarizes the history of a company's net income that has been accumulated and reinvested in the business, and which has not been distributed to its stockholders as a dividend. Retained earnings at the end of a fiscal period is calculated as retained earnings at the start of the period, plus net income for the period, less any dividends paid during the period.

**LEARNING OBJECTIVE 4**

Explain the components of the statement of stockholders' equity.

> **Retained earnings, beginning of period**
> **+ Net income**
> **− Dividends**
> _____
> **Retained earnings, end of period**

The statement of stockholders' equity is a more comprehensive statement, reporting on both the changes in a company's common stock *and* changes in its retained earnings. The statement of stockholders' equity consists of two parts—contributed capital and earned capital. **Contributed capital** is a measure of the capital contributed by the stockholders of a company when they purchase ownership shares in the company. Ownership shares are called common shares or common stock. **Earned capital** is a measure of the capital that is earned by the company, reinvested in the business, and not distributed to its stockholders—that is, its retained earnings.

Exhibit 2-8 presents the statement of stockholders' equity for Apple. The column labeled Common Stock represents the change in Apple's contributed capital during the period covered by the statement. The largest change to common stock is the issuance of additional shares. The newly issued shares may have been sold to Apple's existing stockholders, to new stockholders, or possibly to Apple's employees. "Other adjustments" to contributed capital are covered in later chapters.

The column labeled Retained Earnings in Exhibit 2-8 represents Apple's earned capital. Because Apple does not pay a dividend, the primary adjustment to this column is the addition of net income for the period. Why has Apple's management decided not to distribute any of its net income as a dividend? There are many factors that go into that decision, but one consideration is the investment opportunities that a company has for the money that it earns. As we saw earlier, Apple is able to generate a high return on each dollar of sales, so Apple might feel that it is better to retain its net income and invest it in the business than to make distributions to its stockholders who may have difficulty finding investments with equal or higher rates of return.

| **EXHIBIT 2-8**  Statement of Stockholders' Equity | | | |
| --- | --- | --- | --- |
| **APPLE INC.** **Statement of Stockholders' Equity** | | | |
| **(in millions)** | **Common Stock** | **Retained Earnings** | **Other Equity** |
| Balance at September 27, 2008 .......................................... | $ 7,177 | $15,129 | $ (9) |
| Issuance of common stock............................................. | 1,033 | | |
| Net income........................................................ | | 8,235 | |
| Other adjustments ................................................. | | (11) | 86 |
| Balance at September 26, 2009 .......................................... | 8,210 | 23,353 | 77 |
| Issuance of common stock............................................. | 2,458 | | |
| Net income........................................................ | | 14,013 | |
| Other adjustments ................................................. | | (197) | (123) |
| Balance at September 25, 2010 .......................................... | $10,668 | $37,169 | $(46) |

| **CORPORATE SOCIAL RESPONSIBILITY** | **Investing with a Social Conscience** |
| --- | --- |

Not all investors are singularly focused on the financial performance of businesses they invest in. For a segment of the investing community, corporate social responsibility goes hand in hand with financial performance in choosing an investment. **Socially responsible investing (SRI)**, also known as sustainable investing, considers a firm's environmental stewardship, consumer protection, human rights, and diversity, along with its financial performance. Investments in SRI funds are near $3 trillion and have grown in recent years at a pace almost six times greater than the growth of professionally managed investments.

## WORKING WITH THE STATEMENT OF CASH FLOWS

LEARNING OBJECTIVE 5

**Explain** use of the statement of cash flows to help assess solvency.

A common refrain heard from business people is that we do not pay bills with net income, we pay bills with cash! While net income is eventually converted into cash, it is the cash available that a company uses to run its business and pay its bills. Where can we find information about a company's cash resources? The answer is the statement of cash flows, which provides information on a company's sources and uses of cash.

The statement of cash flows aids us in understanding the change in cash reported by a company over a period of time. The statement explains the change in the cash reported between two balance sheet dates. The statement of cash flows is segmented into three activity categories: (1) cash flow from operating activities, (2) cash flow from investing activities, and (3) cash flow from financing activities. The separation into these three activities increases the statement's usefulness. For example, knowing that cash increased is not as useful as knowing that cash increased because of increased operating cash flow or because of a bank loan.

Exhibit 2-9 shows a simplified version of Apple's statement of cash flows. Apple reported an increase of $5,998 million in cash in 2010, increasing from $5,263 million in 2009 to $11,261 million in 2010. These cash balances are on Apple's balance sheet in Exhibit 2-2. Most of Apple's cash flow in 2010 was generated from operating activities ($18,595 million), with another $1,257 million from financing activities such as the sale of equity securities. Apple used much of its cash flow in its investing activities, with $11,093 million used for purchase of investments and $2,643 used to purchase additional property, plant, and equipment.

**Hint:** When calculating a firm's free cash flow, the "capital expenditures" amount is net of the cash spent for purchases of PP&E less the cash proceeds received from the sale of PP&E. Both amounts are reported on a company's statement of cash flows.

### Free Cash Flow

The level of cash flow provided by operating activities is valuable information on a company's ability to generate cash from its day-to-day operations. One measure of cash flow health is **free cash flow**. Free cash flow is calculated by subtracting a company's capital expenditures for PP&E from its cash flow provided by operating activities. A company's free cash flow is an indicator of its ability to expand operations, repay lenders, or pay stockholders a dividend after replacing the value of any property, plant and equipment used in operations. In general, the larger a company's free cash flow, the healthier a company is in terms of operating cash flow.

$$\text{Free cash flow} = \text{Cash flow from operations} - \text{Capital expenditures}$$

We calculate Apple's free cash flow in 2010 and 2009 with information reported in Apple's statement of cash flows in Exhibit 2-9.

| (in millions) | 2010 | 2009 |
|---|---|---|
| Cash flow provided by operating activities | $18,595 | $10,159 |
| Less: Expenditures on property, plant, and equipment | (2,643) | (1,144) |
| Free cash flow | $15,952 | $ 9,015 |

Apple's free cash flow of $15,952 in 2010 and $9,015 in 2009 indicates that it generates a healthy free cash flow. It also suggests that Apple should have no trouble financing future purchases of property, plant, and equipment, repaying its lenders, or paying dividends to its stockholders, using its operating cash flow.

| Concept ⟶ | Method ⟶ | Assessment |
|---|---|---|
| How much free cash flow does a company generate? | Cash provided by operating activities less cash expended on purchases of property, plant, and equipment.<br><br>Cash provided by operations<br>− Capital expenditures<br>―――――――――――<br>= Free cash flow | Larger free cash flow indicates a greater ability to expand operations, repay debt, or pay dividends without external financing. |

TAKEAWAY 2.4

| EXHIBIT 2-9 | Statement of Cash Flows |
|---|---|

**APPLE INC.**
**Statement of Cash Flows**
**For Years Ended September 25, 2010, and September 26, 2009**

| (in millions) | 2010 | 2009 |
|---|---|---|
| Cash flow provided by operating activities | | |
| Cash receipts from operating activities | $63,076 | $41,966 |
| Cash payments for operating activities | (44,481) | (31,807) |
| Net cash provided by operations | 18,595 | 10,159 |
| Cash flow provided by investing activities | | |
| Net purchases of investments | (11,093) | (16,147) |
| Net payments for property, plant, and equipment | (2,643) | (1,144) |
| Other cash payments | (118) | (143) |
| Net cash used by investing | (13,854) | (17,434) |
| Cash flow provided by financing activities | | |
| Issuance of equity securities | 1,663 | 745 |
| Other payments | (406) | (82) |
| Net cash provided by financing | 1,257 | 663 |
| Net increase in cash | 5,998 | (6,612) |
| Cash at beginning of year | 5,263 | 11,875 |
| Cash at year-end | $11,261 | $ 5,263 |

## Your Turn!                                                      2.2

The following information is available from the financial statements of the Philips Company.

|                                                    | 2010      | 2009      |
|----------------------------------------------------|-----------|-----------|
| Net sales                                          | $120,000  | $110,000  |
| Net income                                         | 20,000    | 15,000    |
| Cash provided by operating activities              | 25,000    | 22,000    |
| Expenditures on property, plant, and equipment     | 7,000     | 6,000     |
| Current assets                                     | 75,000    | 65,000    |
| Current liabilities                                | 50,000    | 45,000    |
| Total assets                                       | 220,000   | 190,000   |
| Total liabilities                                  | 150,000   | 145,000   |

Compute the following ratios and comment on any trends observed between 2009 and 2010: (1) return on sales, (2) current ratio, (3) debt-to-total-assets ratio, and (4) free cash flow.

**The solution is on page 96.**

# GENERALLY ACCEPTED ACCOUNTING PRINCIPLES

**LEARNING OBJECTIVE 6**

**Discuss the development of generally accepted accounting principles and the conceptual framework.**

Generally accepted accounting principles—like common law—originate from problem situations such as changes in tax regulations, business law, organizational forms, or financing techniques. In response to the effects that such changes have on financial reports, new or revised accounting methods are devised. Through comparative use and analysis, one or more of these methods are judged suitable, obtaining authoritative support, and are then considered generally accepted. Organizations such as the Financial Accounting Standards Board (FASB), the American Institute of Certified Public Accountants (AICPA), and the U.S. Securities and Exchange Commission (SEC) have been instrumental in development of generally accepted accounting principles (GAAP) in the United States.

### IFRS ALERT!

Until recently, most countries maintained their own set of generally accepted accounting principles. This situation made it expensive for global companies to raise capital in the various countries where they maintained operations because they were required to produce financial statements using local GAAP. Consequently, the global accounting community began work to develop a single, worldwide set of accounting principles. Today, the International Financial Reporting Standards (IFRS) promulgated by the International Accounting Standards Board (IASB) are used in more than 100 countries. While IFRS is not yet permitted for use by all U.S. companies, the FASB is working with the IASB to "harmonize" U.S. GAAP and IFRS through a joint convergence project. Both groups recognize that a global set of accounting principles would provide financial benefits and cost savings to companies that operate on a global basis. A single set of global GAAP would also facilitate efficient allocation of financial resources by global investors. In 2009, the SEC approved 110 U.S. firms as potential early adopters of IFRS. The SEC, however, will not make a final decision until 2011 as to whether to allow, or require, all U.S. firms to adopt IFRS.

An accounting principle must have substantial authoritative support to qualify as generally accepted. References to a particular accounting principle in authoritative accounting literature constitute substantive evidence of its general acceptance. The FASB completed a major restructuring in 2009, called the FASB Accounting Standards Codification, concerning how U.S. GAAP is organized and communicated. This codification represents authoritative U.S. GAAP for nongovernmental entities and is easily researched through an online database maintained by the FASB. A major justification for the codification project was to ease the convergence of U.S. GAAP and IFRS standards.

As a federal agency, the SEC's primary focus is to regulate the sale of stocks and bonds. The SEC requires companies under its jurisdiction to submit audited annual financial statements to the agency which it makes available to the general public. The SEC has the power to set accounting principles used by these companies, but the agency has largely delegated that principle-setting responsibility to the FASB (and earlier, the AICPA).

## CONCEPTUAL FRAMEWORK

The FASB has developed a conceptual framework to guide the formulation of U.S. generally accepted accounting principles. The **conceptual framework** is a cohesive set of interrelated objectives and fundamentals for external financial reporting. This framework, outlined in Exhibit 2-10, consists of (1) financial reporting objectives, (2) financial statement elements, (3) recognition criteria for financial statement items, and (4) qualitative characteristics of accounting information. A recurrent theme in the conceptual framework is the importance of providing information that is useful to financial statement users.

The **financial reporting objectives** of the conceptual framework focus on information useful to investors and creditors. Accordingly, financial statements have the principal objective of providing information that is (1) useful in making investment, credit, and similar decisions and (2) helpful in assessing the ability of enterprises to generate future cash flows. Financial statements should also (3) contain information about a company's economic resources, the claims on those resources, and the effects of events that change those resources and claims. This helps to identify a company's financial strengths and weaknesses, predict future performance, and evaluate earlier expectations.

The **financial statement elements** of the conceptual framework are the components of financial statements. These elements include assets, liabilities, stockholders' equity,

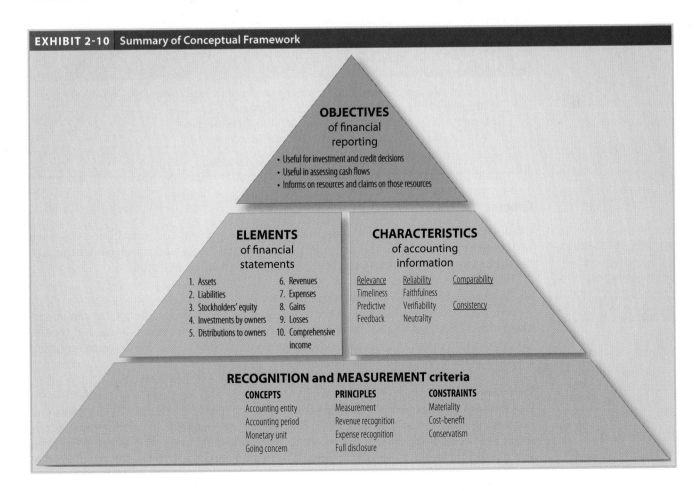

**EXHIBIT 2-10** Summary of Conceptual Framework

**OBJECTIVES**
of financial
reporting
- Useful for investment and credit decisions
- Useful in assessing cash flows
- Informs on resources and claims on those resources

**ELEMENTS**
of financial
statements

1. Assets
2. Liabilities
3. Stockholders' equity
4. Investments by owners
5. Distributions to owners
6. Revenues
7. Expenses
8. Gains
9. Losses
10. Comprehensive income

**CHARACTERISTICS**
of accounting
information

| Relevance | Reliability | Comparability |
| Timeliness | Faithfulness | |
| Predictive | Verifiability | Consistency |
| Feedback | Neutrality | |

**RECOGNITION and MEASUREMENT criteria**

| CONCEPTS | PRINCIPLES | CONSTRAINTS |
|---|---|---|
| Accounting entity | Measurement | Materiality |
| Accounting period | Revenue recognition | Cost-benefit |
| Monetary unit | Expense recognition | Conservatism |
| Going concern | Full disclosure | |

investments by owners, distributions to owners, revenues, expenses, gains, losses, and comprehensive income.

The **qualitative characteristics of accounting information** are qualities that contribute to decision usefulness. The two primary qualities are **relevance** and **reliability**. To be relevant, information must contribute to the predictive and evaluative decisions made by investors and creditors. Reliable information must contain no bias or material error and must faithfully portray what it intends to represent.

The **recognition and measurement criteria** of the framework specify the conditions that must be satisfied before a particular asset, liability, revenue, or expense can be recorded in the financial records. An item under consideration must meet the definition of an element and be measurable, and information about the item must achieve the primary qualitative characteristics of accounting information.

## IFRS ALERT!

There is a debate as to whether accounting principles should be rules-based, as is the case with U.S. GAAP, or principles-based, as is the case with IFRS. A key difference between these approaches is that principles-based accounting provides a conceptual basis to follow instead of a list of detailed rules. The Sarbanes-Oxley legislation called for the SEC to investigate the possible adoption of principles-based standards for U.S. GAAP. The subsequent SEC staff report recommended that U.S. GAAP move toward a principles-based approach. The audit firm PricewaterhouseCoopers wrote: "A rules-based system encourages creativity (and not the good kind) in financial reporting. A principles-based system requires companies to report, and auditors to audit, the substance or business purpose of transactions, not merely whether they can qualify as acceptable under incredibly complex or overly technical rules. A rules-based system allows managers to ignore the substance and instead ask *Where in the rules does it say that I can't do this?*" If the SEC decides in 2011 to permit, or require, U.S. businesses to adopt IFRS, this would be an implicit acceptance of principles-based accounting.

## Your Turn!                                             2.3

1. What are the four key components making up the conceptual framework? What is the main objective of accounting according to this framework?
2. Identify the ten elements that make up the financial statements.
3. What are the two primary qualities of accounting information?

**The solution is on page 96.**

## CHARACTERISTICS OF ACCOUNTING INFORMATION

LEARNING OBJECTIVE 7

Describe the concepts, principles, and constraints of financial accounting.

Qualitative characteristics of accounting information are depicted in Exhibit 2-11. Each of the qualities listed is important and the conceptual framework does not distinguish between primary or secondary qualities. Thus, we view all as essential.

### Understandability and Decision Usefulness

Accounting information should be presented so that a knowledgeable reader can understand how it relates to the decision problem at hand. Because different users will require different information, suppliers (standard setters) must tread a fine line between reporting (requiring) too much or too little information.

### Relevance

The overriding objective that the FASB considers when developing U.S. GAAP is that accounting information must be useful. To be useful, accounting information must be relevant, reliable, comparable, and consistent. To be relevant, accounting information must make a difference in a user's decisions. For example, Apple's financial statements are

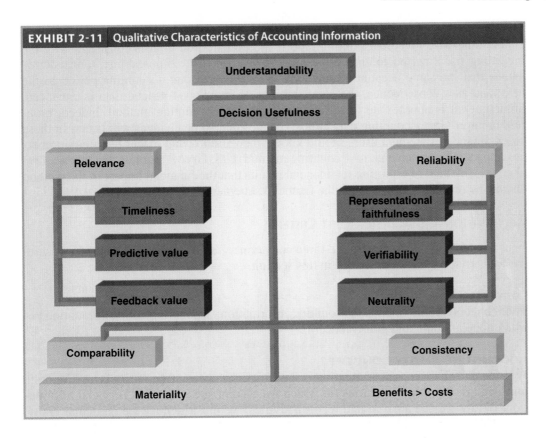

**EXHIBIT 2-11** Qualitative Characteristics of Accounting Information

considered to have *relevance* if they help a potential lender evaluate Apple's profitability, liquidity, and solvency. In addition, financial statements help investors make predictions about Apple's future performance, and help them assess how much they are willing to pay for a share of Apple stock. To be relevant, it is also important that accounting information be timely; consequently, the SEC requires that companies like Apple provide their annual reports to investors within 90 days following the end of a company's fiscal year-end.

### Reliability

*Reliability* dictates that recording of accounting transactions be based on reliable and verifiable evidence. The amounts recorded should be supported by actual order invoices, physical counts of inventory, and other relatively bias-free evidence whenever possible. Undocumented opinions of management or other employees do not provide a good basis for accounting determinations. However, it is often necessary to incorporate estimates into accounting data because some future events are not currently measurable. It is important that these estimates be supported by some type of objective analysis. Reliability also requires that the reported information be a faithful representation of what is reported. If Apple's inventory balance is $400 million, but Apple reports an inventory value of $509 million, the reported number is not a faithful representation of the value of Apple's inventory. Reliability also requires that accounting information be neutral, meaning that it cannot favor one set of financial statement users over another.

### Comparability

Under U.S. GAAP, the uniform use of accounting methods is not required, and firms are allowed flexibility to choose among alternative accounting methods when accounting for business activities. This flexibility is necessary because all firms are not alike, although it must be acknowledged that this flexibility does make financial data comparability more difficult. To enable users to most effectively compare financial results across companies, U.S. GAAP requires that companies disclose in the notes to financial statements the accounting policy choices they elected to use in the preparation of their financial statements.

## Consistency

Unless otherwise noted, accounting reports are prepared on a basis consistent with the preceding fiscal period to ensure the highest level of data comparability. **Consistency** means that the same accounting methods are used from one accounting period to the next, and as a consequence, the comparability of company financial data is enhanced. Sometimes it is appropriate for a firm to change an accounting method. Indeed, progress in improving accounting data almost dictates that some changes will occur. In these cases, financial statement users should know when and to what extent reported numbers are impacted by the change in accounting method. U.S. GAAP requires that when a firm changes a method of reporting its financial results that the financial impact of the method change be revealed in its notes to the financial statements.

## RECOGNITION AND MEASUREMENT CRITERIA

Four concepts, four principles, and three constraints frame the recognition and measurement criteria, which are described in this section.

## Concepts

Four concepts frame financial accounting information: accounting entity, accounting period, monetary unit, and going concern.

### ACCOUNTING ENTITY CONCEPT

A fundamental concept in accounting is the entity. An **accounting entity** is an economic unit with identifiable boundaries for which we accumulate and report financial information. Before we can analyze and report activities, we must identify the particular entity. Each sole proprietorship, partnership, and corporation is an entity, and separate accounting records must be maintained for each unit. In accumulating financial information, we maintain a record of the activities of the accounting entity separately from the economic and personal activities of its owners.

---

**ACCOUNTING IN PRACTICE**    **Johnson & Johnson Accounting Entity**

**Johnson & Johnson**, a manufacturer of health care products, produces such familiar consumer goods as Tylenol and Band-Aids. In a recent annual report to stockholders, it revealed that it had 118,700 employees working in 250 operating companies located in more than 50 different countries. For purposes of reporting, Johnson & Johnson viewed this cluster of companies as a single accounting entity, and consequently, consolidated the financial data of the 250 companies into one set of financial statements. The process of preparing consolidated statements is beneficial for stockholders who would be overwhelmed to receive, and try to comprehend, 250 individual income statements, balance sheets, and statements of cash flows.

---

### ACCOUNTING PERIOD CONCEPT

The operations of most businesses are virtually continuous. Yet, the economic life of a company can be divided into specific periods of time, which is typically one year for purposes of preparing financial statements. Although the division of the total life of a business into segments based on annual periods is artificial, the concept of the **accounting period** is useful. Many taxes are assessed by the government on an annual basis, and reports to corporate stockholders are prepared and distributed annually. In addition, many other noneconomic factors consider the year as a natural division of time. Accounting reports can cover periods other than one year. For instance, investors and creditors can receive quarterly, or *interim*, financial reports and management can receive weekly or monthly reports.

**A.K.A.** A company's accounting period is also referred to as its fiscal period.

### MONETARY UNIT CONCEPT

The **monetary unit concept** specifies that a monetary unit (the dollar in the United States and the euro in the European Union) is to be used to measure and record an entity's eco-

| ACCOUNTING IN PRACTICE | Accounting (or Fiscal) Year-End |
| --- | --- |

Not all companies choose to end their accounting year in December. Companies are allowed to choose any month of the year as their accounting year-end so long as they are consistent from year to year. Choosing a different accounting year-end is one example where data comparability between companies can be difficult.

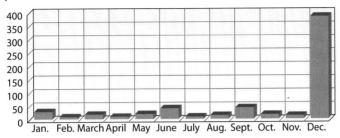

[Following year-ends from a sample of 600 companies; *Accounting Trends & Techniques*]

nomic activity. When all assets, liabilities, and stockholders' equity are stated in monetary terms, they can be added or subtracted to prepare financial statements. Also, relations among financial statement components can be calculated and presented to help interpret the statements. Recording and reporting in monetary terms imposes two limitations. First, only items that can be expressed in monetary terms are brought into the information system. Some economic resources and obligations may be excluded because there is no agreement on how to express them monetarily. For example, the value of a business's workforce—that is, a firm's employees—is not reported as an asset on a balance sheet. The second limitation is that the U.S. dollar (and the currencies of other countries) is not a stable unit of measure. Inflation causes a currency's purchasing power to decline over time. Failure to adjust for this can cause distorted financial statements because amounts are expressed in dollars of different vintages. For example, in calculating total assets at December 31, 2010, supplies purchased in 2010 may be added to land purchased in 1970. Both supplies and land are measured in U.S. dollars, but they are dollars from two different points in time (2010 and 1970), representing quite different units of purchasing power. The measuring unit concept assumes that the purchasing power of the dollar is sufficiently stable such that no adjustments are necessary.

### GOING CONCERN CONCEPT

In the absence of evidence to the contrary, a business is assumed to have an indefinite life. The **going concern concept** presumes that an enterprise will continue to operate indefinitely and will not be sold or otherwise liquidated. This concept often supports use of the cost principle to measure such assets as supplies and equipment. In essence, the going concern concept assumes that a firm will operate long enough to use up its supplies and equipment.

## Principles

Four principles frame financial accounting information: measurement, revenue recognition, expense recognition, and full disclosure.

### MEASUREMENT PRINCIPLE

U.S. GAAP is a mixed measurement system. It is primarily founded on the **cost principle**, meaning assets and liabilities are initially recorded at the amount paid or obligated to pay. Historical acquisition cost is considered the proper initial measurement because, for example, at the time an asset is acquired, it represents the fair value of the asset as agreed upon by both the buyer and seller. However, the fair value principle is sometimes applied after acquisition, which is a "market-based" measurement system for assets and liabilities.

**A.K.A.** An asset's acquisition cost is also called its historical cost.

### REVENUE RECOGNITION PRINCIPLE

Business enterprises exist to provide services and/or sell goods to their customers. The **revenue recognition principle** states that sales revenue should be recorded when services are performed or goods are sold. The revenue recognition principle requires two conditions to exist before sales revenue is recorded on the income statement: (1) the revenue must be *earned* and (2) it must be *realized or realizable.* Normally, both conditions are not met until services are performed or goods are sold.

### EXPENSE RECOGNITION (MATCHING) PRINCIPLE

To the extent feasible, all expenses related to a company's earned sales revenue should be recognized (matched) with, or deducted from, that revenue in the determination of net income. The **expense recognition (matching) principle** states that net income is determined by linking any expenses incurred with the related earned sales revenues. Thus, expenses are recorded in the period that they help to generate the revenues.

Together, the revenue recognition principle and the expense recognition principle define the accrual basis of accounting. Under the **accrual basis of accounting**, sales revenue is recognized when it is both earned and realized (revenue recognition principle) and expenses are recorded in the period in which they help to generate the earned revenue (expense recognition principle). It is important to observe that recording revenues and expenses do not depend upon the receipt or payment of cash. The accrual basis of accounting is widely used. Under the **cash basis of accounting**, revenues are recorded when cash is received from operating activities and expenses are recorded when cash payments are made for operating activities. Net income, therefore, becomes the difference between operating cash receipts and operating cash payments. The cash basis is not considered generally accepted.

### FULL DISCLOSURE PRINCIPLE

All information necessary for a user's understanding of financial statements should be disclosed in a company's annual report. The purpose of accounting is to provide useful information to those parties interested in a firm's financial health. Sometimes, facts or conditions exist that, although not specifically part of the data in the accounting system, have considerable influence on a full understanding and interpretation of financial statements. For example, if a corporation is a defendant in a $500 million product liability lawsuit, this information may be relevant to financial statement users as they evaluate a company's financial health. To properly inform financial statement users, the **full disclosure principle** requires that a business disclose all significant financial facts and circumstances, including pending lawsuits.

**FORENSIC ACCOUNTING** **Cash Fraud Schemes**

Frauds involving cash are the most common frauds, and are more common than corruption or fraudulent financial statements. The more common cash schemes include (1) skimming, where an employee accepts cash from a customer but does not record a sales transaction, (2) cash larceny, where an employee steals cash from the daily receipts before they are deposited in a bank, (3) check tampering, where an employee steals blank company checks and makes them out to themselves or an accomplice, and (4) cash register disbursement, where an employee fraudulently voids a sale on his or her cash register and steals the cash.

## Constraints

Three factors constrain the qualitative characteristics of accounting information: (1) Materiality, (2) Cost-Benefit, and (3) Conservatism.

### MATERIALITY CONSTRAINT

Applying accounting procedures requires effort and costs money. When amounts involved are too small to affect the financial picture, the application of theoretically correct accounting procedures is hardly worth its cost. For example, assets represent items with future economic benefit to an entity. Yet the cost of some assets is so small that it makes little sense to track them. The concept of **materiality** permits a firm to expense the cost of such assets as small tools, office equipment, and furniture when acquired because their cost is "immaterial" in amount. Many firms set dollar limits—such as $500 or $1,000—below which the cost of all assets are immediately expensed on grounds of immateriality.

### COST-BENEFIT CONSTRAINT

The *cost-benefit constraint* requires that the benefit derived from the information outweigh the costs of providing it.

### CONSERVATISM CONSTRAINT

Accounting measurements take place in a context of significant uncertainty, and consequently, there is an accepted realization that errors in the measurement of assets and net income may occur. In today's business world, **conservatism** is the accountant's reaction to situations in which significant uncertainties exist about the outcome of transactions still in progress—that is, accountants follow conservative accounting procedures when they are unsure about the proper measurement to use. For example, if two estimates of future amounts to be received are equally likely, conservatism suggests that the less optimistic estimate be used. Thus, conservatism suggests that the measurement of assets and net income should tend toward an understatement of assets and sales revenues and an overstatement of liabilities and expenses.

---

**Your Turn!**                                                                                 **2.4**

Match the following list of accounting concepts, principles, and constraints with definitions below.

| | | |
|---|---|---|
| Comparability | Relevance | Materiality |
| Reliability | Monetary unit concept | Expense recognition |

1.  Being able to evaluate two different firms in a comparative analysis.
2.  Limit items on financial statements to those that can be expressed in units of money.
3.  Items recorded in the financial statements should be based on verifiable evidence.
4.  Only amounts big enough to matter should be subject to detailed accounting rules.
5.  The idea that accounting information should make a difference to the user.
6.  Record an expense in the same time period as the corresponding revenue is recorded.

**The solution is on page 96.**

---

**WORKING WITH THE TAKEAWAYS**

Throughout this chapter we have considered the financial statements of Apple Inc. and have undertaken select financial analysis using the Takeaways. Utilize these same tools to analyze the financial data of **Logitech International**, a manufacturer of computer peripherals. The following information was reported by Logitech in the company's financial statements as of year-end 2010:

| March 31 (in millions) | 2010 | 2009 |
|---|---|---|
| Current assets . . . . . . . . . . . . . . . . . . . . . . . . . . . . . . . . . . . . . . . . . . . . . . . . . . . . . . . . . . | $ 999 | $1,166 |
| Total assets. . . . . . . . . . . . . . . . . . . . . . . . . . . . . . . . . . . . . . . . . . . . . . . . . . . . . . . . . . . . | 1,422 | 1,527 |
| Current liabilities . . . . . . . . . . . . . . . . . . . . . . . . . . . . . . . . . . . . . . . . . . . . . . . . . . . . . . . | 289 | 443 |
| Total liabilities. . . . . . . . . . . . . . . . . . . . . . . . . . . . . . . . . . . . . . . . . . . . . . . . . . . . . . . . . . | 424 | 567 |
| Net sales . . . . . . . . . . . . . . . . . . . . . . . . . . . . . . . . . . . . . . . . . . . . . . . . . . . . . . . . . . . . . . | 1,518 | 1,521 |
| Net income. . . . . . . . . . . . . . . . . . . . . . . . . . . . . . . . . . . . . . . . . . . . . . . . . . . . . . . . . . . . | 107 | 231 |
| Cash provided by operating activities . . . . . . . . . . . . . . . . . . . . . . . . . . . . . . . . . . . . | 201 | 393 |
| Expenditures on property, plant, and equipment . . . . . . . . . . . . . . . . . . . . . . . . . . . | 48 | 58 |

### Required

1. Calculate return on sales for each year and comment on Logitech's profitability.
2. Calculate the current ratio for each year and comment on Logitech's liquidity.
3. Calculate the debt-to-total-assets ratio for each year and comment on Logitech's solvency.
4. Calculate the free cash flow for each year and comment on what this means for Logitech.
5. Apple's fiscal year-end occurs near the end of September, whereas Logitech uses a March year-end. How might this affect a comparison of the financial results of the two companies?

### Solution

1. Return on sales:

   3/31/2010: $\dfrac{\$107}{\$1,518} = 7.0$ percent      3/31/2009: $\dfrac{\$231}{\$1,521} = 15.2$ percent

   This trend is disappointing. Logitech went from earning over 15 cents of net income for each dollar of sales revenue in 2009 to earning only seven cents on each dollar of sales revenue in 2010. Moreover, Logitech's return on sales compares poorly with Apple's return on sales of 21.5 percent (but is quite favorable when compared to that of Dell Computer).

2. Current ratio:

   3/31/2010: $\dfrac{\$999}{\$289} = 3.46{:}1$         3/31/2009: $\dfrac{\$1,166}{\$443} = 2.63{:}1$

   Logitech appears to be sufficiently liquid, and the company's liquidity is improving.

3. Debt-to-total-assets ratio:

   3/31/2010: $\dfrac{\$424}{\$1,422} = 29.8$ percent      3/31/2009: $\dfrac{\$567}{\$1,527} = 37.1$ percent

   Logitech financed less than one-third of its assets with debt in 2010, and this percentage declined over the two-year period. Consequently, it does not appear that Logitech is exposed to any solvency risk.

4. Free cash flow:

   3/31/2010: $201 - \$48 = \$153$        3/31/2009: $393 - \$58 = \$335$

   Logitech experienced a decline in its free cash flow from 2009 to 2010, but still reported $153 million of free cash flow for the year ended March 31, 2010. This suggests that Logitech's management has considerable operating cash flow available to finance such actions as a business expansion, debt repayment, or dividend distributions to stockholders.

5. As a consequence of the differing fiscal year-end, the information in Logitech's financial statements contains six months of activity not reflected in the financial statements of Apple. Thus, if economic conditions differed dramatically during this time period, it would significantly reduce the comparability of the two companies' financial data. In fact, during this time period there was an economic recession in the United States, making a comparison of the financial performance of the two firms of questionable merit.

## SUMMARY OF LEARNING OBJECTIVES

**Describe a classified balance sheet. (p. 52)**

■ A classified balance sheet contains two subgroups of assets (current assets and long-term assets) and two subgroups of liabilities (current liabilities and long-term liabilities).

■ A classified balance sheet can be presented in account form or report form.

**Discuss use of a balance sheet and ratios to assess liquidity and solvency. (p. 57)**

■ Liquidity refers to a company's ability to pay those obligations that are expected to come due in the next year.

■ The current ratio, or current assets divided by current liabilities, provides a measure of a company's liquidity.

■ Solvency refers to a company's ability to repay its debts over the long term.

■ The debt-to-total-assets ratio, calculated as total debt divided by total assets, provides one measure of a company's solvency.

**Discuss use of the income statement and ratios to assess profitability. (p. 59)**

■ Ratio analysis involves expressing the relation of one relevant accounting number with another relevant accounting number through the process of division. This process helps to provide a context to interpret a particular number.

■ Two techniques that are often used in ratio analysis are (1) trend analysis where ratios are examined over time and (2) benchmarking analysis where a company's ratios are compared to those of another company or to an average of an industry as a whole.

■ Return on sales, or net income divided by net sales, provides a measure of a company's profitability by indicating how much net income a company earns on each dollar of sales revenue.

**Explain the components of the statement of stockholders' equity. (p. 61)**

■ Stockholders' equity comprises two parts: (1) contributed capital and (2) earned capital.

■ Contributed capital is the capital contributed to a firm by stockholders when they purchase ownership shares in the company.

■ Earned capital represents the net income that has been earned by a company and not distributed to stockholders as a dividend.

■ The statement of retained earnings is usually reported as part of the statement of stockholders' equity.

**Explain use of the statement of cash flows to help assess solvency. (p. 62)**

■ The statement of cash flows provides information regarding a company's sources and uses of cash.

■ Free cash flow, calculated as cash provided from operating activities less cash expended on property, plant, and equipment, provides information regarding management's ability to expand operations, repay debt, or make distributions to stockholders, using a firm's operating cash flow.

**Discuss the development of generally accepted accounting principles and the conceptual framework. (p. 64)**

■ The FASB, the AICPA, and the SEC have been instrumental in the development of generally accepted accounting principles in the United States.

■ The conceptual framework is a cohesive set of interrelated objectives, elements, and recognition and measurement criteria for external financial reporting.

**Describe the concepts, principles, and constraints of financial accounting. (p. 66)**

■ Each of the following is an important accounting principle: measurement; revenue recognition; expense recognition; and full disclosure.

■ Each of the following is an important accounting concept: accounting entity; accounting period; monetary unit; and going concern.

■ Each of the following is an important accounting constraint: materiality; cost-benefit; and conservatism.

■ Together, the revenue recognition principle and the expense recognition principle define the accrual basis of accounting.

LO1

LO2

LO3

LO4

LO5

LO6

LO7

REVIEW

REVIEW

## TAKEAWAY: SUMMARY CHART

| | | Concept | Method | Assessment |
|---|---|---|---|---|
| **TAKEAWAY 2.1** | | Can a company meet its short-term obligations? | Current assets and current liabilities from the balance sheet.<br><br>$\text{Current ratio} = \dfrac{\text{Current assets}}{\text{Current liabilities}}$ | A larger current ratio implies greater liquidity and a greater ability to pay short-term obligations. |
| **TAKEAWAY 2.2** | | Can a company meet its long-term obligations? | Total assets and total liabilities from the balance sheet.<br><br>$\text{Debt-to-total-assets ratio} = \dfrac{\text{Total liabilities}}{\text{Total assets}}$ | A larger ratio implies reduced solvency and a reduced ability to repay outstanding obligations over the long term. |
| **TAKEAWAY 2.3** | | How much net income does a company generate from each dollar of sales revenue? | Net sales and net income from the income statement.<br><br>$\text{Return on sales} = \dfrac{\text{Net income}}{\text{Net sales}}$ | A larger ratio indicates that a company is more profitable on each sales dollar; this is because it commands a premium price for its products and/or is more operationally efficient. |
| **TAKEAWAY 2.4** | | How much free cash flow does a company generate? | Cash provided by operating activities less cash expended on purchases of property, plant, and equipment.<br><br>　Cash provided by operations<br>− Capital expenditures<br>　Free cash flow | Larger free cash flow indicates a greater ability to expand operations, repay debt, or pay dividends without external financing. |

## GLOSSARY OF KEY TERMS

**Account form** A format of the classified balance sheet in which assets are displayed on the left side and liabilities and stockholders' equity are displayed on the right side (p. 55).

**Accounting entity** An economic unit with identifiable boundaries that is the focus for the accumulation and reporting of financial information (p. 68).

**Accounting period** The time period, usually one year, to which periodic accounting reports are related; also known as the fiscal period (p. 68).

**Accrual basis of accounting** Accounting procedures whereby sales revenue is recorded when earned and realized and expenses are recorded in the period in which they help to generate the sales revenue (p. 70).

**Benchmarking analysis** A technique where the analyst or investor compares a firm's performance, or a ratio like the ROA, to that of the firm's principal competitors or to an industry average (p. 57).

**Cash basis of accounting** Accounting procedures whereby sales revenue is recorded when cash is received from operating activities and expenses are recorded when cash payments related to operating activities are made (p. 70).

**Classified balance sheet** A balance sheet in which items are classified into subgroups to facilitate financial analysis and management decision making (p. 52).

**Conceptual framework** A cohesive set of interrelated objectives, elements, and recognition and measurement criteria for the GAAP developed by the FASB (p. 65).

**Conservatism** An accounting principle stating that judgmental determinations should tend toward understatement rather than overstatement of assets and net income (p. 71).

**Consistency** An accounting principle stating that accounting reports should be prepared on a basis consistent with the prior periods (p. 68).

**Contributed capital** The capital contributed to a company by stockholders when they purchase shares of stock from the company (p. 61).

**Cost principle** An accounting principle stating that asset measures should be based on the price paid to acquire an asset (p. 69).

**Current assets** Cash and other assets that will be converted to cash or used up during the normal operating cycle of a business or one year, whichever is longer (p. 52).

**Current liabilities** Liabilities that must be settled within the normal operating cycle or one year, whichever is longer (p. 54).

**Current ratio** A measure of a firm's liquidity, calculated as current assets divided by current liabilities (p. 58).

**Debt-to-total-assets ratio** A measure of a firm's solvency, calculated as total liabilities divided by total assets (p. 59).

**Earned capital** Capital that is earned by a company and not distributed to its stockholders as a dividend; referred to as retained earnings (p. 61).

**Expense recognition (matching) principle** An accounting guideline that states that net income is determined by relating expenses to the sales revenues generated by the expenses (p. 70).

**Financial reporting objectives** A component of the conceptual framework which specifies that financial statements should provide information that is (1) useful for investment and credit decisions, (2) helpful in assessing an entity's ability to generate future cash flows, and (3) about an entity's resources, claims on those resources, and the effects of events causing changes in these items (p. 65).

**Financial statement elements** A component of the conceptual framework that identifies the significant components—assets, liabilities, stockholders' equity, revenues, and expenses—used to prepare financial statements (p. 65).

**Free cash flow** A measure of a firm's cash flow health, calculated as cash provided by operating activities less cash expenditures for property, plant, and equipment. Free cash flow is a measure of a firm's operating cash flow available for general corporate purposes such as debt retirement or dividend payment (p. 63).

**Full disclosure principle** An accounting principle stipulating that all facts necessary to make financial statements useful should be disclosed in a firm's annual report (p. 70).

**Going concern concept** An accounting principle that assumes that, in the absence of evidence to the contrary, a business enterprise will have an indefinite life (p. 69).

**Intangible asset** An asset lacking a physical presence; examples of intangible assets include patents, copyrights, and brand names (p. 53).

**Liquidity** A measure of a company's ability to pay its obligations expected to come due in the next year (pp. 53, 58).

**Long-term liabilities** Debt obligations not due to be repaid within the normal operating cycle or one year, whichever is longer (p. 55).

**Materiality** An accounting guideline that states that insignificant data that would not affect a financial statement user's decisions may be recorded in the most expedient manner (p. 71).

**Monetary unit concept** An accounting guideline that reports assets, liabilities and stockholders' equity in the basic unit of money (p. 68).

**Normal operating cycle** The average period of time between the use of cash to buy goods for resale or to provide services and the subsequent collection of cash from customers (p. 53).

**Objectivity** An accounting notion requiring that, whenever possible, accounting data should be based on objectively determined evidence (p. 66).

**Property, plant, and equipment** The land, buildings, equipment, vehicles, furniture, and fixtures that a firm uses in its operations; often referred to as PP&E (p. 53).

**Qualitative characteristics of accounting information** The characteristics of accounting information that contribute to decision usefulness; the primary qualities are *relevance* and *reliability* (p. 66).

**Ratio analysis** The process of expressing the relationship of one accounting number to another accounting number through the process of division (p. 57).

**Recognition and measurement criteria** The criteria that must be met before a financial statement element may be recorded in the accounts. Essentially, the item must meet the definition of an element and must be measurable, and the resultant information about the item must be relevant and reliable (p. 66).

**Relevance** A qualitative characteristic of accounting information; relevant information contributes to the predictive and evaluative decisions made by financial statement users (p. 66).

**Reliability** A qualitative characteristic of accounting information; reliable information contains no bias or error and faithfully portrays what it intends to represent (p. 66).

**Report form** A format of the classified balance sheet where assets are displayed on the top and liabilities and stockholders' equity are displayed below the assets (p. 55).

**Return on assets (ROA)** A measure of profitability; defined as net income divided by average total assets (or period-end assets). (p. 57).

**Return on sales ratio** A measure of a firm's profitability, calculated as net income divided by net sales (p. 60).

**Revenue recognition principle** An accounting principle requiring that sales revenues be recognized when services are performed or goods are sold (p. 70).

**Socially responsible investing (SRI)** An investment strategy that considers not just financial performance but also the social concepts of environmental stewardship, consumer protection, human rights, and diversity (p. 62).

**Solvency** A measure of a company's ability to repay its debts in the long term (p. 58).

**Stockholders' equity** The residual interest in the assets of a business after all liabilities have been paid off; stockholders' equity is equal to a firm's net assets, or total assets less total liabilities (p. 55).

**Trend analysis** A process in which an analyst or investor compares a company's results, or the results of a ratio, over time (p. 57).

## COMPREHENSIVE PROBLEM

Following are items reported on the financial statements of Microsoft Corporation as of June 30, 2009. (Some of the reported accounts have been combined for simplicity.) Amounts given are in millions of dollars.

| | |
|---|---|
| Cash flow provided by operating activities | $19,037 |
| Cash at June 30, 2008 | 10,339 |
| Cash at June 30, 2009 | 6,076 |
| Net revenue | 58,437 |
| Cash flow from investing activities | (15,770) |
| Inventory | 717 |
| Accounts receivable | 13,405 |
| Cost of goods sold | 12,155 |
| Cash flow from financing activities | (7,530) |
| Other current assets | 29,082 |
| Property, plant, and equipment | 7,535 |
| Operating expenses | 25,919 |
| Other expenses | 542 |
| Intangible assets | 14,262 |
| Other long-term assets | 6,811 |
| Income tax expense | 5,252 |
| Accounts payable | 8,889 |
| Other current liabilities | 18,145 |
| Long-term liabilities | 11,296 |
| Common stock | 62,382 |
| Retained earnings | (22,824) |

Prepare an income statement, a classified balance sheet, and a statement of cash flows using the accounts listed above.

### Solution

**MICROSOFT CORPORATION**
**Income Statement**
**For Year Ended June 30, 2009 (in millions)**

| | | |
|---|---|---|
| Net sales | | $58,437 |
| Cost of goods sold | $12,155 | |
| Operating expenses | 25,919 | |
| Other expenses | 542 | |
| Income tax expense | 5,252 | |
| Total expenses | | 43,868 |
| Net income | | $14,569 |

**MICROSOFT CORPORATION**
**Balance Sheet**
**June 30, 2009 (in millions)**

| | | |
|---|---|---|
| **Assets** | | |
| Current assets | | |
| Cash | $ 6,076 | |
| Account receivable | 13,405 | |
| Inventory | 717 | |
| Other current assets | 29,082 | |
| Total current assets | | $49,280 |
| Property, plant, and equipment | | 7,535 |
| Intangible assets | | 14,262 |
| Other long-term assets | | 6,811 |
| Total assets | | $77,888 |
| **Liabilities and Stockholders' Equity** | | |
| Current liabilities | | |
| Accounts payable | $8,889 | |
| Other current liabilities | 18,145 | |
| Total current liabilities | | $27,034 |
| Long-term liabilities | | 11,296 |
| Total liabilities | | 38,330 |

*continued*

Stockholders' equity

| | | |
|---|---|---|
| Common stock........................................................ | 62,382 | |
| Retained earnings.................................................. | (22,824) | |
| Total stockholders' equity ................................... | | 39,558 |
| Total liabilities and stockholders' equity ............................ | | $77,888 |

| MICROSOFT CORPORATION<br>Statement of Cash Flows<br>For Year Ended June 30, 2009 (in millions) | |
|---|---|
| Cash flow provided by operating activities ............................................ | $19,037 |
| Cash flow from investing activities ...................................................... | (15,770) |
| Cash flow from financing activities ..................................................... | (7,530) |
| Net decrease in cash.......................................................................... | (4,263) |
| Cash at June 30, 2008......................................................................... | 10,339 |
| Cash at June 30, 2009......................................................................... | $ 6,076 |

## SELF-STUDY QUESTIONS

(Answers to Self-Study Questions are at the end of this chapter.)

1. Which of the following items will not be reported on a classified balance sheet?    LO1
   a. Current assets
   b. Net income
   c. Total liabilities
   d. Common stock

2. Which of the following would not be considered a current asset?    LO1
   a. Inventory
   b. Accounts receivable
   c. Property, plant, and equipment
   d. Cash

3. For the balance sheet to be in balance, the following must exist:    LO1
   a. Total assets must be greater than total liabilities
   b. Total assets must be less than total liabilities
   c. Total assets must equal total liabilities plus stockholders' equity
   d. Total liabilities must equal total stockholders' equity

4. Which of the following would be considered an intangible asset?    LO1
   a. Cash
   b. Land
   c. Accounts payable
   d. Patents

5. Which of the following would most likely be classified as a long-term liability?    LO1
   a. Accounts payable
   b. Notes payable
   c. Accounts receivable
   d. Common stock

6. Ratio analysis always involves which type of arithmetic operation?    LO4
   a. Addition
   b. Subtraction
   c. Multiplication
   d. Division

7. Which of the following is a not true statement?    LO4
   a. Benchmarking analysis involves comparing a company to its industry's averages.
   b. Benchmarking analysis involves comparing a company to its competitors.
   c. Trend analysis involves comparing a company's ratios over time.
   d. Benchmarking analysis involves comparing a company's ratios over time.

| | |
|---|---:|
| Cash | $ 400 |
| Accounts receivable | 1,200 |
| Inventory | 2,500 |
| Property, plant, and equipment | 10,000 |
| Accounts payable | 800 |
| Other current liabilities | 600 |
| Long-term notes payable | 8,000 |
| Stockholders' equity | 4,700 |

Prepare a classified balance sheet for Dino Company as of January 31, 2010.

**LO3    SE2-2.    Evaluating Firm Profitability**

The following financial information is taken from the annual reports of the Smith Company and the Wesson Company:

| | Smith | Wesson |
|---|---:|---:|
| Net income | $10,000 | $100,000 |
| Net sales | 50,000 | 400,000 |

Calculate the return on sales for each company and determine which firm is more profitable.

**LO2    SE2-3.    Evaluating Firm Liquidity**

The following financial information is taken from the balance sheets of the Drucker Company and the Ito Company:

| | Drucker | Ito |
|---|---:|---:|
| Current assets | $250,000 | $50,000 |
| Current liabilities | 100,000 | 15,000 |

Calculate the current ratio for each company and determine which firm has the higher level of liquidity.

**LO2    SE2-4.    Evaluating Firm Solvency**

The following financial information is taken from the balance sheets of the Lambeth Company and the Maritza Company:

| | Lambeth | Maritza |
|---|---:|---:|
| Total debt | $350,000 | $ 850,000 |
| Total assets | 550,000 | 1,000,000 |

Calculate the debt-to-total-assets ratio and determine which firm has the higher level of solvency.

**LO5    SE2-5.    Calculating Free Cash Flows**

The following financial information is taken from the annual reports of the Jackson Company and the Pearce Company:

| | Jackson | Pearce |
|---|---:|---:|
| Cash flow from operating activities | $250,000 | $750,000 |
| Cash investment in property & equipment | 75,000 | 240,000 |

Calculate the free cash flow for each company and determine which firm has better cash flow health.

**LO6    SE2-6.    Statement of Cash Flows**

Which of the following would not appear on a company's statement of cash flow?

*a.* Cash flow from operating activities
*b.* Net change in cash
*c.* Total assets
*d.* Cash flow for investing activities

**LO7    SE2-7.    Principles of Accounting**

Which of the following accounting principles applies to the income statement?

*a.* Cost principle
*b.* Revenue recognition principle

    *c.*   Matching principle
    *d.*   Both b. and c.

**SE2-8.  Principles of Accounting**                                          LO7

Which of the following accounting principles applies to the statement of cash flows?

    *a.*   Materiality
    *b.*   Conservatism
    *c.*   Accrual basis of accounting
    *d.*   Cash basis of accounting

**SE2-9.  Generally Accepted Accounting Principles**                  LO6, LO7

Select the best answer to each of the following questions:

   1.  Accounting rules are developed for their:
     *a.*   Simplicity
     *b.*   Useful information
     *c.*   Complexity
     *d.*   Ability to change over time
   2.  The conceptual framework consists of each of the following except:
     *a.*   Financial reporting objectives
     *b.*   Financial statement elements
     *c.*   Ratio analysis guidelines for analysts
     *d.*   Recognition criteria for financial statement items
   3.  Which of the following is a financial statement element?
     *a.*   Income statement
     *b.*   Liabilities
     *c.*   Balance sheet
     *d.*   Statement of cash flows

**SE2-10.  Basic Accounting Principles**                                 LO6

Match the following list of accounting concepts, principles, and assumptions with the definitions below:

| | | |
|---|---|---|
| Conservatism constraint | Consistency | Cost principle |
| Accounting period concept | Materiality constraint | Reliability |
| Going concern concept | Comparability | Full disclosure principle |

   1.  Ability to compare the financial performance of different companies.
   2.  Assumption that a company will continue to operate beyond the current period.
   3.  Items recorded in the financial statements should be based on objective evidence.
   4.  Only items large enough to make a difference to a user must be disclosed in the financial statements.
   5.  Prepare financial statements at set time intervals.
   6.  Record assets on the balance sheet at an amount equal to what was paid for them.
   7.  A company prepares its financial statements using the same methods used in prior periods.
   8.  When in doubt, use conservative assumptions when valuing items on the financial statements.
   9.  All items of importance to the users of financial statements should be disclosed in the annual report.

**SE2-11.  Debt-to-Total-Assets Ratio**                                          LO2

Ruby Company's balance sheet reports the following totals: Assets = $40,000; Liabilities = $25,000; Stockholders' Equity = $15,000. Determine the company's debt-to-total-assets ratio.

    *a.*   1.5:4
    *b.*   2.5:4
    *c.*   $15,000
    *d.*   2.5:1.5

LO5    **SE2-12.** **Free Cash Flow**

Lester Linens reports the following items on its statement of cash flows:

     Cash flow provided by operating activities = $100,000
     Cash flow used by investing activities = $50,000
     Cash flow used by financing activities = $25,000
     Capital expenditures = $40,000
     Determine Lester's free cash flow:

a.   $40,000
b.   $5,000
c.   40%
d.   $60,000

LO6    **SE2-13.** **FASB Codification**

A major reason for the codification project completed by the FASB in 2009 was to:

a.   ease the convergence between financial and managerial accounting
b.   ease the convergence between U.S. GAAP and IFRS
c.   ease the convergence between financial and tax accounting
d.   ease the convergence between U.S. GAAP and GASB

LO7    **SE2-14.** **Basic Accounting Principles**

Which of the following is not considered a qualitative characteristic of accounting information?

a.   decision usefulness
b.   consistency
c.   assets must equal liabilities and stockholders' equity
d.   timeliness

LO3    **SE2-15.** **Return on Sales**

The following data are from the financial statements of Burkee Wines, Inc. Compute Burkee's return on sales ratio for 2011.

     Total revenues for 2011: $3,500,000
     Total expenses for 2011: $2,800,000

a.   125%
b.   80%
c.   25%
d.   20%

# EXERCISES—SET A

LO1    **E2-1A.** **Preparing a Classified Balance Sheet**

From the following accounts, listed in alphabetical order, prepare a classified balance sheet for Berkly Wholesalers as of December 31, 2010. All accounts have normal balances.

| | | | |
|---|---|---|---|
| Accounts Payable. . . . . . . . . . . . . . . . . . . . . . . | $43,000 | Inventory . . . . . . . . . . . . . . . . . . . . . . . | $117,000 |
| Accounts Receivable. . . . . . . . . . . . . . . . . . . . | 40,000 | Land . . . . . . . . . . . . . . . . . . . . . . . . . . . . | 45,000 |
| Accumulated Depreciation—Building. . . . . | 23,000 | Mortgage Payable (long term) . . . . . | 78,000 |
| Building. . . . . . . . . . . . . . . . . . . . . . . . . . . . . . | 90,000 | Office Supplies . . . . . . . . . . . . . . . . . . . | 2,000 |
| Cash . . . . . . . . . . . . . . . . . . . . . . . . . . . . . . . . . | 26,000 | Retained Earnings . . . . . . . . . . . . . . . . | ? |
| Common Stock. . . . . . . . . . . . . . . . . . . . . . . . | 111,000 | Salaries Payable . . . . . . . . . . . . . . . . . . | 7,000 |

LO1    **E2-2A.** **Preparing a Classified Balance Sheet**

From the following accounts, listed in alphabetical order, prepare a classified balance sheet for Balford Wholesalers as of December 31, 2010. All accounts have normal balances.

| | | | |
|---|---|---|---|
| Accounts Payable.............................. | $ 52,000 | Inventory ............................. | 142,000 |
| Accounts Receivable........................... | 54,000 | Land .................................. | 58,000 |
| Accumulated Depreciation—Building........... | 28,000 | Mortgage Payable (long-term)......... | 100,000 |
| Accumulated Depreciation—Office Equipment... | 7,000 | Office Equipment...................... | 26,000 |
| Building....................................... | 100,000 | Office Supplies ....................... | 2,000 |
| Cash .......................................... | 40,000 | Retained Earnings..................... | ? |
| Common Stock................................. | 136,000 | Salaries Payable ...................... | 8,000 |

**E2-3A.  The Conceptual Accounting Framework**          LO6

The Financial Accounting Standards Board worked many years to develop a conceptual framework for U.S. GAAP.

*a.* What is the purpose of a conceptual framework?

*b.* Identify the financial reporting objectives that are specified in the conceptual framework.

**E2-4A.  Basic Accounting Principles**          LO7

Indicate the basic principle or principles of accounting that underlie each of the following independent situations:

*a.* Dr. Kline is a practicing pediatrician. Over the years, she has accumulated a personal investment portfolio of securities, virtually all of which have been purchased from her earnings as a pediatrician. The investment portfolio is not reflected in the accounting records of her medical practice.

*b.* A company purchases a desk tape dispenser for use by the office secretary. The tape dispenser cost $10 and has an estimated useful life of 15 years. The purchase is immediately expensed on the company's income statement.

*c.* A company sells a product that has a two-year warranty covering parts and labor. In the same period that revenues from product sales are recorded, an estimate of future warranty costs is recorded on the company's income statement.

*d.* A company is sued for $1 million by a customer claiming that a defective product caused an accident. The company believes that the lawsuit is without merit. Although the case will not be tried for a year, the company adds a note describing the lawsuit to its current financial statements.

**E2-5A.  Revenue Recognition Principle**          LO7

For each of the following situations, determine whether the criteria for revenue recognition have been met by December 31, 2010.

*a.* A manufacturing company received $50,000 cash on December 31, 2010, as an advance payment on a special order for a piece of equipment. The equipment will be manufactured by March 31, 2011.

*b.* A television dealer acquired six new high-definition television sets for $8,400 cash on December 31, 2010, and advertised their availability, at $2,000 each, in that evening's newspaper.

*c.* A snow removal service signed a contract on November 15, 2010, with a shopping mall to clear its parking lot of all snowfalls over 1 inch during the months of December 2010 through March 2011. The cost is $600 per month and payment is due in two $1,200 installments: January 2, 2011, and February 1, 2011. By December 31, 2010, no snowfall over 1 inch had occurred.

**E2-6A.  Basic Accounting Principles**          LO7

Identify whether the following statements are true or false.

1. Together the revenue recognition principle and the matching principle define the accrual basis of accounting.

2. The cash basis of accounting is only used in the preparation of the statement of cash flows.

3. The accrual basis of accounting is used in the preparation of the income statement and the balance sheet.

4. The conservatism principle only applies to the income statement.

LO1 **E2-7A.** **Classified Balance Sheet**

The Werthman Company collected the following information for the preparation of its December 31, 2010, classified balance sheet:

| | | | |
|---|---|---|---|
| Accounts receivable | $15,000 | Property, plant, and equipment | $200,000 |
| Cash | 17,000 | Inventory | 65,000 |
| Other current assets | 25,000 | Other long-term assets | 40,000 |
| Accounts payable | 21,000 | Common stock | 95,000 |
| Long-term liabilities | 55,000 | Retained earnings | ? |
| Other current liabilities | 18,000 | | |

Prepare a classified balance sheet for Werthman Company.

LO2, LO3, LO5 **E2-8A.** **Profitability, Liquidity, and Solvency Ratios**

Shannon Corporation gathered the following information from its 2010 financial statements:

| | |
|---|---|
| Net sales | $180,000 |
| Net income | 25,200 |
| Cash provided by operating activities | 35,000 |
| Expenditures on property, plant, and equipment | 14,000 |
| Current assets | 40,500 |
| Current liabilities | 27,000 |
| Total assets | 130,000 |
| Total liabilities | 97,500 |

Using the above data, calculate the following: (1) return on sales, (2) current ratio, (3) debt-to-total-assets ratio, and (4) free cash flow.

LO1 **E2-9A.** **Return on Assets**

The following information was taken from recent Apple Inc. financial statements. Numbers are in millions.

| | 2010 | 2009 |
|---|---|---|
| Total revenue | $65,225 | $42,905 |
| Net income | 14,013 | 8,235 |
| Total assets | 75,183 | 47,501 |

**Required**

a. What was Apple's return on assets for 2010 and 2009?
b. Based on your answer from part a., how did the company's performance change from 2009 to 2010?

LO4 **E2-10A.** **Statement of Stockholders' Equity**

You have been asked to assist with the preparation of a statement of stockholders' equity for Maxx Company for the year ended December 31, 2011. You determine the following balances:

| | |
|---|---|
| Common stock at December 31, 2010 | $5,000 |
| Retained earnings at December 31, 2010 | 7,500 |
| Net income during 2011 | 2,500 |
| Dividends during 2011 | 250 |
| Issuance of common stock during 2011 | 400 |

**Required**

Prepare a statement of stockholders' equity for Maxx Company for 2011.

# EXERCISES—SET B

LO7 **E2-1B.** **The Conceptual Framework**

The Financial Accounting Standards Board worked many years to develop a conceptual framework for U.S. GAAP.

a. Identify the financial statement elements that are specified in the conceptual framework.

 *b.* Before a financial statement element may be recorded in the accounts, certain recognition criteria must be met. What are those recognition criteria?

**E2-2B.** **Basic Accounting Principles**            LO7

Indicate the basic principle or principles of accounting that underlie each of the following independent situations:

 *a.* Ford Motor Company reports in its annual report to stockholders that revenues from automotive sales "are recorded by the company when products are shipped to dealers."

 *b.* The annual financial report of Chrysler Corporation and subsidiaries includes the financial data of its significant subsidiaries, including Chrysler Financial Corporation (which provides financing for dealers and customers), Chrysler Technologies Corporation (which manufactures high-technology electronic products), and Pentastar Transportation Group, Inc. (which includes Thrifty Rent-A-Car System, Inc., and Dollar Rent A Car Systems, Inc.).

 *c.* A company purchased a parcel of land several years ago for $65,000. The land's estimated current market value is $80,000. The Land account balance is not increased but remains at $65,000.

 *d.* A company has a calendar-year fiscal year-end. On January 8, 2010, a tornado destroyed its largest warehouse, causing a $1,800,000 loss. This information is reported in a footnote to the 2009 financial statements.

**E2-3B.** **Accrual Basis of Accounting versus Cash Basis of Accounting**   LO6

On December 31, Jayne Leigh completed her first year as a financial planner. The following data are available from her accounting records:

| | | | |
|---|---|---|---|
| Fees billed to clients for services rendered... | $97,000 | Rent expense for year just ended..... | 10,800 |
| Cash received from clients ................. | 85,000 | Utility expense incurred ............. | 2,500 |
| Supplies purchased for cash ............... | 4,500 | Utility bills paid..................... | 2,200 |
| Supplies used during the year.............. | 3,300 | Salary earned by assistant ........... | 30,000 |
| Cash paid for rent (rent is paid through | | Salary paid to assistant .............. | 27,500 |
|  Feb. of next year)...................... | 12,600 | | |

 *a.* Compute Leigh's net income for the year just ended using the accrual basis of accounting.

 *b.* Compute Leigh's net income for the year just ended using the cash basis of accounting.

 *c.* Which net income amount is computed in accordance with generally accepted accounting principles?

**E2-4B.** **Basic Accounting Principles**            LO7

The following are unrelated accounting practices:

 1. A recession has caused a slowing of business activity and lower profits for Balke Company. Consequently, the firm delays making its payments for December's rent and utilities until January and does not record either of these expenses in December.

 2. Gail Derry, a consultant operating as a sole proprietorship, used her business car for a personal, month-long vacation. A full year's gas and oil expenditures on the car are charged to the firm's gas and oil expense account.

 3. Vine Company purchased a new $18 snow shovel that is expected to last six years. The shovel is used to clear the firm's front steps during the winter months. The shovel's cost is recorded on the company's balance sheet as an asset.

 4. Filene Corporation has been named as the defendant in a $40 million pollution lawsuit. Because the lawsuit will take several years to resolve and the outcome is uncertain, Filene's management decides not to mention the lawsuit in the current year financial statements.

 5. The management of Newell Corporation, a U.S. company, prepares its financial statements in constant units of purchasing power rather than the U.S. dollar unadjusted for the effect of inflation.

**Required**

For each of the given practices, indicate which generally accepted accounting principles apply and whether they have been applied appropriately. For each inappropriate accounting practice, indicate the proper accounting procedure.

**LO2** **E2-5B.** **Evaluating the Liquidity and Solvency of a Company**

Identify whether the following statements are true or false.

a.  The current ratio is a measure of a firm's liquidity.
b.  Free cash flow is a measure of a firm's solvency.
c.  The return on sales is a measure of a firm's liquidity.
d.  The debt-to-total-assets ratio is a measure of a firm's liquidity.

**LO5** **E2-6B.** **Statement of Cash Flows**

Identify whether the following statements are true or false.

a.  The statement of cash flows reveals whether a firm is "rich" or not.
b.  The statement of cash flows reveals a firm's financial health.
c.  The statement of cash flows reveals a firm's liquidity.
d.  The statement of cash flows reveals a firm's solvency.

**LO1** **E2-7B.** **Classified Balance Sheet**

The Cambridge Company collected the following information for the preparation of its December 31, 2010, classified balance sheet:

| | | | |
|---|---|---|---|
| Accounts receivable | $15,000 | Property, plant, and equipment | $200,000 |
| Cash | 20,000 | Inventory | 65,000 |
| Other current assets | 30,000 | Other long-term assets | 40,000 |
| Accounts payable | 21,000 | Common stock | 105,000 |
| Long-term liabilities | 55,000 | Retained earnings | ? |
| Other current liabilities | 18,000 | | |

Prepare a classified balance sheet for Cambridge Company.

**LO2, LO3, LO5** **E2-8B.** **Profitability, Liquidity, and Solvency Ratios**

O'Neill Corporation gathered the following information from its 2010 financial statements:

| | | | |
|---|---|---|---|
| Net sales | $280,000 | Current assets | 40,500 |
| Net income | 75,000 | Current liabilities | 27,000 |
| Cash provided by operating activities | 85,000 | Total assets | 130,000 |
| Expenditures on property, plant, and equipment | 14,000 | Total liabilities | 97,500 |

Using the above data, calculate the following: (1) return on sales, (2) current ratio, (3) debt-to-total-assets ratio, and (4) free cash flow.

**LO1** **E2-9B.** **Return on Assets**

Daisy Company reports the following information in its financial statements. Numbers are in thousands.

| | 2010 | 2011 |
|---|---|---|
| Net sales | $52,200 | $48,750 |
| Net income | 10,750 | 8,400 |
| Total assets | 63,900 | 61,450 |

There were 3,500 outstanding shares at December 31, 2010.

**Required**

a.  What was Daisy's return on assets ratio for 2010 and 2011?
b.  Based on your answer from part a., how did the company's performance change from 2010 to 2011?

**LO4** **E2-10B.** **Statement of Stockholders' Equity**

You have been asked to assist with the preparation of a statement of stockholders' equity for Palatin Company for the year ended December 31, 2011. You determine the following balances:

| | |
|---|---|
| Common stock at December 31, 2010 | $45,000 |
| Retained earnings at December 31, 2010 | 17,500 |
| Net income during 2011 | 22,500 |
| Dividends during 2011 | 9,250 |
| Issuance of common stock during 2011 | 4,000 |

**Required**

Prepare a statement of stockholders' equity for Palatin Company for 2011.

# PROBLEMS—SET A

**P2-1A. Preparing a Classified Balance Sheet**                                                  LO1

The following financial data for Crane Distributors was collected as of December 31, 2010. All accounts have normal balances.

| | | | |
|---|---|---|---|
| Cash | $ 15,200 | Delivery Equipment | 80,000 |
| Accounts Receivable | 110,200 | Accumulated Depreciation | 35,000 |
| Inventory | 114,000 | Accounts Payable | 70,000 |
| Prepaid Insurance | 2,400 | Common Stock | 100,000 |
| Supplies | 6,400 | Retained Earnings | ? |

**Required**

Prepare a classified balance sheet as of December 31, 2010, for Crane Distributors.

**P2-2A. Preparing a Classified Balance Sheet**                                                  LO1

The following financial data for the Marshall Corporation was collected as of December 31, 2010. All accounts have normal balances.

| | | | |
|---|---|---|---|
| Cash | $ 46,400 | Delivery Equipment | 65,000 |
| Accounts Receivable | 95,200 | Accumulated Depreciation— | |
| | | Delivery Equipment | 32,000 |
| Inventory | 90,000 | Accounts Payable | 17,400 |
| Prepaid Insurance | 300 | Common Stock | 200,000 |
| Furniture and Fixtures | 32,000 | Retained Earnings | ? |
| Accumulated Depreciation— | | | |
| Furniture and Fixtures | 6,800 | | |

**Required**

Prepare a classified balance sheet as of December 31, 2010.

**P2-3A. Basic Accounting Principles**                                                  LO7

The following are unrelated accounting situations and the accounting treatment that was followed in each firm's records:

1. Martin Company mounts a $600,000 year-long advertising campaign on a national cable television network. The firm's annual accounting period is the calendar year. The television network required full payment in December at the beginning of the campaign. Accounting treatment is

    Increase Advertising Expense, $600,000
    Decrease Cash, $600,000

2. Because of a local bankruptcy, machinery worth $200,000 was acquired at a "bargain" purchase price of $180,000. Accounting treatment is

    Increase Machinery, $180,000
    Decrease Cash, $180,000

3. Tim Vagly, a consultant operating a sole proprietorship, withdrew $20,000 from the business and purchased stocks as an investment gift to his wife. Accounting treatment is

    Increase Investments, $20,000
    Decrease Cash, $20,000

4. The Solid State Bank, by action of the board of directors, wrote down the recorded amount of its home office building from its cost of $2,500,000 to the amount of $100. The objective was to bolster its customers' confidence in the bank's financial strength by obviously understating bank assets. Accounting treatment is

    Increase Building Write-Down Expense, $2,499,900
    Decrease Buildings, $2,499,900

5. Sioux Company received a firm offer of $96,000 for a parcel of land it owns that cost $68,000 two years ago. The offer was refused, but the indicated gain was recorded in the accounts. Accounting treatment is

    Increase Land, $28,000
    Increase Revenue from Change in Land Value, $28,000

**Required**

In each of the given situations, indicate which generally accepted accounting principles apply and whether they have been applied appropriately. If you decide the accounting treatment is not generally accepted, discuss the effect of the departure on the balance sheet.

**LO1, LO5**

**P2-4A.** **Preparing the Financial Statements**

Listed below are items reported on the financial statements of the Huntington Company as of June 30, 2010:

| | | | |
|---|---|---|---|
| Cash flow provided by operating activities . . . | $21,000 | Other long-term assets . . . . . . . . . . . . . . . . . . . . . . | 17,500 |
| Cash at June 30, 2009. . . . . . . . . . . . . . . . . . . . . . | 9,000 | Cash flow from financing activities . . . . . . . . . . | 1,300 |
| Cash at June 30, 2010. . . . . . . . . . . . . . . . . . . . . . | 16,000 | Current liabilities . . . . . . . . . . . . . . . . . . . . . . . . . . | 22,000 |
| Inventory . . . . . . . . . . . . . . . . . . . . . . . . . . . . . . . . | 5,500 | Long-term liabilities . . . . . . . . . . . . . . . . . . . . . . . | 18,250 |
| Accounts receivable . . . . . . . . . . . . . . . . . . . . . . . | 12,200 | Intangible assets . . . . . . . . . . . . . . . . . . . . . . . . . | 9,500 |
| Cash flow from investing activities . . . . . . . . . . | (15,300) | Common stock . . . . . . . . . . . . . . . . . . . . . . . . . . . | 51,000 |
| Other current assets . . . . . . . . . . . . . . . . . . . . . . | 1,500 | Retained earnings . . . . . . . . . . . . . . . . . . . . . . . . | ? |
| Property, plant and equipment . . . . . . . . . . . . . | 40,000 | | |

**Required**

Prepare a classified balance sheet as of June 30, 2010, and statement of cash flows for 2010.

**LO2, LO3**    **P2-5A.** **Assessing a Firm's Profitability, Liquidity and Solvency**

Presented below is financial data for the Forrester Company as of year-end 2009 and 2010:

| | 2009 | 2010 |
|---|---|---|
| Current assets . . . . . . . . . . . . . . . . . . . . . . . . . . . . . . . . . . . . . . . . . . . . . . . . . | $ 35,000 | $ 55,000 |
| Total assets. . . . . . . . . . . . . . . . . . . . . . . . . . . . . . . . . . . . . . . . . . . . . . . . . . . . | 120,000 | 170,000 |
| Current liabilities . . . . . . . . . . . . . . . . . . . . . . . . . . . . . . . . . . . . . . . . . . . . . . | 29,000 | 70,000 |
| Total liabilities. . . . . . . . . . . . . . . . . . . . . . . . . . . . . . . . . . . . . . . . . . . . . . . . . | 72,000 | 112,000 |
| Net sales . . . . . . . . . . . . . . . . . . . . . . . . . . . . . . . . . . . . . . . . . . . . . . . . . . . . . . | 132,000 | 187,000 |
| Net income. . . . . . . . . . . . . . . . . . . . . . . . . . . . . . . . . . . . . . . . . . . . . . . . . . . . | 17,500 | 25,200 |

**Required**

Calculate Forrester's current ratio, debt-to-total-assets ratio, and return on sales. Comment on the trend in the company's profitability, liquidity, and solvency from 2009 to 2010.

**LO3**

**P2-6A.** **Profitability and the Income Statement**

Presented below is income statement data for Longo & Company as of year-end 2010:

| | | | |
|---|---|---|---|
| Income tax expense . . . . . . . . . . . . . . . . . . | $ 5,400 | Net revenue. . . . . . . . . . . . . . . . . . . . . . . . . | 58,500 |
| Cost of goods sold. . . . . . . . . . . . . . . . . . . . | 12,300 | Operating expenses . . . . . . . . . . . . . . . . . . | 26,000 |
| Other expenses . . . . . . . . . . . . . . . . . . . . . . | 700 | | |

**Required**

Prepare an income statement for 2010 and calculate the company's return on sales. If Longo's return on sales was 20 percent in 2009, is the company's profitability improving or declining?

**LO4**

**P2-7A.** **Preparing the Statement of Stockholders' Equity**

Presented below is financial data for Likert & Co. as of year-end 2010:

| | | | |
|---|---|---|---|
| Cash . . . . . . . . . . . . . . . . . . . . . . . . . . . . . . . | $ 6,000 | Accumulated depreciation. . . . . . . . . . . . . | (14,000) |
| Retained earnings, Jan. 1, 2010. . . . . . . . | 13,000 | Net income. . . . . . . . . . . . . . . . . . . . . . . . . | 30,000 |
| Intangible assets . . . . . . . . . . . . . . . . . . . . | 22,000 | Stockholders' equity, Jan. 1, 2010. . . . . . . | 63,000 |
| Common stock . . . . . . . . . . . . . . . . . . . . . . | 50,000 | Retained earnings, Dec. 31, 2010. . . . . . . . | 31,000 |
| Accounts payable . . . . . . . . . . . . . . . . . . . | 4,000 | Stockholders' equity, Dec. 31, 2010. . . . . | 81,000 |
| Dividends paid . . . . . . . . . . . . . . . . . . . . . . | 12,000 | | |

**Required**

Prepare a statement of stockholders' equity for Likert & Co. as of December 31, 2010.

**P2-8A.  Interpreting Liquidity, Solvency, and Profitability Ratios**    LO2, LO3

Presented below are financial data for two retail companies:

|  | Company A | Company B |
|---|---|---|
| Return on sales........................................................ | 15.5% | 13.9% |
| Current ratio ........................................................... | 0.5 | 2.0 |
| Debt-to-total-assets ................................................. | 65% | 30% |

**Required**

Consider the financial ratio data for the two companies. Which company represents the better investment opportunity in your view and why?

**P2-9A.  Evaluating Firm Liquidity, Solvency, Profitability and Free Cash Flow: IFRS Financial Statements**    LO2, LO3, LO5

Tesco PLC is the world's third largest retailer and is headquartered in the United Kingdom. Tesco's IFRS financial statements are presented in Appendix C at the end of this textbook. Using this financial data, calculate the company's (a) return on sales, (b) current ratio, (c) debt-to-total-assets ratio, and (d) free cash flow for 2008 and 2009. Comment on the trend in Tesco's liquidity, solvency, profitability, and free cash flow from 2008 to 2009.

**P2-10A. Ratio Analysis**    LO2, LO3, LO5

The following balances were reported in the financial statements for Nafooz Company.

|  | 2011 | 2010 |
|---|---|---|
| Net sales ........................................................ | $800,000 | $700,000 |
| Net income....................................................... | 80,000 | 65,000 |
| Current assets .................................................. | 200,000 | 175,000 |
| Current liabilities ............................................. | 80,000 | 100,000 |
| Total liabilities................................................. | 250,000 | 225,000 |
| Total assets...................................................... | 750,000 | 600,000 |
| Average shares outstanding ................................ | 29,000 | 26,000 |

**Required**

1. Compute the following ratios for 2011 and 2010 for Nafooz Company.
   a.  Return on sales
   b.  Earnings per share
   c.  Current ratio
   d.  Debt-to-total-assets ratio
2. Comment on changes to Nafooz Company's profitability, liquidity, and solvency.

# PROBLEMS—SET B

**P2-1B.  Preparing a Classified Balance Sheet**    LO1

The following financial data for McKensie & Company was collected as of December 31, 2010. All accounts have normal balances.

| | | | |
|---|---|---|---|
| Cash ..................................... | $ 30,400 | Delivery Equipment ................... | 160,000 |
| Accounts Receivable................... | 221,000 | Accumulated Depreciation ............ | 70,000 |
| Inventory ............................ | 228,000 | Accounts Payable..................... | 140,000 |
| Prepaid Insurance .................... | 4,800 | Common Stock........................ | 200,000 |
| Supplies............................. | 12,800 | Retained Earnings .................... | ? |

**Required**

Prepare a classified balance sheet as of December 31, 2010, for McKensie & Company.

**LO1**    **P2-2B.**    **Preparing a Classified Balance Sheet**

The following financial data for the St. John Corporation was collected as of December 31, 2010. All accounts have normal balances.

| | | | |
|---|---|---|---|
| Cash | $ 92,800 | Delivery Equipment | 130,000 |
| Accounts Receivable | 190,400 | Accumulated Depreciation— | |
| | | Delivery Equipment | 64,000 |
| Inventory | 180,000 | Accounts Payable | 34,800 |
| Prepaid Insurance | 600 | Common Stock | 400,000 |
| Furniture and Fixtures | 64,000 | Retained Earnings | ? |
| Accumulated Depreciation— | | | |
| Furniture and Fixtures | 13,600 | | |

**Required**

Prepare a classified balance sheet as of December 31, 2010.

**LO7**    **P2-3B.**    **Basic Accounting Principles**

The following are unrelated accounting situations and the accounting treatment that was followed in each firm's records:

1.  The Baldwin Company mounts an $800,000 year-long advertising campaign on a new national cable television network. The firm's annual accounting period is the calendar year. The television network required full payment in December at the beginning of the campaign. Accounting treatment is

    Increase Advertising Expense, $800,000
    Decrease Cash, $800,000

2.  Because of a local bankruptcy, machinery worth $300,000 was acquired at a "bargain" purchase price of $150,000. Accounting treatment is

    Increase Machinery, $150,000
    Decrease Cash, $150,000

3.  J.P. Smith, a consultant operating a sole proprietorship, withdrew $40,000 from the business and purchased stocks as an investment gift to his wife. Accounting treatment is

    Increase Investments, $40,000
    Decrease Cash, $40,000

4.  The Tucson State Bank, by action of the board of directors, wrote down the recorded amount of its home office building from its cost of $3,500,000 to the amount of $100,000. The objective was to bolster its customers' confidence in the bank's financial strength by obviously understating bank assets. Accounting treatment is

    Increase Building Write-Down Expense, $3,400,000
    Decrease Buildings, $3,400,000

5.  Morongo Company received a firm offer of $106,000 for a parcel of land it owns that cost $75,000 two years ago. The offer was refused, but the indicated gain was recorded in the accounts. Accounting treatment is

    Increase Land, $31,000
    Increase Revenue from Change in Land Value, $31,000

**Required**

In each of the given situations, indicate which generally accepted accounting principles apply and whether they have been applied appropriately. If you decide the accounting treatment is not generally accepted, discuss the effect of the departure on the balance sheet.

**LO1, LO5**    **P2-4B.**    **Preparing the Financial Statements**

Listed below are items reported on the financial statements of the Manhattan Company as of June 30, 2010:

| | |
|---|---|
| Cash flow provided by operating activities .. $ 42,000 | Other long-term assets ..................... 35,000 |
| Cash at June 30, 2009....................... 18,000 | Cash flow from financing activities ......... 2,600 |
| Cash at June 30, 2010....................... 32,000 | Current liabilities .......................... 44,000 |
| Inventory ................................... 11,000 | Long-term liabilities ....................... 36,500 |
| Accounts receivable ........................ 24,400 | Intangible assets .......................... 19,000 |
| Cash flow from investing activities ......... (30,600) | Common stock............................. 102,000 |
| Other current assets ....................... 3,000 | Retained earnings ......................... ? |
| Property, plant and equipment ............. 80,000 | |

### Required
Prepare a classified balance sheet as of June 30, 2010, and statement of cash flows for 2010.

**P2-5B. Assessing a Firm's Profitability, Liquidity and Solvency**    **LO2, LO3**

Presented below is financial data for the Miller Company as of year-end 2009 and 2010:

| | 2009 | 2010 |
|---|---|---|
| Current assets ......................................................... | $ 70,000 | $110,000 |
| Total assets............................................................ | 240,000 | 340,000 |
| Current liabilities ..................................................... | 58,000 | 140,000 |
| Total liabilities........................................................ | 144,000 | 224,000 |
| Net sales ............................................................. | 264,000 | 374,000 |
| Net income........................................................... | 35,000 | 50,400 |

### Required
Calculate Miller's current ratio, debt-to-total-assets ratio, and return on sales. Comment on the trend in the company's profitability, liquidity, and solvency from 2009 to 2010.

**P2-6B. Profitability and the Income Statement**    **LO3**

Presented below are income statement data for VanPool & Company for 2010:

| | | | |
|---|---|---|---|
| Operating expenses ................. | $ 52,000 | Cost of goods sold.................... | 25,200 |
| Other expenses ..................... | 1,000 | Sales revenue ........................ | 116,500 |
| Income taxes........................ | 10,500 | | |

### Required
Prepare an income statement for 2010 and calculate the company's return on sales. If VanPool's return on sales was 26 percent in 2009, did the company's profitability increase or decrease in 2010?

**P2-7B. Preparing a Statement of Stockholders' Equity**    **LO4**

Presented below is financial data for Thomas & Co. as of December 31, 2010:

| | | | |
|---|---|---|---|
| Cash ................................. | $ 16,000 | Inventory ............................. | 14,000 |
| Retained earnings, Jan. 1, 2010......... | 26,000 | Net income............................ | 60,000 |
| Building............................. | 44,000 | Stockholders' equity, Jan. 1, 2010...... | 126,000 |
| Common stock...................... | 100,000 | Retained earnings, Dec. 31, 2010....... | ? |
| Accrued expenses payable............ | 8,000 | Stockholders' equity, Dec. 31, 2010..... | 162,000 |
| Dividends paid ...................... | 24,000 | | |

### Required
Prepare a statement of stockholders' equity as of December 31, 2010.

**P2-8B. Interpreting Profitability, Liquidity, and Solvency Ratios**    **LO2, LO3**

Presented below is financial data for two furniture manufacturing companies:

| | Company B | Company D |
|---|---|---|
| Return on sales....................................................... | 9% | 10.9% |
| Current ratio ......................................................... | 1.9 | 1.0 |
| Debt-to-total-assets ratio ............................................. | 41% | 59% |

**Required**

Consider the financial data of the two companies. Which company represents the better invest-ment opportunity in your opinion and why?

**LO2, LO3** **P2-9B.** **Ratio Analysis**

The following balances were reported in the financial statements for Ruby Company.

|  | 2011 | 2010 |
| --- | --- | --- |
| Net sales | $1,600,000 | $1,700,000 |
| Net income | 160,000 | 195,000 |
| Current assets | 400,000 | 525,000 |
| Current liabilities | 160,000 | 200,000 |
| Total liabilities | 500,000 | 675,000 |
| Total assets | 1,500,000 | 2,400,000 |

**Required**

1. Compute the following ratios for 2011 and 2010 for Ruby Company.
   a. Return on sales
   b. Current ratio
   c. Debt-to-total-assets ratio
2. Comment on changes to Ruby Company's profitability, liquidity, and solvency.

# SERIAL PROBLEM: KATE'S CARDS

(*Note:* **This is a continuation of the Serial Problem: Kate's Cards from Chapter 1.**)

**SP2.** After investigating different organizational forms, Kate Collins decided to operate her business as a corporation, Kate's Cards Inc. Having made that decision, Kate began the process of getting her business up and running.

In order to learn more about the industry and to meet people who could give her advice, Kate attended several industry trade shows. At the most recent trade show, Kate was introduced to Fred Abbott, operations manager of "Sentiments," a national card distributor. After much discussion, Fred asked Kate to consider being one of Sentiments' card suppliers. He provided Kate with a copy of the company's recent financial statements. Fred indicated that he expects that Kate will need to supply Sentiments with approximately 50 card designs per month. Kate is to send Sentiments a monthly invoice, and she will be paid approximately 30 days from the date the invoice is received in Sentiments' corporate office.

Naturally, Kate was thrilled with this offer, since this will certainly give her business a big boost. However, she recently read in the newspaper that Sentiments has a reputation for selling some obscene cards marketed at young singles, and as a result, some conservative groups have boycotted the brand.

**Required**

Kate has several questions. Answer the following questions for Kate.

a. What type of information does each of Sentiments' financial statements provide to Kate?

b. What financial statements would Kate need to evaluate whether Sentiments will have enough cash to meet its current liabilities? Explain what to look for.

c. What financial statement would Kate need to evaluate whether Sentiments will be able to survive over a long period of time? Explain what to look for.

d. What financial statement would Kate need to evaluate Sentiments' profitability? Explain what to look for.

e. Where can Kate find out whether Sentiments has outstanding debt? How can Kate deter-mine whether Sentiments will be able to meet its interest and principal payments on any debts that it has?

f. How could Kate determine whether Sentiments pays a dividend?

g. In deciding whether to go ahead with this opportunity, are there other areas of concern that Kate should be aware of?

# EXTENDING YOUR KNOWLEDGE

## REPORTING AND ANALYSIS

**EYK2-1.** **Financial Reporting Problem: Columbia Sportswear Company**

The financial statements for **Columbia Sportswear** can be found in Appendix A at the end of this textbook.

**COLUMBIA SPORTSWEAR COMPANY**

**Required**

Answer the following questions using the Consolidated Balance Sheet and the Notes to the consolidated financial statements:

*a.* What were the combined totals of Columbia's liabilities and stockholders' equity for 2009 and 2008?

*b.* How do these amounts compare with Columbia's total assets for each year?

*c.* What was the largest, in dollar value, of Columbia's assets each year? What does this asset represent?

*d.* What is the balance of accrued liabilities made up of?

**EYK2-2.** **Comparative Analysis Problem: Columbia Sportswear Company vs. The Timberland Company**

The financial statements for **Columbia Sportswear** can be found in Appendix A and **The Timberland Company**'s financial statements can be found in Appendix B at the end of this textbook.

**COLUMBIA SPORTSWEAR COMPANY**

**THE TIMBERLAND COMPANY**

**Required**

*a.* Calculate for each company the following ratios for 2009:
1. Current ratio
2. Debt-to-total-assets ratio
3. Return on sales

*b.* Comment on the companies' relative profitability, liquidity, and solvency.

**EYK2-3.** **Business Decision Problem**

**SanDisk**, a maker of computer memory devices, reports the following information in its financial statements. Assume that you are a loan officer at a major bank and have been assigned the task of evaluating whether to extend a loan for a plant expansion to the company.

**SANDISK**

| (in millions) | 2010 | 2009 | 2008 |
|---|---|---|---|
| Current assets | $ 2,703 | $3,300 | $4,242 |
| Total assets | 5,927 | 7,235 | 6,968 |
| Current liabilities | 1,263 | 914 | 896 |
| Total liabilities | 2,752 | 2,275 | 2,200 |
| Retained earnings | (927) | 1,130 | 1,106 |
| Net sales | 3,351 | 3,896 | 3,258 |
| Cost of goods sold | 3,288 | 2,694 | 2,018 |
| Net income | (2,057) | 218 | 199 |
| Cash flow from operating activities | 87 | 653 | 598 |
| Cash flow from investing activities | 29 | (1,218) | (978) |
| Cash flow from financing activities | 11,854 | (181) | 1,197 |
| Expenditures for property, plant, and equipment | (184) | (259) | (176) |

**Required**

*a.* Calculate the company's current ratio, debt-to-total-assets ratio, return on sales, and free cash flow for each year.

*b.* Comment on SanDisk's liquidity, solvency, and profitability.

*c.* Based on what you have learned about SanDisk, would you recommend offering the company a loan?

**EYK2-4.** **Financial Analysis Problem**

As part of your internship at Walleys Inc. you have been assigned the job of developing a few important ratios from the company's financial statements. This information is intended to be used by the company to help Walleys obtain a large bank loan. In particular, the data will need to convince the bank that Walleys is a good loan risk based on its liquidity, solvency, and profitability. Below are the data you pulled together:

**ASSIGNMENTS**

| | 2010 | 2009 |
|---|---|---|
| Current ratio | 2.2:1 | 1.5:1 |
| Debt-to-total-assets ratio | 55 percent | 63 percent |
| Return on sales | 9.3 percent | 9.1 percent |
| Free cash flow | Up 17 percent | Up 19 percent |
| Net income | Up 15 percent | Down 12 percent |

**Required**

Prepare brief comments that discuss how each of these items can be used to support the argument that Walleys is showing improving financial health.

## CRITICAL THINKING

GENERAL MILLS, INC.

**EYK2-5.** **Accounting Research Problem**

Go to this book's Website and locate the annual report of **General Mills, Inc.** for the year ending May 30, 2010 (fiscal year 2010).

**Required**

1. Calculate the company's return on sales for 2008, 2009, and 2010. What is the trend?
2. Calculate the company's current asset ratio for 2009 and 2010. What is the trend?
3. Calculate the company's debt-to-total-assets ratio for 2009 and 2010. What is the trend?
4. Calculate the company's free cash flow for 2008, 2009, and 2010. What is the trend?

**EYK2-6.** **Accounting Communication Activity**

V. J. Simmons is the President of Forward Engineering Associates. He is a very good engineer, but his accounting knowledge is quite limited.

**Required**

V. J. has heard that ratio analysis can help him determine the financial condition of his company. In particular, he would like you to explain to him in a memo how to calculate and interpret the following three ratios: (1) return on sales, (2) current ratio, and (3) debt-to-total-assets ratio. Prepare a memo for V.J.

**EYK2-7.** **Accounting Ethics Case**

Go to the web and read the Strategic Finance journal article "ERC Says Ethics Risk Landscape Still Treacherous" at https://www.imanet.org/pdf/01-08-ethics.pdf

**Required**

a. The article reports that many employees in a 2007 survey indicated they had observed violations of company ethics standards, policy, or the law. How did this percentage of employees observing these lapses compare in 2007 with prior surveys in 2005 and 2003?
b. What type of misconduct was observed most often?
c. Did the employees usually report what they observed? If not, what were the two most commonly given reasons for failure to report the observed misconduct?
d. What are some of the most important elements necessary for an effective ethics program?

**EYK2-8.** **Corporate Social Responsibility Problem**

Many investors consider past performance, fees, and investment objectives as the sole criteria for selecting a mutual fund for investment purposes. A growing number of investors are also asking about the actions and philosophies of the companies that form a fund's underlying investment portfolio. Socially responsible mutual funds have been developed to fill this need. These funds are designed for investors who want to align their investments with their religious, political, or social convictions.

Because there is no universally accepted definition as to what makes a company responsible or an investment a socially responsible investment, socially responsible funds are quite diverse. Not surprisingly different funds may take opposite positions on certain controversial issues such as family planning, gay rights, or animal testing.

For the most part, socially responsible funds select their underlying investment firms through either a negative filter or a positive filter. A negative filter is used to screen out firms that are not considered acceptable to the positions advocated by the fund. Examples of firms that may be screened out include firms that are involved in gambling, alcohol, tobacco, or weapons. A positive filter is used to include firms that are seen to be leaders in areas advocated by the fund, such as environmental, diversity, or human rights records.

**Required**

a.   Go to the Websites of three socially responsible mutual funds
   1.   Calvert Signature Funds: http://www.calvertgroup.com/sri-signature.html
   2.   Domini Social Equity Fund: http://www.domini.com/domini-funds/Domini-Social-Equity-Fund/index.htm
   3.   Green Century Balanced Fund: http://www.greencentury.com/funds/Green-Century-Balanced-Fund
b.   Compare the screening criteria used by each fund. How do they differ and how are they alike?

**EYK2-9.**   **Forensic Accounting Problem**

Debra Day, a business major at a local college, was recently hired for the summer at Sweet Delights, a popular ice cream parlor near the campus. Debra spent most of her time tending the cash register where she noticed that most of the customers paid in cash and never seemed to care about getting a receipt. Debra soon figured out that she could ring up a much lesser amount on the register, charge the customer the full amount, then toss the receipt. For example, on a $7 order she would charge and collect the full $7 from the customer, but only ring up $5. She would then deposit $5 in the register so that it would agree with the register tape and pocket the $2.

**Required**

a.   What type of fraud is Debra committing?
b.   The store manager recently hired you as a forensic accountant to critique the controls at Sweet Delights. He has noticed that while the store seems as busy as ever, and the cash in the register agrees with the tapes, the store is not as profitable as it previously was. What control would you recommend to help prevent the type of fraud being committed by Debra?

**EYK2-10.**   **Analyzing IFRS Financial Statements**

Tesco PLC is the world's third largest retailer. Tesco is based in the United Kingdom but also maintains operations in the United States. Tesco's IFRS financial statements are presented in Appendix C at the end of this book, and the complete annual report for year-ended February 28, 2009 is available on this book's Website.
. After reviewing the company's financial statements, consider the following questions:

a.   What basic financial statement is missing from Tesco's annual report?
b.   Using Tesco's group balance sheet, identify the key account changes in the Equity section of the balance sheet.
c.   Using Tesco's group cash flow statement, identify the key changes in the company's Equity accounts.
d.   Do the figures from questions b and c reconcile with each other?

## ANSWERS TO SELF-STUDY QUESTIONS:

1. b, (pp. 52–56)  2. c, (p. 53)  3. c, (p. 12)  4. d, (p. 53)  5. b, (p. 53)  6. d, (p. 57)  7. d, (p. 57)
8. b, (p. 60)  9. c, (p. 60)  10. d, (p. 61)  11. a, (p. 58)  12. b, (p. 61)

## Your Turn! Solutions

### Solution 2.1

| MUSICLAND COMPANY Balance Sheet December 31, 2010 | | | | |
|---|---|---|---|---|
| **Assets** | | | **Liabilities and Stockholders' Equity** | |
| Current assets | | | Current liabilities | |
| Cash.............................. | $ 300 | | Accounts payable ...................... | $2,500 |
| Accounts receivable................ | 3,000 | | Other current liabilities................. | 2,000 |
| Inventory ........................ | 12,200 | | Total current liabilities................. | 4,500 |
| Other current assets............... | 1,500 | | | |
| Total current assets ............. | 17,000 | | Long-term notes payable ................ | 20,000 |
| | | | Total liabilities........................... | 24,500 |
| Property, plant, & equipment ......... | 25,000 | | Stockholders' equity ..................... | 17,500 |
| Total assets.......................... | $42,000 | | Total liabilities and stockholders' equity ... | $42,000 |

### Solution 2.2

| | 2010 | 2009 |
|---|---|---|
| Return on sales.................. | $\frac{\$20,000}{\$120,000} = 16.67\%$ | $\frac{\$15,000}{\$110,000} = 13.6\%$ |
| Current ratio .................... | $\frac{\$75,000}{\$50,000} = 1.50{:}1$ | $\frac{\$65,000}{\$45,000} = 1.44{:}1$ |
| Debt-to-total-assets ratio ........ | $\frac{\$150,000}{\$220,000} = 68.2\%$ | $\frac{\$145,000}{\$190,000} = 76.3\%$ |
| Free cash flow ................... | $\$25,000 - \$7,000 = \$18,000$ | $\$22,000 - \$6,000 = \$16,000$ |

The Philips Company has improved its performance on every measure. The company is earning a higher amount of net income on every dollar of sales revenue as indicated by its return on sales and has more cash for a possible plant expansion as seen in its increasing free cash flow. In addition, both its liquidity as reflected by the current ratio and its solvency as reflected by the debt-to-total-assets ratio are trending in a positive direction.

### Solution 2.3

1. The framework consists of (1) financial reporting objectives, (2) financial statement elements, (3) recognition criteria for financial statement items, and (4) qualitative characteristics of accounting information. The main objective of this framework is to provide information that is useful to the users of the financial statements.
2. The elements include (1) assets, (2) liabilities, (3) owners' equity, (4) investments by owners, (5) distributions to owners, (6) revenues, (7) expenses, (8) gains, (9) losses, and (10) comprehensive income.
3. The two primary qualities are relevance and reliability.

### Solution 2.4

1. Comparability
2. Monetary unit concept
3. Reliability
4. Materiality
5. Relevance
6. Expense recognition

# Processing Accounting Information

## LEARNING OBJECTIVES

1. **Identify** the five major steps in the accounting cycle. (p. 100)

2. **Analyze** and **record** transactions using the accounting equation. (p. 101)

3. **Explain** the nature, format, and purpose of an account. (p. 107)

4. **Describe** the system of debits and credits and its use in recording transactions. (p. 108)

5. **Explain** the process of journalizing and posting transactions. (p. 109)

6. **Describe** the trial balance. (p. 118)

# (AC)COUNTING STARS

Many think accountants and movie stars have little in common. At least one night every year, however, they share the stage at the annual Academy Awards. The global accounting firm **PricewaterhouseCoopers** recently celebrated its 76th year counting and verifying the Oscar ballots to determine the Oscar winners.

Accounting firms such as Pricewaterhouse-Coopers, **Ernst and Young**, **KPMG**, and **Deloitte and Touche** have earned a reputation of honesty and ethical conduct—attributes critical to the accounting profession. Many consider ethics the most fundamental principle underlying financial accounting and the independent accounting firms.

The PricewaterhouseCoopers accountants at the Academy Awards work on the project from a top-secret location. One of the accountants involved explained: "We're proud of our track record and heritage of hand counting every ballot to deliver the utmost level of accuracy and reliability to the Academy."

Although all accounting work is not as glamorous as controlling Oscar ballots, that work is crucial to a successful, global capital market. Businesses as varied as **Disney**, **Lowes**, **Google**, and **McDonald's** all require financial statements for making good business decisions.

This chapter describes the details of the accounting system of debits and credits. That system is applied throughout the world in all business settings. This chapter also explains the process of journalizing and posting transactions so that financial statements can be prepared for both internal and external users of accounting information.

# ACCOUNTING CYCLE

Businesses engage in economic activities. The role of accounting is to analyze these activities for their impact on a company's accounting equation, and then enter the results of that analysis in the company's accounting system. When a company's management team needs financial data for decision-making purposes and for reports to external parties, the company's financial statements are prepared and communicated. At the end of the accounting period, the "books are closed," a process that prepares the accounting records for the next accounting period. The accounting activities described constitute major steps in the **accounting cycle**—a sequence of activities undertaken by accountants to accumulate and report the financial information of a business. Stated succinctly, these steps are analyze, record, adjust, report, and close. Exhibit 3-1 shows the sequence of the major steps in the accounting cycle.

**EXHIBIT 3-1   Five Major Steps in the Accounting Cycle**

**Analyze** Analyze transactions from source documents

**Record** Journalize transactions and prepare unadjusted trial balance

**Adjust** Journalize adjusting entries and prepare adjusted trial balance

**Report** Prepare financial statements

**Close** Journalize closing entries and prepare post-closing trial balance

The five steps in the accounting cycle do not occur with equal frequency. A business analyzes and records financial transactions daily during the accounting period. It adjusts and reports accumulated financial data whenever management needs financial information, usually at weekly, monthly, or quarterly intervals, but at least annually. Closing the books occurs just once, at the end of the accounting period. This chapter focuses on the first two steps of the accounting cycle—analyze and record. In Chapter Four, we examine the final three steps of the cycle.

It is important to know that the steps in the accounting cycle are undertaken whether a business uses a manual accounting system or a computer-based system. This chapter explains the accounting cycle using a manual system for WebWork, a Website development and consulting business launched on December 1, 2011.

---

**ACCOUNTING IN PRACTICE** | **Accounting Periods**

The annual accounting period is known as a **fiscal year**. Businesses with fiscal year-ends on December 31, are said to be on a **calendar year**. About 60 percent of U.S. businesses are on a calendar year. Many companies prefer to have their accounting year coincide with their "natural" year—that is, at a point in time when business activity is at a low point. For example, many retailers conclude their fiscal year when inventory quantities are low and easier to count, as year-end accounting procedures are more efficiently accomplished when there is less inventory. The "natural" year does not necessarily coincide with the calendar year. For example, **Gap**, a retailer, ends its fiscal year on the Friday nearest January 31. The company's busiest period is November through January, when its customers are holiday shopping. Similarly, the **Boston Celtics**, a professional basketball team, concludes its fiscal year on June 30, following completion of the NBA finals.

---

## ANALYZING TRANSACTIONS

Many companies utilize a computer-based accounting system to record their financial transactions. You may have some personal experience using accounting software programs like QuickBooks by **Intuit**. While these computer-based accounting systems are not as sophisticated as the systems used by major corporations, they work in much the same way. Similarly, manual systems might lack the sophistication of large accounting systems utilized by companies like **Ford Motor Company**, but the basic process remains the same.

The accounting equation is written as:

LEARNING OBJECTIVE 2

**Analyze** and **record** transactions using the accounting equation.

$$\text{Assets} = \text{Liabilities} + \text{Stockholders' equity}$$

This accounting equation provides a convenient way to analyze and summarize a company's financial transactions and data. The first step in the accounting cycle—analyze—is to determine just what information (if any) must be recorded in a company's accounting records. Recall from Chapter 2 that only items that can be expressed in monetary terms are recorded in financial statements. For example, the payment of wages to Steve Jobs, the CEO of **Apple**, is recorded because it can be expressed in monetary terms.

An **accounting transaction** is an economic event that must be recorded in the company's accounting records. In general, any event that affects any of the elements of the accounting equation—assets, liabilities, or stockholders' equity—must be recorded in a company's accounting records. Some activities—for example, ordering supplies, bidding on a contract, or negotiating the purchase of an asset—may represent a business activity, but an accounting transaction does not occur until such activities result in a change in one or more amounts of an asset, liability, or stockholders' equity.

An accounting transaction impacts the accounting equation. However, that equation always remains in balance and at least two elements of the equation are always affected. This is where the term **double-entry accounting** comes from. For example, if an asset account such as Cash is increased, one of the following financial events must also occur to keep the accounting equation in balance:

a. Another asset, such as accounts receivable, must decrease; or

b. A liability, such as notes payable, must increase; or

c. Stockholders' equity, such as sales revenue, must increase.

### IFRS ALERT!

Both the FASB in the United States and the FASB's international counterpart, the IASB, are working hard to "harmonize" remaining differences between U.S. GAAP and IFRS. One area that these organizations do not need to worry about is how double-entry accounting works. The same process that is described in this chapter, and uses debits and credits, is universally followed.

## ACCOUNTING EQUATION EXPANDED

Stockholders' equity has two components—the amount invested by stockholders (common stock) and the cumulative net income of the business that has not yet been distributed to stockholders as a dividend (retained earnings). Common stock is increased when the company issues shares of stock, and retained earnings is increased by a company's net income (or decreased by a net loss) and decreased by a company's payment of dividends. Incorporating these two components into stockholders' equity, the *expanded accounting equation* is illustrated in Exhibit 3-2.

**EXHIBIT 3-2    The Accounting Equation Expanded**

## TRANSACTIONS AND THE ACCOUNTING EQUATION: AN ILLUSTRATION

The financial statements of WebWork were introduced in Chapter 1. We return to WebWork to illustrate how its various economic activities and events led to those financial statements.

Steve Gates first established WebWork on December 1, 2011. The company's transactions for December, the first month of operations, are analyzed on the following pages. The accounting equation for WebWork is shown after each transaction so that the financial effects of each transaction can be examined. The accounting equation remains in balance following each transaction. This is not a coincidence; it is the result of the fundamental structure of the accounting system.

The following pages illustrate eleven transactions that occurred during December 2011, at WebWork. Avoid the temptation to skip any of these transactions because each transaction is included to illustrate a particular concept or approach to recording an economic event utilizing the accounting equation.

### Transaction 1. Issued Stock

On December 1, 2011, Steve Gates invested $30,000 cash in exchange for the company's common stock. This transaction increased the company's assets (Cash) by $30,000 and increased its stockholders' equity (Common Stock) by $30,000, as illustrated below using the accounting equation. (For each transaction that impacts equity, we add a brief description—in this case "Issued stock.")

| Assets | = | Liabilities | + | Stockholders' Equity | |
|---|---|---|---|---|---|
| Cash | = | | | Common Stock | |
| (1) +30,000 | = | | | +30,000 | Issued stock |
| $30,000 | | | | $30,000 | |

It is important to verify the equality of the accounting equation following each transaction. After the above transaction is recorded, both sides of the equation total $30,000.

### Transaction 2. Paid Rent in Advance

On December 1, WebWork prepaid its office rent for the next six months, December 2011 through May 2012. WebWork's rent is $1,800 per month; meaning it paid a total of $10,800 cash (6 × $1,800). This transaction decreased Cash by $10,800 and increased Prepaid Rent by $10,800.

| | Assets | | = | Liabilities | + | Stockholders' Equity |
|---|---|---|---|---|---|---|
| | Cash | + Prepaid Rent | = | | | Common Stock |
| | 30,000 | | | | | 30,000 |
| (2) | −10,800 | +10,800 | | | | |
| | 19,200 + | 10,800 | | | | 30,000 |
| | $30,000 | | = | | | $30,000 |

The expenditure for prepaid rent is recorded as an asset because the advance payment is a future economic benefit to the company. This outlay of cash has value to the business beyond the current accounting period, but any rent that is used up in the current accounting period will be recorded as an expense for the month of December.

### Transaction 3. Purchased Office Supplies on Account

On December 1, WebWork purchased office supplies on account totaling $2,850. Businesses often extend credit to their customers. Credit allows businesses to pay for goods or services at a later date. When credit is used to purchase goods or services, the purchase is said to be made *on account*. This transaction increased Office Supplies by $2,850 and it increased Accounts Payable by the same amount.

| | Assets | | | = | Liabilities | + | Stockholders' Equity |
|---|---|---|---|---|---|---|---|
| | Cash + | Office Supplies | + Prepaid Rent | = | Accounts Payable | + | Common Stock |
| | 19,200 | | 10,800 | | | | 30,000 |
| (3) | | +2,850 | | | +2,850 | | |
| | 19,200 + | 2,850 | +10,800 | = | 2,850 | + | 30,000 |
| | $32,850 | | | = | | | $32,850 |

Office supplies are recorded as an asset because they are expected to be used by the business in future periods beyond the current accounting period. Any supplies that are used up in the current accounting period will be recorded as an expense for the month of December. Following the purchase of office supplies, its assets total $32,850, which is equal to the sum of total liabilities ($2,850) plus stockholders' equity ($30,000).

### Transaction 4. Signed Bank Note in Exchange For Cash

On December 1, WebWork obtained a two-year bank loan in the amount of $36,000, after signing a note payable. Annual interest charges on the note amount to 10 percent and are due each November 30. As a consequence of this loan, the company's Cash account increased by $36,000 and the Notes Payable account, a liability, is increased by $36,000.

| | Assets | | | | = | Liabilities | | | + | Stockholders' Equity |
|---|---|---|---|---|---|---|---|---|---|---|
| | Cash | + | Office Supplies | + | Prepaid Rent | = | Accounts Payable | + | Notes Payable | + | Common Stock |
| | 19,200 | | 2,850 | | 10,800 | | 2,850 | | | | 30,000 |
| (4) | +36,000 | | | | | | | | +36,000 | | |
| | 55,200 | + | 2,850 | + | 10,800 | = | 2,850 | + | 36,000 | + | 30,000 |

$68,850                                         $68,850

### Transaction 5. Purchased Equipment With Cash

On December 2, WebWork used cash to purchase office equipment costing $32,400. This transaction decreased Cash by $32,400 and it increased Office Equipment by the same amount. The accounting equation remains in balance because an equal amount ($32,400) is both added to and subtracted from total assets.

| | Assets | | | | | = | Liabilities | | | + | Stockholders' Equity |
|---|---|---|---|---|---|---|---|---|---|---|---|
| | Cash | + | Office Supplies | + | Prepaid Rent | + Equipment = | Accounts Payable | + | Notes Payable | + | Common Stock |
| | 55,200 | | 2,850 | | 10,800 | | 2,850 | | 36,000 | | 30,000 |
| (5) | −32,400 | | | | | +32,400 | | | | | |
| | 22,800 | + | 2,850 | + | 10,800 | + 32,400 = | 2,850 | + | 36,000 | + | 30,000 |

$68,850                                         $68,850

### Transaction 6. Received Customer Prepayment

On December 5, WebWork received a prepayment in the amount of $3,000 for services to be performed over the next few months. Because WebWork has not yet performed the services, and following the revenue recognition principle discussed in Chapter 2, it does not record the $3,000 payment as revenue. Instead, a liability account, **Unearned Revenue**, is increased by $3,000, and the company's Cash account is increased by $3,000. Unearned revenue is a liability because the company accepted payment for goods or services that have not yet been provided and, therefore, the amount cannot be recorded as earned revenue.

**A.K.A.** Unearned revenue is also called *deferred revenue*.

| | Assets | | | | | | = | Liabilities | | | | | + | Stockholders' Equity |
|---|---|---|---|---|---|---|---|---|---|---|---|---|---|---|
| | Cash | + | Office Supplies | + | Prepaid Rent | + Equip-ment | = | Accounts Payable | + | Unearned Revenue | + | Notes Payable | + | Common Stock |
| | 22,800 | | 2,850 | | 10,800 | 32,400 | | 2,850 | | | | 36,000 | | 30,000 |
| (6) | +3,000 | | | | | | | | | +3,000 | | | | |
| | 25,800 | + | 2,850 | + | 10,800 | + 32,400 | = | 2,850 | + | 3,000 | + | 36,000 | + | 30,000 |

$71,850                                         $71,850

### Transaction 7. Provided Services for Customers

On December 6, WebWork performed services for several customers and it was paid $13,510 cash. This transaction increased Cash by $13,510 and it increased Fees Revenue by the same amount.

| Assets | | | | = | Liabilities | | | + | Stockholders' Equity | |
|---|---|---|---|---|---|---|---|---|---|---|
| Cash + | Office Supplies + | Prepaid Rent + | Equipment | = | Accounts Payable + | Unearned Revenue + | Notes Payable + | Common Stock + | Retained Earnings | |
| | | | | | | | | | Rev. − Exp. − Div. | |
| 25,800 | 2,850 | 10,800 | 32,400 | | 2,850 | 3,000 | 36,000 | 30,000 | | |
| (7) +13,510 | | | | | | | | | +13,510 | Fee revenue |
| 39,310 + | 2,850 + | 10,800 + | 32,400 | = | 2,850 + | 3,000 + | 36,000 + | 30,000 + | 13,510 | |
| $85,360 | | | | | $85,360 | | | | | |

## Transaction 8. Performed Services for Both Cash and on Account

On December 8, WebWork performed $4,740 of services and received $1,000 in cash with the remaining $3,740 to be paid to WebWork by customers within 90 days. Businesses often extend credit to customers, allowing them to pay for goods or services at a later date. Under accrual accounting, revenue must be recorded when earned regardless of when payment is received. Consequently, this transaction increased Cash by $1,000, it increased Accounts Receivable by $3,740, and it increased Fees Revenue by $4,740. The accounting equation remains in balance because both sides of the equation are increased by $4,740.

**A.K.A.** Delivering goods or services in advance of payment is referred to as providing goods or services "*on account*" or "on credit."

| Assets | | | | | = | Liabilities | | | + | Stockholders' Equity | |
|---|---|---|---|---|---|---|---|---|---|---|---|
| Cash + | Accounts Receivable + | Office Supplies + | Prepaid Rent + | Equipment | = | Accounts Payable + | Unearned Revenue + | Notes Payable + | Common Stock + | Retained Earnings | |
| | | | | | | | | | | Rev. − Exp. − Div. | |
| 39,310 | | 2,850 | 10,800 | 32,400 | | 2,850 | 3,000 | 36,000 | 30,000 | 13,510 | |
| (8) +1,000 | +3,740 | | | | | | | | | +4,740 | Fee revenue |
| 40,310 + | 3,740 + | 2,850 + | 10,800 + | 32,400 | = | 2,850 + | 3,000 + | 36,000 + | 30,000 + | 18,250 | |
| $90,100 | | | | | | $90,100 | | | | | |

## Non-Accounting Transaction. Hired an Employee

On December 9, WebWork hired an employee to provide administrative help in the office. The employee will be paid $1,620 every two weeks and begins work Monday, December 12. At the time the employee is hired there is no immediate financial effect on the assets, liabilities, or stockholders' equity of the company. There is only an employment agreement between the employee and the company. The employee has not yet performed any work, nor has the employee received any wages.

## Transaction 9. Paid Employee Wages

On December 23, WebWork paid the employee after she completed her first two weeks on the job. This transaction decreased Cash by $1,620, and it increased Wage Expense by $1,620. By definition, an increase in expenses decreases stockholders' equity.

| Assets | | | | | = | Liabilities | | | + | Stockholders' Equity | |
|---|---|---|---|---|---|---|---|---|---|---|---|
| Cash + | Accounts Receivable + | Office Supplies + | Prepaid Rent + | Equipment | = | Accounts Payable + | Unearned Revenue + | Notes Payable + | Common Stock + | Retained Earnings | |
| | | | | | | | | | | Rev. − Exp. − Div. | |
| 40,310 | 3,740 | 2,850 | 10,800 | 32,400 | | 2,850 | 3,000 | 36,000 | 30,000 | 18,250 | |
| (9) −1,620 | | | | | | | | | | −1,620 | Wage expense |
| 38,690 + | 3,740 + | 2,850 + | 10,800 + | 32,400 | = | 2,850 + | 3,000 + | 36,000 + | 30,000 + | 18,250 − 1,620 | |
| $88,480 | | | | | | $88,480 | | | | | |

## Transaction 10. Received Payment on Account from Customer

On December 27, WebWork received a payment of $2,400 cash from a customer that had previously received services performed on account (see Transaction 8). This transaction increased Cash by $2,400, and decreased Accounts Receivable by $2,400.

| Assets | | | | | = | Liabilities | | | + | Stockholders' Equity | |
|---|---|---|---|---|---|---|---|---|---|---|---|
| Cash + | Accounts Receivable + | Office Supplies + | Prepaid Rent + | Equipment | = | Accounts Payable + | Unearned Revenue + | Notes Payable + | Common Stock + | Retained Earnings | |
| | | | | | | | | | | Rev. − Exp. − Div. | |
| 38,690 | 3,740 | 2,850 | 10,800 | 32,400 | | 2,850 | 3,000 | 36,000 | 30,000 | 18,250  1,620 | |
| (10) +2,400 | −2,400 | | | | | | | | | | |
| 41,090 + | 1,340 + | 2,850 + | 10,800 + | 32,400 | = | 2,850 + | 3,000 + | 36,000 + | 30,000 + | 18,250 − 1,620 | |
| $88,480 | | | | | | $88,480 | | | | | |

The balance in Accounts Receivable becomes $1,340. This represents the amount still owed to WebWork for services that were previously performed on account but remain unpaid.

### Transaction 11. Paid Cash Dividend

On December 30, WebWork paid a cash dividend. Dividends are not a business expense, and are not included in the calculation of net income. Rather, dividends are a distribution of the company's accumulated net income to its stockholders. Payment of the dividend decreases Cash by $500 and increases Dividends by $500. (By definition, an increase in dividends causes a decrease in stockholders' equity.)

| | | Assets | | | | = | Liabilities | | | + | | Stockholders' Equity | | | | |
|---|---|---|---|---|---|---|---|---|---|---|---|---|---|---|---|---|
| | | | | | | | | | | | | | Retained Earnings | | | |
| | Cash + | Accounts Receivable + | Office Supplies + | Prepaid Rent + | Equip-ment | = | Accounts Payable + | Unearned Revenue + | Notes Payable + | Common Stock + | | Rev. − | Exp. − | Div. | |
| | 41,090 | 1,340 | 2,850 | 10,800 | 32,400 | | 2,850 | 3,000 | 36,000 | 30,000 | | 18,250 | 1,620 | | |
| (11) | −500 | | | | | | | | | | | | | −500 | Dividends |
| | 40,590 + | 1,340 + | 2,850 + | 10,800 + | 32,400 | = | 2,850 + | 3,000 + | 36,000 + | 30,000 + | | 18,250 − | 1,620 − | 500 | |

$$\$87,980 \qquad\qquad \$87,980$$

## Transaction Summary

Exhibit 3-3 provides a summary of the eleven accounting transactions for WebWork, for the month of December. The exhibit illustrates the financial effect of each transaction using the accounting equation. It is important that the accounting equation remains in balance at all times, and that the equality between total assets and the sum of total liabilities and stockholders' equity is maintained following each transaction.

**EXHIBIT 3-3   Summary of December Business Transactions and Their Effect on the Expanded Accounting Equation**

| | | Assets | | | | = | Liabilities | | | + | | Stockholders' Equity | | | |
|---|---|---|---|---|---|---|---|---|---|---|---|---|---|---|---|
| | | | | | | | | | | | | | Retained Earnings | | |
| | Cash + | Accounts Receivable + | Office Supplies + | Prepaid Rent + | Equip-ment | = | Accounts Payable + | Unearned Revenue + | Notes Payable + | Common Stock + | Rev. − | Exp. − | Div. | |
| (1) | +30,000 | | | | | | | | | +30,000 | | | | Issued stock |
| (2) | −10,800 | | | +10,800 | | | | | | | | | | |
| (3) | | | +2,850 | | | | +2,850 | | | | | | | |
| (4) | +36,000 | | | | | | | | +36,000 | | | | | |
| (5) | −32,400 | | | | +32,400 | | | | | | | | | |
| (6) | +3,000 | | | | | | | +3,000 | | | | | | |
| (7) | +13,510 | | | | | | | | | | +13,510 | | | Fees revenue |
| (8) | +1,000 | +3,740 | | | | | | | | | +4,740 | | | Fees revenue |
| (9) | −1,620 | | | | | | | | | | | −1,620 | | Wage expense |
| (10) | +2,400 | −2,400 | | | | | | | | | | | | |
| (11) | −500 | | | | | | | | | | | | −500 | Dividends |
| | 40,590 + | 1,340 + | 2,850 + | 10,800 + | 32,400 = | 2,850 + | 3,000 + | 36,000 + | 30,000 + | 18,250 − | 1,620 − | 500 | |

$$\$87,980 \qquad\qquad \$87,980$$

| | Concept  ⟶  Method  ⟶  Assessment | | |
|---|---|---|---|
| TAKEAWAY 3.1 | When should an event be recorded in a company's accounting records? | Review the event details.<br><br>Does the event affect the company's assets, liabilities, or stockholders' equity? | If the event affects any of the elements of the accounting equation, it must be recorded in a company's accounting records. |

## Your Turn!                                                    3.1

Ford Aerobics Studio, Inc., operates as a corporation. The firm rents studio space (including a sound system) and specializes in offering aerobics classes to individuals and groups. On January 1, the assets, liabilities, and stockholders' equity of the business were as follows: Cash, $5,000; Accounts Receivable, $5,200; Notes Payable, $2,500; Accounts Payable, $1,000; Common Stock, $5,500; and Retained Earnings, $1,200. The January business activities for the studio were as follows:

(1) Paid $600 cash on accounts payable.
(2) Paid January rent of $3,600 cash.
(3) Billed clients for January classes in the amount of $11,500.
(4) Received a $500 invoice from a supplier for T-shirts given free to January's class members as an advertising promotion.
(5) Collected $10,000 cash on account from clients for prior aerobics classes.
(6) Paid employee wages of $2,400 cash.
(7) Received a $680 invoice for January's utilities.
(8) Paid $20 cash to the bank as January interest on an outstanding note payable.
(9) Paid $900 cash in dividends to stockholders.
(10) Paid $4,000 cash on January 31 to purchase a sound system to replace the rented system.

**Required**

a.  Set up an expanded accounting equation in columnar form with the following individual assets, liabilities, and stockholders' equity accounts: Cash, Accounts Receivable, Equipment, Notes Payable, Accounts Payable, Common Stock, and Retained Earnings. Enter the January 1 balances below each account. (The beginning balance in the Equipment account is $0.)

b.  Record the financial impact (increase or decrease) of each transaction (1) through (10) on the beginning account balances. Then total the columns to demonstrate that total assets equal the sum of total liabilities plus stockholders' equity as of January 31.

*The solution is on page 155.*

# THE "ACCOUNT" SYSTEM

The basic component of an accounting system is the **account**, which is an individual record of the increases and decreases in a specific asset, liability, or stockholders' equity item. An account is created for each individual asset, liability, and stockholders' equity item on a company's financial statements. Some common account titles are Cash, Accounts Receivable, Notes Payable, Fees Revenue, and Rent Expense.

LEARNING OBJECTIVE 3

**Explain** the nature, format, and purpose of an account.

## T-ACCOUNT

A **T-account** is a simplified form of an account. T-accounts are so named because they resemble the letter "T." A T-account with the December changes in the Cash account for WebWork is presented in Exhibit 3-4.

| EXHIBIT 3-4 | Cash T-account | | | |
|---|---|---|---|---|
| | | **Cash** | | |
| (1) | 30,000 | 10,800 | (2) | |
| (4) | 36,000 | 32,400 | (5) | |
| (6) | 3,000 | 1,620 | (9) | |
| (7) | 13,510 | 500 | (11) | |
| (8) | 1,000 | | | |
| (10) | 2,400 | | | |
| **Bal.** | 40,590 | | | |

A T-accounts consists of: (1) the account title (such as Cash), (2) amounts reflecting increases and decreases, and (3) cross-references to other accounting records. It is customary to reference (or link) the data entries in a T-account with a number or a letter to identify the related accounting transaction that originated the data. This permits a systematic review of the data entries in the event of a recording error. It also enables a company, and its independent auditor, to review the company's set of accounts and match the account information with the related accounting transactions. The numerical references in the Cash T-account are the ones used to identify the December transactions for WebWork from Exhibit 3-3.

## SYSTEM OF DEBITS AND CREDITS

**LEARNING OBJECTIVE 4**

**Describe** the system of debits and credits and its use in recording transactions.

One basic characteristic of all accounts is that data entries separately record the increases and decreases to an account. In some accounts, such as the Cash account in Exhibit 3-4, increases are recorded on the left side of the account and decreases are recorded on the right side. In other accounts, the reverse is true. The method of recording data entries in the accounts is a matter of convention; that is, a simple set of rules is followed, which involves debits and credits.

The terms **debit** and **credit** are used to refer to the left side and the right side, respectively, of an account as shown below:

**(Any Type of Account)**

| Debit | Credit |
|---|---|
| Always the left side | Always the right side |

Regardless of what amount is recorded in an account, a data entry made on the left side is a debit to the account; and, a data entry recorded on the right side is a credit to the account. The words *debit* and *credit* are abbreviated *dr.* (from the Latin *debere*) and *cr.* (from the Latin *credere*), respectively.

The system of debits and credits identifies which accounts are increased by debits (or by credits) and which accounts are decreased by debits (or by credits). Exhibit 3-5 summarizes these rules for each of the six primary categories of accounts: assets, liabilities, common stock, dividends, revenues, and expenses. Observe the following relations in Exhibit 3-5:

**Hint:** A "Retained Earnings" account would be included in Exhibit 3-5 for a continuing business that has not paid out its income with dividends. That account would have increases on the right and decreases on the left.

1. *Debit* always refers to the left side of an account; *credit* always refers to the right side.

2. Increases in asset, dividend, and expense accounts are debit entries. Increases in liability, common stock, and revenue accounts are credit entries.

3. Decreases in asset, dividend, and expense accounts are credit entries. Decreases in liability, common stock, and revenue accounts are debit entries.

4. The **normal balance** of an account is the side on which increases to the account are recorded. Thus, asset, dividend, and expense accounts normally have debit balances, whereas liabilities, common stock, and revenue accounts normally have credit balances. This is because increases in an account are usually greater than, or equal to, the decreases to an account.

The pattern of increases and decreases for asset accounts is opposite that for liability, common stock, and revenue accounts. The pattern of increases and decreases for revenue

**EXHIBIT 3-5** System of Increases and Decreases, Debits and Credits, and Normal Balances

accounts is to be expected because revenue is a temporary subdivision of stockholders' equity. Following the same logic, the pattern of increases and decreases for dividends and expenses is opposite that because dividends and expenses reduce stockholders' equity.

### PERMANENT AND TEMPORARY ACCOUNTS

Each account is classified as either a permanent account or a temporary account. The **permanent accounts** are the accounts presented in the balance sheet. They consist of accounts for assets, liabilities, common stock, and retained earnings. The distinguishing feature of a permanent account is that any balance in the account at the end of an accounting period is *carried forward* to the next accounting period. Accounts for revenues, expenses, and dividends are temporary subdivisions of stockholders' equity. These accounts are temporary accounts. **Temporary accounts** are used to gather information for a particular accounting period; at the end of the accounting period, temporary account balances are transferred to a permanent stockholders' equity account. The procedures used to transfer temporary account balances to a permanent stockholders' equity account are explained in Chapter 4.

| Permanent Accounts | Temporary Accounts |
|---|---|
| Assets | Revenues |
| Liabilities | Expenses |
| Common Stock | Dividends |
| Retained Earnings | Income Summary |

### Your Turn!      3.2

For each of the following accounts, identify whether the account's normal balance is a debit or a credit and whether the account is permanent or temporary.

a. Cash
b. Common stock
c. Wage expense
d. Notes payable

e. Dividends
f. Sales revenue
g. Inventory

**The solution is on page 155.**

## RECORDING TRANSACTIONS

Earlier in this chapter we analyzed the transactions of WebWork using the accounting equation. This approach enabled us to see how accounting transactions affect a company's financial position and operations. This approach is not feasible, however, for even a modest-sized business because of the large number of transactions. Consequently, we now explain the process of analyzing and recording accounting information in an actual accounting system.

**LEARNING OBJECTIVE 5**

**Explain** the process of journalizing and posting transactions.

An initial step in the analysis and recording process is to identify evidence of a business transaction. This usually comes in the form of a source document. **Source documents** are printed forms or computer records that are generated when a firm engages in a business transaction. At a minimum, a source document usually specifies the dollar amount involved, the date of the transaction, and possibly the party dealing with the firm. Some examples of source documents include (1) a supplier's invoice showing evidence of a purchase of supplies on account, (2) a bank check indicating the payment of an obligation, (3) a deposit slip showing the amount of cash deposited in a bank, and (4) a cash receipt indicating the amount of cash received from a customer for services rendered. One example follows. Regardless of its form, the source document serves as the basis for the analysis of the underlying business event.

---

**WebWork, Inc.**                                                    **INVOICE**

137 Technology Lane
Irvine, CA. 92614
Phone (949) 727-3555                                   INVOICE # [**100**]
                                                       DATE: DECEMBER 10, 2011
**TO:**                                      **FOR:**
Pick Enterprises                             Web design
1055 Kinrose Ave
Los Angeles, CA 90024
(310) 208-5570

| DESCRIPTION | HOURS | RATE | AMOUNT |
| --- | --- | --- | --- |
| Design work for Website, including motion graphics | 17.5 | $125 | $2,187.50 |
| | | TOTAL | $2,187.50 |

Make all checks payable to WebWork, Inc.
Total due in 15 days. Overdue accounts subject to a service charge of 1% per month.

**Thank you for your business!**

---

Once the source document has been analyzed to determine the accounts affected and the amounts involved, we then record the transaction. All accounting transactions are initially recorded in a journal. A **journal**, or *book of original entry*, is a tabular record in which a business's activities are reflected in terms of debits and credits and recorded in chronological order. A journal organizes information by date, and thus, serves as a chronological diary of a company's business activities. The word *journalize* means to record a transaction in a journal; and, an entry in a journal is called a **journal entry**.

> **A.K.A.** A company's journals are also referred to as its *"books."*

> **A.K.A.** Another term often used to describe the recording of a transaction is to *"book"* the transaction.

## CHART OF ACCOUNTS

Businesses maintain a chart of accounts to facilitate the analysis of a company's business activities and to assist in the preparation of journal entries. A **chart of accounts** is a list of the titles of all accounts in a business's accounting system. Account titles are grouped by, and in the order of, the five major components of the expanded accounting equation: assets, liabilities, stockholders' equity, revenues, and expenses. Exhibit 3-6 shows the chart of accounts for WebWork and indicates the account numbers that will be used throughout this illustration. Temporary accounts are outlined by a red dashed box. (Each company maintains its own unique set of accounts and its own numbering system.)

## GENERAL JOURNAL

The **general journal** is a record with enough flexibility that any type of business transaction can be recorded in it. Like all journals in an accounting system, the general journal is a book of original entry in which accounting data are entered into a company's accounting system.

**EXHIBIT 3-6** | Chart of Accounts for WebWork, Inc.

| Assets | Equity |
|---|---|
| 110 Cash | 310 Common Stock |
| 120 Accounts Receivable | 320 Retained Earnings |
| 130 Office Supplies | 330 Dividends |
| 150 Prepaid Rent | |
| 170 Office Equipment | **Revenues** |
| 175 Accumulated Depreciation— Office Equipment | 410 Fees Revenue |
| | **Expenses** |
| **Liabilities** | 510 Supplies Expense |
| 210 Accounts Payable | 520 Wage Expense |
| 220 Interest Payable | 530 Rent Expense |
| 230 Wages Payable | 540 Depreciation Expense—Office Equipment |
| 250 Unearned Revenue | 550 Interest Expense |
| 260 Notes Payable | |

**Hint:** The number of specific accounts used by a business depends on the complexity of its operations and the degree of detail demanded.

Exhibit 3-7 shows the first transaction as it is recorded in WebWork's general journal. The procedure for recording entries in the general journal follows:

❶ Indicate the year, month, and date of entry. (Usually the year and month are rewritten only at the top of each page of the journal or at the point in the journal where the year and month change.)

❷ Enter the titles of accounts affected (from the chart of accounts) in the Description column. Accounts to receive debits are entered close to the left margin and are recorded first. Accounts to receive credits are recorded next and indented slightly to the right.

❸ Enter dollar amounts in the left (Debit) and right (Credit) columns.

❹ Record an explanation of the transaction below the account titles; it should be brief, disclosing information necessary to understand the event recorded.

**EXHIBIT 3-7** | General Journal with First Entry of WebWork, Inc.

**GENERAL JOURNAL**

| Date | Description | Debit | Credit |
|---|---|---|---|
| 2011 ❶ Dec. 1 | Cash ❷ | 30,000 | |
| | Common stock | | 30,000 |
| | *Issued stock in exchange for cash.* ❹ | | |

A journal entry that involves more than two accounts is called a **compound journal entry**. (The journal entry for Transaction 8 is an example of a compound journal entry involving three accounts. The credit of $4,740 to the Fees Revenue account is offset by debits of $1,000 to the Cash account and $3,740 to the Accounts Receivable account.) Any number of accounts can appear in a compound entry; but, regardless of how many accounts are used, the sum of the debit amounts always equals the sum of the credit amounts. Accordingly, each transaction entered in the general journal is recorded with equal dollar amounts of debits and credits. The account titles cited in the Description column should correspond to those from the chart of accounts. (To delineate between journal entries made in the general journal, we leave a blank line between each transaction entry.)

## POSTING JOURNAL ENTRIES TO THE GENERAL LEDGER

After an accounting transaction is journalized in the general journal, the debits and credits in each journal entry are immediately transferred to another component of the accounting system called the general ledger. This transfer of data from the general journal to a company's general ledger is undertaken to facilitate the preparation of the company's financial statements. Although businesses can use various ledgers to accumulate detailed accounting information, all firms have a general ledger. A **general ledger** is a listing of each account of a company and the amounts making up each account.

The process of transferring the debit and credit information from the general journal to the general ledger is called **posting**. It is important to be able to trace each data entry appearing in a general ledger account to the general journal location from which it was posted; consequently, both the general journal and general ledger accounts have a **posting reference** code. The posting reference of the general journal indicates the account to which the related debit or credit has been posted. The posting references in the general journal and ledger accounts are entered when the journal entries are posted to the ledger accounts (automatically when computerized, or by hand for a manual system).

## ILLUSTRATION OF THE RECORDING PROCESS

We now apply the recording process to the transactions of WebWork, Inc., that were summarized in Exhibit 3-3. For each transaction, we **(1) analyze** the transaction using the accounting equation, **(2) journalize** the transaction, and **(3) post** journal entries to the general ledger (for simplicity, we use the T-account structure for each ledger account).

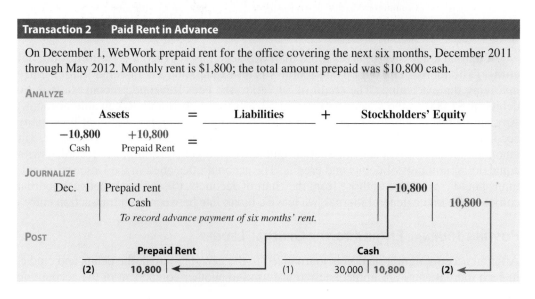

## Transaction 3 | Purchased Office Supplies on Account

On December 1, WebWork purchased $2,850 of office supplies on account.

ANALYZE

| Assets | = | Liabilities | + | Stockholders' Equity |
|---|---|---|---|---|
| +2,850 | = | +2,850 | | |
| Office Supplies | | Accounts Payable | | |

JOURNALIZE

Dec. 1 | Office supplies ⌐2,850
            Accounts payable 2,850 ⌐
            *To record purchase of office supplies.*

POST

| Office Supplies | | Accounts Payable | |
|---|---|---|---|
| (3) | 2,850 | 2,850 | (3) |

## Transaction 4 | Signed Bank Note in Exchange for Cash

On December 1, WebWork obtained a two-year bank loan for $36,000, signing a note payable. Annual interest of 10 percent is due each November 30.

ANALYZE

| Assets | = | Liabilities | + | Stockholders' Equity |
|---|---|---|---|---|
| +36,000 | = | +36,000 | | |
| Cash | | Notes Payable | | |

JOURNALIZE

Dec. 1 | Cash ⌐36,000
            Notes payable 36,000 ⌐
            *To record borrowing of funds.*

POST

| Cash | | | | Notes Payable | |
|---|---|---|---|---|---|
| (1) | 30,000 | 10,800 | (2) | 36,000 | (4) |
| (4) | 36,000 | | | | |

## Transaction 5 | Purchased Office Equipment

On December 2, WebWork used cash to purchase $32,400 of office equipment.

ANALYZE

| Assets | | = | Liabilities | + | Stockholders' Equity |
|---|---|---|---|---|---|
| −32,400 | +32,400 | = | | | |
| Cash | Office Equipment | | | | |

JOURNALIZE

Dec. 2 | Office equipment ⌐32,400
            Cash 32,400 ⌐
            *To record purchase of office equipment.*

POST

| Office Equipment | | | Cash | | |
|---|---|---|---|---|---|
| (5) | 32,400 | (1) | 30,000 | 10,800 | (2) |
| | | (4) | 36,000 | 32,400 | (5) |

### Transaction 6 Received Customer Prepayment

On December 5, WebWork received $3,000 cash for services to be performed in the future.

ANALYZE

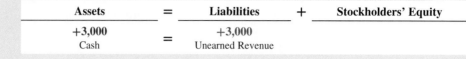

| Assets | = | Liabilities | + | Stockholders' Equity |
|---|---|---|---|---|
| +3,000 | = | +3,000 | | |
| Cash | | Unearned Revenue | | |

JOURNALIZE

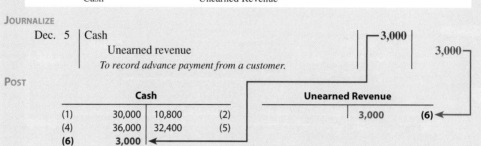

Dec. 5 | Cash ................................................ 3,000
        Unearned revenue ............................ 3,000
        *To record advance payment from a customer.*

POST

| | Cash | | | | Unearned Revenue | |
|---|---|---|---|---|---|---|
| (1) | 30,000 | 10,800 | (2) | | 3,000 | (6) |
| (4) | 36,000 | 32,400 | (5) | | | |
| **(6)** | **3,000** | | | | | |

### Transaction 7 Performed Services for Customers

On December 6, WebWork performed services for several customers and was paid $13,510 cash.

ANALYZE

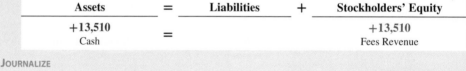

| Assets | = | Liabilities | + | Stockholders' Equity |
|---|---|---|---|---|
| +13,510 | = | | | +13,510 |
| Cash | | | | Fees Revenue |

JOURNALIZE

Dec. 6 | Cash ................................................ 13,510
        Fees revenue ................................... 13,510
        *To record fee revenue earned.*

POST

| | Cash | | | | Fees Revenue | |
|---|---|---|---|---|---|---|
| (1) | 30,000 | 10,800 | (2) | | 13,510 | (7) |
| (4) | 36,000 | 32,400 | (5) | | | |
| (6) | 3,000 | | | | | |
| **(7)** | **13,510** | | | | | |

### Transaction 8 Performed Services for Cash and on Account

On December 8, WebWork performed $4,740 of services for which it received $1,000 cash with the remaining $3,740 to be paid in the future.

ANALYZE

| Assets | | = | Liabilities | + | Stockholders' Equity |
|---|---|---|---|---|---|
| +1,000 | +3,740 | = | | | +4,740 |
| Cash | Accounts Receivable | | | | Fees Revenue |

JOURNALIZE

Dec. 8 | Cash ................................................ 1,000
        Accounts receivable ......................... 3,740
        Fees revenue ................................... 4,740
        *To record fee revenue earned.*

POST

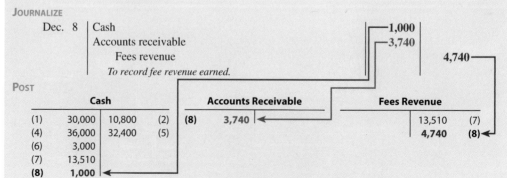

| | Cash | | | | Accounts Receivable | | | | Fees Revenue | |
|---|---|---|---|---|---|---|---|---|---|---|
| (1) | 30,000 | 10,800 | (2) | **(8)** | **3,740** | | | | 13,510 | (7) |
| (4) | 36,000 | 32,400 | (5) | | | | | | 4,740 | (8) |
| (6) | 3,000 | | | | | | | | | |
| (7) | 13,510 | | | | | | | | | |
| **(8)** | **1,000** | | | | | | | | | |

## Transaction 9 — Paid Employee Wages

On December 23, WebWork paid its employee $1,620 cash upon completion of her first two weeks on the job.

**ANALYZE**

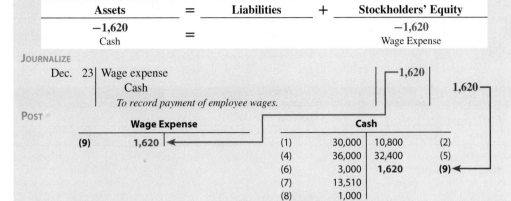

**JOURNALIZE**

Dec. 23 | Wage expense
        Cash
        *To record payment of employee wages.*

**POST**

## Transaction 10 — Received Payment on Account from Customer

On December 27, WebWork received $2,400 cash from a customer for services previously performed on account.

**ANALYZE**

**JOURNALIZE**

Dec. 27 | Cash
        Accounts receivable
        *To record receipt of payment on account.*

**POST**

## Transaction 11 — Paid Cash Dividend

On December 30, WebWork paid a $500 cash dividend.

**ANALYZE**

**JOURNALIZE**

Dec. 30 | Dividends
        Cash
        *To record payment of cash dividends.*

**POST**

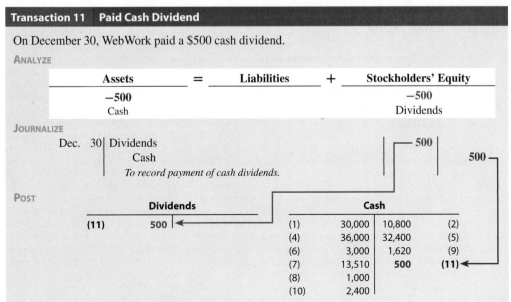

## Summary Illustration of Journalizing and Posting Transactions

Exhibit 3-8 presents the general journal for WebWork for the month of December 2011. Also, Exhibit 3-9 presents the general ledger for WebWork as of December 31, 2011. All journal entries appearing in Exhibit 3-8 have been posted to the general ledger accounts in Exhibit 3-9. The accounts in WebWork's general ledger are grouped by category as follows: (1) assets, (2) liabilities, (3) stockholders' equity, (4) dividends, (5) revenues, and (6) expenses. Each general ledger account in Exhibit 3-9 has been totaled with the ending balance appearing in green.

| **EXHIBIT 3-8** | General Journal for WebWork, Inc. | | |
|---|---|---|---|
| | **General Journal** | | |
| **Date** | **Account Titles and Explanation** | **Debit** | **Credit** |
| 2011<br>Dec. 1 **(1)** | Cash | 30,000 | |
| |     Common stock | | 30,000 |
| | *To record issuance of common stock for cash.* | | |
| 1 **(2)** | Prepaid rent | 10,800 | |
| |     Cash | | 10,800 |
| | *To record advance payment of six months' rent.* | | |
| 1 **(3)** | Office supplies | 2,850 | |
| |     Accounts payable | | 2,850 |
| | *To record purchase of office supplies.* | | |
| 1 **(4)** | Cash | 36,000 | |
| |     Notes payable | | 36,000 |
| | *To record a bank loan, with a signed note payable.* | | |
| 2 **(5)** | Office equipment | 32,400 | |
| |     Cash | | 32,400 |
| | *To record purchase of office equipment.* | | |
| 5 **(6)** | Cash | 3,000 | |
| |     Unearned revenue | | 3,000 |
| | *To record a prepayment from a customer.* | | |
| 6 **(7)** | Cash | 13,510 | |
| |     Fees revenue | | 13,510 |
| | *To record fee revenue earned.* | | |
| 8 **(8)** | Cash | 1,000 | |
| | Accounts receivable | 3,740 | |
| |     Fees revenue | | 4,740 |
| | *To record fee revenue earned.* | | |
| 23 **(9)** | Wage expense | 1,620 | |
| |     Cash | | 1,620 |
| | *To record payment of employee wages.* | | |
| 27 **(10)** | Cash | 2,400 | |
| |     Accounts receivable | | 2,400 |
| | *To record receipt of payment on account.* | | |
| 30 **(11)** | Dividends | 500 | |
| |     Cash | | 500 |
| | *To record payment of cash dividends.* | | |

**EXHIBIT 3-9** General Ledger for WebWork, Inc.

### General Ledger

**Assets**  =  **Liabilities**  +  **Stockholders' Equity**

**Cash**

| | | | |
|---|---|---|---|
| (1) | 30,000 | 10,800 | (2) |
| (4) | 36,000 | 32,400 | (5) |
| (6) | 3,000 | 1,620 | (9) |
| (7) | 13,510 | 500 | (11) |
| (8) | 1,000 | | |
| (10) | 2,400 | | |
| **Bal.** | **40,590** | | |

**Accounts Receivable**

| | | | |
|---|---|---|---|
| (8) | 3,740 | 2,400 | (10) |
| **Bal.** | **1,340** | | |

**Office Supplies**

| | | |
|---|---|---|
| (3) | 2,850 | |
| **Bal.** | **2,850** | |

**Prepaid Rent**

| | | |
|---|---|---|
| (2) | 10,800 | |
| **Bal.** | **10,800** | |

**Office Equipment**

| | | |
|---|---|---|
| (5) | 32,400 | |
| **Bal.** | **32,400** | |

**Accounts Payable**

| | | |
|---|---|---|
| | 2,850 | (3) |
| | **2,850** | **Bal.** |

**Unearned Revenue**

| | | |
|---|---|---|
| | 3,000 | (6) |
| | **3,000** | **Bal.** |

**Notes Payable**

| | | |
|---|---|---|
| | 36,000 | (4) |
| | **36,000** | **Bal.** |

**Common Stock**

| | | |
|---|---|---|
| | 30,000 | (1) |
| | **30,000** | **Bal.** |

**Dividends**

| | | |
|---|---|---|
| (11) | 500 | |
| **Bal.** | **500** | |

**Fees Revenue**

| | | |
|---|---|---|
| | 13,510 | (7) |
| | 4,740 | (8) |
| | **18,250** | **Bal.** |

**Wage Expense**

| | | |
|---|---|---|
| (9) | 1,620 | |
| **Bal.** | **1,620** | |

**Assets = $87,980**  =  **Liabilities = $41,850**  +  **Stockholders' Equity = $46,130**

## Your Turn! 3.3

For each of the transactions below, complete the following requirements.

1. Record the effect of each transaction using the accounting equation.
2. Prepare journal entries for each transaction.
3. Post the journal entries for each transaction to the appropriate T-accounts.

**Transactions:**
a. The company received $1,300 cash from clients for services rendered.
b. The company paid $2,400 cash for wages to employees.
c. The company collected $600 cash from clients on account.
d. The company paid a $400 cash dividend.
e. The company purchased $700 of office supplies on account.
f. The company billed clients $900 for services rendered, which were unpaid.
g. The company paid $500 cash to suppliers on account.

The solution is on pages 155–156.

# TRIAL BALANCE

A **trial balance** is a listing of all accounts from the general ledger with their respective debit or credit balance. A trial balance is prepared at the end of an accounting period after all transactions have been recorded. Exhibit 3-10 shows a trial balance for WebWork, Inc., as of December 31, 2011. The sequence of the accounts and the dollar amounts are taken directly from the general ledger T-accounts in Exhibit 3-9 (which follow the order of the account numbering system). The debit and credit columns from the trial balance are in balance; that is, the $90,100 sum of the debit account balances equals the $90,100 sum of the credit account balances.

Two principal reasons for preparing a trial balance are:

1. To serve as an interim check on whether the sum of the debit balances and the sum of the credit balances from the general ledger accounts are equal. If the totals are not equal, it would indicate the presence of some type of recording error.

2. To show all general ledger account balances in one location, which facilitates the preparation of financial statements. The trial balance, however, is *not* a financial statement.

A trial balance must be dated. In Exhibit 3.10, the trial balance of WebWork, Inc., was prepared as of December 31, 2011.

While it is required that a trial balance be in balance—that is, that the total of the debit column equal the total of the credit column—this equality does not guarantee that the accounting data is error-free. Potential data errors could still exist as a consequence of (1) transactions not being journalized, (2) journal entries not being posted, (3) journal entries being posted in the wrong amount, and (4) journal entries being posted to the wrong accounts.

---

**EXHIBIT 3-10**    Unadjusted Trial Balance for WebWork, Inc.

**WEBWORK, INC.**
**Unadjusted Trial Balance**
**December 31, 2011**

| | Debit | Credit |
|---|---|---|
| Cash | $40,590 | |
| Accounts receivable | 1,340 | |
| Office supplies | 2,850 | |
| Prepaid rent | 10,800 | |
| Office equipment | 32,400 | |
| Accounts payable | | $ 2,850 |
| Unearned revenue | | 3,000 |
| Notes payable | | 36,000 |
| Common stock | | 30,000 |
| Dividends | 500 | |
| Fees revenue | | 18,250 |
| Wage expense | 1,620 | |
| Totals | $90,100 | $90,100 |

---

**FORENSIC ACCOUNTING** **Fraudulent Reporting**

Verifying that the sum of the debit account balances from the general ledger is equal to the sum of the credit account balances is not sufficient to guarantee accuracy of financial records. The infamous accounting scandal at **WorldCom** provides a case in point. To inflate its net income, WorldCom improperly "capitalized expenses"—that is, they inappropriately debited property, plant, and equipment, an asset account, when they should have debited an expense account. While the sum of the debit account balances on WorldCom's books did equal the sum of the credit account balances, assets were overstated and expenses were understated by almost $7 billion. WorldCom's CEO Bernard Ebbers, the mastermind of its fraudulent accounting, was convicted of conspiracy to commit fraud, securities fraud, and making false filings with the SEC. Mr. Ebbers was sentenced to 25 years in prison.

## Your Turn!                                                                      3.4

Each of the following accounts from the Devin Company has a normal balance. The balances are as of December 31, 2011, the end of Devin's first year of operations:

| | | | |
|---|---|---|---|
| Cash | 1,500 | Common stock | 7,500 |
| Accounts receivable | 4,500 | Sales revenue | 12,000 |
| Inventory | 3,750 | Salary expense | 4,500 |
| Property, plant, and equipment | 11,250 | Administrative expenses | 750 |
| Accounts payable | 2,250 | Dividends | 1,500 |
| Notes payable | 6,000 | | |

Prepare a trial balance for the Devin Company as of December 31, 2011.

**The solution is on page 156.**

| Concept ⟶ | Method ⟶ | Assessment |
|---|---|---|
| Is the trial balance in balance? | Ending balances for all of the general ledger accounts entered on the trial balance.<br><br>Total the debit column and the credit column on the trial balance. | Verify the equality of the sum of the debit account balances and the sum of the credit account balances. |

TAKEAWAY 3.2

## WORKING WITH THE TAKEAWAYS

### Part A

Each of the following accounts from the Furst Company has a normal balance as of December 31, 2011, the end of Furst's first year of operations.

| | | | |
|---|---|---|---|
| Cash | $100 | Common stock | $500 |
| Accounts receivable | 300 | Sales revenue | 800 |
| Inventory | 250 | Selling expenses | 300 |
| Property, plant, and equipment | 750 | Administrative expenses | 50 |
| Accounts payable | 150 | Dividends | 100 |
| Notes payable | 400 | | |

### Required
Prepare a trial balance for Furst Company as of December 31, 2011.

### Part B
Lampe Distributors was formed to serve as a distributor of fine furnishings imported from overseas manufacturers. Assume the following trial balance was prepared as of December 31, 2011, at the end of Lampe's first year of operations:

| LAMPE DISTRIBUTORS<br>Unadjusted Trial Balance<br>December 31, 2011 | | |
|---|---|---|
| | **Debit** | **Credit** |
| Cash | $ 23,000 | |
| Accounts receivable | 4,500 | |
| Buildings | 72,000 | |
| Equipment | 20,500 | |
| Inventory | 38,000 | |
| Accounts payable | | $ 5,500 |
| Notes payable | | 47,750 |
| Common stock | | 42,000 |
| Sales revenue | | 280,250 |
| Wage expense | 100,000 | |
| Selling expenses | 31,000 | |
| Rent expense | 23,000 | |
| Administrative expenses | 15,750 | |
| Tax expense | 23,000 | |
| Dividends | 6,000 | |
| Totals | $356,750 | $375,500 |

It is apparent that there is an error somewhere in the company's accounts since the sum of the debit account balances ($356,750) does not equal the sum of the credit account balances ($375,500). After further research, we learn the following:

1. A cash purchase of $20,000 in inventory, occurring near year-end, was not recorded.
2. By mistake, $5,000 that should have been recorded as Accounts Payable was recorded as Notes Payable.
3. A credit of $26,000 was accidentally recorded in the Wage Expense account rather than in Sales Revenue.
4. A sale on account of $18,750 was correctly recorded as Sales Revenue, but the other side of the entry was mistakenly never recorded.

### Required

a. Which of the four errors, if any, is the reason that the trial balance is not in balance? Explain.
b. Which of the errors, if any, must be corrected?
c. Prepare a corrected trial balance.

### Solution

#### Part A

| FURST COMPANY Trial Balance December 31, 2011 | Debit | Credit |
|---|---|---|
| Cash | $ 100 | |
| Accounts receivable | 300 | |
| Inventory | 250 | |
| Property, plant, and equipment | 750 | |
| Accounts payable | | $ 150 |
| Notes payable | | 400 |
| Common stock | | 500 |
| Dividends | 100 | |
| Sales revenue | | 800 |
| Selling expenses | 300 | |
| Administrative expenses | 50 | |
| Totals | $1,850 | $1,850 |

#### Part B

a. Only item #4 caused the trial balance to be out of balance.
b. All of the items are errors, and therefore, all of the errors should be corrected. Just because a trial balance is in balance does not imply that the accounting data is free of recording errors. Each of the four items is an error that will cause incorrect financial statements to be prepared if the errors are not corrected.

c.

| LAMPE DISTRIBUTORS Trial Balance December 31, 2011 | Debit | Credit |
|---|---|---|
| Cash | $ 3,000 | |
| Accounts receivable | 23,250 | |
| Buildings | 72,000 | |
| Equipment | 20,500 | |
| Inventory | 58,000 | |
| Accounts payable | | $ 10,500 |
| Notes payable | | 42,750 |
| Common stock | | 42,000 |
| Sales revenue | | 306,250 |
| Wage expense | 126,000 | |
| Selling expenses | 31,000 | |
| Rent expense | 23,000 | |
| Administrative expenses | 15,750 | |
| Tax expense | 23,000 | |
| Dividends | 6,000 | |
| | $401,500 | $401,500 |

## SUMMARY OF LEARNING OBJECTIVES

**Identify the five major steps in the accounting cycle. (p. 100)**    LO1

- Five major steps in the accounting cycle are:
  1. Analyze.
  2. Record.
  3. Adjust.
  4. Report.
  5. Close.

**Analyze and record transactions using the accounting equation. (p. 101)**    LO2

- The accounting equation provides a convenient way to summarize the recording of financial information.
- An initial step in the accounting process—analyze—is to determine just which transactions (if any) need to be recorded.
- An *accounting transaction* is an economic event that requires accounting recognition. An event that affects any of the elements of the basic accounting equation (assets, liabilities, or stockholders' equity) must be recorded.

**Explain the nature, format, and purpose of an account. (p. 107)**    LO3

- An account is an individual record of the increases and decreases in specific assets, liabilities, permanent stockholders' equity, dividends, revenues, or expenses.
- Information provided by the account includes its title, amounts reflecting increases and decreases, cross-references to other accounting records, and dates and descriptive notations.
- Permanent accounts are the balance sheet accounts—assets, liabilities, and stockholders' equity; any balance in a permanent account at the end of an accounting period is carried forward to the following period.
- Temporary accounts consist of revenue, expense, and dividend accounts; these accounts gather information for an accounting period, but these account balances are not carried forward into the next accounting period.

**Describe the system of debits and credits and its use in recording transactions. (p. 108)**    LO4

- The left side of an account is always the debit side; the right side of an account is always the credit side.
- Increases in assets, dividends, and expenses are debit entries; increases in liabilities, permanent stockholders' equity, and revenues are credit entries. Decreases are the opposite.
- The normal balance of any account appears on the account side used for recording account increases.
- Each accounting transaction should be analyzed into equal amounts of debits and credits.
- All accounting transactions are analyzed using one or more of the basic account categories: (1) assets, (2) liabilities, (3) common stock, (4) dividends, (5) revenues, and (6) expenses. Retained earnings can also be included here.

**Explain the process of journalizing and posting transactions. (p. 109)**    LO5

- Source documents provide the basis for analyzing business transactions.
- Accounting entries are initially recorded in a journal in chronological order; the journal is a book of original entry and acts like a diary of a business's activities.
- A general ledger is a grouping of all of the accounts that are used to prepare the basic financial statements.
- Posting is the transfer of information from a journal to the general ledger accounts.
- Posting references are used to cross-reference the information in journals and the general ledger accounts.

**Describe the trial balance. (p. 118)**    LO6

- A trial balance is a list of the accounts in the general ledger with their respective debit or credit balance. A trial balance is prepared after all transactions have been recorded for an accounting period.
- A trial balance serves as a mechanical check to evaluate the equality of the sum of the debit account balances and the sum of the credit account balances.
- A trial balance facilitates the preparation of the financial statements by showing all account balances in one concise record.

**REVIEW**

| TAKEAWAYS: SUMMARY CHART | | | |
|---|---|---|---|
| | **Concept** ⟶ | **Method** ⟶ | **Assessment** |
| **TAKEAWAY 3.1** | When should an event be recorded in a company's accounting records? | Review the event details.<br><br>Does the event affect the company's assets, liabilities, or stockholders' equity? | If the event affects any of the elements of the accounting equation, it must be recorded in a company's accounting records. |
| **TAKEAWAY 3.2** | Is the trial balance in balance? | Ending balances for all of the general ledger accounts entered on the trial balance.<br><br>Total the debit column and the credit column on the trial balance. | Verify the equality of the sum of the debit account balances and the sum of the credit account balances. |

# GLOSSARY OF KEY TERMS

**Account** A record of the additions, deductions, and balances of individual assets, liabilities, permanent stockholders' equity, dividends, revenues, and expenses (p. 107).

**Accounting cycle** A sequence of activities undertaken by company accountants to accumulate and report the financial information of a business (p. 100).

**Accounting transaction** An economic event that requires accounting recognition; an event that affects any of the elements of the accounting equation—assets, liabilities, or stockholders' equity (p. 101).

**Calendar year** A fiscal year that ends on December 31 (p. 101).

**Chart of accounts** A list of all of the general ledger account titles and their numerical code (p. 110).

**Compound journal entry** A journal entry containing more than one debit and one credit (p. 111).

**Credit (entry)** An entry on the right side (or in the credit column) of an account (p. 108).

**Debit (entry)** An entry on the left side (or in the debit column) of an account (p. 108).

**Double-entry accounting** A method of accounting that results in the recording of equal amounts of debits and credits (p. 101).

**Fiscal year** The annual accounting period used by a business (p. 101).

**General journal** An accounting record with enough flexibility so that any type of business transaction may be recorded in it; a diary of a business's accounting transactions (p. 110).

**General ledger** A grouping of all of a business's accounts that are used to prepare the basic financial statements (p. 112).

**Journal** A tabular record in which business transactions are analyzed in debit and credit terms and recorded in chronological order (p. 110).

**Journal entry** An entry of accounting information into a journal (p. 110).

**Normal balance** The side on which increases to the account are recorded. (p. 108)

**Permanent account** An account used to prepare the balance sheet—that is, an asset, liability, or stockholders' equity account; any balance in a permanent account at the end of an accounting period is carried forward to the following accounting period (p. 109).

**Posting** The transfer of information from the journal to the general ledger accounts (p. 112).

**Posting references** A series of abbreviations used in posting to indicate to where or from where a journal entry is posted (p. 112).

**Source document** Any written document or computer record evidencing an accounting transaction, such as a bank check, deposit slip, sales invoice, or cash register tape (p. 110).

**T-account** An abbreviated form of the formal account in the shape of a *T* (p. 107).

**Temporary account** An account used to gather information for an accounting period; revenue, expense, and dividend accounts are temporary accounts (p. 109).

**Trial balance** A list of the account titles in the general ledger, their respective debit or credit balances, and the totals of the debit and credit balances (p. 118).

**Unearned revenue** A liability representing revenues received in advance; also called *deferred revenue* (p. 104).

# COMPREHENSIVE PROBLEM

Juan Rios acted upon his entrepreneurial spirit and started a graphic design business called Juan's Designs. Based on an excellent business plan, Juan was able to raise sufficient capital to begin operations in October 2011. During the month of October, the following events occurred related to the business.

1. Stockholders invested $40,000 cash in the business in exchange for common stock.
2. Paid $2,500 cash for rent on an office suite.
3. Purchased two desktop computers, software, and a printer for $10,000 cash.
4. Purchased miscellaneous supplies for $500 cash that will be used during the month, all on account.
5. Purchased an advertisement in a local newspaper for $300 cash, announcing the opening of his new business.
6. Performed $5,500 of design work on account.
7. Received $3,500 cash from customers for design work previously completed.

8. Paid $350 cash toward the company's accounts payable balance.
9. Paid $2,500 cash for wages of Juan Rios.

**Required**

a. Use the following accounts to create a general ledger using T-accounts.

| | | |
|---|---|---|
| Cash | Common Stock | Wage Expense |
| Accounts Receivable | Service Revenue | Advertising Expense |
| Equipment | Supplies Expense | Rent Expense |
| Accounts Payable | | |

Post the above accounting transactions to their general ledger T-accounts.

b. Prepare a trial balance as of October 31, 2011.

**Solution**

**Cash**

| | | | | |
|---|---|---|---|---|
| (1) | 40,000 | 2,500 | (2) |
| (7) | 3,500 | 10,000 | (3) |
| | | 300 | (5) |
| | | 350 | (8) |
| | | 2,500 | (9) |
| **Bal.** | 27,850 | | |

**Equipment**

| | |
|---|---|
| (3) | 10,000 |

**Common Stock**

| | | |
|---|---|---|
| | 40,000 | (1) |

**Supplies Expense**

| | |
|---|---|
| (4) | 500 |

**Advertising Expense**

| | |
|---|---|
| (5) | 300 |

**Accounts Receivable**

| | | | | |
|---|---|---|---|---|
| (6) | 5,500 | 3,500 | (7) |
| **Bal.** | 2,000 | | |

**Accounts Payable**

| | | | |
|---|---|---|---|
| (8) | 350 | 500 | (4) |
| | | 150 | **Bal.** |

**Service Revenue**

| | | |
|---|---|---|
| | 5,500 | (6) |

**Wage Expense**

| | |
|---|---|
| (9) | 2,500 |

**Rent Expense**

| | |
|---|---|
| (2) | 2,500 |

| JUAN'S DESIGNS | | |
|---|---|---|
| Unadjusted Trial Balance | | |
| October 31, 2011 | | |
| | **Debit** | **Credit** |
| Cash .......................................................................... | $27,850 | |
| Accounts receivable ................................................... | 2,000 | |
| Equipment ................................................................. | 10,000 | |
| Accounts payable ....................................................... | | $ 150 |
| Common stock ........................................................... | | 40,000 |
| Service revenue .......................................................... | | 5,500 |
| Supplies expense ........................................................ | 500 | |
| Wage expense ............................................................ | 2,500 | |
| Advertising expense .................................................... | 300 | |
| Rent expense ............................................................. | 2,500 | |
| Totals ....................................................................... | $45,650 | $45,650 |

# SELF-STUDY QUESTIONS

(Answers to Self-Study Questions are at the end of this chapter.)

1. Which of the following transactions does not affect the balance sheet totals?   **LO2**
   a. Purchased $500 supplies on account.
   b. Paid off a $3,000 note payable.
   c. Received $4,000 cash from a bank after signing a note payable.
   d. Ordered a new machine that will be paid for upon its delivery in two months.

2. Tobias Company purchased inventory on account. This transaction will affect:   **LO2**
   a. Only the balance sheet.
   b. Only the income statement.
   c. The income statement and the statement of retained earnings.
   d. The income statement, balance sheet, and statement of retained earnings.

REVIEW

LO2 **3.** If assets increase by $100 and liabilities decrease by $30, stockholders' equity must:
    *a.* Remain unchanged.
    *b.* Increase by $130.
    *c.* Decrease by $70.
    *d.* Decrease by $130.

LO3 **4.** An account consists of how many parts?
    *a.* One.
    *b.* Two.
    *c.* Three.
    *d.* It depends if it is a permanent account or a temporary account.

LO3 **5.** Which of the following is true?
    *a.* The debit is on the right side of an asset account.
    *b.* The debit is on the left side of an asset account.
    *c.* The credit is on the left side of a liability account.
    *d.* The debit is on the right side of an expense account.

LO3 **6.** Which of the following accounts is a temporary account?
    *a.* Accounts Receivable.
    *b.* Notes Payable.
    *c.* Common Stock.
    *d.* Advertising Expense.

LO3 **7.** Which of the following accounts is a permanent account?
    *a.* Accounts Receivable.
    *b.* Sales Revenue.
    *c.* Dividends.
    *d.* Advertising Expense.

LO4 **8.** Which of the following is true?
    *a.* A debit will increase a liability account.
    *b.* A credit will increase an asset account.
    *c.* A credit will increase a revenue account.
    *d.* A debit will decrease an expense account.

LO4 **9.** In applying the rules of debits and credits, which of the following statements is correct?
    *a.* The word *debit* means to increase and the word *credit* means to decrease.
    *b.* Asset, expense, and common stock accounts are debited for increases.
    *c.* Liability, revenue, and common stock accounts are debited for increases.
    *d.* Asset, expense, and dividends are debited for increases.

LO4 **10.** Which of these accounts has a normal debit balance?
    *a.* Assets, expenses, dividends.
    *b.* Assets, revenues, common stock.
    *c.* Liabilities, revenues, common stock.
    *d.* Assets, liabilities, dividends.

LO5 **11.** The general ledger includes accounts for all but which of the following?
    *a.* Assets.
    *b.* Expenses.
    *c.* Dividends.
    *d.* All of the above are in the general ledger.

LO6 **12.** Which of the following will cause a trial balance to be out of balance:
    *a.* Mistakenly debiting an asset account instead of an expense account.
    *b.* Posting $123 as $213 to both a debit and a credit account.
    *c.* Posting the same transaction twice by mistake.
    *d.* Posting only the debit part of a transaction.

LO5 **13.** A journal entry that contains more than just two accounts is called:
    *a.* A posted journal entry.
    *b.* An adjusting journal entry.
    *c.* An erroneous journal entry.
    *d.* A compound journal entry.

**14.** Posting refers to the process of transferring information from:   LO5
  *a.* A journal to the general ledger accounts.
  *b.* General ledger accounts to a journal.
  *c.* Source documents to a journal.
  *d.* A journal to source documents.

**15.** Which of the following is not one of the five steps in the accounting cycle?   LO1
  *a.* Analyze.
  *b.* Adjust.
  *c.* Eliminate.
  *d.* Report.

**16.** The purchase of $500 of supplies on account will:   LO2
  *a.* Increase both assets and stockholders' equity by $500.
  *b.* Increase assets and decrease liabilities by $500.
  *c.* Increase assets and decrease stockholders' equity by $500.
  *d.* Increase both assets and liabilities by $500.

## DISCUSSION QUESTIONS

**1.** List the five major steps in the accounting cycle in their proper order.
**2.** Define the term *fiscal year*.
**3.** Provide three examples of source documents that underlie business transactions.
**4.** Provide an example of a transaction that would:
  *a.* Increase one asset account but not change the amount of total assets.
  *b.* Decrease an asset account and a liability account.
  *c.* Decrease an asset account and a stockholders' equity account.
  *d.* Increase an asset account and a liability account.
**5.** Explain the financial effect (increase, decrease, or no effect) of each of the following transactions on stockholders' equity:
  *a.* Purchased supplies for cash.
  *b.* Paid an account payable.
  *c.* Paid salaries.
  *d.* Purchased equipment for cash.
  *e.* Invested cash in business.
  *f.* Rendered services to customers, on account.
  *g.* Rendered services to customers, for cash.
**6.** The retained earnings on a balance sheet are $80,000. Without seeing the rest of the balance sheet, can you conclude that stockholders should be able to receive a dividend in the amount of $80,000 cash from the business? Justify your answer.
**7.** On December 31, 2010, the Miller Company had $700,000 in total assets and owed $220,000 to creditors. If the corporation's common stock amounted to $300,000, what amount of retained earnings should appear on the company's December 31, 2010, balance sheet?
**8.** Some accounting students believe that debits are good and credits are bad. Explain why this is not an accurate way to think about debits and credits.
**9.** What is an account?
**10.** What information is recorded in an account?
**11.** What does the term *debit* mean? What does the term *credit* mean?
**12.** What type of account—asset, liability, permanent stockholders' equity, dividend, revenue, or expense—is each of the following accounts? Indicate whether a debit entry or a credit entry increases the balance of the account.

| | |
|---|---|
| Professional Fees Earned | Common Stock |
| Accounts Receivable | Advertising Expense |
| Accounts Payable | Supplies |
| Cash | Dividends |

**13.** How is the normal side of an account determined?
**14.** What is the normal balance (debit or credit) of each of the accounts in Discussion Question 12?
**15.** Describe the nature and purpose of a general journal.
**16.** What is the justification for the use of posting references?

17. Describe a compound journal entry.
18. What is a chart of accounts?
19. Explain the terms *general ledger* and *trial balance*. What are the primary reasons for preparing a trial balance?
20. Explain how it is possible for a trial balance to be in balance but still be in error.
21. What is a T-account and how is it used?
22. Is it possible for an accounting transaction to only affect the left side of the accounting equation and still leave the equation in balance? If so, provide an example.
23. Would a company record a transaction in its general ledger when an order is placed for the purchase of a machine that will be paid for at the time of its delivery in three months? Explain your answer.

## SHORT EXERCISES

**LO4** **SE3-1.** **Normal Balances**  Indicate for each of the following accounts whether the normal balance is a debit or a credit:
   *a.* Accounts Receivable
   *b.* Accounts Payable
   *c.* Dividends
   *d.* Wage Expense
   *e.* Inventory
   *f.* Interest Income
   *g.* Retained Earnings

**LO4** **SE3-2.** **Debit and Credit Effects**  Indicate the account that will be debited for each of the following transactions:
   *a.* Issued common stock for cash
   *b.* Borrowed money from a bank
   *c.* Provided services on account
   *d.* Purchased inventory on account
   *e.* Collected cash from customers that owed a balance due

**LO4** **SE3-3.** **Debit and Credit Effects**  Indicate the account that will be credited for each of the following transactions:
   *a.* Issued common stock for cash
   *b.* Borrowed money from a bank
   *c.* Provided services on account
   *d.* Purchased inventory on account
   *e.* Collected cash from customers that owed a balance due

**LO4** **SE3-4.** **Determine a Transaction**  The Pearce Company recorded a transaction by debiting Accounts Receivable and crediting Sales Revenue. What event was being recorded?

**LO4** **SE3-5.** **Determine the Cash Balance**  The beginning-of-the-period cash balance for the Travis Company was a $10,000 debit. Cash sales for the month were $5,000 and sales on account were $6,000. The company paid $3,500 cash for current-period purchases and also paid $2,000 cash for amounts due from last month. What is the ending debit or credit balance in the Cash account?

**LO2** **SE3-6.** **Recording Transactions with the Accounting Equation**  During the year, the Decker Company experienced the following accounting transactions:
   1. Issued common stock in the amount of $100,000
   2. Paid a $30,000 cash dividend
   3. Borrowed $25,000 from a bank
   4. Made a principal payment of $2,500 on an outstanding bank loan
   5. Made an interest payment of $1,200 on an outstanding bank loan
Using the accounting equation, record each of the transactions in columnar format using the following template:

| Assets | = | Liabilities | + | Stockholders' Equity | | |
|---|---|---|---|---|---|---|
| Cash | = | Notes Payable | + | Common Stock | + | Retained Earnings |

**SE3-7.** **Recording Transactions with the Accounting Equation**    During the year, the Decker    **LO2**
Company experienced the following accounting transactions:

1. Purchased equipment with cash in the amount of $100,000
2. Purchased supplies on account in the amount of $10,000
3. Collected $21,000 cash from customers
4. Paid a cash dividend of $15,000

Using the accounting equation, record each of the transactions in columnar format using the following template:

| Assets | | | | = | Liabilities | + | Stockholders' Equity |
|---|---|---|---|---|---|---|---|
| Cash + | Accounts Receivable | + Supplies + | Equipment = | | Accounts Payable | + | Retained Earnings |

**SE3-8.** **Posting Transactions to T-accounts**    Using the data from short exercise SE3-6, post your    **LO5**
transaction analysis to the appropriate T-accounts.

**SE3-9.** **Posting Transactions to T-accounts**    Using the data from short exercise SE3-7, post your    **LO5**
transaction analysis to the appropriate T-accounts.

**SE3-10.** The following balances were taken from the general ledger of Howser Corporation as of    **LO6**
December 31. All balances are normal. Prepare a trial balance.

| | | | |
|---|---|---|---|
| Cash .............................. | $ 6,000 | Accounts receivable ................. | $10,800 |
| Accounts payable .................. | 6,000 | Common stock ..................... | 36,000 |
| Equipment ........................ | 30,000 | Dividends .......................... | 2,400 |
| Utilities expense ................... | 2,000 | Administrative expense ............. | 8,000 |
| Sales revenue ..................... | 17,200 | | |

**SE3-11.** **Prepare a Corrected Trial Balance**    The following trial balance for Magill Company has    **LO6**
errors that cause it to be out of balance. Prepare a corrected version of the trial balance for
Magill Company.

**MAGILL COMPANY**
**Unadjusted Trial Balance**
**December 31, 2010**

| | Debit | Credit |
|---|---|---|
| Cash ..................................................... | $ 20,000 | |
| Inventory ................................................. | | $ 85,000 |
| Accounts receivable ....................................... | 30,000 | |
| Accounts payable ......................................... | | 12,000 |
| Common stock ............................................ | | 40,000 |
| Retained earnings ......................................... | | 58,000 |
| Sales revenue ............................................ | 100,000 | |
| Cost of goods sold ........................................ | 60,000 | |
| Selling expenses .......................................... | 15,000 | |
| Totals ................................................... | $225,000 | $195,000 |

**SE3-12.** **The Accounting Cycle**    The following is the correct order of the five steps in the    **LO1**
accounting cycle:

*a.* Analyze; adjust; record; report; close
*b.* Analyze; record; adjust; report; close
*c.* Analyze; record; adjust; close; report
*d.* Analyze; report; adjust; record; close

**SE3-13.** **The Account**    Which of the following is not part of the T-account?    **LO3**

*a.* Title
*b.* Amount
*c.* Cross-reference
*d.* Analysis

# EXERCISES—SET A

**LO2**   **E3-1A.   Accounting Equation**

Determine the missing amount in each of the following cases:

|  | Assets | Liabilities | Stockholders' Equity |
|---|---|---|---|
| a. | $200,000 | $85,000 | ? |
| b. | ? | $32,000 | $28,000 |
| c. | $93,000 | ? | $52,000 |

**LO2**   **E3-2A.   Transaction Analysis**

Following the example shown in (a) below, indicate the accounting effects of the listed transactions on the assets, liabilities, and stockholders' equity of Martin & Company, a corporation:

(a)  Purchased, for cash, a desktop computer for use in the office.
   ANSWER: Increase assets (Office Equipment)
         Decrease assets (Cash)

(b)  Rendered services and billed the client.

(c)  Paid rent for the month.

(d)  Rendered services to a client for cash.

(e)  Received amount due from a client in Transaction (b).

(f)  Purchased an office desk on account.

(g)  Paid employees' salaries for the month.

(h)  Paid for desk purchased in Transaction (f).

(i)  The company paid a dividend.

**LO2**   **E3-3A.   Analysis of Accounts**

Calculate the unknown amount in each of the following five independent situations. The answer to situation (a) is given as an example.

|  | Account | Beginning Balance | Ending Balance | Other Information |
|---|---|---|---|---|
| (a) | Cash ................. | $ 6,100 | $ 5,250 | Total cash disbursed, $5,400. |
| (b) | Accounts receivable ... | 8,500 | 9,300 | Services on account, $16,500. |
| (c) | Notes payable......... | 15,000 | 20,000 | Borrowed funds by issuing a note, $30,000. |
| (d) | Accounts payable ..... | 3,280 | 1,720 | Payments on account, $2,900. |
| (e) | Common stock........ | 32,000 | 46,000 | Capital contribution, $5,000. |

| | Unknown Amounts Required | |
|---|---|---|
| (a) | Total cash received ............................................ | $4,550 |
| (b) | Total cash collected from credit customers ....................... | _____ |
| (c) | Notes payable repaid during the period .......................... | _____ |
| (d) | Goods and services received from suppliers on account .......... | _____ |
| (e) | Net income, assuming that no dividends were paid............... | _____ |

**LO2, LO5**   **E3-4A.   Transaction Analysis**

The accounts below are from the general ledger of The Bast Company. For each letter given in the T-accounts, describe the type of business transaction(s) or event(s) that would most likely be reflected by entries on that side of the account. For example, the answer to (a) is amounts for services performed for clients on account.

**E3-5A.  Transaction Analysis**

Match each of the following transactions of Lesch & Company with the appropriate letters, indicating the debits and credits to be made. The key for the letters follows the list of transactions. The correct answer for Transaction (1) is given as an illustration:

|  | **Answer** |
|---|---|
| (1)  Purchased supplies on account. | a, d |
| (2)  Paid interest on note payable. | _____ |
| (3)  Cash dividend was paid to stockholders. | _____ |
| (4)  Returned some defective supplies and received a reduction in the amount owed. | _____ |
| (5)  Made payment to settle note payable. | _____ |
| (6)  Received an invoice for utilities used. | _____ |
| (7)  Received payment in advance from client for work to be done next month. | _____ |
| (8)  The stockholders contributed additional capital to the business. | _____ |

**Financial Effect of Transaction**

| | |
|---|---|
| a.  Debit an asset | g.  Debit dividends |
| b.  Credit an asset | h.  Credit dividends |
| c.  Debit a liability | i.  Debit a revenue |
| d.  Credit a liability | j.  Credit a revenue |
| e.  Debit stockholders' equity | k.  Debit an expense |
| f.  Credit stockholders' equity | l.  Credit an expense |

**E3-6A.  Transaction Entries**

Creative Designs, a firm providing art services for advertisers, began business on June 1. The following accounts in its general ledger are needed to record the transactions for June: Cash; Accounts Receivable; Supplies; Office Equipment; Accounts Payable; Common Stock; Dividends; Service Fees Earned; Rent Expense; Utilities Expense; and Salaries Expense. Record the following transactions for June in the general journal:

June  1  Lisa Ryan invested $12,000 cash to begin the business; she received common stock for her investment.

2  Paid rent for June, $950.

3  Purchased office equipment on account, $6,400.

6  Purchased art materials and other supplies costing $3,800; paid $1,800 down with the remainder due within 30 days.

11  Billed clients for services, $4,700.

17  Collected $3,250 from clients on account.

19  Paid $3,000 on account to office equipment company (see June 3 transaction).

25  Lisa Ryan received a $2,000 dividend.

30  Paid utility bill for June, $350.

30  Paid salaries for June, $2,500.

**E3-7A.  Source Documents**

For each transaction in E3-6A, indicate the related source document or documents that provide evidence supporting the transaction.

**E3-8A.  Nature of Accounts, Debit and Credit Rules**

For each of the accounts listed below, indicate whether the account (1) is increased by a debit or a credit and (2) is a permanent account or a temporary account:

| | |
|---|---|
| Accounts Payable | Common Stock |
| Advertising Expense | Dividends |
| Cash | Land |
| Equipment | Service Fees Earned |

**E3-9A.  Nature of Accounts, Debit and Credit Rules**

In the first column, enter *permanent* or *temporary* to describe the nature of the account shown on the left. In the last three columns, enter *debit* or *credit* to describe the journal entry necessary to increase and decrease the account shown on the left, and which side of the account represents its normal balance.

| | Permanent or Temporary | Increase | Decrease | Normal Balance |
|---|---|---|---|---|
| Asset............... | _____ | _____ | _____ | _____ |
| Liability ............. | _____ | _____ | _____ | _____ |
| Common stock ....... | _____ | _____ | _____ | _____ |
| Dividends ........... | _____ | _____ | _____ | _____ |
| Revenue ............ | _____ | _____ | _____ | _____ |
| Expense............. | _____ | _____ | _____ | _____ |

**LO4, LO5**   **E3-10A. Nature of Accounts, Debit and Credit Rules**

For each of the accounts listed below, indicate whether the account (1) is increased by a debit or a credit and (2) is a permanent account or temporary account:

Accounts Receivable          Notes Payable
Advertising Revenue          Retained Earnings
Building                     Supplies
Common Stock                 Utilities Expense

**LO2, LO4**   **E3-11A. Transaction Analysis**

Match each of the following transactions of L. Boyd & Company with the appropriate letters, indicating the debits and credits to be made. The key for the letters follows the list of transactions. The correct answer for Transaction 1 is given as an illustration:

|  | **Answer** |
|---|---|
| (1) Stockholders contributed cash to the business. | a, f |
| (2) Purchased equipment on account. | _____ |
| (3) Received and immediately paid advertising bill. | _____ |
| (4) Purchased supplies for cash. | _____ |
| (5) Borrowed money from a bank, giving a note payable. | _____ |
| (6) Billed customers for services rendered. | _____ |
| (7) Made a partial payment on account for equipment. | _____ |
| (8) Paid employee's salary. | _____ |
| (9) Collected amounts due from customers billed in Transaction 6. | _____ |

**Financial Effect of Transaction**

a. Debit an asset                 f. Credit common stock
b. Credit an asset                g. Debit a revenue
c. Debit a liability              h. Credit a revenue
d. Credit a liability             i. Debit an expense
e. Debit common stock             j. Credit an expense

**LO5, LO6**   **E3-12A. Transaction Analysis and Trial Balance**

Make T-accounts for the following accounts that appear in the general ledger of Daniel Kelly, an attorney: Cash; Accounts Receivable; Office Equipment; Legal Database Subscription; Accounts Payable; Stockholders' Equity; Dividends; Legal Fees Earned; Salaries Expense; Rent Expense; and Utilities Expense. Record the following October transactions in the T-accounts and key all entries with the number identifying the transaction. Determine the balance in each account and prepare a trial balance sheet as of October 31.

Oct.  1  Kelly started his law practice by contributing $19,500 cash to the business on October 1, receiving shares of common stock in the company.
2  Purchased office equipment on account, $10,400.
3  Paid office rent for October, $700.
4  Paid $9,600 to access online legal database for two years.
5  Billed clients for services rendered, $11,300.
6  Made $6,000 payment on account for the equipment purchased on October 2.
7  Paid legal assistant's salary, $2,800.
8  Collected $9,400 from clients previously billed for services.
9  Received invoice for October utilities, $180; it will be paid in November.
10  The company paid stockholders $1,500 as a cash dividend.

**E3-13A. Transaction Analysis and Trial Balance**                                    LO5, LO6

Make T-accounts for the following accounts that appear in the general ledger of Mead Pet Hospital, owned by R. Mead, a veterinarian: Cash; Accounts Receivable; Supplies; Office Equipment; Accounts Payable; Stockholders' equity; Dividends; Professional Fees Earned; Salaries Expense; and Rent Expense. Record the following December transactions in the T-accounts and key all entries with the number identifying the transaction. Finally, determine the balance in each account and prepare a trial balance as of December 31.

Dec. 1 Mead opened a checking account on December 1 at United Bank in the name of Mead Pet Hospital and deposited $20,000 cash. Mead received common stock for his investment.

2 Paid rent for December, $1,100.

3 Purchased office equipment on account, $2,900.

4 Purchased supplies for cash, $1,700.

5 Billed clients for services rendered, $7,300.

6 Paid secretary's salary, $1,950.

7 Paid $1,500 on account for the equipment purchased on December 3.

8 Collected $5,800 from clients previously billed for services.

9 The company paid stockholders $2,200 as a cash dividend.

**E3-14A. The Account**                                                              LO3

The following transactions occurred during December, the first month of operations for Harris Company. Create a T-account for accounts payable that includes the following five transactions.

1. Purchased $500 of inventory on account.
2. Purchased $300 of inventory on account.
3. Paid suppliers $600.
4. Purchased $400 of inventory on account.
5. Paid suppliers $300.

# EXERCISES—SET B

**E3-1B. Accounting Equation**                                                       LO2

Determine the missing amount in each of the following cases:

|    | Assets | Liabilities | Stockholders' Equity |
|----|--------|-------------|----------------------|
| a. | $400,000 | $85,000 | ? |
| b. | ? | $54,000 | $28,000 |
| c. | $193,000 | ? | $104,000 |

**E3-2B. Transaction Analysis**                                                      LO2

Following the example shown in (a) below, indicate the effects of the listed transactions on the assets, liabilities, and stockholders' equity of John Dallmus, certified public accountant, a corporation:

(a) Purchased, for cash, a desktop computer for use in the office.
    ANSWER: Increase assets (Office Equipment)
            Decrease assets (Cash)

(b) Rendered accounting services and billed client.

(c) Paid utilities for month.

(d) Rendered tax services to client for cash.

(e) Received amount due from client in Transaction (b).

(f) Purchased a copying machine on account.

(g) Paid employees' salaries for month.

(h) Paid for copying machine purchased in Transaction (f).

(i) The company paid a dividend.

**E3-3B. Analysis of Accounts**                                                      LO2

Compute the unknown amount required in each of the following five independent situations. The answer to situation (a) is given as an illustration:

| Account | Beginning Balance | Ending Balance | Other Information |
|---|---|---|---|
| (a) | Cash ................. | $ 8,100 | $ 5,250 | Total cash disbursed, $5,400. |
| (b) | Accounts receivable ... | 10,500 | 9,300 | Services on account, $16,500. |
| (c) | Notes payable......... | 17,000 | 20,000 | Borrowed funds by issuing a note, $30,000. |
| (d) | Accounts payable ..... | 5,280 | 1,720 | Payments on account, $3,900. |
| (e) | Common stock ........ | 34,000 | 46,000 | Capital contribution, $5,000. |

| | Unknown Amounts Required | |
|---|---|---|
| (a) | Total cash received ............................................. | $2,550 |
| (b) | Total cash collected from credit customers ....................... | _____ |
| (c) | Notes payable repaid during the period .......................... | _____ |
| (d) | Goods and services received from suppliers on account .......... | _____ |
| (e) | Net income, assuming that no dividends were paid............... | _____ |

**LO2, LO5**  **E3-4B.  Transaction Analysis**

The accounts below are from the general ledger of Andrew Miller & Company, an architectural firm. For each letter given in the T-accounts, describe the type of business transaction(s) or event(s) that would most likely be reflected by entries on that side of the account. For example, the answer to (a) is amounts for services performed for clients on account.

**LO4**  **E3-5B.  Transaction Analysis**

Match each of the following transactions of Ardon Peralta & Company, a landscape design firm, with the appropriate letters, indicating the debits and credits to be made. The key for the letters follows the list of transactions. The correct answer for Transaction 1 is given as an illustration:

|  |  | **Answer** |
|---|---|---|
| (1) | Purchased supplies on account. | a, d |
| (2) | Paid interest on a bank loan. | _____ |
| (3) | The business paid the stockholders a dividend. | _____ |
| (4) | Returned some defective supplies and received a reduction in the amount owed. | _____ |
| (5) | Made payment to repay bank loan. | _____ |
| (6) | Received an invoice for supplies used. | _____ |
| (7) | Received payment in advance from client for work to be done next month. | _____ |
| (8) | Paid employee's salary. | _____ |
| (9) | Peralta contributed additional capital to the business. | _____ |

**Financial Effect of Transaction**

| | | | |
|---|---|---|---|
| a. | Debit an asset | g. | Debit dividends |
| b. | Credit an asset | h. | Credit dividends |
| c. | Debit a liability | i. | Debit a revenue |
| d. | Credit a liability | j. | Credit a revenue |
| e. | Debit stockholders' equity | k. | Debit an expense |
| f. | Credit stockholders' equity | l. | Credit an expense |

ASSIGNMENTS

**E3-6B. Transaction Entries**

Thoro Clean, a firm providing house-cleaning services, began business on April 1. The following accounts in its general ledger are needed to record the transactions for April: Cash; Accounts Receivable; Supplies; Prepaid Van Lease; Equipment; Notes Payable; Accounts Payable; Common Stock; Retained Earnings; Dividends; Cleaning Fees Earned; Wage Expense; Advertising Expense; and Fuel Expense. Record the following transactions for April in the general journal:

April  1  Randy Storm invested $9,000 cash to begin the business; he received common stock for his investment.
2  Paid six months' lease on a van, $2,850.
3  Borrowed $10,000 from a bank and signed a note payable agreeing to repay the $10,000 in one year plus 10 percent interest.
3  Purchased $5,500 of cleaning equipment; paid $2,500 down with the remainder due within 30 days.
4  Purchased cleaning supplies for $4,300 cash.
7  Paid $350 for newspaper advertisements to run during April.
21  Billed customers for services, $3,500.
23  Paid $3,000 on account to cleaning equipment firm (see April 3 transaction).
28  Collected $2,300 from customers on account.
29  Randy Storm received a $1,000 cash dividend.
30  Paid wages for April, $1,750.
30  Paid service station for gasoline used during April, $95.

**E3-7B. Source Documents**

For each transaction in E3-6B indicate the related source document or documents that provide evidence supporting the transaction.

**E3-8B. Nature of Accounts, Debit and Credit Rules**

For each of the accounts listed below, indicate whether the account (1) is increased by a debit or a credit and (2) is a permanent account or a temporary account:

| | |
|---|---|
| Accounts Receivable | Common Stock |
| Supplies Expense | Dividends |
| Cash | Building |
| Equipment | Professional Fees Earned |

**E3-9B. Nature of Accounts, Debit and Credit Rules**

In the first column, enter *permanent* or *temporary* to describe the nature of the account shown to the left. In the last three columns, enter *debit* or *credit* to describe the journal entry necessary to increase and decrease the account shown to the left, and indicate which side of the account represents its normal balance.

| | Permanent or Temporary | Increase | Decrease | Normal Balance |
|---|---|---|---|---|
| Asset.............. | _____ | _____ | _____ | _____ |
| Liability............ | _____ | _____ | _____ | _____ |
| Common stock....... | _____ | _____ | _____ | _____ |
| Retained earnings.... | _____ | _____ | _____ | _____ |
| Revenue............ | _____ | _____ | _____ | _____ |
| Expense............. | _____ | _____ | _____ | _____ |

**E3-10B. Nature of Accounts, Debit and Credit Rules**

For each of the accounts listed below, indicate whether the account (1) is increased by a debit or a credit and (2) is a permanent account or a temporary account:

| | |
|---|---|
| Accounts Receivable | Notes Payable |
| Sales Revenue | Retained Earnings |
| Equipment | Inventory |
| Common Stock | Rent Expense |

**LO2, LO4** **E3-11B. Transaction Analysis**

Match each of the following transactions of R. Couche & Company, a printing company, with the appropriate letters, indicating the debits and credits to be made. The key for letters follows the list of transactions. The correct answer for Transaction (1) is given as an illustration:

|  | | **Answer** |
|---|---|---|
| (1) | Stockholders contributed cash to the business. | a, f |
| (2) | Purchased inventory on account. | _____ |
| (3) | Received and immediately paid a utility bill. | _____ |
| (4) | Purchased supplies for cash. | _____ |
| (5) | Borrowed money from a bank, giving a note payable. | _____ |
| (6) | Billed customers for services rendered. | _____ |
| (7) | Made a partial payment on account for equipment. | _____ |
| (8) | Paid employee's salary. | _____ |
| (9) | Collected amounts due from customers billed in Transaction 6. | _____ |

**Financial Effect of Transaction**

| a. Debit an asset | f. Credit common stock |
|---|---|
| b. Credit an asset | g. Debit a revenue |
| c. Debit a liability | h. Credit a revenue |
| d. Credit a liability | i. Debit an expense |
| e. Debit common stock | j. Credit an expense |

**LO5, LO6** **E3-12B. Transaction Analysis and the Trial Balance**

Make T-accounts for the following accounts that appear in the general ledger of Matthew Thomas, an attorney: Cash; Accounts Receivable; Office Equipment; Legal Database Subscription; Accounts Payable; Common Stock; Dividends; Legal Fees Earned; Salaries Expense; Rent Expense; and Utilities Expense. Record the following October transactions in the T-accounts and key all entries with the number identifying the transaction. Determine the balance in each account and prepare a trial balance as of October 31.

Oct.  1 Thomas started his law practice by contributing $20,000 cash to the business on October 1; he received common stock for his investment.
2 Purchased office equipment on account, $12,400.
3 Paid office rent for October, $700.
4 Paid $11,600 to access online legal database for two years.
5 Billed clients for services rendered, $11,300.
6 Made $6,000 payment on account for the equipment purchased on October 2.
7 Paid legal assistant's salary, $2,800.
8 Collected $9,400 from clients previously billed for services.
9 Received invoice for October utilities, $180; it will be paid in November.
10 The firm paid stockholders $2,000 cash as a dividend.

**LO5, LO6** **E3-13B. Transaction Analysis and Trial Balance**

Make T-accounts for the following accounts that appear in the general ledger of The Dog & Cat Hospital, owned by Kate Miller, a veterinarian: Cash; Accounts Receivable; Supplies; Office Equipment; Accounts Payable; Common Stock; Dividends; Professional Fees Earned; Salaries Expense; and Rent Expense. Record the following December transactions in the T-accounts and key all entries with the number identifying the transaction. Finally, determine the balance in each account and prepare a trial balance as of December 31.

Dec. 1 Miller opened a checking account on December 1 at Biltmore Bank in the name of The Dog & Cat Hospital and deposited $25,000 cash; Miller received common stock for her investment.
2 Paid rent for December, $1,500.
3 Purchased office equipment on account, $2,900.
4 Purchased supplies for cash, $1,900.
5 Billed clients for services rendered, $7,300.
6 Paid secretary's salary, $1,950.
7 Paid $1,500 on account for the equipment purchased on December 3.
8 Collected $5,800 from clients previously billed for services.
9 The firm paid stockholders $3,000 cash as a dividend.

### E3-14B. The Account

LO3

The following transactions occurred during January, the first month of operations for Ruby Corporation. Create a T-account for inventory that includes the following five transactions.

1. Purchased $1,500 of inventory on account.
2. Purchased $1,300 of inventory on account.
3. Sold inventory with an original cost of $1,600.
4. Purchased $1,400 of inventory on account.
5. Sold inventory with an original cost of $1,300.

## PROBLEMS—SET A

### P3-1A. Transaction Analysis

LO2

The accounting equation of L. Chen & Company as of the beginning of the accounting period is given below, followed by seven transactions whose effects on the accounting equation are shown. Describe each transaction that occurred. Of the transactions affecting Retained Earnings, transaction (e) had no effect on net income for the period.

| | Cash | + | Accounts Receivable | + | Supplies | = | Notes Payable | + | Accounts Payable | + | Common Stock | + | Retained Earnings |
|---|---|---|---|---|---|---|---|---|---|---|---|---|---|
| Balance | $4,100 | + | $9,000 | + | $700 | = | $2,500 | + | $800 | + | $2,000 | + | $8,500 |
| (a) | +6,500 | | −6,500 | | | | | | | | | | |
| (b) | −400 | | | | +400 | | | | | | | | |
| (c) | | | +7,000 | | | | | | | | | | +7,000 |
| (d) | −800 | | | | | | | | −800 | | | | |
| (e) | −4,900 | | | | | | | | | | | | −4,900 |
| (f) | −300 | | | | +300 | | | | | | | | |
| (g) | +1,200 | | | | | | +1,200 | | | | | | |

### P3-2A. Transaction Analysis

LO2

An analysis of the transactions of Hewitt Detective Agency for the month of May appears below. Line 1 summarizes the company's accounting equation data as of May 1; lines 2–10 represent the transactions for May:

| | Cash | + | Accounts Receivable | + | Supplies | + | Equipment | = | Notes Payable | + | Accounts Payable | + | Common Stock | + | Retained Earnings |
|---|---|---|---|---|---|---|---|---|---|---|---|---|---|---|---|
| (1) | $2,400 | + | $7,600 | + | $500 | + | $8,000 | = | $5,000 | + | $300 | + | $10,000 | + | $3,200 |
| (2) | +2,000 | | | | | | | | +2,000 | | | | | | |
| (3) | +6,100 | | −6,100 | | | | | | | | | | | | |
| (4) | | | | | +980 | | | | | | +980 | | | | |
| (5) | | | +6,800 | | | | | | | | | | | | +6,800 |
| (6) | −300 | | | | | | | | | | −300 | | | | |
| (7) | +1,500 | | | | | | | | | | | | | | +1,500 |
| (8) | −800 | | | | | | | | | | | | | | −800 |
| (9) | −750 | | | | | | +750 | | | | | | | | |
| (10) | −2,500 | | | | | | | | −2,500 | | | | | | |

#### Required

*a.* Show that assets equal liabilities plus stockholders' equity as of May 1.

*b.* Describe the apparent transaction indicated by each line. (For example, line 2: Borrowed $2,000, giving a note payable.) If any line could reasonably represent more than one type of transaction, describe each type.

*c.* Show that assets equal liabilities plus stockholders' equity as of May 31.

### P3-3A. Transaction Analysis

LO2

Grant Appraisal Service provides commercial and industrial appraisals and feasibility studies. On January 1, the assets and liabilities of the business were the following: Cash, $6,700; Accounts Receivable, $14,800; Notes Payable, $2,500; and Accounts Payable, $600. Common Stock had a balance of $18,400. Assume that Retained Earnings as of January 1, 2010, were zero. The following transactions occurred during the month of January:

Jan.  1  Paid rent for January, $950.
2  Received $8,800 payment on customers' accounts.
3  Paid $500 on accounts payable.
4  Received $1,600 for services performed for cash customers.
5  Borrowed $5,000 from a bank and signed a note payable for that amount.
6  Billed the city $6,200 for a feasibility study performed; billed various other credit customers, $1,900.
7  Paid the salary of an assistant, $4,000.
8  Received invoice for January utilities, $410.
9  Paid $6,000 cash for employee salaries.
10  Purchased a van (on January 31) for business use, $9,800.
11  Paid $50 to bank as January interest on the outstanding notes payable.

### Required

a.  Set up an accounting equation in columnar form with the following individual assets, liabilities, and stockholders' equity accounts: Cash, Accounts Receivable, Van, Notes Payable, Accounts Payable, Common Stock, and Retained Earnings. Enter the January 1 balances below each item. (*Note:* The beginning Van account balance is $0.)
b.  Show the impact (increase or decrease) of transactions 1–11 on the beginning balances, and total the columns to show that assets equal liabilities plus stockholders' equity as of January 31.

LO2    **P3-4A.    Transaction Analysis**

On June 1, 2010, a group of bush pilots in Thunder Bay, Ontario, Canada, formed the Outpost Fly-In Service, Inc., by selling $50,000 of common stock for cash. The group then leased several amphibious aircraft and docking facilities, equipping them to transport campers and hunters to outpost camps owned by various resorts. The following transactions occurred during June 2010:

June   1  Sold common stock for cash, $50,000.
2  Paid June rent for aircraft, dockage, and dockside office, $4,800.
3  Received invoice for the cost of a reception the firm gave to entertain resort owners, $1,600.
4  Paid for June advertising in various sports magazines, $900.
5  Paid insurance premium for June, $1,800.
6  Rendered fly-in services for various groups for cash, $22,700.
7  Billed the Canadian Ministry of Natural Resources for transporting mapping personnel, $2,900, and billed various firms for fly-in services, $13,000.
8  Paid $1,500 on accounts payable.
9  Received $13,200 on account from clients.
10  Paid June wages, $16,000.
11  Received invoice for the cost of fuel used during June, $3,500.
12  Paid a cash dividend, $3,000.

### Required

a.  Set up an accounting equation in columnar form with the following column headings: Cash, Accounts Receivable, Accounts Payable, Common Stock, and Retained Earnings.
b.  Show how the June transactions affect the items in the accounting equation, and total all columns to show that assets equal liabilities plus stockholders' equity as of June 30. (*Note:* Revenues, expenses, and dividends affect Retained Earnings.)

LO2    **P3-5A.    Accounting Equation**

Determine the following:

a.  The stockholders' equity of a company that has assets of $450,000 and liabilities of $326,000.

b. The retained earnings of a company that has assets of $618,000, liabilities of $225,000, and common stock of $165,000.

c. The assets of a corporation that has liabilities of $400,000, common stock of $200,000, and retained earnings of $185,000.

**P3-6A. Transaction Analysis**

Following the example shown in (a) below, indicate the effects of the listed transactions on the assets, liabilities, and stockholders' equity of Martin Andrews & Company.

(a) Rendered legal services to clients for cash.

   ANSWER:  Increase assets (Cash)

               Increase stockholders' equity (Retained Earnings)

(b) Purchased office supplies on account.

(c) Andrews invested cash into the firm and received stock for his investment.

(d) Paid amount due on account for office supplies purchased in (b).

(e) Borrowed cash from a bank and signed a six-month note payable.

(f) Rendered services and billed clients.

(g) Purchased, for cash, a desk lamp for the office.

(h) Paid interest on a note payable to the bank.

(i) Received invoice for the current month's utilities.

**P3-7A. Transaction Analysis**

On October 1, Alice Bloom started a consulting firm. The asset, liability, and stockholders' equity account balances after each of her first six transactions are shown below. Describe each of these six transactions:

| | | | Accounts | | | | | | Notes | | Common | | Retained |
| | Cash | + | Receivable | + | Supplies | + | Equipment | = | Payable | + | Stock | + | Earnings |
|---|---|---|---|---|---|---|---|---|---|---|---|---|---|
| (a) | $6,000 | + | $ 0 | + | $ 0 | + | $ 0 | = | $ 0 | + | $6,000 | + | $ 0 |
| (b) | 4,000 | + | 0 | + | 2,000 | + | 0 | = | 0 | + | 6,000 | + | 0 |
| (c) | 7,500 | + | 0 | + | 2,000 | + | 0 | = | 3,500 | + | 6,000 | + | 0 |
| (d) | 2,500 | + | 0 | + | 2,000 | + | 5,000 | = | 3,500 | + | 6,000 | + | 0 |
| (e) | 2,500 | + | 1,000 | + | 2,000 | + | 5,000 | = | 3,500 | + | 6,000 | + | 1,000 |
| (f) | 3,000 | + | 500 | + | 2,000 | + | 5,000 | = | 3,500 | + | 6,000 | + | 1,000 |

**Amounts after Transaction**

**P3-8A. Determination of Omitted Financial Statement Data**

For the four unrelated situations, A-D, calculate the unknown amounts indicated by the letters appearing in each column:

| | A | B | C | D |
|---|---|---|---|---|
| **Beginning** | | | | |
| Assets.......................................... | $28,000 | $12,000 | $28,000 | $ (d) |
| Liabilities...................................... | 18,600 | 5,000 | 19,000 | 9,000 |
| **Ending** | | | | |
| Assets.......................................... | 30,000 | 26,000 | 34,000 | 40,000 |
| Liabilities...................................... | 17,300 | (b) | 15,000 | 19,000 |
| **During the Year** | | | | |
| Common stock............................... | 2,000 | 4,500 | (c) | 3,500 |
| Sales revenues ............................. | (a) | 28,000 | 18,000 | 24,000 |
| Dividends...................................... | 5,000 | 1,500 | 1,000 | 6,500 |
| Expenses...................................... | 8,500 | 21,000 | 11,000 | 17,000 |

**P3-9A. Transaction Analysis**

Appearing below is an analysis of the June transactions for Rhode Consulting Services. Line 1 summarizes Rhode's accounting equation data as of June 1; lines 2-10 are the transactions for the month of June:

| | Cash | + | Accounts Receivable | + | Supplies | + | Equipment | = | Notes Payable | + | Accounts Payable | + | Common Stock | + | Retained Earnings |
|---|---|---|---|---|---|---|---|---|---|---|---|---|---|---|---|
| (1) | $3,500 | + | $5,200 | + | $820 | + | $9,000 | = | $3,000 | + | $600 | + | $10,920 | + | $4,000 |
| (2) | | | | | +670 | | | | | | +670 | | | | |
| (3) | | | | | | | +5,000 | | +5,000 | | | | | | |
| (4) | +4,200 | | −4,200 | | | | | | | | | | | | |
| (5) | | | +7,800 | | | | | | | | | | | | +7,800 |
| (6) | −600 | | | | | | | | | | −600 | | | | |
| (7) | −200 | | | | +200 | | | | | | | | | | |
| (8) | −4,600 | | | | | | | | | | | | | | −4,600 |
| (9) | +2,000 | | | | | | | | +2,000 | | | | | | |
| (10) | | | | | | | +750 | | | | | | | | +750 |

**Required**

a.  Show that assets equal liabilities plus stockholders' equity as of June 1.

b.  Describe the transaction indicated by each line. For example, line 2: Purchased supplies on account, $670. If any line could reasonably represent more than one type of transaction, describe each type.

c.  Show that assets equal liabilities plus stockholders' equity as of June 30.

**LO2**   **P3-10A. Transaction Analysis**

Grace Main began the Main Answering Service in December 2010. The firm provides services for professional people and is currently operating with leased equipment. On January 1, 2011, the assets and liabilities of the business were: Cash, $4,400; Accounts Receivable, $6,900; Notes Payable, $1,500; and Accounts Payable, $600. Assume that Retained Earnings as of January 1, 2011, were zero. The balance of Common Stock was $9,200. The following transactions occurred during the month of January:

Jan.  1  Paid rent on office and equipment for January, $800.
     2  Collected $4,500 on account from clients.
     3  Borrowed $2,000 from a bank and signed a note payable for that amount.
     4  Billed clients for work performed on account, $9,500.
     5  Paid $400 on accounts payable.
     6  Received invoice for January advertising, $550.
     7  Paid January salaries, $3,800.
     8  Paid January utilities, $430.
     9  Paid stockholders a dividend of $2,600 cash.
    10  Purchased fax machine (on January 31) for business use, $1,400.
    11  Paid $30 to the bank as January interest on the outstanding notes payable.

**Required**

a.  Set up an accounting equation in columnar form with the following individual assets, liabilities, and stockholders' equity accounts: Cash, Accounts Receivable, Equipment, Notes Payable, Accounts Payable, Common Stock, and Retained Earnings. Enter the January 1 balances below each item. (*Note:* The beginning Equipment account balance is $0.)

b.  Show the impact (increase or decrease) of the January transactions on the beginning balances, and total all columns to show that assets equal liabilities plus stockholders' equity as of January 31.

**LO2**   **P3-11A. Transaction Analysis**

On December 1, Peter Allen started Career Services Inc., providing career and vocational counseling services. The following transactions took place during the month of December:

Dec.  1  Allen invested $7,000 in the business, receiving common shares.
     2  Paid rent for December on furnished office space, $750.
     3  Received invoice for December advertising, $500.
     4  Borrowed $15,000 from a bank and signed a note payable for that amount.
     5  Received $1,200 for counseling services rendered for cash.

6   Billed certain governmental agencies and other clients for counseling services, $6,800.

7   Paid secretary's salary, $2,200.

8   Paid December utilities, $370.

9   Paid stockholders a dividend of $900 cash.

10   Purchased land for cash to use as a site for a new facility, $13,000.

11   Paid $100 to the bank as December interest on a note payable.

**Required**

a.   Set up an accounting equation in columnar form with the following column headings: Cash, Accounts Receivable, Land, Notes Payable, Accounts Payable, Common Stock, and Retained Earnings.

b.   Show how the December transactions affect the items in the accounting equation, and total all columns to show that assets equal liabilities plus stockholders' equity as of December 31.

**P3-12A.** **Transaction Analysis and the Effect of Errors on the Trial Balance**          LO4, LO5, LO6

The following T-accounts contain numbered entries for the May transactions of Carol Marsh, a market analyst, who opened her business on May 1, 2010:

| | **Cash** | | | | | **Common Stock** | | |
|---|---|---|---|---|---|---|---|---|
| **(1)** | 13,000 | 4,800 | **(2)** | | | 13,000 | **(1)** | |
| **(9)** | 3,700 | 810 | **(4)** | | | | | |
| | | 1,950 | **(6)** | | | | | |
| | | 600 | **(8)** | | | | | |

| | **Accounts Receivable** | | | | | **Dividends** | | |
|---|---|---|---|---|---|---|---|---|
| **(5)** | 6,400 | 3,700 | **(9)** | **(8)** | 600 | | | |

| | **Office Supplies** | | | | **Professional Fees Earned** | | |
|---|---|---|---|---|---|---|---|
| **(3)** | 2,800 | | | | | 6,400 | **(5)** |

| | **Office Equipment** | | | | **Rent Expense** | | |
|---|---|---|---|---|---|---|---|
| **(2)** | 4,800 | | **(4)** | 810 | | | |

| | **Accounts Payable** | | | | | **Utilities Expense** | | |
|---|---|---|---|---|---|---|---|---|
| **(6)** | 1,950 | 2,800 | **(3)** | **(7)** | 270 | | | |
| | | 270 | **(7)** | | | | | |

**Required**

a.   Give a description of each of the nine numbered transactions entered in the above T-accounts. Example: (1) Carol Marsh invested $13,000 of her personal funds in her business.

b.   The following trial balance, prepared from Marsh's data as of May 31, contains several errors. Itemize the errors and indicate the correct totals for the trial balance.

| **CAROL MARSH & COMPANY**<br>**Unadjusted Trial Balance**<br>**May 31, 2010** | | |
|---|---|---|
| | **Debit** | **Credit** |
| Cash | $ 8,450 | |
| Accounts receivable | 3,700 | |
| Office supplies | 2,800 | |
| Office equipment | 4,800 | |
| Accounts payable | | $ 1,120 |
| Common stock | | 13,000 |
| Dividends | | 600 |
| Professional fees earned | | 6,400 |
| Rent expense | 810 | |
| Totals | $20,560 | $21,120 |

**P3-13A.** **Transaction Analysis and Trial Balance**          LO4, LO5, LO6

Pam Brown owns Art Graphics, a firm providing designs for advertisers and market analysts. On July 1, the business's general ledger showed the following normal account balances:

| | | | | |
|---|---|---|---|---|
| Cash ................... | $ 8,500 | Notes payable............................. | | $ 5,000 |
| Accounts receivable ..... | 9,800 | Accounts payable ......................... | | 2,100 |
| | | Common stock............................ | | 2,000 |
| | | Retained earnings ........................ | | 9,200 |
| Total Assets ............ | $18,300 | Total Liabilities and Stockholders' Equity .... | | $18,300 |

The following transactions occurred during the month of July:

July 1 Paid July rent, $670.
2 Collected $7,100 on account from customers.
3 Paid $2,500 installment due on the $5,000 noninterest-bearing note payable.
4 Billed customers for design services rendered on account, $16,550.
5 Rendered design services and collected from cash customers, $1,200.
6 Paid $1,400 to creditors on account.
7 Collected $12,750 on account from customers.
8 Paid a delivery service for delivery of graphics to commercial firms, $400.
9 Paid July salaries, $4,600.
10 Received invoice for July advertising expense, to be paid in August, $600.
11 Paid utilities for July, $350.
12 Paid stockholders a dividend of $2,000 cash.
13 Received invoice for supplies used in July, to be paid in August, $2,260.
14 Purchased computer for $4,300 cash to be used in the business starting next month.

### Required

a. Set up accounts for the general ledger accounts with July 1 balances and enter the beginning balances. Also provide the following accounts: Equipment; Service Fees Earned; Rent Expense; Salaries Expense; Delivery Expense; Advertising Expense; Utilities Expense; Supplies Expense; and Dividends. Record the listed transactions in the accounts.
b. Prepare a trial balance as of July 31.

**LO4, LO5, LO6** **P3-14A. Transaction Analysis and Trial Balance**

Outpost Fly-In Service, Inc., operates leased amphibious aircraft and docking facilities, equipping the firm to transport campers and hunters from Vancouver, Canada, to outpost camps owned by various resorts. On August 1, 2010, the firm's trial balance was as follows:

| OUTPOST FLY-IN SERVICE, INC. Unadjusted Trial Balance August 1, 2010 | | |
|---|---|---|
| | **Debit** | **Credit** |
| Cash ......................................................... | $52,600 | |
| Accounts receivable ................................................ | 23,200 | |
| Notes payable...................................................... | | $ 3,000 |
| Accounts payable .................................................. | | 1,700 |
| Common stock..................................................... | | 50,000 |
| Retained earnings .................................................. | | 21,100 |
| Totals ......................................................... | $75,800 | $75,800 |

During the month of August, the following transactions occurred:

Aug. 1 Paid August rental cost for aircraft, dockage, and dockside office, $5,000.
2 Paid insurance premium for August, $1,800.
3 Paid for August advertising in various sports magazines, $1,000.
4 Rendered fly-in services for various groups for cash, $13,750.
5 Billed the Canadian Ministry of Natural Resources for services in transporting mapping personnel, $3,200.
6 Received $17,400 on account from clients.
7 Paid $1,500 on accounts payable.
8 Billed various clients for services, $16,400.
9 Paid interest on a note payable for August, $25.
10 Paid August wages, $12,800.

11  Received invoice for the cost of fuel used during August, $3,200.

12  Paid a cash dividend, $4,500 (debit Retained Earnings).

**Required**

a.  Set up accounts for each item in the August 1 trial balance and enter the beginning balances. Also provide accounts for the following items: Service Fees Earned, Wage Expense, Advertising Expense, Rent Expense, Fuel Expense, Insurance Expense, and Interest Expense. Record the transactions for August in the accounts, using the dates given.

b.  Prepare a trial balance as of August 31.

**P3-15A. Transaction Analysis and Trial Balance**

Mary Aker opened a tax practice on June 1. The following accounts will be needed to record her transactions for June: Cash; Accounts Receivable; Office Supplies; Tax Library; Office Furniture and Fixtures; Notes Payable; Accounts Payable; Common Stock; Dividends; Professional Fees Earned; Rent Expense; Salaries Expense; Advertising Expense; Utilities Expense; and Interest Expense. The following transactions occurred during the month of June:

June  1  Aker opened a business checking account at a local bank, investing $16,000 in her practice in exchange for common stock.

2  Purchased office furniture and fixtures for $9,800, paid $2,800 cash, and gave a note payable for the balance.

3  Purchased books and software for a tax library on account, $3,700.

4  Purchased office supplies for cash, $560.

5  Paid rent for June, $750.

6  Returned $300 of books with defective bindings. The return reduced the amount owed to the supplier.

7  Billed clients for professional services rendered, $7,600.

8  Paid $1,700 on account for the library items purchased on June 3.

9  Collected $5,900 on account from clients billed on June 7.

10  Paid June salaries, $2,900.

11  Received invoice for June advertising, to be paid in July, $300.

12  Paid stockholders $800 cash as a dividend.

13  Paid utilities for June, $160.

14  Paid interest for June on note payable, $60.

**Required**

a.  Record the above transactions in T-accounts, and key entries with the number of the transactions.

b.  Prepare a trial balance as of June 30.

**P3-16A. Transaction Analysis and the Effect of Errors on the Trial Balance**

The following T-accounts contain numbered entries for the May transactions of Flores Corporation, an architectural firm, which opened its offices on May 1:

| | Cash | | | | Accounts Payable | | |
|---|---|---|---|---|---|---|---|
| **(1)** | 20,000 | 1,400 | **(4)** | **(5)** | 310 | 1,530 | **(3)** |
| **(10)** | 5,200 | 5,950 | **(7)** | **(8)** | 1,000 | 290 | **(9)** |
| | | 1,000 | **(8)** | | | | |

| | Accounts Receivable | | | | Common Stock | | |
|---|---|---|---|---|---|---|---|
| **(6)** | 8,750 | 5,200 | **(10)** | | | 20,000 | **(1)** |

| | Supplies | | | | Professional Fees Earned | | |
|---|---|---|---|---|---|---|---|
| **(3)** | 1,530 | 310 | **(5)** | | | 8,750 | **(6)** |

| | Office Equipment | | | | Rent Expense | |
|---|---|---|---|---|---|---|
| **(2)** | 5,000 | | **(4)** | 1,400 | |

| | Notes Payable | | | | Utilities Expense | |
|---|---|---|---|---|---|---|
| | | 5,000 | **(2)** | **(9)** | 290 | |

| | Salaries Expense | |
|---|---|---|
| **(7)** | 5,950 | |

**Required**

a. Give a description of each of the 10 numbered transactions entered in the above accounts. Example: (1) Flores Corporation issued common stock for cash, $20,000.

b. The following trial balance, prepared for Flores Corporation as of May 31, contains several errors. Itemize the errors, and indicate the correct totals for the trial balance.

| FLORES CORPORATION Unadjusted Trial Balance May 31, 2010 | | |
|---|---|---|
| | **Debit** | **Credit** |
| Cash | $61,850 | |
| Accounts receivable | 3,550 | |
| Supplies | 1,220 | |
| Office equipment | | $ 5,000 |
| Notes payable | | 50,000 |
| Accounts payable | | 510 |
| Common stock | | 2,000 |
| Professional fees earned | | 8,570 |
| Rent expense | 1,400 | |
| Utilities expense | 290 | |
| Salaries expense | 5,950 | |
| Totals | $74,260 | $66,080 |

LO5, LO6 **P3-17A. Transaction Analysis and Trial Balance**

James Behm, electrical contractor, began business on May 1. The following transactions occurred during the month of May:

May 1 Behm invested $18,000 of his personal funds in the business in exchange for common stock.

2 Purchased equipment on account, $4,200.

3 Returned $200 of equipment that was not satisfactory. The return reduced the amount owed to the supplier.

4 Purchased supplies on account, $860.

5 Purchased a truck for $10,500. Behm paid $5,500 cash and gave a note payable for the balance.

6 Paid rent for May, $875.

7 Paid fuel cost for truck, $60.

8 Billed customers for services rendered, $13,700.

9 Paid $3,000 on account for equipment purchased on May 2.

10 Paid utilities for May, $210.

11 Received invoice for May advertising, to be paid in June, $280.

12 Paid employees' wages, $3,350.

13 Collected $8,600 on accounts receivable.

14 Paid stockholders $1,500 cash as a dividend.

15 Paid interest for May on an outstanding note payable, $40.

**Required**

a. Record the above transactions in T-accounts, and key entries with the numbers of the transactions. The following accounts will be needed to record the transactions for May: Cash; Accounts Receivable; Supplies; Equipment; Truck; Notes Payable; Accounts Payable; Common Stock; Dividends; Service Revenue; Rent Expense; Wages Expense; Utilities Expense; Truck Expense; Advertising Expense; and Interest Expense.

b. Prepare a trial balance as of May 31.

# PROBLEMS—SET B

LO2 **P3-1B. Transaction Analysis**

The accounting equation of Matthew Thomas, attorney, at the beginning of an accounting period is given below, followed by seven transactions whose effects on the accounting equation are shown. Describe each transaction that occurred. Of the transactions affecting retained earnings, transaction (e) had no effect on net income for the period.

| | Cash | + | Accounts Receivable | + | Supplies | = | Notes Payable | + | Accounts Payable | + | Common Stock | + | Retained Earnings |
|---|---|---|---|---|---|---|---|---|---|---|---|---|---|
| Balance | $4,100 | + | $9,000 | + | $900 | = | $2,500 | + | $1,000 | + | $7,500 | + | $3,000 |
| (a) | +7,500 | | −7,500 | | | | | | | | | | |
| (b) | | | | | +400 | | | | +400 | | | | |
| (c) | | | +8,000 | | | | | | | | | | +8,000 |
| (d) | −800 | | | | | | | | −800 | | | | |
| (e) | −4,900 | | | | | | | | | | | | −4,900 |
| (f) | −300 | | | | +300 | | | | | | | | |
| (g) | +3,200 | | | | | | +3,200 | | | | | | |

**P3-2B. Transaction Analysis**     LO2

An analysis of the transactions of Likert Shipping Services for the month of May appears below. Line 1 summarizes Likert's accounting equation data as of May 1; lines 2–10 represent the transactions for the month of May:

| | Cash | + | Accounts Receivable | + | Supplies | + | Equipment | = | Notes Payable | + | Accounts Payable | + | Common Stock | + | Retained Earnings |
|---|---|---|---|---|---|---|---|---|---|---|---|---|---|---|---|
| (1) | $2,400 | + | $7,600 | + | $900 | + | $9,000 | = | $6,000 | + | $700 | + | $3,200 | + | $10,000 |
| (2) | +2,000 | | | | | | | | +2,000 | | | | | | |
| (3) | +6,100 | | −6,100 | | | | | | | | | | | | |
| (4) | | | | | +980 | | | | | | +980 | | | | |
| (5) | | | +6,800 | | | | | | | | | | | | +6,800 |
| (6) | −300 | | | | | | | | | | −300 | | | | |
| (7) | +1,500 | | | | | | | | | | | | | | +1,500 |
| (8) | −800 | | | | | | | | | | | | | | −800 |
| (9) | −750 | | | | | | +750 | | | | | | | | |
| (10) | −2,500 | | | | | | | | −2,500 | | | | | | |

**Required**

a. Show that assets equal liabilities plus stockholders' equity as of May 1.

b. Describe the apparent transaction indicated by each line. (For example, line 2: Borrowed $2,000, giving a note payable.) If any line could reasonably represent more than one type of transaction, describe each type.

c. Show that assets equal liabilities plus stockholders' equity as of May 31.

**P3-3B. Transaction Analysis**     LO2

Smith Appraisal Service provides commercial and industrial appraisals and feasibility studies. On January 1, the assets and liabilities of the business were the following: Cash, $8,700; Accounts Receivable, $16,800; Notes Payable, $6,500; and Accounts Payable, $3,600. Assume that Retained Earnings as of January 1, were zero. The balance of Common Stock was $15,400. The following transactions occurred during the month of January:

Jan.  1  Paid rent for January, $1,000.

2  Received $9,800 on customers' accounts.

3  Paid $900 on accounts payable.

4  Received $1,600 for services performed for cash customers.

5  Borrowed $8,000 from a bank and signed a note payable for that amount.

6  Billed the city $8,200 for a feasibility study performed; billed various other credit customers, $2,900.

7  Paid salary of assistant, $4,500.

8  Received invoice for January utilities, $410.

9  Paid $6,000 cash dividends.

10  Purchased an automobile (on January 31) for business use, $9,800 cash.

11  Paid $150 to the bank as January interest on an outstanding note payable.

**Required**

a. Set up an accounting equation in columnar form with the following individual assets, liabilities, and stockholders' equity accounts: Cash, Accounts Receivable, Automobile, Notes Payable, Accounts Payable, Common Stock, and Retained Earnings. Enter January 1 balances below each item. (*Note:* The beginning Automobile amount is $0.)

b. Show the impact (increase or decrease) of transactions 1–11 on the beginning balances, and total the columns to show that assets equal liabilities plus stockholders' equity as of January 31.

LO2  **P3-4B.** **Transaction Analysis**

On June 1, a group of bush pilots in British Columbia, Canada, formed the BC Back-Country Airlines, Inc., by selling $80,000 of common stock for cash. The group then leased several aircraft and docking facilities, equipping them to transport campers and hunters to outpost camps owned by various resorts. The following transactions occurred during June:

June    1  Sold common stock for cash, $80,000.
        2  Paid June rent for aircraft, dockage, and dockside office, $5,500.
        3  Received invoice for the cost of a reception the firm gave to entertain resort owners, $2,600.
        4  Paid for June advertising in various sports magazines, $1,900.
        5  Paid insurance premium for January, $2,800.
        6  Rendered services for various groups for cash, $25,000.
        7  Billed the Canadian Ministry of Natural Resources for transporting mapping personnel, $3,900, and billed various firms for services, $15,000.
        8  Paid $1,500 on accounts payable.
        9  Received $13,200 on account from clients.
        10 Paid June wages, $16,000.
        11 Received an invoice for the cost of fuel used during June, $3,500.
        12 Paid a cash dividend, $5,000.

**Required**

a. Set up an accounting equation in columnar form with the following column headings: Cash, Accounts Receivable, Accounts Payable, Common Stock, and Retained Earnings.

b. Show how the June transactions affect the items in the accounting equation, and total all columns to show that assets equal liabilities plus stockholders' equity as of June 30.

LO2  **P3-5B.** **Accounting Equation**

Determine the following:

a. The stockholders' equity of a company that has assets of $480,000 and liabilities of $330,000.

b. The retained earnings of a company that has assets of $675,000, liabilities of $225,000, and common stock of $165,000.

c. The assets of a corporation that has liabilities of $500,000, common stock of $300,000, and retained earnings of $255,000.

LO2  **P3-6B.** **Transaction Analysis**

Following the example shown in (a) below, indicate the effects of the listed transactions on the assets, liabilities, and stockholders' equity of McKay & Company:

(a) Rendered services to clients for cash.
    ANSWER: Increase assets (Cash)
            Increase stockholders' equity (Retained Earnings)

(b) Purchased office supplies on account.

(c) Invested cash in the firm in exchange for common stock.

(d) Paid amount due on account for supplies purchased in (b).

(e) Borrowed cash from a bank and signed a six-month note.

(f) Rendered services and billed clients.

(g) Purchased, for cash, a desk lamp for the office.

(h) Paid interest on note payable to bank.

(i) Received an invoice for the current month's utilities.

**P3-7B.  Transaction Analysis**                                                                    LO2

On October 1, Deloitte & Coopers started a consulting firm. The asset, liability, and stockholders' equity account balances after each of the firm's first six transactions are shown below. Describe each of these six transactions.

| | Cash | + | Accounts Receivable | + | Supplies | + | Equipment | = | Notes Payable | + | Common Stock | + | Retained Earnings |
|---|---|---|---|---|---|---|---|---|---|---|---|---|---|
| (a) | $6,000 | + | $ 0 | + | $ 0 | + | $ 0 | = | $ 0 | + | $6,000 | + | $ 0 |
| (b) | 4,000 | + | 0 | + | 2,000 | + | 0 | = | 0 | + | 6,000 | + | 0 |
| (c) | 7,500 | + | 0 | + | 2,000 | + | 0 | = | 3,500 | + | 6,000 | + | 0 |
| (d) | 2,500 | + | 0 | + | 2,000 | + | 5,000 | = | 3,500 | + | 6,000 | + | 0 |
| (e) | 2,500 | + | 2,000 | + | 2,000 | + | 5,000 | = | 3,500 | + | 6,000 | + | 2,000 |
| (f) | 3,000 | + | 1,500 | + | 2,000 | + | 5,000 | = | 3,500 | + | 6,000 | + | 2,000 |

**P3-8B.  Determination of Omitted Financial Statement Data**                                       LO2

For the four unrelated situations, A-D, below, calculate the unknown amounts indicated by the letters appearing in each column:

| | A | B | C | D |
|---|---|---|---|---|
| **Beginning** | | | | |
| Assets.......................................... | $38,000 | $12,000 | $28,000 | $ (d) |
| Liabilities..................................... | 18,600 | 5,000 | 10,000 | 9,000 |
| **Ending** | | | | |
| Assets.......................................... | 30,000 | 36,000 | 34,000 | 40,000 |
| Liabilities..................................... | 17,300 | (b) | 15,000 | 15,000 |
| **During the Year** | | | | |
| Common stock............................. | 2,000 | 4,500 | (c) | 3,500 |
| Revenues .................................... | (a) | 28,000 | 18,000 | 24,000 |
| Dividends..................................... | 5,000 | 1,500 | 1,000 | 6,500 |
| Expenses...................................... | 8,500 | 21,000 | 11,000 | 17,000 |

**P3-9B.  Transaction Analysis**                                                                    LO2

Appearing below is an analysis of the June transactions for Carlton Communications Company. Line 1 summarizes Carlton's accounting equation data as of June 1; lines 2-10 are the transactions for June:

| | Cash | + | Accounts Receivable | + | Supplies | + | Equipment | = | Notes Payable | + | Accounts Payable | + | Common Stock | + | Retained Earnings |
|---|---|---|---|---|---|---|---|---|---|---|---|---|---|---|---|
| (1) | $3,500 | + | $5,200 | + | $820 | + | $12,000 | = | $3,000 | + | $600 | + | $10,920 | + | $7,000 |
| (2) | | | | | +670 | | | | | | +670 | | | | |
| (3) | | | | | | | +6,000 | | +6,000 | | | | | | |
| (4) | +4,200 | | −4,200 | | | | | | | | | | | | |
| (5) | | | +7,800 | | | | | | | | | | | | +7,800 |
| (6) | −600 | | | | | | | | | | −600 | | | | |
| (7) | −200 | | | | +200 | | | | | | | | | | |
| (8) | −4,600 | | | | | | | | | | | | | | −4,600 |
| (9) | +3,000 | | | | | | | | +3,000 | | | | | | |
| (10) | −750 | | | | | | +750 | | | | | | | | |

**Required**

*a.*  Show that assets equal liabilities plus stockholders' equity as of June 1.
*b.*  Describe the apparent transaction indicated by each line. For example, line 2: Purchased supplies on account, $670. If any line could reasonably represent more than one type of transaction, describe each type.
*c.*  Show that assets equal liabilities plus stockholders' equity as of June 30.

**P3-10B.  Transaction Analysis**                                                                   LO2

Torrey Mann began the Mann Word Processing Service in December 2009. The firm provides word-processing services for businesses and is currently operating with leased equipment. On January 1, 2010, the assets and liabilities of the business were: Cash, $6,400; Accounts Receivable, $8,900; Notes Payable, $3,500; and Accounts Payable, $900. Assume that Retained Earnings as of January 1, 2010, were zero. Common Stock balance was $10,900. The following transactions occurred during the month of January:

ASSIGNMENTS

Jan.   1   Paid rent on office and equipment for January, $900.
    3   Collected $6,500 on account from clients.
    3   Borrowed $5,000 from a bank and signed a note payable for that amount.
    4   Billed clients for work performed on account, $8,500.
    5   Paid $400 on accounts payable.
    6   Received invoice for January advertising, $750.
    7   Paid January salaries, $4,800.
    8   Paid January utilities, $230.
    9   Paid stockholders a dividend in the amount of $2,600.
  10   Purchased fax machine (on January 31) for business use, $1,400.
  11   Paid $130 to bank as January interest on the outstanding notes payable.

### Required

*a.*   Set up an accounting equation in columnar form with the following individual assets, liabilities, and stockholders' equity accounts: Cash, Accounts Receivable, Equipment, Notes Payable, Accounts Payable, Common Stock, Retained earnings. Enter the January 1 balances below each item. (*Note:* The beginning Equipment amount is $0.)

*b.*   Show the impact (increase or decrease) of the January transactions on the beginning balances, and total all columns to show that assets equal liabilities plus stockholders' equity as of January 31.

**LO2**   **P3-11B.   Transaction Analysis**

On December 1, Judy Johnson started Adult Career Services, which provided career and vocational counseling services to individuals. The following transactions took place during the month of December:

Dec.   1   Johnson invested $9,000 in the business in exchange for common stock.
    2   Paid rent for December on furnished office space, $950.
    3   Received invoice for December advertising, $800.
    4   Borrowed $25,000 from a bank and signed a note payable for that amount.
    5   Received $4,200 for counseling services rendered for cash.
    6   Billed certain governmental agencies and other clients for counseling services, $9,800.
    7   Paid secretary's salary, $3,200.
    8   Paid December utilities, $370.
    9   Paid stockholders a dividend in the amount of $900.
  10   Purchased land for cash to use as a site for the company's future offices, $23,000.
  11   Paid $100 to the bank as December interest on the outstanding note payable.

### Required

*a.*   Set up an accounting equation in columnar form with the following column headings: Cash, Accounts Receivable, Land, Notes Payable, Accounts Payable, Common stock, and Retained Earnings.

*b.*   Show how the December transactions affect the items in the accounting equation, and total all columns to show that assets equal liabilities plus stockholders' equity as of December 31.

**LO4, LO5, LO6**   **P3-12B.   Transaction Analysis and the Effect of Errors on Trial Balance**

The following T-accounts contain numbered entries for the May transactions of Valerie Rankine who opened a consulting services business on May 1:

| Cash | | | | | Common Stock | | |
|---|---|---|---|---|---|---|---|
| (1) | 20,000 | 4,800 | (2) | | | 20,000 | (1) |
| (9) | 3,700 | 810 | (4) | | | | |
| | | 1,950 | (6) | | | | |
| | | 600 | (8) | | | | |

| Accounts Receivable | | | | | Dividends | | |
|---|---|---|---|---|---|---|---|
| (5) | 6,400 | 3,700 | (9) | | (8) | 600 | |

| Office Supplies | | | | | Professional Fees Earned | | |
|---|---|---|---|---|---|---|---|
| (3) | 2,800 | | | | | 6,400 | (5) |

| Office Equipment | | | | Rent Expense | |
|---|---|---|---|---|---|
| (2) | 4,800 | | | (4) | 810 |

| Accounts Payable | | | | Utilities Expense | |
|---|---|---|---|---|---|
| (6) | 1,950 | 2,800 | (3) | (7) | 270 |
| | | 270 | (7) | | |

### Required

a. Give a description of each of the nine numbered transactions entered in the above accounts. Example: (1) Valerie Rankine invested $20,000 of her personal funds in the business in exchange for common stock.

b. The following trial balance, prepared for Rankine's firm as of May 31, contains several errors. Itemize the errors and indicate the correct totals for the trial balance.

| RANKINE CONSULTING SERVICES Unadjusted Trial Balance May 31, 2010 | | |
|---|---|---|
| | **Debit** | **Credit** |
| Cash ........................................................... | $15,450 | |
| Accounts receivable ..................................... | 3,700 | |
| Office supplies ............................................ | 2,800 | |
| Office equipment......................................... | 4,800 | |
| Accounts payable ........................................ | | $ 1,120 |
| Common stock............................................. | | 20,000 |
| Dividends.................................................... | | 600 |
| Professional fees earned .............................. | | 6,400 |
| Rent expense............................................... | 810 | |
| Totals ......................................................... | $27,560 | $28,120 |

## P3-13B. Transaction Analysis and Trial Balance

LO4, LO5, LO6

Ashley Somers owns San Diego Art Company, a firm providing designs for advertisers, market analysts, and others. On July 1, the business's general ledger showed the following normal account balances:

| Cash ...................... | $10,500 | Notes payable............................... | $ 5,000 |
|---|---|---|---|
| Accounts receivable ........ | 9,800 | Accounts payable ........................... | 2,100 |
| | | Common stock............................... | 11,200 |
| | | Retained earnings ........................... | 2,000 |
| Total assets................ | $20,300 | Total Liabilities and Stockholders' Equity ..... | $20,300 |

The following transactions occurred during the month of July:

July 1 Paid July rent, $670.
  2 Collected $8,100 on account from customers.
  3 Paid $2,500 installment due on the $5,000 noninterest-bearing note payable to a relative.
  4 Billed customers for design services rendered on account, $19,550.
  5 Rendered design services and collected from cash customers, $1,200.
  6 Paid $1,700 to creditors on account.
  7 Collected $14,750 on account from customers.
  8 Paid a delivery service for delivery of graphics to commercial firms, $400.
  9 Paid July salaries, $4,600.
  10 Received invoice for July advertising expense, to be paid in August, $600.
  11 Paid utilities for July, $350.
  12 The business paid a $2,000 cash dividend.
  13 Received invoice for supplies used in July, to be paid in August, $2,260.
  14 Purchased a computer for $4,300 cash to be used in the business starting next month.

### Required

a. Set up accounts for the general ledger accounts with July 1 balances and enter the beginning balances. Also provide the following accounts: Equipment; Dividends; Service Fees

Earned; Rent Expense; Salaries Expense; Delivery Expense; Advertising Expense; Utilities Expense; and Supplies Expense. Record the listed transactions in the accounts.

b.   Prepare a trial balance as of July 31.

**LO4, LO5, LO6**   **P3-14B.   Transaction Analysis and Trial Balance**

BC Back-Country Airlines, Inc., operates leased amphibious aircraft and docking facilities, equipping the firm to transport campers and hunters from British Columbia, Canada, to outpost camps owned by various resorts. On August 1, the firm's trial balance was as follows:

| BC BACK-COUNTRY AIRLINES, INC. Unadjusted Trial Balance August 1, 2010 | | |
|---|---|---|
| | **Debit** | **Credit** |
| Cash .................................................................. | $ 82,600 | |
| Accounts receivable ............................................... | 23,200 | |
| Notes payable...................................................... | | $   3,000 |
| Accounts payable .................................................. | | 1,700 |
| Common stock...................................................... | | 80,000 |
| Retained earnings ................................................. | | 21,100 |
| Totals ............................................................... | $105,800 | $105,800 |

During August the following transactions occurred:

Aug.  1   Paid August rental cost for aircraft, dockage, and dockside office, $6,000.

2   Paid the insurance premium for August, $2,800.

3   Paid for August advertising in various sports magazines, $1,500.

4   Rendered services for various groups for cash, $16,750.

5   Billed the Canadian Ministry of Natural Resources for services in transporting mapping personnel, $3,900.

6   Received $20,400 on account from clients.

7   Paid $1,700 on accounts payable.

8   Billed various clients for services, $19,400.

9   Paid interest on an outstanding note payable for August, $75.

10   Paid August wages, $14,800.

11   Received invoice for the cost of fuel used during August, $3,600.

12   Paid a cash dividend, $4,500 (debit Retained Earnings).

### Required

a.   Set up accounts for each item in the August 1 trial balance and enter the beginning balances. Also provide similar accounts for the following items: Service Fees Earned, Wages Expense, Advertising Expense, Rent Expense, Fuel Expense, Insurance Expense, and Interest Expense. Record the transactions for August in the accounts, using the dates given.

b.   Prepare a trial balance as of August 31, 2010.

**LO4, LO5, LO6**   **P3-15B.   Transaction Analysis and Trial Balance**

William Groff opened a tax practice on June 1. The following accounts will be needed to record the business's transactions for June: Cash; Accounts Receivable; Office Supplies; Tax Library; Office Furniture and Fixtures; Notes Payable; Accounts Payable; Common Stock; Dividends; Professional Fees Earned; Rent Expense; Salaries Expense; Advertising Expense; Utilities Expense; and Interest Expense. The following transactions occurred in June:

June  1   Groff opened a business checking account at a local bank, investing $20,000 in his practice in exchange for common stock.

2   Purchased office furniture and fixtures for $9,800, paid $2,800 cash, and gave a note payable for the balance.

3   Purchased books and software for a tax library on account, $5,700.

4   Purchased office supplies for cash, $560.

5   Paid rent for June, $950.

6   Returned $300 of books with defective bindings. The return reduced the amount owed to the supplier.

7   Billed clients for professional services rendered, $17,600.

8 Paid $1,700 on account for the library items purchased on June 3.
9 Collected $15,900 on account from clients billed on June 7.
10 Paid June salaries, $4,900.
11 Received an invoice for June advertising, to be paid in July, $300.
12 The business paid stockholders a cash dividend of $800.
13 Paid utilities for June, $160.
14 Paid interest for June on an outstanding note payable, $60.

**Required**

a. Record the above transactions in T-accounts, and key entries with the numbers of the transactions.
b. Prepare a trial balance from the general ledger as of June 30.

**P3-16B. Transaction Analysis and the Effect of Errors on Trial Balance**    LO4, LO5, LO6

The following T-accounts contain numbered entries for the May transactions of the Claremont Corporation, an architectural firm, which opened its offices on May 1:

| | Cash | | |
|---|---|---|---|
| **(1)** | 50,000 | 1,400 | **(4)** |
| **(10)** | 5,200 | 5,950 | **(7)** |
| | | 1,000 | **(8)** |

| | Accounts Payable | | |
|---|---|---|---|
| **(5)** | 310 | 1,530 | **(3)** |
| **(8)** | 1,000 | 290 | **(9)** |

| | Accounts Receivable | | |
|---|---|---|---|
| **(6)** | 8,750 | 5,200 | **(10)** |

| | Common Stock | | |
|---|---|---|---|
| | | 50,000 | **(1)** |

| | Supplies | | |
|---|---|---|---|
| **(3)** | 1,530 | 310 | **(5)** |

| | Professional Fees Earned | | |
|---|---|---|---|
| | | 8,750 | **(6)** |

| | Office Equipment | |
|---|---|---|
| **(2)** | 5,000 | |

| | Rent Expense | |
|---|---|---|
| **(4)** | 1,400 | |

| | Notes Payable | | |
|---|---|---|---|
| | | 5,000 | **(2)** |

| | Utilities Expense | |
|---|---|---|
| **(9)** | 290 | |

| | Salaries Expense | |
|---|---|---|
| **(7)** | 5,950 | |

**Required**

a. Give a description of each of the 10 numbered transactions entered in the above accounts. Example: (1) Claremont Corporation issued common stock for cash, $50,000.
b. The following trial balance, prepared for Claremont Corporation as of May 31, contains several errors. Itemize the errors, and indicate the correct totals for the trial balance.

**CLAREMONT CORPORATION**
**Unadjusted Trial Balance**
**May 31, 2010**

| | Debit | Credit |
|---|---|---|
| Cash ............................................................. | $ 91,850 | |
| Accounts receivable ...................................... | 3,550 | |
| Supplies......................................................... | 1,220 | |
| Office equipment............................................ | | $ 5,000 |
| Notes payable................................................. | | 50,000 |
| Accounts payable ........................................... | | 510 |
| Common stock................................................ | | 50,000 |
| Professional fees earned ................................ | | 8,570 |
| Rent expense................................................... | 1,400 | |
| Utilities expense............................................. | 290 | |
| Salaries expense.............................................. | 5,950 | |
| Totals ........................................................... | $104,260 | $114,080 |

**P3-17B. Transaction Analysis and Trial Balance**    LO5, LO6

Walsh & Company, electrical contractors, began operations on May 1. The following transactions occurred during the month of May:

# Accrual Basis of Accounting

## LEARNING OBJECTIVES

*1* **Explain** the accrual basis of accounting and contrast it with the cash basis with reference to revenue and expense recognition. (p. 160)

*2* **Describe** the adjusting process and **illustrate** the four major types of adjusting entries. (p. 162)

*3* **Explain** the adjusted trial balance and use it to prepare financial statements. (p. 170)

*4* **Describe** the closing process and **summarize** the accounting cycle. (p. 173)

*5* Appendix 4A: **Describe** the process of closing directly to Retained Earnings and **summarize** the accounting cycle. (p. 178)

*6* Appendix 4B: **Explain** how to use a worksheet in the adjusting and closing process. (p. 181)

# MAKING DOUGH

**Krispy Kreme** is similar to other companies when it comes to the end-of-year accounting processes. As it closes its books for the year, its employees must get the accounting information organized to prepare the financial statements for its annual report. That process normally requires several accounting adjustments to properly determine how well a company performed and its financial condition.

Many estimates, assumptions, and judgments make up these accounting adjustments. Krispy Kreme's recent annual report had a fiscal year-end of February 1. However, because of those adjustments and other year-end procedures, it did not file its audited financial statements until April 17, nearly two-and-a-half months later.

Accounting adjustments are important to investors and others that rely on financial statements for valuing company stock. Not long ago, Krispy Kreme was a high-flying company with a stock price of nearly $50 per share. Today, its stock is selling for just $4 per share.

What precipitated such a dramatic drop in its stock price? One reason suggested by Wall Street pundits is Krispy Kreme's accounting methods. It appears that some adjustments that Krispy Kreme made for its estimate of doubtful accounts, and its method of accounting for the purchase of franchise stores, propped up its earnings much like the yeast in its donuts. When investors began to question the "quality" of Krispy Kreme's earnings, a sharp sell-off of its stock followed as worried stockholders moved their money to alternative investments.

Why are accounting adjustments so important? This chapter focuses on that question. It explains the importance of those adjustments for financial statements. It also shows how companies account for adjustments and how financial statements are prepared from final adjusted numbers.

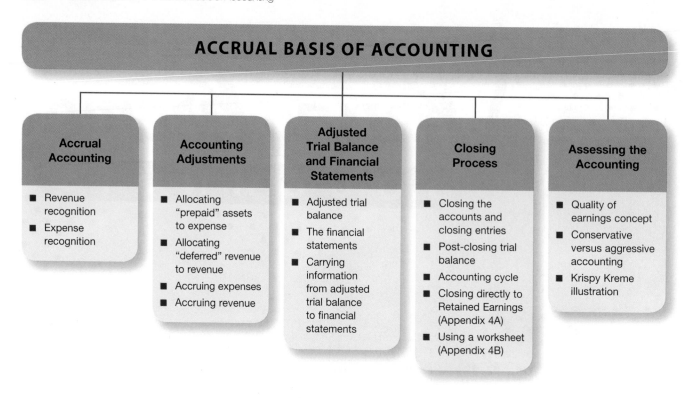

# ACCRUAL BASIS OF ACCOUNTING

Most individuals, and some small businesses, measure their financial performance by looking at their cash flow. For example, an individual who pays for all of her purchases from a checking account is likely to evaluate her financial well-being in terms of her available cash. If she ends the period with a higher cash balance than she started with, she is likely to conclude that she generated a profit.

This cash basis of accounting is not considered generally accepted for most businesses. Generally accepted accounting principles require that companies use the accrual basis of accounting. The accrual basis of accounting requires a business to measure and report its operating performance without the necessity of insuring that all revenues have been collected in cash and all expenses have been paid with cash.

## REVENUE RECOGNITION PRINCIPLE

Under the cash basis of accounting, the receipt and payment of cash is the determining factor for when sales revenue is recognized and when expenses are deducted. Under the accrual basis of accounting, sales revenue is recognized when it is earned, regardless of when the related cash is collected; and, expenses are recognized when incurred, regardless of whether cash has been paid. For most businesses, this means that its sales revenue is recognized at the time that goods and services are delivered to a customer. This may occur before, after, or at the same time that cash is received.

### Cash Received When Revenue Is Earned

For most sales, **Krispy Kreme** will receive cash at the same time that the customer receives donuts. Under these circumstances, accrual accounting recognizes sales revenue at the same time that the company receives payment for its product. As a consequence, Krispy Kreme will debit Cash and credit Sales Revenue.

| April | Cash | 100 | |
| |     Sales revenue | | 100 |
| | *To record revenue at time of cash receipt.* | | |

| A | = | L | + | SE |
|---|---|---|---|---|
| +100 | | | + | 100 Rev. |

## Cash Received *After* Revenue Is Earned

**Safeway** purchases large quantities of Krispy Kreme donuts for resale in their grocery stores. Assume that Safeway agrees to pay for the donuts in thirty days following each purchase. Even though Krispy Kreme has not received any payment for the delivered donuts, the company has earned the right to receive the cash, and consequently, Krispy Kreme must recognize the sales revenue prior to cash collection. In this case, it will debit Accounts Receivable and credit Sales Revenue.

| April | Accounts receivable | 100 | |
| |     Sales revenue | | 100 |
| | *To recognize revenue earned.* | | |

| A | = | L | + | SE |
|---|---|---|---|---|
| +100 | | | + | 100 Rev. |

| May | Cash | 100 | |
| |     Accounts receivable | | 100 |
| | *To recognize cash received.* | | |

| A | = | L | + | SE |
|---|---|---|---|---|
| +100 | | | | |
| −100 | | | | |

## Cash Received *Before* Revenue Is Earned

Assume that **Albertsons** prepays for its donut purchases by giving Krispy Kreme a cash payment prior to receiving any donuts. Even though Krispy Kreme has received cash, it has not earned the revenue, and thus, will defer the recognition of any sales revenue until earned, which is at the time of product delivery. Krispy Kreme will record a liability account, Unearned Revenue, until such time as the donuts are delivered to Albertsons and when it earns the revenue. As these examples demonstrate, it is the earning of sales revenue that determines when revenue is recognized by a company under the accrual basis of accounting, and not the timing of the cash collection.

| April | Cash | 100 | |
| |     Unearned revenue | | 100 |
| | *To recognize the receipt of cash prior to revenue being earned.* | | |

| A | = | L | + | SE |
|---|---|---|---|---|
| +100 | | +100 | | |

| May | Unearned revenue | 100 | |
| |     Sales revenue | | 100 |
| | *To recognize earned revenue.* | | |

| A | = | L | + | SE |
|---|---|---|---|---|
| | | −100 | + | 100 Rev. |

| Concept ➤ | Method ➤ | Assessment |
|---|---|---|
| When should sales revenue be recognized? | Understand the nature of a company's earning process.<br><br>Record revenue when it is earned. | Early recognition of revenue overstates current period revenue; recognizing revenue too late understates current period revenue. |

**TAKEAWAY 4.1**

## EXPENSE RECOGNITION (MATCHING) PRINCIPLE

Accounting requires that the expenses incurred to generate revenues be recognized (matched) in the same period. In other words, business expenses are recognized (matched) with sales revenues so that they are reported on the same income statement. Like the recognition of revenue, the recognition of expenses can occur prior to, simultaneously with, or subsequent to the receipt of cash. It is the recognition of revenue, and not the payment of cash, that determines when expenses are recognized under the accrual basis of accounting.

Referring again to Krispy Kreme, assume that the company pays cash to acquire baking materials for its donuts. A cash purchase of raw materials is not considered to be a business expense until Krispy Kreme sells the donuts that it produces. The cash payment for baking materials precedes the revenue recognition. But what happens if the materials are purchased on account and used in sold donuts prior to being paid for? In this case, the accrual basis of accounting dictates the recognition of the expense prior to the cash payment for the materials so that the expense is properly matched with the earned revenue in the same accounting period.

| | Concept | → | Method | → | Assessment |
|---|---|---|---|---|---|
| TAKEAWAY 4.2 | When should expenses be recognized? | | Understand the nature of the company's earning process.<br><br>Expenses should be recognized with the related revenue in the same accounting period. | | Early recognition of expenses overstates current period expenses; recognizing expenses too late understates current period expenses. |

# ADJUSTING ACCOUNTS

LEARNING OBJECTIVE 2

**Describe** the adjusting process and **illustrate** the four major types of adjusting entries.

In Chapter 3, we analyzed a series of accounting transactions for WebWork, Inc., that occurred during the month of December. We prepared journal entries for those transactions and recorded them in the general journal. We then posted the company's journal entry data to the appropriate general ledger, which we set up in T-account form. Many of the general ledger account balances from Chapter 3, however, require an end-of-period adjustment to bring them to the correct balance for the preparation of WebWork's financial statements. For example, WebWork prepaid six months of rent for its office space on December 1. By December 31, one month's rent has expired, and thus, the prepaid rent account must be adjusted so that the account balance reflects the remaining amount of rent that is still prepaid. When it is time to prepare a company's financial statements, the company must review account balances and make any necessary end-of-period adjustments to bring those (unadjusted) accounts to their proper balance.

## UNADJUSTED TRIAL BALANCE

The end-of-period adjustment process begins with the preparation of a trial balance of all general ledger accounts. Because this trial balance reports the account balances before any adjustments have been made, it is referred to as the **unadjusted trial balance**. An unadjusted trial balance is prepared to insure that the general ledger is in balance before the end-of-period adjusting process begins. Accumulating all general ledger account balances in one location makes it easier to review the accounts and determine which account balances must be adjusted. The unadjusted trial balance of WebWork, Inc., as of December 31 is in Exhibit 4-1.

| EXHIBIT 4-1 | The Unadjusted Trial Balance for WebWork, Inc. | | |
|---|---|---|---|
| | **WEBWORK, INC.**<br>**Unadjusted Trial Balance**<br>**December 31, 2011** | | |
| | | **Debit** | **Credit** |
| Cash | | $40,590 | |
| Accounts receivable | | 1,340 | |
| Office supplies | | 2,850 | |
| Prepaid rent | | 10,800 | |
| Office equipment | | 32,400 | |
| Accounts payable | | | $ 2,850 |
| Unearned revenue | | | 3,000 |
| Notes payable | | | 36,000 |
| Common stock | | | 30,000 |
| Dividends | | 500 | |
| Fees revenue | | | 18,250 |
| Wage expense | | 1,620 | |
| Totals | | $90,100 | $90,100 |

## TYPES OF ADJUSTMENTS

There are four types of accounting adjustments made at the end of an accounting period:

1. **Prepaid Expenses** Allocating previously recorded assets to expenses, to reflect the proper expenses incurred during that period.

2. **Unearned Revenues** Allocating previously recorded unearned revenue to earned revenue, to reflect revenues earned during the period.

3. **Accrued Expenses** Recording operating expenses that have not yet been paid or recorded, to reflect expenses incurred during the period.

4. **Accrued Revenues** Recording revenues that have not yet been received or recorded, to reflect revenue earned during the period.

Journal entries to record accounting adjustments are known as **adjusting entries**. Each adjusting entry affects one or more balance sheet accounts (an asset or liability account) and one or more income statement accounts (an expense or revenue account).

Adjustments in the first two categories—allocating "prepaid" assets to expense, and allocating "unearned" revenues to revenue—are referred to as **deferrals**. The distinguishing characteristic of a deferral is that the adjustment deals with an amount that has previously been recorded in a balance sheet account. The adjusting entry, in effect, decreases the balance sheet account and increases an income statement account. Adjustments in the last two categories—increasing expenses and increasing revenues—are referred to as **accruals**. The unique characteristic of an accrual is that the adjustment deals with an amount that has not previously been recorded in an account. Consequently, the adjusting entry increases both a balance sheet account and an income statement account.

## ALLOCATING PREVIOUSLY RECORDED ASSETS TO EXPENSES

Many expenditures benefit multiple accounting periods. These expenditures must be allocated over the periods benefited. Common examples include purchases of buildings, equipment, and supplies; prepayments of rent and advertising; and payments of insurance premiums covering more than one year. Outlays for these expenditures are normally debited to an asset account at the time of payment. Then, at the end of each accounting period, the estimated portion of the expenditure that has expired, or that has been used up, during the period is transferred from the asset account to an expense account to achieve a proper recognition of sales revenue and expenses.

These adjustments are commonly identified by inspecting the unadjusted trial balance for costs that benefit multiple accounting periods. For example, by looking at the December 31 trial balance of WebWork (Exhibit 4-1), we observe that adjustments are required to allocate costs of the purchased office supplies, the prepaid rent, and the office equipment to the current period (December) and subsequent accounting periods that benefit from these expenditures. The next three sections illustrate those adjustments.

### Office Supplies

WebWork purchased office supplies on account and recorded the expenditure in an asset account, Office Supplies, as follows:

| Dec. 1 | Office supplies | 2,850 | |
| |     Accounts payable | | 2,850 |
| | *To record the purchase of office supplies.* | | |

| A | = | L | + | SE |
|---|---|---|---|---|
| +2,850 | | + 2,850 | | |

During December, office supplies were used up as services were provided. The cost of office supplies used is an expense for December that reduces the amount of supplies available. It is unnecessary to record an expense as each individual supply item, such as a copier cartridge or LCD cleaner, is used up. Instead, at the end of December, the company physically counts the supplies still available and then subtracts that amount from the total amount purchased to determine the amount used up. For example, assume that a physical count of the office supplies reveals that $1,530 worth of WebWork's office supplies are available at the end of the month. This implies that $1,320 ($2,850 − $1,530) worth of supplies were used up during December. An adjusting entry is needed to transfer this amount to an expense account, Supplies Expense, as follows:

| Dec. 31 | Supplies expense | 1,320 | |
| | Office supplies | | 1,320 |
| | *To record expense of office supplies used in December.* | | |

When this adjusting entry is posted, it properly shows the $1,320 December expense for office supplies and reduces the asset account, Office Supplies, to $1,530, the actual amount of the asset remaining as of December 31.

## Prepaid Rent

On December 1, WebWork paid six months' rent in advance and debited the $10,800 payment to Prepaid Rent, an asset account. As each day passes and the rented space is occupied, rent expense is being incurred, and the balance of the prepaid rent is decreasing. It is unnecessary to record rent expense on a daily basis because financial statements are not prepared daily; however, at the end of the accounting period, an adjusting entry is necessary to recognize the correct amount of rent expense for the period and to decrease the Prepaid Rent account. Specifically, on December 31, one month of WebWork's prepaid rent has been used up; consequently, WebWork will transfer $1,800 ($10,800/6 months) from the Prepaid Rent account to the Rent Expense account, as follows:

| Dec. 31 | Rent expense | 1,800 | |
| | Prepaid rent | | 1,800 |
| | *To record rent expense for December.* | | |

The posting of this adjusting entry shows the correct rent expense ($1,800) for December in the Rent Expense account and reduces the Prepaid Rent account balance to the correct balance ($9,000) that remains prepaid as of December 31. (Examples of other prepaid expenses for which similar adjustments are made include prepaid insurance and prepaid advertising.)

## Depreciation

The process of allocating the cost of buildings, equipment, and vehicles to the periods benefiting from their use is called **depreciation**. Because these long-lived assets help generate revenue for a company over many years, each accounting period in which the assets are used must reflect a portion of their cost as an expense. The allocation of a company's costs in these revenue-generating assets over the many periods that they help produce revenues is an application of the expense recognition principle; and, this periodic expense is known as *depreciation expense*.

There is no exact way to measure the amount by which these assets are used up each period, which means that the periodic depreciation expense is an estimate. The procedure used in this chapter estimates the annual amount of depreciation expense by dividing the acquisition cost of the asset by its estimated useful life in years. This method is called **straight-line depreciation**. (We will explore other depreciation methods in a later chapter.)

When recording depreciation expense, the asset account is not reduced directly. Instead, the reduction is recorded in a contra account called **Accumulated Depreciation**. The **contra accounts** are so named because they are used to record reductions in, or offsets against, a controlling account. The Accumulated Depreciation account has a normal credit balance and appears in the balance sheet as a deduction against its related asset account balance. Use of the contra account Accumulated Depreciation allows the original cost of the related asset to be reported in the company's balance sheet, followed by the accumulated amount of depreciation taken to date. Users of financial statements want to see both of these amounts so that they can estimate how much of an asset has been used up and how much remains to benefit the business in future periods.

**Hint:** A contra account is increased and decreased in the opposite way of its controlling account. Also, the normal balance of a contra account is opposite to the normal balance of its controlling account.

To illustrate, assume that the office equipment purchased by WebWork for $32,400 is expected to last six years. Straight-line depreciation is $5,400 per year ($32,400/6 years), or $450 per month ($5,400/12 months). At the end of December, WebWork would make the following adjusting entry:

| | | | |
|---|---|---|---|
| Dec. 31 | Depreciation expense | 450 | |
| |    Accumulated depreciation—Office equipment | | 450 |
| | *To record December depreciation.* | | |

| A | = | L | + | SE |
|---|---|---|---|---|
| −450 | | | | −450 Exp |

When the preceding adjusting entry is posted, it shows the estimated cost of using the asset during December, and shows the estimated expense ($450) in the company's December income statement. On the balance sheet, the accumulated depreciation is subtracted from the related asset account (Office Equipment). The resulting balance (acquisition cost less accumulated depreciation) is called the asset's **book value** and represents the unexpired asset cost to be applied as an expense against future periods. For example, the December 31, 2011, balance sheet shows WebWork's office equipment with a book value of $31,950, presented as follows:

**A.K.A.** Book value is also called *carrying value.*

| | |
|---|---|
| Office equipment. . . . . . . . . . . . . . . . . . . . . . . . . . . . . . . . . . . . . . . . . . . . . . . . . . . . . . . . . . | $32,400 |
| Less: Accumulated depreciation. . . . . . . . . . . . . . . . . . . . . . . . . . . . . . . . . . . . . . . . . . . . | 450 |
| Office equipment, net . . . . . . . . . . . . . . . . . . . . . . . . . . . . . . . . . . . . . . . . . . . . . . . . . . . . | $31,950 |

## ALLOCATING PREVIOUSLY RECORDED UNEARNED REVENUE TO REVENUE

Sometimes a business receives fees for services or products before the services or products are rendered. Such transactions are initially recorded by debiting the Cash account and crediting a liability account called **Unearned Revenue**. The Unearned Revenue account is also called **Deferred Revenue** and represents an obligation to perform a service, or provide a product, in the future. Once the service or product is provided, the revenue is earned; and, this is recognized in the accounts by an adjusting entry with a debit to the Unearned Revenue account, which reduces the liability account, and a credit to the Revenue account for the amount of revenue earned in the current period.

### Deferred Service Revenue

On December 5, WebWork signed a four-month contract to perform work for $750 per month, with the entire contract price of $3,000 received in advance. The journal entry made on December 5 was:

| | | | |
|---|---|---|---|
| Dec. 5 | Cash | 3,000 | |
| |    Unearned revenue | | 3,000 |
| | *Received $3,000 advance payment on a four-month contract.* | | |

| A | = | L | + | SE |
|---|---|---|---|---|
| +3,000 | | +3,000 | | |

On December 31, the following adjusting entry transfers $750, the revenue earned in December, to Fees Revenue and it reduces the liability Unearned Revenue by the same amount:

| | | | |
|---|---|---|---|
| Dec. 31 | Unearned revenue | 750 | |
| |    Fees revenue | | 750 |
| | *To record portion of advance earned in December.* | | |

| A | = | L | + | SE |
|---|---|---|---|---|
| | | −750 | | +750 Rev. |

After the journal entry is posted to the general ledger accounts, the liability account shows a balance of $2,250, the amount of future services still owed by WebWork and the Fees Revenue account reflects the $750 earned in December.

Other examples of revenues received in advance include rental prepayments by real estate management companies, insurance premiums received in advance by insurance companies, subscription revenues received in advance by magazine and newspaper publishers, and membership fees received in advance by health and fitness clubs. In each case, a liability account is established when the prepayment is initially received. Later, an adjusting entry is made to reflect the revenues earned from the services provided or products delivered during the current accounting period.

### RECORDING PREVIOUSLY UNRECORDED EXPENSES

A company often incurs expenses before paying for them. Employee wages, utilities, and income taxes are all examples of expenses that are typically incurred by a business before payment is made. Usually the cash payments are made at regular time intervals, such as weekly, monthly, quarterly, or annually. If the accounting period ends on a date that does not coincide with a scheduled cash payment date, an adjusting entry must be recorded to reflect the expense incurred during the period. Such expenses are referred to as **accrued expenses**. WebWork has two such adjustments to make on December 31: for its employee wages and the interest on its bank loan.

### Accrued Wages

WebWork's employee is paid every two weeks at the rate of $810 per week. The employee was paid $1,620 on Friday, December 23. At the close of business on Friday, December 30, the employee has worked one week during December for which wages are not paid until January. Because the employee's wages are $810 per week, an additional wage expense of $810 must be reflected in WebWork's income statement for December. The adjusting entry at the end of December to accrue one week of wage expense follows:

| A | = | L | + | SE |
|---|---|---|---|---|
| | | +810 | | −810 Exp |

| Dec. 31 | Wage expense | 810 | |
| | Wages payable | | 810 |
| | *To record accrued wages for the final week of December.* | | |

This adjustment enables WebWork's December income statement to show the cost of all wages *incurred* during the month rather than just the wages *paid*. Also, its balance sheet will correctly show a liability for unpaid wages at the end of December.

When the employee is paid on the next regular payday in January, WebWork must insure that the one week of accrued wages for December are not again charged to expense. When the employee is paid $1,620 on Friday, January 6, the following entry is made:

| A | = | L | + | SE |
|---|---|---|---|---|
| −1,620 | | −810 | | −810 Exp. |

| Jan. 6 | Wages payable | 810 | |
| | Wage expense | 810 | |
| | Cash | | 1,620 |
| | *To record two weeks wages paid.* | | |

This entry eliminates the liability recorded in Wages Payable at the end of December and debits January Wage Expense for only those wages earned by the employee in January.

### Accrued Interest

On December 1, 2011, WebWork obtained a bank loan in the amount of $36,000 and signed a two-year note payable. The annual interest rate on the note is 10 percent, with interest payable each November 30. The first year's interest of $3,600 ($36,000 × 10 percent) is due on November 30, 2012. Because interest accumulates as time passes, an adjusting entry is needed on December 31, 2011, to reflect the interest expense for December. December's interest is $300 ($3,600/12 months), and the adjusting entry at December 31 follows:

| A | = | L | + | SE |
|---|---|---|---|---|
| | | +300 | | −300 Exp |

| Dec. 31 | Interest expense | 300 | |
| | Interest payable | | 300 |
| | *To record accrued interest expense for December.* | | |

When this adjusting entry is posted to the general ledger, the correct interest expense for December is shown as well as a liability for one month's interest that has accrued as of December 31.

When the first year's interest of $3,600 is paid on November 30, 2012, WebWork must remember that $300 of that amount relates to 2011. On November 30, 2012, the following entry records the interest payment:

| A | = | L | + | SE |
|---|---|---|---|---|
| −3,600 | | −300 | | −3,300 Exp. |

| Nov. 30 | Interest payable | 300 | |
| | Interest expense | 3,300 | |
| | Cash | | 3,600 |
| | *To record payment of annual interest.* | | |

This entry eliminates the interest payable that was accrued on December 31, 2011, and debits the Interest Expense account for $3,300 ($300 times 11 months), the correct interest expense for the first 11 months of 2012.

## RECORDING PREVIOUSLY UNRECORDED REVENUES

Revenues from selling a product or providing a service must be recognized in the period in which the goods are sold or the services are performed. A company, however, may provide services during a period that are neither paid for by customers nor billed at the end of the period. The value of these services represents revenue that must be included in the current period income statement. To accomplish this, end-of-period adjusting entries are made to reflect any revenues for the period that have been earned, but have not yet been paid or billed. Such accumulated revenue is often called **accrued revenue**.

### Accrued Fees

WebWork entered into a contract with a local company on December 2 that requires a December 31 adjusting entry to accrue revenue. Under the one-year contract, WebWork agreed to maintain that company's Website in exchange for a monthly fee of $150, payable at the end of every three months. By December 31, WebWork has earned one month of Fees revenue, and the following adjusting entry is made:

| Dec. 31 | Accounts receivable | 150 | |
| | Fees revenue | | 150 |
| | *To record accrued fees revenue earned in December.* | | |

| A | = | L | + | SE |
|---|---|---|---|---|
| +150 | | | | +150 Rev. |

When WebWork receives the first $450 payment on February 28, 2012, the company must remember that $150 was previously earned and recorded in 2011. The following entry records the payment received on that date:

| Feb. 28 | Cash | 450 | |
| | Accounts receivable | | 150 |
| | Fees revenue | | 300 |
| | *To record receipt of quarterly payment.* | | |

| A | = | L | + | SE |
|---|---|---|---|---|
| +450 | | | | +300 Rev. |
| −150 | | | | |

This entry eliminates the accounts receivable established on December 31, 2011, and records $300 of fees revenue earned for the first two months of 2012.

### Accrued Interest

Another example of accrued revenue involves a company that has loaned money to another entity on which interest has been earned but that has not yet been collected at the end of the accounting period. The amount of the earned interest must be reflected in net income for the period. In this situation, the following adjusting entry is made:

| Dec. 31 | Interest receivable | # | |
| | Interest revenue | | # |

| A | = | L | + | SE |
|---|---|---|---|---|
| +# | | | | +# Rev. |

## SUMMARY OF ACCOUNTING ADJUSTMENTS

Exhibit 4-2 summarizes the adjusting entries for WebWork as recorded in its general journal. These adjustments are posted to the company's general ledger.

Exhibit 4-3 lists the four types of accounting adjustments along with showing (1) examples of how this type of adjustment arises, (2) the generic adjusting entry for each type of adjustment, and (3) what accounts are overstated or understated *prior to* any adjustment. As we explained, each adjustment affects one (or more) balance sheet (asset or liability) account and one (or more) income statement account (expense or revenue).

> **4.** Record $500 of accrued interest expense that applies to the company's bank loan. The $500 is part of the company's annual cash interest payment that is due next period.
>
> **The solution is on page 216.**

## PREPARING FINANCIAL STATEMENTS

**LEARNING OBJECTIVE 3**

**Explain** the adjusted trial balance and use it to prepare financial statements.

The adjusted trial balance is used to prepare the income statement, the statement of stockholders' equity, and the balance sheet. (It is also helpful in preparing the statement of cash flows; although other information is also necessary for it.) We illustrate the preparation of financial statements for WebWork in Exhibit 4-5.

## INCOME STATEMENT

The income statement presents a company's revenues and expenses and discloses whether the company operated at a profit or a loss. WebWork's adjusted trial balance contains one revenue account and five expense accounts. The revenue and expense accounts are reported in WebWork's income statement located in the lower right side of Exhibit 4-5. As shown in this income statement, its net income for December is $12,850.

## STATEMENT OF STOCKHOLDERS' EQUITY

The statement of stockholders' equity reports the transactions and events causing a company's stockholders' equity to increase or decrease during an accounting period. The middle right side of Exhibit 4-5 presents WebWork's statement of stockholders' equity for December. The stockholders' equity accounts in the general ledger provides some of the information for this statement: the common stock and retained earnings balances at the beginning of the period, new common stock issuances, and dividends during the period. Since December was the first month of operations for WebWork, the beginning retained earnings balance is zero. The net income (or net loss) amount is obtained from the company's income statement.

## BALANCE SHEET

The balance sheet reports a company's assets, liabilities, and stockholders' equity. The assets and liabilities for WebWork as of December 31, 2011, shown in the upper right side of Exhibit 4-5, come from the adjusted trial balance. The $12,350 amount reported as retained earnings is taken from the statement of stockholders' equity as of December 31.

---

**PRINCIPLE ALERT**    **Accounting Period Concept**

The income statement, the statement of stockholders' equity, and the statement of cash flows are financial statements covering periods of time. These statements illustrate the *accounting period concept;* the concept that useful financial statements can be prepared for arbitrary time periods within a company's total life span. Since a company does not complete all of its transactions by the end of an accounting period, accounting principles must provide a process to account for a company's continuing transactions. The end-of-period adjusting procedures provided by the accrual basis of accounting are that process. A major purpose of adjusting entries is to ensure that correct amounts of revenue and expense are reported for each accounting period.

---

## STATEMENT OF CASH FLOWS

The statement of cash flows reports information regarding a company's cash inflows and outflows. The statement of cash flows classifies cash flows into three activity categories: operating, investing, and financing. The procedures for preparing a statement of cash flows are discussed in a future chapter. WebWork's statement of cash flows for December

**EXHIBIT 4-5** | **Financial Statements Prepared From the Adjusted Trial Balance**

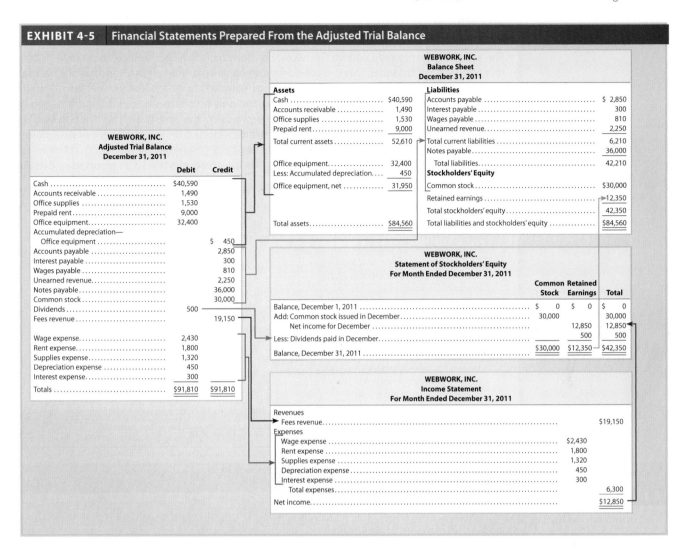

is presented in Exhibit 4-6, and reveals that its operating cash flows were $7,490, its investing cash flows were $(32,400), and its financing cash flows were $65,500. The statement also reveals that its cash balance increased by $40,590 during December.

**EXHIBIT 4-6** | **Statement of Cash Flows**

**WEBWORK, INC.**
**Statement of Cash Flows**
**For Month Ended December 31, 2011**

| | | |
|---|---|---|
| **Cash Flows from Operating Activities** | | |
| Cash received from clients............................................... | $19,910 | |
| Cash paid to employees .................................................... | (1,620) | |
| Cash paid for rent ........................................................... | (10,800) | |
| Cash provided by operating activities................................ | | $ 7,490 |
| **Cash Flows from Investing Activities** | | |
| Purchase of furniture and equipment ................................ | | (32,400) |
| **Cash Flows from Financing Activities** | | |
| Stock issued ................................................................... | 30,000 | |
| Borrowing from bank........................................................ | 36,000 | |
| Cash dividends................................................................. | (500) | |
| Cash provided by financing activities ................................ | | 65,500 |
| Net increase in cash ........................................................ | | 40,590 |
| Cash at December 1, 2011 ................................................ | | 0 |
| Cash at December 31, 2011 .............................................. | | $40,590 |

**ACCOUNTING IN PRACTICE** **Spotlight on Cash**

The adjusting entries prepared for WebWork are used to bring its account balances to their correct accrual-basis balances. This is required for companies that follow GAAP and use the accrual basis to prepare financial statements. By way of contrast, some smaller businesses maintain their records using the cash basis of accounting and only record those accounting transactions that involve cash inflows or outflows. For businesses using the cash basis, their "net income" is equivalent to the cash flow from operating activities reported on the statement of cash flows. The following table illustrates how WebWork's net cash generated by operating activities of $7,490 in Exhibit 4-6 differs from the company's net income of $12,850 as reported in Exhibit 4-5 using the accrual basis.

| | Net cash used by operating activities | Net income |
|---|---|---|
| Payment of rent .............................................. | $(10,800) | $ 0 |
| Advance payment from customers .......................... | 3,000 | 0 |
| Customer payment for services ............................. | 13,510 | 13,510 |
| Payment of wages ........................................... | (1,620) | (1,620) |
| Customer payment from amount on account ................ | 2,400 | 0 |
| Customer partial payment for services ..................... | 1,000 | 4,740 |
| Use of supplies ............................................. | 0 | (1,320) |
| Recognition of rent ......................................... | 0 | (1,800) |
| Depreciation ................................................ | 0 | (450) |
| Recognition of fees earned ................................. | 0 | 900 |
| Wages incurred, but not paid .............................. | 0 | (810) |
| Interest incurred, but not paid ............................. | 0 | (300) |
| Totals ...................................................... | $ 7,490 | $12,850 |

**Your Turn!** **4.2**

Cassi Company prepared the following adjusted trial balance to assist in the preparation of its December 31, 2011, financial statements.

| CASSI COMPANY Adjusted Trial Balance December 31, 2011 | | |
|---|---|---|
| | **Debit** | **Credit** |
| Cash ........................................................ | $ 4,000 | |
| Accounts receivable ....................................... | 15,000 | |
| Inventory .................................................. | 18,000 | |
| Prepaid rent ............................................... | 5,000 | |
| Equipment ................................................. | 50,000 | |
| Accumulated depreciation ................................. | | $ 10,000 |
| Accounts payable .......................................... | | 8,000 |
| Salaries payable ........................................... | | 9,000 |
| Dividends payable .......................................... | | 2,000 |
| Unearned revenue .......................................... | | 5,000 |
| Long-term debt ............................................ | | 35,000 |
| Common stock ............................................. | | 15,000 |
| Retained earnings .......................................... | | 5,000 |
| Sales revenue .............................................. | | 52,000 |
| Cost of goods sold ......................................... | 30,000 | |
| Salaries expense ........................................... | 5,000 | |
| Rent expense ............................................... | 6,000 | |
| Depreciation expense ...................................... | 6,000 | |
| Dividends .................................................. | 2,000 | |
| Totals ...................................................... | $141,000 | $141,000 |

**Required**
Prepare an income statement, a statement of stockholders' equity, and a balance sheet for Cassi Company using its December 31, 2011, adjusted trial balance. There were no changes in stockholders' equity during the year other than for net income and dividends.

**The solution is on page 217.**

*The following section illustrates the closing process using the Income Summary account. Appendix 4A presents an alternative process that closes temporary accounts directly to Retained Earnings. Your instructor can choose to cover either one or both processes. If the process using the Income Summary account is skipped, then read Appendix 4A and return to the section (four pages ahead) titled, "Quality of Accounting Numbers."*

## CLOSING PROCESS

All accounts can be identified as either permanent accounts or temporary accounts. **Permanent accounts** are the accounts presented on the balance sheet. They consist of the asset, liability, and stockholders' equity accounts. The distinguishing feature of a permanent account is that any balance in the account at the end of an accounting period is carried forward to the following accounting period. **Temporary accounts** are used to gather information for a particular accounting period. Revenue, expense, and dividend accounts are temporary subdivisions of stockholders' equity. At the end of the accounting period, temporary account balances are transferred to retained earnings, which is a permanent stockholders' equity account. The process of transferring the balances in temporary accounts to retained earnings is referred to as the **closing process** or **closing procedures**.

A temporary account is *closed* when an entry is made that changes its account balance to zero—that is, the entry is equal in amount to the account's ending balance but is opposite to the balance as a debit or credit. An account that is closed is said to be closed *to* the account that receives the offsetting debit or credit. Thus, a closing entry simply transfers the balance of one account to another account. Because closing entries bring temporary account balances to zero, the temporary accounts are then ready to start accumulating data for the next accounting period. In essence, closing the temporary accounts prevents information from the current accounting period from being carried forward to a subsequent period; and as a consequence, enables financial statement users to make meaningful comparisons of revenue and expenses from one period to the next. The following summarizes the classification of permanent and temporary accounts.

> **LEARNING OBJECTIVE 4**
>
> **Describe** the closing process and **summarize** the accounting cycle.

> **A.K.A.** Closing procedures are also known as *closing the books*.

| Permanent Accounts | Temporary Accounts |
|---|---|
| Assets | Revenues |
| Liabilities | Expenses |
| Common Stock | Dividends |
| Retained Earnings | Income Summary |

### Your Turn! 4.3

For each of the following accounts, identify whether the account is either a permanent account or a temporary account:

*a.* Cash
*b.* Common Stock
*c.* Wage Expense
*d.* Notes Payable

*e.* Dividends
*f.* Sales Revenue
*g.* Inventory
*h.* Prepaid Expense

**The solution is on page 217.**

## JOURNALIZING AND POSTING THE CLOSING ENTRIES

A summary account is traditionally used to close the temporary revenue and expense accounts. We use an account titled Income Summary (alternative titles for this account include Revenue and Expense Summary, Income and Expense Summary, and Profit and Loss Summary). The closing entries occur only at the end of an accounting period and consist of four steps, which are graphically shown below.

1.  **Close the revenue accounts.** Debit each revenue account for an amount equal to its current credit balance, and credit the Income Summary account for the total amount of earned revenue.

2.  **Close the expense accounts.** Credit each expense account for an amount equal to its current debit balance, and debit the Income Summary account for the total amount of expenses.

After steps 1 and 2, the balance of the Income Summary account equals the current period net income (if a credit balance) or net loss (if a debit balance).

3.  **Close the Income Summary account.** In the case of net income, debit the Income Summary account and credit the Retained Earnings account for an amount equal to net income. In the case of a net loss, debit the Retained Earnings account and credit the Income Summary account for an amount equal to the net loss.

4.  **Close the Dividends account.** Debit the Retained Earnings account and credit the Dividends account for an amount equal to the balance in the Dividends account.

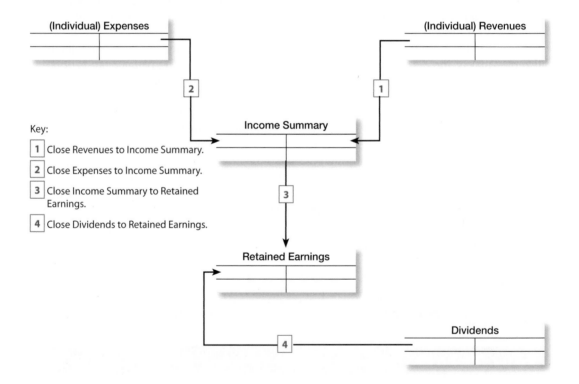

### Closing Process for WebWork

Exhibit 4-7 illustrates the closing entries for the revenue and expense accounts for WebWork as recorded in the company's general journal. The financial information in these entries is posted to the appropriate general ledger accounts, which is represented using T-accounts.

After steps 1 and 2, the Income Summary account has a credit balance equal to WebWork's net income of $12,850. Steps 3 and 4 close the Income Summary account and the Dividends account to the Retained Earnings account. These two entries are recorded

| EXHIBIT 4-7 | Closing Revenue and Expense Accounts—WebWork, Inc. | | |
|---|---|---|---|
| **GENERAL JOURNAL** | | | |
| Date | Description | Debit | Credit |
| 2011 | | | |
| Dec. 31 | Fees revenue | 19,150 | |
| |     Income summary | | 19,150 |
| |     *To close the revenue accounts.* | | |
| | | | |
| Dec. 31 | Income summary | 6,300 | |
| |     Wage expense | | 2,430 |
| |     Rent expense | | 1,800 |
| |     Supplies expense | | 1,320 |
| |     Depreciation expense | | 450 |
| |     Interest expense | | 300 |
| |     *To close the expense accounts.* | | |

in WebWork's general journal in Exhibit 4-8. The financial effect of posting these entries on the general ledger is diagrammed below.

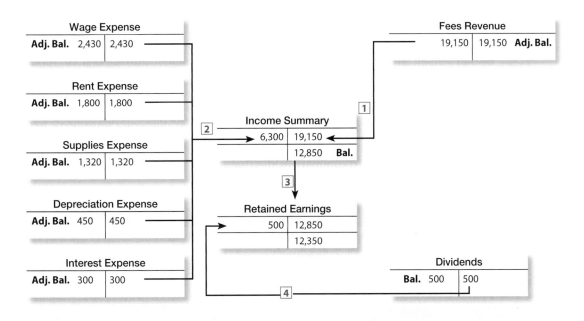

| EXHIBIT 4-8 | Closing the Income Summary and Dividends Accounts—WebWork, Inc. | | |
|---|---|---|---|
| **GENERAL JOURNAL** | | | |
| Date | Description | Debit | Credit |
| 2011 | | | |
| Dec. 31 | Income summary | 12,850 | |
| |     Retained earnings | | 12,850 |
| |     *To close the Income Summary account.* | | |
| Dec. 31 | Retained earnings | 500 | |
| |     Dividends | | 500 |
| |     *To close the Dividends account.* | | |

## Preparing the Post-Closing Trial Balance

After closing entries are recorded in the general journal and posted to the general ledger, all of the temporary accounts have zero balances. At this point a **post-closing trial balance**

**EXHIBIT 4A-1**   Closing Revenue, Expense, and Dividends Accounts—WebWork, Inc.

**GENERAL JOURNAL**

| Date | Description | Debit | Credit |
|---|---|---|---|
| 2011 | | | |
| Dec. 31 | Fees revenue | 19,150 | |
| **1** | Retained earnings | | 19,150 |
| | *To close the revenue accounts.* | | |
| Dec. 31 | Retained earnings | 6,300 | |
| | Wage expense | | 2,430 |
| | Rent expense | | 1,800 |
| **2** | Supplies expense | | 1,320 |
| | Depreciation expense | | 450 |
| | Interest expense | | 300 |
| | *To close the expense accounts.* | | |
| **3** Dec. 31 | Retained earnings | 500 | |
| | Dividends | | 500 |
| | *To close the dividends account.* | | |

## Preparing the Post-Closing Trial Balance

After closing entries are recorded in the general journal and posted to the general ledger, all of the temporary accounts have zero balances. At this point a **post-closing trial balance** is prepared. The post-closing trial balance provides evidence that an equality of debits and credits has been maintained in the general ledger throughout the adjusting and closing processes, and that the general ledger is in balance to start the next accounting period. Because the temporary accounts have been closed, only the balance sheet (or permanent) accounts appear in the post-closing trial balance. Exhibit 4A-2 presents the post-closing trial balance for WebWork.

**EXHIBIT 4A-2**   Post-Closing Trial Balance for WebWork, Inc.

**WEBWORK, INC.**
**Post-Closing Trial Balance**
**December 31, 2011**

| | Debit | Credit |
|---|---|---|
| Cash | $40,590 | |
| Accounts receivable | 1,490 | |
| Office supplies | 1,530 | |
| Prepaid rent | 9,000 | |
| Office equipment | 32,400 | |
| Accumulated depreciation—Office equipment | | $    450 |
| Accounts payable | | 2,850 |
| Interest payable | | 300 |
| Wages payable | | 810 |
| Unearned revenue | | 2,250 |
| Notes payable | | 36,000 |
| Common stock | | 30,000 |
| Retained earnings | | 12,350 |
| Totals | $85,010 | $85,010 |

## Summary of the Accounting Cycle

The sequence of accounting procedures known as the *accounting cycle* occurs each fiscal period and represents a systematic process for accumulating and reporting the financial data of a business. Exhibit 4A-3 summarizes the five major steps in the accounting cycle as described in this and the preceding chapter.

**EXHIBIT 4A-3**   The Accounting Cycle: A Summary

| **Analyze** Analyze transactions from source documents | → | **Record** Journalize transactions and prepare unadjusted trial balance | → | **Adjust** Journalize adjusting entries and prepare adjusted trial balance | → | **Report** Prepare financial statements | → | **Close** Journalize closing entries and prepare post-closing trial balance |

## Your Turn!                                              4A.2

Prior to closing its books, the Morgan Company has the following balances in its temporary accounts as of December 31.

|  | Debit | Credit |
| --- | --- | --- |
| Sales revenue | | 79,000 |
| Cost of goods sold | 41,000 | |
| Wage expense | 22,000 | |
| Rent expense | 3,000 | |
| Depreciation expense | 2,000 | |
| Interest expense | 4,000 | |
| Dividends | 5,000 | |

**Required**
Prepare closing entries as of December 31 for the Morgan Company.

**The solution is on page 218.**

# APPENDIX 4B: Using a Worksheet

A worksheet can be used to facilitate the adjusting and closing processes, and ultimately, the preparation of a company's financial statements. A **worksheet** is an informal document that helps accumulate the accounting information needed to prepare the financial statements. A worksheet is a tool; it is not part of a company's formal accounting records. In this section, we explain how a worksheet can be used to help compile information for a set of financial statements. Computer programs such as Microsoft Excel can simplify the preparation of a worksheet.

## PREPARING A WORKSHEET

A worksheet is prepared at that stage in the accounting cycle when it is time to adjust the accounts and prepare the financial statements. The basic structure of a worksheet is illustrated in Exhibit 4B-1, which includes an explanation of the format used. The worksheet is prepared in the order indicated by the red colored numbers in the exhibit.

**1 Heading**   The worksheet *heading* includes (1) the name of the entity, (2) the term *Worksheet* to indicate the type of analysis being performed, and (3) a date describing the period covered. The worksheet includes both income statement data (for the period described) and balance sheet data (for the end of the period described). Exhibit 4B-2 illustrates the heading for WebWork's worksheet. The worksheet

**APPENDIX 4B**

**EXHIBIT 4B-1**

| | | | 1 | | | | | | |
|---|---|---|---|---|---|---|---|---|---|
| | | | **(HEADING FOR WORKSHEET)** | | | | | | |
| | **Unadjusted Trial Balance** | | **Adjustments** | | **Adjusted Trial Balance** | | **Income Statement** | | **Balance Sheet** |
| **Description** | **Debit** | **Credit** | **Debit** | **Credit** | **Debit** | **Credit** | **Debit** | **Credit** | **Debit** | **Credit** |

2
Unadjusted trial balance

3
Adjustment amounts

4
Adjusted account balances

5
Classify adjusted balances into either the income statement or balance sheet columns

Accounts that arise for adjustments

6 Balancing of columns for each statement

has a description column and 10 amount (monetary) columns. A set of Debit and Credit columns is provided for each of the five headings: Unadjusted Trial Balance, Adjustments, Adjusted Trial Balance, Income Statement, and Balance Sheet.

**2 Unadjusted Trial Balance** The unadjusted trial balance is the starting point for the accounting analysis on the worksheet. It is entered in the worksheet's Description column and the first pair of monetary columns. Once the trial balance is entered in the worksheet and double-ruled, it reflects the general ledger at the time the worksheet is prepared. Exhibit 4B-2 shows the worksheet placement of WebWork's unadjusted trial balance as of December 31, 2011.

**3 Adjustments** *When a worksheet is used, all adjustments are first entered on the worksheet.* This procedure permits the adjustments to be reviewed for completeness and accuracy. To adjust accounts already appearing in the unadjusted trial balance, we simply enter the amounts in the appropriate side (debit or credit) of the Adjustments columns on the lines containing the accounts. When accounts not appearing in the unadjusted trial balance require adjustment, their titles are listed as needed in the Description column below the accounts already listed. Adjustments entered on the worksheet are not yet journalized; journalizing the adjustments occurs later. The adjustments recorded on WebWork's worksheet in Exhibit 4B-2 are identical to those illustrated in the chapter (see Exhibit 4-2). After recording all the adjusting entries on the worksheet, we total the adjustments columns to verify that the sum of the debit entries equals the sum of the credit entries.

**4 Adjusted Trial Balance** Once the adjustments have been entered on the worksheet, there is sufficient information available to complete an adjusted trial balance. The adjusted figures are determined by combining horizontally, line by line, the amounts in the first four money columns—that is, the unadjusted trial balance and the adjustments. We review the calculations for two lines of Exhibit 4B-2 to illustrate this process. The first line shows the Cash account with a debit amount of $40,590 in the unadjusted trial balance. Because Cash is not affected by any of the adjustments, the $40,590 appears in the Debit column of the adjusted trial balance. On the third line, the Office Supplies account begins with a debit of $2,850 in the unadjusted trial balance and then shows a credit of $1,320 in the Adjustments column. The $1,320 credit is subtracted from the $2,850 debit, and the remaining $1,530 is shown as a debit in the adjusted trial balance.

After calculating the adjusted trial balance amounts for all accounts on the worksheet, we total the two columns of the adjusted trial balance to verify that they are equal and that our worksheet is in balance.

**EXHIBIT 4B-2**

**WEBWORK, INC.**
**Worksheet**
**For Month Ended December 31, 2011**

| | Unadjusted Trial Balance | | Adjustments | | Adjusted Trial Balance | | Income Statement | | Balance Sheet | |
| --- | --- | --- | --- | --- | --- | --- | --- | --- | --- | --- |
| | Debit | Credit | Debit | Credit | Debit | Credit | Debit | Credit | Debit | Credit |
| Cash .............................. | $40,590 | | | | $40,590 | | | | $40,590 | |
| Accounts receivable ............... | 1,340 | | (g) $ 150 | | 1,490 | | | | 1,490 | |
| Office supplies .................... | 2,850 | | | (a) $1,320 | 1,530 | | | | 1,530 | |
| Prepaid rent...................... | 10,800 | | | (b) 1,800 | 9,000 | | | | 9,000 | |
| Office equipment.................. | 32,400 | | | | 32,400 | | | | 32,400 | |
| Accumulated depreciation— | | | | | | | | | | |
|   Office equipment ............... | | | | (c) 450 | | $ 450 | | | | 450 |
| Accounts payable ................. | | $ 2,850 | | | | 2,850 | | | | 2,850 |
| Interest payable ................... | | | | (f) 300 | | 300 | | | | 300 |
| Wages payable .................... | | | | (e) 810 | | 810 | | | | 810 |
| Unearned revenue................. | | 3,000 | (d) 750 | | | 2,250 | | | | 2,250 |
| Notes payable..................... | | 36,000 | | | | 36,000 | | | | 36,000 |
| Common stock .................... | | 30,000 | | | | 30,000 | | | | 30,000 |
| Dividends ........................ | 500 | | | | 500 | | | | 500 | |
| Fees revenue ..................... | | 18,250 | | (d) 750 | | 19,150 | | 19,150 | | |
| | | | | (g) 150 | | | | | | |
| Rent expense...................... | | | (b) 1,800 | | 1,800 | | 1,800 | | | |
| Wage expense..................... | 1,620 | | (e) 810 | | 2,430 | | 2,430 | | | |
| Supplies expense.................. | | | (a) 1,320 | | 1,320 | | 1,320 | | | |
| Depreciation expense ............. | | | (c) 450 | | 450 | | 450 | | | |
| Interest expense................... | | | (f) 300 | | 300 | | 300 | | | |
|   Totals......................... | $90,100 | $90,100 | $5,580 | $5,580 | $91,810 | $91,810 | 6,300 | 19,150 | 85,510 | 72,660 |
| Net income....................... | | | | | | | 12,850 | | | 12,850 |
|   Totals......................... | | | | | | | $19,150 | $19,150 | $85,510 | $85,510 |

**5 Extension of the Adjusted Trial Balance**   The amounts in the Adjusted Trial Balance columns are extended into the two remaining pairs of columns as follows:

| | |
| --- | --- |
| Expenses | → Debit column of income statement |
| Revenues | → Credit column of income statement |
| Assets and cash dividends | → Debit column of balance sheet |
| Liabilities, Common Stock, Retained Earnings, and contra assets | → Credit column of balance sheet |

Expense and revenue account balances are extended to the Income Statement columns because these accounts will be used to prepare the income statement. Similarly, asset, contra asset, liability, and stockholders' equity accounts are balance sheet accounts, so their balances are extended to the Balance Sheet columns. In addition, the Dividends debit balance is extended to the Balance Sheet Debit column, and the credit balances in the Common Stock and Retained Earnings accounts are extended to the Balance Sheet Credit column. Exhibit 4B-2 shows the extension of WebWork's adjusted trial balance to the worksheet's Income Statement and Balance Sheet columns. Once the proper extensions are made, the worksheet is complete except for balancing the two pairs of statement columns containing the adjusted balances.

**6 Balancing the Worksheet**   The first step in balancing is to add each of the Income Statement and Balance Sheet columns and record their respective totals on the same line as the totals of the Adjusted Trial Balance columns. The difference between the total debits and total credits in the Income Statement columns is the difference between total revenues and total expenses—that is, the net income or net loss for the period. The net income or net loss must be the amount by which the Debit and Credit columns for the balance sheet differ. This is true because the Retained Earnings account balance, as extended, does not yet reflect the net income or net loss for the current period.

When revenues exceed expenses, we balance the two pairs of statement columns by adding the net income figure to both the Debit column of the income statement and the Credit column of the balance sheet. Exhibit 4B-2 illustrates this balancing situation with WebWork's net income for December of $12,850. If expenses exceed revenues, we add the amount of net loss to the Credit column of the income statement and to the Debit column of the balance sheet. After we have added the net income (or loss) to the proper columns, we total and double-rule the four columns. The worksheet is now complete.

A completed worksheet aids in the last three steps of the accounting cycle—adjust, report, and close.

*Adjust:* The adjusting entries to be journalized and posted can be taken from the information in the Adjustments columns. Because adjustments have first been entered on the worksheet, they can be reviewed for their financial effects before being journalized. Thus, the likelihood of incorrect adjustments appearing in the formal accounting records is reduced.

*Report:* The income statement can be prepared from the data in the Income Statement columns. Two pieces of information for the statement of stockholders' equity are available in the worksheet—the net income (or net loss) and dividends. The assets and liabilities needed for the balance sheet are available in the Balance Sheet columns (the ending Common Stock balance for the balance sheet is obtained from the statement of stockholders' equity).

*Close:* The closing entries to be journalized and posted can be prepared from data in the worksheet because it displays all of the temporary account balances. The revenue and expense account balances are shown in the Income Statement columns and the cash dividends account balance is shown in the Balance Sheet Debit column.

## SUMMARY OF LEARNING OBJECTIVES

**LO1** **Explain the accrual basis of accounting and contrast it with the cash basis with reference to revenue and expense recognition. (p. 160)**

- Revenue is recognized on an accrual basis at the time that it is earned. This may be prior to the receipt of cash, at the same time as the receipt of cash, or following the receipt of cash.
- Expenses are matched against revenues in the same accounting period that the associated revenue is recognized. This may be prior to cash payment, at the same time as cash payment, or following cash payment.
- Revenue recognition and the corresponding matching of expenses may differ in timing on an accrual basis versus on a cash basis.

**LO2** **Describe the adjusting process and illustrate the four major types of adjusting entries. (p. 162)**

- Adjusting entries are made to achieve the appropriate recognition of revenues and matching of expenses with revenues, and consist of four general types of adjustments:
  1. Allocating assets to operating expenses to reflect the total expenses incurred during the period.
  2. Allocating unearned revenue received in advance to revenue to reflect revenues earned during the period.
  3. Increasing operating expenses to reflect expenses incurred during the period that have not yet been paid or recorded.
  4. Increasing revenues to reflect revenue earned during the period that has not yet been received or recorded.

**LO3** **Explain the adjusted trial balance and use it to prepare financial statements. (p. 170)**

- An income statement, statement of stockholders' equity, balance sheet, and statement of cash flows may be prepared from an adjusted trial balance and other information.
- The stockholders' equity account may need to be reviewed to obtain information regarding the beginning balances and additional capital contributions during the period for the statement of stockholders' equity.

**LO4** **Describe the closing process and summarize the accounting cycle. (p. 173)**

- *Closing the books* means closing the revenue, expense, and other temporary accounts. Revenue and expense account balances are transferred to the Income Summary account. The balances of the Income Summary account and the Dividends account are closed to the Retained Earnings account.

**LO5** **Appendix 4A: Describe the process of closing directly to Retained Earnings and summarize the accounting cycle. (p. 178)**

- *Closing the books* means closing the revenue, expense, and other temporary accounts. Revenue and expense account balances are transferred to the Retained Earnings account as is the balance in the Dividends account.

**Appendix 4B: Explain how to use a worksheet in the adjusting and closing process. (p. 181)**    LO6

A worksheet is an informal document that helps in compiling the information needed for the preparation of the financial statements. A worksheet is a tool of the accountant; it is not part of a company's formal accounting records. The worksheet consists of a heading, along with the following columns:

    *a.*   Unadjusted trial balance
    *b.*   Adjustments
    *c.*   Adjusted trial balance
    *d.*   Income statement
    *e.*   Balance sheet

A completed worksheet aids in the last three steps of the accounting cycle: adjust, report, and close.

## TAKEAWAYS: SUMMARY CHART

| Concept ⟶ | Method ⟶ | Assessment | |
|---|---|---|---|
| When should sales revenue be recognized? | Understand the nature of a company's earning process.<br><br>Record revenue when it is earned. | Early recognition of revenue overstates current period revenue; recognizing revenue too late understates current period revenue. | TAKEAWAY 4.1 |
| When should expenses be recognized? | Understand the nature of the company's earning process.<br><br>Expenses should be recognized with the related revenue in the same accounting period. | Early recognition of expenses overstates current period expenses; recognizing expenses too late understates current period expenses. | TAKEAWAY 4.2 |
| When should an adjusting entry be made? | Individual account balances and transaction details such as contracts and agreements.<br><br>Knowledge of the proper account balance is needed. Adjustments involve (1) allocating assets to expense, (2) allocating unearned revenue to revenue, (3) accruing expenses, or (4) accruing revenues. | Record an adjusting entry so that accounts are correctly reported; otherwise income and assets (and/or liabilities) are incorrectly reported. | TAKEAWAY 4.3 |

## GLOSSARY OF KEY TERMS

**Accruals** Adjustments that reflect revenues earned but not received or recorded and expenses incurred but not paid or recorded (p. 163).

**Accrued expense** An expense incurred but not yet paid; recognized with an adjusting entry (p. 166).

**Accrued revenue** Revenue earned but not yet billed or received; recognized with an adjusting entry (p. 167).

**Accumulated depreciation** The cumulative amount of depreciation expense taken in prior periods; subtracted from the related asset account (p. 164).

**Adjusted trial balance** A list of general ledger accounts and their balances prepared after all adjustments have been made (p. 169).

**Adjusting entries** Entries made at the end of an accounting period under accrual accounting to ensure the proper matching of expenses incurred with revenues earned for the period (p. 163).

**Book value** The dollar amount carried in the accounts for a particular asset. The book value of a depreciable asset is derived by deducting the contra account Accumulated Depreciation from the balance in the depreciable asset account (p. 165).

**Closing process** A step in the accounting cycle in which the balances of all temporary accounts are transferred to the Retained Earnings account, leaving the temporary accounts with zero balances (pp. 173, 178).

**Contra account** An account related to, and deducted from, another account when financial statements are prepared or when book values are computed (p. 164).

**Deferrals** Adjustments that allocate various assets and revenues received in advance to the proper accounting periods as expenses and revenues (p. 163).

**Deferred revenue** A liability representing revenues received in advance; also called *unearned revenue* (p. 165).

**Depreciation** The process of allocating the cost of buildings, equipment, and vehicles to expense over the time periods benefiting from their use (p. 164).

**Earnings quality** The degree to which reported financial results reflect the actual financial condition and performance of the reporting company (p. 177).

**Permanent account** An account used to prepare the balance sheet—that is, an asset, liability, or stockholders' equity account; any balance in a permanent account at the end of an accounting period is carried forward to the following accounting period (pp. 173, 178).

**Post-closing trial balance** A list of general ledger accounts and their balances after closing entries have been recorded and posted (pp. 175, 180).

**Straight-line depreciation** A depreciation procedure that allocates uniform amounts of depreciation expense to each period of an asset's useful life (p. 164).

**Temporary account** An account used to gather information for an accounting period; revenue, expense, and dividend accounts are temporary accounts (pp. 173, 178).

**Unadjusted trial balance** A list of general ledger accounts and their balances taken before adjustments have been made (p. 162).

**Unearned revenue** A liability representing revenues received in advance; also called *deferred revenue* (p. 165).

**Worksheet** An informal accounting document used to facilitate the preparation of financial statements (p. 181).

## COMPREHENSIVE PROBLEM

Balke Laboratory began operations on July 1, 2009, and provides diagnostic services for physicians and medical clinics. The company's fiscal year ends on June 30, and the accounts are adjusted annually on this date. Balke's unadjusted trial balance as of June 30, 2011, is as follows:

| BALKE LABORATORY<br>Unadjusted Trial Balance<br>June 30, 2011 | | |
| --- | --- | --- |
| | Debit | Credit |
| Cash | $ 1,000 | |
| Accounts receivable | 9,200 | |
| Prepaid insurance | 6,000 | |
| Supplies | 31,300 | |
| Laboratory equipment | 270,000 | |
| Accumulated depreciation—Laboratory equipment | | $ 60,000 |
| Accounts payable | | 3,100 |
| Diagnostic fees received in advance | | 4,000 |
| Common stock | | 90,000 |
| Retained earnings | | 20,000 |
| Diagnostic fee revenue | | 220,400 |
| Wage expense | 58,000 | |
| Rent expense | 22,000 | |
| Totals | $397,500 | $397,500 |

The following information is also available:

1. The Prepaid Insurance account balance represents a premium paid on January 1, 2011, for two years of fire and casualty insurance coverage. Before 2011, Balke Laboratory had no insurance protection.
2. The supplies were physically counted at June 30, 2011. The count totaled $6,300.
3. All laboratory equipment was purchased on July 1, 2009. It is expected to last nine years.
4. Balke Laboratory received a $4,000 cash payment on April 1, 2011, from Boll Clinic for diagnostic services to be provided uniformly over the four months beginning April 1, 2011. Balke credited the payment to Diagnostic Fees Received in Advance. The services for April, May, and June have been provided to Boll Clinic.
5. Unpaid wages at June 30, 2011, were $600.
6. Balke Laboratory rents facilities for $2,000 per month. Because of cash flow problems, Balke was unable to pay the rent for June 2011. The landlord gave Balke permission to delay the payment until July.

### Required
Make the necessary adjusting entries as of June 30, 2011.

### Solution

| | | | |
| --- | --- | --- | --- |
| June 30 | Insurance expense | 1,500 | |
| | Prepaid insurance | | 1,500 |
| | *To record 6 months' insurance expense.* | | |
| | *($6.000/4 = $1,500).* | | |
| 30 | Supplies expense | 25,000 | |
| | Supplies | | 25,000 |
| | *To record supplies expense for the year.* | | |
| | *($31,300 − $6,300 = $25,000).* | | |

| 30 | Depreciation expense—Laboratory equipment | 30,000 | |
| | Accumulated depreciation—Laboratory equipment | | 30,000 |
| | *To record depreciation for the year.* | | |
| | *($270,000/9 years = $30,000).* | | |
| 30 | Diagnostic fees received in advance | 3,000 | |
| | Diagnostic fee revenue | | 3,000 |
| | *To record portion of advance payment that has been earned.* | | |
| | *($4,000 × 3/4 = $3,000).* | | |
| 30 | Wage expense | 600 | |
| | Wages payable | | 600 |
| | *To record unpaid wages at June 30.* | | |
| 30 | Rent expense | 2,000 | |
| | Rent payable | | 2,000 |
| | *To record rent expense for June.* | | |

## SELF-STUDY QUESTIONS

(Answers to the Self-Study Questions are available at the end of the chapter.)

1. Which of the following is an example of an adjusting entry?  LO2
   a. Recording the purchase of supplies on account.
   b. Recording depreciation expense on a truck.
   c. Recording the billing of customers for services rendered.
   d. Recording the payment of wages to employees.

2. An adjusting entry to record utilities used during a month for which no bill has yet been received  LO2
   is an example of
   a. Allocating assets to expense to reflect the actual operating expenses incurred during the accounting period.
   b. Allocating revenues received in advance to revenue to reflect actual revenues earned during the accounting period.
   c. Accruing expenses to reflect expenses incurred during the accounting period that are not yet paid or recorded.
   d. Accruing revenues to reflect revenues earned during the accounting period that are not yet received or recorded.

3. Which of the following is not an example of a closing entry?  LO4
   a. Close each revenue account to the Income Summary account.
   b. Close each expense account to the Income Summary account.
   c. Close the Income Summary account to the Retained Earnings account.
   d. Close Unearned Revenue to Retained Earnings.

4. Which of the following transactions does not affect the balance sheet totals?  LO2
   a. Purchasing $500 supplies on account.
   b. Paying a $3,000 note payable.
   c. Collecting $4,000 from customers on account.
   d. Payment of an $800 dividend.

5. The beginning and ending balances of stockholders' equity for the year were $30,000 and  LO2
   $35,000, respectively. If yearly dividends totaled $3,000, what was the net income or net loss for the year?
   a. $8,000 net loss.
   b. $14,000 net income.
   c. $2,000 net income.
   d. $8,000 net income.

6. The ending balance of the Accounts Receivable account was $12,000. Services billed to  LO2
   customers for the period were $21,500, and collections on account from customers were $23,600. What was the beginning balance of Accounts Receivable?
   a. $33,500.
   b. $14,100.
   c. $9,900.
   d. $33,100.

LO2 7. Kelly Corporation received an advanced payment of $20,000 in 2010 from Rufus Company for consulting services. Kelly performed half of the consulting in 2010 and the remainder in 2011. Kelly reports using the accrual basis of accounting. How much revenue from this consulting project will Kelly report in 2010?

    *a.* $20,000.

    *b.* $10,000.

    *c.* $0.

    *d.* $15,000.

## DISCUSSION QUESTIONS

1. Why is the adjusting step of the accounting cycle necessary?

2. What four different types of adjustments are frequently necessary at the close of an accounting period? Provide an example of each type.

3. On January 1, Prepaid Insurance was debited with the cost of a two-year premium in the amount of $1,872. What adjusting entry should be made on January 31 before the January financial statements are prepared?

4. What is a contra account? What contra account is used in reporting the book value of a depreciable asset?

5. At the beginning of January, the first month of the accounting year, the Supplies account had a debit balance of $825. During January, purchases of $260 of supplies were debited to the account. Although only $630 of supplies was on hand at the end of January, the necessary adjusting entry was omitted. How will the omission affect (a) the income statement for January and (b) the balance sheet prepared as of January 31?

6. The publisher of *International View*, a monthly magazine, received two-year subscriptions totaling $9,720 on January 1. (a) What entry should be made to record the receipt of the $9,720? (b) What entry should be made at the end of January before financial statements are prepared for the month?

7. Globe Travel Agency pays an employee $475 in wages each Friday for a five-day work week ending on that day. The last Friday of January falls on January 27. What adjusting entry should be made on January 31, the fiscal year-end?

8. The Bayou Company earns interest amounting to $360 per month on its investments. The company receives the interest every six months, on December 31 and June 30. Monthly financial statements are prepared. What adjusting entry should be made on January 31?

9. Define *permanent account*. Provide an example.

10. Define *temporary account*. Provide an example.

11. Which group of accounts is closed at the end of the accounting year? Why?

12. What is the purpose of a post-closing trial balance? Which of the following accounts should not appear in the post-closing trial balance: Cash, Unearned Revenue, Dividends, Depreciation Expense, Utilities Payable, Supplies Expense, Retained Earnings?

## SHORT EXERCISES

LO4 **SE4-1.** **Steps in the Accounting Cycle**

Listed below, out of order, are the steps in an accounting cycle.

1. Prepare the unadjusted trial balance.
2. Post journal entries to general ledger accounts.
3. Analyze transactions from source documents.
4. Journalize and post adjusting entries.
5. Prepare the financial statements.
6. Record transactions in a journal.
7. Prepare the post-closing trial balance.
8. Prepare the adjusted trial balance.
9. Journalize and post closing entries.

(a) Place the numbers from the above list in the order in which the steps in the accounting cycle are performed, and (b) identify the steps in the accounting cycle that occur daily.

**SE4-2.** **Accrual Accounting** LO1

Evan Corporation provided consulting services for Kensington Company in 2010. Evan incurred costs of $60,000 associated with the consulting and billed Kensington $90,000. Evan paid $40,000 of its costs in 2010 and the remaining $20,000 in 2011. Evan received $45,000 of its billing in 2010. Kensington paid the remaining $45,000 in 2011. Evan reports on the accrual basis of accounting. How much is Evan's 2010 and 2011 profit related to the Kensington consulting?

**SE4-3.** **Adjusting Accounts** LO2

MacKenzie Enterprises includes the following accounts in its general ledger. Explain why each of these accounts may need to be adjusted.

*a.* Rent Payable
*b.* Unearned Revenue
*c.* Prepaid Subscriptions
*d.* Depreciation Expense

**SE4-4.** **Adjusting Entry for Depreciation** LO2

Cowley Company just completed its first year of operations. The December 31 equipment account has a balance of $20,000. There is no balance in the Accumulated Depreciation—Equipment account or in the Depreciation Expense account. The accountant estimates the yearly equipment depreciation to be $4,000. Prepare the required adjusting entry to record the yearly depreciation for equipment.

**SE4-5.** **Adjusting Entry for Prepaid Insurance** LO2

Cooper Inc. recorded the purchase of a three-year insurance policy on July 1 in the amount of $3,600 by debiting Prepaid Insurance and crediting Cash. Prepare the necessary December 31 year-end adjusting entry.

**SE4-6.** **Accrual Adjusting Entries** LO2

Sparky Electronics requires adjusting entries for the following items:

*a.* Salaries for employees in the amount of $2,500 have not been paid.
*b.* Interest expense of $1,200 for an outstanding note.
*c.* Work performed but not yet billed for $3,500.

**SE4-7.** **Analyze an Adjusted Trial Balance** LO2

The trial balance of Fisher Supplies contains the following balance sheet accounts that require adjustment. Identify the likely income statement account that will be used to adjust these accounts.

*a.* Prepaid Insurance
*b.* Accumulated Depreciation
*c.* Supplies
*d.* Unearned Revenue
*e.* Interest Payable

**SE4-8.** **Prepare an Income Statement from an Adjusted Trial Balance** LO3

The Century Company's adjusted trial balance contains the following balances as of December 31: Retained Earnings $8,500; Dividends $2,000; Sales $20,000; Cost of Goods Sold $8,000; Selling and Administrative Expenses $3,000; Interest Expense $1,500. Prepare an income statement for the year.

**SE4-9.** **Prepare Closing Entries** LO4

Use the data from SE4-8 to prepare the closing entries for The Century Company. The balance of $8,500 in the retained earnings account is from the beginning of the year. What is the ending retained earnings balance after posting the closing entries?

**SE4-10.** **Identify Financial Statements from Adjusted Trial Balance Accounts** LO3

Trowel Corp reports the following balances in its adjusted trial balance. Identify which financial statement each account would appear on:

*a.* Cash
*b.* Sales
*c.* Accounts Payable
*d.* Unearned Revenue
*e.* Retained Earnings
*f.* Interest Income

ASSIGNMENTS

LO5 **SE4-11. The Accounting Worksheet**

The adjusted trial balance section of Menlo Company's worksheet shows a $1,500 debit balance in utility expense. At the end of the accounting period the accounting manager accrues an additional $300 of utility expense for the last week of the period. This will result in the following amounts appearing on Menlo's worksheet for utilities expense:

a. $300 debit adjustment; $1,800 debit adjusted trial balance; $1,800 debit balance sheet

b. $300 debit adjustment; $1,800 debit adjusted trial balance; $1,800 debit income statement

c. $300 credit adjustment; $1,200 debit adjusted trial balance; $1,800 debit income statement

d. $300 credit adjustment; $1,800 debit adjusted trial balance; $1,800 debit income statement

# EXERCISES—SET A

LO2 **E4-1A. Transaction Entries and Adjusting Entries**

Deluxe Building Services offers janitorial services on both a contract basis and an hourly basis. On January 1, Deluxe collected $20,100 in advance on a six-month contract for work to be performed evenly during the next six months.

a. Provide the general journal entry on January 1 to record the receipt of $20,100 for contract work.

b. Provide the adjusting entry to be made on January 31, for the contract work done during January.

c. At January 31, a total of 30 hours of hourly rate janitor work was unbilled. The billing rate is $19 per hour. Provide the adjusting entry needed on January 31. (*Note:* The firm uses the account Fees Receivable to reflect amounts due but not yet billed.)

LO2 **E4-2A. Adjusting Entries**

Selected accounts of Ideal Properties Inc., a real estate management firm, are shown below as of January 31, before any adjusting entries have been made:

| | Debit | Credit |
|---|---|---|
| Prepaid insurance | $6,660 | |
| Supplies | 1,930 | |
| Office equipment | 5,952 | |
| Unearned rent revenue | | $ 5,250 |
| Salaries expense | 3,100 | |
| Rent revenue | | 15,000 |

Monthly financial statements are prepared. Using the following information, record in a general journal the adjusting entries necessary on January 31:

a. Prepaid Insurance represents a three-year premium paid on January 1.

b. Supplies of $850 were on hand January 31.

c. Office equipment is expected to last eight years. Depreciation is recorded monthly.

d. On January 1, the firm collected six months' rent in advance from a tenant renting space for $875 per month.

e. Accrued salaries not recorded as of January 31 are $490.

LO2 **E4-3A. Adjusting Entries**

For each of the following unrelated situations, prepare the necessary adjusting entry in general journal form:

a. Unrecorded depreciation on equipment is $610.

b. The Supplies account has a balance of $2,990. Supplies on hand at the end of the period totaled $1,100.

c. On the date for preparing financial statements, an estimated utilities expense of $390 has been incurred, but no utility bill has been received.

d. On the first day of the current month, rent for four months was paid and recorded as a $2,800 debit to Prepaid Rent and a $2,800 credit to Cash. Monthly statements are now being prepared.

e. Nine months ago, Solid Insurance Company sold a one-year policy to a customer and recorded the receipt of the premium by debiting Cash for $624 and crediting Unearned Premium Revenue for $624. No adjusting entries have been prepared during the nine-month period. Annual financial statements are now being prepared.

f. At the end of the accounting period, employee wages of $965 have been incurred but not paid.

g. At the end of the accounting period, $300 of interest has been earned but not yet received on notes receivable that are held.

**E4-4A. Statement of Stockholders' Equity**   LO3

On January 1, the credit balance of the Retained Earnings account was $48,000. The company's Common Stock account had an opening balance of $70,000, and $6,000 in new capital contributions were made during the year. On December 31, at year-end, the Dividends account had a debit balance of $9,700 before closing. After revenue and expense accounts were closed, the Income Summary account had a credit balance of $29,900. Prepare a Statement of Stockholders' Equity for Strife & Company, architectural design firm.

**E4-5A. Closing Entries**   LO4

The adjusted trial balance prepared as of December 31, for Phyllis Howell & Company, Consultant, contains the following revenue and expense accounts:

|  | Debit | Credit |
|---|---|---|
| Service fees earned................................................... |  | $80,300 |
| Rent expense......................................................... | $20,800 |  |
| Salaries expense..................................................... | 45,700 |  |
| Supplies expense..................................................... | 5,600 |  |
| Depreciation expense ............................................... | 10,200 |  |
| Retained earnings................................................... |  | 67,000 |
| Dividends............................................................ | 9,000 |  |

Prepare journal entries to close the accounts using the Income Summary account. After these entries are posted, what is the balance in the Retained Earnings account?

**E4-6A. Closing Entries**   LO5
**(Appendix 4A)**

Use the information provided in E4-5A to prepare journal entries to close the accounts directly to Retained Earnings. After these entries are posted, what is the balance in the Retained Earnings account?

**E4-7A. Closing Entries**   LO4

In the midst of closing procedures, Echo Corporation's accountant became ill and was hospitalized. You have volunteered to complete the closing of the books, and you find that all revenue and expense accounts have zero balances and that the Income Summary account has a single debit entry for $308,800 and a single credit entry for $347,400. The Dividends account has a debit balance of $18,000, and the Retained Earnings account has a credit balance of $117,000. Prepare journal entries to complete the closing procedures as of year-end.

**E4-8A. Closing Entries**   LO5
**(Appendix 4A)**

In the midst of closing procedures, Echo Corporation's accountant became ill and was hospitalized. You have volunteered to complete the closing of the books. You find that all the revenue and expense accounts have zero balances. The Dividends account has a debit balance of $18,000. The Retained Earnings account has a beginning credit balance of $117,000. Expenses total $308,500, and revenues total $347,400. Prepare journal entries to complete the closing procedures as of year-end directly to Retained Earnings. After these entries are posted, what is the balance in the Retained Earnings account?

**E4-9A. Worksheet**   LO6
**(Appendix 4B)**

Identify each of the 10 amount columns of the worksheet and indicate to which column the adjusted balance of the following accounts would be extended:

a. Accounts Receivable
b. Accumulated Depreciation
c. Dividends
d. Wages Payable
e. Depreciation Expense
f. Rent Receivable
g. Prepaid Insurance
h. Service Fees Earned
i. Common Stock
j. Retained Earnings

**ASSIGNMENTS**

**LO2** **E4-10A. Analysis of Adjusted Data**

Selected T-account balances for Coyle Company are shown below as of January 31; adjusting entries have already been posted. The firm uses a calendar-year accounting period and makes monthly adjustments.

| Supplies | | Supplies Expense | |
|---|---|---|---|
| Jan. 31 Bal. 800 | | Jan. 31 Bal. 960 | |

| Prepaid Insurance | | Insurance Expense | |
|---|---|---|---|
| Jan. 31 Bal. 574 | | Jan. 31 Bal. 82 | |

| Wages Payable | | Wages Expense | |
|---|---|---|---|
| | Bal. 500 Jan. 31 | Jan. 31 Bal. 3,200 | |

| Truck | | Accumulated Depreciation—Truck | |
|---|---|---|---|
| Jan. 31 Bal. 8,700 | | | Bal. 2,610 Jan. 31 |

a. If the amount in Supplies Expense represents the January 31 adjustment for the supplies used in January, and $620 worth of supplies were purchased during January, what was the January 1 balance of Supplies?

b. The amount in the Insurance Expense account represents the adjustment made at January 31 for January insurance expense. If the original insurance premium was for one year, what was the amount of the premium and on what date did the insurance policy start?

c. If we assume that no balance existed in Wages Payable or Wages Expense on January 1, how much cash was paid as wages during January?

d. If the truck has a useful life of five years, what is the monthly amount of depreciation expense and how many months has Coyle owned the truck?

**LO2** **E4-11A. Analysis of the Impact of Adjustments on Financial Statements**

At the end of the first month of operations, the Bradley Company's accountant prepared financial statements that showed the following amounts:

| | |
|---|---|
| Assets.............................................................................. | $60,000 |
| Liabilities........................................................................... | 20,000 |
| Stockholders' equity............................................................... | 40,000 |
| Net income........................................................................ | 9,000 |

In preparing the statements, the accountant overlooked the following items:

a. Depreciation for the month, $1,000.

b. Service revenue earned but unbilled at month-end, $1,500.

c. Employee wages earned but unpaid at month-end, $250.

Determine the correct amounts of assets, liabilities, and stockholders' equity at month-end and net income for the month.

**LO4** **E4-12A. Closing Entries**

The adjusted trial balance of the Rose Corporation, prepared as of December 31, contains the following accounts:

| | Debit | Credit |
|---|---|---|
| Service fees earned....................................................... | | $92,500 |
| Interest income............................................................ | | 2,200 |
| Salaries expense.......................................................... | $41,800 | |
| Advertising expense...................................................... | 4,300 | |
| Depreciation expense .................................................... | 8,700 | |
| Income tax expense ...................................................... | 9,900 | |
| Common stock............................................................. | | 75,000 |
| Retained earnings ........................................................ | | 57,700 |
| Cash dividends............................................................. | 15,000 | |

Prepare journal entries to close the accounts using the Income Summary account. After these entries are posted, what is the ending balance in the Retained Earnings account?

**LO5**
**(Appendix 4A)**

**E4-13A. Closing Entries**

Use the information provided in E4-12A to prepare journal entries to close the accounts directly to retained earnings. After these entries are posted, what is the balance in the Retained Earnings account?

### E4-14A. Worksheet

**LO6**
**(Appendix 4B)**

The adjusted trial balance columns of a worksheet for Bonn Corporation are shown below. The worksheet is prepared for the year ended December 31.

| | Adjusted Trial Balance | |
|---|---|---|
| | Debit | Credit |
| Cash | $ 4,000 | |
| Accounts receivable | 6,500 | |
| Equipment | 78,000 | |
| Accumulated depreciation | | $ 14,000 |
| Notes payable | | 10,000 |
| Common stock | | 43,000 |
| Retained earnings | | 20,600 |
| Cash dividends | 8,000 | |
| Service fees earned | | 71,000 |
| Rent expense | 18,000 | |
| Salaries expense | 37,100 | |
| Depreciation expense | 7,000 | |
| Totals | $158,600 | $158,600 |

Complete the worksheet by (a) entering the adjusted trial balance, (b) putting in the worksheet income statement and balance sheet columns, (c) extending the adjusted trial balance to the income statement and balance sheet columns, and (d) balancing the worksheet.

### E4-15A. Revenue Recognition

**LO1**

Identify the proper point to recognize revenue for each of the following transactions.

a.  Napoleon Industries sells a machine in January with terms of no payment due until six months later.
b.  Emma Company collects an advance deposit of $700 in July toward the purchase of a $3,000 piece of equipment that is delivered to the customer the following September.
c.  Ashley Corporation receives payment in October at the time of delivery of a rebuilt engine for a tractor.

# Exercises—Set B

### E4-1B. Transaction Entry and Adjusting Entries

**LO2**

Beale Building Services offers janitorial services on both a contract basis and an hourly basis. On January 1, Beale collected $30,000 in advance on a six-month contract for work to be performed evenly during the next six months.

a.  Provide the general journal entry on January 1 to record the receipt of $30,000 for contract work.
b.  Provide the adjusting entry to be made on January 31, for the contract work done during January.
c.  At January 31, a total of 30 hours of hourly rate janitor work was unbilled. The billing rate is $25 per hour. Provide the adjusting entry needed on January 31. (*Note:* The firm uses the account Fees Receivable to reflect amounts due but not yet billed.)

### E4-2B. Adjusting Entries

**LO2**

Judy Brock began Brock Refinishing Service on July 1. Selected accounts are shown below as of July 31, before any adjusting entries have been made:

| | Debit | Credit |
|---|---|---|
| Prepaid rent | $5,700 | |
| Prepaid advertising | 630 | |
| Supplies | 3,000 | |
| Unearned refinishing fees | | $ 600 |
| Refinishing fees revenue | | 2,500 |

Using the following information, record in a general journal the necessary adjusting entries on July 31:

a.  On July 1, the firm paid one year's rent of $5,700.
b.  On July 1, $630 was paid to a local newspaper for an advertisement to run daily for the months of July, August, and September.

c. Supplies on hand at July 31 total $1,100.

d. At July 31, refinishing services of $800 have been performed but not yet billed to customers. The firm uses the account Fees Receivable to reflect amounts due but not yet billed.

e. One customer paid $600 in advance for a refinishing project. At July 31, the project is one-half complete.

**LO2** **E4-3B. Adjusting Entries**

For each of the following unrelated situations, prepare the necessary adjusting entry in general journal form:

a. Unrecorded depreciation on equipment is $900.

b. The Supplies account has a balance of $3,000. Supplies on hand at the end of the period total $1,000.

c. On the date for preparing financial statements, an estimated utilities expense of $400 has been incurred, but no utility bill has been received.

d. On the first day of the current month, rent for four months was paid and recorded as a $2,800 debit to Prepaid Rent and a $2,800 credit to Cash. Monthly statements are now being prepared.

e. Nine months ago, Macke Insurance Company sold a one-year policy to a customer and recorded the receipt of the premium by debiting Cash for $624 and crediting Unearned Premium Revenue for $624. No adjusting entries have been prepared during the nine-month period. Annual financial statements are now being prepared.

f. At the end of the accounting period, employee wages of $600 have been incurred but not paid.

g. At the end of the accounting period, $500 of interest has been earned but not yet received on notes receivable that are held.

**LO3** **E4-4B. Statement of Stockholders' Equity**

On January 1, the credit balance of the Retained Earnings account was $50,000. The company's common stock account had an opening balance of $60,000 and new contributions during the year totaled $7,000. On December 31, at year-end, the Dividends account had a debit balance of $5,700. After revenue and expense accounts were closed, the Income Summary account had a credit balance of $30,000. Prepare a Statement of Stockholders' Equity for A. Miller & Company, architectural design firm.

**LO4** **E4-5B. Closing Entries**

The adjusted trial balance prepared December 31, for Cheryl Fontaine & Company, shipping agent, contains the following accounts:

| | Debit | Credit |
|---|---|---|
| Commissions earned | | $84,900 |
| Wages expense | $36,000 | |
| Insurance expense | 1,900 | |
| Utilities expense | 8,200 | |
| Depreciation expense | 9,800 | |
| Dividends | 12,000 | |
| Common stock | | 50,000 |
| Retained earnings | | 22,100 |

Prepare journal entries to close the accounts using the Income Summary account. After these entries are posted, what is the ending balance in the Retained Earnings account?

**LO5** **E4-6B. Closing Entries**
**(Appendix 4A)**

Use the information provided in E4-5B to prepare journal entries to close the accounts directly to Retained Earnings. After these entries are posted, what is the balance in the Retained Earnings account?

**LO4** **E4-7B. Closing Entries**

In the midst of closing procedures, Claremont Corporation's accountant became ill. You have volunteered to complete the closing of the books, and you find that all revenue and expense accounts have zero balances and that the Income Summary account has a single debit entry for $318,800 and a single credit entry for $347,400. The Cash Dividends account has a debit balance of $29,000, and the Retained Earnings account has a credit balance of $117,000. Prepare journal entries to complete the closing procedures as of year-end.

**E4-8B. Closing Entries**

LO5 (Appendix 4A)

In the midst of closing procedures, Claremont Corporation's accountant became ill and was hospitalized. You have volunteered to complete the closing of the books. The Dividends account has a debit balance of $29,000. The Retained Earnings account has a beginning credit balance of $117,000. Expenses total $318,800, and revenues total $347,400. Prepare journal entries to complete the closing procedures as of year-end directly to Retained Earnings. After these entries are posted, what is the balance in the Retained Earnings account?

**E4-9B. Worksheet**

LO6 (Appendix 4B)

Identify each of the 10 amount columns of the worksheet and indicate to which column the adjusted balance of the following accounts would be extended:

|   |   |   |   |
|---|---|---|---|
| a. | Accounts Receivable | f. | Interest Receivable |
| b. | Accumulated Depreciation | g. | Prepaid Rent |
| c. | Dividends | h. | Service Fees Earned |
| d. | Salaries Payable | i. | Common Stock |
| e. | Wages Expense | j. | Retained Earnings |

**E4-10B. Analysis of Adjusted Data**

LO2

Selected T-account balances for the Parris Company are shown below as of January 31; adjusting entries have already been posted. The firm uses a calendar-year accounting period and makes monthly adjustments.

| Supplies | | Supplies Expense | |
|---|---|---|---|
| Jan. 31  Bal. 800 | | Jan. 31  Bal. 1,960 | |

| Prepaid Insurance | | Insurance Expense | |
|---|---|---|---|
| Jan. 31  Bal. 910 | | Jan. 31  Bal. 182 | |

| Wages Payable | | Wages Expense | |
|---|---|---|---|
| | Bal. 500  Jan. 31 | Jan. 31  Bal. 3,200 | |

| Truck | | Accumulated Depreciation—Truck | |
|---|---|---|---|
| Jan. 31  Bal. 8,700 | | | Bal. 2,610  Jan. 31 |

a. If the amount in Supplies Expense represents the January 31 adjustment for the supplies used in January, and $620 worth of supplies were purchased during January, what was the January 1 balance of Supplies?

b. The amount in the Insurance Expense account represents the adjustment made at January 31 for January insurance expense. If the original insurance premium was for one year, what was the amount of the premium and on what date did the insurance policy start?

c. If we assume that no balance existed in Wages Payable or Wages Expense on January 1, how much cash was paid as wages during January?

d. If the truck has a useful life of five years, what is the monthly amount of depreciation expense and how many months has Parris owned the truck?

**E4-11B. Analysis of the Impact of Adjustments on Financial Statements**

LO2

At the end of the first month of operations, the Omar Company's accountant prepared financial statements that showed the following amounts:

| | |
|---|---|
| Assets. | $80,000 |
| Liabilities. | 30,000 |
| Stockholders' equity. | 50,000 |
| Net income. | 11,000 |

In preparing the statements, the accountant overlooked the following items:

a. Depreciation for the month, $3,000.

b. Service revenue earned but unbilled at month-end, $1,500.

c. Employee wages earned but unpaid at month-end, $250.

Determine the correct amounts of assets, liabilities, and stockholders' equity at month-end and net income for the month.

**E4-12B. Closing Entries**

LO4

The adjusted trial balance of the Matthews Corporation, prepared December 31, contains the following accounts:

ASSIGNMENTS

| | Debit | Credit |
|---|---|---|
| Service fees earned..................................................... | | $97,500 |
| Interest income......................................................... | | 5,200 |
| Salaries expense........................................................ | $49,800 | |
| Advertising expense.................................................... | 4,300 | |
| Depreciation expense .................................................. | 8,700 | |
| Income tax expense .................................................... | 9,900 | |
| Common stock.......................................................... | | 75,000 |
| Retained earnings ...................................................... | | 57,700 |
| Cash dividends ......................................................... | 15,000 | |

Prepare journal entries to close the accounts using the Income Summary account. After these entries are posted, what is the ending balance in the Retained Earnings account?

**LO5**
**(Appendix 4A)**

**E4-13B. Closing Entries**

Use the information provided in E4-12B to prepare journal entries to close the accounts directly to Retained Earnings. After these entries are posted, what is the balance in the Retained Earnings account?

**LO6**
**(Appendix 4B)**

**E4-14B. Worksheet**

The adjusted trial balance columns of a worksheet for Frankfurt Corporation are shown below. The worksheet is prepared for the year ended December 31.

| | Adjusted Trial Balance | |
|---|---|---|
| | Debit | Credit |
| Cash ................................................................. | $ 14,000 | |
| Accounts receivable .................................................. | 16,500 | |
| Equipment............................................................ | 78,000 | |
| Accumulated depreciation............................................ | | $ 24,000 |
| Notes payable......................................................... | | 10,000 |
| Common stock........................................................ | | 43,000 |
| Retained earnings .................................................... | | 20,600 |
| Cash dividends........................................................ | 8,000 | |
| Service fees earned................................................... | | 81,000 |
| Rent expense.......................................................... | 18,000 | |
| Salaries expense....................................................... | 37,100 | |
| Depreciation expense ................................................. | 7,000 | |
| Totals ................................................................ | $178,600 | $178,600 |

Complete the worksheet by (a) entering the adjusted trial balance, (b) putting in the worksheet income statement and balance sheet columns, (c) extending the adjusted trial balance to the income statement and balance sheet columns, and (d) balancing the worksheet.

**LO1**

**E4-15B. Expense Matching**

Identify the proper point to recognize expenses for each of the following transactions.

a.  Garner Inc. purchases for cash five custom dining tables for $1,000 each in March. Three tables are later sold for $1,750 each in April, and the remaining two tables are sold for $1,500 each in May.

b.  Peyton Company purchases $300 of office supplies that are both paid for and used in August.

c.  Kerra Company purchases $500 of inventory on account in July. The inventory is sold for $650 in August. Kerra pays its suppliers the $500 due in September.

# PROBLEMS—SET A

**LO2**

**P4-1A.  Transaction Entries, Posting, Trial Balance, and Adjusting Entries**

Mark Ladd opened Ladd Roofing Service on April 1. Transactions for April are as follows:

April 1   Ladd contributed $11,500 of his personal funds in exchange for common stock to begin the business.

2   Purchased a used truck for $6,100 cash.

3   Purchased ladders and other equipment for a total of $3,100, paid $1,000 cash, with the balance due in 30 days.

4   Paid two-year premium on liability insurance, $2,880.

5   Purchased supplies on account, $1,200.

6  Received an advance payment of $1,800 from a customer for roof repair work to be done during April and May.
7  Billed customers for roofing services, $5,500.
8  Collected $4,900 on account from customers.
9  Paid bill for truck fuel used in April, $75.
10  Paid April newspaper advertising, $100.
11  Paid assistants' wages, $2,500.
12  Billed customers for roofing services, $4,000.

**Required**

a.  Set up a general ledger with the following accounts: Cash; Accounts Receivable; Supplies; Prepaid Insurance; Trucks; Accumulated Depreciation—Trucks; Equipment; Accumulated Depreciation—Equipment; Accounts Payable; Unearned Roofing Fees; Common Stock; Retained Earnings; Roofing Fees Earned; Fuel Expense; Advertising Expense; Wages Expense; Insurance Expense; Supplies Expense; Depreciation Expense—Trucks; and Depreciation Expense—Equipment.
b.  Record these transactions in the general journal and post to the ledger accounts.
c.  Prepare an unadjusted trial balance as of April 30.
d.  Prepare the journal entries to adjust the books for insurance expense, supplies expense, depreciation expense on the truck, depreciation expense on the equipment, and roofing fees earned. Supplies on hand on April 30 amounted to $400. Depreciation for April was $125 on the truck and $35 on the equipment. One-fourth of the roofing fee received in advance was earned by April 30. Post the adjusting entries.

**P4-2A.  Transaction Entries, Posting, Trial Balance, and Adjusting Entries**

LO2

The Wellness Catering Service had the following transactions in July, its first month of operations:

July  1  Kelly Foster contributed $15,000 of personal funds to the business in exchange for common stock.
2  Purchased the following items for cash from a catering firm that was going out of business (make a compound entry): delivery van, $3,780; equipment, $3,240; and supplies, $1,600.
3  Paid premium on a one-year liability insurance policy, $1,080.
4  Entered into a contract with a local service club to cater weekly luncheon meetings for one year at a fee of $750 per month. Received six months' fees in advance.
5  Paid rent for July, August, and September, $2,340.
6  Paid employee's two weeks' wages (five-day week), $1,700.
7  Billed customers for services rendered, $4,500.
8  Purchased supplies on account, $3,400.
9  Paid employee's two weeks' wages, $1,700.
10  Paid July bill for gas, oil, and repairs on delivery van, $690.
11  Collected $3,700 from customers on account.
12  Billed customers for services rendered, $4,800.
13  Foster received a $1,900 dividend.

**Required**

a.  Set up a general ledger that includes the following accounts: Cash; Accounts Receivable; Supplies; Prepaid Rent; Prepaid Insurance; Delivery Van; Accumulated Depreciation—Delivery Van; Equipment; Accumulated Depreciation—Equipment; Accounts Payable; Wages Payable; Unearned Catering Fees; Common Stock; Dividends; Retained Earnings; Catering Fees Revenue; Wages Expense; Rent Expense; Supplies Expense; Insurance Expense; Delivery Van Expense; Depreciation Expense—Delivery Van; and Depreciation Expense—Equipment.
b.  Record July transactions in the general journal and post to the ledger accounts.
c.  Prepare an unadjusted trial balance as of July 31.
d.  Record adjusting journal entries in the general journal and post to the ledger accounts. The following information is available on July 31:

Supplies on hand, $1,500
Accrued wages, $510
Estimated life of delivery van, three years
Estimated life of equipment, six years

Also, make any necessary adjusting entries for insurance, rent, and catering fees indicated by the July transactions.

**LO2**  **P4-3A.**  **Trial Balance and Adjusting Entries**

Photomake, Inc., a commercial photography studio, has just completed its first full year of operations on December 31. The general ledger account balances before year-end adjustments follow. No adjusting entries have been made to the accounts at any time during the year. Assume that all balances are normal.

| | | | |
|---|---|---|---|
| Cash | $ 2,150 | Accounts payable | $ 1,910 |
| Accounts receivable | 3,800 | Unearned photography fees | 2,600 |
| Prepaid rent | 12,600 | Common stock | 24,000 |
| Prepaid insurance | 2,970 | Photography fees earned | 34,480 |
| Supplies | 4,250 | Wages expense | 11,000 |
| Equipment | 22,800 | Utilities expense | 3,420 |

An analysis of the firm's records discloses the following items:

1. Photography services of $925 have been rendered, but customers have not yet been billed. The firm uses the account Fees Receivable to reflect amounts due but not yet billed.
2. The equipment, purchased January 1, has an estimated life of 10 years.
3. Utilities expense for December is estimated to be $400, but the bill will not arrive until January of next year.
4. The balance in Prepaid Rent represents the amount paid on January 1, for a two-year lease on the studio.
5. In November, customers paid $2,600 in advance for pictures to be taken for the holiday season. When received, these fees were credited to Unearned Photography Fees. By December 31, all fees are earned.
6. A three-year insurance premium paid on January 1, was debited to Prepaid Insurance.
7. Supplies on hand at December 31 are $1,520.
8. At December 31, wages expense of $375 has been incurred but not paid.

**Required**

*a.* Prove that the sum of the debits equals the sum of the credits for Photomake's unadjusted account balances by preparing an unadjusted trial balance as of December 31.
*b.* Record adjusting entries in the general journal.

**LO2**  **P4-4A.**  **Adjusting Entries**

Dole Carpet Cleaners ended its first month of operations on June 30. Monthly financial statements will be prepared. The unadjusted account balances are as follows:

| DOLE CARPET CLEANERS Unadjusted Trial Balance June 30, 2010 | | |
|---|---|---|
| | **Debit** | **Credit** |
| Cash | $ 1,180 | |
| Accounts receivable | 450 | |
| Prepaid rent | 3,100 | |
| Supplies | 2,520 | |
| Equipment | 4,440 | |
| Accounts payable | | $ 760 |
| Common stock | | 2,500 |
| Retained earnings | | 5,000 |
| Dividends | 200 | |
| Service fees earned | | 4,650 |
| Wages expense | 1,020 | |
| | $12,910 | $12,910 |

The following information is also available:

1. The balance in Prepaid Rent was the amount paid on June 1 for the first four months' rent.
2. Supplies on hand at June 30 were $820.
3. The equipment, purchased June 1, has an estimated life of five years.
4. Unpaid wages at June 30 were $210.
5. Utility services used during June were estimated at $300. A bill is expected early in July.

6. Fees earned for services performed but not yet billed on June 30 were $380. The firm uses the account Fees Receivable to reflect amounts due but not yet billed.

**Required**

Prepare the adjusting entries needed at June 30 for the general journal.

**P4-5A. Adjusting Entries**                                                      LO2

The following information relates to December 31 adjustments for Finest Print, a printing company. The firm's fiscal year ends on December 31.

1. Weekly salaries for a five-day week total $1,800, payable on Fridays. December 31 of the current year is a Tuesday.
2. Finest Print has $20,000 of notes payable outstanding at December 31. Interest of $200 has accrued on these notes by December 31, but will not be paid until the notes mature next year.
3. During December, Finest Print provided $900 of printing services to clients who will be billed on January 2. The firm uses the account Fees Receivable to reflect amounts due but not yet billed.
4. Starting December 1, all maintenance work on Finest Print's equipment is handled by Prompt Repair Company under an agreement whereby Finest Print pays a fixed monthly charge of $90. Finest Print paid six months' service charge in advance on December 1, debiting Prepaid Maintenance for $540.
5. The firm paid $900 on December 15 for a series of radio commercials to run during December and January. One-third of the commercials have aired by December 31. The $900 payment was debited to Prepaid Advertising.
6. Starting December 16, Finest Print rented 400 square feet of storage space from a neighboring business. The monthly rent of $0.80 per square foot is due in advance on the first of each month. Nothing was paid in December, however, because the neighbor agreed to add the rent for one-half of December to the January 1 payment.
7. Finest Print invested $5,000 in securities on December 1 and earned interest of $38 on these securities by December 31. No interest will be received until January.
8. The annual depreciation on the firm's equipment is $2,175. No depreciation has been recorded during the year.

**Required**

Prepare the required December 31 adjusting entries in the general journal.

**P4-6A. Adjusting Entries**                                                      LO2

The following selected accounts appear in the Shaw Company's unadjusted trial balance as of December 31, the end of the fiscal year (all accounts have normal balances):

| | | | |
|---|---|---|---|
| Prepaid advertising.................. | $ 1,200 | Unearned service fees ............... | $ 5,400 |
| Wages expense...................... | 43,800 | Service fees earned.................. | 87,000 |
| Prepaid insurance ................... | 3,420 | Rental income....................... | 4,900 |

**Required**

Prepare the necessary adjusting entries in the general journal as of December 31, assuming the following:

1. Prepaid advertising at December 31 is $800.
2. Unpaid wages earned by employees in December are $1,300.
3. Prepaid insurance at December 31 is $2,280.
4. Unearned service fees at December 31 are $3,000.
5. Rent revenue of $1,000 owed by a tenant is not recorded at December 31.

**P4-7A. Adjusting Entries**                                                      LO2

The following selected accounts appear in the Birch Company's unadjusted trial balance as of December 31, the end of the fiscal year (all accounts have normal balances):

| | | | |
|---|---|---|---|
| Prepaid maintenance................. | $2,700 | Commission fees earned............. | $84,000 |
| Supplies............................ | 8,400 | Rent expense........................ | 10,800 |
| Unearned commission fees .......... | 8,500 | | |

**Required**

Prepare the necessary adjusting entries in the general journal as of December 31, assuming the following:

1. On September 1, the company entered into a prepaid equipment maintenance contract. Birch Company paid $2,700 to cover maintenance service for six months, beginning September 1. The $2,700 payment was debited to Prepaid Maintenance.
2. Supplies on hand at December 31 are $3,200.
3. Unearned commission fees at December 31 are $4,000.
4. Commission fees earned but not yet billed at December 31 are $2,800. (*Note:* Debit Fees Receivable.)
5. Birch Company's lease calls for rent of $900 per month payable on the first of each month, plus an annual amount equal to 1 percent of annual commissions earned. This additional rent is payable on January 10 of the following year. (*Note:* Be sure to use the adjusted amount of commissions earned in computing the additional rent.)

**LO3, LO4**    **P4-8A.**   **Financial Statements and Closing Entries**

The adjusted trial balance shown below is for Fine Consulting Service as of December 31. Byran Fine made no capital contributions during the year.

|  | Adjusted Trial Balance | |
|---|---|---|
|  | Debit | Credit |
| Cash | $ 2,700 | |
| Accounts receivable | 3,270 | |
| Supplies | 3,060 | |
| Prepaid insurance | 1,500 | |
| Equipment | 6,400 | |
| Accumulated depreciation—Equipment | | $ 1,080 |
| Accounts payable | | 845 |
| Long-term notes payable | | 7,000 |
| Common stock | | 2,000 |
| Retained earnings | | 5,205 |
| Dividends | 2,900 | |
| Service fees earned | | 58,400 |
| Rent expense | 12,000 | |
| Salaries expense | 33,400 | |
| Supplies expense | 4,700 | |
| Insurance expense | 3,250 | |
| Depreciation expense—Equipment | 720 | |
| Interest expense | 630 | |
| Totals | $74,530 | $74,530 |

**Required**

a.   Prepare an income statement and a statement of stockholders' equity for the year, and a balance sheet as of December 31.
b.   Prepare closing entries in general journal form using the Income Summary account.

**LO3, LO5**    **P4-9A.**   **Financial Statements and Closing Entries**
**(Appendix 4A)**     Use the information provided in P4-8A.

**Required**

a.   Prepare an income statement, a statement of stockholders' equity, and a balance sheet as of December 31.
b.   Prepare closing entries directly to Retained Earnings in general journal form.

**LO4**    **P4-10A.**   **Closing Entries**

The adjusted trial balance shown below is for Bayou, Inc., at December 31:

| | Adjusted Trial Balance | |
|---|---|---|
| | Debit | Credit |
| Cash ......................................................... | $ 3,500 | |
| Accounts receivable ...................................... | 8,000 | |
| Prepaid insurance ........................................ | 3,600 | |
| Equipment.................................................. | 72,000 | |
| Accumulated depreciation............................... | | $ 12,000 |
| Accounts payable ......................................... | | 600 |
| Common stock............................................. | | 30,000 |
| Retained earnings ........................................ | | 14,100 |
| Cash dividends............................................. | 5,000 | |
| Service fees earned....................................... | | 97,200 |
| Miscellaneous income .................................... | | 4,200 |
| Salaries expense........................................... | 42,800 | |
| Rent expense............................................... | 13,400 | |
| Insurance expense......................................... | 1,800 | |
| Depreciation expense .................................... | 8,000 | |
| Income tax expense ...................................... | 8,800 | |
| Income tax payable........................................ | | 8,800 |
| Totals ....................................................... | $166,900 | $166,900 |

### Required

a. Prepare closing entries in general journal form using the Income Summary account.

b. After the closing entries are posted, what is the ending balance in the Retained Earnings account?

**P4-11A. Closing Entries**    LO5 (Appendix 4A)

Use the information provided in P4-10A.

### Required

a. Prepare closing entries directly to Retained Earnings in general journal form.

b. After the closing entries are posted, what is the ending balance in the Retained Earnings account?

**P4-12A. Balance Sheet and Net Income**    LO3

At the beginning of 2010, Flynn's Parking Lots had the following balance sheet:

| Assets | | Liabilities | |
|---|---|---|---|
| Cash ............................... | $ 4,800 | Accounts payable .................... | $12,000 |
| Accounts receivable ................. | 14,700 | | |
| Land ............................... | 60,000 | **Stockholders' Equity** | |
| | | Common stock....................... | 20,000 |
| | | Retained earnings ................... | 47,500 |
| | | Total Liabilities and | |
| Total Assets ........................ | $79,500 | Stockholders' Equity .............. | $79,500 |

a. At the end of 2010, Flynn had the following assets and liabilities: Cash, $8,800; Accounts Receivable, $17,400; Land, $60,000; and Accounts Payable, $7,500; and Common Stock, $20,000. Prepare a year-end balance sheet for Flynn's Parking Lots.

b. Assume that stockholders did not invest any money in the business during the year but received $12,000 as a dividend; what was Flynn's net income or net loss for 2010?

**P4-13A. Determination of Retained Earnings and Net Income**    LO3

The following information appears in the records of Bock Corporation at the end of 2010:

| | | | |
|---|---|---|---|
| Accounts receivable ................. | $ 23,000 | Retained earnings .................... | $ ? |
| Accounts payable ................... | 11,000 | Supplies............................. | 9,000 |
| Cash ............................... | 8,000 | Equipment........................... | 138,000 |
| Common stock..................... | 110,000 | | |

a. Calculate the amount of retained earnings at the end of 2010.

b. Using your answer from part *a*, if the amount of the retained earnings at the beginning of 2010 was $30,000, and $12,000 in dividends were paid during 2010, what was the company's net income for 2010?

**LO2, LO3    P4-14A. Transaction Analysis, Trial Balance, and Financial Statements**

Angela Mehl operates the Mehl Dance Studio. On June 1, the business's general ledger contained the following information:

| | | | |
|---|---|---|---|
| Cash | $ 5,930 | Notes payable | $ 3,000 |
| Accounts receivable | 7,420 | Accounts payable | 480 |
| | | Common stock | 7,870 |
| | | Retained earnings | 2,000 |
| | $13,350 | | $13,350 |

The following transactions occurred during the month of June:

June   1   Paid June rent for practice studio, $975.
2   Paid June piano rental, $90 (Rent Expense).
3   Collected $5,320 from students on account.
4   Borrowed $1,500 and signed a promissory note payable due in six months.
5   Billed students for June instructional fees, $5,600.
6   Paid interest for June on notes payable, $30.
7   Paid $350 for advertising ballet performances.
8   Paid costume rental, $400 (Rent Expense).
9   Collected $2,100 admission fees from ballet performances given during the month.
10   Paid $480 owed on account.
11   Received invoice for June utilities, to be paid in July, $280.
12   Paid stockholders $750 cash as a dividend.
13   Purchased piano for $5,000 cash, to be used in business starting in July.

**Required**

a. Set up accounts for the general ledger with June 1 balances and enter the beginning balances. Also provide the following accounts: Piano; Dividends; Instructional Fees Earned; Performance Revenue; Rent Expense; Utilities Expense; Advertising Expense; and Interest Expense. Record the listed transactions in the accounts.
b. Prepare a trial balance as of June 30.
c. Prepare an income statement for the month of June.
d. Prepare a statement of stockholders' equity for the month of June.
e. Prepare a balance sheet as of June 30.

**LO2, LO3    P4-15A. Transaction Analysis, Trial Balance, and Financial Statements**

On December 1, a group of individuals formed a corporation to establish the *Beeper,* a neighborhood weekly newspaper featuring want ads of individuals and advertising of local firms. The free paper will be mailed to about 8,000 local residents; revenue will be generated from advertising and want ads. The December transactions are summarized below:

Dec.   1   Sold common stock of Beeper, Inc., for cash, $25,000.
2   Paid December rent on furnished office, $1,000.
3   Purchased for $750, on account, T-shirts displaying company logo. The T-shirts were distributed at a grand opening.
4   Paid to creditor on account, $750.
5   Collected "Help wanted" ad revenue in cash, $2,800.
6   Paid post office for cost of bulk mailing, $910.
7   Billed various firms for advertising in the first two issues of the newspaper, $5,300.
8   Paid Acme Courier Service for transporting newspapers to post office, $50.
9   Paid for printing newspaper, $2,900.
10   Collected "Help wanted" ad revenue in cash, $2,570.
11   Received invoice for December utilities, to be paid in January, $310.
12   Paid for printing newspaper, $2,900.
13   Paid December salaries, $4,100.
14   Billed various firms for advertising in two issues of the newspaper, $6,850.
15   Paid post office for cost of bulk mailing, $930.

16  Paid Acme Courier Service for transporting newspapers to post office, $50.
17  Collected $5,100 on accounts receivable.
18  Purchased fax machine for office in exchange for a six-month note payable, $1,100.

**Required**
a.  Set up accounts for the following items: Cash, Accounts Receivable, Office Equipment, Notes Payable, Accounts Payable, Common Stock, Advertising Revenue, Want Ad Revenue, Printing Expense, Advertising Expense, Utilities Expense, Salaries Expense, Rent Expense, and Delivery Expense. Record the foregoing transactions in the accounts.
b.  Prepare a trial balance as of December 31.
c.  Prepare an income statement for the month of December.
d.  Prepare a balance sheet as of December 31. (*Note:* In this problem, the net income for December becomes the amount of retained earnings at December 31.)

**P4-16A. Balance Sheets for a Corporation**                    LO3
The following balance sheet data are given for Normandy Catering Service, a corporation, as of May 31:

| | | | |
|---|---|---|---|
| Accounts receivable | $18,300 | Accounts payable | $ 5,200 |
| Notes payable | 20,000 | Cash | 12,200 |
| Equipment | 55,000 | Common stock | 42,500 |
| Supplies | 16,400 | Retained earnings | ? |

Assume that on June 1, the following transactions occurred:

June 1  Purchased additional equipment costing $15,000, giving $2,000 cash and a $13,000 note payable.
     1  Paid a cash dividend of $7,000.

**Required**
a.  Prepare a classified balance sheet as of May 31.
b.  Prepare a classified balance sheet as of June 2.

**P4-17A. Determination of Net Income and Retained Earnings**                    LO3
The following selected income statement and balance sheet information is available for Lloyd Appraisers at the end of the current month:

| | | | |
|---|---|---|---|
| Supplies | $ 4,900 | Accounts payable | $ 4,000 |
| Accounts receivable | 18,000 | Salaries expense | 15,000 |
| Utilities expense | 700 | Appraisal fees earned | 31,000 |
| Supplies expense | 1,300 | Common stock | 10,000 |
| Rent expense | 2,500 | Retained earnings (beginning) | 8,000 |
| Cash | 3,600 | | |

a.  Calculate the net income or net loss for the month.
b.  If Mr. Lloyd made no additional investment in the business during the month but received $7,000 as a dividend, what is the balance in Retained Earnings at the end of the month?

**P4-18A. Trial Balance and Financial Statements**                    LO3
The following account balances were taken (out of order) from the general ledger of R. Ladd & Company as of January 31. Ladd trains dogs for competitive championship field trials. The firm's accounting year began on January 1. All accounts have normal balances.

| | | | |
|---|---|---|---|
| Land | $21,000 | Office rent expense | $ 800 |
| Maintenance expense | 460 | Supplies expense | 760 |
| Supplies | 1,640 | Utilities expense | 200 |
| Advertising expense | 350 | Fees earned | 16,470 |
| Common stock | 20,000 | Accounts receivable | 8,200 |
| Retained earnings | 9,000 | | |
| Cash | 7,300 | Salaries expense | 4,480 |
| Accounts payable | 820 | Dividends | 1,100 |

**Required**
a.  Prepare a trial balance from the given data.
b.  Prepare an income statement for the month of January.
c.  Prepare a statement of stockholders' equity for the month of January.
d.  Prepare a balance sheet as of January 31.

ASSIGNMENTS

ASSIGNMENTS

**LO3** **P4-19A.** **Trial Balance and Financial Statements**

The following account balances, in alphabetical order, are from the general ledger of Morgan's Waterproofing Service at January 31. The firm began business on January 1. All accounts have normal balances.

| | | | |
|---|---|---|---|
| Accounts payable | $ 2,600 | Notes payable | $ 6,000 |
| Accounts receivable | 21,000 | Rent expense | 1,700 |
| Advertising expense | 420 | Salaries expense | 8,000 |
| Cash | 10,400 | Service fees earned | 25,760 |
| Common stock | 29,740 | Supplies | 8,960 |
| Dividends | 3,000 | Supplies expense | 10,250 |
| Interest expense | 50 | Utilities expense | 320 |

**Required**

a.  Prepare a trial balance from the given data.
b.  Prepare an income statement for the month of January.
c.  Prepare a statement of stockholders' equity for the month of January.
d.  Prepare a balance sheet as of January 31.

**LO6**
**(Appendix 4B)**

**P4-20A.** **Worksheet**

The following unadjusted trial balance was prepared as of March 31:

| FOCUS TRAVEL AGENCY Unadjusted Trial Balance March 31, 2010 | Debit | Credit |
|---|---|---|
| Cash | $ 2,400 | |
| Commissions receivable | 5,000 | |
| Supplies | 1,750 | |
| Prepaid insurance | 1,800 | |
| Equipment | 13,000 | |
| Accumulated depreciation | | $ 2,600 |
| Accounts payable | | 550 |
| Unearned commissions | | 600 |
| Common stock | | 4,000 |
| Retained earnings | | 6,000 |
| Dividends | 900 | |
| Commissions earned | | 18,990 |
| Salaries expense | 4,500 | |
| Rent expense | 1,770 | |
| Advertising expense | 1,000 | |
| Utilities expense | 620 | |
| Totals | $32,740 | $32,740 |

Focus Travel Agency's fiscal year ends on March 31. The following additional information is available:

1.  Depreciation for the year is $1,300.
2.  Supplies on hand at March 31 amount to $820.
3.  By March 31, $400 of the unearned commissions was earned. The remainder will be earned in the next year.
4.  Insurance expense for the year is $1,200.
5.  Accrued salaries payable total $600 at March 31.

**Required**

Enter the trial balance on a worksheet and complete the worksheet using the adjustment data given above.

# PROBLEMS—SET B

**LO2** **P4-1B.** **Transaction Entries, Posting, Trial Balance, Adjusting Entries**

Huang Karate School began business on June 1. Transactions for June were as follows:

June  1  Po Huang contributed $7,500 of his personal funds in exchange for common stock to begin the business.
      2  Purchased equipment for $2,750, paying $750 cash, with the balance due in 30 days.

3 Paid six months' rent, $3,450.

4 Paid one-year premium on liability insurance, $876.

5 Paid June newspaper advertising, $225.

6 Billed participants for karate lessons to date, $2,200.

7 Received $555 from a local company to conduct a special three-session class on self-defense for its employees. The three sessions will be held on June 29, July 6, and July 13, at $185 per session.

8 Collected $1,800 on account from participants

9 Paid $275 to repair damage to wall caused by an errant kick.

10 Billed participants for karate lessons to date, $2,000.

11 Paid assistant's wages, $650.

### Required

*a.* Set up a general ledger with the following accounts: Cash; Accounts Receivable; Prepaid Rent; Prepaid Insurance; Equipment; Accumulated Depreciation—Equipment; Accounts Payable; Utilities Payable; Unearned Karate Fees; Common Stock; Retained Earnings; Karate Fees Earned; Advertising Expense; Repairs Expense; Wages Expense; Rent Expense; Insurance Expense; Depreciation Expense—Equipment; and Utilities Expense.

*b.* Record these transactions in general journal form and post to the ledger accounts.

*c.* Prepare an unadjusted trial balance as of June 30.

*d.* Prepare the adjusting entries for rent expense, insurance expense, depreciation expense, utilities expense, and karate fees earned. Depreciation expense for June is $50, and estimated utilities expense for June is $120. Post the adjusting entries.

**P4-2B.** **Transaction Entries, Posting, Trial Balance, and Adjusting Entries**

LO2

Market-Probe, a market research firm, had the following transactions in June, its first month of operations.

June 1 J. Witson invested $24,000 of personal funds in the firm in exchange for common stock.

2 The firm purchased the following from an office supply company: office equipment, $11,040; office supplies, $2,840. Terms called for a cash payment of $4,000, with the remainder due in 60 days. (Make a compound entry.)

3 Paid June rent, $875.

4 Contracted for three months' advertising in a local newspaper at $310 per month and paid for the advertising in advance.

5 Signed a six-month contract with an electronics firm to provide research consulting services at a rate of $3,200 per month. Received two months' fees in advance. Work on the contract started immediately.

6 Billed various customers for services rendered, $5,800.

7 Paid two weeks' salaries (five-day week) to employees, $3,600.

8 Paid J. Witson's travel expenses to business conference, $1,240.

9 Paid $520 cash for postage to mail questionnaire.

10 Paid two weeks' salaries to employees, $3,600.

11 Billed various customers for services rendered, $5,200.

12 Collected $7,800 from customers on account.

13 J. Witson received a $1,500 cash dividend.

### Required

*a.* Set up a general ledger that includes the following accounts: Cash; Accounts Receivable; Office Supplies; Prepaid Advertising; Office Equipment; Accumulated Depreciation— Office Equipment; Accounts Payable; Salaries Payable; Unearned Service Fees; Common Stock; Dividends; Retained Earnings; Service Fees Earned; Salaries Expense; Advertising Expense; Supplies Expense; Rent Expense; Travel Expense; Depreciation Expense—Office Equipment; and Postage Expense.

*b.* Record June transactions in general journal form and post to the ledger accounts.

*c.* Prepare an unadjusted trial balance as of June 30.

*d.* Record adjusting journal entries in general journal form, and post to the ledger accounts. The following information is available on June 30:

Office supplies on hand, $1,530.

Accrued salaries, $725.

Estimated life of office equipment, eight years.

Also, make any necessary adjusting entries for advertising and for service fees indicated by the June transactions.

**LO2** **P4-3B.** **Trial Balance and Adjusting Entries**

Deliverall, a mailing service, has just completed its first full year of operations on December 31, 2010. The firm's general ledger account balances before year-end adjustments are given below. No adjusting entries have been made to the accounts at any time during the year. Assume that all balances are normal.

| | | | |
|---|---|---|---|
| Cash ................................ | $ 2,300 | Accounts payable ..................... | $ 2,700 |
| Accounts receivable .................. | 5,120 | Common stock........................ | 3,000 |
| Prepaid advertising................... | 1,680 | Mailing fees earned................... | 86,000 |
| Supplies.............................. | 6,270 | Wages expense....................... | 38,800 |
| Equipment........................... | 42,240 | Rent expense......................... | 6,300 |
| Notes payable........................ | 7,500 | Utilities expense...................... | 3,020 |
| Retained earnings .................... | 6,530 | | |

An analysis of the firm's records reveals the following:

1. The balance in Prepaid Advertising represents the amount paid for newspaper advertising for one year. The agreement, which calls for the same amount of space each month, covers the period from February 1, 2010, to January 31, 2011. Deliverall did not advertise during its first month of operations.
2. The equipment, purchased January 1, has an estimated life of eight years.
3. Utilities expense does not include expense for December, estimated at $325. The bill will not arrive until January 2011.
4. At year-end, employees have earned $1,200 in wages that will not be paid until January.
5. Supplies on hand at year-end amounted to $1,520.
6. At year-end, unpaid interest of $450 has accrued on the notes payable.
7. The firm's lease calls for rent of $525 per month payable on the first of each month, plus an amount equal to ½ percent of annual mailing fees earned. The rental percentage is payable within 15 days after the end of the year.

**Required**

a. Demonstrate that the sum of the debits equals the sum of the credits for the unadjusted account balances shown above by preparing an unadjusted trial balance as of December 31, 2010.

b. Record adjusting entries in general journal form.

**LO2** **P4-4B.** **Adjusting Entries**

The Wheel Place, Inc., began operations on March 1 to provide automotive wheel alignment and balancing services. On March 31, 2010, the unadjusted balances of the firm's accounts are as follows:

| THE WHEEL PLACE, INC. Unadjusted Trial Balance March 31, 2010 | | |
|---|---|---|
| | **Debit** | **Credit** |
| Cash ........................................................... | $ 1,900 | |
| Accounts receivable ...................................... | 3,820 | |
| Prepaid rent................................................. | 4,770 | |
| Supplies....................................................... | 3,700 | |
| Equipment................................................... | 36,180 | |
| Accounts payable ......................................... | | $ 2,510 |
| Unearned service revenue .............................. | | 1,000 |
| Common stock.............................................. | | 38,400 |
| Service revenue ............................................ | | 12,360 |
| Wages expense.............................................. | 3,900 | |
| Totals .......................................................... | $54,270 | $54,270 |

The following information is also available.

1. The balance in Prepaid Rent was the amount paid on March 1 to cover the first six months' rent.
2. Supplies on hand on March 31 amounted to $1,720.
3. The equipment has an estimated life of nine years.
4. Unpaid wages at March 31 were $560.

5. Utility services used during March were estimated at $390. A bill is expected early in April.

6. The balance in Unearned Service Revenue was the amount received on March 1 from a new car dealer to cover alignment and balancing services on all new cars sold by the dealer in March and April. The Wheel Place agreed to provide the services at a fixed fee of $500 each month.

**Required**

Prepare the adjusting entries needed at March 31 in general journal form.

**P4-5B. Adjusting Entries**                                                      LO2

The following information relates to the December 31 adjustments for Water Barrier, a firm providing waterproofing services for commercial and residential customers. The firm's fiscal year ends December 31; no adjusting entries have been made during the year.

1. The firm paid a $2,340 premium for a three-year insurance policy, coverage to begin October 1. The premium payment was debited to Prepaid Insurance.

2. Weekly wages for a five-day work week total $1,225, payable on Fridays. December 31 is a Thursday.

3. Water Barrier received $3,600 in November for services to be performed during December through February of the following year. When received, this amount was credited to Unearned Service Fees. By December 31, one-third of this amount was earned.

4. Water Barrier receives a 5 percent commission from the manufacturer on sales of a waterproofing agent to Water Barrier's customers. By December 31, Water Barrier had sales of $9,000 (during November and December) for which no commissions had been received or recorded.

5. During December, fuel oil costs of $495 were incurred to heat the firm's buildings. Because the monthly bill from the oil company has not yet arrived, no entry has been made for this amount (fuel oil costs are charged to Utilities Expense).

6. The Supplies account has a balance of $16,900 on December 31. A count of supplies on December 31 indicates that $3,500 worth of supplies are still on hand.

7. On December 1, Water Barrier borrowed $9,000 from the bank, giving a note payable. Interest is not payable until the note is due near the end of the following January. However, the interest for December is $75.

8. Water Barrier rents parking spaces in its lot to firms in the office building next door. On December 1, Water Barrier received $10,000 as advance payments to cover parking privileges in the lot for December through March of the following year. When received, the $10,000 was credited to Unearned Parking Fees.

**Required**

Prepare the necessary December 31 adjusting entries in general journal form.

**P4-6B. Adjusting Entries**                                                      LO2

The following selected accounts appear in the Albany Company's unadjusted trial balance as of December 31, the end of the fiscal year (all accounts have normal balances):

| | | | | |
|---|---|---|---|---|
| Prepaid advertising................... | $ 2,200 | Unearned service fees ................ | $ 5,400 |
| Wages expense...................... | 43,800 | Service fees earned.................. | 87,000 |
| Prepaid insurance ................... | 5,420 | Rental income....................... | 4,900 |

**Required**

Make the necessary adjusting entries in general journal form as of December 31 assuming the following:

a. Prepaid advertising at December 31 is $800.

b. Unpaid wages earned by employees in December are $1,700.

c. Prepaid insurance at December 31 is $2,280.

d. Unearned service fees at December 31 are $2,000.

e. Rent revenue of $3,500 owed by a tenant is not recorded at December 31.

**P4-7B. Adjusting Entries**                                                      LO2

The following selected accounts appear in the Burns Company's unadjusted trial balance as of December 31, the end of the fiscal year (all accounts have normal balances):

| | | | |
|---|---|---|---|
| Prepaid maintenance................ | $ 3,000 | Commission fees earned.............. | $97,000 |
| Supplies........................... | 10,400 | Rent expense........................ | 10,800 |
| Unearned commission fees .......... | 10,500 | | |

### Required

Make the necessary adjusting entries in general journal form at December 31, assuming the following:

1. On September 1, the company entered into a prepaid equipment maintenance contract. The Burns Company paid $3,000 to cover maintenance service for six months, beginning September 1. The $3,000 payment was debited to Prepaid Maintenance.
2. Supplies on hand at December 31 are $3,200.
3. Unearned commission fees at December 31 are $4,000.
4. Commission fees earned but not yet billed at December 31 are $3,500. (*Note:* Debit Fees Receivable.)
5. The Burns Company's lease calls for rent of $900 per month payable on the first of each month, plus an annual amount equal to 1 percent of annual commissions earned. This additional rent is payable on January 10 of the following year. (*Note:* Be sure to use the adjusted amount of commissions earned in calculating the additional rent.)

**LO3, LO4**   **P4-8B.**   **Financial Statements and Closing Entries**

Outdoors, Inc., publishes magazines for skiers and hikers. The firm has the following adjusted trial balance at December 31:

| OUTDOORS, INC. Adjusted Trial Balance December 31, 2010 | Debit | Credit |
|---|---|---|
| Cash ...................................................... | $ 5,400 | |
| Accounts receivable ..................................... | 18,600 | |
| Supplies.................................................. | 4,200 | |
| Prepaid insurance ....................................... | 930 | |
| Office equipment........................................ | 66,000 | |
| Accumulated depreciation................................ | | $ 13,000 |
| Accounts payable ....................................... | | 12,100 |
| Unearned subscription revenue........................... | | 10,000 |
| Salaries payable ......................................... | | 3,500 |
| Common stock........................................... | | 25,000 |
| Retained earnings ....................................... | | 23,220 |
| Subscription revenue.................................... | | 188,300 |
| Advertising revenue ..................................... | | 49,700 |
| Salaries expense......................................... | 120,230 | |
| Printing and mailing expense ............................ | 85,600 | |
| Rent expense............................................ | 8,800 | |
| Supplies expense........................................ | 6,100 | |
| Insurance expense....................................... | 1,860 | |
| Depreciation expense ................................... | 5,500 | |
| Income tax expense ..................................... | 1,600 | |
| Totals ................................................... | $324,820 | $324,820 |

### Required

*a.* Prepare an income statement for 2010 and a balance sheet as of December 31.
*b.* Prepare closing entries in general journal form using the Income Summary account.

**LO3, LO5**   **P4-9B.**   **Financial Statements and Closing Entries**

**(Appendix 4A)**   Use the information provided in P4-8B.

### Required

*a.* Prepare an income statement for 2010 and a balance sheet as of December 31.
*b.* Prepare closing entries directly to Retained Earnings in general journal form.

**P4-10B. Closing Entries**                                                    LO4

The adjusted trial balance for Okay Moving Service as of December 31 is shown below:

|  | Adjusted Trial Balance | |
|---|---|---|
|  | Debit | Credit |
| Cash | $ 3,800 | |
| Accounts receivable | 5,250 | |
| Supplies | 2,300 | |
| Prepaid advertising | 3,000 | |
| Trucks | 28,300 | |
| Accumulated depreciation—Trucks | | $ 10,000 |
| Equipment | 7,600 | |
| Accumulated depreciation—Equipment | | 2,100 |
| Accounts payable | | 1,200 |
| Unearned service fees | | 2,700 |
| Common stock | | 10,000 |
| Retained earnings | | 16,050 |
| Dividends | 5,500 | |
| Service fees earned | | 72,500 |
| Wages expense | 29,800 | |
| Rent expense | 10,200 | |
| Insurance expense | 2,900 | |
| Supplies expense | 5,100 | |
| Advertising expense | 6,000 | |
| Depreciation expense—Trucks | 4,000 | |
| Depreciation expense—Equipment | 800 | |
| Totals | $114,550 | $114,550 |

**Required**

*a.* Prepare the closing entries at December 31 in general journal form using the Income Summary account.

*b.* After the closing entries are posted, calculate the ending balance in the Retained Earnings account.

*c.* Prepare a post-closing trial balance.

**P4-11B. Closing Entries**                                                    LO5

Use the information provided in P4-10B.                                   **(Appendix 4A)**

**Required**

*a.* Prepare closing entries directly to Retained Earnings at December 31 in general journal form.

*b.* After the closing entries are posted, calculate the ending balance in the Retained Earnings account.

*c.* Prepare a post-closing trial balance.

**P4-12B. Balance Sheet and Net Income Determination**                         LO3

At the beginning of 2010, Luxury Parking Services had the following balance sheet:

| Assets | | Liabilities | |
|---|---|---|---|
| Cash | $ 5,800 | Accounts payable | $13,500 |
| Accounts receivable | 14,700 | | |
| Land | 60,500 | **Stockholders' Equity** | |
| | | Common stock | 60,000 |
| | | Retained earnings | 7,500 |
| | | Total Liabilities and | |
| Total Assets | $81,000 | Stockholders' Equity | $81,000 |

*a.* At the end of 2010, Luxury Parking Services had the following assets and liabilities: Cash, $8,800; Accounts Receivable, $17,400; Land, $60,500; and Accounts Payable, $9,500. Prepare a year-end balance sheet for Luxury Parking Services assuming that no additional stock was issued.

*b.* Assuming that stockholders did not invest any money in the business during the year but received a $12,000 dividend, what was the company's net income or net loss for 2010?

LO3 **P4-13B. Determination of Retained Earnings and Net Income**

The following information appears in the records of the Wellington Corporation at year-end 2010:

| | | | |
|---|---|---|---|
| Accounts receivable | $ 33,000 | Retained earnings | $ ? |
| Accounts payable | 10,000 | Supplies | 7,000 |
| Cash | 8,000 | Equipment | 140,000 |
| Common stock | 130,000 | | |

a. Calculate the amount of retained earnings at the end of 2010.

b. Using your answer to part *a*, if the amount of the retained earnings at the beginning of 2010 was $30,000, and $9,000 in dividends were paid during 2010, what was the net income for 2010?

LO2, LO3 **P4-14B. Transaction Analysis, Trial Balance, and Financial Statements**

Kate Miller operates the Miller Dance Studio. On June 1, the studio's general ledger contained the following information:

| | | | |
|---|---|---|---|
| Cash | $ 8,930 | Notes payable | $ 3,000 |
| Accounts receivable | 17,420 | Accounts payable | 480 |
| | | Common stock | 9,870 |
| | | Retained earnings | 13,000 |
| | $26,350 | | $26,350 |

The following transactions occurred during the month of June:

June 1 Paid June rent for practice studio, $1,075.
2 Paid June piano rental, $900 (Rent Expense).
3 Collected $12,320 from students on account.
4 Borrowed $5,500 and signed a promissory note payable due in six months.
5 Billed students for June instructional fees, $7,600.
6 Paid interest for June on the outstanding notes payable, $60.
7 Paid $350 for advertising ballet performances.
8 Paid costume rental, $600 (Rent Expense).
9 Collected $4,100 admission fees from ballet performances given during June.
10 Paid $480 owed on account.
11 Received invoice for June utilities, to be paid in July, $280.
12 The studio paid stockholders a cash dividend of $750.
13 Purchased piano for $5,000 cash, to be used in business starting in July.

**Required**

a. Set up accounts for the general ledger with June 1 balances and enter the beginning balances. Also provide the following accounts: Piano; Dividends; Instructional Fees Earned; Performance Revenue; Rent Expense; Utilities Expense; Advertising Expense; and Interest Expense. Record the listed transactions in the accounts.

b. Prepare a trial balance as of June 30.

c. Prepare an income statement for the month of June.

d. Prepare a statement of stockholders' equity for the month of June.

e. Prepare a balance sheet as of June 30.

LO2, LO3 **P4-15B. Transaction Analysis, Trial Balance, and Financial Statements**

On December 1, a group of individuals formed a corporation to establish the *Arcadia News,* a neighborhood newspaper featuring "Help wanted" ads by individuals and advertising by local firms. The free paper will be mailed to about 20,000 local residents; revenue will be generated from advertising and the want ads. The December transactions are summarized below:

Dec. 1 Sold common stock for cash, $50,000.
2 Paid December rent on furnished office, $3,000.
3 Purchased for $750, on account, T-shirts displaying company logo. The T-shirts were distributed at a grand opening.
4 Paid to creditor on account, $750.

5 Collected want ad revenue in cash, $3,800.
6 Paid post office for cost of bulk mailing, $910.
7 Billed various firms for advertising in the first two issues of the newspaper, $7,300.
8 Paid Tucson Courier Service for transporting newspapers to the post office, $50.
9 Paid for printing newspaper, $2,900.
10 Collected want ad revenue in cash, $2,570.
11 Received invoice for December utilities, to be paid in January, $310.
12 Paid for printing newspaper, $2,900.
13 Paid December salaries, $4,100.
14 Billed various firms for advertising in two issues of the newspaper, $6,950.
15 Paid post office for cost of bulk mailing, $930.
16 Paid Tucson Courier Service for transporting newspapers to the post office, $50.
17 Collected $6,100 on accounts receivable.
18 Purchased fax machine for the office in exchange for a six-month note payable, $2,100.

### Required

a. Set up accounts for the following: Cash, Accounts Receivable, Office Equipment, Notes Payable, Accounts Payable, Common Stock, Advertising Revenue, Want Ad Revenue, Printing Expense, Advertising Expense, Utilities Expense, Salaries Expense, Rent Expense, and Delivery Expense. Record the foregoing transactions in the accounts.
b. Prepare a trial balance as of December 31.
c. Prepare an income statement for the month of December.
d. Prepare a balance sheet as of December 31. (*Note:* In this problem, the net income for December becomes the amount of retained earnings at December 31.)

**P4-16B. Balance Sheets**                                                                 LO3

The following balance sheet data are given for Cornell Catering Service, a corporation, at May 31:

| | | | |
|---|---|---|---|
| Accounts receivable | $28,300 | Accounts payable | $ 5,200 |
| Notes payable | 20,000 | Cash | 12,200 |
| Equipment | 55,000 | Common stock | 62,500 |
| Supplies | 16,400 | Retained earnings | ? |

Assume that on June 1, the following transactions occurred:

June 1 Purchased additional equipment costing $25,000, giving $5,000 cash and a $20,000 note payable.
2 Paid a cash dividend of $7,000.

### Required

a. Prepare a classified balance sheet as of May 31.
b. Prepare a classified balance sheet as of June 2.

**P4-17B. Determination of Net Income and Stockholders' Equity**                            LO3

The following selected income statement and balance sheet information is available for Zerbst Land Appraisers at the end of the current month:

| | | | |
|---|---|---|---|
| Supplies | $ 4,900 | Accounts payable | $ 4,000 |
| Accounts receivable | 18,000 | Salaries expense | 15,000 |
| Utilities expense | 700 | Appraisal fees earned | 31,000 |
| Supplies expense | 1,300 | Common stock | 15,000 |
| Rent expense | 2,500 | Retained earnings (beginning) | 3,000 |
| Cash | 3,600 | | |

a. Calculate the net income or net loss for the month.
b. If stockholders made no additional investment during the month but received $5,000 as a dividend, what is the amount of stockholders' equity at the end of the month?

**P4-18B. Trial Balance and Financial Statements**                                          LO3

The following account balances were prepared (out of order) from the general ledger of The Dog Whisperer Inc. as of January 31. The company trains dogs having behavioral problems. The firm's business began on January 1. All accounts have normal balances.

| | | | |
|---|---|---|---|
| Facilities.................... | $31,000 | Office rent expense.............. | $ 800 |
| Maintenance expense .......... | 460 | Supplies expense.............. | 760 |
| Supplies.................... | 1,640 | Utilities expense............. | 200 |
| Advertising expense............ | 350 | Fees earned ............... | 16,470 |
| Common stock............. | 39,000 | Accounts receivable .......... | 8,200 |
| Cash ...................... | 7,300 | Salaries expense.............. | 4,480 |
| Accounts payable ........... | 820 | Dividends............... | 1,100 |

### Required
a. Prepare a trial balance from the given data.
b. Prepare an income statement for the month of January.
c. Prepare a statement of stockholders' equity for the month of January.
d. Prepare a balance sheet as of January 31.

**LO3** **P4-19B. Trial Balance and Financial Statements**

The following account balances, in alphabetical order, are from the general ledger of The Columbus Service Company at January 31. The firm's business began on January 1. All accounts have normal balances.

| | | | |
|---|---|---|---|
| Accounts payable ............ | $ 2,600 | Notes payable.............. | $ 6,000 |
| Accounts receivable .......... | 21,000 | Rent expense.............. | 1,700 |
| Advertising expense......... | 420 | Salaries expense.............. | 8,000 |
| Cash .................... | 10,400 | Service fees earned.......... | 25,760 |
| Common stock............. | 29,740 | Supplies.............. | 8,960 |
| Dividends............... | 3,000 | Supplies expense.............. | 10,250 |
| Interest expense............. | 50 | Utilities expense.............. | 320 |

### Required
a. Prepare a trial balance from the given data.
b. Prepare an income statement for the month of January.
c. Prepare a statement of stockholders' equity for the month of January.
d. Prepare a balance sheet as of January 31.

**LO6**
**(Appendix 4B)**

**P4-20B. Worksheet**

The July 31 unadjusted trial balance of Sharp Outfitters, a firm renting various types of equipment to canoeists and campers, follows.

| SHARP OUTFITTERS Unadjusted Trial Balance July 31, 2011 | | |
|---|---|---|
| | **Debit** | **Credit** |
| Cash .......................................................... | $ 3,750 | |
| Supplies....................................................... | 8,600 | |
| Prepaid insurance ............................................. | 3,200 | |
| Equipment..................................................... | 95,000 | |
| Accumulated depreciation....................................... | | $ 16,500 |
| Accounts payable .............................................. | | 3,500 |
| Unearned rental fees .......................................... | | 8,850 |
| Common stock................................................. | | 30,000 |
| Retained earnings ............................................. | | 9,000 |
| Dividends...................................................... | 1,200 | |
| Rental fees earned............................................. | | 78,150 |
| Wages expense................................................ | 27,800 | |
| Rent expense.................................................. | 3,300 | |
| Advertising expense............................................ | 2,300 | |
| Travel expense ................................................ | 850 | |
| | $146,000 | $146,000 |

Sharp Outfitters' fiscal year ends on July 31. The following additional information is available:

1. Supplies on hand at July 31 amount to $3,300.
2. Insurance expense for the year is $1,600.
3. Depreciation for the year is $8,250.
4. The unearned rental fees consist of deposits received from customers in advance when reservations are made. During the year, $4,850 of the unearned rental fees were earned. The remaining deposits apply to rentals for August and September 2011.
5. At July 31, revenue from rental services earned during July but not yet billed or received amounts to $2,500. (*Note:* Debit Fees Receivable.)
6. Accrued wages payable for equipment handlers and guides amounts to $900 at July 31.

**Required**

Enter the trial balance in a worksheet and complete the worksheet using the adjustment data given above.

## SERIAL PROBLEM: KATE'S CARDS

(*Note:* **This is a continuation of the Serial Problem: Kate's Cards from Chapters 1 through 3.**)

**SP4.** Getting ready for the upcoming holiday season is traditionally a busy time for greeting card companies, and it was no exception for Kate. The following transactions occurred during the month of October:

1. Hired an assistant at an hourly rate of $10 per hour to help with some of the computer layouts and administrative chores.
2. Supplements her business by teaching a class to aspiring card designers. She charges and receives a total of $450.
3. Delivers greeting cards to several new customers. She bills them a total of $1,500.
4. Pays a utility bill in the amount of $250 that she determines is the business portion of her utility bill.
5. Receives an advance deposit of $500 for a new set of cards she is designing for a new customer.
6. Pays her assistant $200 for the work done this month.
7. Determines that the assistant has worked 10 additional hours this month that have not yet been paid.
8. Ordered and receives additional supplies in the amount of $1,000. These were paid for during the month.
9. Counts her remaining inventory of supplies at the end of the month and determines the balance to be $300. (*Hint:* This expense will be a debit to Cost of Goods Sold.)
10. Records the adjusting entries for depreciation and insurance expense for the month.
11. Pays herself a salary of $1,000.
12. Deciding she needs a little more cash, Kate pays herself a $500 dividend.
13. Receives her next utility bill during December and determines $85 applies to October's operations.

**Required**

Using the information that you gathered and the general ledger accounts that you prepared through Chapter 3, plus the new information above, complete the following:

a. Journalize the above transactions and adjusting entries.
b. Post the October transactions and adjusting entries. (Use the general ledger accounts prepared in Chapter 3 and add any new accounts that you may need.)
c. Prepare a trial balance as of October 31, 2010.
d. Prepare an income statement and a statement of retained earnings for the two-month period ending October 31, 2010, and a classified balance sheet as of October 31, 2010.
e. Prepare the closing entries as of October 31, 2010.
f. Prepare a post-closing trial balance.

**ASSIGNMENTS**

# EXTENDING YOUR KNOWLEDGE

## REPORTING AND ANALYSIS

COLUMBIA SPORTSWEAR
COMPANY

**EYK4-1.** **Financial Reporting Problem: Columbia Sportswear Company**

The financial statements for the **Columbia Sportswear Company** can be found in Appendix A at the end of this book.

**Required**

Answer the following questions using Columbia's Consolidated Financial Statements and the Notes to the consolidated financial statements:

a.  Identify an item that likely requires adjusting entries for prepayments.
b.  Identify an item that likely requires an adjusting accrual.
c.  Examine the statement of cash flows and identify the amount of depreciation expense for 2009. Where on the balance sheet was this accrual likely also shown?
d.  Identify the items that will require closing entries. What account will they be ultimately closed to?

COLUMBIA SPORTSWEAR
COMPANY
THE TIMBERLAND COMPANY

**EYK4-2.** **Comparative Analysis Problem: Columbia Sportswear Company vs. The Timberland Company**

The financial statements for the **Columbia Sportswear Company** can be found in Appendix A, and **The Timberland Company's** financial statements can be found in Appendix B at the end of this book.

**Required**

a.  Examine the balance sheet of Columbia Sportswear and identify three items that indicate that the company uses the accrual method of accounting. In each case, identify the likely income statement account that is affected by these accruals.
b.  Examine the balance sheet of The Timberland Company and identify three items that indicate the company uses the accrual method of accounting. In each case, identify the likely income statement account that is affected by these accruals.

**EYK4-3.** **Business Decision Problem**

Wyland Consulting Services, a firm started three years ago by Bruce Wyland, offers consulting services for material handling and plant layout. The balance sheet prepared by the firm's accountant at the close of 2010 is shown here.

| WYLAND CONSULTING SERVICES | | | | |
|---|---|---|---|---|
| **Balance Sheet** | | | | |
| **As of December 31, 2010** | | | | |
| **Assets** | | | **Liabilities** | |
| Cash ................................ | | $ 3,400 | Notes payable | $30,000 |
| Accounts receivable ................. | | 22,875 | Accounts payable | 4,200 |
| Supplies............................. | | 13,200 | Unearned consulting fees | 11,300 |
| Prepaid insurance ................... | | 4,500 | Wages payable | 400 |
| Equipment......................... | $68,500 | | Total Liabilities | $45,900 |
| Less: Accumulated depreciation....... | 23,975 | 44,525 | **Stockholders' Equity** | |
| | | | Common stock | 20,000 |
| | | | Retained earnings | 22,600 |
| | | | Total Stockholders' Equity | 42,600 |
| | | | Total Liabilities and | |
| Total Assets ........................ | | $88,500 | Stockholders' Equity | $88,500 |

Earlier in the year, Wyland obtained a bank loan of $30,000 for the firm. One of the provisions of the loan is that the year-end debt-to-equity ratio (ratio of total liabilities to total stockholders' equity) shall not exceed 1.0. Based on the above balance sheet, the ratio at the end of 2010 is 1.08 ($45,900/$42,600).

Wyland is concerned about being in violation of the loan agreement and asks your assistance in reviewing the situation. Wyland believes that his rather inexperienced accountant may have overlooked some items at year-end.

In discussions with Wyland and the accountant, you learn the following:

1. On January 1, 2010, the firm paid a $4,500 insurance premium for two years of coverage. The amount in Prepaid Insurance has not been adjusted.
2. Depreciation on the equipment should be 10 percent of cost per year. The accountant inadvertently recorded 15 percent for 2010.
3. Interest on the bank loan has been paid through the end of 2010.
4. The firm concluded a major consulting engagement in December, doing a plant layout analysis for a new factory. The $6,000 fee has not been billed or recorded in the accounts.
5. On December 1, 2010, the firm received an $11,300 advance payment from Croy Corporation for consulting services to be rendered over a two-month period. This payment was credited to the Unearned Consulting Fees account. One-half of this fee was earned by December 31, 2010.
6. Supplies costing $4,800 were on hand on December 31. The accountant filed the record of the count but made no entry in the accounts.

**Required**

*a.* What is the correct debt-to-equity ratio at December 31, 2010? Is the firm in violation of the loan agreement? Prepare a schedule to support your computation of the correct total liabilities and total stockholders' equity as of December 31, 2010.
*b.* Why might the loan agreement have contained the debt-to-equity provision?

**EYK4-4.** **Financial Analysis Problem**
Purpose: To learn more about the Financial Accounting Standards Board (FASB)
Address: http://www.fasb.org

**Required**
Use the information on the FASB site to answer the following questiuons:

*a.* When was the FASB established?
*b.* What is the mission of the FASB?
*c.* Who has oversight responsibility for the FASB?
*d.* What are some of the current projects of the FASB?

## CRITICAL THINKING

**EYK4-5.** **Accounting Research Problem**
Refer to the annual report of **General Mills, Inc.** for the year ending May 30, 2010 (fiscal year 2010), available on this book's Website. Review the consolidated balance sheets.

GENERAL MILLS, INC.

**Required**
*a.* Identify two assets listed in the consolidated balance sheets that indicate that General Mills uses the accrual basis of accounting. Which income statement accounts of General Mills are affected by adjustments to these assets accounts?
*b.* Identify two liabilities listed in the consolidated balance sheets that indicate that General Mills uses the accrual basis of accounting. Which income statement accounts of General Mills are affected by these adjustments?

**EYK4-6.** **Accounting Communications Activity**
Many people do not understand the concept of accrual accounting and how it differs from accounting on a cash basis. In particular, they are confused as to why a company's results in any one accounting period can differ so much between the two methods of accounting. Because the cash basis is understood to a far larger degree, many people argue that the cash basis should be the primary basis of accounting.

**Required**
Write a short memorandum that explains the difference between accrual accounting and the cash basis of accounting. In your memo give a simple example of how the accrual basis can give a clearer picture of a company's performance in a given period.

**EYK4-7.** **Accounting Ethics Case**
It is the end of an accounting year for Juliet Kravetz, controller of a medium-sized, publicly held corporation specializing in toxic waste cleanup. Within the corporation, only Kravetz and the president know that the firm has been negotiating for several months to land a very large contract for waste cleanup in Western Europe. The president has hired another firm with excellent contacts in Western Europe to help with the negotiations. The outside firm charges

an hourly fee plus expenses, but has agreed not to submit a bill until the negotiations are in their final stages (expected to occur in another three to four months). Even if the contract falls through, the outside firm is entitled to receive payment for its services. Based upon her discussion with a member of the outside firm, Kravetz knows that its charge for services provided to date will be $150,000. This is a material amount for the company.

Kravetz knows that the president wants the negotiations to remain as secret as possible so that competitors will not learn of the European contract that the company is pursuing. Indeed, the president recently stated to her, "This is not the time to reveal our actions in Western Europe to other staff members, our auditors, or readers of our financial statements; securing this contract is crucial to our future growth." No entry has been made in the accounting records for the cost of the contract negotiations. Kravetz now faces an uncomfortable situation. The company's outside auditor has just asked her if she knows of any year-end adjustments that have not yet been recorded.

**Required**

What are the ethical considerations that Kravetz faces in answering the auditor's question? How should she respond to the question?

**EYK4-8.** **Corporate Social Responsibility Problem**

Unlike financial reporting that requires all reported amounts to be expressed in monetary terms, Corporate Social Responsibility (CSR) reporting is often more qualitative than quantitative. This has caused some individuals to discount the CSR reports as too subjective.

**Required**

a. Can you identify any subjective areas within a financial statement prepared under GAAP?
b. Discuss the reasons both financial reporting, and to a larger extent CSR reporting, allow subjective estimates to be part of the report.

**EYK4-9.** **Forensic Accounting Problem**

Most employees that choose to commit fraud against their employers feel justified in doing so. For example, a demotion with a corresponding pay cut can provide motivation to produce what is called "wages in kind," where the employee creates his or her own wages.

**Required**

What actions might an organization take to prevent "wages in kind"?

---

# ANSWERS TO SELF-STUDY QUESTIONS:

1. b, (pp. 163–166)  2. c, (pp. 163–166)  3. d, (p. 174)  4. c, (p. 167)  5. d, (p. 170)
6. b, (p. 167)  7. b, (p. 165)

## Your Turn! Solutions

### Solution 4.1

**1.** Dec. 31 | Depreciation expense | 700 |
|     Accumulated depreciation—Buildings | | 700 |
| *To record depreciation on buildings.* | | |

**2.** Dec. 31 | Rent expense | 1,500 |
|     Prepaid rent | | 1,500 |
| *To record rent expense.* | | |

**3.** Dec. 31 | Unearned revenue | 400 |
|     Revenue | | 400 |
| *To recognize revenue earned on a previously recorded advance payment from a customer.* | | |

**4.** Dec. 31 | Interest expense | 500 |
|     Interest payable | | 500 |
| *To accrue interest expense.* | | |

**Solution 4.2**

| THE CASSI COMPANY<br>Income Statement<br>For the Year Ended December 31, 2011 | | |
|---|---|---|
| Sales revenues . . . . . . . . . . . . . . . . . . . . . . . . . . . . . . . . . . . . . . . . . . . . . . . . | | $52,000 |
| Expenses . . . . . . . . . . . . . . . . . . . . . . . . . . . . . . . . . . . . . . . . . . . . . . . . . . . . . | | |
|   Cost of goods sold . . . . . . . . . . . . . . . . . . . . . . . . . . . . . . . . . . . . . . . | $30,000 | |
|   Salaries expense . . . . . . . . . . . . . . . . . . . . . . . . . . . . . . . . . . . . . . . . | 5,000 | |
|   Rent expense . . . . . . . . . . . . . . . . . . . . . . . . . . . . . . . . . . . . . . . . . . . | 6,000 | |
|   Depreciation expense . . . . . . . . . . . . . . . . . . . . . . . . . . . . . . . . . . . . | 6,000 | |
|     Total expenses. . . . . . . . . . . . . . . . . . . . . . . . . . . . . . . . . . . . . . . | | 47,000 |
| Net income. . . . . . . . . . . . . . . . . . . . . . . . . . . . . . . . . . . . . . . . . . . . . . . . . | | $ 5,000 |

| THE CASSI COMPANY<br>Statement of Stockholders' Equity<br>For the Year Ended December 31, 2011 | Common<br>Stock | Retained<br>Earnings | Total |
|---|---|---|---|
| Balance, December 1, 2011 . . . . . . . . . . . . . . . . . . . . . . . . . . . | $15,000 | $5,000 | $20,000 |
| Add: Net income for December . . . . . . . . . . . . . . . . . . . . . . . | | 5,000 | 5,000 |
| Less: Dividends in December. . . . . . . . . . . . . . . . . . . . . . . . . . | | 2,000 | 2,000 |
| Balance, December 31, 2011 . . . . . . . . . . . . . . . . . . . . . . . . . . | $15,000 | $8,000 | $23,000 |

| THE CASSI COMPANY<br>Balance Sheet<br>As of December 31, 2011 | | | | | |
|---|---|---|---|---|---|
| **Assets** | | | **Liabilities** | | |
| Current assets | | | Current liabilities | | |
| Cash . . . . . . . . . . . . . . . . . . . . . . . . . . . . . | $ 4,000 | | Accounts payable . . . . . . . . . . . . | $ 8,000 | |
| Accounts receivable . . . . . . . . . . . . . . . . . | 15,000 | | Salaries payable . . . . . . . . . . . . . . | 9,000 | |
| Inventory . . . . . . . . . . . . . . . . . . . . . . . . . | 18,000 | | Dividends payable. . . . . . . . . . . . | 2,000 | |
| Prepaid rent. . . . . . . . . . . . . . . . . . . . . . . . | 5,000 | | Unearned service. . . . . . . . . . . . . | 5,000 | |
|   Total current assets. . . . . . . . . . . . . . . | | $42,000 |   Total current liabilities. . . . . . | | $24,000 |
| | | | Long-term debt . . . . . . . . . . . . . . | | 35,000 |
| Equipment . . . . . . . . . . . . . . . . . . . . . . . . . | 50,000 | | Total liabilities . . . . . . . . . . . . . . . . | | 59,000 |
| Less: Accumulated depreciation. . . . . . | 10,000 | 40,000 | **Stockholders' Equity** | | |
| | | | Common stock . . . . . . . . . . . . . . . | 15,000 | |
| | | | Retained earnings . . . . . . . . . . . . | 8,000 | |
| | | |   Total stockholders' equity . . . . . | | 23,000 |
| Total Assets . . . . . . . . . . . . . . . . . . . . . . . | | $82,000 | Total Liabilities and<br>  Stockholders' Equity. . . . . . . . | | $82,000 |

**Solution 4.3**

*a.* Permanent      *e.* Temporary
*b.* Permanent      *f.* Temporary
*c.* Temporary      *g.* Permanent
*d.* Permanent      *h.* Permanent

**Solution 4.4**

| | | | |
|---|---|---|---|
| Dec. 31 | Sales revenue | 79,000 | |
| |     Income summary | | 79,000 |
| | *To close the revenue account.* | | |
| Dec. 31 | Income summary | 72,000 | |
| |     Cost of goods sold | | 41,000 |
| |     Wage expense | | 22,000 |
| |     Rent expense | | 3,000 |
| |     Depreciation expense | | 2,000 |
| |     Interest expense | | 4,000 |
| | *To close the expense accounts.* | | |

| Dec. 31 | Income summary | 7,000 | |
| |     Retained earnings | | 7,000 |
| | *To close the Income Summary account.* | | |
| Dec. 31 | Retained earnings | 5,000 | |
| |     Dividends | | 5,000 |
| | *To close the Dividends account.* | | |

### Solution 4A.1

*a.* Permanent             *e.* Temporary
*b.* Permanent             *f.* Temporary
*c.* Temporary           *g.* Permanent
*d.* Permanent             *h.* Permanent

### Solution 4A.2

| Dec. 31 | Sales revenue | 79,000 | |
| |     Retained earnings | | 79,000 |
| | *To close the revenue account.* | | |
| Dec. 31 | Retained earnings | 72,000 | |
| |     Cost of goods sold | | 41,000 |
| |     Wage expense | | 22,000 |
| |     Rent expense | | 3,000 |
| |     Depreciation expense | | 2,000 |
| |     Interest expense | | 4,000 |
| | *To close the expense accounts.* | | |
| Dec. 31 | Retained earnings | 5,000 | |
| |     Dividends | | 5,000 |
| | *To close the dividends account.* | | |

# 5 Accounting for Merchandising Operations

| PAST | PRESENT | FUTURE |
|---|---|---|
| Chapters 1 through 4 explained the five-step accounting cycle: analyze, record, adjust, report, and close. | This chapter focuses on analyzing and recording merchandising transactions. We also introduce the classified income statement. | Chapter 6 describes the accounting for inventory, including cost assumptions, the lower of cost or market approach, and inventory analysis. |

## LEARNING OBJECTIVES

**1** **Explain** the operations of a merchandise company and **contrast** that with the operations of a service company. (p. 222)

**2** **Describe** the accounting for purchases of merchandise. (p. 225)

**3** **Describe** the accounting for sales of merchandise. (p. 230)

**4** **Describe** and **illustrate** a classified income statement. (p. 233)

**5** **Compute** cost of goods sold (periodic system). (p. 236)

**6** **Define** the gross profit percentage and the return on sales ratio, and **explain** their use in profitability analysis. (p. 237)

**7** Appendix 5A: **Describe** and **illustrate** a periodic inventory system. (p. 240)

# RIGHT ON TARGET

**Target Corporation** is one of the largest merchandising companies in the world with more than 1,500 stores and with sales exceeding $65 billion. Target sells products, often referred to as *inventory*. However, Target does not manufacture or make its inventory. Instead, it buys this inventory from manufacturers such as **Sony** and **Panasonic**, and then resells that inventory to consumers. Some refer to companies such as Target as "middlemen."

Target's recent balance sheet reports that it carries over $7 billion in inventory, which is about 39 percent of its total current assets. Further, Target's income statement shows that its cost of goods (or inventory) sold of $44 billion makes up more than 72 percent of its total operating expenses. Target must track all of these purchases and sales of its inventory.

This chapter describes the most common inventory system that merchandisers apply in today's business world. This system *perpetually* tracks all purchases and sales of inventory. Such tracking is important for managers to effectively manage this key asset and to regularly compute measures that report on management's ability to generate profit from inventory.

# THE NATURE OF MERCHANDISING

Manufacturers, wholesalers, and retailers are companies that sell products rather than services. Wholesalers and retailers are both merchandising firms. **Merchandising firms** buy finished products, warehouse and display the products for varying periods of time, and then resell the products. Merchandising firms do not manufacture products nor do they consume the products that they purchase. Merchandising firms provide additional services to their customers, but their primary business is the resale of goods produced by other companies. Exhibit 5-1 illustrates the typical relationship among these three types of companies and the final consumer.

**Manufacturers** convert raw materials and component parts into a finished product through the application of skilled labor and machine operations. **Ford Motor Company,** for example, converts raw materials such as sheets of steel and components such as tires into automobiles and trucks. Similarly, **Del Monte** converts such raw materials as fresh peaches and such components as metal cans into canned peaches. Manufacturers typically only sell their products to wholesale distributors. This process is referred to as a business-to-business (B2B) transaction.

**Wholesalers** buy finished products from manufacturing firms in large quantities. After warehousing the product for a period of time, the wholesale distributor sells and ships the product to various retailers in smaller quantities to satisfy the local demand for the product. Some wholesalers handle the products of only one manufacturer, while others handle the products of many manufacturers. **Retailers** typically buy products from wholesale distributors and resell the finished products to individual consumers in what is referred to as a business-to-consumer transaction (a B2C transaction). Retailers often have multiple store locations, including the Internet, where they display the products they are offering for sale, enabling customers to view and buy the products. Radio, television,

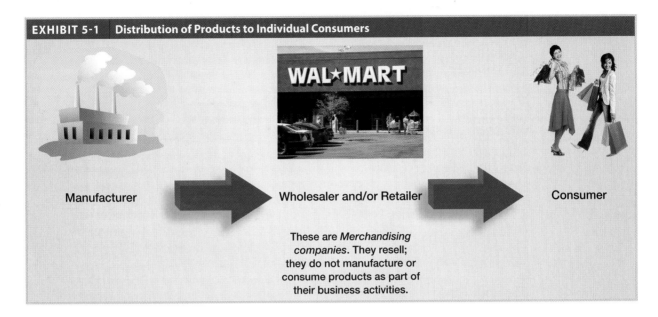

**EXHIBIT 5-1** **Distribution of Products to Individual Consumers**

Manufacturer → Wholesaler and/or Retailer → Consumer

These are *Merchandising companies*. They resell; they do not manufacture or consume products as part of their business activities.

newspaper, and online advertisements inform potential customers of product availability and price. Retailers may range in size from small, with only one store location, to large, with thousands of store locations along with an online Website, such as **Target.com**.

## OPERATING CYCLE OF A MERCHANDISING FIRM

Exhibit 5-2 presents the **operating cycle** of a merchandising firm. There are three primary transactions involved in a merchandising firm's operating cycle: (1) the purchase of merchandise and its placement in inventory; (2) the removal of merchandise from inventory when sold and delivered to the customer; and (3) the receipt of cash from the customer in payment for a cash-and-carry or prior credit purchase. These transactions involve three current asset accounts: cash, accounts receivable, and inventory. The purchased merchandise becomes part of the retailer's inventory until sold; an account receivable is created when the inventory is sold to a customer on credit; and, cash is received when the customer pays for the previously purchased goods. In those cases where a customer pays immediately with cash for the purchased merchandise, no accounts receivable is created.

In contrast, there are only two primary transactions involved in the operating cycle of a service firm: (1) performing a service, and (2) receiving cash from the customer. Service firms have no inventory to warehouse or display, and consequently, the length of their operating cycle is typically much shorter than that of a merchandising firm.

The three primary transactions for a merchandising firm repeat frequently, creating the cycle depicted in Exhibit 5-2. The timing of the cash collection (in Exhibit 5-2) depends upon the credit terms associated with the sale. When a wholesaler sells to a retailer, a B2B transaction, the sale is usually concluded on a credit basis. That is, the retailer is allowed some period of time following the sale, frequently 30 days or more, to pay the wholesaler for the purchased goods. Some retailers call a credit sale a **sale on account** (also referred to as **sale on credit**). "On account" means on a credit basis.

When retailers such as **Nordstrom** sell to individual consumers, the consumer can (1) pay cash at the time of the sale; (2) use a credit card such as **Discover**, **MasterCard**, or **Visa** or (3) use an "open account" with the retailer. An **open account** is a charge account provided by a retailer for its customers. Many retailers such as Target have their own branded credit card to facilitate open account sales. If a customer pays cash, the retailer receives cash immediately. If the customer uses a major credit card issued by a financial institution like **Citibank**, the retailer turns the credit card slip over to the card-issuing financial institution and collects the cash either on the same day or within a few days following the credit-sale transaction. If the customer uses an open account,

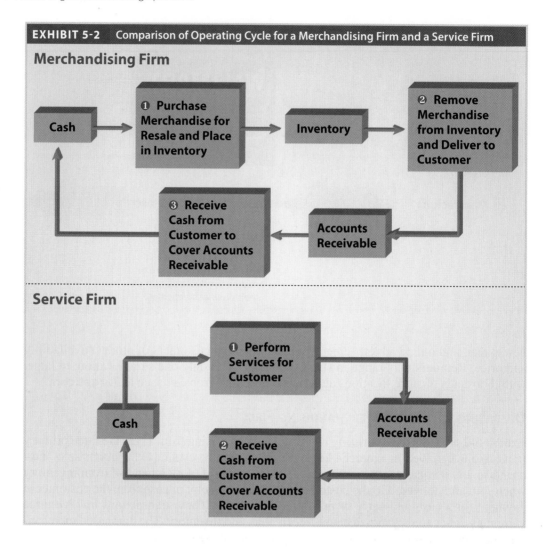

**EXHIBIT 5-2** Comparison of Operating Cycle for a Merchandising Firm and a Service Firm

the retailer may not collect the cash from the customer for 30 to 60 days, depending upon the length of the credit terms allowed by the retailer.

## COST FLOWS

The costs of inventory for merchandisers all flow through its accounting system as diagrammed below. Specifically, a company records its *costs of goods purchased* and adds this to any *beginning inventory* it might have. These two components make up the company's *cost of goods available for sale*. From that total, a company either sells part or all of this inventory, which is recorded in *cost of goods sold*, or carries some of its inventory into the next period, referred to as its *ending inventory*.

| CORPORATE SOCIAL RESPONSIBILITY | Governance and Conflicts of Interest |

An important component of good corporate responsibility is strong corporate governance. **Target** publishes a Business Conduct Guide for its employees as part of its governance program. Included in this handbook are guidelines concerning conflicts of interest. The list below provides examples of potential conflicts of interest:

- Owning a substantial amount of stock in any competing business or in any organization that does business with us.
- Serving as a director, manager, consultant, employee or independent contractor for any organization that does business with us, or is a competitor—except with our company's specific prior knowledge and consent.
- Accepting or receiving gifts of any value or favors, compensation, loans, excessive entertainment or similar activities from any individual or organization that does business or wants to do business with us, or is a competitor.
- Representing the company in any transaction in which you or a related person has a substantial interest.
- Disclosing or using for your benefit confidential or non-public information about Target or other organizations with which we do business.
- Taking personal advantage of a business opportunity that is within the scope of Target's business—such as by purchasing property that Target is interested in acquiring.

## INVENTORY SYSTEMS

There are two basic inventory systems available for merchandisers to account for their merchandise inventory: the **perpetual inventory system** and the **periodic inventory system**. The perpetual inventory system is discussed in the chapter, and the periodic inventory system is discussed in Appendix 5A at the end of this chapter.

As a consequence of the growing use of computerized accounting systems, most merchandising firms use the perpetual inventory system. The main difference between the two inventory systems is the timing of when the cost of merchandise inventory sold is calculated. Under a perpetual system, the cost of merchandise sold is calculated after every sale, and consequently, the inventory balance is kept "perpetually" up-to-date. By way of contrast, under a periodic system, the cost of merchandise sold is only calculated "periodically," specifically when a physical count of the inventory is undertaken, which usually occurs only at the end of a fiscal period. As a consequence, the actual inventory balance remains unknown until the end of a fiscal period.

A major advantage of the perpetual system is the increased control it provides over the inventory. Since the inventory is being continuously updated, management is able to determine whether current inventory levels are adequate to satisfy pending or expected sales. In addition, having a record of exactly how much inventory is available allows management to compare these amounts to a physical count of the inventory. Management can then investigate any difference between the amounts to identify the presence of theft or spoilage (in the case of perishable goods).

## ACCOUNTING FOR PURCHASES OF MERCHANDISE

When a company using the perpetual inventory system purchases merchandise, it debits the Inventory account for the acquisition cost of the merchandise purchased to reflect an increase in the amount of inventory and credits the Accounts Payable account to reflect an increase in the amount owed to the supplying company. For example, the Barton Wholesale Electronics purchase invoice for inventory shown in Exhibit 5.3 requires Barton's to record the company's purchase of merchandise from Malibu Manufacturing on November 10 with the following journal entry:

LEARNING OBJECTIVE 2

**Describe** the accounting for purchases of merchandise.

| Nov 10 | Inventory | 21,000 | | |
| | Accounts payable | | 21,000 | |
| | *To record the purchase of 100 disk drives from Malibu* | | | |
| | *Manufacturing with credit terms of 2/10, n/30.* | | | |

| A | = | L | + | SE |
|---|---|---|---|---|
| +21,000 | | +21,000 | | |

**EXHIBIT 5-3**  Invoice for Inventory Purchase

# INVOICE

Date: November 10, 2011
Invoice # 1050

Malibu Manufacturing
100 Computer Way
Claremont, CA 91711
909-607-6064
Fax 909-610-1234
sales@malibu.com

TO:
Barton Wholesale Electronics
100 Main Street
Anytown, CA 91234
123-456-7890
Customer ID ABC12345

SHIP TO:
George Jones
Barton Wholesale Electronics
100 Main Street
Anytown, CA 91234
123-456-7890
Cutomer ID ABC12345

| SALESPERSON | SHIPPING METHOD | SHIPPING TERMS | DELIVERY DATE | PAYMENT TERMS |
|---|---|---|---|---|
| Kate Kanzu | UPS | FOB Shipping Point | Nov 12, 2011 | 2/10, n/30 |

| QUANTITY | ITEM # | DESCRIPTION | UNIT PRICE | DISCOUNT | LINE TOTAL |
|---|---|---|---|---|---|
| 100 | A30 | 1.5 TB Disk Drives | 210 | | $21,000 |
| | | | | Total | $21,000 |

Make all checks payable to Malibu Manufacturing
Thank you for your business.

## TRANSPORTATION COSTS

**Transportation Costs Incurred by Buyer**  Transportation costs are sometimes incurred by a merchandising company when it acquires goods, and this cost is included as part of the acquisition cost of the inventory. When the buyer pays for shipping, it is referred to as **FOB shipping point**. FOB stands for **free on board**. Assume Barton pays $126 to a freight company on November 11, for transportation costs on the 100 disk drives purchased from Malibu Manufacturing. Barton makes the following journal entry to record the payment of $126:

| A | = | L | + | SE |
|---|---|---|---|---|
| +126 | | | | |
| −126 | | | | |

| Nov 11 | Inventory | 126 | |
|---|---|---|---|
| | Cash | | 126 |
| | *To record the payment of $126 of transportation costs for the purchase of 100 disk drives.* | | |

**PRINCIPLE ALERT**  **Cost Principle**

The inclusion of transportation cost in the acquisition cost of inventory is consistent with the *cost principle*. The cost principle states that an asset is initially recorded at the amount paid to acquire the asset. There can be multiple expenditures associated with an asset acquisition, and all expenditures that are reasonable and necessary to acquire an asset are added to the asset's initial recorded cost.

**Transportation Costs Incurred by Seller**  Instead of the facts above, assume that the seller, Malibu Manufacturing, paid the $126 transportation costs. In this case the transaction cost would be considered an operating expense of the seller, and Malibu Manufacturing would debit an expense account titled Freight-out Expense as follows:

| Nov 11 | Freight-out expense | 126 | |
| | Cash | | 126 |
| | *To record payment for the transportation cost for goods sold.* | | |

| A | = | L | + | SE |
|---|---|---|---|---|
| −126 | | | | −126 Exp |

When the seller pays for shipping, it is referred to as **FOB destination**. Malibu paid the freight charges on the Barton purchase of disk drives, and it will attempt to pass on this cost to the buyer in the form of a higher sales price for the items purchased.

## PURCHASE RETURNS AND ALLOWANCES

Occasionally, a purchaser is dissatisfied with some or all of the merchandise purchased because the merchandise was, for example, manufactured poorly, the wrong merchandise was shipped, or because the merchandise was damaged during shipping. When such circumstances are encountered, the purchaser and the seller can remedy the problem by agreeing to treat the value of the unwanted items either as a purchase return or as a purchase allowance.

With a **purchase return**, the purchaser ships the unsatisfactory merchandise back to the seller and receives a credit against the amount due equal to the **invoice price** of the returned merchandise. With a **purchase allowance**, the purchaser retains the merchandise, and the seller reduces the amount that the purchaser owes the seller for the shipment, in effect reducing the sales price.

A retailer can also return merchandise even though there is nothing wrong with the items. For example, textbook publishers often allow college bookstores to return any unsold textbooks to publishers at the conclusion of a term. When publishers allow bookstores to return unsold books, merchandise returns and merchandise allowances occur. In this case, the publisher increases its Inventory account balance by the invoice price of the returned textbooks.

As an example of a purchase return, assume that on November 15, Barton returns 10 of the 100 disk drives purchased on November 10. Barton has not yet paid Malibu Manufacturing for the goods purchased. Accordingly, Barton makes the following journal entry on November 15 to record the purchase return:

| Nov 15 | Accounts payable | 2,100 | |
| | Inventory | | 2,100 |
| | *To record a purchase return of 10 disk drives at an invoice price of* | | |
| | *$210 each to Malibu Manufacturing.* | | |

| A | = | L | + | SE |
|---|---|---|---|---|
| −2,100 | | −2,100 | | |

This entry reduces the Inventory account balance and reduces the amount owed. When the purchaser and seller reach agreement on how to handle a purchase return, they also must agree on which party pays the freight charges on the returned merchandise. (Usually the seller pays freight charges when goods are returned, in an attempt to maintain a positive customer relationship and to increase the likelihood of future repeat business.)

---

**ACCOUNTING IN PRACTICE** **Bar Codes**

Merchandisers often use bar codes with computerized inventory systems to account for inventory. The merchandiser prints bar codes on the outside of cartons containing the merchandise, enabling clerks with bar code scanners or robots with built-in scanners to read the codes to identify and trace the contents of cartons as they move into and out of warehouses and trucks.

---

## PURCHASE DISCOUNTS

**Credit Period**   When merchandise is sold on credit, the **credit period** is the maximum amount of time, often stated in days, that a purchaser can take to pay a seller for the purchased items. A typical credit period for a wholesale distributor is 30 days. The credit period is frequently described as the *net credit period*, or net terms. Merchandisers use the notation "**n/**" followed by the number of days in the credit period to designate the time period that a customer can take before paying cash for purchased goods. For example, **n/30** indicates a credit period of 30 days, and n/45 indicates a credit period of 45 days.

To encourage the early payment of unpaid bills, many firms offer their customers a cash discount if payment is made within a designated discount period. A **cash discount**, or **sales discount**, is the amount that the seller deducts from the invoice price if payment is made within the allowed discount period. Some refer to the cash discount offered to credit customers as a "quick-pay incentive." Sellers usually state cash discounts as a percent of the invoice price. The **discount period** is the maximum amount of time, stated in days, that a purchaser has within which to pay the seller if the purchaser wants to claim the cash discount. The discount period is always shorter than the credit period. Most merchandisers use the format "cash discount percent/discount period" to designate the cash discount and the discount period. For example, 1/10 indicates a cash discount of one percent of the invoice price and a discount period of ten days following the invoice date. Finally, merchandisers usually combine the notation for the cash discount and the discount period with the notation for the credit period. For example, 1/10, n/30 represents a cash discount of one percent if paid within ten days of the sale with a total credit period of 30 days following the date of the sale.

As an example let's return to the Barton example and assume that Malibu Manufacturing and Barton agree on terms of 2/10, n/30, for the sale on November 10. Barton deducts two percent of the $21,000 invoice price ($420) if it pays Malibu by November 20. In that case, Barton pays $20,580 cash (computed as 21,000 × [1 − .02]). If Barton pays Malibu after November 20 but no later than December 10, the amount that Barton must pay is $21,000. After December 10, the $21,000 amount would become overdue and often incurs additional interest cost depending on the invoice terms.

Discounts are normally attractive to merchandisers. For instance, if Barton did not take the discount offered by Malibu, this is like Barton paying an interest rate of 2 percent on the $21,000 for 20 days (30-day credit period − 10-day discount period). This is similar to paying an annual interest rate of 36.5 percent, computed as 2 percent × 365/20. Barton can borrow money at lower rates.

**Accounting for Discounts**   Let's extend the prior example where Barton owes $18,900 to Malibu Manufacturing; recall that Barton made a $21,000 purchase, then had a $2,100 purchase return, yielding an amount owed of $18,900.

**PAY WITHIN DISCOUNT PERIOD**   Assume that Barton makes a cash payment to Malibu on November 20, the last day of the discount period. (November 11, the first day following the date of sale, is the first day of the discount period, and November 20 is the tenth or last day of the discount period.) Barton records the cash payment, less the cash discount, with the following journal entry:

| A | = | L | + | SE |
|---|---|---|---|---|
| −378 | | −18,900 | | |
| −18,522 | | | | |

| Nov 20 | Accounts payable | 18,900 | |
|---|---|---|---|
| | Inventory | | 378 |
| | Cash | | 18,522 |
| | *To record the purchase discount and payment to Malibu* | | |
| | *Manufacturing within the discount period.* | | |

This entry reduces to zero the amount that Barton owes Malibu Manufacturing. It also records the purchase discount of two percent ($18,900 × 2 percent = $378) as a reduction of the cost in the Inventory account. The entry reveals that $18,522 in cash was paid by Barton to Malibu Manufacturing ($18,900 − $378 = $18,522). Two aspects of this transaction should be noted. First, the cash discount applies only to the cost of the merchandise and not to the transportation cost. Second, the invoice price of the returned merchandise is subtracted from the total invoice price before the cash discount is calculated.

The net total cost reflected in Barton's Inventory account for the disk drives follows:

| | | **Inventory** | | | |
|---|---|---|---|---|---|
| **Purchase (+ 100 units)** | **Nov 10** | 21,000 | | | |
| **Freight-in** | **Nov 11** | 126 | | | |
| | | | 2,100 | **Nov 15** | **Purchase return (−10 units)** |
| | | | 378 | **Nov 20** | **Purchase discount** |
| **Balance** | | 18,648 | | | |

A total cost of $18,648 is assigned to the 90 disk drives in Barton's inventory (100 purchased − 10 returned). This results in an average cost per disk drive of $207.20 ($18,648/90).

**PAY AFTER DISCOUNT PERIOD** If Barton made a cash payment to Malibu sometime between November 21 and December 10, after the discount period expired, Barton is not eligible to receive the two percent purchase discount. Consequently, Barton would record a full cash payment on November 25 with the following journal entry:

| Nov 25 | Accounts payable | 18,900 | |
| |     Cash | | 18,900 |
| | *To record full payment to Malibu Manufacturing following expiration of the discount period.* | | |

| A | = | L | + | SE |
|---|---|---|---|---|
| −18,900 | | −18,900 | | |

When Barton makes the payment to Malibu outside of the allowed discount period, the net total cost in Barton's Inventory account for the 90 disk drives is:

| | | **Inventory** | | | |
|---|---|---|---|---|---|
| **Purchase (+ 100 units)** | **Nov 10** | 21,000 | | | |
| **Freight-in** | **Nov 11** | 126 | | | |
| | | | 2,100 | **Nov 15** | **Purchase return (−10 units)** |
| **Balance** | | 19,026 | | | |

A total cost of $19,026 is assigned to the 90 disk drives in Barton's inventory, resulting in an average cost per disk drive of $211.40 ($19,026/90). The cost per disk drive is higher in this situation because Barton did not make the payment for the inventory in a timely fashion to make it eligible for the cash discount.

## Your Turn!      5.1

On June 1, Musicland Inc. purchases 125 CDs at $4.08 each on account from its distributor for a total of $510. The credit terms of the purchase were 2/10 n/30. Also on June 1, Musicland paid freight charges of $22.18 cash for delivery of the CDs. On June 4, Musicland returned 15 defective CDs for an account credit of $61.20. On June 8, Musicland paid $439.82 for the remaining 110 CDs.

Record these transactions in journal entry form for Musicland.

**The solution is on page 263.**

# ACCOUNTING FOR SALES OF MERCHANDISE

Manufacturing firms and merchandising firms credit Sales Revenue when they sell products, regardless of whether the sales transaction is on credit or for cash. The Sales Revenue account has a normal credit balance.

Let's return to our example and assume that Barton sells 15 disk drives purchased from Malibu Manufacturing (the assumed cost per unit = $18,648/90 disk drives = $207.20 per disk drive) to The Computer Outlet Store at a sales price of $280 per unit. Barton makes the credit sale on December 12, with terms of 1/10, n/15, and The Computer Outlet Store pays shipping cost. Barton makes the following *two* journal entries to record the sale:

| A | = | L | + | SE |
|---|---|---|---|---|
| +4,200 | | | | +4,200 Rev |

| Dec 12 | Accounts receivable | 4,200 | |
|---|---|---|---|
| | Sales revenue | | 4,200 |
| | *To record sale of 15 disk drives at a sales price of $280 each to The Computer Outlet Store with credit terms of 1/10, n/15.* | | |

| A | = | L | + | SE |
|---|---|---|---|---|
| −3,108 | | | | −3,108 Exp |

| Dec 12 | Cost of goods sold | 3,108 | |
|---|---|---|---|
| | Inventory | | 3,108 |
| | *To record sale of 15 disk drives with a unit cost of $207.20 to The Computer Outlet Store.* | | |

**REVENUE SIDE**   The first journal entry records $4,200 of sales revenue ($280 × 15 disk drives) from the sale to Computer Outlet. The debit to Accounts Receivable increases the amount due from customers, and the credit to Sales Revenue increases the total revenue from sales of merchandise during the accounting period.

**COST SIDE**   The second journal entry transfers the $3,108 cost of merchandise sold ($207.20 × 15 disk drives) from the Inventory account, an asset account, to the Cost of Goods Sold account, an expense account. The debit to Cost of Goods Sold increases the total cost of merchandise sold during the accounting period, and the credit to Inventory removes the cost of the merchandise sold from the Inventory account. **Cost of goods sold** is the total cost of merchandise sold to customers during the accounting period.

After recording this sale, the net cost in Barton's Inventory account related to the disk drives is $15,540, as follows:

| | | Inventory | | | |
|---|---|---|---|---|---|
| Purchase (+ 100 units) | Nov 10 | 21,000 | 2,100 | Nov 15 | Purchase return (−10 units) |
| Freight-in | Nov 11 | 126 | 378 | Nov 20 | Purchase discount |
| | | | 3,108 | Dec 12 | Cost of goods sold (−15 units) |
| Balance | | 15,540 | | | |

The $15,540 cost relates to the 75 disk drives (100 purchased − 10 returned − 15 sold) remaining in inventory. The average cost per disk drive remains $207.20 ($15,540/75 disk drives).

---

**PRINCIPLE ALERT** **Revenue and Expense Recognition**

The entry to record sales revenue when 15 disk drives are sold to The Computer Outlet Store illustrates the *revenue recognition principle*. For a merchandising firm, the revenue recognition principle states that revenue is recorded when goods are sold. Normally, this is the earliest point in time that the revenue is both earned (the company has made the economic effort to sell goods) and realized (the company has received payment or has a claim to receive payment for the goods sold). The entry to record the cost of goods sold illustrates the *expense recognition (matching) principle*. Expense recognition states that expenses should be recorded in the same accounting period as the revenues they help generate.

## SALES RETURNS AND ALLOWANCES

When buyers have returns and allowances, there are sellers that must record those same returns and allowances. With a sales return, the customer ships the merchandise back to the seller and the customer receives a reduction in the amount due to the seller. With a sales allowance, the customer retains the merchandise, and the seller reduces the amount the customer owes, in effect reducing the sales price.

Accounting for **sales returns and allowances** requires two journal entries. The first entry offsets the sales revenue generated from the transaction and reduces the amount owed by the customer. The second entry transfers the cost of merchandise from cost of goods sold back to the Inventory account. Extending the previous example, assume that on December 15, The Computer Outlet Store returned five of the disk drives that it had purchased on December 12. Computer Outlet returned the units because it ordered five units too many; there is nothing wrong with the disk drives. Barton records the sales return by making the following two journal entries:

| | | | |
|---|---|---|---|
| Dec 15 | Sales returns and allowances | 1,400 | |
| |     Accounts receivable | | 1,400 |
| | *To record the return of 5 disk drives by The Computer Outlet Store, with a sales price of $280 each.* | | |

| | | | |
|---|---|---|---|
| Dec 15 | Inventory | 1,036 | |
| |     Cost of goods sold | | 1,036 |
| | *To record the return of 5 disk drives with a unit cost of $207.20 from The Computer Outlet Store.* | | |

The first entry offsets the revenue generated from the sale by debiting Sales Returns and Allowances and it reduces the amount the customer owes by crediting Accounts Receivable. The Sales Returns and Allowances account is a *contra-revenue account* and is subtracted from gross sales revenue on the income statement.

The second journal entry transfers the cost of the merchandise from Cost of Goods Sold back to the Inventory account by debiting Inventory (increasing it) and by crediting Cost of Goods Sold (decreasing it). After recording the transfer from Cost of Goods Sold to Inventory, the net total cost in Barton's Inventory account related to the disk drives is:

**Hint:** Contra accounts, such as the contra-revenue account, are useful because they provide more information than if the related account were used by itself. For example, by using both the revenue and the contra-revenue accounts, it is possible to track how much of the original sales have had associated returns or allowances.

**Inventory**

| | | | | | |
|---|---|---|---|---|---|
| Purchase (+ 100 units) | Nov 10 | 21,000 | 2,100 | Nov 15 | Purchase return (− 10 units) |
| Freight-in | Nov 11 | 126 | 378 | Nov 20 | Purchase discount |
| Sales return (+ 5 units) | Dec 15 | 1,036 | 3,108 | Dec 12 | Cost of goods sold (− 15 units) |
| Balance | | 16,576 | | | |

The $16,576 total cost relates to 80 units (100 purchased − 10 purchase return − 15 sold + 5 sales return); and, the average cost of the inventory remains $207.20 ($16,576/80).

---

**ACCOUNTING IN PRACTICE**   **Monitoring Sales Returns and Allowances**

Companies accumulate sales revenue in one account and sales returns and allowances in another account so that they can monitor the two. A high ratio of sales returns and allowances to sales revenue is undesirable, often indicating a problem in the quality of the merchandise or its packaging. A company can compare the ratio for the current year to prior-year ratios or to a target ratio set for the current year to determine how well the company is managing its product and packaging quality.

---

## SALES DISCOUNTS

When making a cash payment for purchased goods, a customer is entitled to take a cash discount only if the payment is made during the allowed discount period. If a cash discount is taken, the seller records it in a separate account called Sales Discounts.

**PAY WITHIN DISCOUNT PERIOD** Returning to the previous example, assume that The Computer Outlet Store agrees to terms of 1/10, n/15, and it then pays the amount due Barton after deducting the 1 percent cash discount on December 22, the last day of the cash discount period. (December 13 is the first day of the discount period, and December 22 is the tenth or last day of the discount period.) Barton makes the following journal entry to record the cash received from Computer Outlet:

| Dec 22 | Cash | 2,772 | |
| | Sales discounts | 28 | |
| | Accounts receivable | | 2,800 |
| | *To record the sales discount and cash payment from The Computer Outlet Store within the allowed discount period.* | | |

This entry reduces the amount the customer, Computer Outlet, owes the seller, Barton, to zero. The total undiscounted amount due from The Computer Outlet Store was $2,800 ($4,200 sale − $1,400 sales return). With terms of 1/10, n/15, the sales discount is $28 ($2,800 × 1 percent); and, the cash collected is $2,772 ($2,800 − $28).

Companies accumulate sales discounts in a separate account. This enables management to monitor the dollar amount of sales discounts being taken by customers. Sales Discounts is a *contra-revenue account* like Sales Returns and Allowances. Both accounts are contra to, or subtracted from, gross Sales Revenue on the income statement. There are two important aspects of the sales discount calculation. First, the cash discount applies only to the sales price of the merchandise sold and not to any transportation cost. Second, the sales price of any merchandise returned must be subtracted from the total amount before calculating the cash discount.

**PAY AFTER DISCOUNT PERIOD** If The Computer Outlet Store makes a cash payment after December 22 (after the discount period has expired), the cash discount does not apply. For example, if cash is received in full payment from Computer Outlet on December 27, Barton would record the following journal entry:

| Dec 27 | Cash | 2,800 | |
| | Accounts receivable | | 2,800 |
| | *To record cash received from The Computer Outlet Store outside the allowed discount period.* | | |

## NET SALES

**Net sales** is the gross sales revenue generated through merchandise sales less any sales revenue given up through sales returns and allowances and any earned sales (cash) discounts. A company calculates its net sales for the period by subtracting the balances of the Sales Returns and Allowances account (normal debit balance) and the Sales Discounts account (normal debit balance) from the balance of the Sales Revenue account (normal credit balance).

---

### Your Turn! 5.2

On June 15, a customer buys 75 CDs on account from Musicland for $10 each, for a total of $750. The **list price** of the CDs is $12 each, but Musicland gave the customer a $2 per CD discount because of the large order. On June 20, the customer returned, unopened, five of the CDs and was given a purchase credit of $50. The customer paid its full balance of $700 on June 25. Record these transactions in journal entry form for Musicland. The unit cost of the CDs in inventory is $4.20 each.*

  *$4.20 is calculated from the prior Your Turn! as follows:

  Inventory cost = $510.00 + $ 22.18 − $61.20 − $8.98 = $462.00
  Inventory quantity = 125 − 15 = 110
  Cost per unit = $462.00/110 = $4.20

**The solution is on page 264.**

# CLASSIFIED INCOME STATEMENT

LEARNING OBJECTIVE 4

**Describe and illustrate a classified income statement.**

In Chapter 2, the classified balance sheet was introduced. On a classified balance sheet, the assets, liabilities and stockholders' equity accounts are grouped into well-defined subgroups to make the balance sheet more informative for creditors, managers, stockholders, and potential investors. In this chapter, we introduce the classified income statement, with a similar objective.

A **classified income statement** presents revenues and expenses in distinct categories to facilitate financial analysis and management decision making. A classified income statement provides financial statement users with more information, and thus, enables them to make better and more informed decisions about a business. Exhibit 5-4 presents the components of a classified income statement for a service company and for a merchandising company. For a service company, Total Operating Expenses are subtracted from Sales Revenues to determine Income from Operations. Operating expenses are those expenses that relate to the primary operating activities of a business. Operating expenses are commonly classified as either Selling Expenses or Administrative Expenses. Revenue and expense items that do not relate to the primary operating activities of the company appear in a separate category called *Other Income and Expense.* The net amount of other income and expense is either added to or subtracted from Income from Operations to determine a company's Net Income.

| **EXHIBIT 5-4** | **Components of a Classified Income Statement** |
| --- | --- |

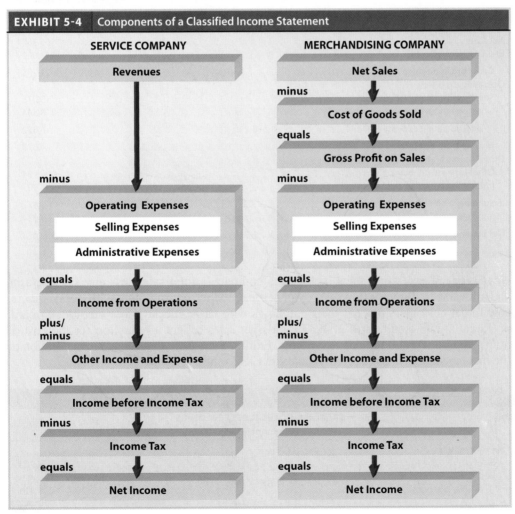

For a merchandising company, the Cost of Goods Sold is subtracted from the firm's Net Sales to determine its gross profit on sales. **Gross profit,** or **gross profit on sales,** is defined as the difference between Net Sales and Cost of Goods Sold and reveals the amount of sales revenue remaining after subtracting the cost of products sold. (Recall that

**A.K.A.** Gross profit is often referred to as *gross margin.*

net sales equals gross sales revenue less any sales returns and allowances and sales discounts.) Gross profit also reveals how much sales revenue remains to cover a business's operating expenses. The remainder of the structure of a merchandising company's classified income statement (following gross profit) is the same as the structure of the service company's classified income statement.

Exhibit 5-5 presents a classified income statement for the **Target Corporation** for the year ended January 30, 2010. Target's classified income statement provides the financial statement user with four measures of company performance: gross profit on sales, income from operations, income before income taxes, and net income. Gross profit on sales indicates just how well the company performed in terms of purchasing goods, warehousing those goods, and pricing the goods for sale. Income from operations reports Target's performance after considering the cost of running its stores, paying its employees, advertising to its customers, and administering the business. The income before income taxes reports the company's performance after considering various nonoperating items like interest expense and interest income but before subtracting the expected cost of income taxes. Net income reports Target's bottom-line performance—that is, after all costs of running the business are subtracted.

| EXHIBIT 5-5 | Classified Income Statement for a Merchandising Company |
| --- | --- |

**TARGET CORPORATION**
**Income Statement (in millions)**
**For Year Ended January 30, 2010**

| | |
| --- | --- |
| Net sales ...................... | $65,357 |
| Less cost of goods sold ................... | 44,062 |
| **Gross profit on sales** .................. | 21,295 |
| Operating expenses | |
| Selling and administrative.................. | 13,078 |
| Other operating expenses.................. | 3,544 |
| Total operating expenses ............... | 16,622 |
| **Income from operations** .............. | 4,673 |
| Other income and expense | |
| Other expense (income)................... | 94 |
| Interest expense ...................... | 707 |
| Income before income taxes................ | 3,872 |
| Income tax expense ..................... | 1,384 |
| **Net income**...................... | $ 2,488 |

**Net Sales**    Target's net sales include the company's total sales less any sales returns and allowances. Target follows a very generous product-return policy with its customers, and Target customers pay for their purchases with cash, check, major credit/debit card, or Target's own credit card. Thus, Target's net sales reflect a reduction for the cost of returned products and for sales discounts. Exhibit 5-6 shows the sales revenue section of the income statement for Barton Wholesale Electronics.

| EXHIBIT 5-6 | Sales Revenue Section |
| --- | --- |

**BARTON WHOLESALE ELECTRONICS**
**Income Statement (sales section)**

| | | |
| --- | --- | --- |
| Sales revenues | | |
| Sales........................ | | $4,200 |
| Less: Sales returns and allowances ............... | $1,400 | |
| Sales discounts ...................... | 28 | 1,428 |
| **Net sales** ...................... | | **$2,772** |

**Gross Profit**    Cost of goods sold is typically the largest expense for a merchandising company. It is subtracted directly from net sales to highlight the gross profit on sales. The gross profit on sales is an important financial indicator for investment professionals who follow retail companies like **Target**. Analysts compare the gross profit on sales between retailers as a way to assess the effectiveness of the retailer's pricing and purchasing policies. Following is the gross profit section of the income statement for Barton Wholesale Electronics.

| BARTON WHOLESALE ELECTRONICS Income Statement (gross profit section) | |
| --- | --- |
| Net sales .......................................................................... | $2,772 |
| Cost of goods sold.............................................................. | 2,072 |
| **Gross profit**...................................................................... | **$ 700** |

**Operating Expenses** The operating expenses section includes those expenses that relate to the primary operating activities of a business. Operating expenses consist primarily of selling expenses and administrative expenses. In Exhibit 5-5, examples of Target's selling and administrative expenses include sales salaries expense, delivery expense, advertising expense, depreciation expense, rent expense, office salaries expense, and supplies expense. Following is the operating expenses section of the income statement for Barton Wholesale Electronics.

| BARTON WHOLESALE ELECTRONICS Income Statement (operating expenses section) | |
| --- | --- |
| Gross profit....................................................................... | $700 |
| **Operating expenses**........................................................... | **450** |
| Income from operations ....................................................... | $250 |

**Other Income and Expenses** This section of the income statement is sometimes labeled Nonoperating activities. Examples of revenues and expenses that do not relate to the primary operating activities of a merchandising firm include:

| Other Expenses and Losses | Other Revenues and Gains |
| --- | --- |
| —Interest expense | —Interest revenue |
| —Losses on asset sales | —Gains on asset sales |
| | —Dividend revenue |

These items are reported in the Other Income and Expense section that follows the financial information regarding a business's primary operating activities.

**IFRS ALERT!**

Appendix C at the end of this book presents the classified income statement for **Tesco PLC**. Tesco is a United Kingdom-based company and is the world's third largest retailer. Tesco is the parent company of Fresh and Easy Neighborhood Markets, a chain of small supermarkets located principally in the western United States. Tesco uses IFRS to prepare its classified income statement. Make a list of the similarities and any differences between Tesco's classified income statement and **Target's** classified income statement in Exhibit 5.5. Like Target, Tesco reports four measures of company performance: gross profit, operating profit, profit before tax, and profit for the year. Differences include: (1) Tesco uses the word "profit" instead of "income"; (2) Tesco lumps all of its noninventory operating expenses into one category called "administrative expenses"; and (3) Tesco refers to its interest income as "finance income" and its interest expense as "finance expense." Other than these labeling differences, Tesco's classified income statement under IFRS is strikingly similar to Target's U.S. GAAP classified income statement.

---

## Your Turn! 5.3

Musicland provides the following information and requests that we prepare a classified income statement for the year ended December 31, 2010. Musicland pays income tax at the rate of 30 percent of income.

| | | | |
|---|---|---|---|
| Net sales ............................. | $100,000 | Other operating expense ........ | 10,000 |
| Cost of goods sold........................ | 45,000 | Other income and expense* ..... | 5,000 |
| Selling and administrative expenses ....... | 25,000 | | |

*Other income and expense consists of $10,000 in interest expense and a $5,000 gain from sale of equipment.

**The solution is on page 264.**

---

**LEARNING OBJECTIVE 5**

**Compute** cost of goods sold (periodic system).

**Cost of Goods Sold Using a Periodic System**   If a firm uses a periodic system rather than a perpetual system, it does not record cost of goods sold at the time sales revenue is recorded. Instead, cost of goods sold is calculated periodically at the end of the accounting period when the inventory is physically counted. Cost of goods sold is then backed into by subtracting the ending inventory from the **cost of goods available for sale**, which represents the total inventory that was available to be sold. The calculation of cost of goods sold using the periodic method is shown in Exhibit 5-7.

| **EXHIBIT 5-7** | Cost of Goods Sold Computation Using the Periodic Method |
|---|---|

|   | |
|---|---|
| | Beginning inventory |
| + | Cost of goods purchased during the period |
| | Cost of goods available for sale |
| − | Ending inventory |
| = | Cost of goods sold |

One additional difference between the periodic method and the perpetual method is how a company keeps track of items that affect the Inventory account. Under the perpetual system, items such as transportation charges, purchase returns, and purchase discounts, are debited and credited directly to the Inventory account. Under the periodic system, separate accounts are used for each of these items, which are then added to beginning inventory to arrive at the cost of goods available for sale. An illustration of this is shown in Exhibit 5-8, assuming that there was no beginning inventory.

| **EXHIBIT 5-8** | Cost of Goods Sold Illustration Using the Periodic Method |
|---|---|

**BARTON WHOLESALE ELECTRONICS**
**Cost of Goods Sold**
**For Year Ended December 31, 2011**

| | | | |
|---|---|---|---|
| Cost of goods sold | | | |
| Inventory, January 1............................................. | | | $ 0 |
| Purchases....................................................... | | $21,000 | |
| Less: Purchase returns and allowances........................... | $2,100 | | |
| Purchase discounts......................................... | 378 | 2,478 | |
| Net purchases ................................................ | | 18,522 | |
| Add: Freight-in................................................. | | 126 | |
| Cost of goods purchased........................................ | | | 18,648 |
| Cost of goods available for sale ................................... | | | 18,648 |
| Less: Inventory, December 31..................................... | | | 16,576 |
| Cost of goods sold........................................... | | | $ 2,072 |

# PROFITABILITY ANALYSIS

## GROSS PROFIT PERCENTAGE

Managers, investment professionals, and stockholders closely monitor a company's gross profit on sales. They know that if gross profit on sales declines from one year to the next, net income for the current and following year is also likely to decline. A declining gross profit can indicate problems in a company's purchasing activities or problems selling its goods at an acceptable price. Financial statement users who monitor a company's gross profit on sales are also usually interested in its **gross profit percentage**—that is, the rate at which a company earns gross profit on its sales revenue. A merchandising company measures its gross profit percentage as follows:

$$\text{Gross profit percentage} = \frac{\text{Gross profit on sales}}{\text{Net sales}}$$

The 2009 gross profit percentage for **Target** is 32.6 percent, computed as $21,295/$65,357.

Financial analysis of the gross profit percentage frequently involves benchmarking the company against competitor companies. Profit margins for a two-year period are presented in Exhibit 5-9 for both **Target Corporation** and one of its chief competitors, **Walmart Corporation**.

| **EXHIBIT 5-9** | **Gross Profit Percentage for Target Corporation and Walmart Corporation** | |
|---|---|---|
| **(in millions)** | **2008** | **2009** |
| Target | $20,791/$64,948 = 32.0 percent | $21,295/$ 65,357 = 32.6 percent |
| Walmart | $99,449/$405,607 = 24.5 percent | $95,086/$401,244 = 23.7 percent |

Target's gross profit percentage increased 0.6 percent, from 32.0 percent in 2008 to 32.6 percent in 2009. In addition, Target has a higher gross profit percentage than Walmart. The likely reason for this result is Walmart's decision to increase its sales of groceries. Groceries typically have a very low gross profit percentage and thus would drag down a company's overall gross profit percentage. Walmart's gross profit percentage is only 24.5 percent in 2008 and 23.7 percent in 2009. Another explanation for the large difference between the gross profit percentages of the two companies is their different business strategies. Target attempts to sell higher-quality products at a reasonable price, whereas Walmart focuses more on low prices and less on product quality.

## COST OF GOODS SOLD PERCENTAGE

Another measure of a company's performance that investors and managers consider is the **cost of goods sold percentage**, calculated as:

$$\text{Cost of goods sold percentage} = \frac{\text{Cost of goods sold}}{\text{Net sales}}$$

For Target in 2009, this percentage is 67.4 percent (computed as $44,062/$65,357). The cost of goods sold percentage indicates how much of each dollar of sales revenue must go to pay for the cost of product sold. Stated alternatively, 67.4 cents of each dollar of Target's sales revenue is needed to cover the company's cost of merchandise sold and only 32.6 cents is available to cover the other expenses of the business and provide for net income. The following summarizes these percentages for Target:

| | | |
|---|---:|---:|
| Net sales | $65,357 | 100.0% |
| Cost of goods sold | 44,062 | 67.4% |
| Gross profit on sales | $21,295 | 32.6% |

| | Concept ➜ | Method ➜ | Assessment |
|---|---|---|---|
| **TAKEAWAY 5.1** | Is a company able to maintain prices on its goods consistent with changes in the cost of its inventory? | Gross profit and net sales<br><br>$\text{Gross profit percentage} = \dfrac{\text{Gross profit on sales}}{\text{Net sales}}$ | A higher ratio suggests the company has market power to command higher retail prices. A lower ratio suggests competitive pressures on price setting. |

## RETURN ON SALES RATIO

First introduced in Chapter 2, the **return on sales ratio** reveals the net income earned on each dollar of net sales and is computed by dividing net income by net sales:

$$\text{Return on sales ratio} = \frac{\text{Net income}}{\text{Net sales}}$$

Target's return on sales ratio is 3.8 percent, computed as $2,488/$65,357. A company has a number of ways to improve its return on sales ratio, for example, by raising its retail prices or by purchase discounts by buying in larger quantities. It could also reduce operating expenses by reducing salaries, administrative costs, or selling and marketing costs. Analysts like to compare return on sales ratios for a company over time to detect any trends. They also like to compare the ratio with those of competitors. Return on sales ratios are presented in Exhibit 5-10 for **Target Corporation** and **Walmart Corporation**.

| **EXHIBIT 5-10**    Return on Sales Ratios for Target Corporation and Walmart Corporation | | |
|---|---|---|
| **(in millions)** | **2008** | **2009** |
| Target | $2,214/$64,948 = 3.4 percent | $2,488/$65,357 = 3.8 percent |
| Walmart | $13,400/$405,607 = 3.3 percent | $13,400/$401,244 = 3.3 percent |

Both Target and Walmart have similar return on sales ratios for 2009, with each company realizing net income of over 3 cents for each dollar of sales. This ratio allows us to compare a company's ability to earn profits on its sales regardless of company size. Walmart generates over six times the sales revenue as does Target ($65,357 million for Target versus $401,244 for Walmart), yet Target has a higher return on sales ratio. The return on sales for both companies increased from 2008 to 2009, although Target's increase was greater.

| Concept | → | Method | → | Assessment | |
|---|---|---|---|---|---|
| Is a company able to maintain prices on its goods consistent with changes in its total expenses? | | Net income and net sales<br><br>Return on sales ratio $= \dfrac{\text{Net income}}{\text{Net sales}}$ | | A higher ratio suggests the company is providing a higher net income on each dollar of net sales. | TAKEAWAY 5.2 |

## Your Turn! 5.5

The President of Musicland has asked for help to evaluate the company's performance during 2010. In particular, we are requested to calculate Musicland's gross profit percentage and its return on sales ratio and then explain what these measures indicate. The following information is from Musicland's financial statements:

| | |
|---|---|
| Net sales .................................................................... | $100,000 |
| Cost of goods sold......................................................... | 45,000 |
| Net income................................................................. | 10,500 |

**The solution is on page 265.**

## WORKING WITH THE TAKEAWAYS

**Costco Wholesale Corporation** is the largest membership warehouse club chain in the world based on sales volume. It is the fifth largest general retailer in the United States. Costco is also one of the fastest growing retailers, having grown to over 500 locations since its start in 1983. A look at Costco's income statement reveals the following data:

| COSTCO WHOLESALE CORPORATION | | |
|---|---|---|
| (in millions) | 2009 | 2008 |
| Net sales .................................................................... | $72,483 | $64,400 |
| Cost of goods sold......................................................... | 63,503 | 56,450 |
| Net income................................................................. | 1,283 | 1,082 |

**Required:**
Evaluate Costco's performance in terms of gross profit percentage and return on sales ratio. How does Costco compare to **Target** and **Walmart**?

**Solution:**

| (in millions) | 2009 | 2008 |
|---|---|---|
| Gross profit percentage............ | $8,980*/$72,483 = 12.4 percent | $7,950/$64,400* = 12.3 percent |
| Profit margin ratio ................ | $1,283/$72,483 = 1.8 percent | $1,082/$64,400 = 1.7 percent |
| | *$72,483 − $63,503 | *$64,400 − $56,450 |

Costco's gross profit percentage improved slightly from 12.3 percent in 2008 to 12.4 percent in 2009; however, this percentage was well below the gross profit percentage for both Target (32.6 percent) and Walmart (23.7 percent) in 2009. This suggests that Costco does not mark up the prices it charges its customers as much as either Target or Walmart.

Costco's return on sales ratio improved slightly from 1.7 percent in 2008 to 1.8 percent in 2009. Again, however, this percentage is well below that of either Target (3.8 percent) or Walmart (3.3 percent) in 2009. On a more positive note, it appears that Costco does a better job of controlling its operating expenses than does either Target or Walmart. This is evident because the difference between Costco's gross profit percentage (12.4 percent − 1.8 percent = 10.6 percent in 2009) is much smaller than for either Target (32.6 percent − 3.8 percent = 28.8 percent) or Walmart (23.7 percent − 3.3 percent = 20.4 percent). One possible explanation for this relates to advertising and marketing costs. Both Target and Walmart have significant advertising and marketing expenditures to attract and retain customers. Costco is able to advertise much less because its business model is based on a membership fee.

APPENDIX 5A

# APPENDIX 5A:  Periodic Inventory System

An alternative to the perpetual inventory system is the periodic inventory system. The **periodic inventory system** does not update the Inventory account or the Cost of Goods Sold account as merchandise transactions occur during the year. Instead, the Inventory account and the Cost of Goods Sold account are updated only at the end of the accounting period when a physical count of the inventory on hand is undertaken. The periodic inventory system is unacceptable for most companies because up-to-date inventory amounts are not available during the year for managerial decision making. The following section illustrates the journal entries that Barton Wholesale Electronics would make if it used the periodic inventory system. We utilize the same data used in the chapter to illustrate the perpetual inventory system to facilitate an easy comparison of the two systems.

## ACCOUNTING FOR PURCHASES OF MERCHANDISE

When a company uses the periodic inventory system, it records the purchase of merchandise by debiting the cost of the merchandise to the Purchases account, rather than the Inventory account, and crediting the cost to Accounts Payable. (The Purchases account has a normal debit balance.) On November 10, Barton records the purchase of 100 disk drives with a list price of $210 each and terms of 2/10, n/30 by making the following journal entry:

| A | = | L | + | SE |
|---|---|---|---|---|
| | | +21,000 | | −21,000 |

| Nov 10 | Purchases | 21,000 | |
| |     Accounts payable | | 21,000 |
| | *To record the purchase of 100 disk drives from Malibu* | | |
| | *with 2/10, n/30 terms.* | | |

**Transportation Costs**   When a purchaser using the periodic inventory system bears the cost of transporting the merchandise from the seller, the purchaser records the transportation cost in the Freight In account, rather than in the Inventory account. (The Freight In account has a normal debit balance.) Barton makes the following journal entry on November 12 to record payment of $126 of transportation costs on the purchase of 100 disk drives:

| A | = | L | + | SE |
|---|---|---|---|---|
| −126 | | | | −126 |

| Nov 12 | Freight in | 126 | |
| |     Cash | | 126 |
| | *To record the payment of $126 of transportation costs on the* | | |
| | *purchase of 100 disk drives.* | | |

**Purchase Returns and Allowances**   If a purchaser is dissatisfied with merchandise that was purchased and a purchase return or allowance is granted, the purchaser records the purchase return or allowance using the Purchase Returns and Allowances account, rather than the Inventory account. (Purchase Returns and Allowances is a contra-purchases account with a normal credit balance.) On November 15, Barton records the return of 10 disk drives to Malibu Manufacturing by making the following journal entry:

| A | = | L | + | SE |
|---|---|---|---|---|
| | | −2,100 | | +2,100 |

| Nov 15 | Accounts payable | 2,100 | |
| |     Purchase returns and allowances | | 2,100 |
| | *To record the return of 10 disk drives at a list price of $210.* | | |

**Purchase Discounts**   If a purchaser makes a cash payment to the seller before the end of the allowed discount period, the purchaser deducts a cash discount. Otherwise, the purchaser pays the full invoice price. When a purchaser takes a cash discount, the purchaser credits the Purchase Discounts account, rather than the Inventory account. (Purchase Discounts is a contra-purchases account with a normal credit balance.) Barton makes the following journal entry on November 20 to record its cash payment to Malibu Manufacturing after deducting the cash discount:

| A | = | L | + | SE |
|---|---|---|---|---|
| −18,522 | | −18,900 | | +378 |

| Nov 20 | Accounts payable | 18,900 | |
| |     Purchase discounts | | 378 |
| |     Cash | | 18,522 |
| | *To record the payment to Malibu Manufacturing within the* | | |
| | *allowed discount period.* | | |

If Barton makes payment between November 21 and December 10, after the discount period has expired, the cash discount does not apply. In this case, Barton records a cash payment on November 25 with the following journal entry:

| Nov 25 | Accounts payable | 18,900 | |
| | Cash | | 18,900 |
| | *To record the payment to Malibu Manufacturing outside the allowed discount period.* | | |

| A | = | L | + | SE |
|---|---|---|---|---|
| −18,900 | | −18,900 | | |

## ACCOUNTING FOR SALES OF MERCHANDISE

Under the periodic inventory system, a seller makes only one journal entry to record a sale of merchandise. The entry records an account receivable from the customer and the sales revenue from the sale by debiting Accounts Receivable and crediting Sales Revenue. Barton records the December 12 sale of 15 disk drives to The Computer Outlet Store at a sales price of $280 each with terms of 1/10, n/15 by making the following entry:

| Dec 12 | Accounts receivable | 4,200 | |
| | Sales revenue | | 4,200 |
| | *To record the sale of 15 disk drives at a sales price of $280 each to The Computer Outlet Store with credit terms of 1/10, n/15.* | | |

| A | = | L | + | SE |
|---|---|---|---|---|
| +4,200 | | | | +4,200 Rev |

The same journal entry is made under the perpetual inventory system. Under the periodic inventory system, however, there is no concurrent entry to transfer the cost of merchandise sold from the Inventory account to the Cost of Goods Sold account.

**Sales Returns and Allowances**   Under the periodic inventory system, only one journal entry is used to record a sales return or allowance. The entry records the reduction of the revenue from the sale and the reduction of the account receivable from the customer by debiting Sales Returns and Allowances and crediting Accounts Receivable. Barton records the December 15 return by The Computer Outlet Store of five disk drives by making the following journal entry:

| Dec 15 | Sales returns and allowances | 1,400 | |
| | Accounts receivable | | 1,400 |
| | *To record the return of 5 disk drives by The Computer Outlet Store; sales price was $280 each.* | | |

| A | = | L | + | SE |
|---|---|---|---|---|
| −1,400 | | | | −1,400 Rev |

This entry is the same as the first journal entry under the perpetual inventory system; however, Barton does not make the second journal entry that was made under the perpetual inventory system. Under the periodic inventory system, there is no immediate reinstatement of the returned merchandise to the Inventory account or corresponding reduction in the Cost of Goods Sold account.

**Sales Discounts**   The journal entry to record the receipt of a cash payment from a customer is exactly the same under either the perpetual inventory system or the periodic inventory system. If the payment is made within the allowed discount period, the entry includes a debit to Sales Discounts, a contra-sales account. Barton records the cash received from The Computer Outlet Store on December 22 (within the discount period) as follows:

| Dec 22 | Cash | 2,772 | |
| | Sales discounts | 28 | |
| | Accounts receivable | | 2,800 |
| | *To record the cash payment from The Computer Outlet Store within the discount period.* | | |

| A | = | L | + | SE |
|---|---|---|---|---|
| +2,772 | | | | −28 Rev |
| −2,800 | | | | |

If The Computer Outlet Store makes its cash payment any time between December 23 and December 27 (after the discount period), the cash discount does not apply. Barton records the cash received from Computer Outlet on December 27 with the following journal entry:

| Dec 27 | Cash | 2,800 | |
| | Accounts receivable | | 2,800 |
| | *To record the cash payment from The Computer Outlet Store outside the discount period.* | | |

| A | = | L | + | SE |
|---|---|---|---|---|
| +2,800 | | | | |
| −2,800 | | | | |

Exhibit 5.11 summarizes all key journal entries under both the perpetual and periodic inventory systems for purchases and sales of merchandise.

**APPENDIX 5A**

**EXHIBIT 5-11** Comparison of Journal Entries under the Perpetual and Periodic Systems

| Date | Transaction | Perpetual Inventory System | | | Periodic Inventory System | | |
|------|-------------|---------------------------|---|---|---------------------------|---|---|
| Nov 10 | Purchase of merchandise on credit | Inventory<br>    Accounts payable | 21,000 | 21,000 | Purchases<br>    Accounts payable | 21,000 | 21,000 |
| Nov 11 | Freight cost | Inventory<br>    Cash | 126 | 126 | Freight In<br>    Cash | 126 | 126 |
| Nov 15 | Purchase returns | Accounts payable<br>    Inventory | 2,100 | 2,100 | Accounts payable<br>    Purchase returns | 2,100 | 2,100 |
| Nov 20 | Purchase discount and payment | Accounts payable<br>    Inventory<br>    Cash | 18,900 | 378<br>18,522 | Accounts payable<br>    Purchase discounts<br>    Cash | 18,900 | 378<br>18,522 |
| Dec 12 | Sale of merchandise on credit | Accounts receivable<br>    Sales revenue | 4,200 | 4,200 | Accounts receivable<br>    Sales revenue | 4,200 | 4,200 |
| | | Cost of goods sold<br>    Inventory | 3,108 | 3,108 | No entry | | |
| Dec 15 | Return of sales merchandise | Sales returns and allowances<br>    Accounts receivable | 1,400 | 1,400 | Sales returns and allowances<br>    Accounts receivable | 1,400 | 1,400 |
| | | Inventory<br>    Cost of goods sold | 1,036 | 1,036 | No entry | | |
| Dec 22 | Sales discount and payment | Cash<br>Sales discounts<br>    Accounts receivable | 2,772<br>28 | 2,800 | Cash<br>Sales discounts<br>    Accounts receivable | 2,772<br>28 | 2,800 |

## Your Turn! 5.6

Assume that Musicland uses the *periodic system*. On June 1, Musicland purchased 125 CDs at $4.08 each on account from its distributor for $510. The terms of the purchase were 2/10, n/30. Also on June 1, Musicland paid in cash a freight charge of $22.18 for delivery of the CDs. On June 4, Musicland returned 15 defective CDs for a credit of $61.20. On June 8, Musicland paid $439.82 for the remaining 110 CDs. Record the transactions in journal entry form for Musicland.

The solution is on page 265.

## Your Turn! 5.7

Assume Musicland uses the *periodic system*. On June 15, a customer buys on account 75 CDs from Musicland for $10 each, for a total of $750. The list price of the CDs is $12 each, but Musicland provided the customer with a $2 per CD discount because of the large order. On June 20, the customer returned, unopened, five of the CDs and was given a credit of $50. The customer paid its full balance of $700 on June 25. Record these transactions on Musicland's books. The unit cost of the CDs in inventory is $4.20 each.*

    *$4.20 is computed from Your Turn 5.1 as follows:

      Inventory cost = $510.00 + $ 22.18 − $61.20 − $8.98 = $462.00
      Inventory quantity = 125 − 15 = 110
      Cost per unit = $462.00 / 110 = $4.20

The solution is on page 265.

## SUMMARY OF LEARNING OBJECTIVES

**LO1** **Explain the operations of a merchandise company and contrast that with the operations of a service company. (p. 222)**

- Merchandise inventory is a stock of products that a company buys from another company and makes available for sale to its customers.
- Merchandising firms sell merchandise. There are two types of merchandising firms: wholesale distributors and retailers.

- Manufacturing companies convert raw materials and components into finished products through the application of skilled labor and machine operations; wholesale distributors buy finished product from manufacturing firms in large quantities and sell smaller quantities to retailers; retailers sell the products to individual consumers.
- The operating cycle of a merchandising firm consists of three types of transactions: purchase merchandise for resale and warehouse the inventory, remove goods from inventory and ship to the customer at sale, and receive cash from the customer.
- The primary revenue source for a service firm is from providing services to customers, rather than manufacturing or selling a physical product.

## Describe the accounting for purchases of merchandise. (p. 225) LO2

- The perpetual inventory system records the cost of merchandise in the Inventory account at the time of purchase and updates the Inventory account for subsequent transactions as they occur.
- When the perpetual inventory system is used, the Inventory account is affected by merchandise transactions as follows:
  - Debited for the invoice price of purchases.
  - Debited for transportation costs.
  - Credited for the cost of purchase returns and allowances.
  - Credited for cash discounts taken.
  - Credited for the cost of the merchandise sold.
  - Debited for the cost of any sales returns.

## Describe the accounting for sales of merchandise. (p. 230) LO3

- When a perpetual inventory system is used, the following procedure is followed to account for the sale of merchandise:
  - Credit Sales Revenue at the time of the sale, and debit Cash or Accounts Receivable.
  - Debit Cost of Goods Sold and credit Inventory at the time of sale to match expenses with revenue and to update the inventory balance.

## Describe and illustrate a classified income statement. (p. 233) LO4

- A classified income statement for a merchandising firm often includes one section for sales revenues; two sections for expenses: cost of goods sold and operating expenses; and a section for other income and expenses.
- A classified income statement for a service firm is similar but only includes two sections—sales revenues and operating expenses.

## Compute cost of goods sold (periodic system). (p. 236) LO5

- The periodic inventory system does not update the Inventory account or the Cost of Goods Sold account as merchandise transactions occur during the year. Instead, the Inventory account and the Cost of Goods Sold account are updated only at the end of the accounting period when a physical count of the inventory is taken. Other accounts are used to record purchases, transportation costs, purchase returns and allowances, and purchase discounts.
- The year-end physical count of inventory is taken to verify the inventory balance. It consists of three steps:
  - Count the number of individual items of merchandise on hand at the end of the year.
  - Determine the unit cost of each individual item and multiply the unit cost times the quantity on hand to obtain the total cost for each individual item of merchandise.
  - Add together the total cost of all the individual items to obtain the total cost of the inventory on hand.
- Cost of goods sold is calculated by subtracting the remaining inventory on hand from the cost of goods available for sale, which represents the aggregate inventory that was available to be sold.
- The basic formula for calculating the cost of goods sold under the periodic system is to calculate goods available for sale consisting of beginning inventory plus net purchases during the period, and then subtract ending inventory from this amount.

## Define the gross profit percentage and the return on sales ratio, and explain their use in profitability analysis. (p. 237) LO6

- The gross profit percentage is the rate at which a company earns gross profit on net sales.
- The gross profit percentage is calculated as net sales less the cost of goods sold, all divided by net sales.
- The return on sales ratio reveals how much of each dollar of net sales is earned by the company after subtracting all expenses.
- The return on sales ratio is calculated by dividing net income by net sales.

REVIEW

**Appendix 5A: Describe and illustrate a periodic inventory system. (p. 240)**

■ The periodic inventory system updates both the Inventory account and the Cost of Goods Sold account at the end of the accounting period when a physical count of the inventory is taken.

■ Under the periodic inventory system separate accounts are used to record merchandise purchases, transportation costs, purchase returns and allowances, and purchase discounts, rather than recording these items to the Inventory account.

### TAKEAWAYS: SUMMARY CHART

| | Concept ⟶ | Method ⟶ | Assessment |
|---|---|---|---|
| **TAKEAWAY 5.1** | Is a company able to maintain prices on its goods consistent with changes in the cost of its inventory? | Gross profit and net sales $$\text{Gross profit percentage} = \frac{\text{Gross profit on sales}}{\text{Net sales}}$$ | A higher ratio suggests the company has market power to command higher retail prices. A lower ratio suggests competitive pressures on price setting. |
| **TAKEAWAY 5.2** | Is a company able to maintain prices on its goods consistent with changes in its total expenses? | Net income and net sales $$\text{Return on sales ratio} = \frac{\text{Net income}}{\text{Net sales}}$$ | A higher ratio suggests the company is providing a higher of net income on each dollar of net sales. |

## GLOSSARY OF KEY TERMS

**Cash discount** An amount that a purchaser of merchandise may deduct from the purchase price for paying within the allowed discount period (p. 228).

**Classified income statement** An income statement in which items are classified into subgroups to facilitate financial analysis and management decision making (p. 233).

**Cost of goods available for sale** An amount that represents the inventory available to be sold, consisting of the beginning inventory plus purchases during the period (p. 236).

**Cost of goods sold** The total cost of merchandise sold to customers during the accounting period; often abbreviated as COGS (p. 230).

**Cost of goods sold percentage** The ratio of cost of goods sold divided by net sales (p. 238).

**Credit period** The maximum time period, stated in days, that a purchaser of merchandise has to pay a seller (p. 227).

**Discount period** The maximum amount of time, stated in days, that a purchaser of merchandise has to pay a seller if the purchaser wants to claim any available cash discount (p. 228).

**FOB destination** Free on board destination indicates that the items being shipped are owned by the seller while the items are in transit (p. 227).

**FOB shipping point** Free on board shipping point indicates that the items being shipped are owned by the buyer while the items are in transit (p. 226).

**Free on board** A term for determining ownership for items in transit (p. 226).

**Gross profit** The difference between net sales and cost of goods sold; also called gross margin (p. 233).

**Gross profit percentage** The ratio of gross profit divided by net sales (p. 238).

**Inventory shrinkage** The cost associated with an inventory shortage; the amount by which the perpetual inventory exceeds the physical inventory (p. 237).

**Invoice price** The price that a seller charges a purchaser for merchandise (p. 227).

**List price** The suggested price or reference price of merchandise in a catalog or price list (p. 232).

**Manufacturer** A company that converts raw materials and components into finished goods through the application of skilled labor and machine operations (p. 222).

**Merchandise inventory** A stock of goods that a company buys from another company and makes available for sale to its customers (p. 222).

**Merchandising firm** A company that buys finished goods, stores the goods for varying periods of time, and then resells the goods (p. 222).

**Net sales** The total revenue generated by a company through merchandise sales less the revenue given up through sales returns and allowances and less the revenue given up through sales discounts (p. 232).

**Open account** A charge account provided by a retailer for its customers (p. 223).

**Operating cycle** For a particular business, the average period of time between the use of cash in its typical operating activity and the subsequent collection of cash from customers (p. 223).

**Periodic inventory system** A system that records merchandise transactions in a variety of accounts; the Inventory account and Cost of Goods Sold account are not updated until the end of the period when a physical count of the inventory is taken (p. 225).

**Perpetual inventory system** A system that records the cost of merchandise inventory in the Inventory account at the time of purchase and updates the Inventory account for subsequent purchases and sales of merchandise as they occur (p. 225).

**Physical count of inventory** A year-end procedure that involves counting the quantity of each inventory item, determining the unit cost of each item, multiplying the unit cost times the quantity on hand, and summing the costs of all the items to determine the total inventory at cost (p. 237).

**Purchase allowance** A reduction in the selling price of merchandise granted by a seller due to dissatisfaction by the purchaser (p. 227).

**Purchase return** Shipping unsatisfactory merchandise from a purchaser back to the seller for a purchase allowance (p. 227).

**Retailer** A company that buys goods from wholesale distributors and sells the goods to individual customers (p. 222).

**Return on sales ratio** The ratio of net income divided by net sales, representing the net profit earned on each dollar of net sales (p. 239).

**Sale on account** A sale of merchandise made on a credit basis (p. 223).

**Sale on credit** See sale on account (p. 223).

**Sales discounts** An account used by a seller to record cash discounts taken by a buyer when payment is made during the allowed discount period (p. 228).

**Sales returns and allowances** An account used by a seller to record either the return of merchandise by a buyer or an allowance given to the buyer in lieu of a return (p. 231).

**Service company** A firm whose primary revenue source is from providing services to a customer rather than manufacturing or selling a physical product. (p. 222)

**Wholesaler** A company that buys finished products from manufacturing firms in large quantities and resells the products to retailers (p. 222).

## COMPREHENSIVE PROBLEM

Williams Distributing Company is a merchandising company. Williams uses the perpetual inventory system. Record each of the following transactions related to the company's purchasing and selling of merchandise:

March 1  Purchased merchandise on account for $6,000; terms were 2/10, n/30.
     3  Paid $200 cash for freight on the March 1 purchase.
     6  Returned merchandise costing $300 (part of the $6,000 purchase).
   10  Paid for merchandise purchased on March 1.
   12  Sold merchandise on account costing $8,000 for $10,000; terms were 2/10, n/30.
   15  Accepted returned and undamaged merchandise from a customer costing $400 that had been sold on account for $500 (part of the $10,000 sale).
   20  Received payment from customer for merchandise sold on March 12.

### Solution

| Date | Account | Debit | Credit |
|---|---|---|---|
| March 1 | Inventory | 6,000 | |
| |     Accounts payable | | 6,000 |
| | *Purchased merchandise with 2/10, n/30 terms.* | | |
| 3 | Inventory | 200 | |
| |     Cash | | 200 |
| | *Paid freight on March 1 purchase.* | | |
| 6 | Accounts payable | 300 | |
| |     Inventory | | 300 |
| | *Returned merchandise from March 1 purchase.* | | |
| 10 | Accounts payable | 5,700 | |
| |     Inventory | | 114 |
| |     Cash | | 5,586 |
| | *Paid for merchandise purchased on March 1 within the discount period [($6,000 − $300) × 2% = $114].* | | |
| 12 | Accounts receivable | 10,000 | |
| |     Sales revenue | | 10,000 |
| | *To record revenue from sale of merchandise.* | | |
| 12 | Cost of goods sold | 8,000 | |
| |     Inventory | | 8,000 |
| | *To record cost of merchandise sold and to reduce inventory.* | | |
| 15 | Sales returns and allowances | 500 | |
| |     Accounts receivable | | 500 |
| | *To record revenue lost from return by customer.* | | |
| 15 | Inventory | 400 | |
| |     Cost of goods sold | | 400 |
| | *To record cost of goods returned by customer.* | | |
| 20 | Cash | 9,310 | |
| | Sales discounts | 190 | |
| |     Accounts receivable | | 9,500 |
| | *To record receipt of cash from customer within the discount period.* | | |

# SELF-STUDY QUESTIONS

**(Answers to the Self-Study Questions can be found at the end of this chapter.)**

LO4    **1.** A merchandising company's classified income statement differs from that of a service company in what way?
  - *a.* There is no difference.
  - *b.* A service company does not include a line for cost of goods sold.
  - *c.* A service company has a line for selling expenses whereas a merchandising company does not.
  - *d.* A merchandising company will have a line for income from operations whereas a service company will not.

LO2    **2.** On March 1, Troy Company purchased merchandise with an invoice price of $2,700 and 2/10, n/30 terms. On March 3, Troy pays $100 transportation cost on the purchased goods. On March 10, Troy pays for the merchandise. What is Troy's total cost of the purchased merchandise?
  - *a.* $2,700
  - *b.* $2,744
  - *c.* $2,746
  - *d.* $2,800

LO2    **3.** Newman Company started business on January 1. During the year, the company purchased merchandise with an invoice price of $500,000. Newman also paid $20,000 freight on the merchandise. During the year, Newman also returned $80,000 of the merchandise to its suppliers. All purchases were paid for in a timely manner, and a $10,000 cash discount was taken. $418,000 of the merchandise was sold for $627,000. What is the December 31, balance in the Inventory account?
  - *a.* $82,000
  - *b.* $32,000
  - *c.* $12,000
  - *d.* $2,000

LO3    **4.** Saber Company uses the perpetual inventory system. Saber purchased merchandise with an invoice price of $800, terms 2/10, n/30. If Saber returns merchandise with an invoice price of $200 to the supplier, what should the journal entry to record the return include?
  - *a.* Debit to Inventory of $200
  - *b.* Debit to Inventory of $196
  - *c.* Credit to Inventory of $200
  - *d.* Credit to Inventory of $100

LO6    **5.** Ira Company reports net sales of $500, cost of sales of $300, and net income of $50. What is the gross profit percentage and return on sales ratio for Ira?
  - *a.* Gross profit percentage is 10 percent and return on sales ratio is 40 percent.
  - *b.* Gross profit percentage is 60 percent and return on sales ratio is 10 percent.
  - *c.* Gross profit percentage is 40 percent and return on sales ratio is 10 percent.
  - *d.* Gross profit percentage is 40 percent and return on sales ratio is 25 percent.

LO3    **6.** Smith & Sons purchased $5,000 of merchandise from the Claremont Company with terms of 3/10, n/30. How much discount is Smith & Sons entitled to take if it pays within the allowed discount period of 10 days?
  - *a.* $50
  - *b.* $100
  - *c.* $150
  - *d.* $300

LO3    **7.** Moonitz Inc. purchased merchandise with a list price of $6,000 from the Sprague Company. Sprague offers its customers credit terms of 2/10, n/30. What amount should Moonitz pay if the cash discount is taken?
  - *a.* $5,940
  - *b.* $6,060
  - *c.* $6,120
  - *d.* $5,880

LO5    **8.** Kali Company began the period with $20,000 in inventory. The company also purchased an additional $20,000 of inventory and returned $2,000 for a full credit. A physical count of the inventory at year-end revealed an inventory on hand of $16,000. What was Kali's cost of goods sold for the period?
  - *a.* $16,000
  - *b.* $22,000
  - *c.* $48,000
  - *d.* $50,000

9. The Arcadia Company is a merchandiser and reports the following data at year-end:   **LO6**

| | |
|---|---|
| Net sales........................................... | $100,000 |
| Cost of goods sold ................................ | 60,000 |
| Net income ........................................ | 15,000 |

What is the company's gross profit percentage?
- *a.* 40 percent
- *b.* 60 percent
- *c.* 15 percent
- *d.* None of the above

10. Using the data in Question 9, what is The Arcadia Company's return on sales ratio?   **LO6**
- *a.* 40 percent
- *b.* 60 percent
- *c.* 15 percent
- *d.* None of the above

11. Denald Co. uses the periodic inventory system. When goods are purchased, Denald will:   **LO7**
- *a.* debit freight costs to Inventory.
- *b.* debit purchase returns and allowance for returned items.
- *c.* debit the Purchases account for purchases on account.
- *d.* debit the Inventory account for purchases on account.

12. Which of the following statements regarding cost flows is true?   **LO1**
- *a.* Cost of goods available for sale is equal to beginning inventory minus cost of goods purchased.
- *b.* Cost of goods available for sale is equal to beginning inventory plus cost of goods purchased.
- *c.* CGAS = beginning inventory minus ending inventory.
- *d.* CGAS = cost of goods sold minus cost of goods purchased.

## DISCUSSION QUESTIONS

1. Describe the differences between (a) a manufacturer, (b) a wholesale distributor, and (c) a retailer.
2. Describe the three primary transactions in the operating cycle of a merchandising firm.
3. What is the difference between a credit period and a discount period? What is a cash discount?
4. Sprague Company purchased merchandise with a list price of $2,000 from the Thompson Company. Thompson offers a two percent cash discount if payment is received within 10 days. What is the payment amount if the cash discount is taken?
5. Krane Company purchased $4,000 of merchandise and paid $250 in transportation costs to deliver the merchandise. Krane then returned $1,000 of the merchandise before paying the supplier within the discount period. Krane was entitled to a two percent cash discount. How much did Krane pay the supplier?
6. What is the primary difference between a merchandise return and a merchandise allowance?
7. What are the three steps that make up the year-end physical count of inventory?
8. Define the *return on sales ratio*. What does this ratio measure?
9. What are the components of a classified income statement for a merchandising firm?
10. Define *gross profit on sales.*
11. For each item listed below, indicate whether it is an element of (a) cost of goods sold, (b) selling expense, (c) administrative expense, (d) both selling and administrative expense—allocated between them—or (e) other income and expense: insurance expense, transportation cost on merchandise purchases, interest expense, office salaries expense, depreciation expense, and advertising expense.
12. Define *normal operating cycle.*
13. Define *gross profit percentage.* How is this percentage used by analysts and investors?
14. When merchandisers and manufacturers prepare income statements for their annual reports to shareholders, they usually begin the statement with net sales. For internal reporting purposes, however, the income statements will show gross sales and the related contra-revenue accounts of sales returns and allowances and sales discounts. What might explain this difference in the financial information disclosed to external parties and management? Do you consider the more limited disclosure in the annual reports to be inconsistent with the full disclosure principle? Briefly explain your point of view.

## Short Exercises

**LO1** **SE5-1.** **Merchandising versus Service Firm**

For each of the following accounts, indicate whether it would be found in the records of a merchandising firm, a service firm, or both.

a. Cost of goods sold.
b. Service revenue.
c. Purchase returns and allowances.
d. Inventory.
e. Accounts receivable.
f. Accounts payable.
g. Sales revenue.
h. Freight-out.

**LO2** **SE5-2.** **Accounting for Purchase Transactions**

Debra Company began operations on June 1. The following transactions took place in June:

a. Purchases of merchandise on account were $600,000.
b. The cost of freight to receive the inventory was $20,000. This was paid in cash.
c. Debra returned $10,000 of the merchandise due to an ordering error. Debra received a full credit for the return.
d. Debra paid the remaining balance for the merchandise.

Calculate the dollar amount that Debra will have in inventory at the end of the month. Assume Debra uses the perpetual inventory system and there were no sales.

**LO2** **SE5-3.** **Accounting for Purchase Transactions**

Use the data from SE5-2 and prepare the journal entries to record the June transactions.

**LO2** **SE5-4.** **Accounting for Purchase Discounts**

Ken Company purchased $5,000 of merchandise from Marilyn Company with terms of 3/10 n/45. What percent discount will Ken Company get if it pays within the allowed discount period? If Ken Company fails to pay within the discount period, how many days does Ken Company have from the date of purchase before the payment is considered to be late?

**LO2** **SE5-5.** **Accounting for Purchase Discounts**

Using the information in SE5-4, what amount will Ken Company pay to Marilyn Company if Ken Company takes advantage of the purchase discount?

**LO3** **SE5-6.** **Accounting for Sales Transactions**

Kate Company uses the perpetual inventory system. Record the journal entries for the following transactions:

a. On July 16, Kate sold $600 of merchandise with terms of 2/10 n/30. The cost of the merchandise was $360.
b. On July 19, the customer returned $100 of the merchandise from (a). The cost of the merchandise was $60.
c. On July 22, the customer paid the entire balance due to Kate.

**LO4** **SE5-7.** **The Classified Income Statement**

Dino Company, a merchandising firm, reports the following data for the month ended January 31:

| | |
|---|---:|
| Net sales | $10,000 |
| Cost of goods sold | 4,000 |
| Operating expenses | 3,000 |
| Other income | 500 |
| Income tax expense | 1,200 |

Prepare a classified income statement for Dino Company for the month of January.

**LO5** **SE5-8.** **Cost of Goods Sold and the Periodic System**

Kanzu Company uses the periodic inventory system. Kanzu started the period with $10,000 in inventory. The Company purchased an additional $25,000 of merchandise, and returned $1,000 for a full credit. A physical count of inventory at the end of the period revealed that there was an ending inventory balance of $8,000. What was Kanzu's cost of goods sold during the period?

**SE5-9. Cost of Goods Sold and the Periodic System**  LO5

Hermani Company uses the periodic inventory system. Hermani started the period with $20,000 in inventory. The Company purchased an additional $25,000 of merchandise and returned $3,000 for a full credit. If Hermani's cost of goods sold during the period was $35,000, what must have been the total of the physical inventory count?

**SE5-10. Gross Profit Percentage**  LO6

Using the data in SE5-7, compute Dino's gross profit percentage for the month of January.

**SE5-11. Return on Sales Ratio**  LO6

Using the data in SE5-7, compute Dino's return on sales ratio for the month of January.

**SE5-12. Journalize Periodic Inventory Entries**  LO7

Prepare the journal entries to record the following transactions for the Walbright Company using a periodic inventory system.  **(Appendix 5A)**

*a.* On June 2, Walbright purchased $350,000 of merchandise from the Ferway Company with terms, 3/15, n/30.
*b.* On June 5, Walbright returned $50,000 of the merchandise purchased on June 2.
*c.* On June 13, Walbright paid the balance due to Ferway.

# EXERCISES—SET A

**E5-1A. Cash Discount Calculations**  LO3

On June 1, Forest Company sold merchandise with a list price of $24,000. For each of the sales terms below, determine the proper amount of cash received:

| | Credit Terms | Date Paid |
|---|---|---|
| 1. | 2/10, n/30 | June 8 |
| 2. | 1/10, n/30 | June 15 |
| 3. | 1/15, n/30 | June 14 |
| 4. | n/30 | June 28 |

**E5-2A. Journal Entries for Sale, Return, and Remittance—Perpetual System**  LO3

On September 13, Brady Company sold merchandise with an invoice price of $900 ($600 cost), with terms of 2/10, n/30, to Dalton Company. On September 17, $150 of the merchandise ($100 cost) was returned because it was the wrong model. On September 23, Brady Company received a check for the amount due from Dalton Company.

**Required**
Prepare the journal entries made by Brady Company for these transactions. Brady uses the perpetual inventory system.

**E5-3A. Journal Entries for Purchase, Return, and Remittance—Perpetual System**  LO2

On April 13, the Kesselman Company purchased $22,000 of merchandise from the Krausman Company, with terms of 1/10, n/30. On April 15, Kesselman paid $300 to Ace Trucking Company for freight on the shipment. On April 18, Kesselman Company returned $1,000 of merchandise for credit. Final payment was made to Krausman on April 22. Kesselman Company records purchases using the perpetual inventory system.

**Required**
Prepare the journal entries that Kesselman Company should make on April 13, 15, 18, and 22.

**E5-4A. Journal Entries for Merchandise Transactions on Seller's and Buyer's Books—**  LO3
**Perpetual System**

The following are selected transactions for Lamont, Inc., during the month of June:

June 21 Sold and shipped on account to Lowery Company, $2,880 ($2,000 cost) of merchandise, with terms of 2/10, n/30.

28 Lowery Company returned defective merchandise billed at $280 on June 21 ($210 cost).

30 Received from Lowery Company a check for full settlement of the June 21 transaction.

**Required**

Prepare the necessary journal entries for (a) Lamont, Inc., and (b) Lowery Company. Both companies use the perpetual inventory system.

**LO2** **E5-5A.** **Recording Purchases—Perpetual System**

On July 1, Alvarez, Inc. purchased merchandise for $1,800, with terms of 2/10, n/30. On July 5, the firm returned $600 of the merchandise to the seller. Payment of the account occurred on July 8. Alvarez uses the perpetual inventory system.

**Required**

a. Prepare the journal entries for July 1, July 5, and July 8.

b. Assuming that the account was paid on July 14, prepare the journal entry for payment on that date.

**LO2, LO5** **E5-6A.** **Year-End Physical Inventory**

The December 31 inventory for the Hayes Company included five products. The year-end physical count revealed the following:

| Product | Quantity available |
|---------|--------------------|
| A | 26 |
| B | 50 |
| C | 34 |
| D | 75 |
| E | 40 |

The related unit costs were: A, $10; B, $6; C, $5; D, $8; and E, $7.

**Required**

Calculate the total cost of the December 31 physical inventory.

**LO4** **E5-7A.** **Classified Income Statement**

From the following accounts, listed in alphabetical order, prepare a classified income statement for Karlman Distributors for the year ended December 31. All accounts have normal balances.

| | | | | |
|---|---|---|---|---|
| Advertising expense | $ 18,000 | Salaries expense (office) | $ 35,000 |
| Cost of goods sold | 330,000 | Salaries expense (sales) | 83,000 |
| Delivery expense | 25,000 | Sales revenue | 560,000 |
| Interest expense | 3,000 | Sales discounts | 10,000 |
| Rent expense (office) | 21,000 | Supplies expense (office) | 4,000 |
| Income tax expense | 10,000 | | |

**LO6** **E5-8A.** **Profitability Analysis**

Shannon Enterprises reports the following information on its year-end income statement:

| | | | |
|---|---|---|---|
| Net sales | $150,000 | Operating expenses | 30,000 |
| Cost of goods sold | 90,000 | Other income | 10,000 |

**Required**

Calculate Shannon's gross profit percentage and return on sales ratio.

**LO5** **E5-9A.** **Journal Entries for Sale, Return, and Remittance—Periodic System**

On June 8, Stevens Company sold merchandise listing for $1,600 to Dalton Company, terms 2/10, n/30. On June 12, $400 worth of the merchandise was returned because it was the wrong color. On June 18, Stevens Company received a check for the amount due.

**Required**

Record the journal entries made by Stevens Company for these transactions. Stevens uses the periodic inventory system.

**E5-10A. Journal Entries for Purchase, Return, and Remittance—Periodic System**

LO7 (Appendix 5A)

On March 10, Horton Company purchased $18,000 worth of merchandise from James Company, terms 1/10, n/30. On March 12, Horton paid $160 freight on the shipment. On March 15, Horton returned $200 of merchandise for credit. Final payment was made to James on March 19. Horton Company uses the periodic inventory system.

**Required**

Prepare the journal entries that Horton should make on March 10, March 12, March 15, and March 19.

**E5-11A. Journal Entries for Merchandise Transactions on Seller's and Buyer's Records—Periodic System**

LO7 (Appendix 5A)

The following are selected transactions for Franklin, Inc., during the month of April:

April 20 Sold and shipped on account to Lind Stores merchandise for $2,400, with terms of 2/10, n/30.

    27 Lind Stores returned defective merchandise billed at $200 on April 20.

    29 Received from Lind Stores a check for full settlement of the April 20 transaction.

**Required**

Prepare the necessary journal entries for (a) Franklin, Inc., and (b) Lind Stores. Both companies use the periodic inventory system.

# EXERCISES—SET B

**E5-1B. Cash Discount Calculations**

LO3

On April 1, the Fitzgerald Company sold merchandise with a list price of $40,000. For each of the sales terms below, determine the proper amount of cash received:

| | Credit Terms | Date Paid |
|---|---|---|
| 1. | 1/15, n/30.... | April 14 |
| 2. | n/30 ......... | April 28 |
| 3. | 2/10, n/30.... | April 8 |
| 4. | 1/10, n/30.... | April 15 |

**E5-2B. Journal Entries for Sale, Return, and Remittance—Perpetual System**

LO3

On October 14, the Patrick Company sold merchandise with an invoice price of $1,000 ($750 cost), with terms of 2/10, n/30, to the Baxter Company. On October 18, $200 of merchandise ($150 cost) was returned because it was the wrong size. On October 24, the Patrick Company received a check for the amount due from the Baxter Company.

**Required**

Prepare the journal entries for the Patrick Company using the perpetual inventory system.

**E5-3B. Journal Entries for Purchase, Return, and Remittance—Perpetual System**

LO3

On May 15, Monique Company purchased $25,000 of merchandise from the Terrell Company, with terms of 1/10, n/30. On May 17, Monique paid $260 to Swift Trucking Company for freight on the shipment. On May 20, Monique Company returned $500 of merchandise for credit. Final payment was made to Terrell on May 24. Monique Company records purchases using the perpetual inventory system.

**Required**

Prepare the journal entries that Monique Company should make on May 15, 17, 20, and 24.

**E5-4B. Journal Entries for Merchandise Transactions on Seller's and Buyer's Books—Perpetual System**

LO3

The following are selected transactions of Candello, Inc., during the month of June:

June 18 Sold and shipped on account to Dante Company $4,000 ($3,000 cost) of merchandise, with terms of 2/10, n/30.

    25 Dante Company returned defective merchandise billed at $400 on June 18 ($300 cost).

    27 Received from Dante Company a check for full settlement of the June 18 transaction.

**Required**

Prepare the necessary journal entries for (a) Candello, Inc., and (b) Dante Company. Both companies use the perpetual inventory system.

**LO2  E5-5B.  Recording Purchases—Perpetual System**

On September 12, Evans, Inc., purchased merchandise for $3,000, with terms of 2/10, n/30. On September 16, the firm returned $900 of the merchandise to the seller. Payment of the account occurred on September 19. Evans uses the perpetual inventory system.

**Required**

a.  Prepare the journal entries for September 12, September 16, and September 19.
b.  Assuming that the account was paid on September 25, prepare the journal entry for payment on that date.

**LO3  E5-6B.  Year-End Physical Inventory**

The December 31, inventory for the Simmons Company included five products. The year-end physical count revealed the following quantities on hand:

| Product | Quantity on Hand |
|---------|------------------|
| K | 40 |
| L | 36 |
| M | 60 |
| N | 52 |
| P | 55 |

The related unit costs are K, $7; L, $10; M, $8; N, $5; and P, $4.

**Required**

Calculate the total cost of the December 31, physical inventory.

**LO4  E5-7B.  Classified Income Statement**

From the following accounts, listed in alphabetical order, prepare a classified income statement for Kokomo Wholesale for the year ended December 31. All accounts have normal balances.

| | | | |
|---|---|---|---|
| Advertising expense | $ 22,000 | Salaries expense (office) | $ 45,000 |
| Cost of goods sold | 400,000 | Salaries expense (sales) | 95,000 |
| Delivery expense | 30,000 | Sales revenue | 670,000 |
| Interest expense | 4,000 | Sales discounts | 12,000 |
| Rent expense (office) | 26,000 | Supplies expense (office) | 5,000 |
| Income tax expense | 8,000 | | |

**LO6  E5-8B.  Profitability Analysis**

Alex Enterprises reports the following information on its year-end income statement:

| | | | |
|---|---|---|---|
| Net sales | $300,000 | Operating expenses | 60,000 |
| Cost of goods sold | 180,000 | Other income | 20,000 |

**Required**

Calculate Alex's gross profit percentage and return on sales ratio.

**LO5  E5-9B.  Journal Entries for Sale, Return, and Remittance—Periodic System**

On March 10, the Sharon Company sold merchandise listing for $2,000 to the Dillard Company with terms of 2/10, n/30. On March 14, $500 of merchandise was returned because it was the wrong size. On March 20, Sharon Company received a check for the amount due.

**Required**

Prepare the journal entries made by Sharon Company for these transactions. Sharon uses the periodic inventory system.

**LO7  E5-10B.  Journal Entries for Purchase, Return, and Remittance—Periodic System**
**(Appendix 5A)**

On August 15, the Harris Company purchased $20,000 of merchandise from Jason Company with terms of 2/10, n/30. On August 17, Harris paid $200 freight on the shipment. On August 20, Harris returned $300 worth of the merchandise for credit. Final payment was made to Jason on August 24. Harris Company records purchases using the periodic inventory system.

**Required**

Prepare the journal entries that Harris should make on August 15, August 17, August 20, and August 24.

**E5-11B.** **Journal Entries for Merchandise Transactions on Seller's and Buyer's Books—Periodic System**

LO7
(Appendix 5A)

The following are selected transactions of Fenton, Inc., during the month of January:

Jan  18  Sold and shipped on account to Lawrence Stores merchandise listing for $1,500 with terms of 2/10, n/30.

25  Lawrence Stores was granted a $200 allowance on goods shipped January 18.

27  Received from Lawrence Stores a check for full settlement of the January 18 transaction.

**Required**

Prepare journal entries for (a) Fenton, Inc., and (b) Lawrence Stores. Both companies use the periodic inventory system.

## PROBLEMS—SET A

**P5-1A.** **Journal Entries for Merchandise Transactions on Seller's and Buyer's Books—Perpetual System**

LO2

The following transactions occurred between the Decker Company and Mann Stores, Inc., during March:

Mar  8  Decker sold $13,200 worth of merchandise ($8,800 cost) to Mann Stores with terms of 2/10, n/30.

10  Mann Stores paid freight charges on the shipment from Decker Company, $200.

12  Mann Stores returned $1,200 of the merchandise ($800 cost) shipped on March 8.

17  Decker received full payment for the net amount due from the March 8 sale.

20  Mann Stores returned goods that had been billed originally at $600 ($400 cost). Decker issued a check for $588.

**Required**

Prepare the necessary journal entries for (a) the books of Decker Company and (b) the books of Mann Stores, Inc. Assume that both companies use the perpetual inventory system.

**P5-2A.** **Journal Entries for Merchandise Transactions—Perpetual System**

LO3

Rockford Corporation, which began business on August 1, sells on terms of 2/10, n/30. Credit terms for its purchases vary with the supplier. Selected transactions for August are given below. Unless noted, all transactions are on account and involve merchandise held for resale. The perpetual inventory system is used.

Aug  1  Purchased merchandise from Norris, Inc., $3,400, terms 2/10, n/30.

5  Paid freight on shipment from Norris, Inc., $160.

7  Sold merchandise to Denton Corporation, $4,800 ($3,400 cost).

7  Paid $240 freight on August 7 shipment and billed Denton for the charges.

9  Returned $600 worth of the merchandise purchased August 1 from Norris, Inc., because it was defective. Norris approved the return.

9  Received $800 of returned merchandise ($600 cost) from Denton Corporation. Rockford approved the return.

10  Paid Norris, Inc., the amount due.

14  Purchased from Chambers, Inc., goods with a price of $8,000. Terms 1/10, n/30.

15  Paid freight on shipment from Chambers, Inc., $280.

17  Received the amount due from Denton Corporation.

18  Sold merchandise to Weber, Inc., $9,600 ($6,600 cost).

20  Paid $320 freight on August 18 shipment and billed Weber for the charges.

24  Paid Chambers, Inc., the amount due.

28  Received the amount due from Weber, Inc.

**Required**

Prepare journal entries for these transactions for Rockford Corporation.

**LO2　P5-3A.　Effects of Transactions on the Inventory Account—Perpetual System**

Watt Wholesale Company purchases merchandise from a variety of manufacturers and sells the merchandise to a variety of retailers. All sales are subject to a cash discount (2/10, n/30). Watt uses a perpetual inventory system. The May 1 balance in Watt's Inventory account was a $60,000 debit. The following transactions occurred during May:

May　2　Purchased $4,500 of merchandise from Ajax Manufacturing; terms are 1/10, n/30.
　　　4　Paid $160 freight on the May 2 purchase.
　　12　Paid Ajax for the May 2 purchase.
　　14　Purchased $3,000 of merchandise from Baker Manufacturing; terms are 2/10, n/45.
　　16　Received a $200 allowance on the May 14 purchase since some of the merchandise was the wrong color. All of the merchandise is salable at regular prices.
　　18　Purchased $2,500 of merchandise from Charles Industries; terms are 2/10, n/30.
　　19　Sold merchandise with a list price of $2,000 ($1,200 cost) to Daytime Industries.
　　22　Daytime Industries returned 30 percent of the merchandise from the May 19 sale.
　　26　Paid Baker Manufacturing for the May 14 purchase.
　　29　Paid Charles Industries for the May 18 purchase.

**Required**
Prepare a schedule that shows the impact of these transactions on Watt's Inventory account. Use the following headings:

| Date | Transaction | Debit Amount | Credit Amount | Account Balance |
| --- | --- | --- | --- | --- |

**LO3　P5-4A.　Journal Entries for Merchandise Transactions—Perpetual System**

Cushing Distributing Company uses the perpetual inventory system. Cushing had the following transactions related to merchandise during the month of June:

June　1　Purchased on account merchandise for resale for $8,000; terms were 2/10, n/30.
　　　3　Paid $350 cash for freight on the June 1 purchase.
　　　7　Returned merchandise costing $500 (part of the $8,000 purchase).
　　10　Paid for merchandise purchased on June 1.
　　13　Sold merchandise on account costing $7,000 for $10,000; terms were 2/10, n/30.
　　16　Customer returned merchandise costing $650 that had been sold on account for $900 (part of the $10,000 sale).
　　22　Received payment from customer for merchandise sold on June 13.

**Required**
Prepare journal entries for each of the transactions for the Cushing Distributing Company.

**LO3, LO5　P5-5A.　Physical Inventory Count and Adjusting Entry**

Apache Stores conducted a physical inventory at December 31. The items counted during the physical inventory are listed below. Apache's accountant provided the unit costs.

| Item Description | December 31, 2010 | |
| --- | --- | --- |
| | Count | Unit Cost |
| Colorado wool sweaters | 48 | $32 |
| Magnum wool sweaters | 27 | 34 |
| Johnson jackets | 50 | 28 |
| Magnum caps | 45 | 12 |
| Evans caps | 26 | 10 |
| Colorado shirts | 72 | 18 |
| Johnson shirts | 68 | 15 |
| Magnum boots | 40 | 60 |

**Required**
Prepare a schedule to determine the total cost of each item in the inventory and the total cost of the complete inventory at December 31.

**LO4　P5-6A.　Classified Income Statements**

The adjusted trial balance of Crane Distributors on December 31, 2010, is shown below; the perpetual inventory system has been used.

| CRANE DISTRIBUTORS<br>Adjusted Trial Balance<br>December 31, 2010 | Debit | Credit |
|---|---|---|
| Cash ............................................................ | $ 15,200 | |
| Accounts receivable ......................................... | 110,200 | |
| Inventory ...................................................... | 84,000 | |
| Prepaid insurance .......................................... | 2,400 | |
| Supplies........................................................ | 6,400 | |
| Delivery equipment ........................................ | 80,000 | |
| Accumulated depreciation................................ | | $ 35,000 |
| Accounts payable ........................................... | | 70,000 |
| Common stock................................................ | | 100,000 |
| Retained earnings .......................................... | | 42,000 |
| Sales revenue ................................................ | | 812,000 |
| Sales returns and allowances............................ | 11,600 | |
| Sales discounts.............................................. | 14,600 | |
| Cost of goods sold.......................................... | 513,400 | |
| Salaries expense (60% selling) .......................... | 118,000 | |
| Rent expense (30% selling) .............................. | 40,000 | |
| Supplies expense (100% administrative)............... | 8,400 | |
| Utilities expense (40% selling)........................... | 4,000 | |
| Depreciation expense (100% selling) ................... | 16,000 | |
| Insurance expense (50% selling) ........................ | 4,800 | |
| Income tax expense ........................................ | 30,000 | |
| | $1,059,000 | $1,059,000 |

**Required**

Prepare a classified income statement for the year ended December 31, 2010.

**P5-7A.** **Classified Income Statement and Adjusting Entries**

The Boston Trading Company, whose accounting year ends on December 31, had the following normal balances in its general ledger at December 31:

| | | | |
|---|---|---|---|
| Cash ............................... | $ 13,000 | Sales revenue ........................ | $640,000 |
| Accounts receivable ................ | 56,600 | Sales returns and | |
| Inventory ......................... | 73,000 | allowances ........................ | 4,400 |
| Prepaid insurance ................... | 6,000 | Sales discounts....................... | 5,600 |
| Office supplies ..................... | 4,200 | Cost of goods sold.................... | 404,000 |
| Furniture and fixtures .............. | 21,000 | Utilities expense..................... | 4,800 |
| Accumulated depreciation— | | Sales salaries expense .............. | 82,000 |
| furniture and fixtures ............. | 5,000 | Delivery expense .................... | 10,800 |
| Delivery equipment ................. | 84,000 | Advertising expense................. | 5,600 |
| Accumulated depreciation— | | Rent expense........................ | 14,400 |
| delivery equipment............... | 12,000 | Office salaries expense.............. | 56,000 |
| Accounts payable ................... | 41,000 | Income tax expense ................. | 9,000 |
| Long-term notes payable ............ | 30,000 | | |
| Common stock..................... | 75,000 | | |
| Retained earnings .................. | 51,400 | | |

Rent expense and utilities expense are 60 percent administrative and 40 percent selling. During the year, the accounting department prepared monthly statements but no adjusting entries were made in the journals and ledgers. Data for the year-end procedures are as follows:

1. Prepaid insurance, December 31 (75 percent of insurance expense is classified as selling expense, and 25 percent is classified as administrative expense) $1,200
2. Depreciation expense on furniture and fixtures for the year (an administrative expense) was $1,800
3. Depreciation expense on delivery equipment for the year was $13,000
4. Salaries payable, December 31 ($1,800 sales and $1,200 office) was $ 3,000
5. Unused office supplies on December 31 were $1,000

**Required**

*a.* Record the necessary adjusting entries at December 31.

*b.* Prepare a classified income statement for the year.

LO4

**LO6**  **P5-8A.**  **Profitability Analysis**

Kolby Enterprises reports the following information on its 2010 income statement:

| | | | |
|---|---|---|---|
| Net sales ......................... | $220,000 | Administrative expenses............. | $10,000 |
| Cost of goods sold.................. | 140,000 | Other income ...................... | 15,000 |
| Selling expenses................... | 40,000 | Other expense ..................... | 5,000 |

**Required**

Calculate Kolby's gross profit percentage and return on sales ratio for 2010. Explain what each ratio tells us about Kolby's performance. Kolby is planning to add a new product and expects net sales to be $30,000 and cost of goods to be $25,000. No other income or expenses are expected to change. How will this affect Kolby's gross profit percentage and return on sales ratio? What do you advise regarding the new product offering?

**LO5**  **P5-9A.**  **Journal Entries for Merchandise Transactions on Seller's and Buyer's Books— Periodic System**

The following transactions occurred between Southwick Company and Mann Stores, Inc., during March:

Mar  8  Southwick sold $6,600 worth of merchandise to Mann Stores, terms 2/10, n/30.
    10  Mann Stores paid freight charges on the shipment from Southwick Company, $100.
    12  Mann Stores returned $600 of the merchandise shipped on March 8.
    17  Southwick received full payment for the net amount due from the March 8 sale.
    20  Mann Stores returned goods that had been billed originally at $200. Southwick issued a check for $196.

**Required**

Prepare the necessary journal entries for (a) the books of Southwick Company and (b) the books of Mann Stores, Inc. Assume that both companies use the periodic inventory system.

**LO5**  **P5-10A.**  **Journal Entries for Merchandise Transactions—Periodic System**

The Malvado Corporation sells goods on terms of 2/10, n/30. Credit terms for its purchases vary with the supplier. Selected transactions for August are given below. Unless noted, all transactions are on account and involve merchandise held for resale. The periodic inventory system is used.

Aug  1  Purchased merchandise from Norris, Inc., $1,700; terms 2/10, n/30.
    5  Paid freight on shipment from Norris, Inc., $80.
    7  Sold merchandise to Denton Corporation, $2,400.
    7  Paid freight on shipment to Denton Corporation, $120, and billed Denton for the charges.
    9  Returned $300 worth of the merchandise purchased August 1 from Norris, Inc., because it was defective. Norris approved the return.
    9  Received $400 of returned merchandise from Denton Corporation.
    10  Paid Norris, Inc., the amount due.
    14  Purchased from Chambers, Inc., goods with a price of $3,000. Terms 1/10, n/30.
    15  Paid freight on shipment from Chambers, Inc., $140.
    17  Received the amount due from Denton Corporation.
    18  Sold merchandise to Weber, Inc., $4,800.
    20  Paid freight on August 18 shipment to Weber, Inc., $160 and billed Weber.
    24  Paid Chambers, Inc., the amount due.
    28  Received the amount due from Weber, Inc.

**Required**

Prepare the necessary journal entries for the Malvado Corporation.

# PROBLEMS—SET B

**LO3**  **P5-1B.**  **Journal Entries for Merchandise Transactions on Seller's and Buyer's Books— Perpetual System**

Riggs Distributing Company had the following transactions with Arlington, Inc., during the month of November:

Nov  10  Riggs sold and shipped $6,000 worth of merchandise ($4,200 cost) to Arlington, terms 2/10, n/30.
    12  Arlington, Inc., paid freight charges on the shipment from Riggs Company, $320.

Nov 14 Riggs received $600 of merchandise returned by Arlington ($420 cost) from the November 10 sale.

19 Riggs received payment in full for the net amount due on the November 10 sale.

24 Arlington returned goods that had originally been billed at $300 ($210 cost). Riggs issued a check for $294.

**Required**

Prepare the necessary journal entries (a) on the books of Riggs Distributing Company and (b) on the books of Arlington, Inc. Assume that both companies use the perpetual inventory system.

**P5-2B.** **Journal Entries for Merchandise Transactions—Perpetual System**     LO3

Webster Company was established on July 1. Its sales terms are 2/10, n/30. Credit terms for its purchases vary with the supplier. Selected transactions for the first month of operations are given below. Unless noted, all transactions are on account and involve merchandise held for resale. Webster Company uses the perpetual inventory system.

July   1 Purchased goods from Dawson, Inc., $1,900; terms 1/10, n/30.

2 Purchased goods from Penn Company, $4,200; terms 2/10, n/30.

3 Paid freight on shipment from Dawson, $100.

5 Sold merchandise to Ward, Inc., $1,300 ($975 cost).

5 Paid freight on shipment to Ward, Inc., $60.

8 Returned $300 worth of the goods purchased July 1 from Dawson, Inc., because some goods were damaged. Dawson approved the return.

9 Received returned goods from Ward, Inc., worth $200 ($150 cost).

10 Paid Dawson, Inc., the amount due.

10 Purchased goods from Dorn Company with a list price of $2,400. Terms 2/10, n/30.

11 Paid freight on shipment from Dorn Company, $130.

15 Received the amount due from Ward, Inc.

15 Sold merchandise to Colby Corporation, $3,200 ($2,400 cost).

16 Mailed a check to Penn Company for the amount due on its July 2 invoice.

18 Received an allowance of $100 from Dorn Company for defective merchandise purchased on July 10.

19 Paid Dorn Company the amount due.

25 Received the amount due from Colby Corporation.

**Required**

Prepare the necessary journal entries for the Webster Company.

**P5-3B.** **Effects of Transactions on the Inventory Account—Perpetual System**     LO2, LO3

Rand Wholesale Company purchases merchandise from a variety of manufacturers and sells the merchandise to a variety of retailers. All sales are subject to a cash discount (2/10, n/30). Rand has a perpetual inventory. The February 1, 2010, balance in Rand's Inventory account was a $50,000 debit. The following transactions occurred during February:

Feb   2 Purchased $7,600 of merchandise from Sweet Manufacturing; terms are 1/10, n/30.

5 Paid $270 freight on the February 2 purchase.

11 Paid Sweet for the February 2 purchase.

13 Purchased $5,000 of merchandise from Tayler Manufacturing; terms are 2/10, n/45.

16 Received a $300 allowance on the February 13 purchase since some of the merchandise was the wrong size. All of the merchandise is salable at regular prices.

17 Purchased $4,200 of merchandise from Zorn Industries; terms are 2/10, n/30.

20 Sold merchandise with a list price of $4,000 ($2,200 cost) to Valley Mart.

22 Valley Mart returned 20 percent of the merchandise from the February 20 sale.

23 Paid Tayler Manufacturing for the February 13 purchase.

28 Paid Zorn Industries for the February 17 purchase.

**Required**

Prepare a schedule that shows the impact of these transactions on Rand's Inventory account. Use the following headings:

| Date | Transaction | Debit Amount | Credit Amount | Account Balance |
| --- | --- | --- | --- | --- |

**P5-4B.** **Journal Entries for Merchandise Transactions**     LO2, LO3

Janetto Distributing Company uses the perpetual inventory system. Janetto had the following transactions related to merchandise during the month of August:

Aug 10 Purchased on account merchandise for resale for $3,000; terms were 2/10, n/30.
   12 Paid $120 cash for freight on the August 10 purchase.
   16 Returned merchandise costing $200 (part of the $3,000 purchase).
   19 Paid for merchandise purchased on August 10.
   22 Sold merchandise on account costing $1,000 for $1,600; terms were 2/10, n/30.
   25 Customer returned merchandise costing $65 that had been sold on account for $100 (part of the $1,600 sale).
   31 Received payment from customer for merchandise sold on August 22.

**Required**

Record each of the transactions related to purchasing and selling merchandise for the Janetto Distributing Company.

**LO1** **P5-5B.** **Physical Inventory Calculations and Adjusting Entry—Periodic System**

Furniture City conducted a physical inventory at December 31. The items counted during the physical inventory are listed below. Furniture City's accountant provided the unit costs.

| Item Description | December 31, 2010 | |
| --- | --- | --- |
| | Count | Unit Cost |
| Taylor sofas.......................................... | 10 | $250 |
| Georgia sofas........................................ | 8 | 300 |
| Taylor chairs......................................... | 22 | 175 |
| Taylor recliners ..................................... | 12 | 200 |
| Georgia recliners ................................... | 4 | 210 |
| Carolina lamps ...................................... | 16 | 30 |
| Chicago lamps ....................................... | 18 | 28 |
| Georgia tables....................................... | 8 | 150 |

**Required**

Prepare a schedule to determine the total cost of each item in the inventory and the total cost of the complete inventory at December 31.

**LO4** **P5-6B.** **Classified Income Statement**

The adjusted trial balance of Marshall Corporation on December 31, 2010, is shown below; the perpetual inventory system has been used. Marshall had no stock transactions during 2010.

| MARSHALL CORPORATION Adjusted Trial Balance December 31, 2010 | | |
| --- | --- | --- |
| | Debit | Credit |
| Cash ................................................................ | $ 46,400 | |
| Accounts receivable ............................................... | 95,200 | |
| Inventory .......................................................... | 87,000 | |
| Prepaid insurance ................................................. | 300 | |
| Furniture and fixtures............................................. | 32,000 | |
| Accumulated depreciation—furniture and fixtures ..................... | | $ 6,800 |
| Delivery equipment ............................................... | 65,000 | |
| Accumulated depreciation—delivery equipment........................ | | 32,000 |
| Accounts payable ................................................. | | 17,400 |
| Common stock..................................................... | | 200,000 |
| Retained earnings ................................................. | | 59,600 |
| Sales revenue ..................................................... | | 374,000 |
| Sales returns and allowances....................................... | 4,800 | |
| Sales discounts.................................................... | 4,000 | |
| Cost of goods sold................................................. | 214,800 | |
| Salaries expense (70% selling) ..................................... | 92,000 | |
| Rent expense (40% selling) ........................................ | 20,800 | |
| Utilities expense (30% selling)...................................... | 6,800 | |
| Insurance expense (60% administrative).............................. | 1,500 | |
| Depreciation expense—furniture and fixtures (100% administrative)....... | 3,200 | |
| Depreciation expense—delivery equipment (100% selling)............... | 13,000 | |
| Income tax expense ............................................... | 3,000 | |
| | $689,800 | $689,800 |

**Required**

Prepare a classified income statement for the year ended December 31, 2010.

**P5-7B.  Classified Income Statement and Adjusting Entries**

LO4

Oregon Distributors, whose accounting year ends on December 31, had the following normal balances in its ledger accounts at December 31:

| | | | |
|---|---|---|---|
| Cash | $ 32,800 | Common stock | $ 100,000 |
| Accounts receivable | 92,000 | Retained earnings | 42,000 |
| Inventory | 82,000 | Sales revenue | 1,180,000 |
| Prepaid insurance | 7,200 | Sales returns and | |
| Office supplies | 4,800 | allowances | 9,600 |
| Furniture and fixtures | 28,000 | Sales discounts | 16,400 |
| Accumulated depreciation— | | Cost of goods sold | 821,200 |
| furniture and fixtures | 10,800 | Utilities expense | 8,600 |
| Delivery equipment | 70,000 | Sales salaries expense | 108,000 |
| Accumulated depreciation— | | Delivery expense | 36,800 |
| delivery equipment | 24,400 | Advertising expense | 26,200 |
| Accounts payable | 69,400 | Rent expense | 30,000 |
| Long-term notes payable | 30,000 | Office salaries expense | 72,000 |
| Income tax expense | 11,000 | | |

Rent expense and utilities expense are 70 percent administrative and 30 percent selling. During the year, the accounting department prepared monthly statements, but no adjusting entries were made in the journals and ledgers. Data for the year-end procedures are as follows:

1.  Prepaid insurance, December 31 (insurance expense is classified as a selling expense) $2,400
2.  Depreciation expense on furniture and fixtures for the year (an administrative expense) $2,000
3.  Depreciation expense on delivery equipment for the year was $10,000
4.  Salaries payable, December 31 ($1,000 sales and $600 office) $1,600
5.  Office supplies on hand, December 31, $1,800

**Required**

*a.*  Record the necessary adjusting entries in general journal form at December 31.
*b.*  Prepare a classified income statement for the year.

**P5-8B.  Profitability Analysis**

LO6

Ashley Enterprises reports the following information on its 2010 income statement:

| | | | |
|---|---|---|---|
| Net sales | $440,000 | Administrative expenses | $20,000 |
| Cost of goods sold | 280,000 | Other income | 30,000 |
| Selling expenses | 80,000 | Other expense | 10,000 |

**Required**

Compute Ashley's gross profit percentage and return on sales ratio for 2010. Explain what each ratio tells us about Ashley's performance. Ashley is planning to add a new product and expects net sales to be $30,000 and cost of goods to be $25,000. No other income or expenses are expected to change. How will this affect Ashley's gross profit percentage and return on sales ratio? What do you advise regarding the new product offering?

**P5-9B.  Journal Entries for Merchandise Transactions on Seller's and Buyer's Books— Periodic System**

LO5

Fortune Distributing Company had the following transactions with Arlington, Inc., during November:

Nov 10  Fortune sold and shipped $6,000 worth of merchandise to Arlington, terms 2/10, n/30.
  12  Arlington, Inc., paid freight charges on the shipment from Fortune Company, $360.
  14  Fortune received $600 of merchandise returned by Arlington from the November 10 sale.
  19  Fortune received payment in full for the net amount due on the November 10 sale.
  24  Arlington returned goods that had originally been billed at $500. Fortune issued a check for $490.

ASSIGNMENTS

**Required**

Prepare the necessary journal entries (a) on the books of Fortune Distributing Company and (b) on the books of Arlington, Inc. Assume that both companies use the periodic inventory system.

**LO5**  **P5-10B. Journal Entries for Merchandise Transactions—Periodic System**

Polidor Company was established on July 1. Its sales terms are 2/10, n/30. Credit terms for its purchases vary with the supplier. Selected transactions for the first month of operations are given below. Unless noted, all transactions are on account and involve merchandise held for resale. All purchases are recorded using the periodic inventory system.

July   1   Purchased goods from Dawson, Inc., $1,900; terms 1/10, n/30.
        2   Purchased goods from Penn Company, $4,200; terms 2/10, n/30.
        3   Paid freight on shipment from Dawson, $80.
        5   Sold merchandise to Ward, Inc., $1,300.
        5   Paid freight on shipment to Ward, Inc., $60.
        8   Returned $300 worth of the goods purchased July 1 from Dawson, Inc., because some goods were damaged. Dawson approved the return.
        9   Received returned merchandise from Ward, Inc., $200.
      10   Paid Dawson, Inc., the amount due.
      10   Purchased goods from Dorn Company with a price of $1,600. Terms 2/10, n/30.
      11   Paid freight on shipment from Dorn Company, $130.
      15   Received the amount due from Ward, Inc.
      15   Sold merchandise to Colby Corporation, $3,200.
      16   Mailed a check to Penn Company for the amount due on its July 2 invoice.
      18   Received an allowance of $100 from Dorn Company for defective merchandise purchased on July 10.
      19   Paid Dorn Company the amount due.
      25   Received the amount due from Colby Corporation.

**Required**

Prepare the necessary journal entries for Polidor Company.

## SERIAL PROBLEM: KATE'S CARDS

(*Note:* **This is a continuation of the Serial Problem: Kate's Cards from Chapters 1 through 4.**)

**SP5.**   As expected, November saw a boom in Kate's greeting card business. She invested in additional computer graphics equipment, which she partially funded with a bank loan of $15,000 and an additional investment of her own funds into the business. The loan carries an interest rate of six percent with interest payments required semiannually. The entire principal balance is due in one balloon payment in two years. As of December 2, 2010, Kate's Cards had the following account balances:

| | | | |
|---|---|---|---|
| Cash | $11,900 | Accumulated depreciation | $ 1,600 |
| Accounts receivable | 16,800 | Accounts payable | 13,800 |
| Inventory | 16,000 | Other current liabilities | 900 |
| Other current assets | 3,600 | Long-term note payable | 15,000 |
| | | Common stock | 25,000 |
| Computer equipment | 38,900 | Retained earnings | 30,900 |

The company had the following transactions during December 2010:

Dec   7   Paid $1,800 to employees. Of this amount, $900 was for an amount owed from November. Salaries due to employees at the end of each month are recorded as Other Current Liabilities.
      9   Received $5,400 from customers as payment on account.
    12   Sold, for cash, $9,000 of greeting cards. This merchandise had cost $6,000 to produce.
    14   Purchased additional inventory totaling $7,000 on account with terms of 2/10, n/45.
    15   Paid cash for supplies (listed as Other Current Assets) in the amount of $600.

19 Sold, on account with terms of 2/10, n/30, greeting cards totaling $6,000. The merchandise had cost $4,000 to produce.

21 Paid additional salaries of $1,400.

25 Paid the total owed for the merchandise that was purchased on December 14.

28 Received payment in full from the customer that purchased the merchandise on June 19. Granted the discount of two percent since payment was within the allowed discount period.

31 Depreciation for the month totaled $900.

31 A physical count of inventory and supplies revealed that $13,000 and $2,000, respectively, were on hand at year-end. Assume that Other Current Assets consists only of the cost of supplies.

### Required

a.  Prepare journal entries for the December transactions.

b.  Prepare a classified income statement for the month of December 2010.

## EXTENDING YOUR KNOWLEDGE

### REPORTING AND ANALYSIS

**EYK5-1.   Financial Reporting Problem: The Columbia Sportswear Company**

The financial statements for the **Columbia Sportswear Company** are in Appendix A at the end of this book.

COLUMBIA SPORTSWEAR
COMPANY

#### Required

Using the company's Consolidated Statement of Operations (which is another name for Income Statement), answer the following questions.

a.  What was the change in net sales and in net income from 2008 to 2009?

b.  What was the gross profit percentage in each of the three years, 2007 through 2009? Comment on the trend in this ratio.

c.  What was the return on sales ratio in each of the three years, 2007 through 2009? Comment on the trend in this ratio.

**EYK5-2.   Comparative Analysis Problem: The Columbia Sportswear Company vs. The Timberland Company**

The financial statements for the **Columbia Sportswear Company** and **The Timberland Company** are in Appendix A and B, respectively, at the end of this book.

COLUMBIA SPORTSWEAR
COMPANY

TIMBERLAND COMPANY

#### Required

a.  Based on the information you find in these financial statements, determine the following values for each company:

1.  Gross profit for 2009
2.  Gross profit percentage for 2009
3.  Net income for 2009
4.  Return on sales ratio for 2009

b.  Based on this information, what can you say about the relative performance of these two companies?

**EYK5-3.   Business Decision Problem**

Northwestern Corporation started a retail clothing business on July 1, 2010. During 2010, Northwestern Corporation had the following summary transactions related to merchandise inventory:

|           | Purchases | Sales       |
| --------- | --------- | ----------- |
| July      | $240,000  | $ 360,000   |
| August    | 384,000   | 696,000     |
| September | 312,000   | 576,000     |
| October   | 360,000   | 660,000     |
| November  | 900,000   | 1,020,000   |
| December  | 264,000   | 1,344,000   |

ASSIGNMENTS

On average, Northwestern's cost of goods sold is 50 percent of sales. Assume that there were no sales returns and allowances or purchases returns and allowances during this six-month time period.

**Required**

*a.* Calculate the ending merchandise inventory for each of the six months.

*b.* Northwestern's purchases peaked during November; its sales peaked during December. Did Northwestern plan its purchases wisely? Should Northwestern expect a similar pattern in future years?

JOHNSON & JOHNSON

**EYK5-4.** **Financial Analysis Problem**

**Johnson & Johnson** is a worldwide manufacturer of health care products, including Band-Aid bandages and Mylanta antacid. It reported the following results for three recent years (Year 3 is the most recent):

| (in millions) | Year 3 | Year 2 | Year 1 |
|---|---|---|---|
| Net sales ........................................... | $63,747 | $61,095 | $53,324 |
| Cost of goods sold..................................... | 18,511 | 17,751 | 15,057 |

Assume that similar-sized companies in the same basic industries have experienced an average gross profit percentage of 70 percent each year.

**Required**

*a.* Calculate the gross profit percentage for Johnson & Johnson for the three years.

*b.* Compare the three-year trend in gross profit percentage for Johnson & Johnson to the assumed industry average. Analyze the trend and evaluate the performance of Johnson & Johnson compared to the assumed industry average.

## CRITICAL THINKING

GENERAL MILLS, INC.

**EYK5-5.** **Accounting Research Problem**

Refer to the fiscal year 2010 annual report of **General Mills, Inc.**, available on this book's Website.

**Required**

*a.* How much sales revenue did General Mills report in 2009 and 2010?

*b.* What was the company's gross profit percentage in 2009 and 2010?

*c.* How much net income did the company earn in 2009 and 2010?

*d.* What was the company's return on sales for 2009 and 2010? What can we conclude about the company's performance over the two-year period?

**EYK5-6.** **Accounting Communication Activity**

Nobel Company produces custom machinery that has few competitors. As such, Nobel is able to charge a large markup that is reflected in its large gross profit percentage. Recently the marketing director proposed offering a new set of products that are more generic in nature, and therefore will not allow large markups. The accounting department has, however, determined the products will add to Nobel's overall net income. The following table provides estimates of Nobel's profitability both with and without the new product:

| | Without New Product | With New Product |
|---|---|---|
| Net sales ..................................... | $250,000 | $350,000 |
| Cost of goods sold........................... | 125,000 | 210,000 |
| Net income.................................... | 25,000 | 31,500 |

**Required**

The President of Nobel, Jack Towne, has asked you to write a memo answering the following questions.

*a.* How will the new product line affect the company's profitability as measured by its gross profit percentage and the return on sales ratio?

*b.* How is it possible for net income to improve, while at the same time these profitability ratios may deteriorate?

*c.* Should the company expand by offering this new product line?

**EYK5-7.** **Accounting Ethics Case**

During the last week of 2009, George Connors, controller of We 'R' Appliances, received a memorandum from the firm's president, Jane Anderson. The memorandum stated that Anderson had negotiated a very large sale with a new customer and directed Connors to see that the order was processed and the goods shipped before the end of the year. Anderson noted that she had to depart from the usual credit terms of n/30 and allow terms of n/60 to clinch the sale. Although the credit terms were unusual for the company, Connors was particularly pleased with the news because business had been somewhat slow. The goods were shipped on December 29 and the sale was incorporated into the 2009 financial data.

It is now mid-February 2010, and two events have occurred recently that, together, cause concern for Connors. First, he was inadvertently copied on a letter from the firm's bank to Anderson. The letter stated that the bank had reconsidered its decision to deny a loan to the company and is now granting the loan based on the new, and favorable, sales data supplied by the president. The bank was "particularly impressed with the sales improvement shown in December." Although Connors had been involved in the initial loan application that was denied, he had been unaware that the president had reapplied for the loan.

The second event was that all of the goods shipped on December 29, 2009, to the new customer had just been returned.

**Required**

What are the ethical considerations George Connors faces as a result of the recent events?

**EYK5-8.** **Corporate Social Responsibility Problem**

**Target** is one of a large growing number of companies that publish an annual corporate social responsibility report. Go to the Target Website and navigate to the section on corporate responsibility in order to download Target's latest corporate responsibility report. Discuss some of the ways that Target documents its good citizenship.

TARGET

**EYK5-9.** **Profitability Analysis: IFRS Financial Statements**

LO6

Tesco PLC is the world's third largest retailer and is based in the United Kingdom. Tesco's IFRS financial statements are presented in Appendix C at the end of this textbook. Using the company's financial statements, calculate the company's (a) gross profit percentage and (b) return on sales for 2008 and 2009. Comment on the trend in the company's profitability over the two-year period.

---

## ANSWERS TO SELF-STUDY QUESTIONS:

1. b, (p. 233)   2. c, (pp. 226–229)   3. c, (pp. 226–229)   4. c, (p. 231)   5. c, (p. 237)
6. c, (p. 232)   7. d, (p. 232)   8. b, (p. 236) 9. a, (p. 237)   10. c, (p. 238)   11. c, (p. 240)
12. b, (p. 224)

## Your Turn! Solutions

**Solution 5.1**

| | | | |
|---|---|---|---|
| June 1 | Inventory | 510.00 | |
| | Accounts payable | | 510.00 |
| | *To record merchandise purchased on account (125 CDs @ $4.08 each)* | | |
| June 1 | Inventory | 22.18 | |
| | Cash | | 22.18 |
| | *To record payment of freight charges on merchandise purchased.* | | |
| June 4 | Accounts payable | 61.20 | |
| | Inventory | | 61.20 |
| | *To record the return of defective merchandise (15 units @ $4.08 per unit).* | | |
| June 8 | Accounts payable | 448.80 | |
| | Cash | | 439.82 |
| | Inventory | | 8.98 |
| | *To record full payment within discount period. Cash discount earned = $8.98.* | | |

ANSWERS

**Solution 5.2**

| | | | |
|---|---|---|---|
| June 15 | Accounts receivable | 750.00 | |
| | Sales revenue | | 750.00 |
| | *To record the sale of 75 CDs on account.* | | |
| | | | |
| June 15 | Cost of goods sold | 315.00 | |
| | Inventory | | 315.00 |
| | *To record cost of goods sold for 75 CDs.* | | |
| | | | |
| June 20 | Sales revenue | 50 | |
| | Inventory | 21 | |
| | Accounts receivable | | 50 |
| | Cost of goods sold | | 21 |
| | *To record the return of 5 CDs for credit.* | | |
| | | | |
| June 25 | Cash | 700 | |
| | Accounts receivable | | 700 |
| | *To record cash payment from customer.* | | |

The third journal entry for the return of merchandise has the effect of reversing a portion of the first two entries.

**Solution 5.3**

| MUSICLAND COMPANY |
|---|
| **Income Statement** |
| **For Year Ended December 31, 2010** |

| | |
|---|---:|
| Net sales . . . . . . . . . . . . . . . . . . . . . . . . . . . . . . . . . . . . . . . . . . . . . . . . . . . . . . . . . . . . . . . . . . . | $100,000 |
| Less Cost of goods sold . . . . . . . . . . . . . . . . . . . . . . . . . . . . . . . . . . . . . . . . . . . . . . . . . . . . . | 45,000 |
| Gross profit on sales. . . . . . . . . . . . . . . . . . . . . . . . . . . . . . . . . . . . . . . . . . . . . . . . . . . . . . . | 55,000 |
| Operating expenses | |
| Selling and administrative. . . . . . . . . . . . . . . . . . . . . . . . . . . . . . . . . . . . . . . . . . . . . . . . . | 25,000 |
| Other operating expenses. . . . . . . . . . . . . . . . . . . . . . . . . . . . . . . . . . . . . . . . . . . . . . . . . | 10,000 |
| Total operating expenses . . . . . . . . . . . . . . . . . . . . . . . . . . . . . . . . . . . . . . . . . . . . . | 35,000 |
| Income from operations. . . . . . . . . . . . . . . . . . . . . . . . . . . . . . . . . . . . . . . . . . . . . . . . . . | 20,000 |
| Other income and expense | |
| Other income . . . . . . . . . . . . . . . . . . . . . . . . . . . . . . . . . . . . . . . . . . . . . . . . . . . . . . . . . . . . | 5,000 |
| Interest expense . . . . . . . . . . . . . . . . . . . . . . . . . . . . . . . . . . . . . . . . . . . . . . . . . . . . . . . . . | 10,000 |
| Income before income taxes . . . . . . . . . . . . . . . . . . . . . . . . . . . . . . . . . . . . . . . . . . . . . . . . | 15,000 |
| Income tax expense . . . . . . . . . . . . . . . . . . . . . . . . . . . . . . . . . . . . . . . . . . . . . . . . . . . . . . . . | 4,500 |
| Net income. . . . . . . . . . . . . . . . . . . . . . . . . . . . . . . . . . . . . . . . . . . . . . . . . . . . . . . . . . . . . . . . . | $10,500 |

**Solution 5.4**

| MUSICLAND COMPANY |
|---|
| **Cost of Goods Sold** |
| **For Year Ended December 31, 2010** |

| | | | |
|---|---:|---:|---:|
| Cost of goods sold | | | |
| Inventory, January 1. . . . . . . . . . . . . . . . . . . . . . . . . . . . . . . . . . . . . . . . . . | | | $10,000 |
| Purchases. . . . . . . . . . . . . . . . . . . . . . . . . . . . . . . . . . . . . . . . . . . . . . . . . . . . | | $50,000 | |
| Less: Purchase returns and allowances. . . . . . . . . . . . . . . . . . . . . . . | $2,000 | | |
| Purchase discounts. . . . . . . . . . . . . . . . . . . . . . . . . . . . . . | 1,000 | 3,000 | |
| Net purchases. . . . . . . . . . . . . . . . . . . . . . . . . . . . . . . . . . . . . . . . . . . . . . . . | | 47,000 | |
| Add: Freight-in. . . . . . . . . . . . . . . . . . . . . . . . . . . . . . . . . . . . . . . . . . . . . . . | | 200 | |
| Cost of goods purchased . . . . . . . . . . . . . . . . . . . . . . . . . . . . . . . . . . . . . | | | 47,200 |
| Cost of goods available for sale . . . . . . . . . . . . . . . . . . . . . . . . . . . . . . . | | | 57,200 |
| Less: Inventory, December 31. . . . . . . . . . . . . . . . . . . . . . . . . . . . . . . . . | | | 12,200 |
| Cost of goods sold . . . . . . . . . . . . . . . . . . . . . . . . . . . . . . . . . . . . . . . . . | | | $45,000 |

**Solution 5.5**

Gross profit percentage = ($100,000 − $45,000)/$100,000 = 55 percent

Return on sales ratio = $10,500/$100,000 = 10.5 percent

A gross profit percentage of 55 percent indicates that Musicland was able to earn 55 cents for each dollar of net sales after considering just its cost of goods sold. In other words, Musicland still has 55 cents available from each dollar of net sales to cover its remaining expenses and to earn a net profit.

A return on sales ratio of 10.5 percent indicates that Musicland was able to earn 10.5 cents in net income from each dollar of net sales after subtracting all of the business's expenses.

**Solution 5.6**

| | | | |
|---|---|---|---|
| June 1 | Purchases | 510.00 | |
| |     Accounts payable | | 510.00 |
| | *To record merchandise purchased on account (125 @ $4.08 each).* | | |
| June 1 | Freight in | 22.18 | |
| |     Cash | | 22.18 |
| | *To record payment of freight charge on merchandise purchase.* | | |
| June 4 | Accounts payable | 61.20 | |
| |     Purchase returns | | 61.20 |
| | *To record the return of defective merchandise (15 units).* | | |
| June 8 | Accounts payable | 448.80 | |
| |     Cash | | 439.82 |
| |     Purchase discounts | | 8.98 |
| | *To record payment for merchandise purchased.* | | |

**Solution 5.7**

| | | | |
|---|---|---|---|
| June 15 | Accounts receivable | 750 | |
| |     Sales revenue | | 750 |
| | *To record the sale of 75 CDs on account.* | | |
| June 20 | Sales returns | 50 | |
| |     Accounts receivable | | 50 |
| | *To record the return of 5 CDs for credit.* | | |
| June 25 | Cash | 700 | |
| |     Accounts receivable | | 700 |
| | *To record cash payment from customer.* | | |

The third entry for the return of merchandise has the effect of reversing a portion of the first entry.

# Accounting for Inventory

| | PAST | PRESENT | FUTURE |
|---|---|---|---|
| | Chapter 5 focused on accounting for merchandising transactions, including how a classified income statement is prepared. | This chapter explains the accounting for inventory and the cost flow assumptions we make to simplify computations. | Chapter 7 focuses on fraud risks faced by businesses and internal controls used to combat fraud and errors. |

## LEARNING OBJECTIVES

# ACHIEVING THE BEST BUY

The recent years leading up to 2011 will likely be remembered as some of the most difficult years ever in the retail industry. Retail company bankruptcies during this time period include **Linens 'n Things**, **Mervyn's**, **Sharper Image**, **Steve and Barry's**, and **Wickes Furniture**. However, the bankruptcy of **Circuit City** was perhaps the biggest surprise. Circuit City had over 500 stores throughout the United States that were full of the latest flat screen TVs and electronics. What could explain the failure of Circuit City when the company's biggest rival, **Best Buy**, reported nearly $5 million in profits during the same time period? One key explanation, according to *Time* magazine, was ineffective inventory management.

Circuit City was unable to sell its existing inventory quickly enough, thereby failing to generate the necessary cash flow to enable the company to pay off its huge debt load and creating a backlog that prevented the company from ordering the newer models that consumers preferred. Best Buy, on the other hand, spent considerable time and effort revamping its supply chain and inventory management system to avoid such a fate. The Vice President of Logistics and Transportation with Best Buy observed that "Without better inventory management, Best Buy would have been a thing of the past."

With inventory comprising approximately one-third of Best Buy's assets, it is readily apparent why effective inventory management is so crucial to its financial health (and that of Circuit City). But how is Best Buy's inventory valued and recorded on its balance sheet? What measures exist for management and financial statement users to evaluate how effectively those inventories are being managed? We discuss answers to both of these important questions and others in this chapter.

"Why Circuit City Busted, While Best Buy Boomed," by Anita Hamilton, Time.com, November 11, 2008; Best Buy 10-K report; Circuit City 10-K report.

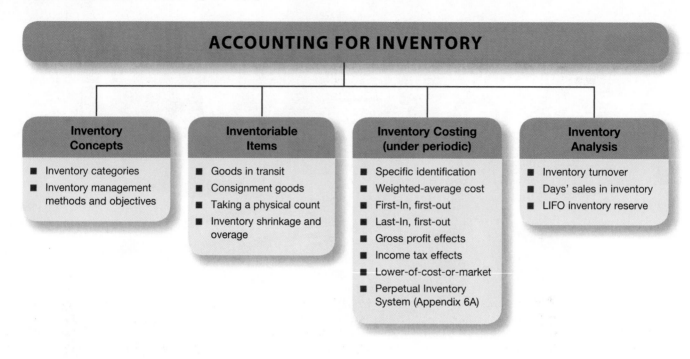

# INVENTORY CATEGORIES AND CONCEPTS

This section explains the basic categories of inventory and introduces basic concepts of inventory management.

## CATEGORIES OF INVENTORY

We define *merchandise inventory* as the inventory of goods that a merchandising company buys from a manufacturing company and makes available for sale to its customers. All necessary costs incurred to acquire the merchandise inventory and deliver it to the buyer's place of business are included in the buyer's cost of inventory. This includes the purchase price of the merchandise, plus any transportation or freight-in costs, less any purchase returns and allowances and any purchase discounts. Wholesale distributors and retailing firms are two major types of merchandising firms.

Unlike merchandising firms, manufacturing firms do not purchase merchandise that is ready for sale. Instead, they purchase various raw materials and components and convert them into salable merchandise in their factories. At any point in time, manufacturing firms have units of merchandise at various stages of completion. Consequently, a manufacturing firm usually maintains three separate categories of inventory: raw materials inventory, work-in-process inventory, and finished goods inventory.

The **raw materials inventory** includes raw materials and components that have been purchased for use in the production of a product but that have not yet been placed into the production process. Sheets of steel are an example of raw material, and computer chips are an example of a component. A *component* is an item in the raw materials inventory account that was a finished product for the manufacturer that produced it. For example, **Intel Corporation** manufactures computer chips that other manufacturers incorporate into their final products. **Dell Inc.**, a computer manufacturer, is an example of a company that incorporates the finished goods of Intel into the computers that it manufactures.

The **work-in-process inventory** consists of units of product that have been placed into production in a factory but that are not fully assembled. All of the costs related to raw materials and components, human labor in the factory, factory utilities, and other factory-related resources are included in the work-in-process inventory. Items in this inventory category are not ready for sale since they are not yet a finished product.

The **finished goods inventory** includes all units that have been fully manufactured and are ready to be sold to customers. The cost of each item in the finished goods inventory is accumulated in the work-in-process inventory account and is then transferred to the finished goods inventory when the inventory is ready for sale.

## CONCEPTS OF INVENTORY MANAGEMENT

Merchandising and manufacturing companies often find it desirable to maintain a large and varied inventory of merchandise to satisfy the diverse needs and preferences of their customers. Consequently, the diversity of customer needs and preferences forces most companies to maintain high levels of inventory.

### Just-in-Case Inventory

Manufacturing companies have traditionally maintained inventories as a buffer against unforeseen shipping delays and unforeseen demand by customers. For example, a manufacturer might maintain an extra supply of raw materials to protect against a supplier being late in the delivery of materials needed to produce a particular product or to provide materials in case a manufacturer decides to produce units that it had not previously planned to manufacture. This extra quantity is known as **just-in-case inventory**—that is, raw material inventory that is just in case the supplier does not deliver when scheduled or just in case the manufacturer decides to produce previously unplanned quantities of inventory. Just-in-case inventories create substantial inventory carrying costs for a manufacturer. **Inventory carrying costs** include insurance, building usage costs, and the cost of the capital invested in the inventory. Higher levels of just-in-case inventories cause higher levels of inventory carrying costs.

### Just-in-Time Manufacturing

Just-in-time (JIT) manufacturing seeks to eliminate or minimize just-in-case inventory quantities and their related costs. A manufacturing company following **just-in-time manufacturing** would, under optimal conditions, have no inventory on hand at the end of each business day. Under the JIT manufacturing approach, raw materials and components are ordered such that only the materials and components necessary for production on a given day would be received. Production would be scheduled so that all units started during the day would be completed by the end of the day, resulting in no work-in-process inventory at the end of the day. And, all completed products would be shipped to customers the same day that they are completed, resulting in no finished goods inventory. The key to just-in-time manufacturing involves careful raw material purchase planning and close management of the manufacturing process. Managerial accounting covers the details of this planning and management process. Most manufacturing companies have been unable to attain the goal of absolute zero inventories; however, many companies have been able to significantly reduce the just-in-case quantities, and hence, reduce their inventory carrying costs.

---

**ACCOUNTING IN PRACTICE** **Quick Response Systems**

Many retailers have installed point-of-sale checkout systems to assist in inventory management. These systems either read Universal Product Code bar codes or specially-formed characters using either a plate scanner built into the checkout counter or a handheld scanner (or "wand") to identify the product being sold. Retailers also use a quick response system to optimize their inventory. A **quick response system** is designed to ensure that the retailer quickly reorders items that are being sold and quickly eliminates from inventory any items that are not selling. Special software on a business's computer identifies fast-selling and slow-selling items. The retailer reviews the list and orders more of the highly desirable items that are selling quickly. A retailer typically uses one (or both) of the following approaches to eliminate slow-moving items: (1) return the item to the supplier (if possible) and (2) reduce the unit selling price to (hopefully) induce a quick sale. Quick response systems tend to reduce both the size of inventory that a company must maintain and increase the dollar amount of its sales revenue.

# INVENTORY OWNERSHIP AND PHYSICAL COUNT

To determine the quantity of inventory, it is necessary to take a physical count of the inventory at the end of a fiscal period. This involves not only physically counting the inventory, but also determining the ownership of the inventory.

## OWNERSHIP OF INVENTORY

### Goods in Transit

Goods in transit can present some uncertainty when trying to determine the end-of-period inventory quantities. It is important to include all inventory items that are owned by a company and exclude any items that are no longer owned, regardless of whether a company has the merchandise in its physical possession or not. When merchandise is shipped by a common carrier—a railroad, trucking company, or an airline—the carrier prepares a *freight bill* in accordance with the instructions of the party making the transportation arrangements. The freight bill designates which party bears the shipping costs and which party has owner-ship of the merchandise that is being shipped, referred to as **goods in transit**.

Freight bills usually show shipping terms of **F.O.B. shipping point** or **F.O.B. destination**. *F.O.B.* is an abbreviation for "free on board." When the freight terms are F.O.B. shipping point, the buyer assumes ownership of the merchandise at the time the common carrier accepts the items from the seller. When the terms are F.O.B. destination, the seller maintains ownership of the merchandise until the buyer takes possession at delivery. In sum, ownership of goods in transit is directly linked to the freight terms when goods are shipped from a seller to a buyer as illustrated in Exhibit 6-1.

**EXHIBIT 6-1**    Ownership of Goods In Transit

| Freight Terms | Ownership |
|---|---|
| F.O.B. Shipping Point . . . . . . . . . . . . | Buyer takes ownership when carrier accepts goods |
| F.O.B. Destination . . . . . . . . . . . . . . | Buyer takes ownership when carrier delivers goods |

### Consignment Goods

Another uncertainty when assessing inventory ownership involves consignment goods. **Consignment goods** are items held for sale by parties other than the item's owner. An example of a consignment good is used cars held for sale at a used car lot specializing in selling cars for private parties. The car lot owner does not assume ownership of the cars, but simply attempts to sell the cars, collecting a commission on any completed sales. Since consignment goods do not involve a transfer of title, they are included in the deter-mination of the end-of-period inventory quantity by the seller until sold.

## PHYSICAL COUNT OF INVENTORY

A company takes a **physical count of inventory** to verify the balance of inventory. It is possible that changes in the quantity of particular items could have taken place without a transaction being recognized. For example, quantities of various items may have been stolen, damaged, or destroyed. Also, the seller might have shipped an incorrect quantity to a customer even though the seller reflected the correct quantity in a journal entry. The physical count of inventory is often taken at year-end and consists of the following steps:

1. Count the number of individual items of merchandise inventory available at the end of the period.
2. Determine the unit cost of each individual item and multiply the unit cost times the quantity to obtain the total cost for each individual inventory item.
3. Add the total cost of all the individual inventory items to obtain the total cost of the aggregate inventory available.

In a perpetual inventory system, the physical count of inventory results in a total that does not agree with the balance in the Inventory account, the company makes a year-end adjusting entry. If the physical inventory total is less than the Inventory account balance, the company makes an adjusting entry debiting Cost of Goods Sold and crediting Inventory for the difference between the physical inventory total and the balance in the Inventory account. This entry decreases the balance in the Inventory account and adds the cost of the inventory shortage to Cost of Goods Sold. The cost associated with an inventory shortage is known as **inventory shrinkage**.

If the physical inventory total is greater than the Inventory account balance, the company makes an adjusting entry debiting Inventory and crediting Cost of Goods Sold for the difference between the physical inventory and the Inventory account balance. This entry increases the balance in the Inventory account and subtracts the cost of this **inventory overage** from Cost of Goods Sold.

To illustrate shrinkage (the usual situation), assume that the December 31 balance of the Inventory account (including all items) is $120,600. Also assume that a physical count of the inventory produced a total cost at December 31 of $120,000. The following period-end adjusting entry is required at December 31 to adjust the balance in the Inventory account from $120,600 to $120,000:

| Dec 31 | Cost of Goods Sold | 600 | |
| | Inventory | | 600 |
| | *To adjust the inventory account balance to the total cost determined by a physical inventory count in a perpetual inventory system.* | | |

| A | = | L | + | SE |
| −600 | | | | −600 Exp |

## Forensic Accounting   Employee Theft

Most of us have encountered stories of an employee at a company or a store stealing from the business. Companies take such risks seriously. For example, **Target** operates two state-of-the-art forensic laboratories to reduce employee theft. A few statistics drive home the magnitude of this problem:

- The FBI calls employee theft "the fastest growing crime in America!"
- The U.S. Chamber of Commerce estimates that 75 percent of employees steal from the workplace and that most do so repeatedly.
- The American Society of Employers estimates that 20 percent of every dollar earned by a U.S. company is lost to employee theft.

## Your Turn!   6.1

The Counter Company just completed the year-end physical count of its inventory. The total value of inventory was determined to be $300,000. The following additional information came to light following the conclusion of the physical count:

1. The company included $20,000 of inventory that was shipped F.O.B. destination.
2. The company included $15,000 of inventory that was shipped F.O.B. shipping point.
3. The company did not include $25,000 of inventory that was being sold on consignment by Johnson Sales, a consignment dealer.

Discuss how this additional information affects the $300,000 value that The Counter Company initially determined to be the value of its ending inventory.

**The solution is on page 313.**

---

**CORPORATE SOCIAL RESPONSIBILITY**  **Best Buy and an Ethical Supply Chain**

Many businesses strive to not only do well financially, but also to do good environmentally and socially. **Best Buy** serves as the ultimate seller of many products manufactured by other companies, such as TVs by **Sony**, cameras by **Nikon**, and computers by **Dell**. Best Buy also sells its Exclusive Brands. As the manufacturer of these products, Best Buy faces decisions on how and where these products are produced. Best Buy's Corporate Responsibility Report states, "While manufacturing expertise, lower labor costs and an efficient global supply chain make production in southeastern Asia a viable proposition, our operations there have not been without challenges." Best Buy meets these challenges through their ethical manufacturing program that includes Supplier Compliance Standards that embody standards of the Fair Labor Association Workplace Code of Conduct and the core labor standards of the International Labor Organization. Best Buy also has a factory audit program to identify environmental and social problems at its suppliers.

---

# INVENTORY COSTING METHODS

LEARNING OBJECTIVE 2

**Describe** inventory costing under specific identification, weighted-average cost, FIFO, and LIFO.

In general, the value of a company's inventory is entered into the accounting records at its acquisition cost. Inventory costing is simple when the acquisition cost remains constant. For example, assume that the Fletcher Motor Company purchased electric motors four times during the year:

| **EXHIBIT 6-2**  Illustration of Cost Flows When Prices Do Not Change | |
|---|---|
| February 10 purchase................................ | 100 motors at $180 each |
| April 25 purchase..................................... | 150 motors at $180 each |
| July 16 purchase...................................... | 150 motors at $180 each |
| October 8 purchase................................... | 200 motors at $180 each |
| December 31 ending inventory ....................... | 40 motors at $ _?_ each |

The December 31 ending inventory for Fletcher Motor Company includes 40 electric motors, some from the July 16 purchase and some from the October 8 purchase. In this case, it is easy to determine the cost to be assigned to the 40 motors ($40 \times \$180 = \$7,200$) since all of the inventory purchases were made at the exact same purchase price of $180. In real business situations, however, the purchase price of an item of inventory often changes. The trend is usually toward increasing prices, but some purchase prices may actually decline. When purchase prices change during the year, a company must either keep track of the acquisition cost of each specific unit or make an assumption about which units have been sold and which units remain in inventory. Most companies choose the latter option and make an assumption about which units have been sold and which are still available because the cost of keeping track of exactly which units are sold can be prohibitively expensive.

## GOODS FLOW VS. COST FLOW

Two concepts that are helpful in understanding the problem of assigning a cost to inventory when purchase prices are changing are Goods Flow and Cost Flow. **Goods flow** describes the actual physical movement of inventory through a business. **Cost flow** is the actual or assumed assignment of costs to goods sold and to ending inventory. The cost flow need not, and often does not, reflect the actual goods flow through a business.

Generally accepted accounting principles permit businesses to use a cost flow that does not reflect the company's actual goods flow. For example, the goods flow in a grocery store chain like **Safeway** will almost always be such that the goods brought in first will be the first goods to be sold. This physical goods flow results in the least amount of loss due to spoilage. However, just because Safeway operates with this physical goods flow through its stores does not mean that the company is required to adopt a similar cost flow to calculate the value of its inventory. The *cost flow assumption* adopted could be one in which the most recent goods added to inventory are assumed to be the first goods sold.

*The following sections on inventory costing use the periodic system. Appendix 6A uses the perpetual system. Your instructor can choose to cover either one or both systems. If the following periodic system is skipped, then read Appendix 6A and return to the section (five pages ahead) titled "Income Tax Effects."*

## DATA FOR ILLUSTRATION OF COST FLOW ASSUMPTIONS

In this section, we introduce and illustrate four generally accepted methods of costing inventories: (1) specific identification, (2) first-in, first-out (FIFO), (3) last-in, first-out (LIFO), and (4) weighted-average cost. Following an illustration of the four methods, a comparative analysis of the financial results of the methods is presented. To facilitate a comparison of their results, we use a common set of data. Assume that the Claremont Company had the following purchases and sales of inventory during the year.

| EXHIBIT 6-3 | Purchases and Sales for Application of Cost Flow Assumptions | | | | |
|---|---|---|---|---|---|
| **Date** | **Event** | **No. of Units** | **Unit Cost** | | **Total Cost** |
| Jan. 1 | Beginning inventory | 60 | @ $10 | = | $ 600 |
| Mar. 27 | Purchase inventory | 90 | @ $11 | = | $ 990 |
| **May 2** | **Sell inventory** | **(130)** | | | |
| Aug. 15 | Purchase inventory | 100 | @ $13 | = | $1,300 |
| Nov. 6 | Purchase inventory | 50 | @ $16 | = | $ 800 |
| **Dec. 10** | **Sell inventory** | **(90)** | | | |
| Dec. 31 | Ending inventory | 80 | | | |

The four inventory costing methods differ in the way they assign costs to the 80 units in ending inventory and the 220 units in cost of goods sold. Under the periodic inventory system, the Inventory account and the Cost of Goods Sold account are updated only at the end of the period, following a physical count of the ending inventory. Once the total cost of ending inventory is determined, the ending inventory amount is subtracted from cost of goods available for sale to derive the period's cost of goods sold.

## SPECIFIC IDENTIFICATION METHOD

The **specific identification method** involves (1) keeping track of the purchase cost of each specific unit available for sale and (2) costing the ending inventory at the actual costs of the specific units not sold. Assume that the 80 unsold units consist of 10 units

| This information is used to compute ending inventory |

from beginning inventory, 20 units from the August 15 purchase, and all 50 of the units purchased on November 6. The cost assigned to the ending inventory and cost of goods sold is shown in Exhibit 6-4. Observe that the entire $3,690 of cost of the goods available for sale is assigned as either ending inventory or as cost of goods sold.

**EXHIBIT 6-4**  Specific Identification Method

| Date | Event | Goods Available Units | Cost | Total | Ending Inventory Units | Cost | Total |
|------|-------|-------|------|-------|-------|------|-------|
| Jan. 1 | Beginning inventory...... | 60 | @ $10 = | $ 600 | 10 | @ $10 = | $ 100 |
| Mar. 27 | Purchase ................. | 90 | @ 11 = | 990 | | | |
| Aug. 15 | Purchase ................ | 100 | @ 13 = | 1,300 | 20 | @ 13 = | 260 |
| Nov. 6 | Purchase ................. | 50 | @ 16 = | 800 | 50 | @ 16 = | 800 |
| | | 300 | | $3,690 | 80 | | $1,160 |

Cost of goods available for sale .... $3,690
Less: Ending inventory............. 1,160
Cost of goods sold................ **$2,530**

Seller $1,160 — $100 $500 $990 $260 $1,040 $800 — Buyer $2,530

## FIRST-IN, FIRST-OUT (FIFO) METHOD

The **first-in, first-out (FIFO) method** assumes that the oldest goods (or earliest purchased) are sold first. This implies that ending inventory is *always* made up of the most recent purchases. FIFO results in the cost allocations as shown in Exhibit 6-5. This method assumes the first 220 units acquired are sold first and that the last 80 units purchased are those remaining.

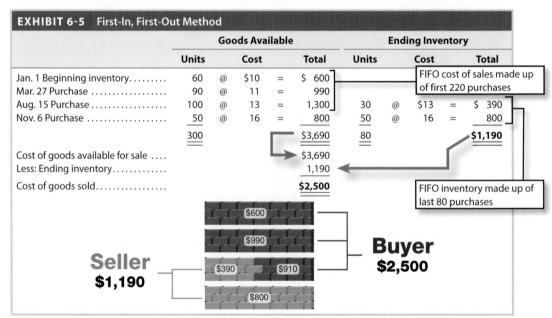

**EXHIBIT 6-5**  First-In, First-Out Method

| | Goods Available Units | Cost | Total | Ending Inventory Units | Cost | Total |
|---|-------|------|-------|-------|------|-------|
| Jan. 1 Beginning inventory......... | 60 | @ $10 = | $ 600 | | | |
| Mar. 27 Purchase ................. | 90 | @ 11 = | 990 | | | |
| Aug. 15 Purchase ................. | 100 | @ 13 = | 1,300 | 30 | @ $13 = | $ 390 |
| Nov. 6 Purchase ................... | 50 | @ 16 = | 800 | 50 | @ 16 = | 800 |
| | 300 | | $3,690 | 80 | | $1,190 |

> FIFO cost of sales made up of first 220 purchases

Cost of goods available for sale .... $3,690
Less: Ending inventory............. 1,190
Cost of goods sold................ **$2,500**

> FIFO inventory made up of last 80 purchases

Seller $1,190 — $600 $990 $390 $910 $800 — Buyer $2,500

## LAST-IN, FIRST-OUT (LIFO) METHOD

The **last-in, first-out (LIFO) method** assumes that the most recent purchases are sold first. Exhibit 6-6 illustrates the calculation of LIFO cost of goods sold. LIFO assumes that the 220 units last (most recently) purchased are sold first, and that the 80 oldest units available for sale remain at the end of the period.

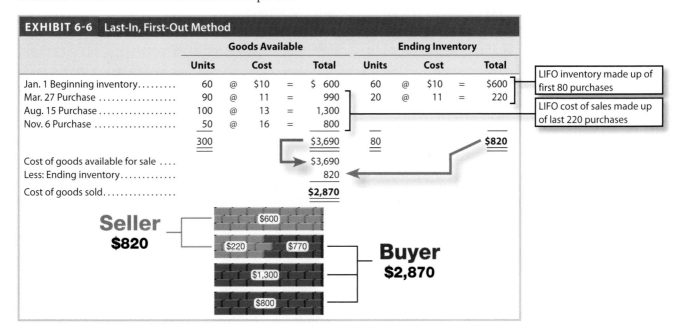

**EXHIBIT 6-6** Last-In, First-Out Method

| | Goods Available | | | Ending Inventory | | |
|---|---|---|---|---|---|---|
| | Units | Cost | Total | Units | Cost | Total |
| Jan. 1 Beginning inventory......... | 60 @ | $10 = | $ 600 | 60 @ | $10 = | $600 |
| Mar. 27 Purchase .................. | 90 @ | 11 = | 990 | 20 @ | 11 = | 220 |
| Aug. 15 Purchase ................. | 100 @ | 13 = | 1,300 | | | |
| Nov. 6 Purchase ................... | 50 @ | 16 = | 800 | | | |
| | 300 | | $3,690 | 80 | | $820 |

LIFO inventory made up of first 80 purchases

LIFO cost of sales made up of last 220 purchases

Cost of goods available for sale .... $3,690
Less: Ending inventory............ 820
Cost of goods sold................ $2,870

**Seller $820**

$600
$220 $770
$1,300
$800

**Buyer $2,870**

## WEIGHTED-AVERAGE COST METHOD

The **weighted-average cost method** spreads the total dollar cost of the goods available for sale equally among all units. In our illustration, the weighted-average cost per unit is $12.30, computed as $3,690/300. Exhibit 6-7 diagrams the assignment of costs under this method. The entire cost of goods available for sale is allocated between ending inventory and cost of goods sold.

**A.K.A.** The weighted-average cost method is often referred to as the average cost method.

**EXHIBIT 6-7** Weighted-Average Method

| Date | Event | No. of Units | Cost | Total |
|---|---|---|---|---|
| Jan. 1 | Beginning inventory ..................................... | 60 @ | $10 = | $ 600 |
| Mar. 27 | Purchase inventory ..................................... | 90 @ | 11 = | 990 |
| Aug. 15 | Purchase inventory ..................................... | 100 @ | 13 = | 1,300 |
| Nov. 6 | Purchase inventory ..................................... | 50 @ | 16 = | 800 |
| | Goods available for sale ................................ | 300 | | $3,690 |

| | Units | Cost | Total |
|---|---|---|---|

$$\frac{\text{Cost of goods available for sale}}{\text{Total units available for sale}} = \text{Average Unit Cost}$$

$$\frac{\$3,690}{300} = \$12.30$$

Ending inventory........................................ 80 @ $12.30 = **$984**
Cost of goods available for sale ......................... $3,690
Less: Ending inventory.................................. 984
Cost of goods sold...................................... **$2,706**

**Seller $984**
($12.30 x 80 units)

**$12.30 per unit**
$$\left(\frac{\$3,690}{300 \text{ units}}\right)$$

**Buyer $2,706**
($12.30 x 220 units)

It would be incorrect to use a *simple* average of the unit costs. The simple average unit cost is $12.50, or ($10 + $11 + $13 + $16)/4). This figure fails to take into account the different number of units purchased and available at the various prices. The simple average cost yields the same result as the weighted-average cost only when the exact same number of units is purchased at each unit price.

**ACCOUNTING IN PRACTICE**    **Inventory Costing Methods**

The following chart identifies the inventory costing method used by a sample of 600 U.S. firms. The most frequently used method is FIFO, followed by LIFO and then weighted-average cost. (The total exceeds 100% because some firms use more than one method to value their inventory, which is permitted under GAAP.) [Source: Accounting Trends and Techniques]

## COMPARATIVE ANALYSIS OF INVENTORY COSTING METHODS

**LEARNING OBJECTIVE 3**

**Analyze** the financial effects of different inventory costing methods on company profit.

The purchase price data used in the Claremont Company illustration has an important characteristic: the purchase price of the inventory increased each time that a purchase was made, from $11 per unit to $13 per unit to $16 per unit. Increasing inventory prices are frequently encountered in the real world where price inflation is common and price deflation is uncommon. Exhibit 6-8 summarizes the results of applying the four inventory costing methods to the Claremont Company data and reveals that the FIFO method produces the lowest cost of goods sold ($2,500), while the LIFO method produces the highest cost of goods sold ($2,870). The exhibit also reveals that FIFO produces the highest year-end value of ending inventory ($1,190), while LIFO produces the lowest year-end value of ending inventory ($820). Specific identification and weighted-average cost produce ending inventory values and cost of goods sold values that fall in between the results obtained using FIFO and LIFO.

These results, however, are highly dependent on the purchase prices for the inventory. If the inventory's purchase price had been decreasing rather than increasing, the financial effects would have been just the opposite, with LIFO producing the lowest cost of goods sold and FIFO the highest. If, on the other hand, the purchase prices had been perfectly stable, there would be no difference between the cost of goods sold or the ending inventory for any of the four methods.

| EXHIBIT 6-8    Results of Different Inventory Costing Methods | | |
| --- | --- | --- |
| **Costing Method** | **Ending Inventory** | **Cost of Goods Sold** |
| Specific identification................ | $1,160 | $2,530 |
| FIFO ............................... | 1,190 | 2,500 |
| LIFO................................ | 820 | 2,870 |
| Weighted-average cost .............. | 984 | 2,706 |

## IMPACTS OF COST FLOW ASSUMPTIONS

Under generally accepted accounting principles, a company is permitted to select one or more of the four methods for purposes of assigning cost to its ending inventory and its cost of goods sold. Which method (or methods, since a company may elect to value some of its inventory using FIFO, some using LIFO, and some using weighted-average cost) is selected by a company depends upon a number of factors—the type of product produced, the cost of producing the product, whether the product is perishable, whether the company desires to report a high or a low net income, and income tax considerations.

### Specific Identification Method

Specific identification is typically used by companies that manufacture a small volume of products with relatively high unit values. Airplanes, jewelry, and construction equipment are examples of products that would justify the cost of tracking the specific unit cost of each inventory item. Specific identification is usually not cost-justified for companies that manufacture products that have a low unit cost or involve high volumes of production. It can be very expensive to trace the exact costs of producing a product, especially a product manufactured in high volumes.

### FIFO Method

Many companies, especially those with perishable, time-dated, or style-affected merchandise, attempt to sell their oldest merchandise first. This is especially true for companies that sell food products, chemicals, and drugs. For these types of companies, the cost flow produced by the FIFO method most closely matches the actual goods flow. However, a company is not required to use the cost flow assumption that most closely matches its actual goods flow. When costs are rising, FIFO will result in the lowest cost of goods sold, and therefore, the highest net income. The desire to show a higher net income by some companies partly explains the popularity of the FIFO method.

### LIFO Method

Although LIFO does not reflect the actual goods flow for most businesses, its popularity is likely linked to the potential income tax savings associated with its use. For some industries, however, LIFO does depict the actual goods flow. For example, in industries that extract natural resources, such as mining, the product is frequently dumped onto a storage pile from an overhead trestle, and sold inventory is taken from the top of the pile. One disadvantage of using LIFO when beginning inventories have been maintained or increased is that a firm's ending inventory can be substantially undervalued since old purchase prices tend to be retained on a company's books under the LIFO method. This, in turn, will cause a firm's current assets and total assets to likewise be undervalued.

### Weighted-Average Cost Method

Weighted-average cost is best suited for businesses that warehouse a large volume of undifferentiated goods in a common area. Liquid fuels, grains, and other commodities are examples. Weighted-average cost typically generates a cost of goods sold amount that is neither high nor low as compared to the other methods, as is revealed in Exhibit 6-8.

### Summary of Impacts

We can broadly summarize the impacts of the cost flow assumptions as follows:

1. Specific identification most closely identifies the actual cost of goods sold and ending inventory.
2. FIFO approximates the actual physical goods flow for most firms.
3. LIFO is popular because of the income tax savings associated with its use.
4. Weighted-average cost is most often associated with businesses in which undifferentiated goods are commingled in a common area like a warehouse.

## ANALYSIS OF COSTING METHODS AND GROSS PROFIT

To illustrate the financial effects of the different inventory costing methods, assume that the 220 units sold by the Claremont Company were sold for $20 each, producing sales of $4,400 ($20 × 220). Exhibit 6-9 shows the difference in gross profit under each of the four inventory costing methods. Remember that the difference in reported gross profit results from the assumptions made about cost flows, not from any difference in actual goods flows. In each case, 220 units were sold and 80 units remained. Each of the inventory costing methods is in accord with generally accepted accounting principles, yet one method's financial impact on gross profit and net income is different from the financial impact of another method.

| **EXHIBIT 6-9**   Gross Profit Using Alternative Inventory Costing Methods | | | | |
| --- | --- | --- | --- | --- |
| | Specific Identification | FIFO | LIFO | Weighted-Average |
| Sales (220 units @ $20)........................................ | $4,400 | $4,400 | $4,400 | $4,400 |
| Cost of goods sold....................................... | 2,530 | 2,500 | 2,870 | 2,706 |
| Gross profit............................................ | $1,870 | $1,900 | $1,530 | $1,694 |
| Increased gross profit compared with LIFO............. | $  340 | $  370 | | $  164 |

### Income Statement and Balance Sheet Effects

As Exhibit 6-9 reveals, LIFO results in the smallest gross profit ($1,530), with FIFO producing the highest ($1,900) gross profit. This result occurs because the purchase price of inventory was increasing throughout the year, from $11 per unit to $13 per unit to $16 per unit. Most agree that when costs are rising, FIFO tends to overstate gross profit (and income) because older, lower unit costs are included in the cost of goods sold and matched with current sales prices. In other words, in the illustration, all of the units sold are charged to costs of goods sold under FIFO at unit costs of $10, $11, and $13. If the latest purchase price reflects the inventory's current acquisition cost, the units sold must be replaced by units costing $16 (or more if costs continue to rise).

It is frequently argued that LIFO provides a better matching of current costs with current revenues since the cost of the most recent purchases constitutes the LIFO cost of goods sold. While LIFO associates the current, higher unit costs with cost of goods sold, it assigns costs to ending inventory using the older, lower unit costs. As a consequence, the value of the LIFO ending inventory on the balance sheet is often undervalued in terms of the inventory's current value. When inventory quantities are maintained or increased, the LIFO method prevents older costs from appearing in the cost of goods sold. No doubt, some firms still carry LIFO inventories at unit costs that existed more than 10 years ago. Under FIFO, the ending inventory is measured at relatively recent costs.

*For readers skipping the periodic system, please resume reading here.*

**PRINCIPLE ALERT**   **Consistency and Full Disclosure**

Inventory costing requires the application of *consistency* and *full disclosure*. Because of the possible variation in gross profit and ending inventory values that result from the use of different inventory costing methods, it is important that a firm use the same inventory costing method from one fiscal period to the next. This application of consistency enhances the comparability of a firm's cost of goods sold, gross profit, net income, inventory, current assets, and total assets over time. In addition, a firm should disclose which inventory costing method it is using, either in its financial statements or in the notes to the statements. This information is required by the full disclosure principle and is important to users who compare financial data across firms.

### Income Tax Effects

During periods of rising purchase prices, LIFO results in a lower gross profit than any of the alternative inventory costing methods. A lower gross profit, and net income, means that lower amounts of income taxes need to be paid. Hence, the desire to reduce current income tax payments is a major reason for widespread use of LIFO.

To illustrate LIFO's income tax advantage, assume that the Huntington Corporation has beginning inventory of 10 units costing $500 each, and that only two transactions occur. In the first transaction, it purchases 10 more units costing $630 each, for a total cash purchase price of $6,300. In the second transaction, it sells 10 units for $700 each, for a total cash sale of $7,000. Both transactions are for cash and, for simplicity, we assume that the company's operating expenses are zero and the applicable income tax rate is 35 percent. Exhibit 6-10 presents the income statements and cash flows for Huntington under both FIFO and LIFO.

| **EXHIBIT 6-10** | **FIFO vs. LIFO Comparison: Phantom Profit Effect and Tax Benefit** | | | | |
|---|---|---|---|---|---|
| | | **FIFO** | | **LIFO** | |
| | | Income Statement | Cash In (Out) | Income Statement | Cash In (Out) |
| Sales (10 @ $700) | | $ 7,000 | $7,000 | $ 7,000 | $7,000 |
| Cost of goods sold | | | | | |
| Beginning inventory (10 @ $500) | | 5,000 | | 5,000 | |
| Purchases (10 @ $630) | | 6,300 | (6,300) | 6,300 | (6,300) |
| Goods available (20 units) | | 11,300 | | 11,300 | |
| Ending inventory | | | | | |
| 10 @ FIFO | | 6,300 | | | |
| 10 @ LIFO | | | | 5,000 | |
| Cost of goods sold | | 5,000 | | 6,300 | |
| Pretax income | | 2,000 | | 700 | |
| Income tax (at 35%) | | 700 | (700) | 245 | (245) |
| Net income | | $ 1,300 | | $ 455 | |
| Net cash proceeds | | | $ 0 | | $ 455 |

Under FIFO, it reports $1,300 of net income, but cash from sales ($7,000) is only enough to replace the inventory sold ($6,300) and pay the income tax ($700) on the $2,000 in FIFO pretax net income. The net income of $1,300 is not realized in cash, and consequently, is unavailable to pay dividends, or be reinvested in the business, or replace the sold inventory. As a consequence, FIFO net income is sometimes referred to as *phantom profit*.

Under LIFO, it reports net income of $455 as a consequence of its larger cost of goods sold ($6,300). With a lower net income, it incurs a smaller cash outflow ($245) for income taxes. The attractiveness of LIFO during periods of rising inventory purchase prices is evidenced by LIFO's more favorable net cash flow ($455) as compared with FIFO ($0). Use of LIFO during times of falling inventory purchase prices, however, has the opposite income tax effect.

Management is usually free to select different accounting treatments for financial reporting to shareholders and for income tax reporting to the Internal Revenue Service (IRS). For example, it is acceptable for a business to use different methods of computing inventory when reporting under GAAP on the income statement and for reporting under income tax regulations on a company's income tax return. This situation has led some individuals to correctly infer that U.S. corporations effectively maintain two sets of financial records—one for reporting to shareholders and one for reporting to the IRS. An exception to this flexibility occurs when a company chooses to use LIFO for income tax reporting to benefit from the lower income taxes that result from the use of LIFO when purchase prices are rising. A U.S. federal tax regulation known as the **LIFO conformity rule** requires any company that selects LIFO for income tax reporting to also use LIFO for financial reporting to shareholders. It is currently not possible to report lower taxable income to the IRS using LIFO while also reporting higher net income to shareholders using FIFO. (President Obama's 2011 U.S. budget proposal called for the elimination of LIFO for income tax purposes in an effort to generate additional tax revenues to help close the U.S. budget deficit.)

The following inventory information is gathered from the accounting records of a company:

| | |
|---|---|
| Beginning inventory......................................... | 4,000 units at $5 each |
| Purchases ................................................. | 6,000 units at $7 each |
| Sales..................................................... | 9,000 units at $10 each |

Calculate (a) ending inventory, (b) cost of goods sold, and (c) the gross profit using each of the following methods (i) FIFO, (ii) LIFO, and (iii) weighted-average cost.

**The solution is on page 314.**

### Errors in the Inventory Count

A physical count of a business's inventory is necessary to determine the value of a company's ending inventory regardless of what inventory method is used. Unfortunately, errors in the inventory count, for example failing to count some items or counting some items twice, can occur. These errors affect not only the value of ending inventory reported on the balance sheet in the period of the error, but also cost of goods sold and current net income. Further, the error is not limited to only the current period—net income in the following period is also affected. To illustrate, assume that the Arrow Company began operations in 2010. Exhibit 6.11 summarizes Arrow's 2010 and 2011 transactions. For simplicity, assume that the only expense that it incurs is its cost of goods sold.

**EXHIBIT 6-11** Inventory Transactions for Arrow Company

| | | Inventory Units | Inventory Balance | Sales |
|---|---|---|---|---|
| **2010** | | | | |
| (1) | Purchased 1,000 units of merchandise inventory for $3 per unit........ | 1000 | $3,000 | |
| (2) | Sold 400 units of merchandise inventory for $7 per unit............... | (400) | (1,200) | $ 2,800 |
| | Ending inventory................................................ | 600 | $1,800 | |
| **2011** | | | | |
| | Beginning inventory............................................. | 600 | $1,800 | |
| (1) | Purchased 2,000 units of merchandise inventory for $3 per unit........ | 2,000 | 6,000 | |
| (2) | Sold 1,500 units of merchandise inventory for $7 per unit.............. | (1,500) | (4,500) | $10,500 |
| | Ending inventory................................................ | 1,100 | $3,300 | |

Assume that Arrow Company made an error in its physical count of inventory at the end of 2010, mistakenly double-counting 40 units of inventory, and consequently, overstating ending inventory by $120 (40 units × $3). As illustrated in Exhibit 6-12, both the value of ending inventory and cost of goods sold in 2010 are affected. Further, because ending inventory in 2010 becomes beginning inventory in 2011, cost of goods sold in 2011 is also misstated. Exhibit 6-12 illustrates these effects on both the 2010 and 2011 Arrow Company income statements.

In sum, an error in the ending inventory account in the current year affects the value of ending inventory in the current year, as well as current year net income through cost of goods sold. The error also affects, in an opposite direction, net income in the following year (through its effect on cost of goods sold). In the case of the company in Exhibit 6-12, ending inventory was overstated in 2010 by $120. This resulted in 2010 ending inventory being overstated by $120, 2010 cost of goods sold being understated by $120, and 2010 net income being overstated by $120. The same $120 error is carried through to 2011 where it causes cost of goods sold to be overstated by $120 (because of the overstatement of beginning inventory), and net income to be understated by $120.

| **EXHIBIT 6-12** | **Inventory Error Effects** | | | | | | |
|---|---|---|---|---|---|---|---|
| **Cost of goods sold** | **=** | **Beginning Inventory** | **+** | **Purchases** | **−** | **Ending Inventory** |
| 2010: $1,080.......................... | = | $ 0 | + | $ 3,000 | − | $1,920 |
| 2011: $4,620.......................... | = | $ 1,920 | + | $ 6,000 | − | $3,300 |

| **Key financial figures** | **Without Error** | **With Error** |
|---|---|---|
| 2010 | | |
| Sales............................... | $ 2,800 | $ 2,800 |
| Cost of goods sold ................. | 1,200 | 1,080 |
| Net income ....................... | $ 1,600 | $ 1,720 |
| 2011 | | |
| Sales............................... | $10,500 | $10,500 |
| Cost of goods sold ................. | 4,500 | 4,620 |
| Net income ....................... | $ 6,000 | $ 5,880 |

---

**FORENSIC ACCOUNTING** **Fraudulent Overstatement of Inventory**

Most errors in Inventory result from honest mistakes; however, there are inventory counts that have been intentionally overstated. One such case involved a retail company called **Crazy Eddie**, which was a discount electronics store. Court records indicate that Eddie, the founder, hired his nephew, Sammy, who had earned a degree in accounting, to inflate sales by $15 to $20 million per year, and falsified inventories to justify the inflated figures. The U.S. Securities and Exchange Commission ultimately charged Eddie with securities fraud and he was sentenced to 8 years in prison and ordered to pay more than $150 million in fines.

# LOWER-OF-COST-OR-MARKET METHOD

LEARNING OBJECTIVE 4

**Apply** the lower-of-cost-or-market method.

In general, inventory is valued at its acquisition cost using the common inventory costing methods explained in this chapter. However, it can be necessary to report inventory at a lower value if there is evidence that the inventory's utility to a business—that is, the inventory's revenue-generating ability—has fallen below its acquisition cost. Such *inventory write-downs* can occur when (1) merchandise must be sold at reduced prices because it is damaged or otherwise not in normal salable condition or when (2) the cost of replacing the ending inventory has declined below the inventory's recorded acquisition cost.

## NET REALIZABLE VALUE

Damaged, physically deteriorated, or obsolete merchandise should be measured and reported at its net realizable value on the balance sheet when this value is less than the inventory's acquisition cost. **Net realizable value** is an item's estimated selling price less the expected cost of disposal. For example, assume that an inventory item cost $300 but can be sold for only $200 because it is damaged. If the related selling costs are estimated to be $20, the inventory should be written down to $180 ($200 estimated selling price less $20 estimated disposal cost) and a $120 inventory write-down loss ($300 − $180) should be reported on the income statement for the current period.

## LOWER-OF-COST-OR-MARKET METHOD

The **lower-of-cost-or-market (LCM)** method provides for the recognition of an inventory write-down loss when the inventory's replacement cost declines below its recorded acquisition cost. Under LCM, a loss is reported in the period when the inventory's replacement cost declines, rather than during a subsequent period when the actual sale of the inventory takes place. *Market, for purposes of applying the LCM method,* is defined as the current replacement cost of the inventory. This procedure assumes that decreases in the replacement cost of inventory will be accompanied by proportionate decreases in the selling price of the inventory. The LCM method values the ending inventory at its lower (replacement) market value. Consequently, income decreases by the amount that the ending inventory is written down. When the ending inventory becomes part of the cost of goods sold in a future period, its reduced carrying value helps maintain normal profit margins in the period when sold.

To illustrate, assume that an inventory item that cost $80 has been selling at a retail price of $100, yielding a gross profit percentage of 20 percent. Assume also that by year-end, the item's replacement cost has declined to $60—a 25 percent decline—and a proportionate reduction in its selling price from $100 to $75 is expected in the following period. In this case, the inventory is written down to its $60 replacement cost, reducing the current period's net income by a $20 write-down loss ($80 − $60 = $20). When the inventory is sold in a subsequent period for $75, the normal gross profit percentage of 20 percent on sales is reported ($75 − $60 = $15 gross profit). The LCM method may be applied to (1) each individual inventory item, (2) the totals of major inventory classes or categories, or (3) the total inventory. Exhibit 6-13 illustrates these alternatives and shows that the value of ending inventory depends on how the LCM method is applied.

| | | **Per Unit** | | **Total** | | **Lower-of-Cost-or-Market by** | | |
|---|---|---|---|---|---|---|---|---|
| **Inventory Item** | **Quantity** | **Cost** | **Market** | **Cost** | **Market** | **Individual Item** | **Major Category** | **Total Inventory** |
| Cameras | | | | | | | | |
| Model V70 ........ | 40 | $80 | $75 | $3,200 | $3,000 | $3,000 | | |
| Model V85 ........ | 30 | 60 | 64 | 1,800 | 1,920 | 1,800 | | |
| Subtotal........ | | | | $5,000 | $4,920 | | $4,920 | |
| | | | | | | | | |
| Calculators | | | | | | | | |
| Model C20........ | 90 | 13 | 15 | $1,170 | $1,350 | 1,170 | | |
| Model C40........ | 50 | 20 | 17 | 1,000 | 850 | 850 | | |
| Subtotal........ | | | | $2,170 | $2,200 | | 2,170 | |
| Total ............... | | | | $7,170 | $7,120 | $6,820 | $7,090 | $7,120 |

**EXHIBIT 6-13** Application of the Lower-of-Cost-or-Market

In Exhibit 6-13, if we apply LCM to the *total inventory*, the ending inventory is valued at $7,120. If LCM is applied on an *individual item-by-item* basis, the value of ending inventory is $6,820; and, if applied by *major category*, the LCM value of ending inventory is $7,090. Although the item-by-item procedure is used most often by businesses, any of the three approaches is generally accepted. Inventory replacement costs are in such sources as current catalogs, purchase contracts with suppliers, and other forms of price quotations.

**PRINCIPLE ALERT**     **Conservatism**

The lower-of-cost-or-market method for inventory is a good illustration of *conservatism*. When the current replacement cost for an inventory item falls below its acquisition cost, there is increased uncertainty about the future profitability of the item. Conservatism is the reaction to significant uncertainties in the measurement of net assets and net income. In choosing between alternative financial measures, conservatism causes the least optimistic measure to be selected. When an item's market value (current replacement cost of inventory) falls below its historical acquisition cost, the least optimistic measure is its lower market value.

## IFRS ALERT!

Under IFRS, LIFO is *not* generally accepted. Further, under U.S. GAAP inventory may not be revalued above its acquisition cost. IFRS permits inventory to be revalued upwards if the inventory's fair value appreciates above acquisition cost. When inventory is revalued upward under IFRS a parallel increase is made to an equity account called Asset Revaluation Reserve. To illustrate, assume that **Tesco**'s ending inventory at year-end is valued on its books at 2,669 million British pounds. Also assume that a review by management concluded that the fair value of its inventory had appreciated to 3,000 million British pounds. Under IFRS, we make the following journal entry to revalue inventory:

| | | |
|---|---|---|
| Inventories | 331 | |
|    Asset revaluation reserve | | 331 |
|    *To write up inventory to its fair market value.* | | |

| A | = | L | + | SE |
|---|---|---|---|---|
| +331 | | | | +331 |

Appendix C at the end of this book presents the IFRS financial statements of Tesco. Tesco's asset revaluation reserve is in the equity section of its balance sheet.

## Your Turn! 6.3

The Images Company sells three types of video equipment—DSLR cameras, Point and Shoot cameras, and Camcorders. The cost and market value of its inventory of video equipment follow:

| | Cost | Market |
|---|---|---|
| DSLR | $110,000 | $125,000 |
| Point and Shoot | 73,000 | 92,000 |
| Camcorders | 57,000 | 48,000 |

Compute the value of the Images Company's ending inventory under the lower-of-cost-or-market method applied on an item-by-item basis.

**The solution is on page 314.**

## Forensic Accounting    Employee Theft of Inventory

Inventory shrinkage arises from employee and/or customer theft, physical damage or deterioration, and obsolescence. Shrinkage is typically discovered following a physical count of inventory. Shrinkage for U.S. retailers is estimated at over $40 billion, and the largest part, nearly $20 billion, is employee theft. Preventing inventory theft is difficult; however, there are ways to reduce it. Here are tips from AskDeb.com:

- Give different passwords to each cashier; using separate passwords and log-ins reveals which employee was manning the cash register at the times when theft occurs.
- Verify any transaction that is voided or canceled. This is a common way for inventory to be removed from a store.
- Review inventory reports daily to be sure sales match current inventory quantities.
- Install an alarm system on a store's back door that is activated each time the door is opened without authorization.
- Inspect the garbage nightly; use clear, plastic bags so that the contents are easily inspected to ensure that no inventory is hidden inside.
- Install security cameras in the store and in the back storage; this allows a store manager to keep an eye on items on the store racks as well as in stock.

# INVENTORY ANALYSIS

## INVENTORY TURNOVER AND DAYS' SALES IN INVENTORY

The **inventory turnover ratio** indicates how many times a year, on average, a firm sells its inventory, and it is calculated as:

$$\text{Inventory turnover} = \frac{\text{Cost of goods sold}}{\text{Average inventory}}$$

This ratio relates data from two financial statements: the income statement and the balance sheet. Cost of goods sold is taken from the income statement, while the average inventory is calculated from balance sheet data—that is, the beginning and ending inventories are summed and the total is divided by two.

In general, the faster a company can turn over its inventory, the more profitable the company will be. Further, the higher the inventory turnover ratio, the less time a firm has its funds tied up in its inventory and the less risk the firm faces from trying to sell out-of-date merchandise. What is considered to be a satisfactory inventory turnover varies from industry to industry. A grocery store chain like **Safeway**, for example, should have a much higher inventory turnover than a jewelry store like **Zales**.

To illustrate the inventory turnover ratio, **Best Buy** reported the following financial data:

| ($ millions) | 2009 | 2008 | 2007 |
|---|---|---|---|
| Cost of goods sold..................................................... | $37,534 | $34,017 | $30,477 |
| Beginning inventory.................................................... | 4,753 | 4,708 | 4,028 |
| Ending inventory....................................................... | 5,486 | 4,753 | 4,708 |

Best Buy's inventory turnover in 2009 is 7.33, computed as $37,534/[($4,753 + $5,486)/2]. Similar calculations reveal that Best Buy's inventory turnover in 2008 was 7.19 and it was 6.98 in 2007, indicating that its inventory turnover was relatively stable over the three-year period.

The inventory turnover ratio can be influenced by a firm's choice of inventory costing method. Inventory amounts calculated using LIFO, for example, will typically be smaller than the same inventory calculated using FIFO. An investor comparing inventory turnover ratios between different firms will need to verify that the firms are using the same inventory costing method; otherwise, any ratio comparisons will be apples-to-oranges rather than apples-to-apples.

An extension of the inventory turnover ratio is the **days' sales in inventory**, calculated as:

$$\text{Days' sales in inventory} = \frac{365}{\text{Inventory turnover}}$$

This ratio indicates how many days it takes, on average, for a firm to sell its inventory. During 2009, for example, Best Buy's days' sales in inventory was 49.8 days, or 365/7.33; that is, Best Buy took almost 50 days to sell its inventory. Similar calculations reveal it took an average of 50.8 days for Best Buy to sell its inventory in 2008 and 52.3 days in 2007. Do these ratio results indicate that Best Buy is doing a good job of managing its investment in inventory? Without comparable ratio data from a competitor like Target Corporation, it is difficult to conclude whether a days' sales in inventory ratio of 49.8 days indicates that Best Buy is doing a good or bad job of managing its inventory.

Flip Company installed a new inventory management system at the beginning of 2011. Shown below are financial data from the company's accounting records:

|  | 2010 | 2011 |
|---|---|---|
| Sales revenue | $4,000,000 | $4,400,000 |
| Cost of goods sold | 2,000,000 | 2,300,000 |
| Beginning inventory | 450,000 | 430,000 |
| Ending inventory | 430,000 | 320,000 |

Calculate the inventory turnover and days' sales in inventory for 2010 and 2011. Discuss your findings.

**The solution is on page 314.**

| Concept | Method | Assessment |
|---|---|---|
| How long, on average, does it take to sell the inventory? | Cost of goods sold, beginning inventory, and ending inventory $$\text{Inventory turnover} = \frac{\text{Cost of goods sold}}{\text{Average inventory}}$$ $$\text{Days' sales in inventory} = \frac{365}{\text{Inventory turnover}}$$ | A higher inventory turnover or a lower days' sales in inventory indicates that the company is able to sell its inventory more quickly. |

TAKEAWAY 6.1

## LIFO RESERVE

LEARNING OBJECTIVE 6

**Define** the LIFO reserve and **explain** how it is used to compare the performance of companies using different inventory costing methods.

As shown in this chapter, the LIFO inventory costing method can produce significantly different results relative to other inventory costing methods for both cost of goods sold, and therefore gross profit and net income, and ending inventory. The difference is greatest when compared to results obtained using FIFO. When costs are rising, FIFO will result in higher reported ending inventory, lower cost of goods sold, and higher net income.

To make comparisons between companies using LIFO and companies using FIFO, we need to use the **LIFO inventory reserve**, or simply *LIFO reserve*. Companies that use LIFO are required under generally accepted accounting principles to report the difference between ending inventory using LIFO and the inventory that would have been reported under FIFO. This difference is called the LIFO inventory reserve and is disclosed in notes to financial statements.

Referring again to Exhibit 6-8, FIFO ending inventory is valued at $1,190 and LIFO ending inventory at $820. The LIFO reserve is $370 ($1,190 − $820). Use of LIFO can have a material impact on many ratios, and one way to compensate for these effects is to use the LIFO reserve to restate the reported inventory. To illustrate, assume that Claremont Company, whose inventory costing method results are contrasted in Exhibit 6-8, has current assets of $2,100 and current liabilities of $1,400 under the LIFO method. Exhibit 6-14 calculates the current ratio (current assets divided by current liabilities) under both LIFO and FIFO. (The current ratio is discussed in Chapter 2.)

| **EXHIBIT 6-14** | **Impact of the LIFO Inventory Reserve on the Current Ratio** | |
|---|---|---|
|  | **LIFO** | **FIFO** |
| Current ratio | $\frac{\$2,100}{\$1,400} = 1.5$ | $\frac{(\$2,100 + \$370)}{\$1,400} = 1.76$ |

**Hint:** The LIFO reserve is also used to restate the LIFO cost of goods sold to that under FIFO. The change in the LIFO reserve from the beginning to the end of the period minus the LIFO cost of goods sold equals FIFO cost of goods sold.

As shown in Exhibit 6-14, the current ratio is much higher under FIFO (1.76) than under LIFO (1.5). Differences occur between LIFO and FIFO companies for many ratios, with FIFO resulting in more favorable ratios in most cases since FIFO generally results in higher inventory values and higher net earnings. For some ratios, however, LIFO produces more favorable results. Two examples are the inventory turnover ratio and the days' sales in inventory ratio. Because LIFO results in lower inventory values, the inventory turnover (and consequently, the days' sales in inventory) under LIFO appears higher (lower) than it does under FIFO. (The LIFO reserve also affects cost of goods sold and therefore the numerator of the inventory turnover ratio; in most cases the adjustment to cost of goods sold is much smaller than the adjustment to average inventory, leading to a higher inventory turnover under LIFO than under FIFO.)

| | Concept ———→ | Method ———→ | Assessment |
|---|---|---|---|
| **TAKEAWAY 6.2** | What effect does the use of LIFO have on ending inventory relative to the use of FIFO? | Ending inventory and the LIFO inventory reserve<br><br>The value of LIFO ending inventory + the LIFO inventory reserve = The value of FIFO ending inventory | If the LIFO reserve is material it can have a significant impact on many ratios when compared to FIFO. The calculation of these ratios can be adjusted using the LIFO inventory reserve to provide a more comparable set of results. |

### WORKING WITH THE TAKEAWAYS

Felix Company uses the LIFO inventory costing method to value inventory. The following financial data was obtained from its accounting records for the current year:

| | |
|---|---:|
| Current assets (including inventory) | $4,000 |
| Current liabilities | 2,000 |
| Inventory under LIFO | 575 |
| Inventory under FIFO | 775 |

Compute (a) the LIFO inventory reserve and (b) the current ratio assuming (i) LIFO and (ii) FIFO.

**Solution:**

a.  LIFO inventory reserve = $775 − $575 = $200

b.  (i)   Current ratio under LIFO = $4,000/$2,000 = 2.0:1

    (ii)  Current ratio under FIFO = ($4,000 + $200)/$2,000 = 2.1:1

# APPENDIX 6A:  Inventory Costing Methods and the Perpetual Inventory System

**LEARNING OBJECTIVE 7**

**Describe** inventory costing under a perpetual inventory system using specific identification, weighted-average cost, FIFO, and LIFO.

This appendix illustrates the accounting for inventories using the perpetual inventory system under the four costing methods of: (1) specific identification; (2) first-in, first-out; (3) last-in, first-out; and (4) weighted-average cost. All four methods are illustrated using the following data for Claremont Company.

| Date | | Event | No. of Units | | Unit Cost | | Total Cost |
|---|---|---|---:|---|---:|---|---:|
| Jan. | 1 | Beginning inventory | 60 | @ | $10 | = | $ 600 |
| Mar. | 27 | Purchase inventory | 90 | @ | 11 | = | 990 |
| Aug. | 15 | Purchase inventory | 100 | @ | 13 | = | 1,300 |
| Nov. | 6 | Purchase inventory | 50 | @ | 16 | = | 800 |
| | | Goods available for sale | 300 | | | | $3,690 |
| | | Sales of inventory | 220 | | | | |
| Dec. | 31 | Ending inventory | 80 | | | | |

Under all four inventory costing methods, the Inventory account is increased each time a purchase occurs for the amount of the purchase and is decreased each time a sale occurs by an amount equal to the cost of goods sold. The methods differ only in the computation of cost of goods sold, consisting of 220 units (130 + 90 = 220), and the year-end Inventory account balance, consisting of 80 units remaining.

## SPECIFIC IDENTIFICATION METHOD

Under the **specific identification method**, the actual cost of the specific units sold is identified and used to compute the cost of goods sold. To illustrate, assume that (1) 50 of the 130 units sold on May 2 came from the beginning inventory of 60 units and the remaining 80 units sold (50 + 80 = 130) came from the purchase of 90 units on March 27, and that (2) 10 of the 90 units sold on December 10 came from the purchase of 90 units on March 27 and the remaining 80 units sold (10 + 80 = 90) came from the purchase of 100 units on August 15. Exhibit 6A-1 illustrates the calculation of cost of goods sold and ending inventory using specific identification. The cost of goods sold is $2,530 (sum of the Sold total column), and the ending inventory of 80 units is valued at $1,160 (final amount in the Inventory Balance total column).

| EXHIBIT 6A-1 | Specific Identification Method (Perpetual Inventory System) | | | | | | | | |
|---|---|---|---|---|---|---|---|---|---|
| | **Purchased** | | | **Sold** | | | **Inventory Balance** | | |
| **Date** | **Units** | **Unit Cost** | **Total** | **Units** | **Unit Cost** | **Total** | **Units** | **Unit Cost** | **Total** |
| Jan. 1 . . . . . . . . . . . | | | | | | | 60 | $10 | $ 600 |
| Mar. 27 . . . . . . . . . . . | 90 | $11 | $ 990 | | | | 60 | 10 | 1,590 |
| | | | | | | | 90 | 11 | |
| **May 2** . . . . . . . . . | | | | 50 | $10 | $ 500 | 10 | 10 | 210 |
| | | | | 80 | 11 | 880 | 10 | 11 | |
| Aug. 15 . . . . . . . . . . . | 100 | 13 | 1,300 | | | | 10 | 10 | |
| | | | | | | | 10 | 11 | 1,510 |
| | | | | | | | 100 | 13 | |
| Nov. 6 . . . . . . . . . . . | 50 | 16 | 800 | | | | 10 | 10 | |
| | | | | | | | 10 | 11 | 2,310 |
| | | | | | | | 100 | 13 | |
| | | | | | | | 50 | 16 | |
| **Dec. 10** . . . . . . . . . | | | | 10 | 11 | 110 | **10** | **10** | |
| | | | | 80 | 13 | 1,040 | **20** | **13** | **1,160** |
| | | | | | | | **50** | **16** | |
| Total . . . . . . . . . . . . . | | | | | | **$2,530** | | | |

## FIRST-IN, FIRST-OUT (FIFO) METHOD

Under the **first-in, first-out (FIFO) method**, each time that a sale is made the cost of the oldest goods are charged to cost of goods sold. Visually, the FIFO method appears like a conveyor belt. Items of inventory are placed on the belt and then move along to the end. As items reach the end of the conveyor belt, they are assumed to be sold. Those items still on the belt (which are the last items placed on the belt) are assumed to remain in inventory until they reach the end of the conveyor belt. This visualization is illustrated in Exhibit 6A-2.

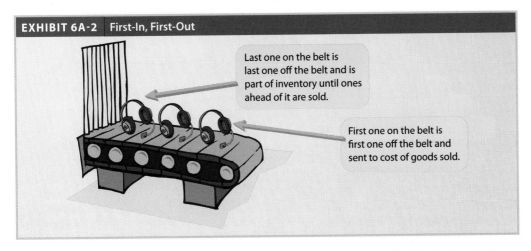

**EXHIBIT 6A-2** First-In, First-Out

Last one on the belt is last one off the belt and is part of inventory until ones ahead of it are sold.

First one on the belt is first one off the belt and sent to cost of goods sold.

Results of the FIFO method are in Exhibit 6A-3. FIFO handles the May 2 sale of 130 units as follows: The oldest units are the units in the January 1 beginning inventory. These are the first 60 units assumed to be sold. The next oldest units are the units purchased on March 27 and 70 units are needed from this purchase (130 sold – 60 from January 1) to provide all of the units sold on May 2. After the May 2 sale, only 20 units remain, all from the March 27 purchase.

The December 10 sale of 90 units is handled in a similar manner. The oldest units at December 10 are the 20 units remaining from the March 27 purchase. These are the first units assumed to be sold. The next oldest units are the 100 units purchased on August 15 and 70 additional units are needed for the sale (90 sold − 20 from the March 27 purchase). Therefore, 70 of the 100 units purchased on August 15 are assumed to be included in the units sold on December 10. After the December 10 sale, 30 units remain from the August 15 purchase and 50 units remain from the November 6 purchase.

Cost of goods sold using the FIFO method is $2,500 (sum of the Sold total column), and the ending inventory is $1,190 (final amount in the Inventory Balance total column).

| EXHIBIT 6A-3 | First-In, First-Out Method (Perpetual Inventory System) | | | | | | | | |
|---|---|---|---|---|---|---|---|---|---|
| | **Purchased** | | | **Sold** | | | **Inventory Balance** | | |
| **Date** | **Units** | **Unit Cost** | **Total** | **Units** | **Unit Cost** | **Total** | **Units** | **Unit Cost** | **Total** |
| Jan. 1 . . . . . . . . . . . | | | | | | | 60 | $10 | $ 600 |
| Mar. 27 . . . . . . . . . . | 90 | $11 | $ 990 | | | | 60 | 10 | 1,590 |
| | | | | | | | 90 | 11 | |
| **May 2** . . . . . . . . . | | | | 60 | $10 | $ 600 | | | |
| | | | | 70 | 11 | 770 | 20 | 11 | 220 |
| Aug. 15 . . . . . . . . . . | 100 | 13 | 1,300 | | | | 20 | 11 | 1,520 |
| | | | | | | | 100 | 13 | |
| Nov. 6 . . . . . . . . . . | 50 | 16 | 800 | | | | 20 | 11 | 2,320 |
| | | | | | | | 100 | 13 | |
| | | | | | | | 50 | 16 | |
| **Dec. 10** . . . . . . . . | | | | 20 | 11 | 220 | 30 | 13 | 1,190 |
| | | | | 70 | 13 | 910 | 50 | 16 | |
| Total . . . . . . . . . . . . . | | | | | | $2,500 | | | |

## LAST-IN, FIRST-OUT (LIFO) METHOD

When the **last-in, first-out (LIFO) method** is used, the cost of the most recent inventory purchased is charged to cost of goods sold when a sale occurs. Visually, the LIFO method appears like a stack of bricks. Each new brick entered into inventory is placed on top of the existing stack of bricks. When a brick is sold, the last brick placed on the stack is pulled from the top of the stack and given to the customer. The bricks at the bottom of the stack are assumed to remain in inventory until the newer bricks from the top of the stack are first sold. This visualization is illustrated in Exhibit 6A-4.

**EXHIBIT 6A-4**    Last-In, First-Out

Last brick placed on the stack is first one sold.

First brick placed in the stack remains in inventory and is last one sold.

Exhibit 6A-5 illustrates the results using LIFO. The LIFO method handles the May 2 sale of 130 units as follows: The most recently purchased units (newest units) are the units from the March 27 purchase. These are the first 90 units assumed to be sold. The next newest units are the units in the January 1 beginning inventory and 40 units from the January 1 units are needed (130 sold − 90 from the March 27 purchase) to provide all of the units sold on May 2. After the May 2 sale, only 20 units remain, all from the January 1 beginning inventory.

The December 10 sale of 90 units is handled in a similar manner. The newest units at December 10 are the 50 units purchased on November 6. These are the first units assumed to be sold. The next newest units are the 100 units purchased on August 15 and 40 additional units are needed for the sale

(90 sold − 50 from the November 6 purchase). Therefore, 40 of the 100 units purchased on August 15 are assumed to be included in the units sold on December 10. After the sale, 20 units remain from the January 1 inventory and 60 units remain from the August 15 purchase.

Cost of goods sold using LIFO is $2,710 (sum of the Sold total column), and the ending inventory is $980 (final amount in the Inventory Balance total column).

**EXHIBIT 6A-5** Last-In, First-Out Method (Perpetual Inventory System)

| | Purchased | | | Sold | | | Inventory Balance | | |
|---|---|---|---|---|---|---|---|---|---|
| Date | Units | Unit Cost | Total | Units | Unit Cost | Total | Units | Unit Cost | Total |
| Jan. 1 ............. | | | | | | | 60 | $10 | $ 600 |
| Mar. 27............. | 90 | $11 | $ 990 | | | | 60 | 10 | 1,590 |
| | | | | | | | 90 | 11 | |
| **May 2 .........** | | | | 90 | $11 | $ 990 | | | |
| | | | | 40 | 10 | 400 | 20 | 10 | 200 |
| Aug. 15............ | 100 | 13 | 1,300 | | | | 20 | 10 | 1,500 |
| | | | | | | | 100 | 13 | |
| Nov. 6............. | 50 | 16 | 800 | | | | 20 | 10 | 2,300 |
| | | | | | | | 100 | 13 | |
| | | | | | | | 50 | 16 | |
| **Dec. 10 .........** | | | | 50 | 16 | 800 | 20 | 10 | 980 |
| | | | | 40 | 13 | 520 | 60 | 13 | |
| Total ............. | | | | | | $2,710 | | | |

## WEIGHTED-AVERAGE COST METHOD

When the **weighted-average cost method** is used, a new weighted-average unit cost is calculated for the goods (**total cost divided by total units**) each time that goods are purchased and added to inventory. The cost of goods sold for each sale is calculated by multiplying the weighted-average unit cost at the time of sale by the number of units sold. Exhibit 6A-6 illustrates the calculation of cost of goods sold and ending inventory under the weighted-average cost method. The weighted-average unit cost is calculated three times in Exhibit 6A-6. On March 27, 90 units were purchased at a unit cost of $11, and the updated weighted-average unit cost on this date is:

$$[\$600 + \$990]/[\,60\text{ Units} + 90\text{ Units}] = \$10.60$$

On August 15, 100 units were purchased at a unit cost of $13. The updated weighted-average unit cost on this date is:

$$[\$212 + \$1,300]/[20\text{ Units} + 100\text{ Units}] = \$12.60$$

On November 6, 50 units were purchased at a unit cost of $16. The updated weighted-average unit cost on this date is:

$$[\$1,512 + \$800]/[120\text{ Units} + 50\text{ Units}] = \$13.60$$

The cost of goods sold is $2,602 (sum of the Sold total column), and the ending inventory is $1,088 (final amount in the Inventory Balance total column).

**EXHIBIT 6A-6** Weighted-Average Cost Method (Perpetual Inventory System)

| | Purchased | | | Sold | | | Inventory Balance | | |
|---|---|---|---|---|---|---|---|---|---|
| Date | Units | Unit Cost | Total | Units | Unit Cost | Total | Units | Unit Cost | Total |
| Jan. 1 .............. | | | | | | | 60 | $10.00 | $ 600 |
| Mar. 27.............. | 90 | $11 | $ 990 | | | | 150 | 10.60 | 1,590 |
| **May 2 ............** | | | | 130 | $10.60 | $1,378 | 20 | 10.60 | 212 |
| Aug. 15.............. | 100 | 13 | 1,300 | | | | 120 | 12.60 | 1,512 |
| Nov. 6.............. | 50 | 16 | 800 | | | | 170 | 13.60 | 2,312 |
| **Dec. 10 ...........** | | | | 90 | 13.60 | 1,224 | 80 | 13.60 | 1,088 |
| Total ............... | | | | | | $2,602 | | | |

## COMPARATIVE ANALYSIS OF INVENTORY COSTING METHODS

The purchase price data used in the Claremont Company illustration has an important characteristic: the purchase price of the inventory increased each time that a purchase was made, from $11 per unit to $13 per unit to $16 per unit. Increasing inventory prices are frequently encountered in the real world where price inflation is common and price deflation is uncommon. Exhibit 6A-7 summarizes the results of applying the four inventory costing methods to the Claremont Company data and reveals that the FIFO method produces the lowest cost of goods sold ($2,500), while the LIFO method produces the highest cost of goods sold ($2,710). The exhibit also reveals that FIFO produces the highest year-end value of ending inventory ($1,190), while LIFO produces the lowest year-end value of ending inventory ($980). Specific identification and weighted-average cost produce ending inventory values and cost of goods sold values that fall in between the results obtained using FIFO and LIFO.

These results, however, are highly dependent on the purchase prices for the inventory. If the inventory's purchase price had been decreasing rather than increasing, the financial effects would have been just the opposite, with LIFO producing the lowest cost of goods sold and FIFO the highest. If, on the other hand, the purchase prices had been perfectly stable, there would be no difference between the cost of goods sold or the ending inventory for any of the four methods.

| EXHIBIT 6A-7    Results of Different Inventory Costing Methods | | |
|---|---|---|
| **Costing Method** | **Ending Inventory** | **Cost of Goods Sold** |
| Specific identification................ | $1,160 | $2,530 |
| FIFO ............................. | 1,190 | 2,500 |
| LIFO................................. | 980 | 2,710 |
| Weighted-average cost .............. | 1,088 | 2,602 |

## IMPACTS OF COST FLOW ASSUMPTIONS

Under generally accepted accounting principles, a company is permitted to select one or more of the four methods for purposes of assigning cost to its ending inventory and its cost of goods sold. Which method (or methods, since a company may elect to value some of its inventory using FIFO, some using LIFO, and some using weighted-average cost) is selected by a company depends upon a number of factors—the type of product produced, the cost of producing the product, whether the product is perishable, whether the company desires to report a high or a low net income, and income tax considerations.

### Specific Identification Method

Specific identification is typically used by companies that manufacture a small volume of products with relatively high unit values. Airplanes, jewelry, and construction equipment are examples of products that would justify the cost of tracking the specific unit cost of each inventory item. Specific identification is usually not cost-justified for companies that manufacture products that have a low unit cost or involve high volumes of production. It can be very expensive to trace the exact costs of producing a product, especially a product manufactured in high volumes.

### FIFO Method

Many companies, especially those with perishable, time-dated, or style-affected merchandise, attempt to sell their oldest merchandise first. This is especially true for companies that sell food products, chemicals, and drugs. For these types of companies, the cost flow produced by the FIFO method most closely matches the actual goods flow. However, a company is not required to use the cost flow assumption that most closely matches its actual goods flow. When costs are rising, FIFO will result in the lowest cost of goods sold, and therefore, the highest net income. The desire to show a higher net income by some companies partly explains the popularity of the FIFO method.

### LIFO Method

Although LIFO does not reflect the actual goods flow for most businesses, its popularity is likely linked to the potential income tax savings associated with its use. For some industries, however, LIFO does depict the actual goods flow. For example, in industries that extract natural resources, such as mining, the product is frequently dumped onto a storage pile from an overhead trestle, and sold inventory is taken from the top of the pile. One disadvantage of using LIFO when beginning inventories have been maintained or increased is that a firm's ending inventory can be substantially undervalued since old purchase prices tend to be retained on a company's books under the LIFO method. This, in turn, will cause a firm's current assets and total assets to likewise be undervalued.

## Weighted-Average Cost Method

Weighted-average cost is best suited for businesses that warehouse a large volume of undifferentiated goods in a common area. Liquid fuels, grains, and other commodities are examples. Weighted-average cost typically generates a cost of goods sold amount that is neither high nor low as compared to the other methods, as is revealed in Exhibit 6A-7.

## Summary of Impacts

We can broadly summarize the impacts of the cost flow assumptions as follows:

1. Specific identification most closely identifies the actual cost of goods sold and ending inventory.
2. FIFO approximates the actual physical goods flow for most firms.
3. LIFO is popular because of the income tax savings associated with its use.
4. Weighted-average cost is most often associated with businesses in which undifferentiated goods are commingled in a common area like a warehouse.

## ANALYSIS OF COSTING METHODS AND GROSS PROFIT

To illustrate the financial effects of the different inventory costing methods, assume that the 220 units sold by the Claremont Company were sold for $20 each, producing sales of $4,400 ($20 × 220). Exhibit 6A-8 shows the difference in gross profit under each of the four inventory costing methods. Remember that the difference in reported gross profit results from the assumptions made about cost flows, not from any difference in actual goods flows. In each case, 220 units were sold and 80 units remained. Each of the inventory costing methods is in accord with generally accepted accounting principles, yet one method's financial impact on gross profit and net income is different from the financial impact of another method.

| EXHIBIT 6A-8 | Gross Profit Using Alternative Inventory Costing Methods | | | |
|---|---|---|---|---|
| | Specific Identification | FIFO | LIFO | Weighted-Average |
| Sales (220 units @ $20).................................. | $4,400 | $4,400 | $4,400 | $4,400 |
| Cost of goods sold....................................... | 2,530 | 2,500 | 2,710 | 2,602 |
| Gross profit............................................ | $1,870 | $1,900 | $1,690 | $1,798 |
| Increased gross profit compared with LIFO............. | $ 180 | $ 210 | | $ 108 |

## Income Statement and Balance Sheet Effects

As Exhibit 6A-8 reveals, LIFO results in the smallest gross profit ($1,690) with FIFO producing the highest ($1,900) gross profit. This result occurs because the purchase price of inventory was increasing throughout the year, from $11 per unit to $13 per unit to $16 per unit. Most agree that when costs are rising, FIFO tends to overstate gross profit (and income) because older, lower unit costs are included in the cost of goods sold and matched with current sales prices. In other words, in the illustration, all of the units sold are charged to costs of goods sold under FIFO at unit costs of $10, $11, and $13. If the latest purchase price reflects the inventory's current acquisition cost, the units sold must be replaced by units costing $16 (or more if costs continue to rise).

It is frequently argued that LIFO provides a better matching of current costs with current revenues since the cost of the most recent purchases constitutes the LIFO cost of goods sold. While LIFO associates the current, higher unit costs with cost of goods sold, it assigns costs to ending inventory using the older, lower unit costs. As a consequence, the value of the LIFO ending inventory on the balance sheet is often undervalued in terms of the inventory's current value. When inventory quantities are maintained or increased, the LIFO method prevents older costs from appearing in the cost of goods sold. No doubt, some firms still carry LIFO inventories at unit costs that existed more than 10 years ago. Under FIFO, the ending inventory is measured at relatively recent costs.

## Comparison of Inventory Costing Methods

Exhibit 6A-9 summarizes the results of applying the periodic and perpetual costing methods to the same Claremont data. The specific identification method and the FIFO method yield the exact same results for ending inventory and cost of goods sold regardless of whether the periodic or the perpetual method

**REVIEW**

is being used. For specific identification, ending inventory and cost of goods sold are identical under both the periodic and perpetual inventory systems. The same is true for FIFO. Only LIFO and weighted-average methods produce different results under the periodic and perpetual systems.

| EXHIBIT 6A-9    Summary Results of Different Inventory Costing Methods | | |
|---|---|---|
| **Costing Method** | **Ending Inventory** | **Cost of Goods Sold** |
| Specific identification | | |
| Periodic | $1,160 | $2,530 |
| Perpetual | 1,160 | 2,530 |
| FIFO | | |
| Periodic | 1,190 | 2,500 |
| Perpetual | 1,190 | 2,500 |
| LIFO | | |
| Periodic | 820 | 2,870 |
| Perpetual | 980 | 2,710 |
| Average | | |
| Periodic | 984 | 2,706 |
| Perpetual | 1,088 | 2,602 |

Choice of a periodic vs perpetual system does *not* impact specific identification or FIFO

Choice of a periodic vs perpetual system does impact LIFO and weighted-average results

## SUMMARY OF LEARNING OBJECTIVES

**LO1**    **Explain inventory concepts and modern inventory practices. (p. 268)**

- Merchandise inventory is a stock of inventory that a merchandising company buys from a manufacturer and makes available for sale to its customers.
- A manufacturing firm maintains three different inventory categories: raw materials inventory, work-in-process inventory, and finished goods inventory.
- Traditionally, manufacturers have maintained just-in-case inventories of raw materials and components to provide for unplanned production or delayed raw material shipments, resulting in high levels of inventory carrying costs.
- Today, many manufacturers have adopted the just-in-time (JIT) manufacturing philosophy which is designed to eliminate or minimize raw materials, work-in-process, and finished goods inventories. The key to JIT manufacturing is careful inventory order planning and sophisticated production management.
- Ownership of goods in transit depends on the shipping terms. The buyer assumes ownership of goods in transit shipped F.O.B. shipping point, whereas the seller maintains ownership of goods shipped F.O.B. destination until the buyer assumes possession at delivery.
- Consignment goods are goods held for sale by parties other than the seller. The seller maintains legal ownership of these inventory items while they are held for sale by the consignment seller.

**LO2**    **Describe inventory costing under specific identification, weighted-average cost, FIFO, and LIFO. (p. 272)**

- To assign cost to units sold (cost of goods sold) and units available (inventory), a company must either keep track of the cost of each specific unit (specific identification method) or make an assumption about which units have been sold (weighted-average cost, FIFO, and LIFO methods).
- The weighted-average cost method assumes that a mix of the goods available is sold; the FIFO method assumes that the oldest goods are sold first; and, the LIFO method assumes that the newest goods are sold first.

**LO3**    **Analyze the financial effects of different inventory costing methods on company profit. (p. 276)**

- Each of the alternative inventory costing methods produces a different cost of goods sold and gross profit.
- When costs are rising, the LIFO method does the best job of matching current costs with revenues; LIFO also produces a lower gross profit and lower income taxes than either weighted-average cost or FIFO.

**Apply the lower-of-cost-or-market method. (p. 281)** LO4

■ Damaged, physically deteriorated, or obsolete merchandise should be valued and reported at its net realizable value—that is, its estimated selling price less the expected cost of disposal.

■ The lower-of-cost-or-market method provides for inventory write-downs to be recorded in the period that the replacement cost of inventory declines below the inventory's acquisition cost.

■ The lower-of-cost-or-market method may be applied to (a) each inventory item, (b) major inventory categories, or (c) the total inventory.

**Define *inventory turnover* and *day's sales in inventory* and explain the use of these ratios. (p. 284)** LO5

■ Inventory turnover and days' sales in inventory indicate, respectively, how many times on average during the year a firm sells its inventory and how many days on average it takes a firm to sell its inventory.

■ Inventory turnover and days' sales in inventory provide evidence regarding a firm's ability to sell its inventory and its ability to effectively manage its investment in inventory.

**Define the LIFO reserve and explain how it is used to compare the performance of companies using different inventory costing methods. (p. 285)** LO6

■ The LIFO inventory reserve represents the difference between the value of LIFO ending inventory and what the ending inventory would have been valued at under FIFO.

■ The LIFO inventory reserve can cause a material effect on many ratios. These ratios should be adjusted for the LIFO inventory reserve when comparing a company using LIFO with a FIFO company.

**Appendix 6A: Describe inventory costing under a perpetual inventory system using specific identification, weighted-average cost, FIFO, and LIFO. (p. 286)** LO7

■ To assign cost to units sold (cost of goods sold) and units available (inventory), a company must either keep track of the cost of each specific unit (specific identification method) or make an assumption about which units have been sold (weighted-average cost, FIFO, and LIFO methods).

■ The weighted-average cost method assumes that a mix of the goods available is sold; the FIFO method assumes that the oldest goods are sold; and, the LIFO method assumes that the newest goods are sold.

■ The specific identification method and the FIFO method yield the exact same results for ending inventory and for cost of goods sold regardless of whether the periodic or the perpetual method is being used. Only LIFO and weighted-average methods produce different results.

## TAKEAWAY: SUMMARY CHART

| Concept | Method | Assessment | |
|---|---|---|---|
| How long, on average, does it take to sell the inventory? | Cost of goods sold, beginning inventory, and ending inventory<br><br>$\text{Inventory turnover} = \dfrac{\text{Cost of goods sold}}{\text{Average inventory}}$<br><br>$\text{Days' sales in inventory} = \dfrac{365}{\text{Inventory turnover}}$ | A higher inventory turnover or a lower days' sales in inventory indicates that the company is able to sell its inventory more quickly. | TAKEAWAY 6.1 |
| What effect does the use of LIFO have on ending inventory relative to the use of FIFO? | Ending inventory and the LIFO inventory reserve<br><br>The value of LIFO ending inventory + the LIFO inventory reserve = The value of FIFO ending inventory | If the LIFO reserve is material it can have a significant impact on many ratios when compared to FIFO. The calculation of these ratios can be adjusted using the LIFO inventory reserve to provide a more comparable set of results. | TAKEAWAY 6.2 |

## GLOSSARY OF KEY TERMS

**Consignment goods** Items held for sale by parties other than the item's owner (p. 270).

**Cost flow** The actual or assumed assignment of costs to goods sold and to ending inventory (p. 273).

**Days' sales in inventory** A ratio computed by dividing 365 by Inventory Turnover; this ratio indicates the number of days it takes, on average, for a company to sell its inventory (p. 284).

**Finished goods inventory** A manufacturer's inventory that includes all products that have been completed and are ready for sale to customers (p. 269).

**First-in, first-out (FIFO) method** An inventory costing method that assumes that the oldest (earliest purchased) goods are sold first (p. 274).

**F.O.B. destination** Free-on-board destination indicates that the items being shipped are owned by the seller while the items are in transit (p. 270).

**F.O.B. shipping point** Free-on-board shipping point indicates that the items being shipped are owned by the buyer while the items are in transit (p. 270).

**Goods flow** The actual physical movement of inventory through a business (p. 273).

**Goods in transit** Items that are being shipped by a common carrier (p. 270).

**Inventory carrying costs** Costs created by just-in-case inventories, including casualty insurance, building usage costs, and the cost of capital invested in the inventory (p. 269).

**Inventory overage** The increase in the inventory account that occurs when the physical inventory count is greater than the inventory account balance (p. 271).

**Inventory shrinkage** The decrease in the inventory account that occurs when the physical inventory count is less than the inventory account balance (p. 271).

**Inventory turnover ratio** A ratio computed by dividing cost of goods sold by the average ending inventory (p. 284).

**Just-in-case inventory** The extra quantity of inventory that a firm carries just in case suppliers do not deliver when scheduled or just in case the company decides to make previously unplanned quantities of product for sale to customers (p. 269).

**Just-in-time manufacturing** A manufacturing philosophy that seeks to minimize or eliminate just-in-case inventory quantities through careful planning of raw material purchases and manufacturing management (p. 269).

**Last-in, first-out (LIFO) method** An inventory costing method that assumes that the newest (most recently purchased) goods are sold first (p. 274).

**LIFO conformity rule** A section of the Internal Revenue Code requiring that any company that selects LIFO for income tax reporting must also use LIFO for financial reporting to stockholders (p. 279).

**LIFO inventory reserve** The difference between the value of ending inventory reported under LIFO and what the inventory would have been valued at under FIFO (p. 285).

**Lower-of-cost-or-market (LCM)** A measurement method that, when applied to inventory, provides for ending inventory to be valued on the balance sheet at the lower of its acquisition cost or current replacement cost (p. 281).

**Net realizable value** An asset measure calculated by subtracting the expected disposal cost from an asset's expected selling price (p. 281).

**Physical count of inventory** The counting of inventory used to verify the balance of inventory (p. 270).

**Quick response system** A system used with a point-of-sale system that is designed to insure that a retailer quickly orders more of the items that are selling and quickly eliminates those items that are not selling (p. 269).

**Raw materials inventory** A manufacturer's inventory that includes raw materials and components that have been purchased for use in the factory but have not yet been placed into production (p. 268).

**Specific identification method** An inventory costing method involving the physical identification of goods sold and goods remaining and costing these amounts at their actual costs (p. 273).

**Weighted-average cost method** An inventory costing method that calculates an average unit purchase cost, weighted by the number of units purchased at each price, and uses that weighted-average unit cost to determine the cost of goods sold for all sales (p. 275).

**Work-in-process inventory** A manufacturer's inventory that consists of units of product that have been entered into production in the factory but have not yet been completed (p. 268).

# COMPREHENSIVE PROBLEM

The Montclair Corporation had the following inventory transactions for its only product during 2010:

| Purchases | |
|---|---|
| February 15 ................. | 2,000 units @ $27.00 each |
| April 20 ..................... | 3,000 units @ $28.40 each |
| October 25 .................. | 1,200 units @ $31.25 each |
| Sales | |
| March 1 ..................... | 1,200 units @ $50.00 each |
| June 12 ..................... | 2,000 units @ $52.00 each |
| August 10 ................... | 1,000 units @ $53.00 each |
| December 14 ................ | 1,600 units @ $55.00 each |

The Montclair Corporation had 1,000 units in its January 1, 2010, beginning inventory with a unit cost of $24 each. Montclair uses the periodic inventory system.

**Required**

a. Determine the cost assigned to Montclair's December 31, 2010, ending inventory and Montclair's cost of goods sold for 2010 under each of the following inventory costing methods:
   1. Weighted-average cost
   2. FIFO
   3. LIFO

b. Determine Montclair's gross profit for 2010 under each of the following inventory costing methods:
   1. Weighted-average cost
   2. FIFO
   3. LIFO

c.  Determine Montclair's LIFO inventory reserve at year-end 2010.

d.  Determine Montclair's inventory turnover and days' sales in inventory for 2010 under each of the following inventory costing methods:
   1. Weighted-average cost
   2. FIFO
   3. LIFO

**Solution**

a.  Units available:

|  |  |  |
|---|---|---|
| 1,000 units @ $24.00 = | $ 24,000 | |
| 2,000 units @ $27.00 = | 54,000 | |
| 3,000 units @ $28.40 = | 85,200 | |
| 1,200 units @ $31.25 = | 37,500 | |
| 7,200 | $200,700 | |

1. **Weighted-average cost:**

   Weighted-average unit cost:   $200,700/7,200 units = $ 27.875

   Ending inventory:        1,400 units × $27.875 = $ 39,025

   Cost of goods sold:      $200,700 − $39,025 = $161,675

2. **FIFO:**

   Ending inventory:   1,200 units @ $31.25 = $ 37,500
                        200 units @ $28.40 =    5,680
                      1,400                    $ 43,180

   Cost of good sold:  $200,700 − $43,180 =    $157,520

3. **LIFO:**

   Ending inventory:   1,000 units @ $24.00 = $ 24,000
                        400 units @ $27.00 =    10,800
                      1,400                    $ 34,800

   Cost of good sold:  $200,700 − $34,800 =    $165,900

b.  Sales revenue:

|  |  |
|---|---|
| 1,200 units @ $50.00 = | $ 60,000 |
| 2,000 units @ $52.00 = | 104,000 |
| 1,000 units @ $53.00 = | 53,000 |
| 1,600 units @ $55.00 = | 88,000 |
| 5,800 | $305,000 |

   1. Weighted-average gross profit = $305,000 − $161,675 = $143,325
   2. FIFO gross profit = $305,000 − $157,520 = $147,480
   3. LIFO gross profit = $305,000 − $165,900 = $139,100

c.  LIFO inventory reserve = $43,180 − $34,800 = $8,380

d.

|  | Inventory Turnover | Days' Sales in Inventory |
|---|---|---|
| Weighted-average cost .......... | 5.13 | 71.15 days |
| FIFO ........................... | 4.69 | 77.83 days |
| LIFO........................... | 6.42 | 56.85 days |

# SELF-STUDY QUESTIONS

(Answers to Self-Study Questions are at the end of this chapter.)

1.  Which of the following concepts relates to the elimination or minimization of inventories by a manufacturing firm?     LO1
    a.  Quick response
    b.  Just-in-time
    c.  Just-in-case
    d.  Specific identification

LO2    **2.** Which inventory costing method assumes that the most recently purchased merchandise is sold first?
- *a.* Specific identification
- *b.* Weighted-average cost
- *c.* FIFO
- *d.* LIFO

LO3    **3.** Which inventory costing method results in the highest-valued ending inventory during a period of rising unit costs?
- *a.* Specific identification
- *b.* Weighted-average cost
- *c.* FIFO
- *d.* LIFO

LO1    **4.** Under which of the following freight terms does the seller retain ownership of the shipped goods?
- *a.* F.O.B. shipping point
- *b.* F.O.B. destination

LO3    **5.** When should ending inventory be written down below its acquisition cost on the balance sheet?
- *a.* When units are damaged, physically deteriorated, or obsolete.
- *b.* When the inventory's replacement cost exceeds its acquisition cost.
- *c.* When the inventory's replacement cost is below its acquisition cost.
- *d.* Both a and c.

LO3    **6.** Which inventory costing method results in the highest net income during a period of rising unit prices?
- *a.* Specific identification
- *b.* Weighted-average cost
- *c.* FIFO
- *d.* LIFO

LO2    **7.** Which inventory costing method is expensive to implement?
- *a.* Specific identification
- *b.* Weighted-average cost
- *c.* FIFO
- *d.* LIFO

LO2    **8.** Which inventory costing method is frequently used when undifferentiated units are stored in a common area?
- *a.* Specific identification
- *b.* Weighted-average cost
- *c.* FIFO
- *d.* LIFO

LO3    **9.** Which inventory costing method results in the lowest net income during a period of rising unit prices?
- *a.* Specific identification
- *b.* Weighted-average cost
- *c.* FIFO
- *d.* LIFO

LO4    **10.** Which inventory costing method does not require the use of the lower-of-cost-or-market method?
- *a.* Specific identification
- *b.* Weighted-average cost
- *c.* FIFO
- *d.* All methods require the use of LCM.

LO5    **11.** Tracker Corp. reported annual cost of goods sold of $30,000 and average inventory on hand during the year of $3,750. What was Tracker's inventory turnover?
- *a.* 0.125 times
- *b.* 8.0 times
- *c.* $26,250
- *d.* 8.0%

LO6    **12.** The Avner Company reports ending inventory under the LIFO method of $15,000. Had Avner used FIFO, the ending inventory would have been reported as $16,500. Avner's LIFO inventory reserve is:
- *a.* $31,500
- *b.* $15,000
- *c.* $1,500
- *d.* 91%

13. The periodic inventory system differs from the perpetual inventory system:
    a.  because the periodic system is not compatible with modern technology.
    b.  because the perpetual system continually updates inventory, while the periodic inventory system only updates inventory at the end of the period.
    c.  because the periodic system continually updates inventory, while the perpetual inventory system only updates inventory at the end of the period.
    d.  because the periodic system is more complex and costly.

**LO7**

**(Appendix 6A)**

## DISCUSSION QUESTIONS

1.  What are the three inventory accounts maintained by a manufacturing firm? Define each.

2.  ShopMart Stores uses point-of-sale equipment at its checkout counters to read universal bar codes. It also uses a quick response system. What is a quick response system?

3.  What are *just-in-case inventory* and *inventory carrying costs?*

4.  What is the *just-in-time manufacturing philosophy?* Describe it.

5.  What is meant by *goods flow* and *cost flow?*

6.  Describe how each of the following inventory costing methods is used with the perpetual inventory system: (a) Specific identification; (b) Weighted-average cost; (c) First-in, first-out; and (d) Last-in, first-out.

7.  What is an appropriate operating situation (that is, goods flow corresponds with cost flow) for each of the following approaches to inventory costing: Specific identification, Weighted-average cost, FIFO, and LIFO?

8.  Why do relatively stable purchase prices reduce the significance of the choice of an inventory costing method?

9.  What is the nature of FIFO *phantom profits* during periods of rising inventory purchase prices?

10. If costs have been rising, which inventory costing method—weighted-average cost; first-in, first-out; or last-in, first-out—yields (a) the lowest ending inventory value? (b) the lowest net income? (c) the largest ending inventory value? (d) the largest net income?

11. Even though it does not represent their goods flow, why might firms adopt last-in, first-out inventory costing during periods when inventory costs are rising?

12. Describe two situations in which merchandise may be valued on the balance sheet at an amount less than its acquisition cost.

13. Which of the following is not an inventory costing method?
    a.  Specific identification
    b.  Weighted-average cost
    c.  Just-in-time manufacturing
    d.  FIFO

14. What is the effect on reported net income of applying the lower-of-cost-or-market method to ending inventory?

15. How do the accounting principles of consistency and full disclosure apply to inventory costing?

16. Which party, the seller or the buyer, bears the freight cost when the terms are F.O.B. shipping point? When the terms are F.O.B. destination?

17. What is a LIFO inventory reserve and how can it be useful to an analyst?

18. Moyer Company has an inventory turnover of 4.51. What is Moyer's days' sales in inventory?

19. In a recent annual report, Craftmade International, Inc., describes its inventory accounting policies as follows:

> Inventories are stated at the lower-of-cost-or-market, with inventory cost determined using the First-in, first-out (FIFO) method. The cost of inventory includes freight-in and duties on imported goods.

Also in a recent annual report, Kaiser Aluminum Corporation made the following statement in discussing its inventories:

> The Company recorded pretax charges of approximately $19.4 million because of a reduction in the carrying values of its inventories caused principally by prevailing lower prices for alumina, primary aluminum, and fabricated products.

**ASSIGNMENTS**

What accounting principle did Craftmade International follow when it included the costs of freight-in and duties on imported goods in its Inventory account? Briefly describe how a firm determines which costs to include in its inventory account. What accounting principle did Kaiser Aluminum follow when it recorded the $19.4 million pretax charge? Briefly describe the rationale for this principle.

## SHORT EXERCISES

**LO4**  **SE6-1.**  **Departures from Acquisition Cost**
At year-end, The Appliance Shop has a refrigerator that has been used as a demonstration model. The refrigerator cost $350 and sells for $500 when new. In its present condition, the refrigerator will be sold for $325. Related selling costs are an estimated $15. At what amount should the refrigerator be carried in inventory?

    *a.*   $350
    *b.*   $335
    *c.*   $325
    *d.*   $310

**LO2**  **SE6-2.**  **Inventory Costing Methods**
Which inventory costing method requires that a company keep track of the cost of each specific unit of inventory?

    *a.*   Specific identification
    *b.*   Lower-of-cost-or-market method
    *c.*   LIFO
    *d.*   All of the above

**LO6**  **SE6-3.**  **LIFO Inventory Reserve**
Lamil Company reports ending inventory of $150,000 on a LIFO basis and also reports a LIFO inventory reserve of $27,000. If Lamil had used FIFO rather than FIFO, ending inventory would have been:

    *a.*   $123,000.
    *b.*   $150,000.
    *c.*   $177,000.
    *d.*   $182,500.

**LO4**  **SE6-4.**  **Lower-of-Cost-or-Market Method**
The Claremont Company's ending inventory is composed of 50 units that had cost $20 each and 100 units that had cost $15 each. If the company can replace all 150 units at a price of $16 each, what value should be assigned to the company's ending inventory assuming that it applies LCM to the total inventory?

**LO4**  **SE6-5.**  **Lower-of-Cost-or-Market Method**
The McQuenny Company's ending inventory is composed of 100 units that had an acquisition cost of $25 per unit and 50 units that had an acquisition cost of $30 per unit. If the company can replace all 150 units at a replacement cost of $27 per unit, what value should be assigned to the company's ending inventory assuming that it applies the LCM method to the total inventory?

**LO5**  **SE6-6.**  **Inventory Turnover and Days' Sales in Inventory**
W. Glass & Company reported the following information in its recent annual report:

|  | 2010 | 2011 |
| --- | --- | --- |
| Cost of goods sold........................................... | $4,000,000 | $4,600,000 |
| Beginning inventory.......................................... | 900,000 | 860,000 |
| Ending inventory............................................. | 860,000 | 640,000 |

Calculate the company's inventory turnover and days' sales in inventory for both years.

**LO5**  **SE6-7.**  **Inventory Turnover and Days' Sales in Inventory**
Herberger & Company disclosed the following information in its recent annual report:

|  | 2010 | 2011 |
| --- | --- | --- |
| Cost of goods sold........................................... | $16,000,000 | $20,000,000 |
| Beginning inventory.......................................... | 2,000,000 | 4,000,000 |
| Ending inventory............................................. | 4,000,000 | 5,000,000 |

Calculate the company's inventory turnover and days' sales in inventory for both years.

**SE6-8. Inventory Costing Methods and the Periodic Method**

LO2

Lambeth Company experienced the following events in January:

| Date | Event | Units | | Unit Cost | Total Cost |
|------|-------|-------|---|-----------|------------|
| Jan. 10 | Purchased inventory............................ | 100 | @ | $12 | $1,200 |
| Jan. 20 | Purchased inventory............................ | 200 | @ | 14 | 2,800 |
| Jan. 30 | Sold inventory.................................... | 150 | | | |

If the Lambeth Company uses the FIFO inventory costing method, calculate the company's cost of goods sold and its ending inventory as of January 31 assuming the periodic method.

**SE6-9. Inventory Costing Methods and the Periodic Method**

LO2

Lambeth Company experienced the following events in February:

| Date | Event | Units | | Unit Cost | Total Cost |
|------|-------|-------|---|-----------|------------|
| Feb. 1 | Purchased inventory............................ | 100 | @ | $20 | $2,000 |
| Feb. 4 | Sold inventory.................................... | 50 | | | |
| Feb. 9 | Purchased inventory............................ | 100 | @ | $22 | $2,200 |
| Feb. 27 | Sold inventory.................................... | 100 | | | |

If the Lambeth Company uses the LIFO inventory costing method, calculate the company's cost of goods sold and ending inventory as of February 28 assuming the periodic method.

**SE6-10. Inventory Costing Methods and the Perpetual Method**

LO7
(Appendix 6A)

Refer to the information in SE6-9 and assume the perpetual inventory system is used. Use the LIFO inventory costing method to calculate the company's cost of goods sold and ending inventory as of February 28.

**SE6-11. Inventory Costing Methods and the Periodic Method**

LO2

McKay & Company experienced the following events in March:

| Date | Event | Units | | Unit Cost | Total Cost |
|------|-------|-------|---|-----------|------------|
| Mar. 1 | Purchased inventory............................ | 100 | @ | $15 | $1,500 |
| Mar. 3 | Sold inventory.................................... | 60 | | | |
| Mar. 15 | Purchased inventory............................ | 100 | @ | $18 | $1,800 |
| Mar. 20 | Sold inventory.................................... | 40 | | | |

If McKay & Company uses the weighted-average cost method, calculate the company's cost of goods sold and ending inventory as of March 31 assuming the periodic method.

**SE6-12. Inventory Costing Methods and the Perpetual Method**

LO7
(Appendix 6A)

Refer to the information in SE6-11 and assume the perpetual inventory system is used. Use the weighted-average inventory costing method to calculate the company's cost of goods sold and ending inventory as of March 31.

**SE6-13. Identify Goods to Be Included in Inventory**

LO1

Patterson Company has the following items at year-end. Identify which items should be included in Patterson's year-end inventory count.

1. Goods held on consignment by Sell For You Company.
2. Goods held by Patterson on consignment that will be sold for another company.
3. Goods in transit sent to a client F.O.B. shipping point.
4. Goods in transit sent to a client F.O.B. destination.

**SE6-14. Errors in Inventory Count**

LO3

Bow Corp. accidentally overstated its 2010 ending inventory by $750. Assume that ending 2011 inventory is accurately counted. The error in 2010 will have what effect on Bow Corp.?

a. 2010 net income is understated by $750.
b. 2010 net income is overstated by $750.
c. 2011 net income is understated by $750.
d. Both b and c are correct.

# EXERCISES—SET A

**E6-1A. Just-in-Time Inventories**

LO1

Raymond Manufacturing Company uses the perpetual inventory system and plans to use raw materials costing $600,000 in manufacturing its products during 2010. Raymond will operate its

ASSIGNMENTS

factory 300 days during 2010. Currently, Raymond follows the just-in-case philosophy with its raw materials inventory, keeping raw materials costing $15,000 in its raw materials inventory. Raymond plans to switch to the just-in-time manufacturing philosophy by keeping only the raw materials needed for the next two days of production. Calculate the new raw materials inventory level after Raymond implements the just-in-time manufacturing philosophy in its factory.

**LO2** **E6-2A.** **Inventory Costing Methods—Periodic Method**

The Lippert Company uses the periodic inventory system. The following July data are for an item in Lippert's inventory:

July 1 Beginning inventory, 30 units @ $8 per unit.
10 Purchased 50 units @ $9 per unit.
15 Sold 60 units.
26 Purchased 25 units @ $10 per unit.

Calculate the cost of goods sold for July and ending inventory at July 31 using (a) first-in, first-out, (b) last-in, first-out, and (c) the weighted-average cost methods.

**LO7** **E6-3A.** **Inventory Costing Methods—Perpetual Method**
**(Appendix 6A)**

Refer to the information in E6-2A and assume the perpetual inventory system is used. Calculate the cost of goods sold for the July 15 sale using (a) first-in, first-out, (b) last-in, first-out, and (c) the weighted-average cost methods.

**LO2** **E6-4A.** **Inventory Costing Methods—Periodic Method**

Archer Company is a retailer that uses the periodic inventory system. On August 1, it had 80 units of product A at a total cost of $1,600. On August 5, Archer purchased 100 units of A for $2,116. On August 8, it purchased 200 units of A for $4,416. On August 11, it sold 150 units of A for $4,800. Calculate the August cost of goods sold and the ending inventory at August 31 using (a) first-in, first-out, (b) last-in, first-out, and (c) the weighted-average cost methods.

**LO7** **E6-5A.** **Inventory Costing Methods—Perpetual Method**
**(Appendix 6A)**

Refer to the information in E6-4A and assume the perpetual inventory system is used. Calculate the inventory cost of item A on August 11 (after the sale) using (a) first-in, first-out, (b) last-in, first-out, and (c) the weighted-average cost methods.

**LO4** **E6-6A.** **Departures from Acquisition Cost**

Determine the proper total inventory value for each of the following items in Viking Company's ending inventory:

a. Viking has 600 video games in stock. The games cost $36 each, but their year-end replacement cost is $30. Viking has been selling the games for $60, but competitors are now selling them for $50. Viking plans to drop its price to $50. Viking's normal gross profit on video games is 40 percent.
b. Viking has 300 rolls of camera film that are past the expiration date marked on the film's box. The films cost $1.65 each and are normally sold for $3.30. New replacement films still cost $1.65. To clear out these old films, Viking will drop their selling price to $1.40. There are no related selling costs.
c. Viking has five cameras in stock that have been used as demonstration models. The cameras cost $180 and normally sell for $280. Because these cameras are in used condition, Viking has set the selling price at $160 each. Expected selling costs are $10 per camera. New models of the camera (on order) will cost Viking $200 and will be priced to sell at $320.

**LO2** **E6-7A.** **Inventory Costing Methods—Periodic Method**

The following information is for the Bloom Company for 2010; the company sells just one product:

|  |  | Units | Unit Cost |
|---|---|---|---|
| Beginning inventory............................................ | | 200 | $10 |
| Purchases: | Feb. 11........................................... | 500 | 14 |
| | May 18........................................... | 400 | 16 |
| | October 23....................................... | 100 | 20 |

At December 31, 2010, there was an ending inventory of 360 units. Assume the use of the periodic inventory method. Calculate the value of ending inventory and the cost of goods sold for the year using (a) first-in, first-out, (b) last-in, first-out, and (c) the weighted-average cost method.

**E6-8A. Inventory Costing Methods—Periodic Method**                              LO2

The following data are for the Bloom Company, which sells just one product:

|  |  | Units | Unit Cost |
|---|---|---|---|
| Beginning inventory, January 1 ..................................... | | 200 | $10 |
| Purchases: | February 11 ...................................... | 500 | 14 |
| | May 18.......................................... | 400 | 16 |
| | October 23....................................... | 100 | 20 |
| Sales | March 1 ......................................... | 400 | |
| | July 1 ........................................... | 400 | |

Calculate the value of ending inventory and cost of goods sold using the periodic method and (a) first-in, first-out, (b) last-in, first-out, and (c) weighted-average cost method.

**E6-9A. Inventory Costing Methods—Perpetual Method**                          LO7

Refer to the information in E6-8A and assume the perpetual inventory system is used. Calculate   **(Appendix 6A)**
the value of ending inventory and cost of goods sold using the perpetual method and (a) first-in, first-out, (b) last-in, first-out, and (c) weighted-average cost method.

**E6-10A. Lower-of-Cost-or-Market (LCM) Method**                               LO4

The following data are taken from the Browning Corporation's inventory accounts:

| Item Code | Quantity | Unit Cost | Replacement Cost |
|---|---|---|---|
| ACE.................................... | 100 | $25 | $24 |
| BDF.................................... | 300 | 30 | 31 |
| GHJ.................................... | 400 | 20 | 18 |
| MBS.................................... | 200 | 23 | 27 |

Calculate the value of the company's ending inventory using the lower-of-cost-or-market method applied to (a) each item of inventory and (b) the total inventory.

**E6-11A. Inventory Turnover and Days' Sales in Inventory**                    LO5

The Southern Company installed a new inventory management system at the beginning of 2010. Shown below are data from the company's accounting records as reported out by the new system:

|  | 2010 | 2011 |
|---|---|---|
| Sales revenue ........................................... | $8,000,000 | $10,000,000 |
| Cost of goods sold...................................... | 4,000,000 | 4,900,000 |
| Beginning inventory..................................... | 500,000 | 530,000 |
| Ending inventory........................................ | 530,000 | 600,000 |

Calculate the company's (a) inventory turnover and (b) days' sales in inventory for 2010 and 2011. Comment on your results.

**E6-12A. The LIFO Inventory Reserve**                                         LO6

Midwestern Steel Company uses the LIFO inventory costing method to value its ending inventory. The following data were obtained from the company's accounting records:

| | |
|---|---|
| Current assets (under FIFO) ........................................ | $8,000,000 |
| Current liabilities ................................................ | 5,500,000 |
| Inventory under LIFO.............................................. | 2,000,000 |
| Inventory under FIFO.............................................. | 2,700,000 |

Calculate the company's (a) LIFO inventory reserve and (b) the current ratio assuming (i) FIFO and (ii) LIFO.

**E6-13A. Applying IFRS**                                                      LO4

LVMH is a Paris-based manufacturer of luxury goods that prepares its financial statements using IFRS. During the year, the management of the company undertook a review of the fair value of its inventory and found that the inventory had appreciated above its book value of 10 million euros. According to the company's management, the inventory was undervalued by 1 million euros. Prepare the journal entry to revalue the company's inventory. How would the revaluation immediately affect the company's (a) current ratio, (b) inventory turnover, and (c) days' sales in inventory?

**LO3**  **E6-14A.** **Errors in Inventory Counts**

The following information was taken from the records of Taylor Enterprises:

|  | 2011 | 2010 |
|---|---|---|
| Beginning inventory | $ 60,000 | $ 50,000 |
| Cost of goods purchased | 420,000 | 400,000 |
| Cost of goods available for sale | 480,000 | 450,000 |
| Ending inventory | 55,000 | 60,000 |
| Cost of goods sold | $425,000 | $390,000 |

The following two errors were made in the physical inventory counts:

1. 2010 inventory was understated by $10,000.
2. 2011 ending inventory was overstated by $5,000.

Compute the correct cost of goods sold for both 2010 and 2011.

# EXERCISES—SET B

**LO1**  **E6-1B.** **Just-in-Time Inventories**

Carson Manufacturing Company uses the perpetual inventory system and plans to use raw material costing $1,650,000 in making its products during 2010. Carson will operate its factory 275 days during 2010. Currently, Carson follows the just-in-case philosophy with its raw materials inventory, keeping raw materials costing $35,000 in its raw materials inventory. Carson plans to switch to the just-in-time manufacturing philosophy by keeping only the raw materials needed for the next two days of production. Calculate the new raw materials inventory level after Carson implements the just-in-time manufacturing philosophy.

**LO2**  **E6-2B.** **Inventory Costing Methods—Periodic Method**

Merritt Company uses the periodic inventory system. The following May data are for an item in Merritt's inventory:

May  1 Beginning inventory, 150 units @ $30 per unit.
     12 Purchased 100 units @ $35 per unit.
     16 Sold 180 units.
     24 Purchased 160 units @ $36 per unit.

Calculate the cost of goods sold for May and ending inventory at May 31 using (a) first-in, first-out, (b) last-in, first-out, and (c) the weighted-average cost method.

**LO7**  **E6-3B.** **Inventory Costing Methods—Perpetual Method**
**(Appendix 6A)**

Refer to the information in E6-2B and assume the perpetual inventory system is used. Calculate the cost of goods sold for the May 16 sale using (a) first-in, first-out, (b) last-in, first-out, and (c) the weighted-average cost method.

**LO2**  **E6-4B.** **Inventory Costing Methods—Periodic Method**

Spangler Company is a retailer that uses the periodic inventory system. On March 1, it had 100 units of product M at a total cost of $1,590. On March 6, Spangler purchased 200 units of M for $3,600. On March 10, it purchased 150 units of M for $3,000. On March 15, it sold 180 units of M for $5,400. Calculate the March cost of goods sold and the ending inventory at March 31 using (a) first-in, first-out, (b) last-in, first-out, and (c) the weighted-average cost method.

**LO7**  **E6-5B.** **Inventory Costing Methods—Perpetual Method**
**(Appendix 6A)**

Refer to the information in E6-4B and assume the perpetual inventory system is used. Calculate the ending inventory cost of item M on March 15 (after the sale) using (a) first-in, first-out, (b) last-in, first-out, and (c) the weighted-average cost method.

**LO4**  **E6-6B.** **Lower-of-Cost-or-Market (LCM) Method**

The following data refer to the Froning Company's ending inventory:

| Item Code | Quantity | Unit Cost | Unit Market |
|---|---|---|---|
| LXC | 60 | $45 | $48 |
| KWT | 210 | 38 | 34 |
| MOR | 300 | 22 | 20 |
| NES | 100 | 27 | 32 |

Calculate the value of the company's ending inventory by using the lower-of-cost-or-market method applied to (a) each item of inventory and (b) the total inventory.

**E6-7B. Inventory Costing Methods—Periodic Method**     LO2

The Toon Company, which uses the periodic inventory system, has the following records for 2010:

| | | Units | Unit Cost |
|---|---|---|---|
| Beginning inventory. | | 100 | $49 |
| Purchases: | Jan. 6 | 650 | 42 |
| | July 15 | 550 | 38 |
| | Dec. 28 | 200 | 36 |

Ending inventory at December 31, 2010, was 350 units. Compute the ending inventory and the cost of goods sold for the year using (a) first-in, first out, (b) weighted-average cost, and (c) last-in, first-out.

**E6-8B. Inventory Costing Methods—Periodic Method**     LO2

The following data are for the Miller Corporation, which sells just one product:

| | | Units | Unit Cost |
|---|---|---|---|
| Beginning inventory, January 1 | | 200 | $12 |
| Purchases | February 11 | 500 | 13 |
| | May 18 | 400 | 15 |
| | October 23 | 100 | 18 |
| Sales | March 1 | 400 | |
| | July 1 | 400 | |

Calculate the value of ending inventory and cost of goods sold using the periodic method and (a) first-in, first-out, (b) last-in, first-out, and (c) weighted-average cost method.

**E6-9B. Inventory Costing Methods—Perpetual Method**     LO7
**(Appendix 6A)**

Refer to the information in E6-8B and assume the perpetual inventory system is used. Calculate the value of ending inventory and cost of goods sold using the perpetual method and (a) first-in, first-out, (b) last-in, first-out, and (c) weighted-average cost method.

**E6-10B. Lower-of-Cost-or-Market (LCM) Method**     LO4

The following data are taken from the Smith & Wesson Corporation's inventory accounts:

| Item Code | Quantity | Unit Cost | Replacement Cost |
|---|---|---|---|
| ZKE | 100 | $22 | $20 |
| XYF | 300 | 33 | 34 |
| MNJ | 400 | 22 | 20 |
| UBS | 200 | 33 | 37 |

Calculate the value of the company's ending inventory using the lower-of-cost-or-market method applied to (a) each item of inventory and (b) the total inventory.

**E6-11B. Inventory Turnover and Days' Sales in Inventory**     LO5

The Northern Company installed a new inventory management system at the beginning of 2010. Shown below are data from the company's accounting records as reported by the new system:

| | 2010 | 2011 |
|---|---|---|
| Sales revenue | $9,000,000 | $11,000,000 |
| Cost of goods sold | 5,000,000 | 5,900,000 |
| Beginning inventory | 600,000 | 630,000 |
| Ending inventory | 630,000 | 700,000 |

Calculate the company's (a) inventory turnover and (b) days' sales in inventory for 2010 and 2011. Comment on your results.

**E6-12B. The LIFO Inventory Reserve**     LO6

Midwestern Steel Company uses the LIFO inventory costing method to value its ending inventory. The following data were obtained from the company's accounting records for 2010:

| | |
|---|---|
| Current assets (under LIFO) | $9,000,000 |
| Current liabilities | 7,500,000 |
| Inventory under LIFO | 4,000,000 |
| Inventory under FIFO | 4,700,000 |

Calculate the company's (a) LIFO inventory reserve and (b) current ratio assuming (i) FIFO and (ii) LIFO.

**LO4** **E6-13B. Applying IFRS**

The French Petroleum Company is a Paris-based oil and gas company that prepares its financial statements using IFRS. During the year, the management of the company undertook a review of the fair value of its oil and gas inventory and found that the inventory had appreciated above its book value of 50 million euros. According to the company's management, the oil and gas inventory was undervalued by 5 million euros. Prepare the journal entry to revalue the company's inventory. How would the revaluation immediately affect the company's (a) current ratio, (b) inventory turnover, and (c) days' sales in inventory?

**LO3** **E6-14B. Errors in Inventory Counts**

The following information was taken from the records of Spencer Enterprises:

| | 2011 | 2010 |
|---|---|---|
| Beginning inventory | $ 55,000 | $ 75,000 |
| Cost of goods purchased | 540,000 | 500,000 |
| Cost of goods available for sale | 595,000 | 575,000 |
| Ending inventory | 85,000 | 55,000 |
| Cost of goods sold | $510,000 | $520,000 |

The following two errors were made in the physical inventory counts:

1. 2010 inventory was overstated by $25,000.
2. 2011 ending inventory was understated by $20,000.

Compute the correct cost of goods sold for both 2010 and 2011.

# PROBLEMS—SET A

**LO1** **P6-1A. Just-in-Time Inventory**

The Dixon Manufacturing Company uses the perpetual inventory system with its raw material inventory. During 2010, Dixon plans to include raw material costing $1,960,000 in the products that it manufactures. John Dixon, president of the company, wants to adopt the just-in-time manufacturing philosophy for the raw materials inventory during 2010. He wants to have only the raw material needed for the next day's production at the end of each day. The factory operates 280 days each year. Historically, the raw materials inventory balance at the end of the day has averaged $50,000 cost. Dixon has an annual inventory carrying cost equal to 20 percent of total inventory cost.

**Required**

a. What is the anticipated inventory carrying cost (in dollars) if Dixon does not adopt the just-in-time manufacturing philosophy?
b. Calculate the average level (in dollars) for the raw materials inventory if Dixon adopts the just-in-time manufacturing philosophy.
c. Calculate the reductions in the raw materials inventory level and the raw materials inventory annual carrying cost if Dixon adopts the just-in-time manufacturing philosophy.
d. What other factors or situations should Dixon consider before deciding to have only one day's supply of raw material? (*Hint:* Consider factors and situations related to environment, supplier problems, labor problems, etc.)

**LO2** **P6-2A. Inventory Costing Methods—Periodic Method**

Fortune Stores uses the periodic inventory system for its merchandise inventory. The April 1 inventory for one of the items in the merchandise inventory consisted of 120 units with a unit cost of $325. Transactions for this item during April were as follows:

April 9 Purchased 40 units @ $345 per unit.
14 Sold 80 units @ $550 per unit.
23 Purchased 20 units @ $350 per unit.
29 Sold 40 units @ $550 per unit.

**Required**

a. Calculate the cost of goods sold and the ending inventory cost for the month of April using the weighted-average cost method.

*b.* Calculate the cost of goods sold and the ending inventory cost for the month of April using the first-in, first-out method.

*c.* Calculate the cost of goods sold and the ending inventory cost for the month of April using the last-in, first-out method.

**P6-3A. Inventory Costing Methods—Perpetual Method**
Refer to the information in P6-2A and assume the perpetual inventory system is used.

LO7
(Appendix 6A)

**Required**

*a.* Calculate the cost of goods sold and the ending inventory cost for the month of April using the weighted-average cost method.

*b.* Calculate the cost of goods sold and the ending inventory cost for the month of April using the first-in, first-out method.

*c.* Calculate the cost of goods sold and the ending inventory cost for the month of April using the last-in, first-out method.

**P6-4A. Inventory Costing Methods—Periodic Method**
Chen Sales Corporation uses the periodic inventory system. On January 1, 2010, Chen had 1,000 units of product A with a unit cost of $20 per unit. A summary of purchases and sales during 2010 follows:

LO2, LO3

| | Unit Cost | Units Purchased | Units Sold |
|---|---|---|---|
| Feb. 2 | | | 400 |
| Apr. 6 | $22 | 1,800 | |
| July 10 | | | 1,600 |
| Aug. 9 | 26 | 800 | |
| Oct. 23 | | | 800 |
| Dec. 30 | 29 | 1,200 | |

**Required**

*a.* Assume that Chen uses the first-in, first-out method. Compute the cost of goods sold for 2010 and the ending inventory balance at December 31, 2010, for product A.

*b.* Assume that Chen uses the last-in, first-out method. Compute the cost of goods sold for 2010 and the ending inventory balance at December 31, 2010, for product A.

*c.* Assume that Chen uses the weighted-average cost method. Compute the cost of goods sold for 2010 and the ending inventory balance at December 31, 2010, for product A.

*d.* Assuming that Chen's products are perishable items, which of the three inventory costing methods would you choose to:
1. Reflect the likely goods flow through the business?
2. Minimize income taxes for the period?
3. Report the largest amount of net income for the period?
Explain your answers.

**P6-5A. Inventory Costing Methods—Perpetual Method**
Refer to the information in P6-4A and assume the perpetual inventory system is used.

LO7
(Appendix 6A)

**Required**

*a.* Assume that Chen uses the first-in, first-out method. Compute the cost of goods sold for 2010 and the ending inventory balance at December 31, 2010, for product A.

*b.* Assume that Chen uses the last-in, first-out method. Compute the cost of goods sold for 2010 and the ending inventory balance at December 31, 2010, for product A.

*c.* Assume that Chen uses the weighted-average cost method. Compute the cost of goods sold for 2010 and the ending inventory balance at December 31, 2010, for product A.

**P6-6A. Goods in Transit**
The Cardinal Wholesale Company sells merchandise to a variety of retailers. Cardinal uses different freight terms with its various customers and suppliers. All sales are made on account.

LO1

**Required**

For each of the following transactions, indicate which company has ownership of the goods in transit:

*a.* Cardinal sold merchandise to X-Mart Stores, with shipping terms of F.O.B. shipping point.

b. Cardinal purchased merchandise from Zendo Manufacturing Company, with shipping terms of F.O.B. destination.

c. Cardinal sold merchandise to Mary's Boutique, with shipping terms of F.O.B. destination.

d. Sunshine Manufacturing Company sold merchandise to Cardinal, with shipping terms of F.O.B. shipping point.

e. Cardinal purchased merchandise from Warfield Manufacturing Company, with freight terms of F.O.B. shipping point.

f. Stevenson Stores purchased merchandise from Cardinal, with shipping terms of F.O.B. shipping point.

**LO4**　**P6-7A.**　**Lower-of-Cost-or-Market (LCM) Method**

The Venner Company had the following inventory at year-end:

| | | Unit Price | |
| --- | --- | --- | --- |
| | Quantity | Cost | Market |
| Fans | | | |
| Model X1 | 300 | $18 | $19 |
| Model X2 | 250 | 22 | 24 |
| Model X3 | 400 | 29 | 26 |
| Heaters | | | |
| Model B7 | 500 | 24 | 28 |
| Model B8 | 290 | 35 | 32 |
| Model B9 | 100 | 41 | 38 |

**Required**

a. Determine the value of ending inventory after applying the lower-of-cost-or-market method to:
  1. Each item of inventory.
  2. Each major category of inventory.
  3. The total inventory.

b. Which of the LCM procedures from requirement (a) results in the lowest net income for the year? Explain.

**LO2**　**P6-8A.**　**Inventory Costing Methods—Periodic Method**

The following data are for the Portet Corporation, which sells just one product:

| | | Units | Unit Cost |
| --- | --- | --- | --- |
| Beginning inventory, January 1 | | 1,200 | $ 8 |
| Purchases | February 11 | 1,500 | 9 |
| | May 18 | 1,400 | 10 |
| | October 23 | 1,100 | 12 |
| Sales | March 1 | 1,400 | |
| | July 1 | 1,400 | |
| | October 29 | 1,000 | |

Calculate the value of ending inventory and cost of goods sold at year-end using the periodic method and (a) first-in, first-out, (b) last-in, first-out, and (c) weighted-average cost method. If the replacement cost of the inventory at year-end is $13, how will the cost of goods sold under each method be affected?

**LO7**　**P6-9A.**　**Inventory Costing Methods—Perpetual Method**
**(Appendix 6A)**　Using the data in P6-8A, assume that Portet Corporation uses the perpetual inventory system. Calculate the value of ending inventory and cost of goods sold at year-end using the perpetual method and (a) first-in, first-out, (b) last-in, first-out, and (c) weighted-average cost method. If the replacement cost of the inventory at year-end is $13, how will the cost of goods sold under each method be affected?

**LO4**　**P6-10A.**　**Lower-of-Cost-or-Market (LCM) Method**
The following data are taken from the Simpson Corporation's inventory accounts:

| Item Code | Quantity | Unit Cost | Replacement Cost |
|---|---|---|---|
| Product 1 | | | |
| ZKE............................. | 100 | $22 | $20 |
| ZKF............................. | 300 | 33 | 34 |
| Product 2 | | | |
| MNJ ............................. | 400 | 22 | 19 |
| MNS............................. | 200 | 33 | 37 |

Calculate the value of the company's ending inventory using the lower-of-cost-or-market method applied to (a) each item of inventory, (b) the total inventory, and (c) the two categories of inventory.

### P6-11A. Inventory Turnover and Days' Sales in Inventory

LO5

The Eastern Corporation installed a new inventory management system at the beginning of 2010. Shown below are data from the company's accounting records as reported by the new system:

| | 2010 | 2011 |
|---|---|---|
| Sales revenue ............................................. | $18,000,000 | $20,000,000 |
| Cost of goods sold....................................... | 8,000,000 | 8,900,000 |
| Beginning inventory...................................... | 2,500,000 | 2,530,000 |
| Ending inventory.......................................... | 2,530,000 | 2,600,000 |

Calculate the company's (a) inventory turnover and (b) days' sales in inventory for 2010 and 2011. Comment on your results.

### P6-12A. The LIFO Inventory Reserve

LO6

Waterloo Manufacturing Company uses the LIFO inventory costing method to value its ending inventory. The following data were obtained from the company's accounting records for 2010:

| | |
|---|---|
| Current assets (under FIFO) ......................................................... | $18,000,000 |
| Current liabilities ...................................................................... | 15,500,000 |
| Inventory under LIFO.................................................................. | 7,000,000 |
| Inventory under FIFO.................................................................. | 7,700,000 |

Calculate the company's (a) LIFO inventory reserve and (b) current ratio assuming (i) FIFO and (ii) LIFO. If the company's LIFO gross profit was $10,000,000 and the change in the LIFO inventory reserve from 2009 to 2010 was $1,200,000, calculate the company's gross profit under FIFO.

## PROBLEMS—SET B

### P6-1B. Just-in-Time Inventory

LO1

The Field Manufacturing Company uses the perpetual inventory system for its raw materials inventory. During 2010, Field plans to include raw material costing $2,400,000 in the products that it manufactures. Henry Field, president of the company, wants to adopt the just-in-time manufacturing philosophy for the raw materials inventory during 2010. He wants to have only the raw material needed for the next day's production at the end of each day. The factory operates 300 days each year. Historically, the raw materials inventory balance at the end of the day has averaged $60,000 cost. Field has an annual inventory carrying cost equal to 22 percent of total inventory cost.

**Required**

a. What is the anticipated annual inventory carrying cost (in dollars) if Field does not adopt the just-in-time manufacturing philosophy?

b. Calculate the average level (in dollars) for the raw materials inventory if Field adopts the just-in-time manufacturing philosophy.

c. Calculate the reduction in the raw materials inventory level and the raw materials inventory annual carrying cost if Field adopts the just-in-time manufacturing philosophy.

d. What other factors or situations should Field consider before deciding to have only one day's supply of material? (*Hint:* Consider factors and situations related to environment, supplier problems, labor problems, etc.)

LO2 **P6-2B.** **Inventory Costing Methods—Periodic Method**

The Shiloh Company uses the periodic inventory system for its merchandise inventory. The June 1 inventory for one of the items in the merchandise inventory consisted of 60 units with a unit cost of $40. Transactions for this item during June were as follows:

June 5 Purchased 40 units @ $50 per unit.
　 13 Sold 50 units @ $90 per unit.
　 25 Purchased 30 units @ $52 per unit.
　 29 Sold 20 units @ $100 per unit.

**Required**
a. Compute the cost of goods sold and the ending inventory cost for the month of June using the weighted-average cost method.
b. Compute the cost of goods sold and the ending inventory cost for the month of June using the first-in, first-out method.
c. Compute the cost of goods sold and the ending inventory cost for the month of June using the last-in, first-out method.

LO7
(Appendix 6A)
**P6-3B.** **Inventory Costing Methods—Perpetual Method**

Refer to the information in P6-2B and assume the perpetual inventory system is used.

**Required**
a. Compute the cost of goods sold and the ending inventory cost for the month of June using the weighted-average cost method.
b. Compute the cost of goods sold and the ending inventory cost for the month of June using the first-in, first-out method.
c. Compute the cost of goods sold and the ending inventory cost for the month of June using the last-in, first-out method.

LO2, LO3 **P6-4B.** **Inventory Costing Methods—Periodic Method**

The Gleem Sales Corporation uses the periodic inventory system. On January 1, 2010, Gleem had 2,600 units of product B with a unit cost of $40 per unit. A summary of purchases and sales during 2010 follows:

| | Unit Cost | Units Purchased | Units Sold |
|---|---|---|---|
| Jan. 3 ................................................... | | | 1,600 |
| Mar. 8 ................................................... | $44 | 3,000 | |
| June 13 ................................................. | | | 2,000 |
| Sept. 19 ................................................ | 50 | 800 | |
| Nov. 23 ................................................. | 55 | 1,200 | |
| Dec. 28 ................................................. | | | 1,800 |

**Required**
a. Assume that Gleem uses the first-in, first-out method. Compute the cost of goods sold for 2010 and the ending inventory balance at December 31, 2010, for product B.
b. Assume that Gleem uses the last-in, first-out method. Compute the cost of goods sold for 2010 and the ending inventory balance at December 31, 2010, for product B.
c. Assume that Gleem uses the weighted-average cost method. Compute the cost of goods sold for 2010 and the ending inventory balance at December 31, 2010, for product B.
d. Assuming that Gleem sells items that quickly become obsolete, which of these three inventory costing methods would you choose to:
　1. Reflect the likely goods flow through the business?
　2. Minimize income tax for the period?
　3. To report the largest amount of net income for the period?
　Explain your answers.

LO7
(Appendix 6A)
**P6-5B.** **Inventory Costing Methods—Perpetual Method**

Refer to the information in P6-4B and assume the perpetual inventory system is used.

**Required**
a. Assume that Gleem uses the first-in, first-out method. Compute the cost of goods sold for 2010 and the ending inventory balance at December 31, 2010, for product B.

    *b.* Assume that Gleem uses the last-in, first-out method. Compute the cost of goods sold for 2010 and the ending inventory balance at December 31, 2010, for product B.

    *c.* Assume that Gleem uses the weighted-average cost method. Compute the cost of goods sold for 2010 and the ending inventory balance at December 31, 2010, for product B.

**P6-6B.** **Goods in Transit**  LO1

Marshall Distributors sells merchandise to a variety of retailers. Marshall uses different freight terms with its various customers and suppliers. All sales are made on account.

### Required

For each of the following transactions, indicate which company has ownership of the goods in transit:

    *a.* Marshall sold merchandise to Clay Boutique, with shipping terms of F.O.B. destination.

    *b.* Marshall purchased merchandise from Campbell Manufacturing Company, with freight terms of F.O.B. shipping point.

    *c.* Marshall sold merchandise to Save-A-Lot Stores, with shipping terms of F.O.B. shipping point.

    *d.* Marshall purchased merchandise from Central Manufacturing Company, with shipping terms of F.O.B. destination.

    *e.* Levinson Stores purchased merchandise from Marshall, with shipping terms of F.O.B. shipping point.

    *f.* Connor Manufacturing Company sold merchandise to Marshall, with shipping terms of F.O.B. shipping point.

**P6-7B.** **Lower-of-Cost-or-Market (LCM) Method**  LO4

The Crane Company had the following inventory at year-end:

| | | Unit Price | |
| --- | --- | --- | --- |
| | Quantity | Cost | Market |
| Desks | | | |
|    Model 9001 | 70 | $190 | $210 |
|    Model 9002 | 45 | 280 | 268 |
|    Model 9003 | 20 | 350 | 360 |
| Cabinets | | | |
|    Model 7001 | 120 | 60 | 64 |
|    Model 7002 | 80 | 95 | 88 |
|    Model 7003 | 50 | 130 | 126 |

### Required

    *a.* Determine the value of the ending inventory after applying the lower-of-cost-or-market method to:

       1. Each item of inventory.

       2. Each major category of inventory.

       3. The total inventory.

    *b.* Which of the LCM procedures from requirement (a) results in the lowest net income for the year? Explain.

**P6-8B.** **Inventory Costing Methods—Periodic Method**  LO2

The following data are for the Graham Corporation, which sells just one product:

| | | Units | Unit Cost |
| --- | --- | --- | --- |
| Beginning inventory, January 1 | | 1,200 | $18 |
| Purchases | February 11 | 1,500 | 19 |
| | May 18 | 1,400 | 20 |
| | October 23 | 1,100 | 22 |
| Sales | March 1 | 1,400 | |
| | July 1 | 1,400 | |
| | October 29 | 1,000 | |

Calculate the value of ending inventory and cost of goods sold for the year using the periodic method and (a) first-in, first-out, (b) last-in, first-out, and (c) weighted-average cost method. If the replacement cost of the inventory at year-end is $23, how will the cost of goods sold under each method be affected?

**LO7**
**(Appendix 6A)**

**P6-9B.   Inventory Costing Methods—Perpetual Method**

Using the data in P6-8B, assume that Graham Corporation uses the perpetual inventory system. Calculate the value of ending inventory and cost of goods sold for the year using the perpetual method and (a) first-in, first-out, (b) last-in, first-out, and (c) weighted-average cost method. If the replacement cost of the inventory at year-end is $23, how will the cost of goods sold under each method be affected?

**LO4**

**P6-10B.   Lower-of-Cost-or-Market (LCM) Method**

The following data are taken from the Smithfield Corporation's inventory accounts:

| Item Code | Quantity | Unit Cost | Replacement Cost |
|---|---|---|---|
| Product 1 | | | |
| XKE................................ | 100 | $32 | $30 |
| XKF................................ | 300 | 43 | 44 |
| Product 2 | | | |
| ZNJ................................ | 400 | 32 | 29 |
| ZNS................................ | 200 | 43 | 47 |

Calculate the value of the company's ending inventory using the lower-of-cost-or-market method applied to (a) each item of inventory, (b) the total inventory, and (c) the two categories of inventory.

**LO5**

**P6-11B.   Inventory Turnover and Days' Sales in Inventory**

The Western States Corporation installed a new inventory management system at the beginning of 2010. Shown below are data from the company's accounting records as reported by the new system:

| | 2010 | 2011 |
|---|---|---|
| Sales revenue ............................................. | $48,000,000 | $40,000,000 |
| Cost of goods sold......................................... | 28,000,000 | 28,900,000 |
| Beginning inventory....................................... | 16,500,000 | 16,530,000 |
| Ending inventory.......................................... | 16,530,000 | 20,600,000 |

Calculate the company's (a) inventory turnover and (b) days' sales in inventory for 2010 and 2011. Comment on your results.

**LO6**

**P6-12B.   The LIFO Inventory Reserve**

The Peoria Manufacturing Company uses the LIFO inventory costing method to value its ending inventory. The following data were obtained from the company's accounting records for 2010:

| | |
|---|---|
| Current assets (under LIFO) ......................................................... | $48,000,000 |
| Current liabilities ................................................................... | 35,500,000 |
| Inventory under LIFO................................................................ | 15,000,000 |
| Inventory under FIFO................................................................. | 18,700,000 |

Calculate the company's (a) LIFO inventory reserve and (b) current ratio assuming (i) FIFO and (ii) LIFO. If the company's LIFO gross profit was $18,000,000 and the change in the LIFO inventory reserve from 2009 to 2010 was $2,200,000, calculate the company's gross profit under FIFO.

# SERIAL PROBLEM: KATE'S CARDS

*(Note:* **This is a continuation of the Serial Problem: Kate's Cards from Chapters 1 through 5.)**

**SP6.**

As expected, the holiday season was very busy for Kate and her greeting card company. In fact, most of her supplies were fully depleted by year-end, necessitating a restocking of inventory. The following transactions occurred for Kate's Cards during January of the New Year:

| Purchases | Units | | Unit Cost | Total Cost |
|---|---|---|---|---|
| Jan. 10 ............................................... | 400 | @ | $3.00 per unit | $1,200 |
| Jan. 17 ............................................... | 500 | @ | $3.50 per unit | 1,750 |
| Jan. 23 ............................................... | 300 | @ | $4.00 per unit | 1,200 |
| Total ................................................ | 1,200 | | | $4,150 |

| Sales | |
|---|---|
| Jan. 15 ............................................... | 360 |
| Jan. 21 ............................................... | 420 |
| Jan. 27 ............................................... | 380 |
| Total ................................................. | 1,160 |

**Required**

a. Calculate the company's cost of goods sold and value of ending inventory for the month of January using (1) FIFO, (2) LIFO, and (3) the weighted-average cost method.

b. If the replacement cost of Kate's inventory is $4.00 per unit on January 31, what value should be reported for her ending inventory on the January 31 balance sheet under each of the three inventory costing methods?

## EXTENDING YOUR KNOWLEDGE

### REPORTING AND ANALYSIS

**EYK6-1. Financial Reporting Problem: The Columbia Sportswear Company**

The financial statements for the **Columbia Sportswear Company** can be found in Appendix A at the end of this textbook.

COLUMBIA SPORTSWEAR COMPANY

**Required**

Answer the following questions using Columbia's Consolidated Financial Statements:

a. How much inventory does Columbia carry on its balance sheet? What percentage of Columbia's total assets does inventory represent in 2009 and 2008?

b. Compute the inventory turnover and days' sales in inventory for 2009 and 2008. Inventory at December 31, 2007, was $265,874.

c. Is Columbia's inventory management improving?

**EYK6-2. Comparative Analysis Problem: Columbia Sportswear Company vs The Timberland Company**

The financial statements for **Columbia Sportswear Company** can be found in Appendix A at the end of this textbook, and the financial statements of **The Timberland Company** can be found in Appendix B.

COLUMBIA SPORTSWEAR COMPANY THE TIMBERLAND COMPANY

**Required**

a. Compare the dollar value of inventory carried on the balance sheet by each company in 2009 and 2008. Which company carries the greatest dollar amount of inventory? Compare the ratio of inventory divided by total assets for each company for 2009 and 2008. Which company carries the largest relative investment in inventory?

b. Calculate the inventory turnover and days' sales in inventory for 2009 and 2008 for each company. Inventory at December 31, 2007, for Columbia and Timberland was $265,874 and $201,932, respectively.

c. Which company appears to be doing the better job of managing its investment in inventory?

**EYK6-3. Business Decision Problem**

Mackenzie Company is a wholesaler that uses the perpetual inventory system. On January 1, 2010, Mackenzie had 3,000 units of its product at a cost of $5 per unit. Transactions related to inventory during 2010 were as follows:

| Purchases | | | | Sales | | | |
|---|---|---|---|---|---|---|---|
| Feb. 5 ............. | 9,000 units | @ | $6 | March 8 ........... | 8,000 units | @ | $ 9 |
| May 19 ........... | 20,000 units | @ | 7 | June 21 ........... | 19,000 units | @ | 10 |
| Dec. 15 ........... | 3,000 units | @ | 9 | Dec. 28 ........... | 4,000 units | @ | 12 |

Mackenzie is trying to decide whether to use the first-in, first-out (FIFO) inventory costing method or the last-in, first-out (LIFO) inventory costing method.

**Required**

a. Assume that Mackenzie decides to use the FIFO inventory costing method.
   1. What would gross profit be for 2010?

2.  How would Mackenzie's gross profit and ending inventory for 2010 change if the December 15, 2010, purchase had been made on January 3, 2011, instead?

3.  How would Mackenzie's gross profit and ending inventory for 2010 change if the December 15, 2010, purchase had been for 6,000 units instead of 3,000 units?

b.  Assume that Mackenzie decides to use the LIFO inventory costing method.

1.  What would gross profit be for 2010?

2.  How would Mackenzie's gross profit and ending inventory for 2010 change if the December 15, 2010, purchase had been made on January 3, 2011, instead?

3.  How would Mackenzie's gross profit and ending inventory for 2010 change if the December 15, 2010, purchase had been for 6,000 units instead of 3,000 units?

c.  Which inventory costing method should Mackenzie choose and why?

**EYK6-4.   Financial Analysis Problem**

Purpose: To use annual financial report filings to learn about how a company accounts for its inventory.

Select any publicly traded company not discussed in this chapter and go to its Website. Find the section on investor information and download its latest annual report (you may download its 10K report rather than the annual report).

### Required

Using this report, answer the following questions.

a.  What is the name of the company you chose and what is the primary industry that it operates in?

b.  Does the company list inventory on its balance sheet? If so, where on the balance sheet does it appear?

c.  Does the company have a separate note in the notes to the financial statements that provides a more detailed breakdown of the amount of inventory listed? If so, what is that breakdown?

d.  What inventory method does the company use?

e.  Calculate the inventory turnover ratio and days' sales in inventory for the most current year shown.

## CRITICAL THINKING

GENERAL MILLS, INC.

**EYK6-5.   Accounting Research Problem**

The fiscal year 2010 annual report of **General Mills, Inc.** is available on this book's Website.

### Required

a.  What percentage of total assets are represented by General Mills' investment in inventory in 2010 and 2009?

b.  Compute the inventory turnover and days' sales in inventory for General Mills for 2010 and 2009.

c.  Is the company doing a better job of managing its investment in inventory in 2010?

d.  What inventory costing method does General Mills use?

e.  What is the value of the company's LIFO reserve at year-end 2010?

PACTIV CORPORATION

**EYK6-6.   Accounting Communications Activity**

**Pactiv Corporation** is a leader in the consumer and foodservice packaging market. In December 2009 the company announced a change in the accounting for inventories. www.businesswire.com/news/home/20091221005622/en/Pactiv-Announces-Inventory-Accounting-Change-LIFO-FIFO

### Required

Sarah Jenkins, CEO of a competing firm, read this announcement, but was confused about what exactly Pactiv was doing. She asked that you write a memo explaining the following items.

a.  What about its accounting for inventory was Pactiv changing?

b.  Why does Pactiv believe the new method is preferable?

c.  What benefit does Pactiv believe will be realized from the change?

**EYK6-7. Accounting Ethics Case**

Reed Kohler is in his final year of employment as controller for Quality Sales Corporation; he hopes to retire next year. As a member of top management, Kohler participates in an attractive company bonus plan. The overall size of the bonus is a function of the firm's net income before bonus and income taxes—the larger the net income, the larger the bonus.

Due to a slowdown in the economy, Quality Sales Corporation has encountered difficulties in managing its cash flow. To improve its cash flow by reducing cash payments for income taxes, the firm's auditors have recommended that the company change its inventory costing method from FIFO to LIFO. This change would cause a significant increase in the cost of goods sold for the year. Kohler believes the firm should not switch to LIFO this year because its inventory quantities are too large. He believes that the firm should work to reduce its inventory quantities and then switch to LIFO (the switch could be made in a year or two). After expressing this opinion to the firm's treasurer, Kohler is stunned when the treasurer replies: "Reed, I can't believe that after all these years with the firm, you put your personal interests ahead of the firm's interests."

Explain why Kohler may be viewed as holding a position that favors his personal interests. What can Kohler do to increase his credibility when the possible change to LIFO is discussed at a meeting of the firm's top management next week?

**EYK6-8. Corporate Social Responsibility Problem**

The Corporate Social Responsibility highlight in this chapter discussed how **Best Buy** is working to make sure its supply chain complies with the company's high ethical standards. One of the ways this is done is through a factory audit program of the factories that supply Best Buy with its many products.

BEST BUY

Go to the Best Buy Website and navigate to the section on corporate responsibility at http://www.bestbuyinc.com/corporate_responsibility/. From there you can download a copy of the company corporate responsibility report. Use this report to explain how the factory audit program works.

**EYK6-9. Forensic Accounting Problem**

The chapter highlights an inventory fraud case at **Crazy Eddie**. Unfortunately there have been many other serious inventory frauds where the auditors were fooled by illegal acts. A few of these cases include (1) **Comptronix Corporation**, (2) **Leslie Fay Company**, (3) **Laribee Manufacturing Company**, and (4) **Phar-Mor** drug stores.

CRAZY EDDIE
COMPTRONIX CORPORATION
LESLIE FAY COMPANY
LARIBEE MANUFACTURING COMPANY
PHAR-MOR

Do a computer search of one of these cases and explain how inventory was used to commit the fraud. List some ways the auditors can lessen the chance such frauds could go undetected.

**EYK6-10. Inventory Turnover and Days' Sales in Inventory: IFRS Financial Statements**

LO5

Tesco PLC is the world's third largest retailer and is based in the United Kingdom. Tesco's IFRS financial statements are presented in Appendix C at the end of this textbook. Using these financial statements, calculate the company's (a) inventory turnover and (b) days' sales in inventory for 2008 and 2009. Tesco's 2007 ending inventory was 1,931 million British pounds. Comment on the company's trend in inventory management effectiveness.

IFRS

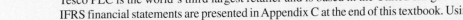

## ANSWERS TO SELF-STUDY QUESTIONS:

## Your Turn! Solutions

**Solution 6.1**

The $15,000 of goods shipped F.O.B. shipping point should be deducted from the inventory valuation, and the $25,000 of consignment goods should be included in the inventory valuation. The corrected ending inventory total should be $310,000 ($300,000 − $15,000 + $25,000).

**Solution 6.2**

*a.* Ending inventory using:

    *i.* FIFO: 1,000 × $7 = $7,000

    *ii.* LIFO: 1,000 × $5 = $5,000

    *iii.* Weighted-average cost: 1,000 × [(4,000 × $5) + (6,000 × $7)]/10,000 = 1,000 × $6.20 = $6,200

*b.* Cost of goods sold using:

    *i.* FIFO: (4,000 × $5) + (5,000 × $7) = $55,000

    *ii.* LIFO: (6,000 × $7) + (3,000 × $5) = $57,000

    *iii.* Weighted-average cost: 9,000 × [(4,000 × $5) + (6,000 × $7)]/10,000 = 9,000 × $6.20 = $55,800

*c.* Gross profit using:

    *i.* FIFO: $90,000 − $55,000 = $35,000

    *ii.* LIFO: $90,000 − $57,000 = $33,000

    *iii.* Weighted-average cost: $90,000 − $55,800 = $34,200

**Solution 6.3**

The lowest value for each inventory item is: DSLR $110,000, Point and Shoot $73,000, and Camcorders $48,000. The total of the inventory is therefore valued under LCM at $231,000 ($110,000 + $73,000 + $48,000).

**Solution 6.4**

| | 2010 | 2011 |
|---|---|---|
| Inventory turnover ............. | $\dfrac{\$2,000,000}{(\$450,000 + \$430,000)/2} = 4.55$ | $\dfrac{\$2,300,000}{(\$430,000 + 320,000)/2} = 6.13$ |
| Days' sales in inventory ........ | 365/4.55 = 80.22 days | 365/6.13 = 59.54 days |

The company increased its sales by $400,000 from 2010 to 2011, and at the same time, decreased its average inventory by $65,000 ($440,000 − $375,000) as a consequence of improved inventory management. This resulted in a significantly improved inventory turnover (6.13 versus 4.55) and 20.68 (80.22 – 59.54) less days' sales in inventory. It appears that the new inventory management system is a financial success.

# INTERNAL CONTROL

**Define** the three elements of fraud and **discuss** the role of internal control in a business to prevent fraud.

The feature story involving **Enron Corporation** illustrates the potential cost that fraud can have on so many people. Unfortunately, it is nearly impossible to completely prevent fraud; however, we do know much about why fraud is committed and what can be done to lower the risk of it occurring. Research has shown that any individual, under the right circumstances, can commit fraud. This does not mean, however, that everyone will commit fraud. What it does mean is that it is very difficult to determine prior to the commission of a fraud exactly which employee will be the one to commit fraud.

**Fraud** refers to any act by the management or employees of a business involving an intentional deception for personal gain. Fraud may include, among other acts, embezzlement of a business's cash, theft of assets, filing false insurance claims, filing false health claims, and financial statement fraud. Fraud is a punishable crime and is also a violation of civil law. Research has shown that three elements are almost always present when a fraud occurs. These elements are often referred to as the **fraud triangle** and include (1) a perceived pressure, (2) some way to rationalize the fraudulent act, and (3) a perceived opportunity. Reducing or suppressing any of the three elements of the fraud triangle reduces the likelihood of fraud occurring in a business.

Unfortunately, the fraud triangle is not well understood. Because of this, nearly all fraud prevention efforts by businesses are devoted to the third element—reducing the opportunity to commit fraud. As we will discuss in this chapter, this often involves implementing a system of internal control, including such measures as physical control over cash and proper authorization over cash disbursements. Too often, little effort is expended on the other elements of fraud even though it has been shown that efforts in any one area can reduce the effort needed in the other two areas.

## PRESSURE

Research has shown that nearly all frauds are committed by individuals under either financial or vice pressure, with financial pressure being more common. Financial statement fraud, such as the overstatement of revenues or the understatement of expenses, usually occurs because of the pressure on management to "make the numbers," either to satisfy Wall Street analyst expectations or to attain a company-sponsored monetary bonus.

While it is not possible to completely eliminate this element of fraud, numerous methods have proven successful at lowering the risk of financial statement fraud. An obvious action is to perform careful personnel screening before hiring any employee to reduce the likelihood of employing individuals with known histories of fraud.

## RATIONALIZATION

Very few individuals want to commit fraud since they recognize that it is wrong. In order to overcome this tremendous feeling of guilt, most employees need to come up with some form of rationalization so that they can live with the knowledge of what they did. Common rationalizations include such attitudes as (1) I am underpaid and the company owes it to me; (2) Everyone else is doing it; or (3) I am only borrowing the money and I will pay it back later.

The best way to reduce this element of fraud is to create an environment in which it is difficult to rationalize unethical behavior. A company that promotes a culture of honesty and integrity, within which unethical behavior is considered unacceptable, is much less likely to encounter fraudulent behavior by management or its employees. The key to building organization-wide attitudes regarding ethical behavior starts with the "tone at the top"—that is, the behaviors and attitudes displayed by a company's CEO or president.

## OPPORTUNITY

The third element of the fraud triangle is perceived opportunity. An individual will only attempt to commit a fraud if he or she perceives that there is an opportunity to succeed. Of course this element is related to the other two elements. For example, if an employee is under tremendous pressure either at work or outside the workplace, he may attempt to commit a fraud even if he perceives only a small chance of success, while an individual under much less pressure will likely only attempt the fraud if it is perceived to be easy to commit.

| CORPORATE SOCIAL RESPONSIBILITY | More Than Just Following the Law! |
|---|---|

Much of what was done at **Enron** was perfectly legal. Enron's management became very skilled at staying within the letter of the law, even if it meant violating the spirit of the law. Examples include the use of specialized accounting rules that allowed Enron to mask the true level of its debt so that financial statement users would be unable to obtain a transparent view of the company's financial position. Top executives at Enron created a culture of deceit within the company that provided employees with an easy rationalization for their own misdeeds. Corporate Social Responsibility, by way of contrast, espouses the notion that not only is it important to make money, but it is important to do so in a responsible way. Cutting corners and playing fast and loose with the rules may work in the short term, but it is not sustainable as the Enron saga reveals. Creating a culture of ethical behavior within a business is perhaps the most important internal control that exists to not only prevent fraud, but to provide a foundation for a sustainable enterprise.

The accounting system represents a cornerstone of the control environment that is necessary to reduce the opportunity for, and success of, fraudulent behavior. A critical aspect of the accounting system is a strong system of internal control. **Internal controls** are the measures undertaken by a business to ensure the reliability of its accounting data, protect its assets from theft or unauthorized use, ensure that employees are following the company's policies and procedures, and evaluate the performance of employees, departments, divisions, and the company as a whole. A company implements internal controls to improve the chances that employees will function according to the plans and standard operating procedures developed by the management team. Internal controls are meant to reduce the likelihood that errors will occur, and if they do occur, that any errors will be caught.

Management is responsible for designing, installing, and monitoring internal controls throughout a business. In designing the controls, management tries to attain "reasonable assurance," rather than "absolute assurance," that the controls will meet their objectives.

Internal control exists in many forms, including policies, standard operating procedures, records, equipment, supervision, and insurance. An internal control can be either a prevention control or a detection control. A **prevention control** is intended to deter a problem or fraud before it can arise. A **detection control**, on the other hand, is designed to discover any problems or fraud shortly after it arises. Prevention controls are generally more desirable and preferred than detection controls, reflecting the old saying that "an ounce of prevention is worth a pound of detection."

A company should incorporate the following elements when it designs its prevention and detection controls:

1. Establish clear lines of authority and responsibility.
2. Implement segregation of duties.
3. Hire competent personnel.
4. Use control numbers on all business documents.
5. Develop plans and budgets.
6. Maintain adequate accounting records.
7. Provide physical and electronic controls.
8. Conduct internal audits.

We consider each of these elements in the following paragraphs and provide examples of their use.

### Establish Clear Lines of Authority and Responsibility

The organizational structure of a company defines the lines of authority and responsibility within the company. When a company assigns authority to an employee to perform certain functions, it also makes that employee responsible for accomplishing certain objectives. This structure provides the overall framework for planning, directing, and controlling the company's operations. It informs employees about who is in charge of which functions and to whom each person reports.

Supervision is an important internal control. The existence of an identified supervisor is a preventive control. Employees know that the supervisor is evaluating their performance; consequently, they are more likely to perform according to a company's established policies and rules. Supervision is also a detection control. A supervisor is likely to discover errors or irregularities when he or she reviews the work performance of employees.

Management must also make sure that all employees understand a company's philosophy and operating style as well as the authority and responsibility relationships. To guide employees in performing their duties, top management should develop written policy statements, procedure manuals, and job descriptions.

---

**ACCOUNTING IN PRACTICE** | **Proper Authorization as an Internal Control**

It is important that proper authorization be maintained, and this means that only those employees with proper authorization should be given access to items that they have the authority to possess. In one documented case, over $900,000 was stolen from a business because of a breach of this internal control. In this particular case, the defrauded company went to considerable lengths to maintain proper authorization to access its automated payment system. This involved, among other things, authorized users obtaining a special code that could be used only once from the internal control register clerk. Unfortunately, the control was circumvented when a charismatic employee gained the trust of fellow employees, including the internal control register clerk. The employee explained to the clerk that one of the authorized users had asked him to pick up access codes for him. The employee then went on to use the codes to access the system, submitting false documents for building maintenance services and eventually stealing over $900,000 from the company.

Source: Davia, *Fraud 101* (2000), pp. 45-46.

## IMPLEMENT SEGREGATION OF DUTIES

**Segregation of duties** requires that when allocating various duties within the accounting system, management should make sure that no employee is assigned too much responsibility. As a general rule, no individual employee should be able to perpetrate and conceal irregularities in the transaction processing system. To accomplish this, management must separate three functions: the authorization function, the recording function, and the custody function. Ideally, for any particular transaction, an individual employee should have the authority to perform only one of the three functions.

For example, if an employee "authorizes" a sales transaction by approving a customer's credit, that employee should not "record" the transaction in the accounting records or have physical "custody" of the merchandise sold or the cash received from the customer. This separation of duties is an important preventive control. When an employee prepares a purchase order to buy merchandise, that employee is effectively "authorizing" the transaction. When the merchandise is received, a second employee should prepare the receiving report when he or she gains "custody" of the merchandise. And, neither of these two employees should be allowed to "record" either the purchase order, the receipt of the merchandise, or the payment of cash for the goods in the accounting records. The separation of work functions in this manner will reduce the likelihood of fraud occurring because committing a fraud when work duties are separated requires collusion among multiple employees.

---

**ACCOUNTING IN PRACTICE** Segregation of Duties Functions as an Internal Control

In a case of a company giving a salesman too much responsibility, an advertising salesman not only sold the ads, but also had the authority to bill the customer and collect on the accounts receivable. In addition, the salesman was authorized to offer discounts to customers. This authority proved too much of a temptation, and resulted in free travel, lodging, and other gifts in return for greatly reduced, and sometimes even free, ads. In total, it was determined that the salesman gave away over $20,000 in advertising revenues in return for the bribes that he was given.

Source: Well, *Principles of Fraud Examination* (2005), p. 264.

---

## HIRE COMPETENT PERSONNEL

Because people are the most important element of an accounting system, it is vital that a company hire competent personnel. Management must screen each job applicant to determine that he or she has sufficient education, training, and experience to qualify for the job. After hiring an employee, the company should provide specific formal training so that the employee is able to complete all of the tasks that the job requires. The training should refer to written policy statements, procedure manuals, and job descriptions so that the employee can become familiar with all aspects and expectations of his or her job.

Some companies routinely rotate personnel among various jobs. For example, a company might switch jobs between an employee working exclusively with the accounts receivable and an employee working exclusively with accounts payable. This rotation may disclose errors or irregularities resulting from over-familiarity with a job or just carelessness. Requiring employees to take vacations of at least one week in duration may also disclose errors or irregularities when another employee performs the vacationing employee's duties.

---

**ACCOUNTING IN PRACTICE** Job Rotation and Mandatory Vacations as Internal Controls

Job rotation and mandatory vacations is one of the best internal controls for uncovering fraud. For many frauds, it is necessary for the perpetrator to actively cover up their misdeeds through the falsification of accounting records. Requiring job rotation and vacations allows another employee to perform these job responsibilities, often leading to the discovery of fraud. And you thought your employer was only giving you that vacation to be nice!

Source: Association of Certified Fraud Examiners 2008 Report.

## USE CONTROL NUMBERS ON ALL BUSINESS DOCUMENTS

All business documents such as purchase orders, sales invoices, credit memos, and checks should have **control numbers** preprinted on them. Each control number should be unique for that type of document. For example, the bank checks that you use to pay your personal expenses have control numbers on them, usually in the upper right-hand corner of the check, referred to as a *check number*. These numbers are an internal control enabling you to track each check written, and to insure that no one has written an improper check against your account.

To provide proper control to the accounting process, a company should use the following three rules related to control numbers on business documents. First, have a commercial printer place the control numbers on the documents when they are printed. Second, use the documents in strict numerical sequence. That is, use check number 101 first, then check 102, then 103, and so on. Third, for each type of business document, periodically account for all the numbers in the sequence to make sure that all were processed. Use of control numbers with this type of reconciliation helps to ensure that a company records all transactions and does not record a transaction multiple times.

## DEVELOP PLANS AND BUDGETS

Top management should initiate the planning and budgeting process to establish forward thinking about the business and to provide a basis for evaluating department and employee performance. Every company should prepare an annual operating plan and budget. These items provide guidance for all levels of management regarding how to respond to various situations. The **budget** also provides a basis for comparing actual operating results to planned results when management evaluates operating unit performance. An example of evaluating performance involves comparing the actual advertising expense to the budgeted advertising expense. When variances between actual and budgeted amounts are observed, those variances should be investigated by management. This type of internal control is both a prevention control and a detection control.

## MAINTAIN ADEQUATE ACCOUNTING RECORDS

Previously we discussed a number of internal controls that help ensure that a business has adequate accounting records. These controls include using the double-entry approach to record transactions (debits must equal credits), preparing trial balances (total debits must equal total credits), and taking a physical count of the inventory on hand (physical inventory total should equal perpetual inventory total).

Many internal controls related to maintaining accurate accounting records involve comparisons of various amounts. For instance, each business should periodically make a physical inspection of its plant assets to compare the data in the plant assets' ledger account to the plant assets actually in use. This inspection identifies any missing assets and any assets not recorded in the asset account. Similarly, a business should periodically confirm the amounts owed to suppliers (Accounts Payable) and the amounts due from customers (Accounts Receivable) by contacting the suppliers and customers to verify any amounts owing and to be received. This internal control process is known as accounts receivable confirmation and accounts payable confirmation.

## PROVIDE PHYSICAL AND ELECTRONIC CONTROLS

Physical and electronic controls take many forms. Locked doors are an important physical control. Locked doors help prevent the theft of assets and protect the integrity of the accounting system. Many companies install safes and vaults to store cash prior to depositing it in a bank and to hold important business documents such as mortgages and securities. Any installed safes and vaults should be of sufficient quality that they can withstand fire and such natural disasters as flooding and tornados. Fencing off company property and assigning security guards at the gates are other commonly used physical controls.

---

**ACCOUNTING IN PRACTICE** | **Physical Control of Assets as an Internal Control**

Failure to adequately maintain physical control of assets is especially risky when it comes to items like cash. In one documented case, checks were left overnight on the desks of employees because processing was not complete. This proved too tempting of a target for a member of the overnight janitorial cleaning crew. The janitor found the checks, forged the endorsements of the payees, and then cashed the checks at a local liquor store.

Source: Well, *Principles of Fraud Examination* (2005), p. 139.

---

Electronic controls are also widely used by businesses. Merchandising firms use electronic cash registers to ensure that each salesperson records each transaction as it occurs and that the salesperson stores cash in a locked drawer. Retailers, convenience stores, and banks use observation cameras to monitor their operations. Retailers also attach special plastic tags to merchandise, which activate electronic sensors and set off alarms if an individual attempts to leave a store without having the plastic tag removed by a salesperson.

## CONDUCT INTERNAL AUDITS

In a small company, internal auditing is a function typically assigned to an employee who has other duties as well. In a large company, internal auditing is an activity assigned to an independent department that reports to top management or the board of directors of the corporation. **Internal auditing** is a company function that provides independent appraisals of the company's financial statements, its internal control, and its operations.

---

**ACCOUNTING IN PRACTICE** | **Internal Audit as an Internal Control**

Sometimes it takes a little luck to uncover a fraud; however, having a strong internal audit department helps that luck to happen. That was exactly the case at **Deerfield College's School of Dentistry**, when a married supervisor in the business office took his girlfriend on a business trip using school funds. In order to cover up the identity of his actual traveling partner, the supervisor unwisely named a senior internal control auditor as the person he was traveling with. As luck would have it, the named auditor was the individual who reviewed the bogus travel report as part of a routine audit of employee expense reports. Because of the unexpected discovery, a larger audit was performed on the business office. During the audit, a much larger unrelated fraud was discovered involving an administrative assistant who had been issuing checks to a bogus vendor and taking the money for herself. The administrative assistant had a drug addiction and was under tremendous pressure to pay for her habit.

Source: McNeal, One fraud leads to another, *Internal Auditor Magazine,* December 2008.

---

The evaluation of a company's internal control involves two phases. First, the internal auditor determines whether sufficient internal controls are in place. Second, the internal auditor determines whether the internal controls in place are actually functioning as planned. After completing the appraisal, the internal auditor makes recommendations to management regarding additional controls that are needed or improvements that are required for existing controls.

### Control Failures

Occasionally, internal controls fail. For example, an employee may forget to lock an exterior door and a thief will steal some merchandise. Or, an employee with custody responsibilities steals cash received from customers. A company cannot completely prevent these types of incidents from occurring. Consequently, many businesses purchase insurance to compensate the company if any of these types of incidents do occur. Casualty insurance provides financial compensation to a business for losses from fire, natural disasters, and theft. A **fidelity bond** is an insurance policy that provides financial compensation for theft by employees specifically covered by the insurance.

Another reason that internal controls fail is **employee collusion**. When two or more employees work together to circumvent or avoid prescribed internal controls, this act is known as *employee collusion*. For example, an employee with custody of an asset (like cash) can work with an employee with recording responsibilities to steal the asset and cover up the theft in the accounting records. Employee collusion is difficult to prevent or detect. Hiring high-quality employees and paying them market wages is the best approach to avoid collusion. Close employee supervision is also important.

### THINKING GLOBALLY

While it might appear that financial fraud occurs only in the United States, that is far from the truth. In 2003, the Italian agricultural conglomerate **Parmalat SpA** filed for bankruptcy after revealing that it had massively underreported its outstanding net debt—that is, its debt minus its liquid current assets—by approximately $16 billion. The financial fraud had been perpetuated for over a decade and had gone undetected by the company's independent auditor, **Grant Thorton**. The underreporting of Parmalat net debt had been achieved by overreporting the amount of cash on hand and by retaining worthless accounts receivable on the company's balance sheet. In a similar situation, in 2008, India's leading software services firm, **Satyam Computer Services**, was found to have defrauded stockholders for over a decade by overstating the company's revenues and its cash by over $1 billion. The company's independent auditors, **PricewaterhouseCoopers**, were arrested shortly thereafter on charges of being an accomplice to the financial fraud.

### THE SARBANES-OXLEY ACT

For public companies, strong internal control like that described above is no longer simply a matter of good business practice, it is required by law. Following the **Enron** and **WorldCom** accounting scandals, the U.S. Congress passed landmark legislation called the Sarbanes-Oxley Act (SOX). This Act mandates that all publicly traded U.S. corporations maintain an adequate system of internal control. Further, top management must ensure the reliability of these controls and outside independent auditors must attest to the adequacy of the controls. Failing to do so can result in prison sentences of up to 20 years and/or monetary fines of up to $5 million.

### Your Turn! 7.1

Identify which internal control concept is being violated and explain how this may cause an opportunity for fraud to occur within a business:

1. The supervisor for the purchasing department has not taken a vacation in three years.
2. Inventory is left in a receiving area at the back of the store by an open door.
3. The purchasing supervisor has the authority to order a purchase and also to receive the merchandise, record its receipt, and authorize the accounting department to issue a check.
4. Order slips are used to order meals at a restaurant; however, the slips are not prenumbered.

**The solution is on page 361.**

| | Concept | Method | Assessment |
|---|---|---|---|
| TAKEAWAY 7.1 | Are the internal controls adequate? | Independent auditors' attestation report.<br><br>The principles of good internal control include: (1) Establish clear lines of authority and responsibility; (2) Segregation of duties; (3) Hire competent personnel; (4) Use control numbers on all business documents; (5) Develop plans and budgets; (6) Maintain adequate accounting records; (7) Provide physical and electronic controls; (8) Conduct internal audits. | Be sure that the report does not indicate any weaknesses in the company's internal control. If weaknesses are reported, be cautious in relying on the reported financial statements. |

# ACCOUNTING FOR CASH

**Cash** includes coins, currency (paper money), checks, money orders, traveler's checks, and funds on deposit at a financial institution in a company's checking accounts and savings accounts. An item is considered to be an element of cash if (1) it is accepted by a bank or other financial institution (brokerage firm or credit union) for deposit, and (2) it is free from restrictions that would prevent its use for paying debts.

LEARNING OBJECTIVE 2

**Define** cash and **discuss** the accounting for cash.

Many near-cash items such as certificates of deposit, postdated checks, not-sufficient-funds checks, and IOUs are not considered to be cash. **Certificates of deposit** (CDs) are securities issued by a bank when cash is invested for a short period of time, typically three months to one year. CDs pay a fixed rate of interest on any deposited funds. A **postdated check** is a check from another person or company with a date that is later than the current date. A postdated check does not become equivalent to cash until the actual calendar date on the check. A **not-sufficient-funds check** (NSF check) is a check from an individual or company that had an insufficient cash balance in the bank when the holder of the check presented it to the bank for payment. IOU is a slang term for a note receivable—that is, a written document that states that one party promises to pay another party a certain amount of cash on a certain date. CDs are accounted for as investments, whereas postdated checks, NSF checks, and IOUs are accounted for as Other Receivables.

## REPORTING CASH

A company may have only one Cash account in the general ledger or it may have multiple cash accounts, such as Cash in Bank, Cash on Hand, and Petty Cash. Cash in Bank includes any cash held in a company's checking accounts and savings accounts, while Cash on Hand includes cash items not yet deposited in the bank. Petty Cash is an example of cash on hand that is used for small disbursements and is maintained at the company's business location.

When a company has several bank accounts, it may maintain a separate general ledger account for each account or use a single Cash in Bank account. Although a company may prepare for internal use only a balance sheet that shows each individual bank account separately, the balance sheet that the company prepares for external users typically shows the combined balances of all bank accounts and other cash accounts under a single heading of Cash. Management is likely to want to see the detail involving the multiple

---

**ACCOUNTING IN PRACTICE** | **Balance Sheet Title for Cash**

Cash is cash, or is it? Companies often include many other items, such as certificates of deposit, that are very similar to cash in their Cash account. Companies also vary in the title they use for their Cash account on their balance sheet. In fact, Cash is not the most common term used. Cash and Cash Equivalents is by far the most commonly used label. The following table identifies the label used by a sample of 600 large U.S. firms for their Cash account on the balance sheet:

Source: Accounting Trends and Techniques

cash accounts that the company maintains so that it can monitor and control the various accounts and on hand amounts. Most external users, however, are only interested in the total amount of cash and its relationship to other items on the balance sheet.

Cash is a current asset and is shown first in the balance sheet listing of assets. Some of a company's cash may be **restricted cash**, in which case it is restricted for a special purpose. For example, a company may have a restriction on its cash to cover a litigation settlement. Restricted cash should be reported separately on the balance sheet as either a current or noncurrent asset depending on the length of the restriction. Sometimes a company's total cash includes one or more compensating balances. A **compensating balance** is a minimum cash balance that a bank requires a firm to maintain in its bank account as part of a borrowing arrangement. Compensating balances related to short-term borrowings are current assets, which, if significant, are reported separately from the cash amount among the current assets. Compensating balances related to long-term borrowings are reported as long-term assets.

## CASH AND CASH EQUIVALENTS

A company may combine certain short-term, highly liquid investments with cash and present a single amount called **cash and cash equivalents** on the balance sheet. Cash equivalents are highly liquid, short-term investments of 90 days maturity or less in such risk-free securities as U.S. Treasury bills and money market funds. A company presents this combined amount on the balance sheet so that it reconciles with the change in cash and cash equivalents appearing on the company's statement of cash flows. The statement of cash flows explains the changes in a firm's total cash and cash equivalents during an accounting period.

| | Concept ➡ | Method ➡ | Assessment |
|---|---|---|---|
| **TAKEAWAY 7.2** | Are there any restrictions on a company's use of its cash and cash equivalents? | Balance sheet and the notes to the financial statements. Are there any restrictions to cash or compensating cash balances reported? | Any assessments of liquidity should consider any existing cash restrictions. |

# INTERNAL CONTROL OF CASH RECEIPTS TRANSACTIONS

LEARNING OBJECTIVE 3

**Describe** the internal controls for cash.

Most companies develop elaborate internal controls to protect their cash because it is their most liquid asset, and in all likelihood, their most important asset. Cash is highly desirable, easily taken and concealed, and quickly converted into other assets. In addition, a high percentage of a company's transactions involve cash. Cash is received from customers following a sale and cash is paid to suppliers and employees for goods and services. A company receives cash from customers, for example, as payment on account and as payment for cash sales. The following sections describe cash handling procedures and the related internal controls for these two types of cash receipts.

## CASH RECEIVED ON ACCOUNT

A company receives cash through the mail from customers who are making payments on their accounts receivable balance. Four departments play major roles in processing cash receipts that arrive via the mail: the mailroom, the treasurer's department, the controller's department, and the internal audit department. Exhibit 7-1 and the following paragraphs describe the role that each department plays in processing mailed cash receipts.

### Mailroom

A company often sets up a separate post office box and requests that its customers mail any cash payments on account to that post office box. All other mail and company correspondence are directed to another company address or a different post office box. This approach automatically sorts a company's mail into two groups: (1) cash receipts from customers and (2) all other mail.

Mailroom employees open the envelopes containing cash receipts from customers. Each envelope should contain two items: a check and a remittance advice. A **remittance advice** is a form that accompanies a check to inform the company receiving the check about the purpose of the check. The remittance advice includes the customer's name, the amount paid, and such reference numbers as the invoice number and the customer account number.

Mailroom employees ensure that the dollar amount on each check and the related remittance advice are the same and then place the two documents in separate piles. An employee then endorses each check "For Deposit Only" so that no one can cash the check. The mailroom employees also prepare a remittance list. A **remittance list** is a list of all of the checks received on a given day. For each check, the remittance list includes the customer name and/or account number, the check number, and the amount received.

| EXHIBIT 7-1 | Processing Cash Received on Account Through the Mail |
| --- | --- |

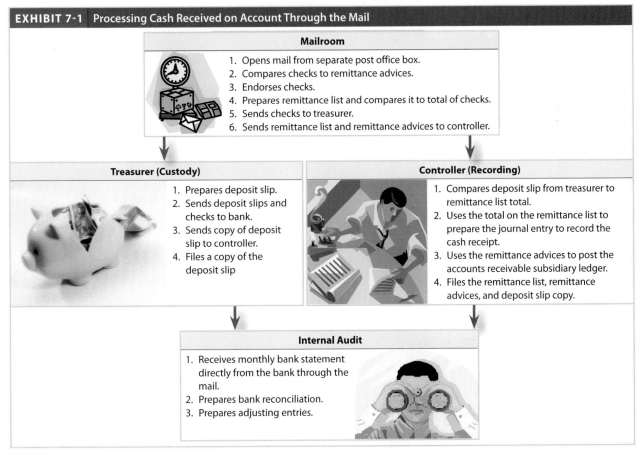

**Mailroom**
1. Opens mail from separate post office box.
2. Compares checks to remittance advices.
3. Endorses checks.
4. Prepares remittance list and compares it to total of checks.
5. Sends checks to treasurer.
6. Sends remittance list and remittance advices to controller.

**Treasurer (Custody)**
1. Prepares deposit slip.
2. Sends deposit slips and checks to bank.
3. Sends copy of deposit slip to controller.
4. Files a copy of the deposit slip

**Controller (Recording)**
1. Compares deposit slip from treasurer to remittance list total.
2. Uses the total on the remittance list to prepare the journal entry to record the cash receipt.
3. Uses the remittance advices to post the accounts receivable subsidiary ledger.
4. Files the remittance list, remittance advices, and deposit slip copy.

**Internal Audit**
1. Receives monthly bank statement directly from the bank through the mail.
2. Prepares bank reconciliation.
3. Prepares adjusting entries.

A separate mailroom employee compares the remittance list total to a list totaling the checks and another list totaling the remittance advices to ensure that the check amounts are listed correctly and that they agree with the remittance advices. The mailroom then sends the checks to the treasurer's department and the remittance list and the remittance advices to the controller's department.

### Treasurer

The treasurer's department is a *custodial* department. It maintains custody of the received customer checks. *It has no responsibilities for any recording or posting activities.* The duties of this department include preparing a bank deposit slip (original plus two copies) for each batch of checks received and sending the original deposit slip and the customer checks to the bank. One copy of the deposit slip is forwarded to the controller's department; and, the treasurer's department files the second copy for future reference.

### Controller

The controller's department is a *recording* department. It records the cash receipts in a journal and posts the cash receipts to the company's general ledger and the Accounts Receivable account. *The controller's department never has access to, or custody of, the received customer checks.*

Before recording and posting the cash receipts, the controller's department compares the total on the deposit slip copy from the treasurer's department to the remittance list obtained from the mailroom to ensure that the treasurer's department deposited all of the checks sent from the mailroom. The controller's department then prepares a journal entry (debit Cash and credit Accounts Receivable) to record the cash receipts. The dollar amount of the debit and credit is the total from the deposit slip.

The controller's department uses the individual remittance advices to post the cash payments to the Accounts Receivable account of each individual customer. After processing, the remittance list, the remittance advices, and the deposit slip copy are filed in the controller's department for future reference.

### Internal Audit

Internal audit is an independent department; it has no recurring custody, recording, or authorization duties related to accounting transactions. Once each month, the internal audit department performs its independent review and reconciliation duties related to the cash received. The internal auditor receives the monthly bank statement directly from the bank through the mail. This ensures that no one can alter the information returned with the bank statement. The internal audit department uses the bank statement to prepare the monthly bank reconciliation and create any needed journal entries. The preparation of the bank reconciliation and related journal entries are discussed later in this chapter.

## CASH RECEIVED FROM RETAIL CASH SALES

A retailer receives cash from customers when the retailer sells merchandise. The retailer must design internal controls to protect any cash received. Five groups play major roles in collecting, protecting, processing, and recording cash received from retail customers: the retail sales area, the retail sales supervisor, the treasurer's department, the controller's department, and the internal audit department. Exhibit 7-2 and the following paragraphs describe the role that each group plays.

### Retail Sales Area

Sales associates use cash registers to record cash sales and to control and protect the cash collected from customers. Some retailers such as **Safeway Food Stores** place all of the company's cash registers near the store exit. Other retailers such as **Macy's Department Stores** place the cash registers throughout the store in the various departments such as men's clothing, cosmetics, and women's shoes.

Each sales associate uses a unique **password** or key to identify him or herself to the cash register. Each associate should have a separate cash drawer for collecting cash from customers and making change. Each sales associate begins each business day with a fixed amount of change in his or her cash drawer. The sales associates enter details of each sale into the cash register and place any cash received from customers into the assigned cash drawer. The cash register prints a paper tape listing the description and price of the items sold and the total amount due. The cash register also records this information either in the memory of the cash register or in a computer memory that the cash register accesses.

### Retail Sales Supervisor

The retail sales supervisor oversees the retail sales operations of a business. Throughout the day, the supervisor approves any unusual transactions such as merchandise returns. At the end of the day, the supervisor counts the contents of each cash drawer. He or she compares the amount of cash in each drawer in excess of the beginning amount of change to the sales total accumulated by the cash register for each sales associate. The supervisor then prepares a written report (three copies) to document the total sales and the total cash received.

**EXHIBIT 7-2** | Processing Cash Received from Retail Cash Sales

**Retail Sales Area**

1. Begin each day with a fixed amount of change in drawer of each cash register.
2. Sales associate enters details of each sale into a cash register and places cash received from the customer into the cash register drawer assigned to that sales associate.

**Retail Sales Supervisor**

1. Observes the sales operation during the day.
2. Approves any unusual transactions during the day.
3. At the end of the day, counts the contents of each drawer with the sales associate responsible for the drawer.
4. Compares the amount in the drawer in excess of the beginning amount to the sales total accumulated by the cash register for that sales associate.
5. Prepares written report of sales and cash received.
6. Sends cash and a copy of the written report to the treasurer.
7. Sends cash register tape and a copy of the report to the controller.

**Treasurer (Custody)**

1. Prepares deposit slip.
2. Sends deposit slip and cash to bank.
3. Sends copy of deposit slip to controller.
4. Files a copy of the deposit slip.

**Controller (Recording)**

1. Compares deposit slip from treasurer to written report and cash register tape.
2. Uses the written report to prepare the journal entry to record cash sales.
3. Files written report and deposit slip.

**Internal Auditor**

1. Receives monthly bank statement directly from the bank through the mail.
2. Prepares bank reconciliation.
3. Prepares adjusting entries.

The supervisor delivers the cash in excess of the initial change amount and a copy of the written report to the treasurer's department. The cash register tape and another copy of the written report are taken to the controller's department. The supervisor files the third copy of the written report for future use if needed.

### Treasurer

The treasurer's department takes custody of any cash from the retail sales supervisor after signing a receipt that the supervisor retains as proof of the cash delivery. Employees of the treasurer's department count the cash and prepare a deposit slip (original plus two copies). The employees then send the original deposit slip and cash to the bank for deposit. One copy of the deposit slip is sent to the controller's department; and, the treasurer's department files the final copy for future reference.

### Controller

The controller's department is responsible for recording cash sales. The controller's department never has access to or custody of the cash or any checks. Before recording and posting the cash receipts, the controller's department compares the total on the deposit slip copy from the treasurer's department to the written report from the retail sales supervisor to ensure that the treasurer's department deposited all of the cash received. The controller's department then prepares a journal entry to record the cash sales. This entry also reflects any shortage or overage of cash, should this occur.

### Internal Audit

The duties of the internal audit department with respect to cash received from retail sales are identical to its duties with respect to cash received on account. Note again that the bank sends the monthly bank statement directly to a company's internal auditor. If a company does not have an internal auditor, the bank sends the monthly bank statement to an appropriate person designated by the company, usually someone who does not have custody or recording responsibilities for cash. The internal audit department prepares a bank reconciliation statement and makes any needed journal entries.

## CHECKS

When a company opens a checking account at a bank, the bank requires each company employee who will sign checks to sign a signature card. Occasionally, a bank employee compares the signatures on the checks presented for payment by various parties to the authorized signatures on the signature cards. This comparison provides an internal control for the bank that it is not cashing a check written by an unauthorized employee. The bank is responsible for any amounts erroneously paid out of a company's checking account.

A **check** is a written order signed by a checking account owner (also known as the *maker*) directing the bank (called the *payer*) to pay a specified amount of money to the person or company named on the check (called the *payee*). A check is a negotiable instrument; it can be transferred to another person or company by writing "pay to the order of" and the name of the other person or company on the back of the check and then signing the back of the check.

---

**ACCOUNTING IN PRACTICE** | **Magnetic Characters on Checks**

The routing number on a check tells the various banks handling the check how to route it through the U.S. Federal Reserve System to properly transfer the cash between bank accounts. The routing number has two formats: the fraction format (item 3 in Exhibit 7-3) and the MICR format (item 4 in Exhibit 7-3). Both formats are printed on each check. In the fraction format in Exhibit 7-3, the number 79 represents the state in which the bank is located, the number 123 represents the number of the bank where the checking account is located, and the number 759 represents the Federal Reserve District and bank through which the check must clear. In the MICR format, the number 0759 identifies the Federal Reserve District and bank, the number 0123 identifies the specific bank, and the number 8 is the check digit.

---

Exhibit 7-3 presents a sample check. As noted previously, proper internal control requires that business documents such as checks be prenumbered in numerical sequence. The printed check number appears in two locations in Exhibit 7-3: in standard type in the upper right corner ❶ and in MICR (magnetic ink character recognition) form on the bottom of the check ❷. Also printed twice on the check are alternative formats of the routing number for the check, a fraction format ❸ and an MICR format ❹. (See Accounting in Practice.) The check printer also places the customer's account number on the check in MICR form ❺. When the check is processed by the banking system, the MICR check amount ❻ is added at the bottom right of the check. Banks use special equipment that reads MICR codes directly into computer files.

## USING ELECTRONIC FUNDS TRANSFER

Many companies use electronic funds transfer to pay suppliers rather than writing and mailing checks. **Electronic funds transfer**, commonly known as EFT, involves sending

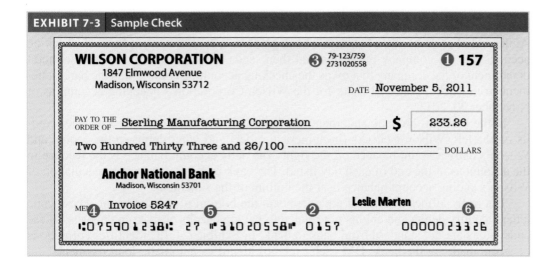

**EXHIBIT 7-3** | Sample Check

an electronic message from one computer to another to cause a transfer of money from one financial institution to another, or directly to a company. Actually, two electronic messages are sent. To illustrate, assume that a company wants to use EFT to transfer money to a second company to pay an invoice. The paying company has its computer send a message to its bank's computer to request the funds transfer. This is known as *retail EFT*. Then, the paying company's bank uses EFT to transfer funds to the receiving company's bank. This is known as *wholesale EFT* or *bank-to-bank EFT*. Wholesale EFT usually involves a central bank (such as a Federal Reserve Bank) that acts as an automated clearinghouse by increasing the balance of one bank and decreasing the balance of the other bank.

## THE PETTY CASH FUND

Most businesses find it inconvenient and expensive to write checks for small expenditures. Instead, these businesses establish a petty cash fund. A **petty cash fund** is a small amount of cash, for example $300, that is placed in a secure location on a business's premises to be used to pay for small expenditures such as postage, delivery service charges, and minor purchases of supplies. The size of the petty cash fund depends on how often it is used and the amount of the disbursements. Firms often select an amount that will last for three or four weeks.

Although the use of a petty cash fund violates the rule that all cash payments should be made by check, control can be maintained by handling the fund on an imprest basis with documented procedures. An imprest fund contains a fixed amount of cash. A business establishes a petty cash fund by writing a check against the firm's checking account and cashing the check at the bank. All replenishments of the petty cash fund are also made by check. As a result, all expenditures are ultimately controlled by check, providing a paper trail of all cash transfers to the petty cash fund.

### Your Turn!                                                          7.2

Match the internal control function from the left-hand column with the area of responsibility in the right-hand column:

|   |   |
|---|---|
| **1.** Prepares deposit receipt. | *a.* Retail sales supervisor |
| **2.** Approves unusual transactions. | *b.* Mailroom |
| **3.** Prepares remittance list. | *c.* Treasurer's department |
| **4.** Prepares bank reconciliation. | *d.* Controller's department |
| **5.** Compares deposit receipt to remittance list. | *e.* Internal audit department |

The solution is on page 361.

## THE BANK STATEMENT

At the end of each month, a business's bank prepares a bank statement for each checking account that the company maintains and then sends the statement to the internal audit department of the company that owns the checking account. Exhibit 7-4 is the bank statement from Anchor National Bank for the Wilson Corporation's checking account as of November 30, 2011.

In the body of the bank statement, the bank lists Wilson's deposits and other credits on the left, Wilson's checks (in numerical order) and other debits in the center, and Wilson's daily account balance on the right. The daily account balance is the balance in the account as of the end of each day listed. The bank presents a summary calculation of Wilson's ending account balance near the bottom of the statement.

The bank defines a series of code letters at the bottom of the statement. These code letters identify debits and credits not related to paying checks or making deposits. These code letters are not standard from bank to bank. In Exhibit 7-4, EC identifies corrections of errors made by the bank; DM (debit memo) identifies automatic loan payments and bank charges for items such as collecting notes; CM (credit memo) identifies amounts collected by the bank for the depositor; SC (service charge) identifies fees charged by the bank for the checking account; OD (overdraft) indicates a negative balance in the account; RT (returned item) identifies items such as posted checks and NSF checks for which the bank could not collect cash; and IN (interest earned) identifies interest added to the account. The bank statement for the Wilson Corporation does not show any interest because federal regulations do not allow corporate checking accounts to earn interest.

## THE BANK RECONCILIATION

The internal audit department prepares a bank reconciliation as of the end of each month. A **bank reconciliation** is a schedule that (1) accounts for all differences between the ending cash balance on the bank statement and the ending cash balance in the Cash account in the company's general ledger and (2) determines the reconciled cash balance as of the end of the month. The internal audit department employee preparing the bank reconciliation needs access to the bank statement, the general ledger, cash receipts records, and cash disbursements records to prepare the reconciliation.

---

**ACCOUNTING IN PRACTICE** **Debits or Credits?**

Debit and credit terminology may seem backward on a bank statement. Debits decrease a bank account balance and credits increase a bank account balance. When a company deposits cash in its checking account, the bank debits Cash and credits a liability account called a Customer Deposit. The bank statement sent to a company each month is a statement of its Customer Deposit account held by the bank. As with any liability, debits decrease its balance and credits increase its balance.

---

### Bank Reconciliation Structure

Exhibit 7-5 outlines the structure of a company's bank reconciliation. The bank reconciliation is really two schedules prepared side by side. The schedule on the left includes bank items, and the schedule on the right includes items related to the company's general ledger.

The schedule on the left begins with the ending cash balance from the bank statement (the month-end balance according to the bank's records). The internal audit department employee preparing the reconciliation adds (1) deposits not yet recorded by the bank, called **deposits in transit**, and (2) any corrections not yet made by the bank that will increase the bank balance. The preparer then subtracts (1) checks not yet recorded by the bank, called **outstanding checks**, and (2) any corrections not yet made by the bank that will decrease the bank balance. The resulting total is the *reconciled cash balance at the end of the month.*

**EXHIBIT 7-4**   Bank Statement of Wilson Corporation

**ANCHOR NATIONAL BANK**
**123 Center Street**
**Madison, Wisconsin 53701**

Wilson Corporation
1847 Elmwood Avenue
Madison, Wisconsin 53712

Account Number   27-310205581847
Statement Date   November 30, 2011

| Deposits and Credits | | Checks and Debits | | | Daily Balance | |
|---|---|---|---|---|---|---|
| Date | Amount | Number | Date | Amount | Date | Amount |
| Nov. 01 | 420.00 | 149 | Nov. 02 | 125.00 | Nov. 01 | 6,060.30 |
| Nov. 02 | 630.00 | 154 | Nov. 03 | 56.25 | Nov. 02 | 6,565.30 |
| Nov. 07 | 560.80 | 155 | Nov. 10 | 135.00 | Nov. 03 | 6,509.05 |
| Nov. 10 | 480.25 | 156 | Nov. 08 | 315.10 | Nov. 07 | 6,801.19 |
| Nov. 14 | 525.00 | 157 | Nov. 07 | 233.26 | Nov. 08 | 6,486.09 |
| Nov. 17 | 270.25 | 158 | Nov. 11 | 27.14 | Nov. 10 | 6,831.34 |
| Nov. 21 | 640.20 | 159 | Nov. 18 | 275.00 | Nov. 11 | 6,804.20 |
| Nov. 26 | 300.00CM | 160 | Nov. 15 | 315.37 | Nov. 14 | 7,329.20 |
| Nov. 26 | 475.00 | 161 | Nov. 17 | 76.40 | Nov. 15 | 7,013.83 |
| Nov. 30 | 471.40 | 162 | Nov. 21 | 325.60 | Nov. 17 | 7,207.68 |
| | | 163 | Nov. 21 | 450.00 | Nov. 18 | 6,932.68 |
| | | 164 | Nov. 23 | 239.00 | Nov. 21 | 6,731.58 |
| | | 165 | Nov. 21 | 65.70 | Nov. 23 | 6,492.58 |
| | | 166 | Nov. 28 | 482.43 | Nov. 26 | 7,262.58 |
| | | 169 | Nov. 28 | 260.00 | Nov. 28 | 6,520.15 |
| | | 170 | Nov. 30 | 122.50 | Nov. 30 | 6,488.95 |
| | | 171 | Nov. 30 | 370.10 | | |
| | | | Nov. 07 | 35.40RT | | |
| | | | Nov. 26 | 5.00DM | | |
| | | | Nov. 30 | 10.00SC | | |

| Beginning Balance | + | Deposits and Credits | − | Checks and Debits | = | Ending Balance |
|---|---|---|---|---|---|---|
| $5,640.30 | + | $4,772.90 | − | $3,924.25 | = | $6,488.95 |

**Item Codes:**  EC: Error Correction   DM: Debit Memo   CM: Credit Memo
SC: Service Charge   OD: Overdraft   RT: Returned Item
IN: Interest Earned

**EXHIBIT 7-5**   Structure of a Company's Bank Reconciliation

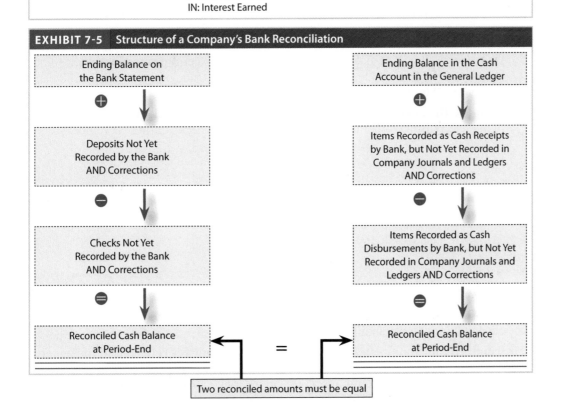

The schedule on the right begins with the ending balance in the Cash account in the company's general ledger. The internal audit department employee adds (1) items recorded as cash receipts by the bank but not yet recorded in the company's journals and (2) any corrections not yet made by the company that will increase the general ledger cash balance. The preparer subtracts (1) items recorded as cash disbursements by the bank but not yet recorded in the company's journals and (2) any corrections not yet made by the company that will decrease the general ledger cash balance. The resulting total is the *reconciled cash balance at the end of the month.* The totals of the two schedules should be the same.

**BANK RECONCILIATION ILLUSTRATED** Assume that the internal auditor of the Wilson Corporation is preparing the November 30, 2011, bank reconciliation. She uses the following procedures to reconcile the November 30 bank statement balance of $6,488.95 to the November 30 general ledger Cash account balance of $5,322.69:

1. **Trace outstanding items on the bank reconciliation for the previous month to the current bank statement.** Any items on the previous bank reconciliation that have still not been processed by the bank must appear on the current bank reconciliation. The October 31 reconciliation included the following:

| | | |
|---|---|---:|
| Deposit in transit | | $420.00 |
| Outstanding checks: | Number 149 | $125.00 |
| | Number 154 | 56.25 |
| | Number 155 | 135.00 |

The November 30 bank statement includes the $420 deposit and all three checks listed above. Therefore, none of these items will appear on the November 30 bank reconciliation.

2. **Compare the deposits made during the month to the deposits on the bank statement.** The Wilson Corporation made the following deposits during November:

| | | | |
|---|---:|---|---:|
| November 2............. | $630.00 | November 21............. | $640.20 |
| November 7............. | 560.80 | November 26............. | 475.00 |
| November 10............ | 480.25 | November 29............. | 471.40 |
| November 14............ | 525.00 | November 30............. | 225.00 |
| November 17............ | 270.25 | | |

All of these deposits appear on the bank statement except for the November 30 deposit of $225. The $225 deposit will appear on the left side of the November 30 bank reconciliation as a deposit in transit.

3. **Compare the checks issued during the month to the checks on the bank statement.** The Wilson Corporation issued the following checks during November:

| | | | |
|---|---:|---|---:|
| Number 156............. | $315.10 | Number 165............. | $ 65.70 |
| Number 157............. | 233.26 | Number 166............. | 482.43 |
| Number 158............. | 27.14 | Number 167............. | 301.66 |
| Number 159............. | 275.00 | Number 168............. | 149.50 |
| Number 160............. | 315.37 | Number 169............. | 260.00 |
| Number 161............. | 76.40 | Number 170............. | 122.50 |
| Number 162............. | 325.60 | Number 171............. | 370.10 |
| Number 163............. | 450.00 | Number 172............. | 450.00 |
| Number 164............. | 239.00 | Number 173............. | 240.50 |

Four of the checks—numbers 167, 168, 172, and 173—do not appear on the bank statement. These four checks will appear on the left side of the November 30 bank reconciliation as outstanding checks.

4. **Scan the bank statement for charges and credits not yet reflected in the general ledger.** The Wilson Corporation's bank statement contains a charge of $35.40 for a returned item, a debit memo of $5.00, and a service charge of $10.00 in the checks and other debits column. The deposits and other credits column contains a credit

memo for $300.00. Supplemental information sent by the bank with the bank statement reveals that the bank charged a $35.40 NSF check against Wilson's account, collected a $300.00 note for Wilson and charged a $5.00 collection fee, and that the service charge for the month of November was $10.00. These four items have not yet been recorded by Wilson Corporation. Therefore, they must be listed on the right side of the bank reconciliation.

After the four preceding procedures have been completed, the November 30 bank reconciliation for the Wilson Corporation appears as shown in Exhibit 7-6. Note that both the left side and the right side of the reconciliation end with a reconciled cash balance and that the two amounts are the same. This reconciled cash balance is the amount that will appear on the November 30 balance sheet for the company.

| EXHIBIT 7-6 | November 30, 2011, Bank Reconciliation for Wilson Corporation |
|---|---|

**WILSON CORPORATION**
**Bank Reconciliation**
**November 30, 2011**

| | | | | | |
|---|---|---|---|---|---|
| Ending balance from bank statement . . . | | $6,488.95 | Balance from general ledger . . . | | $5,322.69 |
| Add: Deposits in transit . . . . . . . . . . . . . . . . | | 225.00 | Add: Collection of note . . . . . . . . | $300.00 | |
| | | | Less: Collection fee . . . . . . . . . . . . | 5.00 | 295.00 |
| | | 6,713.95 | | | 5,617.69 |
| Less: Outstanding checks: | | | Less: NSF check. . . . . . . . . . . . . . . | 35.40 | |
| No. 167 . . . . . . . . . . . . . . . . . . . . . . . . . . | $301.66 | | Service charge . . . . . . . . . . . | 10.00 | 45.40 |
| No. 168 . . . . . . . . . . . . . . . . . . . . . . . . . | 149.50 | | | | |
| No. 172 . . . . . . . . . . . . . . . . . . . . . . . . . | 450.00 | | | | |
| No. 173 . . . . . . . . . . . . . . . . . . . . . . . . . | 240.50 | 1,141.66 | | | |
| Reconciled cash balance | | $5,572.29 | Reconciled cash balance . . . . . . . | | $5,572.29 |

Before the Wilson Corporation prepares its financial statements for November, Wilson must make journal entries to bring the balance in the Cash account into agreement with the reconciled cash balance on the bank reconciliation. These entries incorporate the items on the company's side of the bank reconciliation as follows:

| | | | | |
|---|---|---|---|---|
| Nov. 30 | Cash | 295.00 | | |
| | Miscellaneous expense | 5.00 | | |
| | Notes receivable | | 300.00 | |
| | *To record a note collected by the bank, less a collection fee.* | | | |

| | A | = | L | + | SE |
|---|---|---|---|---|---|
| | +295.00 | | | | |
| | | | | | −5.00 Exp |
| | −300.00 | | | | |

| | | | | |
|---|---|---|---|---|
| Nov. 30 | Accounts receivable | 35.40 | | |
| | Cash | | 35.40 | |
| | *To reclassify an NSF check as an account receivable.* | | | |

| | A | = | L | + | SE |
|---|---|---|---|---|---|
| | +35.40 | | | | |
| | −35.40 | | | | |

| | | | | |
|---|---|---|---|---|
| Nov. 30 | Miscellaneous expense | 10.00 | | |
| | Cash | | 10.00 | |
| | *To record bank service charge for November.* | | | |

| | A | = | L | + | SE |
|---|---|---|---|---|---|
| | | | | | −10.00 Exp |
| | −10.00 | | | | |

## Your Turn! 7.3

Match the reconciling items from the left-hand column with the proper reconciling action from the right-hand column:

| | |
|---|---|
| **1.** Deposits in transit | *a.* Add to bank statement balance |
| **2.** Outstanding checks | *b.* Subtract from bank statement balance |
| **3.** Bank service charge | *c.* Add to cash general ledger account |
| **4.** Cash collected by bank on note | *d.* Subtract from cash general ledger account |

The solution is on page 361.

# EFFECTIVE CASH MANAGEMENT

Cash is a company's most important asset. Without cash, a company would be unable to pay its employees or its suppliers. In short, a company would be unable to continue operating. As a consequence, managers spend considerable time and effort managing and monitoring this key asset. Similarly, investors and lenders spend considerable time understanding where a company's cash came from and how the company spent it.

## MONITORING CASH

The most effective tool for monitoring a company's cash is the statement of cash flows.[1] As discussed in Chapter 1, the statement of cash flows identifies a company's cash inflows and cash outflows, segmenting them into the three business activities of operating, investing, and financing. Exhibit 7-7 presents the statement of cash flows for WebWork Inc. for the month ended December 31, 2011.

| EXHIBIT 7-7 | Statement of Cash Flows for WebWork, Inc. | | |
|---|---|---|---|
| **WEBWORK, INC.** | | | |
| **Statement of Cash Flows** | | | |
| **For Month Ended December 31, 2011** | | | |
| **Cash flow from operating activities** | | | |
| Cash received from clients | | $19,910 | |
| Cash paid to employees and suppliers | | (1,620) | |
| Cash paid for rent | | (10,800) | |
| Cash provided by operating activities | | | $ 7,490 |
| **Cash flow from investing activities** | | | |
| Purchase of office equipment | | (32,400) | |
| Cash used by investing activities | | | (32,400) |
| **Cash flow from financing activities** | | | |
| Stock issued | | 30,000 | |
| Borrowing from bank | | 36,000 | |
| Cash dividends | | (500) | |
| Cash provided by financing activities | | | 65,500 |
| Net increase in cash | | | 40,590 |
| Cash at December 1, 2011 | | | 0 |
| Cash at December 31, 2011 | | | $40,590 |

The positive numbers on the statement of cash flows represent a company's cash inflows and the negative numbers represent a company's cash outflows. The larger positive numbers represent the major cash inflows and the larger negative numbers represent the major cash outflows. WebWork's primay cash inflows involved the sale of stock ($30,000) and its bank borrowings ($36,000). The company's primary uses of cash involved the purchase of office equipment ($32,400) and the payment of rent ($10,800). Not only does the statement of cash flows identify the sources and uses of cash, but it also identifies whether a company's cash balance increased or decreased for the period. Exhibit 7-7 reveals that WebWork's cash account increased by $40,590 for the month of December.

While having some cash on hand is important to enable a company to pay its employees and its suppliers on a timely basis, having too much cash on hand may indicate that a company is not maximizing the return on its assets. Thus, it is important for managers to not only monitor a company's cash but also to manage it effectively to insure that the company is earning an adequate return on this key asset.

---

[1] The statement of cash flows provides an after-the-fact monitoring of cash sources and uses. Many companies use a cash budget in order to plan anticipated cash inflows and outflows so that they are able to manage the amount of cash on hand at an appropriate level. Cash budgets are covered in most managerial accounting textbooks.

## PRIMARY ACTIVITIES OF EFFECTIVE CASH MANAGEMENT

Effective cash management generally involves four primary activities:

1. Manage accounts receivable. Since accounts receivable rarely include interest charges for late payment, the sooner that cash from sales can be collected, the sooner the cash can be used to pay suppliers, pay debt, or be invested in operations. Thus, managers should try to increase the rate at which accounts receivable are collected.

2. Manage inventory levels. Inventory should be maintained at levels that allow a company to satisfy customer needs while also avoid having too much of the company's resources tied up in inventory for extended periods of time. Thus, managers should try to keep inventory levels as low as possible without losing any sales.

3. Manage accounts payable. Since accounts payable rarely include an interest charge for late payment, the longer a manager takes to pay off these accounts, the longer a company can use its cash to fund operations. Thus, managers should delay the payment of accounts payable; however they should not be delayed beyond the point that their credit rating may be harmed. Where accounts payable have credit terms that provide a discount for prompt payment, managers must evaluate the trade-off involved by delaying the payment of accounts payable versus the reduced purchase price that results from timely payment.

4. Invest excess cash. Since cash on hand or in a bank account yields a very low rate of return, it is important to invest any excess cash. Thus, an important management activity is forecasting a company's cash needs by constructing a cash budget each period. Only a sufficient amount of cash necessary to cover a company's day-to-day needs should be kept on hand; any excess amounts should be invested in an effort to earn an adequate rate of return on this asset.

### WORKING WITH THE TAKEAWAYS

The following conditions of material weaknesses were reported in the independent auditors' report on internal control of the U.S. Department of Transportation Highway Trust Fund (HTF) for fiscal year 2006:

1. Weaknesses with respect to journal entry preparation:
   a. Lack of indication of preparer
   b. Lack of supporting documentation
   c. Lack of proper review and approval
2. Weaknesses with respect to the consolidated financial statement preparation and analysis process:
   a. Inadequate analysis of abnormal balances
   b. Inadequate analysis of account relationships
   c. Inadequate controls over journal entry processing
   d. Lack of oversight related to allocation transfers

**Required**
A. What is the possible negative effect of these material weaknesses?
B. If you were the reporting auditor, what would you recommend be done?

**Solution**
A. The agency's financial statements may be misstated. In addition, failure to correct these material internal control weaknesses increases the risk of fraud.
B. The auditor should recommend the following actions:
   a. Develop effective policies and procedures that ensure the proper preparation of journal entry forms.
   b. Develop effective policies and procedures that will strengthen controls over the journal entry review and approval process to ensure that all journal entries are complete, accurate, properly supported and approved prior to posting in the general ledger.
   c. Develop effective policies and procedures that will ensure that all routine or recurring journal entries are properly prepared and posted each month and that all journal entries are properly maintained.

    *d.* Develop effective policies and procedures to ensure that the preparation of quarterly and annual financial statements, note disclosures, and related information are in compliance with accounting standards.

    *e.* Develop effective policies and procedures to review and document the resolution of any abnormal balances and account relationship discrepancies that exist on a monthly basis.

    *f.* Be required to report significant abnormal balances and account relationship discrepancies on a monthly basis including a status of researching and resolving the balances.

    *g.* Develop policies and procedures to determine if any journal entries processed in the current fiscal year have a prior period impact.

    *h.* Develop effective policies and procedures to ensure that other Federal agencies that receive material amounts of the HTF budget authority via the allocation transfer process provide sufficient evidence that the transactions processed exist, are accurate and that all transactions have been reported (i.e., completeness).

# APPENDIX 7A: Auditing and Internal Control

**LEARNING OBJECTIVE 5**

**Appendix 7A Describe financial statement audits and operational audits.**

One of the internal control concepts previously discussed was conducting internal company audits. Internal audits provide appraisals of a company's financial statements, its internal control, and its operations. Internal auditors, who are employees of the company that they audit, conduct internal audits under the direction of top management or a company's board of directors. Parties outside the company, such as bankers and stockholders, prefer independent appraisals of a company's performance. These parties are usually unwilling to accept an audit report prepared by company-employed internal auditors because of possible bias and conflicts of interest.

    Consequently, creditors and stockholders usually require that an independent, professional auditing firm conduct an audit of the annual financial statements. Moreover, U.S. securities law requires that all corporations whose common stock is publicly traded have an independent firm of certified public accountants (CPAs) audit the company's annual financial statements.

---

**FORENSIC ACCOUNTING**    **Not Your Ordinary Audit**

The financial statement audit is performed to enable the independent auditor to express an opinion regarding whether the financial statements present fairly, in all material respects, the financial position and results of operations of a company. In so doing, the independent auditor is looking for material errors, whether the errors are a result of unintentional misstatement or fraud. To perform the audit, the auditor will perform statistical sampling of the reported transactions to make judgments regarding the fairness of the reported statements. The auditor is not specifically looking for fraud, and likely will not find it even if present, because the financial statement audit is not designed to uncover fraud. The forensic accountant, by way of contrast, is specifically looking for fraud. Forensic accountants concentrate their efforts where fraud is likely to occur or is suspected, rather than on the financial statements as a whole. The forensic accountant will also utilize additional investigative techniques and follow leads suggested by what appear to be immaterial items. The forensic accountant will often have additional skills not common to financial statement auditors, such as surveillance tactics and interviewing and interrogation skills.

---

## FINANCIAL STATEMENT AUDITS

A **financial statement audit** is an examination of a company's annual financial statements by a firm of independent certified public accountants. (The quarterly financial reports of U.S. publicly traded companies are "reviewed" by an independent audit firm but they are not subject to a full audit like the annual financial statements.) The independent audit firm conducts this examination so it can prepare a report that expresses an opinion regarding whether (or not) the financial statements fairly present the results of operations, cash flows, and financial position of a company.

| PRINCIPLE ALERT | Going Concern Concept |
| --- | --- |

The *going concern concept* assumes that a business entity will continue to operate indefinitely. As part of the annual audit, a company's independent auditors must assess the likelihood that the company that they are auditing will continue as a going concern for a reasonable period. Events such as recurring losses, pending litigation, and the loss of a major customer or supplier may raise concern about a firm's ability to maintain its going-concern status. In such cases, the independent auditors should assess management's response to the problem and the type of financial statement disclosure being made about the problem. When substantial doubt exists about a company's going-concern status, the independent auditors may include a paragraph in the audit report expressing their concern regarding this issue.

## AUDIT PROCEDURES

The independent audit firm conducts the annual financial statement audit according to standards established by the **Public Company Accounting Oversight Board (PCAOB)**, a quasi-governmental agency established by the Sarbanes-Oxley Act. The PCAOB is responsible for establishing auditing standards, inspecting the auditing practices of independent audit firms, and disciplining those firms that fail to maintain acceptable audit standards and practices.

The annual financial statement audit includes many different stages of work. During the early stage of an audit, the independent auditor reviews and evaluates the internal controls imbedded in a company's accounting system and other systems. This review and evaluation helps the auditor determine what additional investigative steps, if any, should be included in the audit. The auditor then collects and analyzes data that substantiates the amounts in the financial statements. The auditor obtains most of these data from accounting records (such as journals and ledgers), business documents (such as purchase orders, sales invoices, and payment approval forms), and outside sources (such as banks, insurance companies, and suppliers).

## THE AUDIT REPORT

The **audit report** that the independent auditor issues following the annual audit specifies the financial statements that were audited, summarizes the audit process, and states the auditor's opinion regarding the financial statement data. The opinion usually states that the financial statements "fairly present" the results of operations, cash flow, and financial position of the company. The independent auditor does not conduct the audit to determine whether the financial statements are absolutely correct. Instead, the audit is conducted to determine whether the financial statements are a fair representation of operating results, cash flow, and financial position.

The primary purpose of the annual financial statement audit is *not* the discovery of fraudulent acts by management or employees of the company. Many audit procedures use statistical samples of transactions and data rather than examining the complete population of transactions. The auditors use samples to minimize the time required to conduct the audit, and consequently, to minimize its cost. As a result, there is the possibility that some errors or irregularities will exist in the transactions and data that the auditor does not review or evaluate. However, the independent auditor carefully designs the sampling procedures to detect errors and irregularities that are material in relation to the financial statements.

## OPERATIONAL AUDITS

Both internal audit departments and independent audit firms perform operational audits. An **operational audit** is an evaluation of activities, systems, and internal controls within a company to determine their efficiency, effectiveness, and economy. Operational auditing goes beyond accounting records and financial statements to obtain a full understanding of the operations of a company. Companies dedicated to continuous quality improvement often use operational audits to identify specific areas where they need to improve the quality of their operations or products.

Auditors design operational audits to assess the quality and efficiency of operational performance, identify opportunities for improvement, and develop specific recommendations for improvement. The scope of an operational audit can be very narrow, such as a review and evaluation of the procedures for processing cash receipts, or quite broad, such as a review and evaluation of all of the internal controls in a computerized accounting system.

APPENDIX 7A

REVIEW

**Your Turn!**                                                                 7.4

Match the description in the left-hand column with the type of audit in the right-hand column:

1. Conducted by company employees
2. Conducted by independent auditors
3. Conducted by both independent auditors and internal auditors
4. Primary purpose is to report on the fairness of a company's financial statements
5. Evaluation of the efficiency and effectiveness of company activities

   *a.* Internal audit
   *b.* Financial statement audit
   *c.* Operational audit

The solution is on page 361.

## Summary of Learning Objectives

**LO1**  **Define the three elements of fraud and discuss the role of internal control in a business to prevent fraud (p. 318).**

- The fraud triangle consists of three parts: (1) pressure, (2) rationalization, and (3) opportunity.
- Internal controls are the measures undertaken by a company to ensure the reliability of its accounting data, protect its assets from theft or unauthorized use, insure that employees follow the company's policies and procedures, and evaluate the performance of employees, departments, divisions, and the company as a whole.
- A prevention control is designed to deter problems before they arise. A detection control is designed to discover problems soon after they arise. Prevention controls are generally more desirable than detection controls.
- A company should incorporate the following concepts when it designs its internal control:
  - Establish clear lines of authority and responsibility.
  - Implement segregation of duties.
  - Hire competent personnel.
  - Use control numbers on all business documents.
  - Develop plans and budgets.
  - Maintain adequate accounting records.
  - Conduct internal audits.

**LO2**  **Define cash and discuss the accounting for cash (p. 325).**

- Cash includes coins, currency (paper money), checks, money orders, traveler's checks, and funds on deposit at a financial institution in a company's checking accounts and savings accounts.
- A company can have one or more cash accounts in its general ledger. Cash is a current asset.
- A company may combine certain short-term, highly liquid investments with cash and present a single amount called *cash and cash equivalents.*
- Not all of the company's cash may be available for general use. Restricted cash represents cash that has been restricted for specific uses. A compensating balance is an amount that a company must maintain in a bank account as part of a loan agreement.

**LO3**  **Describe the internal controls for cash (p. 326).**

- Companies develop elaborate internal controls to protect cash, their most liquid asset.
- Four departments play major roles in processing cash received on account: the mailroom (open mail, endorse checks, list checks), the treasurer's department (deposit checks), the controller's department (update general ledger accounts), and the internal audit department (reconcile bank statement).
- Five departments play major roles in processing cash received from retail sales: the retail sales area (enter sales in cash register and place cash in drawer), the retail sales supervisor (count cash and prepare reports), the treasurer's department (deposit cash), the controller's department (update general ledger), and the internal audit department (reconcile bank statement).
- A petty cash fund is a small amount of cash placed in a secure location on a company's premises to be used to pay for small expenditures such as postage and delivery service.

- A bank reconciliation is a schedule that (1) accounts for all differences between the ending cash balance of the bank statement and the ending cash balance of the Cash account in a company's general ledger and (2) determines the reconciled cash balance as of the end of the month.
- The procedure used to prepare the bank reconciliation involves four steps:
  ○ Trace outstanding items on the bank reconciliation from the previous month to the current bank statement.
  ○ Compare the deposits made during the month to the deposits on the bank statement.
  ○ Compare the checks issued during the month to the checks on the bank statement.
  ○ Scan the bank statement for charges and credits not yet reflected in the general ledger.

**Describe the four primary activities of effective cash management (p. 336).**    LO4

- Cash should be monitored using the statement of cash flows.
- Effective cash management includes monitoring and managing accounts receivable, inventory, and accounts payable, and investing any excess cash.

**Appendix 7A:  Describe financial statement audits and operational audits (p. 338).**    LO5

- A financial statement audit is an examination of a company's financial statements by a firm of independent certified public accountants. The firm issues an audit report upon completion of the audit.
- An operational audit is an evaluation of activities, systems, and internal controls within a company to determine their efficiency, effectiveness, and economy.

## TAKEAWAYS: SUMMARY CHART

| Concept ⟶ | Method ⟶ | Assessment | |
|---|---|---|---|
| Are the internal controls adequate? | Independent auditors' attestation report.<br><br>The principles of good internal control include: (1) Establish clear lines of authority and responsibility, (2) Segregation of duties, (3) Hire competent personnel, (4) Use control numbers on all business documents, (5) Develop plans and budgets, (6) Maintain adequate accounting records, (7) Provide physical and electronic controls, (8) Conduct internal audits. | Be sure that the report does not indicate any weaknesses in a company's internal control. If weaknesses are reported, be cautious in relying on the reported financial statements. | TAKEAWAY 7.1 |
| Are there any restrictions on a company's use of its cash and cash equivalents? | Balance sheet and the notes to the financial statements. Are there any restrictions to cash or compensating cash balances reported? | Any assessments of liquidity should consider any cash restrictions. | TAKEAWAY 7.2 |

## GLOSSARY OF KEY TERMS

**Audit report**  A report issued by an independent auditor that reports the auditor's opinion regarding a company's financial statements (p. 339).

**Bank reconciliation**  A procedure explaining the various items—such as deposits in transit, checks outstanding, bank charges, and errors—that lead to differences between the balance shown on a bank statement and the related Cash account in a company's general ledger (p. 332).

**Budget**  A planning device that forecasts a business's future operating activities using financial data. The budget serves as an internal control device by providing a benchmark to compare actual performance against so that material deviations can be investigated (p. 322).

**Cash**  An asset category representing the amount of a firm's paper money, coins, checks, money orders, traveler's checks, and funds on deposit at a bank in a company's checking accounts and savings accounts (p. 325).

**Cash and cash equivalents**  The sum of cash plus short-term, highly liquid investments such as U.S. Treasury bills and money market funds (p. 326).

**Certificate of deposit (CD)**  An investment security offering a fixed rate of return for a specified period of time (p. 325).

**Check** A written order signed by a checking account owner directing the bank to pay a specified amount of money to the person or company named on the check (p. 330).

**Compensating balance** A minimum amount that a financial institution requires a firm to maintain in its bank account as a condition of a borrowing arrangement (p. 326).

**Control numbers** Preprinted numbers on documents such as purchase orders, invoices, credit memos, and checks used to provide an internal control that all documents are accounted for (p. 322).

**Deposits in transit** Cash deposits made to a bank account near the end of a month that do not appear on that month's bank statement (p. 332).

**Detection control** An internal control designed to discover problems soon after they arise (p. 320).

**Electronic funds transfer** Sending an electronic message from one computer to another to cause a transfer of money from one financial institution to another (p. 330).

**Employee collusion** When one or more employees work together to circumvent an internal control (p. 323).

**Fidelity bond** An insurance policy that provides financial compensation for theft by employees specifically covered by the insurance (p. 323).

**Financial statement audit** An examination of a company's financial statements by a firm of independent certified public accountants (p. 338).

**Fraud** Any act by the management or employees of a business involving an intentional deception for personal gain (p. 318).

**Fraud triangle** The three elements of fraud, consisting of (1) pressure, (2) rationalization, and (3) opportunity (p. 318).

**Internal auditing** A company function that provides independent appraisals of the company's financial statements, its internal control, and its operations (p. 323).

**Internal control** The measures undertaken by a company to ensure the reliability of its accounting data, protect its assets from theft or unauthorized use, insure that employees follow the company's policies and procedures, and evaluate the performance of employees, departments, divisions, and the company as a whole (p. 319).

**Not-sufficient-funds check** A check from an individual or company that had an insufficient cash balance in the bank when the holder of the check presented it to the bank for payment (p. 325).

**Operational audit** An evaluation of activities, systems, and internal controls within a company to determine their efficiency, effectiveness, and economy (p. 339).

**Outstanding checks** Checks issued by a firm that have not yet been presented to its bank for payment (p. 332).

**Password** A string of characters that a user enters into a device to prove that the user is actually the user that is allowed to use the device (p. 328).

**Petty cash fund** A special, relatively small cash fund established for making minor cash disbursements in the operation of a business (p. 331).

**Postdated check** A check from another person or company with a calendar date that is later than the current date. A postdated check does not become cash until the calendar date of the check (p. 325).

**Prevention control** An internal control designed to discover problems before they arise (p. 320).

**Public Company Accounting Oversight Board (PCAOB)** A quasi-governmental agency established by the Sarbanes-Oxley Act to overhaul auditing standards, inspect the work of accounting firms, and discipline independent auditors that fail to meet and maintain acceptable standards of audit performance (p. 339).

**Remittance advice** A form that accompanies a check to inform the person receiving the check about the purpose of the check (p. 327).

**Remittance list** A list of the checks received from customers to pay their accounts receivable (p. 327).

**Restricted cash** Cash that is restricted for a specific use and not available for general use (p. 326).

**Segregation of duties** An internal control principle that requires that duties should be allocated to separate individuals (p. 321).

# COMPREHENSIVE PROBLEM

At December 31, 2011, the Cash account in the Tyler Company's general ledger had a debit balance of $18,434.27. The December 31, 2011, bank statement showed a balance of $19,726.40. In reconciling the two amounts, you discover the following:

1. Bank deposits made by Tyler on December 31 amounting to $2,145.40 do not appear on the bank statement.

2. A non-interest-bearing note receivable from the Smith Company for $2,000, left with the bank for collection, was collected by the bank at the end of December. The bank credited the proceeds, less a $5 collection charge, on the bank statement. Tyler Company has not recorded the collection.

3. Accompanying the bank statement is a debit memorandum indicating that John Miller's check for $450 was charged against Tyler's bank account on December 30 because of insufficient funds.

4. Check No. 586, written for advertising expense of $869.10, was recorded as $896.10 by Tyler Company.

5. A comparison of the paid checks returned by the bank with the recorded disbursements revealed that the following checks are still outstanding as of December 31:

| No. 561.................. | $306.63 | No. 591.................. | $190.00 |
| No. 585.................. | 440.00 | No. 592.................. | 282.50 |
| No. 588.................. | 476.40 | No. 593.................. | 243.00 |

6. The bank mistakenly charged Tyler Company's account for check printing costs of $30.50, which should have been charged to Taylor Company.

7. The bank charged Tyler Company's account $42.50 for the rental of a safe deposit box. No entry has been made in Tyler's records for this expense.

**Required**

a. Prepare a bank reconciliation as of December 31, 2011.

b. Prepare any necessary journal entries at December 31, 2011.

a.

| TYLER COMPANY Bank Reconciliation December 31, 2011 | | | | | |
|---|---|---|---|---|---|
| Ending balance from bank statement ... | | $19,726.40 | Balance from general ledger ..... | | $18,434.27 |
| Add: Deposits not credited by bank ..... | | 2,145.40 | Add: Collection of note .......... | $2,000.00 | |
| Error by bank (Check printing | | | Less: Collection charge .......... | 5.00 | 1,995.00 |
| charge of Taylor Co.)................. | | 30.50 | Error in recording check No. 586 . | | 27.00 |
| | | 21,902.30 | | | 20,456.27 |
| Less: Outstanding checks: | | | Less: | | |
| No. 561 ............................. | $306.63 | | NSF check .................... | 450.00 | |
| No. 585 ............................. | 440.00 | | Charge for safe deposit box.... | 42.50 | 492.50 |
| No. 588 ............................. | 476.40 | | | | |
| No. 591 ............................. | 190.00 | | | | |
| No. 592 ............................. | 282.50 | | | | |
| No. 593 ............................. | 243.00 | 1,938.53 | | | |
| Reconciled cash balance............... | | $19,963.77 | Reconciled cash balance......... | | $19,963.77 |

b. Dec. 31

| | | | |
|---|---|---|---|
| Cash | | 1,995.00 | |
| Miscellaneous expense | | 5.00 | |
| Notes receivable—Smith Company | | | 2,000.00 |
| *To record collection of Smith Company's note by bank, less collection charge.* | | | |

| A | = | L | + | SE |
|---|---|---|---|---|
| +1,995.00 | | | | |
| | | | | −5.00 |
| −2,000.00 | | | | |

31

| | | | |
|---|---|---|---|
| Cash | | 27.00 | |
| Advertising expense | | | 27.00 |
| *To correct error in recording advertising expense.* | | | |

| A | = | L | + | SE |
|---|---|---|---|---|
| +27.00 | | | | |
| | | | | +27.00 |

31

| | | | |
|---|---|---|---|
| Accounts receivable—John Miller | | 450.00 | |
| Cash | | | 450.00 |
| *To reclassify NSF check as an account receivable.* | | | |

| A | = | L | + | SE |
|---|---|---|---|---|
| +450.00 | | | | |
| −450.00 | | | | |

31

| | | | |
|---|---|---|---|
| Miscellaneous expense | | 42.50 | |
| Cash | | | 42.50 |
| *To record rental expense of safety deposit box.* | | | |

| A | = | L | + | SE |
|---|---|---|---|---|
| | | | | −42.50 |
| −42.50 | | | | |

# SELF-STUDY QUESTIONS

(Answers to the Self-Study Questions are available at the end of the chapter.)

1. Which of the following is not one of the three elements of the fraud triangle?
   a. Pressure
   b. Rationalization
   c. Embezzlement
   d. Opportunity

2. Which of the following is not a common internal control concept?
   a. Establish clear lines of responsibility
   b. Provide physical and electronic controls
   c. Collusion among employees
   d. Separate work functions

3. Which of the following are considered good internal control practice?
   a. Job rotation
   b. Required vacations
   c. Only promoting from within
   d. Both *a* and *b*

     *c.* The company being audited cannot pay the external auditing firm since this would violate their independence.

     *d.* Outside parties prefer appraisals by internal auditors over those of external auditors since they know more about the company being audited.

**LO5**
**(Appendix 7A)**

**SE7-5.  Financial Statement Audit**
The financial statement audit is:
*a.* conducted by the internal auditors.
*b.* conducted by auditors overseen by the American Institute of Certified Public Accountants.
*c.* conducted by auditors overseen by the Public Company Accounting Oversight Board.
*d.* only necessary if fraud is suspected.

**LO2**

**SE7-6.  Cash**
Cash includes each of the following except:
*a.* a postdated check.
*b.* currency.
*c.* money orders.
*d.* funds in a checking account.

**LO2**

**SE7-7.  Restricted Cash**
Restricted cash:
*a.* must be shown as a current asset.
*b.* must be shown as a noncurrent asset.
*c.* is shown as a liability.
*d.* is reported separate from unrestricted cash.

**LO3**

**SE7-8.  Electronic Funds Transfer**
Electronic funds transfer (EFT) involves transferring cash from one location to another using:
*a.* armored trucks.
*b.* computers.
*c.* bicycle messengers.
*d.* the mail service.

**LO3**

**SE7-9.  Cash Internal Control**
Good internal control over cash received on account involves the mailroom doing each of the following activities except:
*a.* Open the mail.
*b.* Prepare the deposit receipt.
*c.* Prepare the remittance list.
*d.* Send checks to the treasurer.

**LO4**

**SE7-10.  Cash Management**
Effective cash management involves all the following except:
*a.* Manage accounts receivable.
*b.* Manage inventory.
*c.* Invest excess cash.
*d.* Conduct internal audits.

# EXERCISES—SET A

**LO1**

**E7-1A.  Internal Control**
Explain how each of the following procedures strengthens a company's internal control:
*a.* After preparing a check for a cash disbursement, the accountant for Travis Lumber Company cancels the supporting business documents (purchase order, receiving report, and invoice) by stamping them PAID.
*b.* The salespeople for Davis Department Store give each customer a cash register receipt along with the proper change. A sign on each cash register states that no refunds or exchanges are allowed without the related cash register receipt.
*c.* The ticket-taker at the Esquire Theater tears each admission ticket in half and gives one half back to the ticket purchaser. The seat number is printed on each half of the ticket.

d. John Renaldo's restaurant provides servers with prenumbered customers' checks. The servers are to void checks with mistakes on them and issue new ones rather than make corrections on them. Voided checks must be given to the manager every day.

**E7-2A.** **Internal Controls for Cash Received on Account** LO3

Hudson Company sells supplies to restaurants. Most sales are made on open account (credit sales). Hudson has requested your help in designing procedures for processing checks received from its customers. Briefly describe the procedures that should be used in each of the following departments:

a. Mailroom
b. Treasurer's department
c. Controller's department

**E7-3A.** **Bank Reconciliation** LO3

Use the following information to prepare a bank reconciliation for Young Company at June 30:

1. Balance per Cash account, June 30, $7,055.80.
2. Balance per bank statement, June 30, $7,300.25.
3. Deposits not reflected on bank statement, $725.
4. Outstanding checks, June 30, $1,260.45.
5. Service charge on bank statement not recorded in books, $11.
6. Error by bank—Yertel Company check charged on Young Company's bank statement, $550.
7. Check for advertising expense, $250, incorrectly recorded in books as $520.

**E7-4A.** **Bank Reconciliation Components** LO3

Identify the requested amount in each of the following situations:

a. Munsing Company's May 31 bank reconciliation shows deposits in transit of $1,400. The general ledger Cash in Bank account shows total cash receipts during June of $57,300. The June bank statement shows total cash deposits of $55,900 (and no credit memos). What amount of deposits in transit should appear in the June 30 bank reconciliation?
b. Sandusky Company's August 31 bank reconciliation shows outstanding checks of $2,100. The general ledger Cash in Bank account shows total cash disbursements (all by check) during September of $50,300. The September bank statement shows $49,200 of checks clearing the bank. What amount of outstanding checks should appear in the September 30 bank reconciliation?
c. Fremont Corporation's March 31 bank reconciliation shows deposits in transit of $800. The general ledger Cash in Bank account shows total cash receipts during April of $38,000. The April bank statement shows total cash deposits of $37,100 (including $1,300 from the collection of a note; the note collection has not yet been recorded by Fremont). What amount of deposits in transit should appear in the April 30 bank reconciliation?

**E7-5A.** **External versus Internal Audit** LO5 (Appendix 7A)

Explain why parties outside the company, such as bankers and stockholders, prefer an independent appraisal of the company's financial results rather than relying on the work of internal auditors.

**E7-6A.** **Operational Audits** LO5 (Appendix 7A)

Explain the nature of an operational audit.

**E7-7A.** **Cash and Cash Equivalents** LO2

Identify each of the following items as either cash (C), cash equivalents (CE), or neither (N):

a. Coin
b. U.S. treasury bills
c. Checks
d. Six-month certificate of deposit
e. Currency

| Bank Statement | | | | | | |
|---|---|---|---|---|---|---|
| **TO Winton, Inc.** | | | | | | **September 30** |
| **St. Louis, MO** | | | | | | **STATE BANK** |
| **Date** | **Deposits** | **No.** | **Date** | **Charges** | **Date** | **Balance** |
| | | | | | Aug. 31.......... | $14,300 |
| Sept. 1.......... | $1,280 | 597 | Sept. 1.......... | $ 830 | Sept. 1.......... | 14,750 |
| 2.......... | 1,120 | 607 | 5.......... | 1,850 | 2.......... | 15,870 |
| 5.......... | 850 | 608 | 5.......... | 1,100 | 5.......... | 13,770 |
| 9.......... | 744 | 609 | 9.......... | 552 | 8.......... | 13,130 |
| 15.......... | 1,360 | 610 | 8.......... | 640 | 9.......... | 13,322 |
| 17.......... | 1,540 | 611 | 17.......... | 488 | 15.......... | 14,008 |
| 25.......... | 1,028 | 612 | 15.......... | 674 | 17.......... | 15,060 |
| 30.......... | 680 | 614 | 25.......... | 920 | 25.......... | 15,168 |
| | | NSF | 29.......... | 1,028 | 29.......... | 14,140 |
| | | SC | 30.......... | 36 | 30.......... | 14,784 |

A list of deposits made and checks written during September is shown below:

| Deposits Made | | Checks Written | |
|---|---|---|---|
| Sept. 1 ................. | $1,120 | No. 607 ................. | $1,850 |
| 4 ................. | 850 | 608 ................. | 1,100 |
| 8 ................. | 744 | 609 ................. | 552 |
| 12 ................. | 1,360 | 610 ................. | 640 |
| 16 ................. | 1,540 | 611 ................. | 488 |
| 24 ................. | 1,028 | 612 ................. | 746 |
| 29 ................. | 680 | 613 ................. | 310 |
| 30 ................. | 1,266 | 614 ................. | 920 |
| | $8,588 | 615 ................. | 386 |
| | | 616 ................. | 420 |
| | | | $7,412 |

The Cash in Bank account balance on September 30 was $15,286. In reviewing checks returned by the bank, the accountant discovered that check No. 612, written for $674 for advertising expense, was recorded in the cash disbursements journal as $746. The NSF check for $1,028, which Winton deposited on September 24, was a payment on account from customer D. Walker.

**Required**

a. Prepare a bank reconciliation for Winton, Inc., at September 30.
b. Prepare the necessary journal entries to bring the Cash in Bank account into agreement with the reconciled cash balance on the bank reconciliation.

LO2   **P7-6A.   Reporting Cash**

Jenkins Company has the following items at year-end.

| | |
|---|---|
| Currency and coin in safe ......................................................................... | $ 3,500 |
| Funds in savings account (requires $2,000 compensating balance) ......................... | 25,250 |
| Funds in checking account........................................................................ | 6,750 |
| Traveler's checks.................................................................................. | 500 |
| Postdated check.................................................................................... | 1,250 |
| Not-sufficient-funds check........................................................................ | 850 |
| Money market fund ............................................................................... | 32,400 |

**Required**

Identify the amount of the above items that should be reported as cash and cash equivalents on Jenkins Company's balance sheet.

LO1   **P7-7A.   Internal Control**

Bart Simons has worked for Dr. Homer Spring for many years. Bart has been a model employee. He has not taken a vacation in over four years, always stating that work was too important. One of Bart's primary jobs at the clinic is to open mail and list the checks received. He also collects cash from patients at the cashier's window as patients leave. There are times that things are so hectic that Bart does not bother to give the patient a receipt; however, he assures them that he will make sure their account is properly credited. When things slow down at the clinic Bart often offers to help Lisa post payments to the patients' accounts receivable ledger. Lisa is always happy to receive help since she is also quite busy and because Bart is such a careful worker.

**Required**

Identify any internal control principles that may be violated in Dr. Spring's clinic.

**P7-8A.    Internal Control**    LO1, LO3

Listed below are (a) four potential errors or problems that could occur in the processing of cash transactions and (b) internal control principles. Review each error or problem and identify an internal control principle that could reduce the chance of the error or problem occurring. You may also cite more than one principle if more than one applies, or write none if none of the principles will correct the error or problem.

1. An employee steals cash collected from a customer's accounts receivable and hides the theft by issuing a credit memorandum indicating the customer returned the merchandise.
2. An official with authority to sign checks is able to steal blank checks and issue them without detection.
3. Due to a labor shortage many employees are hired without sufficient skills with the thought they can "learn on the job."
4. A salesperson often rings up a sale for less than the actual amount and then pockets the additional cash collected from the customer.

Internal control principles:

a.  Establish clear lines of authority and responsibility.
b.  Segregation of duties.
c.  Hire competent personnel.
d.  Use control numbers on all business documents.
e.  Develop plans and budgets.
f.   Maintain adequate accounting records.
g.  Provide physical and electronic controls.
h.  Conduct internal audits.

**P7-9A.    Bank Reconciliation**    LO3

The Seattle Boat Company's bank statement for the month of September indicated a balance of $14,000. The company's cash account in the general ledger showed a balance of $11,318 on September 30. Other relevant information includes the following:

1. Deposits in transit on September 30 total $10,400.
2. The bank statement shows a debit memorandum for an $80 check printing charge.
3. Check number 238 payable to Simon Company was recorded in the accounting records for $496 and cleared the bank for this same amount. A review of the records indicated that the Simon account now has a $72 credit balance and the check to them should have been $568.
4. Outstanding checks as of September 30 totaled $11,600.
5. Check No. 276 was correctly written and paid by the bank for $818. The check was recorded in the accounting records as a debit to accounts payable and a credit to cash for $980.
6. The bank returned a NSF check in the amount of $1,120.
7. The bank included a credit memorandum for $2,520 representing a collection of a customer's note. The principle portion was $2,400 and the interest portion was $120. The interest had not been accrued.

**Required**

a.  Prepare the September bank reconciliation for Seattle Boat Company.
b.  Prepare any necessary adjusting entries.

LO4    **P7-10A. Effective Cash Management**

Longo LLP is a new law firm struggling to manage its cash flow. Like all new businesses, the firm has not yet developed a sufficient client base to cover its operating costs. Additionally, the firm faced a number of large initial, but nonrecurring, start-up costs at the beginning of the year. Ongoing monthly costs include office rent and salary for a paralegal staff member. Another problem that the firm faces is that several of its major clients have failed to pay their current, but overdue, bills. Mick Longo, one of the two founding partners, has not taken any salary since the firm began operations over eight months ago, and has decided to maintain a part-time job bartending on weekends at a local resort to insure that he has some cash to cover day-to-day expenses like travel.

**Required**

What suggestions would you make to Mick Longo to improve his firm's cash management practices?

# PROBLEMS—SET B

LO1, LO3    **P7-1B.    Internal Control**

Wheeler Company encountered the following situations:

*a.*   Jenny Farrell, head of the receiving department, created a fictitious company named Quick Forms and used it to send invoices to Wheeler Company for business documents that Wheeler never ordered or received. Farrell prepared receiving reports that stated that the business documents had been received. Wheeler's controller compared the receiving reports to the invoices and paid each one.

*b.*   Wheeler Company lost one day's cash receipts. An employee took the receipts to the bank after the bank's closing hours to deposit them in the night depository slot. A creative thief had placed a sign on the slot saying it was out of order and all deposits should be placed in a metal canister placed next to the building. Wheeler's employee placed the deposit in the canister and left. Employees from two other companies did the same thing. Later that night, the thief returned and stole the deposits from the canister. (This is an actual case.)

*c.*   Wheeler Company does not prenumber the sales invoices used for over-the-counter sales. A cashier pocketed cash receipts and destroyed all copies of the related sales invoices.

**Required**

For each situation, describe any violations of good internal control procedures and identify the steps that you would take to prevent each situation.

LO1, LO3    **P7-2B.    Internal Control**

The Mountain Twister amusement ride has the following system of internal control over cash receipts. All persons pay the same price for a ride. A person taking the ride pays cash to the cashier and receives a prenumbered ticket. The tickets are issued in strict number sequence. The individual then walks to the ride site, hands the ticket to a ticket-taker (who controls the number of people getting on each ride), and passes through a turnstile. At the end of each day, the beginning ticket number is subtracted from the ending ticket number to determine the number of tickets sold. The cash is counted and compared with the number of tickets sold. The turnstile records how many people pass through it. At the end of each day, the beginning turnstile count is subtracted from the ending count to determine the number of riders that day. The number of riders is compared with the number of tickets sold.

**Required**

Which internal control feature would reveal each of the following irregularities?

*a.*   The ticket-taker lets her friends on the ride without tickets.

*b.*   The cashier gives his friends tickets without receiving cash from them.

*c.*   The cashier gives too much change.

*d.*   The ticket-taker returns the tickets she has collected to the cashier. The cashier then re-sells these tickets and splits the proceeds with the ticket-taker.

*e.*   A person sneaks into the ride line without paying the cashier.

**P7-3B.** **Internal Controls for Cash Received from Retail Sales** LO3

Midland Stores is a retailer of men's clothing. Most customers pay cash for their purchases. The procedures that Midland uses for handling cash are described below:

a.  Each department begins the day with whatever amount of cash remains in the cash register from the prior day. This is not a predetermined amount.
b.  All sales associates share one cash drawer.
c.  Each sales associate can handle all transactions, including returns and unusual transactions, without approval from a supervisor.
d.  At the end of each day, one of the sales associates takes the cash drawer and the cash register totals to a private area where no one can observe what is being done, counts the cash in the drawer, and prepares a written report of sales and cash received. The cash, the register tape, and a copy of the report are sent to the controller's department.
e.  The controller prepares the deposit slip and sends the deposit to the bank. The controller then prepares the journal entry to record the cash sales.
f.  The controller does not keep any copies of the written report or the deposit slip.
g.  The bank statement is sent to the controller, who prepares the bank reconciliation.

**Required**

For each of these procedures, indicate how Midland could improve it. (Refer to Exhibit 7-2 in the chapter to help you generate ideas.)

**P7-4B.** **Bank Reconciliation** LO3

On May 31, the Cash in Bank account of Wallace Company, a sole proprietorship, had a balance of $6,122.50. On that date, the bank statement indicated a balance of $7,933.50. A comparison of returned checks and bank advices revealed the following:

1.  Deposits in transit May 31 totaled $2,709.05.
2.  Outstanding checks May 31 totaled $3,088.25.
3.  The bank added to the account $27.80 of interest income earned by Wallace during May.
4.  The bank collected a $2,400 note receivable for Wallace and charged a $20 collection fee. Both items appear on the bank statement.
5.  Bank service charges in addition to the collection fee, not yet recorded, were $20.
6.  Included with the returned checks is a memo indicating that L. Ryder's check for $686 had been returned NSF. Ryder, a customer, had sent the check to pay an account of $700 less a 2% discount.
7.  Wallace Company incorrectly recorded the payment of an account payable as $690; the check was for $960.

**Required**

a.  Prepare a bank reconciliation for Wallace Company at May 31.
b.  Prepare the journal entry (or entries) necessary to bring the Cash in Bank account into agreement with the reconciled cash balance on the bank reconciliation.

**P7-5B.** **Bank Reconciliation** LO3

The bank reconciliation made by Sandler Company, a sole proprietorship, on March 31 showed a deposit in transit of $1,100 and two outstanding checks, No. 797 for $450 and No. 804 for $890. The reconciled cash balance on March 31 was $11,720.

The following bank statement is available for April 2010:

| **Bank Statement** | | | | | | |
|---|---|---|---|---|---|---|
| **TO Sandler Company** | | | | | | **April 30** |
| Fairbanks, AK | | | | | **FAIRBANKS NATIONAL BANK** | |
| **Date** | **Deposits** | **No.** | **Date** | **Charges** | **Date** | **Balance** |
| | | | | | Mar. 31 . . . . . . . . . . . | $11,960 |
| Apr. 1 . . . . . . . . . . . | $1,100 | 804 | Apr. 2 . . . . . . . . . . . | $ 890 | Apr. 1 . . . . . . . . . . . | 13,060 |
| 3 . . . . . . . . . . . | 1,680 | 807 | 3 . . . . . . . . . . . | 730 | 2 . . . . . . . . . . . | 12,170 |
| 7 . . . . . . . . . . . | 1,250 | 808 | 7 . . . . . . . . . . . | 1,140 | 3 . . . . . . . . . . . | 13,120 |
| 13 . . . . . . . . . . . | 1,020 | 809 | 7 . . . . . . . . . . . | 838 | 7 . . . . . . . . . . . | 12,392 |
| 18 . . . . . . . . . . . | 840 | 810 | 16 . . . . . . . . . . . | 1,040 | 13 . . . . . . . . . . . | 13,086 |
| 23 . . . . . . . . . . . | 790 | 811 | 13 . . . . . . . . . . . | 326 | 16 . . . . . . . . . . . | 12,046 |
| 27 . . . . . . . . . . . | 1,340 | 813 | 27 . . . . . . . . . . . | 540 | 18 . . . . . . . . . . . | 12,386 |
| 30 . . . . . . . . . . . | 1,160 | 814 | 23 . . . . . . . . . . . | 600 | 23 . . . . . . . . . . . | 12,576 |
| 30 . . . . . . . . . . . | 60IN | NSF | 18 . . . . . . . . . . . | 500 | 27 . . . . . . . . . . . | 13,376 |
| | | SC | 30 . . . . . . . . . . . | 40 | 30 . . . . . . . . . . . | 14,556 |

A list of deposits made and checks written during April is shown below:

| Deposits Made | | Checks Written | |
|---|---:|---|---:|
| Apr. 2 . . . . . . . . . . . . . . . . | $1,680 | No. 807 . . . . . . . . . . . . . . . . | $ 730 |
| 6 . . . . . . . . . . . . . . . . | 1,250 | 808 . . . . . . . . . . . . . . . . | 1,140 |
| 10 . . . . . . . . . . . . . . . . | 1,020 | 809 . . . . . . . . . . . . . . . . | 838 |
| 17 . . . . . . . . . . . . . . . . | 840 | 810 . . . . . . . . . . . . . . . . | 1,040 |
| 22 . . . . . . . . . . . . . . . . | 790 | 811 . . . . . . . . . . . . . . . . | 272 |
| 24 . . . . . . . . . . . . . . . . | 1,340 | 812 . . . . . . . . . . . . . . . . | 948 |
| 29 . . . . . . . . . . . . . . . . | 1,160 | 813 . . . . . . . . . . . . . . . . | 540 |
| 30 . . . . . . . . . . . . . . . . | 1,425 | 814 . . . . . . . . . . . . . . . . | 600 |
| | $9,505 | 815 . . . . . . . . . . . . . . . . | 372 |
| | | 816 . . . . . . . . . . . . . . . . | 875 |
| | | | $7,355 |

The Cash in Bank account balance on April 30 was $13,870. In reviewing checks returned by the bank, the accountant discovered that check No. 811, written for $326 for delivery expense, was recorded in the cash disbursements journal as $272. The NSF check for $500 was that of customer R. Koppa, deposited in April. Interest for April added to the account by the bank was $60.

### Required

*a.* Prepare a bank reconciliation for Sandler Company at April 30.

*b.* Prepare the necessary journal entries to bring the Cash in Bank account into agreement with the reconciled cash balance on the bank reconciliation.

**LO2   P7-6B.  Reporting Cash**

Jenkins Company has the following items at year-end:

| | |
|---|---:|
| Currency and coin in safe . . . . . . . . . . . . . . . . . . . . . . . . . . . . . . . . . . . . . . . . . . . . . . . . . . . . . . . . . . . . . . . . | $ 5,500 |
| Funds in savings account (requires $3,000 compensating balance) . . . . . . . . . . . . . . . . . . . . . . . . . | 15,250 |
| Funds in checking account. . . . . . . . . . . . . . . . . . . . . . . . . . . . . . . . . . . . . . . . . . . . . . . . . . . . . . . . . . . . . | 1,750 |
| Traveler's checks. . . . . . . . . . . . . . . . . . . . . . . . . . . . . . . . . . . . . . . . . . . . . . . . . . . . . . . . . . . . . . . . . . . . . . | 1,500 |
| Postdated check. . . . . . . . . . . . . . . . . . . . . . . . . . . . . . . . . . . . . . . . . . . . . . . . . . . . . . . . . . . . . . . . . . . . . . . | 2,250 |
| Not-sufficient-funds check. . . . . . . . . . . . . . . . . . . . . . . . . . . . . . . . . . . . . . . . . . . . . . . . . . . . . . . . . . . . | 450 |
| Money market fund . . . . . . . . . . . . . . . . . . . . . . . . . . . . . . . . . . . . . . . . . . . . . . . . . . . . . . . . . . . . . . . . . . . | 12,600 |

### Required

Identify the amount of the above items that should be reported as cash and cash equivalents on Jenkins Company's balance sheet.

**LO1   P7-7B.  Internal Control**

Jerry Finch has worked for Jones Hardware for many years. Jerry has been a model employee. He has not taken a vacation in over three years, always stating that work was too important. One of Jerry's primary jobs at the store is to open mail and list the checks received. He also collects cash from customers at the store's outdoor nursery area. There are times that things are so hectic that Jerry does not bother to use the register, simply making change from cash he carries with him. When things slow down at the store Jerry often offers to help Cindy post payments to the customer's accounts receivable ledger. Cindy is always happy to receive help since she is also quite busy and because Jerry is such a careful worker.

### Required

Identify any internal control principles that may be violated in Jones Hardware store.

**LO1, LO3   P7-8B.  Internal Control**

Listed below are (a) four potential errors or problems that could occur in the processing of cash transactions and (b) internal control principles. For each error or problem, identify an internal control principle that could reduce the chance of the error or problem occurring. You may also cite more than one principle if more than one applies, or write none if none of the principles will correct the error or problem.

1.  Three cashiers use one cash register and the cash in the drawer is often short of the recorded balance.

2. The same employee is responsible for opening the mail, listing any checks received, preparing the deposit receipt, and recording to the accounts receivable journal. Several customers have complained that their balances are incorrect.

3. In an effort to save printing costs, generic receipts without numbers are used for customer sales.

4. Because things have been hectic, no budgets were prepared this year. One department seems to be doing less volume in revenue, but cost of goods sold appear to be high relative to sales.

Internal control principles:

*a.* Establish clear lines of authority and responsibility.
*b.* Segregation of duties.
*c.* Hire competent personnel.
*d.* Use control numbers on all business documents.
*e.* Develop plans and budgets.
*f.* Maintain adequate accounting records.
*g.* Provide physical and electronic controls.
*h.* Conduct internal audits.

**P7-9B. Bank Reconciliation**

LO3

The Chicago Scooter Company's bank statement for the month of June indicated a balance of $3,500. The company's cash account in the general ledger showed a balance of $2,890 on June 30. Other relevant information includes the following:

1. Deposits in transit on June 30 total $2,600.

2. The bank statement shows a debit memorandum for a $20 check printing charge.

3. Check number 160 payable to Simon Company was recorded in the accounting records for $124 and cleared the bank for this same amount. A review of the records indicated that the Simon account now has an $18 credit balance and the check to them should have been $142.

4. Outstanding checks as of September 30 totaled $2,900.

5. Check No. 176 was correctly written and paid by the bank for $203. The check was recorded in the accounting records as a debit to accounts payable and a credit to cash for $245.

6. The bank returned a NSF check in the amount of $342.

7. The bank included a credit memorandum for $630 representing a collection of a customer's note. The principal portion was $600 and the interest portion was $30. The interest had not been accrued.

**Required**

*a.* Prepare the June bank reconciliation for the Chicago Scooter Company.
*b.* Prepare any necessary adjusting entries.

## SERIAL PROBLEM: KATE'S CARDS

(*Note:* **This is a continuation of the Serial Problem: Kate's Cards from Chapters 1 through 6.**)

**SP7.** On February 15, 2011, Kate Collins, owner of Kate's Cards, asks you to investigate the cash handling activities in her business. She believes that a new employee might be stealing funds. "I have no proof," she says, "but I'm fairly certain that the January 31, 2011, undeposited receipts amounted to more than $12,000, although the January 31 bank reconciliation prepared by the cashier (who works in the treasurer's department) shows only $7,238.40. Also, the January bank reconciliation doesn't show several checks that have been outstanding for a long time. The cashier told me that these checks needn't appear on the reconciliation because he had notified the bank to stop payment on them and he had made the necessary adjustment on the books. Does that sound reasonable to you?"

At your request, Kate shows you the following January 31, 2011, bank reconciliation prepared by the cashier:

ASSIGNMENTS

| KATE'S CARDS | | | | | |
|---|---|---|---|---|---|
| **Bank Reconciliation** | | | | | |
| **January 31, 2011** | | | | | |
| Ending balance from bank statement ... | | $ 4,843.69 | Balance from general ledger ..... | | $10,893.89 |
| Add: Deposits in transit ................ | | 7,238.40 | | | |
| | | $12,082.09 | | | |
| Less: | | | Less: | | |
| Outstanding checks: | | | Bank service charge ........... | $ 60.00 | |
| No. 2351 ......................... | $1,100.20 | | Unrecorded credit ............. | 1,200.00 | (1,260.00) |
| No. 2353 ......................... | 578.32 | | | | |
| No. 2354 ......................... | 969.68 | (2,448.20) | | | |
| Reconciled cash balance ............... | | $ 9,633.89 | Reconciled cash balance ......... | | $ 9,633.89 |

You discover that the $1,200 unrecorded bank credit represents a note collected by the bank on Kate's behalf; it appears in the deposits column of the January bank statement. Your investigation also reveals that the December 31, 2010, bank reconciliation showed three checks that had been outstanding longer than 10 months: No. 1432 for $600, No. 1458 for $466.90, and No. 1512 for $253.10. You also discover that these items were never added back into the Cash account in Kate's books. In confirming that the checks shown on the cashier's January 31 bank reconciliation were outstanding on that date, you discover that check No. 2353 was actually a payment of $1,658.32 and had been recorded on the books for that amount.

To confirm the amount of undeposited receipts at January 31, you request a bank statement for February 1–12 (called a cutoff bank statement). This indeed shows a January 1 deposit of $7,238.40.

**Required**

a.   Calculate the amount of funds stolen by the employee.

b.   Describe how the employee concealed the theft.

c.   What sort of journal entry (or entries) should be made when a business decides that checks outstanding for a long time should no longer be carried in the bank reconciliation?

d.   What suggestions would you make to Kate about cash control procedures?

## EXTENDING YOUR KNOWLEDGE

### REPORTING AND ANALYSIS

**COLUMBIA SPORTSWEAR COMPANY**

**EYK7-1.   Financial Reporting Problem: Columbia Sportswear Company**

The financial statements for the **Columbia Sportswear Company** can be found in Appendix A at the end of this book.

**Required**

Use the financial statements and the accompanying notes to the financial statements to answer the following questions about Columbia Sportswear:

a.   What title is used on Columbia's consolidated balance sheet for cash?

b.   According to the information given in Note 2, what is the makeup of the cash and cash equivalents account?

c.   According to information in Item 9A. Controls and Procedures, who is responsible for establishing and maintaining adequate internal control over financial reporting?

d.   Deloitte and Touche, the independent auditor of Columbia Sportswear, issued a report on their audit of Columbia's internal control. What did they conclude?

**COLUMBIA SPORTSWEAR COMPANY**

**THE TIMBERLAND COMPANY**

**EYK7-2.   Comparative Analysis Problem: Columbia Sportswear Company vs. The Timberland Company**

The financial statements for **Columbia Sportswear Company** can be found in Appendix A and **The Timberland Company**'s financial statements can be found in Appendix B at the end of this book.

**Required**

Use the information in the companies' financial statements to answer the following questions:

*a.* What is the balance in cash and cash equivalents as of December 31, 2008?

*b.* What percentage of each company's total assets is made up of cash and cash equivalents as of December 31, 2008?

*c.* How much did cash and cash equivalents change during 2008 for each firm?

*d.* For each company, how did the change in cash for 2008 compare to its cash provided by operating activities?

**EYK7-3.** **Business Decision Problem**

Qualitec Electronics Company is a distributor of microcomputers and related electronic equipment. The company has grown very rapidly. It is located in a large building near Chicago, Illinois. Jack Flanigan, the president of Qualitec, has hired you to perform an internal control review of the company. You conduct interviews of key employees, tour the operations, and observe various company functions. You discover the following:

1. Qualitec has not changed its ordering procedures since it was formed eight years ago. Anyone in the company can prepare a purchase order and send it to the vendor without getting any managerial approval. When the invoice arrives from the vendor, it is compared only to the purchase order before authorizing payment.

2. Qualitec does not have an organization chart. In fact, employees are encouraged to work on their own, without supervision. Flanigan believes that this approach increases creativity.

3. Business documents have been carefully designed by the controller. When the printer prints the documents, no control numbers are printed on them. Instead, employees using a form write the next sequential number on the form. The controller believes that this approach ensures that a proper sequencing of numbers will be maintained.

4. No budgets are prepared for the company.

5. All doors to the building remain unlocked from 7:00 a.m. to 11:00 p.m. Employees normally work from 7:30 a.m. to 5:00 p.m. A private security firm drives to the building to unlock it each morning and lock it each night. The security firm's employee leaves immediately after unlocking or locking. The company does not use time clocks or employee badges.

6. Flanigan believes that audits (either external or internal) are a waste of time. He has resisted the bank president's urging to hire a CPA firm to conduct an audit.

**Required**

Analyze the findings listed above. Then list all the internal control weaknesses that you can identify. For each weakness, describe one or more internal controls that Qualitec should install to overcome the weakness.

**EYK7-4.** **Financial Analysis Problem**

The **Public Company Accounting Oversight Board (PCAOB)** was created as part of the Sarbanes-Oxley legislation to provide oversight over U.S. accounting firms. The PCAOB's address is http://www.pcaobus.org

**Required**

Answer the following questions:

*a.* What is the mission of the PCAOB?

*b.* What is the title of the first auditing standard issued by the PCAOB?

*c.* According to the rules section of the site, what is required for a PCAOB rule to take effect?

## CRITICAL THINKING

**EYK7-5.** **Accounting Research Problem**

Refer to the consolidated balance sheets in the fiscal year 2010 annual report of **General Mills, Inc.** available on this book's Website.

GENERAL MILLS, INC.

**Required**

*a.* What was the amount of cash and cash equivalents as of May 30, 2010?

*b.* By what amount did cash and cash equivalents increase or decrease during the year?

*c.* What statement elsewhere in the annual report contains an explanation of the increase or decrease in the cash and cash equivalents amount? In that statement, what amount of cash was provided or used by (1) operating activities, (2) investment activities, and (3) financing activities?

d. What members of the company signed off as to the assessment of the company's internal control (see Reports of management and Independent Registered Public Accounting Firm)?

e. What firm conducted the audit of General Mills?

f. What opinion did the accounting firm express about General Mills' financial statements?

g. In addition to their audit of the financial statements, what else did the auditing firm audit?

**EYK7-6.** **Accounting Communication Activity**

You were recently hired as the head of a company's ethics division. As one of your first acts, you decide to prepare a letter to the company's Chairman of the Board explaining the importance of ethics within the company. What are some of the items that should be included in your letter?

**EYK7-7.** **Accounting Ethics Case**

Gina Pullen is the petty cash cashier for a large family-owned restaurant. She has been presented on numerous occasions with properly approved receipts for reimbursement from petty cash that she believes are personal expenses of one of the five owners of the restaurant. She reports to the controller of the company. The controller is also a family member and is the person who approves the receipts for payment out of petty cash.

**Required**

What are the accounting implications if Pullen is correct? What alternatives should she consider?

**EYK7-8.** **Corporate Social Responsibility Problem**

Corporate Social Responsibility and fraud prevention are often related. One way that the two are connected is in the creation of a culture of honesty and the ethical treatment of employees. This is often the result of the tone from the top, where the company leaders not only talk about these concepts, but also practice them.

**Required**

Discuss how a culture of honesty and the ethical treatment of employees can reduce the risk of fraud.

**EYK7-9.** **Forensic Accounting Problem**

Internal control follows the concept of reasonable assurance. Pete Simmons, the chief compliance officer of Salem Company, stated that he does not want simply reasonable assurance. He wants absolute assurance in all aspects that apply to the financial statements of the company. Specifically, Pete stated, "As long as I am working here, we will run a perfectly tight system that ensures absolutely no fraud in our financial statements." Betty Flint, the controller, disagreed with Pete and argued that anything more than reasonable assurance is both financially and practically impossible.

**Required**

Do you agree with Pete or Betty, and why?

**EYK7-10.** **Analyzing IFRS Financial Statements**

Tesco PLC is the world's third largest retailer and is headquartered in the United Kingdom. The complete annual report for **Tesco PLC** for year-ended February 28, 2009 is available on this book's Website.

**Required**

a. What was the amount of cash and cash equivalents as of 28 February, 2009?

b. By what amount did cash and cash equivalents increase or decrease during the year?

c. What statement elsewhere in the annual report contains an explanation of the increase or decrease in the cash and cash equivalents amount? In that statement, what amount of cash was provided or used by (1) operating activities, (2) investment activities, and (3) financing activities?

d. What firm conducted the audit of Tesco's financial statements?

e. What opinion did the accounting firm express about Tesco's financial statements?

f. In addition to their audit of the financial statements, what else did the auditing firm audit?

## ANSWERS TO SELF-STUDY QUESTIONS:

1. c, (p. 318)   2. c, (p. 320)   3. d, (p. 321)   4. a, (p. 322)   5. c, (p. 339)   6. b, (p. 325)
7. c, (p. 328)   8. d, (p. 332)   9. a, (p. 333)   10. c, (p. 331)

## Your Turn! Solutions

### Solution 7.1
1. This is a human resources control violation. The supervisor may be committing a fraud and covering up his acts. If the supervisor were forced to take a vacation, the employee filling in might observe some suspicious activity and uncover the fraud.
2. This is a physical control violation. The unattended inventory could be stolen through the open door.
3. This is a segregation of duties violation. The supervisor is in a position to order an improper purchase, receive the goods for his own purposes, record the goods as received by the company, and then have the company pay for the purchase.
4. This is a violation of the use of control numbers. An employee could defraud the company by writing up a meal purchase, receiving the cash from the customer, then destroying the order slip and keep the cash.

### Solution 7.2
1. Treasurer's department
2. Retail sales supervisor
3. Mailroom
4. Internal audit department
5. Controller's department

### Solution 7.3
1. Add to bank statement balance
2. Subtract from bank statement balance
3. Subtract from cash general ledger account
4. Add to cash general ledger account

### Solution 7.4
1. Internal audit
2. Financial statement audit
3. Operational audit
4. Financial statement audit
5. Operational audit

# Accounting for Receivables

| Past | Present | Future |
|------|---------|--------|
| In Chapter 7 we studied how companies can prevent errors and fraud with the use of internal controls. | In this chapter we turn our attention to the accounting for two important assets—accounts and notes receivable. | In Chapter 9 we will continue our study of a company's assets by looking at long-lived assets. |

## LEARNING OBJECTIVES

1 **Define** accounts receivable, explain losses from uncollectible accounts, and **describe** the allowance method of accounting for doubtful accounts. (p. 364)

2 **Describe** and **illustrate** the percentage of net sales method and the accounts receivable aging method for estimating a business's bad debts expense. (p. 368)

3 **Illustrate** the direct write-off method and **contrast** it with the allowance method for accounting for doubtful accounts. (p. 372)

4 **Discuss** the accounting treatment of credit card sales. (p. 373)

5 **Illustrate** a promissory note receivable, **discuss** the calculation of interest on notes receivable, and **present** journal entries to record notes receivable and interest. (p. 374)

6 **Define** accounts receivable turnover and average collection period and **explain** their use in the analysis and management of accounts and notes receivable. (p. 378)

# MGM Resorts International—
# Managing Credit for Bigger Profits

**MGM Resorts International** is among the largest gaming companies in the world. The company owns, operates, and has investments in 30 casino resorts, including Bellagio, MGM Grand Las Vegas, Mandalay Bay, Luxor, Excalibur, Monte Carlo, New York-New York, Circus Circus, and The Mirage. These establishments provide gaming, hotel accommodations, dining, and other entertainment for their clientele. Gaming, however, is the primary revenue-producing activity for these businesses.

Casino credit is an important marketing tool for gaming companies like MGM Resorts International. When used intelligently, it can result in significant increases in revenue since high-end casinos like Bellagio and The Mirage rely heavily on clientele that gamble on credit. Granting credit to gamblers also increases player loyalty because gamblers are inclined to play at casinos where they have a line of credit. Once credit is established, the gambler is allowed to write a marker and withdraw money to use

to gamble. The credit, however, is only granted to clientele who utilize it. While there is no requirement that a gambler lose in order to maintain a line of credit, the credit is lost if it is not used. In other words, a casino grants credit to its clientele with the expectation that the more a gambler uses the line of credit, the more likely the casino is to win.

While credit lines clearly provide a boost to a casino's revenue, it is critical that the casino carefully manage these receivables. MGM Resorts International, for example, maintains strict controls over the issuance of markers and "aggressively pursues collection from those customers who fail to repay their markers on a timely basis." GAAP requires MGM Resorts International to recognize the likelihood that a casino may be unable to collect all of its outstanding markers on its financial statements. At year-end 2008, despite aggressive collection efforts, MGM Resorts International reported nearly $100 million dollars in doubtful collections.

Credit losses are considered to be an operating expense of a business, and consequently, they are debited to an account called **Bad Debts Expense**. Normally, the Bad Debts Expense account is classified as a selling expense on the income statement, although some companies include it as part of their administrative expenses.

---

**ACCOUNTING IN PRACTICE** | **Credit Scoring Systems**

Most companies use a computerized credit scoring system to decide whether to extend credit to their customers. The credit scoring system is based on a set of formulas with multiple variables. Data from a customer's credit application and from credit reporting agencies are used by the system to calculate a credit score. The system then compares the score to predetermined limits and recommends whether or not credit be extended.

If credit is extended, the scoring system often recommends an upper limit on the amount of credit to be extended. Scoring systems focus on a customer's ability to generate net income and cash flow, the customer's current level of debt and required repayment schedule, and current assets. Many of the financial statement ratios discussed throughout this text are incorporated into credit scoring systems.

---

## ALLOWANCE METHOD

Credit losses are an unfortunate but predictable consequence of extending credit to a business's customers. At the time that a credit sale is made, the seller does not know whether the account receivable will be collected in full, in part, or not at all. Further, any loss from an uncollectible account may not be known for several months, or even a year or more, following the credit sale. To achieve a proper matching of sales revenues and expenses, however, a company's accountants must estimate the amount of the bad debts expense to report on the income statement. This estimate is reported in an end-of-period adjusting entry. The process of estimating and recording the bad debts expense for a business is often executed using the **allowance method**.

---

**PRINCIPLE ALERT** | **Matching Concept**

The *matching concept* states that expenses should be linked with, or matched with, the revenues that they help to generate. A company sells its goods and services on credit because this business practice attracts more customers and, therefore, more sales revenue than if the company only permitted cash transactions. One of the costs associated with extending credit to customers is the bad debts expense. The matching concept requires that this expense be reported in the same accounting period as the related sales revenue. To accomplish the appropriate matching of sales revenue and expenses, accountants must estimate the bad debts expense because the specific accounts that will be uncollectible may not be known until a later time period.

---

The allowance method receives its name because the end-of-period adjusting entry credits a contra-asset account called the *Allowance for Doubtful Accounts*. The allowance method not only matches credit losses with the related credit sales in the same time period in which the sale occurs, but it also reports accounts receivable at their estimated realizable value in the end-of-period balance sheet. To illustrate, assume that the Claremont Corporation estimates its bad debts expense for 2011 to be $4,000 and makes the following adjusting entry in its general journal:

| A | = | L | + | SE | | | | |
|---|---|---|---|---|---|---|---|---|
| −4,000 | | | | −4,000 Exp | | | | |

| **2011** | | | |
|---|---|---|---|
| Dec. 31 | Bad debts expense | 4,000 | |
| | Allowance for doubtful accounts | | 4,000 |
| | *To record the bad debts expense for the year.* | | |

Notice that the credit entry is made to the **Allowance for Doubtful Accounts** rather than directly against the Accounts Receivable account. The reason for this is because when a firm records its estimate of the amount of its uncollectible accounts, it does not know precisely which of its customer accounts will be uncollectible.

The Allowance for Doubtful Accounts is a contra-asset account with a normal credit balance. To report the expected collectible amount of accounts receivable on the balance sheet, the Allowance for Doubtful Accounts is subtracted from the Accounts Receivable account. Assuming that the Claremont Corporation had $100,000 of accounts receivable (and a zero balance in the Allowance for Doubtful Accounts prior to the December 31, 2011, adjusting entry), the year-end balance sheet presentation would appear as follows:

**A.K.A.** The Allowance for Doubtful Accounts is also often referred to as the Allowance for Uncollectible Accounts.

| Current Assets | | |
|---|---|---|
| Cash | | $ 52,000 |
| Accounts receivable | $100,000 | |
| Less: Allowance for doubtful accounts | 4,000 | 96,000 |
| Inventory | | 125,000 |
| Other current assets | | 31,000 |
| Total Current Assets | | $304,000 |

**PRINCIPLE ALERT** **Going Concern Concept**

Accounts receivable are reported on the balance sheet at the amount that a company expects to collect in the future from its credit customers. This presentation assumes that the company will be in existence long enough to collect its accounts receivable, and therefore, it is an example of the *going concern concept*. As a principle of accounting, the going concern concept assumes that a business entity will continue to operate indefinitely in the future.

### Writing Off Specific Accounts Receivable under the Allowance Method

A company's credit department manager is usually the employee with the authority to determine when an account receivable is uncollectible, and hence, when a specific account receivable should be written off and removed from a company's balance sheet. Assume, for example, that the credit manager of the Claremont Corporation authorizes a $300 write off of the Monroe Company's account receivable. When the accounting department is notified of the credit department manager's decision, it will make the following journal entry:

| 2012 | | | |
|---|---|---|---|
| Jan. 5 | Allowance for doubtful accounts | 300 | |
| | Accounts receivable—Monroe Company | | 300 |
| | *To write off the Monroe Company's account receivable.* | | |

A = L + SE
+300
−300

The journal entry to write off an account receivable does not affect a company's net income or total assets. By means of the year-end adjusting entry, the bad debts expense is reported in the period when the related sales revenue is recorded. Because the Allowance for Doubtful Accounts is deducted from the Accounts Receivable account on the balance sheet, the *net* realizable value of accounts receivable is unchanged by the account write off. After the Monroe Company's account receivable has been written off, the Accounts Receivable and the Allowance for Doubtful Accounts T-accounts appear as follows:

| Accounts Receivable | | | | Allowance for Doubtful Accounts | | | |
|---|---|---|---|---|---|---|---|
| Beg. | 100,000 | 300 | Jan. 5 | Jan. 5 | 300 | 4,000 | Beg. |
| Bal. | 99,700 | | | | | 3,700 | Bal. |

As can be seen in the above T-accounts, the net realizable value of Claremont's accounts receivable as of January 1, 2012, is $96,000 ($100,000 less $4,000 allowance for doubtful accounts). Following the January 5, 2012, account write off, the net realizable value of the Claremont Corporation's accounts receivable remains $96,000 ($99,700 less $3,700 allowance for doubtful accounts) since both the Accounts Receivable account and the Allowance for Doubtful Accounts are reduced by the same amount ($300).

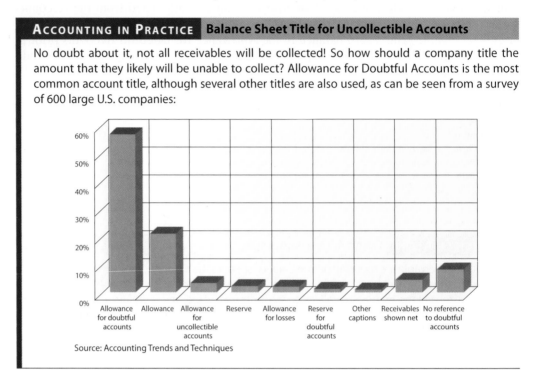

**ACCOUNTING IN PRACTICE** | **Balance Sheet Title for Uncollectible Accounts**

No doubt about it, not all receivables will be collected! So how should a company title the amount that they likely will be unable to collect? Allowance for Doubtful Accounts is the most common account title, although several other titles are also used, as can be seen from a survey of 600 large U.S. companies:

Source: Accounting Trends and Techniques

# ESTIMATING CREDIT LOSSES

When the allowance method is used, estimates of a company's expected credit losses are generally based on past business experience, with additional consideration given to forecasts of future sales activity, economic conditions, and any planned changes to a company's credit-granting policy. The most commonly used estimates of expected credit losses are related either to a company's credit sales for the period, or to the amount of accounts receivable outstanding at the end of a fiscal period.

## PERCENTAGE OF NET SALES METHOD

LEARNING OBJECTIVE 2

**Describe** and **illustrate** the percentage of net sales method and the accounts receivable aging method for estimating a business's bad debts expense.

Through years of business experience, some companies have learned to estimate their expected credit losses as a percentage of their credit sales for a given period. Under this approach, the amount of the end-of-period adjusting entry for a business's expected bad debts expense is determined by multiplying the company's total credit sales for the period by a historical percentage that reflects past credit losses. For example, suppose that credit sales for 2011 for the Claremont Corporation are $500,000 and that past experience indicates that the company is likely to sustain a two percent loss on its credit sales. The adjusting entry for Claremont's expected credit losses for 2011 (2 percent × $500,000) would be recorded as follows in the general journal:

| A | = | L | + | SE |
|---|---|---|---|---|
| −10,000 | | | | −10,000 |
| | | | | Exp |

| **2011** | | | |
|---|---|---|---|
| Dec. 31 | Bad debts expense | 10,000 | |
| |     Allowance for doubtful accounts | | 10,000 |
| | *To record the bad debts expense for the year.* | | |

Because the periodic estimate for doubtful accounts under this procedure is related to credit sales, a firm should review its allowance account regularly to ensure that the account maintains a reasonable balance. If the allowance account balance is too large or too small, the percentage used to estimate the periodic credit losses should be revised accordingly.

A company that uses the **percentage of net sales method** usually applies the estimated uncollectible percentage only to its credit sales, excluding cash sales, since only credit sales are subject to credit losses. Further, any sales discounts and sales returns and allowances should be deducted from total credit sales before applying the historical uncollectible percentage.

---

**Your Turn!** 8.1

Taylor Company estimates three percent of its $600,000 credit sales will prove uncollectible. What journal entry will Taylor Company use to record this estimate?

**The solution is on page 403.**

---

## ACCOUNTS RECEIVABLE AGING METHOD

A second approach to estimating a company's bad debts expense is to determine the appropriate balance for the Allowance for Doubtful Accounts account at year-end, and then determine the appropriate estimate of the bad debts expense. The year-end balance in the Allowance for Doubtful Accounts represents a firm's estimate of the year-end accounts receivable that will prove uncollectible. By adding any existing debit balance or subtracting any existing credit balance in the allowance account to the year-end projected Allowance for Doubtful Accounts balance, it is possible to indirectly determine the appropriate current period estimate of the company's bad debts expense. This approach is called the **accounts receivable aging method**.

When using the accounts receivable aging method, a company determines the amount needed in the allowance account by analyzing the age structure of its outstanding accounts receivable balances. An aging schedule similar to the one in Exhibit 8-1 would be used. An **aging schedule** is simply an analysis that reveals how much time has elapsed since a credit sale originally occurred, and consequently, how long a customer's account receivable has remained unpaid. Assume, for example, that the firm whose aging schedule appears in Exhibit 8-1 sells its goods on credit with a credit period of 30 days. The exhibit reveals that the Alton account is current, which means that the $320 billing was made within the last 30 days; however, the Bailey account is 0–30 days *past due,* which means that the account receivable is from 31 to 60 days old. The aging schedule also reveals that the Wall balance consists of a $50 billing made from 91 to 150 days ago and a $100 billing made from 151 days to seven months ago, and so on.

**EXHIBIT 8-1** Aging Schedule of Customer Balances, December 31. 2011

| | | | Past Due | | | | |
|---|---|---|---|---|---|---|---|
| Customer | Account Balance | Current | 0–30 Days | 31–60 Days | 61–120 Days | 121 Days –6 Mos. | Over 6 Mos. |
| Alton, J. | 320 | $ 320 | | | | | |
| Bailey, C. | 400 | | $ 400 | | | | |
| ... | ... | ... | ... | ... | ... | ... | ... |
| Wall, M. | 150 | | | | | 50 | 100 |
| Zorn, W | 210 | | | 210 | | | |
| | $50,000 | $42,000 | $4,000 | $2,000 | $1,000 | $800 | $200 |

Companies that analyze their uncollectible accounts experience using aged account balances develop probability-of-collection percentages to correspond with each age category. The probability of collection is subtracted from 100 percent to arrive at the probability of noncollection. At the end of each period, the probability-of-noncollection percentages are applied to the totals of each age category to determine the appropriate allowance account balance for a given category. For our example, these percentages are shown in the table below. Applying the percentages to the totals in our aging schedule, we can calculate the required balance for the Allowance for Doubtful Accounts—that is, $1,560:

| | Amount | Probability of Noncollection | Allowance Required |
|---|---|---|---|
| Current........................................................... | $42,000 | 2 | $ 840 |
| 0–30 days past due............................................. | 4,000 | 3 | 120 |
| 31–60 days past due............................................ | 2,000 | 5 | 100 |
| 61–120 days past due........................................... | 1,000 | 20 | 200 |
| 121-180 days past due.......................................... | 800 | 25 | 200 |
| Over 180 days past due......................................... | 200 | 50 | 100 |
| Total allowance required ......................................... | | | $1,560 |

Since the aging method is just an estimation process, estimation errors are likely to occur, causing the allowance account to sometimes be over or underestimated. If, for example, the Allowance for Doubtful Accounts has an existing $400 credit balance (implying an overestimation error in the prior period), the year-end adjusting entry is:

| A | = | L | + | SE |
|---|---|---|---|---|
| −1,160 | | | | −1,160 |
| | | | | Exp |

| 2011 | | | |
|---|---|---|---|
| Dec. 31 | Bad debts expense | 1,160 | |
| | Allowance for doubtful accounts | | 1,160 |
| | *To record the bad debts expense for the period.* | | |

This entry brings the credit balance in the Allowance for Doubtful Accounts account to the required amount—$1,560, as shown below:

**Allowance for Doubtful Accounts**

| | 400 | Beg. |
|---|---|---|
| | 1,160 | Dec. 31 |
| | 1,560 | Bal. |

It is also possible to have a debit balance in the allowance account before the year-end adjustment, implying an underestimation error in the prior period. This would occur whenever the write-off of specific accounts receivable during the year exceeded the credit balance in the account as of the beginning of the year. Assume, for example, that the Allowance for Doubtful Accounts had a $350 debit balance prior to the recording of the December 31, 2011, adjusting entry, and that the aging schedule showed that the allowance account should have a $1,560 credit balance. The year-end adjusting entry would then be as follows:

| A | = | L | + | SE |
|---|---|---|---|---|
| −1,910 | | | | −1,910 |
| | | | | Exp |

| 2011 | | | |
|---|---|---|---|
| Dec. 31 | Bad debts expense | 1,910 | |
| | Allowance for doubtful accounts | | 1,910 |
| | *To record the bad debts expense for the period.* | | |

The following Allowance for Doubtful Accounts T-account shows that this entry creates the desired year-end credit balance in the allowance account of $1,560:

**Allowance for Doubtful Accounts**

| | | | |
|---|---|---|---|
| Beg. | 350 | 1,910 | Dec. 31 |
| | | 1,560 | Bal. |

---

### THINKING GLOBALLY

Just when an account receivable is judged to be uncollectible is very much a cultural issue. In some Central and South American countries, buying goods and services on credit is almost unheard of! In these countries, it is considered in bad taste to owe someone money, and consequently, to preserve a company's good reputation and standing in the business community, companies pay cash for their purchases and avoid buying goods and services on credit. Therefore, in these countries it is extremely rare to see accounts receivable on the financial statements of businesses. In the U.S., on the other hand, buying goods and services on credit is considered to be a normal business activity. In fact, a business manager would be chastised for failing to take advantage of any offered trade credit by paying cash for purchased goods or services. In the United States, most large businesses consider an account receivable to be uncollectible when it becomes 120 days old. Buying goods and services on credit in China is, likewise, quite common; however, buyers often take several years to pay for purchased goods, and consequently, accounts receivable are not considered to be uncollectible until 2 to 3 years have elapsed since the original credit sales transaction.

---

**Recoveries of Accounts Written Off under the Allowance Method**  Occasionally, an account written off against the allowance for doubtful accounts as uncollectible will later prove to be wholly or partially collectible. In such situations, a firm should first reinstate the customer's account receivable for the amount recovered before recording the collection of cash. Then the cash payment can be recorded in the customer's account. The journal entry made for the original account write off is reversed to the extent of the recovery amount and the receipt of cash is recorded in the usual manner. For example, assume that the Claremont Corporation is using the allowance method and wrote off the Monroe Company's $300 account on January 5, 2012, but subsequently received a $200 payment on April 20, 2012. The following journal entries (including write-off) illustrate the recovery procedure:

**To write off the account**

| 2012 | | | | |
|---|---|---|---|---|
| Jan. 5 | Allowance for doubtful accounts | 300 | | |
| | Accounts receivable—Monroe Company | | 300 | |
| | *To write off the Monroe Company's account.* | | | |

| A | = | L | + | SE |
|---|---|---|---|---|
| +300 | | | | |
| −300 | | | | |

**To reinstate the account**

| Apr. 20 | Accounts receivable—Monroe Company | 200 | | |
|---|---|---|---|---|
| | Allowance for doubtful accounts | | 200 | |
| | *To reinstate the Monroe Company's account to the extent of the recovery.* | | | |

| A | = | L | + | SE |
|---|---|---|---|---|
| +200 | | | | |
| −200 | | | | |

**To record receipt of cash**

| Apr. 20 | Cash | 200 | | |
|---|---|---|---|---|
| | Accounts receivable—Monroe Company | | 200 | |
| | *To record collection of cash on account.* | | | |

| A | = | L | + | SE |
|---|---|---|---|---|
| +200 | | | | |
| −200 | | | | |

These last two journal entries are prepared the same way even if the recovery occurs more than a year following the period in which the account was originally written off.

**Your Turn!** **8.2**

Phisher, Inc., analyzed its accounts receivable at the end of its first year of operations, and arrived at the aged balances listed below, along with the percentage that is estimated to be uncollectible:

| Age Group | Balance | Estimated Loss Percentage |
|---|---|---|
| 0–30 days past due...................................................... | $100,000 | 1 |
| 31–60 days past due...................................................... | 15,000 | 3 |
| 61–120 days past due..................................................... | 10,000 | 5 |
| Over 120 days past due................................................... | 20,000 | 10 |
| | $145,000 | |

The company handles credit losses with the allowance method.

*a.* Prepare the adjusting entry for estimated credit losses on December 31, 2011.
*b.* Prepare the journal entry to write off Phorest Company's account on May 12, 2012, in the amount of $480.

**The solution is on page 404.**

## DIRECT WRITE-OFF METHOD

LEARNING OBJECTIVE 3

**Illustrate** the direct write-off method and **contrast** it with the allowance method for accounting for doubtful accounts.

The direct write-off method of accounting for credit losses is an alternative to the allowance method. Under the **direct write-off method**, doubtful accounts are charged to the bad debts expense on the income statement in the period in which the accounts are determined to be uncollectible. Under this approach, there is no attempt to estimate the bad debts expense, nor is there any attempt to match this expense with sales revenues in the period in which the credit sales transaction originally occurred. As a consequence, U.S. GAAP does not permit the use of the direct write-off method unless the amount of the credit losses is immaterial. The reason for this is because the direct write-off method does not properly match credit losses with credit sales in the appropriate time period, violating the matching concept.

For example, an account receivable may not be determined to be uncollectible, and therefore written off, until several periods after the actual credit sales revenue is recorded. By way of contrast, the allowance method, through the use of an estimate of the bad debt expense, properly matches this expense with the associated sales revenue in the same period. The use of the direct write-off method also causes a consistent overstatement of accounts receivable on the balance sheet. Although not generally accepted for accounting purposes for most businesses, the direct write-off method is used by all companies for U.S. federal income tax purposes.

The journal entries made when the direct write-off method is used are illustrated below using data from the Claremont Corporation illustration:

**To write off the account**

| | | | | |
|---|---|---|---|---|
| A = L + SE | **2012** | | | |
| −300 −300 Exp | Jan. 5 | Bad debts expense | 300 | |
| | |     Accounts receivable—Monroe Company | | 300 |
| | | *To write off the Monroe Company's account.* | | |

**To reinstate the account**

| | | | | |
|---|---|---|---|---|
| A = L + SE | Apr. 20 | Accounts receivable—Monroe Company | 200 | |
| +200 +200 Exp | |     Bad debts expense | | 200 |
| | | *To reinstate the Monroe Company's account to the extent of the recovery.* | | |

**To record receipt of cash**

| | | | | |
|---|---|---|---|---|
| Apr. 20 | Cash | | 200 | |
| | Accounts receivable—Monroe Company | | | 200 |
| | *To record collection of cash on account.* | | | |

| A | = | L | + | SE |
|---|---|---|---|---|
| +200 | | | | |
| −200 | | | | |

If an account receivable written off in a prior year is reinstated during the current year and the Bad Debts Expense account has no existing balance from other write-offs (and no more write-offs are expected), then the account credited in the reinstatement entry is the Doubtful Accounts Recovery, a revenue account.

---

### FORENSIC ACCOUNTING | Lapping

 One type of fraud that forensic accountants are trained to detect is "lapping." Lapping is not actually a fraud, but rather is a technique that a fraudster uses to cover up a fraud, typically involving the theft of funds. Under lapping, an employee who has access to incoming payments from the collection of accounts receivables will steal some of the cash received from credit customers. The employee then applies another customer's payment to the outstanding balance from the individual's account whose payment was stolen, in order to cover up the theft. The process is repeated in an effort to cover up the original misappropriation. In other words, after the initial theft, the fraudster must continually "rob Peter to pay Paul." One audit procedure that may detect a lapping scheme involves the confirmation of accounts receivable. As part of the year-end independent audit, or as part of a regular internal audit, a company's accountant will send out confirmation letters to a sample of customers from the list of outstanding accounts receivable and pay particular attention to replies from customers disputing the timing of their payments.

---

### Your Turn! 8.3

Harley Company has determined an account receivable in the amount of $750 from Rhea Inc. will be uncollectible and has decided to write the account off. Harley Company uses the direct write-off method because write-offs are considered immaterial. Provide the journal entry to write off the Rhea account.

The solution is on page 404.

---

| Concept | ➝ | Method | ➝ | Assessment | |
|---|---|---|---|---|---|
| Are the accounts receivable being collected in a timely manner? | | List of accounts receivable along with how long they have been outstanding.<br><br>Prepare an aging schedule. | | Accounts in the older categories require additional collection attention. | TAKEAWAY 8.1 |

---

## CREDIT CARD SALES

Many businesses, especially retailers, allow their customers to use credit cards for their purchase transactions. Popular credit cards include VISA, MasterCard, Discover, and American Express. When a customer uses a credit card to make a purchase, the seller collects cash from the credit card company, and the customer pays cash to the credit card company when billed at a later date. To facilitate this process, the seller prepares a sales slip using the credit card. The seller either imprints the card number on a slip using the card or uses an electronic device such as a cash register with a card reader to read the card number from the magnetic strip on the back of the credit card, and then prints a sales slip

**LEARNING OBJECTIVE 4**

**Discuss** the accounting treatment of credit card sales.

with the card number on it. The second approach also allows for the electronic accumulation and transmission of credit card sales data. In either case, the customer is usually asked to sign the sales slip to authenticate the transaction.

The issuer of a credit card, frequently a financial institution like **Chase Bank** or **Citibank**, will charge the seller a fee each time a card is used. The **credit card fee** usually ranges from one percent to five percent of the amount of the credit card purchase. Businesses are willing to incur this fee because credit cards provide considerable benefits to a seller. For example, the seller does not have to evaluate the creditworthiness of the customer using a credit card, and the business avoids any risk of noncollection of the account since this risk remains with the credit-card issuer. Finally, the seller typically receives the cash from the credit card issuer faster than if the customer were granted trade credit by the seller.

Depending upon the type of credit card, there are two ways that a seller may collect from the credit card issuer: (1) immediately upon deposit of the credit card sales slip or (2) on a delayed basis after the credit card slips have been processed by the credit card issuer. For cards issued by a financial institution, cash is received immediately upon deposit of the sales slip at the financial institution. The journal entry to record a $1,000 credit card sale of this type on March 15, with a three percent credit card fee, is as follows:

| A | = | L | + | SE |
|---|---|---|---|---|
| +970 | | | | −30 Exp |
| | | | | +1,000 |
| | | | | Rev |

| Mar. 15 | Cash | 970 | |
| | Credit card fee expense | 30 | |
| |     Sales revenue | | 1,000 |
| | *To record credit card sales and collection, less a three percent fee.* | | |

If, instead, sales slips are sent to a credit card company for subsequent cash settlement, the journal entries to record the $1,000 credit card sale with subsequent collection on March 23 are as follows:

| A | = | L | + | SE |
|---|---|---|---|---|
| +970 | | | | −30 Exp |
| | | | | +1,000 |
| | | | | Rev |

| Mar. 15 | Accounts receivable—Credit Card Company | 970 | |
| | Credit card fee expense | 30 | |
| |     Sales revenue | | 1,000 |
| | *To record credit card sales.* | | |

| A | = | L | + | SE |
|---|---|---|---|---|
| +970 | | | | |
| −970 | | | | |

| 23 | Cash | 970 | |
| |     Accounts receivable—Credit Card Company | | 970 |
| | *To record collection from credit card company.* | | |

---

## Your Turn!                                                        8.4

Nafooz Company pays a two percent credit card fee on all credit sales, and receives a cash deposit immediately following each credit card transaction. If credit sales for the company total $50,000, what journal entry should be recorded to recognize the receipt of cash and the credit card fee expense?

**The solution is on page 404.**

---

# NOTES RECEIVABLE

**LEARNING OBJECTIVE 5**

**Illustrate** a promissory note receivable, **discuss** the calculation of interest on notes receivable, and **present** journal entries to record notes receivable and interest.

Promissory notes receivable are often used in sale transactions when the credit period is longer than the 30 to 60 day credit period that is typical for accounts receivable. Promissory notes are also used frequently in sales involving equipment and property because the dollar amount of these transactions can be quite large. Occasionally, a note will be substituted for an account receivable when an extension of the usual credit period is granted. Also, promissory notes are normally prepared when financial institutions make a loan to a business or an individual.

A **promissory note** is a written promise to pay a certain sum of money on demand or at a fixed (or determinable) future date. The note is signed by the **maker** and made payable to the order of either a specific **payee** or to the **bearer**. The interest rate specified on the note is typically an annual rate. Exhibit 8.2 illustrates a promissory note.

**EXHIBIT 8-2 A Promissory Note**

| | | |
|---|---|---|
| $2,000.00 | Los Angeles, CA | May 3, 2011 |

Sixty days                                        after date                              I promise to pay to

the order of                              Susan Robinson

Two thousand and no/100 · · · · · · · · · · · · · · · · · · · · · · · · · · · · · · · · · · · · · · · · · · · · · · · · · · dollars

for value received with interest at                    9%

payable at                          First Bank of Los Angeles, CA

*James Stone* · ·

A note from a debtor is called a **note receivable** by the noteholder. A note is usually regarded as a stronger claim against a debtor than an account receivable because the terms of payment are specified in writing.

## INTEREST ON NOTES RECEIVABLE

Interest is a charge for the use of money over time. Interest incurred on a promissory note receivable is interest income to the noteholder or payee of the note and interest expense to the maker of the note. Businesses are required to distinguish between operating and non-operating items in their income statements; consequently, they place any interest expense or interest income on outstanding notes under the other income and expense heading in the income statement so that financial statement users will readily identify interest income or expense as being nonoperating in nature. Interest expense is a financing expense, not an operating expense, and interest income is financing income, not operating income.

Interest on a short-term promissory note is paid at the maturity date of the note. The formula for determining the amount of interest expense to the maker and interest income to the noteholder is as follows:

$$\textbf{Interest = Principal} \times \textbf{Interest rate} \times \textbf{Interest time}$$

The principal is the face amount of a note; and, the interest rate is the annual rate of interest specified in the note agreement. Interest time is the fraction of a year that a note receivable is outstanding.

When a note is written for a certain number of months, interest time is expressed in twelfths of a year. For example, interest on a six-month note for $2,000 with a nine percent annual interest rate is calculated as:

$$\textbf{Interest} = \$2,000 \times 0.09 \times 6/12 = \$90$$

When a note's duration, or time to maturity, is given in days, interest time is expressed as a fraction of a year; the numerator is the number of days that the note receivable will be outstanding and the denominator is 360 days. (Some lenders use 360 days, while others use 365 days; we use 360 days in our examples, exercises, and problems.) For example, interest on a 60 day note for $2,000 with a nine percent annual interest rate is:

$$\textbf{Interest} = \$2,000 \times 0.09 \times 60/360 = \$30$$

### Determining Maturity Date

When a note's duration is expressed in days, it is customary to count the exact number of days in each calendar month to determine the note's **maturity date**. For example, a 90 day note dated July 21 has an October 19 maturity date, which is determined as follows:

| | |
|---|---|
| 10 | days in July (remainder of month—31 days minus 21 days) |
| 31 | days in August |
| 30 | days in September |
| 19 | days in October (number of days required to total 90) |
| 90 | |

If the duration of a note is expressed in months, the maturity date is calculated simply by counting the number of months from the date of issue. For example, a two-month note dated January 31 would mature on March 31, a three-month note of the same date would mature on April 30 (the last day of the month), and a four-month note would mature on May 31.

### Recording Notes Receivable and Interest

When a note is exchanged to settle an account receivable, a journal entry is made to reflect the note receivable and to reduce the balance of the related account receivable. For example, suppose that Jordon Company sold $12,000 of merchandise on account to Bowman Company. On October 1, after the regular credit period had elapsed, the Bowman Company gave the Jordon Company a 60 day, nine percent note receivable for $12,000. Jordon Company makes the following journal entry to record receiving the note:

| A = L + SE |
|---|
| +12,000 |
| −12,000 |

| | | | |
|---|---|---|---|
| Oct. 1 | Notes receivable—Bowman Company | 12,000 | |
| |     Accounts receivable—Bowman Company | | 12,000 |
| | *Received 60 day, nine percent note in payment of account.* | | |

If the Bowman Company pays its note receivable on the November 30 maturity date, the Jordon Company makes the following journal entry:

| A = L + SE |
|---|
| +12,180    +180 Rev |
| −12,000 |

| | | | |
|---|---|---|---|
| Nov. 30 | Cash | 12,180 | |
| |     Interest income | | 180 |
| |     Notes receivable—Bowman Company | | 12,000 |
| | *Collected Bowman Company note.* | | |
| | *($12,000 × 0.09 × 60/360 = $180).* | | |

### Recording Dishonored Notes

In the prior example, interest for 60 days at nine percent is recorded on the maturity date of the note even if the maker of the note (Bowman Company) defaults on or dishonors the note. When a note is dishonored at maturity, the amount of the combined principal plus interest is converted to an account receivable. This procedure leaves only the current, unmatured notes in the noteholder's Notes Receivable account. If the Bowman Company, for example, failed to pay its note on November 30 as expected, the Jordon Company would make the following journal entry:

| A = L + SE |
|---|
| +12,180    +180 Rev |
| −12,000 |

| | | | |
|---|---|---|---|
| Nov. 30 | Accounts receivable—Bowman Company | 12,180 | |
| |     Interest income | | 180 |
| |     Notes receivable—Bowman Company | | 12,000 |
| | *To record the dishonoring of a note by Bowman Company.* | | |

### ADJUSTING ENTRY FOR INTEREST

When the term of a promissory note extends beyond the end of an accounting period, a year-end adjusting entry is necessary to reflect the interest earned. To illustrate, assume that Jordon Company has a note receivable outstanding at December 31, 2011. The note receivable from the Garcia Company is dated December 21, 2011, has a principal amount of $6,000, an interest rate of 12 percent, and a maturity date of February 19, 2012. The adjusting entry that Jordon Company makes at December 31, 2011, to record the earned, but uncollected, interest income is as follows:

| Dec. 31 | Interest receivable | 20 | |
|---|---|---|---|
| | Interest income | | 20 |
| | *To accrue interest income on the note from Garcia Company* | | |
| | *($6,000 × 0.12 × 10/360 = $20).* | | |

| A | = | L | + | SE |
|---|---|---|---|---|
| +20 | | | | +20 Rev |

When the note is subsequently paid on February 19, 2012, Jordon Company makes the following journal entry:

| Feb. 19 | Cash | 6,120 | |
|---|---|---|---|
| | Interest income | | 100 |
| | Interest receivable | | 20 |
| | Notes receivable—Garcia Company | | 6,000 |
| | *Received payment of principal and interest from Garcia Company* | | |
| | *($6,000 × 0.12 × 50/360 = $100).* | | |

| A | = | L | + | SE |
|---|---|---|---|---|
| +6,120 | | | | +100 Rev |
| −20 | | | | |
| −6,000 | | | | |

## REPORTING NOTES RECEIVABLE ON THE BALANCE SHEET

Short-Term Notes Receivable are a current asset on the balance sheet. Since these notes can normally be readily converted into cash, they are often placed below Accounts Receivable in the current asset section. As with accounts receivable, notes receivable are reported separately from other notes receivable from officers and employees and notes representing advances to affiliated companies. If the notes are not short term, they should be classified as noncurrent assets. Interest Receivable on a note receivable is also a current asset.

Sometimes companies with a large volume of notes receivable must provide for possible losses on the outstanding notes. Frequently, the Allowance for Doubtful Accounts also covers potential credit losses on notes as well. In such cases, the Allowance for

Doubtful Accounts account is deducted from the aggregate total of Accounts Receivable and Notes Receivable on the balance sheet. Estimating the potential credit losses on outstanding notes receivable follows the same procedures as for accounts receivable.

---

**Your Turn!**         **8.5**

Ruby Company received a four month, five percent note receivable for $40,000 on October 1, 2011. How much interest income should be accrued on December 31, 2011?

**The solution is on page 404.**

---

# ANALYZING AND MANAGING RECEIVABLES

LEARNING OBJECTIVE 6

**Define** *accounts receivable turnover* and *average collection period* and **explain** their use in the analysis and management of accounts and notes receivable.

Most companies transact the majority of their sales on credit, and doing so creates accounts receivable. Management and financial analysts closely monitor a company's accounts receivable using a variety of financial measures, including the accounts receivable turnover ratio and the average collection period. **Accounts receivable turnover** indicates how many times a year a firm collects its average accounts receivable, and thus, measures how fast accounts receivable are being converted into cash. Accounts receivable turnover is calculated as follows:

$$\text{Accounts receivable turnover} = \frac{\text{Net sales}}{\text{Average accounts receivable}}$$

The numerator in this ratio is net sales. Ideally, the numerator should be net credit sales, but financial information available to financial statement users does not usually divide net sales into credit sales and cash sales. For many businesses like the **Johnson & Johnson Company**, the maker of Band-Aids and baby shampoo, over 99 percent of the company's sales are credit sales; and thus, it is common to assume that a company's net sales is a good proxy for its credit sales. Average accounts receivable (net of the allowance for doubtful accounts) is calculated by summing the beginning and ending accounts receivable (net) balances and dividing the sum by two.

To illustrate these financial indicators, consider the financial results for the Claremont Corporation.

| | 2011 | 2010 |
|---|---|---|
| Net sales . . . . . . . . . . . . . . . . . . . . . . . . . . . . . . . . . . . . . . . . . . . . . . . . . . . . . . . | $40,831 | $33,548 |
| Beginning accounts receivable (net). . . . . . . . . . . . . . . . . . . . . . . . . . . . . . . . . . . | 1,848 | 1,948 |
| Ending accounts receivable (net). . . . . . . . . . . . . . . . . . . . . . . . . . . . . . . . . . . . . . | 1,799 | 1,848 |

Claremont's accounts receivable turnover for 2011 is 22.39, or $40,831/[$1,848 + $1,799)/2], and for 2010 is 17.68, or $33,548/[($1,948 + $1,848)/2]. In general, the higher the accounts receivable turnover ratio, the faster a company is converting its receivables into cash. The increase in accounts receivable turnover from 2010 to 2011 is a positive sign regarding how well the Claremont Corporation is managing its accounts receivable.

An extension of the accounts receivable turnover ratio is the **average collection period**, calculated as follows:

$$\text{Average collection period} = \frac{365}{\text{Accounts receivable turnover}}$$

This ratio indicates how many days it takes on average to collect an account receivable. During 2011, Claremont's average collection period was 16.3 days, or 365/22.39. During 2010, Claremont's average collection period was 20.6 days, or 365/17.68. The ratio reveals that Claremont is taking four fewer days to collect its accounts receivable in 2011 than in 2010, another sign of improved accounts receivable management.

The average collection period may also be used to evaluate the effectiveness of a company's credit policies. One rule of thumb states that the average collection period should not exceed a business's allowed credit period by more than 15 days. Thus, if a firm grants credit terms of 30 days to its customers, its average collection period should not exceed 45 days.

| Your Turn! | 8.6 |
|---|---|

The Forrester Corporation disclosed the following financial information (in millions) in its recent annual report:

| | 2011 |
|---|---|
| Net sales . . . . . . . . . . . . . . . . . . . . . . . . . . . . . . . . . . . . . . . . . . . . . . . . . . . . . . . . . . . . . . . . . . . . . . . . . . . | $30,000 |
| Beginning accounts receivable (net). . . . . . . . . . . . . . . . . . . . . . . . . . . . . . . . . . . . . . . . . . . . . . . . . . . . . | 2,800 |
| Ending accounts receivable (net). . . . . . . . . . . . . . . . . . . . . . . . . . . . . . . . . . . . . . . . . . . . . . . . . . . . . . . | 3,200 |

a. Calculate the accounts receivable turnover ratio for 2011.
b. Calculate the average collection period for 2011.

The solution is on page 404.

## FACTORING AND DISCOUNTING

A company can accelerate the collection of cash on an account receivable or a note receivable by selling the receivable to a finance company or a financial institution. Selling an account receivable is called **factoring** and selling a note receivable is called **discounting**. Finance companies and financial institutions that buy receivables are called **factors**.

When receivables are sold, the factor pays the selling company the amount of the account receivable or note receivable less a fee, often ranging from two percent to five percent of the value of the sold receivable. The factor then collects the cash payments directly from the customer who originally purchased the goods or services on credit. This approach speeds the collection of cash to the selling company and releases it from the work of billing and collecting the account.

Accounts and notes receivable may be sold under two conditions—with recourse and without recourse. "With recourse" indicates that in the event that a factor is unable to collect a specific customer's account or note receivable, the factor has the right to request that the selling company return the amount of the uncollected receivable. "Without recourse" indicates that a factor is unable to request reimbursement from the selling company if the factor is unable to collect a specific account or note receivable. Selling receivables without recourse is more expensive than selling receivables with recourse because the factor is forced to assume additional collection risk.

| Concept | ⟶ | Method | ⟶ | Assessment |
|---|---|---|---|---|
| Are any of the existing accounts receivable in need of further attention? | | Net sales and average accounts receivable<br><br>$\text{Accounts receivable turnover} = \dfrac{\text{Net sales}}{\text{Average accounts receivable}}$<br><br>$\text{Average collection period} = \dfrac{365}{\text{Accounts receivable turnover}}$ | | Compare the average collection period to the company credit policy. Longer collection periods suggest the need for management attention. |

TAKEAWAY 8.2

**WORKING WITH THE TAKEAWAYS**

Below are selected data from a recent MGM Resorts International financial statement. Amounts are in thousands.

| | |
|---|---:|
| Net sales:.................................................................... | $7,208,767 |
| Beginning of year accounts receivable:............................................. | 412,933 |
| End of year accounts receivable: ................................................ | 303,416 |

**Required:**

Calculate the MGM Resorts International (a) accounts receivable turnover, and (b) average collection period.

**Solution**

(a)  Accounts receivable turnover = $7,208,767/[($412,933 + $303,416)/2] = 20.1

(b)  Average collection period = 365/20.1 = 18.2 days

# SUMMARY OF LEARNING OBJECTIVES

**LO1**  **Define accounts receivable, explain losses from uncollectible accounts, and describe the allowance method of accounting for doubtful accounts. (p. 364)**

- Accounts receivable is a current asset created when a sales transaction is executed on a credit basis.

- Accounts receivable does not include such receivables as loans to affiliate companies or advances to employees.

- The credit department of a company is responsible for conducting credit investigations of customers, establishing credit limits, and following up on overdue accounts.

- The allowance method is designed to record the bad debts expense in the same accounting period as the related credit sale.

- When the allowance method is used, specific accounts are written off by debiting the Allowance for Doubtful Accounts and crediting the Accounts Receivable account.

**LO2**  **Describe and illustrate the percentage of net sales method and the accounts receivable aging method for estimating a business's bad debts expense. (p. 368)**

- The percentage of net sales method is used to determine estimated credit losses directly. Estimated credit losses are determined by multiplying credit sales (net of any sales discounts and sales returns and allowances) times the estimated percentage of uncollectible credit sales.

- The accounts receivable aging method determines the estimated credit loss indirectly. The balance in the Accounts Receivable account is segmented into age categories. Then the balance of each category is multiplied by the estimated uncollectible percentage for that age category. The results are added to obtain the desired balance in the Allowance for Doubtful Accounts. The desired balance is then compared to the existing balance in the Allowance for Doubtful Accounts to determine the estimated credit losses and bad debts expense for the period.

- Occasionally, accounts written off against the Allowance for Doubtful Accounts later prove to be wholly or partially collectible. When this happens, the Accounts Receivable account is first reinstated to the extent of the recovery, and then the cash collection is recorded.

**LO3**  **Illustrate the direct write-off method and contrast it with the allowance method for accounting for doubtful accounts. (p. 372)**

- Under the direct write-off method, uncollectible accounts are charged to the bad debts expense in the period in which they are determined to be uncollectible.

- For most companies, the direct write-off method is not a generally accepted method of accounting for credit losses; however, most companies use the direct write-off method for income tax purposes.

**LO4**  **Discuss the accounting treatment of credit card sales. (p. 373)**

- The credit card issuer can reimburse the merchant accepting the credit card immediately upon deposit of any sales slips or subsequently after processing the sales slips.

- In both situations, the credit card fee expense is recognized when the credit card sales slips are remitted to the credit card issuer.

**Illustrate a promissory note receivable, discuss the calculation of interest on notes receivable, and present journal entries to record notes receivable and interest. (p. 374)**  LO5

- Interest on a short-term promissory note is determined using the following formula:

$$\text{Interest} = \text{Principal} \times \text{Interest rate} \times \text{Interest time}$$

- When a note is received in payment of an account receivable balance, the Notes Receivable account is debited and the Accounts Receivable account is credited.
- The noteholder recognizes interest income at the maturity date or in an end-of-period adjusting entry if the financial statements are prepared before the note matures.

**Define *accounts receivable turnover* and *average collection period* and explain their use in the analysis and management of accounts and notes receivable. (p. 378)**  LO6

- Accounts receivable turnover = Net sales/Average accounts receivable
- Average collection period = 365/Accounts receivable turnover
- *Accounts receivable turnover* indicates how many times a year, on average, that a firm collects its accounts receivable. *Average collection period* indicates how many days it takes, on average, to collect an account receivable.

## TAKEAWAYS: SUMMARY CHART

| Concept | ➡ Method | ➡ Assessment | |
|---|---|---|---|
| Are the accounts receivable being collected in a timely manner? | List of accounts receivable along with how long they have been outstanding.  Prepare an aging schedule. | Accounts in the older categories require additional collection attention. | TAKEAWAY 8.1 |
| Are any of the existing accounts receivable in need of further attention? | Net sales and average accounts receivable  $\text{Accounts receivable turnover} = \dfrac{\text{Net sales}}{\text{Average accounts receivable}}$  $\text{Average collection period} = \dfrac{365}{\text{Accounts receivable turnover}}$ | Compare the average collection period to the company credit policy. Longer collection periods suggest the need for management attention. | TAKEAWAY 8.2 |

## GLOSSARY OF KEY TERMS

**Accounts receivable** A current asset that is created by a sale of merchandise or the provision of a service on a credit basis. It represents the amount owed the seller by a customer (p. 364).

**Accounts receivable aging method** A procedure that uses an aging schedule to determine the year-end balance needed in the Allowance for Doubtful Accounts account (p. 369).

**Accounts receivable turnover** A ratio calculated as annual net sales divided by the average balance of accounts receivable (p. 378).

**Aging schedule** An analysis that shows how long a business's accounts receivable balances have remained unpaid (p. 369).

**Allowance for doubtful accounts** A contra-asset account with a normal credit balance shown on the balance sheet as a deduction from accounts receivable to reflect the expected uncollectible amount of accounts receivable (p. 366).

**Allowance method** An accounting procedure whereby the amount of bad debts expense is estimated and recorded in the period in which the related credit sales occur (p. 366).

**Average collection period** A ratio calculated by dividing 365 days by the accounts receivable turnover ratio (p. 378).

**Bad debts expense** The expense stemming from the inability of a business to collect an amount previously recorded as receivable. It is normally classified as a selling or administrative expense (p. 366).

**Bearer** One of the terms that may be used to designate the payee on a promissory note; it means that a note is payable to whoever holds the note (p. 374).

**Credit card fee** A fee charged to retailers for credit card services provided by a financial institution. The fee is usually stated as a percentage of credit card sales (p. 374).

**Credit-granting policy** A policy to determine which customers to grant credit and how much credit to grant those customers (p. 365).

**Credit-collection policy** A policy establishing the amount of time that customers are allowed before they must pay their outstanding accounts receivable (p. 365).

**Direct write-off method** An accounting procedure whereby the amount of bad debts expense is not recorded until specific uncollectible customer accounts are identified (p. 372).

**Discounting** Selling a note receivable for cash at a financial institution (p. 379).

**Factoring** Selling an account receivable for cash to a financial institution (p. 379).

**Factors** Finance companies and financial institutions that buy receivables (p. 379).

**Maker** The signer of a promissory note (p. 374).

**Maturity date** The date on which a note or bond matures (p. 375).

**Note receivable** A promissory note held by the note's payee (p. 375).

**Payee** The company or individual to whom a promissory note is made payable (p. 374).

**Percentage of net sales method** A procedure that determines the bad debts expense for the year by multiplying net credit sales by an estimated uncollectible percentage (p. 369).

**Promissory note** A written promise to pay a certain sum of money on demand or at a determinable future time (p. 374).

## COMPREHENSIVE PROBLEM

At December 31, 2010, the following selected accounts appeared in Delta Company's unadjusted trial balance:

| | |
|---|---|
| Accounts receivable . . . . . . . . . . . . . . . . . . . . . . . . . . . . . . . . . . . . . . . . . | $81,000 |
| Allowance for doubtful accounts . . . . . . . . . . . . . . . . . . . . . . | 1,200 (credit) |
| Notes receivable (Jason, Inc.) . . . . . . . . . . . . . . . . . . . . . . . . . | 12,000 |

Net credit sales for 2010 were $250,000. The $12,000 note receivable was a 90 day, eight percent note dated December 13, 2010. The following adjusting entries and transactions occurred at the end of 2010 and during 2011:

**2010**

Dec. 31 Recorded the adjusting entry for the bad debts expense, at $1\frac{1}{2}$ percent of net credit sales.

31 Recorded the adjusting entry for interest on the $12,000 note receivable.

**2011**

Mar. 12 Received payment on the $12,000 note receivable from Jason, Inc., plus interest.

Apr. 5 Wrote off the account of Abilene Company, $2,850.

July 9 Wrote off the account of Acme Suppliers, $1,450.

Sept. 5 Received payment from Acme Suppliers, which is in bankruptcy proceedings, for $450 in final settlement of the account written off on July 9.

Dec. 6 Wrote off the account of Walton, Inc., $1,300.

31 Changed from the percentage-of-net-sales method of providing for uncollectible accounts to an estimate based on the accounts receivable aging method. The account analysis indicated a desired credit balance of $4,500 in the Allowance for Doubtful Accounts.

**Required**

Prepare the journal entries for these adjustments and transactions.

**Solution**

**2010**

| | | | |
|---|---|---|---|
| Dec. 31 | Bad debts expense | 3,750 | |
| | Allowance for doubtful accounts | | 3,750 |
| | *To provide for bad debts expense at $1\frac{1}{2}$ percent of net credit sales, $250,000.* | | |
| 31 | Interest receivable | 48 | |
| | Interest income | | 48 |
| | *To accrue interest on Jason, Inc., note receivable ($12,000 × 0.08 × 18/360 = $48).* | | |

**2011**

| | | | |
|---|---|---|---|
| Mar. 12 | Cash | 12,240 | |
| | Interest income | | 192 |
| | Interest receivable | | 48 |
| | Notes receivable—Jason, Inc. | | 12,000 |
| | *To record receipt of payment of Jason, Inc., note receivable ($12,000 × 0.08 × 72/360 = $192).* | | |
| Apr. 5 | Allowance for doubtful accounts | 2,850 | |
| | Accounts receivable—Abilene Company | | 2,850 |
| | *To write off the account of Abilene Company as uncollectible.* | | |
| July 9 | Allowance for doubtful accounts | 1,450 | |
| | Accounts receivable—Acme Suppliers | | 1,450 |
| | *To write off the account of Acme Suppliers as uncollectible.* | | |

| | | | |
|---|---|---|---|
| Sept. 5 | Accounts receivable—Acme Suppliers | 450 | |
| | Allowance for doubtful accounts | | 450 |
| | *To reinstate $450 of the account of Acme Suppliers that proved* | | |
| | *collectible.* | | |
| 5 | Cash | 450 | |
| | Accounts receivable—Acme Suppliers | | 450 |
| | *To record payment of Acme Suppliers' account.* | | |
| Dec. 6 | Allowance for doubtful accounts | 1,300 | |
| | Accounts receivable—Walton, Inc. | | 1,300 |
| | *To write off the account of Walton, Inc., as uncollectible.* | | |
| Dec. 31 | Bad debts expense | 4,700 | |
| | Allowance for doubtful accounts | | 4,700 |
| | *To provide for bad debts expense* | | |
| | *($4,500 desired balance + $200 existing debit balance = $4,700).* | | |

## SELF-STUDY QUESTIONS

**(Answers to the Self-Study Questions are available at the end of this chapter.)**

**1.** A firm, using the allowance method of recording credit losses, wrote off a customer's account in the amount of $500. Later, the customer paid the account. The firm reinstated the account by means of a journal entry and then recorded the collection. What is the result of these procedures? **LO1**

   *a.* Increases total assets by $500
   *b.* Decreases total assets by $500
   *c.* Decreases total assets by $1,000
   *d.* Has no effect on total assets

**2.** A firm has accounts receivable of $90,000 and a debit balance of $900 in the Allowance for Doubtful Accounts. Two-thirds of the accounts receivable are current and one-third is past due. The firm estimates that two percent of the current accounts and five percent of the past due accounts will prove to be uncollectible. The adjusting entry to provide for the bad debts expense under the aging method should be for what amount? **LO2**

   *a.* $2,700
   *b.* $3,600
   *c.* $1,800
   *d.* $4,500

**3.** A firm receives a six-month note from a customer. The note has a face amount of $4,000 and an interest rate of nine percent. What is the total amount of interest to be received? **LO5**

   *a.* $1,080
   *b.* $30
   *c.* $360
   *d.* $180

**4.** A business has net sales of $60,000, a beginning balance in Accounts Receivable of $5,000, and an ending balance in Accounts Receivable of $7,000. What is the company's accounts receivable turnover? **LO6**

   *a.* 10.0
   *b.* 12.0
   *c.* 8.6
   *d.* 9.2

**5.** A business has an accounts receivable turnover of ten. What is the company's average collection period? **LO6**

   *a.* 36.0
   *b.* 30.8
   *c.* 34.6
   *d.* 36.5

LO5  **6.** Miller Company received a 90 day, six percent note receivable for $10,000 on December 1. How much interest should be accrued on December 31?
   *a.* $150
   *b.* $90
   *c.* $50
   *d.* $25

LO1  **7.** Smith Company uses the allowance method to record its expected credit losses. It estimates its losses at one percent of credit sales, which were $750,000 during the year. The Accounts Receivable balance was $220,000 and the Allowance for Doubtful Accounts had a credit balance of $1,000 at year-end. What amount is the debit to the Bad Debt Expense?
   *a.* $7,500
   *b.* $8,500
   *c.* $6,500
   *d.* $3,200

LO4  **8.** Rankine & Company pays a three percent credit card fee on all credit sales, and receives a cash deposit immediately following each credit card transaction. If credit sales for the company total $15,000 on December 13, what journal entry should be recorded to recognize the receipt of cash and the credit card fee expense?
   *a.* Debit Cash $14,550; debit Credit Card Fee Expense $450.
   *b.* Debit Cash $15,000; credit Credit Card Fee Expense $450.
   *c.* Debit Cash $15,450; debit Credit Card Fee Expense $450.
   *d.* Debit Cash $15,450; credit Credit Card Fee Expense $450.

LO1, LO2, LO3  **9.** Which of the following statements is true?
   *a.* The direct write-off method is generally accepted.
   *b.* The percentage of net sales method estimates the bad debts expense indirectly.
   *c.* The accounts receivable aging method estimates the bad debts expense indirectly.
   *d.* None of the above is true.

LO5  **10.** On September 1, the Pavoreal Company accepted a $24,000, 60 day, nine percent, promissory note in exchange for overdue accounts receivable balance for the same amount from the Wagner Company. On November 30, the Wagner Company dishonored the note. What journal entry should be recorded on November 30?
   *a.* Debit Dishonored Note Receivable Expense; credit Notes Receivable.
   *b.* Debit Allowance for Doubtful Accounts; credit Notes Receivable.
   *c.* Debit Accounts Receivable; credit Interest Income; credit Notes Receivable.
   *d.* None of the above entries is correct.

# DISCUSSION QUESTIONS

1. In dealing with receivables, what do the terms *factoring* and *discounting* mean?
2. How does a credit scoring system work?
3. How do the allowance method and the direct write-off method of handling credit losses differ with respect to the timing of bad debt expense recognition?
4. When a firm provides for credit losses under the allowance method, why is the Allowance for Doubtful Accounts credited rather than Accounts Receivable?
5. What are the two most commonly used methods of estimating the bad debts expense when the allowance method is employed? Describe them.
6. Murphy Company estimates its bad debts expense by aging its accounts receivable and applying percentages to various age groups of the accounts. Murphy calculated a total of $2,100 in possible credit losses as of December 31. Accounts Receivable has a balance of $98,000, and the Allowance for Doubtful Accounts has a credit balance of $500 before adjustment at December 31. What is the December 31 adjusting entry to provide for credit losses? What is the net amount of accounts receivable that should be included in current assets?
7. On June 15, 2011, Rollins, Inc. sold $750 worth of merchandise to Dell Company. On November 20, 2011, Rollins, Inc., wrote off Dell's account. On March 10, 2012, Dell Company paid the account in full. What are the journal entries that Rollins, Inc. should make for the write-off and the recovery assuming that Rollins, Inc., uses (a) the allowance method of handling credit losses and (b) the direct write-off method?
8. Wood Company sold a $675 refrigerator to a customer who charged the sale using a VISA credit card. Wood Company deposits credit card sales slips daily; cash is deposited in Wood Company's

checking account at the same time. Wood Company's bank charges a credit card fee of four percent of sales revenue. What journal entry should Wood Company make to record the sale?

9. Volter Inc. received a 60 day, nine percent note for $15,000 on March 5 from a customer. What is the maturity date of the note?

10. Stanley Company received a 150 day, eight percent note for $15,000 on December 1. What adjusting entry is needed to accrue the interest due on December 31?

11. Define *accounts receivable turnover* and explain its use. How is the *average collection period* determined?

12. At a recent board of directors meeting of Ascot, Inc., one of the directors expressed concern over the Allowance for Doubtful Accounts appearing on the company's balance sheet. "I don't understand this account," he said. "Why don't we just show accounts receivable at the amount we would receive if we sold them to a financial institution and get rid of that allowance account?"

     Prepare a written response to the director. Include in your response (1) an explanation of why the company has an allowance account, (2) what the balance sheet presentation of accounts receivable is supposed to show, and (3) how the basic principles of accounting relate to the analysis and presentation of accounts receivable.

13. What generally accepted accounting principle is being implemented when a company estimates its potential credit losses from its outstanding accounts receivable?

14. Why is the direct write-off method of accounting for credit losses not generally accepted?

15. When a previously written-off account receivable is collected, it must first be reinstated by debiting the Accounts Receivable account and crediting the Allowance for Doubtful Accounts. Explain the credit portion of the reinstatement journal entry.

## SHORT EXERCISES

**SE8-1. Accounting for Doubtful Accounts**                                       LO1, LO2
Rankine Company estimates its bad debts expense by aging its accounts receivable and applying percentages to various age groups of the accounts. Rankine calculated a total of $4,000 in possible credit losses as of December 31. Accounts Receivable has a balance of $128,000, and the Allowance for Doubtful Accounts has a credit balance of $500 before adjustment at December 31. What is the December 31 adjusting entry to provide for credit losses? What is the net amount of accounts receivable that should be included in current assets?

**SE8-2. Reinstating Written-Off Accounts**                                       LO2
The Watergate Company uses the allowance method of recording credit losses and wrote off a customer's account in the amount of $800. Later, the customer paid the account. The company reinstated the account by means of a journal entry and then recorded the collection. What is the result of these procedures?

   *a.* Increases total assets by $800
   *b.* Decreases total assets by $800
   *c.* Decreases total assets by $1,600
   *d.* Has no effect on total assets

**SE8-3. Estimating the Bad Debts Expense**                                       LO2
Winstead & Company has accounts receivable of $120,000 and a debit balance of $1,000 in the Allowance for Doubtful Accounts. Two thirds of the accounts receivable are current and one third is past due. The firm estimates that two percent of the current accounts and five percent of the past due accounts will prove to be uncollectible. The adjusting entry to provide for the bad debts expense under the aging method should be for what amount?

   *a.* $3,600
   *b.* $4,600
   *c.* $2,600
   *d.* $1,600

**SE8-4. Direct Write-Off Method**                                                LO3
The direct write-off method is not generally accepted because:

   *a.* The method overstates the bad debt expense.
   *b.* It is too complex.
   *c.* The method fails to match sales revenue with expenses in the appropriate time period.
   *d.* The method causes liabilities to be overstated.

ASSIGNMENTS

**LO5** **SE8-5.** **Recording Dishonored Promissory Notes Receivable**

On September 30, the Camelback Company accepted a $50,000, 60 day, nine percent, promissory note in exchange for an overdue accounts receivable balance for the same amount from the Schwartz Company. On November 30, the Schwartz Company dishonored the note. What journal entry should be recorded on November 30?

 *a.* Debit Dishonored Note Receivable Expense; credit Notes Receivable.
 *b.* Debit Allowance for Doubtful Accounts; credit Notes Receivable.
 *c.* Debit Accounts Receivable; credit Interest Income; credit Notes Receivable.
 *d.* None of the above entries is correct.

**LO4** **SE8-6.** **Accounting for Credit Card Sales**

Chassoul & Company pays a three percent credit card fee on all credit sales, and receives a cash deposit immediately following each credit card transaction. If credit sales for the company total $30,000 on January 15, what journal entry should be recorded to recognize the receipt of cash and the credit card fee expense?

 *a.* Debit Cash $29,100; debit Credit Card Fee Expense $900.
 *b.* Debit Cash $29,100; credit Credit Card Fee Expense $900.
 *c.* Debit Cash $30,900; debit Credit Card Fee Expense $900.
 *d.* Debit Cash $30,900; credit Credit Card Fee Expense $900.

**LO5** **SE8-7.** **Calculating Accrued Interest Income on Promissory Notes Receivable**

Likert Company received a 90 day, six percent note receivable for $20,000 on November 1. How much interest income should be accrued on December 31?

 *a.* $100
 *b.* $200
 *c.* $300
 *d.* $400

**LO5** **SE8-8.** **Calculating Interest on Promissory Notes Receivable**

Dallas Company receives a six-month note from a customer. The note has a face amount of $8,000 and an interest rate of nine percent. What is the total amount of interest income to be received?

 *a.* $720
 *b.* $540
 *c.* $360
 *d.* $180

**LO6** **SE8-9.** **Accounts Receivable Turnover**

Tarrant Company has net sales of $120,000, a beginning balance in Accounts Receivable of $10,000, and an ending balance in Accounts Receivable of $14,000. What is the company's accounts receivable turnover?

 *a.* 10.0
 *b.* 12.0
 *c.* 8.6
 *d.* 9.2

**LO6** **SE8-10.** **Average Collection Period**

Smith & Sons has an accounts receivable turnover of 20. What is the company's average collection period?

 *a.* 18.25 days
 *b.* 20.0 days
 *c.* 22.25 days
 *d.* 24.25 days

# EXERCISES—SET A

**LO2** **E8-1A.** **Credit Losses Based on Credit Sales**

Lewis Company uses the allowance method for recording its expected credit losses. It estimates credit losses at 1 percent of credit sales, which were $900,000 during the year. On December

31, the Accounts Receivable balance was $150,000, and the Allowance for Doubtful Accounts had a credit balance of $10,200 before adjustment.

a. Prepare the adjusting entry to record the credit losses for the year.
b. Show how Accounts Receivable and the Allowance for Doubtful Accounts would appear in the December 31 balance sheet.

**E8-2A. Credit Losses Based on Accounts Receivable**                                                   LO1, LO2

Hunter, Inc., analyzed its accounts receivable balances at December 31, and arrived at the aged balances listed below, along with the percentage that is estimated to be uncollectible:

| Age Group | Balance | Probability of Noncollection |
|---|---|---|
| 0–30 days past due | $ 90,000 | 1 |
| 31–60 days past due | 20,000 | 2 |
| 61–120 days past due | 11,000 | 5 |
| 121–180 days past due | 6,000 | 10 |
| Over 180 days past due | 4,000 | 25 |
| | $131,000 | |

The company handles credit losses using the allowance method. The credit balance of the Allowance for Doubtful Accounts is $520 on December 31, before any adjustments.

a. Prepare the adjusting entry for estimated credit losses on December 31.
b. Prepare the journal entry to write off the Rose Company's account on April 10 of the following year in the amount of $425.

**E8-3A. Allowance Method versus Direct Write-Off Method**                                              LO3

On March 10, Gardner, Inc., declared a $900 account receivable from the Gates Company as uncollectible and wrote off the account. On November 18, Gardner received a $400 payment on the account from Gates.

a. Assume that Gardner uses the allowance method of handling credit losses. Prepare the journal entries to record the write-off and the subsequent recovery of Gates's account.
b. Assume that Gardner uses the direct write-off method of handling credit losses. Prepare the journal entries to record the write-off and the subsequent recovery of Gates's account.
c. Assume that the payment from Gates arrives on February 5 of the following year rather than on November 18 of the current year. (1) Prepare the journal entries to record the write-off and subsequent recovery of Gates's account under the allowance method. (2) Prepare the journal entries to record the write-off and subsequent recovery of Gates's account under the direct write-off method.

**E8-4A. Credit Card Sales**                                                                            LO4

Ruth Anne's Fabrics accepts cash, personal checks, and two credit cards when customers buy merchandise. With the Great American Bank Card, Ruth Anne's Fabrics receives an immediate deposit in its checking account when credit card sales slips are deposited at the bank. The bank charges a four percent fee. With the United Merchants Card, Ruth Anne's Fabrics mails the credit card sales slips to United Merchants' regional processing center each day. United Merchants accumulates these slips for three days and then mails a check to Ruth Anne's Fabrics, after deducting a three percent fee. Prepare journal entries to record the following:

a. Sales for March 15 were as follows:

| | |
|---|---|
| Cash and checks | $ 850 |
| Great American Bank Card (Deposited at the end of the day) | 1,100 |
| United Merchants Card (Mailed at the end of the day) | 700 |
| | $2,650 |

b. Received a check for $3,978 from United Merchants on March 20.

**E8-5A. Maturity Dates of Notes Receivable**                                                           LO5

Determine the maturity date and compute the interest for each of the following notes:

| | Date of Note | Principal | Interest Rate (%) | Term |
|---|---|---|---|---|
| a. | August 5 ................................. | $ 6,000 | 8 | 120 days |
| b. | May 10 .................................... | 16,800 | 7 | 90 days |
| c. | October 20 ............................... | 24,000 | 9 | 45 days |
| d. | July 6 .................................... | 4,500 | 10 | 60 days |
| e. | September 15 ............................ | 9,000 | 8 | 75 days |

**LO5** **E8-6A.** **Computing Accrued Interest**

Compute the interest accrued on each of the following notes receivable held by Northland, Inc., on December 31:

| Maker | Date of Note | Principal | Interest Rate (%) | Term |
|---|---|---|---|---|
| Maple ................................ | 11/21 | $18,000 | 10 | 120 days |
| Wyman ............................. | 12/13 | 14,000 | 9 | 90 days |
| Nahn ................................ | 12/19 | 21,000 | 8 | 60 days |

**LO6** **E8-7A.** **Accounts Receivable Turnover and Average Collection Period**

The Forrester Corporation disclosed the following financial information (in millions) in its recent annual report:

| | 2010 | 2011 |
|---|---|---|
| Net sales ........................................................ | $67,096 | $81,662 |
| Beginning accounts receivable (net) ......................... | 3,896 | 3,696 |
| Ending accounts receivable (net) ............................ | 3,696 | 3,598 |

a. Calculate the accounts receivable turnover ratio for both years.
b. Calculate the average collection period for both years.
c. Is the company's accounts receivable management improving or deteriorating?

**LO2** **E8-8A.** **Credit Losses Based on Credit Sales**

Smith & Sons uses the allowance method of handling its credit losses. It estimates credit losses at one percent of credit sales, which were $1,800,000 during the year. On December 31, the Accounts Receivable balance was $300,000, and the Allowance for Doubtful Accounts had a credit balance of $20,400 before adjustment.

a. Prepare the adjusting entry to record the credit losses for the year.
b. Show how Accounts Receivable and the Allowance for Doubtful Accounts would appear in the December 31 balance sheet.

**LO1, LO2** **E8-9A.** **Credit Losses Based on Accounts Receivable**

Miller, Inc., analyzed its accounts receivable balances at December 31 and arrived at the aged balances listed below, along with the percentage that is estimated to be uncollectible:

| Age Group | Balance | Probability of Noncollection |
|---|---|---|
| 0–30 days past due ............................................. | $180,000 | 1 |
| 31–60 days past due ............................................ | 40,000 | 2 |
| 61–120 days past due ........................................... | 22,000 | 5 |
| 121–180 days past due ......................................... | 12,000 | 10 |
| Over 180 days past due ......................................... | 8,000 | 25 |
| | $262,000 | |

The company handles credit losses using the allowance method. The credit balance of the Allowance for Doubtful Accounts is $1,040 on December 31, before any adjustments.

a. Prepare the adjusting entry for estimated credit losses on December 31.
b. Prepare the journal entry to write off the Lyons Company's account on April 10 of the following year in the amount of $425.

**LO3** **E8-10A.** **Allowance Method versus Direct Write-Off Method**

On March 10, Mize, Inc., declared a $1,800 account receivable from Anders Company as uncollectible and wrote off the account. On November 18, Mize received an $800 payment on the account from Anders.

a. Assume that Mize uses the allowance method of handling credit losses. Prepare the journal entries to record the write-off and the subsequent recovery of Anders's account.

b. Assume that Mize uses the direct write-off method of handling credit losses. Prepare the journal entries to record the write-off and the subsequent recovery of Anders's account.

c. Assume that the payment from Anders arrives on the following February 5, rather than on November 18 of the current year. (1) Prepare the journal entries to record the write-off and subsequent recovery of Anders's account under the allowance method. (2) Prepare the journal entries to record the write-off and subsequent recovery of Anders's account under the direct write-off method.

**E8-11A. Credit Card Sales**      LO4

The Tin Roof accepts cash, personal checks, and two credit cards when customers buy merchandise. With the Great American Bank Card, The Tin Roof receives an immediate deposit in its checking account when credit card sales slips are deposited at the bank. The bank charges a four percent fee. With the United Merchants Card, The Tin Roof mails the credit card sales slips to United Merchants' regional processing center each day. United Merchants accumulates these slips for three days and then mails a check to The Tin Roof, after deducting a three percent fee. Prepare journal entries to record the following:

a. Sales for March 15 were as follows:

| | |
|---|---:|
| Cash and checks....................................................... | $1,700 |
| Great American Bank Card | |
|    (Deposited at the end of the day)................................... | 2,200 |
| United Merchants Card | |
|    (Mailed at the end of the day) ...................................... | 1,400 |
| | $5,300 |

b. Received a check for $7,956 from United Merchants on March 20.

**E8-12A. Maturity Dates of Notes Receivable**      LO5

Determine the maturity date and compute the interest for each of the following notes:

| | Date of Note | Principal | Interest Rate (%) | Term |
|---|---|---|---|---|
| a. | August 5 ................................. | $12,000 | 8 | 120 days |
| b. | May 10..................................... | 33,600 | 7 | 90 days |
| c. | October 20............................... | 48,000 | 9 | 45 days |
| d. | July 6 ...................................... | 9,000 | 10 | 60 days |
| e. | September 15............................ | 18,000 | 8 | 75 days |

**E8-13A. Computing Accrued Interest**      LO5

Compute the interest accrued on each of the following notes receivable held by Kierland, Inc., on December 31:

| Maker | Date of Note | Principal | Interest Rate (%) | Term |
|---|---|---|---|---|
| Abel ............................... | 11/21 | $36,000 | 10 | 120 days |
| Baker .............................. | 12/13 | 28,000 | 9 | 90 days |
| Charlie............................. | 12/19 | 42,000 | 8 | 60 days |

**E8-14A. Accounts Receivable Turnover and Average Collection Period**      LO6

VanPoole Corporation disclosed the following financial information (in millions) in its recent annual report:

| | 2010 | 2011 |
|---|---|---|
| Net sales ......................................................... | $167,096 | $181,662 |
| Beginning accounts receivable (net)......................... | 13,896 | 13,696 |
| Ending accounts receivable (net)............................. | 13,696 | 13,598 |

a. Calculate the accounts receivable turnover ratio for both years.

b. Calculate the average collection period for both years.

c. Is the company's accounts receivable management improving or deteriorating?

**LO1   E8-15A.   Recognizing Accounts Receivable**

On June 7, Bixby Co. sells $750 of merchandise to Jasmine Co. on account. Jasmine Co. pays for this merchandise on June 21.

*a.*   Prepare the entry on Bixby's books to record the sale.

*b.*   Prepare the entry on Bixby's books to record the receipt of payment.

# EXERCISES—SET B

**LO2   E8-1B.   Credit Losses Based on Credit Sales**

Highland Company uses the allowance method of handling credit losses. It estimates losses at one percent of credit sales, which were $1,200,000 during the year. On December 31, the Accounts Receivable balance was $280,000, and the Allowance for Doubtful Accounts had a credit balance of $1,700 before adjustment.

*a.*   Prepare the adjusting entry to record credit losses for the year.

*b.*   Show how the Accounts Receivable account and the Allowance for Doubtful Accounts would appear on the December 31 balance sheet.

**LO1, LO2   E8-2B.   Credit Losses Based on Accounts Receivable**

Maxwell, Inc. analyzed its accounts receivable balances at December 31 and arrived at the aged balances listed below, along with the percentage that is estimated to be uncollectible:

| Age Group | Balance | Probability of Noncollection |
|---|---|---|
| 0–30 days past due | $100,000 | 1 |
| 31–60 days past due | 18,000 | 3 |
| 61–120 days past due | 20,000 | 6 |
| 121–180 days past due | 7,000 | 10 |
| Over 180 days past due | 2,000 | 20 |
| | $147,000 | |

The company handles credit losses with the allowance method. The credit balance of the Allowance for Doubtful Accounts is $840 on December 31, before any adjustments.

*a.*   Prepare the adjusting entry for estimated credit losses on December 31.

*b.*   Prepare the journal entry to write off Porter Company's account on the following May 12, in the amount of $480.

**LO3   E8-3B.   Allowance Method versus Direct Write-Off Method**

On April 12, Maddox Company declared a $1,000 account receivable from the Ward Company as uncollectible and wrote off the account. On December 5, Maddox received a $700 payment on the account from Ward.

*a.*   Assume that Maddox uses the allowance method of handling credit losses. Prepare the journal entries to record the write-off and the subsequent recovery of Ward's account.

*b.*   Assume that Maddox uses the direct write-off method of handling credit losses. Prepare the journal entries to record the write-off and the subsequent recovery of Ward's account.

*c.*   Assume that the payment from Ward arrives on the following January 18, rather than on December 5 of the current year. (1) Prepare the journal entries to record the write-off and subsequent recovery of Ward's account under the allowance method. (2) Prepare the journal entries to record the write-off and subsequent recovery of Ward's account under the direct write-off method.

**LO4   E8-4B.   Credit Card Sales**

Historically, 60 percent of the customer bills at the Andrews' Supper Club have been paid with cash or check, and 40 percent have been paid using either the Great American Bank Card or the United Merchants Card. Andrews pays a four percent fee with both cards. Great American Bank deposits cash in Andrews' checking account when the credit card sales slips are deposited. United Merchants makes an electronic funds transfer three days after the sales slips are mailed. Prepare journal entries to record the following:

*a.* Sales for September 10 were as follows:

| | |
|---|---|
| Cash and checks..................................................................... | $1,340 |
| Great American Bank Card (Deposited at the end of the day)................................................. | 500 |
| United Merchants Card (Mailed at the end of the day).................................................. | 300 |
| | $2,140 |

*b.* On September 13, Andrews received an electronic funds transfer from United Merchants for the September 10 sales.

**E8-5B.** **Maturity Dates of Notes Receivable**                                                LO5

Determine the maturity date and compute the interest for each of the following notes:

| | Date of Note | Principal | Interest Rate (%) | Term |
|---|---|---|---|---|
| *a.* | July 10 ..................................... | $ 7,200 | 9 | 90 days |
| *b.* | April 14 .................................... | 12,000 | 8 | 120 days |
| *c.* | May 19...................................... | 11,200 | $7\frac{1}{2}$ | 120 days |
| *d.* | June 10 ..................................... | 5,400 | 8 | 45 days |
| *e.* | October 29................................. | 30,000 | 8 | 75 days |

**E8-6B.** **Computing Accrued Interest**                                                         LO5

Compute the interest accrued on each of the following notes receivable held by Galloway, Inc., on December 31:

| Maker | Date of Note | Principal | Interest Rate (%) | Term |
|---|---|---|---|---|
| Barton .............................. | 12/4 | $10,000 | 8 | 120 days |
| Lawson ............................. | 12/13 | 24,000 | 9 | 90 days |
| Riley ................................ | 12/19 | 9,000 | 10 | 60 days |

**E8-7B.** **Accounts Receivable Turnover and Average Collection Period**                         LO6

The Andrew Miller Corporation disclosed the following financial information (in millions) in its recent annual report:

| | 2010 | 2011 |
|---|---|---|
| Net sales ......................................................... | $97,096 | $111,662 |
| Beginning accounts receivable (net)........................... | 6,896 | 6,696 |
| Ending accounts receivable (net)............................... | 6,696 | 6,598 |

*a.* Calculate the accounts receivable turnover ratio for both years.
*b.* Calculate the average collection period for both years.
*c.* Is the company's accounts receivable management improving or deteriorating?

**E8-8B.** **Credit Losses Based on Credit Sales**                                                LO2

Harris Company uses the allowance method of handling its credit losses. It estimates credit losses at one percent of credit sales, which were $2,700,000 during the year. On December 31, the Accounts Receivable balance was $450,000, and the Allowance for Doubtful Accounts had a credit balance of $30,600 before adjustment.

*a.* Prepare the adjusting entry to record the credit losses for the year.
*b.* Show how Accounts Receivable and the Allowance for Doubtful Accounts would appear in the December 31 balance sheet.

**E8-9B.** **Credit Losses Based on Accounts Receivable**                                         LO1, LO2

Graham, Inc., analyzed its accounts receivable balances at December 31 and arrived at the aged balances listed below, along with the percentage that is estimated to be uncollectible:

| Age Group | Balance | Probability of Noncollection |
|---|---|---|
| 0–30 days past due.............................................. | $270,000 | 1 |
| 31–60 days past due............................................. | 60,000 | 2 |
| 61–120 days past due........................................... | 33,000 | 5 |
| 121–180 days past due .......................................... | 18,000 | 10 |
| Over 180 days past due......................................... | 12,000 | 25 |
| | $393,000 | |

The company handles credit losses using the allowance method. The credit balance of the Allowance for Doubtful Accounts is $1,560 on December 31, before any adjustments.

a. Prepare the adjusting entry for estimated credit losses on December 31.

b. Prepare the journal entry to write off the Matthews Company's account on the following April 10, in the amount of $425.

**LO3** **E8-10B. Allowance Method versus Direct Write-Off Method**

On March 10, Barrett, Inc., declared a $2,700 account receivable from Lamas Company as uncollectible and wrote off the account. On November 18, Barrett received a $1,200 payment on the account from Lamas.

a. Assume that Barrett uses the allowance method of handling credit losses. Prepare the journal entries to record the write-off and the subsequent recovery of Lamas's account.

b. Assume that Barrett uses the direct write-off method of handling credit losses. Prepare the journal entries to record the write-off and the subsequent recovery of Lamas's account.

c. Assume that the payment from Lamas arrives on the following February 5, rather than on November 18 of the current year. (1) Prepare the journal entries to record the write-off and subsequent recovery of Lamas's account under the allowance method. (2) Prepare the journal entries to record the write-off and subsequent recovery of Lamas's account under the direct write-off method.

**LO4** **E8-11B. Credit Card Sales**

The Bedroom Store accepts cash, personal checks, and two credit cards when customers buy merchandise. With the Great American Bank Card, The Bedroom Store receives an immediate deposit in its checking account when credit card sales slips are deposited at the bank. The bank charges a four percent fee. With the United Merchants Card, The Bedroom Store mails the credit card sales slips to United Merchants' regional processing center each day. United Merchants accumulates these slips for three days and then mails a check to The Bedroom Store, after deducting a three percent fee. Prepare journal entries to record the following:

a. Sales for March 15 were as follows:

| | |
|---|---|
| Cash and checks........................................................................ | $2,550 |
| Great American Bank Card | |
| (Deposited at the end of the day)................................................ | 3,300 |
| United Merchants Card | |
| (Mailed at the end of the day) ................................................... | 2,100 |
| | $7,950 |

b. Received a check for $11,934 from United Merchants on March 20.

**LO5** **E8-12B. Maturity Dates of Notes Receivable**

Determine the maturity date and compute the interest for each of the following notes:

| | Date of Note | Principal | Interest Rate (%) | Term |
|---|---|---|---|---|
| a. | August 5 .................................. | $18,000 | 8 | 120 days |
| b. | May 10..................................... | 50,400 | 7 | 90 days |
| c. | October 20............................... | 72,000 | 9 | 45 days |
| d. | July 6 ..................................... | 13,500 | 10 | 60 days |
| e. | September 15 ........................... | 27,000 | 8 | 75 days |

**LO5** **E8-13B. Computing Accrued Interest**

Compute the interest accrued on each of the following notes receivable held by Northland, Inc., on December 31:

| Maker | Date of Note | Principal | Interest Rate (%) | Term |
|---|---|---|---|---|
| Delta.............................. | 11/21 | $54,000 | 10 | 120 days |
| Echo ............................... | 12/13 | 42,000 | 9 | 90 days |
| Foxtrot............................ | 12/19 | 63,000 | 8 | 60 days |

**E8-14B. Accounts Receivable Turnover and Average Collection Period**　LO6

The Longo Corporation disclosed the following financial information (in millions) in its recent annual report:

|  | 2010 | 2011 |
|---|---|---|
| Net sales ....................................................................... | $127,096 | $111,662 |
| Beginning accounts receivable (net)........................................... | 8,896 | 7,696 |
| Ending accounts receivable (net).............................................. | 7,696 | 6,598 |

*a.* Calculate the accounts receivable turnover ratio for both years.
*b.* Calculate the average collection period for both years.
*c.* Is the company's accounts receivable management improving or deteriorating?

**E8-15B. Recognizing Accounts Receivable**　LO1

On August 9, Gunner Co. sells $300 of merchandise to Taylor Co. on account. Taylor Co. pays for this merchandise on September 1.

*a.* Prepare the entry on Gunner's books to record the sale.
*b.* Prepare the entry on Gunner's books to record the receipt of payment.

# PROBLEMS—SET A

**P8-1A. Allowance Method versus Direct Write-Off Method**　LO3

Fullerton Company, which has been in business for three years, makes all of its sales on account and does not offer cash discounts. The firm's credit sales, collections from customers, and write-offs of uncollectible accounts for the three-year period are summarized below:

| Year | Sales | Collections | Accounts Written Off |
|---|---|---|---|
| 2010 | $300,000 | $287,000 | $2,100 |
| 2011 | 385,000 | 380,000 | 3,350 |
| 2012 | 420,000 | 407,000 | 3,650 |

**Required**

*a.* If Fullerton Company had used the direct write-off method of recognizing credit losses during the three years, what amount of accounts receivable would appear on the firm's balance sheet at the end of 2012? What total amount of bad debts expense would have appeared on the firm's income statement during the three-year period?
*b.* If Fullerton Company had used the allowance method of recognizing credit losses and had provided for such losses at the rate of 1.2 percent of credit sales, what amounts in accounts receivable and the allowance for doubtful accounts would appear on the firm's balance sheet at the end of 2012? What total amount of bad debts expense would have appeared on the firm's income statement during the three year period?
*c.* Comment on the use of the 1.2 percent rate to provide for credit losses in part *b.*

**P8-2A. Journal Entries for Credit Losses**　LO1, LO2

At the beginning of the year, Whitney Company had the following accounts on its books:

| | |
|---|---|
| Accounts receivable ....................................................... | $122,000 (debit) |
| Allowance for doubtful accounts............................................... | 7,900 (credit) |

During the year, credit sales were $1,173,000 and collections on account were $1,150,000. The following transactions, among others, occurred during the year:

Feb. 17　Wrote off R. Lowell's account, $3,600.
May 28　Wrote off G. Boyd's account, $2,400.
Oct. 13　Received $600 from G. Boyd, who is in bankruptcy proceedings, in final settlement of the account written off on May 28. This amount is not included in the $1,150,000 collections.

Dec. 15 Wrote off K. Marshall's account, $1,500.

31 In an adjusting entry, recorded the allowance for doubtful accounts at 0.8 percent of credit sales for the year.

**Required**

*a.* Prepare journal entries to record the credit sales, the collections on account, and the preceding transactions and adjustment.

*b.* Show how Accounts Receivable and the Allowance for Doubtful Accounts would appear on the December 31 balance sheet.

**LO2** **P8-3A.** **Credit Losses Based on Accounts Receivable**

At December 31, Schuler Company had a balance of $370,000 in its Accounts Receivable account and a credit balance of $4,200 in the Allowance for Doubtful Accounts account. The accounts receivable T-account consisted of $375,000 in debit balances and $5,000 in credit balances. The company aged its accounts as follows:

| | |
|---|---:|
| Current. . . . . . . . . . . . . . . . . . . . . . . . . . . . . . . . . . . . . . . . . . . . . . . . . . . . . . . . . . . . . . . . . . . . . . . . | $304,000 |
| 0–60 days past due . . . . . . . . . . . . . . . . . . . . . . . . . . . . . . . . . . . . . . . . . . . . . . . . . . . . . . . . . . . . . . . | 44,000 |
| 61–180 days past due. . . . . . . . . . . . . . . . . . . . . . . . . . . . . . . . . . . . . . . . . . . . . . . . . . . . . . . . . . . . . . . | 18,000 |
| Over 180 days past due . . . . . . . . . . . . . . . . . . . . . . . . . . . . . . . . . . . . . . . . . . . . . . . . . . . . . . . . . . . . . | 9,000 |
| | $375,000 |

In the past, the company has experienced credit losses as follows: one percent of current balances, five percent of balances 0–60 days past due, 15 percent of balances 61–180 days past due, and 40 percent of balances over six months past due. The company bases its allowance for doubtful accounts on an aging analysis of accounts receivable.

**Required**

*a.* Prepare the adjusting entry to record the allowance for doubtful accounts for the year.

*b.* Show how Accounts Receivable (including the credit balances) and the Allowance for Doubtful Accounts would appear on the December 31 balance sheet.

**LO4** **P8-4A.** **Credit Card Sales**

Valderi's Gallery sells quality art work, with prices for individual pieces ranging from $500 to $25,000. Sales are infrequent, typically only three to five pieces per week. The following transactions occurred during the first week of June 2010. Perpetual inventory is used.

On June 1, sold an $800 framed print ($500 cost) to Kerwin Antiques on account, with 2/10, n/30 credit terms.

On June 2, sold three framed etchings totaling $2,400 ($1,500 cost) to Maria Alvado, who used the United Merchants Card to charge the cost of the etchings. Valderi mailed the credit card sales slip to United Merchants the same day. United Merchants will send a check within seven days after deducting a one percent fee.

On June 4, sold an $1,800 oil painting ($1,000 cost) to Shaun Chandler, who paid with a personal check.

On June 5, sold a $2,000 watercolor ($1,300 cost) to Julie and John Malbie, who used their Great American Bank Card to charge the purchase of the painting. Valderi deposited the credit card sales slip the same day and received immediate credit in the company's checking account. The bank charged a two percent fee.

On June 6, received payment from Kerwin Antiques for its June 1 purchase.

On June 7, received a check from United Merchants for the June 2 sale.

**Required**

Prepare journal entries to record the Valderi Gallery transactions.

**LO2, LO3, LO5** **P8-5A.** **Journal Entries for Accounts and Notes Receivable**

Lancaster Inc. began business on January 1. Certain transactions for the year follow:

June 8 Received a $15,000, 60 day, eight percent note on account from R. Elliot.

Aug. 7 Received payment from R. Elliot on her note (principal plus interest).

Sept. 1 Received an $18,000, 120 day, nine percent note from B. Shore Company on account.

Dec. 16 Received a $14,400, 45 day, ten percent note from C. Judd on account.

30 B. Shore Company failed to pay its note.

31 Wrote off B. Shore's account as uncollectible. Lancaster, Inc. uses the allowance method of providing for credit losses.

31 Recorded expected credit losses for the year by an adjusting entry. Accounts written off during this first year have created a debit balance in the Allowance for Doubtful Accounts of $22,600. An analysis of aged receivables indicates that the desired balance of the allowance account should be $19,500.

31 Made the appropriate adjusting entries for interest.

### Required

Record the foregoing transactions and adjustments in general journal form.

**P8-6A.** **Allowance Method versus Direct Write-Off Method**

LO3

The Huntington Company, which has been in business for three years, makes all of its sales on account and does not offer cash discounts. The firm's credit sales, collections from customers, and write-offs of uncollectible accounts for the three-year period are summarized below:

| Year | Sales | Collections | Accounts Written Off |
|---|---|---|---|
| 2010 | $600,000 | $574,000 | $4,200 |
| 2011 | 770,000 | 760,000 | 6,700 |
| 2012 | 840,000 | 814,000 | 7,300 |

### Required

a. If the Huntington Company had used the direct write-off method of recognizing credit losses during the three years, what amount of accounts receivable would appear on the firm's balance sheet at the end of 2012? What total amount of bad debts expense would have appeared on the firm's income statement during the three-year period?

b. If the Huntington Company had used the allowance method of recognizing credit losses and had provided for such losses at the rate of 1.2 percent of credit sales, what amounts in Accounts Receivable and the Allowance for Doubtful Accounts would appear on the firm's balance sheet at the end of 2012? What total amount of bad debts expense would have appeared on the firm's income statement during the three year period?

c. Comment on the use of the 1.2 percent rate to provide for credit losses in part b.

**P8-7A.** **Journal Entries for Credit Losses**

LO1, LO2

At the beginning of the year, the Houston Company had the following accounts on its books:

| | |
|---|---|
| Accounts receivable . . . . . . . . . . . . . . . . . . . . . . . . . . . . . . . . . . . . . . . . . . . . . . . . . . . . . . . . . . . . . . . | $244,000 (debit) |
| Allowance for doubtful accounts . . . . . . . . . . . . . . . . . . . . . . . . . . . . . . . . . . . . . . . . . . . . . . . . . . . | 15,800 (credit) |

During the year, credit sales were $2,346,000 and collections on account were $2,300,000. The following transactions, among others, occurred during the year:

Feb. 17 Wrote off R. St. John's account, $7,200.

May 28 Wrote off G. Herberger's account, $4,800.

Oct. 13 Received $1,200 from G. Herberger, who is in bankruptcy proceedings, in final settlement of the account written off on May 28. This amount is not included in the $2,300,000 collections.

Dec. 15 Wrote off R. Clancy's account, $3,000.

31 In an adjusting entry, recorded the allowance for doubtful accounts at 0.8 percent of credit sales for the year.

### Required

a. Prepare journal entries to record the credit sales, the collections on account, and the preceding transactions and adjustment.

b. Show how Accounts Receivable and the Allowance for Doubtful Accounts would appear on the December 31 balance sheet.

**P8-8A.** **Credit Losses Based on Accounts Receivable**

LO2

At December 31, the Selling Company had a balance of $740,000 in its Accounts Receivable account and a credit balance of $8,400 in the Allowance for Doubtful Accounts account. The accounts receivable T-account consisted of $750,000 in debit balances and $10,000 in credit balances. The company aged its accounts as follows:

ASSIGNMENTS

| | |
|---|---:|
| Current.............................................................................. | $608,000 |
| 0–60 days past due............................................................. | 88,000 |
| 61–180 days past due.......................................................... | 36,000 |
| Over 180 days past due........................................................ | 18,000 |
| | $750,000 |

In the past, the company has experienced credit losses as follows: one percent of current balances, five percent of balances 0–60 days past due, 15 percent of balances 61–180 days past due, and 40 percent of balances over six months past due. The company bases its allowance for doubtful accounts on an aging analysis of accounts receivable.

**Required**
a. Prepare the adjusting entry to record the allowance for doubtful accounts for the year.
b. Show how Accounts Receivable (including the credit balances) and the Allowance for Doubtful Accounts would appear on the December 31 balance sheet.

**LO4  P8-9A.  Credit Card Sales**
Le Kai Gallery sells quality art work, with prices for individual pieces ranging from $1,000 to $50,000. Sales are infrequent, typically only six to ten pieces per week. The following transactions occurred during the first week of June. Perpetual inventory is used.

On June 1, sold an $1,600 framed print ($1,000 cost) to Likert Antiques on account, with 2/10, n/30 credit terms.

On June 2, sold three framed etchings totaling $4,800 ($3,000 cost) to Annabelle Herrera, who used the United Merchants Card to charge the cost of the etchings. Le Kai mailed the credit card sales slip to United Merchants the same day. United Merchants will send a check within seven days after deducting a one percent fee.

On June 4, sold a $3,600 oil painting ($2,000 cost) to Ryan LaLander, who paid with a personal check.

On June 5, sold a $4,000 watercolor ($2,600 cost) to Julie and Bobby Herman, who used their Great American Bank Card to charge the purchase of the painting. Le Kai deposited the credit card sales slip the same day and received immediate credit in the company's checking account. The bank charged a two percent fee.

On June 6, received payment from Likert Antiques for its June 1 purchase.

On June 7, received a check from United Merchants for the June 2 sale.

**Required**
Prepare journal entries to record the Le Kai Gallery transactions.

**LO2, LO3, LO5  P8-10A.  Journal Entries for Accounts and Notes Receivable**
Pittsburgh, Inc., began business on January 1. Certain transactions for the year follow:

June 8 Received a $30,000, 60 day, eight percent note on account from J. Albert.
Aug. 7 Received payment from J. Albert on his note (principal plus interest).
Sept. 1 Received a $36,000, 120 day, nine percent note from R.T. Matthews Company on account.
Dec. 16 Received a $28,800, 45 day, ten percent note from D. LeRoy on account.
　 30 R.T. Matthews Company failed to pay its note.
　 31 Wrote off R.T. Matthews' account as uncollectible. Pittsburgh, Inc., uses the allowance method of providing for credit losses.
　 31 Recorded expected credit losses for the year by an adjusting entry. Accounts written off during this first year have created a debit balance in the allowance for doubtful accounts of $45,200. An analysis of aged receivables indicates that the desired balance of the allowance account should be $39,000.
　 31 Made the appropriate adjusting entries for interest.

**Required**
Record the foregoing transactions and adjustments in general journal form.

**LO6  P8-11A.  Accounts Receivable Turnover and Average Collection Period: IFRS Financial Statements**

Tesco PLC is the world's third largest retailer and is headquartered in the United Kingdom. Tesco's IFRS financial statements are presented in Appendix C at the end of this book. Using this financial data, calculate the company's (a) accounts receivable turnover and (b) average collection period for 2008 and 2009. Tesco's 2007 accounts receivable were 1,079 million British pounds. Comment on the trend in Tesco's ratios.

# Problems—Set B

**P8-1B.** **Allowance Method versus Direct Write-Off Method** LO3

Steinbrook Company, which has been in business for three years, makes all of its sales on account and does not offer cash discounts. The firm's credit sales, collections from customers, and write-offs of uncollectible accounts for the three-year period are summarized as follows:

| Year | Sales | Collections | Accounts Written Off |
|------|-------|-------------|----------------------|
| 2010 | $751,000 | $733,000 | $5,300 |
| 2011 | 876,000 | 864,000 | 5,800 |
| 2012 | 972,000 | 938,000 | 6,500 |

**Required**

*a.* If Steinbrook Company used the direct write-off method of recognizing credit losses during the three years, what amount of accounts receivable should appear on the firm's balance sheet at the end of 2012? What total amount of bad debts expense should appear on the firm's income statements during the three year period?

*b.* If Steinbrook Company used an allowance method of recognizing credit losses and provided for such losses at the rate of one percent of credit sales, what amounts of accounts receivable and the allowance for doubtful accounts should appear on the firm's balance sheet at the end of 2012? What total amount of bad debts expense should appear on the firm's income statement during the three-year period?

*c.* Comment on the use of the one percent rate to provide for credit losses in part *b*.

**P8-2B.** **Journal Entries for Credit Losses** LO1, LO2

At January 1, the Griffin Company had the following accounts on its books:

| | |
|---|---|
| Accounts receivable . . . . . . . . . . . . . . . . . . . . . . . . . . . . . . . . . . . . . . . . . . . . . . . . . . . . . . . . . . . . . | $126,000 (debit) |
| Allowance for doubtful accounts. . . . . . . . . . . . . . . . . . . . . . . . . . . . . . . . . . . . . . . . . . . . . . . . | 6,800 (credit) |

During the year, credit sales were $811,000 and collections on account were $794,000. The following transactions, among others, occurred during the year:

Jan. 11 Wrote off J. Wolf's account, $2,800.
Apr. 29 Wrote off B. Avery's account, $1,000.
Nov. 15 Received $1,000 from B. Avery to pay a debt that had been written off April 29. This amount is not included in the $794,000 collections.
Dec. 5 Wrote off D. Wright's account, $2,150.
     31 In an adjusting entry, recorded the allowance for doubtful accounts at one percent of credit sales for the year.

**Required**

*a.* Prepare journal entries to record the credit sales, the collections on account, the transactions, and the adjustment.

*b.* Show how Accounts Receivable and the Allowance for Doubtful Accounts appear on the December 31 balance sheet.

**P8-3B.** **Credit Losses Based on Accounts Receivable** LO2

At December 31, Rinehart Company had a balance of $304,000 in its Accounts Receivable account and a credit balance of $2,800 in the Allowance for Doubtful Accounts account. The accounts receivable T-account consisted of $309,600 in debit balances and $5,600 in credit balances. The company has aged its accounts as follows:

| | |
|---|---|
| Current. . . . . . . . . . . . . . . . . . . . . . . . . . . . . . . . . . . . . . . . . . . . . . . . . . . . . . . . . . . . . . . . . . . . . . . . . . | $262,000 |
| 0–60 days past due . . . . . . . . . . . . . . . . . . . . . . . . . . . . . . . . . . . . . . . . . . . . . . . . . . . . . . . . . . . . . | 28,000 |
| 61–180 days past due. . . . . . . . . . . . . . . . . . . . . . . . . . . . . . . . . . . . . . . . . . . . . . . . . . . . . . . . . . . | 11,200 |
| Over 180 days past due . . . . . . . . . . . . . . . . . . . . . . . . . . . . . . . . . . . . . . . . . . . . . . . . . . . . . . . . . | 8,400 |
| | $309,600 |

In the past, the company has experienced credit losses as follows: two percent of current balances, six percent of balances 0–60 days past due, 15 percent of balances 61–180 days past due, and 30 percent of balances more than six months past due. The company bases its allowance for doubtful accounts on an aging analysis of accounts receivable.

**Required**

a. Prepare the adjusting journal entry to record the provision for credit losses for the year.

b. Show how Accounts Receivable (including the credit balances) and the Allowance for Doubtful Accounts appear on the December 31 balance sheet.

**LO4** **P8-4B.** **Credit Card Sales**

Captain Paul's Marina sells boats and other water recreational vehicles (approximately three vehicles are sold each week). The following transactions occurred during the third week of May:

On May 15, sold a $600 boat trailer ($400 cost) to Sam and Myrna Marston, who paid using a personal check.

On May 16, sold a $10,000 boat ($6,500 cost) to the Calumet Lake Patrol on account, with 2/10, n/30 terms.

On May 18, sold a $1,200 water scooter ($700 cost) to Kyle Bronson, who used the United Merchants Card to charge the cost of the water scooter. Captain Paul's mailed the credit card sales slip to United Merchants the same day. United Merchants will send a check within seven days, net of a two percent fee.

On May 19, sold a $5,000 fishing boat ($3,000 cost) to Michael Ferguson, who used the Great American Bank Card to pay for the boat. Captain Paul's deposited the credit card sales slip the same day and received an immediate credit in the company's checking account, net of a two percent fee.

On May 20, received payment from Calumet Lake Patrol for the boat purchased on May 16.

On May 21, received payment from United Merchants for the May 18 transaction.

**Required**

Prepare journal entries to record these transactions. Captain Paul's Marina uses the perpetual inventory system.

**LO2, LO3, LO5** **P8-5B.** **Journal Entries for Accounts and Notes Receivable**

Armstrong, Inc., began business on January 1. Several transactions for the year follow:

May  2  Received a $14,400, 60 day, ten percent note on account from the Holt Company.
July  1  Received payment from Holt for its note plus interest.
     1  Received a $27,000, 120 day, ten percent note from B. Rich Company on account.
Oct. 30  B. Rich failed to pay its note.
Dec.  9  Wrote off B. Rich's account as uncollectible. Armstrong, Inc., uses the allowance method of providing for credit losses.
     11  Received a $21,000, 90 day, nine percent note from W. Maling on account.
     31  Recorded expected credit losses for the year by an adjusting entry. The allowance for doubtful accounts has a debit balance of $28,300 as a result of accounts written off during this first year. An analysis of aged accounts receivables indicates that the desired balance of the allowance account is $5,800.
     31  Made the appropriate adjusting entries for interest.

**Required**

Record the foregoing transactions and adjustments in general journal form.

**LO3** **P8-6B.** **Allowance Method versus Direct Write-Off Method**

The Wallbrook Company, which has been in business for three years, makes all of its sales on account and does not offer cash discounts. The firm's credit sales, collections from customers, and write-offs of uncollectible accounts for the three-year period are summarized below:

| Year | Sales | Collections | Accounts Written Off |
|------|-------|-------------|----------------------|
| 2010 | $1,502,000 | $1,466,000 | $10,600 |
| 2011 | 1,752,000 | 1,728,000 | 11,600 |
| 2012 | 1,944,000 | 1,876,000 | 13,000 |

**Required**

a. If the Wallbrook Company used the direct write-off method of recognizing credit losses during the three years, what amount of accounts receivable should appear on the firm's balance sheet at the end of 2012? What total amount of bad debts expense should appear on the firm's income statements during the three year period?

*b.* If the Wallbrook Company used an allowance method of recognizing credit losses and provided for such losses at the rate of one percent of credit sales, what amounts of accounts receivable and the allowance for doubtful accounts should appear on the firm's balance sheet at the end of 2012? What total amount of bad debts expense should appear on the firm's income statement during the three year period?

*c.* Comment on the use of the one percent rate to provide for credit losses in part *b.*

**P8-7B.**  **Journal Entries for Credit Losses**                                                        LO1, LO2

At January 1, the Chesley Company had the following accounts on its books:

| | |
|---|---|
| Accounts receivable . . . . . . . . . . . . . . . . . . . . . . . . . . . . . . . . . . . . . . . . . . . . . . . . . . . . . . . . . . . . . . . | $252,000 (debit) |
| Allowance for doubtful accounts . . . . . . . . . . . . . . . . . . . . . . . . . . . . . . . . . . . . . . . . . . . . . . . . . . | 13,600 (credit) |

During the year, credit sales were $1,622,000 and collections on account were $1,588,000. The following transactions, among others, occurred during the year:

Jan.  11  Wrote off J. Smith's account, $5,600.
Apr.  29  Wrote off B. Bird's account, $2,000.
Nov.  15  Received $1,000 from B. Bird to pay a debt that had been written off April 29. This amount is not included in the $1,588,000 collections.
Dec.  5  Wrote off D. Finger's account, $4,300.
       31  In an adjusting entry, recorded the allowance for doubtful accounts at one percent of credit sales for the year.

**Required**

*a.* Prepare journal entries to record the credit sales, the collections on account, the transactions, and the adjustment.

*b.* Show how Accounts Receivable and the Allowance for Doubtful Accounts appear on the December 31 balance sheet.

**P8-8B.**  **Credit Losses Based on Accounts Receivable**                                               LO2

At December 31, the Hope Company had a balance of $608,000 in its accounts receivable account and a credit balance of $5,600 in the allowance for doubtful accounts account. The accounts receivable T-account consisted of $619,200 in debit balances and $11,200 in credit balances. The company has aged its accounts as follows:

| | |
|---|---|
| Current. . . . . . . . . . . . . . . . . . . . . . . . . . . . . . . . . . . . . . . . . . . . . . . . . . . . . . . . . . . . . . . . . . . . . . . . . . . . | $524,000 |
| 0–60 days past due . . . . . . . . . . . . . . . . . . . . . . . . . . . . . . . . . . . . . . . . . . . . . . . . . . . . . . . . . . . . . . . . . | 56,000 |
| 61–180 days past due. . . . . . . . . . . . . . . . . . . . . . . . . . . . . . . . . . . . . . . . . . . . . . . . . . . . . . . . . . . . . . . | 22,400 |
| Over 180 days past due . . . . . . . . . . . . . . . . . . . . . . . . . . . . . . . . . . . . . . . . . . . . . . . . . . . . . . . . . . . . | 16,800 |
| | $619,200 |

In the past, the company has experienced credit losses as follows: two percent of current balances, six percent of balances 0–60 days past due, 15 percent of balances 61–180 days past due, and 30 percent of balances more than six months past due. The company bases its allowance for doubtful accounts on an aging analysis of accounts receivable.

**Required**

*a.* Prepare the adjusting journal entry to record the provision for credit losses for the year.

*b.* Show how Accounts Receivable (including the credit balances) and the Allowance for Doubtful Accounts appear on the December 31 balance sheet.

**P8-9B.**  **Credit Card Sales**                                                                        LO4

Lake Pleasant Marina sells boats and other water recreational vehicles (approximately three vehicles are sold each week). The following transactions occurred during the third week of May:

On May 15, sold a $1,200 boat trailer ($800 cost) to Ed and Jane Peeler, who paid using a personal check.

On May 16, sold a $20,000 boat ($13,000 cost) to the Lake Pleasant Lake Patrol on account, with 2/10, n/30 terms.

On May 18, sold a $2,400 water scooter ($1,400 cost) to Bryan Wagner, who used the United Merchants Card to charge the cost of the water scooter. Lake Pleasant Marina mailed the credit card sales slip to United Merchants the same day. United Merchants will send a check within seven days, net of a two percent fee.

**ASSIGNMENTS**

On May 19, sold a $10,000 fishing boat ($6,000 cost) to Michael Moffett, who used the Great American Bank Card to pay for the boat. Lake Pleasant Marina deposited the credit card sales slip the same day and received an immediate credit in the company's checking account, net of a two percent fee.

On May 20, received payment from the Lake Pleasant Lake Patrol for the boat purchased on May 16.

On May 21, received payment from United Merchants for the May 18 transaction.

**Required**

Prepare journal entries to record these transactions. The Lake Pleasant Marina uses a perpetual inventory system.

**LO2, LO3, LO5**  **P8-10B.** **Journal Entries for Accounts and Notes Receivable**

Dallmus, Inc., began business on January 1. Several transactions for the year follow:

May  2  Received a $28,800, 60 day, ten percent note on account from the Haskins Company.
July  1  Received payment from Haskins for its note plus interest.
    1  Received a $54,000, 120 day, ten percent note from R. Longo Company on account.
Oct. 30  R. Longo failed to pay its note.
Dec.  9  Wrote off R. Longo's account as uncollectible. Dallmus, Inc., uses the allowance method of providing for credit losses.
  11  Received a $42,000, 90 day, nine percent note from R. Canal on account.
  31  Recorded expected credit losses for the year by an adjusting entry. The Allowance for Doubtful Accounts has a debit balance of $56,600 as a result of accounts written off during this first year. An analysis of aged accounts receivables indicates that the desired balance of the allowance account is $11,600.
  31  Made the appropriate adjusting entries for interest.

**Required**

Record the foregoing transactions and adjustments in general journal form.

# SERIAL PROBLEM: KATE'S CARDS

(*Note:* **This is a continuation of the Serial Problem: Kate's Cards from Chapters 1 through 7.**)

**SP8.**  Kate has put a lot of time and effort into streamlining the process to design and produce a greeting card. She has documented the entire process in a QuickTime video she produced on her iMac. The video takes the viewer through the step-by-step process of selecting hardware and software, and shows how to design and produce the card. Kate has met many people who would like to get into the production of greeting cards, but are overwhelmed by the process. Kate has decided to sell the entire package (hardware, software, and video tutorial) to aspiring card producers. The cost of the entire package to Kate is $4,500 and she plans to mark it up by $500 and sell it for $5,000.

John Stevens, an individual Kate met recently at a greeting card conference, would like to buy the package from Kate. Unfortunately, John does not have this much cash and would like for Kate to extend credit.

Kate believes that many of her customers will not be able to pay cash and therefore she will need to find some way to provide financing. One option she is exploring is to accept credit cards. She learned that the credit card provider charges a 2.5 percent fee and provides immediate cash upon receiving the sales receipts.

Kate would like you to answer the following questions:

1. What are the advantages and disadvantages of offering credit?
2. What precautions should she take before offering credit to people like John?
3. If Kate grants credit to John, the terms will be 2/10, n/30. Assuming the payment is made during the 10-day discount period, what would be the journal entry to record the sale and then the subsequent payment?
4. If instead of paying early, John pays in 25 days, what would be the journal entry to record the payment?
5. Rather than providing the financing directly, assume that Kate decides to allow the use of credit cards. Further, assume that during the month there is $15,000 worth of credit card sales. Provide the journal entry to record the sales, along with the associated credit card fee. The cost of the goods sold total $13,500.

# EXTENDING YOUR KNOWLEDGE

## REPORTING AND ANALYSIS

**EYK8-1.** **Financial Reporting Problem: Columbia Sportswear Company**

The annual report of the **Columbia Sportswear Company** is presented in Appendix A at the end of this book.

COLUMBIA SPORTSWEAR COMPANY

   *a.* What was the amount of the Accounts Receivables and the Allowance for Doubtful Accounts at the end of 2009 and 2008?

   *b.* What percent of total accounts receivables was the allowance for doubtful accounts at the end of 2009 and 2008?

**EYK8-2.** **Comparative Analysis Problem: Columbia Sportswear Company vs. The Timberland Company**

The annual report of the Columbia Sportswear Company is presented in Appendix A at the end of this book and the complete annual report of **The Timberland Company** is on this book's Website.

THE TIMBERLAND COMPANY

**Required**

   *a.* Calculate the accounts receivable turnover and the average collection period for Columbia Sportswear and The Timberland Company for 2009 and 2008. (To calculate the accounts receivable turnover, use the ending net accounts receivable balance as the denominator rather than average net accounts receivable.)

   *b.* Compare the average collection periods for the two companies and comment on possible reasons for the difference in the average collection periods for the two companies.

**EYK8-3.** **Business Decision Problem**

Sally Smith owned a dance studio in San Francisco, California. Students could buy access to the dance classes by paying a monthly fee. Unfortunately, many of Sally's students were struggling actors and actresses who lacked the ability to pay their bills in a timely manner. And, although the students were expected to pay for classes in advance, Sally had begun offering credit to many of her students in order to grow her business. This, however, created a serious liquidity problem for Sally.

| Age Classification | Trade Receivables Outstanding Balance | Historical Estimate of Noncollection |
|---|---|---|
| 0–30 days | $44,000 | 4% |
| 31–60 days | 31,000 | 8% |
| 61–90 days | 22,000 | 12% |
| 91–120 days | 13,000 | 14% |
| 121–150 days | 9,000 | 20% |
| > 150 days | 5,000 | 50% |

Sally's accountant, Matt Thomas, had tried to help her get a handle on the receivable problem, but to little avail. One trick he had successfully used in the past to make Sally realize the seriousness of the problem was to overestimate the extent of Sally's bad debt problem; consequently, there currently existed a balance in the Allowance for Uncollectible Accounts totaling $2,700.

**Required**

  1. The first step to help get Sally's business back on track is to write off all receivables having a very low probability of collection (i.e., those accounts over 150 days). Which accounts are affected and by what amount, to execute this action?

  2. Prepare an aging of Sally's remaining accounts receivable. What should be the balance in the Allowance for Uncollectible Accounts?

  3. Sally is in need of an immediate cash infusion and Matt has advised her to sell some of her receivables. A local bank has offered her two alternatives:

    *a.* Factor $40,000 of "current" receivables (i.e., 0–30 days old) on a nonrecourse basis at a flat fee of eleven percent of the receivables sold.

    *b.* Factor $40,000 of "current" receivables on a recourse basis at a flat fee of six percent of the receivables sold.

    Which option should Sally choose? Why?

ABBOTT LABORATORIES
PFIZER INC.

### EYK8-4. Financial Analysis Problem

**Abbott Laboratories** is a diversified health care company devoted to the discovery, development, manufacture, and marketing of innovative products that improve diagnostic, therapeutic, and nutritional practices. Abbott markets products in more than 130 countries and employs 50,000 people. **Pfizer Inc.** is a research-based, global health care company. Its mission is to discover and develop innovative, value-added products that improve the quality of life of people around the world. Pfizer manufactures products in 31 countries and markets these products worldwide. These two companies reported the following information in their financial reports:

| (in millions) | 2008 | 2009 |
| --- | --- | --- |
| Abbott Laboratories | | |
| Net sales | $29,528 | $30,765 |
| Beginning accounts receivable (net) | 4,947 | 5,466 |
| Ending accounts receivable (net) | 5,466 | 6,542 |
| Pfizer Inc. | | |
| Net sales | $48,296 | $50,009 |
| Beginning accounts receivable (net) | 9,843 | 8,958 |
| Ending accounts receivable (net) | 8,958 | 14,645 |

**Required**

*a.* Calculate the accounts receivable turnover and the average collection period for Abbott Laboratories and Pfizer Inc. for 2008 and 2009.

*b.* Compare the average collection periods for the two companies and comment on possible reasons for the difference in average collection periods for the two companies.

## CRITICAL THINKING

GENERAL MILLS, INC.

### EYK8-5. Accounting Research Problem

Access the fiscal year 2010 annual report of **General Mills, Inc.**, available on this book's Website.

**Required**

*a.* What was the amount of total Accounts Receivables and the Allowance for Doubtful Accounts at the end of fiscal-year 2010 and 2009? (Note: This information can be found in note 17.)

*b.* What percent of total accounts receivables was the allowance for doubtful accounts at the end of 2010 and 2009?

*c.* Calculate the accounts receivable turnover and the average collection period for General Mills for 2010 and 2009. (For purposes of calculating the accounts receivable turnover, use the ending total accounts receivable balance as the denominator rather than the average total accounts receivable.)

*d.* Comment on whether General Mills' management of accounts receivable improved (or not) over the two year period.

### EYK8-6. Accounting Communications Activity

You have been hired as the accounting manager of Taylor, Inc., a provider of custom furniture. The company recently switched its method of paying its salespeople from a straight salary to a commission basis in order to encourage them to increase sales. The salespeople receive ten percent of the sales price at the time of the sale. You have noticed that the company's accounts receivable balance is growing because the salespeople are granting more credit to their customers.

**Required**

Draft a memorandum explaining why it is important to closely monitor the company's accounts receivable balance and why a large balance could lead to cash flow problems.

### EYK8-7. Accounting Ethics Case

Tractor Motors' best salesperson is Marie Glazer. Glazer's largest sales have been to Farmers Cooperative, a customer she brought to the company. Another salesperson, Bryan Blanchard, has been told in confidence by his cousin (an employee of Farmers Cooperative) that Farmers Cooperative is experiencing financial difficulties and may not be able to pay Tractor Motors what is owed.

Both Glazer and Blanchard are being considered for promotion to a new sales manager position.

**Required**

What are the ethical considerations that face Bryan Blanchard? What alternatives does he have?

**EYK8-8.** **Corporate Social Responsibility Problem**

MGM MIRAGE

**MGM Resorts International** is committed to responsible gaming and strictly adheres to the Code of Conduct established by the American Gaming Association. The company's efforts include employee training, public awareness, and support for research initiatives through the National Center for Responsible Gaming.

Since MGM Resorts International makes money when people gamble, and the more people gamble, the more money the company makes, why would MGM Resorts International work to curtail gambling by some of the people they could make a lot of money from? Does this form of good citizenship run counter to the company's responsibilities to its stockholders?

**EYK8-9.** **Forensic Accounting Problem**

The chapter highlight on forensic accounting discussed the technique of covering up receivables theft by lapping (see Forensic Accounting: Lapping on page 373), where one account is credited with the receipt from another account. The highlight stated that lapping may be detected by an auditor through the confirmation of accounts receivables. While detection is important, it is far better to prevent lapping from occurring in the first place. Can you think of any controls that can be put in place to help prevent lapping?

**EYK8-10.** **Analyzing IFRS Financial Statements**

Tesco PLC is the world's third largest retailer and is headquartered in the United Kingdom. Tesco's IFRS financial statements are presented in Appendix C at the end of this book, and the complete annual report is available on this book's Website. Using this financial data, respond to the following questions. At year-end 2009 (2008), Tesco's allowance for doubtful accounts was 44 (29) million British pounds.

**Required**

*a.* What was the gross amount of Trade and Other Receivables at fiscal year-end 2008 and 2009?

*b.* What percent of total trade and other receivables was the allowance for doubtful accounts as of the end of 2008 and 2009?

*c.* Calculate the accounts receivable turnover and the average collection period for the company for 2008 and 2009. (For purposes of calculating the accounts receivable turnover, the 2007 ending Trade and Other Receivables was 1,079 million pounds.)

*d.* Comment on whether Tesco's management of its trade receivables improved (or not) over the two year period.

## ANSWERS TO SELF-STUDY QUESTIONS:

1. d, (p. 371)   2. b, (p. 370)   3. d, (p. 375)   4. a, (p. 378)   5. d, (p. 378)   6. c, (p. 377)
7. a, (p. 368)   8. a, (p. 374)   9. c, (p. 372)   10. c, (p. 376)

## Your Turn! Solutions

**Solution 8.1**

| | | |
|---|---|---|
| Bad debt expense | 18,000 | |
|     Allowance for doubtful accounts | | 18,000 |
|     *To record the bad debt expense for the period.* | | |

ANSWERS

### Solution 8.2

| | | | |
|---|---|---|---|
| a. | Bad debt expense | 3,950 | |
| |     Allowance for doubtful accounts | | 3,950 |
| | *To record the bad debt expense for the period.* | | |
| b. | Allowance for doubtful accounts | 480 | |
| |     Accounts receivable | | 480 |
| | *To write off the Phorest Company uncollectible account.* | | |

### Solution 8.3

| | | |
|---|---|---|
| Bad debt expense | 750 | |
|     Accounts receivable | | 750 |
| *To write off the Rhea Inc. uncollectible account.* | | |

### Solution 8.4

| | | |
|---|---|---|
| Cash | 49,000 | |
| Credit card fee expense | 1,000 | |
|     Sales revenue | | 50,000 |
| *To record credit sales and collection, less a two percent fee.* | | |

### Solution 8.5

$40,000 \times .05 \times 3/12 = \$500$

### Solution 8.6

a. Accounts receivable turnover $= \$30,000/[(\$2,800 + \$3,200)/2] = 10$

b. Average collection period $= 365/10 = 36.5$ days

# 9 Accounting for Long-Lived and Intangible Assets

| Past | Present | Future |
|---|---|---|
| In Chapter 8 we studied how to account for accounts and notes receivable. | This chapter focuses on another important set of assets—long-lived plant assets and intangible assets. | Chapter 10 begins our study of the accounting for liabilities. |

## LEARNING OBJECTIVES

*1* **Discuss** the nature of long-lived assets and **identify** the accounting guidelines relating to their initial measurement. (p. 409)

*2* **Discuss** the nature of depreciation, **illustrate** three depreciation methods, and **explain** impairment losses. (p. 412)

*3* **Discuss** the distinction between revenue expenditures and capital expenditures. (p. 419)

*4* **Explain** and **illustrate** the accounting for disposals of plant assets. (p. 421)

*5* **Discuss** the nature of, and the accounting for, intangible assets. (p. 422)

*6* **Illustrate** the balance sheet presentation of plant assets and intangible assets. (p. 426)

*7* **Define** the return on assets ratio and the asset turnover ratio and **explain** their use. (p. 426)

# CUMMINS INC.

**Cummins Inc.** is a multinational, Fortune 500 company based in Columbus, Indiana. The company is best known for its production of large diesel engines that power tractor-trailer trucks and buses. Cummins is no longer just an engine manufacturer. Today, the company is a global power manufacturer with over $10 billion in sales. Cummins, however, was not always so big. The company was founded in 1919 as Cummins Engine Company to develop the commercial potential of the unproven diesel engine. The company saw little success over the next decade. In fact, it was not until several decades later when the United States embarked on a national interstate highway construction program that Cummins cemented its place as the principal provider of the engines to power much of the equipment used to build those roads and power the trucks that drove on the roads.

Manufacturers like Cummins require large investments in plant assets such as land, buildings, and equipment in order to produce the products they sell. Companies like Cummins also typically maintain large investments in such intangible assets as trademarks and patents. Plant assets and intangible assets comprised 21.4 percent and 6.7 percent, respectively, of the company's total assets. Because of its large investment in these long-lived, revenue-producing assets, Cummins is referred to as a capital-intensive company. Wall Street analysts evaluate the capital intensity of companies by calculating a capital-intensity ratio, calculated as the value of plant assets plus the value of intangible assets divided by the value of a company's total assets. Cummins' capital-intensity ratio is consistently about 28 percent.

## ACCOUNTING FOR LONG-LIVED AND INTANGIBLE ASSETS

### Plant Assets

- Measuring acquisition cost of plant assets
- Recording plant assets
- Computing depreciation
- Revenue expenditures
- Disposing of plant assets

### Intangible Assets

- Measuring intangible asset costs
- Recording intangible assets
- Computing amortization
- Examples of intangible assets
- Balance sheet presentation of intangible assets

### Analyzing Long-Lived Assets

- Return on assets
- Asset turnover

# OVERVIEW OF LONG-LIVED ASSETS

**A.K.A.** Plant assets are often referred to as fixed assets.

**A.K.A.** Property, plant and equipment is often referred to as simply PP&E.

Consider for a moment the asset structure of Cummins Inc. More than 28 percent of the assets used to fulfill the company's mission of manufacturing and distributing power products are in two long-term asset categories: *plant assets* and *goodwill and other intangible assets*. **Plant assets** refer to a firm's *long-lived property, plant and equipment*. Cummins reports plant assets of nearly $2 billion. Intangible assets, on the other hand, refer to those economic resources that benefit a company's operations but which lack the physical substance that characterizes plant assets. Examples of intangible assets include copyrights, franchises, and patents. The benefits provided to a firm by its plant assets and its intangible assets extend over many accounting periods. In this chapter, we discuss the accounting for these long-lived assets.

The carrying value of long-lived assets is initially based on the asset's historical cost—that is, the cost incurred to acquire and place the asset into a revenue-producing state. The costs related to the use of long-lived assets must be matched with the revenues that they help to generate to insure that a business's net income is correctly determined. The portion of an asset's cost that is consumed or used up in any given period is called *depreciation expense, when referring to plant assets*, and *amortization expense, when referring to intangible assets*. Both of these terms have an equivalent meaning in accounting: that is, amortization and depreciation refer to the process of allocating a portion of an asset's acquisition cost to expense on the income statement to reflect the consumption of the asset as it produces revenue for a business.

Exhibit 9-1 provides several examples of both categories of assets. The exhibit also identifies the appropriate term for the periodic consumption of the asset and its write-off

| EXHIBIT 9-1 | Long-Lived Assets That Require Periodic Write-Off | |
|---|---|---|
| **Asset Category** | **Examples** | **Term for the Periodic Write-Off to Expense** |
| Plant Assets | Buildings, equipment, tools, furniture, fixtures, vehicles | Depreciation |
| Intangible Assets | Patents, copyrights, leaseholds, franchises, trademarks, brand names | Amortization |

to expense. Note that site land—that is, the land on which a business is operated—has an indefinite useful life, and therefore, does not require any periodic write-off to expense.

# ACCOUNTING FOR LONG-LIVED ASSETS

Exhibit 9-2 is a graphic presentation of the accounting issues associated with long-lived assets during an asset's useful life. The accounting issues include: ❶ Identifying the type, and amount, of expenditures that make up the acquisition cost of the asset. ❷ Determining the appropriate amount of an asset's cost to periodically charge against revenue to reflect the asset's consumption. This involves estimating the asset's useful life and its probable salvage value at disposal. ❸ Differentiating those expenditures related to the maintenance of an asset from those expenditures that increase an asset's productive capacity or extend its useful life. ❹ Determining any gain or loss to be recognized when a long-lived asset is disposed of.

**LEARNING OBJECTIVE 1**

**Discuss** the nature of long-lived assets and **identify** the accounting guidelines relating to their initial measurement.

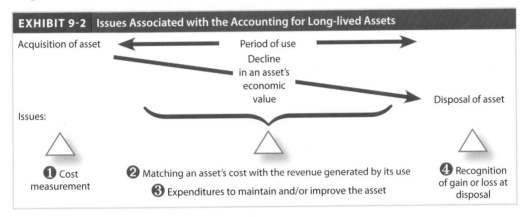

**EXHIBIT 9-2    Issues Associated with the Accounting for Long-lived Assets**

## ACQUISITION COST OF LONG-LIVED ASSETS

Long-lived assets are initially recorded on the balance sheet at their acquisition cost. This measure is also called the asset's *historical cost* because it represents the amount expended when the asset was originally acquired. In general, the acquisition cost of a long-lived asset equals the cash and/or cash equivalent given up to acquire the asset *and* to prepare it for its intended use.

| **PRINCIPLE ALERT**    **Cost Principle** |
| --- |
| The initial valuation of long-lived assets follows directly from the *cost principle* discussed in Chapter 2. To measure an asset's acquisition cost, accountants must not only identify the asset's cash-equivalent purchase price, but also identify whether any additional costs were incurred to get the asset to a company's place of business and in a condition for use by the business. Both costs are added to the asset's balance sheet value and are considered part of the asset's acquisition cost. |

### Cash Purchases

An asset's acquisition cost is often simply the amount of cash paid when the asset is acquired and readied for use by a business. Consider, for example, the following expenditures for a piece of equipment by Smith & Sons:

| | | |
| --- | --- | --- |
| Purchase price components: | | |
| Gross invoice price .................................................... | $10,000 | |
| Less: Cash discount (1/10, n/30)......................................... | 100 | |
| Sales tax ............................................................. | 500 | $10,400 |
| Related expenditures: | | |
| Freight charges ....................................................... | 200 | |
| Installation costs ..................................................... | 500 | |
| Testing of installed machine ........................................... | 300 | 1,000 |
| **Acquisition cost of equipment**......................................... | | **$11,400** |

The total acquisition cost of the Smith & Sons equipment is $11,400, consisting of a cash purchase price of $10,400 and related preparation costs of $1,000. The sales tax is also a necessary component of the purchase price and should be included in the asset's acquisition cost. Similarly, the costs of freight, installation, and testing are expenditures necessary to get the asset to the desired business location and ready for its intended use.

### Deferred Payment Purchases

If an asset's purchase price is not immediately paid in cash, the cash-equivalent purchase price at the date of acquisition is determined and recorded in the asset account. Suppose, for example, that Smith & Sons purchased its equipment under a financing plan requiring a $400 cash down payment and a nine percent, $10,000 note payable due in one year. The implied cash price remains $10,400 even though more than $10,400 is eventually paid under the financing plan ($400 down payment + $10,000 principal payment on note + $900 interest payment = $11,300). Because the equipment is ready for immediate use, the extra $900 paid as interest is charged to interest expense and does not become part of its acquisition cost. The journal entry to record the purchase of the equipment under the financing plan is as follows:

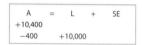

| | | A | = | L | + | SE |
|---|---|---|---|---|---|---|
| | | +10,400 | | | | |
| | | −400 | | +10,000 | | |

| | | |
|---|---|---|
| Equipment | 10,400 | |
|    Cash | | 400 |
|    Notes payable | | 10,000 |
|    *To record purchase of equipment.* | | |

As in the case of a cash purchase, the expenditures for freight, installation, and testing are debited to the Equipment account when incurred.

### Package Purchases

Sometimes several long-lived assets are purchased as a package. For example, assume that Smith & Sons purchased a freight terminal that included land, a building, and some loading equipment for an aggregate price of $190,000. For accounting purposes, the total purchase price should be divided among the three assets because (1) they should be reported in different asset accounts on the balance sheet to properly reflect the company's asset structure, (2) only the building and equipment are subject to depreciation, and (3) the equipment is likely to have an estimated useful life different from that of the building.

    The total package price is allocated among the acquired assets on the basis of their relative market or appraisal values. For example, if the estimated market value of the land, building, and equipment is $60,000, $120,000, and $20,000, respectively, the allocation of the $190,000 acquisition price would be as follows:

| Asset | Estimated Market Value | Percent of Total | Allocation of Purchase Price | Estimated Useful Life |
|---|---|---|---|---|
| Land........................................ | $ 60,000 | 30 | $ 57,000 | Indefinite |
| Building.................................... | 120,000 | 60 | 114,000 | 30 years |
| Equipment............................... | 20,000 | 10 | 19,000 | 8 years |
|   Totals.................................. | $200,000 | 100 | $190,000 | |

### EXPENDITURES RELATED TO LAND

The purchase of land often raises a number of accounting issues. Suppose, for example, that Smith & Sons retains a local real estate broker at a fee of $2,000 to locate an appropriate site for the company's new office building. Assume, also, that the property selected for purchase has an existing building on it which will need to be razed. The terms of the sale include a down payment of $40,000 to the seller, with the buyer paying off an existing mortgage of $10,000 and $300 of accrued interest. In addition, Smith & Sons agrees to pay accrued real estate taxes of $800 owed by the seller. Other related expenditures include legal fees of $400 and a title insurance premium of $500. A local salvage company will be hired to raze the old building, paying Smith & Sons $200 for reclaimed materials. Applying the cost principle, the acquisition cost of the land is calculated as follows:

| | |
|---|---:|
| Payment to the seller | $40,000 |
| Commission to real estate agent | 2,000 |
| Payment of mortgage and accrued interest due at time of sale | 10,300 |
| Payment of property taxes owed by seller | 800 |
| Legal fees | 400 |
| Title insurance premium | 500 |
| | $54,000 |
| Less: Net recovery from material reclamation | 200 |
| Cost of land | $53,800 |

Again, any expenditure for the property taxes, insurance, and legal fees should be capitalized, or added to, the acquisition cost of the land because they are necessary to complete the purchase transaction. Similarly, removing the old building also prepares the land for its intended use. The $200 net recovery from razing the existing structure, therefore, *reduces* the land's cost. A net payment to remove the old building would have *increased* the land's cost.

When a land site is acquired in an undeveloped area, a firm may pay a special assessment to the local government for such property improvements as streets, sidewalks, and sewers. These improvements are considered to be permanent improvements; and consequently, the special assessment is capitalized to (added to) the acquisition cost of the land.

A firm may also make property improvements that have limited lives. Classified as **land improvements**, they include such improvements as paved parking lots, driveways, private sidewalks, and fences. Expenditures for these assets are charged to a separate Land Improvement account on the balance sheet and depreciated over the estimated useful life of the improvements.

### Leasehold Improvements

Expenditures made by a business to alter or improve leased property are called **leasehold improvements**. For example, a merchandising firm may make improvements, with the permission of the owner, to a leased building. **Home Depot**, a home improvement retail chain, leases a significant portion of its more than 2,000 U.S. stores and reports nearly $1.4 billion of leasehold improvements on its balance sheet. The improvements, or alterations, become part of the leased property and revert to the owner of the property at the end of the lease. The cost of the leasehold improvements is capitalized to the Leasehold Improvements account on the balance sheet and is depreciated over the life of the lease or the life of the improvements, whichever is shorter.

---

**Your Turn!** **9.1**

Kelly Company purchased manufacturing equipment for $20,000 cash. In addition to the $20,000 purchase price, Kelly paid sales tax of $1,600, freight costs of $400, installation costs of $600, testing costs of $100, and $300 for a five-year extended warranty. Explain the accounting treatment for each of the expenditures.

**The solution is on page 446.**

---

**CORPORATE SOCIAL RESPONSIBILITY**

It is unlikely that the first company that you think of when asked to name the top companies in an annual ranking of socially-responsible businesses is a manufacturer of diesel engines. Perhaps you may need to revise your thinking. **Cummins Inc.** is a perennial top 10 finisher among Business Ethics 100 Best Corporate Citizens, a prestigious annual ranking by *Business Ethics* magazine. In fact, Cummins placed number one in the ranking in 2005!

Cummins is one of the best manufacturing companies in the world when it comes to air-emissions reduction research. The company's research efforts have paid off with a 90 percent reduction in diesel-engine emissions. Cummins' ten-year goal is to achieve zero, or close to zero, engine emissions.

# THE NATURE OF DEPRECIATION

LEARNING OBJECTIVE 2

**Discuss** the nature of depreciation, **illustrate** three depreciation methods, and **explain** impairment losses.

With the exception of site land, the use of plant assets to generate revenue consumes the economic benefit provided by the assets. At some point—usually before they are totally worthless—these assets are disposed of, and often replaced. A diagram of a typical pattern of plant asset utilization is illustrated below:

Acquisition price, $1,000 ← Useful life → Disposal at $100

Decline in recorded value, $900

In this example, a plant asset is acquired for $1,000, used for several accounting periods, and then sold for $100. The $900 decline in recorded value is called **depreciation** and is an expense of generating the revenues recognized during the periods that the asset was in use. Thus, if a company's net income is to be a meaningful representation of the business's operating performance, $900 of expense must be allocated to the periods of asset use and matched with sales revenue. Failure to do so would overstate the company's net income for these periods.

As part of this allocation process, it is first necessary to estimate the asset's useful life and its expected future salvage value. **Useful life** is the expected period of economic usefulness to a business—that is, the period from the date of acquisition to the expected date of disposal. **Salvage value** (or *residual value*) is the expected net recovery (sales proceeds – disposal costs) when the asset is sold or removed from service. When the salvage value is insignificant, it may be ignored in the depreciation process under the materiality concept.

**A.K.A.** The salvage value of a plant asset is also often referred to as its scrap value.

## ALLOCATION VERSUS VALUATION: DEPRECIATION ACCOUNTING

Although the idea is theoretically appealing, accountants do not base an asset's periodic depreciation expense on changes in the asset's market value or on the measured wear of the asset, primarily because a reliable, objective, and practical source for such data rarely exists. Rather, **depreciation accounting** is simply an attempt to allocate, in a *systematic* and *rational* manner, the difference between an asset's acquisition cost and its estimated salvage value over the *estimated* useful life of the asset. Consequently, depreciation accounting techniques are just convenient expedients for estimating asset utilization and should not be considered precise. Although imprecise, depreciation estimates facilitate a better assessment of a business's net income than would result from expensing the asset at either its date of acquisition or its date of disposal.

> **PRINCIPLE ALERT** **Expense Recognition (Matching) Concept**
>
> Depreciation accounting represents an application of the expense recognition (*matching*) concept. Depreciable plant assets are used in a business's operating activities to help generate revenues. Each period that benefits from the use of a plant asset is assigned part of the asset's cost as depreciation expense. In so doing, the depreciation expense is matched with the sales revenue that the asset helps to generate. The matching that occurs through this allocation process extends throughout the asset's useful life.

Several factors are related to the periodic allocation of depreciation. Depreciation can be caused by wear from use, from natural deterioration, and from technical obsolescence. Each factor reduces the economic value of an asset. To some extent, maintenance (lubrication, adjustments, parts replacements, and cleaning) may partially arrest or offset wear and deterioration. Thus, when an asset's useful life and salvage value are estimated, a given level of maintenance is assumed.

## CALCULATING DEPRECIATION EXPENSE

Estimating the periodic depreciation of a long-lived asset can be achieved in many ways. In this section, three widely used methods for calculating depreciation are illustrated.

1. Straight-line
2. Declining-balance
3. Units-of-production

For each method, we assume that equipment is purchased for $1,000. The equipment is assumed to have an estimated useful life of five years and has an estimated salvage value of $100.

### Straight-Line Method

The **straight-line method** is the easiest depreciation method to understand and calculate. Consequently, this method is the most widely used depreciation method by U.S. businesses. Under the straight-line method, an equal amount of depreciation expense is allocated to each period of an asset's useful life. Straight-line depreciation is calculated as follows:

$$\text{Annual depreciation} = \frac{\text{(Acquisition cost − Salvage value)}}{\text{Estimated useful life (in months or years)}}$$

For the purchased equipment, the annual straight-line depreciation expense is:

$$\frac{(\$1,000 − \$100)}{5 \text{ years}} = \$180 \text{ per year}$$

And, the journal entry to record the annual depreciation expense is:

| | | |
|---|---|---|
| Depreciation expense—Equipment | 180 | |
|     Accumulated depreciation—Equipment | | 180 |
| *To record depreciation expense for the year.* | | |

| A | = | L | + | SE |
|---|---|---|---|---|
| −180 | | | | −180 Exp |

Like other expense accounts, Depreciation Expense is deducted from sales revenue on the income statement and is closed at year-end to the Income Summary account. The offsetting credit entry is posted to a contra-asset account, Accumulated Depreciation, which is deducted from the Equipment account on the balance sheet to calculate the asset's book value. In this manner, the original acquisition cost of the asset is maintained in the asset account, and the cumulative balance of depreciation taken to date is carried in the contra-asset account, as long as the asset is in service. When an asset is disposed of, the asset's acquisition cost and accumulated depreciation are both removed from the accounts.

**A.K.A.** The book value of an asset (acquisition cost less accumulated depreciation) is also referred to as the net book value.

The following table shows the various account balances during the equipment's five-year life under the straight-line method:

| | | | End-of-Period Balance | |
|---|---|---|---|---|
| Year of Useful Life | Balance of Equipment Account | Annual Depreciation Expense | Accumulated Depreciation Account | Asset's Book Value |
|---|---|---|---|---|
| 1................................................ | $1,000 | $180 | $180 | $820 |
| 2................................................ | 1,000 | 180 | 360 | 640 |
| 3................................................ | 1,000 | 180 | 540 | 460 |
| 4................................................ | 1,000 | 180 | 720 | 280 |
| 5................................................ | 1,000 | 180 | 900 | 100 |
| Total ........................................ | | $900 | | |

Notice that (1) the Equipment account always shows the original acquisition cost ($1,000) of the asset; (2) each period reflects $180 of depreciation expense; (3) the Accumulated Depreciation account balance is cumulative and shows the portion of the acquisition cost taken as depreciation to date; (4) the asset's book value is the original acquisition cost of the asset less the accumulated depreciation taken to date; and (5) the asset's book value at the end of the five-year period is equal to the asset's estimated salvage value. Thus, an asset's book value declines to its estimated salvage value as the asset is depreciated over its useful life.

For periods of less than one year, straight-line depreciation amounts are simply proportions of the annual depreciation charge. For example, if an asset is acquired on April 1, depreciation for the period ended December 31 would be $135, or 9/12 × $180. Assets acquired or disposed of during the first half of any month are usually treated as if the acquisition or disposal occurred on the first day of the month. When either event occurs during the last half of any month, it is assumed that the event occurred on the first day of the following month.

---

**PRINCIPLE ALERT** | **Going Concern Concept**

Note the role of the *going concern concept* in depreciation accounting. Absent evidence to the contrary, the going concern concept assumes that a business has an indefinite life. Depreciation accounting allocates an asset's acquisition cost to expense over the asset's useful life. Any depreciation method that allocates an asset's acquisition cost over many years—whether the useful life is five years or 25 years (or more)—implicitly assumes that a business will be in existence for at least that number of years.

---

### Declining-Balance Method

The **declining-balance method** is an **accelerated depreciation method**. It calculates a company's depreciation expense as a constant percentage of an asset's book value as of the beginning of each period. The method takes its name from the fact that, over time, an asset's book value (acquisition cost − accumulated depreciation) declines as the asset is used up, yielding a decreasing depreciation expense. An asset's salvage value is not considered in the calculation of declining-balance depreciation, except that the depreciation of an asset stops when the asset's book value equals its estimated salvage value.

The declining-balance method is considered to be an "accelerated" method because the constant depreciation percentage it uses is a multiple of the straight-line depreciation rate (the straight-line depreciation rate = 100 percent/expected useful life in years). There are many versions of the declining-balance method because different multiples of the straight-line rate may be used. *Double-declining balance depreciation* uses a depreciation rate that is twice the straight-line rate; similarly, *150 percent-declining balance depreciation* uses a depreciation rate that is one and one-half times the straight-line rate.

For example, the straight-line depreciation rate for an asset with a five-year useful life is 20 percent per year (100 percent/5 years). Thus, to depreciate a five-year asset on an accelerated basis, the double-declining balance method uses a 40 percent depreciation rate (2 × 20 percent); and, the 150 percent declining-balance method uses a 30 percent depreciation rate (1.5 × 20 percent).

Under the double-declining balance method, the annual depreciation expense is calculated as follows:

**Annual depreciation = Book value at beginning of year × Double-declining balance rate**

Referring to our example of the equipment purchased for $1,000, with a useful life of five years and an expected salvage value of $100, the periodic double-declining balance depreciation would be calculated as follows (amounts rounded to the nearest dollar):

| Year of Useful Life | Acquisition Cost | Beginning Accumulated Depreciation | Beginning Book Value | | Twice Straight-line Percentage | | Annual Depreciation Expense |
|---|---|---|---|---|---|---|---|
| 1 | $1,000 | $ 0 | $1,000 | × | 40 percent | = | $400 |
| 2 | 1,000 | 400 | 600 | × | 40 percent | = | 240 |
| 3 | 1,000 | 640 | 360 | × | 40 percent | = | 144 |
| 4 | 1,000 | 784 | 216 | × | 40 percent | = | 86 |
| 5 | 1,000 | 870 | 130 | | | | 30 |
| Total | | | | | | | $900 |

Notice in the fifth year that the depreciation expense is only $30, the amount needed to reduce the asset's book value to its estimated salvage value of $100. Assets are not depreciated below their estimated salvage value.

If an asset is purchased during a fiscal period, a pro-rata allocation of the first year's depreciation is calculated. If, for example, an asset is acquired on April 1, depreciation for the period ended December 31 would be $300, or [9/12 × (40 percent × $1,000)]. In subsequent periods, the usual procedure is followed; that is, the asset's book value at the beginning of the period is multiplied by the constant depreciation rate. For example, in the second year, depreciation on the asset would be $280, or [40 percent × ($1,000 − $300)].

**Hint:** An asset's salvage value must be considered when calculating the depreciation expense for an asset using the straight-line method or the units-of-production method; but, an asset's salvage value is not considered when calculating double-declining balance depreciation, until the final year.

### Units-of-Production Method

The **units-of-production method** allocates depreciation in proportion to an asset's use in operations. Under this method, the depreciation per unit of production is first calculated by dividing the total depreciable cost of the asset (in our example, $1000 − $100 = $900) by the asset's projected units-of-production capacity:

$$\text{Depreciation per unit} = \frac{\text{(Acquisition cost − Salvage value)}}{\text{Total estimated units of production}}$$

The total estimated units of production may represent the total expected miles that an asset will be driven, the total tons expected to be hauled, the total hours expected to be used, or the total number of expected cuttings, drillings, or stampings of parts by a piece of equipment. To illustrate, assume that a drilling tool will drill an estimated 45,000 parts during its expected useful life. The tool is purchased for $1,000 and has an expected salvage value of $100. Consequently, the depreciation per unit of production is:

$$\frac{(\$1,000 − \$100)}{45,000 \text{ parts}} = \$0.02 \text{ per part}$$

To find the asset's annual depreciation expense, the depreciation per unit of production is multiplied by the number of units actually produced during a given year:

**Annual depreciation = Depreciation per unit × Units of production for the period**

Assuming that the number of parts drilled over the five years were 8,000, 14,000, 10,000, 4,000, and 9,000, respectively, in Year 1 through Year 5, the units-of-production depreciation expense is calculated as follows:

| Year of Useful Life | Depreciation per Unit | | Annual Units of Production | | Annual Depreciation Expense |
|---|---|---|---|---|---|
| 1 | $0.02 | × | 8,000 | = | $160 |
| 2 | 0.02 | × | 14,000 | = | 280 |
| 3 | 0.02 | × | 10,000 | = | 200 |
| 4 | 0.02 | × | 4,000 | = | 80 |
| 5 | 0.02 | × | 9,000 | = | 180 |
| Total | | | | | $900 |

## A COMPARISON OF ALTERNATIVE DEPRECIATION METHODS

The following charts compare the periodic depreciation expense from our equipment illustration for the straight-line and the double-declining balance methods. The charts visually display the accelerated nature of the double-declining balance method relative to the straight-line method. Notice, for example, that the depreciation expense in

Year 1 under the double-declining balance method is $400 but is only $180 under the straight-line method. In Year 2, the double-declining balance depreciation is $240 but again is only $180 for the straight-line method. It is not until Year 3 that the straight-line method produces a depreciation charge that exceeds the double-declining balance charge. The units-of-production method chart is not shown because there is no general pattern for the annual depreciation expense under this method. The annual depreciation for the units-of-production method depends on the yearly productive activity of an asset, and this activity will vary from asset to asset.

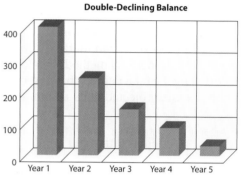

## ACCOUNTING IN PRACTICE | Depreciation Methods

So many assets, so little time. Some accountants may feel that way when it comes to calculating the periodic depreciation expense for a business. They may also feel that variety is the spice of life. At least it appears that way given the various methods that companies choose to calculate the depreciation expense that appears on their income statements. Below are the depreciation methods used by 600 large U.S. companies. As can be seen, the straight-line method is by far the most popular depreciation method used:

- Group/composite 1.8%
- Units-of-production 3.3%
- Accelerated method—not specified 4%
- Sum-of-the-years'-digits <1%
- Declining-balance 2.2%
- Straight-line 99%

*The totals exceed 100 percent because some firms use more than one method.

Source: Accounting Trends and Techniques

## DEPRECIATION METHOD ESTIMATE CHANGES

It is important to remember that a business's periodic depreciation expense is based on estimates of both an asset's useful life and its salvage value. Circumstances change, however, and original estimates of both an asset's useful life and its salvage value may subsequently be found to be too high or too low. Once it is determined that the original estimates of either an asset's useful life or salvage value were incorrect, the calculation of the periodic depreciation expense for an asset's remaining useful life may be revised. When a depreciation estimate revision is found to be warranted, the revision is executed by allocating the undepreciated balance of the asset's book value over the revised remaining useful life. To illustrate this process, refer again to our example of equipment costing $1,000, with a five year life, and an estimated salvage value of $100.

If, based on original estimates, straight-line depreciation of $180 has been recorded for each of the first three years of the asset's useful life, the accumulated depreciation to date would total $540, or 3 × $180. Now, suppose that just before recording the depreciation expense for the fourth year, circumstances indicate that the equipment's useful life will total six years instead of five, and that its salvage value at the end of the sixth year will be $40 instead of $100. The revised depreciation expense to be taken during the revised remaining useful life (Year Four through Year Six) of the equipment is calculated as follows:

| | |
|---|---:|
| Original acquisition cost | $1,000 |
| Depreciation previously recorded (3 years @ $180) | (540) |
| Book value at start of fourth year | $ 460 |
| Revised salvage value | (40) |
| Revised remaining depreciable cost | $ 420 |
| Revised remaining useful life | 3 years |
| Revised periodic depreciation expense for fourth, fifth, and sixth years | $420/3 = $ 140 per year |

## Impairment Losses

Sometimes a change in the circumstances relating to a depreciable asset is so severe that the future cash flows from the asset's use and disposal are estimated to be *less* than its current book value. If an asset's remaining book value cannot be recovered through the future cash flows expected to be generated from the asset's use, the asset's value is said to be *impaired.* Under these circumstances, an impairment loss is recorded on the income statement, and the asset's book value on the balance sheet is reduced. The **impairment loss** is calculated as the difference between the asset's current book value and its current fair value.

To illustrate, assume that two years ago Cummins purchased equipment costing $500,000, with an estimated useful life of six years and a salvage value of $20,000. The equipment's book value is currently $340,000 ($500,000 cost less $160,000 accumulated depreciation). Unanticipated technological advances in equipment used by competitors, however, now severely limits the use of Cummins' equipment. An analysis by the company's CFO indicates that Cummins now expects that the net future cash flows to be generated from the use and disposal of the equipment over the next four years is $300,000. The limited uses for the equipment cause its current fair value to be only $200,000.

Cummins' equipment is impaired because its book value is not recoverable through its expected future cash flows—the $300,000 of expected future cash flows is less than the equipment's $340,000 current book value. Thus, an impairment loss is computed by comparing the equipment's book value with its current fair value, as follows:

| | |
|---|---:|
| Equipment book value | $340,000 |
| Equipment current fair value | (200,000) |
| Impairment loss | $140,000 |

The journal entry to record the impairment loss is as follows:

| | | |
|---|---:|---:|
| Impairment loss on equipment | 140,000 | |
|    Accumulated depreciation—Equipment | | 140,000 |
| *To record impairment loss on equipment.* | | |

| A | = | L | + | SE |
|---|---|---|---|---|
| −140,000 | | | | −140,000 |
| | | | | Loss |

---

### PRINCIPLE ALERT    Conservatism Concept

The accounting for impaired plant assets illustrates the *conservatism concept*. In selecting between alternative accounting measures, the conservatism concept states that the least optimistic measure should be used. When a plant asset is impaired, it is reported on the balance sheet at its current fair value, an amount lower than its book value before any impairment loss is recorded. Unimpaired plant assets remain on the balance sheet at their book value, however, even though current fair values may be higher. U.S. GAAP mandates that asset values be written down when impaired, but prohibits the write-up of assets when their value appreciates.

---

### IFRS ALERT!

While U.S. GAAP requires that long-lived assets be written down in value when they are judged to be impaired, they may not be written up in value if there is a subsequent recovery in their fair market value. Under International Financial Reporting Standards (IFRS), however, the accounting treatment of long-lived asset value recoveries is substantially different. Under IFRS, if an asset's value increases above its current book value, the asset's balance sheet value may be written up to the higher value by debiting the asset account for the amount of the increase. The balancing credit entry is to a stockholders' equity account called the asset revaluation reserve.

To illustrate, assume that Peabody International PLC, based in the United Kingdom, owns land in London that was originally purchased for 20 million British pounds. Current real estate appraisals, however, indicate that the fair market value of the land is now worth 50 million pounds. To recognize the increase in the land's fair market value, Peabody International would record the following journal entry:

| | | |
|---|---|---|
| Land | 30 million pounds | |
|     Asset revaluation reserve—Land | | 30 million pounds |
| *To record the revaluation of land.* | | |

---

### Depreciation for Income Tax Purposes

Depreciation expense may be deducted by a business on its federal income tax return as a normal business expense. As a consequence, some refer to the tax deductibility of depreciation as a "tax shield" since depreciation expense lowers a business's pre-tax net income, and hence, lowers the actual income taxes that must be paid. The depreciation expense deducted on a business's income tax return, however, may differ substantially from the depreciation expense reported on a company's income statement because the calculation of tax depreciation follows income tax regulations referred to as the **modified accelerated cost recovery system (MACRS).**

MACRS establishes eight asset classes with prescribed useful lives ranging from three years to 31.5 years. Most machinery and equipment, for example, are in the seven-year asset class. When acquired, an asset is placed in the appropriate asset class (per MACRS guidelines) and depreciated over the prescribed useful life specified for that class.[1]

MACRS was introduced into U.S. tax law to encourage companies to invest in plant assets. Because the useful life specified under MACRS is usually shorter than an asset's accounting useful life, this method provides larger depreciation deductions during an asset's early years than was previously possible, much like the declining-balance method used for financial statement reporting. In a sense, the accelerated deductions under MACRS provide an interest-free loan to a business because they allow the firm to pay less income tax in the early years of an asset's life and more in the later years. During the

---

[1] Depreciation in most asset classes must follow a half-year convention whereby one-half of the first year's depreciation expense is taken in the first year, regardless of when the asset was acquired, and one-half of the asset's last year's depreciation is taken in the year of disposal. The half-year convention means that assets in the three-year asset class are effectively depreciated over four different accounting periods, assets in the five-year property class are depreciated over six different accounting periods, and so on.

intervening time period, the firm can use the postponed income tax payments to support the business's operations, without incurring any interest charges.

Change and modification characterize U.S. tax law. Tax depreciation guidelines will likely be modified again in the future. Keep in mind, however, that depreciation changes in the tax law do not affect the depreciation method and estimates that a firm may use in preparing its financial statements using U.S. GAAP for its shareholders and lenders.

---

### Your Turn! 9.2

The Salsbury Company purchased equipment costing $10,000 at the start of the year. The equipment has an estimated useful life of five years and a salvage value of $2,000. The CEO is unsure if the company should use the straight-line method or the double-declining balance method to depreciate the new equipment.

**Required:**
Prepare the journal entry for depreciation for the second year under each of the alternative depreciation accounting methods.

The solution is on page 447.

---

# REVENUE EXPENDITURES

**Revenue expenditures** are expenditures relating to plant assets that are expensed when incurred. The following list identifies two common types of revenue expenditures:

1. Expenditures for ordinary maintenance and repairs of existing plant assets.
2. Expenditures to acquire low-cost items that benefit the firm for several periods.

**LEARNING OBJECTIVE 3**

**Discuss** the distinction between revenue expenditures and capital expenditures.

## MAINTENANCE AND REPAIRS

Some level of maintenance and repairs must be assumed when estimating the useful lives and salvage values of property, plant, and equipment. For example, a plant asset that is not maintained or repaired will have a shorter useful life than a similar asset that is properly maintained. Periodic upkeep—such as lubrication, cleaning, and replacement of minor parts—is necessary to maintain an asset's expected level and length of usefulness. These periodic upkeep costs—referred to as maintenance costs—are charged to expense as they are incurred.

## LOW-COST ITEMS

Most businesses purchase items that provide years of service at a relatively small cost, such as paperweights, ashtrays, and wastebaskets. Because of the small dollar amounts involved, establishing these items as assets on the balance sheet and depreciating them over their expected useful lives serves no useful purpose. The effect on the financial statements is insignificant; and consequently, expensing these expenditures at the time of purchase is more efficient. The accounting for such low-cost items is thus completed in the period in which they are acquired.

---

### PRINCIPLE ALERT | Materiality Concept

The practice of accounting for small dollar transactions in the most expedient fashion follows the *materiality concept.* Under this accounting concept, generally accepted accounting principles apply only to items of significance to the users of financial statements. Because the judgment of users will be unaffected by the accounting for immaterial dollar amounts, their immediate expensing does not diminish the usefulness of financial statements.

## CAPITAL EXPENDITURES

**Capital expenditures** increase the book value of long-lived assets. To *capitalize* an amount means to increase an asset's book value by that amount. The following list identifies two typical capital expenditures related to property, plant, and equipment:

**1.** Initial acquisitions and additions.

**2.** Betterments.

### Initial Acquisitions and Additions

At the beginning of this chapter, the accounting guidelines governing the initial measurement of long-lived assets were discussed. At that time, it was noted that expenditures equal to an asset's implied cash purchase price, plus any costs necessary to prepare the asset for use, were debited to the asset account. These amounts are commonly referred to as capital expenditures.

These same accounting guidelines apply for additions to existing plant assets. Adding a new wing to a building or expanding the size of an asphalt parking lot are examples of additions. These capital expenditures should also be debited to an asset account. A separate account (and depreciation schedule) should be used for an addition when its estimated useful life differs from the remaining useful life of the existing plant asset.

### Betterments

**Betterments** are expenditures that (1) extend the useful life of an asset, (2) improve the quality and/or quantity of the asset's output, or (3) reduce the asset's operating expenses. Examples include overhauling the engine or adding a power winch to a highway service truck, improving the precision of a machining device to reduce defects, or converting a building to solar power. Expenditures for betterments are generally debited to the appropriate asset account, and the subsequent periodic depreciation expense is increased to allocate the additional cost over the asset's remaining useful life.

---

**FORENSIC ACCOUNTING** **WorldCom's Bad Accounting**

On the surface, the decision to capitalize or expense an expenditure related to a long-lived asset does not seem like the subject matter for one of the most infamous accounting scandals of all time. Unfortunately, to the many investors in **WorldCom** who saw the value of their investment disappear, this accounting decision had profound consequences.

Beginning in 2001, and continuing through mid-2002, WorldCom, under the direction of its CEO, CFO, Controller, and Director of General Accounting, used fraudulent accounting methods to portray a false picture of the company's financial health. The principal accounting gimmickry used by the company was to misclassify "line costs," a cost that should have been expensed each year, as a capital expenditure, thus, adding to WorldCom's assets rather than adding to its expenses.

A small team of internal auditors working in secret, mostly at night, to investigate and uncover this fraud, brought the fraud to the attention of WorldCom's Board of Directors. The Securities and Exchange Commission followed with its own investigation. The final conclusion—WorldCom's assets and pre-tax net income had been inflated by nearly $11 billion! Following a conviction for filing false financial reports with the SEC, WorldCom's CEO Bernard Ebbers was sentenced to 25 years in prison.

---

## Your Turn! 9.3

Hastings Company recorded the following expenditures during the year with regard to its delivery van:

1. Changed the engine oil
2. Repainted the van
3. Overhauled the engine that is expected to increase the useful life of the van
4. Repaired a dent in a fender
5. Converted the van to run on a biofuel with an estimated annual fuel cost savings of 30 percent.

**Required:**
Determine whether each of the above expenditures is a revenue expenditure or a capital expenditure.

**The solution is on page 447.**

# DISPOSALS OF PLANT ASSETS

A business may dispose of its plant assets in a variety of ways. An asset may be sold, retired, or exchanged as partial payment for a new asset. The asset's usefulness to a firm may also be ended by an unfavorable or unanticipated event—the asset may be stolen or destroyed by a natural disaster.

Depreciation must extend through an asset's total useful life to a business. Consequently, depreciation must be recorded up to the disposal date, regardless of the manner of the asset's disposal. Should the disposal date not coincide with the end of an accounting period, a journal entry must record depreciation for the partial period—that is, the period from the date that depreciation was last recorded to the asset's disposal date.

The following data is used to illustrate the disposal of plant assets:

LEARNING OBJECTIVE 4

**Explain** and **illustrate** the accounting for disposals of plant assets.

| | |
|---|---|
| Equipment's acquisition cost. . . . . . . . . . . . . . . . . . . . . . . . . . . . . . . . . . . . . . . . . . . . . . . . . . . . . . . . . . . . . . . . . . . | $1,000 |
| Estimated salvage value after five years . . . . . . . . . . . . . . . . . . . . . . . . . . . . . . . . . . . . . . . . . . . . . . . . . . . . . | 100 |
| Annual straight-line depreciation . . . . . . . . . . . . . . . . . . . . . . . . . . . . . . . . . . . . . . . . . . . . . . . . . . . . . . . . . . . . | 180 |
| (Unless stated otherwise, assume that depreciation to the date of disposal has been recorded.) | |

## SALE OF PLANT ASSETS

Most sales of plant assets involve the following factors:

1. The sale transaction involves an exchange of a used plant asset for cash. Because the plant asset sold is no longer on hand, a journal entry must remove the asset account and the accumulated depreciation account from the books. These amounts together reflect the asset's book value.

2. Because plant assets are often sold for an amount higher or lower than their book value, a gain or loss will result. Sale proceeds in excess of book value create a gain, whereas book values in excess of sales proceeds create a loss.

### Asset Sales for More Than Book Value

Assume that the equipment is sold for $230 midway through its fifth year of use. Depreciation was last recorded at the end of the fourth year. The journal entries to record the sale are:

| | | | |
|---|---|---|---|
| Depreciation expense—Equipment | 90 | | |
|     Accumulated depreciation—Equipment | | 90 | |
| *To record depreciation expense for six months ($180/2).* | | | |

| A | = | L | + | SE |
|---|---|---|---|---|
| −90 | | | | −90 Exp |

| | | | |
|---|---|---|---|
| Cash | 230 | | |
| Accumulated depreciation—Equipment | 810 | | |
|     Equipment | | 1,000 | |
|     Gain on sale of plant assets | | 40 | |
| *To record the sale of equipment for $230.* | | | |

| A | = | L | + | SE |
|---|---|---|---|---|
| +230 | | | | +40 Gain |
| +810 | | | | |
| −1,000 | | | | |

Note that recording depreciation to the date of sale adds $90 to the Accumulated Depreciation account, which totals $810, calculated as [(4 × $180) + $90]. To reflect the sale properly, it is necessary to remove the entire amount of accumulated depreciation ($810) from the books. The gain of $40 is calculated as the sale proceeds of $230 minus the asset's book value of $190 ($1,000 − $810).

### Asset Sales for Less Than Book Value

Assume that the equipment is sold for $30 at the end of the fifth year. The journal entry to record this sale is:

| | | |
|---|---|---|
| Cash | 30 | |
| Loss on sale of plant assets | 70 | |
| Accumulated depreciation—Equipment | 900 | |
|     Equipment | | 1,000 |
| *To record the sale of equipment for $30.* | | |

The loss on the asset sale equals the book value of $100 minus the sales proceeds of $30. The cash received is recorded, and the balances from both the Equipment account and the Accumulated Depreciation account are removed from the books.

If the equipment is sold for an amount exactly equal to its book value, no gain or loss results. Should the equipment be abandoned, stolen, or destroyed (with no insurance coverage) before the end of its expected useful life, a loss equal to its book value is recorded. Similarly, if the equipment is retired at the end of its useful life and has no salvage value, a loss equal to its book value is recorded.

### Exchange of Plant Assets

A plant asset may be exchanged for another plant asset. The accounting for long-lived asset exchanges can be complex depending upon the relationship between the new asset and the asset being traded in. Consequently, the accounting for asset exchanges is covered in intermediate accounting textbooks.

---

### Your Turn! 9.4

The Jones Company is self-insured; and consequently, the company does not receive any insurance payments if it is involved in an accident. One of the Jones Company trucks was involved in a major accident and the company decided to sell the truck for scrap. At the time of the accident, the truck had a cost basis of $22,500 and accumulated depreciation of $15,000. The proceeds from the sale totaled $750.

**Required:**
Record the journal entry for the disposal of the truck.

The solution is on page 447.

---

# INTANGIBLE ASSETS

**LEARNING OBJECTIVE 5**

**Discuss** the nature of, and the accounting for, intangible assets.

**Intangible assets** are the various resources that benefit a business's operations, but which lack physical characteristics or substance. Intangible assets include, for example, the exclusive rights or privileges obtained from a governmental unit or by legal contract, such as patents, copyrights, franchises, trademarks, and leaseholds. Another intangible asset is goodwill, which reflects the beneficial attributes acquired in the acquisition of another company that cannot be attributed to any other recorded asset.

The term *intangible asset* is not used with precision in accounting. By convention, only certain assets are included in the intangible asset category. Some resources that lack physical substance, such as prepaid insurance, accounts receivable, and investments, are not classified as intangible assets. Because intangible assets lack physical characteristics, the related accounting procedures are more subjective than for such tangible assets as property, plant, and equipment.

## MEASUREMENT OF INTANGIBLE ASSETS

A firm should record intangible assets acquired from outside entities at their acquisition cost. Similarly, some intangible assets created internally by a firm are measured at their cost. For example, the costs to secure a trademark—such as attorney's fees, registration fees, and design costs—are charged to a Trademarks account.

The accounting for other expenditures related to intangible assets varies depending upon the type of expenditure and the nature of the intangible asset. **Research and development costs** are not capitalized to the balance sheet as an intangible asset because GAAP guidelines require that these expenditures be expensed when incurred. As a consequence, many significant costs incurred by a firm associated with developing a patentable product or process are not capitalized to the balance sheet. Legal costs associated with patent work may be capitalized, however. The costs of developing, maintaining, or restoring an intangible asset are also expensed when incurred, provided that the asset is not specifically identifiable or has an indeterminate life. As a result of these accounting procedures, some companies may have important intangible assets that are carried at a nominal amount, or may even fail to appear at all on the firm's balance sheet.

It is noteworthy that one U.S. industry is exempted from the conservative accounting treatment of research and development costs. Under U.S. GAAP, software development companies may capitalize the development of second generation software, although the cost of first generation software must be expensed as incurred.

### IFRS ALERT!

The accounting for some intangible assets under IFRS differs significantly from the accounting under U.S. GAAP. For instance, under U.S. GAAP, all research and development costs must be expensed when incurred; however, under IFRS, development costs may be capitalized if a commercially viable product results from the original research effort. A significant consequence of this alternative accounting treatment is that IFRS-accounted companies enjoy a more fairly presented balance sheet, since most intangible assets are fully disclosed. On the balance sheets of many U.S. GAAP-accounted companies, there are many unreported intangible assets.

To illustrate, assume that British Laboratories PLC, a biotechnology company, spends five million British pounds on research for a cure for diabetes. The research leads to a promising compound that is shown in tests to effectively control the disease. Further testing is needed, however; and consequently, the company spends an additional three million British pounds to develop and test the drug compound before receiving a patent from the British Patent Office. Under these circumstances, the company would record an expense for its initial research effort, and an asset for the subsequent expenditure to develop the drug, as follows:

| | | |
|---|---|---|
| Research expense | 5 million pounds | |
|     Cash | | 5 million pounds |
|     *To record research expense.* | | |
| Development costs | 3 million pounds | |
|     Cash | | 3 million pounds |
|     *To capitalize development costs.* | | |

In short, under IFRS, all research costs must be expensed when incurred; however, development costs may be capitalized to the balance sheet when a commercially viable product is evident.

## AMORTIZATION OF INTANGIBLES

The **amortization** of an intangible asset carried on the balance sheet involves the periodic expensing of the asset's cost over the term of its expected useful life. Because salvage values are ordinarily not involved, the amortization of intangible assets typically entails (1) determining the asset's cost, (2) estimating the period over which it will benefit a company, and (3) allocating the cost in equal amounts to each accounting period involved. Straight-line amortization is typically used for intangible assets unless another method is shown to be more appropriate.

The amortization entry debits the Amortization Expense account, while the credit entry goes directly to the Intangible Asset account. An Accumulated Amortization account could be used for the credit entry, but generally there is no particular benefit to financial statement users from accumulating amortization in a separate contra-asset account. In the following examples, we will reduce the intangible asset account directly for its periodic amortization.

# EXAMPLES OF INTANGIBLE ASSETS

### PATENTS

A **patent** is an exclusive privilege granted to an inventor by the U.S. Patent Office for a period of 20 years from the date the patent application is filed. A patent gives the patent holder the right to exclude others from making, using, or selling the invention. Patent laws were originated to encourage inventors by protecting them from imitators who might usurp the invention for commercial gain. Just what qualifies as a patentable idea, however, has become quite complex in the modern realm of technical knowledge. Consequently, long periods of patent "searching," and frequently, successful defense of infringement suits may precede the validation of a patent. Even though patents have a legal life of 20 years from application date, changes in technology or consumer tastes may shorten their economic life. Because of their uncertain value, patents are accounted for conservatively by most businesses. For example, most businesses amortize patents over a shorter period than 20 years. When patents are purchased, the buyer enjoys patent protection for the patent's remaining legal life.

To illustrate the accounting for patents, assume that a company incurs $30,000 in legal costs to obtain a patent on a new product. The journal entry to recognize the awarding of the patent is:

| A | = | L | + | SE |
|---|---|---|---|---|
| +30,000 | | | | |
| −30,000 | | | | |

| Patents | 30,000 | |
|---|---|---|
| Cash | | 30,000 |
| *To record legal costs of acquiring patent.* | | |

If the company expects the patent to provide benefits for 15 years, the following journal entry is made to record the first year's amortization using the straight-line method:

| A | = | L | + | SE |
|---|---|---|---|---|
| −2,000 | | | | −2,000 Exp |

| Amortization expense—Patents | 2,000 | |
|---|---|---|
| Patents | | 2,000 |
| *To record patent amortization ($30,000/15 years = $2,000).* | | |

Because an accumulated amortization account is not normally used, the intangible asset account balance reflects the asset's book value. The balance sheet presentation of the patent at year-end would appear as follows:

| | |
|---|---|
| Patents (cost less amortization to date)..................................................... | $28,000 |

### COPYRIGHT

A **copyright** protects its owner against the unauthorized reproduction of a specific written work, recorded work, or artwork. A copyright lasts for the life of the author plus 70 years. The purchase price of valuable copyrights can be substantial, and proper measurement and amortization are necessary for valid business income determination.

### FRANCHISES

**Franchises** most often involve exclusive rights to operate or sell a specific brand of products in a given geographic area. Franchises may be for definite or indefinite periods. Although many franchises are agreements between two private firms, various governmental units award franchises for public utility operations within their legal jurisdictions. The right to operate a **Kentucky Fried Chicken (KFC)** restaurant or to sell **Midas Mufflers** in a specific area illustrates franchise agreements in the private sector.

---

**ACCOUNTING IN PRACTICE**　Types of Intangible Assets

Intangible assets are perhaps the most difficult asset category to fully comprehend. Intangible assets appearing on a company's balance sheet represent a varied collection of assets as can be seen from a sample of 600 large U.S. firms:

| Type of Intangible Asset | Number | % |
| --- | --- | --- |
| Goodwill | 542 | 90% |
| Trademarks, brand names, copyrights | 330 | 55% |
| Customer lists/relationships | 320 | 53% |
| Technology | 162 | 27% |
| Patents | 161 | 27% |
| Licenses, franchises, memberships | 114 | 19% |
| Non-compete covenants | 112 | 18.7% |
| Contracts, agreements | 104 | 17.3% |
| Other—described | 65 | 10.8% |

Source: Accounting Trends and Techniques.

---

## TRADEMARKS

**Trademarks** and **trade names** represent the exclusive and continuing right to use certain terms, names, or symbols, usually to identify a brand or family of products. An original trademark or trade name can be registered with the U.S. federal government for a nominal cost. A company may spend considerable time and money to determine an appropriate name or symbol for a product. Also, the purchase of well-known, and thus valuable, trademarks or trade names may involve substantial amounts of money. When the cost of a trademark or trade name is material, the amount is debited to an appropriate intangible asset account—Trademarks—and amortized over the period of expected benefit to a business.

## GOODWILL

**Goodwill** is an often misunderstood concept. In common usage, goodwill may represent the favorable reputation a firm has earned based on its prior operations, quality of service, or positive product characteristics. The term goodwill, however, has a much different meaning when used in accounting and finance. Goodwill represents the amount paid by one company in the acquisition of another company, above the amount that can be attributed to the identifiable net assets of the acquired company. The measurement of goodwill is complex because it can stem from many factors. Examples of such factors include exceptional customer relations, advantageous business location, operating efficiency, superior personnel, favorable financial sources, or perceived synergies between the acquiring company and the acquired company. Unlike most intangible assets, goodwill is not subject to periodic amortization. Instead, goodwill is evaluated annually for any impairment in value. If a company's goodwill is found to be impaired, the Goodwill account is written down to its fair value and an Impairment Loss is recorded on the income statement.

---

**ACCOUNTING IN PRACTICE**　Goodwill Can Be a Significant Asset

Although accountants only record goodwill when another business entity is purchased (to the extent that the purchase price exceeds the fair value of the identifiable net assets acquired), the balance sheets of many major corporations contain significant amounts of goodwill. Recent balance sheets, for example, show the following amounts of goodwill: **Bank of America Corporation**, $86.3 billion; **General Electric Company**, $65.6 billion; **AT&T Inc.**, $73.3 billion; and **Procter & Gamble Company**, $54.0 billion. These amounts are evidence of the active acquisition efforts of these major corporations, and also of the large amounts that may be paid for goodwill in acquisition transactions.

**Your Turn!**                                                                    **9.5**

Match the descriptive explanation below with the correct term:

| Amortization | Patent | Copyright |
|---|---|---|
| Franchise | Trademark | |

1. An exclusive right that protects an owner against the unauthorized reproduction of a specific written work.
2. The periodic write-off of an intangible asset to expense on the income statement.
3. An exclusive and continuing right to use a certain symbol to identify a brand or family of products.
4. An exclusive right to operate or sell a specific brand of products in a given geographic area.
5. An exclusive privilege granted to an inventor that gives the asset holder the right to exclude others from making, using, or selling the invention.

**The solution is on page 447.**

# BALANCE SHEET PRESENTATION

**LEARNING OBJECTIVE 6**

**Illustrate** the balance sheet presentation of plant assets and intangible assets.

Plant assets and intangible assets are presented on the balance sheet below the Long-term Investments category. (Recall that the assets are listed on a classified balance sheet in descending order of liquidity.) For example, Exhibit 9-3 reveals how these assets appear on the balance sheet of **Cummins Inc.** Notice that Cummins lists its intangible assets and goodwill separately. This convention is followed because while Cummins amortizes its intangible assets, it does not amortize its goodwill. Goodwill is subject to an annual impairment test of its current value, but it is not subject to periodic amortization.

**EXHIBIT 9-3**   Cummins Inc.

**CUMMINS INC**
**Balance Sheet**
**December 31, 2008 and 2009**

| (in $ millions) | 2008 | 2009 |
|---|---|---|
| Current Assets | | |
| Cash and cash equivalent | $ 426 | $ 930 |
| Short-term investments | 77 | 190 |
| Net receivables | 1,782 | 2,004 |
| Inventory | 1,783 | 1,341 |
| Other current assets | 645 | 538 |
| Total Current Assets | 4,713 | 5,003 |
| Long-term investments | 588 | 574 |
| Property, plant, and equipment (net) | 1,841 | 1,886 |
| Goodwill | 362 | 364 |
| Intangible assets | 223 | 228 |
| Other assets | 792 | 761 |
| Total Assets | $8,519 | $8,816 |

# RETURN ON ASSETS AND ASSET TURNOVER

**LEARNING OBJECTIVE 7**

**Define** the return on assets ratio and the asset turnover ratio, and **explain** their use.

The ability of a firm to use its assets effectively and efficiently is a sign of a healthy, well-managed company. The rate of return generated on a company's assets, referred to as the *return on assets ratio,* is a widely used indicator that focuses on this dimension of a firm's financial health. In practice, there is some variation in the calculation of this ratio; however, one commonly used definition of the **return on assets** is:

$$\text{Return on assets} = \frac{\text{Net income}}{\text{Average total assets}}$$

This ratio relates data from two financial statements—the income statement and the balance sheet. The numerator consists of the net income for the year from the income statement.[2] The denominator in the ratio is the average balance of total assets for the year (sum the total assets at the beginning of the year with the total assets at the end of the year and divide the sum by two) obtained from the balance sheet.

To illustrate the calculation of the return on assets ratio, we use data from Cummins Inc. The company reported 2009 net income of $428 million, total assets at the beginning of the year of $8,519 million, and year-end total assets of $8,816 million. Cummins' return on assets for the year is 4.9 percent, calculated as $428/[($8,519 + $8,816)/2].

To evaluate a firm's return on assets, it is useful to consider the trend in the ratio, the return for other firms in the same industry, the industry average return on assets, and the economic environment that the company faced. For example, in the same year that Cummins generated a 4.9 percent return on its assets, Caterpillar, Inc., a competitor of Cummins, generated only a 0.8 percent return on assets. These results suggest that, for 2009, Cummins utilized its assets more efficiently and profitably than did Caterpillar.

| Concept ➝ | Method ➝ | Assessment |
|---|---|---|
| How effective is a company in using its assets to produce net income? | Net income and average total assets<br><br>Return on assets ratio = $\frac{\text{Net income}}{\text{Average total assets}}$ | A higher ratio value implies a higher, more effective level of asset utilization. |

TAKEAWAY 9.1

The **asset turnover** ratio is another ratio that evaluates a company's effective use of its assets. This ratio measures how effectively a firm uses its assets to generate sales revenue. The asset turnover ratio is calculated as follows:

$$\text{Asset turnover} = \frac{\text{Net sales}}{\text{Average total assets}}$$

Referring again to the Cummins' data for 2009, the company reported net operating revenues (which is equivalent to net sales), of $10,800 million. Consequently, Cummins' asset turnover for the year is 1.25, or $10,800/[($8,519 + $8,816)/2], indicating that the company was able to generate $1.25 of sales revenue for every dollar invested in assets. A high asset turnover ratio indicates that a company is very effective in using its assets to generate sales revenue. For the preceding year, Cummins' asset turnover was 1.72. Thus, Cummins generated $1.72 in net sales in 2008 for each dollar invested in total assets. The decrease in Cummins' asset turnover from 1.72 to 1.25 indicates that the firm used its assets less effectively in 2009 than in 2008 to generate sales revenue.

| Concept ➝ | Method ➝ | Assessment |
|---|---|---|
| How effective is a company in generating sales revenue using its assets? | Average total assets and net sales<br><br>Asset turnover ratio = $\frac{\text{Net sales}}{\text{Average total assets}}$ | A higher ratio value implies a higher level of sales revenue generated for each dollar invested in assets. |

TAKEAWAY 9.2

[2] An alternative calculation of the return on assets ratio adds interest expense to net income in the ratio's numerator. This calculation keeps the method of financing a company's assets from influencing the calculation of the ratio.

**Units-of-production method** A depreciation method that allocates depreciation expense to each operating period in proportion to the amount of the asset's total expected productive capacity used each period (p. 415).

**Useful life** The period of time that an asset is used by a business, running from the date of acquisition to the date of disposal (or removal from service) (p. 412).

## COMPREHENSIVE PROBLEM

Segman Company purchased a machine on January 2 for $24,300. The machine has an expected useful life of three years and an expected salvage value of $900. The company expects to use the machine for 1,400 hours in the first year, 2,000 hours in the second year, and 1,600 hours in the third year.

### Required

a. Calculate the depreciation expense for each year using each of the following depreciation methods: (1) straight-line, (2) units-of-production (assume that actual usage equals expected usage), (3) double-declining balance.

b. Assume that the machine was purchased June 1. Calculate the depreciation expense for each year using the following depreciation methods: (1) straight-line, (2) double-declining balance.

### Solution

a. 1. Straight-line:
   Year 1: ($24,300 − $900)/3 = $7,800
   Year 2: ($24,300 − $900)/3 = $7,800
   Year 3: ($24,300 − $900)/3 = $7,800

2. Units-of-production:
   Depreciation per hour = ($24,300 − $900)/5,000 hours = $4.68 per hour
   Year 1: 1,400 hours × $4.68 = $6,552
   Year 2: 2,000 hours × $4.68 = $9,360
   Year 3: 1,600 hours × $4.68 = $7,488

3. Double-declining balance:
   Depreciation rate = (100/3) × 2 = 66 2/3 percent
   Year 1: $24,300 × 66 2/3 percent = $16,200
   Year 2: ($24,300 − $16,200) × 66 2/3 percent = $5,400
   Year 3: ($24,300 − $21,600) × 66 2/3 percent = $1,800

b. 1. Straight-line: Refer to calculations in (a)1.
   Year 1: $7,800 × 7/12 = $4,550
   Year 2: $7,800 (full year's depreciation)
   Year 3: $7,800 (full year's depreciation)
   Year 4: $7,800 × 5/12 = $3,250

2. Double-declining balance Refer to calculations in (a)3.
   Year 1: $16,200 × 7/12 = $9,450
   Year 2: ($24,300 − $9,450) × 66 2/3 percent = $9,900
   Year 3: ($24,300 − $19,350) × 66 2/3 percent = $3,300
   Year 4: $750 [This amount reduces the machine's book value to its salvage value of $900 and is the maximum depreciation expense for the year. ($24,300 − $22,650) × 66 2/3 percent = $1,100 gives an amount in excess of the maximum $750 depreciation.]

## SELF-STUDY QUESTIONS

(Answers for the Self-Study Questions are available at the end of this chapter.)

LO1  1. The acquisition cost of a plant asset is equal to the asset's implied cash price and:
   a. The interest paid on any debt incurred to finance the asset's purchase.
   b. The market value of any noncash assets given up to acquire the plant asset.
   c. The reasonable and necessary costs incurred to prepare the asset for its intended use.
   d. The asset's estimated salvage value.

2. On January 1, Rio Company purchased a delivery truck for $10,000. The company estimates the truck will be driven 80,000 miles over its eight-year useful life. The estimated salvage value is $2,000. The truck was driven 12,000 miles in its first year. Which method results in the largest depreciation expense for the first year?    **LO2**
    a. Units-of-production
    b. Straight-line
    c. Double-declining balance

3. On the first day of the current year, Blakely Company sold equipment for less than its book value. Which of the following is part of the journal entry to record the sale?    **LO4**
    a. A debit to Equipment
    b. A credit to Accumulated Depreciation—Equipment
    c. A credit to Gain on Sale of Plant Assets
    d. A debit to Loss on Sale of Plant Assets

4. Accounting for the periodic amortization of intangible assets is similar to which depreciation method?    **LO5**
    a. Straight-line
    b. Units-of-production
    c. Double-declining balance

5. An exclusive right to operate or sell a specific brand of products in a given geographic area is called:    **LO5**

    a. A franchise.           c. A patent.
    b. Goodwill.              d. A copyright.

6. Which of the following statements is true?    **LO5**
    a. Goodwill is subject to amortization.
    b. Research and development costs may be capitalized to the balance sheet.
    c. Intangible assets are amortized to expense on the income statement.
    d. Goodwill arises because of a company's positive corporate image among its customers.

7. Which of the following statements is false?    **LO3**
    a. Expenditures for ordinary repairs are a capital expenditure.
    b. Betterment expenditures are a capital expenditure.
    c. Expenditures to acquire low-cost assets are revenue expenditures.
    d. Material additions to a plant asset are capital expenditures.

8. Which of the following statements is true?    **LO6**
    a. Intangible assets are shown on the balance sheet net of the Accumulated Amortization account.
    b. Goodwill is shown on the balance sheet net of the Accumulated Amortization account.
    c. The Accumulated Depreciation account need not be used for plant assets.
    d. Plant assets are shown on the balance sheet net of the Accumulated Depreciation account.

9. A company reports net income of $6,000, net sales of $15,000, and total assets of $24,000. What is the company's return on assets?    **LO7**
    a. 62.5 percent
    b. 25.0 percent
    c. 40.0 percent
    d. None of the above

10. A company reports net income of $6,000, net sales of $15,000, and average total assets of $24,000. What is the company's asset turnover?    **LO7**
    a. 62.5 percent
    b. 25.0 percent
    c. 40.0 percent
    d. None of the above

11. Harley Company sold one of its worn out delivery trucks on December 31, 2010. The truck was purchased on January 1, 2007, for $50,000 and was depreciated on a straight-line basis over a 5-year life. There was no salvage value associated with the truck. If the truck was sold for $14,000, what was the amount of gain or loss recorded at the time of the sale?    **LO4**
    a. $4,000 loss           c. $4,000 gain
    b. $14,000 gain          d. $6,000 loss

## DISCUSSION QUESTIONS

1. What are the two major types of long-term assets that require a periodic write-off? Present examples of each, and indicate for each type of asset the term that denotes the periodic write-off to expense.

2. In what way is land different from other plant assets?

3. In general, what amounts constitute the acquisition cost of plant assets?

4. Foss Company bought land with a vacant building for $400,000. Foss will use the building in its operations. Must Foss allocate the purchase price between the land and building? Why or why not? Would your answer be different if Foss intends to raze the building and build a new one? Why or why not?

5. Why is the recognition of depreciation expense necessary to match revenue and expense properly?

6. What is the pattern of plant asset utilization (or benefit) that is appropriate for each of the following depreciation methods: (a) straight-line, (b) units-of-production, (c) double-declining balance?

7. How should a revision of depreciation charges due to a change in an asset's estimated useful life or salvage value be handled? Which periods—past, present, or future—are affected by the revision?

8. When is a plant asset considered to be impaired? How is an impairment loss calculated?

9. What is the benefit of accelerating depreciation for income tax purposes when the total depreciation taken is no more than if straight-line depreciation were used?

10. Identify two types of revenue expenditures. What is the proper accounting for revenue expenditures?

11. Identify two types of capital expenditures. What is the proper accounting for capital expenditures?

12. What factors determine the gain or loss on the sale of a plant asset?

13. Folger Company installed a conveyor system that cost $192,000. The system can be used only in the excavation of gravel at a particular site. Folger expects to excavate gravel at the site for 10 years. Over how many years should the conveyor be depreciated if its physical life is estimated at (a) 8 years and (b) 12 years?

14. What are five different types of intangible assets? Briefly explain the nature of each type.

15. How should a firm account for research and development costs?

16. Under what circumstances is goodwill recorded?

17. How is the *return on assets* ratio calculated? What does this ratio reveal about a business?

18. How is the *asset turnover ratio* calculated? What does this ratio reveal about a business?

## SHORT EXERCISES

LO1  **SE9-1.  Calculate Amount to Capitalize**
The Miller Company paid $10,000 to acquire a 100 ton press. Freight charges to deliver the equipment amounted to $1,500 and were paid by Miller. Installation costs amounted to $570, and machine testing charges amounted to $250. Calculate the amount that should be capitalized to the Equipment account.

LO2  **SE9-2.  Depreciation Expense Using the Straight-Line Method**
The Pack Company purchased an office building for $4,500,000. The building had an estimated useful life of 40 years and an expected salvage value of $500,000. Calculate the depreciation expense for the second year using the straight-line method.

LO2  **SE9-3.  Depreciation Expense Using the Double-Declining Balance Method**
The Pack Company purchased an office building for $4,500,000. The building had an estimated useful life of 40 years and an expected salvage value of $500,000. Calculate the depreciation expense for the second year using the double-declining balance method.

LO2  **SE9-4.  Depreciation Expense Using the Units-of-Production Method**
The Likert Company is a coal company based in West Virginia. The company recently purchased a new coal truck for $60,000. The truck had an expected useful life of 200,000 miles and an expected salvage value of $2,000. Calculate the depreciation expense using the units-of-production method assuming the truck travelled 40,000 miles on company business during the year.

**SE9-5. Sale of a Building**          LO4

The Miller Company sold a building for $400,000 that had a book value of $450,000. The building had originally cost the company $12,000,000 and had accumulated depreciation to date of $11,550,000. Prepare a journal entry to record the sale of the building.

**SE9-6. Goodwill Impairment**          LO5

Bruceton Farms Equipment Company had goodwill valued at $80 million on its balance sheet at year-end. A review of the goodwill by the company's CFO indicated that the goodwill was impaired and was now only worth $50 million. Prepare a journal entry to record the goodwill impairment on the books of the company.

**SE9-7. Amortization Expense**          LO5

Smith & Sons obtained a patent for a new optical scanning device. The fees incurred to file for the patent and to defend the patent in court against several companies which challenged the patent amounted to $40,000. Smith & Sons concluded that the expected economic life of the patent was 12 years. Calculate the amortization expense that should be recorded in the second year, and record the journal entry for the amortization expense on the books of Smith & Sons.

**SE9-8. Return on Assets**          LO7

The Kingwood Company reported net income of $50,000 and average total assets of $450,000. Calculate the company's return on assets.

**SE9-9. Asset Turnover**          LO7

The Kingwood Company reported sales revenue of $520,000 and average total assets of $450,000. Calculate the company's asset turnover.

**SE9-10. Return on Assets and Asset Turnover**          LO7

Last year, the Miller Company reported a return on assets of 15 percent and an asset turnover of 1.6. In the current year, the company reported a return on assets of 19 percent but an asset turnover of only 1.2. If sales revenue remained unchanged from last year to the current year, what would explain the two ratio results?

**SE9-11. Sale of Equipment**          LO4

Prepare the journal entry for the following transactions: (1) Geysler Company sold some old equipment that initially cost $30,000 and had $25,000 of accumulated depreciation and received cash in the amount of $3,000. (2) Assume the same facts except Geysler received $9,000.

**SE9-12. Financial Statement Placement**          LO6

Name the financial statement where each of the following will appear: (IS) Income Statement; (BS) Balance Sheet; (SCF) Statement of Cash Flows; (N) None.

   *a.* Book value of equipment purchased five years ago
   *b.* Market value of equipment purchased five years ago
   *c.* Cash proceeds from the sale of land
   *d.* Gain on the sale of buildings
   *e.* Accumulated depreciation on equipment
   *f.* Impairment loss on land

# EXERCISES—SET A

**E9-1A. Acquisition Cost of Long-Lived Asset**          LO1

The following data relate to a firm's purchase of a machine used in the manufacture of its product:

| | |
|---|---:|
| Invoice price | $20,000 |
| Applicable sales tax | 1,200 |
| Cash discount taken for prompt payment | 400 |
| Freight paid | 260 |
| Cost of insurance coverage on machine while in transit | 125 |
| Installation costs | 1,000 |
| Testing and adjusting costs | 475 |
| Repair of damages to machine caused by the firm's employees | 550 |
| Prepaid maintenance contract for first year of machine's use | 300 |

Determine the acquisition cost of the machine.

**LO1** **E9-2A.** **Allocation of Package Purchase Price**

Tamock Company purchased a plant from one of its suppliers. The $975,000 purchase price included the land, a building, and factory machinery. Tamock also paid $5,000 in legal fees to negotiate the purchase of the plant. An appraisal showed the following values for the items purchased:

| Property | Assessed Value |
| --- | --- |
| Land.......................................................................... | $126,000 |
| Building...................................................................... | 486,000 |
| Machinery................................................................... | 288,000 |
| Total........................................................................ | $900,000 |

Using the assessed value as a guide, allocate the total purchase price of the plant to the land, building, and machinery accounts in Tamock Company's records.

**LO2** **E9-3A.** **Depreciation Methods**

A delivery truck costing $18,000 is expected to have a $1,500 salvage value at the end of its useful life of four years or 125,000 miles. Assume that the truck was purchased on January 2. Calculate the depreciation expense for the second year using each of the following depreciation methods: (a) straight-line, (b) double-declining balance, and (c) units-of-production. (Assume that the truck was driven 28,000 miles in the second year.)

**LO2** **E9-4A.** **Revision of Depreciation**

On January 2, 2007, Mosler, Inc., purchased equipment for $66,000. The equipment was expected to have a $6,000 salvage value at the end of its estimated six-year useful life. Straight-line depreciation has been recorded. Before adjusting the accounts for 2011, Mosler decided that the useful life of the equipment should be extended by two years and the salvage value decreased to $4,000.

    *a.*    Prepare a journal entry to record depreciation expense on the equipment for 2011.

    *b.*    What is the book value of the equipment at the end of 2011 (after recording the depreciation expense for 2011)?

**LO2** **E9-5A.** **Impairment Loss**

On July 1, 2007, Okin Company purchased equipment for $225,000; the estimated useful life was 10 years and the expected salvage value was $25,000. Straight-line depreciation is used. On July 1, 2011, economic factors cause the market value of the equipment to decrease to $90,000. On this date, Okin evaluates if the equipment is impaired and estimates future cash flows relating to the use and disposal of the equipment to be $125,000.

    *a.*    Is the equipment impaired at July 1, 2011? Explain.

    *b.*    If the equipment is impaired at July 1, 2011, calculate the amount of the impairment loss.

    *c.*    If the equipment is impaired at July 1, 2011, prepare the journal entry to record the impairment loss.

**LO3** **E9-6A.** **Revenue and Capital Expenditures**

Shively Company built an addition to its chemical plant. Indicate whether each of the following expenditures related to the addition is a revenue expenditure or a capital expenditure:

    *a.*    Shively's initial application for a building permit was denied by the city as not conforming to environmental standards. Shively disagreed with the decision and spent $6,000 in attorney's fees to convince the city to reverse its position and issue the permit.

    *b.*    Due to unanticipated sandy soil conditions, and on the advice of construction engineers, Shively spent $58,000 to extend the footings for the addition to a greater depth than originally planned.

    *c.*    Shively spent $3,000 to send each of the addition's subcontractors a side of beef as a thank-you gift for completing the project on schedule.

    *d.*    Shively invited the mayor to a ribbon-cutting ceremony to open the plant addition. It spent $25 to purchase the ribbon and scissors.

    *e.*    Shively spent $4,100 to have the company logo sandblasted into the concrete above the entrance to the addition.

**LO4** **E9-7A.** **Sale of Plant Asset**

Raine Company has a machine that originally cost $68,000. Depreciation has been recorded for five years using the straight-line method, with a $5,000 estimated salvage value at the end of an expected nine-year life. After recording depreciation at the end of the fifth year, Raine sells the machine. Prepare the journal entry to record the machine's sale for:

a.  $37,000 cash.
b.  $33,000 cash.
c.  $28,000 cash.

**E9-8A. Amortization Expense**                                                                        LO5

For each of the following unrelated situations, calculate the annual amortization expense and prepare a journal entry to record the expense:

a.  A patent with a 15-year remaining legal life was purchased for $270,000. The patent will be commercially exploitable for another nine years.
b.  A patent was acquired on a device designed by a production worker. Although the cost of the patent to date consisted of $42,300 in legal fees for handling the patent application, the patent should be commercially valuable during its entire remaining legal life of 18 years and is currently worth $378,000.
c.  A franchise granting exclusive distribution rights for a new solar water heater within a three-state area for four years was obtained at a cost of $63,000. Satisfactory sales performance over the four years permits renewal of the franchise for another four years (at an additional cost determined at renewal).

**E9-9A. Return on Assets Ratio and Asset Turnover Ratio**                                              LO7

Campo Systems reported the following financial data (in millions) in its annual report:

|  | 2010 | 2011 |
|---|---|---|
| Net income. | $ 8,052 | $ 6,134 |
| Net sales | 39,540 | 36,117 |
| Total assets. | 58,734 | 68,128 |

If the company's total assets are $55,676 in 2009, calculate the company's (a) return on assets and (b) asset turnover for 2010 and 2011.

**E9-10A. Return on Assets Ratio and Asset Turnover Ratio: Using IFRS Financial Statements**           LO7

Tesco PLC is the world's third largest retailer and is headquartered in the United Kingdom. Tesco's IFRS financial statements are presented in Appendix C at the end of this book. Using this financial data, calculate the company's (a) return on assets and (b) asset turnover for 2008 and 2009. Tesco's 2007 total assets were 27,500 million British pounds. Comment on the trend in Tesco's ratios.

**E9-11A. Financial Statement Presentation**                                                            LO6

Vera Corp. reported the following amounts for the year just ended:

| | |
|---|---|
| Land. | $120,000 |
| Patents. | 25,000 |
| Equipment. | 40,000 |
| Buildings. | 150,000 |
| Goodwill. | 35,000 |
| Accumulated amortization. | 10,000 |
| Accumulated depreciation. | 80,000 |

Prepare a partial balance sheet for these amounts.

## EXERCISES—SET B

**E9-1B. Acquisition Cost of Long-Lived Asset**                                                         LO1

Fischer Construction purchased a used front-end loader for $28,000, terms 1/10, n/30, F.O.B. shipping point, freight collect. Fischer paid the freight charges of $270 and sent the seller a check for $27,720 one week after the machine was delivered. The loader required a new battery, which cost Fischer $150. Fischer also spent $240 to have the company name printed on the loader and $375 for one year's insurance coverage on it. Fischer hired a new employee to operate it at a wage of $19 per hour; the employee spent one morning (four hours) practicing with the machine and went to work at a construction site that afternoon. Calculate the amount at which the front-end loader should be reported on the company's balance sheet.

**LO1**    **E9-2B.    Allocation of Package Purchase Price**

Andrew Lupino went into business by purchasing a car lubrication station, consisting of land, a building, and equipment. The seller's original asking price was $210,000. Lupino hired an appraiser for $2,000 to appraise the assets. The appraised valuations were land, $38,000; building, $95,000, and equipment, $57,000. After receiving the appraisal, Lupino offered $175,000 for the business. The seller refused this offer. Lupino then offered $185,000 for the business, which the seller accepted. Using the appraisal values as a guide, allocate the total purchase price of the car lubrication station to the Land, Building, and Equipment accounts.

**LO2**    **E9-3B.    Depreciation Methods**

A machine costing $145,800 was purchased May 1. The machine should be obsolete after three years and, therefore, no longer useful to the company. The estimated salvage value is $5,400. Calculate the depreciation expense for each year of its expected useful life using each of the following depreciation methods: (a) straight-line, (b) double-declining balance.

**LO2**    **E9-4B.    Revision of Depreciation**

Associated Clinic purchased a special machine for use in its laboratory on January 2, 2010. The machine cost $84,000 and was expected to last 10 years. Its salvage value was estimated to be $6,000. By early 2012, it was evident that the machine will be useful for a total of only seven years. The salvage value after seven years was estimated to be $7,500. Associated Clinic uses straight-line depreciation. Compute the proper depreciation expense on the machine for 2012.

**LO2**    **E9-5B.    Impairment Loss**

On May 1, 2008, Silky, Inc., purchased machinery for $315,000; the estimated useful life was eight years and the expected salvage value was $15,000. Straight-line depreciation is used. On May 1, 2010, economic factors cause the market value of the machinery to decrease to $190,000. On this date, Silky evaluates whether the machinery is impaired.

a.    Assume that on May 1, 2010, Silky estimates future cash flows relating to the use and disposal of the machinery to be $260,000. Is the machinery impaired at May 1, 2010? Explain. If it is impaired, what is the amount of the impairment loss?

b.    Assume that on May 1, 2010, Silky estimates future cash flows relating to the use and disposal of the machinery to be $230,000. Is the machinery impaired at May 1, 2010? Explain. If it is impaired, what is the amount of the impairment loss?

**LO3**    **E9-6B.    Revenue and Capital Expenditures**

Indicate whether each of the following expenditures is a revenue expenditure or a capital expenditure for Blare Company:

a.    Paid $280 to replace a truck windshield that was cracked by a stone thrown up by another vehicle while the truck was being used to make a delivery.

b.    Paid $10 for a "No Smoking" sign for the conference room.

c.    Paid $900 to add a hard disk to an employee's computer.

d.    Paid $15 for a dust cover for a computer printer.

e.    Paid $280 to replace a cracked windshield on a used truck that was just purchased for company use. The company bought the truck knowing the windshield was cracked.

f.    Paid $100 for a building permit from the city for a storage shed the company is going to have built.

**LO4**    **E9-7B.    Sale of Plant Asset**

Noble Company has equipment that originally cost $63,000. Depreciation has been recorded for six years using the straight-line method, with a $7,000 estimated salvage value at the end of an expected eight-year life. After recording depreciation at the end of the sixth year, Noble sells the equipment. Prepare the journal entry to record the equipment's sale for:

a.    $27,000 cash.

b.    $21,000 cash.

c.    $18,000 cash.

**LO5**    **E9-8B.    Amortization Expense**

For each of the following unrelated situations, calculate the annual amortization expense and prepare a journal entry to record the expense:

a.    A patent with a 15-year remaining legal life was purchased for $595,000. The patent will be commercially exploitable for another seven years.

b.    A patent was acquired on a device designed by a production worker. Although the cost of the patent to date consisted of $84,600 in legal fees for handling the patent application, the patent should be commercially valuable during its entire remaining legal life of 18 years and is currently worth $720,000.

c.  A franchise granting exclusive distribution rights for a new wind turbine within a three-state area for four years was obtained at a cost of $66,400. Satisfactory sales performance over the four years permits renewal of the franchise for another four years (at an additional cost determined at renewal).

**E9-9B. Return on Assets Ratio and Asset Turnover Ratio**                                LO7

Allied Systems reported the following financial data (in millions) in its annual report:

|  | 2010 | 2011 |
|---|---|---|
| Net income. | $18,052 | $16,134 |
| Net sales | 49,540 | 46,117 |
| Total assets. | 68,734 | 78,128 |

If the company's total assets are $65,676 in 2009, calculate the company's (a) return on assets and (b) asset turnover for 2010 and 2011.

**E9-10B. Financial Statement Presentation**                                LO6

Evae Corp. reported the following amounts for the year just ended:

| | |
|---|---|
| Land | $ 60 |
| Trademarks. | 15 |
| Equipment | 80 |
| Buildings. | 110 |
| Goodwill | 25 |
| Accumulated amortization. | 5 |
| Accumulated depreciation. | 55 |

Prepare a partial balance sheet for these amounts.

# PROBLEMS—SET A

**P9-1A. Acquisition Cost of Long-Lived Assets**                                LO1

The following items represent expenditures (or receipts) related to the construction of a new home office for Lowrey Company.

| | |
|---|---|
| Cost of land site, which included an old apartment building appraised at $75,000 | $  165,000 |
| Legal fees, including fee for title search. | 2,100 |
| Payment of apartment building mortgage and related interest due at time of sale | 9,300 |
| Payment for delinquent property taxes assumed by the purchaser | 4,000 |
| Cost of razing the apartment building. | 17,000 |
| Proceeds from sale of salvaged materials | (3,800) |
| Grading to establish proper drainage flow on land site. | 1,900 |
| Architect's fees on new building | 300,000 |
| Proceeds from sales of excess dirt (from basement excavation) to owner of adjoining property (dirt was used to fill in a low area on property) | (2,000) |
| Payment to building contractor | 5,000,000 |
| Payment of medical bills of employee accidentally injured while inspecting building construction | 1,400 |
| Special assessment for paving city sidewalks (paid to city) | 18,000 |
| Cost of paving driveway and parking lot. | 25,000 |
| Cost of installing lights in parking lot. | 9,200 |
| Premium for insurance on building during construction | 7,500 |
| Cost of open house party to celebrate opening of new building. | 8,000 |

### Required

From the given data, calculate the proper balances for the Land, Building, and Land Improvements accounts of Lowrey Company.

**P9-2A. Allocation of Package Purchase Price and Depreciation Methods**                                LO1, LO2

To expand its business, Small Company paid $754,000 for most of the property, plant, and equipment of a small trucking company that was going out of business. Before agreeing to the price, Small hired a consultant for $6,000 to appraise the assets. The appraised values were as follows:

| Land | $120,000 |
| Building | 440,000 |
| Trucks | 144,000 |
| Equipment | 96,000 |
| Total | $800,000 |

Small issued two checks totaling $760,000 to acquire the assets and pay the consultant on July 1. Small depreciated the assets using the straight-line method on the building and on the equipment, and the double-declining balance method on the trucks. Estimated useful lives and salvage values were as follows:

| | Useful Life | Salvage Value |
| --- | --- | --- |
| Building | 20 years | $42,000 |
| Trucks | 4 years | 15,000 |
| Equipment | 7 years | 10,000 |

### Required

a. Calculate the amounts allocated to the various types of plant assets acquired on July 1.
b. Prepare the July 1 journal entries to record the purchase of the assets and the payment to the consultant.
c. Prepare the December 31 journal entries to record depreciation expense for the year on the building, trucks, and equipment.

**LO2  P9-3A. Depreciation Methods**

On January 2, Roth, Inc. purchased a laser cutting machine to be used in the fabrication of a part for one of its key products. The machine cost $80,000, and its estimated useful life was four years or 1,000,000 cuttings, after which it could be sold for $5,000.

### Required

Calculate the depreciation expense for each year of the machine's useful life under each of the following depreciation methods:

a. Straight-line.
b. Double-declining balance.
c. Units-of-production. Assume annual production in cuttings of 200,000; 350,000; 260,000; and 190,000.

**LO1, LO2, LO3  P9-4A. Accounting for Plant Assets**

Basin Corporation had the following transactions related to its delivery truck:

**Year 1**

Jan.   5   Purchased for $14,300 cash a new truck with an estimated useful life of four years and a salvage value of $2,300.
Feb. 20   Installed a new set of side-view mirrors at a cost of $68 cash.
June  9   Paid $285 for an engine tune-up, wheel balancing, and a periodic chassis lubrication.
Aug.   2   Paid a $250 repair bill for the uninsured portion of damages to the truck caused by Basin's own driver.
Dec. 31   Recorded depreciation on the truck for the year.

**Year 2**

May   1   Installed a set of parts bins in the truck at a cost of $800 cash. This expenditure was not expected to increase the salvage value of the truck.
Dec. 31   Recorded depreciation on the truck for the year.

**Year 3**

Dec. 31   Recorded depreciation on the truck for the year.

Basin's depreciation policies include (1) using straight-line depreciation, (2) recording depreciation to the nearest whole month, and (3) expensing all truck expenditures of $75 or less.

### Required

Prepare journal entries to record these transactions and adjustments.

**P9-5A. Disposal of Plant Asset**

Citano Company has a used executive charter plane that originally cost $800,000. Straight-line depreciation on the plane has been recorded for six years, with an $80,000 expected salvage value at the end of its estimated eight-year useful life. The last depreciation entry was made at the end of the sixth year. Eight months into the seventh year, Citano disposes of the plane.

**Required**

Prepare journal entries to record:

*a.* Depreciation expense to the date of disposal.
*b.* Sale of the plane for cash at its book value.
*c.* Sale of the plane for $215,000 cash.
*d.* Sale of the plane for $195,000 cash.
*e.* Destruction of the plane in a fire. Citano expects a $190,000 insurance settlement.

**P9-6A. Accounting for Intangible Assets and Leasehold Improvements**

Berdahl Company owns several retail outlets. During the year, it expanded operations and entered into the following transactions:

Jan. 2 Signed an eight-year lease for additional retail space for an annual rent of $23,400. Paid the first year's rent on this date. (*Hint:* Debit the first year's rent to Prepaid Rent.)

3 Paid $22,800 to a contractor for installation of a new oak floor in the leased facility. The oak floor's life is an estimated 50 years with no salvage value.

Mar. 1 Paid $45,000 to obtain an exclusive area franchise for five years to distribute a new line of perfume.

July 1 Paid $38,000 to LogoLab, Inc., for designing a trademark for a new line of gourmet chocolates that Berdahl will distribute nationally. Berdahl will use the trademark for as long as the firm remains in business. Berdahl expects to be in business for at least another 50 years.

1 Paid $25,000 for advertisement in a national magazine (June issue) introducing the new line of chocolates and the trademark.

**Required**

*a.* Prepare journal entries to record these transactions.
*b.* Prepare the necessary adjusting entries on December 31 for these transactions. Berdahl makes adjusting entries once a year. Berdahl uses straight-line depreciation and amortization.

**P9-7A. Preparation of Balance Sheet**

Dooley Company's December 31 post-closing trial balance contains the following normal balances:

| | |
|---|---:|
| Cash | $ 9,000 |
| Accounts payable | 18,000 |
| Building | 439,500 |
| Long-term notes payable | 785,000 |
| Common stock | 900,000 |
| Retained earnings | 70,000 |
| Accumulated depreciation—Equipment | 180,000 |
| Land | 829,500 |
| Accounts receivable | 22,500 |
| Accumulated depreciation—Building | 135,000 |
| Wages payable | 6,000 |
| Patent (net of amortization) | 120,000 |
| Notes payable (short term) | 131,000 |
| Inventory | 206,000 |
| Equipment | 600,000 |
| Allowance for doubtful accounts | 1,500 |

**Required**

Prepare a December 31 classified balance sheet for Dooley Company.

LO1, LO2, LO3    **P9-8A.**    **Journal Entries for Plant Assets**

During the first few days of the year, Coast Company entered into the following transactions:

1. Purchased a parcel of land with a building on it for $900,000 cash. The building, which will be used in operations, has an estimated useful life of 25 years and a salvage value of $60,000. The assessed valuations for property tax purposes show the land at $80,000 and the building at $720,000.
2. Paid $30,000 for the construction of an asphalt parking lot for customers. The parking lot is expected to last 12 years and has no salvage value.
3. Paid $25,000 for the construction of a new entrance to the building.
4. Purchased store equipment, paying the invoice price (including seven percent sales tax) of $74,900 in cash. The estimated useful life of the equipment is eight years, and the salvage value is $6,000.
5. Paid $220 freight on the new equipment.
6. Paid $1,500 to repair damages to floor caused when the store equipment was accidentally dropped as it was moved into place.
7. Paid $40 for an umbrella holder to place inside front door (customers may place wet umbrellas in the holder). The holder is expected to last 20 years.

### Required

*a.* Prepare journal entries to record these transactions.
*b.* Prepare the December 31 journal entries to record depreciation expense for the year. Double-declining balance depreciation is used for the equipment, and straight-line depreciation is used for the building and parking lot.

LO1, LO2, LO5    **P9-9A.**    **IFRS**

Sovereign Biotechnology PLC is a U.K.-based biotechnology company. During the year, the company's London office property was appraised at 100 million British pounds, or 20 million pounds more than its current book value on the company's balance sheet. The company also spent 12 million British pounds on original research seeking a cure for cancer. Finally, the company spent 6 million British pounds on development costs associated with a promising new molecule combination that had, in early human tests, shown that it could substantially reduce the likelihood that patients with immune deficiency syndrome would develop pneumonia.

### Required

Prepare journal entries to record the above information.

## PROBLEMS—SET B

LO1    **P9-1B.**    **Acquisition Cost of Long-Lived Assets**

The following items represent expenditures (or receipts) related to the construction of a new home office for Secrest Investment Company.

| | |
|---|---:|
| Cost of land site, which included an abandoned railroad spur | $ 175,000 |
| Legal fees, including title search, relating to land purchase | 4,300 |
| Cost of surveying land to confirm boundaries | 1,100 |
| Cost of removing railroad tracks | 6,500 |
| Payment of delinquent property taxes assumed by the purchaser | 6,000 |
| Proceeds from sale of timber from walnut trees cut down to prepare site for construction | (18,000) |
| Proceeds from sale of salvaged railroad truck | (3,500) |
| Grading to prepare land site for construction | 4,000 |
| Cost of basement excavation (contracted separately) | 3,700 |
| Architect's fees on new building | 128,000 |
| Payment to building contractor—original contract price | 3,200,000 |
| Cost of changes during construction to make building more energy efficient | 91,000 |
| Cost of replacing windows broken by vandals | 2,400 |
| Cost of paving driveway and parking lot | 17,000 |
| Out-of-court settlement for mud slide onto adjacent property | 10,000 |
| Special assessment for paving city sidewalks (paid to city) | 22,000 |
| Cost of brick and wrought iron fence installed across front of property | 16,500 |

### Required

From the given data, compute the proper balances for the Land, Building, and Land Improvements accounts of Secrest Investment Company.

**P9-2B. Allocation of Package Purchase Price and Depreciation Methods**

In an expansion move, Beam Company paid $2,180,000 for most of the property, plant, and equipment of a small manufacturing firm that was going out of business. Before agreeing to the price, Beam hired a consultant for $20,000 to appraise the assets. The appraised values were as follows:

| | |
|---|---|
| Land | $ 384,000 |
| Building | 912,000 |
| Equipment | 960,000 |
| Trucks | 144,000 |
| Total | $2,400,000 |

Beam issued two checks totaling $2,200,000 to acquire the assets and pay the consultant on April 1. Beam depreciated the assets using the straight-line method for the building and equipment, and the double-declining balance method for the trucks. Estimated useful lives and salvage values were as follows:

| | Useful Life | Salvage Value |
|---|---|---|
| Building | 15 years | $86,000 |
| Equipment | 9 years | 70,000 |
| Trucks | 5 years | 13,000 |

**Required**

a. Calculate the amounts allocated to the various types of plant assets acquired on April 1.
b. Prepare the April 1 journal entries to record the purchase of the assets and the payment of the consultant.
c. Prepare the December 31 journal entries to record the depreciation expense on the building, equipment, and trucks for the year.

**P9-3B. Depreciation Methods**

On January 2, 2010, Alvarez Company purchased an electroplating machine to help manufacture a part for one of its key products. The machine cost $218,700 and was estimated to have a useful life of six years or 700,000 platings, after which it could be sold for $23,400.

**Required**

a. Calculate each year's depreciation expense for the period 2010–2015 under each of the following depreciation methods:
   1. Straight-line.
   2. Double-declining balance.
   3. Units-of-production. (Assume annual production in platings of 140,000; 180,000; 100,000; 110,000; 80,000; and 90,000.)
b. Assume that the machine was purchased on September 1, 2010. Calculate each year's depreciation expense for the period 2010–2016 under each of the following depreciation methods:
   1. Straight-line.
   2. Double-declining balance.

**P9-4B. Journal Entries for Plant Assets**

Stellar Delivery Service had the following transactions related to its delivery truck:

**Year 1**
Mar. 1 Purchased for $28,500 cash a new delivery truck with an estimated useful life of five years and a $2,800 salvage value.
     2 Paid $580 for painting the company name and logo on the truck.
Dec. 31 Recorded depreciation on the truck for the year.

**Year 2**
July 1 Installed air conditioning in the truck at a cost of $1,808 cash. Although the truck's estimated useful life was unaffected, its estimated salvage value was increased by $400.
Sept. 7 Paid $430 for truck tune-up and safety inspection.
Dec. 31 Recorded depreciation on the truck for the year.

**Year 3**
Sept. 3 Installed a set of front and rear bumper guards at a cost of $130 cash.
Dec. 31 Recorded depreciation on the truck for the year.

**Year 4**

Dec. 31 Recorded depreciation on the truck for the year.

Stellar's depreciation policies include (1) using straight-line depreciation, (2) recording depreciation to the nearest whole month, and (3) expensing all truck expenditures of $150 or less.

**Required**

Prepare journal entries to record these transactions and adjustments.

**LO2, LO3** **P9-5B.** **Revision of Depreciation and Capital Expenditure**

Richter Company uses straight-line depreciation in accounting for its machines. On January 2, 2005, Richter purchased a new machine for $122,000 cash. The machine's estimated useful life was seven years with a $10,000 salvage value. In 2010, the company decided its original useful life estimate should be increased by three years. Beginning in 2010, depreciation was based on a 10-year total useful life, and no change was made in the salvage value estimate. On January 3, 2011, Richter added an automatic cut-off switch and a self-sharpening blade mechanism to the machine at a cost of $8,800 cash. These improvements did not change the machine's useful life but did increase the estimated salvage value to $11,200.

**Required**

a. Prepare journal entries to record (1) the purchase of the machine, (2) 2005 depreciation expense, (3) 2010 depreciation expense, (4) the 2011 improvements, and (5) 2011 depreciation expense.

b. Calculate the book value of the machine at the end of 2011 (that is, after recording the depreciation expense for 2011).

**LO4** **P9-6B.** **Disposal of Plant Asset**

Canyon Company has a used delivery truck that originally cost $27,200. Straight-line depreciation on the truck has been recorded for three years, with a $2,000 expected salvage value at the end of its estimated six-year useful life. The last depreciation entry was made at the end of the third year. Four months into the fourth year, Canyon disposes of the truck.

**Required**

Prepare journal entries to record:

a. Depreciation expense to the date of disposal.

b. Sale of the truck for cash at its book value.

c. Sale of the truck for $15,000 cash.

d. Sale of the truck for $12,000 cash.

e. Theft of the truck. Canyon carries no insurance for theft.

**LO1, LO2, LO5** **P9-7B.** **Accounting for Plant and Intangible Assets**

Selected transactions of Continental Publishers, Inc., for 2011 are given below:

Jan. 2 Paid $90,000 to purchase copyrights to a series of romantic novels. The copyrights expire in 40 years, although sales of the novels are expected to stop after 10 years.

Mar. 1 Discovered a satellite dish antenna has been destroyed by lightning. The loss is covered by insurance and a claim is filed today. The antenna cost $9,180 when installed on July 1, 2010, and was being depreciated over 12 years with a $900 salvage value. Straight-line depreciation was last recorded on December 31, 2010. Continental expects to receive an insurance settlement of $8,100.

April 1 Paid $120,000 to remodel space to create an employee exercise area on the lower level in a leased building. The building's remaining useful life is 40 years; the lease on the building expires in 12 years.

July 1 Paid $270,000 to acquire a patent on a new publishing process. The patent has a remaining legal life of 15 years. Continental estimates the new process will be utilized for 6 years before it becomes obsolete.

Nov. 1 Paid $63,000 to obtain a four-year franchise to sell a new series of computerized do-it-yourself manuals.

**Required**

a. Prepare journal entries to record these transactions.

b. Prepare the December 31 journal entries to record depreciation and amortization expense for assets acquired during the year. Continental uses straight-line depreciation and amortization.

**P9-8B.** **Preparation of Balance Sheet**                                     LO6

Conlon Corporation's December 31 post-closing trial balance contains the following normal account balances:

| | |
|---|---:|
| Interest payable . . . . . . . . . . . . . . . . . . . . . . . . . . . . . . . . . . . . . . . . . . . . . . . . . . . . . . . . . . . . . . | $ 24,000 |
| Allowance for doubtful accounts . . . . . . . . . . . . . . . . . . . . . . . . . . . . . . . . . . . . . . . . . . . . . . | 1,000 |
| Accumulated depreciation—Equipment . . . . . . . . . . . . . . . . . . . . . . . . . . . . . . . . . . . . . . . | 130,000 |
| Inventory . . . . . . . . . . . . . . . . . . . . . . . . . . . . . . . . . . . . . . . . . . . . . . . . . . . . . . . . . . . . . . . . . . . . | 137,000 |
| Organization costs (net of amortization) . . . . . . . . . . . . . . . . . . . . . . . . . . . . . . . . . . . . . . . | 19,000 |
| Notes payable (short term) . . . . . . . . . . . . . . . . . . . . . . . . . . . . . . . . . . . . . . . . . . . . . . . . . . . | 80,000 |
| Cash . . . . . . . . . . . . . . . . . . . . . . . . . . . . . . . . . . . . . . . . . . . . . . . . . . . . . . . . . . . . . . . . . . . . . . . . | 2,000 |
| Building . . . . . . . . . . . . . . . . . . . . . . . . . . . . . . . . . . . . . . . . . . . . . . . . . . . . . . . . . . . . . . . . . . . . . | 280,000 |
| Accounts receivable . . . . . . . . . . . . . . . . . . . . . . . . . . . . . . . . . . . . . . . . . . . . . . . . . . . . . . . . . | 21,000 |
| Patent (net of amortization) . . . . . . . . . . . . . . . . . . . . . . . . . . . . . . . . . . . . . . . . . . . . . . . . . . | 50,000 |
| Equipment . . . . . . . . . . . . . . . . . . . . . . . . . . . . . . . . . . . . . . . . . . . . . . . . . . . . . . . . . . . . . . . . . . | 266,000 |
| Common stock . . . . . . . . . . . . . . . . . . . . . . . . . . . . . . . . . . . . . . . . . . . . . . . . . . . . . . . . . . . . . . . | 400,000 |
| Retained earnings . . . . . . . . . . . . . . . . . . . . . . . . . . . . . . . . . . . . . . . . . . . . . . . . . . . . . . . . . . . | 353,000 |
| Accumulated depreciation—Building . . . . . . . . . . . . . . . . . . . . . . . . . . . . . . . . . . . . . . . . . | 70,000 |
| Accounts payable . . . . . . . . . . . . . . . . . . . . . . . . . . . . . . . . . . . . . . . . . . . . . . . . . . . . . . . . . . . . | 13,000 |
| Leasehold improvements . . . . . . . . . . . . . . . . . . . . . . . . . . . . . . . . . . . . . . . . . . . . . . . . . . . . . | 140,000 |
| Land . . . . . . . . . . . . . . . . . . . . . . . . . . . . . . . . . . . . . . . . . . . . . . . . . . . . . . . . . . . . . . . . . . . . . . . . | 1,128,000 |
| Long-term notes payable . . . . . . . . . . . . . . . . . . . . . . . . . . . . . . . . . . . . . . . . . . . . . . . . . . . . . | 950,000 |
| Accumulated depreciation—Leasehold improvements . . . . . . . . . . . . . . . . . . . . . . . . . . . | 22,000 |

**Required**

Prepare a December 31 classified balance sheet for Conlon Corporation.

## SERIAL PROBLEM: KATE'S CARDS

(*Note:* **This is a continuation of the Serial Problem: Kate's Cards from Chapters 1 through 8.**)

**SP9.**    Kate's business is growing faster than she had predicted. In order to keep up, she will need to purchase improved computer hardware. Kate has learned that the software that she uses runs much faster if her computer has a lot of memory. In addition, her files are very large and she is running out of free space on her existing hard drive. Finally, Kate has heard horror stories about hard disk drive crashes and the possibility that all of her work will be destroyed. In order to protect against this possibility, she has decided to invest in a large commercial grade backup system.

The cost of the memory and hard disk drive upgrade to Kate's computer will total $420. The cost of the backup system is $3,000. The memory and hard disk upgrade will increase the productivity of Kate's current computer; however, it will not extend its useful life. The backup system is expected to have a 5-year useful life.

Kate would like to know the following items:

1. How should the expenditure for the memory and hard disk drive upgrade be recorded? Provide the journal entry.

2. Kate's current computer has 42 months remaining for depreciation purpose (under the straight-line method). The original cost of the computer was $4,800 and had a four-year useful life. The current monthly depreciation is $100. How will this current expenditure affect the monthly depreciation?

3. Kate would like to know how depreciation on the backup system under both the straight-line method and the double-declining method differ. She is assigning a $500 salvage value to the equipment. Construct a table showing yearly depreciation under both methods.

## EXTENDING YOUR KNOWLEDGE

### REPORTING AND ANALYSIS

**EYK9-1.**    **Financial Reporting Problem: Columbia Sportswear Company**

The financial statements for the **Columbia Sportswear Company** can be found in Appendix A at the end of this book.

**COLUMBIA SPORTSWEAR COMPANY**

**Required**

Answer the following questions.

At the appropriate time, the employer will remit the amounts withheld from employees to the proper recipients. To the extent that any of the payable amounts are not paid at the end of an accounting period, they are reported as current liabilities.

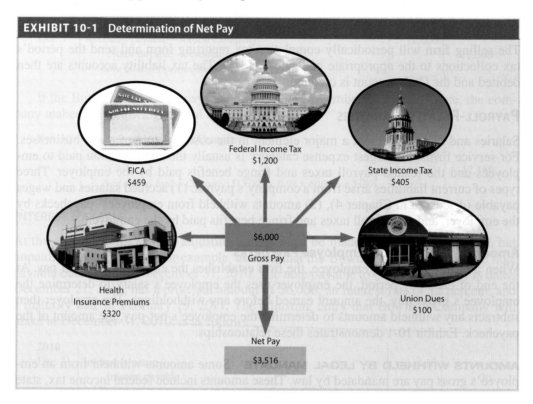

**EXHIBIT 10-1** Determination of Net Pay

FICA $459

Federal Income Tax $1,200

State Income Tax $405

Health Insurance Premiums $320

$6,000 Gross Pay

Union Dues $100

Net Pay $3,516

## Payroll Taxes Paid by the Employer

An employer pays three types of taxes on the gross payroll amount: FICA taxes, federal unemployment tax, and state unemployment tax.

Each employer is required to pay an amount equal to the FICA taxes withheld from the employees' gross pay (2010 rates were 6.2 percent of the first $106,800 of gross pay for Social Security and 1.45 percent of gross pay for Medicare). As a result, the total Social Security collected in 2010 for each employee was 12.4 percent of the first $106,800 of gross pay, and the total Medicare collected was 2.9 percent of all gross pay.

Federal and state unemployment taxes are levied only on employers as a percentage of the gross payroll, subject to various limits. The current federal unemployment tax rate is 6.2 percent of the first $67,000 of an employee's gross pay. However, an employer is entitled to a credit against this tax for unemployment taxes paid to the state. The maximum credit allowed is 5.4 percent of the first $67,000 of gross pay. Many states set their basic unemployment tax rate at this maximum credit. In these states, the effective federal unemployment tax rate is 0.8 percent (6.2 percent − 5.4 percent), and the effective state unemployment tax rate is 5.4 percent.

**RECORDING PAYROLL TAXES PAID BY THE EMPLOYER** Assume that the payroll for the week ended August 15 for Centerline Company totaled $6,000. Amounts withheld included $372 for Social Security and $87 for Medicare. Federal unemployment tax payable for the week was $48 (0.8 percent) and state unemployment tax payable was $324 (5.4 percent). Centerline makes the following journal entry to record its payroll taxes:

| A | = | L | + | SE |
|---|---|---|---|---|
| | | +459 | | −831 Exp |
| | | +48 | | |
| | | +324 | | |

| Aug. 15 | Payroll tax expense | 831 | |
|---|---|---|---|
| | FICA taxes payable | | 459 |
| | Federal unemployment tax payable | | 48 |
| | State unemployment tax payable | | 324 |
| | *To record the payroll taxes for the week ended August 15.* | | |

If payroll taxes have not been remitted to the proper government agency by the end of the accounting period, they are classified as current liabilities in the balance sheet.

**Your Turn!** **10.1**

Archer Corporation had the following payroll data for April:

| | |
|---|---|
| Office salaries | $ 40,000 |
| Sales salaries | 86,000 |
| Federal income taxes withheld | 25,600 |
| Health insurance premiums withheld | 1,850 |
| Union dues withheld | 950 |
| Salaries (included above): | |
| Subject to both FICA taxes | 126,000 |
| Subject to federal unemployment taxes | 76,000 |
| Subject to state unemployment taxes | 88,000 |

The combined FICA tax rate is 7.65 percent (6.2 percent plus 1.45 percent), the federal unemployment compensation tax rate is 0.8 percent, and the state unemployment compensation tax rate is 5.4 percent. The amounts subject to these taxes are given above.

**Required**
Prepare journal entries to record the following on April 30:

a. Accrual of the payroll.
b. Payment of the net payroll.
c. Accrual of the employer's payroll taxes.
d. Payment of all liabilities related to the payroll. (Assume that all liabilities are paid at the same time.)

The solution is on page 496.

## INCOME TAXES PAYABLE

The U.S. Federal Government, most states, and some municipalities levy income taxes against corporations, individuals, estates, and trusts. Sole proprietorships and partnerships are not taxable entities—their owners include any business income on the owner's personal income tax return.

The tax due is determined in accordance with tax law, rulings by taxing agencies, and court decisions. Because the administration of tax law is quite complex and many honest differences exist in their interpretation, the tax obligation reported on a tax return is only an estimate until the government reviews and accepts a firm's (or individual's) calculations.

Because corporations are separate taxable entities, they incur a legal obligation for income taxes whenever income is earned. Therefore, corporate financial statements routinely include income tax liabilities. For example, business income taxes of $8,000 are recorded as follows:

| | | |
|---|---|---|
| Income tax expense | 8,000 | |
|    Income tax payable | | 8,000 |
| *To record estimated income tax.* | | |

| A | = | L | + | SE |
|---|---|---|---|---|
| | | +8,000 | | −8,000 Exp |

Corporations usually pay their estimated income taxes quarterly, with an annual tax return and final payment due within a few months following the end of a calendar year. Thus, any liability for income taxes in the financial statements is classified as a current liability since payment is expected in the short-term.

## ADVANCE PAYMENTS—UNEARNED REVENUE

Airline tickets, cruise-line tickets, season football tickets, and cellular phone connection charges are examples of advance payments for services. A customer pays cash in advance for these services and the service provider agrees to provide future services. As an example, assume that **American Airlines** sells a ticket for $400 on March 20 for travel on May 25. American would make the following journal entry at the time that the airline ticket is sold:

| | A | = | L | + | SE |
|---|---|---|---|---|---|
| | +400 | | +400 | | |

| Mar. 20 | Cash | | 400 | |
|---|---|---|---|---|
| | Unearned ticket revenue | | | 400 |
| | *To record the sale of an airline ticket.* | | | |

When the passenger takes the scheduled flight, the airline makes the following journal entry:

| | A | = | L | + | SE |
|---|---|---|---|---|---|
| | | | −400 | | +400 Rev |

| May 25 | Unearned ticket revenue | | 400 | |
|---|---|---|---|---|
| | Ticket revenue | | | 400 |
| | *To record ticket revenue earned.* | | | |

## LIABILITIES FOR PRODUCT WARRANTIES

Many firms guarantee their products for a period of time following their sale. A proper matching of sales revenue and expenses requires that the estimated cost of honoring and servicing these **product warranties** be recognized as an expense in the period of sale rather than in a later period when the warranty costs may actually be incurred and paid.

To illustrate, assume that a firm sells a product for $300 per unit, which includes a 30-day warranty against defects. Past experience indicates that three percent of the units will prove defective and that the average repair cost will be $40 per defective unit. Furthermore, during a particular month, product sales were $240,000, and 13 of the units sold during the month were defective and were repaired. Using this information, the accrued liability for product warranties at the end of the month can be calculated as follows:

| | |
|---|---|
| Number of units sold ($240,000/$300)............................................................ | 800 |
| Rate of projected defective units.................................................................. | × 0.03 |
| Total units expected to fail........................................................................ | 24 |
| Less: Units that failed in the month of sale..................................................... | 13 |
| Units expected to fail in the remainder of the warranty period ............................ | 11 |
| Average repair cost per unit....................................................................... | × $40 |
| Estimated liability for product warranty at end of month.................................... | $440 |

This accrued liability is recorded at the end of the month of sale as follows:

| | A | = | L | + | SE |
|---|---|---|---|---|---|
| | | | +440 | | −440 |

| | Product warranty expense | | 440 | |
|---|---|---|---|---|
| | Estimated liability for product warranty | | | 440 |
| | *To record estimated warranty expense.* | | | |

When a unit fails in a future period, the repair costs will be recorded by debiting the Estimated Liability for Product Warranty account and crediting Cash, Supplies, and so forth.

---

**PRINCIPLE ALERT** | **Matching Concept**

The accounting for product warranties follows the *matching concept*. This accounting concept states that expenses must be recorded in the same accounting period as the revenues they help generate. Product warranties make a company's products more attractive to buyers; consequently, product warranties help generate incremental sales revenues. Hence, one of the expenses that must be matched with sales revenues is the cost of honoring and servicing a product warranty. Because most warranty costs are incurred in periods following the period of sale, it is necessary to estimate these costs and record them in the same period when the sale of the product occurs, to achieve a proper matching of revenues and expenses.

# BONDS PAYABLE

At various times during a business's operating life, the business will need to secure long-term funds to finance its operations or the acquisition of various operating assets. When a business elects to finance its growth with long-term borrowing, it may do so by issuing bonds. A **bond** is a long-term debt instrument that promises to pay interest periodically as well as a principal amount at maturity, to the bond investor. In the United States, bond interest is usually paid semiannually. The principal amount is referred to as the bond's face value (because it is printed on the face of the bond certificate), par value, or maturity value.

**LEARNING OBJECTIVE 2**

**Illustrate** the accounting for bonds.

## TYPES OF BONDS

Bond agreements may be formulated to capitalize on certain lending situations, appeal to special investor groups, or provide special repayment patterns.

**Secured bonds**, for example, pledge specific property as security for meeting the terms of the bond agreement. The specific title of the bonds may indicate the type of property pledged—for example, real estate mortgage bonds (land or buildings), chattel mortgage bonds (machinery or equipment), and collateral trust bonds (negotiable securities).

Bonds that have no specific property pledged as security for their repayment are called **debenture bonds**. Buyers of debenture bonds rely on a borrower's general credit reputation. Because a lender's risk is usually greater than with secured bonds, the sale of unsecured bonds may require offering a higher rate of interest to attract bond buyers.

The maturity dates of **serial bonds** are staggered over a series of years. For example, a serial bond issue of $15 million may provide for $1 million of the bonds to mature each year for 15 years. An advantage of serial bonds is that bond investors can choose bonds with maturity dates that correspond with their desired length of investment.

**Convertible bonds** grant the bondholder the right to convert the bonds into a company's common stock at some specific exchange (or conversion) ratio. This provision gives an investor the security of being a creditor during a certain stage of a firm's life, with the option of becoming a stockholder if the firm becomes sufficiently profitable. Because the conversion feature is attractive to potential investors, a company may issue convertible bonds at a lower interest rate than it would pay without the conversion feature.

**Zero-coupon bonds** are bonds that pay no periodic interest payments but are issued at a substantial discount from their face value. The face value is paid to the bondholder at maturity. The total interest implicit in the bond contract is the difference between the bond's original issue price and its face value at maturity. For example, a five-year, $1,000 zero-coupon bond issued for $713 will pay the lender $1,000 at the end of the five years. The total interest associated with this bond is $287 ($1,000 − $713). Zero-coupon bonds are particularly helpful to a borrower when the project being financed with the bond proceeds provides no cash inflows until the bond maturity date.

---

**EXHIBIT 10-2** Bond Certificate

**Bond Issuer** → **General Electric Company**

**Interest rate** → **$5,000,000,000** ← **Face value**
**5% Notes due 2013**

**Maturity date** → **Issue price: 99.626%**

We will pay interest on the notes semiannually on February 1 and August 1 of each year, beginning August 1, 2003. The notes will mature on February 1, 2013. We may not redeem the notes prior to maturity.

The notes will be unsecured obligations and rank equally with our other unsecured debt securities that are not subordinated obligations. The notes will be issued in registered form in denominations of $1,000.

Neither the Securities and Exchange Commission nor any state securities commission has approved or disapproved of the notes or determined if this prospectus supplement or the accompanying prospectus is truthful or complete. Any representation to the contrary is a criminal offense.

| | Per Note | Total |
|---|---|---|
| Public Offering Price(1) | 99.626% | $4,981,300,000 |
| Underwriting Discounts | .425% | $ 21,250,000 |
| Proceeds to General Electric Company (before expenses) | 99.201% | $4,960,050,000 |

(1) Plus accrued interest from January 28, 2003, if settlement occurs after that date.

The underwriters expect to deliver the notes in book-entry form only through the facilities of The Depository Trust Company, Clearstream, Luxembourg or the Euroclear System, as the case may be, on or about January 28, 2003.

*Joint Bookrunners*

**Morgan Stanley**        **Salomon Smith Barney**

*Senior Co-Managers*

| Banc of America Securities LLC<br>Goldman. Sachs & Co. | Credit Suisse First Boston<br>JPMorgan<br>UBS Warburg | Deutsche Bank Securities<br>Merrill Lynch & Co. |

*Co-Managers*

| Banc One Capital Markets, Inc.<br>BNP PARIBAN<br>HSBC<br>Utendahl Capital Partners, L.P. | Barclays Capital<br>Dresdner Kleinwort Wasserstein<br>Loop Capital Markets<br>The Williams Capital Group, L.P. | Blaylock & Partners, L.P.<br>Guzman & Company<br>Ormes Capital Markets, Inc. |

---

**ACCOUNTING IN PRACTICE** **Bond Risk Ratings**

The relative riskiness of different bonds may vary considerably. Bond investors who want to know the relative quality of a particular bond issue can consult a bond-rating service. Two major firms that rate the riskiness of bonds are **Standard & Poor's Corporation** (S&P) and **Moody's Investors Service** (Moody's). The rating categories used by these firms are similar. The schedule below shows the relationship between the ratings and the degree of risk using Standard & Poor's rating system:

| Low Risk | | | | | | | High Risk |
|---|---|---|---|---|---|---|---|
| AAA | AA | A | BBB | BB | B | CCC | D |

|----------------------Investment Grade Bonds----------------------------|----------------------Junk Bonds---------------|

Investment grade bonds are highly-rated bonds with little risk that the issuing company will fail to pay interest as scheduled or fail to repay the principal at a bond's maturity. Junk bonds, on the other hand, are low-quality, high-yield bonds. In the S&P rating system, junk bonds are any bond rated BB and lower. Generally, bonds with poor credit ratings must offer higher interest rates than highly-rated bonds to attract potential buyers.

**A.K.A.** Junk bonds are often referred to as high-yield bonds because of the higher yield rates that typically accompany this type of debt investment.

## BOND FEATURES

Bonds with a **call provision** allow the bond issuer to call in the bonds for redemption. Usually, an extra amount or premium must be paid to the holders of a called bond. A call provision offers borrowers additional financing flexibility that may be significant if funds become available at interest rates substantially lower than those currently being paid on the bonds. Borrowers can, in effect, also "call" any of their bonds by buying them in the open market.

A **sinking fund provision** requires that a borrower retire a portion of its outstanding bonds each year or, in some bond issues, make payments each year to a trustee who is responsible for managing the funds needed to retire the bonds at maturity. The orderly retirement of bonds, or the accumulation of funds needed at maturity, as required by a sinking fund provision is generally viewed as making any bond safer (less risky) for the bondholders.

---

**ACCOUNTING IN PRACTICE**   **Microsoft Bond Issuance and Company Value**

As noted in the opening feature story, **Microsoft** was essentially debt free until 2009. Following the $3.75 billion in bonds that Microsoft issued in late 2009, part of a larger $6 billion debt issue that the board of directors approved, analysts weighed in on why they thought this occurred. Noting that Microsoft also authorized a plan to buy back $40 billion of its own stock over the following five years, Sid Parakh, an analyst at McAdams Wright Ragen stated, "They said a few months ago they would like to leverage the balance sheets; that's what they're doing. Lowering the cost of capital will probably benefit shareholder value in the long term."

---

## BOND PRICES

Bonds are typically sold in units of $1,000 face (maturity) value, and the market price is expressed as a percentage of face value. Thus, a $1,000 face value bond that is quoted at 98 will sell for $980. Generally, bond prices fluctuate in response to changes in market interest rates, which are determined by government monetary policies (managing the demand and supply of money) and economic expectations. Bond prices are also affected by the financial outlook for the issuing firm.

**A.K.A.** A bond's face value is also referred to as its maturity value, stated value, or settlement value.

A bond specifies a pattern of future cash flows, usually a series of interest payments and a single payment at maturity equal to the bond's face value. The amount of the periodic interest payment is determined by the **coupon rate** stated on the bond certificate. Interest rates are usually quoted as annual rates, so the coupon rate will need to be converted to a per period interest rate when interest is paid more than once a year. For example, in the U.S., bond interest is usually paid semiannually, with the payments six months apart. Thus, the amount of interest paid semiannually is calculated by multiplying one-half the coupon rate of interest times the bond's face value.

**A.K.A.** A bond's coupon rate of interest is also referred to as its nominal rate or stated rate of interest.

A bond's market price is determined by discounting the bond's future cash flows (both its principal and interest payments) to the present using the current **market rate of interest** for the bond as the discount rate, a process known as *computing the bond's present value*. The market rate is the rate of return investors expect on their investment. Present value factors are available in Appendix E, at the end of this book, to help simplify these calculations.

**A.K.A.** A bond's market rate of interest is also referred to as its real rate of interest or its effective yield rate.

---

**IFRS ALERT!**

U.S. GAAP and IFRS are substantially aligned when it comes to the reporting of liabilities. Under both accounting systems, for example, current liabilities (Accounts Payable) are reported at their settlement or future value, or the amount of money required to satisfy the obligation when it becomes due. Similarly, both systems require that long-term liabilities, like Bonds Payable, be reported at their present value, or the amount of money necessary to currently satisfy the obligation. Where the two systems diverge is in regards to the reporting of some contingent liabilities (to be discussed shortly).

When issued, a bond's price may be equal to, less than, or greater than its face value. Bonds sell at *face value* when the market rate of interest equals the bond's coupon rate. Bonds sell at a *discount* (less than face value) when the market interest rate exceeds the bond's coupon rate; and, bonds sell at a *premium* (more than face value) when the market interest rate is less than the bond's coupon rate.

Since bonds are usually printed and sold at different times, the market rate and coupon rate will often differ. Market rates and coupon rates are frequently stated in percentage terms, although increasingly, these rates are stated as "basis points." One percentage point is equal to one hundred basis points. Thus, a bond with a coupon rate of three percent is said to have a coupon rate of 300 basis points.

Exhibit 10-3 shows the calculation of a bond's selling price using different market rates of interest. (See Appendix E, at the end of this book, for a discussion of the calculation of a bond's present value.) The bond is a $1,000, eight percent annual coupon rate, four-year bond with interest payable semiannually; the periodic interest payment is $40 ($1,000 × 0.08 × 1/2). As shown in the exhibit, the bond will:

1. Sell at a *discount* ($936 bond price) when the market rate (ten percent) exceeds the coupon rate (eight percent).

2. Sell at *face value* ($1,000 bond price) when the market rate (eight percent) equals the coupon rate (eight percent).

3. Sell at a *premium* ($1,070 bond price) when the market rate (six percent) is less than the coupon rate (eight percent).

| EXHIBIT 10-3 | The Calculation of a Bond's Selling Price at Different Market Interest Rates | | |
|---|---|---|---|

The bond being priced is a $1,000, eight percent annual coupon rate, four-year bond with interest payable semiannually. There are eight semiannual interest payments of $40 ($1,000 × 0.08 × 1/2):

| | Priced to Yield an Investor an Interest Rate, Compounded Semiannually, of | | |
|---|---|---|---|
| | 10% | 8% | 6% |
| Present value of $1,000 due at maturity: | | | |
| $1,000 × 0.677 present value factor* ............................ = | $677 | | |
| $1,000 × 0.731 present value factor ............................ = | | $ 731 | |
| $1,000 × 0.789 present value factor ............................ = | | | $ 789 |
| Present value of eight $40 interest payments (rounded to nearest dollar): | | | |
| $40 × 6.463 present value factor* .............................. = | 259 | | |
| $40 × 6.733 present value factor .............................. = | | 269 | |
| $40 × 7.020 present value factor .............................. = | | | 281 |
| Bond selling price ................................................ | $936 | $1,000 | $1,070 |
| Bond priced at.................................................... | Discount | Face value | Premium |

*See Appendix E for a discussion of present value factors.

## Recording Bonds

### Bonds Issued at Face Value

To provide a simple illustration, we will use a bond with a short period to maturity. Assume that on December 31, 2010, Reid, Inc., issues at face value $100,000 of eight percent bonds that mature in four years with interest paid on June 30 and December 31. The following journal entry records the bond, which is sold at its face value:

| 2010 | | | |
|---|---|---|---|
| Dec. 31 | Cash | 100,000 | |
| |     Bonds payable | | 100,000 |
| | *To record the issuance of bonds.* | | |

Interest of $4,000 ($100,000 × 0.08 × 6/12) will be paid on each of the eight payment dates (four years, semiannual payments). For example, the journal entry on June 30, 2011, the first interest payment date, is:

| 2011 | | | |
|---|---|---|---|
| June 30 | Bond interest expense | 4,000 | |
| |     Cash | | 4,000 |
| | *To record the payment of semiannual interest on bonds.* | | |

When the bonds mature, Reid, Inc., records their retirement in the following manner:

| 2014 | | | |
|---|---|---|---|
| Dec. 31 | Bonds payable | 100,000 | |
| |     Cash | | 100,000 |
| | *To record the retirement of bonds.* | | |

## Issuance Between Interest Dates

Not all bonds are sold on the exact day on which their interest payment period begins. Investors who buy bonds after the interest period begins are expected to "buy" any interest that has accrued on the bonds. Such bonds are said to be sold at a given price "plus accrued interest." The accrued interest is returned to the investor at the next interest payment date. This procedure simplifies the bond issuer's administrative work. Regardless of when bonds are issued, a full six months' interest is paid to all bondholders on each interest payment date.

To illustrate, let us assume that Reid, Inc. sold its $100,000, eight percent, four-year bonds at 100 plus accrued interest on February 28, 2011, instead of on December 31, 2010. The following journal entry is made:

| 2011 | | | |
|---|---|---|---|
| Feb. 28 | Cash | 101,333 | |
| |     Bonds payable | | 100,000 |
| |     Bond interest payable | | 1,333 |
| | *To record bond issuance at 100 plus two months' accrued interest.* | | |

The interest accrued on the bonds on February 28 is $1,333 ($100,000 × 0.08 × 2/12, rounded). On the first interest payment date, June 30, 2010, Reid, Inc., makes the following entry:

| 2011 | | | |
|---|---|---|---|
| June 30 | Bond interest payable | 1,333 | |
| | Bond interest expense | 2,667 | |
| |     Cash | | 4,000 |
| | *To record the payment of semiannual interest on bonds payable.* | | |

Note that the bond interest expense recorded by Reid, Inc., relates only to the four months since the bonds were issued.

## Bonds Issued at a Discount

If the coupon rate of interest on the bonds issued is less than the current market rate, the bonds will be sold at a price less than their face value. In such cases, investors "discount" the price of the bonds to enable the buyer to earn the current market rate of interest. For example, assume that Reid, Inc.'s $100,000 issue of eight percent, four-year bonds is sold on December 31, 2010, for $93,552. This price permits investors to earn an interest rate of ten percent. (For calculations, please see Appendix E.) The following journal entry records the issuance of the bonds at a discount:

| A | = | L | + | SE |
|---|---|---|---|---|
| +93,552 | | −6,448 | | |
| | | +100,000 | | |

| 2010 | | | | |
|---|---|---|---|---|
| Dec. 31 | Cash | | 93,552 | |
| | Discount on bonds payable | | 6,448 | |
| |     Bonds payable | | | 100,000 |
| | *To record the issuance of bonds.* | | | |

The $6,448 discount is not an immediate loss or expense to Reid, Inc. Rather, it represents an adjustment of interest expense over the life of the bonds. This can be illustrated by comparing the funds that Reid, Inc., receives with the funds it must pay to the bondholders. Regardless of their selling price, the bonds represent an agreement to pay $132,000 to the bondholders ($100,000 principal plus eight semiannual interest payments of $4,000 each).

| | |
|---|---|
| Total funds paid to bondholders ................................................................ | $132,000 |
| Total funds received from bond sale............................................................ | (93,552) |
| Difference equals total interest expense....................................................... | 38,448 |
| Total semiannual interest payments............................................................ | (32,000) |
| Increase in interest expense beyond semiannual interest payments ............................. | $ 6,448 |

The total interest expense for this four-year bond issue is $38,448[1], the difference between the total cash paid to the bondholders and the proceeds from the sale of the bonds. The semiannual interest payments to bondholders total $32,000, so an additional $6,448 needs to be recognized as interest expense over the life of the bonds. The $6,448 is the amount of the bond discount. To reflect the larger periodic interest expense, the bond discount is *amortized over the eight interest payment periods*. Amortization of a bond discount means that, periodically, an amount is transferred from the Discount on Bonds Payable account to the Bond Interest Expense account.

There are two methods of bond amortization: the straight-line method and the effective interest method. Under the *straight-line method*, equal amounts are transferred from bond discount to interest expense for each interest payment period. The *effective interest method*, on the other hand, reflects a constant rate of interest over the life of the bonds. We use the effective interest method in Appendix E since that is the method more commonly used in the bond market.

### Bonds Issued at a Premium

If the market rate of interest had been below the eight percent offered by Reid, Inc., investors would have been willing to pay a premium to buy the bonds. Suppose that the **effective interest rate** was six percent. Reid Inc.'s $100,000, eight percent, four-year bonds would sell for $106,980 (for calculations, please see Appendix E). The issuance of the bonds on December 31, 2010, is recorded as follows:

| A | = | L | + | SE |
|---|---|---|---|---|
| +106,980 | | +100,000 | | |
| | | +6,980 | | |

| 2010 | | | | |
|---|---|---|---|---|
| Dec. 31 | Cash | | 106,980 | |
| |     Bonds payable | | | 100,000 |
| |     Premium on bonds payable | | | 6,980 |
| | *To record issuance of bonds.* | | | |

When bonds are issued at a premium, the book value of the bond liability is determined by adding the Premium on Bonds Payable account balance to the Bonds Payable account balance.

Like a bond discount, a bond premium is considered an adjustment of interest expense over the life of the bonds. We saw that a bond discount represents the excess of total interest expense over the total semiannual interest payments. A similar analysis shows

---

[1] Calculation of the total cost of borrowing: Bonds sold at a discount

  Annual cash interest payments over four years to maturity:

| | |
|---|---|
|    $100,000 × 8% × 4 years = $8,000 × 4 years = $32,000 | |
|    Add: Bond discount ($100,000 − $93,552) = | 6,448 |
|    Total cost of borrowing | $38,448 |

that a bond premium represents the amount by which the total semiannual interest payments exceed the total interest expense. The analysis begins by comparing the total funds that will be paid to the bondholders over the four years (again, it is $132,000) with the proceeds received when the bonds are issued:

| | |
|---|---:|
| Total funds paid to bondholders .................................................................... | $132,000 |
| Total funds received from bond sale.................................................................. | (106,980) |
| Difference equals total interest expense.......................................................... | 25,020 |
| Total semiannual interest payments.................................................................. | (32,000) |
| Decrease in interest expense below semiannual interest payments................................... | $ 6,980 |

The total interest expense for this four-year bond issue is $25,020^2, an amount that is $6,980 less than the total semiannual interest payments to be made to bondholders. The $6,980 is the amount of the bond premium. The bond premium is amortized to cause the periodic interest expense to be less than the semiannual interest payment.

### Year-End Adjustments

When a periodic interest payment does not correspond with the fiscal year-end, an adjusting entry should be recorded reflecting the amount of interest expense incurred but not yet recorded. The adjusting entry includes a pro rata amortization of bond discount or bond premium for the portion of the year involved.

**PRINCIPLE ALERT** | **Matching Concept**

The adjusting entry to record interest expense incurred but not yet recorded is an application of the *matching concept*. This accounting concept states that all expenses incurred to generate sales revenue must be recorded, regardless of when the expense is paid in cash. Interest is a charge for the use of money, and this charge is incurred every day that a borrower has use of, and benefits from, borrowed funds.

The previous bond discount and bond premium examples assumed that Reid, Inc., was on a calendar year basis. To illustrate the necessary adjusting entries when the fiscal year-end does not correspond with the end of the interest payment period, assume that Reid's fiscal year-end is September 30. Recall that the four-year bonds were issued on December 31, 2010, with semiannual interest payments on June 30 and December 31. On September 30, 2011, for example, Reid is three months into the second six-month interest period. Thus, an adjusting entry to recognize three months of interest expense must be entered in the accounts on September 30, 2011.

**ADJUSTMENT FOR BONDS ISSUED AT A DISCOUNT** For periods of less than six months, the adjustment amounts are proportionate allocations of the six-month amounts. The adjustment at September 30, 2011, covering three months, will be one-half of the amounts for the six-month period ending December 31, 2011. The amounts can be calculated from those shown for the second interest period in the amortization schedule. For our first example (bonds issued at a discount), one-half of the amount shown for the second interest period in Exhibit E-7 (Appendix E), column A. [($4,000/2) = $2,000], is the interest payable. In the same fashion, from column B, [($4,712/2) = $2,356] is the interest expense, and from column C, [($712/2) = $356] is the discount amortization. The year-end adjusting entry is as follows:

---

[2] Calculation of the total cost of borrowing: Bonds sold at a premium

Annual cash interest payments over four years to maturity:

| | |
|---|---:|
| $100,000 × 8% × 4 years = $8,000 × 4 years = $32,000 | |
| Less: Bond premium ($106,980 − $100,000) | 6,980 |
| Total cost of borrowing | $25,020 |

| A | = | L | + | SE |
|---|---|---|---|---|
| | | +356 | | −2,356 Exp |
| | | +2,000 | | |

| | 2011 | | | |
|---|---|---|---|---|
| | Sept. 30 | Bond interest expense | 2,356 | |
| | | Discount on bonds payable | | 356 |
| | | Bond interest payable | | 2,000 |
| | | *To accrue interest for three months and amortize one-half of the* | | |
| | | *discount for the interest period.* | | |

When interest is paid at the next interest payment date, the remaining amounts of the bond interest expense and discount amortization for the six-month period are recognized. The adjusting entry to record the interest payment on December 31, 2011, is as follows:

| A | = | L | + | SE |
|---|---|---|---|---|
| −4,000 | | −2,000 | | −2,356 Exp |
| | | +356 | | |

| | 2011 | | | |
|---|---|---|---|---|
| | Dec. 31 | Bond interest payable | 2,000 | |
| | | Bond interest expense | 2,356 | |
| | | Discount on bonds payable | | 356 |
| | | Cash | | 4,000 |
| | | *To record semiannual interest payment and discount amortization* | | |
| | | *for three months.* | | |

**ADJUSTMENT FOR BONDS ISSUED AT A PREMIUM** For our second example (bonds issued at a premium), we follow the same procedure, using the second interest period in Exhibit E-8 (Appendix E). Again, we use one-half of the amounts shown to derive the amounts for our year-end adjusting entry:

| A | = | L | + | SE |
|---|---|---|---|---|
| | | −407 | | −1,593 Exp |
| | | +2,000 | | |

| | 2011 | | | |
|---|---|---|---|---|
| | Sept. 30 | Bond interest expense | 1,593 | |
| | | Premium on bonds payable | 407 | |
| | | Bond interest payable | | 2,000 |
| | | *To accrue interest for three months and amortize one-half of the* | | |
| | | *premium for the interest period.* | | |

Here, too, the remaining amounts of the bond interest expense and premium amortization for the six-month period are recognized at the next interest payment date. The adjusting entry on December 31, 2011, to record the interest payment is the following:

| A | = | L | + | SE |
|---|---|---|---|---|
| −4,000 | | −2,000 | | −1,593 Exp |
| | | −407 | | |

| | 2011 | | | |
|---|---|---|---|---|
| | Dec. 31 | Bond interest payable | 2,000 | |
| | | Bond interest expense | 1,593 | |
| | | Premium on bonds payable | 407 | |
| | | Cash | | 4,000 |
| | | *To record semiannual interest payment and premium amortization* | | |
| | | *for three months.* | | |

### Bonds Payable Disclosed on the Balance Sheet

Bonds payable that mature more than one year in the future are classified as long-term liabilities on the balance sheet. Bonds payable maturing within the next year, on the other hand, are classified as current liabilities. The Discount on Bonds Payable and Premium on Bonds Payable accounts are classified as a deduction from and as an addition to, respectively, the face value of the bonds reported in the balance sheet. Many companies do not separately disclose the Discount on Bonds Payable account or the Premium on Bonds Payable account on their publicly disseminated balance sheet, but rather net these amounts against the Bonds Payable account.

At December 31, 2011, the Reid, Inc., bonds issued at a discount (see Exhibit E-7) appear on Reid's balance sheet as follows:

| | | |
|---|---|---|
| Bonds payable ................................................................ | $100,000 | |
| Less: Discount on bonds payable.................................................. | 5,058 | $94,942 |

On the same date, the Reid Inc. bonds issued at a premium (see Exhibit E-8) would appear as follows:

| | | |
|---|---|---|
| Bonds payable ............................................................... | $100,000 | |
| Add: Premium on bonds payable.................................................. | 5,375 | $105,375 |

## Retirement of Bonds Before Maturity

Bonds are usually retired at their maturity dates with a journal entry debiting the Bonds Payable account and crediting the Cash account for the face value of the bonds. However, bonds may be retired before maturity—for example, to take advantage of more attractive financing terms.

In accounting for the retirement of bonds before maturity, the following analysis is used:

1. Remove the book value of the bonds being retired from the accounts (that is, remove the Bonds Payable amount and any related bond premium or discount).

2. Record the cash paid to retire the bonds.

3. Recognize any difference between the bonds' book value and the cash paid as a gain or loss on bond retirement.

To illustrate, assume that the Reid, Inc., bonds issued for $106,980 in our previous example were called for retirement at 105 at the end of 2013, after paying the semiannual interest on December 31, 2013. According to Exhibit E-8, the bonds' book value at the end of 2013 is $101,865. The following journal entry would be used to record the bond retirement:

| **2013** | | | |
|---|---|---|---|
| Dec. 31 | Bonds payable | 100,000 | |
| | Premium on bonds payable | 1,865 | |
| | Loss on bond retirement | 3,135 | |
| |     Cash | | 105,000 |
| | *To retire bonds at 105 and record loss on retirement.* | | |

| A | = | L | + | SE |
|---|---|---|---|---|
| −105,000 | | −100,000 | | −3,135 |
| | | −1,865 | | Loss |

## TERM LOANS

When long-term borrowing is arranged with a single lender, the borrower typically signs a note payable and the debt is referred to as a **term loan**. Term loans are often repaid in equal periodic installments. The agreement may require installment payments to be made monthly, quarterly, or semiannually. Each payment contains an interest amount and a partial repayment of principal. Because the installment payments are equal, each installment payment contains different amounts of interest and principal repayment. These

---

**FORENSIC ACCOUNTING**    **Accounting Software**

One definition of forensic accounting is "the use of accounting records and documents to determine the legality of past activities." Possible uses of forensic accounting include financial statements, government investigations, contract disputes, or even culling through a shoebox of receipts in preparation for an IRS audit.

As a business owner, would you rather defend yourself in an investigation with a shoebox full of documents or with a detailed set of accounting records? While some small business owners feel that entry-level accounting systems such as **Intuit's** Quickbooks are fine for their needs, they may want to consider the benefits of a more robust accounting package, such as Microsoft Dynamics GP accounting system.

In today's technology driven society, a security breach is only a few keystrokes away. A hacker will have a much easier time penetrating the single layer of security in most entry-level packages than the eight levels of security in Microsoft Dynamics GP. In addition, the more robust accounting systems provide a richer data repository from which a forensic accountant can data mine in an effort to identify inconsistencies, a major weapon in the detection of fraud.

component amounts change with each installment because the interest is computed on the unpaid principal, and the unpaid principal is reduced with each payment.

To illustrate, assume that on December 31, 2010, Reid, Inc., borrows $100,000 from a bank on a 12 percent, ten-year mortgage note payable. The note is to be repaid with equal quarterly installments of $4,326 (please see Appendix E for calculations). Thus, there will be 40 quarterly payments; and, the quarterly interest rate is three percent (12 percent/4 quarters). Exhibit 10-4 presents the first eight quarterly payments and their division between interest expense and principal repayment. The journal entry to record the first quarterly payment is as follows:

| A | = | L | + | SE |
|---|---|---|---|---|
| −4,326 | | −1,326 | | −3,000 Exp |

| 2011 | | | |
|---|---|---|---|
| Mar. 31 | Interest expense | 3,000 | |
| | Mortgage note payable | 1,326 | |
| | Cash | | 4,326 |
| | *To record quarterly mortgage loan payment.* | | |

**EXHIBIT 10-4**  Partial Mortgage Note Payment Schedule

$100,000 mortgage note payable with quarterly payments of $4,326 and quarterly interest rate of three percent:

| | A | B | C | D |
|---|---|---|---|---|
| | | Interest | Principal | Book Value of Note |
| | Cash | Expense | Repaid | (Unpaid |
| Payment Date | Payment | (3% × D)* | (A − B) | Principal) |
| 2010 | | | | |
| December 31 (issue date)............................ | | | | $100,000 |
| 2011 | | | | |
| March 31 ........................................... | $4,326 | $3,000 | $1,326 | 98,674 |
| June 30............................................. | 4,326 | 2,960 | 1,366 | 97,308 |
| September 30....................................... | 4,326 | 2,919 | 1,407 | 95,901 |
| December 31 ....................................... | 4,326 | 2,877 | 1,449 | 94,452 |
| 2012 | | | | |
| March 31 ........................................... | 4,326 | 2,834 | 1,492 | 92,960 |
| June 30............................................. | 4,326 | 2,789 | 1,537 | 91,423 |
| September 30....................................... | 4,326 | 2,743 | 1,583 | 89,840 |
| December 31 ....................................... | 4,326 | 2,695 | 1,631 | 88,209 |

*3 percent × unpaid principal after previous payment, rounded to the nearest dollar.

**Your Turn!**                                                                      **10.2**

Koby Company issued $300,000 of bonds for $325,000. (a) Prepare the journal entry to record the issuance of the bonds, and (b) illustrate how the bonds will be shown on the Koby Company's balance sheet at the issuance date.

The solution is on page 497.

# CONTINGENT LIABILITIES

**LEARNING OBJECTIVE 3**

**Define** *contingent liabilities* and **explain** their disclosure in the financial statements.

Previously, a *liability* was defined as an obligation resulting from past transactions or events that require a firm to pay money, provide goods, or perform services in the future. Even though a past transaction or event has taken place, the existence of some liabilities still depends on the occurrence of a future event. These types of liability are called **contingent liabilities**. Whether or not a contingent liability is recorded in the accounts depends on the likelihood of the future event occurring and the measurability of the obligation.

If the future event will *probably occur* and the amount of the liability can be *reasonably estimated,* an estimated liability should be recorded in the accounts. The estimated liability for product warranty, discussed earlier in the chapter, is a good example of this situation. The analysis assumed that customers were likely to make claims under a warranty for goods that they had purchased, and that a reasonable estimate of the amount of the warranty obligation could be made.

---

**ACCOUNTING IN PRACTICE**    **Estimated Liabilities Resulting from Lawsuits**

**Walmart Stores, Inc.,** is the world's largest retailer with over 7,000 stores around the globe. Each week, 100 million customers visit a Walmart store to take advantage of the company's notorious low prices. But while Walmart may be cheered by consumers for its low prices, others are more critical of the company. Walmart, for example, has been criticized and sued by community groups, trade unions, and environmental groups for, among other things, its extensive foreign product sourcing, treatment of employees and product suppliers, environmental policies, and store impact on local communities. One such lawsuit alleges that female employees were discriminated against in pay and promotions. The following description of the lawsuit appeared in the company's 2009 annual report:

> . . . The Company is a defendant in Dukes v. Walmart Stores, Inc., a class-action lawsuit . . . The complaint alleges that the Company engaged in a pattern and practice of discriminating against women in promotions, pay, training, and job assignments . . . If the company is not successful in its appeal . . . the resulting liability could be material to the company . . . However, because of the uncertainty of the outcome of the appeal . . . the Company cannot reasonably estimate the possible loss or range of loss which may arise from the litigation.

Walmart's description of its pending litigation illustrates a common problem with measuring and reporting lawsuit liabilities—it is impossible in most cases to arrive at a reasonable estimate of a company's possible losses. For this reason, lawsuit liabilities are most commonly disclosed in the notes to the financial statements and not on the face of the income statement or the balance sheet.

---

Some contingent liabilities are not recorded in the accounts but must be disclosed in a note to the financial statements. Contingent liabilities disclosed in this manner are (1) those for which the likelihood of the future event occurring is probable but no reasonable estimate of the future obligation is determinable or (2) those for which the likelihood of the future event occurring is *reasonably possible* (but not probable), regardless of the ability to measure the future amount. When the future amount is not determinable, the note should state that the amount cannot be estimated.

If the likelihood of the future event occurring is *remote,* the contingent liability is not recorded in the accounts nor disclosed in the notes to the financial statements, regardless of the ability to measure the future amount. One exception to this guideline, however, is when a company guarantees the credit of others (discussed in the following section). Even remote contingent liabilities associated with credit guarantees must be disclosed in the notes to the financial statements.

---

**PRINCIPLE ALERT**    **Measuring Unit Concept and Full Disclosure Principle**

The accounting guidelines for contingent liabilities illustrate the application of two principles of accounting: the *measuring unit concept* and the *full disclosure principle.* The measuring unit concept requires that information reported in the body of the financial statements be expressed in money terms. If a reasonable estimate of a contingent liability's dollar amount cannot be made, the measuring unit concept prevents the item from appearing in the balance sheet, even if its future occurrence is probable. However, the full disclosure principle requires that firms disclose all significant financial facts and circumstances to financial statement users. This principle leads to the reporting of likely, but unmeasurable contingent liabilities in the notes to the financial statements.

## TIMES-INTEREST-EARNED RATIO

A financial ratio of particular interest to current and potential long-term creditors is the times-interest-earned ratio. The **times-interest-earned ratio** is computed as follows:

$$\text{Times-interest-earned ratio} = \frac{\text{Income before interest expense and income taxes}}{\text{Interest expense}}$$

**A.K.A.** The times-interest-earned ratio is also referred to as the interest coverage ratio.

The principal on long-term debt, such as bonds payable, is not due until maturity, which may be many years into the future. Interest payments, however, are due every six months, and possibly monthly on term loans. Thus, creditors examine the times-interest-earned ratio to help assess the ability of a company to meet its periodic interest commitments. The ratio indicates the number of times that the fixed interest charges were earned during the year. Many investment professionals believe that the times-interest-earned ratio should be at least in the range of 3.0–4.0 for the extension of long-term credit to be considered a safe investment. The trend of the ratio in recent years and the nature of the industry (volatile or stable, for example) also influence the interpretation of this ratio.

Both the numerator and denominator in the times-interest-earned ratio are obtained from the income statement. The numerator uses income before interest expense and income taxes because that is the amount available to cover a business's current interest charges. The denominator is the business's total interest expense for the period. To illustrate, Reid, Inc., issued $100,000 of eight percent bonds at face value. The annual interest expense was $8,000. If this was Reid's only interest expense and Reid's income before interest expense and income taxes the first year were $28,000, Reid's times-interest-earned ratio for the year would be 3.5, or $28,000/$8,000.

The times-interest-earned ratio may differ substantially among industries and firms, depending upon a company's decision to use leverage to finance its assets and operations. The following are examples of times-interest-earned ratios for several companies in different industries:

| | |
|---|---|
| Kellogg Company (grocery products) . . . . . . . . . . . . . . . . . . . . . . . . . . . . . . . . . . . . . . . . . . . . . . . . . . | 6.7 |
| MeadWestvaco Corporation (paper and paper products) . . . . . . . . . . . . . . . . . . . . . . . . . . . . | 2.8 |
| Amazon.com Inc. (online retailing) . . . . . . . . . . . . . . . . . . . . . . . . . . . . . . . . . . . . . . . . . . . . . . . | 35.1 |
| Cisco Systems, Inc. (computer communications equip.) . . . . . . . . . . . . . . . . . . . . . . . . . . . . | 16.1 |

**TAKEAWAY 10.3**

| Concept ➡ | Method ➡ | Assessment |
|---|---|---|
| Can a firm pay its current periodic interest payments? | Income before income taxes and interest expense, Interest expense<br><br>Times-interest-earned ratio<br>$= \dfrac{\text{Income before income taxes and interest expense}}{\text{Interest expense}}$ | A higher times-interest-earned ratio indicates that a firm will have less difficulty paying its current interest expense. |

## WORKING WITH THE TAKEAWAYS

Below are selected data from **Microsoft's** 2009 financial statements:

| | 2009 | 2008 |
|---|---|---|
| Net income. . . . . . . . . . . . . . . . . . . . . . . . . . . . . . . . . . . . . . . . . . . . . . . . . . . . . . . | $14,569 | $17,681 |
| Tax expense . . . . . . . . . . . . . . . . . . . . . . . . . . . . . . . . . . . . . . . . . . . . . . . . . . . . . | 5,252 | 6,133 |
| Interest expense. . . . . . . . . . . . . . . . . . . . . . . . . . . . . . . . . . . . . . . . . . . . . . . . . . | 56 | 0 |
| Cash and cash equivalents . . . . . . . . . . . . . . . . . . . . . . . . . . . . . . . . . . . . . . . . . | 6,076 | 10,339 |
| Short-term investments . . . . . . . . . . . . . . . . . . . . . . . . . . . . . . . . . . . . . . . . . . . | 25,371 | 13,323 |
| Accounts receivable . . . . . . . . . . . . . . . . . . . . . . . . . . . . . . . . . . . . . . . . . . . . . . | 11,192 | 13,589 |
| Other current assets . . . . . . . . . . . . . . . . . . . . . . . . . . . . . . . . . . . . . . . . . . . . . . | 6,641 | 5,991 |
| Current liabilities . . . . . . . . . . . . . . . . . . . . . . . . . . . . . . . . . . . . . . . . . . . . . . . . | 27,034 | 29,886 |

**Required**

Calculate the following ratios for 2009 and 2008 and comment on the trend:

*a.* Current ratio

*b.* Quick ratio

*c.* Times-interest-earned ratio

**Solution**

| | | 2009 | 2008 |
|---|---|---|---|
| *a.* | Current ratio ............... | $\frac{\$49,280}{\$27,034} = 1.82$ | $\frac{\$43,242}{\$29,886} = 1.45$ |
| *b.* | Quick ratio ................. | $\frac{(\$6,076 + \$25,371 + \$11,192)}{\$27,034} = 1.58$ | $\frac{(\$10,339 + \$13,323 + \$13,589)}{\$29,886} = 1.25$ |
| *c.* | Times-interest-earned ratio ... | $\frac{(\$14,569 + \$5,252 + \$56)}{\$56} = 354.9$ | N/A* |

Both the current and quick ratios increased in 2009, indicating an increased amount of short-term liquidity. The majority of Microsoft's current assets are in the form of cash or short-term investments, providing even stronger evidence regarding the company's liquidity position. Finally, a times-interest-earned ratio of 354.9 indicates the company is in no danger of being unable to pay its interest expense.

\* Microsoft did not report any interest expense or debt in 2008 (see the Feature Story at the beginning of the chapter).

# APPENDIX 10A: Advantages and Disadvantages of Issuing Bonds

Issuing bonds or issuing common stock are alternative ways for a corporation to obtain needed long-term funds. The advantages of obtaining long-term funds by issuing bonds rather than common stock include the following:

1. **No dilution of ownership interest.** Bondholders are creditors, not shareholders, of a corporation. Issuing bonds rather than common stock maintains the number of outstanding shares of stock at their current level.

2. **Tax deductibility of bond interest expense.** Interest expense is deductible as an expense on a corporation's income tax return. Dividend payments to shareholders are not tax deductible.

3. **Income to common shareholders may increase. Leverage** refers to the use of borrowed funds, particularly long-term debt, to finance a business's growth. When a firm is able to earn a return on its borrowed funds that exceeds the cost of borrowing the funds, then leverage is said to build shareholder value.

For example, assume that a firm can earn 15 percent on $5,000,000 obtained by issuing bonds that have a ten percent interest rate. If the firm pays income taxes at a 40 percent rate, its net income will increase $150,000 each year, as follows:

| | |
|---|---|
| Earnings on funds borrowed: 15 percent × $5,000,000............................................. | $750,000 |
| Interest cost on funds borrowed: 10 percent × $5,000,000 ......................................... | (500,000) |
| Increase in income before income tax expense ...................................................... | $250,000 |
| Income tax expense on increase: 40 percent × $250,000............................................ | (100,000) |
| Increase in net income......................................................................... | $150,000 |

The $150,000 increase in net income accrues exclusively to the company's common stockholders.

Not all aspects of issuing bonds, however, are necessarily desirable for the borrowing company. Among the disadvantages of issuing bonds are the following:

1. **Bond interest expense is a contractual obligation.** In contrast with dividends on common stock, bond interest represents a fixed periodic expenditure that the firm is contractually obligated to pay.

REVIEW

2. **Funds borrowed have a specific repayment date.** Because bonds normally have a defined maturity date, the borrower has a specific obligation to repay the face value of the bonds at maturity.

3. **Borrowing agreement may restrict company actions.** The legal document setting forth the terms of a bond issue is called a *bond indenture*. Some of the provisions in a bond indenture may involve restrictions on dividend payments, restrictions on additional financing, and specification of minimum financial ratios that must be maintained. These provisions, called debt covenants, are intended to provide protection for bondholders by limiting a company's flexibility to act.

## SUMMARY OF LEARNING OBJECTIVES

**LO1** **Describe the nature of liabilities and define *current liabilities*. (p. 450)**
- Liabilities are obligations resulting from past transactions or events that require a business to pay money, provide goods, or perform services in the future.
- Current liabilities are obligations that will require, within the coming year or the normal operating cycle, whichever is longer, (1) the use of existing current assets or (2) the creation of other current liabilities.

**LO2** **Illustrate the accounting for bonds. (p. 457)**
- A bond is a long-term debt instrument used by many businesses to provide financing for operations or asset purchases.
- Discounts and premiums are recorded when the bonds are issued.
- Bonds payable are shown in the long-term liabilities section of the balance sheet, with any unamortized premium added or unamortized discount deducted.
- The entry for the retirement of bonds removes both the bonds payable and any related bond premium or bond discount from the accounts at the date of retirement and recognizes any gain or loss on retirement.

**LO3** **Define *contingent liabilities* and explain their disclosure in the financial statements. (p. 466)**
- Even though a past transaction or event has taken place, the existence of some liabilities, called contingent liabilities, depends on the occurrence of a future event. Whether or not a contingent liability is recorded in the accounts depends on the likelihood of the future event occurring and the measurability of the obligation:
  1. If the future event will probably occur and the amount of the liability can be reasonably estimated, the contingent liability should be recorded in the accounts.
  2. If the likelihood of the future event occurring is probable, but no reasonable estimate of the future obligation is determinable, or the likelihood of the future event occurring is reasonably possible (but not probable), regardless of the ability to measure the future amount, the contingent liability should be disclosed in a note to the financial statements, but not recorded in the accounts.
  3. If the likelihood of the future event occurring is remote, the contingent liability is not recorded in the accounts or disclosed in a note to the financial statements. The only exception is a credit guarantee, which must be disclosed in a note to the financial statements.

**LO4** **Define *capital leases* and *operating leases* and distinguish between them. (p. 468)**
- A capital lease transfers most of the usual risks and rewards of property ownership to the lessee. At the inception of the lease, the lessee records an asset (a leased asset) and a liability (a lease obligation). The asset is depreciated over its expected useful life, and the liability is reduced as the periodic lease payments are made.
- Under an operating lease, the lessor retains the usual risks and rewards of owning the property. The lessee records no leased asset or lease liability at the start of the lease. Each lease payment made by the lessee is charged to rent expense.

**LO5** **Define the *current ratio, quick ratio,* and *times-interest-earned ratio* and explain their use. (p. 470)**
- The current ratio is calculated as follows:

$$\text{Current ratio} = \frac{\text{Current assets}}{\text{Current liabilities}}$$

- The quick ratio is calculated as follows:

$$\text{Quick ratio} = \frac{[\text{Cash and cash equivalents} + \text{Short-term investments} + \text{Accounts receivable}]}{\text{Current liabilities}}$$

■ Both ratios measure a firm's ability to pay its current liabilities, as well as the strength of its working capital position.

■ The times-interest-earned ratio measures the ability of a firm to meet its periodic interest commitments, and is calculated as:

$$\text{Times-interest-earned ratio} = \frac{\text{Income before interest expense and income taxes}}{\text{Interest expense}}$$

## TAKEAWAYS: SUMMARY CHART

| Concept ⟶ | Method ⟶ | Assessment | |
|---|---|---|---|
| Does the company have any contingent or off-balance sheet liabilities? | Notes to the financial statements<br><br>Read the notes to the financial statements to identify contingent liabilities and operating leases | Consider the likely outcome and size of contingent liabilities and the amount of operating leases. If significant, consider these items in the analysis of the firms liabilities. | TAKEAWAY 10.1 |
| Can a firm pay its current liabilities? | Current assets, Quick assets, Current liabilities<br><br>$\text{Current ratio} = \dfrac{\text{Current assets}}{\text{Current liabilities}}$<br><br>$\text{Quick ratio} = \dfrac{\text{Quick assets}}{\text{Current liabilities}}$ | A higher current ratio and quick ratio indicates that a firm can readily pay its current liabilities. | TAKEAWAY 10.2 |
| Can a firm pay its current periodic interest payments? | Income before income taxes and interest expense, Interest expense<br><br>Times-interest-earned ratio<br>$= \dfrac{\text{Income before income taxes and interest expense}}{\text{Interest expense}}$ | A higher times-interest-earned ratio indicates that a firm will have less difficulty paying its current interest expense. | TAKEAWAY 10.3 |

## GLOSSARY OF KEY TERMS

**Bond** A long-term debt instrument that promises to pay interest periodically and a principal amount at maturity. Bonds may incorporate a variety of provisions relating to security for the debt involved, methods of paying the periodic interest, and retirement provisions (p. 457).

**Call provision** A bond feature that allows the borrower to retire (call in) the bonds after a stated date (p. 459).

**Capital lease** A lease that transfers to the lessee substantially all of the usual benefits and risks related to ownership of the property. The lessee records the leased property as an asset and establishes a liability for the lease obligation (p. 468).

**Contingent liabilities** A potential obligation, the eventual occurrence of which usually depends on some future event beyond the control of the firm. Contingent liabilities may originate from such things as lawsuits, credit guarantees, and contested income tax assessments (p. 466).

**Convertible bond** A bond incorporating the holder's right to convert the bond into common stock under prescribed terms (p. 457).

**Coupon rate** The rate of interest stated on a bond certificate (p. 459).

**Credit guarantee** A guarantee of another company's debt by cosigning a note payable; a guarantor's contingent liability must be disclosed in a balance sheet footnote (p. 468).

**Current liabilities** Obligations that will require within the coming year or operating cycle, whichever is longer, (1) the use of existing current assets or (2) the creation of other current liabilities (p. 450).

**Current ratio** Current assets divided by current liabilities (p. 470).

**Debenture bond** A bond that has no specific property pledged as security (or collateral) for the repayment of the borrowed funds (p. 457).

**Effective interest rate** The current rate of interest in the market for a bond or other debt instrument. When issued, a bond is priced to yield the market rate of interest at the date of issuance (p. 462).

**Federal Insurance Contributions Act (FICA)** Under this act, the income of an individual is taxed to support the national social security program providing retirement income, medical care, and death benefits. Employers pay a matching amount of tax on their eligible employees (p. 453).

**Gross pay** The amount an employee earns before any withholdings or deductions (p. 453).

**Lawsuit** A prosecution of a claim in a court of law; may lead to a financial statement footnote disclosure by the defendant as a contingent liability (p. 468).

**Lease** A contract between a lessor (owner) and lessee (tenant) for the rental of property (p. 468).

**Leasehold** The rights transferred from the lessor to the lessee by a lease (p. 468).

**Lessee** The party acquiring the right to the use of property by a lease (p. 468).

**Lessor** The owner of property who transfers the right to use the property to another party by a lease (p. 468).

**Leverage** The use of borrowed funds to finance the assets or operations of a firm (p. 473).

**Liabilities** Present obligations resulting from past transactions that require a firm to pay money, provide goods, or perform services in the future (p. 450).

**Market rate of interest** The rate of interest in the market for a bond or other debt instrument (p. 459).

**Maturity date** The date on which a note payable is due to be paid (p. 451).

**Net pay** The amount of an employee's paycheck, after subtracting withheld amounts (p. 453).

**Off-balance-sheet financing** The structuring of a financing arrangement such that no liability is recorded on the borrower's balance sheet (p. 470).

**Operating lease** A lease by which the lessor retains the usual risks and rewards of owning the property (p. 469).

**Product warranties** Guarantees against product defects for a designated period of time following product sale (p. 456).

**Quick ratio** The sum of (1) cash and cash equivalents, (2) short-term investments, and (3) accounts receivables divided by current liabilities (p. 471).

**Secured bond** A bond that pledges specific property as security (or collateral) for meeting the terms of a bond agreement (p. 457).

**Serial bond** A bond issue that staggers the bond maturity dates over a series of years (p. 457).

**Sinking fund provision** A bond feature that requires the borrower to retire a portion of the outstanding bonds each year or, in some cases, to make payments each year to a trustee who is responsible for managing the resources needed to retire the bonds at maturity (p. 459).

**Term loan** A long-term borrowing, evidenced by a note payable, that is arranged with a single lender (p. 465).

**Times-interest-earned ratio** Income before interest expense and income taxes divided by interest expense (p. 472).

**Working capital** The difference between current assets and current liabilities (p. 470).

**Zero-coupon bond** A bond that offers no periodic interest payments and that is issued at a substantial discount from its face value (p. 457).

## COMPREHENSIVE PROBLEM

The following are selected transactions for Tyler, Inc., for 2011 and 2012. The firm closes its books on December 31.

**2011**

Dec. 31    Issued $500,000 of 12 percent, ten-year bonds for $562,360, yielding an effective rate of ten percent. Interest is payable June 30 and December 31.

**2012**

June 30    Paid semiannual interest and recorded semiannual premium amortization on bonds.

Dec. 31    Paid semiannual interest and recorded semiannual premium amortization on bonds.

    31    Called one-half of the bonds in for retirement at 104.

**Required**

Record the transactions using effective interest amortization. Round amounts to nearest dollar.

**Solution:**

*a.* **2011**

| A | = | L | + | SE |
|---|---|---|---|---|
| +562,360 | | +500,000 | | |
| | | +62,360 | | |

Dec. 31 | Cash | 562,360 | |
|     Bonds payable | | 500,000 |
|     Premium on bonds payable | | 62,360 |
| *Issued $500,000 of 12 percent, ten-year bonds for $562,360.* | | |

*b.* **2012**

| A | = | L | + | SE |
|---|---|---|---|---|
| −30,000 | | −1,882 | | −28,118 Exp |

June 30 | Bond interest expense | 28,118 | |
|     Premium on bonds payable | 1,882 | |
|     Cash | | 30,000 |
| *To record semiannual interest payment and premium amortization* | | |
| *[$562,360 × 0.05 = $28,118].* | | |

| A | = | L | + | SE |
|---|---|---|---|---|
| −30,000 | | −1,976 | | −28,024 Exp |

Dec. 31 | Bond interest expense | 28,024 | |
| Premium on bonds payable | 1,976 | |
|     Cash | | 30,000 |
| *To record semiannual interest payment and premium amortization* | | |
| *[($562,360 − $1,882) × 0.05 = $28,024, rounded].* | | |

| A | = | L | + | SE |
|---|---|---|---|---|
| −260,000 | | −250,000 | | +19,251 |
| | | −29,251 | | Gain |

    31 | Bonds payable | 250,000 | |
| Premium on bonds payable | 29,251 | |
|     Cash | | 260,000 |
|     Gain on bond retirement | | 19,251 |
| *To record retirement of $250,000 of bonds; book value of bonds* | | |
| *retired:* | | |

| | |
|---|---|
| Face amount.......................... | $250,000 |
| Add: Premium (50 percent × $58,502)...... | 29,251 |
| Book value............................ | $279,251 |

*Retirement payment: $250,000 × 1.04 = $260,000.*

# SELF-STUDY QUESTIONS

(Answers to the Self-Study Questions are available at the end of this chapter.)

1. Goldsteen Corporation obtained a $5,000 loan from a bank on April 1. If the bank charges eight percent interest annually, how much interest will be accrued at December 31?                    LO1
   a. $400                                   c. $275
   b. $300                                   d. $250

2. Wong, Inc., sold merchandise on account for $1,840, which is subject to a ten percent excise tax and a five percent sales tax. What would the entry to record this sale include?                    LO1
   a. A debit of $1,600 to Accounts Receivable
   b. A debit of $2,116 to Accounts Receivable
   c. A credit of $1,600 to Sales
   d. A dedit of $1,840 to Sales

3. Jansen Company sells a product for $400 per unit, which includes a 30-day warranty against product defects. Experience indicates that four percent of the units sold will prove defective, requiring an average repair cost of $50 per unit. During the first month of business, product sales were $320,000, and 20 of the units sold were found to be defective and repaired during the month. What is the accrued liability for product warranties at month-end?                    LO1
   a. $1,000                                 c. $1,600
   b. $600                                   d. $2,000

4. Which of the following payroll related taxes are not withheld from an employee's earnings?                    LO1
   a. Medicare taxes
   b. Income taxes
   c. Federal unemployment taxes
   d. Social Security taxes

5. Which of the following is *not* considered to be a contingent liability?                    LO3
   a. Environmental cleanup costs
   b. Notes payable
   c. Credit guarantees
   d. Lawsuit

6. On May 1, 2011, a firm issued $400,000 of 12-year, nine percent bonds payable at 96 1/2 plus accrued interest. The bonds are dated January 1, and interest is payable on January 1 and July 1 of each year. The amount the firm receives on May 1 from the sale of the bonds (see Appendix E) is:                    LO2
   a. $386,000.
   b. $422,000.
   c. $392,000.
   d. $398,000.

7. A firm issued $250,000 of ten-year, 12 percent bonds payable on January 1, for $281,180, yielding an effective rate of ten percent. Interest is payable on January 1 and July 1 each year. The firm records amortization on each interest date. Bond interest expense for the first six months using effective interest amortization (see Appendix E) is:                    LO2
   a. $15,000.
   b. $16,870.80.
   c. $14,059.
   d. $14,331.

8. In financial statement presentations, the Discount on Bonds Payable account is:                    LO2
   a. Added to Bond Interest Expense.
   b. Deducted from Bonds Payable.
   c. Added to Bonds Payable.
   d. Deducted from Bond Interest Expense.

9. An example of off-balance-sheet financing is a(n):                    LO4
   a. Term loan.
   b. Operating lease.
   c. Zero-coupon bond.
   d. Capital lease.

**REVIEW**

**LO5**   **10.** Apolo Company reported year-end current assets of $75,000 and current liabilities of $25,000. The company's current ratio is:

a.   1/3
b.   3
c.   4
d.   $50,000

**LO5**   **11.** Cristo Company reported net income of $50,000 after subtracting $10,000 for interest expense and $20,000 for taxes. Compute the company's times-interest-earned ratio:

a.   2.5
b.   5
c.   8
d.   3

# Discussion Questions

1. For accounting purposes, how are liabilities defined?

2. At what amount are current liabilities presented on the balance sheet?

3. What does the term *current liabilities* mean?

4. What formula should Hardy Company use to calculate the total amount of interest on a note payable that uses add-on interest?

5. Gordon Company signed a note payable on November 20. Gordon has a December 31 year-end. It paid the note, including interest, on the maturity date, February 20. What accounts did Gordon debit and what account did it credit on February 20?

6. Jack Swanson gave a creditor a 90-day, eight percent note payable for $7,200 on December 16. What adjusting entry should Swanson make on December 31?

7. What are two examples of voluntary deductions from an employee's gross pay?

8. On whom is the FICA tax levied? What does the FICA tax finance?

9. What is the difference between accounting for product warranties on (a) failed units repaired in the month of sale and (b) failed units repaired in a subsequent month but that are still covered by warranty?

10. American Paging, Inc., is the seventh largest paging company in the United States. In a recent balance sheet, it reported a current liability of $8,452,379 that was labeled Unearned Revenues and Deposits. A note to the financial statements explained:

    Unearned revenues and deposits primarily represent monthly charges to customers for radio paging rental and dispatch billed in advance. Such revenues and deposits are recognized in the following month when service is provided or are applied against the customer's final bill or last month's rent.

    What basic principle of accounting guides American Paging's handling of its unearned revenues and deposits?

11. What do the following terms mean? (a) term loan, (b) bonds payable, (c) trustee, (d) secured bonds, (e) serial bonds, (f) call provision, (g) convertible bonds, (h) face value, (i) coupon rate, (j) bond discount, (k) bond premium, and (l) amortization of bond premium or discount.

12. What are the advantages and disadvantages of issuing bonds rather than common stock?

13. A $3,000,000 issue of ten-year, nine percent bonds was sold at 98 plus accrued interest three months after the bonds were dated. What net amount of cash is received when the bonds are sold?

14. If the effective interest amortization method is used for bonds payable, how does the periodic interest expense change over the life of the bonds when they are issued (a) at a discount and (b) at a premium?

15. On April 30, one year before maturity, Eastern Company retired $200,000 of nine percent bonds payable at 101. The book value of the bonds on April 30 was $197,600. Bond interest was last paid on April 30. What is the gain or loss on the retirement of the bonds?

16. What are *contingent liabilities*? List three examples of contingent liabilities. When should contingent liabilities be recorded in the accounts?

17. What is the difference between an operating lease and a capital lease?

18. Define the terms *current ratio* and *quick ratio*. What does each ratio tell us?

19. Define the times-interest-earned ratio and explain how it is used.

## SHORT EXERCISES

**SE10-1.** **Contingent Liabilities**                                    LO1
The CEO of Smith & Sons, Inc., negotiated with its principal supplier of raw materials to purchase 10,000 units for a total price of $100,000. The units are to be delivered in 90 days. The CEO is uncertain whether she should record the purchase commitment on the company's balance sheet as a liability or not. She asks for your advice. What would you advise her?

**SE10-2.** **Determining Bond Premium or Discount**                      LO2
Smith & Sons, Inc., decides to sell $1,000,000 in bonds to finance the construction of a new warehouse. The bonds will carry an annual coupon rate of interest of four percent, to be paid semiannually, and will mature in five years. (a) If the market rate of interest at the time of issuance is five percent, will the bonds sell at their face value, a discount, or a premium? (b) If the market rate of interest at the time of issuance is four percent, will the bonds sell at their face value, a discount, or a premium? (c) If the market rate of interest at the time of issuance is three percent, will the bonds sell at their face value, a discount, or a premium?

**SE10-3.** **Contingent Liabilities**                                    LO3
Smith & Sons, Inc., received notification from a local attorney that the company was being sued for $5,000,000 for patent infringement. A review of the situation by the company's CEO led to the conclusion that Smith & Sons had indeed infringed upon the other company's patented product. Nonetheless, the CEO thought the amount of $5,000,000 was excessive and intended to litigate the issue. How should the lawsuit be reported in Smith & Sons' annual report?

**SE10-4.** **Operating and Capital Leases**                             LO4
The CEO of Smith & Sons, Inc., was considering a lease for a new administrative headquarters building. The building was old, but was very well located near the company's principal customers. The leasing agent estimated that the building's remaining useful life was ten years, and at the end of its useful life, the building would probably be worth $100,000. The proposed lease term was eight years, and as an inducement to Smith & Sons' CEO to sign the lease, the leasing agent indicated a willingness to include a statement in the lease agreement that would allow Smith & Sons to buy the building at the end of the lease for only $75,000. As the CEO considered whether or not to sign the lease, she wondered whether the lease could be accounted for as an off-balance-sheet operating lease. What would you advise her?

The following information relates to SE10-5 through SE10-7:

| SMITH & SONS, INC.<br>Income Statement<br>For the Years Ended December 31, 2011 and 2010 | | |
| --- | --- | --- |
| (in millions) | 2011 | 2010 |
| Net sales | $10,000 | $ 9,500 |
| Cost of goods sold | 5,500 | 5,200 |
| Gross profit | 4,500 | 4,300 |
| Selling and administrative expenses | 2,800 | 2,700 |
| Income from operations | 1,700 | 1,600 |
| Interest expense | 300 | 250 |
| Income before income taxes | 1,400 | 1,350 |
| Income tax expense | 420 | 400 |
| Net income | $ 980 | $ 950 |

| SMITH & SONS, INC.<br>Balance Sheet<br>As of December 31, 2011 and 2010 | | |
| --- | --- | --- |
| (in millions) | **2011** | **2010** |
| Assets | | |
| Current assets | | |
| Cash and cash equivalents ......................................... | $ 200 | $ 400 |
| Accounts receivable........................................... | 900 | 800 |
| Inventory....................................................... | 500 | 650 |
| Other current assets.......................................... | 400 | 250 |
| Total current assets .............................................. | 2,000 | 2,100 |
| Property, plant, & equipment (net) ........................... | 2,600 | 2,500 |
| Other assets.................................................... | 5,700 | 5,900 |
| Total Assets ..................................................... | $10,300 | $10,500 |
| Liabilities and Stockholders' Equity | | |
| Current liabilities ............................................... | $ 3,000 | $ 2,900 |
| Long-term liabilities ............................................ | 5,000 | 5,400 |
| Total liabilities.................................................. | 8,000 | 8,300 |
| Stockholders' equity – common.................................... | 2,300 | 2,200 |
| Total Liabilities and Stockholders' Equity ........................... | $10,300 | $10,500 |

**LO5** **SE10-5.** **Current Ratio**

Calculate the current ratio for Smith & Sons, Inc., for 2010 and 2011, and comment on the company's working capital position. Did the company's ability to pay its current liabilities improve over the two years?

**LO5** **SE10-6.** **Quick Ratio**

Calculate the quick ratio for Smith & Sons, Inc., for 2010 and 2011, and comment on the company's working capital position. Did the company's ability to pay its current liabilities improve over the two years?

**LO5** **SE10-7.** **Times-Interest-Earned Ratio**

Calculate the times-interest-earned ratio for Smith & Sons, Inc., for 2010 and 2011, and comment on the company's ability to pay its current interest payments. Did the company's ability to pay its current interest charges improve?

**LO2** **SE10-8.** **Premium and Discount of a Bond or Debenture**

The Johnson & Johnson Company reported the following borrowings in its annual report:

| | Borrowing ($ in millions) | Amount | Effective Interest Rate (%) |
| --- | --- | --- | --- |
| *a.* | 3.00 percent, zero-coupon bond, due 2020 | $202 | 3.00 |
| *b.* | 4.95 percent debentures, due 2033 | 500 | 5.00 |
| *c.* | 3.80 percent debentures, due 2017 | 500 | 3.82 |
| *d.* | 6.95 percent bonds, due 2025 | 293 | 6.90 |

For each borrowing, indicate whether the bond or debenture was originally sold at its face value, a discount, or a premium.

**LO2** **SE10-9.** **Bond Interest Expense**

Smith & Sons, Inc., sold $100,000 face value, six percent coupon rate, four year bonds, for an aggregate issue price of $96,000. Calculate the total interest expense to be recorded by the company over the four year life of the bonds.

**LO2** **SE10-10.** **Bond Interest Expense**

During 2010, Smith & Sons, Inc., issued $400 million of zero-coupon bonds, due in 2020. The proceeds from the bond issuance was $186.6 million. Calculate the total interest expense that the company will incur over the life of the bonds.

## EXERCISES—SET A

**E10-1A. Liabilities on the Balance Sheet**                                                          LO1

For each of the following situations, indicate the amount shown as a liability on the balance sheet of Kane, Inc., at December 31:

a. Kane has accounts payable of $110,000 for merchandise included in the year-end inventory.

b. Kane agreed to purchase a $28,000 drill press in the following January.

c. During November and December of the current year, Kane sold products to a firm and guaranteed them against product failure for 90 days. Estimated costs of honoring this provision next year are $2,200.

d. On December 15, Kane declared a $70,000 cash dividend payable on January 15 of the following year to shareholders of record on December 31.

e. Kane provides a profit-sharing bonus for its executives equal to five percent of the reported before-tax income for the current year. The estimated before-tax income for the current year is $600,000.

**E10-2A. Maturity Dates of Notes Payable**                                                          LO1

Determine the maturity date and compute the interest for each of the following notes payable with add-on interest:

|   | Date of Note | Principal | Interest Rate (%) | Term |
|---|---|---|---|---|
| a. | August 5 ........................................ | $15,000 | 8 | 120 days |
| b. | May 10 .......................................... | 8,400 | 7 | 90 days |
| c. | October 20 ...................................... | 12,000 | 9 | 45 days |
| d. | July 6 ........................................... | 4,500 | 10 | 60 days |
| e. | September 15 ................................... | 13,500 | 8 | 75 days |

**E10-3A. Accrued Interest Payable**                                                          LO1

Compute the interest accrued on each of the following notes payable owed by Northland, Inc., on December 31:

| Lender | Date of Note | Principal | Interest Rate (%) | Term |
|---|---|---|---|---|
| Maple..................... | 11/21 | $18,000 | 10 | 120 days |
| Wyman ................... | 12/13 | 14,000 | 9 | 90 days |
| Nahn..................... | 12/19 | 16,000 | 12 | 60 days |

**E10-4A. Adjusting Entries for Interest**                                                          LO1

The following note transactions occurred during the year for Towell Company:

Nov. 25   Towell issued a 90-day, nine percent note payable for $8,000 to Hyatt Company for merchandise.

Dec.  7   Towell signed a 120-day, $12,000 note at the bank at ten percent.
     22   Towell gave Barr, Inc., a $12,000, ten percent, 60-day note in payment of account.

Prepare the general journal entries necessary to adjust the interest accounts at December 31.

**E10-5A. Excise and Sales Tax Calculations**                                                          LO1

Barnes Company has just billed a customer for $1,044, an amount that includes a ten percent excise tax and a six percent state sales tax.

a. What amount of revenue is recorded?

b. Prepare a general journal entry to record the transaction on the books of Barnes Company.

**E10-6A. Advance Payments for Goods**                                                          LO1

The Chicago Daily Times Corporation (CDT) publishes a daily newspaper. A 52-week subscription sells for $208. Assume that CDT sells 100 subscriptions on January 1. None of the subscriptions are cancelled as of March 31.

*a.* Prepare a journal entry to record the receipt of the subscriptions on January 1.

*b.* Prepare a journal entry to record one week of earned revenue on March 25.

**LO1** **E10-7A.** **Warranty Costs**

Milford Company sells a motor that carries a 60-day unconditional warranty against product failure. Based on a reliable statistical analysis, Milford knows that between the sale and the end of the product warranty period, two percent of the units sold will require repair at an average cost of $50 per unit. The following data reflect Milford's recent experience:

| | October | November | December | Dec. 31 Total |
|---|---|---|---|---|
| Units sold . . . . . . . . . . . . . . . . . . . . . . . . | 23,000 | 22,000 | 25,000 | 70,000 |
| Known product failures from sales in: | | | | |
| October . . . . . . . . . . . . . . . . . . . . . . . | 120 | 180 | 160 | 460 |
| November . . . . . . . . . . . . . . . . . . . . . . | | 130 | 220 | 350 |
| December . . . . . . . . . . . . . . . . . . . . . . | | | 210 | 210 |

Calculate, and prepare a journal entry to record, the estimated liability for product warranties at December 31. Assume that warranty costs of known failures have already been reflected in the records.

**LO2** **E10-8A.** **Bonds Payable Journal Entries; Effective Interest Amortization**

On December 31, 2009, Daggett Company issued $800,000 of ten-year, nine percent bonds payable for $750,232, yielding an effective interest rate of ten percent. Interest is payable semiannually on June 30 and December 31. Prepare journal entries to reflect (a) the issuance of the bonds, (b) the semiannual interest payment and discount amortization (effective interest method) on June 30, 2010, and (c) the semiannual interest payment and discount amortization on December 31, 2010. Round amounts to the nearest dollar.

**LO2** **E10-9A.** **Bonds Payable Journal Entries; Effective Interest Amortization**

On December 31, 2009, Coffey Company issued $300,000 of 15-year, ten percent bonds payable for $351,780, yielding an effective interest rate of eight percent. Interest is payable semiannually on June 30 and December 31. Prepare journal entries to reflect (a) the issuance of the bonds, (b) the semiannual interest payment and premium amortization (effective interest method) on June 30, 2010, and (c) the semiannual interest payment and premium amortization on December 31, 2010. Round amounts to the nearest dollar.

**LO2** **E10-10A.** **Financial Statement Presentation of Bond Accounts**

Indicate the proper financial statement classification for each of the following accounts:

Gain on Bond Retirement (material amount)

Discount on Bonds Payable

Mortgage Notes Payable

Bonds Payable

Bond Interest Expense

Bond Interest Payable

Premium on Bonds Payable

**LO2** **E10-11A.** **Early Retirement of Bonds**

Elston Company issued $400,000 of 11 percent, 20-year bonds at 108 on January 1, 2010. Interest is payable semiannually on July 1 and January 1. Through January 1, 2016, Elston amortized $5,000 of the bond premium. On January 1, 2016, Elston retired the bonds at 103 (after making the interest payment on that date). Prepare the journal entry to record the bond retirement on January 1, 2016.

**LO2** **E10-12A.** **Installment Term Loan**

On December 31, 2009, Thomas, Inc. borrowed $700,000 on a 12 percent, 15-year mortgage note payable. The note is to be repaid in equal semiannual installments of $50,854 (payable on June 30 and December 31). Prepare journal entries to reflect (a) the issuance of the mortgage note payable, (b) the payment of the first installment on June 30, 2010, and (c) the payment of the second installment on December 31, 2010. Round amounts to the nearest dollar.

**E10-13A. Leases**  LO4

On January 1, Spider, Inc., entered into two lease contracts. The first lease contract was a six-year lease for a computer with $15,000 annual lease payments due at the end of each year. Spider took possession of the computer on January 1. The second lease contract was a six-month lease, beginning January 1 for warehouse storage space with $1,000 monthly lease payments due the first of each month. Spider made the first month's payment on January 1. The present value of the lease payments under the first contract is $74,520. The present value of the lease payments under the second contract is $5,853.

a.  The first lease contract is a capital lease. Prepare the journal entry for this lease on January 1.

b.  The second lease contract is an operating lease. Prepare the journal entry for this lease on January 1.

**E10-14A. Contingent Liabilities**  LO3

Determine which of the following transactions represent contingent liabilities for Hermani Rental and indicate the proper accounting treatment at the company's fiscal year-end, by placing the letter of the correct accounting treatment in the space provided.

A.  Accrue a liability and disclose in the financial statement notes
B.  Disclose in the financial statement footnotes only
C.  No disclosure

| | |
|---|---|
| 1. Hermani Rental cosigned a loan for $75,000 due in one year for Wyler Company. Wyler is a very profitable company and is very liquid, making it a remote chance Hermani will have to pay the loan. | |
| 2. One of Hermani's rental tents collapsed at a wedding and injured the bride and groom. Hermani's legal counsel believes it is probable that Hermani will have to pay damages of $400,000. | |
| 3. Hermani Rental is being audited by the Internal Revenue Service. Its tax returns for the past two years are being examined. At the company's year-end, the audit is still in process. Hermani's CPA believes that payment of significant taxes is possible. | |

**E10-15A. Ratio Analysis**  LO5

Presented below are summary financial data from Pompeo's annual report:

| Amounts in millions | |
|---|---|
| **Balance sheet** | |
| Cash and cash equivalents | $ 1,808 |
| Marketable securities | 18,085 |
| Accounts receivable (net) | 9,367 |
| Total current assets | 39,088 |
| Total assets | 123,078 |
| | |
| Current liabilities | 37,724 |
| Long-term debt | 7,279 |
| Shareholders' equity | 68,278 |
| | |
| **Income Statement** | |
| Interest expense | 359 |
| Net income before taxes | 14,007 |

Calculate the following ratios:
a.  Times-interest-earned ratio
b.  Quick ratio
c.  Current ratio

# EXERCISES—SET B

**E10-1B. Liabilities on the Balance Sheet**  LO1

For each of the following situations, indicate the amount shown as a liability on the balance sheet of Anchor, Inc., at December 31:

a. Anchor's general ledger shows a credit balance of $125,000 in Long-Term Notes Payable. Of this amount, a $25,000 installment becomes due on June 30 of the following year.

b. Anchor estimates its unpaid income tax liability for the current year is $34,000; it plans to pay this amount in March of the following year.

c. On December 31, Anchor received a $15,000 invoice for merchandise shipped on December 28. The merchandise has not yet been received. The merchandise was shipped F.O.B. shipping point.

d. During the year, Anchor collected $10,500 of state sales tax. At year-end, it has not yet remitted $1,400 of these taxes to the state department of revenue.

e. On December 31, Anchor's bank approved a $5,000, 90-day loan. Anchor plans to sign the note and receive the money on January 2 of the following year.

**LO1 E10-2B.** **Maturity Dates of Notes Payable**

Determine the maturity date and compute the interest for each of the following notes payable:

| | Date of Note | Principal | Interest Rate (%) | Term |
|---|---|---|---|---|
| a. | July 10 ........................................... | $7,200 | 9 | 90 days |
| b. | April 14 .......................................... | 6,000 | 8 | 120 days |
| c. | May 19 ............................................ | 5,600 | 7 ½ | 120 days |
| d. | June 10 .......................................... | 5,400 | 8 | 45 days |
| e. | October 29 ...................................... | 7,500 | 8 | 75 days |

**LO1 E10-3B.** **Accrued Interest Payable**

Compute the interest accrued on each of the following notes payable owed by Galloway, Inc., on December 31:

| Lender | Date of Note | Principal | Interest Rate (%) | Term |
|---|---|---|---|---|
| Barton ..................... | 12/4 | $10,000 | 12 | 120 days |
| Lawson ................... | 12/13 | 12,000 | 9 | 90 days |
| Riley ...................... | 12/19 | 15,000 | 10 | 60 days |

**LO1 E10-4B.** **Adjusting Entries for Interest**

The following note transactions occurred during the year for Zuber Company:

Nov. 25 Zuber issued a 90-day, 12 percent note payable for $6,000 to Porter Company for merchandise.

Dec. 10 Zuber signed a 120-day, $7,200 note at the bank at ten percent.

23 Zuber gave Dale, Inc., a $9,000, ten percent, 60-day note in payment of account.

Prepare the journal entries necessary to adjust the interest accounts at December 31.

**LO1 E10-5B.** **Excise and Sales Tax Calculations**

Allied Company has just billed a customer for $1,102, an amount that includes a ten percent excise tax and a six percent state sales tax.

a. What amount of revenue is recorded?

b. Prepare a journal entry to record the transaction on the books of Allied Company.

**LO1 E10-6B.** **Advance Payment for Services**

The Columbus Bluebirds football team sells a 12-game season ticket for $180. Assume that the team sells 1,000 season tickets on August 10. The tickets are all used for admission.

a. Prepare a journal entry to record the sale of the season tickets on August 10.

b. Prepare a journal entry to record one game of earned revenue on September 12.

**LO1 E10-7B.** **Warranty Costs**

Brigham Company sells an electric timer that carries a 60-day unconditional warranty against product failure. Based on a reliable statistical analysis, Brigham knows that between the sale and the end of the product warranty period, three percent of the units sold will require repair at an average cost of $35 per unit. The following data reflect Brigham's recent experience:

| | October | November | December | Dec. 31 Total |
|---|---|---|---|---|
| Units sold ........................ | 36,000 | 34,000 | 45,000 | 115,000 |
| Known product failures from sales in: | | | | |
| October ........................ | 320 | 550 | 210 | 1,080 |
| November ...................... | | 230 | 360 | 590 |
| December ...................... | | | 410 | 410 |

Calculate, and prepare a journal entry to record, the estimated liability for product warranties at December 31. Assume that warranty costs of known failures have already been reflected in the records.

**E10-8B.** **Bonds Payable Journal Entries; Effective Interest Amortization**   LO2

On December 31, 2009, Blair Company issued $600,000 of 20-year, 11 percent bonds payable for $554,718, yielding an effective interest rate of 12 percent. Interest is payable semiannually on June 30 and December 31. Prepare journal entries to reflect (a) the issuance of the bonds, (b) the semiannual interest payment and discount amortization (effective interest method) on June 30, 2010, and (c) the semiannual interest payment and discount amortization on December 31, 2010. Round amounts to the nearest dollar.

**E10-9B.** **Bonds Payable Journal Entries; Effective Interest Amortization**   LO2

On December 31, 2009, Kay Company issued $400,000 of five-year, 13 percent bonds payable for $446,372, yielding an effective interest rate of ten percent. Interest is payable semiannually on June 30 and December 31. Prepare journal entries to reflect (a) the issuance of the bonds, (b) the semiannual interest payment and premium amortization (effective interest method) on June 30, 2010, and (c) the semiannual interest payment and premium amortization on December 31, 2010. Round amounts to the nearest dollar.

**E10-10B.** **Bonds Payable on the Balance Sheet**   LO2

The adjusted trial balance for the Lancer Corporation at the end of 2011 contains the following accounts:

| | |
|---|---|
| Bond interest payable ................................................................ | $ 25,000 |
| 9% Bonds payable due 2013 ........................................................ | 600,000 |
| 10% Bonds payable due 2015 ....................................................... | 500,000 |
| Discount on 9% bonds payable ...................................................... | 19,000 |
| Premium on 10% bonds payable ..................................................... | 15,000 |
| Zero coupon bonds payable due 2017 ............................................... | 170,500 |
| 8% Bonds payable due 2019 ........................................................ | 100,000 |

Prepare the long-term liabilities section of the balance sheet. Indicate the balance sheet classification for any accounts listed above that do not belong in the long-term liabilities section.

**E10-11B.** **Early Retirement of Bonds**   LO2

Norwich, Inc., issued $250,000 of 8 percent, 15-year bonds at 96 on June 30, 2009. Interest is payable semiannually on December 31 and June 30. Through June 30, 2015, Norwich amortized $3,000 of the bond discount. On June 30, 2015, Norwich retired the bonds at 101 (after making the interest payment on that date). Prepare the journal entry to record the bond retirement on June 30, 2015.

**E10-12B.** **Installment Term Loan**   LO2

On December 31, 2009, Beam, Inc., borrowed $500,000 on an eight percent, ten-year mortgage note payable. The note is to be repaid in equal quarterly installments of $18,278 (beginning March 31, 2010). Prepare journal entries to reflect (a) the issuance of the mortgage note payable, (b) the payment of the first installment on March 31, 2010, and (c) the payment of the second installment on June 30, 2010. Round amounts to the nearest dollar.

**E10-13B.** **Leases**   LO4

On January 1, Cooper, Inc., entered into two lease contracts. The first lease contract was a seven-year lease for a sound system with $25,000 annual lease payments due at the end of each year. Spider took possession of the sound system on January 1. The second lease contract was a nine-month lease, beginning January 1 for warehouse storage space with $1,500 monthly lease payments due the first of each month. Cooper made the first month's payment on January 1. The present value of the lease payments under the first contract is $140,000. The present value of the lease payments under the second contract is $13,000.

*a.* The first lease contract is a capital lease. Prepare the journal entry for this lease on January 1.

*b.* The second lease contract is an operating lease. Prepare the journal entry for this lease on January 1.

**LO3** **E10-14B. Contingent Liabilities**

Determine which of the following transactions represent contingent liabilities for Koby Leasing and indicate the proper accounting treatment at the company's fiscal year-end, by placing the letter of the correct accounting treatment in the space provided.

*A.* Accrue a liability and disclose in the financial statement notes

*B.* Disclose in the financial statement footnotes only

*C.* No disclosure

| | |
|---|---|
| 1. Koby Leasing was sued by a customer who claimed the equipment they leased was not up to the standards described by Koby. Koby stands by its claims and can support all the item's specifications. Koby plans to vigorously defend itself and believes the chances of losing the lawsuit are remote. | |
| 2. A government audit of Koby found that the company is in violation of several work safety regulations. Koby has been notified that it will be assessed a fine of $25,000. Koby has agreed to make the safety changes so that it will be in compliance with the regulations. | |
| 3. Koby Leasing has been served a lawsuit by a customer that claims he was injured from one of the products leased from Koby. Koby plans to defend itself in court, but its lawyers believe there is a 50/50 chance that they will lose and be forced to pay $50,000. | |

**LO5, LO6** **E10-15B. Ratio Analysis**

Presented below are summary financial data from the Jackson Co. annual report:

| Amounts in millions | |
|---|---:|
| **Balance sheet** | |
| Cash and cash equivalents | $    2,200 |
| Marketable securities | 15,300 |
| Accounts receivable (net) | 10,000 |
| Total current assets | 42,000 |
| Total assets | 155,000 |
| | |
| Current liabilities | 28,000 |
| Long-term debt | 47,500 |
| Shareholders' equity | 79,500 |
| | |
| **Income Statement** | |
| Interest expense | 3,200 |
| Net income before taxes | 36,800 |

Calculate the following ratios:

*a.* Times-interest-earned ratio

*b.* Quick ratio

*c.* Current ratio

# PROBLEMS—SET A

**LO1** **P10-1A. Journal Entries for Accounts and Notes Payable**

Logan Company had the following transactions:

Apr.   8   Issued a $4,800, 75-day, eight percent note payable in payment of an account with Bennett Company.

May  15   Borrowed $36,000 from Lincoln Bank, signing a 60-day note at nine percent.

June  22   Paid Bennett Company the principal and interest due on the April 8 note payable.

July   6   Purchased $12,000 of merchandise from Bolton Company; signed a 90-day note with ten percent interest.

July 14 Paid the May 15 note due Lincoln Bank.

Oct. 2 Borrowed $24,000 from Lincoln Bank, signing a 120-day note at 12 percent.

4 Defaulted on the note payable to Bolton Company.

**Required**

a. Record these transactions in general journal form.

b. Record any adjusting entries for interest in general journal form. Logan Company has a December 31 year-end.

**P10-2A.** **Adjusting Entries for Interest**

LO1

At December 31, 2009, Hoffman Corporation had two notes payable outstanding (notes 1 and 2). At December 31, 2010, Hoffman also had two notes payable outstanding (notes 3 and 4). These notes are described below:

| | Date of Note | Principal Amount | Interest Rate | Number of Days |
|---|---|---|---|---|
| **December 31, 2009** | | | | |
| Note 1 ................ | 11/16/2009 | $12,000 | 8% | 120 |
| Note 2 ................ | 12/4/2009 | 16,000 | 9 | 60 |
| **December 31, 2010** | | | | |
| Note 3 ................ | 12/7/2010 | 9,000 | 9 | 60 |
| Note 4 ................ | 12/21/2010 | 18,000 | 10 | 30 |

**Required**

a. Prepare the adjusting entries for interest at December 31, 2009.

b. Assume that the adjusting entries were made at December 31, 2009. Prepare the 2010 journal entries to record payment of the notes that were outstanding at December 31, 2009.

c. Prepare the adjusting entries for interest at December 31, 2010.

**P10-3A.** **Recording Payroll and Payroll Taxes**

LO1

Beamon Corporation had the following payroll for April:

| | |
|---|---|
| Officers' salaries ........................................................... | $32,000 |
| Sales salaries ............................................................... | 67,000 |
| Federal income taxes withheld............................................ | 19,000 |
| FICA taxes withheld ........................................................ | 7,500 |
| Health insurance premiums withheld .................................... | 1,600 |
| Union Dues withheld ....................................................... | 1,200 |
| Salaries (included above) subject to federal unemployment taxes........................ | 55,000 |
| Salaries (included above) subject to state unemployment taxes .......................... | 60,000 |

**Required**

Prepare journal entries on April 30 to record:

a. Accrual of the monthly payroll.

b. Payment of the net payroll.

c. Accrual of employer's payroll taxes. (Assume that the FICA tax matches the amount withheld, the federal unemployment tax is 0.8 percent, and the state unemployment tax is 5.4 percent.)

d. Payment of all liabilities related to this payroll. (Assume that all are settled at the same time.)

**P10-4A.** **Recording Payroll and Payroll Taxes**

LO1

The following data are taken from Fremont Wholesale Company's May payroll:

| | |
|---|---|
| Administrative salaries........................................................ | $34,000 |
| Sales salaries ................................................................. | 47,000 |
| Custodial salaries............................................................. | 7,000 |
| Total payroll................................................................... | $88,000 |
| Salaries subject to 1.45 percent Medicare tax ........................... | $88,000 |
| Salaries subject to 6.2 percent Social Security tax ....................... | 74,000 |
| Salaries subject to federal unemployment taxes ......................... | 14,000 |
| Salaries subject to state unemployment taxes ........................... | 20,000 |
| Federal income taxes withheld from all salaries.......................... | 17,800 |

Assume that the company is subject to a two percent state unemployment tax (due to a favorable experience rating) and a 0.8 percent federal unemployment tax.

**Required**

Record the following in general journal form on May 31:

a. Accrual of the monthly payroll.
b. Payment of the net payroll.
c. Accrual of the employer's payroll taxes.
d. Payment of these payroll-related liabilities. (Assume that all are settled at the same time.)

**LO1** **P10-5A.** **Excise and Sales Tax Calculations**

Fulton Corporation initially records its sales at amounts that exclude any related excise and sales taxes. During June, Fulton recorded total sales of $400,000. An analysis of June sales indicated the following:

1. Thirty percent of sales were subject to both a ten percent excise tax and a six percent sales tax.
2. Fifty percent of sales were subject only to the sales tax.
3. The balance of sales was for labor charges not subject to either excise or sales tax.

**Required**

a. Calculate the related liabilities for excise and sales taxes for June.
b. Prepare the necessary journal entry at June 30 to record the monthly payment of excise tax and sales tax to the government.

**LO1, LO3** **P10-6A.** **Noncontingent and Contingent Liabilities**

The following independent situations represent various types of liabilities:

1. One of the employees of Martin Company was severely injured when hit by one of Martin's trucks in the parking lot. The 35-year-old employee will never be able to work again. Insurance coverage is minimal. The employee has sued Martin Company and a jury trial is scheduled.
2. A shareholder has filed a lawsuit against Sweitzer Corporation. Sweitzer's attorneys have reviewed the facts of the case. Their review revealed that similar lawsuits have never resulted in a cash award and it is highly unlikely that this lawsuit will either.
3. Armstrong Company signed a 60-day, ten percent note when it purchased merchandise from Fischer Company.
4. Richmond Company has been notified by the Department of Environment Protection (DEP) that a state where it has a plant is filing a lawsuit for groundwater pollution against Richmond and another company that has a plant adjacent to Richmond's plant. Test results have not identified the exact source of the pollution. Richmond's manufacturing process can produce by-products that pollute ground water.
5. Fredonia Company has cosigned a note payable to a bank for one of its customers. The customer received all of the proceeds of the note. Fredonia will have to repay the loan if the customer fails to do so. Fredonia Company believes that it is unlikely that it will have to pay the note.
6. Holt Company manufactured and sold products to Z-Mart, a retailer that sold the products to consumers. The manufacturer's warranty offers replacement of the product if it is found to be defective within 90 days of the sale to the consumer. Historically, 1.2 percent of the products are returned for replacement.

**Required**

Prepare a multicolumn analysis that presents the following information for each of these situations:

a. Number of the situation.
b. Type of liability: (1) noncontingent or (2) contingent.
c. Accounting treatment: (1) record in accounts, (2) disclose in a note to the financial statements, or (3) neither record nor disclose.

**LO2** **P10-7A.** **Bonds Payable Journal Entries; Issued at Par Plus Accrued Interest**

Askew, Inc., which closes its books on December 31, is authorized to issue $500,000 of nine percent, 15-year bonds dated May 1, with interest payments on November 1 and May 1.

**Required**

Prepare journal entries to record the following events, assuming that the bonds were sold at 100 plus accrued interest on October 1:

a. The bond issuance.
b. Payment of the first semiannual period's interest on November 1.
c. Accrual of bond interest expense at December 31.
d. Payment of the semiannual interest on May 1 of the following year.
e. Retirement of $300,000 of the bonds at 101 on May 1, Year 2 (immediately after the interest payment on that date).

**P10-8A. Effective Interest Amortization**  LO2

On December 31, Caper, Inc., issued $250,000 of eight percent, nine-year bonds for $220,900, yielding an effective interest rate of ten percent. Semiannual interest is payable on June 30 and December 31 each year. The firm uses the effective interest method to amortize the discount.

**Required**

a. Prepare an amortization schedule showing the necessary information for the first two interest periods. Round amounts to the nearest dollar.
b. Prepare the journal entry for the bond issuance on December 31.
c. Prepare the journal entry to record the bond interest payment and discount amortization at June 30 of the following year.
d. Prepare the journal entry to record the bond interest payment and discount amortization at December 31 of the following year.

**P10-9A. Effective Interest Amortization**  LO2

On March 31, Eagle, Inc., issued $800,000 of nine percent, 20-year bonds for $878,948, yielding an effective interest rate of eight percent. Semiannual interest is payable on September 30 and March 31 each year. The firm uses the effective interest method to amortize the premium.

**Required**

a. Prepare an amortization schedule showing the necessary information for the first two interest periods. Round amounts to the nearest dollar.
b. Prepare the journal entry for the bond issuance on March 31.
c. Prepare the journal entry to record the bond interest payment and premium amortization at September 30.
d. Prepare the adjusting entry to record interest expense and premium amortization at December 31, the close of the firm's accounting year.
e. Prepare the journal entry to record the bond interest payment and premium amortization at March 31 of the following year.

**P10-10A. Current Ratio, Quick Ratio, and Times-Interest-Earned Ratio**  LO5

The following data is from the current accounting records of Florence Company:

| | |
|---|---:|
| Cash | $120 |
| Accounts receivable (net of allowance of 40) | 200 |
| Inventory | 150 |
| Other current assets | 80 |
| Accounts payable | 110 |
| Other current liabilities | 170 |

The president of the company is concerned that the company is in violation of a debt covenant that requires the company to maintain a minimum current ratio of 2.0. He believes the best way to rectify this is to reverse a bad debt write-off in the amount of $10 that the company just recorded. He argues that the write-off was done too early, and that the collections department should be given more time to collect the outstanding receivables. The CFO argues that this will have no effect on the current ratio, so a better idea is to use $10 of cash to pay accounts payable early.

**Required**

a. Which idea, the president's or the CFO's, is better for attaining a minimum 2.0 current ratio?

b.    Will either the quick ratio or the times-interest-earned ratios be affected by either of these ideas?

**LO5**    **P10-11A.    Current Ratio, Quick Ratio, and Times-Interest-Earned Ratio: IFRS Financial Statements**

Tesco PLC is the world's third largest retailer and is based in the United Kingdom. Tesco also operates a chain of grocery stores in the Western U.S. called Fresh-n-Easy. Tesco prepares its financial statements using IFRS. Selected data from Tesco's 2009 annual report is presented in Appendix C at the end of this book. Using Tesco's financial data for 2008 and 2009, calculate the company's (a) current ratio, (b) quick ratio, and (c) times-interest-earned ratio. Is Tesco's working capital position improving or declining over the two-year period? Can Tesco readily service its interest payments from its income before interest expense and income taxes? (Hint: Tesco's interest expense is labeled "Finance costs" on its group income statement.)

# PROBLEMS—SET B

**LO1**    **P10-1B.    Journal Entries for Accounts Payable and Notes Payable**
Simon Company had the following transactions:

| | | |
|---|---|---|
| Apr. | 15 | Issued a $6,000, 75-day, eight percent note payable in payment of an account with Marion Company. |
| May | 22 | Borrowed $30,000 from Sinclair Bank, signing a 60-day note at nine percent. |
| June | 29 | Paid Marion Company the principal and interest due on the April 15 note payable. |
| July | 13 | Purchased $12,000 of merchandise from Sharp Company; signed a 90-day note with ten percent interest. |
| | 21 | Paid the May 22 note due Sinclair Bank. |
| Oct. | 2 | Borrowed $36,000 from Sinclair Bank, signing a 120-day note at 12 percent. |
| | 11 | Defaulted on the note payable to Sharp Company. |

**Required**
a.    Record these transactions in general journal form.
b.    Record any adjusting entries for interest in general journal form. Simon Company has a December 31 year-end.

**LO1**    **P10-2B.    Adjusting Entries for Interest**

At December 31, 2009, Portland Corporation had two notes payable outstanding (notes 1 and 2). At December 31, 2010, Portland also had two notes payable outstanding (notes 3 and 4). These notes are described below.

| | Date of Note | Principal Amount | Interest Rate | Number of Days |
|---|---|---|---|---|
| **December 31, 2009** | | | | |
| Note 1 ................. | 11/25/2009 | $27,000 | 8% | 90 |
| Note 2 ................. | 12/16/2009 | 16,800 | 9 | 60 |
| **December 31, 2010** | | | | |
| Note 3 ................. | 12/11/2010 | 15,400 | 9 | 120 |
| Note 4 ................. | 12/7/2010 | 18,000 | 10 | 90 |

**Required**
a.    Prepare the adjusting entries for interest at December 31, 2009.
b.    Assume that the adjusting entries were made at December 31, 2009, and that no adjusting entries were made during 2010. Prepare the 2010 journal entries to record payment of the notes that were outstanding at December 31, 2009.
c.    Prepare the adjusting entries for interest at December 31, 2010.

**LO1**    **P10-3B.    Recording Payroll and Payroll Taxes**
Manchester, Inc., had the following payroll for March:

| | |
|---|---|
| Officers' salaries | $39,000 |
| Sales salaries | 65,000 |
| Federal income taxes withheld | 21,000 |
| FICA taxes withheld | 7,900 |
| Health insurance premiums withheld | 2,200 |
| Salaries (included above) subject to federal unemployment unemployment taxes | 65,000 |
| Salaries (included above) subject to state unemployment taxes | 70,000 |

### Required

Prepare journal entries on March 31 to record:

*a.* Accrual of the monthly payroll.

*b.* Payment of the net payroll.

*c.* Accrual of employer's payroll taxes. (Assume that the FICA tax matches the amount withheld, the federal unemployment tax is 0.8 percent, and the state unemployment tax is 5.4 percent.)

*d.* Payment of all liabilities related to this payroll. (Assume that all are settled at the same time.)

**P10-4B.** **Recording Payroll and Payroll Taxes**                                    LO1

The following data are taken from Jefferson Distribution Company's March payroll:

| | |
|---|---|
| Administrative salaries | $29,000 |
| Sales salaries | 55,000 |
| Custodial salaries | 8,000 |
| Total payroll | $92,000 |
| Salaries subject to FICA tax (6.2 percent + 1.45 percent) | $92,000 |
| Salaries subject to federal unemployment taxes | 68,000 |
| Salaries subject to state unemployment taxes | 76,000 |
| Federal income taxes withheld from all salaries | 18,600 |

Assume that the company is subject to a 5.4 percent state unemployment tax and an 0.8 percent federal unemployment tax.

### Required

Record the following in general journal form on March 31:

*a.* Accrual of the monthly payroll.

*b.* Payment of the net payroll.

*c.* Accrual of the employer's payroll taxes.

*d.* Payment of these payroll-related liabilities. (Assume that all are settled at the same time.)

**P10-5B.** **Excise and Sales Tax Calculations**                                     LO1

Madison Corporation initially records its sales at amounts that exclude any related excise and sales taxes. During May, Madison recorded total sales of $600,000. An analysis of May sales indicated the following:

1. Twenty percent of sales were subject to both a ten percent excise tax and a five percent sales tax.
2. Sixty percent of sales were subject only to the sales tax.
3. The balance of sales was for labor charges not subject to either excise or sales tax.

### Required

*a.* Calculate the related liabilities for excise and sales taxes for May.

*b.* Prepare the necessary journal entry at May 31, to record the monthly payment of excise tax and sales tax to the government.

**P10-6B.** **Noncontingent and Contingent Liabilities**                              LO1, LO3

The following independent situations represent various types of liabilities:

1. Marshall Company has a manufacturing plant located in a small, rural community. The only other major employer in the area is Baker Company, which is experiencing financial problems. Marshall agrees to guarantee a loan for Baker, so Baker will remain in the community. Baker will receive all the proceeds of the loan. However, Marshall

ASSIGNMENTS

will have to repay the loan if Baker fails to do so. Marshall believes that Baker will repay the loan.

2. The village of High Creek and the town of Middlebury have been jointly using a rural dump site for 25 years. The state Department of Natural Resources has notified the two municipalities that wells on the nearby farms are polluted and that the dump site will be closed while further testing is done. Cleanup could cost as much as $25 million.

3. Two people walking on the sidewalk in front of the building owned by First United Bank were injured when part of the building collapsed on them. They are 25 years old and both are totally disabled. The building had been in poor condition for a long time. Insurance coverage is minimal. Both are suing First United Bank, and a jury trial is scheduled.

4. Winters Company sells garden tractors through 120 dealers located throughout the United States. Winters provides a two-year warranty for all parts and labor on these tractors. Each year, the average warranty cost per tractor sold is approximately $40.

5. Cronnin Company signed a 90-day note when it bought a new delivery truck for $25,000.

6. The CPA firm of Boyd and Lampe is being sued by one of the owners of an audit client that went bankrupt three years after Boyd and Lampe conducted an audit. The CPA firm has no insurance for this type of lawsuit. The attorneys for the CPA firm have stated that similar cases have never been successful, and they expect the same result here.

**Required**

Prepare a multicolumn analysis that presents the following information for each of these situations:

*a.* Number of the situation.

*b.* Type of liability: (1) noncontingent or (2) contingent.

*c.* Accounting treatment: (1) record in accounts, (2) disclose in a note to the financial statements, or (3) neither record nor disclose.

**LO2** **P10-7B.** **Bonds Payable Journal Entries; Issued at Par Plus Accrued Interest**

Cheney, Inc., which closes its books on December 31, is authorized to issue $800,000 of nine percent, 20-year bonds dated March 1, with interest payments on September 1 and March 1.

**Required**

Prepare journal entries to record the following events, assuming that the bonds were sold at 100 plus accrued interest on July 1.

*a.* The bond issuance.

*b.* Payment of the semiannual interest on September 1.

*c.* Accrual of bond interest expense at December 31.

*d.* Payment of the semiannual interest on March 1 of the following year.

*e.* Retirement of $200,000 of the bonds at 101 on March 1, Year 3 (immediately after the interest payment on that date).

**LO2** **P10-8B.** **Effective Interest Amortization**

On December 31, 2009, Echo, Inc., issued $720,000 of 11 percent, ten-year bonds for $678,852, yielding an effective interest rate of 12 percent. Semiannual interest is payable on June 30 and December 31 each year. The firm uses the effective interest method to amortize the discount.

**Required**

*a.* Prepare an amortization schedule showing the necessary information for the first two interest periods. Round amounts to the nearest dollar.

*b.* Prepare the journal entry for the bond issuance on December 31, 2009.

*c.* Prepare the journal entry to record bond interest expense and discount amortization at June 30, 2010.

*d.* Prepare the journal entry to record bond interest expense and discount amortization at December 31, 2010.

**LO2** **P10-9B.** **Effective Interest Amortization**

On April 30, 2009, Raines, Inc., issued $250,000 of six percent, 15-year bonds for $206,690, yielding an effective interest rate of eight percent. Semiannual interest is payable on October 31 and April 30 each year. The firm uses the effective interest method to amortize the discount.

**Required**

a. Prepare an amortization schedule showing the necessary information for the first two interest periods. Round amounts to the nearest dollar.

b. Prepare the journal entry for the bond issuance on April 30, 2009.

c. Prepare the journal entry to record the bond interest payment and discount amortization at October 31, 2009.

d. Prepare the adjusting entry to record bond interest expense and discount amortization at December 31, 2009, the close of the firm's accounting year.

e. Prepare the journal entry to record the bond interest payment and discount amortization at April 30, 2010.

**P10-10B. Current Ratio, Quick Ratio, and Times-Interest-Earned Ratio** LO5

The following data is from the current accounting records of Sierra Company:

| | |
|---|---|
| Cash .......... | $240 |
| Accounts receivable (net of allowance of 80) .......... | 400 |
| Inventory .......... | 300 |
| Other current assets .......... | 160 |
| Accounts payable .......... | 220 |
| Other current liabilities .......... | 340 |

The president of the company is concerned that the company may be in violation of a debt covenant that requires the company to maintain a minimum current ratio of 2.0. He believes the best way to rectify the problem is to reverse a bad debt write-off in the amount of $20 that the company just recorded. He argues that the write-off was done too early and that the collections department should be given more time to collect the outstanding amounts. The CFO argues that this will have no effect on the current ratio, so a better idea is to use $10 of cash to pay accounts payable early.

**Required**

a. Which idea, the president's or the CFO's, is better for attaining a minimum 2.0 current ratio?

b. Will either the quick ratio or the times-interest-earned ratios be affected by either of these ideas?

# SERIAL PROBLEM: KATE'S CARDS

(*Note:* This is a continuation of the Serial Problem: Kate's Cards from Chapters 1 through 9.)

**SP10.** Recall that Kate previously obtained a $15,000 bank loan, signing a note payable, on November 30th. The note required semiannual interest payments at the rate of six percent. The entire principal balance was due two years from the origination date of the note. Kate has been accruing interest on a monthly basis in the amount of $75. Kate would like to know how she should record the interest in May, the month she makes the first interest payment. She is unsure how much expense will need to be recorded in May.

The upcoming interest payment is really not Kate's main concern right now. She was just notified by a lawyer that she is being sued for copyright infringement. Mega Cards Incorporated, one of the largest greeting card companies, believes that one of Kate's designs is too similar to one of Mega's designs for it to be coincidence, and has, therefore, decided to sue Kate's Cards. Mega has a prior reputation for suing small companies and settling out of court for lesser damages. Kate, however, knows that her design is original and that she had never previously seen the Mega design that is the subject of the lawsuit. She has determined to fight the lawsuit, regardless of the cost. She doesn't know, however, how this will affect her financial statements.

1. Record the May journal entry for Kate's first interest payment. How much interest expense is reported in May?

2. How should Kate report the copyright infringement lawsuit in her financial statements?

ASSIGNMENTS

# EXTENDING YOUR KNOWLEDGE

## REPORTING AND ANALYSIS

**COLUMBIA SPORTSWEAR COMPANY**

**EYK10-1.  Financial Reporting Problem: Columbia Sportswear Company**

The financial statements for the **Columbia Sportswear Company** can be found in Appendix A at the end of this book.

**Required**

Answer the following questions:

*a.*  How much were Columbia's current liabilities as of December 31, 2009?

*b.*  What two items made up the largest percentage of Columbia's December 31, 2009, current liabilities?

*c.*  What was the largest component of Columbia's December 31, 2009, accrued liabilities?

*d.*  What was the largest component of Columbia's December 31, 2009, other long-term liabilities?

**COLUMBIA SPORTSWEAR COMPANY**
**THE TIMBERLAND COMPANY**

**EYK10-2.  Comparative Analysis Problem: Columbia Sportswear Company vs The Timberland Company**

The financial statements for the **Columbia Sportswear Company** can be found in Appendix A at the end of this book, and the financial statements of **The Timberland Company** can be found in Appendix B (the complete annual report is available on this book's Website).

**Required**

Answer the following questions:

*a.*  Compute the current ratio for Columbia Sportswear and The Timberland Company as of December 31, 2009, and comment on what this ratio implies about each company's liquidity and working capital position.

*b.*  Compute the debt-to-total assets ratio for Columbia Sportswear and The Timberland Company as of December 31, 2009, and comment on what this ratio implies about each company's solvency.

**EYK10-3.  Business Decision Problem**

Kingston Corporation has total assets of $5,200,000 and has been earning an average of $800,000 before income taxes the past several years. The firm is planning to expand plant facilities to manufacture a new product and needs an additional $2,000,000 in funds, on which it expects to earn 18 percent before income tax. The income tax rate is expected to be 40 percent for the next several years. The firm has no long-term debt outstanding and presently has 75,000 shares of common stock outstanding. The firm is considering three alternatives:

1.  Obtain the $2,000,000 by issuing 25,000 shares of common stock at $80 per share.

2.  Obtain the $2,000,000 by issuing $1,000,000 of ten percent, 20-year bonds at face value and 12,500 shares of common stock at $80 per share.

3.  Obtain the $2,000,000 by issuing $2,000,000 of ten percent, 20-year bonds at face value.

**Required**

As a shareholder of Kingston Corporation, which of the three alternatives would you prefer if your main concern is enhancing the firm's earnings per share? (Hint: Divide net income by the number of outstanding common shares to determine the company's earnings per share.)

**ABBOTT LABORATORIES**

**EYK10-4.  Financial Analysis Problem**

**Abbott Laboratories** is a diversified health care company devoted to the discovery, development, manufacture, and marketing of innovative products that improve diagnostic, therapeutic, and nutritional practices. The company's balance sheet for three recent years contains the following data:

| | 2009 | 2008 | 2007 |
|---|---|---|---|
| Cash and cash equivalents..................... | $ 8,809,339 | $ 4,112,022 | $ 2,456,384 |
| Investment securities........................... | 1,122,709 | 967,603 | 364,443 |
| Trade receivables (net of allowance)............. | 6,541,941 | 5,465,660 | 4,946,876 |
| Inventories..................................... | 3,264,877 | 2,775,849 | 2,951,442 |
| Other current assets ........................... | 3,575,025 | 3,721,425 | 3,323,588 |
| Total Current Assets ........................... | $23,313,891 | $17,042,559 | $14,042,733 |
| Total Current Liabilities ........................ | $13,049,489 | $11,591,908 | $ 9,103,278 |

**Required**

*a.* Compute the current ratio for 2007–2009.
*b.* Compute the quick ratio for 2007–2009.
*c.* Comment on the three-year trend in these ratios.

## CRITICAL THINKING

**EYK10-5. Financial Analysis on the Web: General Mills, Inc.**

The fiscal year 2010 annual report of **General Mills, Inc.** is available on this book's Website. Refer to the consolidated statement of earnings, the consolidated balance sheets, and Notes 8 and 15.

GENERAL MILLS, INC.

**Required**

*a.* What was the total dollar amount of current liabilities as of May 30, 2010?
*b.* What percent of long-term debt was considered current as of May 30, 2010?
*c.* What were the current ratio and quick ratio as of May 30, 2010?
*d.* What is the total amount of long-term liabilities reported by General Mills as of May 30, 2010?
*e.* How much principal payments on the long-term debt is General Mills anticipating paying in fiscal year 2012?
*f.* Are General Mills' leases capital leases or operating leases? Explain.

**EYK10-6. Accounting Communication Activity**

Cedric Salos is considering different ways to raise money for the expansion of his company's operations. Cedric is not sure about the advantages of issuing bonds versus issuing common stock. In addition, he is not sure which features he should consider including with the bonds if he selects that form of financing. He asks you to explain, in simple terms, the answers to his questions.

**Required**

Write a short memorandum to Cedric explaining the advantages of issuing bonds over issuing common stock and the features that should be considered for inclusion with the bonds.

**EYK10-7. Accounting Ethics Case**

Sunrise Pools, Inc., is being sued by the Crescent Club for negligence when installing a new pool on Crescent Club's property. Crescent Club alleges that the employees of Sunrise Pools damaged the foundation of the clubhouse and part of the golf course while operating heavy machinery to install the pool.

The lawsuit is for $1.5 million. At the time of the alleged incident, Sunrise Pools carried only $600,000 of liability insurance.

While reviewing the draft of Sunrise Pools' annual report, its president deletes all references to this lawsuit. She is concerned that disclosure of this lawsuit in the annual report will be viewed by Crescent Club as admission of Sunrise's wrongdoing, even though she privately admits that Sunrise employees were careless and believes that Sunrise Pools will be found liable for an amount in excess of $1 million. The president sends the amended draft of the annual report to the vice president of finance with a note stating that the lawsuit will not be disclosed in the annual report and that the lawsuit will not be disclosed to the board of directors.

**Required**

Is the president's concern valid? What ethical problems will the vice president of finance face if he follows the president's instructions?

**EYK10-8.** **Corporate Social Responsibility Problem**

The chapter highlight on **Microsoft's** corporate social responsibility efforts (see Page 457) discussed the company's Unlimited Potential partnerships. Go to Microsoft's Website and navigate to the section "About Microsoft;" then navigate to the section on corporate citizenship. Download the Corporate Citizenship Report. In addition to Unlimited Potential, what are some other ways that Microsoft demonstrates its commitment to being a good corporate citizen?

**EYK10-9.** **Forensic Accounting Problem**

Billing schemes are frauds in which an employee causes the victim organization to issue fraudulent payments by submitting invoices for nonexistent goods or services, inflated invoices, or invoices for personal items. One type of billing scheme uses a shell company that is set up for the purpose of committing the fraud. The shell company is often nothing more than a fake corporate name and a post-office mailbox.

What are some of the ways that shell company invoices can be detected?

## ANSWERS TO SELF-STUDY QUESTIONS:

1. b, (p. 451)  2. b, (p. 452)  3. b, (p. 456)  4. c, (p. 454)  5. b, (p. 468)  6. d, (p. 461)
7. c, (p. 464)  8. b, (p. 464)  9. b, (p. 470)  10. b, (p. 471)  11. c, (p. 472)

## Your Turn! Solutions

### Solution 10.1

| | | | | |
|---|---|---|---|---|
| *a.* | Apr. 30 | Office salaries expense | 40,000 | |
| | | Sales salaries expense | 86,000 | |
| | |    Federal income tax withholding payable | | 25,600 |
| | |    FICA tax payable | | 9,639 |
| | |    Health insurance premiums payable | | 1,850 |
| | |    Union dues payable | | 950 |
| | |    Payroll payable | | 87,961 |
| | | *To accrue payroll for April* | | |
| | | *(FICA taxes = 0.0765 × $126,000 = $9,639).* | | |
| | | | | |
| *b.* | 30 | Payroll payable | 87,961 | |
| | |    Cash | | 87,961 |
| | | *To pay April payroll.* | | |
| | | | | |
| *c.* | 30 | Payroll tax expense | 14,999 | |
| | |    FICA tax payable | | 9,639 |
| | |    Federal unemployment tax payable | | 608 |
| | |    State unemployment tax payable | | 4,752 |
| | | *To record employer's payroll taxes (FICA Tax = 0.0765 ×* | | |
| | | *$126,000 = $9,639; Federal Unemployment Tax = 0.008 ×* | | |
| | | *$76,000 = $608; State Unemployment Tax = 0.054 × $88,000* | | |
| | | *= $4,752).* | | |
| | | | | |
| *d.* | 30 | Federal income tax withholding payable | 25,600 | |
| | | FICA tax payable | 19,278 | |
| | | Health insurance premiums payable | 1,850 | |
| | | Union dues payable | 950 | |
| | | Federal unemployment tax payable | 608 | |
| | | State unemployment tax payable | 4,752 | |
| | |    Cash | | 53,038 |
| | | *To record the payment of payroll-related liabilities.* | | |

**Solution 10.2**

(*a*)

| | | | |
|---|---|---|---|
| Cash | | 325,000 | |
|     Bonds payable | | | 300,000 |
|     Premium on bonds payable | | | 25,000 |
|     *To record the issuance of bonds payable* | | | |

(*b*)

Long-term liabilities
Bonds payable . . . . . . . . . . . . . . . . . . . . . . . . . . . . . . . . . . . . . . . . . . . . . . . $300,000
Add: Premium on bonds payable . . . . . . . . . . . . . . . . . . . . . . . . . . . . .  25,000  $325,000

# 11 Stockholders' Equity

| PAST | PRESENT | FUTURE |
|---|---|---|
| Chapter 10 examined the accounting for liabilities. | In this chapter, we turn our attention to the accounting for stockholders' equity. | In Chapter 12, we shift our focus to the statement of cash flows. |

## LEARNING OBJECTIVES

*1* **Define** the corporate form of organization and **discuss** its principal characteristics. (p. 500)

*2* **Explain** the difference between par value stock and no-par value stock. (p. 503)

*3* **Identify** and **discuss** the two types of capital stock and their respective stockholder rights. (p. 504)

*4* **Describe** the accounting for issuances of capital stock. (p. 508)

*5* **Define** and **discuss** the accounting for stock splits. (p. 510)

*6* **Explain** the accounting for treasury stock. (p. 510)

*7* **Identify** and **distinguish** between cash dividends and stock dividends. (p. 512)

*8* **Illustrate** the statement of retained earnings and the statement of stockholders' equity. (p. 515)

*9* **Define** the *return on common stockholders' equity, dividend yield,* and *dividend payout ratio* and **explain** their use. (p. 516)

# STARBUCKS—The Corporate Form of Organization

**Starbucks** is the largest coffeehouse company in the world, with over 16,500 stores in 49 countries. The first Starbucks coffeehouse was opened in Seattle, Washington, in 1971 to sell high quality coffee beans and equipment.

An important event in Starbucks' history occurred in 1982 when Howard Schultz joined the company. Schultz had a different strategic vision for Starbucks. He believed that the company should not only sell coffee beans, but coffee and espresso drinks as well. Starbucks' owners, however, rejected the idea. Schultz was so committed to his vision that he decided to leave the company and start the Il Giornale coffee bar chain in 1985.

In 1987, the Starbucks chain was sold to Schultz's Il Giornale, which was re-branded as Starbucks. Soon after, the company began to rapidly expand at an explosive rate. During the 1990s, Starbucks opened a new store almost every workday!

Where do firms get the necessary capital for expansion? While not every large firm is a corporation, many are; and, one of the most important characteristics of the corporate form of organization is the ability to raise new capital by selling ownership shares in the company. Starbucks had its initial public offering of its common shares in 1992.

Without a doubt, the modern corporation dominates the national and international economic landscape. In the United States, corporations generate well over three-fourths of the combined sales revenue of all forms of business organization, even though less than one of every five businesses is organized as a corporation. The corporate form of organization is used in a variety of business settings—from large multinational corporations with more than a million stockholders operating in countries all over the world, to small, family-owned businesses operating only in their local community.

Why do fast growing firms like Starbucks choose the corporate form of organization? There are several reasons, but certainly one of the primary reasons is the relative ease of attracting large amounts of capital as compared to other organizational forms of business.

# NATURE AND FORMATION OF A CORPORATION

A **corporation** is a legal entity created with the approval of a governmental authority. The right to conduct business as a corporation is a privilege granted by the state in which a corporation is formed (or chartered). All states have laws specifying the requirements for creating a corporation.

To form a corporation, the incorporators (founders) must apply for a charter. The incorporators prepare and file the **articles of incorporation**, which define the basic structure of the corporation, including the purpose for which it is formed and the amount of capital stock to be authorized. If the incorporators meet the requirements of the law, the government issues a charter or certificate of incorporation. After a charter has been granted, the founders hold an organizational meeting to elect the first board of directors and adopt the corporation's bylaws.

Because assets are essential to starting any business, a corporation issues (or sells) *certificates of capital stock* to obtain the necessary funds to acquire its operating assets. As owners of a corporation, capital stock *stockholders* are entitled to a voice in the control and management of the company. Stockholders with voting stock may vote on specific issues at the annual meeting and participate in the election of the board of directors. The board of directors establishes the overall policies of a corporation and declares dividends. Normally, the board also hires a group of corporate officers, including a president, a chief financial officer, one or more vice presidents, a controller, a treasurer, and a secretary, to execute the day-to-day operations of the company. The officers implement the policies of the board of directors and actively manage the affairs of the corporation. Exhibit 11-1 depicts the responsibilities of these stakeholders in a corporation.

## ADVANTAGES OF THE CORPORATE FORM OF ORGANIZATION

A corporation has several advantages when compared with a sole proprietorship or partnership.

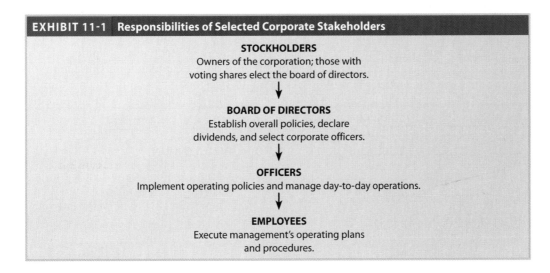

**EXHIBIT 11-1** | **Responsibilities of Selected Corporate Stakeholders**

**STOCKHOLDERS**
Owners of the corporation; those with
voting shares elect the board of directors.

↓

**BOARD OF DIRECTORS**
Establish overall policies, declare
dividends, and select corporate officers.

↓

**OFFICERS**
Implement operating policies and manage day-to-day operations.

↓

**EMPLOYEES**
Execute management's operating plans
and procedures.

### Separate Legal Entity

The corporation, as a separate legal entity, may acquire assets, incur debt, enter into contracts, sue, and be sued—all in its own name. The stockholders of a corporation, however, are separate and distinct from the corporation. This characteristic contrasts with proprietorships and partnerships, which are accounting entities but not legal entities apart from their owners.

### Limited Liability

The liability of stockholders with respect to a company's business affairs is usually limited to the value of their investment in the corporation. By way of contrast, the owners of proprietorships and partnerships can be held financially responsible, separately and collectively, for any unsatisfied obligations of the business. To protect a corporation's creditors, state laws limit the distribution of contributed capital. Distributions of retained earnings (undistributed profits) are not legal unless the board of directors formally votes to declare a dividend. Because of the legal constraints regarding the amount of stockholder capital available for distribution, corporations must maintain clear distinctions in the accounts to identify the various elements of stockholders' equity.

### Transferability of Ownership

Shares in a corporation may be routinely transferred without affecting a company's operations. The corporation merely notes such transfers of ownership in the stockholder records. Although a corporation must have stockholder records to notify stockholders of meetings and to pay dividends, the price at which shares transfer between investors is not recognized in the corporation's accounts.

### Continuity of Existence

Because routine transfers of ownership do not affect a corporation's affairs, the corporation is said to have continuity of existence. In a partnership, any change in ownership technically results in a discontinuation of the old partnership and the formation of a new one.

---

**PRINCIPLE ALERT** | **Entity Concept and Going Concern Concept**

Two characteristics of the corporate form of organization mesh well with the basic principles of accounting. The separate legal status conferred upon a corporation conforms, for example, with the *entity concept*. When the corporation is the unit of focus for accounting purposes, the entity concept requires that the economic activity of the corporation be accounted for separately from the activities of its owners. Legally, the corporate entity is also distinct from its owners. Consequently, the corporation's continuity of existence also aligns well with the *going concern concept*, which assumes that the accounting entity will continue indefinitely into the future.

### Capital Raising Capability

The limited liability of stockholders and the ease with which shares of stock may be transferred from one investor to another are attractive features to potential stockholders. These characteristics enhance the ability of the corporation to raise large amounts of capital by issuing shares of stock. Since both large and small investors may acquire ownership interests in a corporation, there exists a wide spectrum of potential investors. Corporations with thousands of stockholders are not uncommon.

## DISADVANTAGES OF THE CORPORATE FORM OF ORGANIZATION

There are some disadvantages to organizing as a corporation as compared with a proprietorship or partnership.

### Organization Costs

Creating a corporation is more costly than organizing a proprietorship or partnership. The expenditures incurred to organize a corporation are charged to Organization Costs and expensed on the income statement when incurred. These costs include attorney's fees, fees paid to the state, and the costs of promoting the enterprise.

### Taxation

As separate legal entities, corporations are subject to federal income taxes on any earned income. Stockholders are likewise subject to income taxation on any income received from a corporation as dividends, leading to a situation of double taxation of a corporation's distributed earnings.

Usually, corporations are subject to state income taxes in the states in which they are incorporated or are doing business. They may also be subject to real estate, personal property, and franchise taxes.

### Regulation and Supervision

Corporations are subject to greater degrees of regulation and supervision than are proprietorships and partnerships. Each state maintains the right to regulate the corporations it charters. State laws also limit the powers a corporation may exercise, identify reports that must be filed by a corporation, and define the rights and liabilities of stockholders. If shares of stock are issued to the public, the corporation must comply with any securities laws governing the sale of corporate securities. Furthermore, corporations whose shares are listed and traded on organized security exchanges, such as the New York Stock Exchange, are subject to the various reporting and disclosure requirements of these exchanges.

---

**THINKING GLOBALLY**

The equity ownership structure of most U.S. and United Kingdom companies is characterized by small diffuse investors, each of whom owns only a small fraction of the firm. But the ownership structure of public companies in most of the rest of the world is strikingly different, and is more commonly characterized by the presence of a large investor who holds a controlling interest in the company's shares. These large owners usually consist of families and are typically directly involved in managing the company's operations. To illustrate, consider the following seven East Asian countries and the percentage of their public companies that are controlled by families. South Korea has the highest percentage of family-controlled public companies at 78 percent:

| Country | Percentage of Family-Controlled Companies |
| --- | --- |
| Hong Kong | 65 |
| Indonesia | 75 |
| Malaysia | 71 |
| Singapore | 50 |
| South Korea | 78 |
| Taiwan | 55 |
| Thailand | 68 |

| Separate Legal Entity | Limited Liability | Transferability of Ownership | Continuous Existence | Capital Raising Capability |

## ACCOUNTING FOR STOCKHOLDERS' EQUITY IN ALTERNATIVE ORGANIZATIONAL FORMS

Differences exist between the accounting for the stockholders' equity of a corporation and for that of a sole proprietorship or partnership. In a sole proprietorship, only a single owner's capital account is needed to reflect increases from capital contributions and net income as well as decreases from owner withdrawals and net losses. A similar situation exists in most partnerships, which customarily maintain capital and drawing accounts for each partner.

A corporation, on the other hand, is subject to certain legal restrictions imposed by the government approving its creation. These restrictions focus on the distinction between contributed capital and retained earnings and make accounting for stockholders' equity somewhat more complex for corporations than for other types of business organizations.

---

### Your Turn!     11.1

The following attributes are associated with the corporate form of organization. Identify each one as either an advantage or a disadvantage of the corporate form over other forms of organization:

1. Taxation
2. Limited liability
3. Capital raising capability
4. Regulation
5. Cost to organize
6. Transferability of ownership

**The solution is on page 541.**

---

## PAR VALUE STOCK AND NO-PAR VALUE STOCK

A corporate charter may specify a face value, or **par value,** for each share of capital stock. In the early days of corporate stock issuances, par value represented the market value of the stock when it was issued. In more recent times, however, par values have typically been set at amounts well below a stock's fair market value on the date of issue. As a consequence, a stock's par value has no economic significance today.

Par value, however, may have legal implications. In some states, par value may represent the minimum amount that must be paid in per share of stock. If stock is issued at a *discount* (that is, at less than its par value), the stockholder may have a liability for the amount of the discount should any creditor claims remain unsatisfied following a company's liquidation. Issuing stock at a discount rarely occurs, however, because boards of directors have generally established par values below fair market values at the time of issue. For example, **PepsiCo** set the par value of its common stock at $0.0167 and **Charles Schwab Corporation** set the par value of its common stock at $0.01.

Par value may also be used in some states to define a corporation's legal capital. *Legal capital* is the minimum amount of contributed capital that must remain in a corporation as a margin of protection for creditors. However, given the low par values typically assigned

LEARNING OBJECTIVE 2

**Explain** the difference between par value stock and no-par value stock.

to common stock today, this protection has limited usefulness for creditors. Still, given the role that par value may play in defining legal capital, accountants carefully segregate and record the par value of stock transactions in an appropriate capital stock account.

Most states permit the issuance of capital stock without a par value, called **no-par value stock.** The company's board of directors, however, usually sets a **stated value** for the no-par stock. In such cases, the stated value will determine the corporation's legal capital. For accounting purposes, stated value amounts are treated similarly to par value amounts. In the absence of a stated value, the entire proceeds from the issuance of no-par value stock will likely establish a corporation's legal capital.

---

**CORPORATE SOCIAL RESPONSIBILITY** **Starbucks**

To some, corporate social responsibility (CSR) means doing things for non-stockholder stake-holders, even if it means a lower rate of return for stockholders. This sort of thinking pits CSR against stockholder gains, as if the two were competitors for the corporate dollar. Companies that truly understand CSR have come to see CSR in a more strategic light, where doing good can lead to doing well. Further, these companies realize that they would not have the resources to do good if they were not making money. Starbucks is known to be not only a highly profitable company with 2010 profits of nearly $1 billion U.S. dollars, but also a company on the leading edge of social responsibility. Starbucks believes business should have a positive impact on the communities they serve. The company has set goals in such areas as ethical sourcing, recycling, diversity, and philanthropy.

---

# TYPES OF CAPITAL STOCK

The amounts and kinds of capital stock that a corporation may issue are specified in a company's charter of incorporation. Providing for the sale of several classes of capital stock permits a company to raise capital from different types of investors with diverse risk preferences. The charter also specifies a corporation's **authorized shares**—the maximum number of shares of each class of capital stock that may be issued. Shares that have been sold and issued to stockholders constitute the **issued shares** of a corporation. Some of these shares may be repurchased by the corporation. When shares are repurchased, they may be retired and cancelled or held for reissuance. Shares actually held by stockholders are called **outstanding shares,** whereas those reacquired by a corporation (and not cancelled) are called *treasury stock.* We will discuss treasury stock later in the chapter.

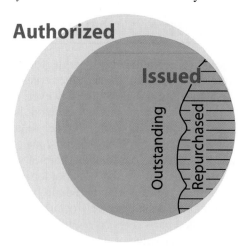

## COMMON STOCK

When only one class of stock is issued, it is called **common stock.** Common stockholders have the right to vote on corporate matters, to share in the corporation's net income, to participate in additional issuances of stock, and in the case of a corporate liquidation, to share in any asset distributions after any prior claims against the corporation by its creditors have been settled.

As the owners of a corporation, the common stockholders elect the board of directors and vote on all matters requiring the approval of the owners. Common stockholders are entitled to one vote for each share of stock they own. Stockholders who do not attend the annual stockholders' meetings may vote by proxy.

A common stockholder has the right to a proportionate share of the corporation's earnings that are distributed as dividends. All earnings belong to the corporation, however, until the board of directors formally votes to declare a dividend.

Each stockholder of a corporation has a **preemptive right** to maintain his or her proportionate ownership interest in the corporation. If a company issues additional shares of stock, the current owners of that type of capital stock receive the first opportunity to acquire, on a pro rata basis, the new shares. In certain situations, management may request stockholders to waive their preemptive right. For example, a corporation may wish to issue additional shares of capital stock for use to acquire another company.

---

**ACCOUNTING IN PRACTICE** | **Preemptive Right Prevents Wealth Transfer**

A major reason for the preemptive right is to protect stockholders against a transfer of their wealth to new stockholders. To illustrate, assume that a firm has 10,000 shares of common stock outstanding with a market price of $20 per share. Thus, the firm's total market value is $200,000 (10,000 shares × $20). If the firm sells another 10,000 common shares at $10 per share (a price below its current market value), the additional $100,000 cash received would raise the firm's total market value to $300,000. With a new market value of $15 per share ($300,000/20,000 shares), the new share issuance causes the old stockholders to lose $5 per share and the new stockholders to gain $5 per share—that is, the sale of the new shares at a lower price caused a wealth transfer from the old stockholders to the new stockholders. The preemptive right protects the existing stockholders from such wealth transfers by enabling them to purchase any newly issued shares.

---

When a corporation liquidates, it converts its assets to a form suitable for distribution, usually cash, which it then distributes to all parties having claims on the corporate assets. Any assets remaining after all claims have been satisfied belong to the residual owners of the corporation—that is, the common stockholders. Common stockholders are entitled to the final distribution of the balance of any remaining assets in a corporate liquidation.

A company may occasionally issue *classified* common stock; that is, it may issue more than one class of common stock. For example, when two classes of common stock are issued, they are often identified as Class A and Class B. The two classes usually differ in either their respective dividend rights or their respective voting powers. Usually, classified common stock is issued when the founders of a corporation wish to acquire funds from the public while retaining voting control of the corporation.

## PREFERRED STOCK

**Preferred stock** is a class of stock with characteristics that differentiate it from common stock. Preferred stock, for example, has one or more preferences over common stock, usually with reference to (1) the payment of dividends and (2) the distribution of assets when a corporation liquidates. To determine the features of a particular preferred stock issue, it is necessary to examine the preferred stock contract. The majority of preferred shares issues, however, have certain typical features, which are discussed below.

### Dividend Preference

When the board of directors declares a distribution of the company's net income, preferred stockholders are entitled to an annual dividend before common stockholders may receive any dividend distribution. The amount is usually specified in the preferred stock contract as a percentage of the par value of the stock or in dollars per share if the stock lacks a par value. Thus, if the preferred stock has a $100 par value and a six percent dividend rate, the preferred stockholders receive $6 per share in dividends. However, the dividend is owed to the stockholders only if, and when, declared by the board of directors.

From both a legal and an accounting standpoint, preferred stock is disclosed as part of stockholders' equity on the balance sheet. Dividends are distributions of earnings and, unlike interest on bonds, are not shown as expenses on the income statement. Also, because of the legal classification of preferred stock as stockholders' equity, the company cannot deduct dividends as expenses for income tax purposes, whereas interest on debt can be deducted as an expense.

Preferred dividends are usually **cumulative**—that is, regular dividends to preferred stockholders omitted in the past must be paid in addition to the current year's dividend before any dividend distribution can be made to the common stockholders. If a preferred stock is noncumulative, omitted dividends do not carry forward.

To illustrate the difference between cumulative and noncumulative preferred stock, assume that a company ending its second year of operations has 1,000 shares of $100 par value, six percent preferred stock and 100,000 shares of $1 par value common stock outstanding. The company declared no dividends last year. This year a dividend of $27,000 is declared. The distribution of the $27,000 between the two stockholder classes depends upon whether the preferred stock is cumulative or noncumulative. If the preferred stock is cumulative, preferred stockholders receive $12 per share before common stockholders receive anything, as illustrated below:

|  | Preferred | Common | Total |
|---|---|---|---|
| Total par value of outstanding shares. . . . . . . . . . . . . . . . . . . . . . . . . . . . . . . . . . . . | $100,000 | $100,000 | $200,000 |
| **Preferred stock is cumulative:** |  |  |  |
| Preferred dividends in arrears (6 percent) . . . . . . . . . . . . . . . . . . . . . . . . . . . . . . . | $ 6,000 |  | $ 6,000 |
| Regular preferred dividend (6 percent). . . . . . . . . . . . . . . . . . . . . . . . . . . . . . . . . . | 6,000 |  | 6,000 |
| Remainder to common. . . . . . . . . . . . . . . . . . . . . . . . . . . . . . . . . . . . . . . . . . . . . . . . . |  | $ 15,000 | 15,000 |
| Total distribution . . . . . . . . . . . . . . . . . . . . . . . . . . . . . . . . . . . . . . . . . . . . . . . | $ 12,000 | $ 15,000 | $ 27,000 |
| **Preferred stock is noncumulative:** |  |  |  |
| Regular preferred dividend (6 percent). . . . . . . . . . . . . . . . . . . . . . . . . . . . . . . . . . | $ 6,000 |  | $ 6,000 |
| Remainder to common. . . . . . . . . . . . . . . . . . . . . . . . . . . . . . . . . . . . . . . . . . . . . . . . . |  | $ 21,000 | 21,000 |
| Total distribution . . . . . . . . . . . . . . . . . . . . . . . . . . . . . . . . . . . . . . . . . . . . . . . | $ 6,000 | $ 21,000 | $ 27,000 |

Dividends in arrears (that is, dividends omitted in past years) on cumulative preferred stock are not an accounting liability and do not appear in the liability section of the balance sheet. They do not become an obligation of the corporation until the board of directors formally declares such dividends. Any dividends in arrears are disclosed to investors in the notes to the financial statements.

### Asset Distribution Preference

Preferred stockholders normally have a preference over common stockholders with respect to the receipt of assets in the event of a corporate liquidation. When a corporation liquidates, any creditor claims are settled first. Preferred stockholders then have the right to receive assets equal to the par value of their shares, or a larger stated liquidation value per share, before any assets are distributed to common stockholders. The preferred stockholders' preference to assets in liquidation also includes any dividends in arrears.

### Other Preferred Stock Features

Although preferred stockholders do not ordinarily have the right to vote in the election of the board of directors, this right can be accorded by contract. Some state laws require that all capital stock issued by a corporation be given voting rights. Further, preferred stock may contain features that cause the shares to resemble common stock. Preferred stock may, for example, be **convertible** into common stock at a specified conversion rate. When this feature is present, the market price of the preferred shares often moves in a fashion consistent with the related common shares; that is, when the price of the common

stock rises, the value of the conversion feature is enhanced, and consequently, the value of the preferred shares should also rise. When preferred stock is converted into a company's common stock, the newly issued common stock assumes the book value of the preferred stock; that is, the Preferred Stock—Par Value and the Paid-in Capital in Excess of Par Value—Preferred Stock are debited while the Common Stock—Par Value and Paid-in Capital in Excess of Par Value—Common Stock are credited.

Preferred stock may be **participating**. A *participating preferred stock* shares any special dividend distributions with common stock beyond the regular preferred stock dividend rate. After receiving its regular dividend preference, preferred stock normally does not participate in any special dividend distribution until the common stock is allowed a dividend amount corresponding to the regular preferred stock dividend rate (Special dividends are discussed on p. 512). At this point, the two classes of stock begin to share the special dividend distribution at the same rate. The preferred stock participation feature may be partial (which limits the participation to a certain amount) or full (which places no limit on the rate of participation).

Preferred stock may be **callable**, which means that a corporation can redeem the shares after a length of time and at a price specified in the stock contract. The call feature makes the preferred stock similar to a bond, since many bonds are callable or have a limited life. Most preferred stocks are callable, with the call or redemption price set slightly above the original preferred stock issuance price.

---

### FORENSIC ACCOUNTING | Benford's Law Aids Accounting Sleuths

 How often should the number 9 appear as the first digit of an amount reported on a financial statement? If you say one out of ten times you, like most people, would be wrong. It turns out the number 9 should appear less than five percent of the time, whereas the number 1 will appear as the first digit of a reported amount over thirty percent of the time! This numerical phenomenon, known as Benford's Law, was discovered by Frank Benford while working as a physicist at the GE Research Laboratories.

An intuitive explanation of Benford's Law appeared in the Journal of Accountancy in the article "I've Got Your Number" written by Mark Nigrini. Nigrini offered an explanation that considered "the total assets of a mutual fund that is growing at 10 percent per year. When the total assets are $100 million, the first digit of total assets is 1. The first digit will continue to be 1 until total assets reach $200 million. This will require a 100 percent increase (from 100 to 200), which, at a growth rate of 10 percent per year, will take about 7.3 years (with compounding). At $500 million the first digit will be 5. Growing at 10 percent per year, the total assets will rise from $500 million to $600 million in about 1.9 years, significantly less time than assets took to grow from $100 million to $200 million. At $900 million, the first digit will be 9 until total assets reach $1 billion, or about 1.1 years at 10 percent. Once total assets are $1 billion the first digit will again be 1, until total assets again grow by another 100 percent. The persistence of a 1 as a first digit will occur with any phenomenon that has a constant (or even an erratic) growth rate."

Benford's Law has been applied to the detection of fraudulent financial statements by forensic accountants with some success. The reasoning is simply that when somebody chooses to make up numbers to produce a fraudulent financial statement they are more likely to choose numbers more randomly than what Benford has shown will occur.

---

### ACCOUNTING IN PRACTICE | Preferred Shares and the Capital Market

Although legally, and from an accounting standpoint, preferred shares are considered to be part of a company's stockholders' equity, the capital market takes a different point of view. Most investment professionals consider a company's preferred stock to be part of the company's debt structure. Thus, from a capital market perspective, the only true stockholders of a business are its common stockholders. This point of view is apparent in the calculation of such ratios as the return on common stockholders' equity, discussed shortly, which excludes a company's preferred stockholders' equity.

**Your Turn!**                                                               **11.2**

Match the description in the right column with the appropriate term in the left column:

1. Authorized
2. Outstanding
3. Common stock
4. Preemptive right
5. Preferred stock
6. Cumulative preference

    *a.* The right to receive dividends omitted in prior years.
    *b.* The most basic class of stock ownership.
    *c.* Stock with one or more preferences over common stock.
    *d.* The maximum number of shares of each class of stock that may be issued.
    *e.* Shares actually held by stockholders.
    *f.* The right to maintain a proportionate ownership interest in a corporation.

**The solution is on page 541.**

# STOCK ISSUANCES FOR CASH

LEARNING OBJECTIVE 4

**Describe** the accounting for issuances of capital stock.

When issuing capital stock to investors, a corporation may use the services of an investment bank, a specialist in marketing securities to the capital market. The investment bank may *underwrite* a stock issue by agreeing to sell the shares on a firm commitment basis—that is, buying the shares from the corporation and then reselling them to investors. Under a firm commitment agreement, a corporation does not risk being unable to sell its stock. The underwriter bears this risk in return for the fees and profits generated by selling the shares to investors at a price higher than it paid to the corporation. An investment bank that is unwilling to underwrite a stock issue may handle the issuance of the shares on a *best efforts* basis. In this case, the investment bank agrees to sell as many shares as possible at a set price, but the corporation bears the risk of any unsold shares.

When capital stock is issued to investors, the appropriate capital stock account is credited for the par value of the stock issued, or if the stock is no-par value stock, with its stated value, if any. The asset received in exchange for the stock (usually cash) is debited, and any difference is credited to the Paid-in Capital in Excess of Par Value account.

To illustrate the journal entries to record various stock issuances in exchange for cash, assume that Smith & Sons issued two different types of capital stock during its first year of operations:

1. Issued 1,000 shares of $100 par value, nine percent preferred stock at $107 cash per share:

| A | = | L | + | SE |
|---|---|---|---|---|
| +107,000 | | | | +100,000 PS |
| | | | | +7,000 PS |

| | | |
|---|---|---|
| Cash | 107,000 | |
|     9 Percent preferred stock | | 100,000 |
|     Paid-in capital in excess of par value—Preferred stock | | 7,000 |

In this transaction, the preferred stock is issued at a price greater than its par value—that is, the shares were sold at a premium. The par value of the preferred stock issued is credited to the nine percent Preferred Stock account and the $7,000 premium is credited to the Paid-in Capital in Excess of Par Value account. If there is more than one class of par value stock, the account title may indicate the class of stock to which the premium relates, in this case Paid-in Capital in Excess of Par Value—Preferred Stock.

2. Issued 30,000 shares of no-par value common stock, stated value $5, at $8 cash per share:

| A | = | L | + | SE |
|---|---|---|---|---|
| +240,000 | | | | +150,000 CS |
| | | | | +90,000 CS |

| | | |
|---|---|---|
| Cash | 240,000 | |
|     Common stock | | 150,000 |
|     Paid-in capital in excess of stated value—Common stock | | 90,000 |

When no-par value stock has a stated value, as in Entry 2, the stated value of the total shares issued is credited to the proper capital stock account, and any additional amount received is credited to the account Paid-in Capital in Excess of Stated Value. If there is no stated value for the no-par value stock, the entire proceeds are credited to the appropriate capital stock account. In the second journal entry, if the common stock had no stated value, the entire $240,000 amount would have been credited to the Common Stock account.

These two stock issuances are reflected in Exhibit 11-2, which presents the stockholders' equity section from Smith & Sons' year-end balance sheet. (Retained earnings are assumed to be $25,000.) The stockholders' equity section is divided into two major categories: ❶ Paid-in Capital and ❷ Retained Earnings. **Paid-in capital** is the amount of capital contributed to the corporation from various capital stock transactions such as the issuance of preferred stock and common stock. The capital contributed by stockholders through the issuance of stock is divided between the legal capital (the par value or stated value of the stock) and the amounts received in excess of the legal capital. Later in this chapter we discuss treasury stock transactions that may affect a corporation's paid-in capital. *Retained earnings* represent the cumulative net income and losses of the company that have not been distributed to stockholders as a dividend.

| EXHIBIT 11-2 | Stockholders' Equity Section of the Balance Sheet | | |
|---|---|---|---|
| ❶ | Paid-in Capital | | |
| | 9% Preferred stock, $100 par value, 1,000 shares authorized, issued, and outstanding......................................... | $100,000 | |
| | No-par common stock, stated value $5, 40,000 shares authorized; 30,000 shares issued and outstanding...................................... | 150,000 | $250,000 |
| | Additional paid-in capital....................................................... | | |
| | In excess of par value—Preferred stock...................................... | 7,000 | |
| | In excess of stated value—Common stock................................... | 90,000 | 97,000 |
| | Total Paid-in Capital ..................................................... | | 347,000 |
| ❷ | Retained earnings........................................................ | | 25,000 |
| | Total Shareholders' Equity ............................................... | | $372,000 |

## NONCASH STOCK ISSUANCES

Sometimes a corporation will exchange its common stock for services, operating assets, or for its own convertible debt. For example, some start-up companies lacking cash will exchange their common stock for professional services provided by attorneys and accountants. When this occurs, a journal entry is made to debit the Professional Services Expense account and a credit is made to Common Stock—Par Value and to the Paid-in Capital in Excess of Par Value—Common Stock account for the fair value of the services received.

When common stock is exchanged for operating assets, a similar journal entry is made, although the debit in this case is to the Land or Equipment account. When common stock is exchanged for convertible bonds (discussed in Chapter 10), the value of the newly issued stock is assumed to be equal to the book value of the bonds. An exchange of convertible bonds for common stock is executed by debiting the Bonds Payable account and the Premium on Bonds Payable account (or crediting the Discount on Bonds Payable account) and crediting the Common Stock account and the Paid-in Capital in Excess of Par Value—Common Stock for any excess of the bonds' book value over the stock's par value.

| **Your Turn!** | **11.3** |
|---|---|

Wyatt Industries began operations on June 1 by issuing 10,000 shares of $1 par value common stock for cash at $9 per share. How much Additional Paid-in Capital will be reported by Wyatt Industries?

The solution is on page 541.

# STOCK SPLITS

Occasionally, a corporation may issue additional shares of common stock to its stockholders through a **forward stock split**. The principal reason that companies execute a forward stock split is to reduce the market price of their shares. A forward stock split increases the number of shares outstanding and is accounted for by reducing the par value or stated value of the stock affected. A forward stock split does not change the balances of any of the stockholders' equity accounts; however, a memorandum entry is made in the general journal to show the altered par value or stated value of the stock and to note the increase in the number of shares issued and outstanding. For example, if Smith & Sons has 10,000 shares of $10 par value common stock outstanding and announces a 2-for-1 forward stock split, it would simply reduce the par value of its common stock to $5 per share and issue to its stockholders 10,000 new common shares. Thus, after the forward stock split, each stockholder would have twice the number of shares held prior to the split, and the value of the Common Stock account would remain unchanged at $100,000 (10,000 shares × $10 = 20,000 shares × $5 = $100,000).

Occasionally, a company may execute a *reverse stock split* by increasing the par value of the stock and reducing the number of shares outstanding. Reverse stock splits are designed to increase a company's stock price. Most major stock exchanges have a minimum trading price that a company must meet or exceed in order to be traded on the exchange. When a company's stock price falls below the minimum trading price, the shares may be delisted, making it difficult for stockholders to find buyers for their shares. Meeting and exceeding an exchange's minimum listing price is one of the principal reasons for reverse stock splits.

# TREASURY STOCK

When a corporation acquires its own outstanding shares for a purpose other than retiring (cancelling) them, the acquired shares are called **treasury stock**. Treasury stock may be purchased for a variety of reasons, to include reissuing them to officers and employees in profit sharing programs or employee stock option plans. Whatever the purpose, treasury stock purchases reduce a company's stockholders' equity. The repurchased shares do not carry voting privileges or preemptive rights, are not paid dividends, and do not receive assets in the event of a corporation's liquidation.

> ### ACCOUNTING IN PRACTICE    Greenmail
>
> Corporations usually purchase their own shares by buying them through a brokerage firm on the open market or by making a tender offer to stockholders. Under a tender offer, the company offers to buy back its shares of stock at a specified price per share. Another way to acquire treasury stock is to negotiate a purchase of shares from a single large stockholder. In some cases, this latter technique may involve greenmail. *Greenmail* is a ploy in which an investor purchases a large number of a company's shares, threatens to take control of the company, and then sells the shares back to the company at a premium. Management pays the premium to entice the investor to "be quiet and go away." Although it is not illegal, payment of an unjustified greenmail premium is likely to upset other stockholders and may lead to legal action against a company.

## ACCOUNTING FOR TREASURY STOCK

Accountants commonly record treasury stock at its acquisition cost, debiting the Treasury Stock account and crediting the Cash account. The Treasury Stock account is a contra-stockholders' equity account, and its balance is deducted when deriving total stockholders' equity on the balance sheet. To illustrate the accounting for the purchase of treasury stock, assume that Smith & Sons had 20,000 shares of $10 par value common stock outstanding and then purchased 1,000 shares at $12 per share. The journal entry to record the purchase is:

| | | |
|---|---|---|
| Treasury stock | 12,000 | |
| Cash | | 12,000 |
| *To record purchase of 1,000 shares of treasury stock at $12 per share.* | | |

| A | = | L | + | SE |
|---|---|---|---|---|
| −12,000 | | | | −12,000 TS |

If a balance sheet is prepared following this transaction, the stockholders' equity section would appear as follows (the values for Paid-in Capital in Excess of Par Value and Retained Earnings are assumed):

| Smith & Sons, Inc. Stockholders' Equity | |
|---|---|
| Paid-in Capital | |
| Common stock, $10 par value, authorized and issued 20,000 shares; | |
| 1,000 shares in treasury, 19,000 shares outstanding . . . . . . . . . . . . . . . . . . . . . . . . . . . . . . . . . . . . . . . . . | $200,000 |
| Paid-in capital in excess of par value . . . . . . . . . . . . . . . . . . . . . . . . . . . . . . . . . . . . . . . . | 20,000 |
| Total Paid-in Capital . . . . . . . . . . . . . . . . . . . . . . . . . . . . . . . . . . . . . . . . . . . . . . . . . | 220,000 |
| Retained earnings . . . . . . . . . . . . . . . . . . . . . . . . . . . . . . . . . . . . . . . . . . . . . . . . . . . | 40,000 |
| | 260,000 |
| Less: Treasury stock (1,000 shares) at cost . . . . . . . . . . . . . . . . . . . . . . . . . . . . . . . . . . . . . . . | 12,000 |
| Total Stockholders' Equity . . . . . . . . . . . . . . . . . . . . . . . . . . . . . . . . . . . . . . . . . . . . . . | $248,000 |

Note that the $200,000 par value of all *issued* stock is disclosed, although the 1,000 treasury shares are no longer outstanding. The total cost of the 1,000 shares, however, is later deducted as the last component in the presentation of total stockholders' equity.

If Smith & Sons subsequently resells 500 shares of its treasury stock at $14 per share, the following journal entry is made:

| | | |
|---|---|---|
| Cash | 7,000 | |
| Treasury stock | | 6,000 |
| Paid-in capital—Treasury stock | | 1,000 |

| A | = | L | + | SE |
|---|---|---|---|---|
| +7,000 | | | | +6,000TS |
| | | | | +1,000TS |

Note that the $1,000 "gain" on the resale of the treasury stock is accounted for as an increase in shareholders' equity and not as net income.

---

**IFRS ALERT!**

Under IFRS and U.S. GAAP, treasury stock is reported on the balance sheet as a contra stockholders' equity account; that is, the repurchase cost of any treasury stock is subtracted from total stockholders' equity. In addition, both IFRS and U.S. GAAP preclude the recognition of any gain or loss by a company from stock transactions involving its own shares—that is, any "gain" or "loss" from trading in a company's own shares is recorded as part of Paid-in Capital in Excess of Par Value. By way of contrast, some countries permit treasury stock to be reported on the asset side of the balance sheet as an investment in marketable securities. Under IFRS and U.S. GAAP, treasury stock does not satisfy the definition of an asset, and therefore, cannot be reported on the balance sheet as marketable securities. It is also noteworthy that in some countries, treasury stock purchases are illegal because they are viewed as a form of stock price manipulation.

---

**Your Turn!**  **11.4**

The Fullerton Corporation purchased 5,000 shares of its outstanding $2 par value common stock for $75,000 cash on November 1. Management anticipates holding the stock in the treasury until it resells the stock. By how much would the Fullerton Corporation debit Treasury Stock for this purchase?

**The solution is on page 541.**

# CASH DIVIDENDS AND STOCK DIVIDENDS

**Dividends** are a distribution of assets or shares of stock from a corporation to its stockholders. A corporation can distribute dividends to stockholders only after its board of directors has formally voted to declare a distribution. Dividends are usually paid in cash but may also be paid as property or additional shares of stock in the firm. Legally, declared dividends are an obligation of the firm, and an entry to record the dividend obligation is made on the *dividend declaration date*. Cash and property dividends payable are carried as liabilities, and stock dividends to be issued are shown in the stockholders' equity section of the balance sheet. At the date of declaration, a *record date* and *payment date* are also established. For example, assume that on April 25 (the declaration date), the board of directors of Smith & Sons declares a cash dividend payable on June 1 (the payment date) to those investors who own shares of stock on May 15 (the record date). Stockholders owning stock on the record date receive the dividend even if they dispose of their shares before the payment date. Therefore, shares sold between the record date and the payment date are sold *ex dividend*— that is, they are sold without the right to receive the dividend.

Most dividend declarations are accounted for by reducing retained earnings. Under certain conditions, however, state laws may permit distributions from additional paid-in capital. Stockholders should be informed of the source of such dividends, because, in a sense, any dividend paid from a company's paid-in capital is a nontaxable return of capital rather than a taxable distribution of earnings.

---

**THINKING GLOBALLY**

While U.S. corporations principally distribute cash and/or stock dividends, property dividend distributions are common among Japanese corporations. For example, **McDonald's Holding Company of Japan** annually distributes to its stockholders coupons for a free Big Mac as a property dividend. And, **DyDo Drinco, Inc.**, distributes to its stockholders samples of its beverage products as a property dividend. Companies that distribute their products or coupons for their products to stockholders as a property dividend believe that by making stockholders more familiar with the company's products, they will retain the investment commitment of their stockholders on a longer term basis than would otherwise be the case.

---

## CASH DIVIDENDS

The majority of dividends distributed by corporations are paid in cash. Although companies may pay such dividends annually, many firms pay quarterly dividends. Dividends that are paid routinely are called regular dividends. The **Johnson & Johnson Company** and **PepsiCo, Inc.**, for example, pay regular quarterly dividends. Some companies occasionally pay a special dividend. Special dividends occur infrequently and represent the distribution of excess cash that has been accumulated by a business and for which the business has no immediate operational need.

When a company declares a cash dividend, the company must have both an appropriate amount of retained earnings and the necessary amount of cash on hand. Uninformed investors often believe that a large retained earnings balance automatically permits generous dividend distributions. A company, however, may successfully accumulate earnings and at the same time not be sufficiently liquid to pay large cash dividends. Many companies, especially new firms in growth industries, finance their expansion from assets generated through earnings and pay out small cash dividends or none at all.

Cash dividends are based on the number of shares outstanding. When a company's directors declare a cash dividend, an entry is made by debiting the Cash Dividends account and crediting the Dividends Payable account. To illustrate, assume that Smith & Sons has 1,000 shares of $100 par value, six percent preferred stock and 6,000 shares of $10 par value common stock outstanding. If the company declares the regular $6 dividend on the preferred stock and a $2 dividend on the common stock, the dividend payment totals $18,000. The following journal entry is made on the declaration date:

| | | | | |
|---|---|---|---|---|
| Cash dividends | 18,000 | | | |
| Dividends payable—Preferred stock | | 6,000 | | |
| Dividends payable—Common stock | | 12,000 | | |

*To record the declaration of $6 dividend on preferred stock and
$2 dividend on common stock.*

| A | = | L | + | SE |
|---|---|---|---|---|
| | | +6,000 | | −18,000 Div |
| | | +12,000 | | |

The Cash Dividends account is a temporary account that is closed to the Retained Earnings account at year-end.[1] Dividends Payable—Preferred Stock and Dividends Payable—Common Stock are reported as current liabilities on the balance sheet until paid. On the dividend payment date, the following journal entry is made:

| | | | |
|---|---|---|---|
| Dividends payable—Preferred stock | 6,000 | | |
| Dividends payable—Common stock | 12,000 | | |
| Cash | | 18,000 | |

*To record the payment of dividends on preferred and common shares.*

| A | = | L | + | SE |
|---|---|---|---|---|
| −18,000 | | −6,000 | | |
| | | −12,000 | | |

## STOCK DIVIDENDS

Companies frequently distribute shares of their own stock as dividends to stockholders in lieu of, or in addition to, cash dividends. A company may issue **stock dividends** when it does not wish to deplete its working capital by paying a cash dividend. Young and growing companies often issue stock dividends because cash is usually needed to acquire new facilities and to expand.

The accounting for a stock dividend results in a transfer of a portion of retained earnings to the paid-in capital accounts. Thus, the distribution of a stock dividend signals investors of management's desire to "plow back" earnings into the company. Although stock dividends may take a number of forms, usually common shares are distributed to common stockholders. We limit our discussion to this type of stock dividend distribution.

### Small Stock Dividends

Small stock dividends are share distributions that involve less than 25 percent of the total number of shares previously outstanding. Small stock dividends are *recorded at the market value* of the shares issued, causing retained earnings to decrease and paid-in capital to increase by this amount. To illustrate the journal entries for a declaration of a small stock dividend, assume that the stockholders' equity of Smith & Sons is as follows prior to the declaration of a ten percent stock dividend:

| | |
|---|---|
| Common stock, $5 par value, 20,000 shares issued and outstanding | $100,000 |
| Paid-in capital in excess of par value | 20,000 |
| Total Paid-in Capital | 120,000 |
| Retained earnings | 65,000 |
| Total Stockholders' Equity | $185,000 |

With 20,000 shares outstanding, the declaration of a ten percent stock dividend requires the issuance of an additional 2,000 shares (10 percent × 20,000 shares). If the current market price per share is $11, the total market value of the shares to be distributed is $22,000 (2,000 shares × $11), resulting in the following journal entry:

| | | | |
|---|---|---|---|
| Stock dividends | 22,000 | | |
| Stock dividend distributable | | 10,000 | |
| Paid-in capital in excess of par value | | 12,000 | |

*To record declaration of 10 percent stock dividend on common shares.*

| A | = | L | + | SE |
|---|---|---|---|---|
| | | | | −22,000 Div |
| | | | | +10,000 CS |
| | | | | +12,000 CS |

The amount of the credit to the Stock Dividend Distributable account is the par value of the shares to be distributed (2,000 shares × $5). If a balance sheet is prepared between

---

[1] Some companies, especially those paying regular dividends, debit the Retained Earnings account directly on the dividend declaration date.

the declaration date and the distribution date of a stock dividend, the Stock Dividend Distributable account is shown in stockholders' equity immediately after the Common Stock account. When the shares are distributed, the following journal entry is made:

| A | = | L | + | SE |
|---|---|---|---|---|
| | | | | −10,000 CS |
| | | | | +10,000 CS |

| | | |
|---|---|---|
| Stock dividend distributable | 10,000 | |
|     Common stock | | 10,000 |
| *To record issuance of stock dividend on common shares.* | | |

The Stock Dividends account is a temporary account that is closed to the Retained Earnings account at year-end, as shown by the following journal entry:

| A | = | L | + | SE |
|---|---|---|---|---|
| | | | | −22,000 RE |
| | | | | +22,000 Div |

| | | |
|---|---|---|
| Retained earnings | 22,000 | |
|     Stock dividends | | 22,000 |
| *To close the Stock Dividends account.* | | |

After the shares are distributed and the Stock Dividends account is closed, a comparison of the stockholders' equity and outstanding shares before and after the stock dividend appears below. Note that retained earnings decreased by $22,000 and paid-in capital increased by $22,000, but total stockholders' equity remains unchanged:

| | Before Stock Dividend | After Stock Dividend |
|---|---|---|
| Common stock, $5 par value............................................... | $100,000 | $110,000 |
| Paid-in capital in excess of par value....................................... | 20,000 | 32,000 |
|   Total Paid-in Capital..................................................... | 120,000 | 142,000 |
| Retained earnings......................................................... | 65,000 | 43,000 |
|   Total Stockholders' Equity ............................................... | $185,000 | $185,000 |
| Common shares issued and outstanding ..................................... | 20,000 | 22,000 |

The relative ownership interest of a common stockholder is unaltered by the receipt of a common stock dividend. If a ten percent stock dividend is distributed, all stockholders increase their proportionate holdings by ten percent, and the total shares outstanding are increased in the same proportion. Small stock dividends rarely affect the market value of the underlying stock.

### Large Stock Dividends

When the number of shares issued as a stock dividend is large enough to impact the stock's market value per share, the stockholders may not perceive the same benefits as they do for a small stock dividend. Accordingly, the accounting for large stock dividends (those over 25 percent) differs from the accounting for small stock dividends. The journal entry to record the declaration of a large stock dividend debits the Stock Dividends account and credits the Stock Dividend Distributable account for the par or stated value of the shares issued. Once the stock is issued, the increase in paid-in capital is reflected in the Common Stock account.[2]

## Your Turn!          11.5

Fango Company's president would like to know the financial impact that a cash dividend and a stock dividend will have on the company's retained earnings account. The current balance in retained earnings is $500,000. The company has 10,000 shares of $1 par value common stock outstanding

---

[2] A large stock dividend is similar in many respects to a stock split (discussed earlier in the chapter). A stock's par value or stated value per share is not changed by a stock dividend; however, a stock split reduces the par value or stated value in proportion to the increase in the number of shares issued. This difference leads to a difference in accounting treatment—only a memorandum entry is made for a stock split, whereas a large stock dividend requires a journal entry to transfer the legal capital of the shares to be issued from retained earnings to paid-in capital.

with a current market value of $20 per share. The potential cash dividend will be $3 per share and the potential stock dividend will be ten percent.

**Required**

Compute the Fango Company retained earnings balance after

*a.* A $3 per share cash dividend
*b.* A ten percent stock dividend

The solution is on page 541.

# RETAINED EARNINGS AND THE STATEMENT OF STOCKHOLDERS' EQUITY

A **statement of retained earnings** presents an analysis of the Retained Earnings account for a given accounting period. An example of a statement of retained earnings is presented in Exhibit 11-3. The statement begins with the retained earnings balance as of the beginning of the period ❶, then reports the items that caused retained earnings to change during the period ❷, and ends with the end-of-period balance in retained earnings ❸.

LEARNING OBJECTIVE 8

**Illustrate** the statement of retained earnings and the statement of stockholders' equity.

| EXHIBIT 11-3 | Statement of Retained Earnings |
|---|---|

**GEYSER CORPORATION**
**Statement of Retained Earnings**
**For the Year Ended December 31, 2011**

| | | |
|---|---|---:|
| ❶ | Retained earnings, January 1, 2011...................................................... | $48,000 |
| ❷ | Add: Net income ...................................................................... | 32,000 |
| | | 80,000 |
| | Less: Cash dividends declared......................................................... | 19,000 |
| ❸ | Retained earnings, December 31, 2011................................................. | $61,000 |

## STATEMENT OF STOCKHOLDERS' EQUITY

Rather than reporting a statement of retained earnings, many corporations integrate the information regarding retained earnings into a more comprehensive statement called a **statement of stockholders' equity**. This statement shows an analysis of all of the stockholders' equity accounts for the period. Exhibit 11-4 presents an example of a statement of stockholders' equity. The statement begins with the beginning balances of the various stockholders' equity accounts ❶, reports the items causing changes in these accounts ❷, and ends with the end-of-period balances ❸.

| EXHIBIT 11-4 | Statement of Stockholders' Equity |
|---|---|

**GEYSER CORPORATION**
**Statement of Stockholders' Equity**
**For the Year Ended December 31, 2011**

| | | Common Stock | Paid-in Capital in Excess of Par Value | Paid-in Capital from Treasury Stock | Retained Earnings | Treasury Stock | Total |
|---|---|---|---|---|---|---|---|
| ❶ | Balance, January 1, 2011........ | $200,000 | $120,000 | $18,000 | $48,000 | $(14,000) | $372,000 |
| ❷ | 6,000 Common shares issued ... | 30,000 | 24,000 | | | | 54,000 |
| | 500 Treasury shares issued...... | | | 2,000 | | 3,500 | 5,500 |
| | Net income.................... | | | | 32,000 | | 32,000 |
| | Cash dividends declared........ | | | | (19,000) | | (19,000) |
| | 200 Treasury shares acquired ... | | | | | (2,000) | (2,000) |
| ❸ | Balance, December 31, 2011 .... | $230,000 | $144,000 | $20,000 | $61,000 | $(12,500) | $442,500 |

The statement of stockholders' equity in Exhibit 11-4 reveals all of the events affecting the Geyser Corporation's stockholders' equity during 2011. These events are the issuance of common stock, the issuance of treasury stock, the earning of net income, the declaration of a cash dividend, and the acquisition of treasury stock. Note that the information in the retained earnings column contains the same information as a statement of retained earnings.

## IFRS ALERT!

There exist a number of significant terminology differences between U.S. GAAP and IFRS with respect to the reporting of stockholders' equity.

| U.S. GAAP | IFRS |
| --- | --- |
| Common stock | Share capital |
| Paid-in capital in excess of par value | Share premium |
| Retained earnings | Retained profits |
| Accumulated other comprehensive income | Other reserve accounts |

## Your Turn!                                              11.6

Dior Company had beginning balances at January 1, 2010, of $100,000 Common Stock, $900,000 Paid-in Capital in Excess of Par Value, and $50,000 Retained Earnings, $(10,000) Treasury Stock. Net income for the year was $30,000. Dior paid a cash dividend of $8,000. Dior also issued 1,000 new $1 par value common shares for $15 each.

**Required**

Prepare a statement of stockholders' equity for the Dior Company for 2010.

**The solution is on page 541.**

# ANALYZING STOCKHOLDERS' EQUITY

LEARNING OBJECTIVE 9

**Define** the *return on common stockholders' equity, dividend yield,* and *dividend payout ratio* and **explain** their use.

## RETURN ON COMMON STOCKHOLDERS' EQUITY

A financial ratio of particular interest to common stockholders is the return on common stockholders' equity. This ratio measures the profitability of the common stockholders' investment in a company. The **return on common stockholders' equity** is calculated as follows:

$$\text{Return on common stockholders' equity} = \frac{\text{(Net income – Preferred stock dividends)}}{\text{Average common stockholders' equity}}$$

By subtracting the preferred stock dividends from net income, the numerator represents the net income available exclusively to the common stockholders. The denominator averages the common stockholders' equity for the year (sum the beginning and ending common stockholders' equity and then divide by 2). If a company has preferred stock outstanding, the common stockholders' equity is calculated by subtracting the preferred stockholders' equity (the sum of the preferred stock par value and the preferred stock paid-in capital in excess of par value) from total stockholders' equity.

To illustrate the calculation of the return on common stockholders' equity, financial data from **Johnson Controls, Inc.**, is used. Johnson Controls manufactures automotive seating systems, environmental control systems, automotive batteries, and plastic packaging. The company's financial data are as follows (in millions of dollars):

| | |
|---|---:|
| Net income. . . . . . . . . . . . . . . . . . . . . . . . . . . . . . . . . . . . . . . . . . . . . . . . . . . . . . . . . . . . . . . . . . . . . . . . . . . . . | $ 979 |
| Preferred stock dividends. . . . . . . . . . . . . . . . . . . . . . . . . . . . . . . . . . . . . . . . . . . . . . . . . . . . . . . . . . . . . . . . | 0 |
| Preferred stockholders' equity, beginning of year . . . . . . . . . . . . . . . . . . . . . . . . . . . . . . . . . . . . . . . . . . . . | 0 |
| Preferred stockholders' equity, end of year. . . . . . . . . . . . . . . . . . . . . . . . . . . . . . . . . . . . . . . . . . . . . . . . . . . | 0 |
| Common stockholders' equity, beginning of year. . . . . . . . . . . . . . . . . . . . . . . . . . . . . . . . . . . . . . . . . . . . . | 9,424 |
| Common stockholders' equity, end of year . . . . . . . . . . . . . . . . . . . . . . . . . . . . . . . . . . . . . . . . . . . . . . . . . . . | 8,907 |

Johnson Controls' return on common stockholders' equity for the year is 10.7 percent, calculated as ($979 − $0) / [($9,424 + $8,907)/2].

| Concept ⟶ | Method ⟶ | Assessment | |
|---|---|---|---|
| How profitable is the stockholders' investment in a company? | Statement of stockholders' equity and the income statement.<br><br>Calculate the return on common stockholders' equity. | The higher the return on common stockholders' equity, the higher the profitability of the stockholders' investment in a business. | **TAKEAWAY 11.1** |

## DIVIDEND YIELD AND DIVIDEND PAYOUT RATIO

Investors differ in their expectations regarding their investments—some investors are primarily interested in appreciation in the market value of their shares, while other investors focus on receiving current income in the form of dividends. Dividend yield and dividend payout ratio are ratios that are helpful to this latter group of investors.

### Dividend Yield

**Dividend yield** measures the current rate of return in cash dividends from an investment in a company's shares. The ratio may be calculated for either common or preferred shares, and is calculated by dividing the latest annual dividend per share by the current market price of the stock:

$$\text{Dividend yield} = \frac{\textbf{Annual dividend per share}}{\textbf{Market price per share}}$$

To illustrate, **Worthington Industries**, a manufacturer of steel and plastic products, declared cash dividends per common share of $0.61. At its fiscal year-end, Worthington's common stock had a market price of $13.99 per share. Consequently, at year-end, the company's dividend yield was 4.4 percent, or $0.61/$13.99.

Dividend yields are included in the stock tables published in *The Wall Street Journal* and *Barrons,* as well as online resources such as Yahoo! Finance, so it is easy for investors to compare current dividend yields for different stocks. The following are dividend yields for several well-known companies:

| | |
|---|---:|
| The Coca-Cola Company . . . . . . . . . . . . . . . . . . . . . . . . . . . . . . . . . . . . . . . . . . . . . . . . . . . . . . . . . | 1.5 percent |
| AT&T . . . . . . . . . . . . . . . . . . . . . . . . . . . . . . . . . . . . . . . . . . . . . . . . . . . . . . . . . . . . . . . . . . . . . . . . . . . | 6.5 percent |
| IBM Corporation. . . . . . . . . . . . . . . . . . . . . . . . . . . . . . . . . . . . . . . . . . . . . . . . . . . . . . . . . . . . . . . . | 1.7 percent |
| J.C. Penney Company . . . . . . . . . . . . . . . . . . . . . . . . . . . . . . . . . . . . . . . . . . . . . . . . . . . . . . . . . . . . | 3.1 percent |
| Chevron Corp.. . . . . . . . . . . . . . . . . . . . . . . . . . . . . . . . . . . . . . . . . . . . . . . . . . . . . . . . . . . . . . . . . . . | 3.4 percent |
| Wal-Mart Stores, Inc. . . . . . . . . . . . . . . . . . . . . . . . . . . . . . . . . . . . . . . . . . . . . . . . . . . . . . . . . . . . . . | 2.0 percent |

| Concept ⟶ | Method ⟶ | Assessment | |
|---|---|---|---|
| What is a company's current rate of return to stockholders in the form of dividends? | Statement of stockholders' equity and a company's current market price per share.<br><br>Calculate the company's dividend yield by dividing the annual dividend per share by the company's market price per share. | The higher a company's dividend yield, the greater the rate of return to stockholders in the form of dividends. | **TAKEAWAY 11.2** |

### Dividend Payout Ratio

The **dividend payout ratio** measures the percentage of net income available to common stockholders that is paid out as dividends. The ratio is calculated as follows:

$$\text{Dividend payout ratio} = \frac{\text{Annual dividend per share}}{\text{Earnings per share}}$$

Dividend payout ratios vary considerably among corporations. Companies that are considered "growth" companies often have low payout ratios because they use the net income generated by operations to help finance their growth. By way of contrast, "mature" companies that lack significant growth opportunities often distribute a high percentage of their net income as dividends. A good example of a mature company is the local utility company whose growth is limited by the net increase of new homes and businesses in the community and the approved rate increases by the local public utility commission.

Some corporations try to maintain a reasonably stable dividend payout ratio, so their payout ratios do not vary much from one year to the next. Other corporations try to keep their dividend per share either constant or increasing each year at a constant rate. If net income fluctuates quite a bit from year to year, these latter corporations will show dividend payout ratios that are quite variable over time.

The following are the dividend payout ratios for some well-known corporations:

| | |
|---|---|
| **Best Buy Co. Inc.** (retail) | 18 percent |
| **Microsoft Corporation** (technology) | 25 percent |
| **Procter & Gamble Co.** (consumer goods) | 44 percent |

| | Concept | ⟶ | Method | ⟶ | Assessment |
|---|---|---|---|---|---|
| TAKEAWAY 11.3 | What percentage of a company's net income is paid out to stockholders as a dividend? | | Statement of stockholders' equity and the income statement.<br><br>Calculate the dividend payout ratio by dividing the annual dividend per share by a company's earnings per share. | | The higher the dividend payout ratio, the higher the percentage of net income paid to stockholders as a dividend. |

### WORKING WITH THE TAKEAWAYS

The following data is from a recent **General Electric Company** annual report. All amounts, except per share data, are in $ millions).

| | |
|---|---|
| Net income | $ 17,410 |
| Preferred stock dividends | 75 |
| Average common stockholders' equity | 110,112 |
| Dividends per share | 1.24 |
| Earnings per share | 1.72 |
| Per share market price of common stock at year-end | 16.20 |

### Required

Compute the following ratios for the General Electric Company:

a. Return on common stockholders' equity
b. Dividend yield
c. Dividend payout

### Solution

a. Return on common stockholders' equity = ($17,410 − $75)/$110,112 = 15.7 percent
b. Dividend yield = $1.24/$16.20 = 7.7 percent
c. Dividend payout = $1.24/$1.72 = 72.1 percent

## SUMMARY OF LEARNING OBJECTIVES

**Define the corporate form of organization and discuss its principal characteristics. (p. 500)**   **LO1**
- A corporation is a separate legal entity chartered by the state in which it is formed.
- The liability of corporate stockholders for the debts of a business is limited to the value of their ownership interest in a corporation, whereas claims against partners and sole proprietors may extend to their personal resources.
- Unlike proprietorships and partnerships, corporations must report paid-in capital separately from the accumulated balance of retained earnings. Distributions to stockholders are limited by the amount of retained earnings and other capital as specified by state law.

**Explain the difference between par value stock and no-par value stock. (p. 503)**   **LO2**
- Par value is the face value printed on a stock certificate. It has no economic significance but may have legal significance.
- No-par value stock has no face value printed on the stock certificate, although generally the board of directors sets a stated value for a corporation's capital stock.

**Identify and discuss the two types of capital stock and their respective stockholder rights. (p. 504)**   **LO3**
- Common stock represents a corporation's basic ownership class of stock; common shares carry the right to vote and may or may not pay a dividend.
- Preferred stocks may differ from common stock in several ways. Typically, preferred stocks have, at a minimum, some type of dividend preference and a prior claim to assets in the event of a corporate liquidation, relative to common stock.

**Describe the accounting for issuances of capital stock. (p. 508)**   **LO4**
- When capital stock is issued, the appropriate capital stock account is credited with the par value or stated value of the shares issued. The asset exchanged for the stock (usually cash) is debited for its fair value. Any difference is placed in the Paid-in Capital in Excess of Par Value account.

**Define and discuss the accounting for stock splits. (p. 510)**   **LO5**
- Stock splits change the par or stated value of capital stock and affect the number of shares outstanding. Only a memorandum notation records stock splits in the general journal. Forward stock splits increase the number of shares outstanding and lower its par or stated value, while reverse stock splits do the opposite.

**Explain the accounting for treasury stock. (p. 510)**   **LO6**
- Treasury stock represents reacquired shares of a firm's capital stock. It is commonly recorded at its acquisition cost and is deducted from total stockholders' equity on the balance sheet.

**Identify and distinguish between cash dividends and stock dividends. (p. 512)**   **LO7**
- Cash dividends reduce retained earnings and are a current liability when declared.
- Stock dividends are accounted for by a transfer of retained earnings to the appropriate capital stock and paid-in capital accounts at the fair market value of the shares distributed for small stock dividends and at par value for large stock dividends.

**Illustrate the statement of retained earnings and the statement of stockholders' equity. (p. 515)**   **LO8**
- A statement of retained earnings presents the financial effect of events causing retained earnings to change during an accounting period.
- A statement of stockholders' equity presents the financial effect of events causing each component of stockholders' equity (including retained earnings) to change during an accounting period.

**Define the *return on common stockholders' equity, dividend yield,* and *dividend payout ratio* and explain their use. (p. 516)**   **LO9**
- The return on common stockholders' equity is computed as (net income − preferred stock dividends)/average common stockholders' equity. It indicates the profitability of the common stockholders' investment in a company.
- Dividend yield is computed by dividing a stock's annual dividend per share by its current market price per share. For investors, this ratio identifies the annual rate of return in dividends from an investment in a company's shares.
- The dividend payout ratio is computed by dividing the annual dividend per share by a company's earnings per share.

## TAKEAWAYS: SUMMARY CHART

| | Concept → | Method → | Assessment |
|---|---|---|---|
| **TAKEAWAY 11.1** | How profitable is the stockholders' investment in a company? | Statement of stockholders' equity and the income statement.<br><br>Calculate the return on common stockholders' equity. | The higher the return on common stockholders' equity, the higher the profitability of the stockholders' investment in a business. |
| **TAKEAWAY 11.2** | What is a company's current rate of return to stockholders in the form of dividends? | Statement of stockholders' equity and a company's current market price per share.<br><br>Calculate the company's dividend yield by dividing the annual dividend per share by the company's market price per share. | The higher a company's dividend yield, the greater the rate of return to stockholders in the form of dividends. |
| **TAKEAWAY 11.3** | What percentage of a company's net income is paid out to stockholders as a dividend? | Statement of stockholders' equity and the income statement.<br><br>Calculate the dividend payout ratio by dividing the annual dividend per share by a company's earnings per share. | The higher the dividend payout ratio, the higher the percentage of net income paid to stockholders as a dividend. |

## GLOSSARY OF KEY TERMS

**Articles of incorporation** A document prepared by the founders of a corporation that sets forth the structure and purpose of the corporation and specifics regarding the type and quantity of capital stock to be issued (p. 500).

**Authorized shares** The maximum number of shares in a class of stock that a corporation may issue (p. 504).

**Callable** A feature associated with preferred stock whereby the preferred stock can be redeemed by the issuing corporation at a price specified in the stock contract (p. 507).

**Common stock** The basic ownership class of capital stock, carrying the right to vote, share in earnings, participate in future share issues, and share in any liquidation proceeds after all more senior claims have been settled (p. 504).

**Convertible** A feature associated with preferred stock whereby the preferred stock can be converted into common stock at a specified conversion rate (p. 506).

**Corporation** A legal entity created by the granting of a charter from an appropriate governmental authority and owned by stockholders who have limited liability for the corporation's debt (p. 500).

**Cumulative** A feature associated with preferred stock whereby any dividends-in-arrears must be paid before any dividends may be paid on common stock (p. 506).

**Dividend payout ratio** A financial ratio showing the percentage of net income available to common stockholders that is paid out as dividends; calculated as the annual dividend per share divided by earnings per share (p. 518).

**Dividend yield** Annual dividend per share divided by the market price per share (p. 517).

**Dividends** Distributions of assets (usually cash) or stock from a corporation to its stockholders (p. 512).

**Forward stock split** Additional shares of capital stock issued by a corporation to its current stockholders in proportion to their current ownership interests without changing the balances in the related stockholders' equity accounts. A forward stock split increases the number of shares outstanding and reduces proportionately the stock's par value per share (p. 510).

**Issued shares** Shares of stock that have been sold and issued to stockholders; issued stock may be either outstanding or held in the treasury (p. 504).

**No-par value stock** Stock that does not have a par value (p. 504).

**Outstanding shares** Shares of stock that are currently held by stockholders (p. 504).

**Paid-in capital** The amount of capital contributed to a corporation by its stockholders in excess of its par value or stated value (p. 509).

**Par value** An amount specified in the corporate charter for each class of stock and imprinted on the face of each stock certificate; often determines the legal capital of a corporation (p. 503).

**Participating** A feature associated with preferred stock whereby the preferred stock can share any special dividend distribution with common stock beyond the regular preferred stock dividend rate (p. 507).

**Preemptive right** The right of a stockholder to maintain his or her proportionate ownership interest in a corporation by having the right to purchase an appropriate quantity of shares in any new share issue (p. 505).

**Preferred stock** A class of capital stock with priority over common stock in dividend payments and in the distribution of assets in the event of a corporation liquidation (p. 505).

**Return on common stockholders' equity** A financial ratio computed as (net income − preferred stock dividends) divided by average common stockholders' equity (p. 516).

**Stated value** A nominal amount that may be assigned to each share of no-par value stock and accounted for much as if it were a par value (p. 504).

**Statement of retained earnings** A financial statement showing the financial changes that occurred in retained earnings during the accounting period (p. 515).

**Statement of stockholders' equity** A financial statement that presents the financial changes that occurred in all components of stockholders' equity during the accounting period (p. 515).

**Stock dividends** Additional shares of capital stock issued by a corporation to its current stockholders in proportion to their existing ownership interest (p. 513).

**Treasury stock** Shares of a corporation that have been acquired for purposes other than retiring (cancelling) the stock. Treasury stock is recorded at cost and is deducted from stockholders' equity on the balance sheet (p. 510).

## COMPREHENSIVE PROBLEM

Following is the stockholders' equity section of Bayside Corporation's December 31 balance sheet:

Paid-in Capital

| | | |
|---|---|---|
| 7 Percent preferred stock, $50 par value, 5,000 shares authorized, issued, and outstanding .................................................... | $ 250,000 | |
| Common stock, $6 par value, 700,000 shares authorized; 200,000 issued, of which 10,000 shares are in the treasury ..................................... | 1,200,000 | $1,450,000 |
| Additional Paid-in Capital | | |
| In excess of par value—Preferred stock......................................... | 80,000 | |
| In excess of par value—Common stock.......................................... | 1,000,000 | |
| From treasury stock................................................. | 22,000 | 1,102,000 |
| Total Paid-in Capital ..................................................... | | 2,552,000 |
| Retained earnings........................................................ | | 2,223,000 |
| | | 4,775,000 |
| Less: Treasury stock (10,000 common shares) at cost............................. | | 140,000 |
| Total Stockholders' Equity................................................... | | $4,635,000 |

### Required

a. What is Bayside's legal capital at December 31?
b. What is the number of common shares outstanding at December 31?
c. What is the average amount per share received from the original issuance of common stock?
d. Assuming that the preferred stock is cumulative with no dividends in arrears, what total dollar amount of preferred dividends needs to be declared at December 31, before the common stock-holders may receive a dividend?
e. Has Bayside ever sold treasury stock for more than the treasury stock cost when it was acquired? Briefly explain.
f. Assume that Bayside splits its common stock 3-for-1 on the following January 1. What is the total amount of paid-in capital immediately after the split?

### Solution

a. $1,450,000 (the par value of the issued preferred stock and common stock).
b. 190,000 shares (200,000 issued common shares less 10,000 shares in the treasury).
c. $11 [($1,200,000 par value of issued shares + $1,000,000 paid-in capital in excess of par value)/200,000 issued shares].
d. $17,500 (7 percent × $250,000).
e. Yes, the stockholders' equity section shows additional paid-in capital of $22,000 from treasury stock. This type of paid-in capital represents the excess of proceeds from the sale of treasury stock over that treasury stock's cost.
f. $2,552,000 (splitting the common stock does not change any of the account balances compos-ing paid-in capital; the common stock's par value will decrease to $2 per share, and the common shares issued will increase to 600,000).

## SELF-STUDY QUESTIONS

(Answers to the Self-Study Questions are available at the end of this chapter.)

1. What is the usual liability of stockholders for corporation actions?          LO1
   a. Unlimited
   b. Limited to the par value or stated value of the shares of stock they hold
   c. Limited to the amount of their investment in the corporation
   d. Limited to the amount of a corporation's retained earnings

2. Which type of stock may have dividends in arrears?          LO3
   a. Cumulative preferred stock
   b. Common stock
   c. Noncumulative preferred stock
   d. Treasury stock

**LO4** **3.** Wyler Company issued 20,000 shares of $10 par value common stock in exchange for a building with a current fair value of $1,000,000. In recording this transaction, what amount should be credited to the Paid-in Capital in Excess of Par Value account?

    *a.* $1,000,000                *c.* $800,000

    *b.* $200,000                 *d.* $980,000

**LO6** **4.** Which of the following accounts has a normal debit balance?

    *a.* Common Stock

    *b.* Paid-in Capital in Excess of Stated Value

    *c.* Preferred Stock

    *d.* Treasury Stock

**LO7** **5.** Which of the following events decreases a corporation's stockholders' equity?

    *a.* A payment of a previously declared cash dividend

    *b.* A declaration of a six percent stock dividend

    *c.* A 2-for-1 forward stock split

    *d.* A declaration of a $1 cash dividend per share on preferred stock

**LO5** **6.** When a company wants to reduce the market price per share of its stock, what action should it take?

    *a.* Issue a cash dividend

    *b.* Issue a stock dividend

    *c.* Do a reverse stock split

    *d.* Do a forward stock split

**LO9** **7.** What type of company is typically characterized by a high dividend payout ratio?

    *a.* Technology company

    *b.* High-growth company

    *c.* Mature, low-growth company

    *d.* All of the above

**LO2** **8.** Which of the following accounts is unneeded when a company issues no-par value common stock?

    *a.* Common Stock—stated value

    *b.* Treasury Stock

    *c.* Retained Earnings

    *d.* Paid-in capital in Excess of Par Value

**LO3** **9.** Preferred stock that may be converted into common stock has which of the following characteristics?

    *a.* Call feature

    *b.* Cumulative feature

    *c.* Participation feature

    *d.* Convertible feature

**LO7** **10.** A dividend that is paid every quarter or every year is called?

    *a.* Regular dividend

    *b.* Special dividend

    *c.* Property dividend

    *d.* Stock dividend

**LO8** **11.** The statement of stockholders' equity includes each of the following except:

    *a.* Retained Earning

    *b.* Treasury Stock

    *c.* Paid-in Capital in Excess of Par Value

    *d.* Accounts Receivable

## DISCUSSION QUESTIONS

**1.** What is the meaning of each of the following terms and, when appropriate, how do they interrelate: *corporation, articles of incorporation, corporate charter, board of directors, corporate officers,* and *organization costs*?

2. What is meant by the limited liability of a stockholder? Does this characteristic enhance or reduce a corporation's ability to raise capital?

3. Contrast the federal income taxation of a corporation with that of a sole proprietorship and a partnership. Which of the three types of organizations must file a federal income tax return?

4. Define *par value stock*. What is the significance of a stock's par value?

5. What is the preemptive right of a stockholder?

6. What are the basic differences between preferred stock and common stock? What are the typical features of preferred stock?

7. What features make preferred stock similar to debt? Similar to common stock?

8. What is meant by dividend in arrears? If dividends are two years in arrears on $500,000 of six percent preferred stock and dividends are declared this year, what amount of total dividends must preferred stockholders receive before any distributions can be made to common stockholders?

9. Distinguish between authorized shares and issued shares. Why might the number of shares issued be more than the number of shares outstanding?

10. What are two different sources of paid-in capital?

11. Define a *forward stock split*. What is the major reason for a forward stock split?

12. Define *treasury stock*. Why might a corporation acquire treasury stock? How is treasury stock shown on the balance sheet?

13. If a corporation purchases 600 shares of its own common stock at $10 per share and resells the shares at $14 per share, where would the $2,400 [($14 − $10) × 600 shares] increase in capital appear in the financial statements? Why is no gain reported?

14. Assume that a corporation has preferred shares outstanding. How is the return on common stockholders' equity computed?

15. What is a stock dividend? How does a common stock dividend paid to common stockholders affect their respective ownership interests?

16. What is the difference between the accounting for a small stock dividend versus the accounting for a large stock dividend?

17. What information is presented in a statement of retained earnings? a statement of stockholders' equity?

18. Where do the following accounts (and their balances) appear in the balance sheet?
    a. Dividends Payable—Common Stock
    b. Stock Dividend Distributable

19. How is a corporation's dividend yield calculated?

20. Bleaker Company declares and pays its annual dividend near the end of its fiscal year. For the current year, Bleaker's dividend payout ratio was 40 percent, its earnings per common share were $5.80, and it had 50,000 shares of common stock outstanding all year. What total amount of dividends did Bleaker declare and pay in the current year?

## SHORT EXERCISES

**SE11-1.** **Issuance of Common Stock**      LO1

Smith & Sons, Inc., is authorized to issue one million shares of $1 par value common stock. In the company's initial public offering, 500,000 shares are sold to the investing public at a price of $5 per share. One month following Smith & Sons' initial public offering, 1,000 of its common shares were sold by one investor to another at a price of $10 per share. How should this transaction be recorded in the accounts of Smith & Sons? Why?

**SE11-2.** **Issuance of No-Par Common Stock**      LO2

Jackson & Company issued 100,000 shares of $1 par value common stock at a price of $5 per share and issued 10,000 shares of no-par value common stock at a price of $10 per share. Prepare the journal entry to record the issuance of the no-par value common stock. How does this entry differ from the entry to record the $1 par value common stock?

**SE11-3.** **Allocating Liquidation Between Common Stockholders and Preferred Stockholders**      LO3

The Arcadia Company is liquidating. After paying off all of its creditors, the company has $1 million to distribute between its preferred stockholders and its common stockholders. The aggregate par value of the preferred stock is $900,000 and the aggregate par value of its common stock is $2 million. How much of the remaining $1 million in assets should be distributed to the preferred stockholders and how much should be distributed to the common stockholders?

**LO4** **SE11-4.** **Issuance of Common Stock**

Smith & Sons, Inc., is authorized to issue one million shares of $1 par value common stock. The company actually sells 500,000 shares at $10 per share. Prepare the journal entry to record the issuance of the 500,000 shares.

**LO5** **SE11-5.** **Outstanding Shares**

Pearce & Company has 10 million shares of $2 par value common stock outstanding. The company believes that its current market price of $100 per share is too high and decides to execute a 4-for-1 forward stock split to lower the price. How many shares will be outstanding following the stock split, and what will be the new par value per share?

**LO6** **SE11-6.** **Treasury Stock Purchase**

Jackson & Company has no-par value common stock outstanding that is selling at $20 per share. The company's CEO believes that the stock price is undervalued and decides to buy back 10,000 shares. Prepare the journal entry to record the purchase of the treasury stock.

**LO7** **SE11-7.** **Dividends Paid and Dividends in Arrears**

The Arcadia Company has 100,000 shares of cumulative, six percent, $100 par value preferred stock outstanding. Last year the company failed to pay its regular dividend, but the board of directors would like to resume paying its regular dividend this year. Calculate the dividends in arrears and the total dividend that must be paid this year.

The following information relates to SE11-8 through SE11-10:

Smith & Sons, Inc., disclosed the following information in a recent annual report:

|  | 2010 | 2011 |
|---|---|---|
| Net income............................................................ | $   35,000 | $   55,000 |
| Preferred stock dividends.............................................. | 3,000 | 3,000 |
| Average common stockholders' equity................................. | 1,200,000 | 1,500,000 |
| Dividend per common share.......................................... | 1.20 | 1.20 |
| Earnings per share................................................... | 1.90 | 2.05 |
| Market price per common share, year-end........................... | 19.50 | 21.00 |

**LO9** **SE11-8.** **Return on Common Stockholders' Equity**

Calculate the return on common stockholders' equity for Smith & Sons for 2010 and 2011. Did the return improve from 2010 to 2011?

**LO9** **SE11-9.** **Dividend Yield**

Calculate the dividend yield for Smith & Sons for 2010 and 2011. Did the dividend yield improve from 2010 to 2011?

**LO9** **SE11-10.** **Dividend Payout Ratio**

Calculate the dividend payout for Smith & Sons for 2010 and 2011. Did the dividend payout increase from 2010 to 2011?

**LO8** **SE11-11.** **Change in Stockholders' Equity**

Nikron Corporation issued 10,000 shares of $0.50 par value common stock during the year for $20 each. Nikron also repurchased treasury stock for $15,000. Net income for the year was $120,000. The company also paid cash dividends of $25,000. What was the total change in Nikron's stockholders' equity for the year?

# EXERCISES—SET A

**LO7** **E11-1A.** **Dividend Distribution**

Lakeside Company has the following shares outstanding: 20,000 shares of $50 par value, six percent cumulative preferred stock and 80,000 shares of $10 par value common stock. The company declared cash dividends amounting to $160,000.

    *a.*    If no dividends in arrears on the preferred stock exist, how much in total dividends, and in dividends per share, is paid to each class of stock?

    *b.*   If one year of dividends in arrears exist on the preferred stock, how much in total dividends, and in dividends per share, is paid to each class of stock?

**E11-2A.**  **Share Issuances for Cash**                                                                 LO4

Finlay, Inc., issued 8,000 shares of $50 par value preferred stock at $68 per share and 12,000 shares of no-par value common stock at $10 per share. The common stock has no stated value. All issuances were for cash.

    *a.*   Prepare the journal entries to record the share issuances.

    *b.*   Prepare the journal entry for the issuance of the common stock assuming that it had a stated value of $5 per share.

    *c.*   Prepare the journal entry for the issuance of the common stock assuming that it had a par value of $1 per share.

**E11-3A.**  **Forward Stock Split**                                                                 LO5

On March 1 of the current year, Sentry Corporation has 400,000 shares of $20 par value common stock that are issued and outstanding. The general ledger shows the following account balances relating to the common stock:

| | |
|---|---:|
| Common stock......................................................................... | $8,000,000 |
| Paid-in capital in excess of par value................................................ | 3,400,000 |

On March 2, Sentry Corporation splits its stock 2-for-1 and reduces the par value to $10 per share.

    *a.*   How many shares of common stock are issued and outstanding immediately following the stock split?

    *b.*   What is the balance in the Common Stock account immediately following the stock split?

    *c.*   What is the balance in the Paid-in Capital in Excess of Par Value account immediately following the stock split?

    *d.*   Is a journal entry required to record the forward stock split? If yes, prepare the entry.

**E11-4A.**  **Treasury Stock**                                                                 LO4, LO6

Coastal Corporation issued 25,000 shares of $5 par value common stock at $17 per share and 6,000 shares of $50 par value, eight percent preferred stock at $78 per share. Later, the company purchased 3,000 shares of its own common stock at $20 per share.

    *a.*   Prepare the journal entries to record the share issuances and the purchase of the common shares.

    *b.*   Assume that Coastal sold 2,000 shares of the treasury stock at $26 per share. Prepare the general journal entry to record the sale of this treasury stock.

    *c.*   Assume that Coastal sold the remaining 1,000 shares of treasury stock at $19 per share. Prepare the journal entry to record the sale of this treasury stock.

**E11-5A.**  **Cash Dividends**                                                                    LO7

Sanders Corporation has the following shares outstanding: 6,000 shares of $50 par value, six percent preferred stock and 40,000 shares of $1 par value common stock. The company has $328,000 of retained earnings. At year-end, the company declares its regular $3 per share cash dividend on the preferred stock and a $2.20 per share cash dividend on the common stock. Three weeks later, the company pays the dividends.

    *a.*   Prepare the journal entry for the declaration of the cash dividends.

    *b.*   Prepare the journal entry for the payment of the cash dividends.

**E11-6A.**  **Stock Dividends**                                                                   LO7

Witt Corporation has 70,000 shares of $5 par value common stock outstanding. At year-end, the company declares a four percent stock dividend. The market price of the stock on the declaration date is $21 per share. Four weeks later, the company issues the shares of stock to stockholders.

    *a.*   Prepare the journal entry for the declaration of the stock dividend.

    *b.*   Prepare the journal entry for the issuance of the stock dividend.

    *c.*   Assume that the company declared a 40 percent stock dividend rather than a four percent stock dividend. Prepare the journal entries for (1) the declaration of the stock dividend and (2) the issuance of the stock dividend.

LO8 **E11-7A.** **Statement of Retained Earnings**

Use the following data to prepare a statement of retained earnings for Shepler Corporation.

| | |
|---|---|
| Total retained earnings originally reported at January 1..................................... | $324,000 |
| Cash dividends declared during the year ................................................ | 75,000 |
| Net income for the year....................................................................... | 193,000 |
| Stock dividend declared during the year ................................................ | 30,000 |

LO3 **E11-8A.** **Conversion of Preferred Stock into Common Stock**

Smith & Sons, Inc., has 12,000 shares of $100 par value, six percent preferred stock and 80,000 shares of $0.50 par value common stock outstanding. The preferred stock is convertible into the company's common stock at a conversion rate of 1-to-20; that is, each share of preferred stock is convertible into 20 shares of common stock. The preferred stock had been sold for its par value when issued. Prepare the journal entry to record the conversion of all of the company's preferred stock into common stock.

LO5 **E11-9A.** **Reverse Stock Split**

Titanium Metals Company had 20,000,000 shares of $0.01 par value common stock outstanding which had been sold for an aggregate amount of $300,000,000. The company's shares are traded on the New York Stock Exchange, which has a minimum listing price of $1 per share. Recently, the company's common stock has been trading on the exchange below $1 per share, and the exchange has notified the company that its common stock would be delisted in 30 days if the stock price did not rebound above its minimum listing price. In response to this notification, Titanium Metals authorized a 1-for-10 reverse stock split. Following the reverse stock split:

a. How many common shares will be outstanding?
b. What will be the new par value per share?
c. How will the reverse stock split be recorded in the company's accounts?

LO9 **E11-10A.** **Return on Common Stockholders' Equity, Dividend Yield, and Dividend Payout**

The following information relates to Waterloo Components, Inc.:

| | 2010 | 2011 |
|---|---|---|
| Net income....................................................... | $ 55,000 | $ 75,000 |
| Preferred stock dividends ........................................... | 5,000 | 5,000 |
| Average common stockholders' equity ............................... | 2,000,000 | 2,100,000 |
| Dividend per common share ....................................... | 1.50 | 1.60 |
| Earnings per share ............................................... | 2.90 | 2.95 |
| Market price per common share, year-end ......................... | 29.50 | 30.00 |

a. Calculate the company's return on common stockholders' equity for 2010 and 2011.
b. Calculate the company's dividend yield for 2010 and 2011.
c. Calculate the company's dividend payout for 2010 and 2011.

LO1 **E11-11A.** **Characteristics of a Corporation**

Label each of the following characteristics of a corporation as either an (A) advantage, or a (D) disadvantage:

a. Limited liability
b. Taxation
c. Regulations
d. Transferability of ownership

# EXERCISES—SET B

LO7 **E11-1B.** **Dividend Distribution**

Bower Corporation has the following shares outstanding: 15,000 shares of $50 par value, eight percent preferred stock and 50,000 shares of $5 par value common stock. During its first three years in business, the firm declared no dividends in the first year, $280,000 of dividends in the second year, and $60,000 of dividends in the third year.

a. If the preferred stock is cumulative, determine the total amount of dividends paid to each class of stock in each of the three years.

b. If the preferred stock is noncumulative, determine the total amount of dividends paid to each class of stock in each of the three years.

**E11-2B.** **Cash and Noncash Share Issuances** LO4

Chavoy Corporation was organized on July 1. The company's charter authorizes 100,000 shares of $10 par value common stock. On August 1, the attorney who helped organize the corporation accepted 800 shares of Chavoy common stock in settlement for the services provided (the services were valued at $9,600). On August 15, Chavoy issued 5,000 common shares for $75,000 cash. On October 15, Chavoy issued 3,000 common shares to acquire a vacant land site appraised at $48,000. Prepare the journal entries to record the stock issuances on August 1, August 15, and October 15.

**E11-3B.** **Forward Stock Split** LO5

On September 1, Oxford Company has 250,000 shares of $15 par value common stock that are issued and outstanding. The general ledger shows the following account balances relating to the common stock:

| | |
|---|---|
| Common stock. . . . . . . . . . . . . . . . . . . . . . . . . . . . . . . . . . . . . . . . . . . . . . . . . . . . . . . . . . . . . . . . . . . . . | $3,750,000 |
| Paid-in capital in excess of par value. . . . . . . . . . . . . . . . . . . . . . . . . . . . . . . . . . . . . . . . . . . . . . . | $2,250,000 |

On September 2, Oxford splits its stock 3-for-2 and reduces the par value to $10 per share.

a. How many shares of common stock are issued and outstanding immediately following the stock split?

b. What is the balance in the Common Stock account immediately following the stock split?

c. What is the likely reason that Oxford Company split its stock?

**E11-4B.** **Stock Issuance and Treasury Stock** LO4, LO6

Diva, Inc., recorded certain capital stock transactions shown in the following journal entries: (1) issued common stock for $19 cash per share, (2) purchased treasury shares at $22 per share, and (3) sold some of the treasury shares:

| | | | |
|---|---|---|---|
| 1. | Cash | 437,000 | |
| | Common stock | | 46,000 |
| | Paid-in capital in excess of par value | | 391,000 |
| 2. | Treasury stock | 77,000 | |
| | Cash | | 77,000 |
| 3. | Cash | 62,400 | |
| | Treasury stock | | 52,800 |
| | Paid-in capital from treasury stock | | 9,600 |

a. How many shares were originally issued?

b. What was the par value of the shares issued?

c. How many shares of treasury stock were acquired?

d. How many shares of treasury stock were sold?

e. At what price per share was the treasury stock sold?

**E11-5B.** **Cash and Stock Dividends** LO7

Mandrich Corporation has 25,000 shares of $10 par value common stock outstanding. The company has $405,000 of retained earnings. At year-end, the company declares a cash dividend of $1.90 per share and a four percent stock dividend. The market price of the stock at the declaration date is $35 per share. Four weeks later, the company pays the dividends.

a. Prepare the journal entry for the declaration of the cash dividend.

b. Prepare the journal entry for the declaration of the stock dividend.

c. Prepare the journal entry for the payment of the cash dividend.

d. Prepare the journal entry for the payment of the stock dividend.

**E11-6B.** **Large Stock Dividend and Forward Stock Split** LO5, LO7

Key Corporation has 40,000 shares of $10 par value common stock outstanding and retained earnings of $820,000. The company declares a 100 percent stock dividend. The market price at the declaration date is $17 per share.

    *a.* Prepare the journal entries for (1) the declaration of the dividend and (2) the issuance of the dividend.

    *b.* Assume that the company splits its stock 2-for-1 and reduces the par value from $10 to $5 rather than declaring a 100 percent stock dividend. How does the accounting for the forward stock split differ from the accounting for the 100 percent stock dividend?

**LO8**  **E11-7B.**  **Statement of Retained Earnings**

Use the following data to prepare a statement of retained earnings for Schauer Corporation.

| | |
|---|---|
| Total retained earnings originally reported as of January 1 | $347,000 |
| Stock dividends declared during the year | 28,000 |
| Cash dividends declared during the year | 35,000 |
| Net income for the year | 94,000 |

**LO3**  **E11-8B.**  **Conversion of Preferred Stock into Common Stock**

Groff & Sons, Inc., has 20,000 shares of $50 par value, nine percent preferred stock and 100,000 shares of $1.00 par value common stock outstanding. The preferred stock is convertible into the company's common stock at a conversion rate of 1-to-40; that is, each share of preferred stock is convertible into 40 shares of common stock. The preferred stock had been sold for its par value when issued. Prepare the journal entry to record the conversion of all of the company's preferred stock into common stock.

**LO5**  **E11-9B.**  **Reverse Stock Split**

The Waterford Company had 50,000,000 shares of $0.10 par value common stock outstanding which had been sold for an aggregate amount of $500,000,000. The company's shares are traded on the New York Stock Exchange, which has a minimum listing price of $1 per share. Recently, the company's common stock has been trading on the exchange below $1 per share, and the exchange has notified the company that its common stock would be delisted in 30 days if the stock price did not rebound above its minimum listing price. In response to this notification, Waterford authorized a 1-for-20 reverse stock split. Following the reverse stock split:

    *a.* How many common shares will be outstanding?

    *b.* What will be the new par value per share?

    *c.* How will the reverse stock split be recorded in the company's accounts?

**LO9**  **E11-10B.**  **Return on Common Stockholders' Equity, Dividend Yield, and Dividend Payout**

The following information relates to Litchfield, Inc.:

| | 2010 | 2011 |
|---|---|---|
| Net income | $ 110,000 | $ 150,000 |
| Preferred stock dividends | 15,000 | 15,000 |
| Average common stockholders' equity | 4,000,000 | 4,200,000 |
| Dividend per common share | 3.00 | 3.20 |
| Earnings per share | 5.80 | 5.90 |
| Market price per common share, year-end | 58.00 | 59.50 |

    *a.* Calculate the company's return on common stockholders' equity for 2010 and 2011.

    *b.* Calculate the company's dividend yield for 2010 and 2011.

    *c.* Calculate the company's dividend payout for 2010 and 2011.

**LO1**  **E11-11B.**  **Characteristics of a Corporation**

Label each of the following characteristics of a corporation as either an (A) advantage, or a (D) disadvantage:

    *a.* Organizational costs

    *b.* Continuity of existence

    *c.* Capital raising capability

    *d.* Separate legal entity

# PROBLEMS—SET A

**P11-1A.** **Dividend Distribution**

LO7

Rydon Corporation began business on March 1, 2010. At that time, it issued 20,000 shares of $60 par value, seven percent cumulative preferred stock and 100,000 shares of $5 par value common stock. Through the end of 2012, there had been no change in the number of preferred and common shares outstanding.

**Required**

a. Assume that Rydon declared dividends of $0 in 2010, $183,000 in 2011, and $200,000 in 2012. Calculate the total dividends and the dividends per share paid to each class of stock in 2010, 2011, and 2012.

b. Assume that Rydon declared dividends of $0 in 2010, $84,000 in 2011, and $150,000 in 2012. Calculate the total dividends and the dividends per share paid to each class of stock in 2010, 2011, and 2012.

**P11-2A.** **Stockholders' Equity: Transactions and Balance Sheet Presentation**

LO4

Tunic Corporation was organized on April 1, with an authorization of 25,000 shares of six percent, $50 par value preferred stock and 200,000 shares of $5 par value common stock. During April, the following transactions affecting stockholders' equity occurred:

Apr. 1 Issued 80,000 shares of common stock at $15 cash per share.
3 Issued 2,000 shares of common stock to attorneys and promoters in exchange for their services in organizing the corporation. The services were valued at $31,000.
8 Issued 3,000 shares of common stock in exchange for equipment with a fair market value of $48,000.
20 Issued 6,000 shares of preferred stock for cash at $55 per share.
30 Closed the $49,000 in net income for April from the Income Summary account to the Retained Earnings account.

**Required**

a. Prepare journal entries to record the above transactions.
b. Prepare the stockholders' equity section of the balance sheet at April 30.

**P11-3A.** **Stockholders' Equity: Transactions and Balance Sheet Presentation**

LO4, LO6

The stockholders' equity accounts of Windham Corporation at January 1 appear below:

| | |
|---|---:|
| 8 Percent preferred stock, $25 par value, 50,000 shares authorized; | |
| 6,800 shares issued and outstanding............................................... | $170,000 |
| Common stock, $10 par value, 200,000 shares authorized; | |
| 50,000 shares issued and outstanding ............................................. | 500,000 |
| Paid-in capital in excess of par value—Preferred stock ................................. | 68,000 |
| Paid-in capital in excess of par value—Common stock ................................. | 200,000 |
| Retained earnings ........................................................................ | 270,000 |

During the year, the following transactions occurred:

Jan. 10 Issued 28,000 shares of common stock for $17 cash per share.
23 Purchased 8,000 shares of common stock as treasury stock at $19 per share.
Mar. 14 Sold one-half of the treasury shares acquired January 23 for $21 per share.
July 15 Issued 3,200 shares of preferred stock in exchange for equipment with a fair market value of $128,000.
Nov. 15 Sold 1,000 of the treasury shares acquired January 23 for $24 per share.
Dec. 31 Closed the net income of $59,000 from the Income Summary account to the Retained Earnings account.

**Required**

a. Set up T-accounts for the stockholders' equity accounts as of the beginning of the year and enter the January 1 balances.
b. Prepare journal entries to record the foregoing transactions and post to T-accounts (set up any additional T-accounts needed). Determine the ending balances for the stockholders' equity accounts.
c. Prepare the December 31 stockholders' equity section of the balance sheet.

**LO4, LO5, LO6**     **P11-4A.**     **Stockholders' Equity: Transactions and Balance Sheet Presentation**

The stockholders' equity of Summit Corporation at January 1 follows:

| | |
|---|---:|
| 7 Percent preferred stock, $100 par value, 20,000 shares authorized; 5,000 shares issued and outstanding.................................... | $ 500,000 |
| Common stock, $15 par value, 100,000 shares authorized; 40,000 shares issued and outstanding............................... | 600,000 |
| Paid-in capital in excess of par value—Preferred stock ............................... | 24,000 |
| Paid-in capital in excess of par value—Common stock .............................. | 360,000 |
| Retained earnings ....................................................................... | 325,000 |
| Total Stockholders' Equity ...................................................... | $1,809,000 |

The following transactions, among others, occurred during the year:

Jan. 12   Announced a 3-for-1 common stock split, reducing the par value of the common stock to $5 per share. The authorization was increased to 300,000 shares.

Mar. 31   Converted $40,000 face value of convertible bonds payable (the book value of the bonds was $43,000) to common stock. Each $1,000 bond converted to 125 shares of common stock.

June 1   Acquired equipment with a fair market value of $60,000 in exchange for 500 shares of preferred stock.

Sept. 1   Acquired 10,000 shares of common stock for cash at $10 per share.

Oct. 12   Sold 1,500 treasury shares at $12 per share.

Nov. 21   Issued 5,000 shares of common stock at $11 cash per share.

Dec. 28   Sold 1,200 treasury shares at $9 per share.

31   Closed the Income Summary account, with net income of $83,000, to the Retained Earnings account.

**Required**

*a.*   Set up T-accounts for the stockholders' equity accounts as of the beginning of the year and enter the January 1 balances.

*b.*   Prepare journal entries for the given transactions and post them to the T-accounts (set up any additional T- accounts needed). Determine the ending balances for the stockholders' equity accounts.

*c.*   Prepare the stockholders' equity section of the balance sheet at December 31.

**LO4, LO6**     **P11-5A.**     **Stockholders' Equity: Information and Entries from Comparative Data**

Comparative stockholders' equity sections from two successive years of balance sheets from Smiley, Inc., are as follows:

| | Dec. 31, 2012 | Dec. 31, 2011 |
|---|---:|---:|
| Paid-in Capital | | |
| 8 Percent preferred stock, $50 par value, authorized 20,000 shares; issued and outstanding, 2011: 8,000 shares; 2012: 12,000 shares..... | $ 600,000 | $ 400,000 |
| Common stock, no-par value, $20 stated value, authorized 80,000 shares; issued, 2011: 32,000 shares; 2012: 40,000 shares ............. | 800,000 | 640,000 |
| Additional Paid-in Capital | | |
| In excess of par value—Preferred stock ........................... | 224,000 | 144,000 |
| In excess of stated value—Common stock........................ | 232,000 | 160,000 |
| From treasury stock.............................................. | 21,000 | |
| Retained earnings .............................................. | 300,000 | 229,000 |
| | | $1,573,000 |
| Less: Treasury stock (7,000 shares common) at cost ..................... | -0- | 196,000 |
| Total Stockholders' Equity..................................... | $2,177,000 | $1,377,000 |

No dividends were declared or paid during 2012.

**Required**

Prepare the journal entries for the transactions affecting stockholders' equity that occurred during 2012. Assume that any share transactions were for cash.

**LO7, LO8**     **P11-6A.**     **Retained Earnings: Transactions and Statement**

The stockholders' equity accounts of Rayburn Corporation as of January 1 appear below:

| Common stock, $5 par value, 400,000 shares authorized; 160,000 shares issued and outstanding | $800,000 |
|---|---|
| Paid-in capital in excess of par value | 920,000 |
| Retained earnings | 513,000 |

During the year, the following transactions occurred:

June 7    Declared a ten percent stock dividend; market value of the common stock was $11 per share.

      28    Issued the stock dividend declared on June 7.

Dec. 5    Declared a cash dividend of $1.25 per share.

      26    Paid the cash dividend declared on December 5.

      31    Closed the net income of $412,000 from the Income Summary account to the Retained Earnings account.

      31    Closed the dividend accounts to the Retained Earnings account.

### Required

*a.*    Prepare journal entries to record the foregoing transactions.

*b.*    Prepare a statement of retained earnings.

**P11-7A.**    **Retained Earnings: Transactions and Statement**

LO7, LO8

The stockholders' equity of Cyclone Corporation at January 1 follows:

| 6 Percent preferred stock, $25 par value, 40,000 shares authorized; 20,000 shares issued and outstanding | $ 500,000 |
|---|---|
| Common stock, $5 par value, 300,000 shares authorized; 80,000 shares issued and outstanding | 400,000 |
| Paid-in capital in excess of par value—Common stock | 560,000 |
| Retained earnings | 830,000 |
| Total Stockholders' Equity | $2,290,000 |

The following transactions, among others, occurred during the year:

June 18    Declared a 50 percent stock dividend on all outstanding shares of common stock. The market value of the stock was $14 per share.

July 1    Issued the stock dividend declared on June 18.

Dec. 20    Declared the annual cash dividend on the preferred stock and a cash dividend of $1.30 per share on the common stock, payable on January 20 to stockholders of record on December 28.

      31    Closed the Income Summary account, with net income of $379,000, to the Retained Earnings account.

      31    Closed the dividend accounts to the Retained Earnings account.

### Required

*a.*    Prepare journal entries to record the foregoing transactions.

*b.*    Prepare a statement of retained earnings.

**P11-8A.**    **Stockholders' Equity Transactions, Journal Entries, and T-Accounts**

LO4, LO5, LO6

The stockholders' equity of Fremantle Corporation at January 1 follows:

| 8 Percent preferred stock, $100 par value, 20,000 shares authorized; 4,000 shares issued and outstanding | $ 400,000 |
|---|---|
| Common stock, $1 par value, 100,000 shares authorized; 40,000 shares issued and outstanding | 40,000 |
| Paid-in capital in excess of par value—Preferred stock | 200,000 |
| Paid-in capital in excess of par value—Common stock | 800,000 |
| Retained earnings | 550,000 |
| Total Stockholders' Equity | $1,990,000 |

The following transactions, among others, occurred during the year:

Jan. 1    Announced a 2-for-1 common stock split, reducing the par value of the common stock to $0.50 per share.

Mar. 31 Converted $80,000 face value of convertible bonds payable (the book value of the bonds was $83,000) to common stock. Each $1,000 bond converted to 125 shares of common stock.

June 1 Acquired equipment with a fair market value of $45,000 in exchange for 300 shares of preferred stock.

Sept. 1 Acquired 10,000 shares of common stock for cash at $20 per share.

Nov. 21 Issued 5,000 shares of common stock at $22 cash per share.

Dec. 28 Sold 1,000 treasury shares at $23 per share.

31 Closed the Income Summary account, with net income of $103,000, to the Retained Earnings account.

**Required**

a. Set up T-accounts for the stockholders' equity accounts as of the beginning of the year and enter the January 1 balances.

b. Prepare journal entries for the given transactions and post them to the T-accounts (set up any additional T-accounts needed). Determine the ending balances for the stockholders' equity accounts.

**LO4, LO5, LO6** **P11-9A.** **Stockholders' Equity Section of the Balance Sheet**

Using your analysis from P11-8A, prepare the stockholders' equity section of the Fremantle Corporation's balance sheet.

**LO9** **P11-10A.** **Return on Common Shareholders' Equity, Dividend Yield, and Dividend Payout: IFRS Financial Statements**

Tesco PLC is the world's third largest retailer and is based in the United Kingdom. Tesco prepares its financial statements using IFRS. The complete annual report for **Tesco PLC** for year-ended February 28, 2009 is available on this book's Website. Calculate Tesco's (a) return on common stockholders' equity, (b) dividend yield, and (c) dividend payout for 2008 and 2009. Additional information that you will need are the following:

| | 2007 | 2008 | 2009 |
|---|---|---|---|
| Total equity (millions of British pounds) ............................. | 10,571 | | |
| Dividend per share (in British pence) ................................. | | 11.27 | 12.28 |
| Market price per share (in British pence) ............................ | | 351.0 | 426.0 |

# PROBLEMS—SET B

**LO7** **P11-1B.** **Dividend Distribution**

Gardner Corporation began business on June 30, 2010. At that time, it issued 18,000 shares of $50 par value, six percent, cumulative preferred stock and 90,000 shares of $10 par value common stock. Through the end of 2012, there had been no change in the number of preferred and common shares outstanding.

**Required**

a. Assume that Gardner declared dividends of $63,000 in 2010, $0 in 2011, and $378,000 in 2012. Calculate the total dividends and the dividends per share paid to each class of stock in 2010, 2011, and 2012.

b. Assume that Gardner declared dividends of $0 in 2010, $108,000 in 2011, and $189,000 in 2012. Calculate the total dividends and the dividends per share paid to each class of stock in 2010, 2011, and 2012.

**LO4** **P11-2B.** **Stockholders' Equity: Transactions and Balance Sheet Presentation**

Beaker Corporation was organized on July 1, with an authorization of 50,000 shares of $4 no-par value preferred stock ($4 is the annual dividend) and 100,000 shares of $10 par value common stock. During July, the following transactions affecting stockholders' equity occurred:

July  1   Issued 31,000 shares of common stock at $17 cash per share.

12   Issued 3,500 shares of common stock in exchange for equipment with a fair
market value of $63,000.

15   Issued 5,000 shares of preferred stock for cash at $44 per share.

31   Closed the $38,000 in net income for July from the Income Summary account to
the Retained Earnings account.

### Required

a.   Prepare journal entries to record the foregoing transactions.

b.   Prepare the stockholders' equity section of the balance sheet at July 31.

**P11-3B.   Stockholders' Equity: Transactions and Balance Sheet Presentation**      LO4, LO6

The stockholders' equity accounts of Scott Corporation at January 1 follow:

| | |
|---|---:|
| Common stock, $5 par value, 350,000 shares authorized; | |
| 150,000 shares issued and outstanding............................................. | $750,000 |
| Paid-in capital in excess of par value................................................. | 600,000 |
| Retained earnings ........................................................................ | 346,000 |

During the year, the following transactions occurred:

Jan.   5   Issued 10,000 shares of common stock for $12 cash per share.

18   Purchased 4,000 shares of common stock as treasury stock at $14 cash per share.

Mar. 12   Sold one-fourth of the treasury shares acquired January 18 for $17 per share.

July 17   Sold 500 shares of the remaining treasury stock for $13 per share.

Oct.   1   Issued 5,000 shares of eight percent, $25 par value preferred stock for $35 cash
per share. These are the first preferred shares issued out of 50,000 authorized
shares.

Dec. 31   Closed the net income of $72,500 from the Income Summary account to the
Retained Earnings account.

### Required

a.   Set up T-accounts for the stockholders' equity accounts as of the beginning of the year
and enter the January 1 balances.

b.   Prepare journal entries to record the foregoing transactions and post to T-accounts (set
up any additional T-accounts needed). Determine the ending balances for the stockholders' equity accounts.

c.   Prepare the December 31 stockholders' equity section of the balance sheet.

**P11-4B.   Stockholders' Equity: Transactions and Balance Sheet Presentation**      LO4, LO5, LO6

The following is the stockholders' equity of Clipper Corporation at January 1:

| | |
|---|---:|
| 8 Percent preferred stock, $50 par value, 10,000 shares authorized; | |
| 7,000 shares issued and outstanding ............................................. | $  350,000 |
| Common stock, $20 par value, 50,000 shares authorized; | |
| 25,000 shares issued and outstanding............................................. | 500,000 |
| Paid-in capital in excess of par value—Preferred stock ................................ | 70,000 |
| Paid-in capital in excess of par value—Common stock ................................ | 385,000 |
| Retained earnings ...................................................................... | 238,000 |
| Total Stockholders' Equity......................................................... | $1,543,000 |

The following transactions, among others, occurred during the year:

Jan. 15   Issued 1,000 shares of preferred stock for $62 cash per share.

20   Issued 4,000 shares of common stock at $36 cash per share.

31   Converted $20,000 face value of convertible bonds payable (the book value
of the bonds is $18,500) to common stock. Each $1,000 bond converted to 25
shares of common stock.

May  18   Announced a 2-for-1 common stock split, reducing the par value of the common
stock to $10 per share. The authorization was increased to 100,000 shares.

June  1   Acquired equipment with a fair market value of $40,000 in exchange for 2,000
shares of common stock.

Sept. 1 Purchased 2,500 shares of common stock as treasury stock at $18 cash per share.
Oct. 12 Sold 900 treasury shares at $21 per share.
Dec. 22 Issued 500 shares of preferred stock for $59 cash per share.
28 Sold 1,100 of the remaining treasury shares at $16 per share.
31 Closed the Income Summary account, with net income of $85,000, to the Retained Earnings account.

**Required**
a. Set up T-accounts for the stockholders' equity accounts as of the beginning of the year and enter the January 1 balances.
b. Prepare journal entries for the given transactions and post them to the T-accounts (set up any additional T-accounts needed). Determine the ending balances for the stockholders' equity accounts.
c. Prepare the stockholders' equity section of the balance sheet at December 31.

**LO4, LO6** **P11-5B.** **Stockholders' Equity: Transaction Descriptions from Account Data**
The following T-accounts contain keyed entries representing five transactions involving the stockholders' equity of Riverview, Inc.:

| | **Cash** | | | | **Paid-in Capital in Excess of Par Value—Common Stock** | | |
|---|---|---|---|---|---|---|---|
| (1) | 80,600 | 12,800 | (4) | | | | |
| (2) | 35,000 | | | | | 33,000 | (3) |
| (5) | 6,080 | | | | | | |

| | **Land** | | | | **Paid-in Capital from Treasury Stock** | | |
|---|---|---|---|---|---|---|---|
| (3) | 93,000 | | | | | 960 | (5) |

| | **Preferred Stock, $50 Par** | | |
|---|---|---|---|
| | | 65,000 | (1) |

| | **Paid-in Capital in Excess of Par Value—Preferred Stock** | | |
|---|---|---|---|
| | | 15,600 | (1) |

| | **Treasury Stock** | | |
|---|---|---|---|
| (4) | (800 shares of common) | 5,120 | (5) |
| | 12,800 | | |

| | **Common Stock, $10 Par** | | |
|---|---|---|---|
| | | 35,000 | (2) |
| | | 60,000 | (3) |

**Required**
Using this information, give detailed descriptions, including number of shares and price per share when applicable, for each of the five transactions.

**LO7, LO8** **P11-6B.** **Retained Earnings: Transactions and Statement**
The stockholders' equity of Striker Corporation at January 1 appears below:

| | |
|---|---|
| Common stock, $10 par value, 200,000 shares authorized; 80,000 shares issued and outstanding.............................................. | $800,000 |
| Paid-in capital in excess of par value..................................................... | 480,000 |
| Retained earnings........................................................................ | 305,000 |

During the year, the following transactions occurred:

May 12 Declared a seven percent stock dividend; market value of the common stock was $18 per share.
June 6 Issued the stock dividend declared on May 12.
Dec. 5 Declared a cash dividend of 75 cents per share.
30 Paid the cash dividend declared on December 5.
31 Closed the net income of $283,000 from the Income Summary account to Retained Earnings.
31 Closed the dividend accounts to Retained Earnings.

**Required**
a. Prepare journal entries to record the foregoing transactions.
b. Prepare a statement of retained earnings.

**P11-7B.   Retained Earnings: Transactions and Statement**

The stockholders' equity of Elson Corporation at January 1 is shown below:

| | |
|---|---:|
| 5 Percent preferred stock, $100 par value, 10,000 shares | |
| authorized; 4,000 shares issued and outstanding ................................. | $ 400,000 |
| Common stock, $5 par value, 200,000 shares | |
| authorized; 50,000 shares issued and outstanding ............................... | 250,000 |
| Paid-in capital in excess of par value—Preferred stock ............................... | 40,000 |
| Paid-in capital in excess of par value—Common stock ............................... | 300,000 |
| Retained earnings ...................................................................... | 656,000 |
| Total Stockholders' Equity ....................................................... | $1,646,000 |

The following transactions, among others, occurred during the year:

Apr.   1   Declared a 100 percent stock dividend on all outstanding shares of common stock. The market value of the stock was $11 per share.

   15   Issued the stock dividend declared on April 1.

Dec.   7   Declared a three percent stock dividend on all outstanding shares of common stock. The market value of the stock was $14 per share.

   17   Issued the stock dividend declared on December 7.

   20   Declared the annual cash dividend on the preferred stock and a cash dividend of 80 cents per common share, payable on January 15 to common stockholders of record on December 31.

   31   Closed the Income Summary account, with net income of $253,000, to the Retained Earnings account.

   31   Closed the dividend accounts to the Retained Earnings account.

**Required**

a.   Prepare journal entries to record the foregoing transactions.

b.   Prepare a statement of retained earnings.

**P11-8B.   Stockholders' Equity: Transactions and Statement**

The stockholders' equity section of Day Corporation's balance sheet at January 1 follows:

| | | |
|---|---:|---:|
| Common stock, $10 par value, 200,000 shares authorized, | | $350,000 |
| 35,000 shares issued, 4,000 shares are in the treasury.................. | | |
| Additional paid-in capital | | |
| In excess of par value............................................... | $315,000 | |
| From treasury stock ................................................ | 18,000 | 333,000 |
| Retained earnings (see note)........................................... | | 298,000 |
| | | 981,000 |
| Less: Treasury stock (4,000 shares) at cost................................ | | 84,000 |
| Total Stockholders' Equity............................................. | | $897,000 |

The following transactions affecting stockholders' equity occurred during the year:

Jan.   8   Issued 10,000 shares of previously unissued common stock for $23 cash per share.

Mar.  12   Sold all of the treasury shares for $26 cash per share.

June 30   Declared a six percent stock dividend on all outstanding shares of common stock. The market value of the stock was $30 per share.

July 10   Issued the stock dividend declared on June 30.

Oct.   7   Acquired 1,500 shares of common stock as treasury stock at $27 cash per share.

Dec. 18   Declared a cash dividend of 90 cents per outstanding common share, payable on January 9 to stockholders of record on December 31.

   31   Closed the Income Summary account, with net income of $186,000, to the Retained Earnings account.

   31   Closed the dividend accounts to the Retained Earnings account.

**Required**

a.   Prepare journal entries to record the foregoing transactions.

b.   Prepare a statement of stockholders' equity.

LO4, LO5, LO6     **P11-9B.**     **Stockholders' Equity Transactions, Journal Entries, and T-Accounts**

The stockholders' equity of Xeltron Corporation at January 1 follows:

| | |
|---|---:|
| 9 Percent preferred stock, $100 par value, 20,000 shares authorized; 6,000 shares issued and outstanding .................................. | $ 600,000 |
| Common stock, $2 par value, 100,000 shares authorized; 40,000 shares issued and outstanding ................................ | 80,000 |
| Paid-in capital in excess of par value—Preferred stock ................................ | 400,000 |
| Paid-in capital in excess of par value—Common stock ............................... | 800,000 |
| Retained earnings ...................................................................... | 750,000 |
| Total Stockholders' Equity ......................................................... | $2,630,000 |

The following transactions, among others, occurred during the year:

Jan.    1    Announced a 2-for-1 common stock split, reducing the par value of the common stock to $1.00 per share.

Mar.   31   Converted $100,000 face value of convertible bonds payable (the book value of the bonds was $103,000) to common stock. Each $1,000 bond converted to 125 shares of common stock.

June    1    Acquired equipment with a fair market value of $30,000 in exchange for 200 shares of preferred stock.

Sept.   1    Acquired 10,000 shares of common stock for cash at $20 per share.

Nov.  21   Issued 5,000 shares of common stock at $22 cash per share.

Dec.  28   Sold 1,000 treasury shares at $23 per share.

         31   Closed the Income Summary account, with net income of $200,000, to the Retained Earnings account.

**Required**

a.    Set up T-accounts for the stockholders' equity accounts as of the beginning of the year and enter the January 1 balances.

b.    Prepare journal entries for the given transactions and post them to the T-accounts (set up any additional T-accounts needed). Determine the ending balances for the stockholders' equity accounts.

LO4, LO5, LO6     **P11-10B.**     **The Stockholders' Equity Section of the Balance Sheet**

Using your analysis from P11-9B, prepare the Stockholders' Equity section of the Xeltron Corporation's balance sheet.

# SERIAL PROBLEM: KATE'S CARDS

(*Note:* **This is a continuation of the Serial Problem: Kate's Cards from Chapters 1 through 10.**)

**SP11.**     Kate's business continues to flourish. It hardly seems that just eleven months ago, in September of 2010, that Kate started the business. She is especially pleased that she was able to successfully defend herself against what turned out to be a mistaken attempt to sue her for copyright infringement. She was able to clearly demonstrate that her card designs were unique and significantly different from the designs sold by Mega Cards.

Kate has decided to take on an investor. Taylor Kasey believes that Kate's Cards represents a good investment and wishes to invest money to help Kate expand the business. Kate, however, is somewhat unsure how to structure Taylor's investment. Taylor wishes to be an equity investor rather than simply providing a loan to Kate. Kate wants to know whether she should issue Taylor common stock or preferred stock for her investment.

1. Discuss the difference between the two classes of stock and suggest which type is more appropriate for Kate to issue.

Kate has decided that she does not want to give up voting control of Kate's Cards. Since Taylor prefers to be a passive investor, but does wish to have a steady income from dividends, the decision is made to issue 50 shares of $100 par value, 6 percent cumulative preferred stock.

2. Provide the journal entry to record the issuance of the preferred stock for cash.

Kate also wishes to pay dividends on both her common shares and the preferred stock. She is a little confused between cash and stock dividends.

3. Explain the difference between a cash dividend and a stock dividend. Since Kate is the only stockholder of the common stock, what would be the effect of issuing a 10 percent stock dividend?

Kate decides to issue cash dividends on both the common stock and the preferred stock. Currently there are 50 outstanding preferred shares and 500 common shares outstanding. The dividends that Kate paid were $6 per share on the preferred shares and $2 per share on the common shares.

4. Provide the journal entry for the payment of the cash dividends.

Kate's Cards has a net income of $1,500 for the current month of August 2011. Kate had decided that the business will have a fiscal year-end of August 31, so this is the completion of the company's first year. Kate will be preparing her annual financial statements; however, she would also like to see a monthly statement of retained earnings for August, 2011. In addition, she would like to see how the stockholders' equity section of the balance sheet will look after the addition of the preferred stock. The stockholders' equity section from July 2011 is shown below:

Stockholders' Equity
Common stock (5,000 shares authorized, 500 shares issued and outstanding) ......... $ 500
Paid-in capital in excess of par value—common stock ............................... 9,500
Retained earnings ...................................................................... 15,000
Total stockholders' equity ............................................................ $25,000

5. Prepare a statement of retained earnings for the month of August 2011 and the stockholders' equity section of the balance sheet as of August 31, 2011.

# EXTENDING YOUR KNOWLEDGE

## REPORTING AND ANALYSIS

**EYK11-1. Financial Reporting Problem: Columbia Sportswear Company**

The financial statements for the **Columbia Sportswear Company** can be found in Appendix A at the end of this book.

**COLUMBIA SPORTSWEAR COMPANY**

**Required**

Answer the following questions:

a. How many shares of common stock are authorized at the end of 2009?
b. What percentage of the common shares authorized are outstanding at the end of 2009?
c. Does Columbia Sportswear have any preferred shares outstanding at the end of 2009?
d. How many shares of common stock did Columbia Sportswear repurchase in 2009? What was the dollar amount of this repurchase?
e. What amount of dividends per share did Columbia Sportswear report for 2009? 2008? 2007?

**EYK11-2. Comparative Analysis Problem: Columbia Sportswear Company vs The Timberland Company**

The financial statements for the **Columbia Sportswear Company** can be found in Appendix A at the end of this book, and the financial statements of **The Timberland Company** can be found in Appendix B (the complete annual report is available on this book's Website).

**COLUMBIA SPORTSWEAR COMPANY**

**THE TIMBERLAND COMPANY**

**Required**

Answer the following questions:

a. Calculate the return on common stockholders' equity for each company for 2009.
b. Calculate the dividend payout ratio for each company for 2009.
c. Based on these ratios, which company performed better for its shareholders during 2009?

**EYK11-3. Business Decision Problem**

Egghead, Inc., was a software chain that had over 100 stores across the U.S. Initially its founders and employees owned the company privately. The company eventually went public with an initial public offering (IPO) of 3.6 million shares (the company had 12 million shares prior to the IPO). The new shares were priced at $15 each. The company did not hold any treasury shares.

**Required**

a. Assume that the common shares had a $1 par value. Provide the journal entry to record the issuance of new shares.
b. Discuss whether you think Egghead's board of directors and existing shareholders had to approve the public issuance before it occurred.
c. Provide some reasons why Egghead wished to raise $54 million with equity rather than debt.

**EYK11-4. Financial Analysis Problem**

GILLETTE COMPANY
PROCTER & GAMBLE
COLGATE-PALMOLIVE COMPANY

The following data was obtained prior to the acquisition of **Gillette Company** by **Procter & Gamble**. Gillette Company, the Procter & Gamble Company, and **Colgate-Palmolive Company** are three firms in the personal care consumer products industry. During the prior year, the average return on common stockholders' equity for the personal care consumer products industry was 28.1 percent. In the same year, the relevant financial data for Gillette, Procter & Gamble, and Colgate-Palmolive were as follows (in millions):

| | Gillette | Procter & Gamble | Colgate-Palmolive |
|---|---|---|---|
| Preferred stockholders' equity, beginning .............. | $ 99.2 | $1,969.0 | $ 418.3 |
| Preferred stockholders' equity, ending.................. | 99.0 | 1,942.0 | 414.3 |
| Preferred dividends..................................... | 4.7 | 102.0 | 21.6 |
| Common stockholders' equity, beginning .............. | 1,397.2 | 5,472.0 | 2,201.5 |
| Common stockholders' equity, ending ................. | 1,380.0 | 6,890.0 | 1,460.7 |
| Net income............................................ | 426.9 | 2,211.0 | 548.1 |

**Required**

a. Calculate Gillette Company's return on common stockholders' equity.
b. Evaluate Gillette Company's return on common stockholders' equity by comparing it with the following:
   1. The average for the personal care consumer products industry.
   2. The return earned by the Procter & Gamble Company.
   3. The return earned by Colgate-Palmolive Company.
   4. The return earned by Gillette Company in the previous year (in the previous year, Gillette's net income was $513.4 million, preferred stock dividends were $4.8 million, and average common stockholders' equity was $1,227.3 million).

## CRITICAL THINKING

**EYK11-5. Financial Analysis on the Web: General Mills, Inc.**

GENERAL MILLS, INC.

The fiscal year 2010 annual report of **General Mills, Inc.** is available on this book's Website.

**Required**

a. How many shares of common stock is General Mills authorized to issue? How many common shares are issued as of May 30, 2010?
b. What is the par value of General Mills' common stock?
c. Does General Mills have any preferred shares? If so, how many shares of preferred stock are outstanding on May 30, 2010?
d. How many treasury shares did General Mills purchase on the open market during the 2010 fiscal year? What did General Mills pay to purchase these shares? How many common shares are in the treasury as of May 30, 2010?
e. What is General Mills' return on common stockholders' equity for the 2010 fiscal year?

*f.* What is the cash dividend per share declared by General Mills in fiscal year 2010? 2009? 2008?

*g.* What are General Mills' basic earnings per share in fiscal year 2010? 2009? 2008?

*h.* What is General Mills' dividend payout ratio for fiscal year 2010? 2009? 2008?

**EYK11-6. Accounting Communication Activity**

Your neighbor, Norman Vetter, has always been tinkering in his garage with his inventions. He believes he has finally come up with one that could really sell well. He is a little concerned about some potential safety issues, but he believes those issues will be worked out. He wants to form a business to manufacture and sell his invention and has come to you for advice. In particular, he would like to know the advantages and disadvantages of forming a corporation, rather than simply organizing as a sole proprietor.

**Required**

Write a brief memorandum to your neighbor explaining the advantages and disadvantages of the corporate form of organization.

**EYK11-7. Accounting Ethics Case**

Colin Agee, chairperson of the board of directors and chief executive officer of Image, Inc., is pondering a recommendation to make to the firm's board of directors in response to actions taken by Sam Mecon. Mecon recently informed Agee and other board members that he (Mecon) had purchased 15 percent of the voting stock of Image at $12 per share and is considering an attempt to take control of the company. His effort to take control would include offering $16 per share to stockholders to induce them to sell shares to him. Mecon also indicated that he would abandon his takeover plans if the company would buy back his stock at a price 50 percent over its current market price of $13 per share.

Agee views the proposed takeover by Mecon as a hostile maneuver. Mecon has a reputation of identifying companies that are undervalued (that is, their underlying net assets are worth more than the price of the outstanding shares), buying enough shares to take control of the company, replacing top management, and, on occasion, breaking up the company (that is, selling off the various divisions to the highest bidder). The process has proven profitable to Mecon and his financial backers. Stockholders of the companies taken over have also benefited because Mecon paid them attractive prices to buy their shares.

Agee recognizes that Image is currently undervalued by the stock market but believes that eventually the company will significantly improve its financial performance to the long-run benefit of its stockholders.

**Required**

What are the ethical issues that Agee should consider in arriving at a recommendation to make to the board of directors regarding Mecon's offer to be "bought out" of his takeover plans?

**EYK11-8. Corporate Social Responsibility Problem**

In the corporate social responsibility highlight regarding Starbucks on page 504 in this chapter, it was stated that Starbucks believes in measuring and monitoring the company's CSR progress. One of Starbucks' commitments is to ethical coffee sourcing. Two of the metrics that the company uses in this regard are the pounds of coffee purchased from C.A.F.E. and the pounds of green coffee purchased from Fair Trade Certified cooperatives. Go to the Starbucks Website and navigate to the section on global responsibility to download the report on Ethical Coffee Sourcing. Identify how the company is doing with respect to these two metrics.

**EYK11-9. Forensic Accounting Problem**

Wayne James Nelson, a manager in the office of the Arizona State Treasurer, was found guilty of trying to defraud the state of nearly $2 million. Nelson's scheme involved issuing checks to bogus vendors. The amounts of the 23 checks issued are shown below:

ASSIGNMENTS

The table lists the checks that a manager in the office of the Arizona State Treasurer wrote to divert funds for his own use. The vendors to whom the checks were issued were fictitious.

| Date of Check | Amount |
|---|---|
| October 9, 1992 | $    1,927.48 |
| | 27,902.31 |
| October 14, 1992 | 86,241.90 |
| | 72,117.46 |
| | 81,321.75 |
| | 97,473.96 |
| October 19, 1992 | 93,249.11 |
| | 89,658.17 |
| | 87,776.89 |
| | 92,105.83 |
| | 79,949.16 |
| | 87,602.93 |
| | 96,879.27 |
| | 91,806.47 |
| | 84,991.67 |
| | 90,831.83 |
| | 93,766.67 |
| | 88,338.72 |
| | 94,639.49 |
| | 83,709.28 |
| | 96,412.21 |
| | 88,432.86 |
| | 71,552.16 |
| **TOTAL** | **$1,878,687.58** |

**Required**

Refer to the chart shown below that reports the occurrences of various digits in a number. Compare the first digit of the fraudulent checks to the table of Benford's Law. How do the two compare? Are there any other unusual patterns you detect in the check amounts?

| Position of digit in number | | | | |
|---|---|---|---|---|
| Digit | First | Second | Third | Fourth |
| 0 | . | .11968 | .10178 | .10018 |
| 1 | .30103 | .11389 | .10138 | .10014 |
| 2 | .17609 | .10882 | .10097 | .10010 |
| 3 | .12494 | .10433 | .10057 | .10006 |
| 4 | .09691 | .10031 | .10018 | .10002 |
| 5 | .07918 | .09668 | .09979 | .09998 |
| 6 | .06695 | .09337 | .09940 | .09994 |
| 7 | .05799 | .09035 | .09902 | .09990 |
| 8 | .05115 | .08757 | .09864 | .09986 |
| 9 | .04576 | .08500 | .09827 | .09982 |

Example: The number 147 has three digits, with 1 as the first digit, 4 as the second digit and 7 as the third digit. The table shows that under Benford's Law the expected proportion of numbers with a first digit 1 is 30.103% and the expected proportion of numbers with a third digit 7 is 9.902%.

Source: "A Taxpayer Compliance Application of Benford's Law," by M. J. Nigrini. The Journal of American Taxation Association 18, 1996.

## ANSWERS TO SELF-STUDY QUESTIONS:

1. c, (p. 501)   2. a, (p. 506)   3. c, (p. 509)   4. d, (p. 510)   5. d, (p. 512)   6. d, (p. 510)
7. c, (p. 518)   8. d, (p. 504)   9. d, (p. 506)   10. a, (p. 512)   11. d, (p. 515)

## Your Turn! Solutions

### Solution 11.1

1. Disadvantage
2. Advantage
3. Advantage
4. Disadvantage
5. Disadvantage
6. Advantage

### Solution 11.2

**1.** d   **2.** e   **3.** b   **4.** f   **5.** c   **6.** a

### Solution 11.3

Paid-in capital in excess of par value = ($9 − $1) × 10,000 shares = $80,000

### Solution 11.4

$75,000

### Solution 11.5

*a.* A cash dividend will lower retained earnings by $30,000 ($3 × 10,000 shares) to $470,000.

*b.* A ten percent stock dividend will lower retained earnings by $20,000 (.10 × 10,000 × $20) to $480,000.

### Solution 11.6

| DIOR COMPANY<br>Statement of Stockholders' Equity<br>For the Year Ended December 31, 2010 | | | | | |
|---|---|---|---|---|---|
| | Common Stock | Paid-in Capital in Excess of Par Value | Retained Earnings | Treasury Stock | Total |
| Balance, January 1, 2010........ | $100,000 | $900,000 | $50,000 | $(10,000) | $1,040,000 |
| 1,000 common shares issued.... | 1,000 | 14,000 | | | 15,000 |
| Net income.................... | | | 30,000 | | 30,000 |
| Cash dividend................. | | | (8,000) | | (8,000) |
| Balance, December 31, 2010 .... | $101,000 | $914,000 | $72,000 | $(10,000) | $1,077,000 |

# 12

# Statement of Cash Flows

| PAST | PRESENT | FUTURE |
|---|---|---|
| Chapter 11 examined the accounting for stockholders' equity. | In this chapter we turn our attention to the statement of cash flows. | Chapter 13 completes our study of financial accounting by looking at the analysis and interpretation of financial statements. |

## LEARNING OBJECTIVES

*1* **Discuss** the content and format of the statement of cash flows. (p. 544)

*2* **Explain** the preparation of a statement of cash flows using the indirect method. (p. 550)

*3* **Explain** the preparation of a statement of cash flows using the direct method. (p. 557)

*4* **Define** *free cash flow, operating-cash-flow-to-current-liabilities ratio,* and the *operating-cash-flow-to-capital-expenditures ratio* and **explain** their use. (p. 560).

# HOME DEPOT: A Company with a Vision

**Home Depot** is the largest home improvement retailer in the United States and ranks only behind Wal-Mart as the second largest U.S. general retailer. Home Depot was founded in 1978 in Atlanta, Georgia, with only a few stores. Today, the company operates over 2,300 stores in the United States and Canada. The company's founders had a vision that led to the company's tremendous growth:

> "We founded [The Home Depot] with a special vision—to create a company that would keep alive the values that were important to us. Values like respect among all people, excellent customer service and giving back to communities and society."

—Arthur Blank, co-founder, Home Depot

It takes a lot of cash to build and operate over 2,300 stores, especially when the average Home Depot store is over 100,000 square feet. Even in fiscal year 2009, a period of economic downturn, Home Depot continued its growth and opened new stores. In the same year, the company's capital expenditures totaled approximately $966 million. While this amount is down from prior years, $966 million is still a lot of money.

How can a financial statement user determine where a company obtained the cash to fund such growth? In this chapter we examine the statement of cash flows and learn how a company discloses both the sources and uses of its cash. Understanding the content, format, and construction of the statement of cash flows will enable a financial statement user to assess just how a company like Home Depot was able to finance its capital expenditures for new store growth.

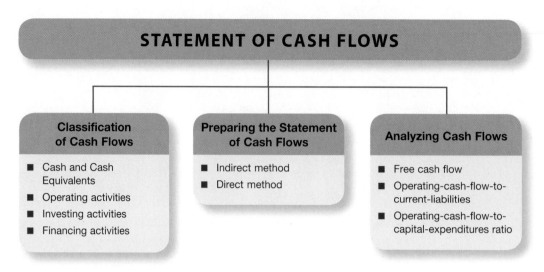

# CASH AND CASH EQUIVALENTS

Do you maintain a checkbook in which you record the checks you write and the bank deposits you make? If so, you are keeping a record of your cash flows—the checks you write are your cash outflows and the bank deposits you make are your cash inflows. Businesses also experience cash inflows and outflows; but, they do more than just record their cash flows because GAAP requires that businesses prepare an entirely separate financial statement explaining where their cash flow came from and how it was used.

The statement of cash flows complements the balance sheet and the income statement. While a balance sheet reports a company's financial position as of a point in time, usually the end of a fiscal period, the statement of cash flows explains the change in one component of a company's financial position—its cash—from one balance sheet date to the next. The income statement, on the other hand, reveals the results of a company's operating activities for the period, and these operating activities are a major source and use of the cash reported in a company's statement of cash flows.

In the eyes of most creditors, investors, and managers, cash is a business's most important asset. Without cash, a business would be unable to pay its employees, its lenders, its suppliers, its service providers, or its shareholders. In short, cash is the only asset that a business can't operate without.

The dilemma for most managers, however, is knowing exactly how much cash to keep on hand. Although managers know that they need to keep some cash on hand in a checking account and/or petty cash fund to pay their immediate bills, they also know that cash is the lowest return generating asset that a business has. Keeping too much cash on hand means that a business is not maximizing the value of its assets. For this reason, most managers spend considerable time assessing their cash needs—an activity called **cash management**. Because the science of cash management is inexact, managers have derived ways to help them minimize the amount of cash that they need to keep on hand while also maximizing the return on a business's assets. One such method is to invest any excess cash in alternative investments that are readily convertible back into cash and earn a higher rate of return than cash, but which do not place the invested cash at risk of loss. These alternative investments are known as cash equivalents.

**Cash equivalents** are short-term, highly liquid investments that are (1) easily convertible into cash and (2) close enough to maturity so that their market value is relatively insensitive to interest rate changes (generally, investments with maturities of three months or less). U.S. Treasury bills, certificates of deposit (CDs), commercial paper (short-term notes issued by corporations), and money market funds are examples of cash equivalents. Because firms may differ as to exactly which investments they consider to be cash equivalents, GAAP requires that each firm disclose in the notes to the financial statements the company's policy regarding which investments are treated as cash equivalents.

When preparing a statement of cash flows, the cash and cash equivalents are added together and treated as a single amount. This is done because the purchase and sale of investments in cash equivalents are considered to be part of a firm's overall cash management strategy rather than a source or use of cash. As financial statement users evaluate a firm's cash flows, it should not matter whether the cash is on hand, deposited in a bank account, or invested in cash equivalents. Transfers back and forth between a firm's Cash account and its investments in cash equivalents, consequently, are not treated as cash inflows or outflows in the statement of cash flows.

When discussing the statement of cash flows, accountants often just use the word *cash* rather than the term *cash and cash equivalents*. We follow that practice in this chapter.

---

**ACCOUNTING IN PRACTICE** | **Definition of Cash Equivalents**

There exist some differences between firms as to just which investments of cash are considered to be cash equivalents. For example, **PepsiCo, Inc.**, the beverage and snack food company, states in the notes to its financial statements that "Cash equivalents are investments with original maturities of three months or less which we do not intend to rollover beyond three months." **International Game Technology**, a manufacturer of gaming machines and proprietory gaming software systems, on the other hand, notes that "Cash and equivalents consist primarily of deposits held at major banks and other marketable securities with original maturities of 90 days or less. The majority of our cash equivalents are in 100 percent U.S. Treasury-backed money market funds." The commonality among all firms, however, is that cash equivalents represent a temporary investment of excess cash in risk-free investments until such time as the cash is needed to support a business's operations.

---

# ACTIVITY CLASSIFICATIONS IN THE STATEMENT OF CASH FLOWS

A statement of cash flows classifies a company's cash receipts and cash payments into three major business activity categories: operating activities, investing activities, and financing activities. Grouping cash flows into these categories identifies the effect on cash of each of the major business activities of a firm (see Chapter 1). The combined effects on cash from all three categories explain the net change in cash for the period. The net change in cash is then reconciled with the beginning and ending balances of cash from the balance sheet. Exhibit 12-1 illustrates the basic format for a statement of cash flows.

---

**EXHIBIT 12-1** | **Format for the Statement of Cash Flows**

**SAMPLE COMPANY**
**Statement of Cash Flows**
**For the Year Ended December 31, 2011**

| | | |
|---|---|---|
| **Cash flow from operating activities** | | |
| (DETAILS OF CASH FLOW FROM OPERATING ACTIVITIES) . . . . . . . . . . . . . . . . . . . . . . . . . . . . . . . . . . . . . | $XXX | |
| Cash provided (used) by operating activities . . . . . . . . . . . . . . . . . . . . . . . . . . . . . . . . . . . . . . . . . . . | | $XXX |
| **Cash flow from investing activities** | | |
| (DETAILS OF INDIVIDUAL INVESTING CASH INFLOWS AND OUTFLOWS) . . . . . . . . . . . . . . . . . . . . . . . | XXX | |
| Cash provided (used) by investing activities. . . . . . . . . . . . . . . . . . . . . . . . . . . . . . . . . . . . . . . . . . . . | | XXX |
| **Cash flow from financing activities** | | |
| (DETAILS OF INDIVIDUAL FINANCING CASH INFLOWS AND OUTFLOWS) . . . . . . . . . . . . . . . . . . . . . . . | XXX | |
| Cash provided (used) by financing activities. . . . . . . . . . . . . . . . . . . . . . . . . . . . . . . . . . . . . . . . . . . | | XXX |
| Net increase (decrease) in cash. . . . . . . . . . . . . . . . . . . . . . . . . . . . . . . . . . . . . . . . . . . . . . . . . . . . . | | XXX |
| Cash at beginning of year. . . . . . . . . . . . . . . . . . . . . . . . . . . . . . . . . . . . . . . . . . . . . . . . . . . . . . . . . . | | XXX |
| Cash at end of year . . . . . . . . . . . . . . . . . . . . . . . . . . . . . . . . . . . . . . . . . . . . . . . . . . . . . . . . . . . . . . . | | $XXX |

## OPERATING ACTIVITIES

A company's income statement reflects the transactions and events that constitute its operating activities. The focus of a firm's operating activities involves selling goods or rendering services. The cash flow from **operating activities** is defined broadly enough, however, to include any cash receipts or payments that are not classified as investing activities or financing activities. For example, cash received from a lawsuit settlement and cash payments to charity are treated as cash flow from operating activities. The following are examples of cash inflows and outflows relating to a firm's operating activities:

| Cash Inflows | Cash Outflows |
|---|---|
| 1. Receipts from customers for sales of goods or services. | 1. Payments to suppliers. |
| 2. Receipts of interest and dividends. | 2. Payments to employees. |
| 3. Other receipts that are not related to investing or financing activities, such as lawsuit settlements and refunds received from suppliers. | 3. Payments of interest to creditors. |
| | 4. Payments of taxes to governmental agencies. |
| | 5. Other payments that are not related to investing or financing activities, such as contributions to charity. |

## INVESTING ACTIVITIES

A firm's **investing activities** include those transactions involving (1) the acquisition or disposal of plant assets and intangible assets, (2) the purchase or sale of stocks, bonds, and other securities (that are not cash equivalents), and (3) the lending and subsequent collection of money.[1] The related cash receipts and cash payments appear in the investing activities section of the statement of cash flows. Examples of these cash flows include:

| Cash Inflows | Cash Outflows |
|---|---|
| 1. Receipts from the sale of plant assets and intangible assets. | 1. Payments to purchase plant assets and intangible assets. |
| 2. Receipts from sales of investments in stocks, bonds, and other securities (other than cash equivalents). | 2. Payments to purchase stocks, bonds, and other securities (other than cash equivalents). |
| 3. Receipts from repayments of loans by borrowers. | 3. Payments made to lend money to borrowers. |

## FINANCING ACTIVITIES

A firm engages in **financing activities** when it obtains cash from shareholders, returns cash to shareholders, borrows from creditors, and repays amounts borrowed from creditors. Cash flows related to these events are reported in the financing activities section of the statement of cash flows. Examples of these cash flows include:

| Cash Inflows | Cash Outflows |
|---|---|
| 1. Receipts from the issuance of common stock and preferred stock and from sales of treasury stock. | 1. Payments to acquire treasury stock. |
| 2. Receipts from the issuance of bonds payable, mortgage notes payable, and other notes payable. | 2. Payments of dividends. |
| | 3. Payments to settle outstanding bonds payable, mortgage notes payable, and other notes payable. |

Observe that paying cash to settle such obligations as accounts payable, wages payable, interest payable, and income tax payable is an operating activity, not a financing activity. Also observe that cash received as interest and dividends and cash paid as interest

[1] There are exceptions to the classification of these events as investing activities. For example, the purchase or sale of mortgage loans by a mortgage banker, like Bank of America, and the purchase or sale of securities in the trading account of a broker/dealer in financial securities, like Merrill Lynch, represent operating activities for these businesses.

are classified as cash flows from operating activities, although cash paid as dividends to a company's stockholders is classified as a financing activity.

### IFRS ALERT!

Although the statement of cash flows under U.S. GAAP has three activity categories—operations, investing, and financing—this is not the case under International Financial Reporting Standards (IFRS). Under IFRS, the statement of cash flows may have either four or five activity categories: Operations, Investing, Debt Financing, Equity Financing, and sometimes a category called the Effect of Foreign Currency Translation. In essence, IFRS segments the financing activities category into two separate categories relating to financing with debt and financing with equity. The sum of these two categories is exactly equivalent to the single category of financing activities under U.S. GAAP.

### AN ILLUSTRATION OF ACTIVITY CLASSIFICATION USEFULNESS

The classification of cash flows into the three business activity categories helps financial statement users analyze and interpret a company's cash flow data. To illustrate, assume that companies D, E, and F operate in the same industry, and that each company reported a $100,000 increase in cash during the period. Information from each company's statement of cash flows is summarized below:

| | Company | | |
|---|---|---|---|
| | D | E | F |
| Cash flow from operating activities..................................... | $100,000 | $ 0 | $ 0 |
| Cash flow from investing activities: | | | |
|    Sale of plant assets............................................... | 0 | 100,000 | 0 |
| Cash flow from financing activities: | | | |
|    Issuance of notes payable ......................................... | 0 | 0 | 100,000 |
| Net increase in cash ................................................ | $100,000 | $100,000 | $100,000 |

Although each company's increase in cash was exactly the same ($100,000), the source of the cash increase varied by company. This variation affects the analysis of the cash flow data, particularly for potential creditors who must evaluate the likelihood of the repayment of funds loaned to a company. Based only on this cash flow data, a potential creditor would feel more comfortable lending money to Company D than to either Company E or F. D's cash increase came from its operating activities, whereas E's cash increase came from the sale of plant assets, a source that is unlikely to recur, and F's cash increase came from borrowed funds. Company F faces additional future uncertainty when the interest and principal payments on the existing notes become due, and for this reason, a potential creditor would be less inclined to extend additional loans to Company F.

## NONCASH INVESTING AND FINANCING ACTIVITIES

A secondary objective of the statement of cash flows is to present summary information about a firm's investing and financing activities. Although many of these activities affect cash and therefore are already included in the investing and financing sections of the statement of cash flows, some significant investing and financing events do not affect current cash flow. Examples of **noncash investing and financing activities** are the issuance of stock or bonds in exchange for plant assets or intangible assets, the exchange of long-term assets for other long-term assets, and the conversion of long-term debt into common stock. A common feature among each of these transactions is that no cash is exchanged between the parties involved in the transaction.

    Noncash investing and financing transactions generally do, however, affect future cash flows. Issuing bonds in exchange for equipment, for example, requires future cash payments for interest and principal on the bonds. On the other hand, converting bonds into common stock eliminates the future cash payments related to the bonds' interest and principal. Knowledge of these types of events, therefore, should be helpful to financial statement users who wish to evaluate a firm's future cash flows.

Information regarding noncash investing and financing transactions is disclosed in a separate accounting schedule. The separate schedule may be placed immediately below the statement of cash flows or it may be placed among the notes to the financial statements.

---

**PRINCIPLE ALERT**    **Objectivity Principle**

The *objectivity principle* asserts that the usefulness of financial statements is enhanced when the underlying data are objective and verifiable. Measuring cash and the changes in cash are among the most objective measurements that accountants make. The statement of cash flows, therefore, is the most objective financial statement required under generally accepted accounting principles. This characteristic of the statement of cash flows is welcomed by investors and creditors interested in evaluating the quality of a firm's net income and assets. Financial statement users often feel more confident about the quality of a company's net income and assets when there is a high correlation between, or relationship with, a company's cash flow from operating activities and its net income.

---

# USING THE STATEMENT OF CASH FLOWS

The Financial Accounting Standards Board believes that one of the principal objectives of financial reporting is to help financial statement users assess the amount, timing, and uncertainty of a business's future cash flows. These assessments, in turn, help users evaluate prospective future cash receipts from their investments in, or loans to, a business. Although the statement of cash flows describes a company's past cash flows, the statement is also useful for assessing future cash flows since the recent past is often a very good predictor of the future.

A statement of cash flows shows the cash effects of a firm's operating, investing, and financing activities. Distinguishing among these different categories of cash flow helps financial statement users compare, evaluate, and predict a business's future cash flows. With cash flow information, creditors and investors are better able to assess a company's ability to repay its liabilities and pay dividends. A firm's need for outside financing can also be evaluated using the statement of cash flows. Further, the statement enables users to observe and analyze management's investing and financing policies, plans, and strategies.

A statement of cash flows also provides information useful in evaluating a firm's financial flexibility. **Financial flexibility** is a company's ability to generate sufficient amounts of cash to respond to unanticipated needs and opportunities. Information about past cash flows, particularly the cash flow from operations, helps in assessing financial flexibility. An evaluation of a firm's ability to survive an unexpected drop in demand for its goods and services, for example, may include a review of its past cash flow from operations. The larger these past cash flows, the greater will be a firm's ability to withstand adverse changes in future economic conditions.

Some investors and creditors find the statement of cash flows useful in evaluating the "quality" of a firm's net income. As we saw in Chapter 2, determining net income under the accrual basis of accounting requires many accruals, deferrals, allocations, and valuations. These adjustment and measurement procedures introduce greater subjectivity into a company's income determination than some financial statement users are comfortable with. Consequently, these users can relate a more objective performance measure—a firm's cash flow from operations—to net income. To these users, the higher the relationship between a company's net income and the cash flow from operations, the higher is the quality of the firm's net income.

# CASH FLOW FROM OPERATING ACTIVITIES

The first section of the statement of cash flows presents a firm's cash flow from operating activities. *Two alternative formats are available to present the cash flow from operating activities: the indirect method and the direct method. Both methods report the same amount of cash flow from operating activities and differ only in how the cash flow from operating activities is presented.*

The **indirect method** starts with net income using the accrual basis of accounting and applies a series of adjustments to convert it to net income under the cash basis of accounting, which is equivalent to the cash flow from operating activities. The adjustments to net income do not represent specific cash flows; consequently, the indirect method does not report any detail concerning individual operating cash inflows and outflows. The process of converting a company's accrual-basis net income to its cash-basis cash flow from operating activities is illustrated below:

By way of contrast, the **direct method** shows individual amounts of cash inflows and cash outflows for the major operating activities. The net difference between these inflows and outflows is the cash flow from operating activities.

*The Financial Accounting Standards Board encourages companies to use the direct method but permits the use of the indirect method.* Despite the FASB's preference for the direct method, *more than 95 percent of companies preparing the statement of cash flows use the indirect method.* The indirect method is popular because (1) it is easier and less expensive to prepare than the direct method and (2) the direct method requires a supplemental disclosure showing the indirect method.

---

**ACCOUNTING IN PRACTICE**  **The Method for Reporting the Cash Flow From Operations**

Do you think a direct approach in communicating with financial statement users is best, or should your approach be more indirect? When it comes to reporting the cash flow from operations, companies appear to favor the indirect approach by a wide margin as evidenced by the responses to a survey of 600 large U.S. companies.

Source: Accounting Trends and Techniques

---

The remainder of this chapter discusses the preparation of the statement of cash flows. *The indirect method is discussed first, followed by the direct method. These discussions are independent of each other; either one provides complete coverage of the preparation of the statement of cash flows.*

---

**ACCOUNTING IN PRACTICE** **A Comparison of Accrual-Basis and Cash-Basis Amounts**

Accountants calculate net income on the income statement using the accrual basis of accounting. The cash flow from operating activities, presented on the statement of cash flows, represents a company's net income using the cash basis of accounting. There is no necessary relationship between the two numbers. Compared with net income, the cash flow from operating activities may be larger, smaller, or about the same amount. Financial data from annual reports of three well-known companies—Chiquita Brands, Levi Strauss, and Harley-Davidson—bear this out.

| | Net Income or (Loss) | Cash Flow Provided (Used) by Operating Activities |
|---|---|---|
| Chiquita Brands Intl. . . . . . . . . . . . . . . . . . . . . | $(323,725,000) | $ 8,204,000 |
| Levi Strauss & Co. . . . . . . . . . . . . . . . . . . . . . . | $ 229,285,000 | $ 224,809,000 |
| Harley-Davidson Inc. . . . . . . . . . . . . . . . . . . . | $ 654,718,000 | $(684,649,000) |

---

**Your Turn!** **12.1**

Classify each of the cash flow events listed below as either an (1) operating activity, (2) investing activity, or (3) financing activity:

1. Cash received from customers
2. Cash sale of land
3. Cash paid to suppliers
4. Cash purchase of equipment
5. Payment on note payable
6. Cash dividend payment
7. Cash wages paid
8. Purchase of treasury stock
9. Cash sale of investments

The solution is on page 550.

# PREPARING THE STATEMENT OF CASH FLOWS USING THE INDIRECT METHOD

**LEARNING OBJECTIVE 2**

**Explain** the preparation of a statement of cash flows using the indirect method.

To prepare a statement of cash flows using the indirect method, the following information is needed: a company's income statement, comparative balance sheets, and possibly additional data taken from the company's financial statements. Exhibit 12-2 presents this information for the Bennett Company. We will use this data to prepare Bennett's 2011 statement of cash flows using the indirect method. As will be seen shortly, Bennett's statement of cash flows will explain the $25,000 increase in the company's cash account that occurred during 2011 (from $10,000 at the beginning of the year to $35,000 at the end of the year) by classifying the firm's cash inflows and outflows into the three business activity categories of operating, investing, and financing.

To see that the statement of cash flows can be prepared using only a company's income statement and the changes in its balance sheet accounts, consider again the balance sheet equation that was first introduced in Chapter 1:

$$\text{Assets (A)} = \text{Liabilities (L)} + \text{Stockholders' equity (SE)} \qquad (1)$$

Separating a firm's assets into its cash (CA) and noncash assets (NCA) gives:

$$\text{CA} + \text{NCA} = \text{L} + \text{SE} \qquad (2)$$

**EXHIBIT 12-2** Financial Data of Bennett Company

| BENNETT COMPANY Income Statement For the Year Ended December 31, 2011 | | |
|---|---|---|
| Sales revenue | | $250,000 |
| Cost of goods sold | $148,000 | |
| Wages expense | 52,000 | |
| Insurance expense | 5,000 | |
| Depreciation expense | 10,000 | |
| Income tax expense | 11,000 | |
| Gain on sale of plant assets | (8,000) | 218,000 |
| Net income | | $ 32,000 |

**Additional Data for 2011**
1. Sold plant assets costing $20,000 for $28,000 cash.
2. Declared and paid cash dividends of $13,000.

| BENNETT COMPANY Balance Sheets | Dec. 31, 2011 | Dec. 31, 2010 |
|---|---|---|
| **Assets** | | |
| Cash ........................... | $ 35,000 | $ 10,000 |
| Accounts receivable ............ | 39,000 | 34,000 |
| Inventory ..................... | 54,000 | 60,000 |
| Prepaid insurance .............. | 17,000 | 4,000 |
| Long-term investments......... | 15,000 | — |
| Plant assets .................... | 180,000 | 200,000 |
| Accumulated depreciation...... | (50,000) | (40,000) |
| Patent......................... | 60,000 | — |
| Total assets.................... | $350,000 | $268,000 |
| **Liabilities and Stockholders' Equity** | | |
| Accounts payable .............. | $ 10,000 | $ 19,000 |
| Income tax payable............. | 5,000 | 3,000 |
| Common stock ................. | 260,000 | 190,000 |
| Retained earnings ............. | 75,000 | 56,000 |
| Total Liabilities and Stockholders' Equity.......... | $350,000 | $268,000 |

And, rewriting the balance sheet equation in changes form yields:

$$\Delta CA + \Delta NCA = \Delta L + \Delta SE \qquad (3)$$

Finally, rearranging the components of the equation shows that the change in cash (which is the end result of the statement of cash flows) can be computed from the change in all of the other balance sheet accounts:

$$\Delta CA = \Delta L - \Delta NCA + \Delta SE \qquad (4)$$

**IFRS ALERT!**

Currently, both U.S. GAAP and IFRS permit a company to present its statement of cash flows using either the direct method or the indirect method. A topic being considered by the FASB/IASB convergence project would limit the preparation of the statement of cash flows to just the direct method. The direct method is currently preferred by both the FASB and the IASB, although most U.S. firms present their statement of cash flows using the indirect method.

## FIVE STEPS TO PREPARING A STATEMENT OF CASH FLOWS

The process to prepare a statement of cash flows using the indirect method involves five steps. The approach begins by focusing initially only on the balance sheet and then proceeds to integrate a business's income statement through a series of systematic adjustments to a preliminary statement of cash flows derived solely from balance sheet data.

### Step One

Using just the beginning and ending balance sheets (see Columns 1 and 2 in Exhibit 12-3), calculate the change in each balance sheet account by subtracting the beginning balance sheet amount from the ending amount. The results of this step for the Bennett Company are presented in Column 3 of Exhibit 12-3. To simplify this step, the change in the Plant Assets account is combined with the Accumulated Depreciation account—that is, the change in the Plant Assets account is calculated on a net of accumulated depreciation basis.

**EXHIBIT 12-3    Preparing a Statement of Cash Flows: The Indirect Method**

**BENNETT COMPANY**
**Balance Sheet**
**2011**

|  | (1) Beginning of Year | (2) End of Year | (3) Change for Year | (4) Cash Flow Classification |
|---|---|---|---|---|
| **Assets** | | | | |
| Cash .......................................... | $ 10,000 | $ 35,000 | **$25,000** | **Cash flow** |
| Accounts receivable ............................. | 34,000 | 39,000 | 5,000 | Operating |
| Inventory ...................................... | 60,000 | 54,000 | (6,000) | Operating |
| Prepaid insurance .............................. | 4,000 | 17,000 | 13,000 | Operating |
| Long-term investments........................... | 0 | 15,000 | 15,000 | Investing |
| Plant assets (net) ............................... | 160,000 | 130,000 | (30,000) | Investing/Operating |
| Patent......................................... | 0 | 60,000 | 60,000 | Investing/Operating |
| Total assets.................................... | $268,000 | $350,000 | $82,000 | |
| **Liabilities and Stockholders' Equity** | | | | |
| Accounts payable .............................. | $ 19,000 | $ 10,000 | $ (9,000) | Operating |
| Income tax payable............................. | 3,000 | 5,000 | 2,000 | Operating |
| Common stock................................. | 190,000 | 260,000 | 70,000 | Financing |
| Retained earnings .............................. | 56,000 | 75,000 | 19,000 | Operating/Financing |
| Total Liabilities and Stockholders' Equity ........... | $268,000 | $350,000 | $82,000 | |

To verify the accuracy of the Step One calculations, simply compare the sum of the changes in the asset accounts ($82,000) with the sum of the changes in the liability and stockholders' equity accounts ($82,000). These totals must be equal. If the totals are not equal, it indicates the presence of a subtraction error that must be identified and corrected before progressing to Step Two.

An important figure identified during Step One is the "bottom line" of the statement of cash flows, namely the change in the cash account. The highlighted area in Exhibit 12-3 reveals that the cash account of the Bennett Company increased by $25,000 from the beginning of the year to the end of the year. Hence, all of the various cash inflows and outflows for the company must aggregate to this figure.

## Step Two

Identify the appropriate business activity category—operating, investing, or financing—for each balance sheet account. The cash flow activity classifications are presented in Column 4 of Exhibit 12-3.

Although measuring the change in the balance sheet accounts in Step 1 is a straightforward arithmetic activity, there can be some confusion over the correct activity classification for some of the balance sheet accounts in Step 2. The change in accounts receivable, inventory, prepaid insurance, accounts payable, and income tax payable are all easily identified as operating activities because they are associated with the day-to-day operations of a business. The change in common stock, on the other hand, is clearly a financing activity because it is associated with raising capital to finance a business. The change in net plant assets, however, can be both an investing activity and an operating activity. Purchases and sales of plant assets are associated with the capital investment needed to run a business, and thus are an investing activity; but, the depreciation expense associated with plant assets is an operating activity since the depreciation of plant assets is deducted as an expense in the calculation of a company's net income. Similarly, the change in intangible assets such as patents can be both an investing activity and an operating activity because the acquisition or sale of intangibles is an investing activity, whereas the amortization of intangibles is an expense deducted in the calculation of net income, and hence, an operating activity. Finally, the change in retained earnings can be both an operating activity and a financing activity because retained earnings is increased by net income, an operating activity, but decreased by the payment of dividends, a financing activity.

As a general rule, the following cash flow activity classifications apply, although exceptions exist:

| Balance Sheet Account | Cash Flow Activity Category |
| --- | --- |
| Current assets | Operating |
| Noncurrent assets | Investing/Operating |
| Current liabilities | Operating |
| Noncurrent liabilities | Financing |
| Capital stock | Financing |
| Retained earnings | Operating/Financing |

Examples of exceptions to the above cash flow activity classifications include the following:

- Marketable securities, a current asset, are an investing activity item.
- Current maturities of long-term debt, a current liability, are a financing activity item.
- Employee pension obligations, a noncurrent liability, are an operating activity item.

### Step Three

Having completed Steps One and Two, you are now ready to build a preliminary statement of cash flows using the calculated increases or decreases in the various balance sheet accounts from Step One and the identified activity classifications from Step Two. The preliminary statement of cash flows for the Bennett Company using the change values from Column 3 of Exhibit 12-3 and the cash flow activity classifications from Column 4 is presented in Exhibit 12-4.

| **EXHIBIT 12-4** An Illustration of a Preliminary Statement of Cash Flows: The Indirect Method | |
| --- | --- |
| **BENNETT COMPANY**<br>**Preliminary Statement of Cash Flows**<br>**For the Year Ended December 31, 2011** | |
| Operating activities | |
| Retained earnings | $19,000 |
| Accounts receivable | (5,000) |
| Inventory | 6,000 |
| Prepaid insurance | (13,000) |
| Accounts payable | (9,000) |
| Income tax payable | 2,000 |
| Cash flow from operating activities | 0 |
| Investing activities | |
| Long-term investments | (15,000) |
| Plant assets (net) | 30,000 |
| Patent | (60,000) |
| Cash flow for investing activities | (45,000) |
| Financing activities | |
| Common stock | 70,000 |
| Cash flow from financing activities | 70,000 |
| Change in cash (from the balance sheet) | $25,000 |

Because a statement of cash flows measures the inflows and outflows of cash for a business, it is important to note that the sign of the asset account changes calculated in Step One must be reversed for purposes of preparing the preliminary statement of cash flows in Exhibit 12-4. This can be seen in equation (4) above in which the change in noncash assets has a negative sign. For instance, Exhibit 12-4 shows that the change in accounts receivable was an increase of $5,000, whereas the change in inventory was a decrease of $6,000. When preparing the indirect method statement of cash flows, a $5,000 increase in accounts receivable represents a subtraction from net income (a cash outflow), and a decline in inventory of $6,000 represents an addition to net income (a cash inflow), to arrive at the cash flow from operations. To illustrate why an increase in accounts receivable must be subtracted from net income to arrive at operating cash flow, consider how sales revenue is initially recorded. Assume that a $2,000 sale of goods is paid for with $1,200 in cash and the remaining amount recorded as an increase in accounts receivable. In this example, net income increases by $2,000, but cash is increased by only $1,200. Therefore, net income must be reduced by the $800 increase in accounts receivable in order to yield the correct cash flow from operations. Hence, when preparing the preliminary statement of cash flows in Step Three, it is important to remember to reverse the sign of the change values for the asset accounts. This is unnecessary for the liability and stockholders' equity accounts as can also be seen from equation (4) above.

Exhibit 12-4 presents the preliminary statement of cash flows for the Bennett Company. This preliminary statement suggests that the firm's cash flow from operating activities was $0, the cash flow from investing activities was negative $45,000, and the cash flow from financing activities was $70,000. As required, the cash inflows and outflows aggregate to the change in cash from the balance sheet, an increase of $25,000.

## Step Four

To this point we have used the balance sheet exclusively to provide the needed inputs to our statement of cash flows. For most businesses, however, cash flow will also be generated by a firm's ongoing operations. Hence, it is now appropriate to introduce the operations related data found on the company's income statement (see Exhibit 12-2).

In this step, we accomplish two important actions involving the preliminary statement of cash flows in Exhibit 12-4. First, the change in retained earnings from the balance sheet will be replaced by net income from the income statement. For the Bennett Company, the change in retained earnings of $19,000 does not equal net income of $32,000. The difference of $13,000 ($32,000 − $19,000) represents a cash dividend paid to Bennett's shareholders. Thus, when we replace retained earnings of $19,000 with net income of $32,000, it is also necessary to report the $13,000 cash dividend payment as a cash outflow under the financing activities section in Exhibit 12-5. Increasing the cash flow from operations and decreasing the cash flow from financing activities by an equivalent amount ($13,000) allows the statement of cash flows to remain in balance with the net change in cash of $25,000.

Second, we adjust the Bennett Company's net income for any **noncash expenses** such as the depreciation of plant assets and the amortization of intangibles that were deducted in the process of calculating the firm's accrual basis net income.[2] These noncash expenses must be added back to net income in the operating activities section to correctly measure the firm's operating cash flow. However, to keep the preliminary statement of cash flows in balance with an increase in cash of $25,000, it is also necessary to subtract equivalent amounts in the investing activities section.

To summarize, the adjustments to the Bennett Company's preliminary statement of cash flows in Exhibit 12-4 are:

1. Net income of $32,000 replaces the change in retained earnings of $19,000 in the operating activities section. This action adds $13,000 to the cash flow from operating activities. To keep the statement of cash flows in balance with the change in cash of $25,000, it is necessary to subtract $13,000 elsewhere on the statement. Since retained earnings is calculated as follows:

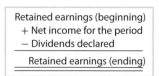

```
Retained earnings (beginning)
 + Net income for the period
 − Dividends declared
 Retained earnings (ending)
```

the outflow of $13,000 is also reflected as a cash dividend to shareholders under the financing activities section.

---

[2] Depreciation expense and amortization expense are called noncash expenses because these expenses do not involve any current period cash outflow. Depreciation expense, for example, represents the allocation of the purchase price of plant assets over the many periods that these assets produce sales revenue for a business. The matching principle requires that the cost of plant assets be matched with the sales revenue produced by these assets, and this is accomplished on the income statement by the deduction of the periodic depreciation charge.

2. Depreciation expense of $10,000, a noncash deduction from net income, is added back to net income to avoid understating the cash flow from operations. However, to keep the statement of cash flows in balance with the change in cash of $25,000, a similar amount is subtracted from plant assets under the investing activities section.

The results of these adjustments are displayed in Exhibit 12-5, which presents the final statement of cash flows for Bennett. Note that the company's statement of cash flows remains in balance with the change in cash of $25,000 after the two adjustments. This result is possible because whatever amount was added to (or subtracted from) net income under the cash flow from operating activities, an equivalent amount was subtracted from (or added to) the investing activities or the financing activities.

**EXHIBIT 12-5** | Statement of Cash Flows—The Indirect Method

**BENNETT COMPANY**
**Statement of Cash Flows**
**For the Year Ended December 31, 2011**

| | | |
|---|---|---|
| **Cash flow from operating activities** | | |
| Net income | $32,000 | |
| Add (deduct) items to convert net income to cash basis | | |
| Depreciation | 10,000 | |
| Gain on sale of plant assets | (8,000) | |
| Accounts receivable increase | (5,000) | |
| Inventory decrease | 6,000 | |
| Prepaid insurance increase | (13,000) | |
| Accounts payable decrease | (9,000) | |
| Income tax payable increase | 2,000 | |
| Cash provided by operating activities | | $15,000 |
| **Cash flow from investing activities** | | |
| Purchase of long-term investments | (15,000) | |
| Sale of plant assets | 28,000 | |
| Purchase of patent | (60,000) | |
| Cash used by investing activities | | (47,000) |
| **Cash flow from financing activities** | | |
| Issuance of common stock | 70,000 | |
| Payment of dividends | (13,000) | |
| Cash provided by financing activities | | 57,000 |
| Net increase in cash | | 25,000 |
| Cash at beginning of year | | 10,000 |
| Cash at end of year | | $35,000 |

**Step Five**

To provide the most useful cash flow data, a final step is required: Make any appropriate adjustments to the operating activities section to calculate a company's operating cash flow. As noted above, a firm's operating cash flow should include only the cash flows from operating activities. Consequently, to calculate the cash flow from operating activities of a business, it is necessary to review a company's income statement to identify and remove the financial effects of any nonoperating transactions included in net income.[3]

To illustrate this point, note that the Bennett Company sold plant assets during the year at a gain of $8,000 ($28,000 sales price less $20,000 cost). This event is an investing activity and therefore properly belongs under the investing activities. To correctly assess Bennett's operating cash flow, it is necessary to remove this gain from the operating activity section and to add it to plant assets under the investing activities section. These actions allow us to correctly measure Bennett's cash flow from operating activities, as well as its cash flow from plant assets.

Exhibit 12-5 presents the final statement of cash flows for Bennett Company and includes not only the adjustments from Step Four, but also the adjustment to remove any nonoperating

[3] An exception is interest expense, which most investment professionals view as a financing activity. Regardless, interest payments are required to be included in the cash flow from operations activities.

gains and losses from the cash flow from operating activities (Step 5). Bennett's statement of cash flows in Exhibit 12-5, using the indirect method, reveals that the cash flow from operating activities is $15,000, the cash flow used for investing activities is negative $47,000, and the cash flow provided by financing activities is $57,000. The resulting cash flow of $25,000 exactly equals the increase in cash on the balance sheet of $25,000, as required.

The following illustration summarizes the five-step process to prepare an indirect method statement of cash flows:

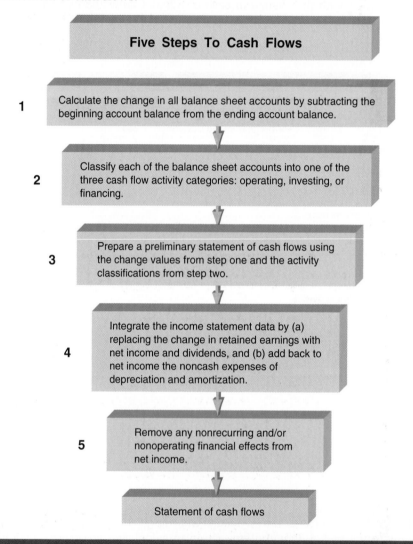

**Five Steps To Cash Flows**

1  Calculate the change in all balance sheet accounts by subtracting the beginning account balance from the ending account balance.

2  Classify each of the balance sheet accounts into one of the three cash flow activity categories: operating, investing, or financing.

3  Prepare a preliminary statement of cash flows using the change values from step one and the activity classifications from step two.

4  Integrate the income statement data by (a) replacing the change in retained earnings with net income and dividends, and (b) add back to net income the noncash expenses of depreciation and amortization.

5  Remove any nonrecurring and/or nonoperating financial effects from net income.

Statement of cash flows

---

## CORPORATE SOCIAL RESPONSIBILITY

According to **Home Depot**, "Our values are our beliefs, principles and standards that do not change over time. Values are the resources we draw on when asked to make decisions. They form the groundwork for our ethical behavior. All that we do at The Home Depot must be consistent with the values of the Company. We believe in *Doing the Right Thing*, having *Respect for all People*, building *Strong Relationships*, *Taking Care of Our People*, *Giving Back*, providing *Excellent Customer Service*, *Encouraging Entrepreneurial Spirit* and providing strong *Shareholder Returns*."

Home Depot believes that "Doing the Right Thing" leads to doing well for all its stakeholders, including its shareholders. As Home Depot states, "We will conduct our business and ourselves in a way that enhances and preserves the reputation of the Company while providing our shareholders with a fair return on their investment." There seems to be a lot of truth in this as Home Depot has managed to stay profitable even as the poor U.S. economy has battered the construction industry. In fiscal years 2008 and 2007, during the height of the construction downturn, the company managed to produce cash flows from operating activities each year in excess of $5 billion.

### Your Turn! 12.2

Husky Company's 2011 income statement and comparative balance sheets as of December 31 of 2011 and 2010 are shown below:

| HUSKY COMPANY | | |
|---|---|---|
| Income Statement | | |
| For the Year Ended December 31, 2011 | | |
| Sales revenue | | $1,270,000 |
| Cost of goods sold | $860,000 | |
| Wages expense | 172,000 | |
| Insurance expense | 16,000 | |
| Depreciation expense | 34,000 | |
| Interest expense | 18,000 | |
| Income tax expense | 58,000 | 1,158,000 |
| Net income | | $ 112,000 |

| HUSKY COMPANY | | |
|---|---|---|
| Balance Sheets | | |
| | Dec. 31, 2011 | Dec. 31, 2010 |
| **Assets** | | |
| Cash | $ 22,000 | $ 10,000 |
| Accounts receivable | 82,000 | 64,000 |
| Inventory | 180,000 | 120,000 |
| Prepaid insurance | 10,000 | 14,000 |
| Plant assets | 500,000 | 390,000 |
| Accumulated depreciation | (136,000) | (102,000) |
| Total assets | $658,000 | $496,000 |
| **Liabilities and Stockholders' Equity** | | |
| Accounts payable | $ 14,000 | $ 20,000 |
| Wages payable | 18,000 | 12,000 |
| Income tax payable | 14,000 | 16,000 |
| Bonds payable | 260,000 | 150,000 |
| Common stock | 180,000 | 180,000 |
| Retained earnings | 172,000 | 118,000 |
| Total Liabilities and Stockholders' Equity | $658,000 | $496,000 |

Cash dividends of $58,000 were declared and paid during 2011. Plant assets were purchased for cash, and bonds payable were issued for cash. Accounts payable relate to merchandise purchases.

**Required**

Prepare a 2011 statement of cash flows for the Husky Company using the indirect method.

The solution is on page 589.

## PREPARING THE STATEMENT OF CASH FLOWS UNDER THE DIRECT METHOD

Although it is quite straightforward to create a direct method statement of cash flows given access to a company's internal accounting records, such access is rarely available to anyone except a company's management team. All that is necessary is to pull the numbers directly off the Cash general ledger account and place them in the appropriate section of the statement of cash flows. This is why, in fact, the direct method is referred to as "direct." The cash flow from operations is taken directly from the

**LEARNING OBJECTIVE 3**

**Explain** the preparation of a statement of cash flows using the direct method.

company's general ledger, rather than being indirectly computed from net income. Unfortunately, investment professionals, lenders, and stockholders rarely have access to such proprietary internal data. Thus, it is necessary to be able to create direct method cash flow information using only such publicly available data as the indirect method statement of cash flows.

The process to convert an indirect method statement of cash flows to the direct method requires two steps. First, replace net income (the first line item under the operating activities section of the indirect method statement format) with the line items appearing on a firm's income statement. For instance, Bennett Company's income statement in Exhibit 12-2 contains the following line items:

| | |
|---|---:|
| Sales revenue | $250,000 |
| Cost of goods sold | (148,000) |
| Wages expense | (52,000) |
| Insurance expense | (5,000) |
| Depreciation expense | (10,000) |
| Income tax expense | (11,000) |
| Gain on sale of plant assets | 8,000 |
| Net income | $ 32,000 |

Thus, for the Bennett Company, we begin by replacing the net income of $32,000 under the operating activities section in Exhibit 12-5 with the seven income statement line items shown above, which aggregate to $32,000.

The second step involves adjusting the income statement line items identified in Step One with the remaining line items from the operating activities section of the indirect method statement of cash flows. Exhibit 12-6 summarizes the procedures for converting individual income statement items to the corresponding cash flows from operating activities.

**EXHIBIT 12-6   Direct Method Conversion Schedule: Adjustments to Convert Income Statement Items to Operating Activity Cash Flows**

Using Bennett Company's data in Exhibit 12-5, those adjustments would appear as follows:

| Income Statement Line Items | Operating Activities Line Items | Direct Method Cash Flow |
|---|---|---|
| Sales Revenue......... $250,000 | Less $5,000 accounts receivable | Cash received from<br>customers ................ $245,000 |
| Cost of goods sold..... (148,000) | Add $6,000 inventory<br>Less $9,000 accounts payable | Cash paid for merchandise.... (151,000) |
| Wage expense........ (52,000) | | Cash paid to employees ...... (52,000) |
| Insurance expense..... (5,000) | Less $13,000 prepaid insurance | Cash paid for insurance....... (18,000) |
| Depreciation expense . (10,000) | Add $10,000 depreciation | |
| Income tax expense ... (11,000) | Add $2,000 income tax payable | Cash paid for income taxes ... (9,000) |
| Gain on sale of plant<br>assets.............. 8,000 | Less $8,000 gain on sale of<br>plant assets | |
| Net income........... $ 32,000 | | Cash flow from operations .... $ 15,000 |

Exhibit 12-7 presents the Bennett Company's direct method statement of cash flows after undertaking the above two steps. As expected, the direct method cash flow from operating activities of $15,000 is exactly equivalent to the indirect method result of $15,000 as reported in Exhibit 12-5. Note that the cash flow from investing activities and the cash flow from financing activities are exactly the same in both Exhibit 12-5 and Exhibit 12-7. The only difference between the two exhibits is the manner in which the cash flow from operating activities is calculated. In Exhibit 12-5, the cash flow from operating activities is calculated by beginning with net income and then adjusting for various noncash expenses (depreciation expense) and nonoperating transactions (gain on sale of plant assets), as well as adjusting for the changes in the various working capital accounts (accounts receivable, inventory, prepaid insurance, accounts payable, and taxes payable). In Exhibit 12-7, net income is replaced with the income statement line items and the noncash expenses and working capital adjustments are disaggregated to the individual line items. But in each case, the operating cash flow of $15,000 remains the same.

| EXHIBIT 12-7 | Statement of Cash Flows under the Direct Method |
|---|---|

**BENNETT COMPANY**
**Statement of Cash Flows**
**For the Year Ended December 31, 2011**

| | | |
|---|---:|---:|
| **Cash flow from operating activities** | | |
| Cash received from customers ................................................... | | $245,000 |
| Cash paid for merchandise purchased............................................ | $(151,000) | |
| Cash paid to employees ....................................................... | (52,000) | |
| Cash paid for insurance....................................................... | (18,000) | |
| Cash paid for income taxes ................................................... | (9,000) | (230,000) |
|    Cash provided by operating activities.......................................... | | 15,000 |
| **Cash flow from investing activities** | | |
| Purchase of long-term investments ............................................. | (15,000) | |
| Sale of plant assets .......................................................... | 28,000 | |
| Purchase of patent ........................................................... | (60,000) | |
|    Cash used by investing activities............................................. | | (47,000) |
| **Cash flow from financing activities** | | |
| Issuance of common stock...................................................... | 70,000 | |
| Payment of dividends ......................................................... | (13,000) | |
|    Cash provided by financing activities ......................................... | | 57,000 |
| Net increase in cash ......................................................... | | 25,000 |
| Cash at beginning of year...................................................... | | 10,000 |
| Cash at end of year .......................................................... | | $ 35,000 |

**Your Turn!**                                                **12.3**

Husky Company's 2011 income statement and comparative balance sheets as of December 31 of 2011 and 2010 are shown below:

**HUSKY COMPANY**
**Income Statement**
**For the Year Ended December 31, 2011**

| | | |
|---|---|---|
| Sales revenue . . . . . . . . . . . . . . . . . . . . . . . . . . . . . . . . . . . . . . . . . . . . . . . . . . . . . | | $1,270,000 |
| Cost of goods sold. . . . . . . . . . . . . . . . . . . . . . . . . . . . . . . . . . . . . . . . . . . . . . | $860,000 | |
| Wages expense. . . . . . . . . . . . . . . . . . . . . . . . . . . . . . . . . . . . . . . . . . . . . . . . . | 172,000 | |
| Insurance expense. . . . . . . . . . . . . . . . . . . . . . . . . . . . . . . . . . . . . . . . . . . . . . | 16,000 | |
| Depreciation expense . . . . . . . . . . . . . . . . . . . . . . . . . . . . . . . . . . . . . . . . . . | 34,000 | |
| Interest expense. . . . . . . . . . . . . . . . . . . . . . . . . . . . . . . . . . . . . . . . . . . . . . . . | 18,000 | |
| Income tax expense . . . . . . . . . . . . . . . . . . . . . . . . . . . . . . . . . . . . . . . . . . . . | 58,000 | 1,158,000 |
| Net income. . . . . . . . . . . . . . . . . . . . . . . . . . . . . . . . . . . . . . . . . . . . . . . . . . . . | | $  112,000 |

**HUSKY COMPANY**
**Balance Sheets**

| | Dec. 31, 2011 | Dec. 31, 2010 |
|---|---|---|
| **Assets** | | |
| Cash . . . . . . . . . . . . . . . . . . . . . . . . . . . . . . . . . . . . . . . . . . . . . . . . . . . . . . . . . . | $  22,000 | $  10,000 |
| Accounts receivable . . . . . . . . . . . . . . . . . . . . . . . . . . . . . . . . . . . . . . . . . . | 82,000 | 64,000 |
| Inventory . . . . . . . . . . . . . . . . . . . . . . . . . . . . . . . . . . . . . . . . . . . . . . . . . . . . | 180,000 | 120,000 |
| Prepaid insurance . . . . . . . . . . . . . . . . . . . . . . . . . . . . . . . . . . . . . . . . . . . . | 10,000 | 14,000 |
| Plant assets . . . . . . . . . . . . . . . . . . . . . . . . . . . . . . . . . . . . . . . . . . . . . . . . . . | 500,000 | 390,000 |
| Accumulated depreciation. . . . . . . . . . . . . . . . . . . . . . . . . . . . . . . . . . . . . | (136,000) | (102,000) |
| Total assets. . . . . . . . . . . . . . . . . . . . . . . . . . . . . . . . . . . . . . . . . . . . . . . . . . | $658,000 | $496,000 |
| **Liabilities and Stockholders' Equity** | | |
| Accounts payable . . . . . . . . . . . . . . . . . . . . . . . . . . . . . . . . . . . . . . . . . . . . | $  14,000 | $  20,000 |
| Wages payable . . . . . . . . . . . . . . . . . . . . . . . . . . . . . . . . . . . . . . . . . . . . . . . | 18,000 | 12,000 |
| Income tax payable. . . . . . . . . . . . . . . . . . . . . . . . . . . . . . . . . . . . . . . . . . . | 14,000 | 16,000 |
| Bonds payable . . . . . . . . . . . . . . . . . . . . . . . . . . . . . . . . . . . . . . . . . . . . . . . | 260,000 | 150,000 |
| Common stock . . . . . . . . . . . . . . . . . . . . . . . . . . . . . . . . . . . . . . . . . . . . . . . | 180,000 | 180,000 |
| Retained earnings . . . . . . . . . . . . . . . . . . . . . . . . . . . . . . . . . . . . . . . . . . . . | 172,000 | 118,000 |
| Total Liabilities and Stockholders' Equity . . . . . . . . . . . . . . . . . . . . . . . . | $658,000 | $496,000 |

Cash dividends of $58,000 were declared and paid during 2011. Plant assets were purchased for cash, and bonds payable were issued for cash. Bond interest is paid semiannually on June 30 and December 31. Accounts payable relate to merchandise purchases.

**Required**
Prepare a 2011 statement of cash flows using the direct method.

**The solution is on page 589.**

# ANALYZING CASH FLOWS

Data from the statement of cash flows are often used to calculate financial measures to evaluate a company's cash flow health. Three such measures include a company's free cash flow, the operating cash flow to current liabilities ratio, and the operating cash flow to capital expenditures ratio.

## FREE CASH FLOW

**Free cash flow (FCF)** is often used by investment professionals and investors to evaluate a company's cash-flow strength. FCF is an important performance reference point for investment professionals because it is less subject to the accounting trickery that often characterizes accrual basis net income. Free cash flow is calculated as follows:

$$\text{FCF} = \text{Cash flow from operating activities} - \text{Capital expenditures}$$

As discussed in Chapter 9, capital expenditures refer to the required reinvestment in a business's plant and intangible assets necessary to enable a firm to remain a going concern. A firm with strong free cash flow will carry a higher stock value than one with weak (or no) free cash flow.

| Concept ⟶ | Method ⟶ | Assessment | |
|---|---|---|---|
| Does a company generate cash flows in excess of its capital expenditure needs? | Statement of cash flows.<br><br>FCF = Cash flow from operating activities − Capital expenditures | The higher the free cash flow, the greater is a company's ability to generate cash for needs other than capital expenditures. | TAKEAWAY 12.1 |

## OPERATING-CASH-FLOW-TO-CURRENT-LIABILITIES RATIO

Two measures previously introduced—the current ratio and the quick ratio—emphasize the relationship of a company's current or quick assets to its current liabilities in an attempt to measure the ability of a firm to pay its current liabilities. The **operating-cash-flow-to-current-liabilities ratio** is another measure of a company's ability to pay its current liabilities. While the current and quick ratios focus on a firm's ability to pay liabilities using existing current or quick assets, the operating cash flow to current liabilities highlights a firm's ability to pay its current liabilities using its operating cash flow. The ratio is calculated as follows:

$$\text{Operating-cash-flow-to-current-liabilities ratio} = \frac{\text{Cash flow from operating activities}}{\text{Average current liabilities}}$$

The cash flow from operating activities is obtained from the statement of cash flows. The denominator is the average of the beginning and ending current liabilities for the year.

The following amounts (in thousands of dollars) were taken from the financial statements of the **Gannett Co., Inc.,** a diversified news and information company that publishes *USA Today:*

| | |
|---|---|
| Cash flow from operating activities...................................................... | $1,017,186,000 |
| Current liabilities at beginning of the year................................................... | 962,163,000 |
| Current liabilities at end of the year ..................................................... | 1,153,141,000 |

The operating cash flow to current liabilities ratio for the Gannett Co. is calculated as follows:

$$\frac{\$1,017,186,000}{\left[\frac{(\$962,163,000 + \$1,153,141,000)}{2}\right]} = 0.96$$

The higher this ratio, the greater is a firm's ability to pay current liabilities using its operating cash flow. A ratio of 0.5 is considered a strong ratio; consequently, Gannett's ratio of 0.96 would be interpreted as very strong. A ratio of 0.96 indicates that Gannett generates $0.96 of operating cash flow for every dollar of current liabilities.

| Concept ⟶ | Method ⟶ | Assessment | |
|---|---|---|---|
| Will a company have sufficient cash to pay its current liabilities as they become due? | Statement of cash flows and balance sheet.<br><br>Operating-cash-flow-to-current-liabilities ratio = $\frac{\text{Cash flow from operating activities}}{\text{Average current liabilities}}$ | The higher the ratio, the higher the probability that a company will have sufficient operating cash flow to pay its current liabilities as they become due. | TAKEAWAY 12.2 |

## OPERATING-CASH-FLOW-TO-CAPITAL-EXPENDITURES RATIO

To remain competitive, a business must be able to replace, and expand when appropriate, its property, plant, and equipment. A ratio that evaluates a firm's ability to finance its capital investments from operating cash flow is the **operating-cash-flow-to-capital-expenditures ratio**. This ratio is calculated as follows:

$$\text{Operating-cash-flow-to-capital-expenditures ratio} = \frac{\text{Cash flow from operating activities}}{\text{Annual capital expenditures}}$$

The numerator in this ratio comes from the statement of cash flows. Information for the denominator may be found in one or more places in the financial statements. Data on capital expenditures are part of the required industry segment disclosures in the notes to the financial statements. Data regarding a company's capital expenditures are also presented in the investing activities section of the statement of cash flows. (When capital expenditures are reported in the statement of cash flows, the amount is often broken into two figures—(1) Proceeds from the sale of property, plant and equipment and (2) Purchases of property, plant and equipment. The appropriate "capital expenditures" figure for purpose of calculating this ratio is the net of the two amounts.) Finally, management's discussion and analysis of the financial statements may identify a company's annual capital expenditures.

A ratio in excess of 1.0 indicates that a firm's current operating activities are providing cash in excess of the amount needed to fund its desired investment in plant and intangible assets and would normally be considered a sign of financial strength. The interpretation of this ratio is influenced by the trend in recent years, the ratio being achieved by other firms in the same industry, and the stage of a firm's life cycle. A firm in the early stages of its life cycle—when periods of rapid expansion may occur—may be expected to experience a lower ratio than a firm in the later stage of its life cycle—when maintenance of plant capacity may be more likely than an expansion of plant capacity.

To illustrate the ratio's calculation, **Abbott Laboratories**, a manufacturer of pharmaceutical and health care products, reported capital expenditures of $1,287,724,000. Abbott's cash flow from operating activities was $6,994,620,000. Thus, Abbott's operating-cash-flow-to-capital-expenditures ratio for the year was 5.43, or ($6,994,620,000/ $1,287,724,000). The following are operating-cash-flow-to-capital-expenditures ratios for other well-known companies:

| | |
|---|---|
| PepsiCo (Consumer foods and beverages) | 2.98 |
| Lockheed Martin Corporation (Aerospace) | 4.77 |
| Norfolk Southern Corporation (Freight transportation services) | 1.87 |
| Federal Mogul Corporation (Precision parts) | 2.04 |

**TAKEAWAY 12.3**

| Concept → | Method → | Assessment |
|---|---|---|
| Does a company generate sufficient operating cash flows to finance its capital expenditure needs? | Statement of cash flows.<br><br>$$\text{Operating-cash-flow-to-capital-expenditures ratio} = \frac{\text{Cash flow from operating activities}}{\text{Annual capital expenditures}}$$ | The higher the ratio, the higher the probability that a company will generate sufficient operating cash flow to finance its capital expenditure needs. |

## Your Turn!        12.4

The following selected data were obtained from the financial statements of Blake Enterprises:

| | |
|---|---|
| Cash flow from operating activities | $40,000 |
| Annual capital expenditures | 12,500 |
| Average current liabilities | 30,000 |

Calculate the following financial measures for Blake Enterprises:

1. Free cash flow
2. Operating-cash-flow-to-current-liabilities ratio
3. Operating-cash-flow-to-capital-expenditures ratio

**The solution is on page 590.**

## WORKING WITH THE TAKEAWAYS

Home Depot reports (in millions) cash provided by operating activities of $5,125. For the same period, average current liabilities were reported to be $10,758 and annual capital expenditures were $966. Calculate the free cash flow, operating-cash-flow-to-current-liabilities ratio, and the operating-cash-flow-to- capital-expenditures ratio for Home Depot and comment on the results.

### Solution

The free cash flow is $4,159 ($5,125 − $966), the operating-cash-flow-to-current-liabilities ratio is 0.48 ($5,125/$10,758), and the operating-cash-flow-to-capital-expenditures ratio is 53.31 ($5,125/$966). Thus, the Home Depot does not generate sufficient cash flow from operating activities to pay all of its current liabilities. The company will need to either increase its operating cash flow or find some alternative means of financing, such as short-term bank financing, to pay its current liabilities. The company is, however, generating sufficient cash flow from operations to fund capital expenditures.

## SUMMARY OF LEARNING OBJECTIVES

**Discuss the content and format of the statement of cash flows. (p. 544)**   LO1
- A statement of cash flows explains the net increase or decrease in cash and cash equivalents during the period.
- A statement of cash flows separates cash flows into operating, investing, and financing activity categories.
- A secondary objective of cash flow reporting is to provide information regarding a firm's investing and financing activities. A required supplemental disclosure reports noncash investing and financing activities.
- A statement of cash flows should help users compare, evaluate, and predict a firm's cash flows and also help evaluate its financial flexibility.

**Explain the preparation of a statement of cash flows using the indirect method. (p. 550)**   LO2
- The indirect method reconciles net income to cash flow from operating activities.
- A firm using the indirect method must separately disclose the cash paid for interest and the cash paid for income taxes.

**Explain the preparation of a statement of cash flows using the direct method. (p. 557)**   LO3
- The direct method shows the major categories of operating cash receipts and payments.
- The FASB encourages use of the direct method but permits use of either the direct or the indirect method.
- A firm using the direct method must separately disclose the reconciliation of net income to cash flow from operating activities.

**Define *free cash flow, operating-cash-flow-to-current-liabilities ratio*, and the *operating-cash-flow-to-capital-expenditures ratio* and explain their use. (p. 560)**   LO4
- Free cash flow is defined as a company's cash flow from operations less its capital expenditures; the metric provides a measure of a firm's cash flow that can be used to fund business activities beyond the replacement of property, plant, and equipment.
- The operating cash flow to current liabilities ratio is calculated by dividing a company's cash flow from operating activities by its average current liabilities for the year; the ratio reveals a firm's ability to repay current liabilities from operating cash flow.
- The operating cash flow to capital expenditures ratio is calculated by dividing a firm's cash flow from operating activities by its annual capital expenditures; the ratio evaluates a firm's ability to fund its capital investment using operating cash flow.

### TAKEAWAYS: SUMMARY CHART

| Concept | Method | Assessment |
|---|---|---|
| Does a company generate cash flows in excess of its capital expenditure needs? | Statement of cash flows.<br><br>FCF = Cash flow from operating activities − Capital expenditures | The higher the free cash flow, the greater is a company's ability to generate cash for needs other than capital expenditures. |

TAKEAWAY 12.1

| TAKEAWAY 12.2 | Will a company have sufficient cash to pay its current liabilities as they become due? | Statement of cash flows and balance sheet.<br><br>$\text{Operating-cash-flow-to-current-liabilities ratio} = \dfrac{\text{Cash flow from operating activities}}{\text{Average current liabilities}}$ | The higher the ratio, the higher the probability that a company will have sufficient operating cash flow to pay its current liabilities as they become due. |
|---|---|---|---|
| TAKEAWAY 12.3 | Does a company generate sufficient operating cash flows to finance its capital expenditure needs? | Statement of cash flows.<br><br>$\text{Operating-cash-flow-to-capital-expenditures ratio} = \dfrac{\text{Cash flow from operating activities}}{\text{Annual capital expenditures}}$ | The higher the ratio, the higher the probability that a company will generate sufficient operating cash flow to finance its capital expenditure needs. |

## GLOSSARY OF KEY TERMS

**Cash equivalents** Short-term, highly liquid investments that firms acquire with temporarily idle cash to earn interest on these funds. To qualify as a cash equivalent, an investment must be readily convertible into cash and be close enough to maturity so that its market value is not sensitive to interest rate changes (p. 544).

**Cash management** Management's efforts to determine cash needs and maintain the proper amount of cash for the company's needs (p. 544).

**Direct method** A presentation of the cash flow from operating activities in a statement of cash flows that shows the major categories of operating cash receipts and payments (p. 549).

**Financial flexibility** A firm's ability to generate sufficient amounts of cash to respond to unanticipated business needs and opportunities (p. 548).

**Financing activities** A section in the statement of cash flows that reports cash flows associated with obtaining cash from owners and creditors, returning cash to owners, and repaying amounts borrowed (p. 546).

**Free cash flow** Calculated as cash flow from operating activities less capital expenditures; this metric provides a measure of a firm's cash flow that can be used to fund business activities beyond the replacement of property, plant, and equipment (p. 560).

**Indirect method** A presentation of cash flow from operating activities in a statement of cash flows that begins with net income and applies a series of adjustments to convert the net income to a cash basis amount (p. 549).

**Investing activities** A section in the statement of cash flows that reports cash flows involving (1) the purchase and sale of plant assets and intangible assets, (2) the purchase and sale of stocks, bonds, and other securities (other than cash equivalents), and (3) the lending and subsequent collection of money (p. 546).

**Noncash expenses** Expenses that do not involve any current period cash outflows and that are deducted in the process of calculating a company's accrual basis net income (p. 554).

**Noncash investing and financing activities** Investing activities and financing activities that do not affect current cash flows; information about these events must be reported as a supplement to the statement of cash flows (p. 547).

**Operating activities** A section in the statement of cash flows that reports cash flows from all activities that are not classified as investing or financing activities (p. 546).

**Operating-cash-flow-to-capital-expenditures ratio** A financial ratio calculated by dividing a firm's cash flow from operating activities by its annual capital expenditures (p. 562).

**Operating-cash-flow-to-current-liabilities ratio** A financial ratio calculated by dividing cash flow from operating activities by the average current liabilities for the year (p. 561).

**Statement of cash flows** A financial statement showing a firm's cash inflows and cash outflows for a specific period, classified into operating, investing, and financing activity categories (p. 544).

## COMPREHENSIVE PROBLEM

Terry Company's income statement and comparative balance sheets at December 31, 2011 and 2010, are as follows:

| TERRY COMPANY<br>Income Statement<br>For the Year Ended December 31, 2011 | | |
|---|---:|---:|
| Sales revenue | | $385,000 |
| Dividend income | | 5,000 |
| | | 390,000 |
| Cost of goods sold | $233,000 | |
| Wages expense | 82,000 | |
| Advertising expense | 10,000 | |
| Depreciation expense | 11,000 | |
| Income tax expense | 17,000 | |
| Loss on sale of investments | 2,000 | 355,000 |
| Net income | | $ 35,000 |

| TERRY COMPANY Balance Sheets | | |
|---|---|---|
| | Dec. 31, 2011 | Dec. 31, 2010 |
| **Assets** | | |
| Cash ........................................................................ | $ 8,000 | $ 12,000 |
| Accounts receivable ...................................................... | 22,000 | 28,000 |
| Inventory ................................................................. | 94,000 | 66,000 |
| Prepaid advertising...................................................... | 12,000 | 9,000 |
| Long-term investments—available for sale ............................... | 30,000 | 41,000 |
| Fair value adjustment to investments .................................... | — | (1,000) |
| Plant assets .............................................................. | 178,000 | 130,000 |
| Accumulated depreciation................................................ | (72,000) | (61,000) |
| Total assets............................................................... | $272,000 | $224,000 |
| **Liabilities and Stockholders' Equity** | | |
| Accounts payable ........................................................ | $ 27,000 | $ 14,000 |
| Wages payable ........................................................... | 6,000 | 2,500 |
| Income tax payable....................................................... | 3,000 | 4,500 |
| Common stock............................................................ | 139,000 | 125,000 |
| Retained earnings ........................................................ | 97,000 | 79,000 |
| Unrealized loss on investments .......................................... | — | (1,000) |
| Total Liabilities and Stockholders' Equity ............................... | $272,000 | $224,000 |

Cash dividends of $17,000 were declared and paid during 2011. Plant assets were purchased for cash, and, later in the year, additional common stock was issued for cash. Investments costing $11,000 were sold for cash at a $2,000 loss; an unrealized loss of $1,000 on these investments had been recorded in 2010 (at December 31, 2011, the cost and fair value of the unsold investments are equal).

### Required

a. Calculate the change in cash that occurred during 2011.
b. Prepare a 2011 statement of cash flows using the indirect method.
c. Prepare a 2011 statement of cash flows using the direct method.

### Solution

a. $8,000 ending balance − $12,000 beginning balance = $4,000 decrease in cash
b. 1. Use the indirect method to determine the cash flow from operating activities.
   - The adjustments to convert Terry Company's net income of $35,000 to the cash provided by operating activities of $38,000 are shown in the following statement of cash flows.
   2. Analyze changes in remaining noncash asset (and contra asset) accounts to determine cash flows from investing activities.
   - Long-term investments: $11,000 decrease resulted from sale of investments for cash at a $2,000 loss. Cash received from sale of investments = $9,000 ($11,000 cost − $2,000 loss).
   - Fair value adjustment to investments: $1,000 decrease resulted from the elimination of this account balance (and the unrealized loss of investments) at the end of 2011. No cash flow effect.
   - Plant assets: $48,000 increase resulted from purchase of plant assets for cash. Cash paid to purchase plant assets = $48,000.
   - Accumulated depreciation: $11,000 increase resulted from the recording of 2011 depreciation. No cash flow effect.
   3. Analyze changes in remaining liability and stockholders' equity accounts to determine cash flows from financing activities.
   - Common stock: $14,000 increase resulted from the issuance of stock for cash. Cash received from issuance of common stock = $14,000.
   - Retained earnings: $18,000 increase resulted from net income of $35,000 and dividend declaration of $17,000. Cash paid as dividends = $17,000.
   - Unrealized loss on investments: $1,000 decrease resulted from the elimination of this account balance (and the fair value adjustment to investments) at the end of 2011. No cash flow effect.

The statement of cash flows (indirect method) is as follows:

| | | |
|---|---:|---:|
| **TERRY COMPANY**<br>**Statement of Cash Flows**<br>**For the Year Ended December 31, 2011** | | |
| **Cash flow from operating activities** | | |
| Net income . . . . . . . . . . . . . . . . . . . . . . . . . . . . . . . . . . . . . . . . . . . . . . . | $35,000 | |
| Add (deduct) items to convert net income to cash basis | | |
| Depreciation . . . . . . . . . . . . . . . . . . . . . . . . . . . . . . . . . . . . . . . . . . . | 11,000 | |
| Loss on sale of investments . . . . . . . . . . . . . . . . . . . . . . . . . . . . . . . . | 2,000 | |
| Accounts receivable decrease . . . . . . . . . . . . . . . . . . . . . . . . . . . . . . . | 6,000 | |
| Inventory increase . . . . . . . . . . . . . . . . . . . . . . . . . . . . . . . . . . . . . . . | (28,000) | |
| Prepaid advertising increase . . . . . . . . . . . . . . . . . . . . . . . . . . . . . . . | (3,000) | |
| Accounts payable increase . . . . . . . . . . . . . . . . . . . . . . . . . . . . . . . . . | 13,000 | |
| Wages payable increase . . . . . . . . . . . . . . . . . . . . . . . . . . . . . . . . . . | 3,500 | |
| Income tax payable decrease . . . . . . . . . . . . . . . . . . . . . . . . . . . . . . . | (1,500) | |
| Cash provided by operating activities . . . . . . . . . . . . . . . . . . . . . . . | | $38,000 |
| **Cash flow from investing activities** | | |
| Sale of investments . . . . . . . . . . . . . . . . . . . . . . . . . . . . . . . . . . . . . . | 9,000 | |
| Purchase of plant assets . . . . . . . . . . . . . . . . . . . . . . . . . . . . . . . . . . . | (48,000) | |
| Cash used by investing activities . . . . . . . . . . . . . . . . . . . . . . . . . . . | | (39,000) |
| **Cash flow from financing activities** | | |
| Issuance of common stock . . . . . . . . . . . . . . . . . . . . . . . . . . . . . . . . . | 14,000 | |
| Payment of dividends . . . . . . . . . . . . . . . . . . . . . . . . . . . . . . . . . . . . . | (17,000) | |
| Cash used by financing activities . . . . . . . . . . . . . . . . . . . . . . . . . . . | | (3,000) |
| Net decrease in cash . . . . . . . . . . . . . . . . . . . . . . . . . . . . . . . . . . . . . . . . | | (4,000) |
| Cash at beginning of year . . . . . . . . . . . . . . . . . . . . . . . . . . . . . . . . . . . . | | 12,000 |
| Cash at end of year . . . . . . . . . . . . . . . . . . . . . . . . . . . . . . . . . . . . . . . . | | $ 8,000 |

*c.* 1. Use the direct method to determine the individual cash flows from operating activities.
   - $385,000 Sales + $6,000 Accounts receivable decrease = $391,000 Cash received from customers
   - $5,000 Dividend income = $5,000 Cash received as dividends
   - $233,000 Cost of goods sold + $28,000 Inventory increase − $13,000 Accounts payable increase = $248,000 Cash paid for merchandise purchased
   - $82,000 Wages expense − $3,500 Wages payable increase = $78,500 Cash paid to employees
   - $10,000 Advertising expense + $3,000 Prepaid advertising increase = $13,000 Cash paid for advertising
   - $17,000 Income tax expense + $1,500 Income tax payable decrease = $18,500 Cash paid for income taxes

2. Analyze changes in remaining noncash asset (and contra asset) accounts to determine cash flows from investing activities.
   - Long-term investments: $11,000 decrease resulted from sale of investments for cash at a $2,000 loss. Cash received from sale of investments = $9,000 ($11,000 cost − $2,000 loss).
   - Fair value adjustment to investments: $1,000 decrease resulted from the elimination of this account balance (and the unrealized loss on investments) at the end of 2011. No cash flow effect.
   - Plant assets: $48,000 increase resulted from purchase of plant assets for cash. Cash paid to purchase plant assets = $48,000.
   - Accumulated depreciation: $11,000 increase resulted from the recording of 2011 depreciation. No cash flow effect.

3. Analyze changes in remaining liability and stockholders' equity accounts to determine cash flows from financing activities.
   - Common stock: $14,000 increase resulted from the issuance of stock for cash. Cash received from issuance of common stock = $14,000.
   - Retained earnings: $18,000 increase resulted from net income of $35,000 and dividend declaration of $17,000. Cash paid as dividends = $17,000.

- Unrealized loss on investments: $1,000 decrease resulted from the elimination of this account balance (and the fair value adjustment to investments) at the end of 2011. No cash flow effect.

The statement of cash flows (direct method) is as follows:

| TERRY COMPANY<br>Statement of Cash Flows<br>For the Year Ended December 31, 2011 | | |
|---|---:|---:|
| **Cash flow from operating activities** | | |
| Cash received from customers............................................ | $391,000 | |
| Cash received as dividends ............................................. | 5,000 | $396,000 |
| Cash paid for merchandise purchased ..................................... | (248,000) | |
| Cash paid to employees.................................................. | (78,500) | |
| Cash paid for advertising................................................ | (13,000) | |
| Cash paid for income taxes.............................................. | (18,500) | (358,000) |
| Cash provided by operating activities ..................................... | | 38,000 |
| **Cash flow from investing activities** | | |
| Sale of investments .................................................... | 9,000 | |
| Purchase of plant assets................................................. | (48,000) | |
| Cash used by investing activities ......................................... | | (39,000) |
| **Cash flow from financing activities** | | |
| Issuance of common stock ............................................... | 14,000 | |
| Payment of dividends .................................................... | (17,000) | |
| Cash used by financing activities ......................................... | | (3,000) |
| Net decrease in cash.................................................... | | (4,000) |
| Cash at beginning of year................................................ | | 12,000 |
| Cash at end of year ..................................................... | | $  8,000 |

# SELF-STUDY QUESTIONS

(Answers to the Self-Study Questions are available at the end of the chapter.)

1. Which of the following is not disclosed in a statement of cash flows?     LO1
   a. A transfer of cash to a cash equivalent investment
   b. The amount of cash at year-end
   c. Cash outflows from investing activities during the period
   d. Cash inflows from financing activities during the period

2. Which of the following events will appear in the cash flows from investing activities section of     LO1
   the statement of cash flows?
   a. Cash received as interest
   b. Cash received from issuance of common stock
   c. Cash purchase of truck
   d. Cash payment of dividends

3. Which of the following events will appear in the cash flows from financing activities section of     LO1
   the statement of cash flows?
   a. Cash purchase of equipment
   b. Cash purchase of bonds issued by another company
   c. Cash received as repayment for funds loaned
   d. Cash purchase of treasury stock

4. Tyler Company has net income of $49,000 and the following related items:     LO2

| | |
|---|---:|
| Depreciation expense ...................................................... | $ 5,000 |
| Accounts receivable increase ............................................... | 2,000 |
| Inventory decrease ........................................................ | 10,000 |
| Accounts payable decrease ................................................. | 4,000 |

Using the indirect method, what is Tyler's cash flow from operations?
   a. $42,000
   b. $46,000
   c. $58,000
   d. $38,000

REVIEW

LO1 **5.** Which of the following methods will disclose the cash received from customers in the statement of cash flows?
  *a.* Indirect method
  *b.* Reconciliation method
  *c.* Direct method
  *d.* Both direct and indirect methods

LO1 **6.** Which of the following events will not appear in the cash flows from financing activities section of the statement of cash flow?
  *a.* Borrowing cash from a bank
  *b.* Issuance of stock in exchange for plant assets
  *c.* Sales of common stock
  *d.* Payment of dividends on preferred stock

LO3 **7.** Smith & Sons reports sales revenue of $1,000,000 on its income statement. Its balance sheet reveals beginning and ending accounts receivable of $60,000 and $92,000, respectively. What is the amount of cash collected from customers of the company?
  *a.* $1,032,000
  *b.* $968,000
  *c.* $1,060,000
  *d.* $1,092,000

LO1 **8.** Which of the following is not a cash equivalent?
  *a.* Short-term U.S. Treasury bill
  *b.* Short-term certificate of deposit
  *c.* Money-market account
  *d.* IBM common stock

LO2 **9.** Which of the following expenses are not added back to net income when using the indirect method to prepare a statement of cash flows?
  *a.* Amortization expense
  *b.* Depletion expense
  *c.* Interest expense
  *d.* Depreciation expense

LO3 **10.** Smith & Sons reports interest expense of $90,000 on its income statement. The beginning and ending balances for interest payable reported on its balance sheet are $10,000 and $15,000, respectively. How much cash did Smith & Sons pay for interest expense this period?
  *a.* $85,000
  *b.* $95,000
  *c.* $100,000
  *d.* $105,000

LO4 **11.** Free cash flow is a measure of a firm's
  *a.* interest free debt.
  *b.* ability to generate net income.
  *c.* ability to generate cash and invest in new capital expenditures.
  *d.* ability to collect accounts receivable in a timely manner.

LO4 **12.** Taylor Company reports free cash flow of $15,000, total cash of $18,000, net income of $50,000, current assets of $90,000, average current liabilities of $60,000, and cash flow from operating activities of $48,000. Compute the operating-cash-flow-to-current-liabilities ratio for Taylor Company.
  *a.* 0.83
  *b.* 0.80
  *c.* 0.30
  *d.* 1.25

## DISCUSSION QUESTIONS

**1.** What is the definition of *cash equivalents?* Give three examples of cash equivalents.
**2.** Why are cash equivalents included with cash in a statement of cash flows?

3. What are the three major types of activities classified on a statement of cash flows? Give an example of a cash inflow and a cash outflow in each classification.

4. In which of the three activity categories of a statement of cash flows would each of the following items appear? Indicate for each item whether it represents a cash inflow or a cash outflow:
   a. Cash purchase of equipment
   b. Cash collection on loans
   c. Cash dividends paid
   d. Cash dividends received
   e. Cash proceeds from issuing stock
   f. Cash receipts from customers
   g. Cash interest paid
   h. Cash interest received

5. Why is a statement of cash flows a useful financial statement?

6. What is the difference between the direct method and the indirect method of presenting the cash flow from operating activities?

7. In determining the cash flow from operating activities using the indirect method, why is it necessary to add depreciation back to net income? Give an example of another item that is added back to net income under the indirect method.

8. Vista Company sold land for $98,000 cash that had originally cost $70,000. The company recorded a gain on the sale of $28,000. How is this event reported in a statement of cash flows using the indirect method?

9. A firm uses the indirect method. Using the following information, what is its cash flow from operating activities?

| | |
|---|---|
| Net income. | $88,000 |
| Accounts receivable decrease | 13,000 |
| Inventory increase. | 9,000 |
| Accounts payable decrease | 3,500 |
| Income tax payable increase | 1,500 |
| Depreciation expense | 6,000 |

10. What separate disclosures are required for a company that reports a statement of cash flows using the indirect method?

11. If a business had a net loss for the year, under what circumstances would the statement of cash flows show a positive cash flow from operating activities?

12. A firm is converting its accrual revenues to corresponding cash amounts using the direct method. Sales revenue on the income statement are $925,000. Beginning and ending accounts receivable on the balance sheet are $58,000 and $44,000, respectively. What is the amount of cash received from customers?

13. A firm reports $86,000 wages expense in its income statement. If beginning and ending wages payable are $3,900 and $2,800, respectively, what is the amount of cash paid to employees?

14. A firm reports $43,000 advertising expense in its income statement. If beginning and ending prepaid advertising are $6,000 and $7,600, respectively, what is the amount of cash paid for advertising?

15. Rusk Company sold equipment for $5,100 cash that had cost $35,000 and had $29,000 of accumulated depreciation. How is this event reported in a statement of cash flows using the direct method?

16. What separate disclosures are required for a company that reports a statement of cash flows using the direct method?

17. How is the *operating-cash-flow-to-current-liabilities ratio* calculated? Explain its use.

18. How is the *operating-cash-flow-to-capital-expenditures ratio* calculated? Explain its use.

19. The statement of cash flows provides information that may be useful in predicting future cash flows, evaluating financial flexibility, assessing liquidity, and identifying a company's financing needs. It is not, however, the best financial statement for learning about a firm's financial performance during a period. Information about a company's financial performance is provided by the income statement. Two basic principles—the revenue recognition principle and the matching concept—work to distinguish the income statement from the statement of cash flows. (a) Define the revenue recognition principle and the matching concept. (b) Briefly explain how these two principles work to make the income statement a better report regarding a firm's periodic financial performance than the statement of cash flows.

# SHORT EXERCISES

Use the following information regarding the Seville Corporation to answer Short Exercises 12-1 through 12-3:

| | |
|---|---:|
| Accounts payable increase | $ 9,000 |
| Accounts receivable increase | 4,000 |
| Accrued liabilities decrease | 3,000 |
| Amortization expense | 6,000 |
| Cash balance, January 1 | 22,000 |
| Cash balance, December 31 | 15,000 |
| Cash paid as dividends | 29,000 |
| Cash paid to purchase land | 90,000 |
| Cash paid to retire bonds payable at par | 60,000 |
| Cash received from issuance of common stock | 35,000 |
| Cash received from sale of equipment | 17,000 |
| Depreciation expense | 29,000 |
| Gain on sale of equipment | 4,000 |
| Inventory decrease | 13,000 |
| Net income | 76,000 |
| Prepaid expenses increase | 2,000 |

**LO1, LO2** **SE12-1.** **Cash Flow from Operating Activities**
Using the information for the Seville Corporation above, calculate the cash flow from operating activities.

**LO1, LO2** **SE12-2.** **Cash Flow from Investing Activities**
Using the information for the Seville Corporation above, calculate the cash flow from investing activities.

**LO1, LO2** **SE12-3.** **Cash Flow from Financing Activities**
Using the information for the Seville Corporation above, calculate the cash flow for financing activities.

**LO3** **SE12-4.** **Direct Method**
Using the following data for Smith & Sons, calculate the cash paid for rent:

| | |
|---|---:|
| Rent expense | $80,000 |
| Prepaid rent, January 1 | 10,000 |
| Prepaid rent, December 31 | 8,000 |

**LO3** **SE12-5.** **Direct Method**
Using the following data for Smith & Sons, calculate the cash received as interest:

| | |
|---|---:|
| Interest income | $26,000 |
| Interest receivable, January 1 | 3,000 |
| Interest receivable, December 31 | 3,700 |

**LO3** **SE12-6.** **Direct Method**
Using the following data for Smith & Sons, calculate the cash paid for merchandise purchased:

| | |
|---|---:|
| Cost of goods sold | $108,000 |
| Inventory, January 1 | 19,000 |
| Inventory, December 31 | 22,000 |
| Accounts payable, January 1 | 11,000 |
| Accounts payable, December 31 | 7,000 |

**LO3** **SE12-7.** **Converting Sales Revenue to Cash**
Smith & Sons is converting its sales revenues to corresponding cash amounts using the direct method. Sales revenue on the income statement are $1,025,000. Beginning and ending accounts receivable on the balance sheet are $58,000 and $34,000, respectively. Calculate the amount of cash received from customers.

The following information for Smith & Sons relates to Short Exercises 12-8 through 12-10:

| | |
|---|---:|
| Cash flow from operating activities. | $1,500,000 |
| Capital expenditures. | 850,000 |
| Current liabilities, beginning of year. | 300,000 |
| Current liabilities, end of year | 360,000 |

LO4

**SE12-8.** **Free Cash Flow**
Using the above data, calculate the free cash flow for Smith & Sons.

LO4

**SE12-9.** **Operating-Cash-Flow-to-Current-Liabilities Ratio**
Using the above data, calculate the operating-cash-flow-to-current-liabilities ratio for Smith & Sons.

LO4

**SE12-10.** **Operating-Cash-Flow-to-Capital-Expenditures Ratio**
Using the above data, calculate the operating-cash-flow-to-capital-expenditures ratio for Smith & Sons.

# EXERCISES—SET A

LO1

**E12-1A.** **Classification of Cash Flows**
For each of the items below, indicate whether the cash flow item relates to an operating activity, an investing activity, or a financing activity:

a. Cash receipts from customers for services rendered
b. Sale of long-term investments for cash
c. Acquisition of plant assets for cash
d. Payment of income taxes
e. Bonds payable issued for cash
f. Payment of cash dividends declared in previous year
g. Purchase of short-term investments (not cash equivalents) for cash

LO1

**E12-2A.** **Classification of Cash Flows**
For each of the items below, indicate whether it is (1) a cash flow from an operating activity, (2) a cash flow from an investing activity, (3) a cash flow from a financing activity, (4) a noncash investing and financing activity, or (5) none of the above:

a. Paid cash to retire bonds payable at a loss
b. Received cash as settlement of a lawsuit
c. Acquired a patent in exchange for common stock
d. Received advance payments from customers on orders for custom-made goods
e. Gave large cash contribution to local university
f. Invested cash in 60-day commercial paper (a cash equivalent)

LO2

**E12-3A.** **Cash Flow From Operating Activities (Indirect Method)**
The Lincoln Company owns no plant assets and had the following income statement for the year:

| | | |
|---|---:|---:|
| Sales revenue | | $750,000 |
| Cost of goods sold. | $470,000 | |
| Wages expense. | 110,000 | |
| Rent expense. | 42,000 | |
| Insurance expense. | 15,000 | 637,000 |
| Net income. | | $113,000 |

Additional information about the company includes:

| | End of Year | Beginning of Year |
|---|---:|---:|
| Accounts receivable | $54,000 | $49,000 |
| Inventory | 60,000 | 66,000 |
| Prepaid insurance | 8,000 | 7,000 |
| Accounts payable | 22,000 | 18,000 |
| Wages payable | 9,000 | 11,000 |

Use the preceding information to calculate the cash flow from operating activities using the indirect method.

b. Prepare a statement of cash flows using the direct method. Use one cash outflow for "cash paid for wages and other operating expenses." Accounts payable relate to inventory purchases only.

**LO3** **P12-8B.** **Statement of Cash Flows (Direct Method)**

Refer to the data given for the Towne Company in Problem P12-4B.

**Required**

a. Compute the change in cash that occurred during 2011.
b. Prepare a statement of cash flows using the direct method. Use one cash outflow for "cash paid for wages and other operating expenses."

**LO4** **P12-9B.** **Analyzing Cash Flow Ratios**

Molly Enterprises reported the following information for the past year of operations:

| | Transaction | Free Cash Flow $300,000 | Operating-Cash-Flow-to-Current-Liabilities Ratio 1.2 times | Operating-Cash-Flow-to-Capital-Expenditures Ratio 4.0 times |
|---|---|---|---|---|
| a. | Recorded credit sales of $10,000 | | | |
| b. | Collected $9,000 owed from customers | | | |
| c. | Purchased $50,000 of equipment on long-term credit | | | |
| d. | Purchased $65,000 of equipment for cash | | | |
| e. | Paid $14,000 of wages with cash | | | |
| f. | Recorded utility bill of $11,500 that has not been paid | | | |

For each transaction, indicate whether the ratio will (I) increase, (D) decrease, or (N) have no effect.

# SERIAL PROBLEM: KATE'S CARDS

(*Note:* **This is a continuation of the Serial Problem: Kate's Cards from Chapter 1 through Chapter 11.**)

**SP12.** Kate has just completed her first year running Kate's Cards. She has been preparing monthly income statements and balance sheets, so she knows that her company has been profitable and that there is cash in the bank. She has not, however, prepared a statement of cash flows. Kate provides you with the year-end income statement and balance sheet and asks that you prepare a statement of cash flows for Kate's Cards.

Additional information:

1. There was no disposals of equipment during the year.
2. Dividends in the amount of $1,300 were paid in cash during the year.
3. Prepaid expenses relate to operating expenses.

**Required**

a. Prepare a statement of cash flows for Kate's Cards for the year ended August 31, 2011, using the indirect method. Hint: Since this was Kate's first year of operations, the beginning balance sheet account balances were zero.
b. Prepare a statement of cash flows for Kate's Cards for the year ended August 31, 2011, using the direct method.

**KATE'S CARDS**
**Income Statement**
**Year Ended August 31, 2011**

| | |
|---|---:|
| Sales revenue | $135,000 |
| Cost of goods sold | 72,000 |
| Gross profit | 63,000 |
| Operating expenses | |
| Wages | 18,000 |
| Consulting | 11,850 |
| Insurance | 1,200 |
| Utilities | 2,400 |
| Depreciation | 3,250 |
| Total operating expenses | 36,700 |
| Income from operations | 26,300 |
| Interest expense | 900 |
| Income before income tax | 25,400 |
| Income tax expense | 8,900 |
| Net income | $16,500 |

**KATE'S CARDS**
**Balance Sheet**
**As of August 31, 2011**

| | |
|---|---:|
| **Assets** | |
| Current assets | |
| Cash | $12,300 |
| Accounts receivable | 11,000 |
| Inventory | 16,000 |
| Prepaid insurance | 1,000 |
| Total current assets | 40,300 |
| Equipment | 17,500 |
| Accumulated depreciation | 3,250 |
| Total assets | $54,550 |
| **Liabilities** | |
| Current liabilities | |
| Accounts payable | $6,200 |
| Unearned revenue | 1,250 |
| Other current liabilities | 1,900 |
| Total current liabilities | 9,350 |
| Note payable | 15,000 |
| Total liabilities | 24,350 |
| Stockholders' equity | |
| Common stock | 500 |
| Additional paid-in-capital | 9,500 |
| Preferred stock | 5,000 |
| Retained earnings | 15,200 |
| Total stockholders' equity | 30,200 |
| Total liabilities and stockholders' equity | $54,550 |

# EXTENDING YOUR KNOWLEDGE

## REPORTING AND ANALYSIS

**EYK12-1.** **Financial Reporting Problem: Columbia Sportswear Company**

The financial statements for the **Columbia Sportswear Company** can be found in Appendix A at the end of this book.

COLUMBIA SPORTSWEAR
COMPANY

**Required**

Answer the following questions:

*a.* How much did Columbia Sportswear's cash and cash equivalents increase in 2009?

*b.* What was the largest source of cash and cash equivalents in 2009?

*c.* What was the single largest use of cash and cash equivalents in 2009?

*d.* How much dividends were paid in 2009?

*e.* Why do depreciation and amortization, both noncash items, appear on Columbia's statement of cash flows?

COLUMBIA SPORTSWEAR
COMPANY

THE TIMBERLAND COMPANY

**EYK12-2.  Comparative Analysis Problem: Columbia Sportswear Company vs The Timberland Company**

The financial statements for the Columbia Sportswear Company can be found in Appendix A at the end of this book, and the financial statements of The Timberland Company can be found in Appendix B (the complete annual report is available on this book's Website).

**Required**

Answer the following questions:

*a.* Compute the free cash flow in 2009 for both Columbia Sportswear and Timberland.

*b.* Compute the operating cash flows to capital expenditures for both Columbia Sportswear and Timberland.

*c.* Comment on the ability of each company to finance its capital expenditures.

**EYK12-3.  Business Decision Problem**

Recently hired as assistant controller for Finite, Inc., you are sitting next to the controller as she responds to questions at the annual stockholders' meeting. The firm's financial statements contain a statement of cash flows prepared using the indirect method. A stockholder raises his hand.

Stockholder: "I notice that depreciation expense is shown as an addition in the calculation of the cash flow from operating activities."

Controller: "That's correct."

Stockholder: "What depreciation method do you use?"

Controller: "We use the straight-line method for all plant assets."

Stockholder: "Well, why don't you switch to an accelerated depreciation method, such as double-declining balance, increase the annual depreciation amount, and thus increase the cash flow from operating activities?"

The controller pauses, turns to you, and replies, "My assistant will answer your question."

**Required**

Prepare an answer to the stockholder's question.

**EYK12-4.  Financial Analysis Problem**

PARKER HANNIFIN CORPORATION

**Parker Hannifin Corporation**, headquartered in Cleveland, Ohio, manufactures motion control and fluid system components for a variety of industrial users. The firm's financial statements contain the following data (Year 3 is the most recent year; dollar amounts are in thousands):

|  | Year 3 | Year 2 | Year 1 |
|---|---|---|---|
| Current assets at year-end ................................ | $1,018,354 | $1,056,443 | $1,055,776 |
| Current liabilities at year-end ............................. | 504,444 | 468,254 | 358,729 |
| Current liabilities at beginning of year..................... | 468,254 | 358,729 | 345,594 |
| Cash provided by operating activities ..................... | 259,204 | 229,382 | 235,186 |
| Capital expenditures....................................... | 99,914 | 91,484 | 84,955 |

*a.* Calculate Parker Hannifin's current ratio (current assets/current liabilities) for Years 1, 2, and 3.

*b.* Calculate Parker Hannifin's operating-cash-flow-to-current-liabilities ratio for Years 1, 2, and 3.

*c.* Comment on the three-year trend in Parker Hannifin's current ratio and operating-cash-flow-to-current-liabilities ratio. Do the trends in these two ratios reinforce each other or contradict each other as indicators of Parker Hannifin's ability to pay its current liabilities?

*d.* Calculate Parker Hannifin's operating-cash-flow-to-capital-expenditures ratio for Years 1, 2, and 3. Comment on the strength of this ratio over the three-year period.

## CRITICAL THINKING

**EYK12-5.** **Accounting Research Problem: General Mills, Inc.**

The fiscal year 2010 annual report of General Mills, Inc. is available on this book's Website.

**Required**

a. Refer to Note 2. How does General Mills define its cash equivalents?

b. What method does General Mills use to report its cash provided by operating activities?

c. What is the change in cash and cash equivalents experienced by General Mills during fiscal 2010? What is the amount of cash and cash equivalents as of May 30, 2010?

d. Refer to the Five Year Summary. What is the trend in General Mills' ratio of operating-cash-flow-to-capital-expenditures ratio during the period 2006–2010?

e. Calculate General Mills' 2010 operating-cash-flow-to-current-liabilities ratio.

**EYK12-6.** **Accounting Communication Activity**

Susan Henderson, the vice president of marketing, was told by the CEO that she needs to understand the numbers because the company's existence depends on making money. It has been a long time since Susan took a class in accounting. She recalls that companies report net income and cash flows in two separate statements. She feels pretty comfortable with the income statement, but is somewhat lost looking at the statement of cash flows. She asks you to help explain this statement.

**Required**

Write a brief memo to Susan explaining the form and content of the statement of cash flows, along with a short discussion of how to analyze the statement.

**EYK12-7.** **Accounting Ethics Case**

Due to an economic recession, Anton Corporation faces severe cash flow problems. Management forecasts that payments to some suppliers will have to be delayed for several months. Jay Newton, controller, has asked his staff for suggestions on selecting the suppliers for which payments will be delayed.

"That's a fairly easy decision," observes Tim Haslem. "Some suppliers charge interest if our payment is late, but others do not. We should pay those suppliers that charge interest and delay payments to the ones that do not charge interest. If we do this, the savings in interest charges will be quite substantial."

"I disagree," states Tara Wirth. "That position is too 'bottom line' oriented. It's not fair to delay payments only to suppliers who don't charge interest for late payments. Most suppliers in that category are ones we have dealt with for years; selecting these suppliers would be taking advantage of the excellent relationships we have developed over the years. The fair thing to do is to make pro-rata payments to each supplier."

"Well, making pro-rata payments to each supplier means that *all* our suppliers will be upset because no one receives full payment," comments Sue Myling. "I believe it is most important to maintain good relations with our long-term suppliers; we should pay them currently and delay payments to our newer suppliers. The interest costs we end up paying these newer suppliers is the price we must pay to keep our long-term relationships solid."

**Required**

Which suppliers should Jay Newton select for delayed payments? Discuss.

**EYK12-8.** **Corporate Social Responsibility Problem**

The corporate social responsibility highlighted in this chapter (see page 556) mentions that **Home Depot** believes in giving back. One of the ways the company has done this is through its Team Depot program of employee volunteerism. Under this program, Home Depot employees volunteer their own time to work together on projects that benefit communities in which the company does business. Each year the program provides millions of hours of employee volunteerism.

One of the many programs that benefits from Team Depot is Habitat for Humanity. Do a computer search and report how Team Depot has helped Habitat for Humanity.

**EYK12-9.** **Forensic Accounting Problem**

Cash larceny involves the fraudulent stealing of an employer's cash. These schemes often target the company's bank deposits. The fraudster steals the money after the deposit has been prepared, but before the deposit is taken to the bank. Most often these schemes involve a deficiency in the internal control system where segregation of duties is not present. The perpetrator is often in charge of recording receipts, preparing the deposit, delivering the deposit to the bank, and verifying the receipted deposit slip. Without proper segregation of duties, the fraudster is able cover up the theft.

In addition to segregation of duties, what internal control procedures might help deter and detect cash larceny?

## ANSWERS TO SELF-STUDY QUESTIONS

1. a, (p. 544)   2. c, (p. 546)   3. d, (p. 546)   4. c, (p. 550)   5. c, (p. 549)   6. b, (p. 546)
7. b, (p. 558)   8. d, (p. 544)   9. c, (p. 554)   10. a, (p. 558)   11. c, (p. 560)   12. b, (p. 561)

## Your Turn! Solutions

### Solution 12.1
1. Operating
2. Investing
3. Operating
4. Investing
5. Financing
6. Financing
7. Operating
8. Financing
9. Investing

### Solution 12.2

| HUSKY COMPANY<br>Statement of Cash Flows<br>For the Year Ended December 31, 2011 | | |
|---|---:|---:|
| **Cash flow from operating activities** | | |
| Net income. | $112,000 | |
| Add (deduct) items to convert net income to cash basis | | |
| Depreciation | 34,000 | |
| Accounts receivable increase | (18,000) | |
| Inventory increase. | (60,000) | |
| Prepaid insurance decrease | 4,000 | |
| Accounts payable decrease | (6,000) | |
| Wages payable increase | 6,000 | |
| Income tax payable decrease | (2,000) | |
| Cash provided by operating activities | | $ 70,000 |
| **Cash flow from investing activities** | | |
| Purchase of plant assets | | (110,000) |
| **Cash flow from financing activities** | | |
| Issuance of bonds payable. | 110,000 | |
| Payment of dividends | (58,000) | |
| Cash provided by financing activities. | | 52,000 |
| Net increase in cash | | 12,000 |
| Cash at beginning of year. | | 10,000 |
| Cash at end of year | | $ 22,000 |

## Solution 12.3

### Supporting calculations:

Cash received from customers:

$1,270,000 Sales revenue − $18,000 Accounts receivable increase = $1,252,000

Cash paid for merchandise purchased:

$860,000 Cost of goods sold + $60,000 Inventory increase + $6,000 Accounts payable decrease = $926,000

Cash paid to employees:

$172,000 Wages expense − $6,000 Wages payable increase = $166,000

Cash paid for insurance:

$16,000 Insurance expense − $4,000 Prepaid insurance decrease = $12,000

Cash paid for interest:

Equal to the $18,000 balance in interest expense

Cash paid for income taxes:

$58,000 Income tax expense + $2,000 Income tax payable decrease = $60,000

Purchase of plant assets:

$500,000 Ending plant assets − $390,000 Beginning plant assets = $110,000

Issuance of bonds payable:

$260,000 Ending bonds payable − $150,000 Beginning bonds payable = $110,000

Payment of dividends

$58,000 given in problem data

### Other analysis

Accumulated depreciation increased by $34,000, which is the amount of depreciation expense.

Common stock account balance did not change.

Retained earnings increased by $54,000, which is the difference between the net income of $112,000 and the dividends declared of $58,000.

| HUSKY COMPANY |
|---|
| **Statement of Cash Flows (Direct Method)** |
| **For the Year Ended December 31, 2011** |

| | | |
|---|---:|---:|
| **Cash flow from operating activities** | | |
| Cash received from customers........................................... | | $1,252,000 |
| Cash paid for merchandise purchased ...................................... | $(926,000) | |
| Cash paid to employees................................................... | (166,000) | |
| Cash paid for insurance................................................... | (12,000) | |
| Cash paid for interest.................................................... | (18,000) | |
| Cash paid for income taxes .............................................. | (60,000) | (1,182,000) |
| Cash provided by operating activities ..................................... | | 70,000 |
| **Cash flow from investing activities** | | |
| Purchase of plant assets................................................. | | (110,000) |
| **Cash flow from financing activities** | | |
| Issuance of bonds payable .............................................. | 110,000 | |
| Payment of dividends .................................................... | (58,000) | |
| Cash provided by financing activities...................................... | | 52,000 |
| Net increase in cash ..................................................... | | 12,000 |
| Cash at beginning of year................................................. | | 10,000 |
| Cash at end of year ...................................................... | | $    22,000 |

## Solution 12.4

Free cash flow: $40,000 − $12,500 = $27,500

Operating-cash-flow-to-current-liabilities-ratio: $40,000/$30,000 = 1.33

Operating-cash-flow-to-capital-expenditures-ratio: $40,000/$12,500 = 3.20

# 13 Analysis and Interpretation of Financial Statements

| PAST | PRESENT |
|---|---|
| In Chapter 12, we examined the statement of cash flows. | In this chapter we complete our study of financial accounting by looking at the analysis and interpretation of financial statements. |

## LEARNING OBJECTIVES

1 **Identify** persistent earnings and **discuss** the content and format of the income statement. (p. 594)

2 **Identify** the sources of financial information used by investment professionals and **explain** horizontal financial statement analysis. (p. 598)

3 **Explain** vertical financial statement analysis. (p. 603)

4 **Define** and **discuss** financial ratios for analyzing a firm. (p. 605)

5 **Discuss** the limitations of financial statement analysis. (p. 617)

6 Appendix 13A **Describe** financial statement disclosures. (p. 620)

# PROCTER & GAMBLE

The **Procter & Gamble Company (P&G)** is one of America's oldest companies, dating back to 1837 when candle maker William Procter and soap maker James Gamble combined their small businesses. Over the next few decades the company introduced such well-known products as Ivory soap and Crisco shortening that are still sold today.

P&G has continued to grow, with annual sales of almost $80 billion. Not all of the company's growth, however, is the result of internally developed products like Crest toothpaste, Head & Shoulders shampoo, and Pampers diapers. A significant part of P&G's growth has come from mergers and acquisitions. P&G's largest acquisition occurred in 2005 when it acquired Gillette for $57 billion.

Acquisitions, such as the one involving Gillette, are complex transactions. Perhaps the hardest part of any merger or acquisition is to determine the appropriate price to pay—in this case $57 billion. How did P&G determine how much to pay for Gillette? Many factors go into such an analysis, but it often comes down to how much a company like Gillette will be able to add to P&G's future persistent earnings.

In this chapter we explore some of the ways that investment professionals determine how much a company is worth. The process involves analyzing a company's persistent earnings potential as well as the various risks associated with a company's day-to-day operations.

# PERSISTENT EARNINGS AND THE INCOME STATEMENT

**LEARNING OBJECTIVE 1**

**Identify** persistent earnings and discuss the content and format of the income statement.

Net income is the "bottom line" measure of firm performance. It is a measure that depends on such accrual accounting procedures as the revenue recognition and expense matching policies selected by a firm's management. Generally accepted accounting practice has historically emphasized the importance of accounting earnings because past accounting earnings have been found to be a good predictor of a firm's future operating cash flow. Modern valuation theory tells us that the economic value of a company is the present value of the company's future operating cash flows. Thus, an important role for accounting numbers is their use by investment professionals when assessing the economic value of a company (like Gillette in the feature story).

One of the determinants of the ability of historical accounting earnings to predict future cash flow is the extent to which earnings recur over time, or what is known as *earnings persistence*. Since the value of a share of common stock today is a function of a firm's ability to consistently generate earnings year in and year out, the persistence (or sustainability) of a company's operating earnings is closely linked to its economic value. **Persistent earnings** are also sometimes referred to as *sustainable earnings* or *permanent earnings*, whereas non-persistent earnings are often referred to as transitory earnings. In general, **transitory earnings** include such single-period events as extraordinary gains/losses, special items, restructuring charges, changes in accounting principle, and discontinued operations.

To assist investors in their assessment of a company's persistent earnings, and hence in assessing a firm's economic value, companies are required under GAAP to classify income statement accounts in a manner that aids a financial statement user in assessing persistent earnings. In Chapter 5, we discussed the classified income statement. In this chapter, we discuss a refinement of the classified income statement called the multi-step income statement.

Exhibit 13-1 illustrates the basic format of the multi-step income statement. While a **single-step income statement** derives the net income of a business in one step by subtracting total expenses from total revenues, a **multiple-step income statement** derives

**AKA** Persistent earnings are also referred to as *sustainable earnings* or *permanent earnings*.

| EXHIBIT 13-1 | The Multi-Step Income Statement |
|---|---|

**KALI COMPANY**
**Income Statement**
**For Year Ended December 31, 2011**

| | | | |
|---|---|---:|---|
| Sales revenue | | $500 | Usual and frequent |
| Cost of goods sold | | 200 | Usual and frequent |
| Gross profit | | 300 | |
| Operating expenses | | 250 | Usual and frequent |
| Net operating income | | 50 | |
| Other income and expense | | | |
| Interest income | 25 | | Unusual |
| Interest expense | (35) | | Unusual |
| Gain on sale of equipment | 15 | 5 | Unusual |
| Net income from continuing operations before tax | | 55 | |
| Income tax | | 20 | Usual and frequent |
| Net income from continuing operations | | 35 | |
| Gain from operations of discontinued division, net of tax | 15 | | Infrequent |
| Loss on disposal of discontinued division (net of tax) | (5) | 10 | |
| Net income before extraordinary item | | 45 | |
| Extraordinary gain (loss), net of tax | | (15) | Unusual and infrequent |
| Net income | | $ 30 | |
| Earning per share (100 shares outstanding): | | $ .30 | |

one or more intermediate performance measures before net income is reported. Examples of such intermediate performance measures are gross profit, net operating income, and net income from continuing operations before taxes.

The income statement is organized in such a way that items with greater persistence are reported higher up in the income statement, whereas items considered more transitory are reported further down in the statement. Thus, accounts representing financial events that are both usual and frequent are reported first. Usual refers to whether an item is central to a firm's core operations, whereas **unusual items** display a high degree of abnormality and/or are unrelated, or only incidentally related to the normal activities of a business. Frequent refers to how often an item is expected to occur, with infrequent items not reasonably expected to recur in the foreseeable future. Usual and frequent items typically consist of such income statement accounts as sales revenue, cost of goods sold, and other operating expenses. Just below these usual and frequent items are items that are either unusual or infrequent, but not both. Examples of these include such financial events as asset write-downs and restructuring charges. While these items are not expected to occur regularly, they are not considered unusual in nature. Income statement accounts such as interest expense, interest income, and gains on sales of equipment are often frequently recurring items; however, they are not considered part of a firm's central operations and therefore are considered unusual.

Each of the above items is reported as part of a company's continuing operations and is shown before any income tax expense. GAAP, however, requires certain single-period items, or one-time events, to be reported on an after-tax basis. For example, discontinued operations, or the part of a business which is being shuttered or sold, are shown net of the financial effect of any applicable income taxes. Reporting discontinued operations on a net-of-tax basis allows the income tax expense reported on the income statement to reflect only the income taxes associated with a firm's continuing operations.

Most believe that the income statement is more useful when certain types of transactions and events are reported in separate sections. For this reason, information about discontinued operations is disclosed separately in the income statement. Segregating these categories of information from the results of continuing operations makes it easier for financial statement users to identify a company's persistent earnings.

The creation of sections within the income statement, however, complicates the reporting of a company's income tax expense. Items affecting the overall amount of income tax expense may appear in more than one section. If this is the case, accountants allocate a company's total income tax expense among those sections of the income statement in which the items affecting the tax expense appear.

The income statement's usefulness is also enhanced if it contains information on a firm's earnings per share. Since stock prices are quoted on the New York Stock Exchange and the NASDAQ exchange on a per share basis, it is customary for businesses to also report their net income on a per common share basis, called earnings per share. Accordingly, earnings per share are also reported on the income statement, immediately following net income.

We now examine these topics in greater detail.

## DISCONTINUED OPERATIONS

When a company sells, abandons, or otherwise disposes of a segment of its operations, a **discontinued operations** section of the income statement reports information about the discontinued business segment. The discontinued operations section presents two categories of information:

1.  The income or loss from the segment's operations for the portion of the year before its discontinuance.
2.  Any gain or loss from the disposal of the segment.

This section is reported on the income statement immediately after information regarding a firm's continuing operations.

To illustrate the reporting of discontinued operations, assume that on July 1, 2011, Kali Company, a diversified manufacturing company, sold its pet food division. Exhibit 13-1 illustrates the income statement for Kali Company, including information regarding its pet food division in the discontinued operations section. From January 1 through June 30, Kali's pet food division operated at a profit, net of income taxes, of $15. The loss, net of income taxes, from the sale of the division's assets and liabilities was $5. Note that when there is a discontinued operations section, the difference between a firm's continuing sales revenues and expenses is labeled net income from continuing operations.

## EXTRAORDINARY ITEMS

**Extraordinary items** are transactions and events that are both *unusual in nature* and *occur infrequently*. An item that is unusual in nature is highly abnormal and significantly different from a firm's typical activities. To determine a firm's typical activities, it is necessary to consider such factors as the type of operations, lines of business, operating policies, and the environment in which the firm operates. The operating environment includes the characteristics of the industry, the geographic location of a firm's facilities, and the type of government regulations imposed on the industry and firm. A transaction or event is considered to occur infrequently if the firm does not expect it to recur in the foreseeable future.

The fact that the two criteria—unusual nature and infrequent occurrence—must *both* be present substantially restricts the events and transactions that qualify as extraordinary. For example, suppose a farmer suffers crop loss from a flood that normally happens every few years. The history of floods creates a reasonable expectation that another flood will occur in the foreseeable future. The crop loss, therefore, does not meet the criteria for classification as an extraordinary item. Now consider a second farmer in a location rarely exposed to flooding and who suffers flood damage to his crop for the first time from a broken dam. The dam is repaired and is not expected to fail again in the foreseeable future. The flood loss in this circumstance would be considered an extraordinary item.

In addition to natural disasters, other events that may generate extraordinary losses include expropriations of property by foreign governments (such as Venezuela's 2007 nationalization of ExxonMobil's assets located in that country), and prohibitions under newly enacted laws (such as a government ban on a currently marketed product).

**ACCOUNTING IN PRACTICE** Earthquake Loss for Dayton Hudson

Dayton Hudson Corporation is a large merchandise retailer with several chains of department stores. In 1994, the firm suffered earthquake damage at 11 of its Target stores and 13 of its Mervyn's stores in the Los Angeles, California, area. The uninsured earthquake losses totaled $22 million. Dayton Hudson reported the losses as an unusual item in its financial statements. Given the frequency of earthquakes in the Los Angeles area, the earthquake loss did not qualify as extraordinary—that is, an earthquake loss in an area frequented by earthquakes would not qualify as both unusual and infrequent.

**IFRS ALERT!**

Like U.S. GAAP, IFRS encourages companies to use a multi-step income statement when presenting a company's periodic performance. Tesco, the world's third largest retailer, presents its IFRS accounted income statement in Appendix C at the end of this book. Examining Tesco's income statement reveals that the retailer presents four measures of firm performance: gross profit, operating profit, profit before tax, and profit for the year. These indicators correspond to the four performance measures reported by the Kali Company in Exhibit 13.1: gross profit, net operating income, net income from continuing operations before tax, and net income. Although the income statements under U.S. GAAP and IFRS are very similar, with only minor labeling differences—like using "profit" instead of "income"—one significant difference relates to extraordinary items, which are separately disclosed on U.S. GAAP income statements but which are not separately disclosed on IFRS accounted income statements.

## CHANGES IN ACCOUNTING PRINCIPLES

Occasionally a company may implement a **change in accounting principle**—that is, a switch from one generally accepted method to another. Examples include a change in inventory costing method, such as from FIFO to weighted-average cost. Such changes are permitted when a business can demonstrate that the reported financial results under the new accounting method are superior to the results reported under the replaced method.

Changing accounting principles can present a problem for financial statement users analyzing a company's performance over time because different accounting principles are likely to produce different financial statement results. This concern led to the adoption of the GAAP practice that financial statements of prior years, issued in comparative form with current year financial statements, should be restated using any new accounting principles. This means that a change in accounting principle is accounted for by restating prior financial statements as if the new method had been used all along.

**PRINCIPLE ALERT** Consistency Principle

The *consistency principle* states that, unless otherwise disclosed, financial statements use the same accounting methods from one period to the next. A consistent use of accounting methods enhances the comparability of financial data across time. The consistency principle impacts the accounting for a change in accounting principles in several ways. First, to change an accounting principle, a company must be able to justify that the reported results under the new principle are preferable. Second, a company must restate its prior year financial statements as though the new principle had been in use all along. In actual practice, only the prior year financial statements presented with the current year financial statements must be restated to reflect the financial effect of the new accounting method. For all financial statements prior to those presented with the current statements, a lump sum financial restatement is made to retained earnings on the statement of retained earnings and the statement of stockholders' equity.

## COMPREHENSIVE INCOME

Most items that generate wealth changes in a business are required to be shown on the income statement. There are, however, a few items that do not appear as part of the regular content of the income statement and instead are classified under a category labeled **comprehensive income**. A business's comprehensive income includes its net income, any changes in the market value of certain marketable securities (see Appendix D at the end of this book), and any unrealized gains and losses from translating foreign currency denominated financial statements into U.S. dollars. This latter topic is covered in more advanced accounting textbooks.

Companies are given some flexibility as to how they report their comprehensive income. They are allowed to utilize three alternative formats under GAAP: (1) appending comprehensive income to the bottom of the income statement; (2) creating a separate statement of comprehensive income; or, (3) including comprehensive income in the statement of stockholders' equity. In addition to comprehensive income for the current period, GAAP requires a company to report accumulated other comprehensive income as part of stockholders' equity on the balance sheet. Accumulated other comprehensive income serves the same role for comprehensive income as retained earnings serves for regular net income—it reports the cumulative amount of comprehensive income as of the balance sheet date.

---

**CORPORATE SOCIAL RESPONSIBILITY** | **Pampers and UNICEF**

Maternal and neonatal tetanus is a disease that kills over 100,000 women and children annually. **P&G**, through its Pampers product, has teamed up with UNICEF to fight this completely preventable disease. For every purchase of a pack of Pampers, P&G donates one dose of the tetanus vaccine for use by vulnerable mothers and their children. Thus far, nearly 50 million women and their babies have been inoculated against the disease. P&G and UNICEF have committed to a goal of completely eliminating the disease by 2012.

P&G and UNICEF have gone even further in their teamwork. P&G offers its western European employees a three-month paid sabbatical to work with UNICEF. The program is aimed at employees who have always desired to perform humanitarian work but have lacked the financial resources to do so.

---

**Your Turn!** 13.1

Conner Company, a retail company, entered into the following transactions during the year:

1. Sold merchandise to customers
2. Settled a major lawsuit
3. Wrote down the book value of a closed warehouse
4. Paid employee wages
5. Disposed of a line of discount stores
6. Paid income taxes

**Required**
Classify each of the above items as either persistent earnings or transitory earnings.

**The solution is on page 653.**

---

# SOURCES OF INFORMATION

LEARNING OBJECTIVE 2

Identify the sources of financial information used by investment professionals and explain horizontal financial statement analysis.

Except for closely held companies, businesses publish their financial statements at least annually. Most large companies also issue quarterly financial data. Normally, annual financial statements are attested to by a certified public accountant, and investment professionals carefully review the independent accountant's opinion to assess the reliability of the published financial data. Companies listed on stock exchanges must also submit annual financial statements, called a 10-K for the annual report and 10-Q for the quarterly report, to the U.S. Securities and Exchange Commission (SEC). These statements are available to any interested party and are generally more useful than annual reports because they contain greater detail.

Investment professionals may also want to compare the performance of a particular firm with that of the other firms in the same industry. Data on industry norms, median ratios by industry, and other relationships are available from such data collection services as Dun & Bradstreet, Moody's, and Standard and Poor's. In addition, some brokerage firms compile industry norms and ratios from their own computer databases.

---

**ACCOUNTING IN PRACTICE** | **SEC EDGAR Database**

An example of a financial database is **EDGAR**, the Electronic Data Gathering, Analysis, and Retrieval system, maintained by the U.S. SEC. This computer database aids financial statement analysis by performing automated data collection, validation, indexing, acceptance, and forwarding of submissions by companies and others who are required by law to file forms with the U.S. Securities and Exchange Commission. The primary intent of the SEC in creating EDGAR was to increase the efficiency of the securities market for the benefit of investors, corporations, and the economy, by accelerating the receipt, acceptance, dissemination, and analysis of corporate information filed with the agency. An "efficient" securities market means that investors are able to make the best possible decisions regarding where and when to invest their funds.

---

## ANALYTICAL TECHNIQUES

The absolute dollar amounts of net income, sales revenue, total assets, and other key data are usually not meaningful when analyzed in isolation. For example, knowing that a company's annual net income is $1 million is of little informational value unless the amount of the income can be related to other factors. A $1 million profit might represent excellent performance for a company with less than $10 million in invested capital. On the other hand, $1 million in net income would be considered meager for a firm that had several hundred million dollars in invested capital. Thus, significant information can be derived by examining the relationship between two or more accounting variables, such as net income and total assets, net income and sales revenue, and net income and stockholders' equity. To describe these relationships clearly and to make comparisons easy, the relationships are often expressed in terms of ratios or percentages.

For example, we might express the relationship of $15,000 in net income to $150,000 in sales revenue as a ten percent ($15,000/$150,000) rate of return on sales. To describe the relationship between sales revenue of $150,000 and inventory of $20,000, we might use a ratio or a percentage; ($150,000/$20,000) may be expressed as 7.5, 7.5:1, or 750 percent.

Changes in selected financial statement items compared in successive financial statements are often expressed as percentages. For example, if a firm's net income increased from $40,000 last year to $48,000 this year, the $8,000 increase related to last year (the base year) is expressed as a 20 percent increase ($8,000/$40,000) in net income. To express a dollar increase or decrease as a percentage, however, the analyst must make the base year amount a positive figure. If, for example, a firm had a net loss of $4,000 in one year and net income of $20,000 in the next, the $24,000 increase cannot be meaningfully expressed as a percentage. Similarly, if a firm reported no marketable securities in last year's balance sheet but showed $15,000 of such securities in this year's statement, the $15,000 increase cannot be expressed as a meaningful percentage.

When evaluating a firm's financial statements for two or more years, analysts often use **horizontal analysis**. Horizontal analysis is a technique that can be useful for detecting an improvement or deterioration in a firm's performance and for spotting trends regarding a firm's financial well-being. The term **vertical analysis** is used describe the analysis of a single year of financial data.

# HORIZONTAL ANALYSIS

## COMPARATIVE FINANCIAL STATEMENTS

The type of horizontal analysis most often used by investment professionals is **comparative financial statement analysis** for two or more years, showing dollar and/or percentage changes for important financial statement items and totals. Dollar increases and decreases are divided by the earliest year's data to obtain percentage changes. To illustrate, the 2008 and 2009 financial statements of Procter & Gamble (P&G) are presented in Exhibits 13-2, 13-3, and 13-4. We will use the data in these statements throughout this chapter to illustrate various analytical techniques.

**EXHIBIT 13-2** Procter & Gamble Income Statement

### THE PROCTER & GAMBLE COMPANY
#### Consolidated Income Statements

| (in millions) | Year Ended 2009 | Common-Size | Year Ended 2008 | Common-Size | $ Change | % Change |
|---|---|---|---|---|---|---|
| Net sales ............................ | $79,029 | 100.0% | $81,748 | 100.0% | $(2,719) | (3.3)% |
| Cost of products sold .................. | 38,898 | 49.2% | 39,536 | 48.4% | (638) | (1.6)% |
| Gross margin........................ | 40,131 | 50.8% | 42,212 | 51.6% | (2,081) | (4.9)% |
| Selling, general, and administrative expense | 24,008 | 30.4% | 25,575 | 31.3% | (1,567) | (6.1)% |
| Operating income..................... | 16,123 | 20.4% | 16,637 | 20.4% | (514) | (3.1)% |
| Interest expense..................... | 1,358 | 1.7% | 1,467 | 1.8% | (109) | (7.4)% |
| Other non-operating income ............ | 560 | 0.7% | 462 | 0.6% | 98 | 21.2% |
| Earnings from continuing operations before taxes | 15,325 | 19.4% | 15,632 | 19.1% | (307) | (2.0)% |
| Income taxes on continuing operations .... | 4,032 | 5.1% | 3,834 | 4.7% | 198 | 5.2% |
| Net earnings from continuing operations .. | 11,293 | 14.3% | 11,798 | 14.4% | (505) | (4.3)% |
| Net earnings from discontinued operations, net of taxes | 2,143 | 2.7% | 277 | 0.3% | 1,866 | 673.6% |
| Net earnings ........................ | $13,436 | 17.0% | $12,075 | 14.8% | $ 1,361 | 11.3 % |
| Earnings per share.................... | 4.49 | | 3.86 | | 0.63 | 16.3% |
| Dividends per share .................. | 1.64 | | 1.45 | | 0.19 | 13.1% |

**EXHIBIT 13-3** Procter & Gamble Balance Sheet

### THE PROCTER & GAMBLE COMPANY
#### Consolidated Balance Sheets

| (in millions) | 2009 | | 2008 | | $ Change | % Change |
|---|---|---|---|---|---|---|
| **Assets** | | | | | | |
| Current assets | | | | | | |
| Cash and cash equivalents......................... | $ 4,781 | 3.6% | $ 3,313 | 2.3% | $1,468 | 44.3% |
| Accounts receivable............................ | 5,836 | 4.3% | 6,761 | 4.7% | (925) | (13.7)% |
| Inventories.................................... | 6,880 | 5.1% | 8,416 | 5.8% | (1,536) | (18.3)% |
| Other current assets............................ | 4,408 | 3.3% | 6,025 | 4.2% | (1,617) | (26.8)% |
| Total Current Assets.......................... | 21,905 | 16.3% | 24,515 | 17.0% | (2,610) | (10.6)% |
| Net plant assets.................................. | 19,462 | 14.4% | 20,640 | 14.3% | (1,178) | (5.7)% |
| Intangible assets ................................ | 89,118 | 66.1% | 94,000 | 65.3% | (4,882) | (5.2)% |
| Other noncurrent assets ........................... | 4,348 | 3.2% | 4,837 | 3.4% | (489) | (10.1)% |
| Total assets ................................ | $134,833 | 100.0% | $143,992 | 100.0% | $(9,159) | (6.4)% |
| **Liabilities and Stockholders' Equity** | | | | | | |
| Current liabilities | | | | | | |
| Accounts payable ............................. | $ 5,980 | 4.4% | $ 6,775 | 4.7% | $(795) | (11.7)% |
| Other current liabilities......................... | 24,921 | 18.5% | 24,183 | 16.8% | 738 | 3.1% |
| Total current liabilities ...................... | 30,901 | 22.9% | 30,958 | 21.5% | (57) | (0.2)% |
| Long-term debt .................................. | 20,652 | 15.3% | 23,581 | 16.4% | (2,929) | (12.4)% |
| Other noncurrent liabilities ........................ | 20,181 | 15.0% | 19,959 | 13.9% | 222 | 1.1% |
| Total liabilities ............................. | 71,734 | 53.2% | 74,498 | 51.7% | (2,764) | (3.7)% |
| Preferred stock .................................. | 1,324 | 1.0% | 1,366 | 0.9% | (42) | (3.1)% |
| Common stock ................................... | 4,007 | 3.0% | 4,002 | 2.8% | 5 | 0.1% |
| Additional paid-in capital.......................... | 61,118 | 45.3% | 60,307 | 41.9% | 811 | 1.3% |
| Accumulated other comprehensive income (loss)....... | (4,698) | (3.5)% | 2,421 | 1.7% | (7,119) | (294.1)% |
| Treasury stock.................................. | (55,961) | (41.5)% | (47,588) | (33.0)% | (8,373) | 17.6% |
| Retained earnings ............................... | 57,309 | 42.5% | 48,986 | 34.0% | 8,323 | 17.0% |
| Total stockholders' equity ..................... | 63,099 | 46.8% | 69,494 | 48.3% | (6,395) | (9.2)% |
| Total stockholders' equity and liabilities............. | $134,833 | 100.0% | $143,992 | 100.0% | $(9,159) | (6.4)% |

**EXHIBIT 13-4** Procter & Gamble Statement of Cash Flows

### THE PROCTER & GAMBLE COMPANY
### Consolidated Statements of Cash Flows

| (in millions) | Year Ended 2009 | Year Ended 2008 | $ Change | % Change |
|---|---|---|---|---|
| **Operating activities** | | | | |
| Net earnings ............................................... | 13,436 | 12,075 | | |
| Depreciation and amortization............................ | 3,082 | 3,166 | | |
| Gain on sale of business ................................... | (2,377) | (284) | | |
| Other noncash items ...................................... | 1,112 | 1,769 | | |
| Change in accounts receivable............................ | 415 | 432 | | |
| Change in inventories ..................................... | 721 | (1,050) | | |
| Change in accounts payable, accrued and other ............ | (742) | 297 | | |
| Change in other operating assets and liabilities............. | (758) | (1,270) | | |
| Other .................................................... | 30 | (127) | | |
|   Net cash flow provided by operating activities ............ | 14,919 | 15,008 | $(89) | (0.6)% |
| **Investing activities** | | | | |
| Capital expenditures....................................... | (3,238) | (3,046) | | |
| Proceeds from asset sales ................................. | 1,087 | 928 | | |
| Acquisitions, net........................................... | (368) | (381) | | |
| Change in investments ..................................... | 166 | (50) | | |
|   Net cash flow provided by investing activities............. | (2,353) | (2,549) | 196 | 7.7% |
| **Financing activities** | | | | |
| Dividends................................................. | (5,044) | (4,655) | | |
| Change in short-term debt................................. | (2,420) | 2,650 | | |
| Additions to long-term debt ............................... | 4,926 | 7,088 | | |
| Reductions of long-term debt.............................. | (2,587) | (11,747) | | |
| Treasury stock purchases .................................. | (6,370) | (10,047) | | |
| Other .................................................... | 681 | 1,867 | | |
|   Net cash flow provided by financing activities............. | (10,814) | (14,844) | 4,030 | 27.1% |
| Effect of exchange rate changes ........................... | (284) | 344 | | |
| Change in cash and cash equivalents....................... | 1,468 | (2,041) | | |
| Beginning cash and cash equivalents ...................... | 3,313 | 5,354 | | |
| Ending cash and cash equivalents.......................... | $ 4,781 | $ 3,313 | | |

When analyzing financial statements, the investment professional is likely to focus his or her immediate attention on those financial statement items or percentages that are significant in amount. Although percentage changes are helpful in identifying significant items, they can sometimes be misleading. An unusually large percentage change may occur simply because the dollar amount of the base year is small. For example, assume that P&G had an increase in interest expense of $25, from $10 in 2008 to $35 in 2009. This increase amounts to a percentage change of 250 percent, yet the dollar amount is quite small and insignificant relative to the other reported dollar amounts on P&G's income statement. The financial statement user's attention should be directed first to changes in key financial statement totals: sales revenue, operating income, net income, total assets, total liabilities, and so on. Next, the changes in significant individual items, such as accounts receivable, inventory, and property, plant and equipment should be examined.

For example, P&G's total assets decreased 6.4 percent from 2008 to 2009 (see Exhibit 13-3), and net sales decreased 3.3 percent over the same time period (see Exhibit 13-2). (Note: Some companies, like P&G, use the label "net sales" to refer to their sales revenue, the top line of the income statement.) A small percentage decrease in net sales coincided with a larger decrease in total assets, reflecting a slowing of the world economy in 2009, and indicating that P&G undertook certain business strategies to remain profitable in the face of slowing consumer spending. Note that P&G's 18.3 percent decrease in inventory levels is consistent with this strategy. One potential note of concern is the relationship between cost of products sold and net sales. While net sales shrank by 3.3 percent, cost of products sold decreased by only 1.6 percent, leading to a deterioration in P&G's gross profit margin of 4.9 percent.

We can also see from P&G's statement of cash flow (Exhibit 13-4) that the company's cash flow from operations declined marginally from 2008 to 2009; and, that P&G increased its capital spending from 2008 to 2009, perhaps in anticipation of a return to a more robust economy. Finally, Exhibit 13-4 reveals that P&G chose to repurchase its common stock (treasury stock) in both 2008 and 2009, perhaps to take advantage of the depressed share prices that characterized the U.S. stock market during this time period.

From this limited analysis of comparative financial statements, an investment professional might conclude that P&G's operating performance for 2009 was slightly worse when compared with that of 2008, mostly the result of slowing sales revenue. Further analysis using some of the techniques summarized later in the chapter, however, may cause that opinion to be modified. The foregoing analysis did reveal one "red flag"—a deteriorating gross profit margin.

## TREND ANALYSIS

To observe percentage changes over time in selected financial data, investment professionals often calculate **trend percentages**. Most companies provide summaries of their key financial data for the past five or ten years in their annual reports. With such information, the financial statement user can examine changes over periods longer than just the past two years. For example, suppose an analyst is interested in the trend in sales and net income for P&G for the past five years. The following are P&G's sales revenue and net income figures for 2005 through 2009:

<table>
<tr><td colspan="11" align="center">**PROCTER & GAMBLE COMPANY**<br>**Annual Performance**</td></tr>
<tr><td></td><td colspan="2" align="center">**2005**</td><td colspan="2" align="center">**2006**</td><td colspan="2" align="center">**2007**</td><td colspan="2" align="center">**2008**</td><td colspan="2" align="center">**2009**</td></tr>
<tr><td></td><td>**Millions of Dollars**</td><td>**Percentage of Base Year**</td><td>**Millions of Dollars**</td><td>**Percentage of Base Year**</td><td>**Millions of Dollars**</td><td>**Percentage of Base Year**</td><td>**Millions of Dollars**</td><td>**Percentage of Base Year**</td><td>**Millions of Dollars**</td><td>**Percentage of Base Year**</td></tr>
<tr><td>Net sales . . . . . . . . . . . . . .</td><td>$55,292</td><td>100</td><td>$66,724</td><td>121</td><td>$74,832</td><td>135</td><td>$81,748</td><td>148</td><td>$79,029</td><td>143</td></tr>
<tr><td>Net income. . . . . . . . . . .</td><td>6,923</td><td>100</td><td>8,684</td><td>125</td><td>10,340</td><td>149</td><td>12,075</td><td>174</td><td>13,436</td><td>194</td></tr>
</table>

These data suggest a fairly healthy growth pattern for the company, but the pattern of change from year to year can be determined more precisely by calculating trend percentages. To do this, we select a *base year* and then divide the data for each of the remaining years by the base-year data. The resultant figures are actually indexes of the changes occurring throughout the period. If, for example, 2005 is selected as the base year, all data for 2006 through 2009 will be related to 2005, which is represented as 100 percent.

To create the table of data displayed above, we divide each year's net sales—from 2006 through 2009—by $55,292, P&G's 2005 net sales (in millions of dollars). Similarly, P&G's net income for 2006 through 2009 is divided by $6,923, the company's 2005 net income (in millions of dollars):

---

### PRINCIPLE ALERT | Consistency Principle

Horizontal analysis is a process of analyzing a firm's financial data across two or more years by examining dollar changes, percentage changes, and/or trend percentages. The utility of horizontal analysis, however, is dependent upon the effective implementation of the *consistency principle*. This accounting principle requires that a firm use the same accounting methods from one period to the next or, if a firm finds it necessary (or required) to change an accounting method, that the financial effects of any change be fully disclosed in the financial statements. The consistency principle assures financial analysts that, unless otherwise noted, changes in the accounts over time represent underlying economic changes in a business, and not the result of an accounting method change.

P&G's trend percentages above reveal that the company's growth in net income outstripped its growth in net sales for the entire five-year period. The horizontal analysis of P&G's financial data also reveals that, while net sales declined in 2009, P&G appeared to take steps to counter the adverse impact on its profitability. The trend data indicate that P&G's performance actually showed a large (20 percent) increase in its net income growth in 2009. This increase was largely attributable to a gain from discontinued operations, and therefore not the result of persistent earnings.

It is important to exercise care when interpreting trend percentages. Since all index percentages are related to a *base year, it must be remembered that* the change between the 2006 net sales index (121 percent) and the 2007 net sales index (135 percent) represents a 14 percent increase in terms of *base year* dollars. To express the increase as a percentage of 2006 dollars, we divide the $8,108 increase in net sales from 2007 to 2006 ($74,832 − $66,724) by 2006 net sales of $66,724 to yield a percentage increase of only 12.2 percent. It is also important to select a *representative* base year. For example, if 2005 was an unusual period for the firm, perhaps because of some large transitory items, its use in the trend analysis would be of limited value.

Other data items that an investment professional may relate to sales revenue and net income over multiple years include total assets, a company's investment in plant assets, and its cash flow from operations, among others.

## Your Turn! 13.2

The following data pertain to the Farrow Company:

|  | 2011 | 2010 |
| --- | --- | --- |
| Sales revenue | $800,000 | $750,000 |
| Net income | 120,000 | 100,000 |
| Total assets | 300,000 | 290,000 |

Calculate both the amount in dollars and the percentage change in 2011 using horizontal analysis and 2010 as the base year.

**The solution is on page 653.**

| Concept ➤ | Method ➤ | Assessment |
| --- | --- | --- |
| How does a company's current performance compare with the prior year? | Income statement and balance sheet for current and prior year.<br><br>The income statement and balance sheet should be compared using the prior year as the base. Percentage changes in net income and total assets can be computed as the change between years divided by the base year amount. | Significant changes should be analyzed to determine the reason for any change. |

TAKEAWAY 13.1

## VERTICAL ANALYSIS

The relative importance of various accounts in a company's financial statements for a single year can be highlighted by showing them as a percentage of a key financial statement figure. A financial statement that presents the various account balances as a percentage of a key figure is called a **common-size financial statement**. Sales revenue (or net sales) is the key figure used to construct a common-size income statement, whereas total assets is the key figure used to construct a common-size balance sheet.

LEARNING OBJECTIVE 3

Explain vertical financial statement analysis.

A financial statement may present both the dollar amounts and common-size percentages. For example, Exhibit 13-2 presents P&G's 2009 income statement in dollars and common-size percentages. The common-size percentages show each item in the income statement as a percentage of the company's net sales.

The common-size income statement allows financial statement users to readily compare P&G's ability to manage and control its various expenses while the level of its sales revenue changes over time. For example, P&G's net earnings increased from 14.8 percent of net sales in 2008 to 17 percent of net sales in 2009. We can also observe that there are only small changes in almost all of the line items as a percentage of net sales and that almost all of the percentage increase in P&G's net income comes from its net earnings from discontinued operations. Common-size income statements are also useful when comparing different firms to one another, especially when the firms are significantly different in size. While we should expect different size firms in similar industries to report dissimilar sales revenues and expenses on a dollar basis, we would expect far more similarities when the comparison is done on a common-size basis.

Common-size percentages can also be used to analyze balance sheet data. For example, by examining a firm's current assets and long-term assets as a percentage of total assets, we can determine whether a company is becoming more or less liquid over time. Another use of common-size percentages with balance sheet data is to evaluate the changing sources of financing used by a business. For example, the proportion of total assets supplied by short-term creditors, long-term creditors, preferred stockholders, and common stockholders of P&G are shown in Exhibit 13-3.

P&G's common-size balance sheets reveal that P&G is relying more on debt financing than equity financing in 2009 as compared to 2008. The primary means that P&G used to make this shift in financing appears to be through the use of treasury stock purchases, growing from 33 percent of total assets in 2008 to 41.5 percent of total assets in 2009. We also see that although P&G experienced a rather large decrease in total assets, the relative composition of those assets remained quite stable between 2008 and 2009.

---

## Your Turn! 13.3

The Sanford Company reported the following income statement in 2010:

| SANFORD COMPANY Income Statement For the Year Ended December 31, 2010 | |
|---|---:|
| Sales revenue | $13,500 |
| Cost of goods sold | 5,400 |
| Gross profit | 8,100 |
| Selling and administrative expenses | 1,350 |
| Income from operations | 6,750 |
| Interest expense | 675 |
| Other expense | 135 |
| Income before income taxes | 5,940 |
| Income tax expense | 2,295 |
| Net income | $ 3,645 |

**Hint:** When preparing common-size income statements, expenses are expressed as a positive percentage of net sales even though they are subtractions on the income statement.

**Required**

Prepare a 2010 common-size income statement for Sanford Company.

The solution is on page 653.

| Concept | → Method → | Assessment | |
|---|---|---|---|
| How do the relationships within a company's income statement and balance sheet compare to those of prior years? | Income statement and balance sheet for current and prior year.<br><br>Each income statement item should be presented as a percentage of sales revenue and each balance sheet item should be presented as a percentage of total assets. Financial statements in this form are called common-size statements. | The percentages should be analyzed for differences between years and significant changes should be analyzed to determine the reason for any change. | TAKEAWAY 13.2 |

### THINKING GLOBALLY

Financial statement analysis is executed, worldwide, in exactly the same way. Common-size financial statements and the financial ratios discussed below are currency neutral and can be effectively used anywhere in the world. Not all ratios are relevant, however, in all countries. For example, in emerging countries that lack the financial infrastructure to support a credit system, ratios involving accounts receivable and accounts payable are likely to be irrelevant since sales transactions in those countries are only executed on a cash basis. Similarly, solvency ratios like the times-interest-earned ratio (discussed shortly) are irrelevant since bank financing in lesser-developed countries is rare (although it is becoming more prevalent with the advent of micro-finance in these countries).

# RATIO ANALYSIS

In prior chapters, a number of financial ratios were introduced. At this juncture, we classify those ratios by their analytical objective and review their analysis and interpretation by calculating them for a single company. P&G's financial statements in Exhibit 13-2 and Exhibit 13-3 provide the data for these calculations (all amounts are in millions). Also, representative industry averages are presented for comparison purposes where available.

**LEARNING OBJECTIVE 4**

**Define** and **discuss** financial ratios for analyzing a firm.

Several ratios assist in evaluating how efficiently a firm has performed in its quest for profits, or what is referred to as firm profitability. These ratios include (1) the gross profit percentage, (2) the return on sales, (3) asset turnover, (4) the return on assets, and (5) the return on common stockholders' equity.

## ANALYZING FIRM PROFITABILITY

### Gross Profit Percentage

The **gross profit percentage** is a closely watched ratio for both retailers and manufacturers. The ratio is calculated as:

$$\text{Gross profit percentage} = \frac{\text{Gross profit on sales}}{\text{Net sales}}$$

This ratio reflects the impact on firm profitability associated with changes in a firm's product pricing structure, sales mix, and merchandise costs.

P&G's common-size income statements (see Exhibit 13-2) reveal that its gross profit percentage decreased from 51.6 percent in 2008 to 50.8 percent in 2009. These percentages are derived using the following figures:

| | 2009 | 2008 |
|---|---|---|
| Gross profit............................................................. | $40,131 | $42,212 |
| Net sales................................................................. | 79,029 | 81,748 |
| Gross profit percentage.............................................. | 50.8 percent | 51.6 percent |
| Industry average ....................................................... | 33.3 percent | |

While P&G's gross profit percentage decreased slightly from 2008 to 2009, its ratio is well above the industry average of 33.3 percent. This suggests that P&G is still able to command premium prices for its well-known consumer products.

### Return on Sales

Another important measure of firm profitability is the **return on sales**. This ratio reveals the percentage of each dollar of net sales that remains as profit after subtracting all operating and nonoperating expenses. The return on sales is calculated as follows:

$$\text{Return on sales} = \frac{\text{Net income}}{\text{Net sales}}$$

When common-size income statements are available, the return on sales equals the net income percentage. P&G's common-size income statements in Exhibit 13-2 reveal that its return on sales increased from 14.8 percent in 2008 to 17.0 percent in 2009. These percentages are calculated using the following figures:

| | 2009 | 2008 |
|---|---|---|
| Net income.............................................. | $13,436 | $12,075 |
| Net sales ................................................ | 79,029 | 81,748 |
| Return on sales......................................... | 17.0 percent | 14.8 percent |
| Industry average ....................................... | 8.7 percent | |

The increase in the return on sales for P&G is quite favorable, however as noted above, P&G's increase in its return on sales is mostly attributable to the company's net earnings from discontinued operations. Additionally, P&G's 2009 return on sales exceeds the industry average of 8.7 percent.

The return on sales and gross profit percentages should be used only when analyzing companies from the same industry or when comparing a firm's performance across multiple time periods (as we did above) since the ratio may vary widely across industries. Retail jewelers, for example, have much larger gross profit percentages (an industry average of 45.0 percent) than do retail grocers (an industry average of 23.0 percent). Industry averages for the asset turnover ratio, discussed next, would also be expected to vary significantly from one industry to another.

### Asset Turnover

The **asset turnover ratio** measures how efficiently a firm uses its assets to generate sales revenue by calculating the amount of sales dollars generated annually for each dollar of assets invested in the company. This ratio is calculated as follows:

$$\text{Asset turnover} = \frac{\text{Net sales}}{\text{Average total assets}}$$

P&G's asset turnover is (total assets were $138,014 at year-end 2007):

| | | 2009 | 2008 |
|---|---|---|---|
| Net sales ..................................................... | | $ 79,029 | $ 81,748 |
| Total assets: | | | |
| Beginning of year ......................................... | (a) | 143,992 | 138,014 |
| End of year.................................................. | (b) | 134,833 | 143,992 |
| Average [(a + b)/2]........................................ | | 139,413 | 141,003 |
| Asset turnover.............................................. | | 0.57 | 0.58 |
| Industry average .......................................... | | 2.2 | |

P&G's asset turnover remained stable from 2008 to 2009, indicating little change in how effectively the company used its assets to generate its sales revenue. Specifically, the company generated $0.57 in net sales for every dollar invested in total assets during 2009. This ratio result, however, is well below the industry average of 2.2 for the same time period, indicating that other firms in the consumer products industry significantly outperformed P&G on this financial metric.

Some industries that are characterized by low gross profit percentages manage to generate relatively high asset turnover ratios. Retail grocery chains, for example, typically turnover their assets five to six times per year. By way of contrast, retail jewelers average only one to two asset turnovers per year. These industry differences largely reflect the high cost of products sold by jewelers versus the low cost of products sold by retail grocers.

### Return on Assets

The rate of return on total assets, called the **return on assets**, is an overall measure of a firm's profitability. It reveals the rate of profit earned per dollar of assets under a firm's control. The return on assets is calculated as follows:[1]

$$\text{Return on assets} = \frac{\text{Net income}}{\text{Average total assets}}$$

P&G's return on assets is:

|  | 2009 | 2008 |
|---|---|---|
| Net income. . . . . . . . . . . . . . . . . . . . . . . . . . . . . . . . . . . . . . . . . . . . . . . . . | $ 13,436 | $ 12,075 |
| Average total assets *(see asset turnover calculation above)* . . . . . . . . . . . . . . . . . . . . . . . . . | 139,413 | 141,003 |
| Return on assets. . . . . . . . . . . . . . . . . . . . . . . . . . . . . . . . . . . . . . . . . . . . | 9.6 percent | 8.6 percent |
| Industry average . . . . . . . . . . . . . . . . . . . . . . . . . . . . . . . . . . . . . . . . . . . | 11.0 percent |  |

P&G improved its return on assets from 8.6 percent in 2008 to 9.6 percent in 2009, a return that is still below the industry average of 11.0 percent. P&G's low asset turnover (see above) is principally responsible for the company falling below the industry average return on assets.

The return on asset ratio summarizes the financial impact of two component ratios: the return on sales and asset turnover; that is, the return on assets is the multiplicative product of these latter two ratios, as follows:

| **Ratio:** | Return on Sales × Asset Turnover = Return on Assets |
|---|---|
| **Ratio calculation:** | Net Income/Net Sales × Net Sales/Average Total Asset = Net Income/Average Total Assets |
| **P&G:** | 17.0 percent × 0.57 = 9.6 percent |

### Return on Common Stockholders' Equity

The **return on common stockholders' equity** measures the profitability of the ownership interest held by a company's common stockholders. The ratio shows the percentage of profit earned on each dollar of common stockholder equity invested in a business. The return is earned on the equity invested throughout the year, and consequently, the ratio uses the average common stockholders' equity as its denominator, as follows:

$$\frac{\text{Return on common}}{\text{stockholders' equity}} = \frac{\text{(Net income − Preferred stock dividends)}}{\text{Average common stockholders' equity}}$$

The return on common stockholders' equity for P&G is (common stockholders' equity was $65,354 at year-end 2007):

---

[1] An alternative calculation adds interest expense to a company's net income in the ratio's numerator. This action prevents the method of financing a company's assets from influencing the ratio result.

|  | 2009 | 2008 |
|---|---|---|
| Net income............................................................ | $13,436 | $12,075 |
| Less: Preferred stock dividends.................................... | 192 | 176 |
| Common stock earnings........................................... | $13,244 | $11,899 |
| Common stockholders' equity: |  |  |
| Beginning of year...................................................... (a) | $68,128 | $65,354 |
| End of year ........................................................... (b) | 61,775 | 68,128 |
| Average [(a + b)/2]..................................................... | 64,952 | 67,741 |
| Return on common stockholders' equity ....................... | 20.4 percent | 17.6 percent |
| Industry average ...................................................... | 16.3 percent | |

P&G's return on common stockholders' equity improved by 2.8 percent, from 17.6 percent in 2008 to 20.4 percent in 2009. Unlike the return on assets, P&G's return on common stockholders' equity exceeds the industry average of 16.3 percent.

## Your Turn! 13.4

The following data was obtained from the current financial statements for Kelly Corporation:

| | |
|---|---|
| Net sales ......................................................................... | $30,000 |
| Cost of goods sold............................................................. | 10,500 |
| Net income....................................................................... | 4,500 |
| Average total assets .......................................................... | 50,000 |
| Average common stockholders' equity .................................... | 35,000 |
| Preferred dividends............................................................ | 500 |

**Required**
Calculate the following ratios for Kelly Corporation:

a. Gross profit percentage
b. Return on sales
c. Asset turnover
d. Return on assets
e. Return on common stockholders' equity

The solution is on page 653.

| | Concept | → | Method | → | Assessment |
|---|---|---|---|---|---|
| TAKEAWAY 13.3 | How much profit is a company generating relative to the amount of assets invested in the company? | | Income statement and balance sheet.<br><br>Calculate the return on assets by dividing net income by the average total assets for the year. | | The higher the return on assets, the better a company is doing in terms of generating profits utilizing the assets under its control. |

## ANALYSIS OF SHORT-TERM FIRM LIQUIDITY

A firm's **working capital** is the difference between its current assets and current liabilities. Maintaining an adequate working capital enables a firm to repay its current obligations on a timely basis and to take advantage of any available purchase discounts associated with the timely payment of accounts payable. Shortages of working capital, on the other hand, can force a company into borrowing at inopportune times and unfavorable interest rates. As a consequence, many long-term debt contracts contain provisions that require the borrowing firm to maintain an adequate working capital position. A firm's working capital is calculated as follows:

**Working capital = Current assets − Current liabilities**

Analysis of a firm's short-term liquidity utilizes several financial ratios that relate to various aspects of a company's working capital. These ratios are (1) the current ratio, (2) the quick ratio, (3) operating-cash-flow-to-current-liabilities ratio, (4) accounts receivable turnover and average collection period, and (5) inventory turnover and days' sales in inventory.

## Current Ratio

The **current ratio** is calculated as a firm's current assets divided by its current liabilities:

$$\text{Current ratio} = \frac{\text{Current assets}}{\text{Current liabilities}}$$

This ratio is a widely used measure of a firm's ability to meet its current obligations and to have funds available for use in daily operations. The following calculations reveal that P&G's current ratio declined from 0.79 in 2008 to 0.71 (or 0.71:1) in 2009:

|  | 2009 | 2008 |
|---|---|---|
| Current assets | $21,905 | $24,515 |
| Current liabilities | 30,901 | 30,958 |
| Current ratio | 0.71 | 0.79 |
| Industry average | 1.0 | |

In essence, P&G had $0.71 in current assets for every $1 in current liabilities at the end of 2009.

In the past, a generally accepted rule of thumb was that a firm's current ratio should be approximately 2:1, indicating that a company should maintain twice the dollar amount of current assets as was needed to satisfy its current liabilities. Improved cash flow management techniques and alternate forms of short-term financing (such as bank lines of credit) have reduced the need for businesses to maintain such a high current ratio. Still, many creditors prefer to see a higher current ratio and consider a low ratio as a potential warning sign of short-term liquidity problems.

Evaluating the adequacy of a firm's current ratio may involve comparing it with the recent past (P&G's current ratio declined slightly from 2008 to 2009) or with an industry average (P&G's ratio is below the industry average of 1.0). What is considered an appropriate current ratio varies by industry. A service firm with little or no inventory, such as a car wash service, would be expected to have a smaller current ratio than would a firm carrying a large inventory, such as a hardware retailer. The composition (or mix) of a firm's current assets significantly influences any evaluation of a firm's short-term liquidity. The quick ratio, discussed next, explicitly considers the composition of a firm's current assets when evaluating short-term liquidity.

## Quick Ratio

The **quick ratio** (or *acid-test ratio*) reveals the relationship between a firm's liquid, or *quick,* assets and its current liabilities. Quick assets include cash and cash equivalents, short-term investments, and accounts receivables. The quick ratio omits a company's inventory and prepaid assets, which may not be particularly liquid. Consequently, the quick ratio may give a more accurate picture of a company's ability to meet its current obligations since the ratio ignores a firm's potentially illiquid inventory and prepaid expenses.

The quick ratio and the current ratio together also indicate the financial impact of a company's inventory on its working capital. For example, a company might have an acceptable current ratio, but if its quick ratio falls to an unacceptable level, a financial analyst is likely to be concerned about the amount of inventory on hand, and consequently, analyze the company's inventory position more thoroughly.

The quick ratio is calculated as follows:

$$\text{Quick ratio} = \frac{(\text{Cash and cash equivalents} + \text{Short-term investments} + \text{Accounts receivables})}{\text{Current liabilities}}$$

The quick ratio for P&G is:

| | 2009 | 2008 |
|---|---|---|
| Cash and cash equivalents, short-term investments, and accounts receivable.............. | $10,617 | $10,074 |
| Current liabilities ................................................................ | 30,901 | 30,958 |
| Quick ratio ..................................................................... | 0.34 | 0.33 |
| Industry average ............................................................... | 0.6 | |

P&G's quick ratio improved slightly from 0.33 in 2008 to 0.34 in 2009; but, its 2009 quick ratio is well below the industry average of 0.6. P&G may feel that it is unnecessary to maintain a higher quick ratio if the company has other sources of liquidity, such as a bank line of credit.

### Operating-Cash-Flow-to-Current-Liabilities Ratio

Ultimately, cash will be needed to settle a business's current liabilities. Another ratio indicating a firm's ability to pay its current liabilities as they come due focuses on a company's operating cash flow. The **operating-cash-flow-to-current-liabilities ratio** is calculated as follows:

$$\text{Operating-cash-flow-to-current-liabilities ratio} = \frac{\text{Cash flow from operating activities}}{\text{Average current liabilities}}$$

The operating-cash-flow-to-current-liabilities ratio relates the net cash available as a result of operating activities to the average current liabilities outstanding during the period. A higher ratio indicates that a firm has a greater ability to settle its current liabilities using its operating cash flow.

P&G's operating-cash-flow-to-current-liabilities ratio is (current liabilities at the end of 2007 were $30,717; no industry average is available):

| | | 2009 | 2008 |
|---|---|---|---|
| Cash flow from operating activities................................................ | | $14,919 | $15,008 |
| Current liabilities ............................................................... | | | |
| Beginning of year.............................................................. | (a) | 30,958 | 30,717 |
| End of year..................................................................... | (b) | 30,901 | 30,958 |
| Average [(a+b)/2] .............................................................. | | 30,930 | 30,838 |
| Operating-cash-flow-to-current-liabilities ratio ..................................... | | 0.48 | 0.49 |

P&G's operating-cash-flow-to-current-liabilities ratio declined slightly from 2008 to 2009, a result of both a small decline in cash provided by operating activities and a slight increase in average current liabilities.

### Accounts Receivable Turnover

The speed with which accounts receivable are collected is of considerable interest to investment professionals when evaluating a firm's short-term liquidity. **Accounts receivable turnover** indicates how many times a year a firm collects its average outstanding accounts receivable, and thus, measures how fast a firm converts its accounts receivable into cash. The quicker a firm is able to convert its accounts receivables into cash, the less cash the company needs to keep on hand to satisfy its current liabilities. Accounts receivable turnover is calculated as follows:

$$\text{Accounts receivable turnover} = \frac{\text{Net sales}}{\text{Average accounts receivable}}$$

The accounts receivable turnover for P&G is (accounts receivable at the end of 2007 were $6,629):

| | | 2009 | 2008 |
|---|---|---|---|
| Net sales | | $79,029 | $81,748 |
| Average accounts receivable (net) | | | |
| Beginning of year | (a) | 6,761 | 6,629 |
| End of year | (b) | 5,836 | 6,761 |
| Average [(a + b)/2] | | 6,299 | 6,695 |
| Accounts receivable turnover | | 12.55 | 12.21 |
| Industry average | | 8.5 | |

The higher the accounts receivable turnover, the faster a company is able to convert its accounts receivable into cash. P&G's accounts receivable turnover increased from 12.21 in 2008 to 12.55 in 2009. Moreover, P&G's 2009 accounts receivable turnover is well above the industry average of 8.5 for the year.

### Average Collection Period

An extension of the accounts receivable turnover is the **average collection period**. The average collection period reveals how many days it takes, on average, for a company to collect an account receivable. The ratio is calculated as follows:

**A.K.A.** The average collection period is also referred to as the days' sales outstanding, or DSO.

$$\text{Average collection period} = \frac{365}{\text{Accounts receivable turnover}}$$

P&G's average collection period is calculated as follows:

| | 2009 | 2008 |
|---|---|---|
| Average collection period | | |
| 2009: 365/12.55; 2008: 365/12.21 | 29.1 days | 29.9 days |
| Industry average | 42.9 days | |

P&G reduced its average collection period by almost a full day during 2009. This may have resulted from such actions as a tightening of the credit standards offered by the company to its customers or by shortening the allowed credit period. Alternatively, it may reflect that P&G's customers have improved their cash flows, and thus, are able to pay their accounts payable more promptly. Knowledge of P&G's credit terms would permit a more complete analysis of these results. If, for example, P&G's credit terms are n/20, then an average collection period of 29.1 days indicates that the company has a problem with slow-paying customers. If, on the other hand, P&G's credit terms are n/30, then the 2009 average collection period shows no particular problem with the company's speed of receivable collection.

### Inventory Turnover

An analyst concerned about a company's inventory position is likely to evaluate the company's **inventory turnover**. This ratio indicates whether the inventory on hand is disproportionate to the amount of sales revenue. Excessive inventories not only tie up company funds and increase storage costs but may also lead to subsequent losses if the goods become outdated or unsalable. The calculation of inventory turnover is as follows:

$$\text{Inventory turnover} = \frac{\text{Cost of goods sold}}{\text{Average inventory}}$$

P&G's inventory turnover is (inventory at the end of 2007 was $6,819):

| | | 2009 | 2008 |
|---|---|---|---|
| Cost of goods sold | | $38,898 | $39,536 |
| Inventory | | | |
| Beginning of year | (a) | 8,416 | 6,819 |
| End of year | (b) | 6,880 | 8,416 |
| Average [(a + b)/2] | | 7,648 | 7,618 |
| Inventory turnover | | 5.09 | 5.19 |
| Industry average | | 6.0 | |

Financial statement users must also be aware of the inherent limitations of financial statement data. Problems of comparability are frequently encountered. Companies within the same industry may use different accounting methods that can cause problems in comparing certain key relationships. For instance, inventory turnover is likely to be quite different for a company using LIFO than for one using FIFO. Inflation may also distort certain financial data and ratios, especially those resulting from horizontal analysis. For example, trend percentages calculated from data unadjusted for inflation may be deceptive.

Financial statement users must also be careful when comparing companies within a particular industry. Factors such as firm size, diversity of product line, and mode of operations can make firms within the same industry completely dissimilar in their reported results. Moreover, some firms, particularly conglomerates, are difficult to classify by industry. If segment information is available, the financial statement user may compare the statistics for several industries. Often, trade associations prepare industry statistics that are stratified by size of firm or type of product, facilitating financial statement analysis.

## FORENSIC ACCOUNTING

It is generally considered more difficult to deter financial statement fraud than it is to deter other types of fraud such as embezzlement. The best approach to fraud deterrence is to put into place a strong set of internal controls. Unfortunately, senior management, such as a firm's CEO and CFO, are the most likely employees to commit financial statement fraud. These individuals are able to use their position of authority to override most internal controls. Thus, it is important to consider alternative approaches to fraud deterrence. Potential alternative approaches are based on the fraud triangle concept, in which fraud is related to the interaction of three factors: (1) pressure, (2) opportunity, and (3) rationalization.

The fraud element of pressure can be reduced by avoiding the practice of setting unachievable financial goals and utilizing compensation systems that are considered fair but which do not create excessive incentives to commit fraud. Although internal controls may be circumvented by senior management, it is still important to maintain a strong system of internal controls and to establish clear and uniform accounting procedures with no exception clauses. In addition, a strong internal control department reporting to the board of directors provides further deterrence. Finally, the creation and promotion of a culture of honesty and integrity throughout an organization makes the rationalization of financial statement fraud much more difficult.

## WORKING WITH THE TAKEAWAYS

Below are income statements and balance sheets for the Fango Company for 2011 and 2010:

| FANGO COMPANY Income Statement For the Years Ended December 31, 2011 and 2010 | | |
| --- | --- | --- |
| (in millions) | 2011 | 2010 |
| Sales revenue | $10,000 | $9,500 |
| Cost of goods sold | 5,500 | 5,200 |
| Gross profit | 4,500 | 4,300 |
| Selling and administrative expenses | 2,800 | 2,700 |
| Income from operations | 1,700 | 1,600 |
| Interest expense | 300 | 250 |
| Income before income taxes | 1,400 | 1,350 |
| Income tax expense | 420 | 400 |
| Net income | $ 980 | $ 950 |

*continued*

**FANGO COMPANY**
**Income Statement**
**For the Years Ended December 31, 2011 and 2010**

**(in millions)**

| | 2011 | 2010 |
|---|---|---|
| **Assets** | | |
| Current assets | | |
| Cash and cash equivalents . . . . . . . . . . . . . . . . . . . . . . . . . . . . . . . . . . . . . . . . . . . . . . . . . . | $ 200 | $ 400 |
| Accounts receivable . . . . . . . . . . . . . . . . . . . . . . . . . . . . . . . . . . . . . . . . . . . . . . . . . . . . . . | 900 | 800 |
| Inventory . . . . . . . . . . . . . . . . . . . . . . . . . . . . . . . . . . . . . . . . . . . . . . . . . . . . . . . . . . . . . | 700 | 650 |
| Other current assets . . . . . . . . . . . . . . . . . . . . . . . . . . . . . . . . . . . . . . . . . . . . . . . . . . . . . | 400 | 250 |
| Total current assets . . . . . . . . . . . . . . . . . . . . . . . . . . . . . . . . . . . . . . . . . . . . . . . . . . . . . | 2,000 | 2,100 |
| Property, plant, & equipment (net) . . . . . . . . . . . . . . . . . . . . . . . . . . . . . . . . . . . . . . . . . | 2,600 | 2,500 |
| Other assets. . . . . . . . . . . . . . . . . . . . . . . . . . . . . . . . . . . . . . . . . . . . . . . . . . . . . . . . . . . | 5,700 | 5,900 |
| Total assets. . . . . . . . . . . . . . . . . . . . . . . . . . . . . . . . . . . . . . . . . . . . . . . . . . . . . . . . . . . | $10,300 | $10,500 |
| **Liabilities and Stockholders' Equity** | | |
| Current liabilities . . . . . . . . . . . . . . . . . . . . . . . . . . . . . . . . . . . . . . . . . . . . . . . . . . . . . . | $ 3,000 | $ 2,900 |
| Long-term liabilities . . . . . . . . . . . . . . . . . . . . . . . . . . . . . . . . . . . . . . . . . . . . . . . . . . . . | 5,000 | 5,400 |
| Total liabilities. . . . . . . . . . . . . . . . . . . . . . . . . . . . . . . . . . . . . . . . . . . . . . . . . . . . . . . . | 8,000 | 8,300 |
| Stockholders' equity – common. . . . . . . . . . . . . . . . . . . . . . . . . . . . . . . . . . . . . . . . . . . | 2,300 | 2,200 |
| Total liabilities and stockholders' equity . . . . . . . . . . . . . . . . . . . . . . . . . . . . . . . . . . . | $10,600 | $10,500 |

**Required**

Calculate the following ratios for the Fango Company for 2011 and 2010 and discuss your findings:

1. Profitability
   a. Return on sales
   b. Return on common stockholders' equity (common stockholders' equity was $2,000 on December 31, 2009)
2. Liquidity
   a. Current ratio
   b. Accounts receivable turnover (accounts receivable was $780 on December 31, 2009)
   c. Inventory turnover (inventory was $620 on December 31, 2009)
3. Solvency
   a. Debt-to-equity ratio
   b. Times-interest-earned ratio

**Solution**

1. Profitability
   a. Return on sales
      2011: $980/$10,000 = 9.8 percent
      2010: $950/$9,500  = 10.0 percent
   b. Return on common stockholders' equity (common stockholders' equity was $2,000 on December 31, 2009)
      2011: ($980 − $0)/(($2,300 + $2,200)/2)) = 43.6 percent
      2010: ($950 − $0)/(($2,200 + $2,000)/2)) = 45.2 percent

Fango Corporation experienced deterioration in both ratios in 2011; however, both the return on sales of 20 percent and the return on common stockholders' equity of 43.6 percent represent very healthy indicators of firm profitability.

2. Liquidity
   a. Current ratio
      2011: $2,000/$3,000 = 0.67
      2010: $2,100/$2,900 = 0.72
   b. Accounts receivable turnover (accounts receivable was $780 on December 31, 2009)
      2011: $10,000/(($900 + $800)/2) = 11.77 times
      2010: $9,500/(($800 + $780)/2)  = 12.03 times
   c. Inventory turnover (inventory was $620 on December 31, 2009)
      2011: $5,500/(($700 + $650)/2) = 8.15 times
      2010: $5,200/(($650 + $620)/2) = 8.19 times

*continued*

Fango Corporation experienced deterioration in all three ratios in 2011; however, the turnover ratios suggest relatively quick cash collection and quick sales of inventory. Thus, even though the current ratio is under 1.0, the company is generating cash quickly.

3. Solvency
   a. Debt-to-equity ratio
      2011: $8,000/$300 = 5.67
      2010: $8,300/$250 = 6.40
   b. Times-interest-earned ratio
      2011: ($980 + $300 + $420)/$300 = 5.67
      2010: ($950 + $250 + $400)/$250 = 6.40

Fango Corporation experienced improvement in the debt-to-equity ratio in 2011; however, the Company uses a large amount of debt financing relative to its equity financing and its times-interest-earned ratio declined in 2011. Combined with the liquidity ratios from Part 2, further analysis of the company's solvency appears warranted.

# APPENDIX 13A: Financial Statement Disclosures

LEARNING OBJECTIVE 6

Appendix 13A
**Describe** financial
statement disclosures

Disclosures related to a company's financial statements fall into one of three categories: (1) parenthetical disclosures on the face of the financial statements, (2) notes to the financial statements, and (3) supplementary information. Most disclosures amplify or explain aggregated information contained in the financial statements. Some disclosures, however, add new information.

## PARENTHETICAL DISCLOSURES

*Parenthetical disclosures* are placed next to an account title or other descriptive label in the financial statements. Their purpose is to provide additional detail regarding the item or account.

An example of parenthetical disclosures follows:

|  | 2010 | 2009 |
|---|---|---|
| Accounts receivable, less allowances for doubtful accounts (2010—$30,000; 2009—$26,500) ........................................... | $215,000 | $174,000 |

## NOTES TO THE FINANCIAL STATEMENTS

Although much information is gathered, summarized, and reported in a company's financial statements, the financial statements alone are limited in their ability to convey a complete picture of a company's financial status. *Notes* are added to the financial statements to help fill in these gaps. In fact, over time, accountants have given so much attention to the financial statement notes that the notes now consume more page space in the annual report than the financial statements themselves. Notes may cover a wide variety of topics. Typically, they deal with significant accounting policies, explanations of complex or special transactions, details of reported amounts, commitments, contingencies, business segments, quarterly data, and subsequent material events.

### Significant Accounting Policies

GAAP contains a number of instances for which alternative accounting procedures are equally acceptable. For example, there are several generally accepted depreciation and inventory valuation methods, and there are different ways to recognize sales revenue. The particular accounting policies selected by a company affect the financial data presented. Knowledge of a firm's specific accounting principles and methods of applying these principles helps users more fully understand a company's financial statements. Accordingly, these principles and methods are disclosed in a **summary of significant accounting policies**.

For example, the annual report of the **Columbia Sportswear Company**, included in Appendix A of this book, contains the following description of its inventory policy:

> Inventories are carried at the lower of cost or market. Cost is determined using the first-in, first-out method. The Company periodically reviews its inventories for excess, close-out or slow moving items and makes provisions as necessary to properly reflect inventory value.

## Explanations of Complex or Special Transactions

The complexity of certain transactions means that not all important aspects are likely to be reflected in the accounts. Financial statement notes, therefore, report additional relevant details about such transactions. Typical examples include notes discussing the financial aspects of pension plans, profit-sharing plans, acquisitions of other companies, borrowing agreements, stock option and other incentive plans, and income taxes.

Transactions with related parties are special transactions requiring disclosure in the financial statement notes. *Related party transactions* include transactions between a firm and its (1) principal owners, (2) members of management, (3) subsidiary companies, or (4) affiliate companies.

## Details of Reported Amounts

Financial statements often summarize several groups of accounts into a single aggregate dollar amount. For example, a balance sheet may show one asset account labeled *Property, Plant, and Equipment,* or it may list *Long-Term Debt* as a single amount among the liabilities. Notes report more detail, presenting schedules that list the types and amounts of property, plant, and equipment and long-term debt. Other items that may be summarized in the financial statements and detailed in the notes include inventories, other current assets, notes payable, accrued liabilities, stockholders' equity, and a company's income tax expense.

The notes to Columbia Sportswear Company's annual report (see Appendix A at the end of this book) contain several examples of financial statement items that are detailed, including inventories (Note 3), property, plant, and equipment (Note 4), short-term borrowing and credit lines (Note 5), accrued liabilities (Note 6), other long-term liabilities (Note 7), and income taxes (Note 9).

## Commitments

A firm may have contractual arrangements existing as of a balance sheet date in which both parties to the contract still have acts yet to be completed. If performance under these **commitments** will have a significant financial impact on a firm, the existence and nature of the commitments should be disclosed in the notes to the financial statements. Examples of commitments reported in the notes include commitments under operating leases, contracts to purchase materials or equipment, contracts to construct facilities, salary commitments to executives, commitments to retire or redeem stock, and commitments to deliver goods.

**Columbia Sportswear Company** reports the following commitments in its annual report:

> During its normal course of business, the Company has made certain indemnities, commitments and guarantees under which it may be required to make payments in relation to certain transactions. These include (i) intellectual property indemnities to the Company's customers and licensees in connection with the use, sale and/or license of Company products, (ii) indemnities to various lessors in connection with facility leases for certain claims arising from such facility or lease, (iii) indemnities to vendors and service providers pertaining to claims based on the negligence or willful misconduct of the Company, (iv) executive severance arrangements and (v) indemnities involving the accuracy of representations and warranties in certain contracts. The duration of these indemnities, commitments and guarantees varies, and in certain cases, may be indefinite. The majority of these indemnities, commitments and guarantees do not provide for any limitation of the maximum potential for future payments the Company could be obligated to make. The Company has not recorded any liability for these indemnities, commitments and guarantees in the accompanying Consolidated Balance Sheets.

## Contingencies

Contingent liabilities were discussed in Chapter 10. As noted there, if the future event that would turn a contingency into an obligation is not likely to occur, or if the liability cannot be reasonably estimated, the **contingency** is disclosed in a note to the financial statements. Typical contingencies disclosed in the notes include pending lawsuits, environmental cleanup costs, possible income tax assessments, credit guarantees, and discounted notes receivable.

The **Timberland Company** reports the following contingencies in its annual report:

> We are involved in various legal matters, including litigation, that have arisen in the ordinary course of business. Management believes that the ultimate resolution of any existing matter will not have a material adverse effect on our business or our consolidated financial statements. In December 2008, we settled certain litigation involving infringement of our intellectual property rights by a third party, which resulted in a pre-tax gain of approximately $2,630. The cash associated with the settlement was received in 2007.

APPENDIX 13A

## Segments

Many firms diversify their business activities and operate in several different industries. A firm's financial statements often combine information from all of a company's operations into aggregate amounts. This complicates the financial statement user's ability to analyze the statements because the interpretation of financial data is influenced by the industry in which a firm operates. Different industries face different types of risk and have different rates of profitability. In making investment and lending decisions, financial statement users evaluate risk and required rates of return. Having financial data available by industry segment is helpful to such evaluations.

The FASB recognizes the usefulness of industry data to investors and lenders. Public companies with significant operations in more than one industry must report certain financial information by industry **segment**. Typically, these disclosures are in the financial statement notes. The major disclosures by industry segment are sales revenue, operating profit or loss, identifiable assets (the assets used by the segment), capital expenditures, and depreciation.

Other types of segment data may also be disclosed. Business operations in different parts of the world are subject to different risks and opportunities for growth. Thus, public companies with significant operations in foreign countries must report selected financial data by foreign geographic area. The required data disclosures include sales revenue, operating profit or loss (or other profitability measure), and identifiable assets. Also, if a firm has export sales or sales revenue to a single customer that are ten percent or more of total sales revenue, the amount of such sales revenue must be separately disclosed.

Note 15 to **Columbia Sportswear's** financial statements in its annual report (see Appendix A at the end of this book) illustrates segment disclosures by foreign versus domestic segments.

## Quarterly Data

Interim financial reports cover periods shorter than one year. Companies that issue interim reports generally do so quarterly. These reports provide financial statement users with timely information on a firm's progress and are useful in predicting a company's annual financial results. The SEC requires that certain companies disclose selected quarterly financial data in their annual reports to stockholders. Included among the notes, the data reported for each quarter include sales revenue, gross profit, net income, and earnings per share. **Quarterly data** permit financial statement users to analyze such things as the seasonal nature of operations, the impact of diversification on quarterly activity, and whether the firm's activities lead or lag general economic trends.

The Columbia Sportswear Company provides quarterly financial information as supplemental data in its annual report (see the Columbia Annual Report in Appendix A).

## Subsequent Events

If a company issues a large amount of securities or suffers a casualty loss after the balance sheet date, this information should be reported in a note, even though the situation arose subsequent to the balance sheet date. Firms are responsible for disclosing any significant events that occur between the balance sheet date and the date the financial statements are issued. This guideline recognizes that it takes several weeks for financial statements to be prepared and audited before they are issued. Events occurring during this period may have a material effect on a firm's operations and should be disclosed. Other examples of **subsequent events** requiring disclosure are sales of assets, significant changes in long-term debt, and acquisitions of other companies.

For example, the **Timberland Company** reported the following subsequent event in its annual report:

> In February 2009, we received notification that our U.S. federal tax examinations for 2006 and 2007 had been completed. Accordingly, in the first quarter of 2009, we will reverse approximately $6,000 of accruals related to uncertain tax positions.

## SUPPLEMENTARY INFORMATION

Supplementing the financial statements are several additional disclosures—management's discussion and analysis of the financial statements and selected financial data covering a five- to ten-year period along with possible other *supplementary* disclosures that are either required of certain companies by the SEC or recommended (but not required) by the FASB.

## Management Discussion and Analysis

**A.K.A.** The management discussion and analysis is also referred to simply as the MD&A.

Management may increase the usefulness of financial statements by sharing some of their knowledge about a company's financial condition and operations. This is the purpose of the disclosure devoted to the management discussion and analysis. In this supplement to the financial statements, management identifies and comments on events and trends influencing a company's liquidity, operating results, and financial resources. Management's position within a company not only provides it with insights unavailable to outsiders, but also may introduce certain biases into the analysis. Nonetheless, management's comments, interpretations, and explanations should contribute to a better understanding of a company's financial statements.

## Comparative Selected Financial Data

The analysis of a company's financial performance is enhanced when financial data for several years are available. By analyzing trends over time, it is possible for a financial statement user to learn much more about a company than would be possible by analyzing only a single year of data. Year-to-year changes may give clues as to a firm's future growth or may highlight areas for concern. Corporate annual reports to stockholders present complete financial statements in comparative form, showing the current year and one or more preceding years. Beyond this, however, the financial statements are supplemented by a summary of selected key financial statistics for a five- or ten-year period. The financial data presented in this historical summary usually include sales revenue, net income, dividends, earnings per share, working capital, and total assets.

## SUMMARY OF LEARNING OBJECTIVES

**Identify persistent earnings and discuss the content and format of the income statement. (p. 594)**   LO1

■ Persistent earnings are earnings that are likely to recur, while transitory earnings are unlikely to recur.

■ The continuing income of a business may be reported in a single-step format or in a multiple-step format.

■ Gains and losses from discontinued operations are reported in a special income statement section following income from continuing operations.

■ Extraordinary items are both unusual *and* nonrecurring; they are reported in a separate section of the income statement.

■ The effect of most changes in accounting principle requires restatement of prior financial statements as if the new method had been applied all along.

■ Companies are required to report other comprehensive income in addition to regular income in their financial statements.

**Identify the sources of financial information used by investment professionals and explain horizontal financial statements analysis. (p. 598)**   LO2

■ Data sources for investment professionals include published financial statements, filings with the U.S. Securities and Exchange Commission, and statistics available from financial data services.

■ A common form of horizontal analysis involves analyzing dollar and percentage changes in comparative financial statements for two or more years.

■ Analyzing trend percentages of key figures, such as sales revenue, net income, and total assets for a number of years, related to a base year, is often useful.

**Explain vertical financial statement analysis. (p. 603)**   LO3

■ Vertical analysis deals with the relationship of financial statement data for a single year.

■ Common-size statements express financial statement items as a percentage of another key item, such as expressing income statement items as a percentage of sales revenue and balance sheet items as a percentage of total assets.

**Define and discuss financial ratios for analyzing a firm. (p. 605)**   LO4

■ Ratios for analyzing firm profitability include the gross profit percentage, the return on sales, asset turnover, the return on assets, and the return on common stockholders' equity.

■ Ratios for analyzing short-term firm liquidity include the current ratio, quick ratio, operating-cash-flow-to-current-liabilities ratio, accounts receivable turnover, average collection period, inventory turnover, and days' sales in inventory.

■ Ratios for analyzing long-term firm solvency include the debt-to-equity ratio, the times-interest-earned ratio, and operating-cash-flow-to-capital-expenditures ratio.

■ Ratios of particular interest to common stockholders include a company's earnings per share, the price-earnings ratio, dividend yield, and the dividend payout ratio.

**LO5** Discuss the limitations of financial statement analysis. (p. 617)

- When analyzing financial statements, financial statement users must be aware of a firm's accounting methods, the effects of inflation, and the difficulty of currently identifying a firm's industry classification.

**LO6** Appendix 13A: Describe financial statement disclosures. (p. 620)

- Parenthetical disclosures on the face of the financial statements provide additional detail regarding the item or account.
- Notes to the financial statements provide information on significant accounting policies, explanations of complex or special transactions, details of reported amounts, commitments, contingencies, segments, quarterly data, and subsequent events.
- Supplemental information includes the management discussion and analysis, and comparable selected financial information.

## SUMMARY OF FINANCIAL STATEMENT RATIOS

### ANALYZING FIRM PROFITABILITY

$$\text{Gross profit percentage} = \frac{\text{Gross profit on sales}}{\text{Net sales}}$$

$$\text{Return on sales} = \frac{\text{Net income}}{\text{Net sales}}$$

$$\text{Asset turnover} = \frac{\text{Net sales}}{\text{Average total assets}}$$

$$\text{Return on assets} = \frac{\text{Net income}}{\text{Average total assets}}$$

$$\text{Return on common stockholders' equity} = \frac{(\text{Net income} - \text{Preferred stock dividends})}{\text{Average common stockholders' equity}}$$

### ANALYZING SHORT-TERM FIRM LIQUIDITY

$$\text{Current ratio} = \frac{\text{Current assets}}{\text{Current liabilities}}$$

$$\text{Quick ratio} = \frac{(\text{Cash and cash equivalents} + \text{Short-term investments} + \text{Accounts receivable})}{\text{Current liabilities}}$$

$$\text{Operating-cash-flow-to-current-liabilities ratio} = \frac{\text{Cash flow from operating activities}}{\text{Average current liabilities}}$$

$$\text{Accounts receivable turnover} = \frac{\text{Net sales}}{\text{Average accounts receivable}}$$

$$\text{Average collection period} = \frac{365}{\text{Accounts receivable turnover}}$$

$$\text{Inventory turnover} = \frac{\text{Cost of goods sold}}{\text{Average inventory}}$$

$$\text{Days' sales in inventory} = \frac{365}{\text{Inventory turnover}}$$

### ANALYZING LONG-TERM FIRM SOLVENCY

$$\text{Debt-to-equity ratio} = \frac{\text{Total liabilities}}{\text{Total stockholders' equity}}$$

$$\text{Times-interest-earned ratio} = \frac{\text{Income before interest expense and income taxes}}{\text{Interest expense}}$$

$$\text{Operating-cash-flow-to-capital-expenditures ratio} = \frac{\text{Cash flow from operating activities}}{\text{Annual net capital expenditures}}$$

## FINANCIAL RATIOS FOR COMMON STOCKHOLDERS

$$\text{Earnings per share} = \frac{\text{(Net income} - \text{Preferred stock dividends)}}{\text{Weighted average common shares outstanding}}$$

$$\text{Price-earnings ratio} = \frac{\text{Market price per share}}{\text{Earnings per share}}$$

$$\text{Dividend yield} = \frac{\text{Annual dividends per share}}{\text{Market price per share}}$$

$$\text{Dividend payout ratio} = \frac{\text{Annual dividends per share}}{\text{Earnings per share}}$$

## TAKEAWAYS: SUMMARY CHART

| Concept ⟶ | Method ⟶ | Assessment | |
|---|---|---|---|
| How does a company's current performance compare with the prior year? | Income statement and balance sheet for current and prior year.<br><br>The income statement and balance sheet should be compared using the prior year as the base. Percentage changes in net income and total assets can be calculated as the change between years divided by the base year amount. | Significant changes should be analyzed to determine the reason for any change. | TAKEAWAY 13.1 |
| How do the relationships within a company's income statement and balance sheet compare to those of the prior year? | Income statement and balance sheet for current and prior year.<br><br>Each income statement item should be presented as a percentage of sales revenue and each balance sheet item should be presented as a percentage of total assets. Financial statements in this form are called common-size statements. | The percentages should be analyzed for differences between years and significant changes should be analyzed to determine the reason for any change. | TAKEAWAY 13.2 |
| How much profit is a company generating relative to the amount of assets invested in the company? | Income statement and balance sheet.<br><br>Calculate the return on assets by dividing net income by the average total assets for the year. | The higher the return on assets, the better a company is doing with respect to generating net income on the assets it has under its control. | TAKEAWAY 13.3 |
| How financially capable is a company to pay its current liabilities as they come due? | Income statement, balance sheet, and statement of cash flows.<br><br>Calculate the current ratio, the quick ratio, and the operating-cash-flow-to-current-liabilities ratio. | The higher the ratios, the higher the probability that the company will have the ability to pay its current liabilities as they come due. | TAKEAWAY 13.4 |
| How solvent is a company? | Income statement, balance sheet, and statement of cash flows.<br><br>Calculate the debt-to-equity ratio, the times-interest-earned ratio, and the operating-cash-flow-to-capital-expenditures ratio. | The higher the times-interest-earned and the operating-cash-flow-to-capital-expenditures ratios, and the lower the debt-to-equity ratio, the greater is a company's solvency. | TAKEAWAY 13.5 |
| How much dividends are common stockholders likely to receive? | Earnings per share, dividends per share, and market price of common stock.<br>Calculate the dividend yield and dividend payout ratio. | The higher the dividend yield and the dividend payout ratio, the greater the company's dividend distribution policy. | TAKEAWAY 13.6 |

REVIEW

# GLOSSARY OF KEY TERMS

**Accounts receivable turnover** Annual net sales divided by average accounts receivable (net) (p. 610).

**Asset turnover ratio** Net sales divided by average total assets (p.606).

**Average collection period** 365 days divided by accounts receivable turnover (p. 611).

**Change in accounting principle** A switch from one generally accepted accounting method to another generally accepted method, such as changing depreciation methods (p. 597).

**Commitments** A contractual arrangement in which both parties to the contract still have acts yet to perform (p. 621).

**Common-size financial statement** A financial statement in which each item is presented as a percentage of a key statement item (p. 603).

**Comparative financial statement analysis** A form of horizontal analysis involving a comparison of two or more periods of financial statement data showing dollar and/or percentage changes (p. 599).

**Comprehensive income** A broader definition of a company's income that includes net income plus any changes in the market value of certain marketable securities and any unrealized gains and losses from translating foreign currency denominated financial statements into U.S. dollars (p. 598).

**Contingency** A possible future event; significant contingent liabilities must be disclosed in the notes to the financial statements (p. 621).

**Current ratio** A firm's current assets divided by its current liabilities (p. 609).

**Days' sales in inventory** 365 days divided by inventory turnover (p. 612).

**Debt-to-equity ratio** A firm's total liabilities divided by its total stockholders' equity (p. 613).

**Discontinued operations** Operating segments of a company that have been sold, abandoned, or disposed of during the accounting period. Related operating income (or loss) and related gains and losses on disposal are reported separately on the income statement (p. 596).

**Dividend payout ratio** Annual dividend per share divided by a company's earnings per share (p. 617).

**Dividend yield** Annual dividend per share divided by the market price per share (p. 616).

**Earnings per share (EPS)** A financial ratio computed as net income less preferred stock dividends divided by the weighted average number of common shares outstanding for the period (p. 615).

**Extraordinary items** Transactions and events that are unusual in nature and occur infrequently. Gains and losses on such items are shown separately, net of tax effects, on the income statement (p. 596).

**Gross profit percentage** Gross profit on sales divided by net sales (p. 605).

**Horizontal analysis** The analysis of a firm's financial statements that covers two or more years (p. 599).

**Inventory turnover** Cost of goods sold divided by average inventory (p. 611).

**Multiple-step income statement** An income statement in which one or more intermediate performance measures, such as gross profit on sales, are derived before the continuing income is reported (p. 594).

**Operating-cash-flow-to-capital-expenditures ratio** A firm's cash flow from operating activities divided by its annual capital expenditures (p. 614).

**Operating-cash-flow-to-current-liabilities ratio** A firm's cash flow from operating activities divided by its average current liabilities (p. 610).

**Persistent earnings** Earnings that are expected to recur over time. Also known as *sustainable earnings* or *permanent earnings* (p. 594).

**Price-earnings ratio** The current market price per common share divided by a company's earnings per share (p. 616).

**Quarterly data** Selected quarterly financial information that is reported in the annual report to stockholders (p. 622).

**Quick ratio** Quick assets (that is, cash and cash equivalents, short-term investments, and accounts receivable) divided by current liabilities (p. 609).

**Return on assets** Net income divided by average total assets (p. 607).

**Return on common stockholders' equity** Net income less preferred stock dividends divided by average common stockholders' equity (p. 607).

**Return on sales** Net income divided by net sales (p. 606).

**Segment** A subdivision of a firm for which supplemental financial information is disclosed (p. 622).

**Single-step income statement** An income statement in which the continuing income is derived in one step by subtracting total expenses from total sales revenues (p. 594).

**Subsequent events** Events occurring shortly after a fiscal year-end that are reported as supplemental information to the financial statements of the year just ended (p. 622).

**Summary of significant accounting policies** A financial statement disclosure, usually the initial note to the financial statements, which identifies the major accounting policies and procedures used by a firm (p. 620).

**Times-interest-earned ratio** Income before interest expense and income taxes divided by interest expense (p. 614).

**Transitory earnings** Single-period events such as extraordinary gains/losses, special items, restructuring charges, changes in accounting principle, and discontinued operations (p. 594).

**Trend percentages** A comparison of the same financial item over two or more years stated as a percentage of a base-year amount (p. 602).

**Unusual items** Items that display a high degree of abnormality and/or are unrelated, or only incidentally related, to the normal activities of a business (p. 595).

**Vertical analysis** Analysis of a firm's financial statements that focuses on the statements of a single year (p. 599).

**Working capital** The difference between a firm's current assets and current liabilities (p. 608).

# COMPREHENSIVE PROBLEM

Knox Instruments, Inc., is a manufacturer of various medical and dental instruments. Financial statement data for the firm follow:

| (thousands of dollars, except per-share amount) | 2011 |
| --- | --- |
| Sales revenue | $200,000 |
| Cost of goods sold | 98,000 |
| Net income | 10,750 |
| Dividends | 4,200 |
| Cash provided by operating activities | 7,800 |
| Earnings per share | 3.07 |

| KNOX INSTRUMENTS, INC. Balance Sheets | | |
|---|---|---|
| (thousands of dollars) | Dec. 31, 2011 | Dec. 31, 2010 |
| **Assets** | | |
| Cash . . . . . . . . . . . . . . . . . . . . . . . . . . . . . . . . . . . . . . . . . . . . . . . . . . . . . . . . . . . . . . . . . . . . . . . . . | $ 3,000 | $ 2,900 |
| Accounts receivable (net) . . . . . . . . . . . . . . . . . . . . . . . . . . . . . . . . . . . . . . . . . . . . . . | 28,000 | 28,800 |
| Inventory . . . . . . . . . . . . . . . . . . . . . . . . . . . . . . . . . . . . . . . . . . . . . . . . . . . . . . . . . . . . . . . . . . . | 64,000 | 44,000 |
| Total current assets . . . . . . . . . . . . . . . . . . . . . . . . . . . . . . . . . . . . . . . . . . . . . . . . . | 95,000 | 75,700 |
| Plant assets (net) . . . . . . . . . . . . . . . . . . . . . . . . . . . . . . . . . . . . . . . . . . . . . . . . . . . . . . . | 76,000 | 67,300 |
| Total Assets . . . . . . . . . . . . . . . . . . . . . . . . . . . . . . . . . . . . . . . . . . . . . . . . . . . . . . . . . . . . . | $171,000 | $143,000 |
| **Liabilities and Stockholders' Equity** | | |
| Current liabilities . . . . . . . . . . . . . . . . . . . . . . . . . . . . . . . . . . . . . . . . . . . . . . . . . . . . . . . . | $ 45,200 | $ 39,750 |
| 10% Bonds payable . . . . . . . . . . . . . . . . . . . . . . . . . . . . . . . . . . . . . . . . . . . . . . . . . . . . . . . | 20,000 | 14,000 |
| Total Liabilities . . . . . . . . . . . . . . . . . . . . . . . . . . . . . . . . . . . . . . . . . . . . . . . . . . . . . . . . . | 65,200 | 53,750 |
| Common stock, $10 par value . . . . . . . . . . . . . . . . . . . . . . . . . . . . . . . . . . . . . . . . . . | 40,000 | 30,000 |
| Retained earnings . . . . . . . . . . . . . . . . . . . . . . . . . . . . . . . . . . . . . . . . . . . . . . . . . . . . . . . | 65,800 | 59,250 |
| Total Stockholders' Equity . . . . . . . . . . . . . . . . . . . . . . . . . . . . . . . . . . . . . . . . . . . . . | 105,800 | 89,250 |
| Total Liabilities and Stockholders' Equity . . . . . . . . . . . . . . . . . . . . . . . . . . . . | $171,000 | $143,000 |

## Required

a. Using the given data, calculate financial ratios one through nine for 2011. Compare the ratio results for Knox Instruments, Inc., with the following industry averages and comment on its operations.

### Median Ratios for the Industry

| | | |
|---|---|---|
| 1. | Current ratio | 2.7 |
| 2. | Quick ratio | 1.6 |
| 3. | Average collection period | 73 days |
| 4. | Inventory turnover | 2.3 |
| 5. | Operating-cash-flow-to-current-liabilities ratio | NA |
| 6. | Debt-to-equity ratio | 0.50 |
| 7. | Return on assets | 4.9 percent |
| 8. | Return on common stockholders' equity | 10.2 percent |
| 9. | Return on sales | 4.1 percent |

b. Calculate the dividends paid per share of common stock. (Use the average number of shares outstanding during the year.) What was the dividend payout ratio?

c. If the 2011 year-end market price per share of Knox's common stock is $25, what is the company's (1) price-earnings ratio and (2) dividend yield?

## Solution

a.

1. Current ratio = $95,000/$45,200 = 2.10
2. Quick ratio = $31,000/$45,200 = 0.69
3. Average collection period:
   Accounts receivable turnover = $200,000/($28,800 + $28,000)/2 = 7.04
   Average collection period = 365/7.04 = 51.8 days
4. Inventory turnover = $98,000/($44,000 + $64,000)/2 = 1.81
5. Operating-cash-flow-to-current-liabilities ratio = $7,800/($39,750 + $45,200)/2 = 0.18
6. Debt-to-equity ratio = $65,200/$105,800 = 0.62
7. Return on assets = $10,750/($143,000 + $171,000)/2 = 6.8 percent
8. Return on common stockholders' equity = $10,750/($89,250 + $105,800)/2 = 11.0 percent
9. Return on sales = $10,750/$200,000 = 5.4 percent

Although the firm's current ratio of 2.10 is below the industry median, it is still acceptable; however, the quick ratio of 0.69 is well below the industry median. This indicates that Knox's inventory (which is omitted from this calculation) is excessive. This is borne out by the firm's inventory turnover of 1.81 times, which compares with the industry median of 2.3 times. The firm's average collection period of 51.8 days is significantly better than the industry median of 73 days. No industry median is available for the operating-cash-flow-to-current-liabilities ratio. Knox's debt-to-equity ratio of 0.62 indicates that the firm has proportionately more debt in its capital structure than the median industry firm, which has a debt-to-equity ratio of 0.50. Knox's operations appear efficient as its return on assets, return on common stockholders' equity, and return on sales all exceed the industry medians.

b. Average number of shares outstanding = (4,000,000 + 3,000,000)/2 = 3,500,000 shares.
$4,200,000 dividends/3,500,000 shares = $1.20 dividend per share.
Dividend payout ratio = $1.20/$3.07 = 39.1 percent.

c. Price-earnings ratio = $25/$3.07 = 8.1.
Dividend yield = $1.20/$25 = 4.8 percent.

## SELF-STUDY QUESTIONS

**(Answers to the Self-Study Questions are available at the end of this chapter.)**

LO1    **1.** Assume that an income statement contains each of the four sections listed below. Which will be the last section presented in the income statement?
     *a.*   Extraordinary items
     *b.*   Gross profit
     *c.*   Income from continuing operations
     *d.*   Discontinued operations

LO3    **2.** When constructing a common-sized income statement, all amounts are expressed as a percentage of:
     *a.*   net income.                      *c.*   net sales.
     *b.*   gross profit.                  *d.*   income from operations.

Questions 3–10 of the Self-Study Questions are based on the following data:

| HYDRO COMPANY<br>Balance Sheet<br>As of December 31, 2010 | | | |
|---|---:|---|---:|
| Cash ......................... | $ 40,000 | Current liabilities ........................... | $ 80,000 |
| Accounts receivable (net) ..... | 80,000 | 10% Bonds payable......................... | 120,000 |
| Inventory .................... | 130,000 | Common stock ............................. | 200,000 |
| Plant and equipment (net) .... | 250,000 | Retained earnings ......................... | 100,000 |
| Total Assets ................. | $500,000 | Total Liabilities and Stockholders' Equity ..... | $500,000 |

Sales revenues for 2010 were $800,000, gross profit was $320,000, and net income was $36,000. The income tax rate was 40 percent. One year ago, accounts receivable (net) were $76,000, inventory was $110,000, total assets were $460,000, and stockholders' equity was $260,000. The bonds payable were outstanding all year and the 2010 interest expense was $12,000.

LO4    **3.** The current ratio of Hydro Company at 12/31/2010, calculated using the above data, was 3.13 and the company's working capital was $170,000. Which of the following would happen if the firm paid off $20,000 of its current liabilities on January 1, 2011?
     *a.*   Both the current ratio and working capital would decrease.
     *b.*   Both the current ratio and working capital would increase.
     *c.*   The current ratio would increase, but working capital would remain the same.
     *d.*   The current ratio would increase, but working capital would decrease.

LO4    **4.** What was the firm's inventory turnover for 2010?
     *a.*   6.67                               *c.*   6
     *b.*   4                                   *d.*   3.69

LO4    **5.** What was the firm's return on common stockholders' equity for 2010?
     *a.*   25.7 percent                 *c.*   17.1 percent
     *b.*   12.9 percent                 *d.*   21.4 percent

LO4    **6.** What was the firm's average collection period for 2010?
     *a.*   36.5 days                    *c.*   35.6 days
     *b.*   37.4 days                    *d.*   18.3 days

LO4    **7.** What was the firm's times-interest-earned ratio for 2010?
     *a.*   4                                    *c.*   5
     *b.*   3                                    *d.*   6

8. What was the firm's return on sales for 2010?  **LO4**
   a. 4.0 percent   c. 5.0 percent
   b. 4.5 percent   d. 5.5 percent

9. What was the firm's return on assets for 2010?  **LO4**
   a. 6.0 percent   c. 7.5 percent
   b. 7.0 percent   d. 8.0 percent

10. When performing trend analysis, each line item is expressed as a percentage of:  **LO2**
    a. net income.   c. the prior year amount.
    b. the base year amount.   d. total assets.

11. Recognized limitations of financial statement analysis include each of the following except:  **LO5**
    a. companies in the same industry using different accounting methods.
    b. inflation.
    c. different levels of profitability between companies.
    d. difficulty of classifying by industry conglomerates.

12. Financial statement disclosures include each of the following except:  **LO6**
    a. notes to the financial statements.   c. supplementary information.
    b. parenthetical disclosures.   d. promotional giveaways.

## Discussion Questions

1. What is the difference between a single-step income statement and a multiple-step income statement?

2. Which of the following amounts would appear only in a multiple-step income statement?
   a. Income from continuing operations.
   b. Income before extraordinary item.
   c. Gross profit on sales.
   d. Net income.

3. What is a business *segment*? Why are gains and losses from a discontinued segment reported in a separate section of the income statement?

4. Define *extraordinary items*. How are extraordinary items disclosed in the income statement?

5. A manufacturing plant of Park Corporation was destroyed by an earthquake, which is rare in the region where the plant was located. Where should this loss be classified on the income statement?

6. A Florida citrus grower incurs substantial frost damage to crops. Frost damage typically is experienced every few years. How should the loss on the crop damage be shown in the income statement?

7. How do horizontal analysis and vertical analysis of financial statements differ?

8. "Financial statement users should focus attention on each item showing a large percentage change from one year to the next." Is this statement correct? Why?

9. What are trend percentages and how are they calculated? What pitfalls must financial statement users avoid when preparing trend percentages?

10. What are common-size financial statements and how are they used?

11. What item is the key figure (that is, 100 percent) in a common-size income statement? a common-size balance sheet?

12. During the past year, Lite Company had net income of $5 million, and Scanlon Company had net income of $8 million. Both companies manufacture electrical components for the construction industry. What additional information would you need to compare the profitability of the two companies?

13. Under what circumstances can the return on sales be used to assess the profitability of a company? Can this ratio be used to compare the profitability of companies from different industries? Explain.

14. What is the relationship between asset turnover, return on assets, and return on sales?

15. Blare Company had a return on sales of 6.5 percent and an asset turnover of 2.40. What is Blare's return on assets?

16. What does the return on common stockholders' equity measure?

17. How does the quick ratio differ from the current ratio?

18. For each of the following ratios, is a high ratio or low ratio considered, in general, a positive sign?
    a. Current ratio
    b. Quick ratio
    c. Operating-cash-flow-to-current-liabilities ratio
    d. Accounts receivable turnover
    e. Average collection period
    f. Inventory turnover
    g. Days' sales in inventory

19. What is the significance of the debt-to-equity ratio and how is it computed?

20. What does the times-interest-earned ratio indicate and how is it calculated?

21. What does the operating-cash-flow-to-capital-expenditures ratio measure?

22. Clair, Inc., earned $4.50 per share of common stock in the current year and paid dividends of $2.34 per share. The most recent market price per share of the common stock is $46.80. What is the company's (a) price-earnings ratio, (b) dividend yield, and (c) dividend payout ratio?

23. What are two inherent limitations of financial statement data?

# SHORT EXERCISES

Use the following financial data for Hi-Tech Instruments to answer Short Exercises 13-1 through 13-10:

| 2011 (Thousands of Dollars, except Earnings per Share) | |
| --- | --- |
| Sales revenue | $210,000 |
| Cost of goods sold | 125,000 |
| Net income | 8,300 |
| Dividends | 2,600 |
| Earnings per share | 4.15 |

| HI-TECH INSTRUMENTS, INC. Balance Sheets | | |
| --- | --- | --- |
| (Thousands of Dollars) | Dec. 31, 2011 | Dec. 31, 2010 |
| **Assets** | | |
| Cash | $ 18,300 | $ 18,000 |
| Accounts receivable (net) | 46,000 | 41,000 |
| Inventory | 39,500 | 43,700 |
| Total Current Assets | 103,800 | 102,700 |
| Plant assets (net) | 52,600 | 50,500 |
| Other assets | 15,600 | 13,800 |
| Total Assets | $172,000 | $167,000 |
| **Liabilities and Stockholders' Equity** | | |
| Notes payable—banks | $ 6,000 | $ 6,000 |
| Accounts payable | 22,500 | 18,700 |
| Accrued liabilities | 16,500 | 21,000 |
| Total Current Liabilities | 45,000 | 45,700 |
| 9% Bonds payable | 40,000 | 40,000 |
| Total Liabilities | 85,000 | 85,700 |
| Common stock, $25 par value (2,000,000 shares) | 50,000 | 50,000 |
| Retained earnings | 37,000 | 31,300 |
| Total Stockholders' Equity | 87,000 | 81,300 |
| Total Liabilities and Stockholders' Equity | $172,000 | $167,000 |

ASSIGNMENTS

| Industry Average Ratios for Competitors | |
| --- | --- |
| Quick ratio | 1.3 |
| Current ratio | 2.4 |
| Accounts receivable turnover | 5.9 times |
| Inventory turnover | 3.5 times |
| Debt-to-equity ratio | 0.73 |
| Gross profit percentage | 42.8 percent |
| Return on sales | 4.5 percent |
| Return on assets | 7.6 percent |

**SE13-1.** **Quick Ratio**                                                                          LO4
Calculate the company's quick ratio for 2011 and compare the result to the industry average.

**SE13-2.** **Current Ratio**                                                                         LO4
Calculate the company's current ratio for 2011 and compare the result to the industry average.

**SE13-3.** **Accounts Receivable Turnover**                                                         LO4
Calculate the company's accounts receivable turnover for 2011 and compare the result to the industry average.

**SE13-4.** **Inventory Turnover**                                                                    LO4
Calculate the company's inventory turnover for 2011 and compare the result to the industry average.

**SE13-5.** **Debit-to-Equity Ratio**                                                                LO4
Calculate the company's 2011 debt-to-equity ratio and compare the result to the industry average.

**SE13-6.** **Gross Profit Percentage**                                                              LO4
Calculate the company's 2011 gross profit percentage and compare the result to the industry average.

**SE13-7.** **Return on Sales**                                                                       LO4
Calculate the company's return on sales for 2011 and compare the result to the industry average.

**SE13-8.** **Return on Assets**                                                                      LO4
Calculate the company's return on assets for 2011 and compare the result to the industry average.

**SE13-9.** **Dividends per Share**                                                                   LO4
Calculate the company's dividend paid per share of common stock. What was the dividend payout ratio?

**SE13-10.** **Earnings per Share**                                                                   LO4
If the company's most recent price per share of common stock is $62.25, what is the company's price-earnings ratio and dividend yield?

**SE13-11.** **Persistent Earnings**                                                                  LO1
Identify each of the following items as either (P) persistent, or (T) transitory.

*a.* Sale of merchandise.
*b.* Settlement of a lawsuit.
*c.* Interest income.
*d.* Payment to vendors.
*e.* Loss from expropriations of property by a foreign government.

**SE13-12.** **Horizontal Analysis**                                                                 LO2
Total assets were $1,000,000 in 2010, $900,000 in 2009, and $950,000 in 2008. What was the percentage change from 2008 to 2009 and from 2009 to 2010? Was the change an increase or a decrease?

**SE13-13.** **Common-Size Income Statement**                                                        LO3
A partial common-size income statement for Prag Company for three years is shown below.

| Item | 2011 | 2010 | 2009 |
|------|------|------|------|
| Net sales . . . . . . . . . . . . . . . . . . . . . . . . . . . . . . . . . . . . . . . . . . . . . . . . . . . . . . . . | 100.0 | 100.0 | 100.0 |
| Cost of goods sold. . . . . . . . . . . . . . . . . . . . . . . . . . . . . . . . . . . . . . . . . . . . . . . | 60.5 | 63.0 | 62.5 |
| Other expenses . . . . . . . . . . . . . . . . . . . . . . . . . . . . . . . . . . . . . . . . . . . . . . . . . | 21.0 | 19.0 | 20.5 |

Did Prag's net income as a percentage of net sales increase, remain the same, or decrease over the three-year period?

# EXERCISES—SET A

**LO1 E13-1A. Income Statement Sections**

During the current year, Dale Corporation incurred an extraordinary tornado loss of $300,000 and sold a segment of its business at a gain of $196,000. Until it was sold, the segment had a current period operating loss of $75,000. Also, the company discovered that an error caused last year's ending inventory to be understated by $31,000 (a material amount). The company had $800,000 income from continuing operations for the current year. Prepare the lower part of the income statement, beginning with the $800,000 income from continuing operations. Follow tax allocation procedures, assuming that all changes in income are subject to a 40 percent income tax rate. Disregard earnings per share disclosures.

**LO4 E13-2A. Earnings per Share**

Lucky Corporation began the year with a simple capital structure consisting of 200,000 shares of outstanding common stock. On April 1, 10,000 additional common shares were issued, and another 30,000 common shares were issued on August 1. The company had net income for the year of $572,000. Calculate the earnings per share of common stock.

**LO2 E13-3A. Comparative Income Statements**

Consider the following income statement data from the Ross Company:

| | 2011 | 2010 |
|------|------|------|
| Sales revenue . . . . . . . . . . . . . . . . . . . . . . . . . . . . . . . . . . . . . . . . . . . . . . . . . . . . . . . | $525,000 | $450,000 |
| Cost of goods sold. . . . . . . . . . . . . . . . . . . . . . . . . . . . . . . . . . . . . . . . . . . . . . . . . . | 336,000 | 279,000 |
| Selling expenses. . . . . . . . . . . . . . . . . . . . . . . . . . . . . . . . . . . . . . . . . . . . . . . . . . . . | 105,000 | 99,000 |
| Administrative expenses. . . . . . . . . . . . . . . . . . . . . . . . . . . . . . . . . . . . . . . . . . . . | 60,000 | 54,000 |
| Income tax expense . . . . . . . . . . . . . . . . . . . . . . . . . . . . . . . . . . . . . . . . . . . . . . . | 7,800 | 5,400 |

*a.* Prepare a comparative income statement, showing increases and decreases in dollars and in percentages.

*b.* Comment briefly on the changes between the two years.

**LO3 E13-4A. Common-Size Income Statements**

Refer to the income statement data given in Exercise E13-3A.

*a.* Prepare common-size income statements for each year.

*b.* Compare the common-size income statements and comment briefly.

**LO4 E13-5A. Ratios Analyzing Firm Profitability**

The following information is available for Buhler Company:

| Annual Data | 2011 | 2010 |
|------|------|------|
| Net sales . . . . . . . . . . . . . . . . . . . . . . . . . . . . . . . . . . . . . . . . . . . . . . . . . . . . . . . . . . | $8,600,000 | $8,000,000 |
| Gross profit on sales . . . . . . . . . . . . . . . . . . . . . . . . . . . . . . . . . . . . . . . . . . . . . . | 3,053,000 | 2,736,000 |
| Net income. . . . . . . . . . . . . . . . . . . . . . . . . . . . . . . . . . . . . . . . . . . . . . . . . . . . . . . | 567,600 | 488,000 |

| Year-End Data | Dec. 31, 2011 | Dec. 31, 2010 |
|------|------|------|
| Total assets. . . . . . . . . . . . . . . . . . . . . . . . . . . . . . . . . . . . . . . . . . . . . . . . . . . . . . . | $6,500,000 | $6,100,000 |
| Stockholders' equity . . . . . . . . . . . . . . . . . . . . . . . . . . . . . . . . . . . . . . . . . . . . . . | 3,800,000 | 3,200,000 |

Calculate the following ratios for 2011:

*a.* Gross profit percentage

*b.* Return on sales

*c.* Asset turnover

*d.* Return on assets

*e.* Return on common stockholders' equity (Buhler Company has no preferred stock.)

**E13-6A.** **Working Capital and Short-Term Liquidity Ratios**    LO4

Bell Company has a current ratio of 2.85 (2.85:1) on December 31. On that date the company's current assets are as follows:

| | |
|---|---|
| Cash | $ 26,400 |
| Short-term investments | 49,000 |
| Accounts receivable (net) | 169,000 |
| Inventory | 200,000 |
| Prepaid expenses | 11,600 |
| Current assets | $456,000 |

Bell Company's current liabilities at the beginning of the year were $135,000 and during the year its operating activities provided a cash flow of $50,000.

a.  What are the firm's current liabilities on December 31?
b.  What is the firm's working capital on December 31?
c.  What is the quick ratio on December 31?
d.  What is Bell's operating-cash-flow-to-current-liabilities ratio?

**E13-7A.** **Accounts Receivable and Inventory Ratios**    LO4

Bell Company, whose current assets at December 31 are shown in Exercise E13-6A, had net sales for the year of $950,000 and cost of goods sold of $552,900. At the beginning of the year, Bell's accounts receivable (net) were $155,000 and its inventory was $194,000.

a.  What is the company's accounts receivable turnover for the year?
b.  What is the company's average collection period for the year?
c.  What is the company's inventory turnover for the year?
d.  What is the company's days' sales in inventory for the year?

**E13-8A.** **Ratios Analyzing Long-Term Firm Solvency**    LO4

The following information is available for Antler Company:

| Annual Data | 2011 | 2010 |
|---|---|---|
| Interest expense | $ 88,000 | $ 82,000 |
| Income tax expense | 203,500 | 185,000 |
| Net income | 496,500 | 395,000 |
| Capital expenditures | 320,000 | 400,000 |
| Cash provided by operating activities | 425,000 | 390,000 |

| Year-End Data | Dec. 31, 2011 | Dec. 31, 2010 |
|---|---|---|
| Total liabilities | $2,200,000 | $1,900,000 |
| Total stockholders' equity | 4,000,000 | 3,600,000 |

Calculate the following:

a.  2011 debt-to-equity ratio.
b.  2011 times-interest-earned ratio.
c.  2011 operating-cash-flow-to-capital-expenditures ratio.

**E13-9A.** **Financial Ratios for Common Stockholders**    LO4

Kluster Corporation has only common stock outstanding. The firm reported earnings per share of $5.10 for the year. During the year, Kluster paid dividends of $2.04 per share. At year end the current market price of the stock was $63 per share. Calculate the following:

a.  Year-end price-earnings ratio
b.  Dividend yield
c.  Dividend payout ratio

**E13-10A.** **Financial Statement Notes**    LO6

The notes to financial statements present information on significant accounting policies, complex or special transactions, details of reported amounts, commitments, contingencies, segments, quarterly data, and subsequent events. Indicate which type of note disclosure is illustrated by each of the following notes:

a.  The company has agreed to purchase seven EMB-120 aircraft and related spare parts. The aggregate cost of these aircraft is approximately $35,500,000, subject to a cost escalation provision. The aircraft are scheduled to be delivered over the next two fiscal years.

*b.* The company has deferred certain costs related to major accounting and information systems enhancements that are anticipated to benefit future years. Upon completion, the related cost is amortized over a period not exceeding five years.

*c.* The company has guaranteed loans and leases of independent distributors approximating $26,800,000 as of December 31 of the current year.

*d.* An officer of the company is also a director of a major raw material supplier of the company. The amount of raw material purchases from this supplier approximated $365,000 in the current year.

**LO5** **E13-11A. Financial Statement Limitations**

You have been asked to perform financial statement analysis on the Patton Company. The Patton Company is a large chain of retail outlets that sells a wide range of household items. Last year the company introduced its own credit card and is pleased that profit from this financing activity now accounts for over twenty percent of the company's total profit. As part of your analysis you have chosen to compare the Patton Company to Johnson Stores, a much larger chain of stores. Johnson Stores sells household items and groceries, but it does not have its own credit card. Your analysis includes both horizontal trend analysis and vertical analysis. Identify some of the limitations from the description above.

# EXERCISES—SET B

**LO1** **E13-1B. Income Statement Sections**

During the current year, Newtech Corporation sold a segment of its business at a loss of $230,000. Until it was sold, the segment had a current period operating loss of $200,000. Also, the company had an extraordinary gain of $90,000 during the year as the result of an expropriation settlement received from a foreign government. The company has $800,000 income from continuing operations for the current year. Prepare the lower part of the income statement, beginning with the $800,000 income from continuing operations. Follow tax allocation procedures, assuming that all changes in income are subject to a 40 percent income tax rate. Disregard earnings per share disclosures.

**LO4** **E13-2B. Earnings per Share**

Ewing Corporation began the year with a simple capital structure consisting of 38,000 shares of common stock outstanding. On May 1, 10,000 additional common shares were issued, and another 1,000 common shares were issued on September 1. The company had a net income for the year of $234,000. Calculate the earnings per share of common stock.

**LO2** **E13-3B. Comparative Balance Sheets**

Consider the following balance sheet data for Great Buy Co., Inc., an electronics and major appliance retailer, at February 26, 2011 and February 27, 2010 (amounts in thousands):

| | Feb. 26, 2011 | Feb. 27, 2010 |
|---|---|---|
| Cash and cash equivalents | $ 59,872 | $ 7,138 |
| Accounts receivables | 52,944 | 37,968 |
| Merchandise inventories | 637,950 | 249,991 |
| Other current assets | 13,844 | 9,829 |
| Current Assets | 764,610 | 304,926 |
| Property and equipment (net) | 172,724 | 126,442 |
| Other assets | 15,160 | 7,774 |
| Total Assets | $952,494 | $439,142 |
| Current Liabilities | $402,028 | $186,005 |
| Long-term liabilities | 239,022 | 70,854 |
| Total Liabilities | 641,050 | 256,859 |
| Common stock | 2,087 | 1,149 |
| Additional paid-in-capital | 224,089 | 137,151 |
| Retained earnings | 85,268 | 43,983 |
| Total Stockholders' Equity | 311,444 | 182,283 |
| Total Liabilities and Stockholders' Equity | $952,494 | $439,142 |

    *a.* Prepare a comparative balance sheet, showing increases in dollars and percentages.

    *b.* Comment briefly on the changes between the two years.

**E13-4B.** **Common-Size Balance Sheets**                                                   **LO3**
Refer to the balance sheet data given in Exercise E13-3B.

    *a.* Prepare common-size balance sheets for each year (use total assets as the base amount for computing percentages).

    *b.* Compare the common-size balance sheets and comment briefly.

**E13-5B.** **Ratios Analyzing Firm Profitability**                                    **LO4**
The following information is available for Crest Company:

| Annual Data | 2011 | 2010 |
|---|---|---|
| Sales revenue | $6,400,000 | $6,000,000 |
| Cost of goods sold | 4,006,400 | 3,720,000 |
| Net income | 307,200 | 264,000 |

| Year-End Data | Dec. 31, 2011 | Dec. 31, 2010 |
|---|---|---|
| Total assets | $2,850,000 | $2,360,000 |
| Common stockholders' equity | 1,900,000 | 1,800,000 |

Calculate the following ratios for 2011:

    *a.* Gross profit percentage

    *b.* Return on sales

    *c.* Asset turnover

    *d.* Return on assets

    *e.* Return on common stockholders' equity (Crest Company declared and paid preferred stock dividends of $25,000 in 2011.)

**E13-6B.** **Working Capital and Short-Term Firm Liquidity Ratios**                    **LO4**
Favor Company has a current ratio of 2.08 (2.08:1) on December 31. On that date its current assets are as follows:

| | |
|---|---|
| Cash and cash equivalents | $ 28,000 |
| Short-term investments | 87,000 |
| Accounts receivable (net) | 125,000 |
| Inventory | 178,500 |
| Prepaid expenses | 9,980 |
| Current assets | $428,480 |

Favor Company's current liabilities at the beginning of the year were $192,000 and during the year its operating activities provided a cash flow of $33,830.

    *a.* What are the firm's current liabilities at December 31?

    *b.* What is the firm's working capital on December 31?

    *c.* What is the quick ratio on December 31?

    *d.* What is the firm's operating-cash-flow-to-current-liabilities ratio?

**E13-7B.** **Accounts Receivable and Inventory Ratios**                              **LO4**
Favor Company, whose current assets at December 31 are shown in Exercise E13-6B, had net sales for the year of $522,750 and cost of goods sold of $345,900. At the beginning of the year, accounts receivable (net) were $121,000 and inventory was $165,700.

    *a.* What is the company's accounts receivable turnover?

    *b.* What is the company's average collection period?

    *c.* What is the company's inventory turnover?

    *d.* What is the company's days' sales in inventory?

**E13-8B.** **Ratios Analyzing Long-Term Firm Solvency**                                **LO4**
The following information is available for Percy Company:

| Annual Data | 2011 | 2010 |
|---|---|---|
| Interest expense......................................................... | $175,000 | $166,000 |
| Income tax expense ...................................................... | 126,000 | 117,000 |
| Net income.............................................................. | 294,000 | 273,000 |
| Capital expenditures...................................................... | 440,000 | 350,000 |
| Cash provided by operating activities ....................................... | 247,000 | 223,000 |

| Year-End Data | Dec. 31, 2011 | Dec. 31, 2010 |
|---|---|---|
| Total liabilities................................................. | $3,300,000 | $2,900,000 |
| Total stockholders' equity....................................... | 2,200,000 | 1,900,000 |

Calculate the following:

*a.* 2011 debt-to-equity ratio
*b.* 2011 times-interest-earned ratio
*c.* 2011 operating-cash-flow-to-capital-expenditures ratio

LO4 **E13-9B.** **Financial Ratios for Common Stockholders**
Henshue Corporation has only common stock outstanding. The firm reported earnings per share of $1.80 for the year. During the year, Henshue paid dividends of $0.81 per share. At year end, the current market price of the stock was $35.15 per share.
Calculate the following:

*a.* Year-end price-earnings ratio
*b.* Dividend yield
*c.* Dividend payout ratio

LO6 **E13-10B.** **Financial Statement Notes**
Notes to the financial statements present information on significant accounting policies, complex or special transactions, details of reported amounts, commitments, contingencies, segments, quarterly data, and subsequent events. Indicate the type of note disclosure that is illustrated by each of the following notes:

*a.* Sales by the Farm and Equipment segment to independent dealers are recorded at the time of shipment to those dealers. Sales through company-owned retail stores are recorded at the time of sale to retail customers.
*b.* Members of the board of directors, the advisory board, and employees are not charged the vendor's commission on property sold at auction for their benefit. (From the notes of an auctioneer company.)
*c.* Sales to an airline company accounted for approximately 43 percent of the company's net sales in the current year.
*d.* The company's product liability insurance coverage with respect to insured events occurring after January 1 of the current year is substantially less than the amount of that insurance available in the recent past. The company is now predominantly self-insured in this area. The reduction in insurance coverage reflects trends in the liability insurance field generally and is not unique to the company.

LO5 **E13-11B.** **Financial Statement Limitations**
You have been asked to perform financial statement analysis on the Anderson Company. The Anderson Company is a large manufacturer of construction machinery and vehicles. Last year the company closed down a segment of the business that produced mining equipment because it was not providing an adequate return on assets. This segment represented fifteen percent of the company's total assets. As part of your analysis you have chosen to compare the Anderson Company to Bertran, Inc., a much smaller manufacturer of equipment, although Bertran, Inc. also performs contract repairs for many other brands of equipment. Your analysis includes both horizontal trend analysis and vertical analysis. Identify some of the limitations from the description above.

# PROBLEMS—SET A

LO1 **P13-1A.** **Income Statement Format**
The following information from Belvidere Company's current operations is available:

| | |
|---|---|
| Administrative expenses | $ 69,000 |
| Cost of goods sold | 464,000 |
| Sales revenue | 772,000 |
| Flood loss (considered unusual and infrequent) | 25,000 |
| Selling expenses | 87,000 |
| Interest expense | 7,000 |
| Loss from operations of discontinued segment | 60,000 |
| Gain on disposal of discontinued segment | 40,000 |
| Income taxes: | |
| Amount applicable to ordinary operations | 58,000 |
| Reduction applicable to loss from operations of discontinued segment | 24,000 |
| Amount applicable to gain on disposal of discontinued segment | 16,000 |
| Reduction applicable to flood loss | 10,000 |

**Required**
a. Prepare a multiple-step income statement. (Disregard earnings per share.)
b. Prepare a single-step income statement. (Disregard earnings per share.)

**P13-2A.** **Earnings per Share**
LO4

Leland Corporation began the year with 120,000 shares of common stock outstanding. On March 1 an additional 10,000 shares of common stock were issued. On August 1, another 16,000 shares of common stock were issued. On November 1, 6,000 shares of common stock were acquired as Treasury Stock. Leland Corporation's net income for the calendar year is $501,000.

**Required**
Calculate the company's earnings per share.

**P13-3A.** **Earnings per Share and Multiple-Step Income Statement**
LO1, LO4
The following information from Bowden Corporation's current operations is available:

| | |
|---|---|
| Sales revenue | $745,000 |
| Cost of goods sold | 450,000 |
| Selling expenses | 58,000 |
| Administrative expenses | 72,000 |
| Loss from earthquake damages (considered unusual and infrequent) | 40,000 |
| Loss on sale of equipment | 5,000 |
| Income tax expense (not allocated) | 48,000 |
| Shares of common stock | |
| Outstanding at January 1 | 15,000 shares |
| Additional issued at May 1 | 7,000 shares |
| Additional issued at November 1 | 2,000 shares |

**Required**
Prepare a multiple-step income statement for Bowden Corporation for the year. Assume a 40 percent income tax rate. Allocate income tax expense within the income statement. Include earnings per share disclosures at the bottom of the income statement.

**P13-4A.** **Trend Percentages**
LO2
Net sales, net income, and total asset figures for Vibrant Controls, Inc., for five consecutive years are given below (Vibrant manufactures pollution controls):

| | Annual Amounts (Thousands of Dollars) | | | | |
|---|---|---|---|---|---|
| | Year 1 | Year 2 | Year 3 | Year 4 | Year 5 |
| Net sales | $71,500 | $79,800 | $84,250 | $88,400 | $94,700 |
| Net income | 3,200 | 3,650 | 3,900 | 4,160 | 4,790 |
| Total assets | 42,500 | 45,400 | 48,700 | 51,000 | 54,900 |

**Required**
a. Calculate trend percentages, using Year 1 as the base year.
b. Calculate the return on sales for each year. (Rates above 2.8 percent are considered good for manufacturers of pollution controls; rates above 6.4 percent are considered very good.)
c. Comment on the results of your analysis.

LO4 **P13-5A.** **Changes in Various Ratios**

Presented below is selected information for Brimmer Company:

|  | 2011 | 2010 |
|---|---|---|
| Sales revenue | $910,000 | $840,000 |
| Cost of goods sold | 575,000 | 542,000 |
| Interest expense | 20,000 | 20,000 |
| Income tax expense | 27,000 | 24,000 |
| Net income | 61,000 | 52,000 |
| Cash flow from operating activities | 65,000 | 55,000 |
| Capital expenditures | 42,000 | 45,000 |
| Accounts receivable (net), December 31 | 126,000 | 120,000 |
| Inventory, December 31 | 196,000 | 160,000 |
| Stockholders' equity, December 31 | 450,000 | 400,000 |
| Total assets, December 31 | 730,000 | 660,000 |

### Required

*a.* Calculate the following ratios for 2011. The 2010 results are given for comparative purposes.

|  |  | 2010 |
|---|---|---|
| 1. | Gross profit percentage | 35.5 percent |
| 2. | Return on assets | 8.3 percent |
| 3. | Return on sales | 6.2 percent |
| 4. | Return on common stockholders' equity | |
|  | (no preferred stock was outstanding) | 13.9 percent |
| 5. | Accounts receivable turnover | 8.00 |
| 6. | Average collection period | 45.6 days |
| 7. | Inventory turnover | 3.61 |
| 8. | Times-interest-earned ratio | 4.80 |
| 9. | Operating-cash-flow-to-capital-expenditures ratio | 1.22 |

*b.* Comment on the changes between the two years.

LO2, LO3, LO4 **P13-6A.** **Ratios from Comparative and Common-Size Data**

Consider the following financial statements for Waverly Company.

During 2011, management obtained additional bond financing to enlarge its production facilities. The company faced higher production costs during the year for such things as fuel, materials, and freight. Because of temporary government price controls, a planned price increase on products was delayed several months.

As a holder of both common and preferred stock, you decide to analyze the financial statements:

| WAVERLY COMPANY Balance Sheets (Thousands of Dollars) | | |
|---|---|---|
|  | Dec. 31, 2011 | Dec. 31, 2010 |
| **Assets** | | |
| Cash and cash equivalents | $ 18,000 | $ 12,000 |
| Accounts receivable (net) | 55,000 | 43,000 |
| Inventory | 120,000 | 105,000 |
| Prepaid expenses | 20,000 | 14,000 |
| Plant and other assets (net) | 471,000 | 411,000 |
| Total Assets | $684,000 | $585,000 |
| **Liabilities and Stockholders' Equity** | | |
| Current liabilities | $ 90,000 | $ 82,000 |
| 10% Bonds payable | 225,000 | 160,000 |
| 9% Preferred stock, $50 Par Value | 75,000 | 75,000 |
| Common stock, $10 Par Value | 200,000 | 200,000 |
| Retained earnings | 94,000 | 68,000 |
| Total Liabilities and Stockholders' Equity | $684,000 | $585,000 |

| WAVERLY COMPANY<br>Income Statements<br>(Thousands of Dollars) | | |
| --- | --- | --- |
| | **2011** | **2010** |
| Sales revenue .......................................... | $820,000 | $678,000 |
| Cost of goods sold...................................... | 541,200 | 433,920 |
| Gross profit on sales.................................. | 278,800 | 244,080 |
| Selling and administrative expenses ................... | 171,400 | 149,200 |
| Income before interest expense and income taxes..... | 107,400 | 94,880 |
| Interest expense....................................... | 22,500 | 16,000 |
| Income before income taxes ........................... | 84,900 | 78,880 |
| Income tax expense ................................... | 22,900 | 21,300 |
| Net income............................................ | $ 62,000 | $ 57,580 |
| Other financial data (thousands of dollars) | | |
| Cash provided by operating activities................ | $ 65,200 | $ 60,500 |
| Preferred stock dividends............................ | 6,750 | 6,750 |

### Required

a. Calculate the following for each year: current ratio, quick ratio, operating-cash-flow-to-current-liabilities ratio (current liabilities were $78,000,000 at January 1, 2010), inventory turnover (inventory was $87,000,000 at January 1, 2010), debt-to-equity ratio, times-interest-earned ratio, return on assets (total assets were $493,000,000 at January 1, 2010), and return on common stockholders' equity (common stockholders' equity was $236,000,000 at January 1, 2010).

b. Calculate common-size percentages for each year's income statement.

c. Comment on the results of your analysis.

**P13-7A.** **Constructing Statements from Ratio Data**                                       **LO4**

The following are the 2010 financial statements for Omicron Company, with almost all dollar amounts missing:

| OMICRON COMPANY<br>Balance Sheet<br>December 31, 2010 | | | | |
| --- | --- | --- | --- | --- |
| Cash ............................. | $ | ? | Current liabilities .................. | $ | ? |
| Accounts receivable (net) .......... | | ? | 8% Bonds payable................. | | ? |
| Inventory ........................ | | ? | Common stock .................... | | ? |
| Equipment (net).................. | | ? | Retained earnings ................. | | 900,000 |
| | | | Total Liabilities and | | |
| Total Assets ...................... | $5,900,000 | | Stockholders' Equity............. | $5,900,000 | |

| OMICRON COMPANY<br>Income Statement<br>For the Year Ended December 31, 2010 | | |
| --- | --- | --- |
| Sales revenue ............................................... | $ | ? |
| Cost of goods sold........................................... | | ? |
| Gross profit ................................................. | | ? |
| Selling and administrative expenses ......................... | | ? |
| Income before interest expense and income taxes............. | | ? |
| Interest expense............................................. | | 80,000 |
| Income before income taxes ................................. | | ? |
| Income tax expense (30%) ................................... | | ? |
| Net income.................................................. | | $560,000 |

The following information is available about Omicron Company's financial statements:

1. Quick ratio, 0.90.
2. Inventory turnover (inventory at January 1 was $924,000), 5 times.
3. Return on sales, 8.0 percent.

4. Accounts receivable turnover (accounts receivable (net) at January 1 were $860,000), 8 times.

5. Gross profit percentage, 32 percent.

6. Return on common stockholders' equity (common stockholders' equity at January 1 was $3,300,000), 16 percent.

7. The interest expense relates to the bonds payable that were outstanding all year.

**Required**

Compute the missing amounts, and complete the financial statements of Omicron Company. *Hint:* Complete the income statement first.

**LO4** **P13-8A.** **Ratios Compared with Industry Averages**

Because you own the common stock of Phantom Corporation, a paper manufacturer, you decide to analyze the firm's performance for the most recent year. The following data are taken from the firm's latest annual report:

| | Dec. 31, 2011 | Dec. 31, 2010 |
|---|---|---|
| Quick assets. . . . . . . . . . . . . . . . . . . . . . . . . . . . . . . . . . . . . . . . . . . | $ 600,000 | $ 552,000 |
| Inventory and prepaid expenses . . . . . . . . . . . . . . . . . . . . . . . . . . . . . | 372,000 | 312,000 |
| Other assets. . . . . . . . . . . . . . . . . . . . . . . . . . . . . . . . . . . . . . . . . . | 4,788,000 | 4,176,000 |
| Total Assets . . . . . . . . . . . . . . . . . . . . . . . . . . . . . . . . . . . . . . . | $5,760,000 | $5,040,000 |
| Current liabilities . . . . . . . . . . . . . . . . . . . . . . . . . . . . . . . . . . . . . | $ 624,000 | $ 540,000 |
| 10% Bonds payable. . . . . . . . . . . . . . . . . . . . . . . . . . . . . . . . . . . . . | 1,440,000 | 1,440,000 |
| 8% Preferred stock, $100 par value . . . . . . . . . . . . . . . . . . . . . . . . . . | 480,000 | 480,000 |
| Common stock, $10 par value. . . . . . . . . . . . . . . . . . . . . . . . . . . . . . | 2,700,000 | 2,160,000 |
| Retained earnings . . . . . . . . . . . . . . . . . . . . . . . . . . . . . . . . . . . . . | 516,000 | 420,000 |
| Total Liabilities and Stockholders' Equity . . . . . . . . . . . . . . . . . . . . . . . | $5,760,000 | $5,040,000 |

For 2011, net sales amount to $11,280,000, net income is $573,600, and preferred stock dividends paid are $38,400.

**Required**

*a.* Calculate the following ratios for 2011:
1. Return on sales
2. Return on assets
3. Return on common stockholders' equity
4. Quick ratio
5. Current ratio
6. Debt-to-equity ratio

*b.* Trade association statistics and information provided by credit agencies reveal the following data on industry norms:

| | Median | Upper Quartile |
|---|---|---|
| Return on sales. . . . . . . . . . . . . . . . . . . . . . . . . . . . . . . . . . . . . . | 4.9 percent | 8.6 percent |
| Return on assets. . . . . . . . . . . . . . . . . . . . . . . . . . . . . . . . . . . . . | 6.5 percent | 11.2 percent |
| Return on common stockholders' equity . . . . . . . . . . . . . . . . . . | 10.6 percent | 17.3 percent |
| Quick ratio . . . . . . . . . . . . . . . . . . . . . . . . . . . . . . . . . . . . . . . | 1.0 | 1.8 |
| Current ratio . . . . . . . . . . . . . . . . . . . . . . . . . . . . . . . . . . . . . . | 1.8 | 3.0 |
| Debt-to-equity-ratio. . . . . . . . . . . . . . . . . . . . . . . . . . . . . . . . . | 1.08 | 0.66 |

Compare Phantom Corporation's performance with industry performance.

**LO4** **P13-9A.** **Ratios Compared with Industry Averages**

Packard Plastics, Inc., manufactures various plastic and synthetic products. Financial statement data for the firm follow:

| | 2011 (Thousands of Dollars, except Earnings per Share) |
|---|---|
| Sales revenue . . . . . . . . . . . . . . . . . . . . . . . . . . . . . . . . . . . . . . | $815,000 |
| Cost of goods sold. . . . . . . . . . . . . . . . . . . . . . . . . . . . . . . . . . . | 540,000 |
| Net income. . . . . . . . . . . . . . . . . . . . . . . . . . . . . . . . . . . . . . . . | 50,500 |
| Dividends . . . . . . . . . . . . . . . . . . . . . . . . . . . . . . . . . . . . . . . . | 14,000 |
| Earnings per share. . . . . . . . . . . . . . . . . . . . . . . . . . . . . . . . . . . | 4.04 |

| PACKARD PLASTICS, INC.<br>Balance Sheets<br>(Thousands of Dollars) | Dec. 31,<br>2011 | Dec. 31,<br>2010 |
|---|---|---|
| **Assets** | | |
| Cash ....................................................... | $ 4,100 | $ 2,700 |
| Accounts receivable (net)................................. | 66,900 | 60,900 |
| Inventory .................................................. | 148,000 | 140,000 |
| Total Current Assets ................................... | 219,000 | 203,600 |
| Plant assets (net) ........................................ | 215,000 | 194,000 |
| Other assets............................................... | 5,300 | 3,900 |
| Total Assets ............................................ | $439,300 | $401,500 |
| **Liabilities and Stockholders' Equity** | | |
| Notes payable—banks.................................... | $ 31,000 | $ 25,000 |
| Accounts payable ........................................ | 27,600 | 23,000 |
| Accrued liabilities........................................ | 25,100 | 24,800 |
| Total Current Liabilities ............................... | 83,700 | 72,800 |
| 10% Bonds payable....................................... | 150,000 | 150,000 |
| Total Liabilities ....................................... | 233,700 | 222,800 |
| Common stock, $10 par value (12,500,000 shares) ...... | 125,000 | 125,000 |
| Retained earnings ....................................... | 80,600 | 53,700 |
| Total Stockholders' Equity ............................ | 205,600 | 178,700 |
| Total Liabilities and Stockholders' Equity ............. | $439,300 | $401,500 |

**Required**

a.  Using the given data, calculate items 1 through 8 below for 2011. Compare the performance of Packard Plastics, Inc., with the following industry averages and comment on its operations.

| | | Median Ratios for Manufacturers<br>of Plastic and Synthetic Products |
|---|---|---|
| 1. | Quick ratio ......................................... | 1.2 |
| 2. | Current ratio ....................................... | 1.9 |
| 3. | Accounts receivable turnover ....................... | 7.9 |
| 4. | Inventory turnover ................................. | 7.8 |
| 5. | Debt-to-equity-ratio................................ | 0.95 |
| 6. | Gross profit percentage............................. | 32.7 percent |
| 7. | Return on sales..................................... | 3.5 percent |
| 8. | Return on assets.................................... | 6.3 percent |

b.  Calculate the dividends paid per share of common stock. What was the dividend payout ratio?

c.  If the most recent price per share of common stock is $47.75, what is the price-earnings ratio? The dividend yield?

**P13-10A. Financial Statement Notes: Quarterly Data**    LO2, LO4

Quarterly data are presented below for Company A and Company B. One of these companies is Gibson Greetings, Inc., which manufactures and sells greeting cards. The other company is Hon Industries, Inc., which manufactures and sells office furniture. Both companies are on a calendar year basis.

| | (Amounts in Thousands) | | | | |
|---|---|---|---|---|---|
| | First<br>Quarter | Second<br>Quarter | Third<br>Quarter | Fourth<br>Quarter | Year |
| **Company A** | | | | | |
| Net sales................. | $186,111 | $177,537 | $203,070 | $213,608 | $780,326 |
| Gross profit ............. | 55,457 | 53,643 | 64,024 | 69,374 | 242,498 |
| **Company B** | | | | | |
| Net sales................. | $ 84,896 | $ 83,796 | $142,137 | $235,336 | $546,165 |
| Gross profit ............. | 53,900 | 52,983 | 66,018 | 104,961 | 277,862 |

**Required**

a.   Compute the percent of annual net sales generated each quarter by Company A. Round to the nearest percent.

b.   Compute the percent of annual net sales generated each quarter by Company B. Round to the nearest percent.

c.   Which company has the most seasonal business? Briefly explain.

d.   Which company is Gibson Greetings, Inc.? Hon Industries, Inc.? Briefly explain.

e.   Which company's interim quarterly data are probably most useful for predicting annual results? Briefly explain.

**LO4**   **P13-11A.   Ratios Using IFRS Financial Statements**

Tesco PLC is the world's third largest retailer. The company is based out of the United Kingdom and prepares its financial statements using IFRS. The complete annual report for **Tesco PLC** is available on this book's Website. Calculate the following ratios for the company for 2008 and 2009 and comment on your results:

a.   Current ratio

b.   Quick ratio

c.   Accounts receivable turnover

d.   Inventory turnover

e.   Debt-to-equity ratio

f.   Times-interest-earned ratio

g.   Return on sales

h.   Return on assets

i.   Return on common stockholders' equity

j.   Dividend payout ratio

*Hint:* Additional 2007 year-end data (in millions of pounds):

| | |
|---|---:|
| Accounts receivable . . . . . . . . . . . . . . . . . . . . . . . . . . . . . . . . . . . . . . . . . . . . . . . . . . . . . . . . . . . . . . . . . . . . | 1,079 |
| Inventories . . . . . . . . . . . . . . . . . . . . . . . . . . . . . . . . . . . . . . . . . . . . . . . . . . . . . . . . . . . . . . . . . . . . . . . . . . . . . . | 1,931 |
| Total assets . . . . . . . . . . . . . . . . . . . . . . . . . . . . . . . . . . . . . . . . . . . . . . . . . . . . . . . . . . . . . . . . . . . . . . . . . . . . . | 27,500 |
| Total stockholders' equity . . . . . . . . . . . . . . . . . . . . . . . . . . . . . . . . . . . . . . . . . . . . . . . . . . . . . . . . . . . . . . . . . | 10,571 |

Dividend per share was 11.29 pence in 2008 and 12.28 pence in 2009.

# PROBLEMS—SET B

**LO1**   **P13-1B.   Income Statement Format**

The following information from Tricon Company's operations is available:

| | |
|---|---:|
| Administrative expenses . . . . . . . . . . . . . . . . . . . . . . . . . . . . . . . . . . . . . . . . . . . . . . . . . . . . . . . . . . . . . . . | $ 138,000 |
| Cost of goods sold . . . . . . . . . . . . . . . . . . . . . . . . . . . . . . . . . . . . . . . . . . . . . . . . . . . . . . . . . . . . . . . . . . . . . | 928,000 |
| Sales revenue . . . . . . . . . . . . . . . . . . . . . . . . . . . . . . . . . . . . . . . . . . . . . . . . . . . . . . . . . . . . . . . . . . . . . . . . . | 1,544,000 |
| Selling expenses . . . . . . . . . . . . . . . . . . . . . . . . . . . . . . . . . . . . . . . . . . . . . . . . . . . . . . . . . . . . . . . . . . . . . . | 174,000 |
| Interest expense . . . . . . . . . . . . . . . . . . . . . . . . . . . . . . . . . . . . . . . . . . . . . . . . . . . . . . . . . . . . . . . . . . . . . . | 14,000 |
| Loss from operations of discontinued segment . . . . . . . . . . . . . . . . . . . . . . . . . . . . . . . . . . . . . . . . | 120,000 |
| Flood loss (considered unusual and infrequent) . . . . . . . . . . . . . . . . . . . . . . . . . . . . . . . . . . . . | 50,000 |
| Gain on disposal of discontinued segment . . . . . . . . . . . . . . . . . . . . . . . . . . . . . . . . . . . . . . . . . . . | 80,000 |
| Income taxes | |
|   Amount applicable to ordinary operations . . . . . . . . . . . . . . . . . . . . . . . . . . . . . . . . . . . . . . . . . . | 116,000 |
|   Reduction applicable to loss from operations of discontinued segment . . . . . . . . . . . . . . . . | 48,000 |
|   Amount applicable to gain on disposal of discontinued segment . . . . . . . . . . . . . . . . . . . . . | 32,000 |
|   Reduction applicable to flood loss . . . . . . . . . . . . . . . . . . . . . . . . . . . . . . . . . . . . . . . . . . . . . . . . | 20,000 |

**Required**

a.   Prepare a multiple-step income statement. (Disregard earnings per share amounts.)

b.   Prepare a single-step income statement. (Disregard earnings per share amounts.)

**LO4**   **P13-2B.   Earnings per Share**

Island Corporation began the year with 25,000 shares of common stock outstanding. On May 1, an additional 9,000 shares of common stock were issued. On July 1, 6,000 shares of common stock were acquired as treasury stock. On September 1, the 6,000 treasury shares of common stock were reissued. Island Corporation's net income for the calendar year is $230,000.

**Required**

Compute earnings per share.

**P13-3B. Earnings per Share and Multiple-Step Income Statement**

LO1, LO4

The following information from Garner Corporation's current operations is available:

| | |
|---|---|
| Sales revenue | $2,220,000 |
| Cost of goods sold | 1,290,000 |
| Selling expenses | 180,000 |
| Administrative expenses | 143,000 |
| Gain from expropriation of property by foreign government | 190,000 |
| Loss from plant strike | 97,000 |
| Shares of common stock | |
| Outstanding at January 1 | 61,000 shares |
| Additional issued at April 1 | 17,000 shares |
| Additional issued at August 1 | 3,000 shares |

**Required**

Prepare a multiple-step income statement for Garner Corporation. Assume a 40 percent income tax rate. Include earnings per share disclosures at the bottom of the income statement. Garner Corporation has no preferred stock.

**P13-4B. Trend Percentages**

LO2

Sales of automotive products for Ford Motor Company and General Motors Corporation for a five-year period are:

| | Net Sales of Automotive Products (Millions of Dollars) | | | | |
|---|---|---|---|---|---|
| | Year 1 | Year 2 | Year 3 | Year 4 | Year 5 |
| Ford Motor Company | $82,879 | $81,844 | $72,051 | $ 84,407 | $ 91,568 |
| General Motors Corporation | 99,106 | 97,312 | 94,828 | 103,005 | 108,027 |

Net sales for Pfizer Inc. and Abbott Laboratories for the same five years follow:

| | Net Sales (Millions of Dollars) | | | | |
|---|---|---|---|---|---|
| | Year 1 | Year 2 | Year 3 | Year 4 | Year 5 |
| Pfizer Inc. | $5,672 | $6,406 | $6,950 | $7,230 | $7,478 |
| Abbott Laboratories | 5,380 | 6,159 | 6,877 | 7,852 | 8,408 |

**Required**

*a.* Calculate trend percentages for all four companies, using Year 1 as the base year.

*b.* Comment on the trend percentage of Ford Motor Company and General Motors Corporation.

*c.* Comment on the trend percentages of Pfizer Inc. and Abbott Laboratories.

**P13-5B. Changes in Various Ratios**

LO2, LO4

Selected information follow for Cycle Company:

| | 2011 | 2010 |
|---|---|---|
| Sales revenue | $675,000 | $520,000 |
| Cost of goods sold | 407,700 | 310,000 |
| Interest expense | 18,000 | 14,000 |
| Income tax expense | 6,200 | 5,100 |
| Net income | 24,600 | 20,300 |
| Cash flow from operating activities | 29,500 | 26,500 |
| Capital expenditures | 40,000 | 25,000 |
| Accounts receivable (net), December 31 | 182,000 | 128,000 |
| Inventory, December 31 | 225,000 | 180,000 |
| Stockholders' equity, December 31 | 205,000 | 165,000 |
| Total assets, December 31 | 460,000 | 350,000 |

**Required**

*a.* Calculate the following ratios for 2011. The 2010 results are given for comparative purposes.

| | | 2010 |
|---|---|---|
| 1. | Gross profit percentage........................................................ | 40.4 percent |
| 2. | Return on assets................................................................ | 6.3 percent |
| 3. | Return on sales................................................................. | 3.9 percent |
| 4. | Return on common stockholders' equity (no preferred stock was outstanding)................................. | 14.0 percent |
| 5. | Accounts receivable turnover ............................................ | 4.77 |
| 6. | Average collection period................................................. | 76.5 days |
| 7. | Inventory turnover ........................................................... | 2.07 |
| 8. | Times-interest-earned ratio .............................................. | 2.81 |
| 9. | Operating-cash-flow-to-capital-expenditures ratio ...................... | 1.06 |

*b.* Comment on the changes between the two years.

**LO2, LO3, LO4**    **P13-6B.**   **Ratios from Comparative and Common-Size Data**

Consider the following financial statements for Vega Company.

During the year, management obtained additional bond financing to enlarge its production facilities. The plant addition produced a new high-margin product, which is supposed to improve the average rate of gross profit and return on sales.

As a potential investor, you decide to analyze the financial statements:

| VEGA COMPANY Balance Sheets (Thousands of Dollars) | Dec. 31, 2011 | Dec. 31, 2010 |
|---|---|---|
| **Assets** | | |
| Cash ........................................................................ | $ 21,000 | $ 16,100 |
| Accounts receivable (net) .......................................... | 39,000 | 21,400 |
| Inventory ................................................................. | 105,000 | 72,000 |
| Prepaid expenses...................................................... | 1,500 | 3,000 |
| Plant and other assets (net) ...................................... | 463,500 | 427,500 |
| Total Assets ............................................................. | $630,000 | $540,000 |
| **Liabilities and Stockholders' Equity** | | |
| Current liabilities ..................................................... | $ 76,000 | $ 45,000 |
| 9% Bonds payable..................................................... | 187,500 | 150,000 |
| 8% Preferred stock, $50 par value ............................... | 60,000 | 60,000 |
| Common stock, $10 par value...................................... | 225,000 | 225,000 |
| Retained earnings ..................................................... | 81,500 | 60,000 |
| Total Liabilities and Stockholders' Equity ...................... | $630,000 | $540,000 |

| VEGA COMPANY Income Statements (Thousands of Dollars) | 2011 | 2010 |
|---|---|---|
| Sales revenue ........................................................... | $840,000 | $697,500 |
| Cost of goods sold...................................................... | 552,000 | 474,000 |
| Gross profit on sales................................................... | 288,000 | 223,500 |
| Selling and administrative expenses .............................. | 231,000 | 174,000 |
| Income before interest expense and income taxes.............. | 57,000 | 49,500 |
| Interest expense........................................................ | 16,800 | 13,500 |
| Income before income taxes ........................................ | 40,200 | 36,000 |
| Income tax expense ................................................... | 14,100 | 12,600 |
| Net income.............................................................. | $ 26,100 | $ 23,400 |
| Other financial data (thousands of dollars):...................... | | |
| Cash provided by operating activities.............................. | $ 30,000 | $ 25,000 |
| Preferred stock dividends............................................ | 4,800 | 4,800 |

**Required**

a. Calculate the following for each year: current ratio, quick ratio, operating-cash-flow-to-current-liabilities ratio (current liabilities were $42 million at January 1, 2010), inventory turnover (inventory was $68 million at January 1, 2010), debt-to-equity ratio, times-interest-earned ratio, return on assets (total assets were $472 million at January 1, 2010), and return on common stockholders' equity (common stockholders' equity was $266 million at January 1, 2010).

b. Calculate common-size percentage for each year's income statement.

c. Comment on the results of your analysis.

**P13-7B.** **Constructing Statements from Ratio Data**                                   LO4

The following are the financial statements for Timber Company, with almost all dollar amounts missing:

| TIMBER COMPANY Balance Sheet December 31 | | | |
|---|---|---|---|
| Cash .............................. | $    ? | Current liabilities ................. | $    ? |
| Accounts receivable (net) .......... | ? | 10% Bonds payable............... | 144,000 |
| Inventory ......................... | ? | Common stock.................... | ? |
| Equipment (net)................... | ? | Retained earnings ................ | 48,000 |
| | | Total Liabilities and | |
| Total Assets ...................... | $576,000 | Stockholders' Equity............. | $576,000 |

| TIMBER COMPANY Income Statement For the Year Ended December 31 | |
|---|---|
| Sales revenue ..................................................................... | $    ? |
| Cost of goods sold................................................................ | ? |
| Gross profit on sales .............................................................. | ? |
| Selling and administrative expenses ................................................ | ? |
| Income before interest expense and income taxes..................................... | ? |
| Interest expense................................................................... | ? |
| Income before income taxes ........................................................ | ? |
| Income tax expense (35%) .......................................................... | ? |
| Net income....................................................................... | $70,200 |

The following information is available about Timber Company's financial statements:

1. Quick ratio, 1.65.
2. Current ratio, 3.15.
3. Return on sales, 7.5 percent.
4. Return on common stockholders' equity (common stockholders' equity at January 1 was $342,000), 20 percent.
5. Gross profit percentage, 30 percent.
6. Accounts receivable turnover (accounts receivable (net) at January 1 were $97,200), 10 times.
7. The interest expense relates to the bonds payable that were outstanding all year.

**Required**

Compute the missing amounts, and complete the financial statements of Timber Company.

**P13-8B.** **Ratios Compared with Industry Averages**                                   LO4

You are analyzing the performance of Lumite Corporation, a manufacturer of personal care products, for the most recent year. The following data are taken from the firm's latest annual report:

| | Dec. 31, 2011 | Dec. 31, 2010 |
|---|---|---|
| Quick assets......................................................... | $ 290,000 | $ 250,000 |
| Inventory and prepaid expenses ........................................ | 945,000 | 820,000 |
| Other assets......................................................... | 4,165,000 | 3,700,000 |
| Total Assets ....................................................... | $5,400,000 | $4,770,000 |
| Current liabilities ................................................... | $ 500,000 | $ 400,000 |
| 10% Bonds payable................................................... | 1,300,000 | 1,300,000 |
| 7% Preferred stock................................................... | 900,000 | 900,000 |
| Common stock, $5 par value........................................... | 1,900,000 | 1,800,000 |
| Retained earnings ................................................... | 800,000 | 370,000 |
| Total Liabilities and Stockholders' Equity ............................... | $5,400,000 | $4,770,000 |

In 2011, net sales amount to $8,600,000, net income is $675,000, and preferred stock dividends paid are $63,000.

**Required**

a. Calculate the following for 2011:
  1. Return on sales
  2. Return on assets
  3. Return on common stockholders' equity
  4. Quick ratio
  5. Current ratio
  6. Debt-to-equity ratio

b. Trade association statistics and information provided by credit agencies reveal the following data on industry norms:

| | Median | Upper Quartile |
|---|---|---|
| Return on sales........................................... | 3.7 percent | 10.6 percent |
| Return on assets.......................................... | 5.8 percent | 14.2 percent |
| Return on common stockholders' equity .................. | 18.5 percent | 34.2 percent |
| Quick ratio ............................................... | 1.0 | 1.8 |
| Current ratio ............................................. | 2.2 | 3.7 |
| Debt-to-equity ratio ...................................... | 1.07 | 0.37 |

Compare Lumite Corporation's performance with industry performance.

**LO4** **P13-9B.** **Ratios Compared with Industry Averages**

Avery Instrument, Inc., is a manufacturer of various measuring and controlling instruments. Financial statement data for the firm are as follows:

| | 2011 (Thousands of Dollars, except Earnings per Share) |
|---|---|
| Sales revenue ...................................................... | $210,000 |
| Cost of goods sold.................................................. | 125,000 |
| Net income........................................................ | 8,300 |
| Dividends ......................................................... | 2,600 |
| Earnings per share................................................. | 4.15 |

| AVERY INSTRUMENTS, INC. Balance Sheets (Thousands of Dollars) | | |
|---|---|---|
| | Dec. 31, 2011 | Dec. 31, 2010 |
| **Assets** | | |
| Cash ......................................................... | $ 18,300 | $ 18,000 |
| Accounts receivable (net).............................................. | 46,000 | 41,000 |
| Inventory ......................................................... | 39,500 | 43,700 |
| Total Current Assets ............................................. | 103,800 | 102,700 |
| Plant assets (net) .................................................. | 52,600 | 50,500 |
| Other assets....................................................... | 15,600 | 13,800 |
| Total Assets ....................................................... | $172,000 | $167,000 |

*continued*

| Liabilities and Stockholders' Equity | | |
|---|---|---|
| Notes payable—banks. . . . . . . . . . . . . . . . . . . . . . . . . . . . . . . . . . . . . . . . . . | $ 6,000 | $ 6,000 |
| Accounts payable . . . . . . . . . . . . . . . . . . . . . . . . . . . . . . . . . . . . . . . . . . . . . | 22,500 | 18,700 |
| Accrued liabilities. . . . . . . . . . . . . . . . . . . . . . . . . . . . . . . . . . . . . . . . . . . . | 16,500 | 21,000 |
| Total Current Liabilities . . . . . . . . . . . . . . . . . . . . . . . . . . . . . . . . . . . | 45,000 | 45,700 |
| 9% Bonds payable. . . . . . . . . . . . . . . . . . . . . . . . . . . . . . . . . . . . . . . . . . . . . | 40,000 | 40,000 |
| Total Liabilities . . . . . . . . . . . . . . . . . . . . . . . . . . . . . . . . . . . . . . . . . . | 85,000 | 85,700 |
| Common stock, $25 par value (2,000,000 shares) . . . . . . . . . . . . . . . . . . . . . | 50,000 | 50,000 |
| Retained earnings . . . . . . . . . . . . . . . . . . . . . . . . . . . . . . . . . . . . . . . . . . . . | 37,000 | 31,300 |
| Total Stockholders' Equity . . . . . . . . . . . . . . . . . . . . . . . . . . . . . . . . | 87,000 | 81,300 |
| Total Liabilities and Stockholders' Equity . . . . . . . . . . . . . . . . . . . . . . . . . . | $172,000 | $167,000 |

## Required

a. Using the given data, calculate ratios 1 through 8 for 2011. Compare the performance of Avery Instruments, Inc., with the following industry averages and comment on its operations.

| | | Median Ratios for Manufacturers of Measuring and Controlling Instruments |
|---|---|---|
| 1. | Quick ratio . . . . . . . . . . . . . . . . . . . . . . . . . . . . . . . . . . . . . . | 1.3 |
| 2. | Current ratio . . . . . . . . . . . . . . . . . . . . . . . . . . . . . . . . . . . | 2.4 |
| 3. | Accounts receivable turnover . . . . . . . . . . . . . . . . . | 5.9 times |
| 4. | Inventory turnover . . . . . . . . . . . . . . . . . . . . . . . . . . . | 3.5 times |
| 5. | Debt-to-equity ratio . . . . . . . . . . . . . . . . . . . . . . . . . . | 0.73 |
| 6. | Gross profit percentage. . . . . . . . . . . . . . . . . . . . . . . | 42.8 percent |
| 7. | Return on sales. . . . . . . . . . . . . . . . . . . . . . . . . . . . . . . | 4.5 percent |
| 8. | Return on assets. . . . . . . . . . . . . . . . . . . . . . . . . . . . . . | 7.6 percent |

b. Calculate the dividends paid per share of common stock. What was the dividend payout ratio?

c. If the most recent price per share of common stock is $62.25, what is the price-earnings ratio? The dividend yield?

**P13-10B. Financial Statement Notes: Quarterly Data**   LO2, LO4

Quarterly data are presented below for Company C and Company D. One of these companies is Toys "R" Us, a children's specialty retail chain. The company's fiscal year ends on the Saturday nearest to January 31. The other company is the Gillette Company prior to its acquisition by Procter & Gamble. Gillette manufactures and sells blades, razors, and toiletries. Gillette was on a calendar year basis.

| | | (Amounts in Thousands) | | | |
|---|---|---|---|---|---|
| | First Quarter | Second Quarter | Third Quarter | Fourth Quarter | Year |
| **Company C** | | | | | |
| Net Sales. . . . . . . . . . . . . . . | $ 1,216.6 | $1,237.3 | $1,339.7 | $1,617.2 | $5,410.8 |
| Gross profit . . . . . . . . . . . . . | 753.1 | 773.6 | 839.0 | 1,000.8 | 3,366.5 |
| **Company D** | | | | | |
| Net Sales. . . . . . . . . . . . . . . | $1,172.5 | $1,249.1 | $1,345.8 | $3,401.8 | $7,169.2 |
| Gross profit . . . . . . . . . . . . . | 362.5 | 384.6 | 423.2 | 1,030.3 | 2,200.6 |

## Required

a. Compute the percentage of annual net sales generated each quarter by Company C. Round to the nearest percent.

b. Compute the percentage of annual net sales generated each quarter by Company D. Round to the nearest percent.

c. Which company has the most seasonal business? Briefly explain.

d. Which company is Toys "R" Us? The Gillette Company? Briefly explain.

# SERIAL PROBLEM: KATE'S CARDS

(*Note:* **This is a continuation of the Serial Problem: Kate's Cards from Chapter 1 through Chapter 12.)**

**SP13.** Kate is very pleased with the results of the first year of operations for Kate's Cards. She ended the year on a high note, with the company's reputation for producing quality cards leading to more business than she can currently manage. Kate is considering expanding and bringing in several employees. In order to do this, she will need to find a larger location and also purchase more equipment. All this means additional financing. Kate has asked you to look at her year-end financial statements as if you were a banker considering giving Kate a loan. Comment on your findings and provide calculations to support your comments.

| KATE'S CARDS<br>Income Statement<br>Year Ended August 31, 2011 | |
|---|---:|
| Sales revenue | $135,000 |
| Cost of goods sold | 72,000 |
| Gross profit | 63,000 |
| Operating expenses | |
| Wages | 18,000 |
| Consulting | 11,850 |
| Insurance | 1,200 |
| Utilities | 2,400 |
| Depreciation | 3,250 |
| Total operating expenses | 36,700 |
| Income from operations | 26,300 |
| Interest expense | 900 |
| Income before income tax | 25,400 |
| Income tax expense | 8,900 |
| Net income | $ 16,500 |

| KATE'S CARDS<br>Balance Sheet<br>As of August 31, 2011 | |
|---|---:|
| Assets | |
| Current assets | |
| Cash | $12,300 |
| Accounts receivable | 11,000 |
| Inventory | 16,000 |
| Prepaid insurance | 1,000 |
| Total current assets | 40,300 |
| Equipment | 17,500 |
| Accumulated depreciation | 3,250 |
| Total assets | $54,550 |
| Liabilities | |
| Current liabilities | |
| Accounts payable | $ 6,200 |
| Unearned revenue | 1,250 |
| Other current liabilities | 1,900 |
| Total current liabilities | 9,350 |
| Note payable | 15,000 |
| Total liabilities | 24,350 |
| Stockholders' equity | |
| Common stock | 500 |
| Additional paid-in-capital | 9,500 |
| Preferred stock | 5,000 |
| Retained earnings | 15,200 |
| Total stockholders' equity | 30,200 |
| Total liabilities and stockholders' equity | $54,550 |

| KATE'S CARDS<br>Statement of Cash Flows<br>Year Ended August 31, 2011 | |
| --- | --- |
| Cash flow from operating activities | |
| Net income ..................................................... | $16,500 |
| Add depreciation ............................................... | 3,250 |
| Increase in accounts receivable .............................. | (11,000) |
| Increase in inventory ......................................... | (16,000) |
| Increase in prepaid expenses ................................. | (1,000) |
| Increase in accounts payable ................................. | 6,200 |
| Increase in unearned revenue ................................ | 1,250 |
| Increase in other current liabilities ........................ | 1,900 |
| Cash provided by operating activities ........................ | 1,100 |
| Cash flow from investing activities | |
| Purchase of equipment........................................ | (17,500) |
| Cash used by investing activities ............................ | (17,500) |
| Cash flow from financing activities | |
| Proceeds from bank note...................................... | 15,000 |
| Issuance of common stock .................................... | 10,000 |
| Issuance of preferred stock .................................. | 5,000 |
| Cash dividends ($300 preferred and $1,000 common) ............ | (1,300) |
| Cash provided by financing activities......................... | 28,700 |
| Net increase in cash ......................................... | 12,300 |
| Cash at beginning of year..................................... | 0 |
| Cash at end of year .......................................... | $12,300 |

# EXTENDING YOUR KNOWLEDGE

## REPORTING AND ANALYSIS

**EYK13-1. Financial Reporting Problem: Columbia Sportswear Company**

The financial statements for the Columbia Sportswear Company can be found in Appendix A at the end of this book.

COLUMBIA SPORTSWEAR COMPANY

You are considering an investment in Columbia Sportswear after a recent outdoor trip in which you really liked some of the clothes you purchased from the company. You decide to do an analysis of the company's financial statements in order to help you make an informed decision.

**Required**

a. Using the five year selected financial data reported in the annual report, produce a 5-year trend analysis, using 2005 as a base year, of (1) net sales, (2) net income, and (3) total assets. Comment on your findings.

b. Calculate the (1) gross profit percentage, (2) return on sales, and (3) return on assets for 2008 and 2009. Comment on Columbia Sportswear's profitability. (2007 total assets = $1,166,481,000)

c. Calculate the (1) current ratio, (2) quick ratio, and (3) operating-cash-flow-to-current-liabilities ratio for 2008 and 2009. Comment on Columbia Sportswear's liquidity. (2007 current liabilities = $166,531,000)

d. Calculate the debt-to-equity ratio for 2008 and 2009. Comment on Columbia Sportswear's solvency.

**EYK13-2. Comparative Analysis Problem: Columbia Sportswear Company vs The Timberland Company**

The financial statements for the Columbia Sportswear Company can be found in Appendix A at the end of this book, and the financial statements of the Timberland Company can be found in Appendix B (the complete annual report is available on this book's Website).

COLUMBIA SPORTSWEAR COMPANY

TIMBERLAND COMPANY

**Required**

Based on the information from the financial statements of each company, do the following.

a. Calculate the percentage change in (1) net sales, (2) net income, (3) cash flow from operating activities, and (4) total assets from 2008 to 2009.

b. What conclusions can you draw from this analysis?

**ASSIGNMENTS**

**EYK13-3.** **Business Decision Problem**

Crescent Paints, Inc., a paint manufacturer, has been in business for five years. The company has had modest profits and has experienced few operating difficulties until this year, 2011, when president Alice Becknell discussed her company's working capital problems with you, a loan officer at Granite Bank. Becknell explained that expanding her firm has created difficulties in meeting obligations when they come due and in taking advantage of cash discounts offered by manufacturers for the timely payment of the company's accounts payable. She would like to borrow $50,000 from Granite Bank. At your request, Becknell submits the following financial data for the past two years:

|  | 2011 | 2010 |
|---|---|---|
| Sales revenue | $2,000,000 | $1,750,000 |
| Cost of goods sold | 1,320,000 | 1,170,000 |
| Net income | 42,000 | 33,600 |
| Dividends | 22,000 | 18,000 |
| December 31, 2009, data |  |  |
| Total assets | 1,100,000 |  |
| Accounts receivable (net) | 205,000 |  |
| Inventory | 350,000 |  |

| CRESCENT PAINTS, INC. Balance Sheets | | |
|---|---|---|
|  | Dec. 31, 2011 | Dec. 31, 2010 |
| **Assets** | | |
| Cash | $ 31,000 | $ 50,000 |
| Accounts receivable (net) | 345,000 | 250,000 |
| Inventory | 525,000 | 425,000 |
| Prepaid expenses | 11,000 | 6,000 |
| Total Current Assets | 912,000 | 731,000 |
| Plant assets (net) | 483,000 | 444,000 |
| Total Assets | $1,395,000 | $ 1,175,000 |
| **Liabilities and Stockholders' Equity** | | |
| Notes payable—banks | $ 100,000 | $ 35,000 |
| Accounts payable | 244,000 | 190,000 |
| Accrued liabilities | 96,000 | 85,000 |
| Total Current Liabilities | 440,000 | 310,000 |
| 10% Mortgage payable | 190,000 | 250,000 |
| Total Liabilities | 630,000 | 560,000 |
| Common stock | 665,000 | 535,000 |
| Retained earnings | 100,000 | 80,000 |
| Total Stockholders' Equity | 765,000 | 615,000 |
| Total Liabilities and Stockholders' Equity | $1,395,000 | $1,175,000 |

You calculate the following items for both years from the given data and then compare them with the median ratios for paint manufacturers provided by a commercial credit firm:

| | | Median Ratios for Paint Manufacturers |
|---|---|---|
| 1. | Current ratio | 2.5 |
| 2. | Quick ratio | 1.3 |
| 3. | Accounts receivable turnover | 8.1 |
| 4. | Average collection period | 44.9 days |
| 5. | Inventory turnover | 4.9 |
| 6. | Debt-to-equity ratio | 0.78 |
| 7. | Return on assets | 4.8% |
| 8. | Return on sales | 2.4% |

**Required**

Based on your analysis, decide whether and under what circumstances you would grant Becknell's request for a loan. Explain the reasons for your decision.

**EYK13-4. Financial Analysis Problem**

Listed below are selected financial data for three corporations: **Honeywell, Inc.** (environmental controls), **The Dow Chemical Company** (chemicals and plastic products), and **Abbott Laboratories** (health care products). These data cover five years (Year 5 is the most recent year; net income in thousands):

| | Year 5 | Year 4 | Year 3 | Year 2 | Year 1 |
|---|---|---|---|---|---|
| **Honeywell, Inc.** | | | | | |
| Net income............................. | $278,900 | $322,200 | $246,800 | $331,100 | $381,900 |
| Earnings per common share ............. | $2.15 | $2.40 | $1.78 | $2.35 | $2.52 |
| Dividend per common share............. | $1.00 | $0.91 | $0.84 | $0.77 | $0.70 |
| **The Dow Chemical Company** | | | | | |
| Net income............................. | $938,000 | $644,000 | $276,000 | $942,000 | $1,384,000 |
| Earnings per common share ............. | $3.88 | $2.33 | $0.99 | $3.46 | $5.10 |
| Dividend per common share............. | $2.60 | $2.60 | $2.60 | $2.60 | $2.60 |
| **Abbott Laboratories** | | | | | |
| Net income*............................. | $1,399,100 | $1,239,100 | $1,088,700 | $965,800 | $859,800 |
| Earnings per common share* ............. | $1.69 | $1.47 | $1.27 | $1.11 | $0.96 |
| Dividend per common share............. | $0.68 | $0.60 | $0.50 | $0.42 | $0.35 |

*Before extraordinary gain and accounting change

**Required**

*a.* Calculate the dividend payout ratio for each company for each of the five years.

*b.* Companies may differ in their dividend policy; that is, they may differ in whether they emphasize a constant dividend amount per share, a steady growth in dividend amount per share, a target or constant dividend payout ratio, or some other criterion. Based on the data available, identify what appears to be each of the above firm's dividend policy over the five-year period.

## CRITICAL THINKING

**EYK13-5. Accounting Research Problem: General Mills, Inc.**

The fiscal year 2010 annual report of General Mills, Inc. is available on this book's Website.

**Required**

*a.* Calculate (or identify) the following financial ratios for 2009 and 2010:
   1. Gross profit percentage
   2. Return on sales
   3. Asset turnover (2008, total assets = $19,041.6 million)
   4. Return on assets (2008, total assets = $19,041.6 million)
   5. Return on common stockholders' equity (2008, total stockholders' equity = $6,215.8 million)
   6. Current ratio
   7. Quick ratio
   8. Operating-cash-flow-to-current-liabilities ratio (2008, current liabilities = $4,856.3 million)
   9. Accounts receivable turnover (2008, accounts receivable = $1,081.6 million)
   10. Average collection period
   11. Inventory turnover (2008, inventory = $1,366.8 million)
   12. Days' sales in inventory
   13. Debt-to-equity ratio
   14. Times-interest-earned ratio
   15. Operating-cash-flow-to-capital-expenditures ratio
   16. Earnings per share
   17. Price-earnings ratio (Use year-end closing stock price of $35.62)
   18. Dividend yield
   19. Dividend payout ratio

*b.* Comment briefly on the changes from fiscal 2009 to fiscal 2010 in the ratios computed above.

**EYK13-6.** **Accounting Communication Activity**

Pete Hollingsworth is currently taking an accounting course and is confused about what his professor told the class about analyzing financial statements. Pete would like you to lead a study session on the topic. In order to help everyone out, you decide to write a short memo describing some of the key points.

**Required**
Include the following items in your memo:
a. What is meant by trend analysis and how is it helpful?
b. How are common-size statements constructed and what are their uses?
c. What are a few common profitability, liquidity, and solvency ratios and how are they interpreted?
d. What are some limitations of financial statement analysis?

**EYK13-7.** **Accounting Ethics Case**

Chris Nelson, the new assistant controller for Grand Company, is preparing for the firm's year-end closing procedures. On December 30, 2010, a memorandum from the controller directed Nelson to make a journal entry debiting Cash and crediting Long-Term Advances to Officers for $1,000,000. Not finding the $1,000,000 in the cash deposit prepared for the bank that day, Nelson went to the controller for a further explanation. In response, the controller took from her desk drawer a check for $1,000,000 payable to Grand Company from Jason Grand, chief executive officer of the firm. Attached to the check was a note from Jason Grand saying that if this check were not needed to return it to him next week.

"This check is paying off a $1,000,000 advance the firm made to Jason Grand six years ago," stated the controller. "Mr. Grand has done this every year since the advance; each time we have returned the check to him in January of the following year. We plan to do so again this time. In fact, when Mr. Grand retires in four years, I expect the board of directors will forgive this advance. However, if the firm really needed the cash, we would deposit the check."

"Then why go through this charade each year?" inquired Nelson.

"It dresses up our year-end balance sheet," replied the controller. "Certain financial statement ratios are improved significantly. Further, the notes to the financial statements don't have to reveal a related-party loan. Lots of firms engage in year-end transactions designed to dress up their financial statements."

**Required**
a. What financial statement ratios are improved by making the journal entry contained in the controller's memorandum?
b. Is the year-end handling of Jason Grand's advance an ethical practice? Discuss.

**EYK13-8.** **Corporate Social Responsibility Problem**

PROCTER & GAMBLE COMPANY

The chapter highlighted one way in which the **Procter & Gamble Company** demonstrates its commitment to being a good corporate citizen (see Page 598). Go to Procter & Gamble's website and navigate to the section on sustainability. From there you can download their annual sustainability report. The report contains a section on social responsibility. In addition to the joint effort with UNICEF, what are some other ways that P&G demonstrates its commitment to being a good corporate citizen?

**EYK13-9.** **Forensic Accounting Problem**

Accrual accounting is based on the principle that revenue should be reported when earned and that expenses associated with that revenue should be matched against the revenue in the same period. Some financial statement frauds violate this fundamental concept in order to overstate net income in the current year. Provide an example of how this may be accomplished.

## ANSWERS TO SELF-STUDY QUESTIONS

1. a, (p. 595)  2. c, (p. 603)  3. c, (p. 609)  4. b, (p. 611)  5. b, (p. 607)  6. c, (p. 611)
7. d (p. 614)  8. b, (p. 606)  9. c, (p. 607)  10. b, (p. 602)  11. c, (p. 618)  12. d, (p. 620)

# Your Turn! Solutions

## Solution 13.1
1. Persistent
2. Transitory
3. Transitory
4. Persistent
5. Transitory
6. Persistent

## Solution 13.2

| | Increase in 2011 | |
|---|---|---|
| | Amount | Percent |
| Sales revenue .......................... | $50,000 | 6.7 percent [($800,000 − $750,000)/$750,000] |
| Net income............................ | 20,000 | 20.0 percent [($120,000 − $100,000)/$100,000] |
| Total assets........................... | 10,000 | 3.4 percent [($300,000 − $290,000)/$290,000] |

## Solution 13.3

| SANFORD COMPANY<br>Income Statement<br>For the Year Ended December 31, 2010 | Amount | Percent |
|---|---|---|
| Sales revenue ...................................................... | $13,500 | 100.0 |
| Cost of goods sold.................................................. | 5,400 | 40.0 |
| Gross profit........................................................ | 8,100 | 60.0 |
| Selling and administrative expenses ............................... | 1,350 | 10.0 |
| Income from operations ........................................... | 6,750 | 50.0 |
| Interest expense................................................... | 675 | 5.0 |
| Other expense ..................................................... | 135 | 1.0 |
| Income before income taxes ....................................... | 5,940 | 44.0 |
| Income tax expense ................................................ | 2,295 | 17.0 |
| Net income......................................................... | $ 3,645 | 27.0 |

## Solution 13.4
a. Gross profit percentage = ($30,000 − $10,500)/$30,000 = 65.0 percent
b. Return on sales = $4,500/$30,000 = 15.0 percent
c. Asset turnover = $30,000/$50,000 = 0.60
d. Return on assets = $4,500/$50,000 = 9.0 percent
e. Return on common stockholders' equity = ($4,500 − $500)/$35,000 = 11.4 percent

## Solution 13.5
a. Working capital = $60,000 − $40,000 = $20,000
b. Current ratio = $60,000/$40,000 = 1.5
c. Operating-cash-flow-to-current-liabilities ratio = $55,000/$40,000 = 1.375
d. Accounts receivable turnover = $100,000/$15,000 = 6.67 times
e. Days' sales in inventory = 365/($70,000/$9,000) = 46.9 days

## Solution 13.6
a. Debt-to-equity ratio = $180,000/$600,000 = 0.30
b. Times-interest-earned ratio = ($55,000 + $5,000 + $25,000)/$5,000 = 17.0 times
c. Operating-cash-flow-to-capital-expenditures ratio = $100,000/$30,000 = 3.33 times

## Solution 13.7
a. Dividend yield = $1.50/$54.00 = 2.8 percent
b. Dividend payout ratio = $1.50/$4.50 = 33.3 percent

# A

# Columbia Sportswear Company: Annual Report and Social Responsibility Report

The law requires publicly traded companies to submit an audited annual report to the Securities and Exchange Commission (SEC) within two months of the close of their fiscal year. This annual report is called Form 10-K. Companies also provide their stockholders with an annual report that contains many of the items included in Form 10-K, along with a letter to the shareholders and public relations and marketing material. Although each annual report is different, all annual reports typically include the following elements:

- Letter to the Shareholders
- Management Discussion and Analysis
- Independent Auditor's Report
- Financial Statements
- Notes to Financial Statements
- Report on Internal Control
- Management's Certification of Financial Statements
- Supplemental Information

In addition, most publicly traded companies also provide a voluntary report on their corporate social responsibility commitments. Because this report is voluntary, its content varies to a greater degree from company to company. Most reports, however, discuss the company's commitment in the areas of both social and environmental impact.

The following pages include data from Columbia Sportswear's 2009 Annual Report, along with highlights from its social responsibility reporting. Appendix A is organized as follows:

Occasionally, companies restate financial data for previous years, which may cause specific amounts to change in their financial statements. The data in this appendix reflect the most current financial data available at the time this book was printed.

# LETTER TO SHAREHOLDERS

**Dear Fellow Shareholders,**

If you know anything about Columbia Sportswear, you know that we are not the kind of company that sits inside and complains about the weather. Our "Welcome to the Greater Outdoors" brand campaign is not a fair-weather call to action. On the contrary, it is a statement about accepting conditions as they are, strapping on gear designed to overcome those conditions, and going outside to embrace the Greater Outdoors in all her variety.

While our 2009 financial results were better than what we expected at the beginning of the year, they were well below the global potential of our portfolio of outdoor brands.

Consolidated sales of $1.24 billion fell six percent compared with 2008 and net income totaled $67.0 million, or $1.97 per share, compared with $95.0 million, or $2.74 per share in 2008.

Just as our innovative products help outdoor consumers overcome external conditions, we have been tapping the talents of our people, and using our financial strength throughout this turbulent economic cycle to invest in critical strategic initiatives designed to elevate our brands, strengthen our competitive position and improve our financial results moving forward.

As a result, we believe we are poised for renewed sales growth in 2010 and to begin reclaiming market share in key markets around the world.

## A Beacon of Innovation to Outdoor Enthusiasts

Of all our strategic initiatives, none is more important than our renewed commitment to innovation that differentiates our brands and our products from competitors'.

Brands that earn a reputation as the leading innovator in their industry invariably attract the most passionate and loyal consumers.

In the past two years, Columbia Sportswear has applied for more patents than in its entire 72-year history.  Our goal is to assemble a portfolio of innovative technologies that deliver benefits of highest importance to outdoor consumers and differentiate our products from our competitors'.

Today, a far greater percentage of our products contain these differentiating technologies, compared with just two years ago.

And the best is yet to come.

For Fall 2010, we will launch the newest addition to our innovation portfolio with the patent-pending Omni-Heat™ suite of warmth technologies – Omni-Heat™ Reflective, Omni-Heat™ Insulated, and Omni-Heat™ Electric.  We believe Omni-Heat is the most innovative warmth technology to hit the outdoor industry in decades.

Unlike many other technologies, Omni-Heat is relevant across outerwear, sportswear, footwear, accessories and equipment.  And it is visible so that consumers can immediately "get it" and understand the benefits they will experience when they use it.

Omni-Heat will be available in over 90 styles across a wide range of prices, forming the nucleus of our Fall 2010 product offering, and will be supported by an aggressive integrated global marketing blitz.

**Wielding Design as a Competitive Weapon**

In addition to being known as category innovators, powerful brands are also known for compelling and elegant design.

Today, more than ever before, the product merchandising and design teams within each of our major brands – Columbia, Mountain Hardwear, Sorel and Montrail – are focused on uncovering real consumer insights and bringing those insights to life through designs that perform and deliver benefits through innovation.

The industry has taken notice, bestowing top design awards on Columbia's Mobex™ backpack, and Bugathermo™ heated boot. Most recently, our Ravenous™ trail-running shoe ran off with *Trail Runner Magazine's* 2010 Editor's Choice Award for Best Debut, while Montrail's Mountain Masochist™ was selected as the best new trail-running shoe in *Outside Magazine's 2009 Annual Buyer's Guide*.

Mountain Hardwear's Intention 75 backpack was honored as the best large-load backpack in *Backpacker Magazine's 2009 Gear Guide* and in the December 2009 *"Gear of the Year"* issue of *Men's Journal*. Our Sorel™ design team infused fun and performance-grounded fashion into this iconoclastic winter boot brand, successfully broadening its appeal to female consumers and elevating the brand's distribution into some of the finest luxury shoe retailers in the world.

Through innovation and design fed by consumer insight, each of our brands is succeeding in redefining and re-energizing its category, strengthening relationships with consumers and building confidence among our wholesale partners around the world.

The strides we are making infusing our products with innovation and design also enable us to segment our product assortments to better match each channel of distribution and the consumers who shop there. A growing number of high-influence specialty and sporting goods retailers are adding our brands to their assortment for the first time, while others with whom our business has contracted in the past decade are showing renewed interest.

We also expanded our direct-to-consumer platform in 2009 with the launch of our first e-commerce sites for Columbia (www.columbia.com) and Sorel (www.sorel.com). Within four months of its launch, www.columbia.com was named one of *Internet Retailer's* "Hot 100" e-commerce sites, proving that our design and innovation talent isn't limited to our product teams.

The company's financial position remains extremely solid and provides us the confidence and flexibility to continue building a world-class organization capable of producing world-class products and marketing every season.

Our global teams are committed to our strategies and optimistic about the significant global opportunities for our brands.

But we are taking nothing for granted.

The economic weather forecast is still cloudy.   Many of our retail customers are weakened. Consumers remain cautious.  Our competitors are formidable.

What a great time to be Columbia Sportswear Company.

I'll meet you outside.

Sincerely,

Timothy P. Boyle
President and Chief Executive Officer

This letter contains forward-looking statements.   Actual results may differ materially from those projected in these forward-looking statements as a result of a number of risks and uncertainties, including those described in the Company's Annual Report on Form 10-K for the year ended December 31, 2009, under the heading "Risk Factors."

# MANAGEMENT DISCUSSION AND ANALYSIS

## Item 7. *MANAGEMENT'S DISCUSSION AND ANALYSIS OF FINANCIAL CONDITION AND RESULTS OF OPERATIONS*

This Annual Report, including Item 1 of Part I and Items 6 and 6A of Part II, contains forward-looking statements. Forward-looking statements include any statements related to our expectations regarding future performance or market position, including any statements regarding anticipated sales across markets, distribution channels and product categories, access to raw materials and factory capacity, financing and working capital requirements and resources and our exposure to market risk associated with interest rates and foreign currency exchange rates.

These forward-looking statements, and others we make from time to time, are subject to a number of risks and uncertainties. Many factors may cause actual results to differ materially from those projected in forward-looking statements, including the risks described above in Item 1A, Risk Factors. We do not undertake any duty to either update forward-looking statements after the date they are made or conform them to actual results or to changes in circumstances or expectations.

### Our Business

As one of the largest outdoor apparel and footwear companies in the world, we design, develop, market and distribute active outdoor apparel, footwear, accessories and equipment under the Columbia, Mountain Hardwear, Sorel, Montrail, and Pacific Trail brands. Our products are sold through a mix of wholesale distribution channels, independent distributors, our own retail channels and licensees.

The popularity of outdoor activities and changing design trends affect consumer desire for our products. Therefore, we seek to anticipate and respond to trends and shifts in consumer preferences by adjusting the mix of available product offerings, developing new products with innovative performance features and designs, and by creating persuasive and memorable marketing communications to drive consumer awareness and demand. Failure to anticipate or respond to consumer needs and preferences in a timely and adequate manner could have a material adverse effect on our sales and profitability.

### Business Environment

Like other branded consumer product companies, our business is heavily dependent upon discretionary consumer spending patterns. Our net sales volumes have been negatively affected by the volatility of the global economy and its impact on consumer purchasing behavior, and retailers' behavior related to advance orders, replenishment orders, order cancellations and seasonal reorders. Consequences of the economic environment during the past 18 months include tightening of credit for some of our wholesale customers and consumers and a significant slowing of retail sales. This has resulted in, and could continue to result in, liquidations and reorganization of several of our wholesale customers and a more cautious approach by many of our wholesale customers when placing advance orders for seasonal products. It also affects decisions regarding reducing, delaying delivery of, or cancelling advance orders prior to shipment. In addition, the effects of foreign currency exchange rates may amplify any revenue declines if the U.S. dollar strengthens compared to local currencies in our direct markets, as we have experienced in some markets.

We believe that we have appropriately factored our historical experiences, incremental sales from our new retail stores and e-commerce platform, and the estimated effect of changes in foreign currency exchange rates into our outlook for fiscal year 2010. However, unfavorable and unprecedented global economic conditions have increased the uncertainty of our planning and forecasts. In this challenging economic environment, we are also mindful of our reliance on the overall financial health of our wholesale customers and their ability to continue to access credit markets to fund their inventory purchases and day-to-day operations.

The business climate continues to present us with a great deal of uncertainty, with a number of variables that we rely on for planning purposes moving in opposing directions and making it more difficult to predict the future. Factors that could significantly affect our 2010 outlook include:

- Fluctuating currency exchange rates;

- Changes in mix and volume of full price sales in contrast with closeout product sales;

- Changes in the volume of order cancellations and reorders;

- Incremental sales through our expanding retail and e-commerce operations, which are not included in backlog;

- Changes in consumer activity and sales fluctuations in our retail stores; and

- Changes in spending levels related to strategic initiatives and cost-containment efforts.

Although we cannot predict future results with certainty and despite current global economic conditions, we are committed to our strategies, which focus on product innovation and using our portfolio of outdoor brands to meet the needs of outdoor consumers. Our direct-to-consumer initiatives include our retail expansion plans and e-commerce platforms. We believe that our commitment to invest in these strategies, while maintaining a well-developed sourcing and distribution infrastructure, positions us well to establish sustainable platforms that will support long-term growth and profitability.

## Overview

The following discussion of our results of operations and liquidity and capital resources, including known trends and uncertainties identified by management, should be read in conjunction with the Consolidated Financial Statements and accompanying Notes that appear elsewhere in this annual report.

All references to years relate to the calendar year ended December 31. Highlights for the year ended December 31, 2009 include the following:

- Net sales decreased $73.8 million, or 6%, to $1,244.0 million in 2009 from $1,317.8 million in 2008. Changes in foreign currency exchange rates compared with 2008 negatively affected the consolidated net sales comparison by approximately one percentage point. The decrease in net sales was primarily the result of decreased sales of Columbia-branded products in the EMEA region and Canada, partially offset by increased sales of Columbia-branded products in the United States and the LAAP region. Difficult economic conditions worldwide negatively affected our net sales during 2009 as initial orders for our wholesale businesses declined for the spring and fall 2009 selling seasons. In addition, customer order cancellation rates were higher and reorder rates were lower for our spring 2009 selling season, with some improvement in cancellation and reorder rates for our fall 2009 selling season.

| | Year Ended December 31, | | |
| --- | --- | --- | --- |
| | **2009** | **2008** | **% Change** |
| | **(In millions, except for percentage changes)** | | |
| Geographical Net Sales to Unrelated Entities: | | | |
| United States | $ 736.9 | $ 727.7 | 1% |
| EMEA | 197.4 | 267.2 | (26)% |
| LAAP | 203.2 | 198.2 | 3% |
| Canada | 106.5 | 124.7 | (15)% |
| | $1,244.0 | $1,317.8 | (6)% |
| Categorical Net Sales to Unrelated Entities: | | | |
| Sportswear | $ 472.5 | $ 540.9 | (13)% |
| Outerwear | 482.5 | 491.7 | (2)% |
| Footwear | 214.6 | 217.2 | (1)% |
| Accessories and Equipment | 74.4 | 68.0 | 9% |
| | $1,244.0 | $1,317.8 | (6)% |
| Brand Net Sales to Unrelated Entities: | | | |
| Columbia | $1,072.5 | $1,162.0 | (8)% |
| Mountain Hardwear | 100.5 | 95.0 | 6% |
| Sorel | 60.6 | 48.1 | 26% |
| Other | 10.4 | 12.7 | (18)% |
| | $1,244.0 | $1,317.8 | (6)% |

- Our wholesale backlog for the spring 2010 selling season as of September 30, 2009 decreased $20.1 million, or 5%, to $350.8 million from $370.9 million as of September 30, 2008, including a benefit of approximately two percentage points from changes in foreign currency exchange rates compared with 2008. The decrease in our spring wholesale backlog consisted of a decline in orders from EMEA distributors, our EMEA direct business and LAAP distributors, partially offset by an increase in orders in Japan. Spring wholesale backlog for the United States and Canada was essentially flat compared to 2008. The decrease in orders, categorically, was driven primarily by a decline in orders of Columbia-branded sportswear. Although we cannot predict with certainty any future results, our reported wholesale backlog is one indicator of our anticipated wholesale net sales for the spring 2010 selling season. Many factors, however, could cause actual sales to differ materially from reported wholesale backlog, including the potential cancellation of orders by customers, which was significant for spring 2009 products, changes in the volume of closeout products sales, changes in foreign currency exchange rates and macroeconomic conditions. In addition, we expect incremental sales through our direct-to-consumer operations, which are not included in wholesale backlog, to affect actual sales comparisons for the spring 2010 season. Our spring 2010 wholesale backlog should not be used as a sole indicator of, or in forecasting, sales beyond the spring 2010 selling season.

- Gross profit decreased 100 basis points to 42.1% in 2009 from 43.1% in 2008. Gross profit margins contracted primarily as a result of a higher volume of close-out product sales at lower gross margins and unfavorable hedge rates.

- Selling, general and administrative expense increased $14.3 million, or 3%, to $444.7 million in 2009 from $430.4 million in 2008. This increase was primarily due to initial investment and incremental operating costs in support of our direct-to-consumer initiatives and increased incentive compensation and professional fees, partially offset by reduced advertising and bad debt expense.

- Net income decreased 29% to $67.0 million in 2009 from $95.0 million in 2008, and diluted earnings per share decreased to $1.97 in 2009 compared to $2.74 in 2008, which included a $0.46 per diluted share after-tax impairment charge. Net income in 2009 was unfavorably affected by lower revenues and gross profit margins and increased selling, general and administrative expenses compared to 2008. Our effective tax rate was 25.4% in 2009 compared to 24.7% in 2008.

- Since the inception of our stock repurchase plan in 2004 through December 31, 2009, our Board of Directors has authorized the repurchase of $500 million of our common stock. As of December 31, 2009, we have repurchased 8,897,957 shares under this program at an aggregate purchase price of approximately $407.4 million. Shares of our common stock may be purchased in the open market or through privately negotiated transactions, subject to market conditions. The repurchase program does not obligate us to acquire any specific number of shares or to acquire shares over any specified period of time.

# OVERVIEW OF FINANCIAL PERFORMANCE

### Results of Operations

Net income decreased $28.0 million, or 29%, to $67.0 million in 2009 from $95.0 million in 2008. Diluted earnings per share decreased to $1.97 in 2009 from $2.74 in 2008, which included a $0.46 per diluted share after-tax impairment charge. Net income decreased $49.5 million, or 34%, to $95.0 million in 2008 from $144.5 million in 2007. Diluted earnings per share decreased to $2.74 in 2008, which included a $0.46 per diluted share after-tax impairment charge, from $3.96 in 2007.

The following table sets forth, for the periods indicated, the percentage relationship to net sales of specified items in our Consolidated Statements of Operations:

|  | 2009 | 2008 | 2007 |
|---|---|---|---|
| Net sales | 100.0% | 100.0% | 100.0% |
| Cost of sales | 57.9 | 56.9 | 57.2 |
| Gross profit | 42.1 | 43.1 | 42.8 |
| Selling, general and administrative expense | 35.7 | 32.7 | 28.5 |
| Impairment of acquired intangible assets | — | 1.9 | — |
| Net licensing income | 0.7 | 0.5 | 0.4 |
| Income from operations | 7.1 | 9.0 | 14.7 |
| Interest income, net | 0.1 | 0.6 | 0.6 |
| Income before income tax | 7.2 | 9.6 | 15.3 |
| Income tax expense | (1.8) | (2.4) | (4.6) |
| Net income | 5.4% | 7.2% | 10.7% |

### *Year Ended December 31, 2009 Compared to Year Ended December 31, 2008*

*Net Sales:*   Consolidated net sales decreased $73.8 million, or 6%, to $1,244.0 million in 2009 from $1,317.8 million in 2008. Changes in foreign currency exchange rates compared with 2008 negatively affected the consolidated net sales comparison by approximately one percentage point. The decrease in net sales was led by the EMEA region and Canada, partially offset by increased net sales in the United States and the LAAP region. By product category, the reduction in net sales was led by sportswear, followed by outerwear and footwear, partially offset by increased net sales of accessories and equipment.

*Sales by Product Category*

Net sales of sportswear decreased $68.4 million, or 13%, to $472.5 million in 2009 from $540.9 million in 2008. The decrease in sportswear net sales consisted of decreased net sales in the United States wholesale business, the EMEA direct and distributor businesses, Canada and the LAAP distributor business, partially offset by increased net sales in our United States retail business, Japan and Korea. By brand, the decrease in net sales of Columbia-branded sportswear was partially offset by increased net sales of Mountain Hardwear-branded sportswear. We primarily attribute the decrease in wholesale net sales of Columbia-branded sportswear to lower initial order volumes.

Net sales of outerwear decreased $9.2 million, or 2%, to $482.5 million in 2009 from $491.7 million in 2008. The decrease in outerwear net sales consisted of decreased net sales in the EMEA direct and distributor businesses, the LAAP distributor business, Canada and the United States wholesale business, partially offset by increased net sales in our United States retail business, Japan and Korea. By brand, the decrease in net sales of Columbia-branded outerwear was partially offset by increased net sales of Mountain Hardwear-branded outerwear. We primarily attribute the decrease in wholesale net sales of Columbia-branded outerwear to lower initial order volumes.

Net sales of footwear decreased $2.6 million, or 1%, to $214.6 million in 2009 from $217.2 million in 2008. The decrease in footwear net sales was concentrated in the EMEA distributor business, followed by the United States wholesale and LAAP distributor businesses, partially offset by increased net sales of footwear in our United States retail business, Japan and Canada. Footwear net sales were essentially flat in the EMEA direct business and Korea. By brand, the decrease in net sales of Columbia-branded footwear was partially offset by increased net sales of Sorel-branded footwear. Net sales of Sorel-branded footwear increased in all regions and businesses except the EMEA distributor business. The decrease in footwear net sales to EMEA distributors primarily reflects lower Columbia-branded product net sales to our largest customer in that region and a shift in the timing of shipments as a smaller percentage of spring 2010 shipments occurred in the fourth quarter of 2009, while a higher percentage of spring 2009 shipments occurred in the fourth quarter of 2008.

Net sales of accessories and equipment increased $6.4 million, or 9%, to $74.4 million in 2009 from $68.0 million in 2008. Accessories and equipment sales growth was concentrated in Columbia-branded accessories and equipment and led by the United States and the LAAP region, followed by Canada, partially offset by a decrease in net sales in the EMEA region.

*Sales by Geographic Region*

Net sales in the United States increased $9.2 million, or 1%, to $736.9 million in 2009 from $727.7 million in 2008. The increase in net sales in the United States was led by outerwear, followed by footwear and accessories and equipment, partially offset by decreased net sales of sportswear. A net sales increase through our retail channels was partially offset by a net sales decrease in our wholesale business. During 2009, we opened 11 new outlet retail stores in the United States, ending the year with 39 outlet retail stores and 6 branded retail stores. In addition, we launched e-commerce websites for the Columbia brand in the third quarter of 2009 and for the Sorel brand in the fourth quarter of 2009.

Net sales in the EMEA region decreased $69.8 million, or 26%, to $197.4 million in 2009 from $267.2 million in 2008. Changes in foreign currency exchange rates compared to 2008 negatively affected the net sales comparison by three percentage points. The decrease in net sales in the EMEA region was led by sportswear and outerwear, followed by footwear and accessories and equipment. Net sales decreased for both the EMEA distributor and EMEA direct businesses. The decrease in net sales to EMEA distributors primarily reflects lower Columbia-branded product net sales to our largest distributor in the region and a shift in the timing of shipments as a smaller percentage of spring 2010 shipments occurred in the fourth quarter of 2009, while a higher percentage of spring 2009 shipments occurred in the fourth quarter of 2008. The decrease in EMEA direct net sales was consistent with lower advance order volumes due in part to continued product assortment and marketing challenges.

Net sales in the LAAP region increased $5.0 million, or 3%, to $203.2 million in 2009 from $198.2 million in 2008. Changes in foreign currency exchange rates contributed two percentage points of benefit to LAAP net sales compared to 2008. The net sales increase in the LAAP region was led by outerwear, followed by accessories and equipment and footwear, partially offset by a net sales decrease in sportswear. Net sales growth in the LAAP region was led by our Japan business, which benefited from foreign currency exchange rates, followed by our Korea business, partially offset by a net sales decrease in our LAAP distributor business.

Net sales in Canada decreased $18.2 million, or 15%, to $106.5 million in 2009 from $124.7 million in 2008. Changes in foreign currency exchange rates compared to 2008 negatively affected the net sales comparison by seven percentage points. The decrease in net sales in Canada was led by sportswear and outerwear, partially offset by increased net sales of footwear and accessories and equipment. The decrease in net sales was consistent with lower advance order volumes of Columbia-branded products due in part to planned reductions in certain channels of distribution.

*Gross Profit:*   Gross profit as a percentage of net sales decreased to 42.1% in 2009 from 43.1% in 2008. Gross profit margins contracted primarily as a result of a higher volume of close-out product sales at lower gross margins and unfavorable hedge rates.

Our gross profits may not be comparable to those of other companies in our industry because some include all of the costs related to their distribution network in cost of sales. We, like others, have chosen to include these expenses as a component of selling, general and administrative expense.

*Selling, General and Administrative Expense:*   Selling, general and administrative expense ("SG&A") includes all costs associated with our design, merchandising, marketing, selling, distribution and corporate functions, including related depreciation and amortization.

SG&A expense increased $14.3 million, or 3%, to $444.7 million in 2009 from $430.4 million in 2008. As a percentage of net sales, SG&A expense increased to 35.7% of net sales in 2009 from 32.7% of net sales in 2008. The increase in SG&A expense as a percentage of net sales was largely the result of reduced net sales in our wholesale business coupled with an increased fixed cost base related to our expanding direct-to-consumer operations and increased incentive compensation and professional fees, partially offset by reduced advertising and bad debt expense.

Selling expenses, including commissions and advertising, decreased $17.0 million, or 14%, to 8.4% of net sales in 2009 from 9.2% of net sales in 2008. We attribute the decrease in selling expenses as a percentage of net sales to lower commission expense as relationships with certain independent sales agencies in the United States and the EMEA region have been discontinued and replaced by in-house sales operations. Operating expenses for the in-house sales organization are included in general and administrative expenses.

General and administrative expenses increased $31.3 million, or 10%, to 27.4% of net sales in 2009 from 23.4% of net sales for the comparable period in 2008. The increase in general and administrative expenses as a percentage of net sales was primarily due to incremental operating costs in support our direct-to-consumer initiatives and the expansion of our in-house sales organization, partially offset by lower bad debt expense. Depreciation and amortization included in SG&A expense totaled $35.5 million for 2009, compared to $30.1 million for the same period in 2008.

*Impairment of Acquired Intangible Assets:*   We did not incur any impairment of acquired intangible assets in 2009. During the fourth quarter of 2008, we incurred a $24.7 million non-cash pre-tax charge, or approximately $0.46 per diluted share after tax, for the write-down of acquired intangible assets related to our acquisitions of the Pacific Trail and Montrail brands in 2006. The impairment charge related primarily to goodwill and trademarks and resulted from our annual evaluation of intangible asset values. These brands had not achieved our sales and profitability objectives and the deterioration in the macro-economic environment and resulting effect on consumer demand have decreased the probability of realizing these objectives in the near future. We remain committed to marketing and distributing Montrail-branded footwear through the outdoor specialty, running specialty and sporting goods channels. Beginning in 2009, Pacific Trail products are sold primarily through licensing arrangements.

*Net Licensing Income:*   Net licensing income increased $2.4 million, or 40%, to $8.4 million in 2009 from $6.0 million in 2008. The increase in net licensing income was primarily due to increased apparel and footwear

30

licensing in the LAAP region. Products distributed by our licensees in 2009 included apparel, footwear, leather accessories, eyewear, socks, insulated products including soft-sided coolers, camping gear, bicycles, home products, luggage, watches and other accessories.

*Interest Income, Net:*   Interest income was $2.1 million in 2009 compared to $7.6 million in 2008. The decrease in interest income was almost entirely due to significantly lower interest rates in 2009 compared to 2008. Interest expense was nominal in 2009 and 2008.

*Income Tax Expense:*   Our provision for income taxes decreased to $22.8 million in 2009 from $31.2 million in 2008. This decrease resulted from lower income before tax, partially offset by an increase in our effective income tax rate to 25.4% in 2009 compared to 24.7% in 2008. Our 2009 effective tax rate varied from the U.S. statutory rate due to foreign tax credits and the favorable settlement of uncertain tax positions.

### Year Ended December 31, 2008 Compared to Year Ended December 31, 2007

*Net Sales:*   Consolidated net sales decreased $38.2 million, or 3%, to $1,317.8 million in 2008 from $1,356.0 million in 2007. Changes in foreign currency exchange rates compared to 2007 contributed one percentage point of benefit to the consolidated net sales comparison. The decrease in net sales was led by the United States, followed by the EMEA region and Canada, partially offset by increased net sales in the LAAP region. By product category, the reduction in net sales was led by sportswear, followed by footwear and outerwear, partially offset by increased net sales of accessories and equipment.

#### Sales by Product Category

Net sales of sportswear decreased $24.7 million, or 4%, to $540.9 million in 2008 from $565.6 million in 2007. The decrease in sportswear net sales was predominantly the result of decreased net sales in the United States, followed by the EMEA region, offset by increased net sales in the LAAP region and Canada. The sportswear net sales decrease was led by the United States wholesale business for the Columbia brand, partially offset by incremental net sales through our expanded base of branded and outlet retail stores. We primarily attribute the decrease in wholesale net sales of sportswear to the lower initial order volumes and the weak U.S. retail environment resulting from difficult macro-economic conditions.

Net sales of outerwear decreased $5.9 million, or 1%, to $491.7 million in 2008 from $497.6 million in 2007. The decrease in outerwear net sales was led by the United States, followed by the EMEA region and Canada, partially offset by an increase in the LAAP region. The decrease in outerwear net sales was predominantly the result of decreased sales of the Columbia brand in the United States wholesale and EMEA direct businesses. The decrease in both regions was primarily the result of lower initial order volumes for the spring and fall 2008 seasons as well as the weak retail environment resulting from difficult macro-economic conditions. The decrease in sales of Columbia-branded outerwear was partially offset by increased sales of Mountain Hardwear-branded outerwear.

Net sales of footwear decreased $10.2 million, or 4%, to $217.2 million in 2008 from $227.4 million in 2007. The decrease in footwear net sales was led by the EMEA region, followed by Canada, partially offset by increased net sales of footwear in the LAAP region and the United States. The decrease in footwear net sales in the EMEA region was led by EMEA direct footwear net sales, followed by EMEA distributor net sales. The decrease in EMEA direct footwear net sales was primarily the result of lower initial order volumes due to continued product assortment and marketing challenges, coupled with economic uncertainty in that region. The decrease in EMEA distributor footwear net sales was primarily a result of earlier shipments of spring 2008 product that occurred in the fourth quarter of 2007.

Net sales of accessories and equipment increased $2.6 million, or 4%, to $68.0 million in 2008 from $65.4 million in 2007. Accessories and equipment sales growth was led by the LAAP region, followed by Canada, partially offset by a decrease in net sales in the United States, while net sales of accessories and equipment remained flat in the EMEA region.

*Sales by Geographic Region*

Net sales in the United States decreased $39.5 million, or 5%, to $727.7 million in 2008 from $767.2 million in 2007. The reduction in net sales in the United States was led by sportswear, followed by outerwear and accessories and equipment, while sales of footwear remained essentially flat. The net sales decrease was led by the wholesale business for the Columbia brand, partially offset by increased net sales through our expanded base of branded and outlet retail stores. During 2008 we opened 15 new outlet retail stores and 5 branded retail stores in the United States, ending the year with 28 outlet retail stores and 6 branded retail stores in the United States.

Net sales in the EMEA region decreased $19.8 million, or 7%, to $267.2 million in 2008 from $287.0 million in 2007. Changes in foreign currency exchange rates contributed five percentage points of benefit to EMEA net sales compared to 2007. The decrease in net sales in the EMEA region was led by footwear, followed by outerwear and sportswear, while net sales of accessories and equipment remained essentially flat. The decrease in net sales in the EMEA region included a decrease in EMEA direct net sales, partially offset by an increase in net sales to EMEA distributors. The decrease in EMEA direct net sales was the result of lower initial order volumes for the spring and fall 2008 seasons due to continued product assortment and marketing challenges, coupled with economic uncertainty in the region. The increase in net sales to EMEA distributors primarily reflects increased Columbia-branded outerwear and sportswear net sales to our largest distributor in the region.

Net sales in the LAAP region increased $22.5 million, or 13%, to $198.2 million in 2008 from $175.7 million in 2007. Changes in foreign currency exchange rates contributed less than one percentage point of benefit to LAAP net sales compared to 2007. Sales growth in the LAAP region was led by our Japan business, which benefited from foreign currency exchange rates, followed by our LAAP distributor business, while net sales in Korea remained essentially flat, including a negative impact from foreign currency exchange rates. The increase in Japan net sales was primarily the result of growth in our retail business as well as continued expansion with key wholesale partners, particularly in the sports chain channel.

Net sales in Canada decreased $1.4 million, or 1%, to $124.7 million in 2008 from $126.1 million in 2007. Changes in foreign currency exchange rates contributed two percentage points of benefit to Canada net sales compared to 2007. The decrease in net sales in Canada was led by outerwear, followed by footwear, partially offset by increased net sales of sportswear and accessories and equipment. The decrease in outerwear was primarily attributable to lower initial order volumes of Columbia-branded products for the fall 2008 season, partially offset by incremental sales of Mountain Hardwear-branded products that were previously sold through third party distributors.

***Gross Profit:***   Gross profit as a percentage of net sales increased to 43.1% in 2008 from 42.8% in 2007. Gross profit margins expanded in all of our product categories primarily due to a lower volume of close-out product sales and an increase in average selling prices, partially offset by the negative effects of an increased mix of sales to distributors, which carry lower margins than wholesale customers, and the effects of changes in foreign currency exchange rates.

A decrease in 2008 close-out product sales at slightly lower gross margins compared to 2007 had a favorable affect on our consolidated gross profits. We primarily attribute this decrease to earlier close-out sales of fall 2007 product in the fourth quarter of 2007.

***Selling, General and Administrative Expense:***   SG&A expense increased $44.6 million, or 12%, to $430.4 million in 2008 from $385.8 million in 2007. Selling expenses increased $8.2 million, or 7%, while general and administrative expenses increased $36.4 million, or 13%. As a percentage of net sales, SG&A expense increased to 32.7% of net sales in 2008 from 28.5% of net sales in 2007.

Selling expenses, including commissions and advertising, increased to 9.2% of net sales in 2008 from 8.3% of net sales in 2007. We attribute the increase in selling expenses as a percentage of net sales to our increased marketing investments to drive consumer demand for our brands, which was amplified by a decrease in consolidated net sales in 2008 compared with the same period in 2007.

The increase in general and administrative expenses primarily resulted from the start-up and operational costs of our new retail stores. Depreciation and amortization included in SG&A expense totaled $30.1 million for 2008, compared to $29.3 million for the same period in 2007.

*Impairment of Acquired Intangible Assets:* We incurred a $24.7 million non-cash pre-tax charge, or approximately $0.46 per diluted share after tax, in 2008 for the write-down of acquired intangible assets related to our acquisitions of the Pacific Trail and Montrail brands in 2006. The impairment charge related primarily to goodwill and trademarks and resulted from our annual evaluation of intangible asset values. These brands have not achieved our sales and profitability objectives and the deterioration in the macro-economic environment and resulting effect on consumer demand decreased the probability of realizing these objectives in the near future.

*Net Licensing Income:* Net licensing income increased $0.8 million, or 15%, to $6.0 million in 2008 from $5.2 million in 2007. In 2008, licensing income was led by Columbia-branded leather accessories, followed by Columbia-branded socks, eyewear, insulated products including soft-sided coolers, and camping gear.

*Interest Income, Net:* Interest income was $7.6 million in 2008 compared to $9.0 million in 2007. The decrease in interest income was primarily due to lower average investment yields compared with the same period in 2007. Interest expense was nominal in 2008 and 2007.

*Income Tax Expense:* Our provision for income taxes decreased to $31.2 million in 2008 from $63.6 million in 2007. This decrease resulted from lower income before tax combined with a decrease in our effective income tax rate to 24.7% in 2008 compared to 30.6% in 2007. The decrease in our tax rate resulted primarily from generating a higher proportion of our income in foreign jurisdictions with lower overall tax rates, increased foreign tax credits and the favorable conclusion of a European tax examination.

**Liquidity and Capital Resources**

Our primary ongoing funding requirements are for working capital, investing activities associated with the expansion of our global operations and general corporate needs. At December 31, 2009, we had total cash and cash equivalents of $386.7 million compared to $230.6 million at December 31, 2008. In addition, we had short-term investments of $22.8 million at December 31, 2009 compared to $22.4 million at December 31, 2008.

Net cash provided by operating activities was $214.4 million in 2009 compared to $144.9 million in 2008. The increase in cash provided by operating activities was primarily the result of significant reductions in accounts receivable and inventory in 2009, partially offset by lower net income and a decrease in accounts payable in 2009, and the non-cash pre-tax charge for the impairment of acquired intangible assets in 2008.

Net cash used in investing activities was $33.2 million in 2009 compared to net cash provided by investing activities of $11.7 million in 2008. In 2009, our investing activities primarily consisted of capital expenditures of $40.9 million, of which $7.8 million was incurred but not yet paid. Capital expenditures in 2009 consisted of approximately $25.7 million related to retail expansion, including e-commerce in the United States and modest investments in Korea and Japan, and approximately $15.2 million in maintenance and infrastructure projects. In 2008, our investing activities primarily consisted of net liquidation of short-term investments of $59.2 million partially offset by capital expenditures of $54.3 million, of which $6.7 million was incurred but not yet paid. Capital expenditures in 2008 consisted of approximately $12.8 million in maintenance capital expenditures and $41.5 million for retail expansion and other capacity initiatives.

Cash used in financing activities was $29.6 million in 2009 compared to $102.4 million in 2008. In 2009, net cash used in financing activities included dividend payments of $22.3 million and the repurchase of common stock at an aggregate price of $7.4 million. In 2008, net cash used in financing activities included the repurchase of common stock at an aggregate price of $83.9 million and dividend payments of $22.1 million, partially offset by proceeds from the issuance of common stock under employee stock plans of $3.5 million.

To fund our domestic working capital requirements, we have available unsecured revolving lines of credit with aggregate seasonal limits ranging from $50 million to $125 million, of which $25 million to $100 million is committed. At December 31, 2009, no balance was outstanding under these lines of credit and we were in compliance with all associated covenants. Internationally, our subsidiaries have local currency operating lines of credit in place guaranteed by us with a combined limit of approximately $105.1 million at December 31, 2009, of which $3.6 million is designated as a European customs guarantee. At December 31, 2009, no balance was outstanding under these lines of credit.

We expect to fund our future capital expenditures with existing cash, operating cash flows and credit facilities. If the need arises for additional expenditures, we may need to seek additional funding. Our ability to obtain additional financing will depend on many factors, including prevailing market conditions, our financial condition, and our ability to negotiate favorable terms and conditions. Financing may not be available on terms that are acceptable or favorable to us, if at all.

Our operations are affected by seasonal trends typical in the outdoor apparel industry, and have historically resulted in higher sales and profits in the third calendar quarter. This pattern has resulted primarily from the timing of shipments to wholesale customers for the fall season. We believe that our liquidity requirements for at least the next 12 months will be adequately covered by existing cash, cash provided by operations and existing short-term borrowing arrangements.

The following table presents our estimated contractual commitments (in thousands):

| | Year ending December 31, | | | | | | |
| | 2010 | 2011 | 2012 | 2013 | 2014 | Thereafter | Total |
|---|---|---|---|---|---|---|---|
| Inventory purchase obligations (1) ..... | 258,069 | — | — | — | — | — | 258,069 |
| Operating leases (2): | | | | | | | |
|    Non-related parties ............. | 28,379 | 27,534 | 26,137 | 25,678 | 23,869 | 128,672 | 260,269 |
|    Related party ................. | 625 | 625 | 72 | 72 | 54 | — | 1,448 |

We have recorded liabilities for net unrecognized tax benefits related to income tax uncertainties in our Consolidated Balance Sheet at December 31, 2009 of approximately $20.9 million; however, they have not been included in the table above because we are uncertain about whether or when these amounts may be settled. See Note 9 of Notes to Consolidated Financial Statements.

(1)  Inventory purchase obligations consist of open production purchase orders for sourced apparel, footwear, accessories and equipment, and materials used to manufacture apparel. The reported amounts exclude product purchase liabilities included in accounts payable on the Consolidated Balance Sheet at December 31, 2009. To support certain inventory purchase obligations, we maintain unsecured and uncommitted lines of credit available for issuing import letters of credit. At December 31, 2009, we had letters of credit outstanding of $7.8 million issued for purchase orders for inventory. See *Off-balance Sheet Arrangements* in Note 5 of Notes to Consolidated Financial Statements for further disclosure.

(2)  Operating lease obligations include retail space operating leases, which often include real estate taxes, insurance, common area maintenance ("CAM"), and other costs in addition to base rent. Operating lease obligations listed above do not include real estate taxes, insurance, CAM, and other costs for which we are obligated. Total expenses for real estate taxes, insurance, CAM, and other costs related to retail space operating leases for the year ended December 31, 2009 was $7.2 million and is included in SG&A expense in the Consolidated Statement of Operations. These operating lease commitments are not reflected on the Consolidated Balance Sheet.

## Quantitative and Qualitative Disclosures About Market Risk

In the normal course of business, our financial position and results of operations are routinely subject to a variety of risks, including market risk associated with interest rate movements on borrowings and investments and exchange rate movements on non-U.S. dollar currency denominated assets, liabilities, income and expenses. We regularly assess these risks and have established policies and business practices that should result in an appropriate level of protection against the adverse effect of these and other potential exposures. We do not engage in speculative trading in any financial market.

Our foreign currency risk management objective is to mitigate the uncertainty of anticipated cash flows attributable to changes in exchange rates. We focus on anticipated cash flows resulting from firmly and non-firmly committed inventory purchases and the related receivables and payables, including third party or intercompany transactions.

We manage this risk primarily by using currency forward, option and swap contracts. Anticipated, but not yet firmly committed, transactions that we hedge carry a high level of certainty and are expected to be recognized within one year. We use cross-currency swaps to hedge foreign currency denominated payments related to intercompany loan agreements. Hedged transactions are denominated primarily in European euros, Canadian dollars, Japanese yen and Korean won.

The fair value of our hedging contracts was unfavorable by approximately $0.4 million and $1.8 million at December 31, 2009 and 2008, respectively. A 10% change in the euro, Canadian dollar, yen and won exchange rates would have resulted in the fair value fluctuating approximately $9.7 million at December 31, 2009 and $6.2 million at December 31, 2008. Changes in fair value resulting from foreign exchange rate fluctuations would be substantially offset by the change in value of the underlying hedged transactions.

Our exposure to market risk for changes in interest rates relates primarily to our debt obligations. We did not have any long-term debt obligations at December 31, 2009 or 2008. We have cash flow exposure on our committed and uncommitted bank lines of credit since the interest is indexed to various reference rates such as Prime and LIBOR. At December 31, 2009 and 2008, our bank lines of credit did not have an outstanding balance.

## Critical Accounting Policies and Estimates

Management's discussion and analysis of our financial condition and results of operations are based on our consolidated financial statements, which have been prepared in accordance with accounting principles generally accepted in the United States. The preparation of these financial statements requires us to make various estimates and judgments that affect reported amounts of assets, liabilities, sales, cost of sales and expenses and related disclosure of contingent assets and liabilities. We believe that the estimates, assumptions and judgments involved in the accounting policies described below have the greatest potential impact on our financial statements, so we consider these to be our critical accounting policies and estimates. Because of the uncertainty inherent in these matters, actual results could differ from the estimates we use in applying the critical accounting policies. We base our ongoing estimates on historical experience and other various assumptions that we believe to be reasonable under the circumstances. Many of these critical accounting policies affect working capital account balances, including the policy for revenue recognition, the allowance for uncollectible accounts receivable, the provision for potential excess, close-out and slow moving inventory, product warranty, income taxes and stock-based compensation.

Management and our independent auditors regularly discuss with our audit committee each of our critical accounting estimates, the development and selection of these accounting estimates, and the disclosure about each estimate in Management's Discussion and Analysis of Financial Condition and Results of Operations. These discussions typically occur at our quarterly audit committee meetings and include the basis and methodology used in developing and selecting these estimates, the trends in and amounts of these estimates, specific matters affecting the amount of and changes in these estimates, and any other relevant matters related to these estimates, including significant issues concerning accounting principles and financial statement presentation.

### Revenue Recognition

We record wholesale and licensed product revenues when title passes and the risks and rewards of ownership have passed to the customer, based on the terms of sale. Title generally passes upon shipment to, or upon receipt by, the customer depending on the country of the sale and the agreement with the customer. Retail store revenues are recorded at the time of sale and e-commerce revenues are recorded upon shipment to the customer.

In some countries outside of the United States where title passes upon receipt by the customer, predominantly in our Western European wholesale business, precise information regarding the date of receipt by the customer is not readily available. In these cases, we estimate the date of receipt by the customer based on historical and expected delivery times by geographic location. We periodically test the accuracy of these estimates based on actual transactions. Delivery times vary by geographic location, generally from one to five days. To date, we have found these estimates to be materially accurate.

At the time of revenue recognition, we also provide for estimated sales returns and miscellaneous claims from customers as reductions to revenues. The estimates are based on historical rates of product returns and claims. However, actual returns and claims in any future period are inherently uncertain and thus may differ from the estimates. If actual or expected future returns and claims are significantly greater or lower than the reserves that we have established, we will record a reduction or increase to net revenues in the period in which we make such a determination. Over the three year period ended December 31, 2009, our actual annual sales returns and miscellaneous claims from customers have averaged approximately two percent of net sales.

### Allowance for Uncollectible Accounts Receivable

We make ongoing estimates of the uncollectibility of our accounts receivable and maintain an allowance for estimated losses resulting from the inability of our customers to make required payments. In determining the amount of the allowance, we consider our historical level of credit losses and we make judgments about the creditworthiness of customers based on ongoing credit evaluations. We analyze specific customer accounts, customer concentrations, credit insurance coverage, standby letters of credit, current economic trends, and changes in customer payment terms. Current credit and market conditions may slow our collection efforts as customers experience increased difficulty in accessing credit and paying their obligations, leading to higher than normal accounts receivable and increased bad debt expense. Because we cannot predict future changes in the financial stability of our customers, actual future losses from uncollectible accounts may differ from our estimates and may have a material effect on our consolidated financial position, results of operations or cash flows. If the financial condition of our customers deteriorates and results in their inability to make payments, a larger allowance may be required. If we determine that a smaller or larger allowance is appropriate, we will record a credit or a charge to SG&A expense in the period in which we make such a determination.

### Inventory Obsolescence and Product Warranty

We make ongoing estimates of potential future excess, close-out or slow moving inventory and product warranty costs. We evaluate our inventory on hand considering our purchase commitments, sales forecasts, and historical experience to identify excess, close-out or slow moving inventory and make provisions as necessary to properly reflect inventory value at the lower of cost or estimated market value. When we evaluate our reserve for warranty costs, we consider our historical claim rates by season, product mix, current economic trends, and the historical cost to repair, replace, or refund the original sale. If we determine that a smaller or larger reserve is appropriate, we will record a credit or a charge to cost of sales in the period in which we make such a determination.

### Long-lived assets:

Long-lived assets are amortized over their useful lives and are measured for impairment only when events or circumstances indicate the carrying value may be impaired. In these cases, we estimate the future

36

undiscounted cash flows to be derived from the asset or asset group to determine whether a potential impairment exists. When reviewing for retail store impairment, identifiable cash flows are measured at the individual store level. If the sum of the estimated undiscounted cash flows is less than the carrying value of the asset, we recognize an impairment loss, measured as the amount by which the carrying value exceeds the estimated fair value of the asset. Our evaluations of impairment require estimates and assumptions about the forecasted amount and duration of future cash flows and residual value, if any, attributable to assets being tested. Impairment charges for long-lived assets are included in SG&A expense.

### *Income Taxes*

We use the asset and liability method of accounting for income taxes. Under this method, we recognize income tax expense for the amount of taxes payable or refundable for the current year and for the amount of deferred tax liabilities and assets for the future tax consequences of events that have been recognized in our financial statements or tax returns. We make assumptions, judgments and estimates to determine our current provision for income taxes, our deferred tax assets and liabilities, and our uncertain tax positions. Our judgments, assumptions and estimates relative to the current provision for income tax take into account current tax laws, our interpretation of current tax laws and possible outcomes of current and future audits conducted by foreign and domestic tax authorities. Changes in tax law or our interpretation of tax laws and the resolution of current and future tax audits could significantly affect the amounts provided for income taxes in our consolidated financial statements. Our assumptions, judgments and estimates relative to the value of a deferred tax asset take into account predictions of the amount and category of future taxable income. Actual operating results and the underlying amount and category of income in future years could cause our current assumptions, judgments and estimates of recoverable net deferred taxes to be inaccurate. Changes in any of the assumptions, judgments and estimates mentioned above could cause our actual income tax obligations to differ from our estimates, which could materially affect our financial position and results of operations.

Our tax provision for interim periods is determined using an estimate of our annual effective tax rate, adjusted for discrete items, if any, that are taken into account in the relevant period. As the calendar year progresses, we periodically refine our estimate based on actual events and earnings by jurisdiction. This ongoing estimation process can result in changes to our expected effective tax rate for the full calendar year. When this occurs, we adjust the income tax provision during the quarter in which the change in estimate occurs so that our year-to-date provision equals our expected annual effective tax rate.

### *Stock-Based Compensation*

Stock-based compensation cost is estimated at the grant date based on the award's fair value and is recognized as expense over the requisite service period using the straight-line attribution method. We estimate stock-based compensation for stock options granted using the Black-Scholes option pricing model, which requires various highly subjective assumptions, including volatility and expected option life. Further, we estimate forfeitures for stock-based awards granted, which are not expected to vest. If any of these inputs or assumptions changes significantly, stock-based compensation expense may differ materially in the future from that recorded in the current period.

### Recent Accounting Pronouncements

See "Recent Accounting Pronouncements" in Note 1 to the notes to the consolidated financial statements.

## Item 7A.   *QUANTITATIVE AND QUALITATIVE DISCLOSURES ABOUT MARKET RISK*

The information required by this item is included in Management's Discussion and Analysis of Financial Condition and Results of Operations and is incorporated herein by this reference.

## Item 8.   *FINANCIAL STATEMENTS AND SUPPLEMENTARY DATA*

Our management is responsible for the information and representations contained in this report. The financial statements have been prepared in conformity with accounting principles generally accepted in the United States of America, which we consider appropriate in the circumstances and include some amounts based on our best estimates and judgments. Other financial information in this report is consistent with these financial statements.

Our accounting systems include controls designed to reasonably assure that assets are safeguarded from unauthorized use or disposition and which provide for the preparation of financial statements in conformity with accounting principles generally accepted in the United States of America. These systems are supplemented by the selection and training of qualified financial personnel and an organizational structure providing for appropriate segregation of duties.

The Audit Committee is responsible for recommending to the Board of Directors the appointment of the independent registered public accounting firm and reviews with the independent registered public accounting firm and management the scope and the results of the annual examination, the effectiveness of the accounting control system and other matters relating to our financial affairs as they deem appropriate.

# REPORT OF INDEPENDENT AUDITORS

## REPORT OF INDEPENDENT REGISTERED PUBLIC ACCOUNTING FIRM

To the Board of Directors and Shareholders
Columbia Sportswear Company
Portland, Oregon

We have audited the accompanying consolidated balance sheets of Columbia Sportswear Company and subsidiaries (the "Company") as of December 31, 2009 and 2008, and the related consolidated statements of operations, shareholders' equity and cash flows for each of the three years in the period ended December 31, 2009. Our audits also included the financial statement schedule listed on the Index at Item 15. These financial statements and financial statement schedule are the responsibility of the Company's management. Our responsibility is to express an opinion on these financial statements and financial statement schedule based on our audits.

We conducted our audits in accordance with the standards of the Public Company Accounting Oversight Board (United States). Those standards require that we plan and perform the audit to obtain reasonable assurance about whether the financial statements are free of material misstatement. An audit includes examining, on a test basis, evidence supporting the amounts and disclosures in the financial statements. An audit also includes assessing the accounting principles used and significant estimates made by management, as well as evaluating the overall financial statement presentation. We believe that our audits provide a reasonable basis for our opinion.

In our opinion, such consolidated financial statements present fairly, in all material respects, the financial position of the Company as of December 31, 2009 and 2008, and the results of its operations and its cash flows for each of the three years in the period ended December 31, 2009, in conformity with accounting principles generally accepted in the United States of America. Also, in our opinion, such financial statement schedule, when considered in relation to the basic consolidated financial statements taken as a whole, presents fairly, in all material respects, the information set forth therein.

We have also audited, in accordance with the standards of the Public Company Accounting Oversight Board (United States), the Company's internal control over financial reporting as of December 31, 2009, based on the criteria established in *Internal Control—Integrated Framework* issued by the Committee of Sponsoring Organizations of the Treadway Commission and our report dated March 12, 2010, expressed an unqualified opinion on the Company's internal control over financial reporting.

DELOITTE & TOUCHE LLP
Portland, Oregon
March 12, 2010

# FINANCIAL STATEMENTS

## COLUMBIA SPORTSWEAR COMPANY
## CONSOLIDATED BALANCE SHEETS
### (In thousands)

|  | December 31, 2009 | December 31, 2008 |
|---|---|---|
| **ASSETS** | | |
| Current Assets: | | |
| Cash and cash equivalents | $ 386,664 | $ 230,617 |
| Short-term investments | 22,759 | 22,433 |
| Accounts receivable, net (Note 2) | 226,548 | 299,585 |
| Inventories, net (Note 3) | 222,161 | 256,312 |
| Deferred income taxes (Note 9) | 31,550 | 33,867 |
| Prepaid expenses and other current assets | 32,030 | 29,705 |
| Total current assets | 921,712 | 872,519 |
| Property, plant, and equipment, net (Note 4) | 235,440 | 229,693 |
| Intangibles and other non-current assets (Notes 2 and 9) | 43,072 | 33,365 |
| Goodwill (Note 2) | 12,659 | 12,659 |
| Total assets | $1,212,883 | $1,148,236 |
| **LIABILITIES AND SHAREHOLDERS' EQUITY** | | |
| Current Liabilities: | | |
| Accounts payable | $ 102,494 | $ 104,354 |
| Accrued liabilities (Note 6) | 67,312 | 58,148 |
| Income taxes payable (Note 9) | 6,884 | 8,718 |
| Deferred income taxes (Note 9) | 2,597 | 1,969 |
| Total current liabilities | 179,287 | 173,189 |
| Income taxes payable (Note 9) | 19,830 | 20,412 |
| Deferred income taxes (Note 9) | 1,494 | — |
| Other long-term liabilities (Note 7) | 15,044 | 10,545 |
| Total liabilities | 215,655 | 204,146 |
| Commitments and contingencies (Note 11) | | |
| Shareholders' Equity: | | |
| Preferred stock; 10,000 shares authorized; none issued and outstanding | — | — |
| Common stock (no par value); 125,000 shares authorized; 33,736 and 33,865 issued and outstanding (Note 8) | 836 | 1,481 |
| Retained earnings (Note 8) | 952,948 | 909,443 |
| Accumulated other comprehensive income (Note 14) | 43,444 | 33,166 |
| Total shareholders' equity | 997,228 | 944,090 |
| Total liabilities and shareholders' equity | $1,212,883 | $1,148,236 |

See accompanying notes to consolidated financial statements.

40

## COLUMBIA SPORTSWEAR COMPANY

## CONSOLIDATED STATEMENTS OF OPERATIONS
### (In thousands, except per share amounts)

| | Year Ended December 31, | | |
| --- | --- | --- | --- |
| | 2009 | 2008 | 2007 |
| Net sales | $1,244,023 | $1,317,835 | $1,356,039 |
| Cost of sales | 719,945 | 750,024 | 776,288 |
| Gross profit | 524,078 | 567,811 | 579,751 |
| Selling, general, and administrative expenses | 444,715 | 430,350 | 385,769 |
| Impairment of acquired intangible assets (Note 2) | — | 24,742 | — |
| Net licensing income | 8,399 | 5,987 | 5,157 |
| Income from operations | 87,762 | 118,706 | 199,139 |
| Interest income, net | 2,088 | 7,537 | 8,888 |
| Income before income tax | 89,850 | 126,243 | 208,027 |
| Income tax expense (Note 9) | (22,829) | (31,196) | (63,575) |
| Net income | $ 67,021 | $ 95,047 | $ 144,452 |
| Earnings per share: | | | |
| Basic | $ 1.98 | $ 2.75 | $ 4.00 |
| Diluted | 1.97 | 2.74 | 3.96 |
| Cash dividends per share: | $ 0.66 | $ 0.64 | $ 0.58 |
| Weighted average shares outstanding (Note 13): | | | |
| Basic | 33,846 | 34,610 | 36,106 |
| Diluted | 33,981 | 34,711 | 36,434 |

See accompanying notes to consolidated financial statements.

## COLUMBIA SPORTSWEAR COMPANY

## CONSOLIDATED STATEMENTS OF CASH FLOWS
### (In thousands)

| | Year Ended December 31, | | |
| --- | --- | --- | --- |
| | 2009 | 2008 | 2007 |
| **Cash flows from operating activities:** | | | |
| Net income | $ 67,021 | $ 95,047 | $ 144,452 |
| Adjustments to reconcile net income to net cash provided by operating activities: | | | |
| Depreciation and amortization | 36,253 | 31,158 | 30,338 |
| Loss on disposal or impairment of property, plant, and equipment | 1,828 | 253 | 237 |
| Deferred income tax (benefit) expense | 55 | (10,338) | 278 |
| Stock-based compensation | 6,353 | 6,302 | 7,260 |
| Excess tax benefit from employee stock plans | (41) | (72) | (1,811) |
| Impairment of acquired intangibles | — | 24,742 | — |
| Changes in operating assets and liabilities: | | | |
| Accounts receivable | 77,490 | (9,689) | (3,093) |
| Inventories | 38,831 | 4,507 | (46,010) |
| Prepaid expenses and other current assets | (1,695) | (15,787) | (1,355) |
| Intangibles and other assets | (5,179) | 101 | 592 |
| Accounts payable | (16,944) | 8,944 | 1,381 |
| Accrued liabilities | 7,563 | (1,047) | (4,400) |
| Income taxes payable | (1,558) | 2,567 | (5,665) |
| Other liabilities | 4,395 | 8,242 | 2,111 |
| Net cash provided by operating activities | 214,372 | 144,930 | 124,315 |
| **Cash flows from investing activities:** | | | |
| Purchases of short-term investments | (25,305) | (72,337) | (305,769) |
| Sales of short-term investments | 25,163 | 131,565 | 379,460 |
| Capital expenditures | (33,074) | (47,580) | (31,971) |
| Proceeds from sale of property, plant, and equipment | 31 | 52 | 32 |
| Net cash provided by (used in) investing activities | (33,185) | 11,700 | 41,752 |
| **Cash flows from financing activities:** | | | |
| Proceeds from notes payable | 57,588 | 33,727 | 30,651 |
| Repayments on notes payable | (57,588) | (33,727) | (34,276) |
| Repayment on long-term debt and other long-term liabilities | (4) | (21) | (22) |
| Proceeds from issuance of common stock under employee stock plans, net | 86 | 3,488 | 14,162 |
| Excess tax benefit from employee stock plans | 41 | 72 | 1,811 |
| Repurchase of common stock | (7,399) | (83,865) | (31,819) |
| Cash dividends paid | (22,331) | (22,098) | (20,915) |
| Net cash used in financing activities | (29,607) | (102,424) | (40,408) |
| **Net effect of exchange rate changes on cash** | 4,467 | (15,539) | 1,411 |
| **Net increase in cash and cash equivalents** | 156,047 | 38,667 | 127,070 |
| **Cash and cash equivalents, beginning of year** | 230,617 | 191,950 | 64,880 |
| **Cash and cash equivalents, end of year** | $386,664 | $ 230,617 | $ 191,950 |
| **Supplemental disclosures of cash flow information:** | | | |
| Cash paid during the year for interest, net of capitalized interest | $     35 | $     47 | $     148 |
| Cash paid during the year for income taxes | 31,284 | 48,521 | 73,293 |
| **Supplemental disclosures of non-cash investing activities:** | | | |
| Capital expenditures incurred but not yet paid | 7,852 | 6,760 | 2,318 |

See accompanying notes to consolidated financial statements.

42

## COLUMBIA SPORTSWEAR COMPANY

## CONSOLIDATED STATEMENTS OF SHAREHOLDERS' EQUITY
### (In thousands)

| | Common Stock | | | Accumulated Other | | |
| | Shares Outstanding | Amount | Retained Earnings | Comprehensive Income | Comprehensive Income | Total |
|---|---|---|---|---|---|---|
| **BALANCE, JANUARY 1, 2007** | 35,998 | $ 24,370 | $771,939 | $ 34,394 | | $830,703 |
| Components of comprehensive income: | | | | | | |
| Net income | — | — | 144,452 | — | $144,452 | 144,452 |
| Cash dividends ($0.58 per share) | — | — | (20,915) | — | — | (20,915) |
| Foreign currency translation adjustment | — | — | — | 25,394 | 25,394 | 25,394 |
| Unrealized holding loss on derivative transactions, net | — | — | — | (2,147) | (2,147) | (2,147) |
| Comprehensive income | — | — | — | — | $167,699 | — |
| Issuance of common stock under employee stock plans, net | 416 | 14,162 | — | — | | 14,162 |
| Tax benefit from stock plans | — | 3,031 | — | — | | 3,031 |
| Stock-based compensation expense | — | 7,260 | — | — | | 7,260 |
| Repurchase of common stock | (590) | (31,819) | — | — | | (31,819) |
| **BALANCE, DECEMBER 31, 2007** | 35,824 | 17,004 | 895,476 | 57,641 | | 970,121 |
| Components of comprehensive income: | | | | | | |
| Net income | — | — | 95,047 | — | $ 95,047 | 95,047 |
| Cash dividends ($0.64 per share) | — | — | (22,098) | — | — | (22,098) |
| Foreign currency translation adjustment | — | — | — | (30,511) | (30,511) | (30,511) |
| Unrealized holding gain on derivative transactions, net | — | — | — | 6,036 | 6,036 | 6,036 |
| Comprehensive income | — | — | — | — | $ 70,572 | — |
| Issuance of common stock under employee stock plans, net | 131 | 3,488 | — | — | | 3,488 |
| Tax adjustment from stock plans | — | (430) | — | — | | (430) |
| Stock-based compensation expense | — | 6,302 | — | — | | 6,302 |
| Repurchase of common stock | (2,090) | (24,883) | (58,982) | — | | (83,865) |
| **BALANCE, DECEMBER 31, 2008** | 33,865 | 1,481 | 909,443 | 33,166 | | 944,090 |
| Components of comprehensive income: | | | | | | |
| Net income | — | — | 67,021 | — | $ 67,021 | 67,021 |
| Cash dividends ($0.66 per share) | — | — | (22,331) | — | — | (22,331) |
| Unrealized holding gains on available-for-sales securities, net | — | — | — | 64 | 64 | 64 |
| Foreign currency translation adjustment | — | — | — | 13,854 | 13,854 | 13,854 |
| Unrealized holding loss on derivative transactions, net | — | — | — | (3,640) | (3,640) | (3,640) |
| Comprehensive income | — | — | — | — | $ 77,299 | — |
| Issuance of common stock under employee stock plans, net | 75 | 86 | — | — | | 86 |
| Tax adjustment from stock plans | — | (870) | — | — | | (870) |
| Stock-based compensation expense | — | 6,353 | — | — | | 6,353 |
| Repurchase of common stock | (204) | (6,214) | (1,185) | — | | (7,399) |
| **BALANCE, DECEMBER 31, 2009** | 33,736 | $ 836 | $952,948 | $ 43,444 | | $997,228 |

See accompanying notes to consolidated financial statements.

# NOTES TO FINANCIAL STATEMENTS

## COLUMBIA SPORTSWEAR COMPANY

## NOTES TO CONSOLIDATED FINANCIAL STATEMENTS

### NOTE 1—BASIS OF PRESENTATION AND ORGANIZATION

*Nature of the business:*

Columbia Sportswear Company is a global leader in the design, development, marketing and distribution of active outdoor apparel, including sportswear, outerwear, footwear, accessories and equipment.

*Principles of consolidation:*

The consolidated financial statements include the accounts of Columbia Sportswear Company and its wholly-owned subsidiaries (the "Company"). All significant intercompany balances and transactions have been eliminated in consolidation.

*Estimates and assumptions:*

The preparation of financial statements in conformity with accounting principles generally accepted in the United States of America requires management to make estimates and assumptions that affect the reported amounts of assets and liabilities and disclosure of contingent assets and liabilities at the date of the consolidated financial statements and the reported amounts of revenues and expenses during the reporting period. Actual results may differ from these estimates and assumptions. Some of these more significant estimates relate to revenue recognition, allowance for doubtful accounts, inventory, product warranty, long-lived and intangible assets and income taxes.

*Reclassifications:*

Certain immaterial reclassifications of amounts reported in the prior period financial statements have been made to conform to classifications used in the current period financial statements.

*Dependence on key suppliers:*

The Company's products are produced by independent factories worldwide. For 2009, the Company sourced nearly all of its products outside the United States, principally in the Southeast Asia. In 2009, the Company's four largest apparel factory groups accounted for approximately 15% of the Company's total global apparel production and the Company's four largest footwear factory groups accounted for approximately 66% of the Company's total global footwear production. In addition, a single vendor supplied substantially all of the zippers used in the Company's products in 2009. From time to time, the Company has had difficulty satisfying its raw material and finished goods requirements. Although the Company believes that it can identify and qualify additional raw material suppliers and independent factories to produce these products, the unavailability of some existing suppliers or independent factories for supply of these products may have a material adverse effect on the Company.

*Concentration of credit risk:*

*Trade Receivables*

At December 31, 2009, the Company had one customer in its Canadian segment that accounted for approximately 15.5% of consolidated accounts receivable. At December 31, 2008, the Company had one customer in its EMEA segment and one customer in its Canadian segment that accounted for approximately 13.5% and 10.2% of consolidated accounts receivable, respectively. No single customer accounted for 10% or more of consolidated revenues for any of the years ended December 31, 2009, 2008 or 2007.

## COLUMBIA SPORTSWEAR COMPANY

## NOTES TO CONSOLIDATED FINANCIAL STATEMENTS—(Continued)

*Cash and Investments*

At December 31, 2009, approximately 80% of the Company's cash and cash equivalents were concentrated in domestic and international money market mutual funds. Substantially all of the Company's money market mutual funds were assigned a AAA or analogous rating from S&P, Moody's Investor Services ("Moody's") or Fitch Ratings.

All the Company's remaining cash and cash equivalents and short-term investments were deposited with various institutions in the Company's primary operating geographies. All institutions were rated investment grade by both S&P and Moody's and most were rated AA- / Aa1 or better.

*Derivatives*

The Company uses derivative instruments primarily to hedge the exchange rate risk of anticipated transactions denominated in non-functional currencies. From time to time, the Company also uses derivative instruments to economically hedge the exchange rate risk of certain investment positions and to hedge balance sheet remeasurement risk. At December 31, 2009, the Company's derivative contracts had a remaining maturity of approximately one year or less. All the counterparties to these transactions had a S&P / Moody's short-term credit rating of A-2 / P-2 or better. The net exposure to any single counterparty, which is generally limited to the aggregate unrealized gain of all contracts with that counterparty, was less than $1,000,000 at December 31, 2009. The majority of the Company's derivative counterparties have strong credit ratings and as a result, the Company does not require collateral to facilitate transactions. See Note 16 for further disclosures concerning derivatives.

## NOTE 2—SUMMARY OF SIGNIFICANT ACCOUNTING POLICIES

### Cash and cash equivalents:

Cash and cash equivalents are stated at cost, which approximates fair value, and include investments with maturities of three months or less from the date of acquisition. At December 31, 2009 and 2008, cash and cash equivalents were $386,664,000 and $230,617,000, respectively, primarily consisting of money market funds and time deposits with maturities ranging from overnight to less than 90 days.

### Investments:

At December 31, 2009 and 2008, short-term investments consisted of shares in a short-term bond fund available for use in current operations and time deposits with maturities of six months or less. All short-term investments are classified as available-for-sale securities and are recorded at fair value with any unrealized gains and losses reported, net of tax, in other comprehensive income. Realized gains or losses are determined based on the specific identification method.

At December 31, 2009, long-term investments consisted of mutual fund shares held to offset liabilities to participants in the Company's deferred compensation plan. The investments are classified as long-term as the related deferred compensation liabilities are not expected to be paid within the next year. These investments are classified as trading securities and are recorded at fair value with unrealized gains and losses reported in operating expenses. These long-term investments are included in intangibles and other non-current assets and totaled $826,000 at December 31, 2009, including unrealized gains of $130,000. There were no long-term investments at December 31, 2008.

### Accounts receivable:

Accounts receivable have been reduced by an allowance for doubtful accounts. The Company makes ongoing estimates of the uncollectibility of accounts receivable and maintains an allowance for estimated losses

## COLUMBIA SPORTSWEAR COMPANY

## NOTES TO CONSOLIDATED FINANCIAL STATEMENTS—(Continued)

resulting from the inability of the Company's customers to make required payments. The allowance for doubtful accounts was $7,347,000 and $9,542,000 at December 31, 2009 and 2008, respectively.

*Inventories:*

Inventories are carried at the lower of cost or market. Cost is determined using the first-in, first-out method. The Company periodically reviews its inventories for excess, close-out or slow moving items and makes provisions as necessary to properly reflect inventory value.

*Property, plant, and equipment:*

Property, plant and equipment are stated at cost, net of accumulated depreciation. Depreciation is provided using the straight-line method over the estimated useful lives of the assets. The principal estimated useful lives are: buildings and building improvements, 15-30 years; land improvements, 15 years; furniture and fixtures, 3-10 years; and machinery and equipment, 3-5 years. Leasehold improvements are depreciated over the lesser of the estimated useful life of the improvement, which is most commonly 7 years, or the remaining term of the underlying lease.

The interest-carrying costs of capital assets under construction are capitalized based on the Company's weighted average borrowing rates if there are any outstanding borrowings. There was no capitalized interest for the years ended December 31, 2009, 2008 and 2007.

*Impairment of long-lived assets:*

Long-lived assets are amortized over their useful lives and are measured for impairment only when events or circumstances indicate the carrying value may be impaired. In these cases, the Company estimates the future undiscounted cash flows to be derived from the asset or asset group to determine whether a potential impairment exists. When reviewing for retail store impairment, identifiable cash flows are measured at the individual store level. If the sum of the estimated undiscounted cash flows is less than the carrying value of the asset, the Company recognizes an impairment loss, measured as the amount by which the carrying value exceeds the estimated fair value of the asset. Impairment charges for long-lived assets are included in selling, general and administrative expense and were immaterial for the years ended December 31, 2009, 2008 and 2007.

*Intangibles and other non-current assets:*

Intangible assets with indefinite useful lives are not amortized and are periodically evaluated for impairment. Intangible assets that are determined to have finite lives are amortized using the straight-line method over their useful lives.

The following table summarizes the Company's identifiable intangible assets (in thousands):

| | December 31, 2009 | | December 31, 2008 | |
| --- | --- | --- | --- | --- |
| | Gross Carrying Amount | Accumulated Amortization | Gross Carrying Amount | Accumulated Amortization |
| Intangible assets subject to amortization: | | | | |
| Patents .................................. | $ 898 | $(643) | $ 898 | $(534) |
| Intangible assets not subject to amortization: | | | | |
| Trademarks and trade names ................ | $26,872 | | $26,872 | |
| Goodwill ............................. | 12,659 | | 12,659 | |
| | $39,531 | | $39,531 | |

46

## COLUMBIA SPORTSWEAR COMPANY

## NOTES TO CONSOLIDATED FINANCIAL STATEMENTS—(Continued)

Amortization expense for the years ended December 31, 2009, 2008, and 2007 was $109,000, $205,000 and $175,000, respectively. Amortization expense for patents is estimated to be $109,000 in 2010 and $73,000 per year in 2011 and 2012. These patents are anticipated to become fully amortized in 2012.

Other non-current assets consisted of the following (in thousands):

| | December 31, | |
| --- | --- | --- |
| | 2009 | 2008 |
| Deferred tax assets | $ 5,435 | $ 723 |
| Long-term deposits | 8,360 | 4,483 |
| Other | 2,150 | 923 |
| | $15,945 | $6,129 |

### Impairment of goodwill and intangible assets:

Goodwill and intangible assets with indefinite useful lives are not amortized but instead are measured for impairment. The Company reviews and tests its goodwill and intangible assets with indefinite useful lives for impairment in the fourth quarter of each year and when events or changes in circumstances indicate that the carrying amount of such assets may be impaired. The Company's intangible assets with indefinite lives consist of trademarks and trade names. Substantially all of the Company's goodwill is recorded in the United States segment and impairment testing for goodwill is performed at the reporting unit level. The two-step process first compares the estimated fair value of reporting unit goodwill with the carrying amount of that reporting unit. The Company estimates the fair value of its reporting units using a combination of discounted cash flow analysis, comparisons with the market values of similar publicly traded companies and other operating performance based valuation methods. If step one indicates impairment, step two compares the estimated fair value of the reporting unit to the estimated fair value of all reporting unit assets and liabilities except goodwill to determine the implied fair value of goodwill. The Company calculates impairment as the excess of carrying amount of goodwill over the implied fair value of goodwill. In the impairment test for trademarks, the Company compares the estimated fair value of the asset to the carrying amount. The fair value of trademarks is estimated using the relief from royalty approach, a standard form of discounted cash flow analysis used in the valuation of trademarks. If the carrying amount of trademarks exceeds the estimated fair value, the Company calculates impairment as the excess of carrying amount over the estimate of fair value. Impairment charges are classified as a component of operating expense. The fair value estimates are based on a number of factors, including assumptions and estimates for projected sales, income, cash flows, discount rates and other operating performance measures. Changes in estimates or the application of alternative assumptions could produce significantly different results. These assumptions and estimates may change in the future due to changes in economic conditions, changes in the Company's ability to meet sales and profitability objectives or changes in the Company's business operations or strategic direction.

Intangible assets that are determined to have finite lives are amortized over their useful lives and are measured for impairment only when events or circumstances indicate the carrying value may be impaired. In these cases, the Company estimates the future undiscounted cash flows to be derived from the asset or asset group to determine whether a potential impairment exists. If the sum of the estimated undiscounted cash flows is less than the carrying value of the asset the Company recognizes an impairment loss, measured as the amount by which the carrying value exceeds the estimated fair value of the asset. Impairment charges are classified as a component of operating expense.

At December 31, 2009, the Company determined that its goodwill and intangible assets were not impaired. At December 31, 2008, the Company determined that its Pacific Trail brand and Montrail brand goodwill and

47

## COLUMBIA SPORTSWEAR COMPANY

## NOTES TO CONSOLIDATED FINANCIAL STATEMENTS—(Continued)

trademarks were impaired. These brands were not achieving their sales and profitability objectives. The deterioration in the macroeconomic environment and the resulting effect on consumer demand decreased the probability of realizing the objectives in the near future. These brands were acquired in 2006. For the year ended December 31, 2008, the Company recorded impairment charges, before income taxes, of $12,250,000 in trademarks and $3,900,000 in goodwill for the Pacific Trail brand. The Pacific Trail brand has $2,300,000 in trademarks and no goodwill after the impairment charge. The Pacific Trail brand is a reporting unit for goodwill impairment testing and Pacific Trail brand intangible assets are included in the United States segment. For the year ended December 31, 2008, the Company recorded impairment charges, before income taxes, of $7,400,000 in trademarks, $714,000 in goodwill and $478,000 in patents for the Montrail brand. The Montrail brand has $2,600,000 in trademarks and no goodwill or patents after the impairment charge. The Montrail brand is a reporting unit for goodwill impairment testing and Montrail brand intangible assets are included in the United States segment. Other than Pacific Trail brand goodwill and trademarks and Montrail brand goodwill, trademarks and patents, at December 31, 2008, the Company determined that its goodwill and intangible assets were not impaired.

### Deferred income taxes:

Income tax expense is provided at the U.S. tax rate on financial statement earnings, adjusted for the difference between the U.S. tax rate and the rate of tax in effect for non-U.S. earnings deemed to be permanently reinvested in the Company's non-U.S. operations. Deferred income taxes have not been provided for the potential remittance of non-U.S. undistributed earnings to the extent those earnings are deemed to be permanently reinvested, or to the extent such recognition would result in a deferred tax asset. Deferred income taxes are provided for the expected tax consequences of temporary differences between the tax bases of assets and liabilities and their reported amounts. Valuation allowances are recorded to reduce deferred tax assets to the amount that will more likely than not be realized.

### Revenue Recognition:

The Company records wholesale and licensed product revenues when title passes and the risks and rewards of ownership have passed to the customer, based on the terms of sale. Title generally passes upon shipment to, or upon receipt by, the customer depending on the country of the sale and the agreement with the customer. Retail store revenues are recorded at the time of sale and e-commerce revenues are recorded upon shipment to the customer.

In some countries outside of the United States where title passes upon receipt by the customer, predominantly in the Company's Western European wholesale business, precise information regarding the date of receipt by the customer is not readily available. In these cases, the Company estimates the date of receipt by the customer based on historical and expected delivery times by geographic location. The Company periodically tests the accuracy of these estimates based on actual transactions. Delivery times vary by geographic location, generally from one to five days. To date, the Company has found these estimates to be materially accurate.

At the time of revenue recognition, the Company also provides for estimated sales returns and miscellaneous claims from customers as reductions to revenues. The estimates are based on historical rates of product returns and claims. However, actual returns and claims in any future period are inherently uncertain and thus may differ from the estimates. If actual or expected future returns and claims are significantly greater or lower than the reserves that had been established, the Company would record a reduction or increase to net revenues in the period in which it made such determination. Over the three year period ended December 31, 2009, the Company's actual annual sales returns and miscellaneous claims from customers have averaged

## COLUMBIA SPORTSWEAR COMPANY

## NOTES TO CONSOLIDATED FINANCIAL STATEMENTS—(Continued)

approximately two percent of net sales. The allowance for outstanding sales returns and miscellaneous claims from customers was approximately $13,889,000 and $10,583,000 as of December 31, 2009 and 2008, respectively.

### Cost of sales:

The expenses that are included in cost of sales include all direct product and conversion-related costs, and costs related to shipping, duties and importation. Product warranty costs and specific provisions for excess, close-out or slow moving inventory are also included in cost of sales.

### Selling, general and administrative expense:

Selling, general and administrative expense consists of commissions, advertising, other selling costs, personnel-related costs, planning, receiving finished goods, warehousing, depreciation and other general operating expenses.

### Shipping and handling costs:

Shipping and handling fees billed to customers are recorded as revenue. The direct costs associated with shipping goods to customers are recorded as cost of sales. Inventory planning, receiving and handling costs are recorded as a component of selling, general, and administrative expenses and were $55,867,000, $57,700,000 and $64,420,000 for the years ended December 31, 2009, 2008 and 2007, respectively.

### Foreign currency translation:

The assets and liabilities of the Company's foreign subsidiaries have been translated into U.S. dollars using the exchange rates in effect at period end, and the net sales and expenses have been translated into U.S. dollars using average exchange rates in effect during the period. The foreign currency translation adjustments are included as a separate component of accumulated other comprehensive income (loss) in shareholders' equity and are not currently adjusted for income taxes when they relate to indefinite net investments in non-U.S. operations.

### Fair value of financial instruments:

The carrying value of substantially all financial instruments potentially subject to valuation risk (principally consisting of cash and cash equivalents, short-term investments, accounts receivable and accounts payable) approximates fair value because of their short-term maturities. See note 17 for more information on fair value measures for financial instruments.

### Derivatives:

Changes in fair values of outstanding cash flow hedges are recorded in other comprehensive income until earnings are affected by the hedged transaction. In most cases amounts recorded in other comprehensive income will be released to earnings some time after maturity of the related derivative. The Consolidated Statement of Operations classification of effective hedge results is the same as that of the underlying exposure. Results of hedges of product costs are recorded in cost of sales when the underlying hedged transaction affects earnings. Unrealized derivative gains and losses, which are recorded in current assets and liabilities, respectively, are non-cash items and therefore are taken into account in the preparation of the Consolidated Statement of Cash Flows based on their respective balance sheet classifications. See note 16 for more information on derivatives and risk management.

49

## COLUMBIA SPORTSWEAR COMPANY

## NOTES TO CONSOLIDATED FINANCIAL STATEMENTS—(Continued)

### Stock-based compensation:

Stock-based compensation cost is estimated at the grant date based on the award's fair value and is recognized as expense over the requisite service period using the straight-line attribution method. The Company estimates stock-based compensation for stock options granted using the Black-Scholes option pricing model, which requires various highly subjective assumptions, including volatility and expected option life. Further, the Company estimates forfeitures for stock-based awards granted, which are not expected to vest. If any of these inputs or assumptions changes significantly, stock-based compensation expense may differ materially in the future from that recorded in the current period.

### Advertising costs:

Advertising costs are expensed in the period incurred and are included in selling, general and administrative expenses. Total advertising expense, including cooperative advertising costs, was $65,204,000, $72,237,000 and $55,290,000 for the years ended December 31, 2009, 2008 and 2007, respectively.

Through cooperative advertising programs, the Company reimburses its wholesale customers for some of their costs of advertising the Company's products based on various criteria, including the value of purchases from the Company and various advertising specifications. Cooperative advertising costs are included in expenses because the Company receives an identifiable benefit in exchange for the cost, the advertising may be obtained from a party other than the customer, and the fair value of the advertising benefit can be reasonably estimated. Cooperative advertising costs were $10,978,000, $16,351,000 and $17,884,000 for the years ended December 31, 2009, 2008 and 2007, respectively.

### Product warranty:

Some of the Company's products carry limited warranty provisions for defects in quality and workmanship. A warranty reserve is established at the time of sale to cover estimated costs based on the Company's history of warranty repairs and replacements and is recorded in cost of sales. The reserve for warranty claims at December 31, 2009 and 2008 was $12,112,000 and $9,746,000, respectively.

### Recent Accounting Pronouncements:

In June 2009, the Financial Accounting Standards Board ("FASB") issued SFAS No. 168, *The FASB Accounting Standards Codification™ and the Hierarchy of Generally Accepted Accounting Principles, as amended,* which was codified into Topic 105 *Generally Accepted Accounting Standards* in the ASC. This standard establishes the FASB ASC as the source of authoritative accounting principles recognized by the FASB to be applied in the preparation of financial statements in conformity with generally accepted accounting principles. This standard is effective for interim and annual financial periods ending after September 15, 2009. The adoption of this standard did not have a material effect on the Company's consolidated financial position, results of operations or cash flows.

In May 2009, the FASB issued SFAS No. 165, *Subsequent Events,* which was codified into Topic 855 *Subsequent Events* in the ASC and updated by Accounting Standards Update No. 2010-09, *Amendments to Certain Recognition and Disclosure Requirements*. This guidance establishes general standards of evaluating and accounting for events that occur after the balance sheet date but before financial statements are issued or are available to be issued. This standard is effective for interim or annual financial periods ending after June 15, 2009. The adoption of this standard did not have a material effect on the Company's consolidated financial position, results of operations or cash flows.

**COLUMBIA SPORTSWEAR COMPANY**

**NOTES TO CONSOLIDATED FINANCIAL STATEMENTS—(Continued)**

In March 2008, the FASB issued SFAS No. 161, *Disclosures about Derivative Instruments and Hedging Activities,* which was codified into Topic 815 *Derivatives and Hedging* in the ASC. This standard is intended to improve financial reporting about derivative instruments and hedging activities by requiring enhanced disclosures to enable investors to better understand their effects on an entity's financial position, financial performance and cash flows. The provisions of this standard are effective for fiscal years and interim quarters beginning after November 15, 2008. The adoption of this standard did not have a material effect on the Company's consolidated financial position, results of operations or cash flows. See Note 16.

### NOTE 3—INVENTORIES, NET

Inventories consist of the following (in thousands):

|  | December 31, | |
|---|---|---|
|  | **2009** | **2008** |
| Raw materials | $ 1,021 | $ 621 |
| Work in process | 163 | 1,065 |
| Finished goods | 220,977 | 254,626 |
|  | $222,161 | $256,312 |

### NOTE 4—PROPERTY, PLANT, AND EQUIPMENT, NET

Property, plant, and equipment consist of the following (in thousands):

|  | December 31, | |
|---|---|---|
|  | **2009** | **2008** |
| Land and improvements | $ 16,557 | $ 16,465 |
| Building and improvements | 147,093 | 143,997 |
| Machinery and equipment | 184,721 | 171,091 |
| Furniture and fixtures | 44,158 | 37,886 |
| Leasehold improvements | 57,866 | 45,231 |
| Construction in progress | 8,932 | 5,929 |
|  | 459,327 | 420,599 |
| Less accumulated depreciation | 223,887 | 190,906 |
|  | $235,440 | $229,693 |

### NOTE 5—SHORT-TERM BORROWINGS AND CREDIT LINES

The Company has available an unsecured and committed revolving line of credit providing for borrowings in an aggregate amount not to exceed, at any time, $100,000,000 during the period of August 15 through November 14 and $25,000,000 at all other times. The maturity date of this agreement is July 1, 2010. Interest, payable monthly, is computed at the bank's prime rate minus 195 to 205 basis points per annum or LIBOR plus 45 to 65 basis points. The unsecured revolving line of credit requires the Company to comply with certain covenants including a Capital Ratio, which limits indebtedness to tangible net worth. At December 31, 2009, the Company was in compliance with all of these covenants. If the Company defaults on its payments, it is prohibited, subject to certain exceptions, from making dividend payments or other distributions. The Company also has available an unsecured and uncommitted revolving line of credit providing for borrowing to a maximum of $25,000,000. The revolving line accrues interest at LIBOR plus 125 basis points. There were no balances outstanding under either of these lines at December 31, 2009 and 2008.

## COLUMBIA SPORTSWEAR COMPANY

## NOTES TO CONSOLIDATED FINANCIAL STATEMENTS—(Continued)

The Company's Canadian subsidiary has available an unsecured and uncommitted line of credit guaranteed by the parent company providing for borrowing to a maximum of C$30,000,000 (US$28,485,000) at December 31, 2009. The revolving line accrues interest at the bank's Canadian prime rate. There was no balance outstanding under this line at December 31, 2009 and 2008.

The Company's European subsidiary has available two separate unsecured and uncommitted lines of credit guaranteed by the parent company providing for borrowing to a maximum of 30,000,000 and 20,000,000 euros respectively (combined US$71,602,000) at December 31, 2009, of which US$3,580,000 of the 20,000,000 euro line is designated as a European customs guarantee. These lines accrue interest based on the ECB refinancing rate plus 50 basis points and EONIA plus 75 basis points, respectively. There was no balance outstanding under either line at December 31, 2009 or 2008.

The Company's Japanese subsidiary has an unsecured and uncommitted line of credit guaranteed by the parent company providing for borrowing to a maximum of US$5,000,000 at December 31, 2009. The revolving line accrues interest at the bank's Best Lending Rate. There was no balance outstanding under this line at December 31, 2009 and 2008.

*Off-Balance Sheet Arrangements*

The Company has arrangements in place to facilitate the import and purchase of inventory through import letters of credit. The Company has available unsecured and uncommitted import letters of credit in the aggregate amount of $65,000,000 subject to annual renewal. At December 31, 2009, the Company had outstanding letters of credit of $7,771,000 for purchase orders for inventory under this arrangement.

### NOTE 6—ACCRUED LIABILITIES

Accrued liabilities consist of the following (in thousands):

|  | December 31, | |
| --- | --- | --- |
|  | **2009** | **2008** |
| Accrued salaries, bonus, vacation and other benefits | $34,711 | $29,437 |
| Accrued product warranty | 12,112 | 9,746 |
| Accrued cooperative advertising | 4,358 | 6,457 |
| Other | 16,131 | 12,508 |
|  | $67,312 | $58,148 |

### NOTE 7—OTHER LONG-TERM LIABILITIES

Other long-term liabilities consist of deferred rent obligations, the effect of straight-line rent under various operating leases, rental asset retirement obligations, liabilities to participants in the Company's nonqualified deferred compensation plan, installment purchase obligations for non-inventory purchases made in the ordinary course of business and long-term severance liabilities. Deferred rent, straight-line rent, and rental asset retirement obligation liabilities were $14,218,000 and $10,126,000 at December 31, 2009 and 2008, respectively. The corresponding lease obligations for these deferred and straight-line rent liabilities are disclosed in Note 11. Principal payments due on other long-term liabilities are immaterial.

## COLUMBIA SPORTSWEAR COMPANY

## NOTES TO CONSOLIDATED FINANCIAL STATEMENTS—(Continued)

### NOTE 8—SHAREHOLDERS' EQUITY

Since the inception of the Company's stock repurchase plan in 2004 through December 31, 2009, the Company's Board of Directors has authorized the repurchase of $500,000,000 of the Company's common stock. As of December 31, 2009, the Company has repurchased 8,897,957 shares under this program at an aggregate purchase price of approximately $407,399,000. During the year ended December 31, 2009, the Company repurchased an aggregate of $7,399,000 of the Company's common stock under the stock repurchase plan, of which $1,185,000 was recorded as a reduction to total retained earnings; otherwise, the aggregate purchase price would have resulted in a negative common stock carrying amount. Shares of the Company's common stock may be purchased in the open market or through privately negotiated transactions, subject to the market conditions. The repurchase program does not obligate the Company to acquire any specific number of shares or to acquire shares over any specified period of time.

### NOTE 9—INCOME TAXES

The Company applies an asset and liability method of accounting for income taxes that requires the recognition of deferred tax assets and liabilities for the expected future tax consequences of events that have been recognized in the Company's financial statements or tax returns. In estimating future tax consequences, the Company generally considers all expected future events other than enactment of changes in the tax laws or rates. Deferred taxes are provided for temporary differences between assets and liabilities for financial reporting purposes and for income tax purposes. Valuation allowances are recorded against net deferred tax assets when it is more likely than not that the asset will not be realized.

The Company had undistributed earnings of foreign subsidiaries of approximately $162,784,000 at December 31, 2009 for which deferred taxes have not been provided. Such earnings are considered indefinitely invested outside of the United States. If these earnings were repatriated to the United States, the earnings would be subject to U.S. taxation. The amount of the unrecognized deferred tax liability associated with the undistributed earnings was approximately $40,011,000 at December 31, 2009. The unrecognized deferred tax liability approximates the excess of the United States tax liability over the creditable foreign taxes paid that would result from a full remittance of undistributed earnings.

The Company recognizes the tax benefit from an uncertain tax position if it is more likely than not that the tax position will be sustained on examination by the relevant taxing authority based on the technical merits of the position. The tax benefits recognized in the financial statements from such positions are then measured based on the largest benefit that has a greater than 50% likelihood of being realized upon ultimate settlement with the relevant tax authority. In making this determination, the Company assumes that the taxing authority will examine the position and that they will have full knowledge of all relevant information. A reconciliation of the beginning and ending amount of gross unrecognized tax benefits is as follows (in thousands):

|  | December 31, | |
|---|---|---|
|  | **2009** | **2008** |
| Balance at January 1 | $21,839 | $20,694 |
| Increases related to prior years tax positions | 1,346 | 583 |
| Decreases related to prior years tax positions | (634) | (2,496) |
| Increases related to current year tax positions | 1,598 | 4,768 |
| Settlements | (1,194) | — |
| Lapses of statute of limitations | (2,772) | (1,710) |
| Balance at December 31 | $20,183 | $21,839 |

53

## COLUMBIA SPORTSWEAR COMPANY

## NOTES TO CONSOLIDATED FINANCIAL STATEMENTS—(Continued)

$18,659,000 and $20,096,000 of the unrecognized tax benefits balance would affect the effective tax rate if recognized at December 31, 2009 and 2008, respectively.

The Company conducts business globally, and as a result, the Company or one or more of its subsidiaries files income tax returns in the U.S. federal jurisdiction and various state and foreign jurisdictions. The Company is subject to examination by taxing authorities throughout the world, including such major jurisdictions as Canada, China, France, Germany, Hong Kong, Italy, Japan, South Korea, Switzerland, the United Kingdom and the United States. The Company has effectively settled U.S. tax examinations of all years through 2005. Internationally, the Company has effectively settled French tax examinations of all years through 2006 and Italian tax examinations of all years through 2007. The Company has effectively settled Canadian tax examinations of all years through 2004 and is currently under examination for the tax years 2005 through 2008. The Company does not anticipate that adjustments relative to this ongoing tax audit will result in a material change to its consolidated financial position, results of operations or cash flows.

Due to the potential for resolution of income tax audits currently in progress, and the expiration of various statutes of limitation, it is reasonably possible that the unrecognized tax benefits balance may change within the twelve months following December 31, 2009 by a range of zero to $9,181,000. At December 31, 2008, the comparable range was zero to $8,645,000. Open tax years, including those previously mentioned, contain matters that could be subject to differing interpretations of applicable tax laws and regulations as they relate to the amount, timing, or inclusion of revenue and expenses or the sustainability of income tax credits for a given examination cycle.

The Company recognizes interest expense and penalties related to income tax matters in income tax expense. The Company recognized a net reversal of accrued interest and penalties of $80,000 during 2009. The Company recognized net interest and penalties related to uncertain tax positions during 2008 of $313,000 and the Company recognized a net reversal of accrued interest and penalties of $117,000 during 2007. The Company had $3,155,000 and $3,234,000 of accrued interest and penalties related to uncertain tax positions at December 31, 2009 and 2008, respectively.

Consolidated income from continuing operations before income taxes consists of the following (in thousands):

|  | Year Ended December 31, | | |
|  | 2009 | 2008 | 2007 |
|---|---|---|---|
| U.S. operations | $59,629 | $ 44,478 | $122,588 |
| Foreign operations | 30,221 | 81,765 | 85,439 |
| Income before income tax | $89,850 | $126,243 | $208,027 |

## COLUMBIA SPORTSWEAR COMPANY

## NOTES TO CONSOLIDATED FINANCIAL STATEMENTS—(Continued)

The components of the provision (benefit) for income taxes consist of the following (in thousands):

| | Year Ended December 31, | | |
| --- | --- | --- | --- |
| | 2009 | 2008 | 2007 |
| Current: | | | |
| Federal | $10,030 | $ 22,576 | $40,490 |
| State and local | 2,088 | 2,459 | 3,685 |
| Non-U.S. | 10,399 | 18,568 | 22,493 |
| | 22,517 | 43,603 | 66,668 |
| Deferred: | | | |
| Federal | 2,377 | (10,444) | (2,726) |
| State and local | 12 | (1,228) | (222) |
| Non-U.S. | (2,077) | (735) | (145) |
| | 312 | (12,407) | (3,093) |
| Income tax expense | $22,829 | $ 31,196 | $63,575 |

The following is a reconciliation of the normal expected statutory federal income tax rate to the effective rate reported in the financial statements:

| | Year Ended December 31, | | |
| --- | --- | --- | --- |
| | 2009 | 2008 | 2007 |
| | (percent of income) | | |
| Provision for federal income taxes at the statutory rate | 35.0% | 35.0% | 35.0% |
| State and local income taxes, net of federal benefit | 1.9 | 0.8 | 1.1 |
| Non-U.S. income taxed at different rates | 0.4 | (4.1) | (1.4) |
| Foreign tax credits | (5.8) | (3.2) | — |
| Reduction of accrued income taxes | (4.1) | (3.3) | (2.8) |
| Tax-exempt interest | (0.5) | (0.8) | (1.0) |
| Other | (1.5) | 0.3 | (0.3) |
| Actual provision for income taxes | 25.4% | 24.7% | 30.6% |

55

## COLUMBIA SPORTSWEAR COMPANY

## NOTES TO CONSOLIDATED FINANCIAL STATEMENTS—(Continued)

Approximate future minimum payments, including rent escalation clauses and stores that are not yet open, on all lease obligations at December 31, 2009, are as follows (in thousands). Future minimum payments listed below do not include percentage rent or operating costs for which the Company is obligated.

|  | Non-related Parties | Related Party | Total |
|---|---|---|---|
| 2010 | $ 28,379 | $ 625 | $ 29,004 |
| 2011 | 27,534 | 625 | 28,159 |
| 2012 | 26,137 | 72 | 26,209 |
| 2013 | 25,678 | 72 | 25,750 |
| 2014 | 23,869 | 54 | 23,923 |
| Thereafter | 128,672 | — | 128,672 |
|  | $260,269 | $1,448 | $261,717 |

*Inventory Purchase Obligations*

Inventory purchase obligations consist of open production purchase orders for sourced apparel, footwear, accessories and equipment, and materials used to manufacture apparel. At December 31, 2009 and 2008 inventory purchase obligations were $258,069,000 and $157,774,000, respectively. To support certain inventory purchase obligations, the Company maintains unsecured and uncommitted lines of credit available for issuing import letters of credit. At December 31, 2009, the Company had letters of credit of $7,771,000 outstanding for inventory purchase obligations. See *Off-Balance Sheet Arrangements* in Note 5 for further disclosure.

*Litigation*

The Company is a party to various legal claims, actions and complaints from time to time. Although the ultimate resolution of legal proceedings cannot be predicted with certainty, management believes that disposition of these matters will not have a material adverse effect on the Company's consolidated financial statements.

*Indemnities and Guarantees*

During its normal course of business, the Company has made certain indemnities, commitments and guarantees under which it may be required to make payments in relation to certain transactions. These include (i) intellectual property indemnities to the Company's customers and licensees in connection with the use, sale and/or license of Company products, (ii) indemnities to various lessors in connection with facility leases for certain claims arising from such facility or lease, (iii) indemnities to vendors and service providers pertaining to claims based on the negligence or willful misconduct of the Company, (iv) executive severance arrangements and (v) indemnities involving the accuracy of representations and warranties in certain contracts. The duration of these indemnities, commitments and guarantees varies, and in certain cases, may be indefinite. The majority of these indemnities, commitments and guarantees do not provide for any limitation of the maximum potential for future payments the Company could be obligated to make. The Company has not recorded any liability for these indemnities, commitments and guarantees in the accompanying Consolidated Balance Sheets.

## COLUMBIA SPORTSWEAR COMPANY

## NOTES TO CONSOLIDATED FINANCIAL STATEMENTS—(Continued)

### NOTE 12—STOCK-BASED COMPENSATION

The following table shows total stock-based compensation expense included in the Consolidated Statement of Operations for the years ended December 31, (in thousands):

|  | 2009 | 2008 | 2007 |
|---|---|---|---|
| Cost of sales | $ 335 | $ 302 | $ 415 |
| Selling, general, and administrative expense | 6,018 | 6,000 | 6,830 |
| Licensing | — | — | 15 |
| Pre-tax stock-based compensation expense | 6,353 | 6,302 | 7,260 |
| Income tax benefits | (2,258) | (2,088) | (2,383) |
| Total stock-based compensation expense, net of tax | $ 4,095 | $ 4,214 | $ 4,877 |

No stock-based compensation costs were capitalized for the years ended December 31, 2009, 2008 and 2007.

The Company realized a tax benefit for the deduction from stock-based award transactions of $851,000, $636,000, and $4,213,000 for the years ended December 31, 2009, 2008 and 2007, respectively.

*1997 Stock Incentive Plan*

The Company's 1997 Stock Incentive Plan (the "Plan") provides for issuance of up to 8,900,000 shares of the Company's Common Stock, of which 2,106,182 shares were available for future grants under the Plan at December 31, 2009. The Plan allows for grants of incentive stock options, non-statutory stock options, restricted stock awards, restricted stock units and other stock-based awards. The Company uses original issuance shares to satisfy share-based payments.

*Stock Options*

Options to purchase the Company's common stock are granted at prices equal to or greater than the fair market value on the date of grant. Options granted prior to 2001 generally vested and became exercisable ratably on a monthly basis over a period of five years from the date of grant and expire ten years from the date of grant. Options granted after 2000 and before 2009 generally vest and become exercisable over a period of four years (twenty-five percent on the first anniversary date following the date of grant and monthly thereafter) and expire ten years from the date of the grant, with the exception of most options granted in 2005. Most options granted in 2005 vested and became exercisable one year from the date of grant and expire ten years from the date of grant. Options granted in 2009 generally vest and become exercisable ratably on an annual basis over a period of four years and expire ten years from the date of the grant.

The Company estimates the fair value of stock options using the Black-Scholes model. Key inputs and assumptions used to estimate the fair value of stock options include the exercise price of the award, the expected option term, the expected volatility of the Company's stock over the option's expected term, the risk-free interest rate over the option's expected term, and the Company's expected annual dividend yield. Assumptions are evaluated and revised as necessary to reflect changes in market conditions and the Company's experience. Estimates of fair value are not intended to predict actual future events or the value ultimately realized by people who receive equity awards.

## COLUMBIA SPORTSWEAR COMPANY

## NOTES TO CONSOLIDATED FINANCIAL STATEMENTS—(Continued)

The following table shows the weighted average assumptions for the year ended December 31:

|  | 2009 | 2008 | 2007 |
|---|---|---|---|
| Expected term | 4.71 years | 4.43 years | 5.04 years |
| Expected stock price volatility | 29.52% | 25.03% | 28.97% |
| Risk-free interest rate | 1.73% | 2.54% | 4.55% |
| Expected dividend yield | 2.17% | 1.57% | 1.01% |
| Weighted average grant date fair value | $ 6.55 | $ 8.60 | $ 18.87 |

The following table summarizes stock option activity under the Plan:

|  | Number of Shares | Weighted Average Exercise Price | Weighted Average Remaining Contractual Life | Aggregate Intrinsic Value (in thousands) |
|---|---|---|---|---|
| Options outstanding at January 1, 2007 | 1,579,150 | $41.93 | 6.78 | $21,761 |
| Granted | 263,272 | 61.44 |  |  |
| Cancelled | (81,160) | 53.11 |  |  |
| Exercised | (402,845) | 36.37 |  |  |
| Options outstanding at December 31, 2007 | 1,358,417 | 46.70 | 6.54 | 4,497 |
| Granted | 640,008 | 40.98 |  |  |
| Cancelled | (228,300) | 49.49 |  |  |
| Exercised | (116,486) | 32.42 |  |  |
| Options outstanding at December 31, 2008 | 1,653,639 | 45.10 | 6.73 | 1,042 |
| Granted | 387,505 | 29.75 |  |  |
| Cancelled | (252,303) | 44.90 |  |  |
| Exercised | (28,668) | 24.76 |  |  |
| Options outstanding at December 31, 2009 | 1,760,173 | $42.08 | 6.25 | $ 4,599 |
| Options vested and expected to vest at December 31, 2009 | 1,707,304 | $42.31 | 6.18 | $ 4,289 |
| Options exercisable at December 31, 2009 | 1,069,713 | $45.56 | 4.94 | $ 1,209 |

The aggregate intrinsic value in the table above represents pre-tax intrinsic value that would have been realized if all options had been exercised on the last business day of the period indicated, based on the Company's closing stock price on that day. Total stock option compensation expense for the years ended December 31, 2009, 2008 and 2007 was $2,861,000, $3,329,000 and $4,417,000, respectively. At December 31, 2009, 2008 and 2007, unrecognized costs related to stock options totaled approximately $4,609,000, $6,473,000 and $6,515,000, respectively, before any related tax benefit. The unrecognized costs related to stock options are being amortized over the related vesting period using the straight-line attribution method. Unrecognized costs related to stock options at December 31, 2009 are expected to be recognized over a weighted average period of 2.46 years. The aggregate intrinsic value of stock options exercised was $333,000, $1,071,000 and $10,953,000 for the years ended December 31, 2009, 2008 and 2007, respectively. The total cash received as a result of stock option exercises for the years ended December 31, 2009, 2008 and 2007 was $710,000, $3,731,000 and $14,604,000, respectively.

## COLUMBIA SPORTSWEAR COMPANY

## NOTES TO CONSOLIDATED FINANCIAL STATEMENTS—(Continued)

*Restricted Stock Units*

Service-based restricted stock units are granted at no cost to key employees and shares granted prior to 2009 generally vest over three years from the date of grant. Service-based restricted stock units granted in 2009 generally vest over a period of four years. Performance-based restricted stock units are granted at no cost to certain members of the Company's senior executive team, excluding the Chairman and the President and Chief Executive Officer, and generally vest over a performance period of between two and one-half and three years with an additional required service period of one year. Restricted stock units vest in accordance with the terms and conditions established by the Compensation Committee of the Board of Directors, and are based on continued service and, in some instances, on individual performance and/or Company performance. For the majority of restricted stock units granted, the number of shares issued on the date the restricted stock units vest is net of the minimum statutory withholding requirements that the Company pays in cash to the appropriate taxing authorities on behalf of its employees. For the years ended December 31, 2009, 2008 and 2007, the Company withheld 19,819, 5,951 and 7,176 shares, respectively, to satisfy $624,000, $243,000 and $442,000 of employees' tax obligations, respectively.

The fair value of service-based and performance-based restricted stock units is discounted by the present value of the estimated future stream of dividends over the vesting period using the Black-Scholes model. The relevant inputs and assumptions used in the Black-Scholes model to compute the discount are the vesting period, dividend yield and closing price of the Company's common stock on the date of grant.

The following table presents the weighted average assumptions for the years ended December 31:

|  | 2009 | 2008 | 2007 |
|---|---|---|---|
| Vesting period | 3.82 years | 3.06 years | 3.11 years |
| Expected dividend yield | 2.19% | 1.56% | 1.01% |
| Estimated average fair value per restricted stock unit granted | $ 27.14 | $ 39.27 | $ 60.16 |

The following table summarizes the restricted stock unit activity under the Plan:

|  | Number of Shares | Weighted Average Grant Date Fair Value Per Share |
|---|---|---|
| Restricted stock units outstanding at January 1, 2007 | 99,688 | $49.06 |
| Granted | 98,422 | 60.16 |
| Vested | (21,622) | 49.79 |
| Forfeited | (16,618) | 53.72 |
| Restricted stock units outstanding at December 31, 2007 | 159,870 | 55.31 |
| Granted | 168,347 | 39.27 |
| Vested | (20,625) | 51.85 |
| Forfeited | (47,083) | 49.25 |
| Restricted stock units outstanding at December 31, 2008 | 260,509 | 46.32 |
| Granted | 136,327 | 27.14 |
| Vested | (65,935) | 53.41 |
| Forfeited | (44,381) | 41.22 |
| Restricted stock units outstanding at December 31, 2009 | 286,520 | $36.35 |

Restricted stock unit compensation expense for the years ended December 31, 2009, 2008 and 2007 was $3,492,000, $2,973,000 and $2,843,000, respectively. At December 31, 2009, 2008 and 2007, unrecognized costs

**COLUMBIA SPORTSWEAR COMPANY**

**NOTES TO CONSOLIDATED FINANCIAL STATEMENTS—(Continued)**

related to restricted stock units totaled approximately $4,216,000, $5,499,000 and $5,963,000, respectively, before any related tax benefit. The unrecognized costs related to restricted stock units are being amortized over the related vesting period using the straight-line attribution method. These unrecognized costs at December 31, 2009 are expected to be recognized over a weighted average period of 1.95 years. The total grant date fair value of restricted stock units vested during the year ended December 31, 2009, 2008 and 2007 was $3,522,000, $1,069,000 and $1,077,000, respectively.

*1999 Employee Stock Purchase Plan*

In 1999, the Company's shareholders approved the 1999 Employee Stock Purchase Plan ("ESPP"). There are 750,000 shares of common stock authorized for issuance under the ESPP, which allows qualified employees of the Company to purchase shares on a quarterly basis up to fifteen percent of their respective compensation. The purchase price of the shares is equal to eighty five percent of the lesser of the closing price of the Company's common stock on the first or last trading day of the respective quarter. Effective July 1, 2005, the Company suspended offerings under the ESPP indefinitely. As of December 31, 2009, a total of 275,556 shares of common stock had been issued under the ESPP.

**NOTE 13—EARNINGS PER SHARE**

Earnings per Share ("EPS"), is presented on both a basic and diluted basis. Basic EPS is based on the weighted average number of common shares outstanding. Diluted EPS reflects the potential dilution that could occur if outstanding securities or other contracts to issue common stock were exercised or converted into common stock. For the calculation of diluted EPS, the basic weighted average number of shares is increased by the dilutive effect of stock options and restricted stock units determined using the treasury stock method.

A reconciliation of the common shares used in the denominator for computing basic and diluted EPS is as follows (in thousands, except per share amounts):

|  | Year Ended December 31, | | |
| --- | --- | --- | --- |
|  | **2009** | **2008** | **2007** |
| Weighted average common shares outstanding, used in computing basic earnings per share | 33,846 | 34,610 | 36,106 |
| Effect of dilutive stock options and restricted stock units | 135 | 101 | 328 |
| Weighted-average common shares outstanding, used in computing diluted earnings per share | 33,981 | 34,711 | 36,434 |
| Earnings per share of common stock: | | | |
| Basic | $ 1.98 | $ 2.75 | $ 4.00 |
| Diluted | 1.97 | 2.74 | 3.96 |

Stock options and service-based restricted stock units representing 1,562,064, 1,410,849 and 354,342 shares of common stock for the years ended December 31, 2009, 2008 and 2007, respectively, were outstanding but were excluded in the computation of diluted EPS because their effect would be anti-dilutive as a result of applying the treasury stock method. In addition, performance-based restricted stock units representing 44,043, 41,799 and 24,318 shares for the years ended December 31, 2009, 2008 and 2007, respectively, were outstanding but were excluded from the computation of diluted EPS because these shares were subject to performance conditions that had not been met.

Since the inception of the Company's stock repurchase plan in 2004 through December 31, 2009, the Company's Board of Directors has authorized the repurchase of $500,000,000 of the Company's common stock.

**COLUMBIA SPORTSWEAR COMPANY**

**NOTES TO CONSOLIDATED FINANCIAL STATEMENTS—(Continued)**

As of December 31, 2009, the Company has repurchased 8,897,957 shares under this program at an aggregate purchase price of approximately $407,399,000. During the year ended December 31, 2009, the Company repurchased an aggregate of $7,399,000 of the Company's common stock under the stock repurchase plan, of which $1,185,000 was recorded as a reduction to total retained earnings; otherwise, the aggregate purchase price would have resulted in a negative common stock carrying amount. Shares of the Company's common stock may be purchased in the open market or through privately negotiated transactions, subject to the market conditions. The repurchase program does not obligate the Company to acquire any specific number of shares or to acquire shares over any specified period of time.

**NOTE 14—COMPREHENSIVE INCOME**

Accumulated other comprehensive income, net of applicable taxes, reported on the Company's Consolidated Balance Sheets consists of foreign currency translation adjustments, unrealized gains and losses on derivative transactions and unrealized gains on available-for-sale securities. A summary of comprehensive income, net of related tax effects, for the year ended December 31, is as follows (in thousands):

|  | 2009 | 2008 | 2007 |
|---|---|---|---|
| Net income | $67,021 | $ 95,047 | $144,452 |
| Other comprehensive income (loss): |  |  |  |
| Unrealized holding gains on available-for-sale securities | 64 | — | — |
| Unrealized derivative holding gains (losses) arising during period (net of tax expense (benefit) of ($1,054), $361 and ($796) in 2009, 2008 and 2007, respectively) | (3,024) | 6,425 | (844) |
| Reclassification to net income of previously deferred gains on derivative transactions (net of tax benefit of $227, $36 and $608 in 2009, 2008 and 2007, respectively) | (616) | (389) | (1,303) |
| Foreign currency translation adjustments | 13,854 | (30,511) | 25,394 |
| Other comprehensive income (loss) | 10,278 | (24,475) | 23,247 |
| Comprehensive income | $77,299 | $ 70,572 | $167,699 |

**NOTE 15—SEGMENT INFORMATION**

The Company operates in four geographic segments: (1) United States, (2) Europe, Middle East and Africa ("EMEA"), (3) Latin America and Asia Pacific ("LAAP"), and (4) Canada, which are reflective of the Company's internal organization, management, and oversight structure. Each geographic segment operates predominantly in one industry: the design, development, marketing and distribution of active outdoor apparel, including sportswear, outerwear, footwear, accessories and equipment.

63

# COLUMBIA SPORTSWEAR COMPANY

## NOTES TO CONSOLIDATED FINANCIAL STATEMENTS—(Continued)

At December 31, 2009, the notional value of outstanding forward contracts designated as hedging anticipated inventory purchases was approximately $82,730,000. At December 31, 2009, insignificant deferred gains and losses (net of tax) on both outstanding and matured derivatives accumulated in other comprehensive income are expected to be reclassified to net income during the next twelve months as a result of underlying hedged transactions also being recorded in net income. Actual amounts ultimately reclassified to net income are dependent on U.S. dollar exchange rates in effect against the European euro, Canadian dollar, Japanese yen and Korean won when outstanding derivative contracts mature.

The classification of effective hedge results in the Consolidated Statements of Operations is the same as that of the underlying exposure. Results of hedges of product costs are recorded in cost of sales when the underlying hedged transaction affects income. Unrealized derivative gains and losses, which are recorded in current assets and liabilities, respectively, are non-cash items and therefore are taken into account in the preparation of the Consolidated Statements of Cash Flows based on their respective balance sheet classifications.

The Company also uses derivative instruments not formally designated as hedges to manage the exchange rate risk associated with the functional currency remeasurement of monetary assets and liabilities. At December 31, 2009, the notional value of outstanding forward contracts not formally designated as hedges was approximately $61,017,000. The change in fair value of these instruments is recognized immediately in cost of sales.

The Company does not hold derivatives featuring credit-related contingent terms. In addition, the Company is not a party to any derivative master agreement featuring credit-related contingent terms. Finally, the Company has not pledged assets or posted collateral as a requirement for entering into or maintaining derivative positions. See "Concentration of credit risk" under Note 1 for more information on credit risk related to financial instruments.

The following table presents the balance sheet classification and fair value of derivative instruments as of December 31, 2009 (in thousands):

| | Classification | Fair Value |
|---|---|---|
| Derivative instruments designated as cash flow hedges(1): | | |
| Derivative instruments in asset positions: | | |
| Currency forward contracts .......... | Prepaid expenses and other current assets | $1,099 |
| Derivative instruments in liability positions: | | |
| Currency forward contracts .......... | Accrued liabilities | 890 |

(1) Includes a $45,000 net liability position attributable to the component excluded from effectiveness testing.

| | Classification | Fair Value |
|---|---|---|
| Derivative instruments not designated as hedges: | | |
| Derivative instruments in asset positions: | | |
| Currency forward contracts .......... | Prepaid expenses and other current assets | $ 453 |
| Derivative instruments in liability positions: | | |
| Currency forward contracts .......... | Accrued liabilities | 1,065 |

## COLUMBIA SPORTSWEAR COMPANY

## NOTES TO CONSOLIDATED FINANCIAL STATEMENTS—(Continued)

The following table presents the effect and classification of derivative instruments for the year ended December 31, 2009 (in thousands):

| | Statement Of Operations Classification | Gain (loss) |
|---|---|---|
| Currency Forward Contracts: | | |
| Derivative instruments designated as cash flow hedges: | | |
| Loss recognized in other comprehensive income, net of tax . . . . . . . . . . . . . . | — | $(3,024) |
| Loss reclassified from accumulated other comprehensive income to income for the effective portion, net of tax . . . . . . . . . . . . . . . . . . . . . . . . . . . . . . . . | Cost of sales | (740) |
| Loss recognized in income for amount excluded from effectiveness testing and for the ineffective portion(1) . . . . . . . . . . . . . . . . . . . . . . . . . . . . . . . . | Cost of sales | (14) |
| Derivative instruments not designated as cash flow hedges: | | |
| Loss recognized in income . . . . . . . . . . . . . . . . . . . . . . . . . . . . . . . . . . . . . | Cost of sales | (130) |

(1) During the periods presented, the Company recognized an immaterial amount of ineffectiveness.

### NOTE 17—FAIR VALUE MEASURES

Certain assets and liabilities are reported at fair value on either a recurring or nonrecurring basis. Fair value is defined as an exit price, representing the amount that would be received to sell an asset or paid to transfer a liability in an orderly transaction between market participants, under a three-tier fair value hierarchy which prioritizes the inputs used in measuring fair value as follows:

Level 1 – observable inputs such as quoted prices in active markets;

Level 2 – inputs, other than the quoted market prices in active markets, which are observable, either directly or indirectly; and

Level 3 – unobservable inputs for which there is little or no market data available, which require the reporting entity to develop its own assumptions.

Assets and liabilities measured at fair value on a recurring basis as of December 31, 2009 are as follows (in thousands):

| | Total | Level 1 (1) | Level 2 (2) | Level 3 |
|---|---|---|---|---|
| Assets: | | | | |
| Cash and cash equivalents . . . . . . . . . . . . . . . . . . . . . . . . . . . . . . | $386,664 | $386,664 | $ — | $— |
| Short-term investments . . . . . . . . . . . . . . . . . . . . . . . . . . . . . . | 22,759 | 22,759 | — | — |
| Long-term investments . . . . . . . . . . . . . . . . . . . . . . . . . . . . . . | 826 | 826 | — | — |
| Derivative financial instruments . . . . . . . . . . . . . . . . . . . . . . . . | 1,552 | — | 1,552 | — |
| Liabilities: | | | | |
| Derivative financial instruments . . . . . . . . . . . . . . . . . . . . . . . . | 1,955 | — | 1,955 | — |

(1) Level 1 assets include cash equivalents consisting of money market funds, ultra-short bond funds, bank deposits and time deposits for which cost approximates fair value and long-term investments consisting of equity-concentrated mutual funds held to offset deferred compensation arrangements.

(2) Level 2 assets and liabilities include derivative financial instruments which are valued based on significant observable inputs. See Note 14 and Note 16 for further discussion.

There were no assets and liabilities measured at fair value on a nonrecurring basis.

# REPORT ON INTERNAL CONTROL

## Item 9A.  *CONTROLS AND PROCEDURES*

### *Evaluation of Disclosure Controls and Procedures*

Our management has evaluated, under the supervision and with the participation of our chief executive officer and chief financial officer, the effectiveness of our disclosure controls and procedures as of the end of the period covered by this report pursuant to Rule 13a-15(b) under the Securities Exchange Act of 1934 (the "Exchange Act"). Based on that evaluation, our chief executive officer and chief financial officer have concluded that, as of the end of the period covered by this report, our disclosure controls and procedures are effective in ensuring that information required to be disclosed in our Exchange Act reports is (1) recorded, processed, summarized and reported in a timely manner, and (2) accumulated and communicated to our management, including our chief executive officer and chief financial officer, as appropriate to allow timely decisions regarding required disclosure.

### *Design and Evaluation of Internal Control Over Financial Reporting*

### Report of Management

Our management is responsible for establishing and maintaining adequate internal control over financial reporting. All internal control systems, no matter how well designed, have inherent limitations. Therefore, even those systems determined to be effective can provide only reasonable assurance with respect to financial statement preparation and presentation.

Under the supervision and with the participation of our management, we assessed the effectiveness of our internal control over financial reporting as of December 31, 2009. In making this assessment, we used the criteria set forth by the Committee of Sponsoring Organizations of the Treadway Commission in Internal Control—Integrated Framework. Based on our assessment we believe that, as of December 31, 2009, the Company's internal control over financial reporting is effective based on those criteria.

There has been no change in our internal control over financial reporting that occurred during our fiscal quarter ended December 31, 2009 that has materially affected, or is reasonably likely to materially affect, our internal control over financial reporting.

Our independent auditors have issued an audit report on the effectiveness of our internal control over financial reporting as of December 31, 2009, which is included herein.

### Report of Independent Registered Public Accounting Firm

To the Board of Directors and Shareholders
Columbia Sportswear Company
Portland, Oregon

We have audited the internal control over financial reporting of Columbia Sportswear Company and subsidiaries (the "Company") as of December 31, 2009, based on criteria established in *Internal Control—Integrated Framework* issued by the Committee of Sponsoring Organizations of the Treadway Commission. The Company's management is responsible for maintaining effective internal control over financial reporting and for its assessment of the effectiveness of internal control over financial reporting, included in the accompanying "Report of Management". Our responsibility is to express an opinion on the Company's internal control over financial reporting based on our audit.

We conducted our audit in accordance with the standards of the Public Company Accounting Oversight Board (United States). Those standards require that we plan and perform the audit to obtain reasonable assurance about whether effective internal control over financial reporting was maintained in all material respects. Our audit included obtaining an understanding of internal control over financial reporting, assessing the risk that a material weakness exists, testing and evaluating the design and operating effectiveness of internal control based on the assessed risk, and performing such other procedures as we considered necessary in the circumstances. We believe that our audit provides a reasonable basis for our opinion.

A company's internal control over financial reporting is a process designed by, or under the supervision of, the company's principal executive and principal financial officers, or persons performing similar functions, and effected by the company's board of directors, management, and other personnel to provide reasonable assurance regarding the reliability of financial reporting and the preparation of financial statements for external purposes in accordance with generally accepted accounting principles. A company's internal control over financial reporting includes those policies and procedures that (1) pertain to the maintenance of records that, in reasonable detail, accurately and fairly reflect the transactions and dispositions of the assets of the company; (2) provide reasonable assurance that transactions are recorded as necessary to permit preparation of financial statements in accordance with generally accepted accounting principles, and that receipts and expenditures of the company are being made only in accordance with authorizations of management and directors of the company; and (3) provide reasonable assurance regarding prevention or timely detection of unauthorized acquisition, use, or disposition of the company's assets that could have a material effect on the financial statements.

Because of the inherent limitations of internal control over financial reporting, including the possibility of collusion or improper management override of controls, material misstatements due to error or fraud may not be prevented or detected on a timely basis. Also, projections of any evaluation of the effectiveness of the internal control over financial reporting to future periods are subject to the risk that the controls may become inadequate because of changes in conditions, or that the degree of compliance with the policies or procedures may deteriorate.

In our opinion, the Company maintained, in all material respects, effective internal control over financial reporting as of December 31, 2009, based on the criteria established in *Internal Control—Integrated Framework* issued by the Committee of Sponsoring Organizations of the Treadway Commission.

We have also audited, in accordance with the standards of the Public Company Accounting Oversight Board (United States), the consolidated financial statements and financial statement schedule as of and for the year ended December 31, 2009 of the Company and our report dated March 12, 2010 expressed an unqualified opinion on those financial statements and financial statement schedule.

DELOITTE & TOUCHE LLP
Portland, Oregon
March 12, 2010

### Item 9B.  *OTHER INFORMATION*

None.

# MANAGEMENT'S CERTIFICATION OF FINANCIAL STATEMENTS

## SECTION 1350 CERTIFICATION

In connection with the Annual Report of Columbia Sportswear Company (the "Company") on Form 10-K for the period ended December 31, 2009, as filed with the Securities and Exchange Commission on the date hereof (the "Form 10-K"), I, Timothy P. Boyle, Chief Executive Officer of the Company, certify, pursuant to 18 U.S.C. Section 1350, as adopted pursuant to Section 906 of the Sarbanes-Oxley Act of 2002, that to my knowledge:

**(1)** The Form 10-K fully complies with the requirements of Section 13(a) or 15(d), as applicable, of the Securities Exchange Act of 1934 as of, and for, the periods presented in the Form 10-K; and

**(2)** The information contained in the Form 10-K fairly presents, in all material respects, the financial condition and results of the operation of the Company.

> Dated: March 12, 2010
> /s/ TIMOTHY P. BOYLE
> Timothy P. Boyle
> President and Chief Executive Officer
> Columbia Sportswear Company

# SUPPLEMENTAL INFORMATION

## STOCK PRICE PERFORMANCE GRAPH

### Performance Graph

The line graph below compares the cumulative total shareholder return of our Common Stock with the cumulative total return of the Standard & Poor's ("S&P") 400 Mid-Cap Index and the Russell 3000 Textiles Apparel Manufacturers for the period beginning December 31, 2004 and ending December 31, 2009. The graph assumes that $100 was invested on December 31, 2004, and that any dividends were reinvested.

Historical stock price performance should not be relied on as indicative of future stock price performance.

**Columbia Sportswear Company**
**Stock Price Performance**
**December 31, 2004—December 31, 2009**

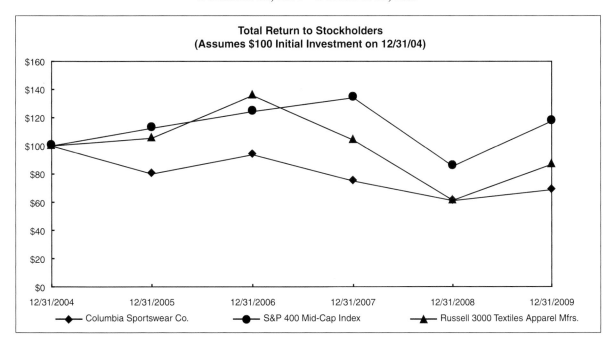

### Total Return Analysis

|  | 12/31/2004 | 12/31/2005 | 12/31/2006 | 12/31/2007 | 12/31/2008 | 12/31/2009 |
|---|---|---|---|---|---|---|
| Columbia Sportswear Co. . . . . . . . . . . . . . | $100.00 | $ 80.07 | $ 93.66 | $ 74.88 | $61.07 | $ 68.74 |
| S&P 400 Mid-Cap Index . . . . . . . . . . . . . . | $100.00 | $112.55 | $124.16 | $134.05 | $85.47 | $117.41 |
| Russell 3000 Textiles Apparel Mfrs. . . . . . . | $100.00 | $105.39 | $135.66 | $104.09 | $61.25 | $ 86.82 |

### Securities Authorized for Issuance Under Equity Compensation Plans

See Part III, Item 12, Security Ownership of Certain Beneficial Owners and Management and Related Stockholder Matters, of this Annual Report on Form 10-K for information regarding our securities authorized for issuance under equity compensation plans.

# CORPORATE RESPONSIBILITY REPORT

### Corporate Responsibility at Columbia Sportswear

At Columbia Sportswear, Corporate Responsibility (CR) is part of what we do every day—for our employees, the communities where we operate, and for the environment. To us, responsible business practices mean balancing our economic goals with social and environmental considerations.

CR involves supporting responsible sourcing practices that promote the values of equality, fairness, and safety in the independent factories that manufacture our products. It means considering our environmental impact from designing products with more eco-friendly material to cutting down on our packaging. It includes empowering communities through partnering, volunteering, and promoting programs that support those in need and enhance quality of life.

*Whether it s working on fair labor in our manufacturing locations or lessening our environmental footprint, we believe corporate responsibility is a companywide effort.*

### Our Code

At the heart of our CR programs are our Standards of Manufacturing Practices (SMP). Columbia manufactures products around the world and values ethical and fair treatment of people and practices. We are committed to assuring that the partners with whom we do business share these values. Each factory producing Columbia Sportswear products is monitored regularly against these *Standards* in addition to local labor laws and International Labor Organization (ILO) conventions.

### Social Responsibility

We see responsible sourcing as multiple gears working together to better the conditions in which people work. From codes of conduct, like our Standard of Manufacturing Practices (SMP), to monitoring and training and collaborating with others in the industry, all the gears have to work together to make a lasting difference. Here's how our gears work:

### Conducting unannounced audits

Columbia employs a team of specialists in the field to conduct regular, unannounced audits of our suppliers against our SMP. All our audits are strictly unannounced, that is, the factory is not notified in advance when an audit will take place. That allows us to see the factory conditions as they are on a typical day.

### Helping factories and their communities

Monitoring alone is not enough. We promote sustainable solutions through consulting and training projects for factory managers and workers. At some factories, we train workers on their rights, how to report grievances confidentially and without fear of retaliation, and how to calculate their pay and benefits. At other factories, we advise management on how to set up stronger human resource management systems. These projects help suppliers find their own solutions that fit the local context and that will therefore be more lasting.

We also engage the communities in which our manufacturing partners operate. We believe that helping factory workers better their lives extends beyond what takes place at the factory. We participate in long-term projects, like providing health education through the HER Project, as well as short-term assistance, like donating products and time to disaster relief such as the China earthquake. More information about our Giving Program can be found under Giving Back.

### Our approach to working with others

Social responsibility is not a statement, it's a conversation. It's about engaging others in the industry for continuous improvement.

Columbia collaborates with other apparel and footwear brands who share our CR approach and whose products are produced in the same factories as ours. At any given time, a factory could be making shirts for ten different companies in the U.S. and Europe, each with its own code of conduct. By sharing audit findings with these other companies, we can reduce redundant auditing and focus on finding solutions.

We also participate in industry-wide initiatives and organizations to explore how we can address complex questions around corporate responsibility as an industry. Please read more in the Industry section.

## Environment

We drive environmental efforts within our own facilities and in our operations, as well as in the field.

### Sustainability efforts in our facilities and operations

Columbia's sustainability program works to reduce the impact on the environment from our facilities and operations, as well as inspiring others to do the same. The focus is on reducing upstream impacts, such as energy and materials usage, then responsibly managing downstream waste.

We've installed solar panels at our headquarters in Portland, Oregon. You can also read what the *Portland Business Journal* thought about our solar panels: Portland Business Journal article.

### Environmental initiatives with our factories

The goals of Columbia's Environment, Health & Safety (EHS) program are to further develop our own staff to effectively monitor for factory conditions harmful to a worker's health and safety, enhance our monitoring of factory environmental performance, and identify opportunities to reduce the impact of manufacturing operations on the environment. Many EHS efforts are facilitated through collaboration with other brands, business partners, and government agencies.

We have multiple factories participating in the Hong Kong Productivity Council's Cleaner Production Partnership Program. This program encourages Hong Kong-owned factories operating in the Pearl River Delta region of China to improve energy efficiency and reduce emissions from their operations.

Find out more information about the Cleaner Production Partnership Program (CPPP or CP3) of the Hong Kong Productivity Council. HK Productivity Council CPPP

## Industry

### Fair Labor Association

Columbia is a proud affiliate of the Fair Labor Association (FLA) as a Collegiate Licensee, Category B. The FLA is an independent nonprofit dedicated to improving the lives of factory workers and providing independent monitoring of factory conditions. FLA is governed by a multi-stakeholder board with equal representation of companies, universities, and civil society organizations. The organization provides a forum where companies can exchange ideas with universities and nonprofits that share a commitment to ethical sourcing. For more information about the FLA, please visit www.fairlabor.org.

Columbia's collegiate apparel and equipment is subjected to FLA's rigorous Independent External Monitoring (IEM) process. Our program is also informed by FLA guidance on challenging issues such as effective grievance systems and migrant labor.

### Outdoor Industry Collaboration

In the outdoor industry, Columbia belongs to the Sustainability Council of the **Outdoor Industry Association (OIA)**. These global CR issues cannot be tackled by a single company working alone. Working together, companies in the outdoor industry can have a much greater impact on factory labor conditions and environmental issues.

**Apparel & Footwear Industry**

Columbia is also active with the Environmental and the Social Responsibility Committees of the **American Apparel & Footwear Association**, creating an even larger base of expertise from which to learn and share information and best practices.

# B

# Financial Statements for Timberland

# THE TIMBERLAND COMPANY

## CONSOLIDATED STATEMENTS OF CHANGES IN STOCKHOLDERS' EQUITY
### For the Years Ended December 31, 2009, 2008 and 2007

| | Class A Common Stock | Class B Common Stock | Additional Paid-in Capital | Retained Earnings | Accumulated Other Comprehensive Income/(Loss) | Treasury Stock | Comprehensive Income | Total Stockholders' Equity |
|---|---|---|---|---|---|---|---|---|
| | | | | (Dollars in thousands) | | | | |
| Balance, January 1, 2007 | $727 | $117 | $224,611 | $838,462 | $ 15,330 | $(517,562) | | $561,685 |
| Impact of adoption of ASC 740 | — | — | — | (3,328) | — | — | | (3,328) |
| Issuance of shares of common stock | 7 | — | 13,096 | — | — | — | | 13,103 |
| Cancellation/surrender of shares of common stock | — | — | 4,381 | — | — | (7,371) | | (2,990) |
| Repurchase of common stock | — | — | — | — | — | (45,060) | | (45,060) |
| Share-based compensation expense | — | — | 8,969 | — | — | — | | 8,969 |
| Tax benefit from share-based compensation | — | — | 6 | — | — | — | | 6 |
| Comprehensive income: | | | | | | | | |
| Net income | — | — | — | 39,999 | — | — | $ 39,999 | 39,999 |
| Translation adjustment | — | — | — | — | 8,401 | — | 8,401 | 8,401 |
| Change in fair value of cash flow hedges, net of taxes | — | — | — | — | (3,625) | — | (3,625) | (3,625) |
| Comprehensive income | — | — | — | — | — | — | $ 44,775 | — |
| Balance, December 31, 2007 | 734 | 117 | 251,063 | 875,133 | 20,106 | (569,993) | | 577,160 |
| Issuance/conversion of shares of common stock | 4 | (2) | 2,121 | — | — | — | | 2,123 |
| Cancellation/surrender of shares of common stock | — | — | — | — | — | (410) | | (410) |
| Repurchase of common stock | — | — | — | — | — | (44,761) | | (44,761) |
| Share-based compensation expense | — | — | 8,166 | — | — | — | | 8,166 |
| Tax deficiency from share-based compensation | — | — | (1,083) | — | — | — | | (1,083) |
| Comprehensive income: | | | | | | | | |
| Net income | — | — | — | 42,906 | — | — | $ 42,906 | 42,906 |
| Translation adjustment | — | — | — | — | (15,955) | — | (15,955) | (15,955) |
| Change in fair value of cash flow hedges, net of taxes | — | — | — | — | 8,254 | — | 8,254 | 8,254 |
| Other adjustment, net of taxes | — | — | — | — | 138 | — | 138 | 138 |
| Comprehensive income | — | — | — | — | — | — | $ 35,343 | — |
| Balance, December 31, 2008 | 738 | 115 | 260,267 | 918,039 | 12,543 | (615,164) | | 576,538 |
| Issuance/conversion of shares of common stock | 8 | (4) | 1,958 | — | — | — | | 1,962 |
| Cancellation/surrender of shares of common stock | — | — | — | — | — | (1,284) | | (1,284) |
| Repurchase of common stock | — | — | — | — | — | (44,980) | | (44,980) |
| Share-based compensation expense | — | — | 6,295 | — | — | — | | 6,295 |
| Tax deficiency from share-based compensation | — | — | (2,063) | — | — | — | | (2,063) |
| Comprehensive income: | | | | | | | | |
| Net income | — | — | — | 56,644 | — | — | $ 56,644 | 56,644 |
| Translation adjustment | — | — | — | — | 5,877 | — | 5,877 | 5,877 |
| Change in fair value of cash flow hedges, net of taxes | — | — | — | — | (3,725) | — | (3,725) | (3,725) |
| Other adjustment, net of taxes | — | — | — | — | 353 | — | 353 | 353 |
| Comprehensive income | — | — | — | — | — | — | $ 59,149 | — |
| Balance, December 31, 2009 | $746 | $111 | $266,457 | $974,683 | $ 15,048 | $(661,428) | | $595,617 |

The accompanying notes are an integral part of these consolidated financial statements.

## THE TIMBERLAND COMPANY

### CONSOLIDATED STATEMENTS OF CASH FLOWS
#### For the Years Ended December 31, 2009, 2008 and 2007

| | 2009 | 2008 | 2007 |
|---|---|---|---|
| | (Dollars in thousands) | | |
| **Cash flows from operating activities:** | | | |
| Net income | $ 56,644 | $ 42,906 | $ 39,999 |
| Adjustments to reconcile net income to net cash provided by operating activities: | | | |
| Deferred income taxes | 450 | 2,784 | 1,007 |
| Share-based compensation | 5,942 | 8,518 | 9,051 |
| Depreciation and amortization | 28,783 | 32,345 | 31,307 |
| Provision for losses on accounts receivable | 3,224 | 7,575 | 7,406 |
| Impairment of intangible asset | 925 | 2,061 | — |
| Impairment of other long-lived assets | 3,023 | 1,154 | 5,817 |
| Litigation settlement | — | (2,630) | — |
| Tax expense from share-based compensation, net of excess benefit | (2,214) | (1,254) | (1,095) |
| Unrealized (gain)/loss on derivatives | 333 | (131) | (2,749) |
| Other non-cash charges/(credits), net | (1,381) | 2,274 | 3,798 |
| Increase/(decrease) in cash from changes in operating assets and liabilities, net of the effect of business combinations: | | | |
| Accounts receivable | 18,206 | 3,847 | 17,247 |
| Inventory | 24,178 | 20,789 | (12,010) |
| Prepaid expenses and other assets | 1,479 | 4,963 | 154 |
| Accounts payable | (17,762) | 11,533 | (26,155) |
| Accrued expense | 11,846 | 3,809 | (16,496) |
| Prepaid income taxes | 4,894 | 674 | (5,008) |
| Income taxes payable | (2,093) | 7,270 | (18,127) |
| Other liabilities | (626) | (767) | 4,462 |
| Net cash provided by operating activities | 135,851 | 147,720 | 38,608 |
| **Cash flows from investing activities:** | | | |
| Acquisition of business and purchase price adjustments, net of cash acquired | (1,554) | 970 | (12,843) |
| Additions to property, plant and equipment | (17,677) | (22,316) | (30,479) |
| Other | (849) | 141 | (1,073) |
| Net cash used by investing activities | (20,080) | (21,205) | (44,395) |
| **Cash flows from financing activities:** | | | |
| Common stock repurchases | (43,905) | (46,261) | (47,748) |
| Issuance of common stock | 1,962 | 1,875 | 12,574 |
| Excess tax benefit from share-based compensation | 151 | 183 | 1,101 |
| Other | (1,284) | — | — |
| Net cash used by financing activities | (43,076) | (44,203) | (34,073) |
| Effect of exchange rate changes on cash and equivalents | (45) | (8,397) | 1,436 |
| Net increase/(decrease) in cash and equivalents | 72,650 | 73,915 | (38,424) |
| Cash and equivalents at beginning of year | 217,189 | 143,274 | 181,698 |
| Cash and equivalents at end of year | $289,839 | $217,189 | $143,274 |
| **Supplemental disclosures of cash flow information:** | | | |
| Interest paid | $ 331 | $ 486 | $ 1,564 |
| Income taxes paid | $ 23,513 | $ 24,863 | $ 40,453 |

The accompanying notes are an integral part of these consolidated financial statements.

# C

# Financial Statements for Tesco PLC

# Independent auditors' report to the members of Tesco PLC

We have audited the Group financial statements of Tesco PLC for the 53 weeks ended 28 February 2009 which comprise the Group Income Statement, the Group Balance Sheet, the Group Cash Flow Statement, the Group Statement of Recognised Income and Expense and the related notes. These Group financial statements have been prepared under the accounting policies set out therein.

We have reported separately on the Parent Company financial statements of Tesco PLC for the 53 weeks ended 28 February 2009 and on the information in the Directors' Remuneration Report that is described as having been audited.

**Respective responsibilities of Directors and auditors**
The Directors' responsibilities for preparing the Annual Report and the Group financial statements in accordance with applicable law and International Financial Reporting Standards (IFRSs) as endorsed by the European Union are set out in the Statement of Directors' Responsibilities.

Our responsibility is to audit the Group financial statements in accordance with relevant legal and regulatory requirements and International Standards on Auditing (UK and Ireland). This report, including the opinion, has been prepared for and only for the Company's members as a body in accordance with Section 235 of the Companies Act 1985 and for no other purpose. We do not, in giving this opinion, accept or assume responsibility for any other purpose or to any other person to whom this report is shown or into whose hands it may come save where expressly agreed by our prior consent in writing.

We report to you our opinion as to whether the Group financial statements give a true and fair view and whether the Group financial statements have been properly prepared in accordance with the Companies Act 1985 and Article 4 of the IAS Regulation. We also report to you whether in our opinion the information given in the Report of the Directors is consistent with the Group financial statements.

In addition we report to you if, in our opinion, we have not received all the information and explanations we require for our audit, or if information specified by law regarding Directors' remuneration and other transactions is not disclosed.

We review whether the Corporate Governance Statement reflects the Company's compliance with the nine provisions of the Combined Code (2006) specified for our review by the Listing Rules of the Financial Services Authority, and we report if it does not. We are not required to consider whether the Board's statements on internal control cover all risks and controls, or form an opinion on the effectiveness of the Group's corporate governance procedures or its risk and control procedures.

We read other information contained in the Annual Report and consider whether it is consistent with the audited Group financial statements. The other information comprises only the Introduction, the Financial highlights, Chairman's statement, Tesco at a glance, the Chief Executive's Q&A, the Report of the Directors, the Corporate governance statement, the unaudited part of the Directors' remuneration report and the Five year record. We consider the implications for our report if we become aware of any apparent misstatements or material inconsistencies with the Group financial statements. Our responsibilities do not extend to any other information.

**Basis of audit opinion**
We conducted our audit in accordance with International Standards on Auditing (UK and Ireland) issued by the Auditing Practices Board. An audit includes examination, on a test basis, of evidence relevant to the amounts and disclosures in the Group financial statements. It also includes an assessment of the significant estimates and judgements made by the Directors in the preparation of the Group financial statements, and of whether the accounting policies are appropriate to the Group's circumstances, consistently applied and adequately disclosed.

We planned and performed our audit so as to obtain all the information and explanations which we considered necessary in order to provide us with sufficient evidence to give reasonable assurance that the Group financial statements are free from material misstatement, whether caused by fraud or other irregularity or error. In forming our opinion we also evaluated the overall adequacy of the presentation of information in the Group financial statements.

**Opinion**
In our opinion:

- the Group financial statements give a true and fair view, in accordance with IFRSs as endorsed by the European Union, of the state of the Group's affairs as at 28 February 2009 and of its profit and cash flows for the 53 weeks then ended;

- the Group financial statements have been properly prepared in accordance with the Companies Act 1985 and Article 4 of the IAS Regulation; and

- the information given in the Report of the Directors is consistent with the Group financial statements.

**PricewaterhouseCoopers LLP**
Chartered Accountants and Registered Auditors
London 1 May 2009

**68**    FINANCIAL STATEMENTS

# Group income statement

| 53 weeks ended 28 February 2009 | notes | 2009 £m | 2008* £m |
|---|---|---|---|
| **Continuing operations** | | | |
| Revenue (sales excluding VAT) | 2 | **54,327** | 47,298 |
| Cost of sales | | **(50,109)** | (43,668) |
| Gross profit | | **4,218** | 3,630 |
| Administrative expenses | | **(1,248)** | (1,027) |
| Profit arising on property-related items | 2/3 | **236** | 188 |
| Operating profit | 2 | **3,206** | 2,791 |
| Share of post-tax profits of joint ventures and associates | 13 | **110** | 75 |
| Finance income | 5 | **116** | 187 |
| Finance costs | 5 | **(478)** | (250) |
| Profit before tax | 3 | **2,954** | 2,803 |
| Taxation | 6 | **(788)** | (673) |
| Profit for the year | | **2,166** | 2,130 |
| | | | |
| **Attributable to:** | | | |
| Equity holders of the parent | 30 | **2,161** | 2,124 |
| Minority interests | 30 | **5** | 6 |
| | | **2,166** | 2,130 |
| | | | |
| **Earnings per share** | | | |
| Basic | 9 | **27.50p** | 26.95p |
| Diluted | 9 | **27.31p** | 26.61p |

**Non-GAAP measure: underlying profit before tax**

| | notes | 2009 £m | 2008* £m |
|---|---|---|---|
| Profit before tax | | **2,954** | 2,803 |
| Adjustments for: | | | |
| IAS 32 and IAS 39 'Financial Instruments' – Fair value remeasurements | 1/5 | **88** | (49) |
| IAS 19 Income Statement charge for pensions | 28 | **403** | 414 |
| 'Normal' cash contributions for pensions | 28 | **(376)** | (340) |
| IAS 17 'Leases' – impact of annual uplifts in rent and rent-free periods | 1 | **27** | 18 |
| IFRS 3 Amortisation charge from intangible assets arising on acquisition | 1 | **32** | – |
| Underlying profit before tax | 1 | **3,128** | 2,846 |

* Results for the year ended 23 February 2008 include 52 weeks of operation.

The notes on pages 72 to 123 form part of these financial statements.

FINANCIAL STATEMENTS                                                                                69

# Group statement of recognised income and expense

| 53 weeks ended 28 February 2009 | notes | 2009 £m | 2008* £m |
|---|---|---|---|
| Change in fair value of available-for-sale investments | | 3 | (4) |
| Foreign currency translation | | (275) | 38 |
| Total (loss)/gain on defined benefit pension schemes | 28 | (629) | 187 |
| Gains/(losses) on cash flow hedges: | | | |
| Net fair value gains | | 505 | 66 |
| Reclassified and reported in the Group Income Statement | | (334) | (29) |
| Tax on items taken directly to equity | 6 | 435 | 123 |
| Net (expense)/income recognised directly in equity | | (295) | 381 |
| Profit for the year | | 2,166 | 2,130 |
| Total recognised income and expense for the year | 30 | 1,871 | 2,511 |
| | | | |
| Attributable to: | | | |
| Equity holders of the parent | | 1,872 | 2,500 |
| Minority interests | | (1) | 11 |
| | | 1,871 | 2,511 |

\* Results for the year ended 23 February 2008 include 52 weeks of operation.

FINANCIAL STATEMENTS

# Group balance sheet

| 28 February 2009 | notes | 2009 £m | 2008 £m |
|---|---|---|---|
| **Non-current assets** | | | |
| Goodwill and other intangible assets | 10 | **4,027** | 2,336 |
| Property, plant and equipment | 11 | **23,152** | 19,787 |
| Investment property | 12 | **1,539** | 1,112 |
| Investments in joint ventures and associates | 13 | **62** | 305 |
| Other investments | 14 | **259** | 4 |
| Loans and advances to customers | 17 | **1,470** | – |
| Derivative financial instruments | 22 | **1,478** | 216 |
| Deferred tax assets | 6 | **21** | 104 |
| | | **32,008** | 23,864 |
| **Current assets** | | | |
| Inventories | 15 | **2,669** | 2,430 |
| Trade and other receivables | 16 | **1,798** | 1,311 |
| Loans and advances to customers | 17 | **1,918** | – |
| Loans and advances to banks and other financial assets | 18 | **2,129** | – |
| Derivative financial instruments | 22 | **382** | 97 |
| Current tax assets | | **9** | 6 |
| Short-term investments | | **1,233** | 360 |
| Cash and cash equivalents | 19 | **3,509** | 1,788 |
| | | **13,647** | 5,992 |
| Non-current assets classified as held for sale | 7 | **398** | 308 |
| | | **14,045** | 6,300 |
| **Current liabilities** | | | |
| Trade and other payables | 20 | **(8,522)** | (7,277) |
| Financial liabilities | | | |
| Borrowings | 21 | **(4,059)** | (2,084) |
| Derivative financial instruments and other liabilities | 22 | **(525)** | (443) |
| Customer deposits | 24 | **(4,538)** | – |
| Deposits by banks | 25 | **(24)** | – |
| Current tax liabilities | | **(362)** | (455) |
| Provisions | 26 | **(10)** | (4) |
| | | **(18,040)** | (10,263) |
| **Net current liabilities** | | **(3,995)** | (3,963) |
| **Non-current liabilities** | | | |
| Financial liabilities | | | |
| Borrowings | 21 | **(12,391)** | (5,972) |
| Derivative financial instruments and other liabilities | 22 | **(302)** | (322) |
| Post-employment benefit obligations | 28 | **(1,494)** | (838) |
| Other non-current payables | 20 | **(68)** | (42) |
| Deferred tax liabilities | 6 | **(696)** | (802) |
| Provisions | 26 | **(67)** | (23) |
| | | **(15,018)** | (7,999) |
| **Net assets** | | **12,995** | 11,902 |
| | | | |
| **Equity** | | | |
| Share capital | 29/30 | **395** | 393 |
| Share premium account | 30 | **4,638** | 4,511 |
| Other reserves | 30 | **40** | 40 |
| Retained earnings | 30 | **7,865** | 6,871 |
| **Equity attributable to equity holders of the parent** | | **12,938** | 11,815 |
| Minority interests | 30 | **57** | 87 |
| **Total equity** | | **12,995** | 11,902 |

**Sir Terry Leahy**
**Laurie McIlwee**

**Directors**
The financial statements on pages 68 to 123 were authorised for issue by the Directors on 1 May 2009 and are subject to the approval of the shareholders at the Annual General Meeting on 3 July 2009.

FINANCIAL STATEMENTS                                                                                                71

# Group cash flow statement

| 53 weeks ended 28 February 2009 | notes | 2009 £m | 2008* £m |
|---|---|---|---|
| **Cash flows from operating activities** | | | |
| Cash generated from operations | 33 | **4,978** | 4,099 |
| Interest paid | | **(562)** | (410) |
| Corporation tax paid | | **(456)** | (346) |
| **Net cash from operating activities** | | **3,960** | 3,343 |
| **Cash flows from investing activities** | | | |
| Acquisition of subsidiaries, net of cash acquired | | **(1,275)** | (169) |
| Purchase of property, plant and equipment and investment property | | **(4,487)** | (3,442) |
| Proceeds from sale of property, plant and equipment | | **994** | 1,056 |
| Purchase of intangible assets | | **(220)** | (158) |
| Increase in loans to joint ventures | | **(242)** | (36) |
| Investments in joint ventures and associates | | **(30)** | (61) |
| Investments in short-term investments | | **(1,233)** | (360) |
| Proceeds from sale of short-term investments | | **360** | – |
| Dividends received | | **69** | 88 |
| Interest received | | **90** | 128 |
| **Net cash used in investing activities** | | **(5,974)** | (2,954) |
| **Cash flows from financing activities** | | | |
| Proceeds from issue of ordinary share capital | | **130** | 138 |
| Proceeds from sale of ordinary share capital to minority interests | | **–** | 16 |
| Increase in borrowings | | **7,387** | 9,333 |
| Repayment of borrowings | | **(2,733)** | (7,593) |
| New finance leases | | **–** | 119 |
| Repayment of obligations under finance leases | | **(18)** | (32) |
| Dividends paid | | **(883)** | (792) |
| Dividends paid to minority interests | | **(3)** | (2) |
| Own shares purchased | | **(265)** | (775) |
| **Net cash from financing activities** | | **3,615** | 412 |
| **Net increase in cash and cash equivalents** | | **1,601** | 801 |
| Cash and cash equivalents at beginning of year | | **1,788** | 1,042 |
| Effect of foreign exchange rate changes | | **120** | (55) |
| **Cash and cash equivalents at end of year** | 19 | **3,509** | 1,788 |

\* Results for the year ended 23 February 2008 include 52 weeks of operation.

# Reconciliation of net cash flow to movement in net debt note

| 53 weeks ended 28 February 2009 | notes | 2009 £m | 2008* £m |
|---|---|---|---|
| Net increase in cash and cash equivalents | | **1,601** | 801 |
| Elimination of net increase in TPF cash and cash equivalents | | **(37)** | – |
| Net cash inflow from debt and lease financing | | **(4,636)** | (1,827) |
| Short-term investments | | **873** | 360 |
| Movement in joint venture loan receivables | | **242** | 36 |
| Debt acquired on acquisition of Homever | | **(611)** | – |
| Transfer of joint venture loan receivable on acquisition of TPF | | **(91)** | – |
| Other non-cash movements | | **(759)** | (691) |
| **Increase in net debt in the year** | | **(3,418)** | (1,321) |
| Opening net debt | 34 | **(6,182)** | (4,861) |
| **Closing net debt** | 34 | **(9,600)** | (6,182) |

\* Results for the year ended 23 February 2008 include 52 weeks of operation.
NB. The reconciliation of net cash flow to movement in net debt note is not a primary statement and does not form part of the cash flow statement and forms part of the notes to the financial statements.

# APPENDIX D

# Accounting for Investments and Consolidated Financial Statements

## LEARNING OBJECTIVES

**1** **Identify** and **define** the investment categories for debt and equity securities. (p. D-2)

**2** **Describe** the accounting for various kinds of debt security investments. (p. D-3)

**3** **Describe** the accounting for various kinds of equity security investments. (p. D-8)

**4** **Define** parent-subsidiary relationships and **discuss** how their balance sheet data are consolidated. (p. D-12)

# INVESTMENTS

## DEBT AND EQUITY SECURITIES

The assets of a business may include investments in one or more types of debt or equity securities. For some businesses, such as insurance companies, investments in debt and equity securities constitute the major portion of a company's total assets. Investments in various debt and equity securities, for example, represent more than 50 percent of the assets of **Aetna Inc.**, a large diversified insurance company and a member of the Fortune 100 companies.

A **debt security** refers to a financial instrument that creates a creditor relationship for the debtholder. Examples of debt securities include U.S. Treasury bills, notes, and bonds; U.S. government agency bonds, such as Fannie Mae and Ginnie Mae bonds; state and local government bonds; corporate bonds; and commercial paper. *Bonds* are long-term debt securities and are discussed in detail in Chapter 10. Some bonds may not mature for 30 to 40 years, while others may have short maturity periods. *Commercial paper*, on the other hand, refers to very short-term (1 to 180 days), unsecured promissory notes issued by large corporations.

An **equity security** is a financial instrument that represents an ownership interest in a company. Shares of stock represent ownership interests in a corporation and are discussed in detail in Chapter 11. Investors owning a company's *common stock* have the most basic ownership rights, whereas owners of a company's *preferred stock* have some rights that take preference over the common stockholders, such as preferential treatment in the receipt of dividends and the receipt of assets in the event that a company liquidates.

Debt and equity securities may be acquired directly from the entity that issues the securities or through a secondary market. When corporations or government agencies need to borrow, they offer their debt securities for sale to the general public. This process is called *floating an issue*. When a corporation initially issues (sells) stock to the general public to raise money, the process is called an *initial public offering* (IPO). When companies need additional cash to fund their operations after initially going public, they may conduct additional sales of their shares through secondary public offerings.

More frequently, investors acquire debt and equity securities through the secondary capital market. The secondary capital market consists of individual and institutional investors desiring to buy or sell securities. Many debt and equity securities are bought and sold on organized exchanges. Stocks and bonds, for example, may trade on a national exchange such as the New York Stock Exchange or the London Stock Exchange. (Despite their names, both exchanges list both bonds and stocks.) Stocks and bonds may also trade in a less formal market known as the *over-the-counter* market. Both the buyer and seller of a security normally use the services of a brokerage firm, such as **Charles Schwab** or **Fidelity Investments**, to facilitate the acquisition and disposition of their investments.

## INVESTMENT CATEGORIES

For accounting purposes, each debt or equity security is placed in one of five investment categories: **trading securities**, **available-for-sale securities**, **held-to-maturity securities**, **influential securities**, and **controlling securities**. Of these categories, three apply to debt securities and four apply to equity securities. Exhibit D-1 presents the five investment categories.

**EXHIBIT D-1** Investment Categories for Debt and Equity Securities

The placement of an investment in the proper investment category depends on (1) management's intent with respect to selling the security and (2) the ability to influence or control another entity's activities as a result of an equity investment. Typical evidence of the latter factor is the ownership percentage represented by the equity investment. Exhibit D-2 defines and explains the five investment categories.

Notice in Exhibit D-2 that the trading securities and available-for-sale securities categories may include noninfluential equity securities. Noninfluential equity securities refer to stock investments that do not permit the investor to exert significant influence over the policies of the investee company (the company whose stock is acquired). Accountants consider stock investments noninfluential if the quantity of stock purchased is less than 20 percent of a company's outstanding voting (common) stock.

An entity that owns 20 percent or more of a company's outstanding voting stock may exert a significant influence on the operating or financial decisions of that company. However, if 50 percent or less of the total voting stock is owned, the investment does not represent a controlling interest. Voting stock investments in the 20 to 50 percent ownership range, therefore, compose the influential securities category.

When more than 50 percent of a corporation's voting stock is owned, the investor is a majority owner and is in a position to control the operating and financial policies of the investee company. These majority-ownership stock investments are classified as controlling securities.[1]

| EXHIBIT D-2 | Definitions of Investment Categories |
|---|---|
| Trading Securities (debt and equity securities) | Debt securities and noninfluential equity securities that management buys with the intent to sell in the near future |
| Available-for-Sale Securities (debt and equity securities) | Debt securities that management neither intends to sell in the near future nor hold to maturity |
| | Noninfluential equity securities that management does not intend to sell in the near future |
| Held-to-Maturity Securities (debt securities only) | Debt securities that management intends to hold to maturity |
| Influential Securities (equity securities only) | Equity securities that represent a 20 percent through 50 percent ownership of the corporation's voting stock |
| Controlling Securities (equity securities only) | Equity securities that represent an ownership of more than 50 percent of the corporation's voting stock |

Debt and equity investments are placed in one of the five different categories because accounting guidelines differ among the categories. We now review those accounting guidelines, considering debt securities first, followed by equity securities.

## INVESTMENTS IN DEBT SECURITIES

Investments in debt securities are placed in one of three investment categories: trading securities, available-for-sale securities, or held-to-maturity securities. The major accounting events concerning investments in debt securities are their purchase, the recognition of interest income, their balance sheet valuation, and their sale or redemption at maturity. Exhibit D-3 summarizes the accounting guidelines for these events. We will illustrate these guidelines with examples.

LEARNING OBJECTIVE 2

**Describe** the accounting for various kinds of debt security investments.

---

[1] The ownership percentages are guidelines only and may be overcome by other factors. In some cases, a company may own more than 20 percent of the outstanding voting shares of another company and still not be able to significantly influence its operating and financial activities. Or, effective control of another entity may exist with less than 50 percent ownership of its voting stock. For example, ownership of a large minority interest (such as 45 percent), with other owners widely dispersed and unorganized, may provide effective control. The key to proper accounting classification is the presence of significant influence on, or effective control over, another entity.

## PURCHASE

Assume that the Warner Company purchases $300,000 face value of Natco Company 8 percent bonds at 98 on July 1, 2010. (Recall from Chapter 10 that bond prices are quoted on a basis of $100 while their base value is actually $1,000. Thus, a bond said to sell for 98 is actually selling for $980. And, for a group of bonds with an aggregate maturity value of $100,000, this would imply a selling price of $98,000.) The bonds pay interest on December 31 and June 30 and mature in 10 years. The brokerage commission is $600. Warner's management considers the bond investment to be divided equally between trading securities, available-for-sale securities, and held-to-maturity securities. Exhibit D-4 shows the entry to record this debt investment. Note that the accounting for the purchase event is the same regardless of the classification of the bond investment.

| **EXHIBIT D-3** Accounting Guidelines for Investments in Debt Securities | | | |
|---|---|---|---|
| **Event/Accounting Guideline** | **Trading Securities** | **Available-for-Sale Securities** | **Held-to-Maturity Securities** |
| **1.  Purchase** Record at cost, which includes any broker's fees. | X | X | X |
| **2.  Recognition of Interest Income** Interest accrues daily and is usually recorded when payment is received. Premium or discount on purchase price is not amortized. | X | | |
| Interest accrues daily and is usually recorded when payment is received. Premium or discount on purchase price is amortized as an adjustment of interest income. | | X | X |
| **3.  Balance Sheet Valuation** Measure securities at fair value at balance sheet date. No valuation account to the asset account is used. Changes in fair value are reported in the income statement. | X | | |
| Measure securities at fair value at balance sheet date. Use a valuation account to the asset account. Changes in fair value are reported in stockholders' equity. | | X | |
| Measure securities at amortized cost at balance sheet date. | | | X |
| **4.  (a) Sale** Sale proceeds less investment's book value is a realized gain or loss. | X | | |
| Sale proceeds less investment's amortized cost is a realized gain or loss. | | X | |
| **(b) Redemption at Maturity** At maturity, the investment's book value will equal the redemption proceeds. | | | X |

The Natco Company bonds are purchased the first day after an interest payment date, so there is no unpaid interest related to the bonds. If any more time had elapsed, however, the bond price would include an amount for the accrued but unpaid interest. This occurs because the bond seller is entitled to receive the interest earned up to the date of sale. As a result, the purchase price of a bond that is sold between interest payment dates includes not only the current market price but also any interest accrued since the last interest payment date. (See Chapter 10 for additional discussion regarding the accrual of interest between interest payment dates.) The bond buyer pays the accrued interest amount to the bond seller, debits the amount to the Bond Interest Receivable account, and then collects it as part of the next interest payment received from the bond issuer. Because the accrued interest purchased by the bond buyer is collected with the next interest payment, the accrued interest is not treated as part of the initial cost of the bond investment.

| EXHIBIT D-4 | Purchase of Debt Securities | | | |
|---|---|---|---|---|

| 2010 | | | | |
|---|---|---|---|---|
| July | 1 | Bond investment—trading (Natco) | 98,200 | |
| | | Bond investment—available for sale (Natco) | 98,200 | |
| | | Bond investment—held to maturity (Natco) | 98,200 | |
| | | Cash | | 294,600 |
| | | *To record purchase of $300,000 of Natco Company bonds at 98 plus $600 commission [($300,000 × 0.98) + $600 = $294,600].* | | |

| A | = | L | + | SE |
|---|---|---|---|---|
| +98,200 | | | | |
| +98,200 | | | | |
| +98,200 | | | | |
| −294,600 | | | | |

## RECOGNITION OF INTEREST INCOME

Each $100,000 of Natco Company bonds acquired on July 1, 2010, was purchased at a $1,800 discount ($100,000 − $98,200). This means that the market rate of interest on July 1, 2010 was higher than the 8 percent coupon rate offered on the bonds. For trading securities, any bond discount (or premium) is ignored in accounting for the periodic interest income because management plans to sell the securities in the near future. As such, the effect on net income from ignoring the bond discount (or premium) is immaterial.

| PRINCIPLE ALERT | Materiality Concept |
|---|---|

Note the role played by the *materiality concept* in determining interest income on trading securities. Because of the short time period that trading securities are held by a company before being resold, accountants do not bother to amortize any discount or premium associated with the debt securities. This simplifies the accounting for these debt securities, yet it causes no significant distortion in the periodic reporting of interest income.

For available-for-sale securities and held-to-maturity securities, any bond discount (or premium) is amortized to interest income. This is done to make periodic interest income more accurately reflect the economic reality of the bond investment. The amortization of bond discount causes the periodic interest income to be higher than the semiannual cash receipt of interest. If the bonds had been purchased at a premium (more than their face value), the premium amortization would cause periodic interest income to be less than the semiannual cash receipt of interest.

Two amortization methods are available for use: the straight-line method and the effective interest method. We use the straight-line method here because the difference in the financial effect between the two methods is immaterial in this case. The *straight-line method* of amortization writes off an equal amount of discount or premium each interest period. The Natco Company bonds, when purchased, had 10 years to maturity, with interest paid semi-annually. Consequently, there are 20 interest periods associated with the bonds. During each interest period, $90 ($1,800/20 periods) of discount will be amortized for the available-for-sale securities and the held-to-maturity securities. Each $100,000 (face value) of Natco bonds pays $4,000 interest semiannually (8 percent × $100,000 × ½ year). The entries to record interest income at December 31, 2010, are shown in Exhibit D-5.

## BALANCE SHEET VALUATION

Debt securities are interest rate sensitive; that is, as market interest rates change, the market values of debt securities also change. Debt securities that management intends to sell (trading securities) or may sell (available-for-sale securities) are reported on the balance sheet at their current fair value. If available, quoted market prices from one of the national bond exchanges provide the best evidence of a bond's fair value. Year-end adjusting entries are made to record these current fair values. Current fair value is not a

| | | | EXHIBIT D-5 | Recognition of Interest Income on Debt Securities | | |
|---|---|---|---|---|---|---|

**EXHIBIT D-5**    **Recognition of Interest Income on Debt Securities**

2010

**Trading Debt Securities**

| | A | = | L | + | SE | |
|---|---|---|---|---|---|---|
| | +4,000 | | | | +4,000 Rev | |

| | | | | | | |
|---|---|---|---|---|---|---|
| Dec. | 31 | Cash | | | 4,000 | |
| | |     Bond interest income | | | | 4,000 |
| | | *To record receipt of semiannual interest on $100,000 of trading bonds.* | | | | |

**Available-for-Sale Debt Securities**

| | A | = | L | + | SE | |
|---|---|---|---|---|---|---|
| | +4,000 | | | | +4,090 Rev | |
| | +90 | | | | | |

| | | | | | | |
|---|---|---|---|---|---|---|
| Dec. | 31 | Cash | | | 4,000 | |
| | | Bond investment—available for sale (Natco) | | | 90 | |
| | |     Bond interest income | | | | 4,090 |
| | | *To record receipt of semiannual interest and discount amortization on* | | | | |
| | |     *$100,000 of available-for-sale bonds.* | | | | |

**Held-to-Maturity Debt Securities**

| | A | = | L | + | SE | |
|---|---|---|---|---|---|---|
| | +4,000 | | | | +4,090 Rev | |
| | +90 | | | | | |

| | | | | | | |
|---|---|---|---|---|---|---|
| Dec. | 31 | Cash | | | 4,000 | |
| | | Bond investment—held to maturity (Natco) | | | 90 | |
| | |     Bond Interest Income | | | | 4,090 |
| | | *To record receipt of semiannual interest and discount amortization on* | | | | |
| | |     *$100,000 of held-to-maturity bonds.* | | | | |

relevant measure for debt securities that management intends to hold to maturity. Thus, no adjustment to fair value is made for held-to-maturity securities.

Assume that a general decline in market interest rates causes the Natco Company bonds to trade at 99.5 as of December 31, 2010. (Remember that 99.5 means that a bond is actually selling for $995; and, for a group of bonds with a maturity value of $100,000, this equates to an aggregate selling price of $99,500.) Exhibit D-6 shows the adjusting entries made on this date to record the relevant fair values.

**EXHIBIT D-6**    **Balance Sheet Valuation for Debt Securities**

2010

**Trading Debt Securities**

| | A | = | L | + | SE | |
|---|---|---|---|---|---|---|
| | +1,300 | | | | +1,300 Gain | |

| | | | | | | |
|---|---|---|---|---|---|---|
| Dec. | 31 | Bond investment—trading (Natco) | | | 1,300 | |
| | |     Unrealized gain on investments (income) | | | | 1,300 |
| | | *To adjust trading debt securities to year-end fair value* | | | | |
| | |     *($99,500 − $98,200 = $1,300 gain).* | | | | |

**Available-for-Sale Debt Securities**

| | A | = | L | + | SE | |
|---|---|---|---|---|---|---|
| | +1,210 | | | | +1,210 | |
| | | | | | Comprehensive | |
| | | | | | Income | |

| | | | | | | |
|---|---|---|---|---|---|---|
| Dec. | 31 | Fair value adjustment to bond investment | | | 1,210 | |
| | |     Unrealized gain/loss on investments (equity) | | | | 1,210 |
| | | *To adjust available-for-sale debt securities to year-end fair value* | | | | |
| | |     *($99,500 − $98,290 = $1,210 gain).* | | | | |

Fair value changes in securities that are still owned are called *unrealized gains and losses*. Unrealized gains and losses that relate to trading securities are reported in the income statement. Thus, the $1,300 unrealized gain shown in Exhibit D-6 is included in Warner's 2010 income statement.

Unrealized gains and losses that relate to available-for-sale securities are excluded from the income statement. Instead, their net amount is reported as a separate component of stockholders' equity called Unrealized Gain/Loss on Investments (Equity). Unrealized Gain/Loss on Investments is included in comprehensive income that was discussed in Chapter 13 (see pages 597–598). Because these unrealized gains and losses are not included in earnings, the investment's cost must be maintained in the accounts so that a total realized gain or loss can be determined when the investment is actually sold. Using the valuation account Fair Value Adjustment to Bond Investment permits the maintenance of the investment's cost in the Bond Investment—Available for Sale account.[2] After the adjustments shown in Exhibit D-6, the December 31, 2010, balance sheet reports the bond investments as follows:

| | | |
|---|---|---|
| Bond investment—trading (fair value) | | $99,500 |
| Bond investment—available for sale (cost) | $98,290 | |
| Add: Fair value adjustment to bond investment | 1,210 | 99,500 |
| Bond investment—held to maturity (cost) | | 98,290 |

## SALE OR REDEMPTION AT MATURITY

To complete our illustration, assume that the trading and available-for-sale bond investments are both sold on July 1, 2011, for $99,800 each (after recognizing interest income on June 30, 2011). The remaining bond investment is held to maturity (June 30, 2020), at which time the issuer redeems the bonds for their maturity value of $100,000. Exhibit D-7 shows the appropriate journal entries related to these events.

> **Hint:** Although the accounting for debt (and equity) trading securities calls for the recognition of any fair value changes as part of a company's current net income, those unrealized gains or losses are not reported as part of a company's net income for income tax purposes. The IRS does not require the reporting of any gains until they are realized and prohibits the reporting of any losses until realized (when a security is sold).

| **EXHIBIT D-7** | Sale or Redemption at Maturity of Debt Securities | | |
|---|---|---|---|
| **2011** | | | |
| | *Trading Debt Securities* | | |
| July | 1 | Cash | 99,800 | |
| | | Bond investment—trading (Natco) | | 99,500 |
| | | Gain on sale of investments | | 300 |
| | | *To record sale of trading debt securities for $99,800* *($99,800 − $99,500 = $300 realized gain).* | | |
| | | *Available-for-Sale Debt Securities* | | |
| July | 1 | Cash | 99,800 | |
| | | Bond investment—available for sale (Natco) | | 98,380 |
| | | Gain on sale of investments | | 1,420 |
| | | *To record sale of available-for-sale debt securities for $99,800* *($99,800 − $98,380 = $1,420 gain).* | | |
| Dec. | 31 | Unrealized gain/loss on investments (equity) | 1,210 | |
| | | Fair value adjustment to bond investment | | 1,210 |
| | | *To adjust these account balances to zero.* | | |
| **2020** | | | |
| | *Held-to-Maturity Debt Securities* | | |
| June | 30 | Cash | 100,000 | |
| | | Bond investment—held to maturity (Natco) | | 100,000 |
| | | *To record redemption of bonds at maturity.* | | |

Accounting equation boxes:

| A | = L + | SE |
|---|---|---|
| +99,800 | | +300 Gain |
| −99,500 | | |

| A | = L + | SE |
|---|---|---|
| +99,800 | | +1,420 Gain |
| −98,380 | | |

| A | = L + | SE |
|---|---|---|
| −1,210 | | −1,210 Comprehensive Income |

| A | = L + | SE |
|---|---|---|
| +100,000 | | |
| −100,000 | | |

In Exhibit D-7, the $300 gain on the sale of the trading securities is the difference between the $99,800 sales proceeds and the last recorded fair value of $99,500. By July 1, 2011, another $90 of discount amortization would have been recorded on the available-for-sale securities, increasing their amortized cost to $98,380 ($98,290 + $90). The $1,420 gain that is recorded on their sale is the difference between the $99,800 sales proceeds and the amortized cost of $98,380. Because all available-for-sale bonds were sold, the related valuation account and unrealized gain/loss account are adjusted to zero balances at the next financial statement closing date (December 31, 2011). The completion of the discount amortization on the held-to-maturity bonds brings their amortized cost to $100,000 on June 30, 2020. Thus, there is no gain or loss associated with the redemption of the bonds at maturity.

---

[2] The cost of trading securities must be maintained for income tax purposes. A fair value valuation account, therefore, may be used for maintaining the income tax records of trading securities.

## INVESTMENTS IN EQUITY SECURITIES

LEARNING OBJECTIVE 3

**Describe** the accounting for various kinds of equity security investments.

Equity security investments fit into one of four categories: trading securities, available-for-sale securities, influential securities, and controlling securities. The major accounting events associated with investments in equity securities are their purchase, the recognition of investment income, their balance sheet valuation, and their sale. Exhibit D-8 summarizes the accounting guidelines for these events. We will illustrate these guidelines with examples.

| **EXHIBIT D-8** | Accounting Guidelines for Investments in Equity Securities | | | | |
|---|---|:---:|:---:|:---:|:---:|
| | **Event/Accounting Guideline** | **Trading Securities** | **Available-for-Sale Securities** | **Influential Securities** | **Controlling Securities** |
| **1.** | **Purchase** Record at cost, which includes any broker's fees. | X | X | X | X |
| **2.** | **Recognition of Investment Income** Record dividend income when dividends are received. | X | X | | |
| | Record equity in investee company's net income as investment income. Decrease investment account for dividends received. | | | X | X |
| **3.** | **Balance Sheet Valuation** Measure securities at fair value at balance sheet date. No valuation account to the investment account is used. Changes in fair value are reported in the income statement. | X | | | |
| | Measure securities at fair value at balance sheet date. Use a valuation account to the investment account. Changes in fair value are reported in stockholders' equity. | | X | | |
| | Report securities at book value (cost plus share of investee net income less dividends). | | | X | |
| | Eliminate investment account as part of consolidation procedures. | | | | X |
| **4.** | **Sale** Sale proceeds less investment's book value is a realized gain or loss. | X | | X | X |
| | Sale proceeds less investment's cost is a realized gain or loss. | | X | | |

## PURCHASE

Assume that Warner Company purchases 1,500 shares of common stock in each of four different companies—Ark, Inc.; Bain, Inc.; Carr, Inc.; and Dot, Inc.—on January 1, 2010. Each investment cost $15,000, including broker's fees. The shares acquired represent 10 percent of Ark's voting stock, 10 percent of Bain's voting stock, 25 percent of Carr's voting stock, and 60 percent of Dot's voting stock.[3] Only the Ark investment is considered by management to be a trading security. Thus, each of these stock investments is placed in a different category. Exhibit D-9 presents the journal entry to record the purchase of these investments. Note that each stock investment is recorded at its acquisition cost.

[3] We assume that the cost of the investments in Carr and Dot are equal to the book value of the underlying net assets of the investee company. This assumption permits us to simplify the illustration of the accounting for these two investments.

| EXHIBIT D-9 | Purchase of Equity Securities | | |
|---|---|---|---|

| 2010 | | | | | | |
|---|---|---|---|---|---|---|
| Jan. | 1 | Stock investment—trading (Ark) | | 15,000 | | |
| | | Stock investment—available for sale (Bain) | | 15,000 | | |
| | | Stock investment—influential (Carr) | | 15,000 | | |
| | | Stock investment—controlling (Dot) | | 15,000 | | |
| | | Cash | | | 60,000 | |
| | | *To record purchase of 1,500 shares each of Ark, Inc., Bain, Inc., Carr, Inc.,* | | | | |
| | | *and Dot, Inc., common stock for $60,000 ($15,000 for each investment),* | | | | |
| | | *including broker's fees.* | | | | |

| A | = | L | + | SE |
|---|---|---|---|---|
| +15,000 | | | | |
| +15,000 | | | | |
| +15,000 | | | | |
| +15,000 | | | | |
| −60,000 | | | | |

## RECOGNITION OF INVESTMENT INCOME

Now assume that each of the four companies earns net income of $10,000 in 2010; and, that each company also declares a cash dividend of $0.50 per share, which is received by Warner on December 31, 2010. Exhibit D-10 shows the journal entries to record this information.

As shown in Exhibit D-10, the dividends of $750 received on both the Ark and Bain investments are reported as Dividend Income. This is the proper treatment for cash dividends received on trading securities (Ark) and available-for-sale securities (Bain).

When the percentage ownership of voting stock reaches 20 percent or more, as is the case with the investment in Carr stock, the **equity method** of accounting is used. Under the equity method, the investor company records as income or loss its proportionate share of the net income or net loss reported for the period by the investee company (Carr), with an offsetting debit or credit going to the Stock Investment account. In addition, the receipt of any cash dividends from the investee company reduces the Stock Investment account. *The equity method prevents an investor company from manipulating its own income by the influence it can exercise on the dividend policies of the investee company.*

In Exhibit D-10, the equity method is used for the Carr stock investment (25 percent ownership) and Dot stock investment (60 percent ownership). At December 31, 2010, the Income from Stock Investments account and the Carr Stock Investment account are increased by 25 percent of Carr's 2010 net income (25 percent × $10,000 = $2,500). The receipt of the $750 cash dividend from Carr reduces the Carr Stock Investment account. Similarly, the equity method causes a $6,000 increase (60 percent × $10,000 net income) in both the Income from Stock Investments account and the Dot Stock Investment account at December 31, 2010. The $750 cash dividend received from Dot decreases the Dot Stock Investment account.

**A.K.A.** Stock investments involving ownership interests of 20 to 50 percent of the outstanding voting shares are often referred to as affiliate companies.

## BALANCE SHEET VALUATION

The balance sheet valuations for equity trading securities and available-for-sale securities are handled in the same manner as the corresponding debt securities. Year-end adjusting entries are made to record these equity securities at their current fair value, with quoted market prices from established exchanges like the New York and London stock exchanges, being the best evidence of a stock's current fair value.

| PRINCIPLE ALERT | Objectivity Principle |
|---|---|

The standard to measure equity trading securities and available-for-sale securities at current fair value applies only to equity securities that have readily determinable fair values. It does not apply to equity investments that would create significant valuation problems, such as equity investments in closely held companies whose shares do not trade on an established stock exchange. This represents an application of the *objectivity principle*, which states that accounting entries should be based on objectively determined evidence.

**EXHIBIT D-10**  Recognition of Investment Income on Equity Securities

2010

| | | | | |
|---|---|---|---|---|
| | | Trading Equity Securities | | |
| Dec. | 31 | Cash | 750 | |
| | |     Dividend income | | 750 |
| | | *To record receipt of cash dividend from Ark, Inc.* | | |
| | | Available-for-Sale Equity Securities | | |
| Dec. | 31 | Cash | 750 | |
| | |     Dividend income | | 750 |
| | | *To record receipt of cash dividend from Bain, Inc.* | | |
| | | Influential Equity Securities | | |
| Dec. | 31 | Stock investment—influential (Carr) | 2,500 | |
| | |     Income from stock investments | | 2,500 |
| | | *To record as income 25% of Carr's 2010 net income of $10,000* | | |
| | | *(investment balance = $17,500).* | | |
| Dec. | 31 | Cash | 750 | |
| | |     Stock investment—influential (Carr) | | 750 |
| | | *To record receipt of cash dividend from Carr, Inc.* | | |
| | | *(investment balance = $16,750).* | | |
| | | Controlling Equity Securities | | |
| Dec. | 31 | Stock investment—controlling (Dot) | 6,000 | |
| | |     Income from stock investments | | 6,000 |
| | | *To record as income 60% of Dot's 2010 net income of $10,000* | | |
| | | *(investment balance = $21,000).* | | |
| Dec. | 31 | Cash | 750 | |
| | |     Stock investment—controlling (Dot) | | 750 |
| | | *To record receipt of cash dividend from Dot, Inc.* | | |
| | | *(investment balance = $20,250).* | | |

Margin notes (left column):

A = L + SE; +750 ; +750 Rev

A = L + SE; +750 ; +750 Rev

A = L + SE; +2,500 ; +2,500 Rev

A = L + SE; +750 / −750

A = L + SE; +6,000 ; +6,000 Rev

A = L + SE; +750 / −750

Assume that at December 31, 2010, the fair values of 1,500 shares of Ark common stock and Bain common stock are each $23,000. Exhibit D-11 shows the adjusting entries made on this date to record the relevant fair values.

**EXHIBIT D-11**  Balance Sheet Valuation for Equity Securities

2010

| | | | | |
|---|---|---|---|---|
| | | Trading Equity Securities | | |
| Dec. | 31 | Stock investment—trading (Ark) | 8,000 | |
| | |     Unrealized gain on investments (income) | | 8,000 |
| | | *To adjust trading stock securities to year-end fair value of $23,000* | | |
| | | *($23,000 − $15,000 = $8,000 gain).* | | |
| | | Available-for-Sale Equity Securities | | |
| Dec. | 31 | Fair value adjustment to stock investment | 8,000 | |
| | |     Unrealized gain/loss on investments (equity) | | 8,000 |
| | | *To adjust available-for-sale equity securities (Bain) to year-end fair* | | |
| | | *value of $23,000 ($23,000 − $15,000 = $8,000 gain).* | | |

Margin notes (left column):

A = L + SE; +8,000 ; +8,000 Gain

A = L + SE; +8,000 ; +8,000 Comprehensive Income

As is true with debt securities, the $8,000 unrealized gain shown in Exhibit D-11 on the trading securities (Ark) is reported in Warner's 2010 income statement, whereas the $8,000 unrealized gain on the available-for-sale securities (Bain) is reported in the stockholders' equity section of the balance sheet of the Warner Company. The valuation account for the Bain stock investment plays the same role as discussed earlier in the accounting for debt securities; it permits the security's cost basis to be maintained in the Stock Investment—Available for Sale account.

Stock investments accounted for by the equity method are not measured at year-end fair values. The year-end account balances remain as calculated using the equity method—that is, $16,750 for the Carr investment and $20,250 for the Dot investment. For controlling investments, the financial statements of the investee company are usually consolidated with the statements of the investor company; consequently, the investment account does not appear in the consolidated statements.

## SALE

To complete our illustration, assume that all four stock investments are sold on July 1, 2011. Each of the stock investments is sold for $22,000. Exhibit D-12 shows the journal entries related to these events. As shown in Exhibit D-12, each sale generates a different gain or loss. Even though the basic events relating to each of the stock investments were the same, the accounting guidelines result in quite different analyses.

| **EXHIBIT D-12** | **Sale of Equity Securities** |
|---|---|

**2011**

**Trading Equity Securities**

| July | 1 | Cash | 22,000 | |
|---|---|---|---|---|
| | | Loss on sale of investments | 1,000 | |
| | |     Stock investment—trading (Ark) | | 23,000 |
| | |     *To record sale of trading equity securities for $22,000* | | |
| | |     *($22,000 − $23,000 = $1,000 loss).* | | |

A = L + SE
+22,000    −1,000 Loss
−23,000

**Available-for-Sale Equity Securities**

| July | 1 | Cash | 22,000 | |
|---|---|---|---|---|
| | |     Stock investment—available for sale (Bain) | | 15,000 |
| | |     Gain on sale of investments | | 7,000 |
| | |     *To record sale of available-for-sale equity securities for $22,000* | | |
| | |     *($22,000 − $15,000 = $7,000 gain).* | | |
| Dec. | 31 | Unrealized gain/loss on investments (equity) | 8,000 | |
| | |     Fair value adjustment to stock investment | | 8,000 |
| | |     *To adjust these account balances to zero.* | | |

A = L + SE
+22,000    +7,000 Gain
−15,000

A = L + SE
−8,000    −8,000
Comprehensive Income

**Influential Equity Securities**

| July | 1 | Cash | 22,000 | |
|---|---|---|---|---|
| | |     Stock investment—influential (Carr) | | 16,750 |
| | |     Gain on sale of investments | | 5,250 |
| | |     *To record sale of influential equity securities for $22,000* | | |
| | |     *($22,000 − $16,750 = $5,250 gain).* | | |

A = L + SE
+22,000    +5,250 Gain
−16,750

**Controlling Equity Securities**

| July | 1 | Cash | 22,000 | |
|---|---|---|---|---|
| | |     Stock investment—controlling (Dot) | | 20,250 |
| | |     Gain on sale of investments | | 1,750 |
| | |     *To record sale of controlling equity securities for $22,000* | | |
| | |     *($22,000 − $20,250 = $1,750 gain).* | | |

A = L + SE
+22,000    +1,750 Gain
−20,250

Because all available-for-sale stock was sold, the second entry in Exhibit D-12 for the Bain stock investment eliminates the balances in the related valuation account and unrealized gain/loss account at the next adjustment date (December 31, 2011).

## CURRENT AND NONCURRENT CLASSIFICATIONS

Each investment in debt and equity securities must be classified as either a current asset or a noncurrent asset in the balance sheet. Trading securities are always classified as *current assets*. Held-to-maturity securities are classified as *noncurrent assets* until the last year before maturity. Available-for-sale securities may be classified as either *current* or

---

**THINKING GLOBALLY!**

In some countries where there are not actively traded markets for debt and equity securities, the balance sheet valuation of debt and equity securities is often at the original acquisition cost of an investment. In other countries, where actively traded markets for securities do exist, a variant of the current fair value approach used under U.S. GAAP, called the lower-of-cost-or-market method, may be used. Under the lower-of-cost-or-market method, a debt or equity security is valued at the lower of two values—its current fair value or its original acquisition cost. When a security's current fair value falls below its acquisition cost, the security's carrying value is written down to the lower amount and an unrealized loss is reported as part of the company's current income.

---

*noncurrent assets*, depending on management's intentions regarding their sale. Influential investments are usually classified as *noncurrent assets*, but a current classification is proper if management intends to sell the investments within the next year or operating cycle, whichever is longer. As mentioned earlier, controlling investments do not appear in consolidated financial statements as a separate account but rather are "consolidated" into the accounts of the parent company.

---

**IN PRACTICE**    **Cherry Picking**

The treatment of unrealized gains and losses on available-for-sale investments permits management to engage in a practice known as "cherry picking." Management may select for sale those available-for-sale securities that have unrealized gains, thereby converting the unrealized gains into realized gains that appear in the company's income statement. Similarly, available-for-sale investments having unrealized losses are not sold, thereby keeping the losses out of the income statement and on the company's balance sheet instead. Cherry picking is a management behavior fostered by accounting principles. Many observers believe that it is a practice that gives management too much control over income statement results.

---

# PARENT-SUBSIDIARY RELATIONSHIP

LEARNING OBJECTIVE 4

**Define** parent-subsidiary relationships and **discuss** how their balance sheet data are consolidated.

A corporation that controls another corporation through ownership of a company's voting stock is known as a **holding company**. Control over another corporation is ensured through ownership of all or a majority of the investee's voting stock. Another name for a holding company is **parent company**, and the wholly owned or majority-held investees are called **subsidiaries**. The parent company and each subsidiary company are separate legal entities.

## CONSOLIDATED FINANCIAL STATEMENTS

As separate legal entities, a parent company and its subsidiaries maintain their own accounting records and prepare separate financial statements primarily for internal purposes. In the parent company's *separate* financial statements, the ownership of a subsidiary's stock is reported as a stock investment accounted for by the equity method. When the parent company prepares financial statements for its stockholders and creditors, however, the financial statements of the parent company and its subsidiaries are combined and reported as a single set of **consolidated financial statements**.

Under consolidated accounting, the individual line item (stock investment – controlling) used to account for an investment in a subsidiary under the equity method is replaced by all the individual asset and liability accounts of the consolidated subsidiary. In other words, the cash account of the subsidiary is combined with the cash account of the parent, the accounts receivable of the subsidiary is combined with the accounts receivable of the parent, the accounts payable of the subsidiary is combined with the accounts payable of the parent, and so on. The financial statements of a parent company and its various subsidiaries are combined using what is known as the acquisition method. When the financial data of these legal entities are consolidated, the resulting statements represent the group as an *economic entity*, as shown in Exhibit D-13.

Consolidated financial statements are prepared to avoid the problem of information overload in which investors and investment professionals receive more financial data than can be purposely processed. For example, the **General Electric Company** is made up of over 2,000 companies worldwide. A shareholder of General Electric would be overwhelmed to receive 2,000 individual company balance sheets, 2,000 individual company income statements, and 2,000 individual company statements of cash flows. Consolidated financial statements avoid this data problem for financial statement users by providing a single set of financial data for the economic entity.

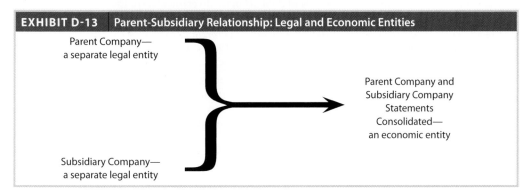

**EXHIBIT D-13** | **Parent-Subsidiary Relationship: Legal and Economic Entities**

Parent Company—
a separate legal entity

Parent Company and
Subsidiary Company
Statements
Consolidated—
an economic entity

Subsidiary Company—
a separate legal entity

Consolidated financial statements present both the total assets controlled by a parent company and the aggregate results of the group's operations and cash flows. These amounts are difficult to perceive when viewing only the separate reports of the individual companies. Consolidated statements are particularly valuable to the managers and stockholders of the parent company. In addition, creditors, government agencies, and the general public are informed of the magnitude and scope of an economic enterprise through consolidated statements.

---

**PRINCIPLE ALERT** **ACCOUNTING ENTITY CONCEPT**

The preparation of consolidated financial statements represents an application of the *accounting entity concept*. By viewing the parent company and its subsidiaries as a single economic entity, accountants ignore the legal boundaries of the separate companies. For consolidated financial statements, the overall economic entity is the accounting entity.

---

## LIMITATIONS OF CONSOLIDATED STATEMENTS

Consolidated statements have certain limitations. The status or performance of weak subsidiaries in a group can be "masked" through consolidation with more successful subunits. Rates of return, other ratios, and trend percentages calculated from consolidated statements may sometimes prove deceptive because they are really composite calculations. Stockholders and creditors of controlled companies who are interested in their legal rights and prerogatives should examine the separate financial statements of the relevant constituent companies.

Supplemental disclosures do improve the quality of consolidated statements, particularly those of *conglomerates – that is,* entities with diversified lines of business. U.S. GAAP stipulates that firms disclose information regarding revenues, income from operations, and identifiable assets for significant business segments.

REVIEW

## SUMMARY OF LEARNING OBJECTIVES

**LO1    Identify and define the investment categories for debt and equity securities. (p. D-2)**

■ Debt and equity security investments are placed in one of five investment categories:
  a. *Trading security,* a debt or equity security that management buys with the intent to sell in the near future.
  b. *Held-to-maturity security,* a debt security that management intends to hold to maturity.
  c. *Available-for-sale security,* a debt security that management neither intends to sell in the near future nor hold to maturity or a noninfluential equity security that management does not intend to sell in the near future.
  d. *Influential security,* an equity security investment that represents a 20 to 50 percent ownership of a company's voting stock.
  e. *Controlling security,* an equity security investment that represents an ownership of more than 50 percent of a company's voting stock.

**LO2    Describe the accounting for various kinds of debt security investments. (p. D-3)**

■ Debt trading securities are initially recorded at their acquisition cost, and interest income is recorded when received. The securities are reported at current fair value on the balance sheet with fair value changes reported on the income statement. When sold, the difference between the sales proceeds and the investment's book value is a realized gain or loss.

■ Debt available-for-sale securities are initially recorded at their acquisition cost. Interest income is recorded when received, with any premium or discount amortized as an adjustment to interest income. The securities are reported at current fair value on the balance sheet with fair value changes reported in stockholders' equity. When sold, the difference between the sales proceeds and the investment's amortized cost is a realized gain or loss.

■ Debt held-to-maturity securities are initially recorded at their acquisition cost. Interest income is recorded when received, with any premium or discount amortized as an adjustment to interest income. At maturity, the investment's book value equals the redemption proceeds.

**LO3    Describe the accounting for various kinds of equity security investments. (p. D-8)**

■ Equity trading securities are initially recorded at their acquisition cost, and dividend income is recorded when received. The securities are reported at current fair value on the balance sheet with fair value changes reported on the income statement. When sold, the difference between the sales proceeds and the investment's book value is a realized gain or loss.

■ Equity available-for-sale securities are initially recorded at their acquisition cost. Dividend income is recorded when received. The securities are reported at current fair value on the balance sheet with fair value changes reported in stockholders' equity. When sold, the difference between the sales proceeds and the investment's cost is a realized gain or loss.

■ Equity influential securities are initially recorded at their acquisition cost. Subsequent accounting uses the equity method: the investment account is increased by a proportionate share of the investee company's net income and decreased by the amount of any dividends received. When sold, the difference between the sales proceeds and the investment's book value is a realized gain or loss.

■ Equity controlling securities are initially recorded at their acquisition cost. Subsequent accounting uses the equity method: the investment account is increased by a proportionate share of the investee company's net income and decreased by the amount of any dividends received. For financial reporting, however, the investment account is replaced by a subsidiary's individual assets and liabilities, producing consolidated financial statements. When sold, the difference between the sales proceeds and the investment's book value is a realized gain or loss.

**LO4    Define parent-subsidiary relationships and discuss how their balance sheet data are consolidated. (p. D-12)**

■ A corporation that controls another corporation (the investee) by virtue of owning all, or a majority, of the investee's common stock is referred to as the parent company. The wholly owned or majority-owned investee is called the subsidiary.

■ When a parent company prepares financial statements for its stockholders, the financial statements of the parent and its subsidiaries are combined and reported as a single set of consolidated financial statements.

## SELF-STUDY QUESTIONS

(Answers to the Self-Study Questions are at the end of the chapter.)

1. Snyder, Inc., purchased $100,000 of Dane Company's 8 percent, 15 year, bonds for $96,400 on **LO2** January 1. Snyder plans to hold the bonds to maturity. Snyder records interest and straight-line amortization on interest dates (June 30 and December 31). At December 31, the bonds have a market value of $97,200. Snyder's balance sheet at December 31 should report the bonds at:
   a. $96,400.
   b. $96,640.
   c. $97,200.
   d. $96,160.

2. A firm purchased noninfluential and noncontrolling stock investments for $65,000. The firm does **LO3** not intend to sell the investments in the near future. During the year, the firm received dividends totaling $4,000 from these stock investments. At year-end, the stock portfolio had a quoted market value of $68,000. The increase in net income for the year (ignore income taxes) from these stock investments is:
   a. $1,000.
   b. $3,000.
   c. $4,000.
   d. $7,000.

3. Artway Company purchased 30 percent of the voting stock of Barton Company for $60,000 on **LO3** January 1. During the year, Barton Company earned $50,000 net income and paid $15,000 in dividends. At the end of the year, Artway Company's account, Stock Investment—Influential (Barton) should have a balance of:
   a. $110,000.
   b. $70,500.
   c. $95,000.
   d. $60,000.

4. The proper category to classify an investment in equity securities depends on: **LO1**
   a. management's intentions with regard to when to sell the investment.
   b. the relative size of the investment to the purchasing company's total assets.
   c. the ability of the purchasing company to influence the investee company.
   d. both *a* and *c*.

5. Where would the account unrealized gain/loss on investment appear for trading security **LO3** investment?
   a. Income Statement
   b. Equity section of the Balance Sheet
   c. Statement of Cash Flows
   d. It does not appear on any statement.

6. Where would the account unrealized gain/loss on investment appear for an available-for-sale **LO3** security investment?
   a. Income Statement
   b. Equity section of the Balance Sheet
   c. Statement of Cash Flows
   d. It does not appear on any statement.

7. Controlling securities typically require the investor to acquire what percent of the investee **LO1** company common stock?
   a. Under 20 percent
   b. Between 20 and 50 percent
   c. Over 50 percent
   d. 100 percent

8. Jeffrey Company invested in debt securities. Jeffrey will initially record this investment at: **LO2**
   a. Cost
   b. Cost plus any accrued interest
   c. Cost less any accrued interest
   d. Maturity value

Dec. 31 Received the semiannual interest payment on the Cynad bonds and amortized the bond discount for six months.

    31 Made the adjusting entry to record the current fair value of the Cynad bonds. At December 31, the market value of the Cynad bonds was $790,000.

2011

June 30 Received the semiannual interest payment on the Cynad bonds and amortized the bond discount for six months.

July 1 Sold the Cynad bond investment for $792,500 cash.

Dec. 31 Made the adjusting entry to eliminate balances from the Fair Value Adjustment to Bond Investment account and the Unrealized Gain/Loss on Investments (Equity) account.

Record the transactions and adjustments of Hilyn Company using journal entries.

**LO2** **ED-3A.** **Accounting for Debt Securities—Held to Maturity**

Kurl Company had the following transactions and adjustments related to a bond investment:

2010

Jan. 1 Purchased $600,000 face value of Sphere, Inc.'s 9 percent bonds at 102 plus a brokerage commission of $900. The bonds pay interest on June 30 and December 31 and mature in 10 years. Kurl expects to hold the bonds to maturity.

June 30 Received the semiannual interest payment on the Sphere bonds and amortized the bond premium for six months. Kurl uses the straight-line method to amortize bond discounts and premiums.

2019

Dec. 31 Received the semiannual interest payment on the Sphere bonds and amortized the bond premium for six months.

    31 Received the principal amount in cash on maturity date of the Sphere bonds.

Record the transactions and adjustments of Kurl Company using journal entries.

**LO3** **ED-4A.** **Accounting for Equity Securities—Trading**

The Glass Company had the following transactions and adjustment related to a stock investment:

2010

Nov. 15 Purchased 6,000 shares of Erie, Inc.'s common stock at $12 per share plus a brokerage commission of $750. Glass expects to sell the stock in the near future.

Dec. 22 Received a cash dividend of $1.10 per share of common stock from Erie.

    31 Made the adjusting entry to reflect year-end fair value of the stock investment in Erie. The year-end market price of the Erie common stock is $11.25 per share.

2011

Jan. 20 Sold all 6,000 shares of the Erie common stock for $66,900.

Record the transactions and adjustment of the Glass Company using journal entries.

**LO3** **ED-5A.** **Accounting for Equity Securities—Available for Sale**

Refer to the data for the Glass Company in ED-4A. Assume that when the shares were purchased, management did not intend to sell the stock in the near future. Record the transactions and adjustment for Glass Company under this assumption using journal entries. In addition, prepare any adjusting entry needed at December 31, 2011.

**LO3** **ED-6A.** **Accounting for Equity Securities—Influential**

The Dunn Company had the following transactions and adjustment related to a stock investment:

2010

Jan. 15 Purchased 12,000 shares of Van, Inc.'s common stock at $9 per share plus a brokerage commission of $900. These shares represent a 30 percent ownership of Van's common stock.

Dec. 31 Received a cash dividend of $1.25 per share of common stock from Van.

    31 Made the adjusting entry to reflect income from the Van stock investment. Van's 2010 net income is $80,000.

2011

Jan. 20 Sold all 12,000 shares of the Van common stock for $120,500.

Record the transactions and adjustment of the Dunn Company using journal entries.

**ED-7A.** **Accounting for Equity Securities**                                                                   LO3

On March 15, Kat Corp. purchased 200 shares of common stock of Scott Company for $15 per share. Kat Corp. is not able to exercise significant influence over Scott. On December 31, the market value of the Scott stock was $14.00 per share. Kat Corp. plans to hold the stock for the unforeseeable future.

   *a.* Upon the purchase of the Scott stock, how should Kat Corp. classify the shares on its balance sheet? Justify your answer.
   *b.* Record all transactions necessary for Kat.

**ED-8A** **Recording Influential Securities**                                                                   LO3

On January 3, Mahony Farm purchased 20% of the outstanding stock of Flepo Company for $80,000. The purchase gave Mahony the ability to exercise significant influence over Flepo. During the year, Flepo paid cash dividends totaling $70,000 and reported net income for the year of $90,000.

   Record all transactions necessary for Mahony Farm.

**ED-9A.** **Accounting for Equity Securities**                                                                   LO3

Microsoft, Inc., maintained a large investment in marketable securities valued at approximately $42 billion as of the beginning of the year. During the year, the securities produced investment income (dividends and interest income) totaling $2 billion. At year-end, the portfolio of marketable securities had appreciated to $43.5 billion.

   Calculate the income statement effect of the marketable securities if:

   1. The entire portfolio is classified as trading securities.
   2. The entire portfolio is classified as available-for-sale securities.

**ED-10A.** **Consolidation Accounting**                                                                   LO4

Fletcher Company, a manufacturer of precision mining equipment, acquired 100 percent of the outstanding common stock of Denfork Company, a small mining company with several mines that extract rare earth materials.

   *a.* How should Fletcher account for this acquisition during the year?
   *b.* What adjustments are needed at year-end?
   *c.* What limitations are present in this method of accounting?

# EXERCISES—SET B

**ED-1B.** **Accounting for Debt Securities—Trading**                                                                   LO2

Sanders, Inc. had the following transactions and adjustments related to a bond investment:

2010

Nov. 1 Purchased $300,000 face value of Batem, Inc.'s 9 percent bonds at 102 plus a brokerage commission of $900. The bonds pay interest on October 31 and April 30 and mature in 15 years. Sanders expects to sell the bonds in the near future.

Dec. 31 Made the adjusting entry to record interest earned on investment in the Batem bonds.

   31 Made the adjusting entry to record the current fair value of the Batem bonds. At December 31, the market value of the Batem bonds was $301,500.

2011

Apr. 30 Received the semiannual interest payment on investment in the Batem bonds.

May 1 Sold the Batem bond investment for $300,900 cash.

Record the transactions and adjustments of the Sanders Company using journal entries.

**ED-2B.** **Accounting for Debt Securities—Available for Sale**                                                                   LO2

The Witt Company had the following transactions and adjustments related to a bond investment:

2010

Jan.  1   Purchased $600,000 face value of Chevy, Inc.'s 8 percent bonds at 101 plus a brokerage commission of $1,400. The bonds pay interest on June 30 and December 31 and mature in 10 years. Witt does not expect to sell the bonds in the near future, nor does it intend to hold the bonds to maturity.

June  30   Received the semiannual interest payment on the Chevy bonds and amortized the bond premium for six months. Witt uses the straight-line method to amortize bond discounts and premiums.

Dec.  31   Received the semiannual interest payment on the Chevy bonds and amortized the bond premium for six months.

      31   Made the adjusting entry to record the current fair value of the Chevy bonds. At December 31, the market value of the Chevy bonds was $609,000.

2011

June  30   Received the semiannual interest payment on the Chevy bonds and amortized the bond premium for six months.

July  1   Sold the Chevy bond investment for $608,500 cash.

Dec.  31   Made the adjusting entry to eliminate balances from the Fair Value Adjustment to Bond Investment account and the Unrealized Gain/Loss on Investments (Equity) account.

Record the transactions and adjustments of the Witt Company using journal entries.

**LO2   ED-3B.   Accounting for Debt Securities—Held to Maturity**

The Shepler Company had the following transactions and adjustments related to a bond investment:

2010

Jan.  1   Purchased $250,000 face value of Lowe, Inc.'s 6 percent bonds at 98 plus a brokerage commission of $500. The bonds pay interest on June 30 and December 31 and mature in 15 years. Shepler expects to hold the bonds to maturity.

June  30   Received the semiannual interest payment on the Lowe bonds and amortized the bond discount for six months. Shepler uses the straight-line method to amortize bond discounts and premiums.

2024

Dec.  31   Received the semiannual interest payment on the Lowe bonds and amortized the bond discount for six months.

      31   Received the principal amount in cash on maturity date of the Lowe bonds.

Record the transactions and adjustments of the Shepler Company using journal entries.

**LO3   ED-4B.   Accounting for Equity Securities—Trading**

The Dale Company had the following transactions and adjustment related to a stock investment:

2010

Nov.  15   Purchased 5,000 shares of Lake, Inc.'s common stock at $16 per share plus a brokerage commission of $900. Dale Company expects to sell the stock in the near future.

Dec.  22   Received a cash dividend of $1.25 per share of common stock from Lake.

      31   Made the adjusting entry to reflect year-end fair value of the stock investment in Lake. The year-end market price of the Lake common stock is $17.50 per share.

2011

Jan.  20   Sold all 5,000 shares of the Lake common stock for $86,400.

Record the transactions and adjustment of the Dale Company using journal entries.

**LO3   ED-5B.   Accounting for Equity Securities—Available for Sale**

Refer to the data for Dale Company in ED-4B. Assume that when the shares were purchased, management did not intend to sell the stock in the near future. Record the transactions and adjustment for Dale Company under this assumption using journal entries. In addition, prepare any adjusting entry needed at December 31, 2011.

**ED-6B.** **Accounting for Equity Securities—Influential**                                LO3

The Prince Company had the following transactions and adjustment related to a stock investment:

2010

Jan. 15 Purchased 15,000 shares of Park, Inc.'s common stock at $8 per share plus a brokerage commission of $1,000. These shares represent a 25 percent ownership of the Park common stock.

Dec. 31 Received a cash dividend of $0.80 per share of common stock from Park.

31 Made the adjusting entry to reflect income from the Park stock investment. Park's 2010 net income is $120,000.

2011

Jan. 20 Sold all 15,000 shares of the Park common stock for $132,000.

Record the above transactions for the Prince Company using journal entries.

**ED-7B.** **Accounting for Equity Securities**                                LO3

On March 15, Kit Corp. purchased 400 shares of common stock of Murat Company for $25 per share. Kit Corp. is not able to exercise significant influence over Murat. On December 31, the market value of the Murat stock was $27.00 per share. Kat Corp. plans to sell the stock soon.

*a.* Upon the purchase of the Murat stock, how should Kit Corp. classify the shares on its balance sheet? Justify your answer.

*b.* Record all transactions necessary for Kit.

**ED-8B.** **Recording Influential Securities**                                LO3

On January 3, Negrito Farm purchased 25% of the outstanding stock of Philip Company for $90,000. The purchase gave Negrito the ability to exercise significant influence over Philip. During the year, Philip paid cash dividends totaling $80,000 and reported net income for the year of $100,000.

Record all transactions necessary for Negrito Farm.

**ED-9B.** **Accounting for Equity Securities**                                LO3

Macroview, Inc., maintained a large investment in marketable securities valued at approximately $60 billion as of the beginning of the year. During the year, the securities produced investment income (dividends and interest income) totaling $3 billion. At year-end, the portfolio of marketable securities had appreciated to $64.5 billion.

Calculate the income statement effect of the marketable securities if:

1. The entire portfolio is classified as trading securities

2. The entire portfolio is classified as available-for-sale securities

**ED-10B.** **Consolidation Accounting**                                LO4

Peyton Company, a manufacturer of silicon chips, acquired 100 percent of the outstanding common stock of Visik Company, a small manufacturer of mobile computing devices.

*a.* How should Peyton account for this acquisition during the year?

*b.* What adjustments are needed at year-end?

*c.* What limitations are present in this method of accounting?

## PROBLEMS—SET A

**PD-1A.** **The Analysis of Bond Investments**                                LO2

Columbia Company began operations in 2010 and by year-end (December 31) had made six bond investments. Year-end information on these bond investments follows:

| Company | Face Value | Cost or Amortized Cost | Year-End Market Value | Classification |
|---|---|---|---|---|
| Ling, Inc. .................... | $100,000 | $102,400 | $105,300 | Trading |
| Wren, Inc. .................... | $250,000 | $262,500 | $270,000 | Trading |
| Olanamic, Inc. ................. | $200,000 | $197,000 | $199,000 | Available for sale |
| Fossil, Inc. .................... | $150,000 | $154,000 | $160,000 | Available for sale |
| Meander, Inc. ................. | $100,000 | $101,200 | $102,400 | Held to maturity |
| Resin, Inc. .................... | $140,000 | $136,000 | $137,000 | Held to maturity |

**Required**

*a.* At what total amount will the trading bond investments be reported on the December 31 balance sheet?

*b.* At what total amount will the available-for-sale bond investments be reported on the December 31 balance sheet?

*c.* At what total amount will the held-to-maturity bond investments be reported on the December 31 balance sheet?

*d.* What total amount of unrealized holding gains or unrealized holding losses related to bond investments will appear on the income statement?

*e.* What total amount of unrealized holding gains or unrealized holding losses related to bond investments will appear in the stockholders' equity section of the December 31 balance sheet?

*f.* What total amount of fair value adjustment to bond investments will appear on the December 31 balance sheet? Which category of bond investments does the fair value adjustment relate to? Does the fair value adjustment increase or decrease the financial statement presentation of these bond investments?

**LO2  PD-2A. Bond Investment Journal Entries**

The following transactions and adjustments relate to bond investments acquired by Bloom Corporation:

2010

June 30 Purchased $200,000 face value of Dynamo, Inc.'s 20-year, 9 percent bonds dated June 30, 2010, for $215,200 cash. Interest is paid December 31 and June 30. The investment is classified as an available-for-sale security.

Dec. 31 Received the semiannual interest payment from Dynamo and amortized the bond premium (straight-line method).

31 Purchased $300,000 face value of Link, Inc.'s 10-year, 7 percent bonds dated December 31, 2010, for $297,000 cash. Interest is paid June 30 and December 31. The investment is classified as a held-to-maturity security.

31 Made an adjusting entry to record the current fair value of the Dynamo bonds. At December 31, the market value was $216,000.

2011

June 30 Received the semiannual interest payment from Dynamo and amortized the bond premium.

30 Received the semiannual interest payment from Link and amortized the bond discount (straight-line method).

July 1 Sold the Dynamo bonds for $216,500.

Oct. 31 Purchased $60,000 face value of Taxco, Inc.'s 5-year, 8 percent bonds dated October 31, 2011, for $60,500. Interest is paid April 30 and October 31. The investment is classified as a trading security.

Dec. 31 Received the semiannual interest payment from Link and amortized the bond discount.

31 Made an adjusting entry to record interest earned on the investment in Taxco bonds.

31 Made an adjusting entry to record the current fair value of the Taxco bonds. At December 31, the market value of the bonds was $59,200.

31 Made an adjusting entry to eliminate balances in the Fair Value Adjustment to Bond Investment account and the Unrealized Gain/Loss on Investments (Equity) account.

**Required**

Prepare the journal entries to record these transactions and adjustments.

**LO3  PD-3A. Stock Investment Journal Entries**

The following transactions and adjustments relate to stock investments made by Steen Corporation:

2010

July 1 Purchased 1,000 shares of Polk, Inc.'s common stock for $66,200 cash. The investment is noninfluential and noncontrolling and is classified as a trading security.

Oct. 1 Purchased 3,000 shares of Wynn, Inc.'s common stock for $78,000 cash and 2,000 shares of Maple, Inc.'s common stock for $64,000 cash. These investments are noninfluential and noncontrolling and are classified as available-for-sale securities. (Note: Use two separate investment accounts.)

Nov. 9 Received a cash dividend of 90 cents per share on the Wynn stock.

Dec. 31 Made an adjusting entry to record the current fair value of the Polk stock. At December 31, the stock has a market value of $63.00 per share.

31 Made an adjusting entry to record the current fair value of the Wynn and Maple stocks. At December 31, the Wynn stock has a market value of $27.50 per share and the Maple stock has a market value of $31.00 per share. (*Note:* Make one adjusting entry for the portfolio of available-for-sale stocks.)

2011

Feb. 1 Sold the Polk stock for $62 per share.

Dec. 31 Made an adjusting entry to record the current fair value of the Wynn and Maple stocks. At December 31, 2011, the per-share market values are Wynn, $30.00, and Maple, $33.00. (*Note:* Be sure to allow for the adjustment made at December 31.)

**Required**

Prepare the journal entries to record these transactions and adjustments.

**PD-4A.** **Contrasting Journal Entries for Stock Investments: Trading and Equity Methods** LO3

On January 2, 2010, Trubek Corporation purchased 10,000 shares of Forge Company common stock for $15 per share, including commissions and taxes. On December 31, 2010, Forge announced its net income of $80,000 for the year and paid a dividend of $1.10 per share. At December 31, 2010, the market value of Forge's stock was $19 per share. Trubek received its dividend on December 31, 2010.

**Required**

*a.* Assume that the stock acquired by Trubek represents 15 percent of Forge's voting stock and is classified as a trading security. Prepare all journal entries appropriate for this investment.

*b.* Assume that the stock acquired by Trubek represents 25 percent of Forge's voting stock. Prepare all journal entries appropriate for this investment.

**PD-5A.** **Recording Influential Securities** LO3

At the beginning of the year, the Carlton and United Brewery (CUB) of Melbourne, Australia, purchased a 30 percent ownership interest in Icehouse Brewery of Brisbane, Australia. The investment cost $30 million. At year-end, Icehouse Brewery declared and paid cash dividends to shareholders totaling $800,000, after reporting earnings of $5 million.

**Required**

*a.* Calculate the income statement effect of CUB's investment in Icehouse Brewery as of year-end.

*b.* Calculate the book value of CUB's equity investment in Icehouse Brewery at year-end.

*c.* Calculate the book value of CUB's equity investment in Icehouse Brewery at year-end assuming that Icehouse reported a loss of $3 million instead of a profit of $5 million and still paid its dividend of $800,000.

**PD-6A.** **Accounting for Equity Securities** LO3

Susan Company has the following securities in its portfolio on December 31, 2011:

| | | Market Values | |
| --- | --- | --- | --- |
| | Cost | Dec. 31, 2011 | Dec. 31, 2010 |
| 5,000 shares of Answa Corp. .................... | $60,000 | $58,000 | $ 0 |
| 10,000 shares of Smiler Co. .................... | 80,000 | 85,300 | 88,400 |

Additional information:

- Susan is not able to exercise significant influence over either of the investments.
- The Smiler Company securities were purchased at the beginning of 2010 and the appropriate year-end adjustments were made at the end of that year. Susan intends to hold the Smiler stock for long-term growth.
- The investment in Answa Corp. was in anticipation of a quick sale during February of 2012.
- During 2011, Susan received cash dividends of $700 from Smiler Corp.

**Required**

a. How will each of the two securities be accounted for by Susan Company? Justify your choices.

b. Prepare a partial balance sheet and partial income statement at December 31, 2011, which reflect the transactions provided.

# PROBLEMS—SET B

**LO3**  **PD-1B.**  **The Analysis of Stock Investments**

The Discovery Company began operations in 2010, and by year-end (December 31), had made six stock investments. Year-end information on these stock investments follows:

| Company | Cost or Equity (as appropriate) | Year-End Market Value | Classification |
|---|---|---|---|
| Lisle, Inc. | $ 68,000 | $ 65,300 | Trading |
| Owl, Inc. | $162,500 | $160,000 | Trading |
| Bionamic, Inc. | $197,000 | $192,000 | Available for sale |
| Foote, Inc. | $157,000 | $154,700 | Available for sale |
| Buckley, Inc. | $100,000 | $102,400 | Influential |
| Riccer, Inc. | $136,000 | $133,200 | Influential |

**Required**

a. At what total amount will the trading stock investments be reported on the December 31 balance sheet?

b. At what total amount will the available-for-sale stock investments be reported on the December 31 balance sheet?

c. At what total amount will the influential stock investments be reported on the December 31 balance sheet?

d. What total amount of unrealized holding gains or unrealized holding losses related to stock investments will appear on the income statement?

e. What total amount of unrealized holding gains or unrealized holding losses related to stock investments will appear in the stockholders' equity section of the December 31 balance sheet?

f. What total amount of fair value adjustment to stock investments will appear on the December 31 balance sheet? Which category of stock investments does the fair value adjustment relate to? Does the fair value adjustment increase or decrease the financial statement presentation of these stock investments?

**LO2**  **PD-2B.**  **Bond Investment Journal Entries**

The following transactions and adjustments relate to bond investments acquired by Jackson Corporation:

2010

June 30   Purchased $100,000 face value of Alamo, Inc.'s 20-year, 7 percent bonds dated June 30, 2010, for $97,200 cash. Interest is paid December 31 and June 30. The investment is classified as an available-for-sale security.

Dec. 31   Received the semiannual interest payment from Alamo and amortized the bond discount (straight-line method).

31   Purchased $300,000 face value of Lyme, Inc.'s 10-year, 8 percent bonds dated December 31, 2010, for $304,000 cash. Interest is paid June 30 and December 31. The investment is classified as a held-to-maturity security.

31   Made an adjusting entry to record the current fair value of the Alamo bonds. At December 31, the market value was $96,400.

2011
June 30   Received the semiannual interest payment from Alamo and amortized the bond discount.

30   Received the semiannual interest payment from Lyme and amortized the bond premium (straight-line method).

July  1   Sold the Alamo bonds for $96,500.

Oct. 31   Purchased $80,000 face value of Weir, Inc.'s 5-year, 7.57 percent bonds dated October 31, 2011, for $79,000. Interest is paid April 30 and October 31. The investment is classified as a trading security.

Dec. 31   Received the semiannual interest payment from Lyme and amortized the bond premium.

31   Made an adjusting entry to record interest earned on investment in the Weir bonds.

31   Made an adjusting entry to record the current fair value of Weir bonds. At December 31, the market value of the bonds was $79,900.

31   Made an adjusting entry to eliminate balances in the Fair Value Adjustment to Bond Investment account and the Unrealized Gain/Loss on Investments (Equity) account.

### Required

Prepare the journal entries to record these transactions and adjustments.

**PD-3B.   Stock Investment Journal Entries**                                                      LO3

The following transactions and adjustments relate to stock investments made by Kramer Corporation:

2010
July  1   Purchased 2,000 shares of Cook, Inc.'s common stock for $96,200 cash. The investment is noninfluential and noncontrolling and is classified as a trading security.

Oct.  1   Purchased 1,000 shares of Fox, Inc.'s common stock for $28,000 cash and 5,000 shares of Dent, Inc.'s common stock for $75,000 cash. These investments are noninfluential and noncontrolling and are classified as available-for-sale securities. (Note: Use two separate investment accounts.)

Nov.  9   Received a cash dividend of 70 cents per share on the Dent stock.

Dec. 31   Made an adjusting entry to record the current fair value of the Cook stock. At December 31, the stock has a market value of $50.50 per share.

31   Made an adjusting entry to record the current fair values of the Fox and Dent stocks. At December 31, the Fox stock has a market value of $26.25 per share and the Dent stock has a market value of $14.00 per share. (Note: Make one adjusting entry for the portfolio of available-for-sale stocks.)

2011
Feb.  1   Sold the Cook stock for $52 per share.

Dec. 31   Made an adjusting entry to record the current fair values of Fox and Dent stocks. At December 31, the per-share market values are Fox, $25.00, and Dent, $12.00. (Note: Be sure to allow for the adjustment made at December 31.)

### Required

Prepare the journal entries to record these transactions and adjustments.

**PD-4B.   Contrasting Journal Entries for Stock Investments: Trading and Equity Methods**       LO3

On January 2, 2010, Clemens, Inc., purchased 20,000 shares of Baer, Inc.'s common stock for $21 per share, including commissions and taxes. On December 31, 2010, Baer announced its net income of $280,000 for the year and paid a dividend of 80 cents per share. At December 31, 2010, the market value of Baer's stock was $18 per share. Clemens received its dividend on December 31, 2010.

**Required**

a. Assume that the stock acquired by Clemens represents 10 percent of Baer's voting stock and is classified as a trading security. Prepare all journal entries appropriate for this investment.

b. Assume that the stock acquired by Clemens represents 40 percent of Baer's voting stock. Prepare all journal entries appropriate for this investment.

**LO3 PD-5B. Recording Influential Securities**

At the beginning of the year, the Frederick and Prince Brewery (FPB) of Auckland, New Zealand, purchased a 40 percent ownership interest in Flanagan Brewery of Belfast, Ireland. The investment cost $40 million. At year-end, Flanagan Brewery declared and paid cash dividends to shareholders totaling $1,200,000, after reporting earnings of $7 million.

**Required**

a. Calculate the income statement effect of FPB's investment in Flanagan Brewery as of year-end.

b. Calculate the book value of FPB's equity investment in Flanagan Brewery at year-end.

c. Calculate the book value of FPB's equity investment in Flanagan Brewery at year-end assuming that Flanagan reported a loss of $4 million instead of a profit of $7 million and still paid its dividend of $1,200,000.

**LO3 PD-6B. Accounting for Equity Securities**

Sally Company has the following securities in its portfolio on December 31, 2011:

| | | Market Values | |
|---|---|---|---|
| | Cost | Dec. 31, 2011 | Dec. 31, 2010 |
| 5,000 shares of Peach Corp. . . . . . . . . . . . . . . . . . . . . | $ 90,000 | $ 85,000 | $      0 |
| 10,000 shares of Gordon Co. . . . . . . . . . . . . . . . . . . . | 120,000 | 130,300 | 133,400 |

Additional information:

- Sally is not able to exercise significant influence over either of the investments.
- The Gordon Company securities were purchased at the beginning of 2010 and the appropriate year-end adjustments were made at the end of that year. Sally intends to hold the Gordon stock for long-term growth.
- The investment in Peach Corp. was in anticipation of a quick sale during February of 2012.
- During 2011, Sally received cash dividends of $900 from Peach Corp.

**Required**

a. How will each of the two securities be accounted for by Sally Company? Justify your choices.

b. Prepare a balance sheet and partial income statement at December 31, 2011, which reflects the transactions provided.

## ANSWERS TO SELF-STUDY QUESTIONS

1. b, (p. D-6)  2. c, (p. D-9)  3. b, (p. D-9)  4. d, (p. D-3)  5. a, (p. D-10)  6. b, (p. D-10)
7. c, (p. D-3)  8. c, (p. D-4)  9. a, (p. D-9)  10. b, (p. D-9)  11. c, (p. D-6)  12. b, (p. D-12)
13. a, (p. D-3)

# E

# Accounting and the Time Value of Money

## LEARNING OBJECTIVES

1 **Describe** the nature of interest and **distinguish** between simple and compound interest. (p. E-2)

2 **Calculate** future values. (p. E-3)

3 **Calculate** present values. (p. E-6)

4 **Calculate** the present value of a bond and a capital lease. (p. E-10)

5 **Determine** the time value of money using a calculator. (p. E-13)

6 **Determine** the time value of money using a spreadsheet. (p. E-15)

In this appendix, we explain the time value of money concepts of future and present values. We then use these concepts to calculate the value of a bond payable and of a lease. Three alternate methods of calculation are illustrated: (1) the use of present value tables, (2) the use of a financial calculator, and (3) the use of an Excel spreadsheet.

## TIME VALUE OF MONEY CONCEPT

Would you rather receive a dollar now or a dollar one year from now? Most persons would answer "a dollar now." Intuition tells us that a dollar received now is more valuable than the same amount received sometime in the future. Sound reasons exist, however, for choosing the option of receiving the money sooner rather than later, the most obvious of which concerns risk. Because the future is always uncertain, some event may prevent you from receiving the dollar at a later date. To avoid this risk, we choose the earlier date.

A second reason for choosing the earlier date is that the dollar has a **time value**—that is, the dollar received now could be invested such that one year from now, you could have not only the original dollar but also the interest income on the dollar for the past year. **Interest** is a payment for the use of money, much like a rent payment for the use of an apartment. Interest is calculated by multiplying an interest rate, usually stated as an annual rate, by a principal amount for a period of time. The **principal** amount represents the amount to be repaid. The amount of interest can be computed as either a simple interest amount or a compound interest amount.

### Time Value of Money: Simple Interest Model

**Simple interest** involves calculating interest on only the principal amount owed without considering any interest already earned. Simple interest is calculated using the following well-known formula:

$$\textbf{Interest} = \textbf{p} \times \textbf{i} \times \textbf{n}$$

where

  p = principal (total amount)
  i = interest rate for one period
  n = time (number of periods)

For example, if you borrow $3,000 for four years at a simple interest rate of six percent annually, the amount of simple interest would total $720, calculated as $3,000 × .06 × 4.

### Time Value of Money: Compound Interest Model

**Compound interest** differs from simple interest because it is calculated on both the principal and any previously earned interest that has not been paid. In other words, compound interest involves computing interest on interest, along with the principal amount.

As we can see in Exhibit E-1, simple interest only uses the original $3,000 principal to compute the annual interest in each of the four years. In contrast, compound interest uses the entire principal balance, including both the original $3,000 principal and the accumulated interest to date, to compute the next year's interest. This results in increasing interest each year, with the result in Exhibit E-1 for compound interest yielding a larger ending balance by $67.43.

Because almost all businesses use compound interest, we will assume the use of compound interest in all of the illustrations in this appendix. Simple interest is generally only used in short-term credit arrangements, typically lasting less than a year.

| **EXHIBIT E-1** | Illustration Comparing Simple Interest to Compound Interest | | | | | | |
|---|---|---|---|---|---|---|---|
| | **Simple Interest Model** | | | | **Compound Interest Model** | | |
| | Interest Calculation | Simple Interest | Principal Balance | | Interest Calculation | Compound Interest | Principal Balance |
| Year 1 ..... | $3,000.00 × 6% | $180.00 | $3,180.00 | | $3,000.00 × 6% | $180.00 | $3,180.00 |
| Year 2 ..... | $3,000.00 × 6% | $180.00 | $3,360.00 | | $3,180.00 × 6% | $190.80 | $3,370.80 |
| Year 3 ..... | $3,000.00 × 6% | $180.00 | $3,540.00 | | $3,370.80 × 6% | $202.25 | $3,573.05 |
| Year 4 ..... | $3,000.00 × 6% | $180.00 | $3,720.00 | | $3,573.05 × 6% | $214.38 | $3,787.43 |
| | | $720.00 | → $67.43 variance ← | | | $787.43 | |

# FUTURE VALUE OF AN AMOUNT

The **future value** of a single sum is the amount that a specified investment will be worth at a future date if invested at a given rate of compound interest. For example, suppose that we decide to invest $6,000 in a savings account that pays six percent annual interest, and that we intend to leave the principal and interest in the account for five years. Assuming that interest is credited to the account at the end of each year, the balance in the account at the end of five years is determined using the following formula:

LEARNING OBJECTIVE 2

**Calculate** future values.

$$FV = PV \times (1 + i)^n$$

where

FV = future value of an amount
PV = present value (today's value)
 i = interest rate for one period
 n = number of periods

The future value in this case is $8,028, computed as [$6,000 × $(1.06)^5$] = ($6,000 × 1.338).

It is often easier to solve time value of money problems with the aid of a time diagram, as illustrated in Exhibit E-2. Time diagrams are drawn to show the timing of the various cash inflows and outflows. Note in Exhibit E-2 that our initial $6,000 cash inflow (the amount deposited in a savings account) allows us to remove $8,028 (a cash outflow) at the end of five years.

| **EXHIBIT E-2** | Solving Future Values with the Aid of a Time Diagram |
|---|---|

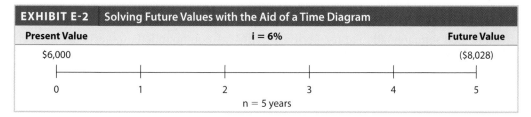

We can also calculate the future value of a single amount with the use of a table like Table I, which presents the future value of a single dollar after a given number of time periods. Simply stated, future value tables provide a multiplier for many combinations of time periods and interest rates that, when applied to the dollar amount of a present value, determines its future value.

| TABLE I | Future Value of $1 | | | | | | | | | | | |
|---|---|---|---|---|---|---|---|---|---|---|---|---|
| **Period** | **1%** | **2%** | **3%** | **4%** | **5%** | **6%** | **7%** | **8%** | **9%** | **10%** | **11%** | **12%** |
| 1 | 1.010 | 1.020 | 1.030 | 1.040 | 1.050 | 1.060 | 1.070 | 1.080 | 1.090 | 1.100 | 1.110 | 1.120 |
| 2 | 1.020 | 1.040 | 1.061 | 1.082 | 1.103 | 1.124 | 1.145 | 1.166 | 1.188 | 1.210 | 1.232 | 1.254 |
| 3 | 1.030 | 1.061 | 1.093 | 1.125 | 1.158 | 1.191 | 1.225 | 1.260 | 1.295 | 1.331 | 1.368 | 1.405 |
| 4 | 1.041 | 1.082 | 1.126 | 1.170 | 1.216 | 1.262 | 1.311 | 1.360 | 1.412 | 1.464 | 1.518 | 1.574 |
| 5 | 1.051 | 1.104 | 1.159 | 1.217 | 1.276 | 1.338 | 1.403 | 1.469 | 1.539 | 1.611 | 1.685 | 1.762 |
| 6 | 1.062 | 1.126 | 1.194 | 1.265 | 1.340 | 1.419 | 1.501 | 1.587 | 1.677 | 1.772 | 1.870 | 1.974 |
| 7 | 1.072 | 1.149 | 1.230 | 1.316 | 1.407 | 1.504 | 1.606 | 1.714 | 1.828 | 1.949 | 2.076 | 2.211 |
| 8 | 1.083 | 1.172 | 1.267 | 1.369 | 1.477 | 1.594 | 1.718 | 1.851 | 1.993 | 2.144 | 2.305 | 2.476 |
| 9 | 1.094 | 1.195 | 1.305 | 1.423 | 1.551 | 1.689 | 1.838 | 1.999 | 2.172 | 2.358 | 2.558 | 2.773 |
| 10 | 1.105 | 1.219 | 1.344 | 1.480 | 1.629 | 1.791 | 1.967 | 2.159 | 2.367 | 2.594 | 2.839 | 3.106 |
| 11 | 1.116 | 1.243 | 1.384 | 1.539 | 1.710 | 1.898 | 2.105 | 2.332 | 2.580 | 2.853 | 3.152 | 3.479 |
| 12 | 1.127 | 1.268 | 1.426 | 1.601 | 1.796 | 2.012 | 2.252 | 2.518 | 2.813 | 3.138 | 3.498 | 3.896 |
| 13 | 1.138 | 1.294 | 1.469 | 1.665 | 1.886 | 2.133 | 2.410 | 2.720 | 3.066 | 3.452 | 3.883 | 4.363 |
| 14 | 1.149 | 1.319 | 1.513 | 1.732 | 1.980 | 2.261 | 2.579 | 2.937 | 3.342 | 3.797 | 4.310 | 4.887 |
| 15 | 1.161 | 1.346 | 1.558 | 1.801 | 2.079 | 2.397 | 2.759 | 3.172 | 3.642 | 4.177 | 4.785 | 5.474 |
| 16 | 1.173 | 1.373 | 1.605 | 1.873 | 2.183 | 2.540 | 2.952 | 3.426 | 3.970 | 4.595 | 5.311 | 6.130 |
| 17 | 1.184 | 1.400 | 1.653 | 1.948 | 2.292 | 2.693 | 3.159 | 3.700 | 4.328 | 5.054 | 5.895 | 6.866 |
| 18 | 1.196 | 1.428 | 1.702 | 2.026 | 2.407 | 2.854 | 3.380 | 3.996 | 4.717 | 5.560 | 6.544 | 7.690 |
| 19 | 1.208 | 1.457 | 1.754 | 2.107 | 2.527 | 3.026 | 3.617 | 4.316 | 5.142 | 6.116 | 7.263 | 8.613 |
| 20 | 1.220 | 1.486 | 1.806 | 2.191 | 2.653 | 3.207 | 3.870 | 4.661 | 5.604 | 6.727 | 8.062 | 9.646 |
| 25 | 1.282 | 1.641 | 2.094 | 2.666 | 3.386 | 4.292 | 5.427 | 6.848 | 8.623 | 10.835 | 13.585 | 17.000 |
| 30 | 1.348 | 1.811 | 2.427 | 3.243 | 4.322 | 5.743 | 7.612 | 10.063 | 13.268 | 17.449 | 22.892 | 29.960 |
| 35 | 1.417 | 2.000 | 2.814 | 3.946 | 5.516 | 7.686 | 10.677 | 14.785 | 20.414 | 28.102 | 38.575 | 52.800 |
| 40 | 1.489 | 2.208 | 3.262 | 4.801 | 7.040 | 10.286 | 14.974 | 21.725 | 31.409 | 45.259 | 65.001 | 93.051 |
| 50 | 1.645 | 2.692 | 4.384 | 7.107 | 11.467 | 18.420 | 29.457 | 46.902 | 74.358 | 117.391 | 184.565 | 289.002 |

Future value tables are used as follows. First, determine the number of interest compounding periods involved (five years compounded annually are five periods, five years compounded semiannually are ten periods, five years compounded quarterly are 20 periods, and so on). The extreme left-hand column indicates the number of periods covered in the table.

Next, determine the interest rate per compounding period. Note that interest rates are usually quoted on an annual or *per year* basis. Therefore, only in the case of annual compounding is the quoted interest rate the interest rate per compounding period. In other cases, the rate per compounding period is the annual rate divided by the number of compounding periods in a year. For example, an interest rate of ten percent per year would be ten percent for one compounding period if compounded annually, five percent for two compounding periods if compounded semiannually, and 2 ½ percent for four compounding periods if compounded quarterly.

Locate the factor that is to the right of the appropriate number of compounding periods and beneath the appropriate interest rate per compounding period. Multiply this factor by the number of dollars involved.

Note the logical progression among the various multipliers in Table I. All values are 1.0 or greater because the future value is always greater than the $1 present amount if the interest rate is greater than zero. Also, as the interest rate increases (moving from left to right in the table) or the number of periods increases (moving from top to bottom), the multipliers become larger.

Continuing with our example of calculating the future value of a $6,000 savings account deposit earning 6 percent annual compound interest for five years, and using the multipliers from Table I, we solve for the future value of the deposit as follows:

$$\textbf{Principal} \quad \times \quad \textbf{Factor} \quad = \quad \textbf{Future Value}$$
$$\textbf{\$6,000} \quad \times \quad \textbf{1.338} \quad = \quad \textbf{\$8,028}$$

The factor 1.338 is in the row for five periods and the column for six percent.

Suppose, instead, that the interest is credited to the savings account semiannually rather than annually. In this situation, there are ten compounding periods, and we use a three percent rate (one-half the annual rate). The future value calculation using the Table I multipliers is as follows:

$$\textbf{Principal} \quad \times \quad \textbf{Factor} \quad = \quad \textbf{Future Value}$$
$$\textbf{\$6,000} \quad \times \quad \textbf{1.344} \quad = \quad \textbf{\$8,064}$$

# FUTURE VALUE OF AN ANNUITY

Using future value tables like Table I, we can calculate the future value of any single future cash flow or series of future cash flows. One frequent pattern of cash flows, however, is subject to a more convenient calculation. This pattern, known as an **annuity**, can be described as *equal amounts equally spaced over a period.*

For example, assume that $100 is to be deposited at the end of each of the next three years as an annuity into a savings account. When annuity cash flows occur at the end of each period, the annuity is called an **ordinary annuity**. As shown below in Exhibit E-3, the future value of this ordinary annuity can be calculated from Table I by calculating the future value of each of the three individual deposits and summing them (assuming eight percent annual interest).

**EXHIBIT E-3** | Future Value of an Ordinary Annuity

| Future Deposits (ordinary annuity) | | | | PV Multiplier (Table I) | | Future Value |
|---|---|---|---|---|---|---|
| Year 1 | Year 2 | Year 3 | | | | |
| $100 | | | × | 1.166 | = | $116.60 |
| | $100 | | × | 1.080 | = | 108.00 |
| | | $100 | × | 1.000 | = | 100.00 |
| | | | | Total future value............. | | $324.60 |

| Present Value | | | Future Value |
|---|---|---|---|
| | $100 | $100 | $100 |
| 0 | 1 | 2 | 3 |

Table II, on the other hand, provides a single multiplier for calculating the future value of a series of future cash flows that reflect an ordinary annuity. Referring to Table II in the three periods row and the eight percent interest column, we see that the multiplier is 3.246. When applied to the $100 annuity amount, the multiplier gives a future value of $324.60, or $100 × 3.246. As shown above, the same future value is derived from the several multipliers of Table I. For annuities of 5, 10, or 20 years, numerous calculations are avoided by using annuity tables like Table II.

| TABLE II | Future Value of an Ordinary Annuity of $1 per period | | | | | | | | | | | |
|---|---|---|---|---|---|---|---|---|---|---|---|---|
| Period | 1% | 2% | 3% | 4% | 5% | 6% | 7% | 8% | 9% | 10% | 11% | 12% |
| 1 | 1.000 | 1.000 | 1.000 | 1.000 | 1.000 | 1.000 | 1.000 | 1.000 | 1.000 | 1.000 | 1.000 | 1.000 |
| 2 | 2.010 | 2.020 | 2.030 | 2.040 | 2.050 | 2.060 | 2.070 | 2.080 | 2.090 | 2.100 | 2.110 | 2.120 |
| 3 | 3.030 | 3.060 | 3.091 | 3.122 | 3.153 | 3.184 | 3.215 | 3.246 | 3.278 | 3.310 | 3.342 | 3.374 |
| 4 | 4.060 | 4.122 | 4.184 | 4.246 | 4.310 | 4.375 | 4.440 | 4.506 | 4.573 | 4.641 | 4.710 | 4.779 |
| 5 | 5.101 | 5.204 | 5.309 | 5.416 | 5.526 | 5.637 | 5.751 | 5.867 | 5.985 | 6.105 | 6.228 | 6.353 |
| 6 | 6.152 | 6.308 | 6.468 | 6.633 | 6.802 | 6.975 | 7.153 | 7.336 | 7.523 | 7.716 | 7.913 | 8.115 |
| 7 | 7.214 | 7.434 | 7.662 | 7.898 | 8.142 | 8.394 | 8.654 | 8.923 | 9.200 | 9.487 | 9.783 | 10.089 |
| 8 | 8.286 | 8.583 | 8.892 | 9.214 | 9.549 | 9.897 | 10.260 | 10.637 | 11.028 | 11.436 | 11.859 | 12.300 |
| 9 | 9.369 | 9.755 | 10.159 | 10.583 | 11.027 | 11.491 | 11.978 | 12.488 | 13.021 | 13.579 | 14.164 | 14.776 |
| 10 | 10.462 | 10.950 | 11.464 | 12.006 | 12.578 | 13.181 | 13.816 | 14.487 | 15.193 | 15.937 | 16.722 | 17.549 |
| 11 | 11.567 | 12.169 | 12.808 | 13.486 | 14.207 | 14.972 | 15.784 | 16.645 | 17.560 | 18.531 | 19.561 | 20.655 |
| 12 | 12.683 | 13.412 | 14.192 | 15.026 | 15.917 | 16.870 | 17.888 | 18.977 | 20.141 | 21.384 | 22.713 | 24.133 |
| 13 | 13.809 | 14.680 | 15.618 | 16.627 | 17.713 | 18.882 | 20.141 | 21.495 | 22.953 | 24.523 | 26.212 | 28.029 |
| 14 | 14.947 | 15.974 | 17.086 | 18.292 | 19.599 | 21.015 | 22.550 | 24.215 | 26.019 | 27.975 | 30.095 | 32.393 |
| 15 | 16.097 | 17.293 | 18.599 | 20.024 | 21.579 | 23.276 | 25.129 | 27.152 | 29.361 | 31.772 | 34.405 | 37.280 |
| 16 | 17.258 | 18.639 | 20.157 | 21.825 | 23.657 | 25.673 | 27.888 | 30.324 | 33.003 | 35.950 | 39.190 | 42.753 |
| 17 | 18.430 | 20.012 | 21.762 | 23.698 | 25.840 | 28.213 | 30.840 | 33.750 | 36.974 | 40.545 | 44.501 | 48.884 |
| 18 | 19.615 | 21.412 | 23.414 | 25.645 | 28.132 | 30.906 | 33.999 | 37.450 | 41.301 | 45.599 | 50.396 | 55.750 |
| 19 | 20.811 | 22.841 | 25.117 | 27.671 | 30.539 | 33.760 | 37.379 | 41.446 | 46.018 | 51.159 | 56.939 | 63.440 |
| 20 | 22.019 | 24.297 | 26.870 | 29.778 | 33.066 | 36.786 | 40.995 | 45.762 | 51.160 | 57.275 | 64.203 | 72.052 |
| 25 | 28.243 | 32.030 | 36.459 | 41.646 | 47.727 | 54.865 | 63.249 | 73.106 | 84.701 | 98.347 | 114.41 | 133.33 |
| 30 | 34.785 | 40.568 | 47.575 | 56.085 | 66.439 | 79.058 | 94.461 | 113.28 | 136.31 | 164.49 | 199.02 | 241.33 |
| 35 | 41.660 | 49.994 | 60.462 | 73.652 | 90.320 | 111.43 | 138.24 | 172.32 | 215.71 | 271.02 | 341.59 | 431.66 |
| 40 | 48.886 | 60.402 | 75.401 | 95.026 | 120.80 | 154.76 | 199.64 | 259.06 | 337.88 | 442.59 | 581.83 | 767.09 |
| 50 | 64.463 | 84.579 | 112.80 | 152.67 | 209.35 | 290.34 | 406.53 | 573.77 | 815.08 | 1,163.9 | 1,668.8 | 2,400.0 |

If we decide to invest $50 at the end of each six months for three years at an eight percent annual rate of return, we would use the factor for 6 periods at four percent, as follows:

$$\text{Periodic Payment} \times \text{Factor} = \text{Future Value}$$
$$\$50 \times 6.633 = \$331.65$$

# PRESENT VALUE OF AN AMOUNT

LEARNING OBJECTIVE 3

**Calculate** present values.

We can generalize that (1) the right to receive an amount of money now—its **present value**—is normally worth more than the right to receive the same amount later—its future value; (2) the longer we must wait to receive an amount, the less attractive the receipt is; and (3) the difference between the present value of an amount and its future value is a function of interest (Principal × Interest Rate × Interest Time). Further, the more risk associated with any situation, the higher the appropriate interest rate.

We support these generalizations with an illustration. What amount should we accept now that would be as valuable as receiving $100 one year from now ($100 represents the future value) if the appropriate interest rate is ten percent? We recognize intuitively that with a ten percent interest rate, we should accept less than $100, or approximately $91. We base this estimate on the realization that the $100 received in the future must equal the present value (100 percent) plus ten percent interest on the present value. Thus, in our example, the $100 future receipt must be 1.10 times the present value. Dividing $100 by 1.10, we obtain a present value of $90.90. In other words, under the given conditions, we would do as well to accept $90.90 now as to wait one year and receive $100. To confirm the equality of a $90.90 payment now with a $100 payment one year later, we calculate the future value of $90.90 at ten percent for one year as follows:

$$\$90.90 \times 1.10 \times 1 \text{ year} = \$100 \text{ (rounded)}$$

Thus, we calculate the present value of a future receipt by discounting (deducting an interest factor) the future receipt back to the present at an appropriate interest rate. We present this schematically below:

| Present value $90.90 | → | Interest for one year at 10% | → | Future value ($100) |
|---|---|---|---|---|
| 0 | | | | 1 |

The formula for calculating the present value of a single amount is determined using the following formula:

$$PV = FV \times [1 \div (1 + i)^n]$$

where

PV = present value of an amount
FV = future value
  i = interest rate for one period
  n = number of periods

As can be seen from this formula, if either the time period or the interest rate is increased, the resulting present value would decrease. If more than one time period is involved, compound interest calculations are appropriate.

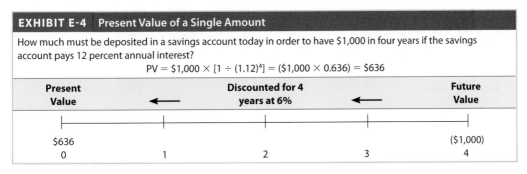

**EXHIBIT E-4    Present Value of a Single Amount**

How much must be deposited in a savings account today in order to have $1,000 in four years if the savings account pays 12 percent annual interest?
$$PV = \$1,000 \times [1 \div (1.12)^4] = (\$1,000 \times 0.636) = \$636$$

| Present Value | | Discounted for 4 years at 6% | | Future Value |
|---|---|---|---|---|
| $636 | ← | | ← | ($1,000) |
| 0 | 1 | 2 | 3 | 4 |

Tables III and IV can be used to calculate the present value amounts in a manner similar to the way we previously calculated future values using Tables I and II. As with the future value tables, present value tables provide a multiplier for many combinations of time periods and interest rates that, when applied to the dollar amount of a future cash flow or annuity, determines its present value.

(single sum)

## TABLE III    Present Value of $1

| Period | 1% | 2% | 3% | 4% | 5% | 6% | 7% | 8% | 9% | 10% | 11% | 12% |
|---|---|---|---|---|---|---|---|---|---|---|---|---|
| 1 | 0.990 | 0.980 | 0.971 | 0.962 | 0.952 | 0.943 | 0.935 | 0.926 | 0.917 | 0.909 | 0.901 | 0.893 |
| 2 | 0.980 | 0.961 | 0.943 | 0.925 | 0.907 | 0.890 | 0.873 | 0.857 | 0.842 | 0.826 | 0.812 | 0.797 |
| 3 | 0.971 | 0.942 | 0.915 | 0.889 | 0.864 | 0.840 | 0.816 | 0.794 | 0.772 | 0.751 | 0.731 | 0.712 |
| 4 | 0.961 | 0.924 | 0.888 | 0.855 | 0.823 | 0.792 | 0.763 | 0.735 | 0.708 | 0.683 | 0.659 | 0.636 |
| 5 | 0.951 | 0.906 | 0.863 | 0.822 | 0.784 | 0.747 | 0.713 | 0.681 | 0.650 | 0.621 | 0.593 | 0.567 |
| 6 | 0.942 | 0.888 | 0.837 | 0.790 | 0.746 | 0.705 | 0.666 | 0.630 | 0.596 | 0.564 | 0.535 | 0.507 |
| 7 | 0.933 | 0.871 | 0.813 | 0.760 | 0.711 | 0.665 | 0.623 | 0.583 | 0.547 | 0.513 | 0.482 | 0.452 |
| 8 | 0.923 | 0.853 | 0.789 | 0.731 | 0.677 | 0.627 | 0.582 | 0.540 | 0.502 | 0.467 | 0.434 | 0.404 |
| 9 | 0.914 | 0.837 | 0.766 | 0.703 | 0.645 | 0.592 | 0.544 | 0.500 | 0.460 | 0.424 | 0.391 | 0.361 |
| 10 | 0.905 | 0.820 | 0.744 | 0.676 | 0.614 | 0.558 | 0.508 | 0.463 | 0.422 | 0.386 | 0.352 | 0.322 |
| 11 | 0.896 | 0.804 | 0.722 | 0.650 | 0.585 | 0.527 | 0.475 | 0.429 | 0.388 | 0.350 | 0.317 | 0.287 |
| 12 | 0.887 | 0.788 | 0.701 | 0.625 | 0.557 | 0.497 | 0.444 | 0.397 | 0.356 | 0.319 | 0.286 | 0.257 |
| 13 | 0.879 | 0.773 | 0.681 | 0.601 | 0.530 | 0.469 | 0.415 | 0.368 | 0.326 | 0.290 | 0.258 | 0.229 |
| 14 | 0.870 | 0.758 | 0.661 | 0.577 | 0.505 | 0.442 | 0.388 | 0.340 | 0.299 | 0.263 | 0.232 | 0.205 |
| 15 | 0.861 | 0.743 | 0.642 | 0.555 | 0.481 | 0.417 | 0.362 | 0.315 | 0.275 | 0.239 | 0.209 | 0.183 |
| 16 | 0.853 | 0.728 | 0.623 | 0.534 | 0.458 | 0.394 | 0.339 | 0.292 | 0.252 | 0.218 | 0.188 | 0.163 |
| 17 | 0.844 | 0.714 | 0.605 | 0.513 | 0.436 | 0.371 | 0.317 | 0.270 | 0.231 | 0.198 | 0.170 | 0.146 |
| 18 | 0.836 | 0.700 | 0.587 | 0.494 | 0.416 | 0.350 | 0.296 | 0.250 | 0.212 | 0.180 | 0.153 | 0.130 |
| 19 | 0.828 | 0.686 | 0.570 | 0.475 | 0.396 | 0.331 | 0.277 | 0.232 | 0.194 | 0.164 | 0.138 | 0.116 |
| 20 | 0.820 | 0.673 | 0.554 | 0.456 | 0.377 | 0.312 | 0.258 | 0.215 | 0.178 | 0.149 | 0.124 | 0.104 |
| 25 | 0.780 | 0.610 | 0.478 | 0.375 | 0.295 | 0.233 | 0.184 | 0.146 | 0.116 | 0.092 | 0.074 | 0.059 |
| 30 | 0.742 | 0.552 | 0.412 | 0.308 | 0.231 | 0.174 | 0.131 | 0.099 | 0.075 | 0.057 | 0.044 | 0.033 |
| 35 | 0.706 | 0.500 | 0.355 | 0.253 | 0.181 | 0.130 | 0.094 | 0.068 | 0.049 | 0.036 | 0.026 | 0.019 |
| 40 | 0.672 | 0.453 | 0.307 | 0.208 | 0.142 | 0.097 | 0.067 | 0.046 | 0.032 | 0.022 | 0.015 | 0.011 |
| 50 | 0.608 | 0.372 | 0.228 | 0.141 | 0.087 | 0.054 | 0.034 | 0.021 | 0.013 | 0.009 | 0.005 | 0.003 |

---

**EXHIBIT E-5**    Present Value of a Single Amount Using Present Value Tables

Calculate the present value of $1,000 four years hence, at twelve percent interest compounded annually:
  Number of periods (one year, annually) = 4
  Interest rate per period (12%/1) = 12%
  Multiplier = 0.636
  Present value = $100.00 × 0.636 = $636
  (This result agrees with our earlier illustration.)
Calculate the present value of $116.99 two years hence, at eight percent compounded semiannually:
  Number of periods (two years, semiannually) = 4
  Interest rate per period (8%/2) = 4%
  Multiplier = 0.855
  Present value = $116.99 × 0.855 = $100 (rounded)

## PRESENT VALUE OF AN ANNUITY

We can also use present value tables like Table III to calculate the present value of any single future cash flow or series of future cash flows. For example, assume $100 is to be received at the end of each of the next three years as an annuity. As shown below, the present value of this ordinary annuity can be calculated from Table III by calculating the present value of each of the three individual receipts and summing them (assuming five percent annual interest).

| Future Receipts (ordinary annuity) | | | | PV Multiplier (Table I) | | Future Value |
|---|---|---|---|---|---|---|
| Year 1 | Year 2 | Year 3 | | | | |
| $100 | | | × | 0.952 | = | $ 95.20 |
| | $100 | | × | 0.907 | = | 90.70 |
| | | $100 | × | 0.864 | = | 86.40 |
| | | | | Total present value............ | | $272.30 |

Table IV, on the other hand, provides a single multiplier for calculating the present value of a series of future cash flows that represent an ordinary annuity. Referring to Table IV in the three periods row and the five percent interest column, we see that the multiplier is 2.723. When applied to the $100 annuity amount, the multiplier gives a present value of $272.30.

(*interest payment*)

| TABLE IV | Present Value of an Ordinary Annuity of $1 per period | | | | | | | | | | | |
|---|---|---|---|---|---|---|---|---|---|---|---|---|
| Period | 1% | 2% | 3% | 4% | 5% | 6% | 7% | 8% | 9% | 10% | 11% | 12% |
| 1 | 0.990 | 0.980 | 0.971 | 0.962 | 0.952 | 0.943 | 0.935 | 0.926 | 0.917 | 0.909 | 0.901 | 0.893 |
| 2 | 1.970 | 1.942 | 1.913 | 1.886 | 1.859 | 1.833 | 1.808 | 1.783 | 1.759 | 1.736 | 1.713 | 1.690 |
| 3 | 2.941 | 2.884 | 2.829 | 2.775 | 2.723 | 2.673 | 2.624 | 2.577 | 2.531 | 2.487 | 2.444 | 2.402 |
| 4 | 3.902 | 3.808 | 3.717 | 3.630 | 3.546 | 3.465 | 3.387 | 3.312 | 3.240 | 3.170 | 3.102 | 3.037 |
| 5 | 4.853 | 4.713 | 4.580 | 4.452 | 4.329 | 4.212 | 4.100 | 3.993 | 3.890 | 3.791 | 3.696 | 3.605 |
| 6 | 5.795 | 5.601 | 5.417 | 5.242 | 5.076 | 4.917 | 4.767 | 4.623 | 4.486 | 4.355 | 4.231 | 4.111 |
| 7 | 6.728 | 6.472 | 6.230 | 6.002 | 5.786 | 5.582 | 5.389 | 5.206 | 5.033 | 4.868 | 4.712 | 4.564 |
| 8 | 7.652 | 7.325 | 7.020 | 6.733 | 6.463 | 6.210 | 5.971 | 5.747 | 5.535 | 5.335 | 5.146 | 4.968 |
| 9 | 8.566 | 8.162 | 7.786 | 7.435 | 7.108 | 6.802 | 6.515 | 6.247 | 5.995 | 5.759 | 5.537 | 5.328 |
| 10 | 9.471 | 8.983 | 8.530 | 8.111 | 7.722 | 7.360 | 7.024 | 6.710 | 6.418 | 6.145 | 5.889 | 5.650 |
| 11 | 10.368 | 9.787 | 9.253 | 8.760 | 8.306 | 7.887 | 7.499 | 7.139 | 6.805 | 6.495 | 6.207 | 5.938 |
| 12 | 11.255 | 10.575 | 9.954 | 9.385 | 8.863 | 8.384 | 7.943 | 7.536 | 7.161 | 6.814 | 6.492 | 6.194 |
| 13 | 12.134 | 11.348 | 10.635 | 9.986 | 9.394 | 8.853 | 8.358 | 7.904 | 7.487 | 7.103 | 6.750 | 6.424 |
| 14 | 13.004 | 12.106 | 11.296 | 10.563 | 9.899 | 9.295 | 8.745 | 8.244 | 7.786 | 7.367 | 6.982 | 6.628 |
| 15 | 13.865 | 12.849 | 11.938 | 11.118 | 10.380 | 9.712 | 9.108 | 8.559 | 8.061 | 7.606 | 7.191 | 6.811 |
| 16 | 14.718 | 13.578 | 12.561 | 11.652 | 10.838 | 10.106 | 9.447 | 8.851 | 8.313 | 7.824 | 7.379 | 6.974 |
| 17 | 15.562 | 14.292 | 13.166 | 12.166 | 11.274 | 10.477 | 9.763 | 9.122 | 8.544 | 8.022 | 7.549 | 7.120 |
| 18 | 16.398 | 14.992 | 13.754 | 12.659 | 11.690 | 10.828 | 10.059 | 9.372 | 8.756 | 8.201 | 7.702 | 7.250 |
| 19 | 17.226 | 15.678 | 14.324 | 13.134 | 12.085 | 11.158 | 10.336 | 9.604 | 8.950 | 8.365 | 7.839 | 7.366 |
| 20 | 18.046 | 16.351 | 14.877 | 13.590 | 12.462 | 11.470 | 10.594 | 9.818 | 9.129 | 8.514 | 7.963 | 7.469 |
| 25 | 22.023 | 19.523 | 17.413 | 15.622 | 14.094 | 12.783 | 11.654 | 10.675 | 9.823 | 9.077 | 8.422 | 7.843 |
| 30 | 25.808 | 22.396 | 19.600 | 17.292 | 15.372 | 13.765 | 12.409 | 11.258 | 10.274 | 9.427 | 8.694 | 8.055 |
| 35 | 29.409 | 24.999 | 21.487 | 18.665 | 16.374 | 14.498 | 12.948 | 11.655 | 10.567 | 9.644 | 8.855 | 8.176 |
| 40 | 32.835 | 27.355 | 23.115 | 19.793 | 17.159 | 15.046 | 13.332 | 11.925 | 10.757 | 9.779 | 8.951 | 8.244 |
| 50 | 39.196 | 31.424 | 25.730 | 21.482 | 18.256 | 15.762 | 13.801 | 12.233 | 10.962 | 9.915 | 9.042 | 8.304 |

# BOND VALUATIONS

In Chapter 10, we explained that (1) a bond agreement specifies a pattern of future cash flows—usually a series of interest payments and a single payment at maturity equal to the face value—and that (2) bonds are sold at premiums or discounts to adjust their effective interest rates to the prevailing market rate of interest when they are issued.

Because of the role played by interest, the selling price of a bond that is necessary to yield a specific rate can be determined as follows:

❶ Use Table III to calculate the present value of the future principal repayment at the bond's effective rate of interest.

❷ Use Table IV to calculate the present value of the future series of interest payments at the bond's effective rate of interest.

❸ Add the two present value calculations obtained in steps one and two.

Exhibit E-6 illustrates the pricing of a $100,000 issue of eight percent, four-year bonds paying interest semiannually and sold on the date of issue to yield (1) eight percent, (2) ten percent, and (3) six percent. Note that the price of the eight-percent bonds sold to yield eight percent is the face (or par) value of the bonds. The bonds will sell for $93,552 to provide a yield of ten percent. And, the bonds will sell for $106,980 to provide a yield of six percent.

**EXHIBIT E-6**    Calculating Bond Issue Price Using Present Value Tables

❶ $100,000 of eight percent, four-year bonds with interest payable semiannually sold to yield eight percent:

| Future Cash Flows | Multiplier (Table III) | Multiplier (Table IV) | Present Values at 4% Semiannually |
|---|---|---|---|
| Principal repayment, $100,000 (a single amount received eight semiannual periods hence) .............................. | 0.731 | | $ 73,100 |
| Interest payments, $4,000 at end of each of eight semiannual interest periods .......... | | 6.733 | 26,900 (rounded) |
| Total present value (or issue price) of bonds ...... | | | $100,000 |

❷ $100,000 of eight percent, four-year bonds with interest payable semiannually sold to yield ten percent:

| Future Cash Flows | Multiplier (Table III) | Multiplier (Table IV) | Present Values at 5% Semiannually |
|---|---|---|---|
| Principal repayment, $100,000 (a single amount received eight semiannual periods hence) .............................. | 0.677 | | $ 67,700 |
| Interest payments, $4,000 at end of each of eight semiannual interest periods .......... | | 6.463 | 25,852 |
| Total present value (or issue price) of bonds ...... | | | $ 93,552 |

❸ $100,000 of eight percent, four-year bonds with interest payable semiannually sold to yield six percent:

| Future Cash Flows | Multiplier (Table III) | Multiplier (Table IV) | Present Values at 3% Semiannually |
|---|---|---|---|
| Principal repayment, $100,000 (a single amount received eight semiannual periods hence) .............................. | 0.789 | | $ 78,900 |
| Interest payments, $4,000 at end of each of eight semiannual interest periods .......... | | 7.020 | 28,080 |
| Total present value (or issue price) of bonds ...... | | | $106,980 |

## EFFECTIVE INTEREST METHOD OF DISCOUNT AMORTIZATION

A bond premium or discount can be amortized to interest expense using the straight-line method or the effective interest method. GAAP requires the effective interest method, except in cases where the differences between the two methods in not material. The **effective interest method** of amortization recognizes a constant percentage of the book value of a bond as interest expense for each interest payment period. For bonds issued at a discount, the book value of a bond is the balance in the Bonds Payable account less the balance in the Discount on Bonds Payable account. To obtain a period's interest expense under the effective interest method, we multiply the bond's book value at the beginning of each period by the effective interest rate. The **effective interest rate** is the market rate of interest used to price the bonds when they are originally issued. The difference between this amount and the amount of interest paid (coupon interest rate × face value of bonds) is the amount of discount amortized. When using the effective interest method of amortization, accountants often prepare an amortization schedule similar to the one in Exhibit E-7. This schedule covers the four-year life of the Reid, Inc., bonds issued at a discount.

| PRINCIPLE ALERT | Materiality Concept |
| --- | --- |

Under U.S. GAAP, the effective interest method is the preferred method of bond amortization. It is generally accepted because it uses the actual market rate of interest when the bonds were originally issued to determine the amount of the periodic amortization. The effective interest method, however, is somewhat more complex than the straight-line method. Accounting standards permit the straight-line method of amortization to be used when the results are not materially different from those achieved under the effective interest method. This exception represents an application of the *materiality concept.* As previously discussed, the materiality concept permits insignificant accounting transactions to be recorded most expediently. Here, the materiality concept permits a simpler (and, thus, more expedient) straight-line method to be used when it results in insignificant differences from the theoretically superior effective interest method.

| EXHIBIT E-7 | Bonds Sold at a Discount: Effective Interest Method |
| --- | --- |

**$100,000 of 8%, four-year bonds with interest payable semiannually issued on December 31, 2010, at $93,552 to yields 10%**

| Year | Interest Period | A<br>Interest Paid<br>(4% of face value) | B<br>Interest Expense<br>(5% of bond book value) | C<br>Periodic Amortization<br>(B − A) | D<br>Balance of Unamortized Discount<br>(D − C) | E<br>Book Value of Bonds, End of Period<br>($100,000 − D) |
| --- | --- | --- | --- | --- | --- | --- |
| At issue | | | | | $6,448 | $ 93,552 |
| 2011......... | 1 | $4,000 | $4,678 | $678 | 5,770 | 94,230 |
| | 2 | 4,000 | 4,712 | 712 | 5,058 | 94,942 |
| 2012......... | 3 | 4,000 | 4,747 | 747 | 4,311 | 95,689 |
| | 4 | 4,000 | 4,784 | 784 | 3,527 | 96,473 |
| 2013......... | 5 | 4,000 | 4,824 | 824 | 2,703 | 97,297 |
| | 6 | 4,000 | 4,865 | 865 | 1,838 | 98,162 |
| 2014......... | 7 | 4,000 | 4,908 | 908 | 930 | 99,070 |
| | 8 | 4,000 | 4,930* | 930 | 0 | 100,000 |

*Adjusted for cumulative rounding error of $24

Exhibit E-7 presents the various components for the Reid, Inc., bonds for the six-month interest payment periods. Note that the interest rates shown in columns A and B are one-half the annual rates. Column A lists the constant amounts of interest paid each six months—that is, the coupon interest rate times the face value (4 percent × $100,000). The amounts in Column B are obtained by multiplying the book value as of the beginning of each period (column E) by the 5 percent effective interest rate. For example, the $4,678 interest expense for the first period is 5 percent times $93,552; for the second period, it is 5 percent times $94,230, or $4,712, and so on. Note that the reported value of the bonds changes each period. For discounted bonds, the value increases each period because the book value increases over the life of the bonds until it reaches the face value on the maturity date. The amount of discount amortization for each period, given in column C, is the difference between the corresponding amounts in columns A and B. Column D lists the amount of unamortized discount at the end of each period.

The amounts recorded for each interest payment can be read directly from the amortization schedule. The following journal entries record the interest expense and discount amortization at the time of the first two interest payments:

| | | | |
|---|---|---:|---:|
| A = L + SE | | | |
| −4,000 +678 −4,678 Exp | | | |

**2011**

| June 30 | Bond interest expense | 4,678 | |
|---|---|---:|---:|
| | Discount on bonds payable | | 678 |
| | Cash | | 4,000 |
| | *To record semiannual interest payment and amortization of bond discount.* | | |

| | | | |
|---|---|---:|---:|
| A = L + SE | | | |
| −4,000 +712 −4,712 Exp | | | |

| Dec. 31 | Bond interest expense | 4,712 | |
|---|---|---:|---:|
| | Discount on bonds payable | | 712 |
| | Cash | | 4,000 |
| | *To record semiannual interest payment and amortization of bond discount.* | | |

Amortizing the bond discount over the four-year life of the bonds leaves a zero balance in the Discount on Bonds Payable account on the maturity date of the bonds. The retirement of the bonds is then recorded by debiting Bonds Payable and crediting Cash for $100,000, the amount of their face value.

## EFFECTIVE INTEREST METHOD OF PREMIUM AMORTIZATION

The effective interest method of amortizing a bond premium is handled the same way as a bond discount amortization. Each interest period, a constant percentage of the bonds' book value as of the beginning of the period is recognized as interest expense; the difference between the interest expense and the semiannual interest payment is the amount of the premium amortization.

Exhibit E-8 shows the amortization schedule for the four-year life of the Reid, Inc., bonds that were issued at a premium. The coupon rate of 4 percent in column A and the effective interest rate of 3 percent in column B are one-half the annual rates because the calculations are for six-month periods.

**EXHIBIT E-8** Bonds Sold at a Premium: Effective Interest Method

$100,000 of 8%, four-year bonds with interest payable semiannually issued on December 31, 2010, at $106,980 to yields 6%

| | | A | B | C | D | E |
|---|---|---|---|---|---|---|
| | | | Interest Expense | Periodic | Balance of Unamortized | Book Value of Bonds, End of |
| Year | Interest Period | Interest Paid (4% of face value) | (3% of bond book value) | Amortization (B − A) | Discount (D − C) | Period ($100,000 − D) |
| At issue | | | | | $6,980 | $106,980 |
| 2011......... | 1 | $4,000 | $3,209 | $791 | 6,189 | 106,189 |
| | 2 | 4,000 | 3,186 | 814 | 5,375 | 105,375 |
| 2012......... | 3 | 4,000 | 3,161 | 839 | 4,536 | 104,536 |
| | 4 | 4,000 | 3,136 | 864 | 3,672 | 103,672 |
| 2013......... | 5 | 4,000 | 3,110 | 890 | 2,782 | 102,782 |
| | 6 | 4,000 | 3,083 | 917 | 1,865 | 101,865 |
| 2014......... | 7 | 4,000 | 3,056 | 944 | 921 | 100,921 |
| | 8 | 4,000 | 3,079* | 921 | 0 | 100,000 |

*Adjusted for cumulative rounding error of $51

The journal entries for each interest payment may be taken directly from the amortization schedule. The entries for the first two interest payments (June 30 and December 31, 2011) follow. Note that the periodic interest expense is less than the semiannual interest payment:

| 2011 | | | | |
|---|---|---|---|---|
| June 30 | Bond interest expense | 3,209 | | |
| | Premium on bonds payable | | 791 | |
| | Cash | | 4,000 | |
| | *To record semiannual interest payment and amortization of bond premium.* | | | |

| A | = | L | + | SE |
|---|---|---|---|---|
| −4,000 | | −791 | | −3,209 Exp |

| | | | | |
|---|---|---|---|---|
| Dec. 31 | Bond interest expense | 3,186 | | |
| | Premium on bonds payable | | 814 | |
| | Cash | | 4,000 | |
| | *To record semiannual interest payment and amortization of bond premium.* | | | |

| A | = | L | + | SE |
|---|---|---|---|---|
| −4,000 | | −814 | | −3,186 Exp |

After amortizing the bond premium over the four-year life of the bonds, the balance in the Premium on Bonds Payable account is zero. When the bonds are retired at the end of four years, the journal entry to record the retirement debits Bonds Payable and credits Cash for the $100,000 face value of the bonds.

## CAPITAL LEASE VALUATION

At the time that a lessee enters into a capital lease, a leased asset and a lease liability are recorded on the lessee's books. The amount of the capitalized lease asset and lease liability is determined by calculating the present value of the future lease payments. Most lease payment schedules take the form of an annuity. The interest rate used in the calculation is usually the lessee's current interest rate on borrowed funds.

Assume, for example, that a firm leases equipment for ten years under a capital lease. Annual lease payments of $40,000 will be made at the end of each year, and the lessee's current interest rate to borrow money is 12 percent. The present value factor to be used in the calculation is for an annuity of $1 for ten periods at 12 percent. From Table IV, this factor is 5.650. The initial valuation of the capital lease, then, is calculated as follows:

| **Annual Lease Payments** | × | **Present Value Factor** | = | **Lease Valuation** |
|---|---|---|---|---|
| **$40,000** | × | **5.650** | = | **$226,000** |

# CALCULATIONS USING A CALCULATOR

While present value tables can provide a handy method to solve some time value of money problems, they are not suitable for many real world situations. For example, many real world interest rates are not even integers like those appearing in Table I through Table IV, nor are many problems limited to the number of time periods appearing in the tables. While it is still possible to solve these problems with the provided formulas, a financial calculator provides a much quicker solution. Financial calculators can be distinguished from other calculators by the presence of dedicated keys for present and future values, along with keys for the number of periods, interest rates, and annuity payments. There exists many brands of financial calculators; however, all of them work in much the same way. We will illustrate the calculation of bond issuance prices from Exhibit E-6 using a Hewlett Packard 10BII financial calculator, as illustrated in Exhibit E-9.[1]

LEARNING OBJECTIVE 5

**Determine** the time value of money using a calculator.

---

[1] It is usually necessary to do some preliminary setup on a financial calculator before performing time value of money calculations. For example, the HP 10BII calculator has a default setting of monthly compounding. This may need to be changed if the problem calls for a different number of compounding periods, such as annual. In addition, the calculator assumes annuity payments occur at the end of each period. This will need to be changed if the problem requires beginning of period payments. See your calculator manual to determine how to make these setting changes.

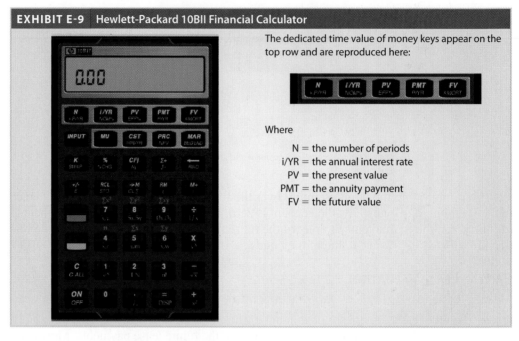

**EXHIBIT E-9** Hewlett-Packard 10BII Financial Calculator

The dedicated time value of money keys appear on the top row and are reproduced here:

Where

N = the number of periods
i/YR = the annual interest rate
PV = the present value
PMT = the annuity payment
FV = the future value

To solve a time value of money problem using a financial calculator, all that is needed is to input all of the known values and then press the key of the unknown value. Exhibit E-10 illustrates the bond value calculations from Exhibit E-6. You should not be concerned if your calculator solutions are slightly different from the solutions that you get using either the tables or the formulas. This difference is due to rounding of the future value and present value multipliers.

**EXHIBIT E-10** Calculating Bond Issue Prices Using a Financial Calculator

(1) $100,000 of eight percent, four-year bonds with interest payable semiannually sold to yield eight percent:

| Enter | | Display | | |
|---|---|---|---|---|
| 8 | N | N | = | 8 |
| 8 | I/YR | I/YR | = | 8 |
| 4,000 | PMT | PMT | = | 4,000 |
| 100,000 | FV | FV | = | 100,000 |
| Press | PV | PV | = | −100,000 |

(2) $100,000 of eight percent, four-year bonds with interest payable semiannually sold to yield ten percent:

| Enter | | Display | | |
|---|---|---|---|---|
| 8 | N | N | = | 8 |
| 10 | I/YR | I/YR | = | 10 |
| 4,000 | PMT | PMT | = | 4,000 |
| 100,000 | FV | FV | = | 100,000 |
| Press | PV | PV | = | −93,537 |

(3) $100,000 of eight percent, four-year bonds with interest payable semiannually sold to yield six percent:

| Enter | | Display | | |
|---|---|---|---|---|
| 8 | N | N | = | 8 |
| 6 | I/YR | I/YR | = | 6 |
| 4,000 | PMT | PMT | = | 4,000 |
| 100,000 | FV | FV | = | 100,000 |
| Press | PV | PV | = | −107,020 |

Note that the calculator needs to be preset to semiannual compounding.

We can also use the calculator to easily solve the capital lease problem from prior page, where a firm leases equipment for ten years under a capital lease with annual lease payments of $40,000, made at the end of each year, and the lessee's current interest rate to borrow money is 12 percent. After setting the calculator to annual compounding we input the following:

| Enter | | Display | | |
|---|---|---|---|---|
| 10 | N | N | = | 10 |
| 12 | I/YR | I/YR | = | 12 |
| 40,000 | PMT | PMT | = | 40,000 |
| 0 | FV | FV | = | 0 |
| Press | PV | PV | = | −226,009 |

Note that the calculator needs to be preset to annual compounding.

It is also possible to solve for more than just the present or future values in a time value of money problem. For example, you may need to compute the quarterly payment required for a ten-year, $100,000 note with 12 percent annual (three percent quarterly) interest (see page 466 in Chapter 10). The $4,326 payment can be solved as follows:

| Enter | | Display | | |
|---|---|---|---|---|
| 40 | N | N | = | 40 |
| 12 | I/YR | I/YR | = | 12 |
| 100,000 | PMT | PMT | = | 100,000 |
| 0 | FV | FV | = | 0 |
| Press | PMT | PV | = | −4,326 |

Note that the calculator needs to be preset to quarterly compounding.

# CALCULATIONS USING A SPREADSHEET

In addition to formulas, tables, and financial calculators, a fourth way to solve time value of money problems is with an electronic spreadsheet such as Excel. Excel has several built-in functions that allow easy calculation of time value of money problems. Depending upon your version of Excel, these functions are accessed differently. Within Excel 2010, you will go to the Insert function *fx* in the Formulas ribbon. The required functions are located under the FINANCIAL option. Below are examples of how to use Excel to solve the same problems we previously solved using a financial calculator.

LEARNING OBJECTIVE 6

**Determine** the time value of money using a spreadsheet.

## Example 1

Find the selling price (present value) of $100,000 of eight percent, four-year bonds with interest payable semiannually sold to yield eight percent.

Use the PV function and enter the values as follows:

### Example 2

Find the selling price (present value) of $100,000 of eight percent, four-year bonds with interest payable semiannually sold to yield ten percent.

Use the PV function and enter the values as follows:

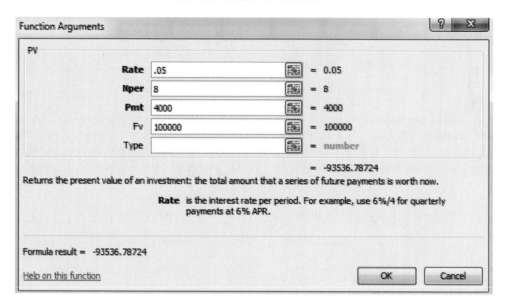

### Example 3

Find the selling price (present value) of $100,000 of eight percent, four-year bonds with interest payable semiannually sold to yield six percent.

Use the PV function and enter the values as follows:

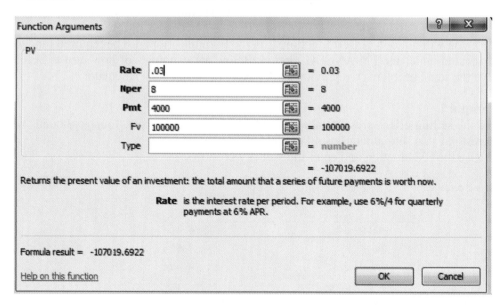

### Example 4

Find the present value of a capital lease involving a ten-year lease with annual payments of $40,000 made at the end of each year, and the lessee's current interest rate to borrow money is 12 percent.

Use the PV function and enter the values as follows:

## Example 5

Find the quarterly payment for a ten-year, $100,000 note with an annual interest rate of 12 percent (3 percent period rate).

Use the PMT function and enter the values as follows:

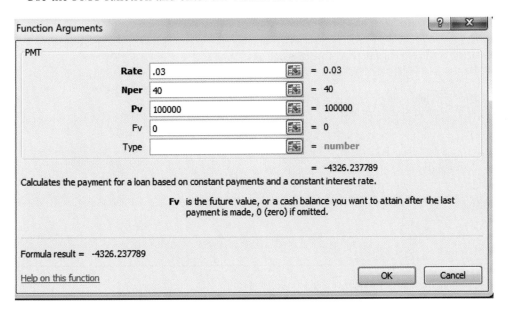

## SUMMARY OF LEARNING OBJECTIVES

**Describe the nature of interest and distinguish between simple and compound interest. (p. E-2)**    LO1

- Interest is payment for the use of money over time.
- Simple interest is computed only on the principal.
- Compound interest is computed on the accumulated principal including any earned interest that has not been paid.

**Calculate future values. (p. E-3)**    LO2

- The future value of a single sum is the amount that a specified investment will be worth at a future date if invested at a given rate of compound interest.
- The formula for calculating the future value of a single amount is $PV = FV \times (1 + i)^n$.

REVIEW

■ Future value tables provide a multiplier for many combinations of time periods and interest rates that, when applied to the dollar amount of a present value, determines its future value.

**LO3** **Calculate the present values. (p. E-6)**
■ The right to receive an amount of money now—its present value—is normally worth more than the right to receive the same amount later—its future value.
■ The formula for calculating the present value of a single amount is $PV = FV \times [1 \div (1 + i)^n]$.

**LO4** **Calculate the present value of a bond and a capital lease. (p. E-10)**
■ At the time that a lessee enters into a capital lease, a leased asset and a lease liability are recorded on the lessee's books; the amount of the capitalized lease asset and lease liability is determined by calculating the present value of the future lease payments.

**LO5** **Determine the time value of money using a calculator. (p. E-13)**
■ Financial calculators can be distinguished from other calculators by the presence of dedicated keys for present and future values, along with keys for the number of periods, interest rates, and annuity payments; there exist many brands of financial calculators; however, all of them work in much the same way.
■ To solve a time value of money problem using a financial calculator, all that is needed is to input all of the known values and then press the key of the unknown value

**LO6** **Determine the time value of money using a spreadsheet. (p. E-15)**
■ In addition to formulas, tables, and financial calculators, a fourth way to solve time value of money problems is with an electronic spreadsheet such as Excel, which has several built-in functions that allow easy calculation of time value of money problems.

## GLOSSARY OF KEY TERMS

**Annuity** A pattern of cash flows in which equal amounts are spaced equally over a number of periods (p. E-5).

**Compound interest** Interest that is computed on the accumulated principal balance plus any interest that has been earned but not yet paid (p. E-2).

**Effective interest method** A method of interest amortization that recognizes a constant percentage of the book value of a bond as interest expense for each interest payment period. (p. E-11).

**Effective interest rate** The current rate of interest in the market for a bond or other debt instrument. When issued, a bond is priced to yield the market rate of interest at the date of issuance (p. E-11).

**Future value** The amount that a specified investment (or series of investments) will be worth at a future date if invested at a given rate of compound interest (p. E-3).

**Interest** A payment for the use of money (p. E-2).

**Ordinary annuity** An annuity where the payments occur at the end of each period (p. E-5).

**Present value** The current worth of amounts to be paid (or received) in the future; calculated by discounting the future payments (or receipts) at a specified interest rate (p. E-6).

**Principal** The amount borrowed or invested (p. E-2).

**Simple interest** Interest that is calculated only on the initial principal and not on any unpaid interest (p. E-2).

**Time value of money** The concept that money can be invested at a positive interest rate and grow to a larger sum in the future (p. E-2).

## SELF-STUDY QUESTIONS

**LO2** 1. Calculate the future value of each of the following items.
    *a.* $50,000 deposited in a savings account for ten years if the annual interest rate is
       1. Twelve percent compounded annually.
       2. Twelve percent compounded semiannually.
       3. Twelve percent compounded quarterly.
    *b.* $5,000 received at the end of each year for the next ten years if the money earns interest at the rate of four percent compounded annually.
    *c.* $3,000 received semiannually for the next five years if the money earns interest at the rate of eight percent compounded semiannually.
    *d.* $1,000 deposited each year for the next ten years plus a single sum of $15,000 deposited today if the interest rate is ten percent per year compounded annually.

**LO3** 2. Calculate the present value of each of the following items.
    *a.* $90,000 ten years hence if the annual interest rate is
       1. Eight percent compounded annually.
       2. Eight percent compounded semiannually.
       3. Eight percent compounded quarterly.

b. $1,000 received at the end of each year for the next eight years if money is worth ten percent per year compounded annually.

c. $600 received at the end of each six months for the next fifteen years if the interest rate is eight percent per year compounded semiannually.

d. $500,000 inheritance ten years hence if money is worth ten percent per year compounded annually.

e. $2,500 received each half year for the next ten years plus a single sum of $85,000 at the end of ten years if the interest rate is twelve percent per year compounded semiannually.

## EXERCISES—SET A

**EE-1A.** **Simple and Compound Interest**                                                    LO1

a. For each of the following notes, calculate the simple interest due at the end of the term.

| Note | Principal | Rate | Term |
|------|-----------|------|---------|
| 1 | $10,000 | 4% | 6 years |
| 2 | $10,000 | 6% | 4 years |
| 3 | $10,000 | 8% | 3 years |

b. Compute the amount of interest due at the end of the term for each of the above notes assuming interest is compounded annually.

**EE-2A.** **Future Value Computation**                                                       LO2

At the beginning of the year you deposit $2,500 in a savings account. How much will accumulate in three years if you earn 8% compounded annually?

**EE-3A.** **Future Value Computation**                                                       LO2

You deposit $2,500 at the end of every year for three years. How much will accumulate in three years if you earn 8% compounded annually?

**EE-4A.** **Present Value Computation**                                                      LO3

You will receive $2,500 in three years. What is the present value if you can earn 8% interest compounded annually?

**EE-5A.** **Present Value Computation**                                                      LO3

You receive $2,500 at the end of every year for three years. What is the present value of these receipts if you earn 8% compounded annually?

**EE-6A.** **Future Value Computation**                                                       LO2

What amount will be accumulated in four years if $10,000 is invested today at 6% interest compounded annually?

**EE-7A.** **Present Value Computation**                                                      LO3

You are scheduled to be paid $10,000 in four years. What amount today is equivalent to the $10,000 to be received in four years assuming interest is compounded annually at 6%?

**EE-8A.** **Future Value Computation**                                                       LO2

What amount will be accumulated in four years if $10,000 is invested every six months beginning in six months and ending four years from today? Interest will accumulate at an annual rate of 10% compounded semiannually.

**EE-9A.** **Future Value Computation**                                                       LO2

You are scheduled to receive $10,000 every six months for ten periods beginning in six months. What amount in five years is equivalent to the future series of payments assuming interest compounds at the annual rate of 10% compounded semiannually?

**EE-10A.** **Present Value Computation**                                                     LO3

Zazzi, Inc., believes it will need $200,000 in seven years to expand its operations. Zazzi can earn 6%, compounded annually, if it deposits its money right now. How large of a deposit must Zazzi make in order to have the necessary $200,000 in seven years?

**EE-11A.** **Future Value Computation**                                                      LO2

Peyton Company deposited $10,000 in the bank today, earning 12% interest. Peyton plans to withdraw the money in five years. How much money will be available to withdraw assuming that interest is compounded (a) annually, (b) semiannually, and (c) quarterly?

ASSIGNMENTS

LO2 **EE-12A.** **Future Value Computation**

Sam Smith deposited $6,000 in a savings account today. The deposit will earn interest at the rate of 8%. How much will be available for Sam to withdraw in three years, assuming interest is compounded (a) annually, (b) semiannually, and (c) quarterly?

LO3 **EE-13A.** **Present Value Computation**

Pete Frost made a deposit into his savings account three years ago, and earned interest at an annual rate of 8%. The deposit accumulated to $20,000. How much was initially deposited assuming that the interest was compounded (a) annually, (b) semiannually, and (c) quarterly?

LO2 **EE-14A.** **Future Value Computation**

Kumari Jennings has decided to start saving for his daughter's college education by depositing $2,500 at the end of every year for 18 years. He has determined that he will be able to earn 5% interest compounded annually. He hopes to have at least $70,000 when his daughter starts college in eighteen years. Will his savings plan be successful?

LO3 **EE-15A.** **Present Value Computation**

Kerry Bales won the state lottery and was given four choices for receiving her winnings.

1. Receive $200,000 right now.
2. Receive $216,000 in one year.
3. Receive $40,000 at the end of each year for eight years.
4. Receive $20,000 at the end of each year for 30 years.

Assuming Kerry can earn interest of 8% compounded annually, which option should Kerry choose?

LO6 **EE-16A.** **Present Value and Payment Calculation**

Dino Evans signed a contract to buy a used car. His annual payments, due at the end of each year for three years, are $3,000. The car dealer charges interest at 12%, compounded annually in order to determine the payment amount.

*a.* What is the current selling price of the car assuming no down payment was made?
*b.* Based on the selling price determined in (a), what would the required payments be if Dino made monthly, rather than annual payments? For part (b), assume interest is compounded monthly.

LO4 **EE-17A.** **Issue Price of a Bond**

Conner Enterprises issued $100,000 of 10%, five-year bonds with interest payable semiannually. Determine the issue price if the bonds are priced to yield (a) 10%, (b) 8%, and (c) 12%.

LO4 **EE-18A.** **Present Value of a Capital Lease**

Hiller Construction Company leases equipment for six years under a capital lease. Annual lease payments of $25,000 will be made at the end of each year, and Hiller's current interest rate to borrow money is 6%. Compute the present value of the leased equipment.

LO6 **EE-19A.** **Payment Computation**

Determine the car payment that would be required if a five-year loan is used to purchase a $30,000 car. The loan terms require monthly payments and the period interest is 1% per month.

LO4 **EE-20A.** **Issue Price of a Bond**

Lunar, Inc., plans to issue $900,000 of 10% bonds that will pay interest semiannually and mature in five years. Assume that the effective interest rate is 12 percent per year compounded semiannually. Calculate the selling price of the bonds.

# Exercises—Set B

LO1 **EE-1B.** **Simple and Compound Interest**

*a.* For each of the following notes, calculate the simple interest due at the end of the term.

| Note | Principal | Rate | Term |
|------|-----------|------|------|
| 1 | $5,000 | 8% | 8 years |
| 2 | $5,000 | 12% | 5 years |
| 3 | $5,000 | 4% | 2 years |

*b.* Compute the amount of interest due at the end of the term for each of the above notes assuming interest is compounded annually.

**EE-2B.** **Future Value Computation**      LO2
At the beginning of the year you deposit $3,500 in a savings account. How much will accumulate in four years if you earn 6% compounded annually?

**EE-3B.** **Future Value Computation**      LO2
You deposit $3,500 at the end of every year for four years. How much will accumulate in four years if you earn 6% compounded annually?

**EE-4B.** **Present Value Computation**      LO3
You will receive $3,500 in four years. What is the present value if you can earn 6% interest compounded annually?

**EE-5B.** **Present Value Computation**      LO3
You receive $3,500 at the end of every year for four years. What is the present value of these receipts if you earn 6% compounded annually?

**EE-6B.** **Future Value Computation**      LO2
What amount will be accumulated in five years if $5,000 is invested today at 4% interest compounded annually?

**EE-7B.** **Present Value Computation**      LO3
You are scheduled to be paid $5,000 in five years. What amount today is equivalent to the $5,000 to be received in five years assuming interest is compounded annually at 4%?

**EE-8B.** **Future Value Computation**      LO2
What amount will be accumulated in five years if $5,000 is invested every six months beginning in six months and ending five years from today? Interest will accumulate at an annual rate of 4% compounded semiannually.

**EE-9B.** **Future Value Computation**      LO2
You are scheduled to receive $5,000 every six months for six periods beginning in six months. What amount in three years is equivalent to the future series of payments assuming interest compounds at the annual rate of 8% compounded semiannually?

**EE-10B.** **Present Value Computation**      LO3
Zumi, Inc., believes it will need $150,000 in nine years to expand its operations. Zumi can earn 5%, compounded annually, if it deposits its money right now. How large of a deposit must Zumi make in order to have the necessary $150,000 in nine years?

**EE-11B.** **Future Value Computation**      LO2
Triton Company deposited $7,500 in the bank today, earning 8% interest. Triton plans to withdraw the money in five years. How much money will be available to withdraw assuming that interest is compounded (a) annually, (b) semiannually, and (c) quarterly?

**EE-12B.** **Future Value Computation**      LO2
Sally Smithton deposited $4,000 in a savings account today. The deposit will earn interest at the rate of 12%. How much will be available for Sally to withdraw in three years, assuming interest is compounded (a) annually, (b) semiannually, and (c) quarterly?

**EE-13B.** **Present Value Computation**      LO3
Raul Gomez made a deposit into his savings account four years ago, and earned interest at an annual rate of 12%. The deposit accumulated to $30,000. How much was initially deposited assuming that the interest was compounded (a) annually, (b) semiannually, and (c) quarterly?

**EE-14B.** **Future Value Computation**      LO2
Herman Lee has decided to start saving for his daughter's college education by depositing $4,000 at the end of every year for 15 years. He has determined that he will be able to earn 6% interest compounded annually. He hopes to have at least $90,000 when his daughter starts college in fifteen years. Will his savings plan be successful?

LO3 **EE-15B.** **Present Value Computation**

Kelly Zales won the state lottery and was given four choices for receiving her winnings.

1. Receive $100,000 right now.
2. Receive $104,000 in one year.
3. Receive $15,000 at the end of each year for eight years.
4. Receive $6,000 at the end of each year for 30 years.

Assuming Kelly can earn interest of 4% compounded annually, which option should Kelly choose?

LO6 **EE-16B.** **Present Value and Payment Calculation**

Dan Peters signed a contract to buy a used car. His annual payments, due at the end of each year for four years, are $5,000. The car dealer charges interest at 12%, compounded annually in order to determine the payment amount.

*a.* What is the current selling price of the car assuming no down payment was made?
*b.* Based on the selling price determined in (a), what would the required payments be if Dan made monthly, rather than annual payments? For part (b), assume interest is compounded monthly.

LO4 **EE-17B.** **Issue Price of a Bond**

Maggie Enterprises issued $100,000 of 6%, five-year bonds with interest payable semiannually. Determine the issue price if the bonds are priced to yield (a) 6%, (b) 8%, and (c) 4%.

LO4 **EE-18B.** **Present Value of a Capital Lease**

Hiller Construction Company leases equipment for eight years under a capital lease. Annual lease payments of $20,000 will be made at the end of each year, and Hiller's current interest rate to borrow money is 8%. Compute the present value of the leased equipment.

LO6 **EE-19B.** **Payment Computation**

Determine the car payment that would be required if a four-year loan is used to purchase a $40,000 car. The loan terms require monthly payments and the period interest is 1% per month.

LO4 **EE-20B.** **Issue Price of a Bond**

Tide, Inc., plans to issue $500,000 of 9% bonds that will pay interest semiannually and mature in ten years. Assume that the effective interest is 8 percent per year compounded semiannually. Calculate the selling price of the bonds.

## ANSWERS TO SELF-STUDY QUESTIONS

**1.** *a.* 1. $50,000 × 3.106 = $155,300
 2. $50,000 × 3.207 = $160,350
 3. $50,000 × 3.262 = $163,100
 *b.* $5,000 × 12.006 = $60,030
 *c.* $3,000 × 12.006 = $36,018
 *d.* $1,000 × 15.937 = $15,937
 $15,000 × 2.594 = $38,910
 $54,847

**2.** *a.* 1. $90,000 × 0.463 = $41,670
 2. $90,000 × 0.456 = $41,040
 3. $90,000 × 0.453 = $40,770
 *b.* $1,000 × 5.335 = $5,335
 *c.* $600 × 17.292 = $10,375.20
 *d.* $500,000 × 0.386 = $193,000
 *e.* $2,500 × 11.470 = $28,675
 $85,000 × 0.312 = $26,520
 $55,195

# Glossary

**10-K** The report filed annually with the U.S. Securities and Exchange Commission by publicly held companies that reports the financial position and operating performance of the company (p. 20).

## A

**Accelerated depreciation method** A depreciation method in which the amounts of depreciation expense taken in the early years of an asset's life are greater than the amounts expensed in later years (p. 414).

**Account** A record of the additions, deductions, and balances of individual assets, liabilities, permanent stockholders' equity, dividends, revenues, and expenses (p. 107).

**Account form** A format of the classified balance sheet in which assets are displayed on the left side and liabilities and stockholders' equity are displayed on the right side (p. 55).

**Accounting cycle** A sequence of activities undertaken by company accountants to accumulate and report the financial information of a business (p. 100).

**Accounting entity** An economic unit with identifiable boundaries that is the focus for the accumulation and reporting of financial information (p. 68).

**Accounting equation** An expression of the equivalency of the economic resources and the claims upon those resources of a business, often stated as Assets = Liabilities + Stockholders' Equity (p. 12).

**Accounting period** The time period, usually one year, to which periodic accounting reports are related; also known as the fiscal period (p. 68).

**Accounting** The process of measuring the economic activity of a business in money terms and communicating those financial results to interested parties. The purpose of accounting is to provide financial information that is useful in economic decision making (p. 10).

**Accounting transaction** An economic event that requires accounting recognition; an event that affects any of the elements of the accounting equation—assets, liabilities, or stockholders' equity (p. 101).

**Accounts receivable** A current asset that is created by a sale of merchandise or the provision of a service on a credit basis. It represents the amount owed the seller by a customer (p. 364).

**Accounts receivable aging method** A procedure that uses an aging schedule to determine the year-end balance needed in the Allowance for Doubtful Accounts account (p. 369).

**Accounts receivable turnover** Annual net sales divided by average accounts receivable (net) (p. 610).

**Accounts receivable turnover** A ratio calculated as annual net sales divided by the average balance of accounts receivable (p. 378).

**Accrual basis of accounting** Accounting procedures whereby sales revenue is recorded when earned and realized and expenses are recorded in the period in which they help to generate the sales revenue (p. 70).

**Accruals** Adjustments that reflect revenues earned but not received or recorded and expenses incurred but not paid or recorded (p. 163).

**Accrued expense** An expense incurred but not yet paid; recognized with an adjusting entry (p. 166).

**Accrued revenue** Revenue earned but not yet billed or received; recognized with an adjusting entry (p. 167).

**Accumulated depreciation** The cumulative amount of depreciation expense taken in prior periods; subtracted from the related asset account (p. 164).

**Adjusted trial balance** A list of general ledger accounts and their balances prepared after all adjustments have been made (p. 169).

**Adjusting entries** Entries made at the end of an accounting period under accrual accounting to ensure the proper matching of expenses incurred with revenues earned for the period (p. 163).

**Aging schedule** An analysis that shows how long a business's accounts receivable balances have remained unpaid (p. 369).

**Allowance for doubtful accounts** A contra-asset account with a normal credit balance shown on the balance sheet as a deduction from accounts receivable to reflect the expected uncollectible amount of accounts receivable (p. 366).

**Allowance method** An accounting procedure whereby the amount of bad debts expense is estimated and recorded in the period in which the related credit sales occur (p. 366).

**Amortization** The periodic write-off of an intangible asset to expense on a company's income statement (p. 423).

**Annual report** A report filed with the U.S. Securities and Exchange Commission by publicly held companies that reports the financial position and operating performance of the company. A less detailed version is mailed to the company's stockholders (p. 20).

**Annuity** A pattern of cash flows in which equal amounts are spaced equally over a number of periods (p. E-5).

**Articles of incorporation** A document prepared by the founders of a corporation that sets forth the structure and purpose of the corporation and specifics regarding the type and quantity of capital stock to be issued (p. 500).

**Assets** The economic resources of a business that can be expressed in money terms (p. 12).

**Asset turnover** Net sales divided by average total assets; it represents a measure of a firm's efficiency in producing sales revenue using its total assets (p. 427).

**Asset turnover ratio** Net sales divided by average total assets (p.606).

**Auditor's report** The report of the independent auditor that describes the activities undertaken by a company's outside auditor and reports the auditor's opinion regarding whether the financial statements fairly present the results of the company's operations and financial health (p. 21).

**Audit report** A report issued by an independent auditor that reports the auditor's opinion regarding a company's financial statements (p. 339).

**Authorized shares** The maximum number of shares in a class of stock that a corporation may issue (p. 504).

**Available-for-sale securities** Debt securities and noninfluential equity securities that management does not intend to sell in the near future or hold to maturity (p. D-2).

**Average collection period** 365 days divided by accounts receivable turnover (p. 611).

**Average collection period** A ratio calculated by dividing 365 days by the accounts receivable turnover ratio (p. 378).

## B

**Bad debts expense** The expense stemming from the inability of a business to collect an amount previously recorded as receivable. It is normally classified as a selling or administrative expense (p. 366).

**Balance sheet** A financial statement showing a business's assets, liabilities, and stockholders' equity as of a specific date (p. 12).

**Bank reconciliation** A procedure explaining the various items—such as deposits in transit, checks outstanding, bank charges, and errors—that lead to differences between the balance shown on a bank statement and the related Cash account in a company's general ledger (p. 332).

**Bearer** One of the terms that may be used to designate the payee on a promissory note; it means that a note is payable to whoever holds the note (p. 374).

**Benchmarking analysis** A technique where the analyst or investor compares a firm's performance, or a ratio like the ROA, to that of the firm's principal competitors or to an industry average (p. 57).

**Betterments** Capital expenditures that improve the quality of services rendered by a plant asset or extend the asset's useful life (p. 420).

**Bond** A long-term debt instrument that promises to pay interest periodically and a principal amount at maturity. Bonds may incorporate a variety of provisions relating to security for the debt involved, methods of paying the periodic interest, and retirement provisions (p. 457).

**Book value** The dollar amount carried in the accounts for a particular asset. The book value of a depreciable asset is derived by deducting the contra account Accumulated Depreciation from the balance in the depreciable asset account (p. 165).

**Budget** A planning device that forecasts a business's future operating activities using financial data. The budget serves as an internal control device by providing a benchmark to compare actual performance against so that material deviations can be investigated (p. 322).

## C

**Calendar year** A fiscal year that ends on December 31 (p. 101).

**Callable** A feature associated with preferred stock whereby the preferred stock can be redeemed by the issuing corporation at a price specified in the stock contract (p. 507).

**Call provision** A bond feature that allows the borrower to retire (call in) the bonds after a stated date (p. 459).

**Capital expenditures** An expenditure that increases the book value of long-term assets (p. 420).

**Capital lease** A lease that transfers to the lessee substantially all of the usual benefits and risks related to ownership of the property. The lessee records the leased property as an asset and establishes a liability for the lease obligation (p. 468).

**Cash** An asset category representing the amount of a firm's paper money, coins, checks, money orders, traveler's checks, and funds on deposit at a bank in a company's checking accounts and savings accounts (p. 325).

**Cash and cash equivalents** The sum of cash plus short-term, highly liquid investments such as U.S. Treasury bills and money market funds (p. 326).

**Cash basis of accounting** Accounting procedures whereby sales revenue is recorded when cash is received from operating activities and expenses are recorded when cash payments related to operating activities are made (p. 70).

**Cash discount** An amount that a purchaser of merchandise may deduct from the purchase price for paying within the allowed discount period (p. 228).

**Cash equivalents** Short-term, highly liquid investments that firms acquire with temporarily idle cash to earn interest on these funds. To qualify as a cash equivalent, an investment must be readily convertible into cash and be close enough to maturity so that its market value is not sensitive to interest rate changes (p. 544).

**Cash management** Management's efforts to determine cash needs and maintain the proper amount of cash for the company's needs (p. 544).

**Certificate of deposit (CD)** An investment security offering a fixed rate of return for a specified period of time (p. 325).

**Certified public accountant (CPA)** A professional designation given to an accountant who has fulfilled stringent licensing requirements (p. 6).

**Change in accounting principle** A switch from one generally accepted accounting method to another generally accepted method, such as changing depreciation methods (p. 597).

**Chart of accounts** A list of all of the general ledger account titles and their numerical code (p. 110).

**Check** A written order signed by a checking account owner directing the bank to pay a specified amount of money to the person or company named on the check (p. 330).

**Classified balance sheet** A balance sheet in which items are classified into subgroups to facilitate financial analysis and management decision making (p. 52).

**Classified income statement** An income statement in which items are classified into subgroups to facilitate financial analysis and management decision making (p. 233).

**Closing process** A step in the accounting cycle in which the balances of all temporary accounts are transferred to the Retained Earnings account, leaving the temporary accounts with zero balances (pp. 173, 178).

**Commitments** A contractual arrangement in which both parties to the contract still have acts yet to perform (p. 621).

**Common-size financial statement** A financial statement in which each item is presented as a percentage of a key statement item (p. 603).

**Common stock** The basic ownership class of capital stock, carrying the right to vote, share in earnings, participate in future share issues, and share in any liquidation proceeds after all more senior claims have been settled (p. 504).

**Comparative financial statement analysis** A form of horizontal analysis involving a comparison of two or more periods of financial statement data showing dollar and/or percentage changes (p. 599).

**Compensating balance** A minimum amount that a financial institution requires a firm to maintain in its bank account as a condition of a borrowing arrangement (p. 326).

**Compound interest** Interest that is computed on the accumulated principal balance plus any interest that has been earned but not yet paid (p. E-2).

**Compound journal entry** A journal entry containing more than one debit and one credit (p. 111).

**Comprehensive income** A broader definition of a company's income that includes net income plus any changes in the market value of certain marketable securities and any unrealized gains and losses from translating foreign currency denominated financial statements into U.S. dollars (p. 598).

**Conceptual framework** A cohesive set of interrelated objectives, elements, and recognition and measurement criteria for the GAAP developed by the FASB (p. 65).

**Conservatism** An accounting principle stating that judgmental determinations should tend toward understatement rather than overstatement of assets and net income (p. 71).

**Consignment goods** Items held for sale by parties other than the item's owner (p. 270).

**Consistency** An accounting principle stating that accounting reports should be prepared on a basis consistent with the prior periods (p. 68).

**Consolidated financial statements** Financial statements prepared to portray the financial position, results of operations, and cash flows of two or more affiliated companies as a single economic entity (p. D-12).

**Contingency** A possible future event; significant contingent liabilities must be disclosed in the notes to the financial statements (p. 621).

**Contingent liabilities** A potential obligation, the eventual occurrence of which usually depends on some future event beyond the control of the firm. Contingent liabilities may originate from such things as lawsuits, credit guarantees, and contested income tax assessments (p. 466).

**Contra account** An account related to, and deducted from, another account when financial statements are prepared or when book values are computed (p. 164).

**Contributed capital** The capital contributed to a company by stockholders when they purchase shares of stock from the company (p. 61).

**Controlling securities** Equity securities that represent an ownership of more than 50 percent of a corporation's voting stock (p. D-2).

**Control numbers** Preprinted numbers on documents such as purchase orders, invoices, credit memos, and checks used to provide an internal control that all documents are accounted for (p. 322).

**Convertible** A feature associated with preferred stock whereby the preferred stock can be converted into common stock at a specified conversion rate (p. 506).

**Convertible bond** A bond incorporating the holder's right to convert the bond into common stock under prescribed terms (p. 457).

**Copyright** An exclusive right that protects an owner against the unauthorized reproduction of a specific written work or artwork (p. 424).

**Corporate social responsibility** The practice that considers how a corporation's behavior affects its various stakeholders to ensure an adherence to ethical standards (p. 18).

**Corporation** A legal entity created by the granting of a charter from an appropriate governmental authority and owned by stockholders who have limited liability for the corporation's debt (p. 500).

**Corporation** A legal entity created under the laws of a state or the federal government. The owners of a corporation receive shares of stock as evidence of their ownership interest in the company (p. 4).

**Cost flow** The actual or assumed assignment of costs to goods sold and to ending inventory (p. 273).

**Cost of goods available for sale** An amount that represents the inventory available to be sold, consisting of the beginning inventory plus purchases during the period (p. 236).

**Cost of goods sold percentage** The ratio of cost of goods sold divided by net sales (p. 238).

**Cost of goods sold** The total cost of merchandise sold to customers during the accounting period; often abbreviated as COGS (p. 230).

**Cost principle** An accounting principle stating that asset measures should be based on the price paid to acquire an asset (p. 69).

**Coupon rate** The rate of interest stated on a bond certificate (p. 459).

**Credit card fee** A fee charged to retailers for credit card services provided by a financial institution. The fee is usually stated as a percentage of credit card sales (p. 374).

**Credit-collection policy** A policy establishing the amount of time that customers are allowed before they must pay their outstanding accounts receivable (p. 365).

**Credit (entry)** An entry on the right side (or in the credit column) of an account (p. 108).

**Credit-granting policy** A policy to determine which customers to grant credit and how much credit to grant those customers (p. 365).

**Credit guarantee** A guarantee of another company's debt by cosigning a note payable; a guarantor's contingent liability must be disclosed in a balance sheet footnote (p. 468).

**Creditor** An individual or financial institution that lends money or services to a company with the expectation of receiving repayment in the future (p. 9).

**Credit period** The maximum time period, stated in days, that a purchaser of merchandise has to pay a seller (p. 227).

**Cumulative** A feature associated with preferred stock whereby any dividends-in-arrears must be paid before any dividends may be paid on common stock (p. 506).

**Current assets** Cash and other assets that will be converted to cash or used up during the normal operating cycle of a business or one year, whichever is longer (p. 52).

**Current liabilities** Liabilities that must be settled within the normal operating cycle or one year, whichever is longer (p. 54).

**Current liabilities** Obligations that will require within the coming year or operating cycle, whichever is longer, (1) the use of existing current assets or (2) the creation of other current liabilities (p. 450).

**Current ratio** A firm's current assets divided by its current liabilities (p. 609).

**Current ratio** A measure of a firm's liquidity, calculated as current assets divided by current liabilities (p. 58).

**Current ratio** Current assets divided by current liabilities (p. 470).

**D**

**Days' sales in inventory** 365 days divided by inventory turnover (p. 612).

**Days' sales in inventory** A ratio computed by dividing 365 by Inventory Turnover; this ratio indicates the number of days it takes, on average, for a company to sell its inventory (p. 284).

**Debenture bond** A bond that has no specific property pledged as security (or collateral) for the repayment of the borrowed funds (p. 457).

**Debit (entry)** An entry on the left side (or in the debit column) of an account (p. 108).

**Debt financing** A source of financing for a company involving the use of debt, such as a bank loan or the issuance of bonds (p. 9).

**Debt security** A security that creates, for the holder, a creditor relationship with an entity (p. D-2).

**Debt-to-equity ratio** A firm's total liabilities divided by its total stockholders' equity (p. 613).

**Debt-to-total-assets ratio** A measure of a firm's solvency, calculated as total liabilities divided by total assets (p. 59).

**Declining-balance method** An accelerated depreciation method that allocates depreciation expense to each year by applying a constant depreciation percentage to the declining book value of a long-lived asset (p. 414).

**Deferrals** Adjustments that allocate various assets and revenues received in advance to the proper accounting periods as expenses and revenues (p. 163).

**Deferred revenue** A liability representing revenues received in advance; also called *unearned revenue* (p. 165).

**Deposits in transit** Cash deposits made to a bank account near the end of a month that do not appear on that month's bank statement (p. 332).

**Depreciation accounting** The process of allocating the cost of long-lived assets (less salvage value) to expense in a systematic and rational manner over the time period benefitting from their use (p. 412).

**Depreciation** The decline in economic potential of long-lived assets originating from wear, deterioration, and obsolescence (p. 412).

**Depreciation** The process of allocating the cost of buildings, equipment, and vehicles to expense over the time periods benefiting from their use (p. 164).

**Detection control** An internal control designed to discover problems soon after they arise (p. 320).

**Direct method** A presentation of the cash flow from operating activities in a statement of cash flows that shows the major categories of operating cash receipts and payments (p. 549).

**Direct write-off method** An accounting procedure whereby the amount of bad debts expense is not recorded until specific uncollectible customer accounts are identified (p. 372).

**Discontinued operations** Operating segments of a company that have been sold, abandoned, or disposed of during the accounting period. Related operating income (or loss) and related gains and losses on disposal are reported separately on the income statement (p. 596).

**Discounting** Selling a note receivable for cash at a financial institution (p. 379).

**Discount period** The maximum amount of time, stated in days, that a purchaser of merchandise has to pay a seller if the purchaser wants to claim any available cash discount (p. 228).

**Dividend payout ratio** A financial ratio showing the percentage of net income available to common stockholders that is paid out as dividends; calculated as the annual dividend per share divided by earnings per share (p. 518).

**Dividend payout ratio** Annual dividend per share divided by a company's earnings per share (p. 617).

**Dividends** Distributions of assets (usually cash) or stock from a corporation to its stockholders (p. 512).

**Dividend yield** Annual dividend per share divided by the market price per share (p. 517).

**Dividend yield** Annual dividend per share divided by the market price per share (p. 616).

**Double-entry accounting** A method of accounting that results in the recording of equal amounts of debits and credits (p. 101).

### E

**Earned capital** Capital that is earned by a company and not distributed to its stockholders as a dividend; referred to as retained earnings (p. 61).

**Earnings per share (EPS)** A financial ratio computed as net income less preferred stock dividends divided by the weighted average number of common shares outstanding for the period (p. 615).

**Earnings quality** The degree to which reported financial results reflect the actual financial condition and performance of the reporting company (p. 177).

**Effective interest method** A method of interest amortization that recognizes a constant percentage of the book value of a bond as interest expense for each interest payment period. (p. E-11).

**Effective interest rate** The current rate of interest in the market for a bond or other debt instrument. When issued, a bond is priced to yield the market rate of interest at the date of issuance (p. 462).

**Effective interest rate** The current rate of interest in the market for a bond or other debt instrument. When issued, a bond is priced to yield the market rate of interest at the date of issuance (p. E-11).

**Electronic funds transfer** Sending an electronic message from one computer to another to cause a transfer of money from one financial institution to another (p. 330).

**Employee collusion** When one or more employees work together to circumvent an internal control (p. 323).

**Equity financing** A source of financing for a company involving the sale of shares of common stock (p. 9).

**Equity method** A method of accounting by a parent company for investments in affiliate companies by which the parent's share of subsidiary income or loss is periodically recorded in the parent company's investment account (p. D-9).

**Equity security** A security that represents an ownership interest in an entity (p. D-2).

**Ethics** An area of inquiry dealing with the values, rules, and justifications that govern an individual's way of life or a corporation's behavior (p. 7).

**Expense recognition (matching) principle** An accounting guideline that states that net income is determined by relating expenses to the sales revenues generated by the expenses (p. 70).

**Expenses** Decreases in stockholders' equity incurred by a firm during the process of generating its sales revenues (p. 14).

**Extraordinary items** Transactions and events that are unusual in nature and occur infrequently. Gains and losses on such items are shown separately, net of tax effects, on the income statement (p. 596).

### F

**Factoring** Selling an account receivable for cash to a financial institution (p. 379).

**Factors** Finance companies and financial institutions that buy receivables (p. 379).

**Federal Insurance Contributions Act (FICA)** Under this act, the income of an individual is taxed to support the national social security program providing retirement income, medical care, and death benefits. Employers pay a matching amount of tax on their eligible employees (p. 453).

**Fidelity bond** An insurance policy that provides financial compensation for theft by employees specifically covered by the insurance (p. 323).

**Financial Accounting Standards Board (FASB)** A private, not-for-profit organization whose task is to develop generally accepted accounting principles in the United States (p. 11).

**Financial accounting** The area of accounting dealing with the preparation of financial statements showing a business's results of operations, financial position, and cash flow (p. 6).

**Financial flexibility** A firm's ability to generate sufficient amounts of cash to respond to unanticipated business needs and opportunities (p. 548).

**Financial reporting objectives** A component of the conceptual framework which specifies that financial statements should provide information that is (1) useful for investment and credit decisions, (2) helpful in assessing an entity's ability to generate future cash flows, and (3) about an entity's resources, claims on those resources, and the effects of events causing changes in these items (p. 65).

**Financial statement audit** An examination of a company's financial statements by a firm of independent certified public accountants (p. 338).

**Financial statement elements** A component of the conceptual framework that identifies the significant components—assets, liabilities, stockholders' equity, revenues, and expenses—used to prepare financial statements (p. 65).

**Financing activities** A section in the statement of cash flows that reports cash flows associated with obtaining cash from owners and creditors, returning cash to owners, and repaying amounts borrowed (p. 546).

**Financing activities** Cash flow activities that include obtaining cash by issuing debt, the repayment of debt, obtaining cash by the issuance of common stock, the repurchase of stock, and the payment of dividends (p. 9).

**Finished goods inventory** A manufacturer's inventory that includes all products that have been completed and are ready for sale to customers (p. 269).

**First-in, first-out (FIFO) method** An inventory costing method that assumes that the oldest (earliest purchased) goods are sold first (p. 274).

**Fiscal year** The annual accounting period used by a business (p. 101).

**FOB destination** Free on board destination indicates that the items being shipped are owned by the seller while the items are in transit (p. 227).

**F.O.B. destination** Free-on-board destination indicates that the items being shipped are owned by the seller while the items are in transit (p. 270).

**FOB shipping point** Free on board shipping point indicates that the items being shipped are owned by the buyer while the items are in transit (p. 226).

**F.O.B. shipping point** Free-on-board shipping point indicates that the items being shipped are owned by the buyer while the items are in transit (p. 270).

**Forensic accounting** A branch of accounting that involves investigations that result from actual or anticipated disputes such as criminal activity (p. 8).

**Forward stock split** Additional shares of capital stock issued by a corporation to its current stockholders in proportion to their current ownership interests without changing the balances in the related stockholders' equity accounts. A forward stock split increases the number of shares outstanding and reduces proportionately the stock's par value per share (p. 510).

**Franchise** An exclusive right to operate or sell a specific brand of products in a given geographic area (p. 424).

**Fraud** Any act by the management or employees of a business involving an intentional deception for personal gain (p. 318).

**Fraud triangle** The three elements of fraud, consisting of (1) pressure, (2) rationalization, and (3) opportunity (p. 318).

**Free cash flow** A measure of a firm's cash flow health, calculated as cash provided by operating activities less cash expenditures for property, plant, and equipment. Free cash flow is a measure of a firm's operating cash flow available for general corporate purposes such as debt retirement or dividend payment (p. 63).

**Free cash flow** Calculated as cash flow from operating activities less capital expenditures; this metric provides a measure of a firm's cash flow that can be used to fund business activities beyond the replacement of property, plant, and equipment (p. 560).

**Free on board** A term for determining ownership for items in transit (p. 226).

**Full disclosure principle** An accounting principle stipulating that all facts necessary to make financial statements useful should be disclosed in a firm's annual report (p. 70).

**Future value** The amount that a specified investment (or series of investments) will be worth at a future date if invested at a given rate of compound interest (p. E-3).

## G

**General journal** An accounting record with enough flexibility so that any type of business transaction may be recorded in it; a diary of a business's accounting transactions (p. 110).

**General ledger** A grouping of all of a business's accounts that are used to prepare the basic financial statements (p. 112).

**Generally accepted accounting principles (GAAP)** A set of standards and procedures that guide the preparation of financial statements (p. 11).

**Going concern concept** An accounting principle that assumes that, in the absence of evidence to the contrary, a business enterprise will have an indefinite life (p. 69).

**Goods flow** The actual physical movement of inventory through a business (p. 273).

**Goods in transit** Items that are being shipped by a common carrier (p. 270).

**Goodwill** The value of all attributes acquired in an acquisition that are not otherwise associated with other specific assets; calculated as the purchase price of the acquired company less the fair market value of the identifiable net assets (p. 425).

**Gross pay** The amount an employee earns before any withholdings or deductions (p. 453).

**Gross profit percentage** Gross profit on sales divided by net sales (p. 605).

**Gross profit percentage** The ratio of gross profit divided by net sales (p. 238).

**Gross profit** The difference between net sales and cost of goods sold; also called gross margin (p. 233).

## H

**Held-to-maturity securities** Debt securities that management intends to hold to maturity (p. D-2).

**Holding company** A corporation that controls another corporation through ownership of the latter's stock (p. D-12).

**Horizontal analysis** The analysis of a firm's financial statements that covers two or more years (p. 599).

## I

**Impairment loss** A loss recognized on an impaired asset equal to the difference between its book value and its current fair value (p. 417).

**Income statement** A financial statement reporting a business's sales revenue and expenses for a given period of time (p. 13).

**Indirect method** A presentation of cash flow from operating activities in a statement of cash flows that begins with net income and applies a series of adjustments to convert the net income to a cash basis amount (p. 549).

**Influential securities** Equity securities that represent a 20 to 50 percent ownership of a corporation's voting stock (p. D-2).

**Intangible asset** An asset lacking a physical presence; examples of intangible assets include patents, copyrights, and brand names (p. 53).

**Intangible assets** A term applied to a group of long-term assets, including patents, copyrights, franchises, trademarks, and goodwill, that benefit an entity but lack physical characteristics or substance (p. 422).

**Interest** A payment for the use of money (p. E-2).

**Internal auditing** A company function that provides independent appraisals of the company's financial statements, its internal control, and its operations (p. 323).

**Internal control** The measures undertaken by a company to ensure the reliability of its accounting data, protect its assets from theft or unauthorized use, insure that employees follow the company's policies and procedures, and evaluate the performance of employees, departments, divisions, and the company as a whole (p. 319).

**International accounting principles** A set of accounting guidelines that are acceptable for the preparation of financial statements worldwide (p. 23).

**International Accounting Standards Board (IASB)** An independent accounting standard-setting agency whose purpose is to develop international financial accounting standards (p. 12).

**International Financial Reporting Standards (IFRS)** An international set of accounting standards, interpretations, and the framework for the preparation and presentation of financial statements used in many countries (p. 12).

**Inventory carrying costs** Costs created by just-in-case inventories, including casualty insurance, building usage costs, and the cost of capital invested in the inventory (p. 269).

**Inventory overage** The increase in the inventory account that occurs when the physical inventory count is greater than the inventory account balance (p. 271).

**Inventory shrinkage** The cost associated with an inventory shortage; the amount by which the perpetual inventory exceeds the physical inventory (p. 237).

**Inventory shrinkage** The decrease in the inventory account that occurs when the physical inventory count is less than the inventory account balance (p. 271).

**Inventory turnover** Cost of goods sold divided by average inventory (p. 611).

**Inventory turnover ratio** A ratio computed by dividing cost of goods sold by the average ending inventory (p. 284).

**Investing activities** A section in the statement of cash flows that reports cash flows involving (1) the purchase and sale of plant assets and intangible assets, (2) the purchase and sale of stocks, bonds, and other securities (other than cash equivalents), and (3) the lending and subsequent collection of money (p. 546).

**Investing activities** Cash flow activities involving the acquisition and disposition of the infrastructure of a company, including land, buildings, and equipment. Also included are cash flows for investments in shares of other companies (p. 9).

**Invoice price** The price that a seller charges a purchaser for merchandise (p. 227).

**Issued shares** Shares of stock that have been sold and issued to stockholders; issued stock may be either outstanding or held in the treasury (p. 504).

### J

**Journal** A tabular record in which business transactions are analyzed in debit and credit terms and recorded in chronological order (p. 110).

**Journal entry** An entry of accounting information into a journal (p. 110).

**Just-in-case inventory** The extra quantity of inventory that a firm carries just in case suppliers do not deliver when scheduled or just in case the company decides to make previously unplanned quantities of product for sale to customers (p. 269).

**Just-in-time manufacturing** A manufacturing philosophy that seeks to minimize or eliminate just-in-case inventory quantities through careful planning of raw material purchases and manufacturing management (p. 269).

### L

**Land improvements** Improvements with limited useful lives made to land sites, such as paved parking lots and driveways (p. 411).

**Last-in, first-out (LIFO) method** An inventory costing method that assumes that the newest (most recently purchased) goods are sold first (p. 274).

**Lawsuit** A prosecution of a claim in a court of law; may lead to a financial statement footnote disclosure by the defendant as a contingent liability (p. 468).

**Lease** A contract between a lessor (owner) and lessee (tenant) for the rental of property (p. 468).

**Leasehold improvements** Expenditures made by a lessee to alter or improve leased property (p. 411).

**Leasehold** The rights transferred from the lessor to the lessee by a lease (p. 468).

**Lessee** The party acquiring the right to the use of property by a lease (p. 468).

**Lessor** The owner of property who transfers the right to use the property to another party by a lease (p. 468).

**Leverage** The use of borrowed funds to finance the assets or operations of a firm (p. 473).

**Liabilities** Present obligations resulting from past transactions that require a firm to pay money, provide goods, or perform services in the future (p. 450).

**Liabilities** The obligations or debts that a business must pay in money or services at some time in the future as a consequence of past transactions or events (p. 13).

**LIFO conformity rule** A section of the Internal Revenue Code requiring that any company that selects LIFO for income tax reporting must also use LIFO for financial reporting to stockholders (p. 279).

**LIFO inventory reserve** The difference between the value of ending inventory reported under LIFO and what the inventory would have been valued at under FIFO (p. 285).

**Liquidity** A measure of a company's ability to pay its obligations expected to come due in the next year (pp. 53, 58).

**List price** The suggested price or reference price of merchandise in a catalog or price list (p. 232).

**Long-term liabilities** Debt obligations not due to be repaid within the normal operating cycle or one year, whichever is longer (p. 55).

**Lower-of-cost-or-market (LCM)** A measurement method that, when applied to inventory, provides for ending inventory to be valued on the balance sheet at the lower of its acquisition cost or current replacement cost (p. 281).

### M

**Maker** The signer of a promissory note (p. 374).

**Management Discussion and Analysis (MD&A)** Part of the annual report that contains management's interpretation of the company's recent past performance along with discussion of possible future opportunities and risks (p. 21).

**Managerial accounting** The accounting activities carried out by a firm's accounting staff primarily to provide management with accounting data for decisions related to a firm's operations (p. 5).

**Manufacturer** A company that converts raw materials and components into finished goods through the application of skilled labor and machine operations (p. 222).

**Market rate of interest** The rate of interest in the market for a bond or other debt instrument (p. 459).

**Materiality** An accounting guideline that states that insignificant data that would not affect a financial statement user's decisions may be recorded in the most expedient manner (p. 71).

**Maturity date** The date on which a note or bond matures (p. 375).

**Maturity date** The date on which a note payable is due to be paid (p. 451).

**Merchandise inventory** A stock of goods that a company buys from another company and makes available for sale to its customers (p. 222).

**Merchandising firm** A company that buys finished goods, stores the goods for varying periods of time, and then resells the goods (p. 222).

**Modified accelerated cost recovery system (MACRS)** A system of accelerated depreciation for U.S. income tax purposes; it prescribes depreciation rates by asset-life classification (p. 418).

**Monetary unit concept** An accounting guideline that reports assets, liabilities and stockholders' equity in the basic unit of money (p. 68).

**Multiple-step income statement** An income statement in which one or more intermediate performance measures, such as gross profit on sales, are derived before the continuing income is reported (p. 594).

## N

**Net assets** The difference between a business's assets and liabilities. Net assets are equal to stockholders' equity (p. 13).

**Net income** The excess of a business's sales revenues over its expenses (p. 14).

**Net pay** The amount of an employee's paycheck, after subtracting withheld amounts (p. 453).

**Net realizable value** An asset measure calculated by subtracting the expected disposal cost from an asset's expected selling price (p. 281).

**Net sales** The total revenue generated by a company through merchandise sales less the revenue given up through sales returns and allowances and less the revenue given up through sales discounts (p. 232).

**New York Stock Exchange (NYSE)** A marketplace, located in New York City, for the buying and selling of corporate shares (p. 5).

**Noncash expenses** Expenses that do not involve any current period cash outflows and that are deducted in the process of calculating a company's accrual basis net income (p. 554).

**Noncash investing and financing activities** Investing activities and financing activities that do not affect current cash flows; information about these events must be reported as a supplement to the statement of cash flows (p. 547).

**No-par value stock** Stock that does not have a par value (p. 504).

**Normal balance** The side on which increases to the account are recorded. (p. 108)

**Normal operating cycle** The average period of time between the use of cash to buy goods for resale or to provide services and the subsequent collection of cash from customers (p. 53).

**Note receivable** A promissory note held by the note's payee (p. 375).

**Notes to the financial statements** The annual report section following the four financial statements that includes a description of the assumptions and estimates that were used in preparing the statements, the measurement procedures that were followed, and the details behind the summary numbers (p. 21).

**Not-sufficient-funds check** A check from an individual or company that had an insufficient cash balance in the bank when the holder of the check presented it to the bank for payment (p. 325).

## O

**Objectivity** An accounting notion requiring that, whenever possible, accounting data should be based on objectively determined evidence (p. 66).

**Off-balance-sheet financing** The structuring of a financing arrangement such that no liability is recorded on the borrower's balance sheet (p. 470).

**Open account** A charge account provided by a retailer for its customers (p. 223).

**Operating activities** A section in the statement of cash flows that reports cash flows from all activities that are not classified as investing or financing activities (p. 546).

**Operating activities** Cash flow activities that are associated with the day-to-day operations of a business, for example the cash received from sales revenues and the cash paid for operating expenses (p. 9).

**Operating-cash-flow-to-capital-expenditures ratio** A financial ratio calculated by dividing a firm's cash flow from operating activities by its annual capital expenditures (p. 562).

**Operating-cash-flow-to-capital-expenditures ratio** A firm's cash flow from operating activities divided by its annual capital expenditures (p. 614).

**Operating-cash-flow-to-current-liabilities ratio** A financial ratio calculated by dividing cash flow from operating activities by the average current liabilities for the year (p. 561).

**Operating-cash-flow-to-current-liabilities ratio** A firm's cash flow from operating activities divided by its average current liabilities (p. 610).

**Operating cycle** For a particular business, the average period of time between the use of cash in its typical operating activity and the subsequent collection of cash from customers (p. 223).

**Operating lease** A lease by which the lessor retains the usual risks and rewards of owning the property (p. 469).

**Operational audit** An evaluation of activities, systems, and internal controls within a company to determine their efficiency, effectiveness, and economy (p. 339).

**Ordinary annuity** An annuity where the payments occur at the end of each period (p. E-5).

**Outstanding checks** Checks issued by a firm that have not yet been presented to its bank for payment (p. 332).

**Outstanding shares** Shares of stock that are currently held by stockholders (p. 504).

## P

**Paid-in capital** The amount of capital contributed to a corporation by its stockholders in excess of its par value or stated value (p. 509).

**Parent company** A company holding all, or a majority, of the voting stock of another company, called a *subsidiary* (p. D-12).

**Participating** A feature associated with preferred stock whereby the preferred stock can share any special dividend distribution with common stock beyond the regular preferred stock dividend rate (p. 507).

**Partnership** A voluntary association of two or more persons for the purpose of conducting a business (p. 4).

**Par value** An amount specified in the corporate charter for each class of stock and imprinted on the face of each stock certificate; often determines the legal capital of a corporation (p. 503).

**Password** A string of characters that a user enters into a device to prove that the user is actually the user that is allowed to use the device (p. 328).

**Patent** An exclusive privilege granted for 20 years to an inventor that gives the patent holder the right to exclude others from making, using, or selling the invention (p. 424).

**Payee** The company or individual to whom a promissory note is made payable (p. 374).

**Percentage of net sales method** A procedure that determines the bad debts expense for the year by multiplying net credit sales by an estimated uncollectible percentage (p. 369).

**Periodic inventory system** A system that records merchandise transactions in a variety of accounts; the Inventory account and Cost of Goods Sold account are not updated until the end of the period when a physical count of the inventory is taken (p. 225).

**Period-in-time** A financial statement accumulating information for a specific period of time; examples include the income statement, the statement of stockholders' equity, the statement of retained earnings, and the statement of cash flows (p. 16).

**Permanent account** An account used to prepare the balance sheet—that is, an asset, liability, or stockholders' equity account; any balance in a permanent account at the end of an accounting period is carried forward to the following accounting period (p. 109).

**Permanent account** An account used to prepare the balance sheet—that is, an asset, liability, or stockholders' equity account; any balance in a permanent account at the end of an accounting period is carried forward to the following accounting period (pp. 173, 178).

**Perpetual inventory system** A system that records the cost of merchandise inventory in the Inventory account at the time of purchase and updates the Inventory account for subsequent purchases and sales of merchandise as they occur (p. 225).

**Petty cash fund** A special, relatively small cash fund established for making minor cash disbursements in the operation of a business (p. 331).

**Physical count of inventory** A year-end procedure that involves counting the quantity of each inventory item, determining the unit cost of each item, multiplying the unit cost times the quantity on hand, and summing the costs of all the items to determine the total inventory at cost (p. 237).

**Physical count of inventory** The counting of inventory used to verify the balance of inventory (p. 270).

**Plant assets** A firm's property, plant, and equipment; also called fixed assets (p. 408).

**Point-in-time** A financial statement presenting information as of a particular date; the balance sheet is a point-in-time statement (p. 16).

**Post-closing trial balance** A list of general ledger accounts and their balances after closing entries have been recorded and posted (pp. 175, 180).

**Postdated check** A check from another person or company with a calendar date that is later than the current date. A postdated check does not become cash until the calendar date of the check (p. 325).

**Posting references** A series of abbreviations used in posting to indicate to where or from where a journal entry is posted (p. 112).

**Posting** The transfer of information from the journal to the general ledger accounts (p. 112).

**Preemptive right** The right of a stockholder to maintain his or her proportionate ownership interest in a corporation by having the right to purchase an appropriate quantity of shares in any new share issue (p. 505).

**Preferred stock** A class of capital stock with priority over common stock in dividend payments and in the distribution of assets in the event of a corporation liquidation (p. 505).

**Present value** The current worth of amounts to be paid (or received) in the future; calculated by discounting the future payments (or receipts) at a specified interest rate (p. E-6).

**Prevention control** An internal control designed to discover problems before they arise (p. 320).

**Price-earnings ratio** The current market price per common share divided by a company's earnings per share (p. 616).

**Principal** As it relates to debt financing, the amount initially borrowed from the creditor (p. 9)

**Principal** The amount borrowed or invested (p. E-2).

**Product warranties** Guarantees against product defects for a designated period of time following product sale (p. 456).

**Promissory note** A written promise to pay a certain sum of money on demand or at a determinable future time (p. 374).

**Property, plant, and equipment** The land, buildings, equipment, vehicles, furniture, and fixtures that a firm uses in its operations; often referred to as PP&E (p. 53).

**Public Company Accounting Oversight Board (PCAOB)** A quasi-governmental agency established by the Sarbanes-Oxley Act to overhaul auditing standards, inspect the work of accounting firms, and discipline independent auditors that fail to meet and maintain acceptable standards of audit performance (p. 339).

**Purchase allowance** A reduction in the selling price of merchandise granted by a seller due to dissatisfaction by the purchaser (p. 227).

**Purchase return** Shipping unsatisfactory merchandise from a purchaser back to the seller for a purchase allowance (p. 227).

## Q

**Qualitative characteristics of accounting information** The characteristics of accounting information that contribute to decision usefulness; the primary qualities are *relevance* and *reliability* (p. 66).

**Quarterly data** Selected quarterly financial information that is reported in the annual report to stockholders (p. 622).

**Quick ratio** Quick assets (that is, cash and cash equivalents, short-term investments, and accounts receivable) divided by current liabilities (p. 609).

**Quick ratio** The sum of (1) cash and cash equivalents, (2) short-term investments, and (3) accounts receivables divided by current liabilities (p. 471).

**Quick response system** A system used with a point-of-sale system that is designed to insure that a retailer quickly orders more of the items that are selling and quickly eliminates those items that are not selling (p. 269).

## R

**Ratio analysis** The process of expressing the relationship of one accounting number to another accounting number through the process of division (p. 57).

**Raw materials inventory** A manufacturer's inventory that includes raw materials and components that have been purchased for use in the factory but have not been placed into production (p. 268).

**Recognition and measurement criteria** The criteria that must be met before a financial statement element may be recorded in the accounts. Essentially, the item must meet the definition of an element and must be measurable, and the resultant information about the item must be relevant and reliable (p. 66).

**Relevance** A qualitative characteristic of accounting information; relevant information contributes to the predictive and evaluative decisions made by financial statement users (p. 66).

**Reliability** A qualitative characteristic of accounting information; reliable information contains no bias or error and faithfully portrays what it intends to represent (p. 66).

**Remittance advice** A form that accompanies a check to inform the person receiving the check about the purpose of the check (p. 327).

**Remittance list** A list of the checks received from customers to pay their accounts receivable (p. 327).

**Report form** A format of the classified balance sheet where assets are displayed on the top and liabilities and stockholders' equity are displayed below the assets (p. 55).

**Research and development costs** Expenditures for the research and development of products or processes. These costs are almost always expensed rather than capitalized (p. 423).

**Restricted cash** Cash that is restricted for a specific use and not available for general use (p. 326).

**Retailer** A company that buys goods from wholesale distributors and sells the goods to individual customers (p. 222).

**Return on assets** A financial ratio computed as net income divided by average total assets (p. 426).

**Return on assets** Net income divided by average total assets (p. 607).

**Return on assets (ROA)** A measure of profitability; defined as net income divided by average total assets (or period-end assets). (p. 57).

**Return on common stockholders' equity** A financial ratio computed as (net income − preferred stock dividends) divided by average common stockholders' equity (p. 516).

**Return on common stockholders' equity** Net income less preferred stock dividends divided by average common stockholders' equity (p. 607).

**Return on sales** Net income divided by net sales (p. 606).

**Return on sales ratio** A measure of a firm's profitability, calculated as net income divided by net sales (p. 60).

**Return on sales ratio** The ratio of net income divided by net sales, representing the net profit earned on each dollar of net sales (p. 239).

**Revenue expenditures** An expenditure related to plant assets that is expensed when incurred (p. 419).

**Revenue recognition principle** An accounting principle requiring that sales revenues be recognized when services are performed or goods are sold (p. 70).

**Sale on account** A sale of merchandise made on a credit basis (p. 223).

**Sale on credit** See sale on account (p. 223).

**Sales discounts** An account used by a seller to record cash discounts taken by a buyer when payment is made during the allowed discount period (p. 228).

**Sales returns and allowances** An account used by a seller to record either the return of merchandise by a buyer or an allowance given to the buyer in lieu of a return (p. 231).

**Sales revenues** Increases in stockholders' equity that result when a firm provides goods or services to its customers (p. 14).

**Salvage value** The expected net recovery when a plant asset is sold or removed from service; also called *residual value* (p. 412).

**Sarbanes-Oxley Act (SOX)** A set of legislative rules enacted in 2002 to provide stricter guidance over corporate behavior. The legislation was a reaction to the infamous accounting scandals at Enron and WorldCom (p. 8).

**Secured bond** A bond that pledges specific property as security (or collateral) for meeting the terms of a bond agreement (p. 457).

**Segment** A subdivision of a firm for which supplemental financial information is disclosed (p. 622).

**Segregation of duties** An internal control principle that requires that duties should be allocated to separate individuals (p. 321).

**Serial bond** A bond issue that staggers the bond maturity dates over a series of years (p. 457).

**Service company** A firm whose primary revenue source is from providing services to a customer rather than manufacturing or selling a physical product. (p. 222)

**Simple interest** Interest that is calculated only on the initial principal and not on any unpaid interest (p. E-2).

**Single-step income statement** An income statement in which the continuing income is derived in one step by subtracting total expenses from total sales revenues (p. 594).

**Sinking fund provision** A bond feature that requires the borrower to retire a portion of the outstanding bonds each year or, in some cases, to make payments each year to a trustee who is responsible for managing the resources needed to retire the bonds at maturity (p. 459).

**Socially responsible investing (SRI)** An investment strategy that considers not just financial performance but also the social concepts of environmental stewardship, consumer protection, human rights, and diversity (p. 62).

**Sole proprietorship** A form of business organization in which one person owns the business (p. 4).

**Solvency** A measure of a company's ability to repay its debts in the long term (p. 58).

**Source document** Any written document or computer record evidencing an accounting transaction, such as a bank check, deposit slip, sales invoice, or cash register tape (p. 110).

**Specific identification method** An inventory costing method involving the physical identification of goods sold and goods remaining and costing these amounts at their actual costs (p. 273).

**Stated value** A nominal amount that may be assigned to each share of no-par value stock and accounted for much as if it were a par value (p. 504).

**Statement of cash flows** A financial statement showing a business's cash inflows and outflows for a specific time period, classified into operating, investing, and financing activities (p. 15).

**Statement of cash flows** A financial statement showing a firm's cash inflows and cash outflows for a specific period, classified into operating, investing, and financing activity categories (p. 544).

**Statement of retained earnings** A financial statement showing the financial changes that occurred in retained earnings during the accounting period (p. 515).

**Statement of retained earnings** A financial statement that presents information regarding the events causing a change in retained earnings during a period, including net income and dividends (p. 14).

**Statement of stockholders' equity** A financial statement presenting information regarding the events that cause a change in stockholders' equity during a period. The statement presents the beginning balance, additions to, deductions from, and the ending balance of stockholders' equity for the period (p. 14).

**Statement of stockholders' equity** A financial statement that presents the financial changes that occurred in all components of stockholders' equity during the accounting period (p. 515).

**Stock dividends** Additional shares of capital stock issued by a corporation to its current stockholders in proportion to their existing ownership interest (p. 513).

**Stockholder** An owner of a corporation as a result of the purchase of the corporation's shares of stock; also known as a shareholder (p. 4).

**Stockholders' equity** The residual interest in the assets of a business after all liabilities have been paid off; stockholders' equity is equal to a firm's net assets, or total assets less total liabilities (p. 55).

**Stockholders' equity** The residual interest of a company's stockholders in the assets of a business; equal to the difference between the company's assets and liabilities (p. 13).

**Straight-line depreciation** A depreciation procedure that allocates uniform amounts of depreciation expense to each period of an asset's useful life (p. 164).

**Straight-line method** A depreciation method that allocates equal amounts of depreciation expense to each period of an asset's expected useful life (p. 413).

**Subsequent events** Events occurring shortly after a fiscal year-end that are reported as supplemental information to the financial statements of the year just ended (p. 622).

**Subsidiaries** Corporations that have at least a majority of their voting stock owned by another company (p. D-12).

**Summary of significant accounting policies** A financial statement disclosure, usually the initial note to the financial statements, which identifies the major accounting policies and procedures used by a firm (p. 620).

**Sustainable earnings** Earnings that are expected to reoccur over time. Also known as permanent earnings (p. 594).

**T**

**T-account** An abbreviated form of the formal account in the shape of a *T* (p. 107).

**Temporary account** An account used to gather information for an accounting period; revenue, expense, and dividend accounts are temporary accounts (p. 109).

**Temporary account** An account used to gather information for an accounting period; revenue, expense, and dividend accounts are temporary accounts (pp. 173, 178).

**Term loan** A long-term borrowing, evidenced by a note payable, that is arranged with a single lender (p. 465).

**Times-interest-earned ratio** Income before interest expense and income taxes divided by interest expense (p. 472).

**Times-interest-earned ratio** Income before interest expense and income taxes divided by interest expense (p. 614).

**Time value of money** The concept that money can be invested at a positive interest rate and grow to a larger sum in the future (p. E-2).

**Trademark** An exclusive and continuing right to use a certain symbol to identify a brand or family of products (p. 425).

**Trade name** An exclusive and continuing right to use a certain term or name to identify a brand or family of products (p. 425).

**Trading securities** Debt securities and noninfluential equity securities that management buys with the intent to sell in the near future (p. D-2).

**Transitory earnings** Single-period events such as extraordinary gains/losses, special items, restructuring charges, changes in accounting principle, and discontinued operations (p. 594).

**Treasury stock** Shares of a corporation that have been acquired for purposes other than retiring (cancelling) the stock. Treasury stock is recorded at cost and is deducted from stockholders' equity on the balance sheet (p. 510).

**Trend analysis** A process in which an analyst or investor compares a company's results, or the results of a ratio, over time (p. 57).

**Trend percentages** A comparison of the same financial item over two or more years stated as a percentage of a base-year amount (p. 602).

**Trial balance** A list of the account titles in the general ledger, their respective debit or credit balances, and the totals of the debit and credit balances (p. 118).

**Triple bottom line** A form of reporting that captures an expanded set of measures in addition to traditional financial reporting. The three bottom lines include economic, ecological, and social (p. 18).

**U**

**Unadjusted trial balance** A list of general ledger accounts and their balances taken before adjustments have been made (p. 162).

**Unearned revenue** A liability representing revenues received in advance; also called *deferred revenue* (p. 104).

**Unearned revenue** A liability representing revenues received in advance; also called *deferred revenue* (p. 165).

**Units-of-production method** A depreciation method that allocates depreciation expense to each operating period in proportion to the amount of the asset's total expected productive capacity used each period (p. 415).

**Unusual items** Items that display a high degree of abnormality and/or are unrelated, or only incidentally related, to the normal activities of a business (p. 595).

**Useful life** The period of time that an asset is used by a business, running from the date of acquisition to the date of disposal (or removal from service) (p. 412).

**V**

**Vertical analysis** Analysis of a firm's financial statements that focuses on the statements of a single year (p. 599).

**W**

**Weighted-average cost method** An inventory costing method that calculates an average unit purchase cost, weighted by the number of units purchased at each price, and uses that weighted-average unit cost to determine the cost of goods sold for all sales (p. 275).

**Wholesaler** A company that buys finished products from manufacturing firms in large quantities and resells the products to retailers (p. 222).

**Working capital** The difference between a firm's current assets and current liabilities (p. 608).

**Working capital** The difference between current assets and current liabilities (p. 470).

**Work-in-process inventory** A manufacturer's inventory that consists of units of product that have been entered into production in the factory but have not yet been completed (p. 268).

**Worksheet** An informal accounting document used to facilitate the preparation of financial statements (p. 181).

**Z**

**Zero-coupon bond** A bond that offers no periodic interest payments and that is issued at a substantial discount from its face value (p. 457).

# Index